Street by Street
HAMPSHIRE

CW00339710

PLUS BOURNEMOUTH, CAMBERLEY, CHRISTCHURCH, FARNHAM, FERNDOWN, HASLEMERE, NEWBURY, NORTH TIDWORTH, POOLE, SOUTHBOURNE, VERWOOD, WIMBORNE MINSTER

Enlarged Areas Aldershot, Andover, Basingstoke, Fareham, Gosport, Havant, Portsmouth, Southampton, Winchester

Ist edition May 2001

© Automobile Association Developments Limited 2001

This product includes map data licensed from Ordnance Survey® with the permission of the Controller of Her Majesty's Stationery Office. © Crown copyright 2000. All rights reserved. Licence No: 399221.

Published by AA Publishing (a trading name of Automobile Association Developments Limited, whose registered office is Norfolk House, Priestley Road, Basingstoke, Hampshire, RG24 9NY. Registered number 1878835).

Mapping produced by the Cartographic Department of The Automobile Association.

ISBN 0 7495 2360 3

A CIP Catalogue record for this book is available from the British Library.

Printed in Italy by Printer Trento srl

The contents of this atlas are believed to be correct at the time of the latest revision. However, the publishers cannot be held responsible for loss occasioned to any person acting or refraining from action as a result of any material in this atlas, nor for any errors, omissions or changes in such material. The publishers would welcome information to correct any errors or omissions and to keep this atlas up to date. Please write to Publishing, The Automobile Association, Fanum House, Basing View, Basingstoke, Hampshire, RG21 4EA.

Ref: MX008

Key to map pages	ii-iii
Key to map symbols	iv-1
Enlarged scale pages	2-23
Street by Street	24-457
Index – towns & villages	458-460
Index – streets	461-506
Index – featured places	506-513

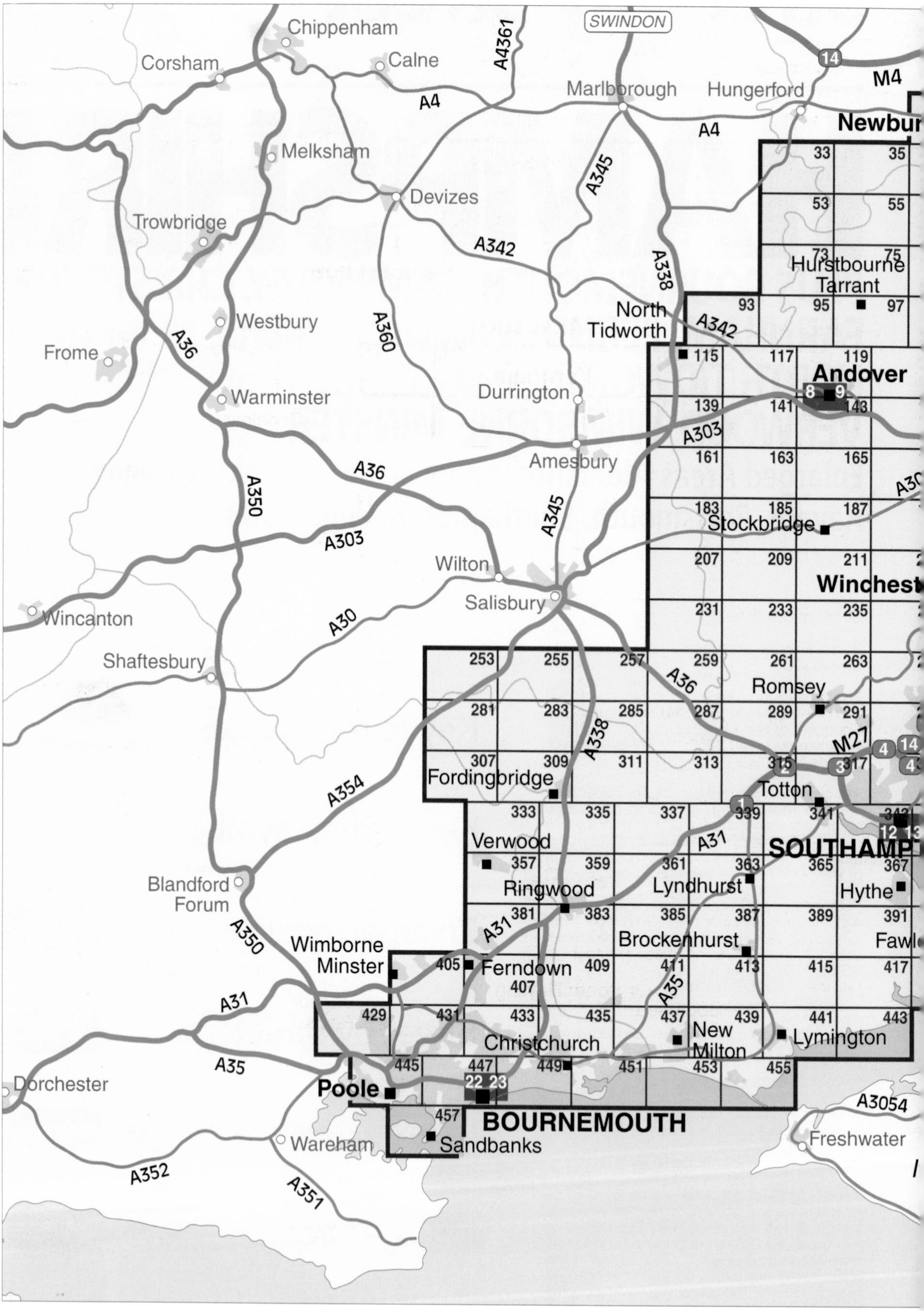

Chippenham · Corsham · Calne · Marlborough · Hungerford · SWINDON · 14 · M4 · Newbur

A4361 · A4 · A4 · A342 · A345 · A338 · Melksham · Devizes

33 · 35 · 53 · 55 · 73 · 75

Trowbridge · A360 · Hurstbourne Tarrant

93 · 95 · 97

Frome · A36 · Westbury · North Tidworth · A342 · 115 · 117 · 119 · Andover

Warminster · Durrington · 139 · 141 · 143 · 8 9

A350 · A36 · A303 · A345 · Amesbury · 161 · 163 · 165 · A30

A303 · 183 · 185 · 187 · Stockbridge

Wincanton · A30 · Wilton · 207 · 209 · 211 · Winchest

Shaftesbury · Salisbury · 231 · 233 · 235

253 · 255 · 257 · 259 · 261 · 263

281 · 283 · 285 · 287 · 289 · 291 · A36 · Romsey · A338

307 · 309 · 311 · 313 · 315 · 317 · M27 · 4 · 14 · 4 · 2 · 3

A354 · Fordingbridge · Totton · 1 · SOUTHAMP · 12 13

333 · 335 · 337 · 339 · 341 · 343 · A31 · Verwood

357 · 359 · 361 · 363 · 365 · 367 · Lyndhurst · Hythe

Blandford Forum · Ringwood · 381 · 383 · 385 · 387 · 389 · 391 · Brockenhurst · Fawl

A31 · A350 · Wimborne Minster · 405 · 407 · 409 · 411 · 413 · 415 · 417 · A35 · Ferndown

429 · 431 · 433 · 435 · 437 · 439 · 441 · 443 · New Milton · Lymington

A31 · A35 · Christchurch · 445 · 447 · 449 · 451 · 453 · 455 · A3054

Dorchester · Poole · 22 23 · 457 · BOURNEMOUTH · Freshwater

Wareham · Sandbanks · A352 · A351

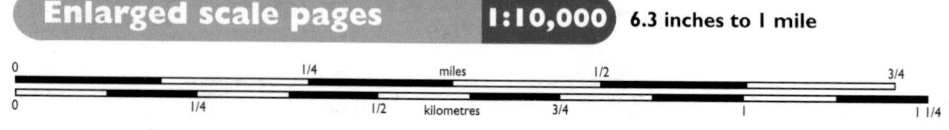

Enlarged scale pages · **1:10,000** · 6.3 inches to 1 mile

0 · 1/4 · miles · 1/2 · 3/4

0 · 1/4 · 1/2 · kilometres · 3/4 · 1 · 1 1/4

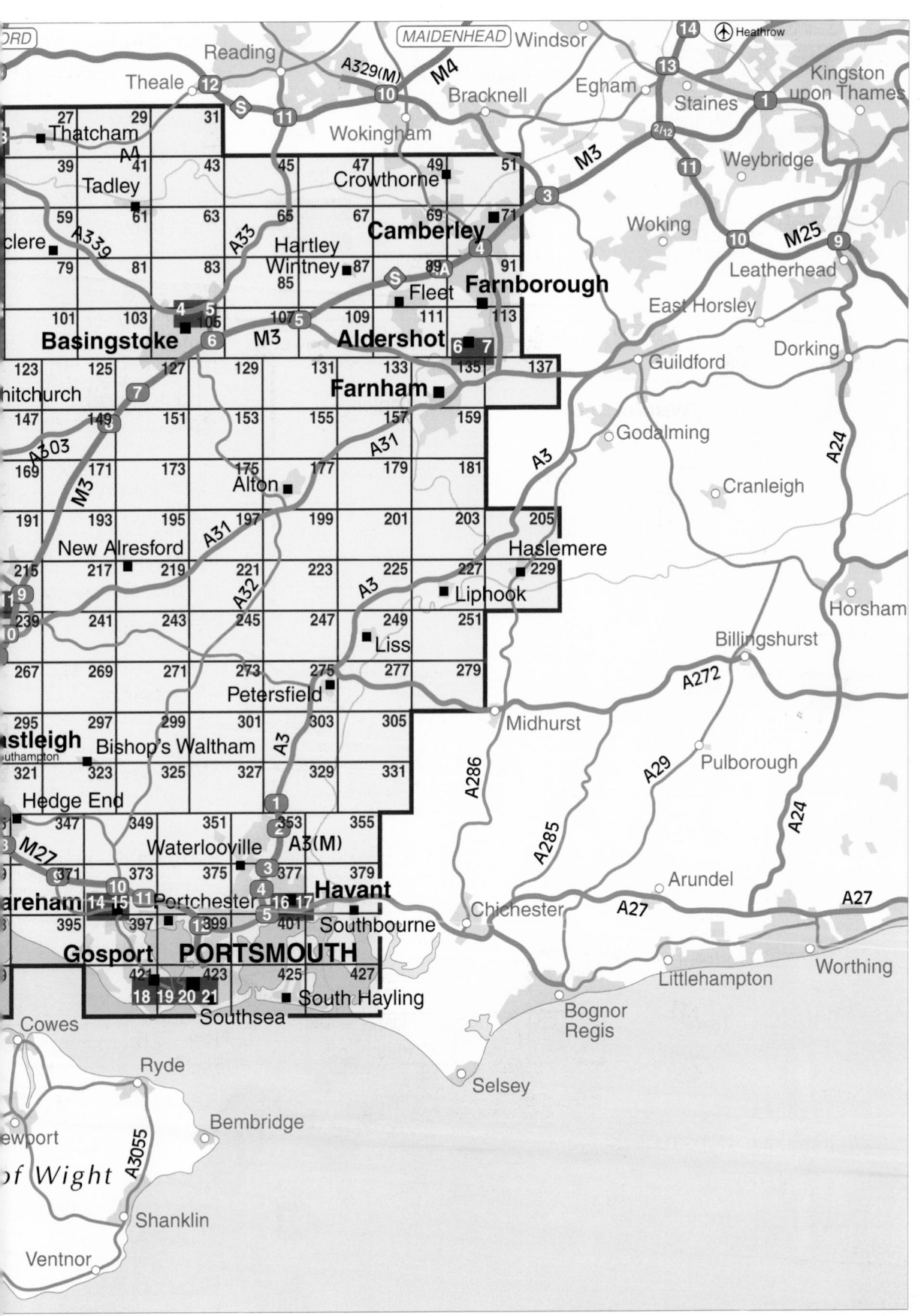

ORD

MAIDENHEAD Windsor

Heathrow 14

Reading

Kingston upon Thames

Theale 12

A329(M) M4

Bracknell

Egham

13

Staines

1

Thatcham 27 29 31

10

Wokingham

Weybridge 2/12

39 41 43 45 47 49 51

Tadley

Crowthorne

M3 3

Woking 11

A4

59 61 63 65 67 69 71

Camberley

Leatherhead

clere 79 81 83 Hartley 85 87 89A 91

A339

Wintney

Farnborough 10 M25 9

East Horsley

Fleet S

Dorking

101 103 105 107 109 111 113

Basingstoke 4 5

6

M3 5

Aldershot 6 7

Guildford

135 137

123 125 127 129 131 133

A33

Farnham

Godalming

hitchurch 7

147 149 151 153 155 157 159

9

A31

A3

Cranleigh

169 171 173 175 177 179 181

A303

Alton

M3

191 193 195 197 199 201 203 205

New Alresford

A31

Haslemere

Horsham

215 217 219 221 223 225 227 229

19

A32

Liphook

Billingshurst

0 239 241 243 245 247 249 251

A3

Liss

A272

267 269 271 273 275 277 279

Petersfield

Midhurst

Pulborough

295 297 299 301 303 305

stleigh

Bishop's Waltham

A3

A286

A29

A24

outhampton

321 323 325 327 329 331

Hedge End

A285

Arundel A27

1

347 349 351 353 355

M27

2

A3(M)

Chichester A27

Worthing

371 373 375 377 379

areham 10 11 Portchester

16 17 Havant

3

14 15

4

Southbourne

Gosport 395 397 399 401

Littlehampton

5

PORTSMOUTH

421 423 425 427

Bognor Regis

18 19 20 21

South Hayling

Southsea

Cowes

Selsey

Ryde

Bembridge

ewport

A3055

of Wight

Shanklin

Ventnor

Junction 9	Motorway & junction	**P+**	Park & Ride
Services	Motorway service area		Bus/coach station
	Primary road single/dual carriageway		Railway & main railway station
Services	Primary road service area		Railway & minor railway station
	A road single/dual carriageway	⊖	Underground station
	B road single/dual carriageway	⊖	Light railway & station
	Other road single/dual carriageway	++++++++++++++	Preserved private railway
	Restricted road	*LC*	Level crossing
	Private road	•–•–•–•–•	Tramway
← ←	One way street	-------------	Ferry route
	Pedestrian street	....	Airport runway
-------------	Track/ footpath	–·–·–·–·–	Boundaries- borough/ district
	Road under construction	▼▼▼▼▼▼▼▼	Mounds
[-------]	Road tunnel	**93**	Page continuation 1:17,500
P	Parking	**7**	Page continuation to enlarged scale 1:10,000

	River/canal lake, pier			Toilet with disabled facilities
	Aqueduct lock, weir			Petrol station
465 ▲ Winter Hill	Peak (with height in metres)		PH	Public house
	Beach		PO	Post Office
	Coniferous woodland			Public library
	Broadleaved woodland		i	Tourist Information Centre
	Mixed woodland			Castle
	Park			Historic house/ building
	Cemetery		Wakehurst Place NT	National Trust property
	Built-up area		M	Museum/ art gallery
	Featured building		†	Church/chapel
⊓⊓⊓⊓⊓⊓	City wall			Country park
A&E	Accident & Emergency hospital			Theatre/ performing arts
	Toilet			Cinema

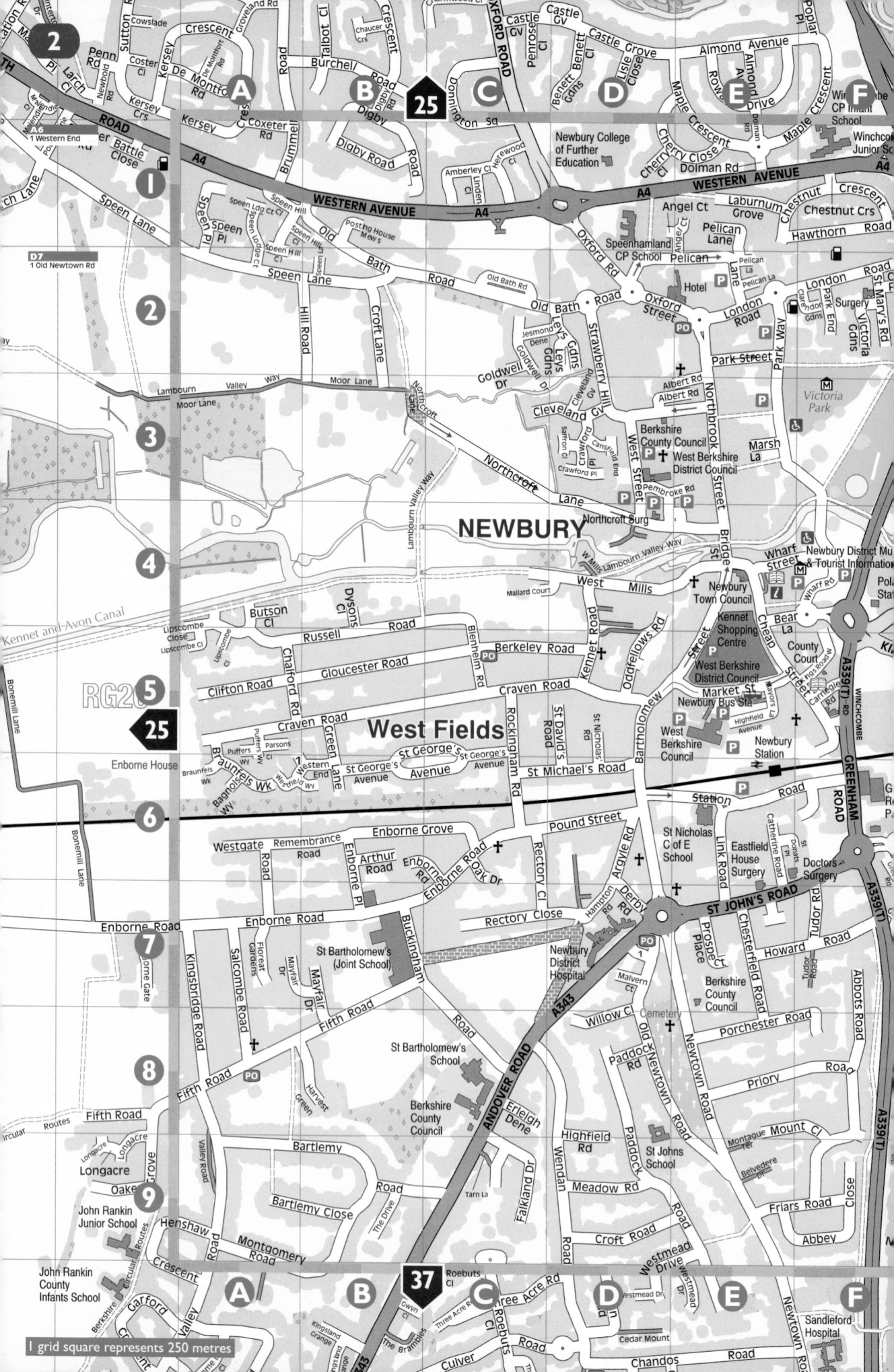

2
25
37
A
B
C
D
E
F
1
2
3
4
5
6
7
8
9
NEWBURY
West Fields
RG20
A6 1 Western End
D7 1 Old Newtown Rd
WESTERN AVENUE
A4
ROAD
Kennet and Avon Canal
Lambourn Valley Way
Moor Lane
Speen Lane
Speen Hill
Speen Pl
Speen Lodge Ct
Old Bath Road
Old Bath Rd
Posting House Mews
Hill Road
Croft Lane
North Croft Lane
Northcroft Lane
Northcroft Surg
Goldwell Dr
Jesmond Dene
Leys Gdns
Strawberry Hill
Cleveland Gv
Saffron Cl
Crawford Pl
Cansfield End
West Street
Berkshire County Council
West Berkshire District Council
Pembroke Rd
Northbrook Street
Albert Rd
Park Street
Park Way
Marsh La
Victoria Park
Oxford Street
Oxford Rd
London Road
Pelican Lane
Pelican La
Speenhamland CP School
Hotel
Angel Ct
Laburnum Grove
Chestnut Crescent
Chestnut Crs
Hawthorn Road
Park End
Victoria Gdns
St Mary's Rd
Surgery
Newbury College of Further Education
Dolman Rd
Cherry Close
Maple Crescent
Almond Avenue
Almond Av
Castle Grove
Castle Gv
Penrose Cl
Benett Cl
Benett Gdns
Lisle Close
Rowe Ct
Drive
Poplar Pl
Winchcombe CP Infant School
Winchcombe Junior School
Donnington Sq
OXFORD ROAD
Amberley Cl
Linden Cl
Herewood Cl
Digby Road
Digby Rd
Burchell Road
Talbot Cl
Chaucer Crs
Crescent
Brummell Road
Coxeter Rd
Kersey Crescent
Kersey Crs
De Montfort Rd
Cowslade
Coster Cl
Penn Rd
Sutton Rd
Larch Cl
Battle Close
Bath Road
Bridge St
Wharf Street
Wharf Rd
Newbury District Museum & Tourist Information
West Mills
W Mills
Mallard Court
Newbury Town Council
Kennet Shopping Centre
West Berkshire District Council
Cheap Street
Bear La
County Court
Kings Road W
Carnegie Rd
Market St
Mayors La
Newbury Bus Sta
Highfield Avenue
West Berkshire Council
Newbury Station
Station Road
GREENHAM ROAD
WINCHCOMBE RD
A339(T)
Kennet Road
Oddfellows Rd
Butson Cl
Dysons Cl
Russell Road
Lipscombe Close
Lipscombe Cl
Berkeley Road
Blenheim Rd
Gloucester Road
Clifton Road
Chalford Rd
Craven Road
Rockingham Rd
St David's Road
St Nicholas Rd
Bartholomew St
St George's Avenue
St Michael's Road
Green Lane
Western End
Braunfels Wk
Bagnols Wy
Puffers Wy
Parsons Cl
Westfield Wy
Enborne House
Bonemill Lane
Pound Street
Enborne Grove
Westgate Road
Remembrance Road
Arthur Road
Enborne Pl
Enborne Rd
Enborne Road
Oak Dr
Rectory Cl
Rectory Close
Argyle Rd
Hampton Rd
Derby Rd
St Nicholas C of E School
Link Road
Eastfield House Surgery
Catherine Road
St Donats Pl
Doctors Surgery
ST JOHN'S ROAD
Prospect Place
Chesterfield Road
Howard Road
Tudor Rd
Tudor Road
Abbots Road
Kingsbridge Road
Salcombe Road
Floreat Gardens
Mayfair Dr
Buckingham Road
St Bartholomew's (Joint School)
Newbury District Hospital
Malvern Ct
Willow Cl
Cemetery
Old Newtown Rd
Newtown Road
Berkshire County Council
Porchester Road
Priory Road
Paddock Rd
Fifth Road
Harvest Green
St Bartholomew's School
ANDOVER ROAD
A343
Erleigh Dene
Highfield Rd
Wendan Road
Paddock Road
St Johns School
Montague Ter
Mount Cl
Belvedere Dr
Friars Road
Abbey Close
Circular Routes
Longacre
Oaken Grove
Valley Road
Bartlemy Road
Bartlemy Close
The Drive
Tarn La
Falkland Dr
Meadow Rd
Croft Road
Westmead Drive
Westmead Dr
John Rankin Junior School
John Rankin County Infants School
Henshaw Crescent
Montgomery Road
Roebuts Cl
Three Acre Rd
Gwyn Cl
The Brambles
Kingsland Grange
Berkshire Circular Routes
Garford Cres
Culver Road
Chandos Road
Cedar Mount
Sandleford Hospital
PO
P
1 grid square represents 250 metres

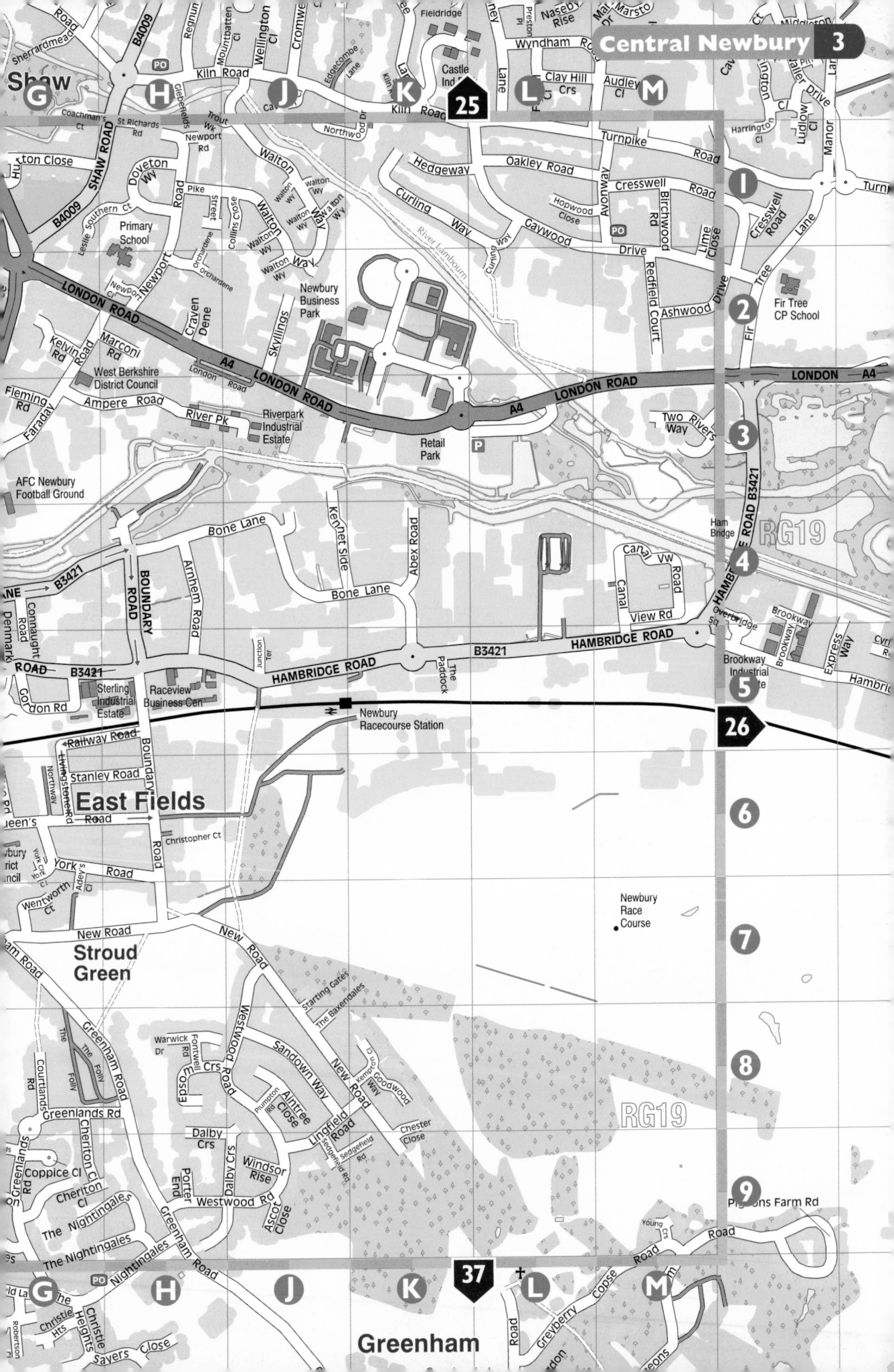
Shaw
East Fields
Stroud Green
Greenham
London Road
Hambridge Road
Newbury Business Park
Retail Park
Newbury Racecourse Station
Newbury Race Course
West Berkshire District Council
Riverpark Industrial Estate
AFC Newbury Football Ground
Fir Tree CP School
Sterling Industrial Estate
Raceview Business Cen
RG19

4
82
104
A
B
C
D
E
F
1
2
3
4
5
6
7
8
9
BASINGSTOKE
Oakridge
South View
Popley Way
Buckfast Cl
Romsey Cl
Fountains Cl
Abbey Road
Tewkesbury Close
Pershore Road
Tintern Close
Merton County Junior School
Glastonbury Close
Priestley Road
North Hampshire Hospital
A&E
A340
ALDERMASTON ROAD
Hotel
RINGWAY NORTH
A339
Vickers Business Centre
Stratfield Rd
Stratfield Road
Lansley Rd
Hallstone Road
Oakridge Road
Normanton Road
Upr Sherborne Road
Upton Crescent
Maple Crs
Scotney Road
Aldermaston Rd S
Millard Close
Oakridge County Junior School
Osborne Cl
Osborne Close
Edison Road
Hamilton Close
Tempus Business Centre
Hubbard Road
Sutton Rd
Dove House School
Maple Ridge School
St Thomas' Cl
Arlott Dr
Joule Road
Joule Rd
Sherborne Road
Hillary Road
Darlington Road
Gower Cl
Marshall Gdns
Telford Road
Kingsclere Road
Merton Road
Lancaster Rd
Lancaster Road
Richmond Road
Queen
Norden Cl
Cromwell Road
Vyne Road
Lyford Rd
Brunel Road
Houndmills Road
Burgess Road
Soper Grove
Phoenix Park Terrace
Cemetery
Holy Ghost Chapel Ruins
Pelton Road
Stephenson Rd
Chapel Hill
Basingstoke Station
Winterthur Way
Clifton Ter
Bunnian Pl
Alencon
Provident Way
The Malls/The Walks Shopping Centre
Town Centre redevelopment due for Completion 2001
VICTORY ROUNDABOUT
Alencon Link
The Anvil Concert Hall
CHURCHILL WAY WEST
A3010
CHURCHILL WAY
A301
Bus Station
Lwr Wote St
Basingstoke Sports Centre
Chute House
Recreation Ground
Welton Ct
Essex Rd
Brookvale Cl
Southend Rd
College Rd
Lower Brook Street
Queen's Road
WAY WEST
RG2
Church Street
Elbow Cnr
Church Sq
George Street
Alexandra Rd
Rochford Road
Raleigh Road
Flaxfield Court
Essex Road
Mortimer La
Hadleigh Pl
Flaxfield Road
Timberlake Road
Hampshire County Council
Deep Lane
Highfield Cha
Wilton Place
Superstore
Basingstoke College of Technology
Mosque
Cross St
Church St
New St
Wote St
Sarum Hill
Feathers
Red Lion
Davy Close
Thorneycroft Industrial Estate
Worting Road
Westdeane Ct
Downsland Rd
Roundmead Rd
Kings School
Haymarket Theatre
Willis Mus
May Pl
Grafton Way
Morse Road
Morse Rd
Winchcombe Rd
Budd's Cl
Penrith Road
Bramblys Drive
Bramblys Dr
Church Grange & Bramblys Grange Health Cen
Winchester St
Market Pl
London Rd
Worting Rd
Overbridge Surgery
Amazon Close
Attwood Cl
Antar Cl
Lawrencedale Court
Townsend Cl
Knight St
Anchor
Victoria Street
New Road
South Ham Rd
Ham Rd
RINGWAY
Knight Street
Goodman Cl
Stukeley Rd
Fletcher Cl
Longmoor Rd
Hamelyn Road
Devonshire Place
Chester Pl
Winchester Road
Frances Road
Southern Road
Jubilee Road
Council Road
Beaconsfield Road
Aldworth Cres
Hardy La
Packenham Rd
Bounty Road
Bounty Rise
Fairfields School & Arts Centre
Primary School
Houndmills
RG22
King's Furlong
1 grid square represents 250 metres

Central Basingstoke
5
Popley
Daneshill
Eastrop
83
105
105
G
H
J
K
L
M
I
2
3
4
5
6
7
8
9
Bilton Industrial Estate
Longfellow Parade Clinic
Doctors Surgery
Chineham Park Primary School
Basingstoke & Deane Borough Council
Hassocks Wood Industrial Estate
Daneshill Industrial Estate
Loddon Business Centre
Daneshill East Industrial Estate
The Hampshire Clinic
The AA - Fanum House
Police Station
Basingstoke County Court
Surrey Hants Borders NHS Trust
The Business Centre
Magistrates Court
Hotel
Harriet Costello School
Basingstoke & Deane Borough Council Offices
War Memorial Park
John Arlott Pavilion
East Barn Surgery
Eastrop Park
READING
A33
RINGWAY EAST
A339
CHURCHILL WAY EAST
A3010
A30 LONDON ROAD
A30
M3
Popley Way
Shetland Road
Lawrence Close
Byron Cl
Keats Cl
Dryden Close
Milton Cl
Shelley Cl
Shakespeare
Browning Cl
Wordsworth Cl
Marlowe Cl
Burns Cl
Hathaway Gdns
Chineham Lane
Oakridge Road
Wateridge Road
Palmer Cl
Mylands Cl
Cowdrey Cl
Coleman Cl
Martin Cl
Gregory Cl
Vivian Road
Lefroy Av
Lefroy Avenue
Bennet Cl
Taverner Cl
Norn Hill
Westray Close
Freemantle Close
Baynard Cl
Pemerton Rd
Brocas Dr
Lewis Cl
Silvester Cl
Gordon Cl
Norn Hl Cl
The Laurels
Coronation Road
Warton Rd
Doswell Way
Deane's Cl
Gresley Road
Basing View
Rutherford Rd
Rankine Road
Enterprise Ct
Faraday Road
Stewart Road
Wade Road
Bond Cl
Stroudley Road
Swing Swang Lane
Armstrong Road
Whitney Rd
Bell Road
Roentgen Rd
Roentgen Road
Blackberry Wk
Cowdrey Heights
Basing Road
Redbridge Lane
Eastrop Way
Frome Cl
Lune Ct
Lea Cl
Buckby La
The Butty
Water Way
Barbel Av
Blackwater Cl
Wevsprings Close
Neath Rd
Roding Cl
Thames Ct
Trent Way
The Moorings
Medway Ct
The Rushes
Loddon Dr
Ribble Way
Test Way
Dudden Way
Damsel Pth
Rothay Ct
Hamble Ct
Waterlily Cl
Irwell Cl
Allnutt Av
Eastfield Av
Eastrop Lane
St Mary's Ct
Lytton Rd
Kennet Cl
Colne Way
Severn Way
London Road
Common Road
White Hart Lane
Crossborough Hill
Dam
Turner Cl
Hogarth
Van Dyck Cl
Reynolds Cl
Badger's Bank
Harvest Way
Elderberry Bank
Cowslip Bank
Dewpond Wk
Rosehip Way
Lambs Row
Saxon Way
Gt Binfields Rd
Great Binfields Rd
Lutyens Close
Clover Fld
PO
P+

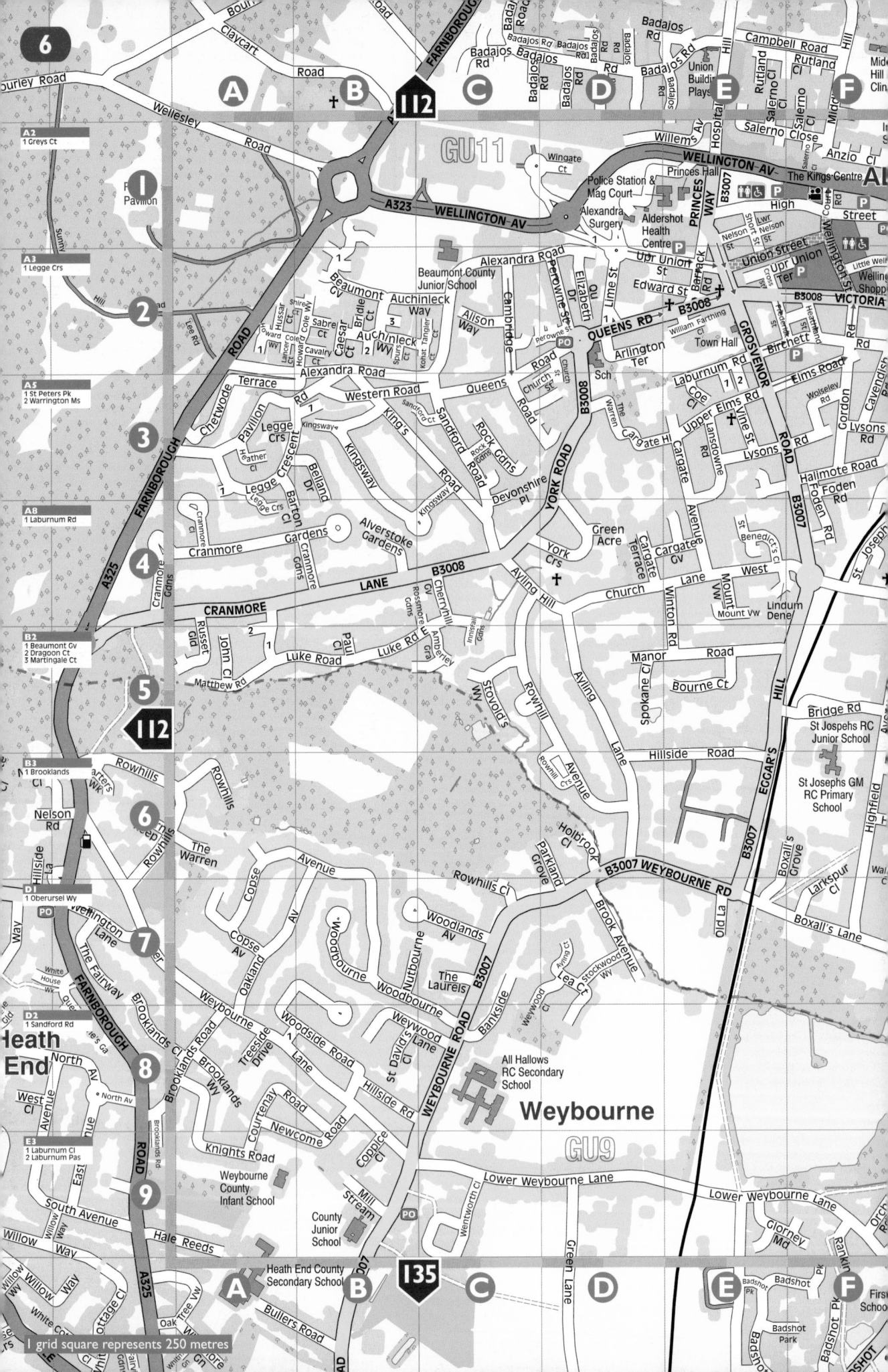
6
112
135
A
B
C
D
E
F
1
2
3
4
5
6
7
8
9
GU11
GU9
A2
1 Greys Ct
A3
1 Legge Crs
A5
1 St Peters Pk
2 Warrington Ms
A8
1 Laburnum Rd
B2
1 Beaumont Gv
2 Dragoon Ct
3 Martingale Ct
B3
1 Brooklands
D1
1 Oberursel Wy
D2
1 Sandford Rd
E3
1 Laburnum Cl
2 Laburnum Pas
Claycart Road
Wellesley Road
FARNBOROUGH ROAD
A325
A323 WELLINGTON AV
WELLINGTON AV
Badajos Rd
Campbell Road
Rutland Cl
Salerno Close
Salerno Cl
Anzio Cl
Willems Av
Hospital Hill
Union Building Plays
Wingate Ct
Police Station & Mag Court
Princes Hall
PRINCES WAY
B3007
The Kings Centre
High Street
Alexandra Surgery
Aldershot Health Centre
Nelson St
Union Street
Upr Union Ter
Little Wellington
Wellington St
Upr Union St
Edward St
Barrack Rd
B3008
VICTORIA
Beaumont County Junior School
Alexandra Road
Perowne St
Elizabeth Dr
Lime St
Beaumont Gv
Auchinleck Way
Auchinleck Wy
Alison Way
Cambridge Road
QUEENS RD
William Farthing Cl
Town Hall
GROSVENOR ROAD
Birchett Rd
Hussar Ct
Shire Ct
Cole Wy
Sabre Ct
Caesar Ct
Bridie Ct
Howard Wy
Cavalry Ct
Lancer Ct
Spurs Ct
Kohat Ct
Tangier Ct
Lee Rd
Arlington Ter
Church St
Sch
Laburnum Rd
Elms Road
Wolseley Rd
Cavendish Rd
Coe Cl
Upper Elms Rd
Vine St
Lansdowne Rd
Gordon Rd
Lysons Rd
Lysons Avenue
Chetwode Terrace
Western Road
Queens Road
Sandford Ct
Sandford Road
Kingsway
King's Road
Rock Gdns
Pavilion Rd
Legge Crs
Heather Cl
Legge Crescent
Belland Dr
Barton Cl
YORK ROAD
Devonshire Pl
The Warren
Cargate Hl
Cargate Avenue
Halimote Road
Foden Rd
St Benedict's Cl
St Joseph's Rd
Cranmore Ct
Cranmore Gardens
Alverstoke Gardens
Cranmore Gdns
Green Acre
York Crs
Cargate Terrace
Cargate Gv
CRANMORE LANE
B3008
Rossmore Gdns
Cherryhill Gv
Innisfail Gdns
Ayling Hill
Church Lane West
Mount Vw
Lindum Dene
Winton Rd
Russet Gld
John Cl
Paul Cl
Luke Road
Luke Rd
Amberley Gra
Matthew Rd
Manor Road
Spokane Cl
Bourne Ct
Stovold's Wy
Rowhill Avenue
Rowhill Crs
Ayling Lane
ECGAR'S HILL
Bridge Rd
St Josephs RC Junior School
St Josephs GM RC Primary School
Hillside Road
Highfield
Rowhills
Carters Wk
Nelson Rd
Hillside La
The Warren
Holbrook Cl
Parkland Grove
B3007 WEYBOURNE RD
Boxall's Grove
Larkspur Cl
Boxall's Lane
Copse Avenue
Copse Av
Oakland Av
Rowhills Cl
Old La
Wellington Lane
The Fairway
White House Wk
Woodbourne
Woodlands Av
Nutbourne
The Laurels
Ayling Ct
Stockwood Wy
Lea Ct
Brook Avenue
Weywood Cl
Weywood Lane
Bankside
WEYBOURNE ROAD
Brooklands Road
Brooklands Cl
Brooklands Wy
Weybourne Road
Treeside Drive
Woodside Road
Woodside Lane
St David's Cl
All Hallows RC Secondary School
Weybourne
Heath End
North Av
West Cl
West Avenue
East Avenue
Courtenay Road
Newcome Road
Hillside Rd
Knights Road
Coppice Cl
Weybourne County Infant School
Mill Stream
County Junior School
Lower Weybourne Lane
Wentworth Cl
Green Lane
Glorney Md
Rankine
South Avenue
Willow Way
Hale Reeds
Heath End County Secondary School
Badshot Pk
Badshot Park
Oak Tree Vw
Bullers Road
Cottage Cl
1 grid square represents 250 metres

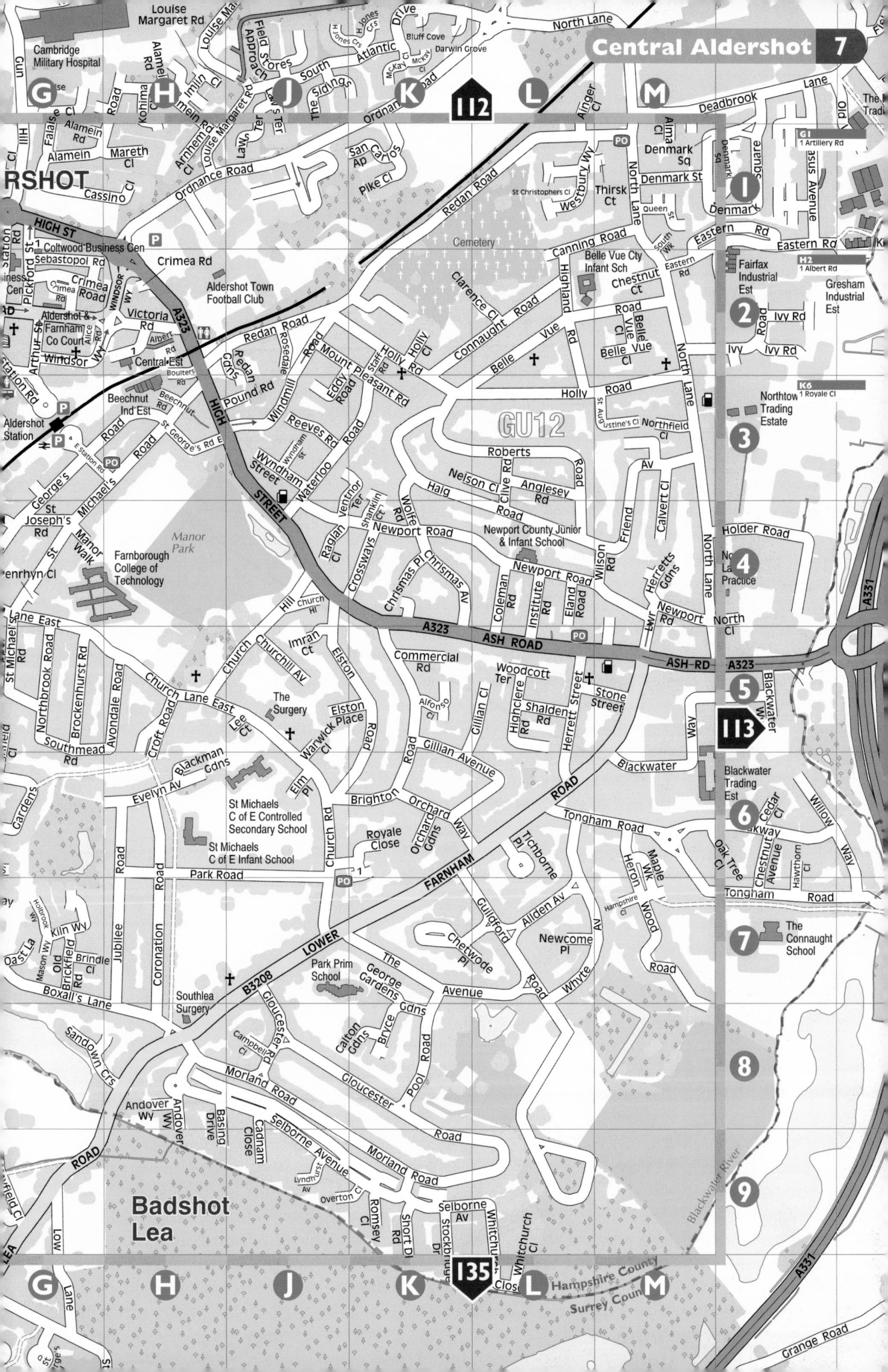

Central Aldershot
7
112
113
135
G
H
J
K
L
M
1
2
3
4
5
6
7
8
9
GU12
Cambridge Military Hospital
Louise Margaret Rd
Field Stores Approach
Atlantic Drive
Bluff Cove
Darwin Grove
North Lane
Deadbrook Lane
Ordnance Road
Alamein Rd
Mareth Cl
Cassino Cl
Arnhem Cl
Kohima Cl
Lawn Ter
San Carlos Ap
Pike Cl
Redan Road
Cemetery
St Christophers Cl
Westbury Wy
Thirsk Ct
Denmark Sq
Denmark St
Alma Cl
Queen St
Eastern Rd
Canning Road
Belle Vue Cty Infant Sch
Chestnut Ct
Fairfax Industrial Est
Gresham Industrial Est
Ivy Rd
1 Artillery Rd
1 Albert Rd
1 Royale Cl
Northtown Trading Estate
HIGH ST
A323
Coltwood Business Cen
Sebastopol Rd
Crimea Road
Crimea Rd
Pickford St
Aldershot & Farnham Co Court
Arthur St
Victoria Rd
Albert Rd
Windsor Wy
Central Est
Aldershot Town Football Club
Redan Gdns
Rosedale
Pound Rd
Windmill Road
Mount Pleasant Rd
Eddy Road
Holly Rd
Holly Cl
Staff Rd
Clarence Cl
Connaught Road
Belle Vue Rd
Belle Vue Cl
Highland Rd
Holly Road
St Augustine's Cl
Northfield Cl
Beechnut Ind Est
Aldershot Station
Station Rd
St George's Rd E
St Michael's Road
St Joseph's Rd
Reeves Rd
Wyndham Street
Waterloo Road
Ventnor Ter
Shanklin Ct
Raglan Cl
Wolfe Rd
Newport Road
Roberts Road
Nelson Cl
Clive Rd
Anglesey Rd
Haig Road
Friend Av
Calvert Cl
Newport County Junior & Infant School
Holder Road
Manor Park
Farnborough College of Technology
Manor Walk
Penrhyn Cl
Crossways
Chrismas Pl
Chrismas Av
Coleman Rd
Institute Rd
Eland Road
Wilson Rd
Herretts Gdns
Newport Rd
North Lane
North Cl
ASH ROAD
ASH RD
A331
Church Hill
Church Lane East
Churchill Av
Imran Ct
Elston Road
Commercial Rd
Woodcott Ter
Stone Street
Herrett Street
Blackwater Way
Blackwater Trading Est
Northbrook Road
Brockenhurst Rd
Avondale Road
Southmead Rd
Croft Road
The Surgery
Lee Ct
Warwick Place
Elston Cl
Alfonso Cl
Gillian Cl
Highclere Rd
Shalden Rd
Gillian Avenue
Blackman Gdns
Evelyn Av
St Michaels C of E Controlled Secondary School
St Michaels C of E Infant School
Elm Pl
Church Rd
Brighton Road
Orchard Way
Orchard Gdns
Royale Close
FARNHAM ROAD
Tongham Road
Tichborne Pl
Maple Wk
Heron Wk
Oak Tree Cl
Cedar Cl
Chestnut Avenue
Hawthorn Cl
Willow Way
Park Road
Jubilee Road
Coronation Road
Kiln Wy
Holbrook Wy
Mason Wy
Old Brickfield Rd
Brindle Cl
Oast La
Boxall's Lane
Guildford Road
Allden Av
Hampshire Cl
Wood Road
Whyte Av
Newcome Pl
The Connaught School
Chetwode Pl
LOWER FARNHAM ROAD
B3208
Park Prim School
The George Gardens
George Gdns
Avenue
Southlea Surgery
Sandown Crs
Gloucester Rd
Campbell Cl
Calton Gdns
Bryce Gdns
Pool Road
Morland Road
Gloucester Road
Andover Wy
Basing Drive
Cadnam Close
Selborne Avenue
Lyndhurst Av
Overton Cl
Romsey Cl
Short Rd
Stockbridge Dr
Selborne Av
Whitchurch Cl
Whitchurch Close
Badshot Lea
Low Lane
Blackwater River
Hampshire County
Surrey County
Grange Road

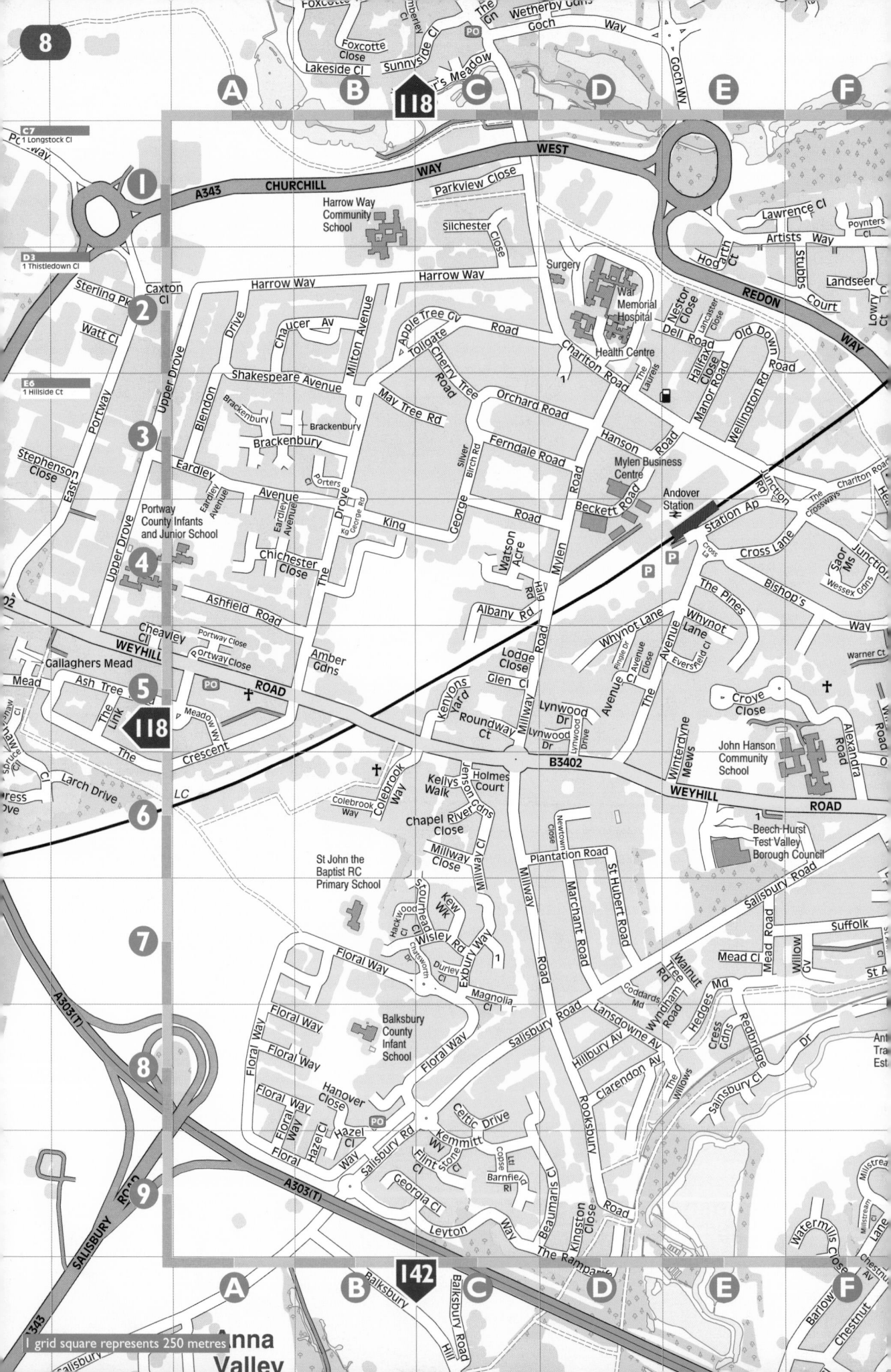
C7
1 Longstock Cl
D3
1 Thistledown Cl
E6
1 Hillside Ct
A343
CHURCHILL
WAY
WEST
REDON
WAY
Parkview Close
Harrow Way Community School
Silchester Close
Lawrence Cl
Poynters Cl
Artists Way
Hogarth Ct
Stubbs Court
Landseer Cl
Surgery
War Memorial Hospital
Health Centre
Harrow Way
Caxton Cl
Sterling Pk
Watt Cl
Chaucer Av
Milton Avenue
Apple Tree Gv
Tollgate Road
Cherry Tree Road
Chariton Road
Nestor Close
Lancaster Close
Dell Road
Old Down Road
The Laurels
Halifax Close
Manor Road
Wellington Rd
Shakespeare Avenue
May Tree Rd
Orchard Road
Portway
Upper Drove
Blendon Drive
Brackenbury
Silver Birch Rd
Ferndale Road
Hanson Road
Mylen Business Centre
Stephenson Close
East
Eardley Avenue
Porters Cl
The Drove
George Rd
Kg
King George Road
Mylen Road
Beckett Road
Andover Station
Junction Rd
Station Ap
The Crossways
Charlton Road
Portway County Infants and Junior School
Chichester Close
Watson Acre
Haig Rd
Cross La
Cross Lane
Saor Ms
Junction
Wessex Gdns
Ashfield Road
Albany Rd
The Pines
Bishop's Way
Whynot Lane
Whynot Lane
Warner Ct
Cheavley Cl
Portway Close
Portway Close
WEYHILL ROAD
Gallaghers Mead
Mead
Ash Tree
The Link
Amber Gdns
Lodge Close
Glen Cl
Millway Road
Lynwood Dr
Lynwood Drive
Avenue Cl
Avenue Close
Eversfield Cl
The Avenue
Croye Close
Kenyons Yard
Roundway Ct
Meadow Wy
The Crescent
Larch Drive
LC
B3402
Winterdyne Mews
John Hanson Community School
Alexandra Road
Colebrook Way
Colebrook Way
Kellys Walk
Jenson Gdns
Holmes Court
Chapel River Close
Millway Close
Millway Cl
Newtown Close
Plantation Road
1
Beech Hurst Test Valley Borough Council
St John the Baptist RC Primary School
Stourhead Cl
Hackwood Cl
Kew Wk
Marchant Road
St Hubert Road
Salisbury Road
Suffolk
Mead Road
Willow Gv
Mead Cl
St A
Floral Way
Wisley Rd
Chatsworth Dr
Durley Cl
Exbury Way
Magnolia Cl
Walnut Tree Rd
Goddards Md
Wyndham Road
Hedges Md
Redbridge
Cress Gdns
Dr
A303(T)
Balksbury County Infant School
Salisbury Road
Lansdowne Av
Hillbury Av
Clarendon Av
The Willows
Salisbury Cl
Hanover Close
Hazel Cl
Hazel Cl
Celtic Drive
Kemmitt Wy
Salisbury Rd
Flint Cl
Stone Cl
Copse Ltt
Barnfield Ri
Georgia Cl
Rooksbury Road
Beaumaris Cl
Kingston Close
Leyton Way
The Ramparts
Watermills Close
Millstream
Chestnut Av
Barlow
Chestnut
SALISBURY ROAD
Balksbury
Balksbury Road
Hill
Anna Valley
A343
Salisbury
Foxcotte Close
Lakeside Cl
Sunnyside Cl
Wetherby Gdns
Goch Way
The Gn
PO
A B C D E F
1 2 3 4 5 6 7 8 9
118
142
1 grid square represents 250 metres

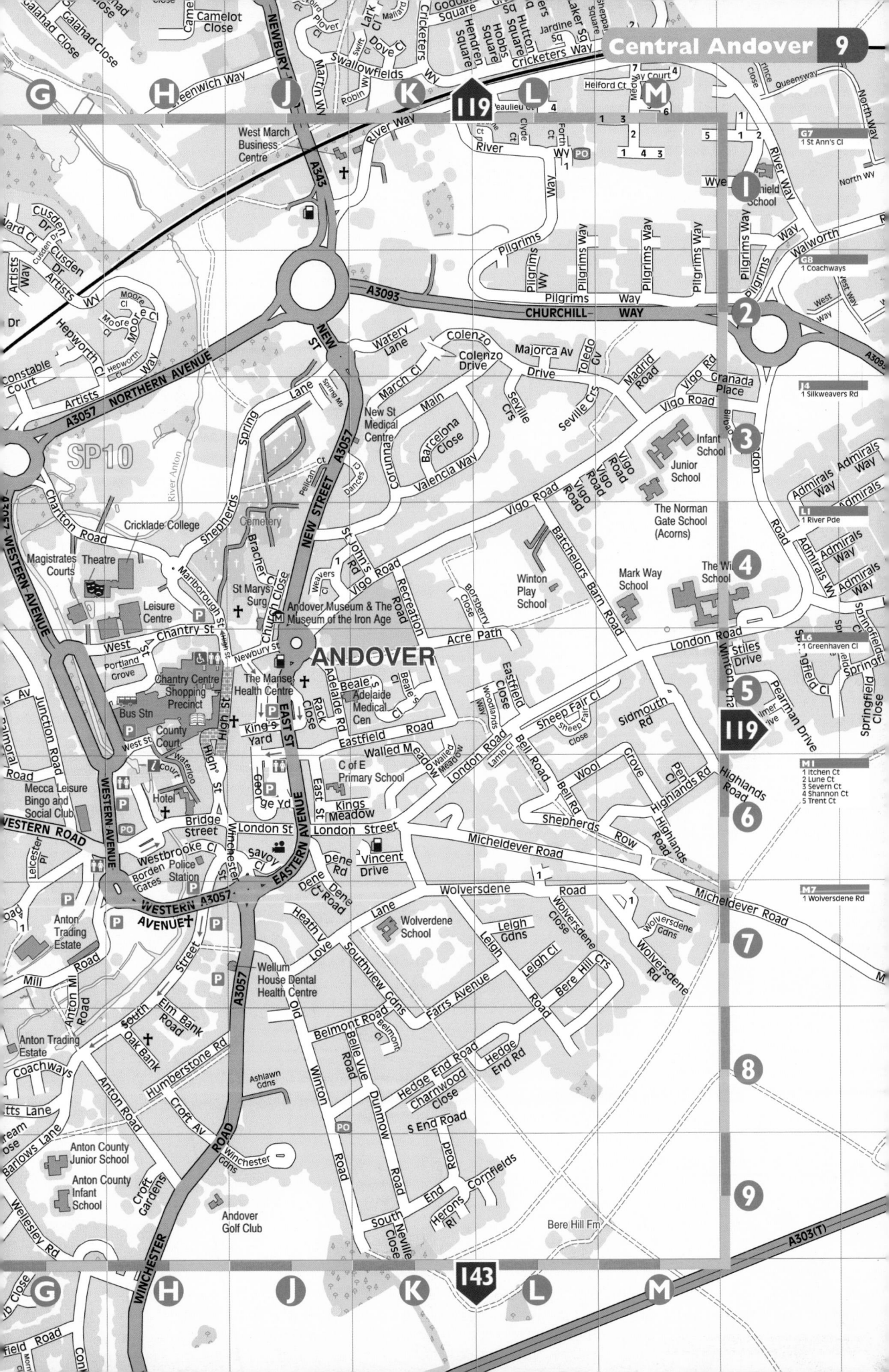

Central Andover
9
119
143
G
H
J
K
L
M
1
2
3
4
5
6
7
8
9
ANDOVER
SP10
Camelot Close
Galahad Close
Greenwich Way
NEWBURY ST
Plover Cl
Lark Cl
Mallard
Dove Cl
Swift Cl
Martin Way
Swallowfields
Robin Wy
Cricketers Wy
Goddard Square
Hendren Square
Hobbs Square
Hutton Square
Jardine Sq
Laker Sq
Cricketers Way
Helford Ct
Medway Court
Beaulieu Ct
River Way
Clyde Ct
Forth Ct
Wye
PO
West March Business Centre
A343
Cusden Dr
Ward Cl
Artists Way
Moore Cl
Hepworth Cl
Constable Court
A3057 NORTHERN AVENUE
A3093
CHURCHILL WAY
Pilgrims Way
Pilgrims Wy
Walworth
Queensway
North Way
North Wy
West Way
Jest Way
G7
1 St Ann's Cl
G8
1 Coachways
J4
1 Silkweavers Rd
L1
1 River Pde
L6
1 Greenhaven Cl
M1
1 Itchen Ct
2 Lune Ct
3 Severn Ct
4 Shannon Ct
5 Trent Ct
M7
1 Wolversdene Rd
NEW ST
Watery Lane
Colenzo Drive
Majorca Av
Toledo Gv
Madrid Road
Vigo Rd
Granada Place
Vigo Road
March Cl
Main
New St Medical Centre
Corunna Main
Barcelona Close
Valencia Way
Seville Crs
Spring Lane
Spring Ms
Pelican Ct
Dances Cl
A3057
NEW STREET
Infant School
Junior School
The Norman Gate School (Acorns)
Admirals Way
Road
Charlton Road
Cricklade College
Shepherds Spring
Cemetery
Bracher Cl
St John's Rd
Weavers Cl
Magistrates Courts
Theatre
Marlborough St
St Marys Surg
Church Close
Andover Museum & The Museum of the Iron Age
Recreation Road
Borsberry Close
Winton Play School
Batchelors Barn Road
Mark Way School
The Winton School
Springfield Close
Springfield Cl
Leisure Centre
Chantry St
West St
Portland Grove
Newbury St
Acre Path
London Road
Stiles Drive
Winton Chase
Pearman Drive
Chantry Centre Shopping Precinct
The Manse Health Centre
Beale's Ct
Adelaide Medical Cen
Beale's Cl
Eastfield Close
Sheep Fair Cl
Sidmouth Rd
Bus Stn
County Court
High St
King's Yard
EAST ST
Rack Close
Adelaide Rd
Eastfield Road
Woodlands Way
Sheep Fair Close
Bell Road
Lamb Cl
Junction Road
Balmoral Road
Waterloo Court
Walled Meadow
C of E Primary School
Wool Grove
Pen Cl
Highlands Rd
Highlands Road
Mecca Leisure Bingo and Social Club
WESTERN AVENUE
WESTERN ROAD
Hotel
George Yd
East St
Kings Meadow
Shepherds Row
Bell Rd
Bridge Street
London St
London Street
Micheldever Road
Leicester Pl
Westbrooke Cl
Borden Gates
Police Station
Winchester St
Savoy Cl
EASTERN AVENUE
Dene Rd
Vincent Drive
Dene Road
Dene Ct
Wolversdene Road
Wolversdene Close
Wolversdene Gdns
Wolversdene Rd
WESTERN A3057 AVENUE
Anton Trading Estate
Heath Vale
Love Lane
Wolverdene School
Leigh Gdns
Leigh Road
Leigh Cl
Bere Hill Crs
Mill Road
Anton Mill Road
South Street
Wellum House Dental Health Centre
Southview Gdns
Farrs Avenue
Old Winton Rd
Elm Bank Road
Oak Bank
Belmont Road
Belmont Cl
Belle Vue Road
Humberstone Rd
Hedge End Road
Hedge End Rd
Coachways
Anton Road
Croft Av
Ashlawn Gdns
Winton Road
Dunmow Road
Charnwood Close
S End Road
Pitts Lane
Barlows Lane
Anton County Junior School
Anton County Infant School
Winchester Gdns
End Road
Cornfields
Croft Gardens
Wellesley Rd
Andover Golf Club
South End
Herons Ri
Neville Close
Bere Hill Fm
A303(T)
WINCHESTER ROAD
A3057
Road

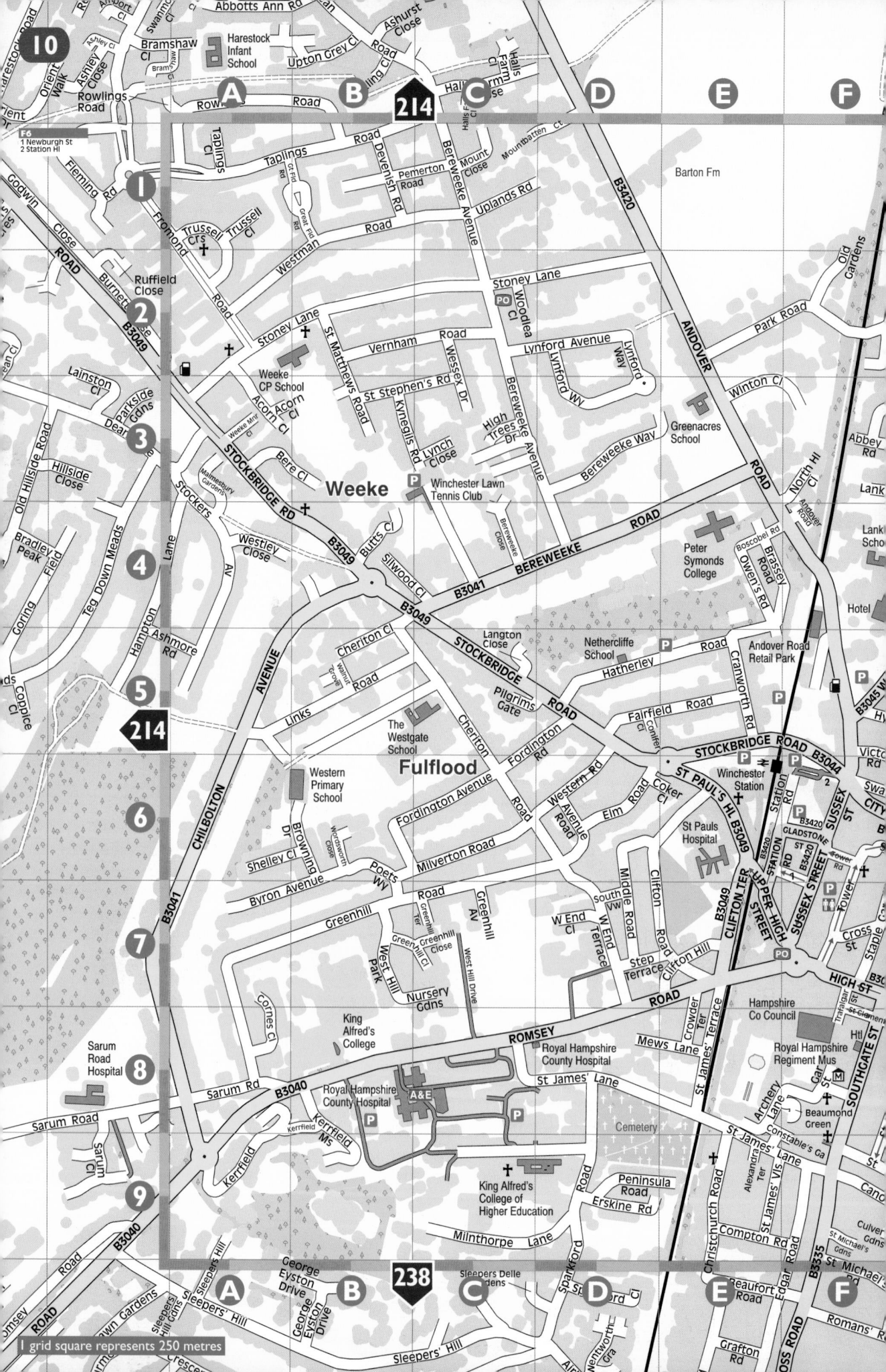

10
214
238
Weeke
Fulflood
Harestock Infant School
Weeke CP School
Winchester Lawn Tennis Club
Greenacres School
Peter Symonds College
Nethercliffe School
Andover Road Retail Park
The Westgate School
Western Primary School
Winchester Station
St Pauls Hospital
King Alfred's College
Royal Hampshire County Hospital
Sarum Road Hospital
Hampshire Co Council
Royal Hampshire Regiment Mus
King Alfred's College of Higher Education
Cemetery
Barton Fm
Beaumond Green
Hotel
Ruffield Close
Stockbridge Road B3049
Andover Road B3420
Bereweeke Road B3041
Chilbolton Avenue B3041
Romsey Road B3040
Sarum Road
St James' Lane
St Paul's Hl B3049
Upper High Street
Clifton Ter
Sussex Street
Southgate St
High St
Stoney Lane
Westman Road
Taplings Road
Fromond Road
Bereweeke Avenue
Milverton Road
Greenhill Road
Byron Avenue
Fordington Avenue
Links Road
Cheriton Road
Hatherley Road
Fairfield Road
Milnthorpe Lane
Sleepers' Hill
Romans' Rd
F6
1 Newburgh St
2 Station Hl
1 grid square represents 250 metres

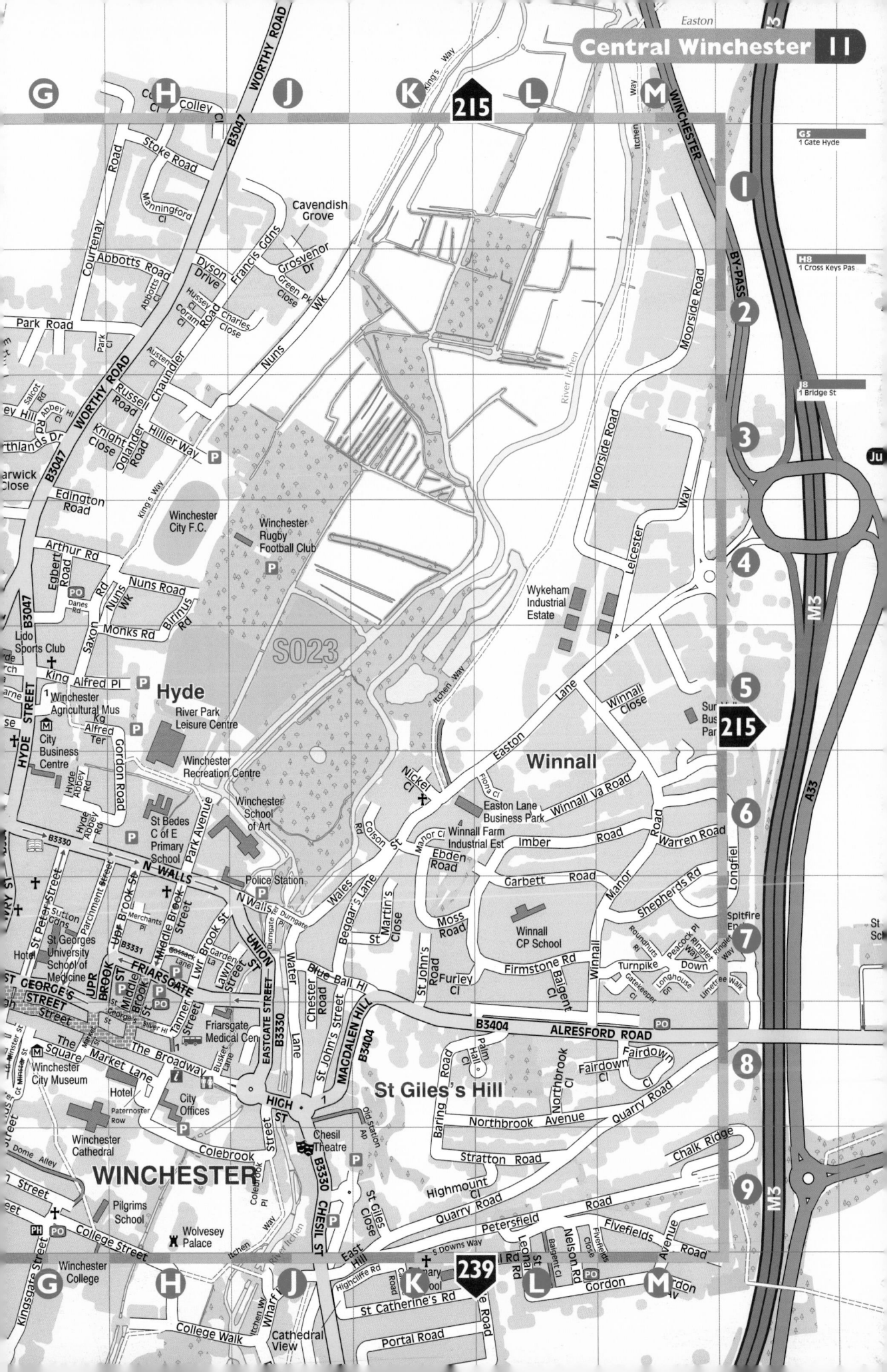
Easton
215
239
G5 1 Gate Hyde
H8 1 Cross Keys Pas
J8 1 Bridge St
Cavendish Grove
Winchester City F.C.
Winchester Rugby Football Club
SO23
Wykeham Industrial Estate
Hyde
River Park Leisure Centre
Winchester Recreation Centre
Winchester School of Art
Winnall
Easton Lane Business Park
Winnall Farm Industrial Est
Lido Sports Club
Winchester Agricultural Mus
City Business Centre
St Bedes C of E Primary School
Police Station
Winnall CP School
St Georges University School of Medicine
Friarsgate Medical Cen
Winchester City Museum
City Offices
St Giles's Hill
Chesil Theatre
Winchester Cathedral
WINCHESTER
Pilgrims School
Wolvesey Palace
Winchester College
Cathedral View
WORTHY ROAD
WINCHESTER BY-PASS
ALRESFORD ROAD
M3
A33
B3047
B3330
B3331
B3404
Easton Lane
Moorside Road
Nuns Wk
Hyde Street
Jewry St
North Walls
Friarsgate
The Broadway
High St
Chesil St
Magdalen Hill
Quarry Road
Petersfield Road
Fivefields Road
St Catherine's Rd
Portal Road
College Street
College Walk
Kingsgate Street

12
Liner Industrial Est
Payne's
Freemantle C of E School
Mansion Rd
Queenstown Road
Road
Kings Rd
Landguard Road
F6
1 French St
2 Vyse La
F5
1 Cement Ter
2 Lansdowne Hl
3 Maddison St
4 Simnel St
F4
1 West Bargate
E2
1 Fitzhugh St
Kenilworth Rd
On Line Gallery
Bedford
Sandhurst Road
Sir George's Rd
Alexandra Road
Almond Rd
Varna Rd
Waterloo Road
PO
A
B
C
D
E
F
343
Hotel
Hill Lane
Grosvenor Sq
Southampton City Council
Roberts Road
Mandela Wy
Tintern Gv
Handel Ter
Morris
Handel Rd
Road
Bridgwater Ct
Dymott Cl
Millbrook Rd East
Edith Haisman Cl
A3057
Bourne Rd
Southampton & New Forest Magistrates Court
The Polygon
A3024
CUMBERLAND PLACE
Cenotaph
West Park
Guildhall
1
Cen
Millbrook Rd East
Commercial Road
BBC South TV & Radio Solent
Commercial Road
Elgin Rd
Waverley Rd
Cracknore Rd
Hewitt's Rd
Four Posts Hl
Wyndham Pl
Mayflower Theatre
Police Stn & Courts
Civic Cen
Cliff Road
Mountbatten Business Cen
West Pk Rd
HAVELOCK RD
MOUNTBATTEN
Saxon Rd
City Council
Trading Est
Blechynden Ter
CTRL STATION
Southampton Central Station
City Council
W Marlands Rd
Gibbs Rd
2
WAY
A33
BR
A3024
WESTERN ESP
CIVIC CENTRE RD
Civic Centre Rd
West Bay Road
SOUTHERN ROAD
Superstore
Western Esp
Superstore
Marlands Shopping Cen
Hotel
Harbour Parade
Hotel
Ogle Rd
3
West Bay Road
Southern Rd
City Ind Park
Regent St
Pirelli St
Pirelli St
Portland Terrace
Portland Ter
WEST QUAY ROAD
West Quay Retail Park
West Quay Shopping Centre
Harbour Parade
Spa Road
Solent Road
4
Herbert Walker Avenue
City Ind Park
W Quay Rd
Odeon Cinema
A33
Western Esplanade
Bargate St
Castle
Albion
W Quay Rd
W Quay Road
Harbour Pde
Forest Vw
Castle La
Hamtun St
Herbert Walker Avenue
5
WEST QUAY RD
Hotel
Hotel
Tudor House Museum
Western Esp
Bugle St
Southampton City Council
343
Herbert Walker Avenue
Westgate St
Mayflower Memorial
6
MAYFLOWER ROUNDABOUT
Mayflower Park
River Test
City Council
Wool House Maritime Mus
A33
Cracknore Hard
Red Funnel Ferry Terminal
7
Cracknore Hard
Royal Pier
City of Southampton
Hampshire County
8
ISLE OF WIGHT
9
SO40
343
A
B
C
D
E
F
1 grid square represents 250 metres

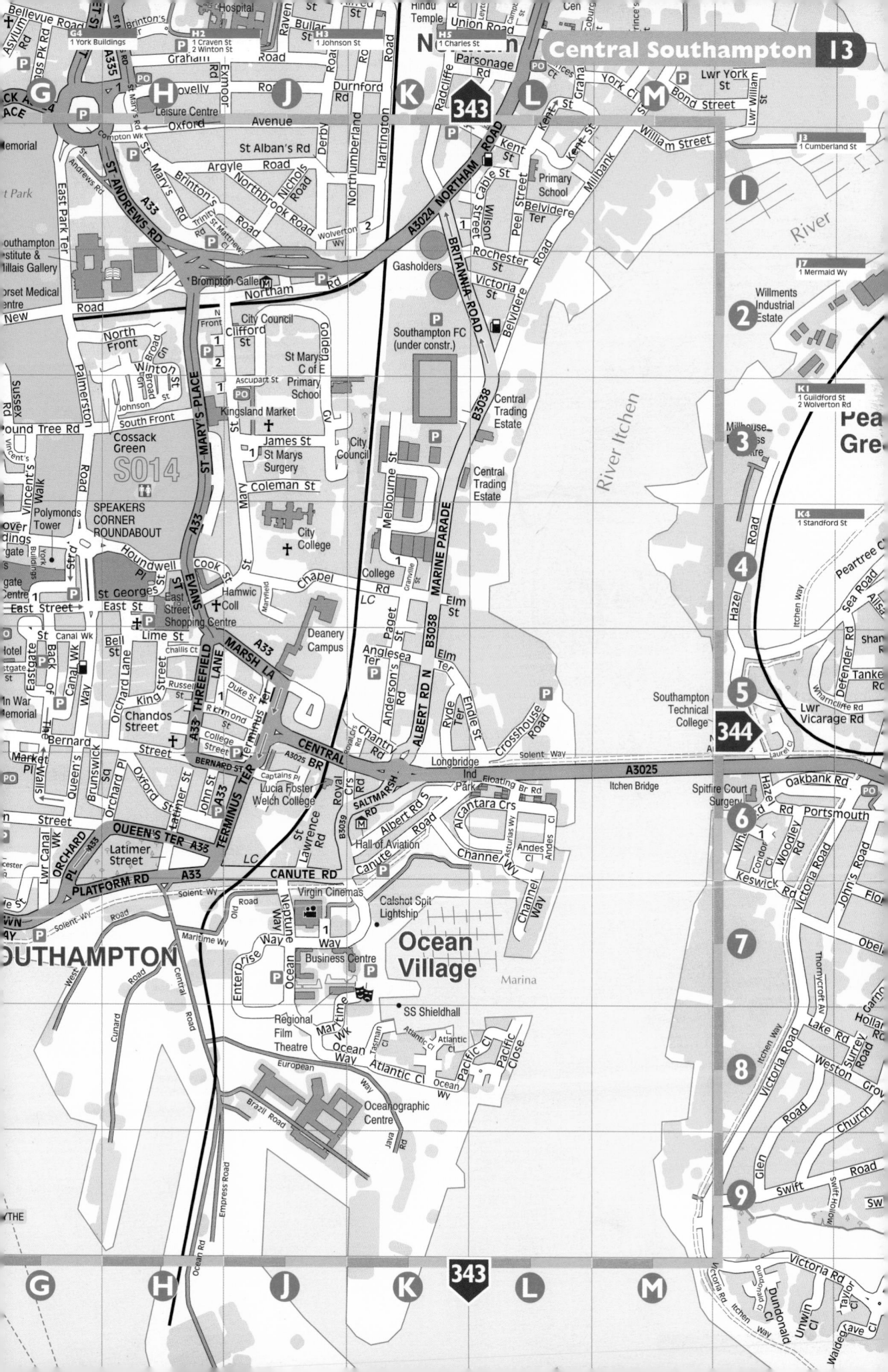
G4 1 York Buildings
H2 1 Craven St 2 Winton St
H3 1 Johnson St
H5 1 Charles St
J3 1 Cumberland St
J7 1 Mermaid Wy
K1 1 Guildford St 2 Wolverton Rd
K4 1 Standford St
343
344
Bellevue Road
Hospital
Hindu Temple
Union Road
Parsonage Rd
Radcliffe
Lwr York St
Bond Street
York Cl
Lwr William St
William Street
Graham Road
Exmoor Rd
Durnford Rd
Leisure Centre
Oxford Avenue
Compton Wk
St Alban's Rd
Argyle Road
Northbrook Road
Nichols Road
Northumberland
Hartington
Brinton's Road
St Mary's Rd
ST ANDREWS RD
East Park Ter
A33
A335
A3024 NORTHAM ROAD
Wolverton Wy
Kent St
Cable St
Primary School
Belvidere Ter
Peel Street
Wilson Street
Millbank
Rochester St
Victoria St
Belvidere Road
BRITANNIA ROAD
Gasholders
Brompton Gallery
Northam Rd
Southampton Institute & Millais Gallery
Dorset Medical Centre
New Road
River
Willments Industrial Estate
City Council
Clifford St
North Front
Winton St
Golden Gv
Southampton FC (under constr.)
St Marys C of E Primary School
Ascupart St
Johnson St
South Front
Kingsland Market
Central Trading Estate
B3038
Palmerston Road
Sussex Rd
Pound Tree Rd
Cossack Green
SO14
James St
St Marys Surgery
City Council
River Itchen
Millhouse Business Centre
Peartree Green
ST MARY'S PLACE
Coleman St
Mary St
Melbourne St
MARINE PARADE
Vincent's Walk
Polymonds Tower
SPEAKERS CORNER ROUNDABOUT
City College
Hazel Road
Peartree Cl
Sea Road
Houndwell Pl
Cook St
Chapel Rd
College
Granville St
Elm St
Itchen Way
St Georges
East Street Shopping Centre
ST EVANS
Hamwic Coll
Maryfield
Deanery Campus
Paget St
B3038
ALBERT RD N
East Street
Canal Wk
Bell St
Lime St
Challis Ct
MARSH LA
Anglesea Ter
Elm Ter
Defender Rd
Tankerville Rd
Hotel
Eastgate St
Back of the Walls
Orchard Lane
King Street
Russell St
Duke St
THREEFIELD LANE
Terminus Ter
Anderson's Rd
Ryde Ter
Endle St
Crosshouse Road
Southampton Technical College
Lwr Vicarage Rd
Wharncliffe Rd
Chandos Street
Richmond St
College St
Bernard Street
BERNARD ST
Chantry Rd
CENTRAL BR
A3025
Longbridge Ind Park
Solent Way
A3025
Itchen Bridge
Laurel Cl
Spitfire Court Surgery
Oakbank Rd
Market Pl
Queen's Way
Brunswick Sq
Orchard Pl
Oxford St
Latimer St
John St
TERMINUS TER
Captains Pl
Lucia Foster Welch College
Royal Crs Rd
SALTMARSH RD
Floating Br Rd
Alcantara Crs
Asturias Wy
Andes Cl
Portsmouth Rd
Condor Cl
Woodley Rd
Victoria Road
St John's Road
Keswick Rd
Street
Lwr Canal Wk
ORCHARD PL
QUEEN'S TER
Latimer Street
St Lawrence Rd
B3039
Albert Rd S
Road
Hall of Aviation
Channel Wy
Channel Way
PLATFORM RD
CANUTE RD
Canute Rd
Solent Wy
Virgin Cinemas
Calshot Spit Lightship
Old Road
Neptune Way
Maritime Wy
SOUTHAMPTON
Enterprise Way
Ocean Way
Business Centre
Ocean Village
Marina
West Road
Central Road
Cunard Road
Regional Film Theatre
Maritime Wk
SS Shieldhall
Tasman Cl
Atlantic Cl
Pacific Cl
Pacific Close
Ocean Way
Ocean Wy
European Way
Oceanographic Centre
Brazil Road
Java Rd
Empress Road
Ocean Rd
Thornycroft Av
Lake Rd
Surrey Road
Weston Grove
Church Road
Glen Road
Swift Road
Swift Hollow
Victoria Rd
Dundonald Cl
Unwin Cl
Taylor Cl
Waldegrave Cl
Itchen Way
River Itchen
LC

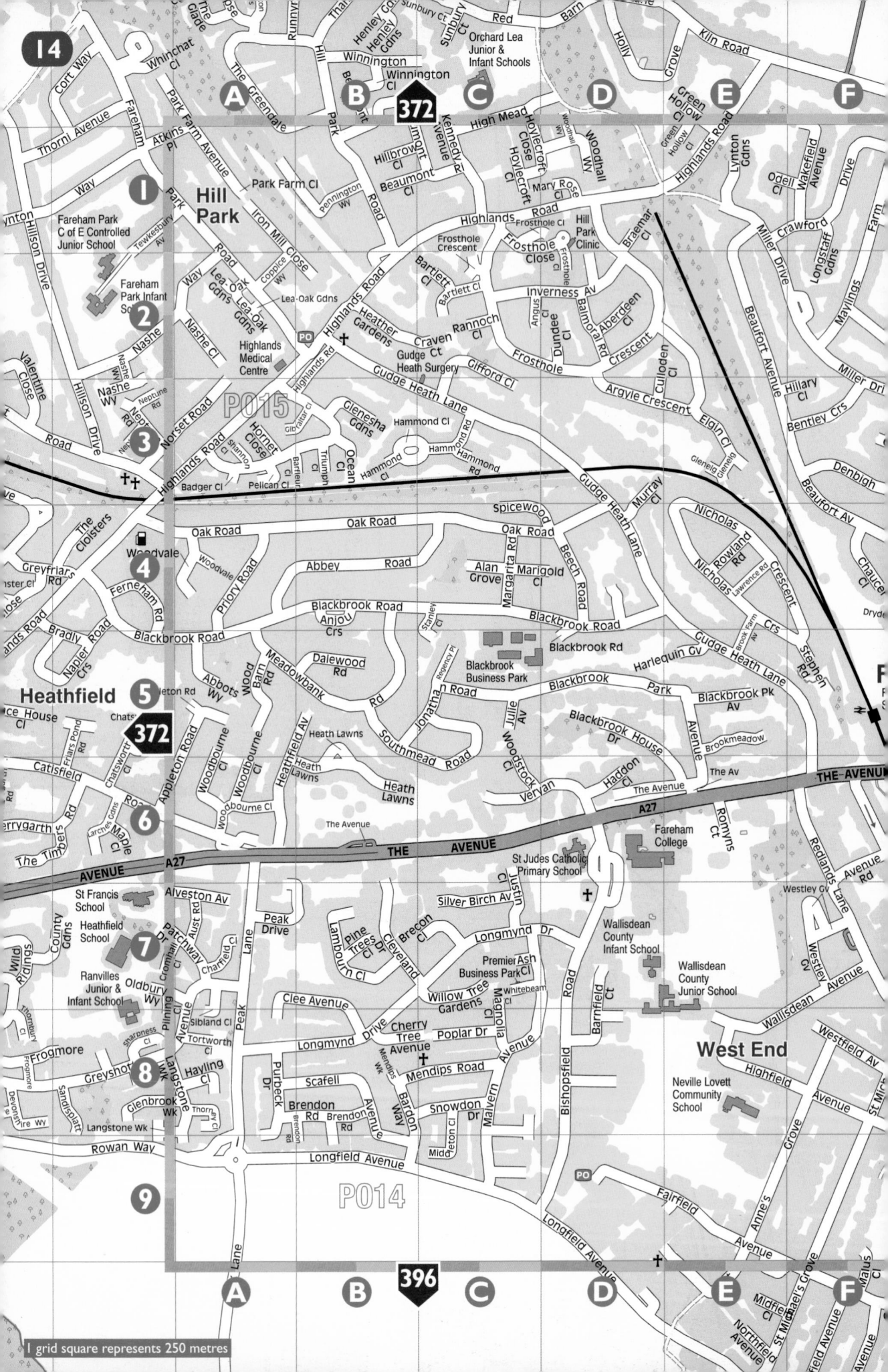

Hill Park
Heathfield
West End
PO15
PO14
372
396
A B C D E F
1 2 3 4 5 6 7 8 9
Fareham Park C of E Controlled Junior School
Fareham Park Infant School
Orchard Lea Junior & Infant Schools
Highlands Medical Centre
Gudge Heath Surgery
Hill Park Clinic
Blackbrook Business Park
St Judes Catholic Primary School
Fareham College
Wallisdean County Infant School
Wallisdean County Junior School
Neville Lovett Community School
St Francis School
Heathfield School
Ranvilles Junior & Infant School
Premier Business Park
Heath Lawns
Whinchat Cl
Cort Way
Thorni Avenue
Fareham Park Road
Park Farm Avenue
Park Farm Cl
Atkins Pl
The Greendale
The Glade
Runnymede
Winnington
Winnington Cl
Henley Gdns
Sunbury Ct
Kennedy Avenue
High Mead
Hoylecroft Close
Woodhall Wy
Kiln Road
Holly Grove
Green Hollow Cl
Highlands Road
Lynton Gdns
Wakefield Avenue
Odell Cl
Miller Drive
Crawford
Longstaff Gdns
Maylings Farm
Hillbrow Cl
Beaumont Cl
Beaumont Ri
Pennington Wy
Mary Rose Cl
Braemar Cl
Iron Mill Close
Coppice Wy
Lea-Oak Gdns
Tewkesbury Av
Frostholle Cl
Frostholle Crescent
Frostholle Close
Bartlett Cl
Inverness Av
Angus Cl
Dundee Cl
Balmoral Rd
Aberdeen Cl
Culloden Cl
Argyle Crescent
Elgin Cl
Gleneig
Rannoch Cl
Heather Gardens
Craven Ct
Gifford Cl
Gudge Heath Lane
Hillson Drive
Valentine Close
Nashe Way
Nashe Cl
Neptune Rd
Norset Road
Glenesha Gdns
Hammond Cl
Hammond Rd
Gibraltar Cl
Hornet Close
Shannon Cl
Ocean Cl
Triumph Cl
Badger Cl
Pelican Cl
Beaufort Avenue
Beaufort Av
Hillary Cl
Bentley Crs
Denbigh
Chaucer Cl
The Cloisters
Greyfriars Rd
Oak Road
Spicewood
Murray Cl
Nicholas Crescent
Rowland Rd
Lawrence Rd
Woodvale
Abbey Road
Priory Road
Alan Grove
Margarita Rd
Marigold Cl
Beech Road
Ferneham Rd
Blackbrook Road
Blackbrook Rd
Anjou Crs
Stanley Cl
Bradly Road
Napier Crs
Meadowbank
Dalewood Rd
Regency Pl
Jonathan Road
Blackbrook Park Avenue
Blackbrook Pk Av
Harlequin Gv
Brook Farm Av
Stephen Rd
Abbots Wy
Wood Barn Rd
Heathfield Av
Southmead Road
Julie Av
Woodstock Cl
Blackbrook House Dr
Brookmeadow
Vervan
Haddon Cl
The Avenue
The Av
Romyns Ct
Redlands Lane
Avenue Rd
Westley Gv
Appleton Road
Woodbourne Cl
Catisfield
Chatsworth Cl
Friars Pond Rd
Larches Gdns
Maple Cl
The Timbers
Ferrygarth
A27
THE AVENUE
Alveston Av
Aust Rd
Patchway Dr
Charfield Cl
Cromhall Cl
Oldbury Wy
County Gdns
Wild Ridings
Thornbury Cl
Peak Drive
Peak Lane
Pine Trees Cl
Lambourn Cl
Cleveland Dr
Brecon Cl
Silver Birch Av
Justin Cl
Longmynd Dr
Longmynd Drive
Ash Cl
Whitebeam Cl
Willow Tree Gardens
Magnolia Cl
Clee Avenue
Cherry Tree Avenue
Poplar Dr
Mendips Road
Mendips Wk
Bishopsfield Road
Barnfield Ct
Wallisdean Avenue
Westfield Av
Highfield Avenue
Frogmore
Greyshott
Sharpness Cl
Sibland Cl
Tortworth Cl
Pilning Cl
Langstone Wk
Hayling Cl
Glenbrook Wk
Thornley Cl
Sandisplatt
Devonshire Wy
Purbeck Dr
Scafell Avenue
Brendon Rd
Bardon Way
Snowdon Dr
Malvern Avenue
Middleton Cl
Rowan Way
Longfield Avenue
Fairfield Avenue
Anne's Grove
St Michael's Grove
Midfield Cl
Northfield Avenue
Malus Cl
1 grid square represents 250 metres

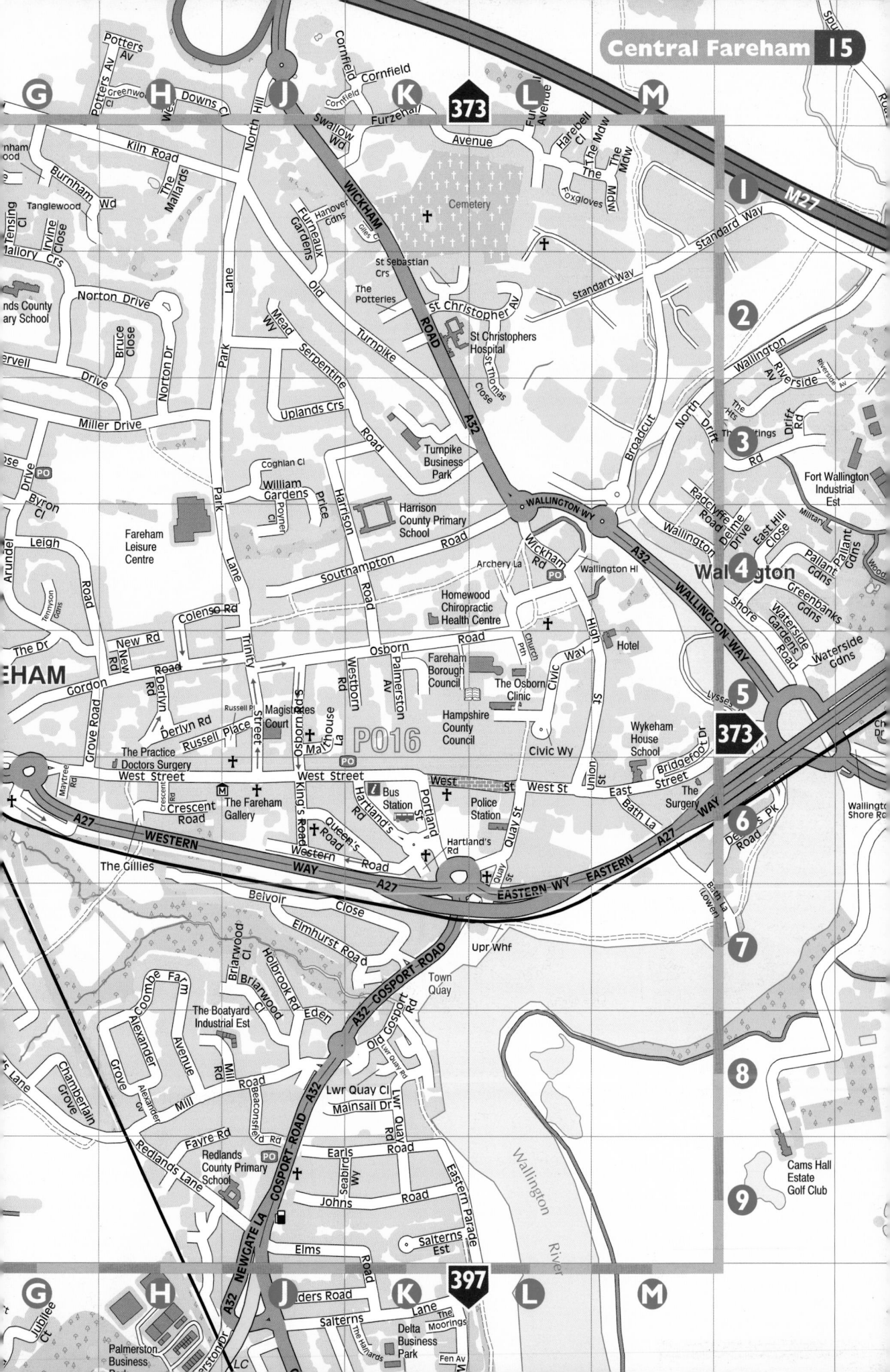
G
H
J
K
373
L
M
Potters Av
Potters Av
Greenwood Cl
Downs Cl
North Hill
Cornfield
Cornfield
Furzehall Avenue
Swallow Wd
Avenue
Harebell Cl
The Mdw
The Mdw
The Mdw
Kiln Road
The Mallards
Burnham Wd
Tanglewood
Tensing Cl
Irvine Close
Mallory Crs
Norton Drive
Bruce Close
Norton Dr
Drive
Miller Drive
Park Lane
Wickham Road
A32
Hanover Gdns
Furneaux Gardens
Gilles Cl
Cemetery
Foxgloves
M27
Standard Way
Standard Way
St Sebastian Crs
The Potteries
St Christopher Av
St Christophers Hospital
St Thomas Close
Old Turnpike
Mead Wy
Serpentine Road
Uplands Crs
Turnpike Business Park
Wallington Av
Riverside Av
Riverside Av
North Drift
Drift Rd
Broadcut
Fort Wallington Industrial Est
Military
Coghlan Cl
William Gardens
Poyner Cl
Price
Harrison Road
Harrison County Primary School
Southampton Road
Wallington Wy
Wickham Rd
Archery La
Wallington Hl
Radclyffe Road
Delme Drive
East Hill Close
Wallington
Pallant Gdns
Pallant Gdns
Greenbanks Gdns
Shore Rd
Waterside Gardens
Waterside Gdns
Fareham Leisure Centre
Byron Cl
Leigh Road
Arundel
Tennyson Gdns
The Dr
PO
Colenso Rd
New Rd
New Rd
Trinity Street
Homewood Chiropractic Health Centre
Osborn Road
Church Pth
High St
Hotel
Civic Way
Fareham Borough Council
The Osborn Clinic
Westborn Rd
Palmerston Av
EHAM
Gordon Road
Derlyn Rd
Derlyn Rd
Russell Pl
Russell Place
Magistrates Court
Osborn Rd
Malthouse La
PO16
Hampshire County Council
Civic Wy
Union St
Wykeham House School
Bridgefoot Dr
Lysses
Grove Road
The Practice Doctors Surgery
Maytree Rd
West Street
West Street
West St
West St
East Street
Bath La
The Surgery
Crescent Rd
Crescent Road
The Fareham Gallery
Bus Station
Portland St
Hartland's Rd
King's Road
Queen's Road
Police Station
Quay St
Hartland's Rd
A27
Western Way
Western Road
Eastern Wy
Eastern Way
The Gillies
Quay St
Belvoir Close
Elmhurst Road
Bath La (Lower)
Upr Whf
Town Quay
A32 Gosport Road
Briarwood Cl
Briarwood Cl
Holbrook Rd
Eden
Coombe Farm Avenue
Alexander Grove
Alexander Gv
The Boatyard Industrial Est
Mill Rd
Mill Road
Old Gosport Rd
Lwr Quay Rd
Lwr Quay Cl
Mainsail Dr
Lwr Quay Rd
Chamberlain Grove
Lane
Fayre Rd
Beaconsfield Rd
Redlands Lane
Redlands County Primary School
Earls Road
Seabird Wy
Johns Road
Eastern Parade
Salterns Est
Wallington River
Elms Road
Newgate La
Gosport Road
Wallington Shore Rd
Dells Pk Road
Cams Hall Estate Golf Club
397
Jubilee Ct
Palmerston Business Park
Palmerston Dr
LC
Alders Road
Salterns Lane
The Moorings
Delta Business Park
The Halliards
Fen Av
1
2
3
4
5
6
7
8
9

16
HAVANT
P09
Bedhampton
Brockhampton
Langstone
377
401
A B C D E F
1 2 3 4 5 6 7 8 9
B2149 BEDHAMPTON ROAD
B2149 NEW ROAD
PARK ROAD NORTH B2149
PARK RD S B2149
B2149 PETERSFIELD ROAD
A27(T)
A3023 LANGSTONE
Havant Station
Bedhampton Station
Havant College
Havant War Memorial Hospital
Havant Sports Club
Havant Leisure Centre
Civic Offices
Magistrates Court
Havant Rugby Football Club
St Thomas Mores RC Primary School
Bidbury Junior & Infant School
Barncroft Infant School
Park Lane Medical Centre
Bosmere Junior School
Havant Business Cen
Solent Way
Wayfarer's Walk
1 grid square represents 250 metres

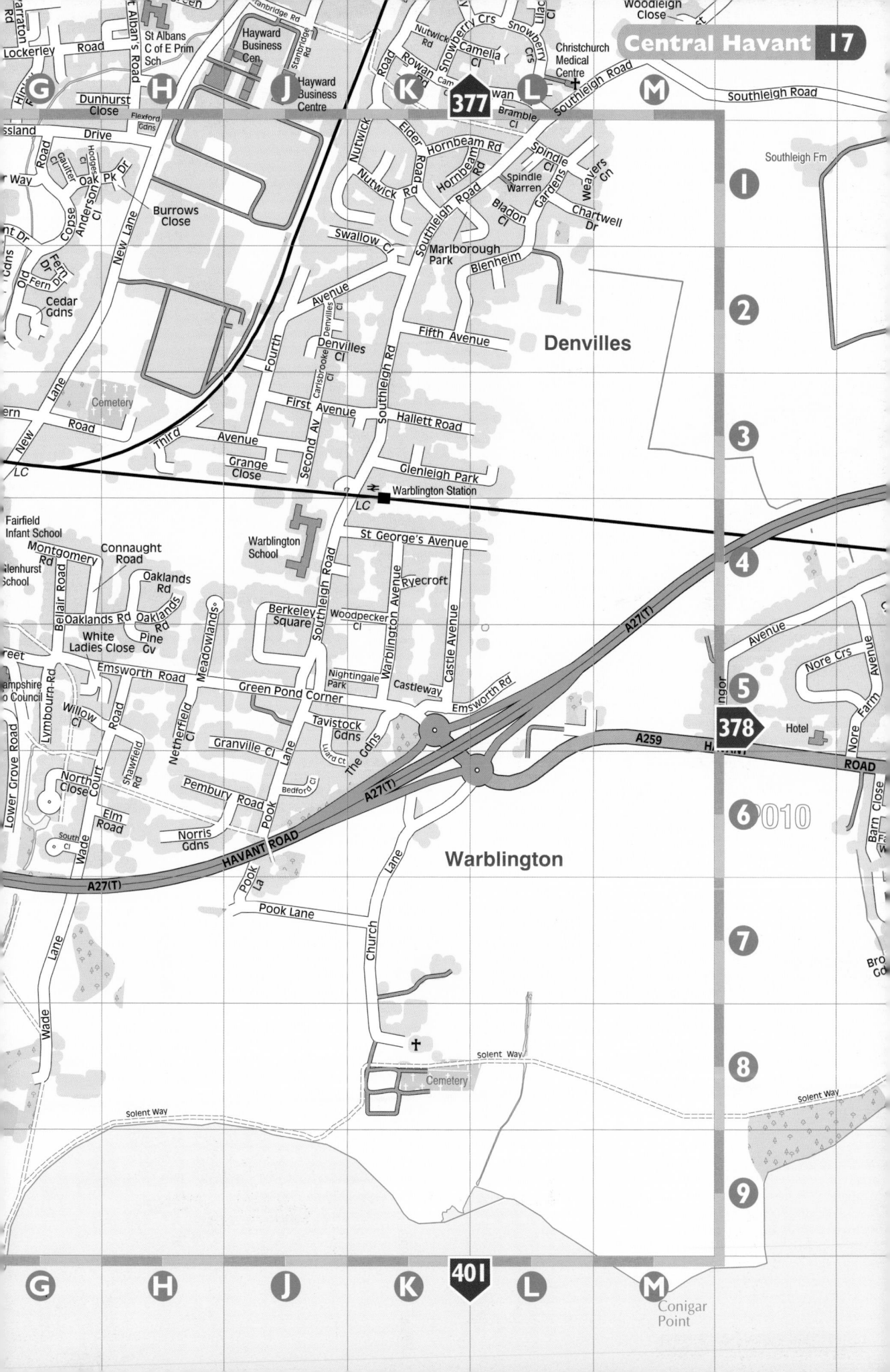

Woodleigh Close

St Albans C of E Prim Sch

Lockerley Road

Hayward Business Cen.

Cranbridge Rd

Stanbridge Rd

Hayward Business Centre

Nutwick Rd

Snowberry Crs

Camelia Cl

Cam...

Snowberry Crs

Lilac Cl

Christchurch Medical Centre

Southleigh Road

G   **H**   **J**   **K**   377   **L**   **M**

Southleigh Road

Dunhurst Close

Flexford Gdns

Drive

Nutwick Rd

Rowan

Elder Road

Nutwick Road

Hornbeam Rd

swan

Bramble Cl

Spindle Gardens

Weavers Gn

Southleigh Fm

I

Hi...

...raton Road

...t Dr

Copse

Oak

Pk

Hodges Cl

Anderson Cl

Fern Dr

Old Fern

Cauter Rd

New Lane

Burrows Close

Swallow C.

Hornbeam Road

Southleigh Road

Spindle Warren

Bladon Cl

Chartwell Dr

2

... Way

Gdns

Cedar Gdns

Cemetery

Lane

New Road

Road

Avenue

Fourth

Denvilles

Carisbrooke

Denvilles Cl

Fifth Avenue

Southleigh Rd

Marlborough Park

Blenheim

Denvilles

2

...ern

Third Avenue

Second Av

First Avenue

Avenue

Grange Close

Hallett Road

Glenleigh Park

3

LC

LC

Warblington Station

3

Fairfield Infant School

Montgomery Rd

Glenhurst School

Connaught Road

Warblington School

St George's Avenue

Ryecroft

A27(T)

Avenue

Nore Crs

Nore Farm Avenue

4

Bellair Road

Oaklands Rd

Oaklands Rd

Pine Gv

White Ladies Close

Berkeley Square

Southleigh Road

Woodpecker Cl

Warblington Avenue

Castle Avenue

Castleway

Emsworth Rd

...ngor

Hotel

5

378

...ampshire ...o Council

Lymbourn Rd

Willow Cl

Road

Meadowlands

Emsworth Road

Green Pond Corner

Nightingale Park

A259

HAVANT

ROAD

5

Lower Grove Road

Court

Shaws Rd

Bellfield

Netherfield

Granville Cl

Tavistock Gdns

The Gdns

Luard Ct

Bedford Cl

Emsworth Rd

A27(T)

010

Barn Close

6

North Close

Elm Road

Wade Rd

South Cl

Pembury Road

Norris Gdns

Pook La

A27(T)

HAVANT ROAD

Pook La

Warblington

Bro...

7

Wade Lane

Pook Lane

Church Lane

Solent Way

7

Cemetery

Solent Way

Solent Way

8

Solent Way

9

G   **H**   **J**   **K**   401   **L**   **M**

Conigar Point

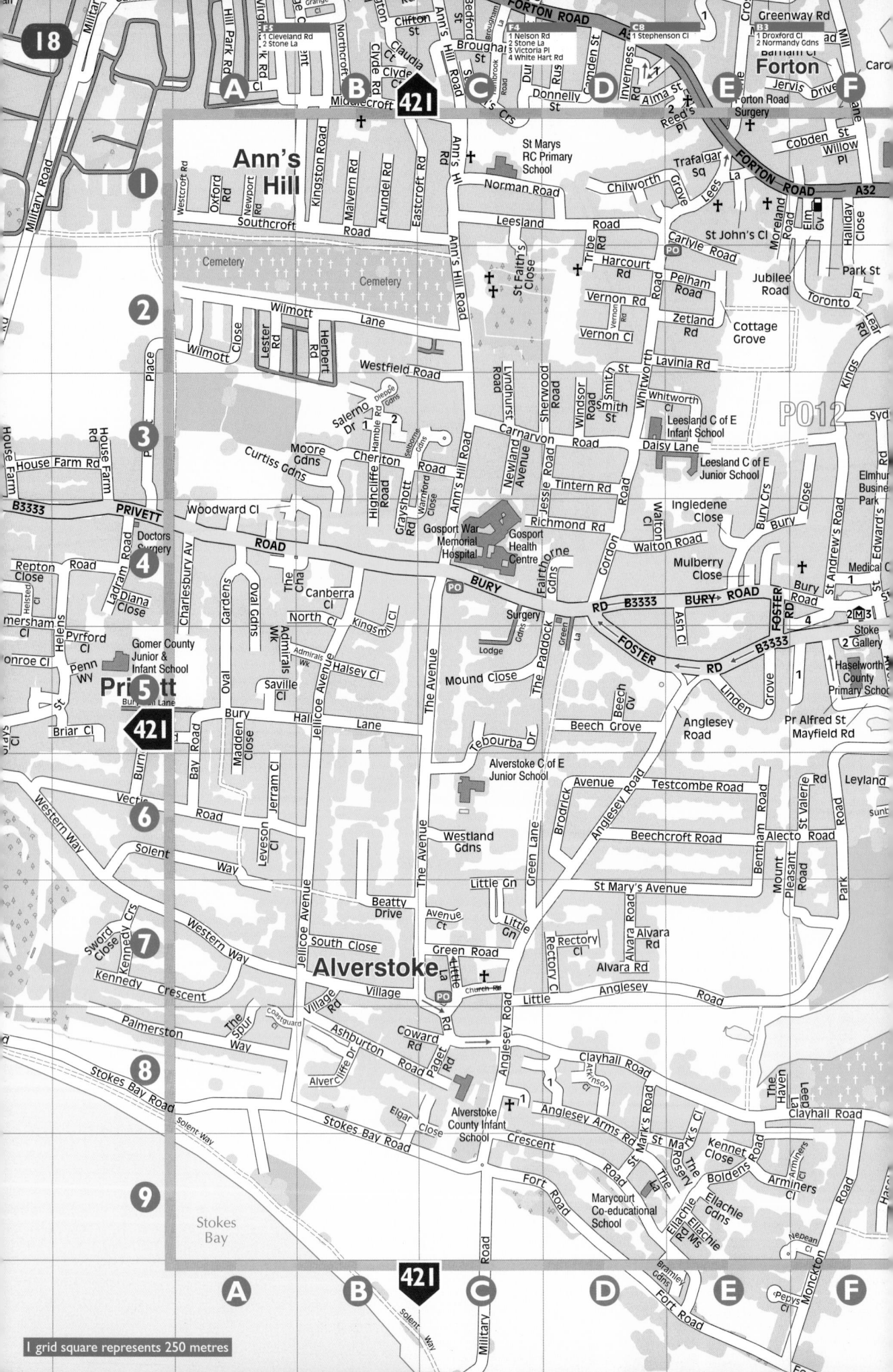
18
Ann's Hill
Forton
Privett
Alverstoke
Stokes Bay
PO12
421
FORTON ROAD
A32
PRIVETT ROAD
BURY ROAD
FOSTER RD
B3333
F5 1 Cleveland Rd 2 Stone La
F4 1 Nelson Rd 2 Stone La 3 Victoria Pl 4 White Hart Rd
C8 1 Stephenson Cl
B3 1 Droxford Cl 2 Normandy Gdns
St Marys RC Primary School
Cemetery
Leesland C of E Infant School
Leesland C of E Junior School
Gosport War Memorial Hospital
Gosport Health Centre
Doctors Surgery
Gomer County Junior & Infant School
Alverstoke C of E Junior School
Alverstoke County Infant School
Marycourt Co-educational School
Haselworth County Primary School
Stoke Gallery
Forton Road Surgery
Elmhurst Business Park
Medical Ctr
Surgery
Lodge
1 grid square represents 250 metres

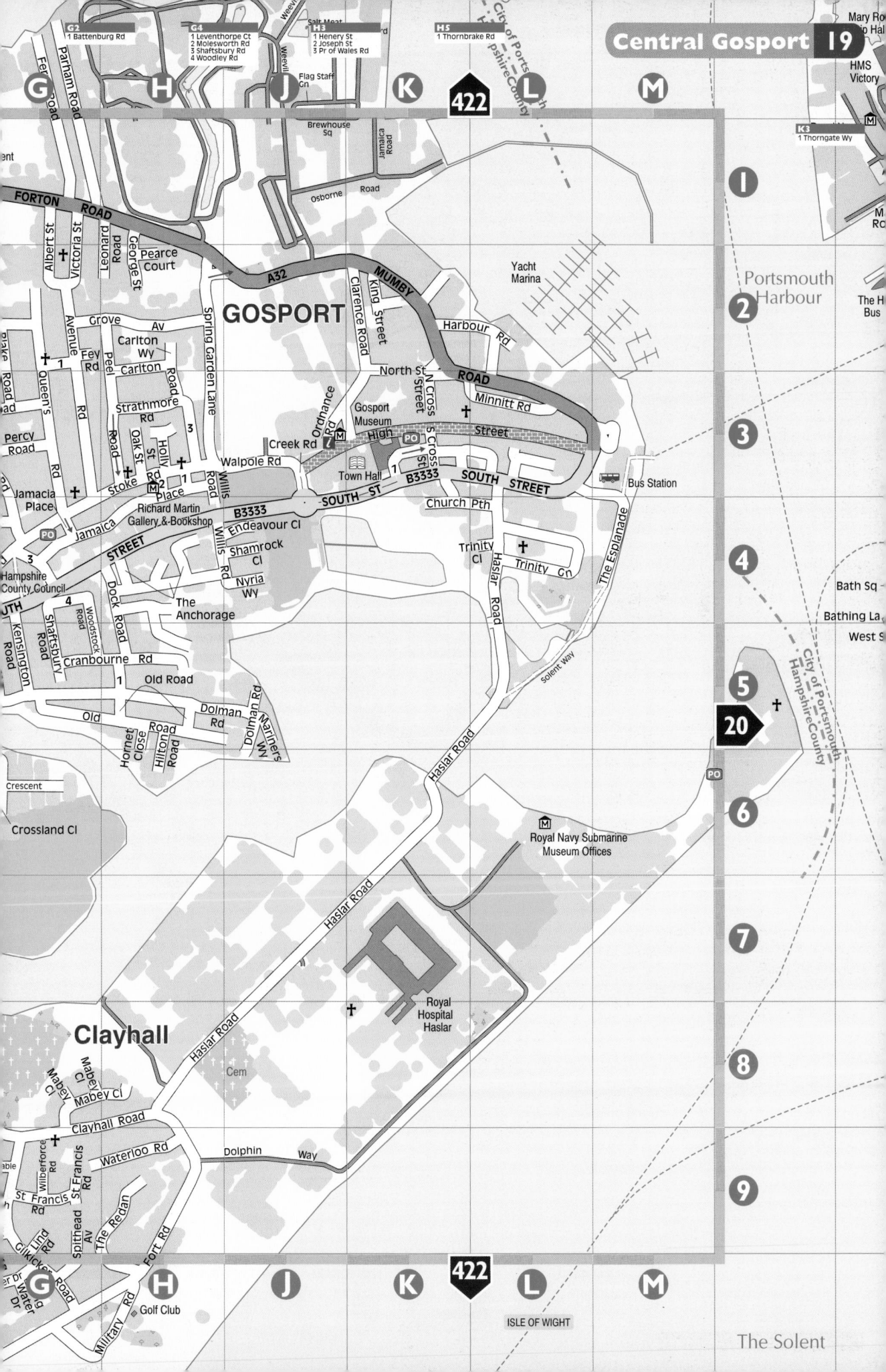
G2
1 Battenburg Rd
G4
1 Leventhorpe Ct
2 Molesworth Rd
3 Shaftsbury Rd
4 Woodley Rd
H3
1 Henery St
2 Joseph St
3 Pr of Wales Rd
H5
1 Thornbrake Rd
K3
1 Thorngate Wy
422
20
GOSPORT
Clayhall
Forton Road
A32
Mumby Road
Harbour Rd
Minnitt Rd
High Street
South Street
South St
B3333
Yacht Marina
Portsmouth Harbour
Bus Station
Gosport Museum
Town Hall
Richard Martin Gallery & Bookshop
Hampshire County Council
The Esplanade
Haslar Road
Royal Navy Submarine Museum Offices
Royal Hospital Haslar
Cem
Dolphin Way
Clayhall Road
Golf Club
Isle of Wight
The Solent
HMS Victory
City of Portsmouth
Hampshire County
Bath Sq
Bathing La
Solent Way
Crossland Cl
The Anchorage
Old Road
Cranbourne Rd
Dolman Rd
Mariners Wy
Hornet Close
Hilton Road
Walpole Rd
Creek Rd
Spring Garden Lane
Clarence Road
King Street
North St
N Cross Street
Church Pth
Trinity Cl
Trinity Grn
Osborne Road
Brewhouse Sq
Jamaica Road
Pearce Court
Grove Av
Carlton Wy
Carlton Road
Strathmore Rd
Percy Road
Jamaica Place
Endeavour Cl
Shamrock Cl
Nyria Wy
Dock Road
Woodstock Road
Shaftsbury Road
Kensington Road
Mabey Cl
Waterloo Rd
St Francis Rd
Wilberforce Rd
Spithead Av
The Redan
Fort Rd
Military Rd
Gilkicker Road
Lind Rd
Albert St
Victoria St
Leonard Road
George St
Avenue
Queen's Road
Fey Rd
Peel Rd
Oak St
Holly St
Stoke Rd
Willis Road
Flag Staff Gn
Ordnance Rd

20
C5
1 French St
2 Lombard St
3 Oyster Ms
C2
1 Beneficial St
2 College La
3 Havant St
4 Rosemary La
5 Ship Leopard St
6 Victory Rd
C1
1 Benbow Pl
2 South Ter
B5
1 Seager's Ct
D1
1 Aylward St
D2
1 Dean St
2 Margery's Ct
3 St Georges Sq
4 Solent Wy
5 Sun St
D4
1 Beehive Wk
2 Nobbs La
D5
1 Halfpenny La
2 Wyndham Ms
D6
1 Pembroke Cl
E1
1 St James's St
E2
1 Purbeck St
E5
1 Poynings Pl
F2
1 Exchange Rd
2 Spring Gdns
F3
1 Kg Richard 1 Rd
2 Lord Monty Wy
3 Meriden Rd
4 St Vincent St
5 Waltham St
F4
1 Landport St
2 Landsdowne St
3 St Paul's Sq
F5
1 Chapel St
2 Diamond St
3 Elm St
4 Gold St
5 Jubilee Ter
cont.
F5 cont.
6 Lt Hambrook St
7 Lt Southsea St
8 Meadow St
9 Nickel St
10 Slingsby Cl
11 South St
F6
1 Cecil Pl
2 Regent Pl
422
19
A
B
C
D
E
F
1
2
3
4
5
6
7
8
9
Mary Rose Hall
Main Road
King's Rd
Sampson Rd
Jago Rd
Stony Lane
Circular Rd
Cumberland St
William St
HMS Victory
HMS Nelson
PO1
Royal Naval Museum
Dockyard Apprentice Exhibition
College Road
Prince George St
Cross St
North Street
Treadgold Museum
Portsea
Queen Street
Edinburgh
Alfred Rd
Anglesea Road A3
Beck St
Doctors Surgery
Lion St
Victoria
Main Road
Mary Rose Exhibition
Wickham Street
Hawke St
Hanover St
Union St
Curzon Howe Road
Bishop St
Aylward St
University of Portsmouth
Old Star
Clock St
Primary School
Hay St
Portland St
Kent Street
Three Tun Cl
St George's Wy
Richmond Place
University of Portsmouth
Kg Henry
Portsmouth Harbour
HMS Warrior
The Hard
B2154
Station Ap
College St
Butcher St
The Hard Interchange Bus & Coach Station
Portsmouth Harbour Station
Ordnance Rw
Britain St
Park Road
St Georges Business Centre
Burnaby Road
United Services Rugby Club
New Theatre
Whitesward
St Michael's Rd
A3
University of Portsmouth
Park Rd
United Services Cricket Ground
St George's Rd
Old Portsmouth
Kin Hon Clinic
Bus Station
The Esplanade
Solent Way
Gunwharf Road
St George's Rd
B2154
HMS Temeraire
Cambridge Rd
A3
Hampshire Terrace
A288
Wiltshire St
Isle of Wight Car Ferry Terminal
Armory La
Grays Ct
University of Portsmouth
Warblington St
King Charles St
Highbury St
The Pascoe Practice
Portsmouth Natural Health
University Practice
Landport Ter
Bath Sq
Bathing La
West St
East Street
Tower St
Broad Street
A3
Captains Rw
Camber Place
White Hart Road
Oyster St
Thomas's St
Street
Portsmouth Grammar School
Museum Road
Portsmouth City Council
City Museum & Art Gallery
City Museum
Chadderton Gdns
B2154 King's Rd
King's Ter
A288
Goldfield Gallery
Peacock La
St Nicholas St
Cathedral Church of St Thomas of Canterbury
High St
St Judes C of E Primary School
Woodville Dr
Blount Rd
Steel St
Silver St
Flint St
Copper St
Hambrook St
University of Portsmouth
Cecil Gv
City of Portsmouth
Hampshire County
Round Tower
Town Walls
Square Tower
Grand Pde
Penny Street
Battery Row
Pembroke Road
Chatham Dr
Hotel
Pembroke Rd
Bellevue Ter
Southsea Terrace
Solent Way
The Long Curtain (Old Town Defences)
Gordon Road
Royal Navy Submarine Museum Offices
Long Curtain Road
A288 Pier Road
Duisburg Way
Western Pde
Clarence Pde
Clarence Pier & Amusement Centre
Clarence Esplanade
Hovercraft Terminal
Clarence Esplanade
Solent Way
Southsea Common
1 grid square represents 250 metres
Solent
GUERNSEY; JERSEY

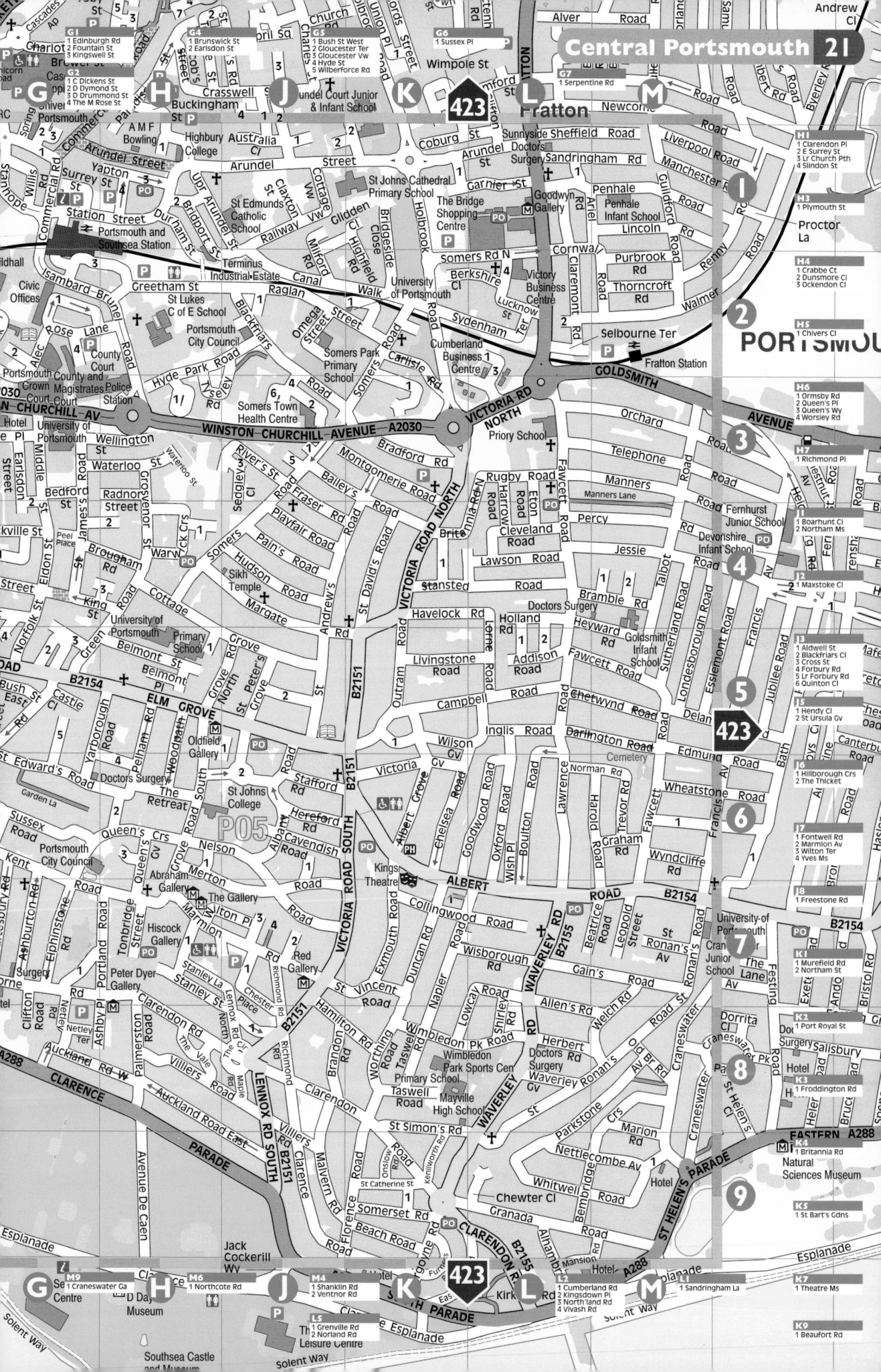
G1
1 Edinburgh Rd
2 Fountain St
3 Kingswell St
G2
1 C Dickens St
2 D Dymond St
3 D Drummond St
4 The M Rose St
G4
1 Brunswick St
2 Earlsdon St
G5
1 Bush St West
2 Gloucester Ter
3 Gloucester Vw
4 Hyde St
5 Wilberforce Rd
G6
1 Sussex Pl
G7
1 Serpentine Rd
H1
1 Clarendon Pl
2 E Surrey St
3 Lr Church Pth
4 Slindon St
H3
1 Plymouth St
H4
1 Crabbe Ct
2 Dunsmore Cl
3 Ockendon Cl
H5
1 Chivers Cl
H6
1 Ormsby Rd
2 Queen's Pl
3 Queen's Wy
4 Worsley Rd
H7
1 Richmond Pl
I1
1 Boarhunt Cl
2 Northam Ms
J2
1 Maxstoke Cl
J3
1 Aldwell St
2 Blackfriars Cl
3 Cross St
4 Forbury Rd
5 Lr Forbury Rd
6 Quinton Cl
J5
1 Hendy Cl
2 St Ursula Gv
J6
1 Hillborough Crs
2 The Thicket
J7
1 Fontwell Rd
2 Marmion Av
3 Wilton Ter
4 Yves Ms
J8
1 Freestone Rd
K1
1 Murefield Rd
2 Northam St
K2
1 Port Royal St
K3
1 Froddington Rd
K4
1 Britannia Rd
K5
1 St Bart's Gdns
K7
1 Theatre Ms
K9
1 Beaufort Rd
M9
1 Craneswater Ga
M6
1 Northcote Rd
M4
1 Shanklin Rd
2 Ventnor Rd
L5
1 Grenville Rd
2 Norland Rd
L2
1 Cumberland Rd
2 Kingsdown Pl
3 North'land Rd
4 Vivash Rd
L1
1 Sandringham La
G
H
J
K
L
M
1
2
3
4
5
6
7
8
9
423
Fratton
PORTSMOU
Portsmouth and Southsea Station
Fratton Station
Winston Churchill Avenue A2030
Goldsmith Avenue
Victoria Road North
Victoria Road South
Elm Grove
B2154
B2151
B2155
A288
Albert Road
Waverley Rd
Lennox Rd South
Clarence Parade
Eastern Parade
St Helen's Parade
Clarendon Rd
South Parade
Esplanade
Solent Way
PO5
St Johns Cathedral Primary School
St Edmunds Catholic School
The Bridge Shopping Centre
Goodwyn Gallery
Penhale Infant School
Victory Business Centre
Terminus Industrial Estate
University of Portsmouth
St Lukes C of E School
Portsmouth City Council
Somers Park Primary School
Cumberland Business Centre
Somers Town Health Centre
Priory School
Portsmouth Crown Court
County and Magistrates Court
Police Station
Civic Offices
Fernhurst Junior School
Devonshire Infant School
Goldsmith Infant School
Sikh Temple
Doctors Surgery
Oldfield Gallery
St Johns College
Kings Theatre
Abraham Gallery
The Gallery
Hiscock Gallery
Peter Dyer Gallery
Red Gallery
Wimbledon Park Sports Cen
Primary School
Mayville High School
Cemetery
Natural Sciences Museum
D Day Museum
Southsea Castle and Museum
The Leisure Centre
Hotel
Highbury College
Bowling
Craneswater Junior School
Chewter Cl
Jack Cockerill Wy
Avenue De Caen

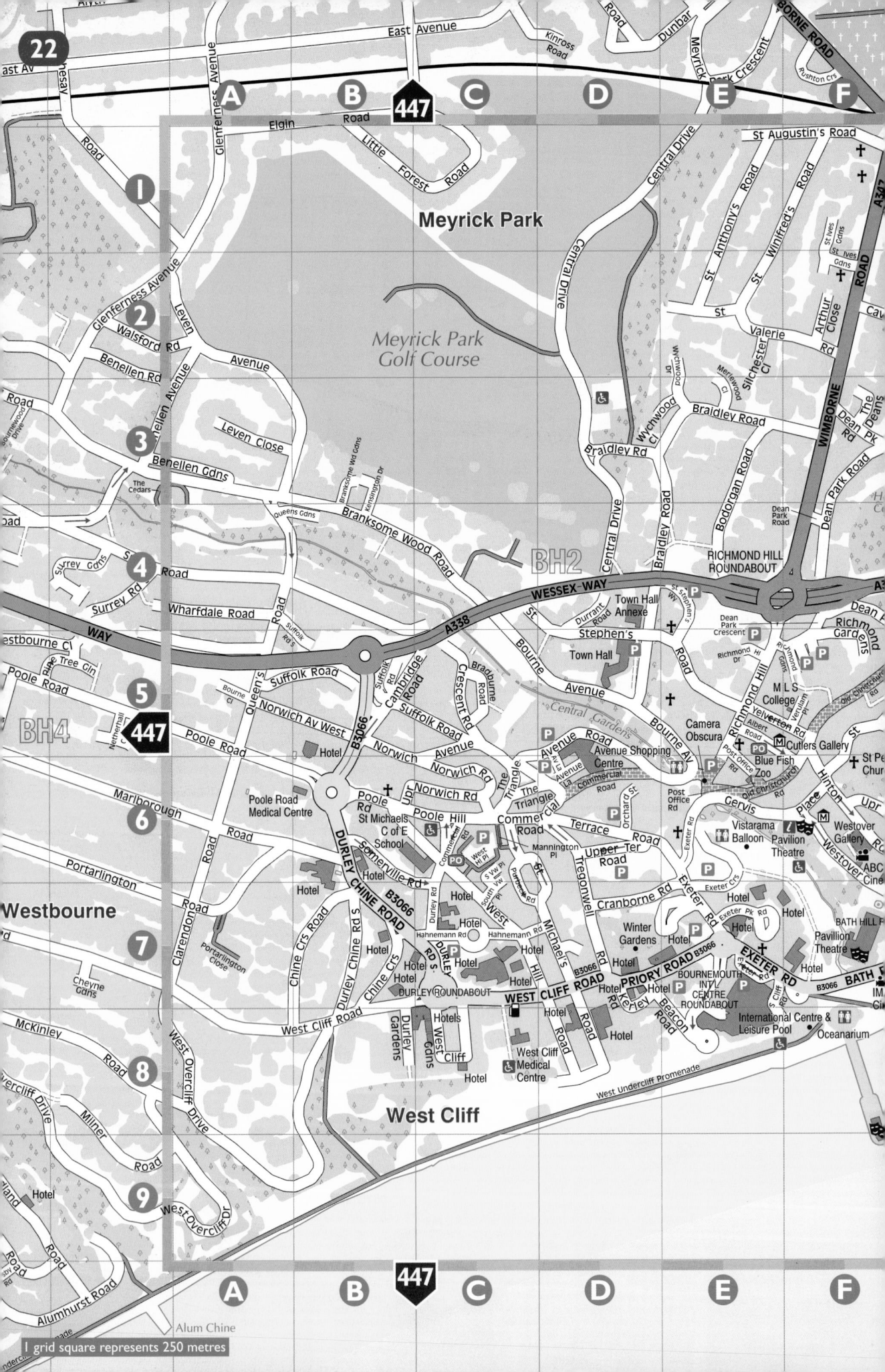
22
447
Meyrick Park
Meyrick Park Golf Course
BH2
BH4
WESSEX WAY
A338
B3066
RICHMOND HILL ROUNDABOUT
DURLEY ROUNDABOUT
BOURNEMOUTH INT'L CENTRE ROUNDABOUT
Westbourne
West Cliff
Central Gardens
Town Hall
Town Hall Annexe
Avenue Shopping Centre
Camera Obscura
M L S College
Cutlers Gallery
Blue Fish Zoo
Vistarama Balloon
Pavilion Theatre
Westover Gallery
Winter Gardens
International Centre & Leisure Pool
Oceanarium
West Cliff Medical Centre
Poole Road Medical Centre
St Michaels C of E School
West Undercliff Promenade
Alum Chine
1 grid square represents 250 metres

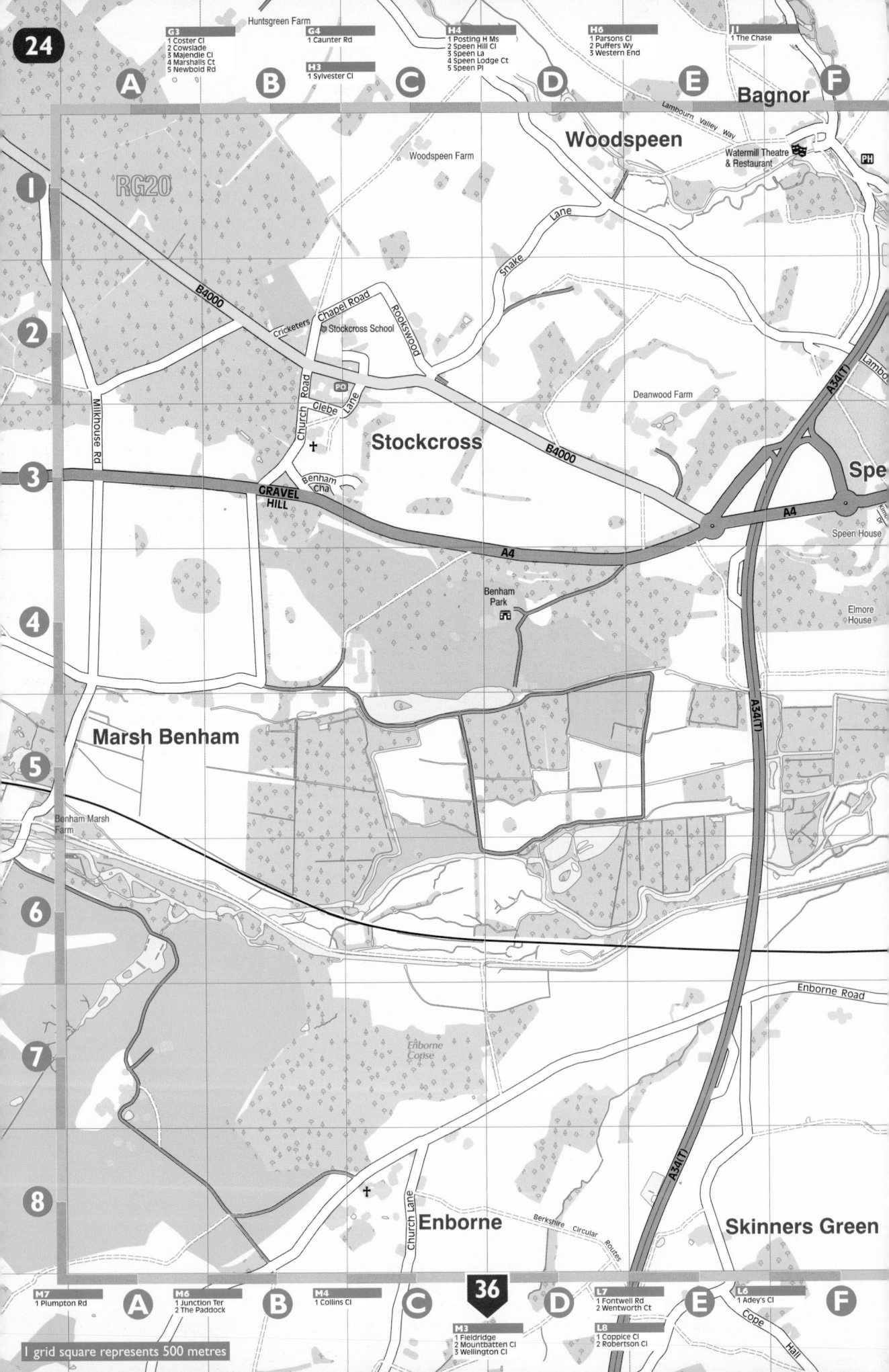
Huntsgreen Farm
G3
1 Coster Cl
2 Cowslade
3 Majendie Cl
4 Marshalls Ct
5 Newbold Rd
G4
1 Caunter Rd
H3
1 Sylvester Cl
H4
1 Posting H Ms
2 Speen Hill Cl
3 Speen La
4 Speen Lodge Ct
5 Speen Pl
H6
1 Parsons Cl
2 Puffers Wy
3 Western End
J1
1 The Chase
A
B
C
D
E
F
Bagnor
Lambourn Valley Way
Woodspeen
Watermill Theatre & Restaurant
PH
Woodspeen Farm
RG20
Snake Lane
B4000
Cricketers
Chapel Road
Rookswood
Stockcross School
Church Road
Glebe
Lane
PO
Milkhouse Rd
Stockcross
Deanwood Farm
A34(T)
Lambo
Spe
GRAVEL HILL
Benham Cha
A4
Speen House
Benham Park
Elmore House
Marsh Benham
Benham Marsh Farm
Enborne Road
Enborne Copse
Church Lane
Enborne
Berkshire Circular Routes
Skinners Green
1
2
3
4
5
6
7
8
M7
1 Plumpton Rd
M6
1 Junction Ter
2 The Paddock
M4
1 Collins Cl
36
M3
1 Fieldridge
2 Mountbatten Cl
3 Wellington Cl
L7
1 Fontwell Rd
2 Wentworth Ct
L8
1 Coppice Cl
2 Robertson Cl
L6
1 Adey's Cl
Cope Hall
1 grid square represents 500 metres

J3
1 Charmwood Cl
J4
1 Herewood Cl
2 Jesmond Dene
3 Linden Cl
4 Old Bath Rd
J5
1 Cansfield End
2 Crawford Pl
3 Saffron Cl
J6
1 Oddfellows Rd
J7
1 Derby Rd
2 Malvern Ct
3 Old Newtown Rd
Donnington Castle
Donnington Holt
Hotel
Red Farm
Brickkiln Wood
Shaw Farm
Castle School
Shaw-cum-Donnington School
The Priory
Donnington
Battlesite 1644
RG14
Trinity School
Shaw
Winchcombe CP Infant School
Newbury College
Speenhamland CP School
Primary School
Newbury Business Park
West Berkshire District Council
Victoria Park
Berkshire Co Council
AFC Newbury Football Ground
Riverpark Industrial Estate
Retail Park
Newbury Town Council
Newbury District Museum & Tourist Information Centre
NEWBURY
Police Stn
Raceview Business Cen
West Fields
Kennet Shopping Centre
West Berkshire District Council
Sterling Industrial Est
Newbury Racecourse Station
Newbury Station
Greenham Road Retail Park
East Fields
Enborne House
St Nicholas C of E Sch
Newbury District Council
St Bartholomew's (Joint) School
Newbury District Hosp
Stroud Green
Berkshire Co Council
St Bartholomew's School
Berkshire County Council
St Johns School
John Rankin Junior School
John Rankin County Infants School
Sandleford Hospital
Greenham
Greenham Lodge
WESTERN AVENUE
BATH ROAD
LONDON ROAD
OXFORD ROAD
SHAW HILL
SHAW ROAD
GREENHAM RD
ST JOHN'S RD
KINGS ROAD
MILL LANE
HAMBRIDGE R
A339(T)
B4494
B4009
A4
A34
26
37
L5
1 Connaught Rd
2 Denmark Rd
L3
1 Coachman's Ct
2 Glebefields
3 Sherrardmead
L4
1 L Southern Ct
2 Newport Cl
3 Newport Rd
K6
1 Carnegie Rd
2 Mayors La
3 St Donats Pl
4 Winchcombe Rd
K5
1 Bear La
K3
1 Dolman Rd
K4
1 Clarendon Gdns
J8
1 Culver Rd
2 The Glade
G H J K L M
1 2 3 4 5 6 7 8

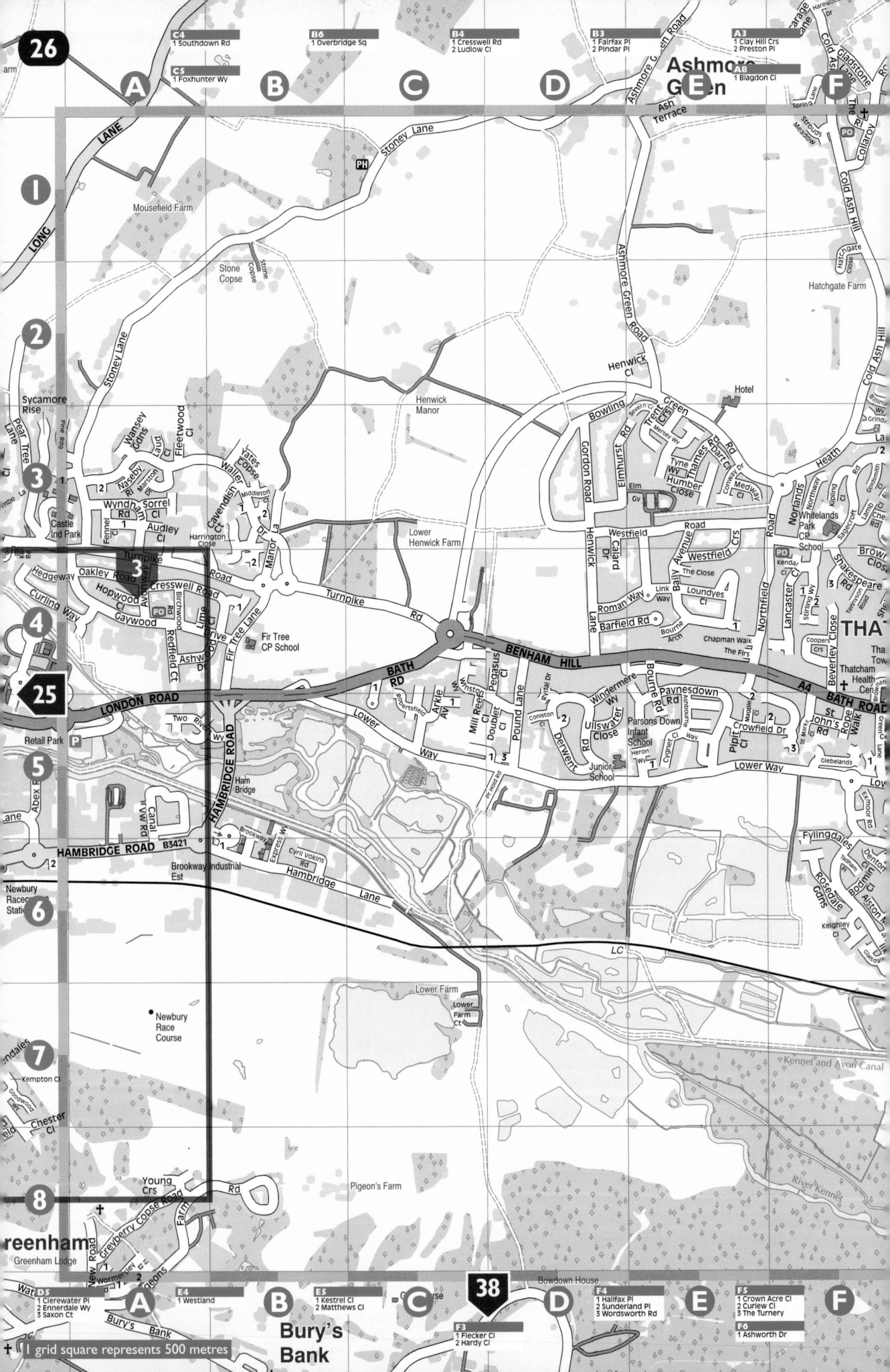
C4
1 Southdown Rd
C5
1 Foxhunter Wy
B6
1 Overbridge Sq
B4
1 Cresswell Rd
2 Ludlow Cl
B3
1 Fairfax Pl
2 Pindar Pl
A3
1 Clay Hill Crs
2 Preston Pl
A8
1 Blagdon Cl
Ashmore Green
Ashmore Green Road
Ash Terrace
Stoney Lane
PH
LONG LANE
Mousefield Farm
Stone Copse
Hatchgate Farm
Cold Ash Hill
Henwick Cl
Hotel
Henwick Manor
Sycamore Rise
Pear Tree Lane
Wansey Gdns
Fleetwood Cl
Yates Copse
Waller Dr
Naseby Rl
Marston Dr
Wyndham Rd
Sorrel Cl
Audley Cl
Cavendish Ct
Middleton Cl
Manor La
Castle Ind Park
Fennel Cl
Harrington Close
Turnpike Road
Lower Henwick Farm
Bowling Green Rd
Gordon Road
Elmhurst Rd
Trent Crs
Thames Rd
Dart Cl
Tyne Wy
Humber Close
Conway Dr
Medway Cl
Elm Gv
Westfield Road
Henwick Lane
Calard Dr
Bally Avenue
Westfield Crs
The Close
Roman Way
Link Way
Loundyes Cl
Barfield Rd
Bourne Arch
Chapman Walk
The Firs
Northfield Road
Norlands
Whitelands Park CP School
Lancaster Cl
Shakespeare Rd
Beverley Close
THA
Thatcham Health Cen
Hedgeway
Oakley Road
Avonway
Cresswell Road
Hopwood Cl
Curling Way
Gaywood
PO
Lime Cl
Drive
Redfield Ct
Ashwood Dr
Fir Tree Lane
Fir Tree CP School
Turnpike Rd
BENHAM HILL
BATH RD
LONDON ROAD
25
Retail Park
P
Two Rivers Wy
HAMBRIDGE ROAD
Robertsfield
Arkle Av
Winston Wy
Pegasus Cl
Mill Reef Cl
Doublet Cl
Pound Lane
Rydal Dr
Coniston Ct
Windermere Wy
Bourne Rd
Paynesdown Rd
Ullswater Close
Derwent Rd
Parsons Down Infant School
Junior School
Cygnet Cl
Heron Wy
Crowfield Dr
Pipit Cl
St John's Rd
Rope Walk
A4 BATH ROAD
Lower Way
Glebelands
Ham Bridge
Canal View Rd
HAMBRIDGE ROAD B3421
Brookway Industrial Est
Express Wy
Cyril Vokins Rd
Hambridge Lane
Abex Rd
Newbury Racecourse Station
Fylingdales
Rosedale Gdns
Keighley Cl
LC
Lower Farm
Lower Farm Ct
Newbury Race Course
Kennet and Avon Canal
River Kennet
Kempton Cl
Goodwood Wy
Chester Cl
Young Crs
Greyberry Copse Road
Farm
Pigeon's Farm
Greenham
Greenham Lodge
New Road
Wormersley
Bowdown House
38
D5
1 Clerewater Pl
2 Ennerdale Wy
3 Saxon Ct
E4
1 Westland
E5
1 Kestrel Cl
2 Matthews Cl
F3
1 Flecker Cl
2 Hardy Cl
F4
1 Halifax Pl
2 Sunderland Pl
3 Wordsworth Rd
F5
1 Crown Acre Cl
2 Curlew Cl
3 The Turnery
F6
1 Ashworth Dr
Bury's Bank
A B C D E F
1 2 3 4 5 6 7 8
1 grid square represents 500 metres

G4
1 The Waverleys
G5
1 Holywell Ct
G6
1 Cairngorm Rd
2 Danvers Cl
3 Glenmore Cl
4 Porlock Cl
5 Snowdon Cl
6 The Thakerays
7 Wenlock Wy
8 Wolsingham Wy
H5
1 Cochrane Cl
2 Goose Green Wy
H6
1 Sargood Cl
2 Thompson Dr
3 Tomlin Cl
Ridge House School
The Ridge
St Fi School
Broad Lane
Turner's Green
Upper Common
Miles's Green
Burdens Heath
Briff Lane
Roundfield
Little Lane
Upper Bucklebury
Harts Hill Road
Bucklebury C of E Primary School
Woodside Close
Blacklands Road
Long Grove
Park Farm
Lawrences Lane
Harts Hill Farm
Blacklands Copse
Floral Way
Bluebell Wy
Blackthorn Dr
Foxglove Wy
Cowslip Crs
Trefoil Dro
Parkside Rd
Junior School
Park Lane
Mount Road
Dunstan Rd
Marsh Rd
The Haywards
Avenue
Vincent Rd
Henrys
Cemetery
CHAPEL ST
LONDON RD
A4 BATH ROAD
High St
Church Gate
Station Rd
The Moors
Hartmead Rd
Stoney Lane
Kennet Secondary School
Falmouth Way
Cropper Cl
Siege Cross Farm
Colthrop Manor
Colthrop
Enterprise Way
Berkshire Drive
Berkshire Business Cen
Pipers Way
Turners Dr
Peachey Drive
Agricola Way
Longcroft Road
Spurcroft Primary School
Burdwood Surgery
Station Rd
Aylesford Wy
Colthrop Wy
Daytona Drive
Gables Way
Colthrop Lane
Horne Road
Urquhart Road
Buchanan Square
Flag Staff Square
Pipers Industrial Est
Pipers Lane
Thatcham Station
Kennet and Avon Canal
River Kennet
Thatcham Town Football Club
Crookham Manor
Bury's Bank Road
Chamberhouse Farm

28
39

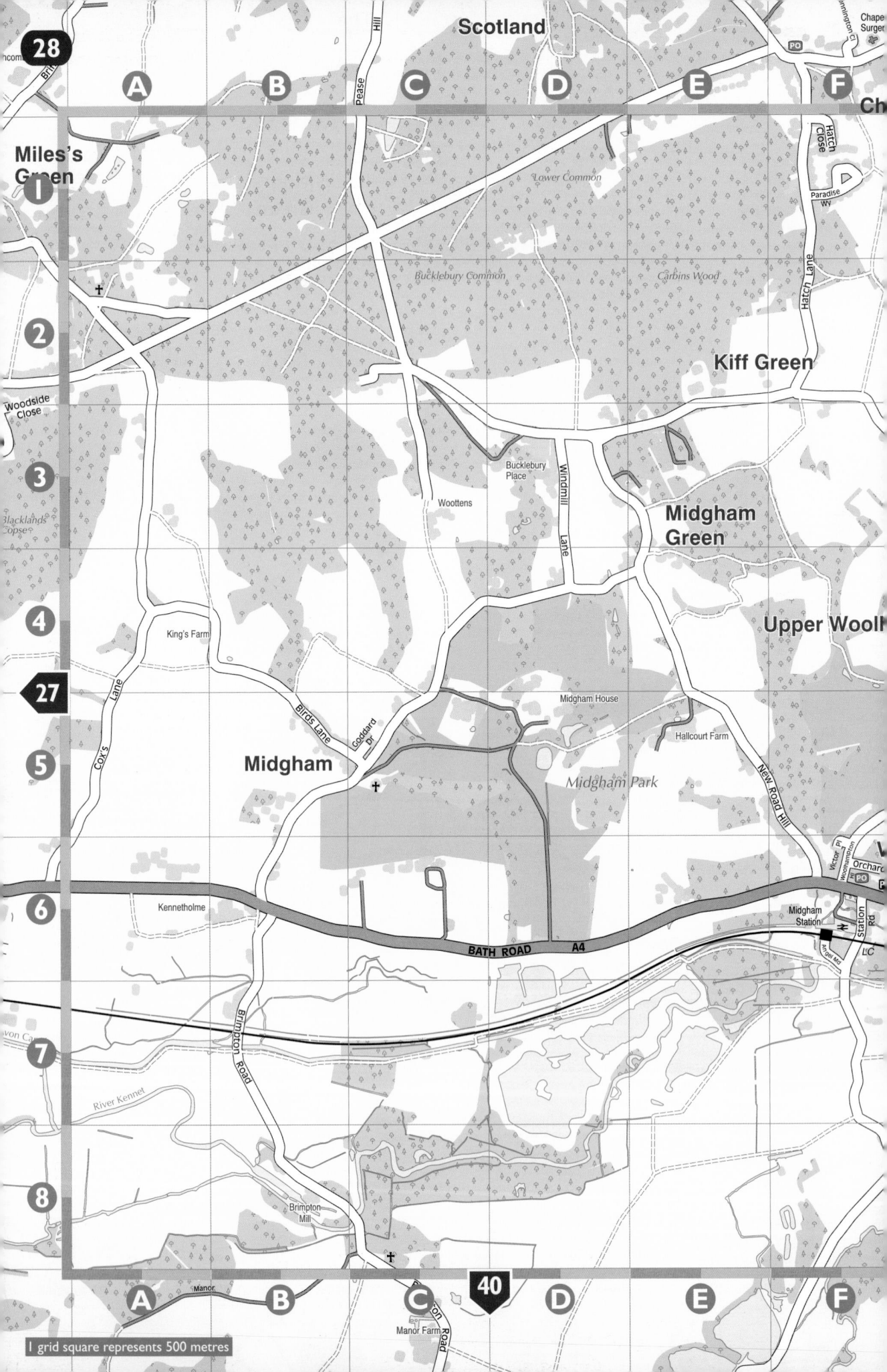

Scotland

28

A   B   C   D   E   F

Miles's
Green

1

Woodside
Close

2

Lower Common

Bucklebury Common

Carbins Wood

Kiff Green

Blacklands
Copse

3

Bucklebury
Place

Woottens

Windmill Lane

**Midgham
Green**

4

King's Farm

Midgham House

Hallcourt Farm

Upper Wooll

27

Cox's Lane

Birds Lane

Goddard Dr

Midgham

Midgham Park

New Road Hill

5

Kennetholme

Victor Pl

Woolhampton

Orchard

PO

Station Rd

6

BATH ROAD   A4

Midgham
Station

Ardell Mdw

LC

Brimpton Road

7

Avon Ca

River Kennet

8

Brimpton
Mill

A   B   C   D   E   F

Manor

40

Manor Farm Road

1 grid square represents 500 metres

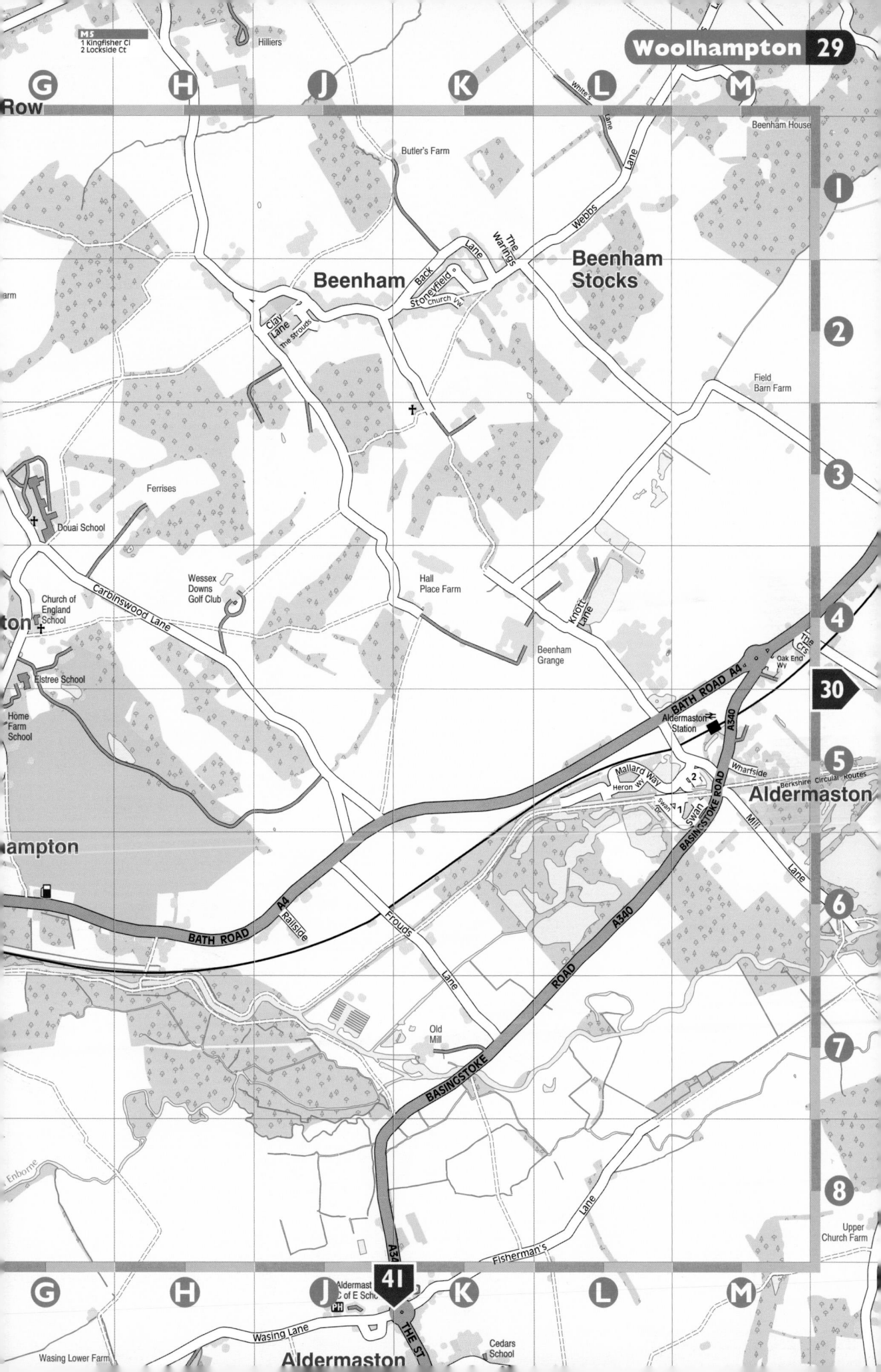

M5
1 Kingfisher Cl
2 Lockside Ct

Hilliers

G   H   J   K   L   M

Row

Butler's Farm

Beenham House

1

The Warings
Back Lane
Stoneyfield
Church Vw

Beenham

Beenham Stocks

2

Clay Lane
The Strouds

Field Barn Farm

3

Douai School

Ferrises

Carbinswood Lane

Church of England School

Wessex Downs Golf Club

Hall Place Farm

Knott Lane

4

The Crs

Oak End Wy

30

Elstree School

Beenham Grange

BATH ROAD A4

Aldermaston Station

A340

Home Farm School

Wharfside

5

Mallard Way
Heron Wy

Berkshire Circular Routes

Aldermaston

2

Swan

1

BASINGSTOKE ROAD

ampton

A4

Railside

Frouds Lane

A340

Mill Lane

6

BATH ROAD

BASINGSTOKE ROAD

A340

Old Mill

7

Enbone

8

Upper Church Farm

G   H   J   K   L   M

Aldermast C of E Sc
PH

41

THE ST

Wasing Lane

Cedars School

Wasing Lower Farm

Aldermaston

A   B   C   D   E   F

I

Beenham House

Lambden's
Farm

Lambdens Hill

2

Field
Barn Farm

BATH   ROAD   A4   Avon Way

LC

Berkshire Circular Routes

Ufton
Bridge

Berkshire Circular Routes

Tyle
Mill

Sulhamstead

Sulhamstead

Kin

3

Bath   Road

LC

Lower Padworth

Berkshire Circular Routes

Hart's   Lane

Ufton Green

Church   Lane

Ufton
Paro
Prim
Scho

4

River Kenner

The
Crs

Oak End
Wv

Berkshire Circular Routes

Middle Farm

29

5

arfside

Berkshire Circular Routes

Aldermaston Wharf

Padworth Lane

Mill   Lane

Berkshire Circular Routes

Green

6

Lodge Farm

7

Berkshire Circular Routes

Padworth
House College

Berkshire Circular Routes

Padworth

The Ark
School

School Road

Old Farm

Silver Lane

8

Upper
Church Farm

The Old
Rectory

A   B   C   D   E   F

Rectory

Hatch

West Berkshire
Hampshire Cour

I grid square represents 500 metres

J5
1 Abbot's Rd
2 Kirkwood Crs
J6
1 Boldrewood
J7
1 Alison Cl
Trash Green
Whitehouse Green
Sulhamstead Bannister Upper End
Sulhamstead Abbots
Burghfield
Burghfield Common
Four Houses Corner
RG7
K5
1 St Mary's Wy
L5
1 Blackbird Cl
2 Granby End
3 Holmdene
4 Robin Cl
5 Sorrel Cl
6 Wheeler Cl
7 Wren Cl
K6
1 Bracken Wy

43

A B C D E F

Stype Grange

Bagshot

Upper Slope End Farm

Prosperous
Home Farm

1

Annett's Lane

The Lilley
Clinic

2

Eastcourt Farm

Polesdon House

Six Acre Lane

3

Bitham Lane

SALISBURY ROAD A338

Cutting Hill

4

Shalbourne
C of E School

Mill Lane

Cemetry

Ham Road

5

Road

Shalbourne

Kingston

Cox's Lane

Manor House

Ham

Church Road

PO

Carvers Hill

Burr Lane

Rivar Road

Little Mead

The Lynch

6

Manor Farm

7

8

Rivar

A B C D E F Wood

1 grid square represents 500 metres

Anvilles

G H J K L M

I

Balsdon Farm

Totterdown House

Little Common

2

Sadlers

Northcroft Farm

Anville's Copse

Folly Road

Inkpen

3

Berkshire Circular Routes

Lower Green

Manor Farm

PH

Bitham Lane

4

Cemetery

†

West Berkshire
Wiltshire County

Lower Spray Farm

34 ▶

Uppe

Spray Road

5

Ham Spray House

6

Combe Gibbet

Test Way

7

Combe Gibbet

8

Town Farm

Downs Lane

G H J **53**▽ K L M

Wright's Farm

Buttermere

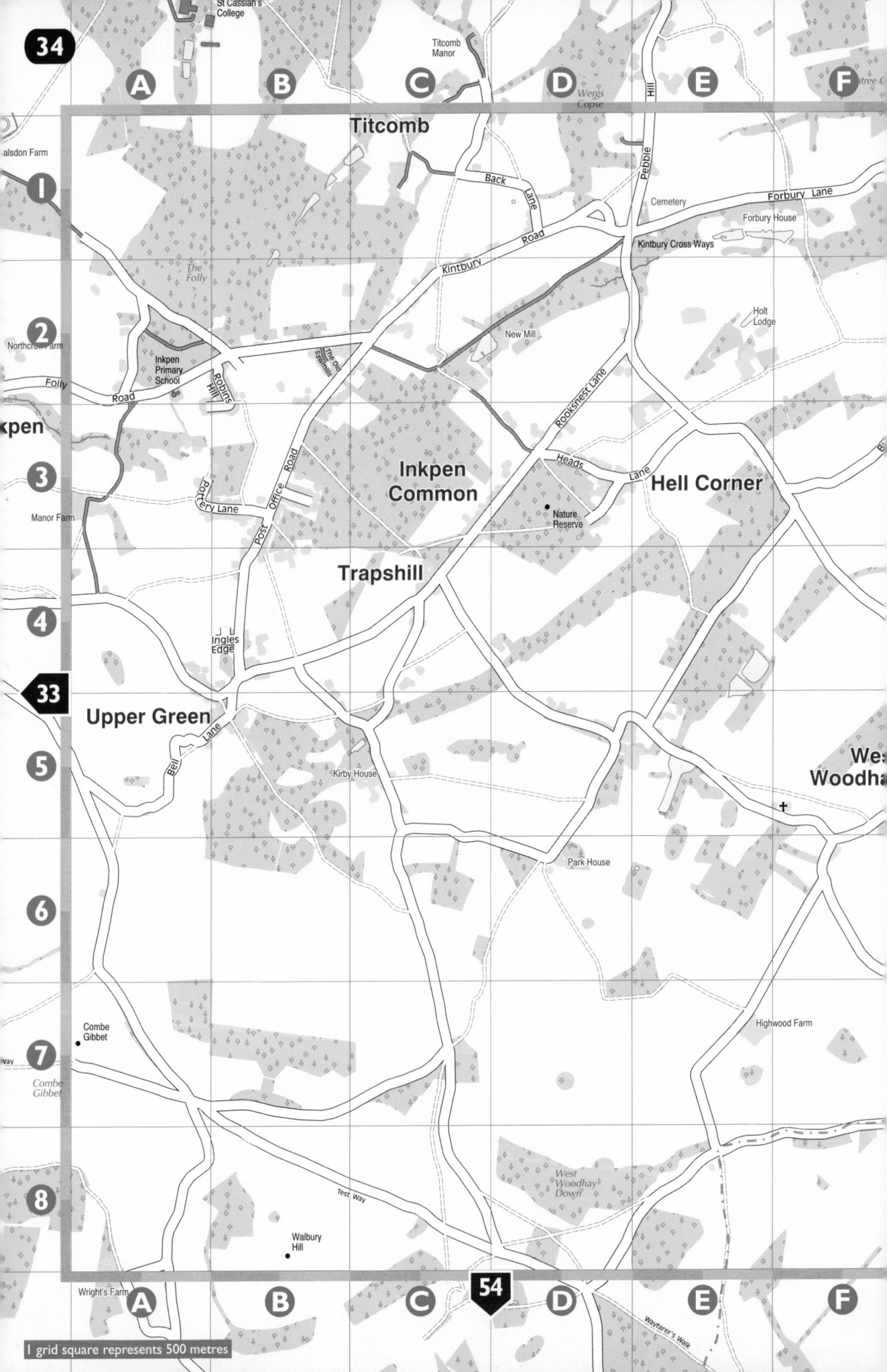

St Cassian's College
Titcomb Manor
Wergs Copse
Titcomb
alsdon Farm
Back Lane
Pebble Hill
Cemetery
Forbury Lane
Forbury House
Kintbury Cross Ways
Kintbury Road
The Folly
Holt Lodge
New Mill
Northcroft Farm
Inkpen Primary School
The Old Sawmills
Folly Road
Robins Hill
Rooksnest Lane
Inkpen
Post Office Road
Inkpen Common
Heads Lane
Hell Corner
Manor Farm
Pottery Lane
Nature Reserve
Trapshill
Ingles Edge
33
Upper Green
Bell Lane
West Woodhay
Kirby House
Park House
Highwood Farm
Combe Gibbet
Combe Gibbet
Test Way
West Woodhay Down
Walbury Hill
Wright's Farm
54
Wayfarer's Walk
1 grid square represents 500 metres

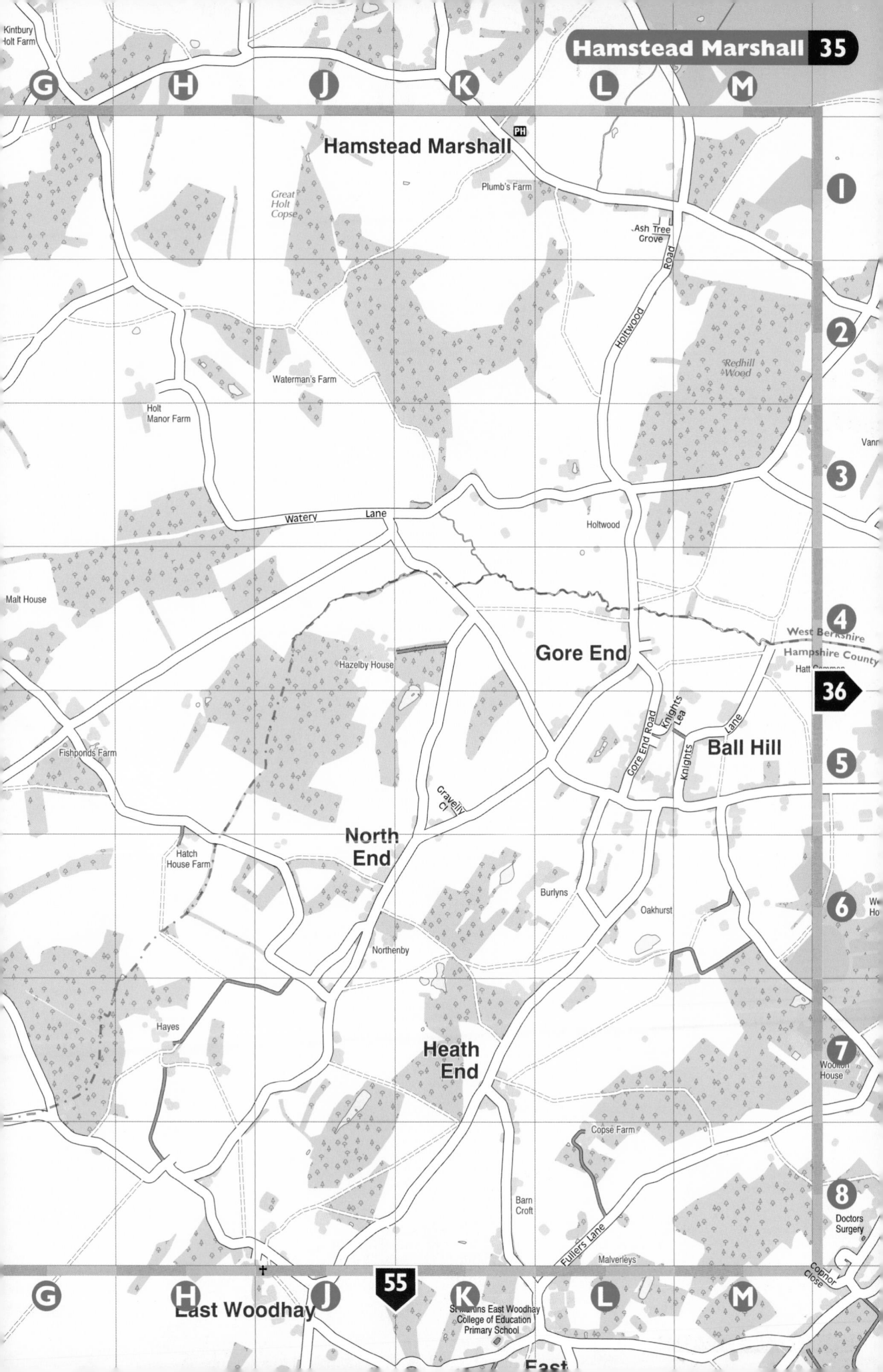

G H J K L M

Hamstead Marshall PH

I

Plumb's Farm

Great Holt Copse

Ash Tree Grove

2

Holtwood Road

Redhill Wood

Waterman's Farm

3

Holt Manor Farm

Vann

Watery Lane

Holtwood

Malt House

Gore End

Hazelby House

4

West Berkshire

Hampshire County

Hatt Common

36

Fishponds Farm

Gravelly Cf

Gore End Road

Knights Lea

Knights Lane

Ball Hill

5

North End

Hatch House Farm

Burlyns

Oakhurst

6

W Ho

Northenby

Hayes

Heath End

7

Woolton House

Copse Farm

8

Doctors Surgery

Barn Croft

Fullers Lane

Malverleys

Copnor Close

G H J K L M

55

East Woodhay

St Martins East Woodhay College of Education Primary School

East

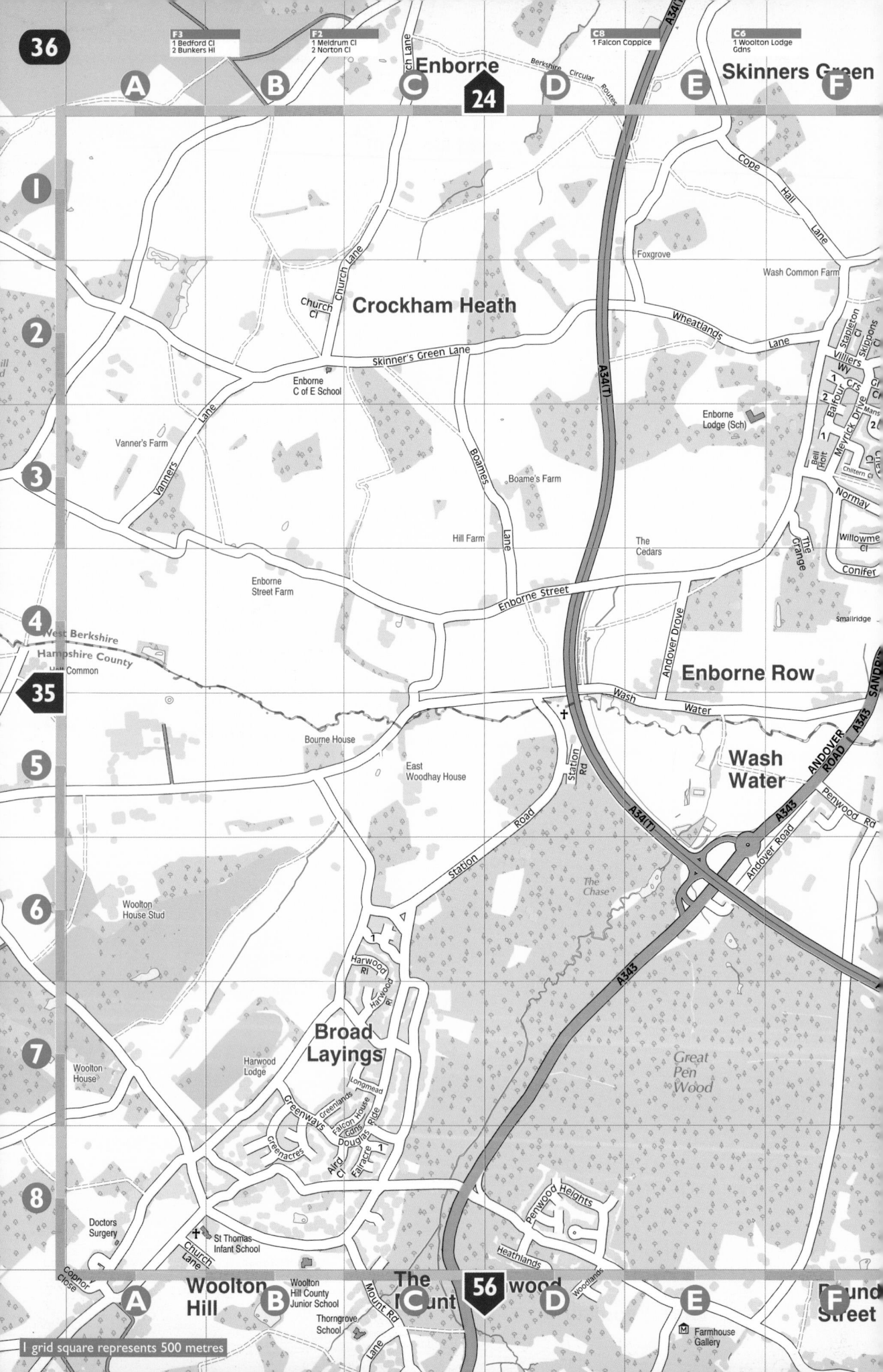

F3
1 Bedford Cl
2 Bunkers Hl
F2
1 Meldrum Cl
2 Norton Cl
C8
1 Falcon Coppice
C6
1 Woolton Lodge Gdns
Enborne
Skinners Green
24
Berkshire Circular Routes
Cope Hall Lane
Foxgrove
Wash Common Farm
Church Lane
Church Cl
Crockham Heath
Skinner's Green Lane
Wheatlands Lane
Enborne C of E School
Vanner's Farm
Vanners Lane
Boames Lane
Boame's Farm
Hill Farm
A34(T)
Enborne Lodge (Sch)
Stapleton Cl
Skippons Cl
Villiers Wy
Balfour Crs
Meyrick Drive
Bell Holt
Chiltern Cl
Normay
The Grange
Willowme Cl
Conifer
The Cedars
Smallridge
Enborne Street Farm
Enborne Street
Andover Drove
Enborne Row
West Berkshire
Hampshire County
35
Wash Water
Bourne House
East Woodhay House
Station Rd
Station Road
Wash Water
ANDOVER ROAD
A343
Penwood Rd
Andover Road
The Chase
Woolton House Stud
Harwood Rl
Broad Layings
Harwood Lodge
Great Pen Wood
Woolton House
Longmead
Greenlands
Greenways
Falcon House Gdns
Douglas Ride
Greenacres
Fairacre
Aird Cl
Penwood Heights
Heathlands
Woodlands
Doctors Surgery
St Thomas Infant School
Church Lane
Copnor Close
Woolton Hill
Woolton Hill County Junior School
The Mount
56
Thorngrove School
Mount Rd
Lane
Farmhouse Gallery
1 grid square represents 500 metres

Wash Common
37
G1
1 Monkswood Cl
2 Monument Cl
G3
1 Bledlow Cl
H1
1 Sutherlands
John Rankin Junior School
John Rankin County Infant School
Bartlemy Cl
Montgomery Rd
Tarn Lane
Croft Road
Friars Rd
Abbey Cl
Springfield La
Nightingales
Bodin Gdns
Christie Hts
Sayers Cl
Greenham Road
Meenham
Greenham Lodge
New Road
Greybery
Wormersley Rd
Water Lane
Bury's
Garford Crs
Valley
Home Mead Cl
Sidestrand Road
AppleTree Cl
Culver Rd
Three Acre Rd
Roberts Cl
The Marrowes
Bruan Rd
Robins Cl
Byron Cl
Rupert Road
Sandleford Rise
Rokeby Cl
Sandleford Hospital
25
Road
Newbury Retail Park
Equine Wy
Pinchington Lane
The Triangle
Deadmans Lane
Priory Pl
Tydehams
Wood Rdg
ANDOVER ROAD
Middle Cl
Avenue
Woodside
Pond Cl
Elizabeth
Hill Cl
Falkland Garth
Barn Crs
Monks Lane
St
The Natural Health Cen
Kennedy Cl
Falkland Memorial
Charles St
Falkland Rd
Dormer Cl
Battery End
Newbury Rugby Football Club Ltd
NEWTOWN ROAD
Falkland P School
Park House School
Spencer Rd
Warren Road
Sunley Cl
Warren Lodge
The Gabriels
Round End
Kendrick Rd
St Gabriels School
The Hollies
A343
Wash Common
Ladwell Cl
Garden Close
Lane
Sandleford Place
A339(T)
B4640
Newtown House
West Berkshire
Hampshire County
River Enborne
Newtown
38
Adbury
kland Farm
Jonathan Hill
Horris Hill Preparatory School
Newtown Common
Broken Way
Sheepwash Lane
Pinewood Dr
Woodbine La
Yeomans La
Deadmoor Lane
Burghclere Common
Adbury Park
Tot Hill
Heatherwold
Earlstone Common
A34(T)
Ayres Lane
57
Burghclere
The Clere Secondary School
Lines Av
Palmer's Hill
L1
1 The Halters
2 Horseshoe End
3 Stirrup Pightle
K1
1 Pinchington La
G H J K L M
1 2 3 4 5 6 7 8

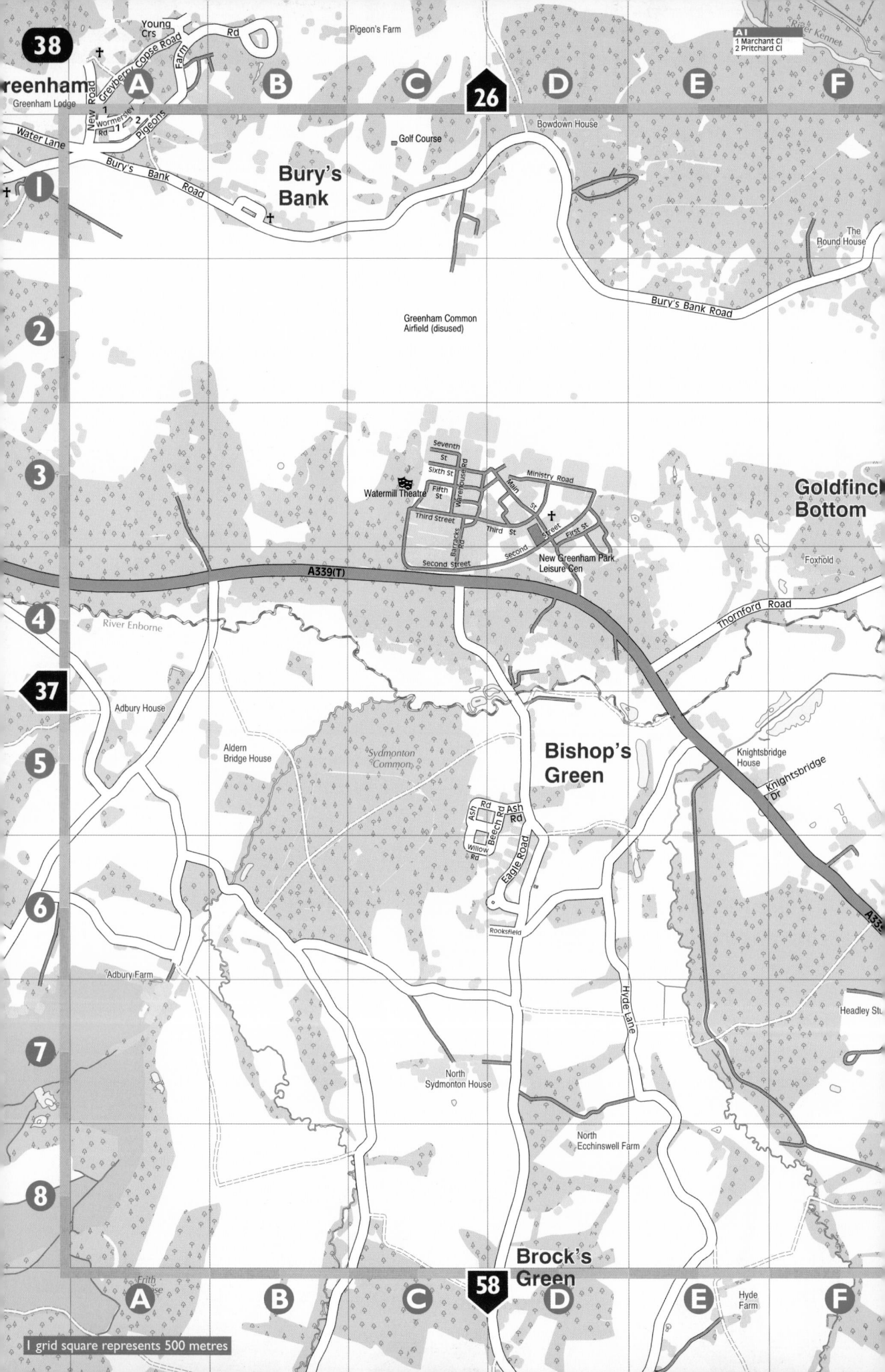

Greenham

A1
1 Marchant Cl
2 Pritchard Cl

A   B   C   **26**   D   E   F

Greenham Lodge
Water Lane
New Road
Greyberry Copse Road
Young Crs
Farm Rd
Pigeon's Farm
Wormsley Rd
Pigeons Farm

Bowdown House

Bury's Bank

Golf Course

Bury's Bank Road

The Round House

Greenham Common
Airfield (disused)

Bury's Bank Road

Seventh St
Sixth St
Fifth St
Waterhouse Rd
Ministry Road
Watermill Theatre
Third Street
Barracks Rd
Third St
Main St
First St
Second St
Second Street
New Greenham Park
Leisure Cen

**Goldfinch
Bottom**

Foxhold

A339(T)

River Enborne

Thornford Road

37

Adbury House

Aldern
Bridge House

Sydmonton
Common

**Bishop's
Green**

Knightsbridge
House

Knightsbridge
Dr

Ash Rd
Beech Rd
Ash Rd
Willow Rd
Eagle Road

Rooksfield

Headley St

Adbury Farm

North
Sydmonton House

Hyde Lane

A33

North
Ecchinswell Farm

Frith
House

**Brock's
Green**

Hyde
Farm

A   B   C   **58**   D   E   F

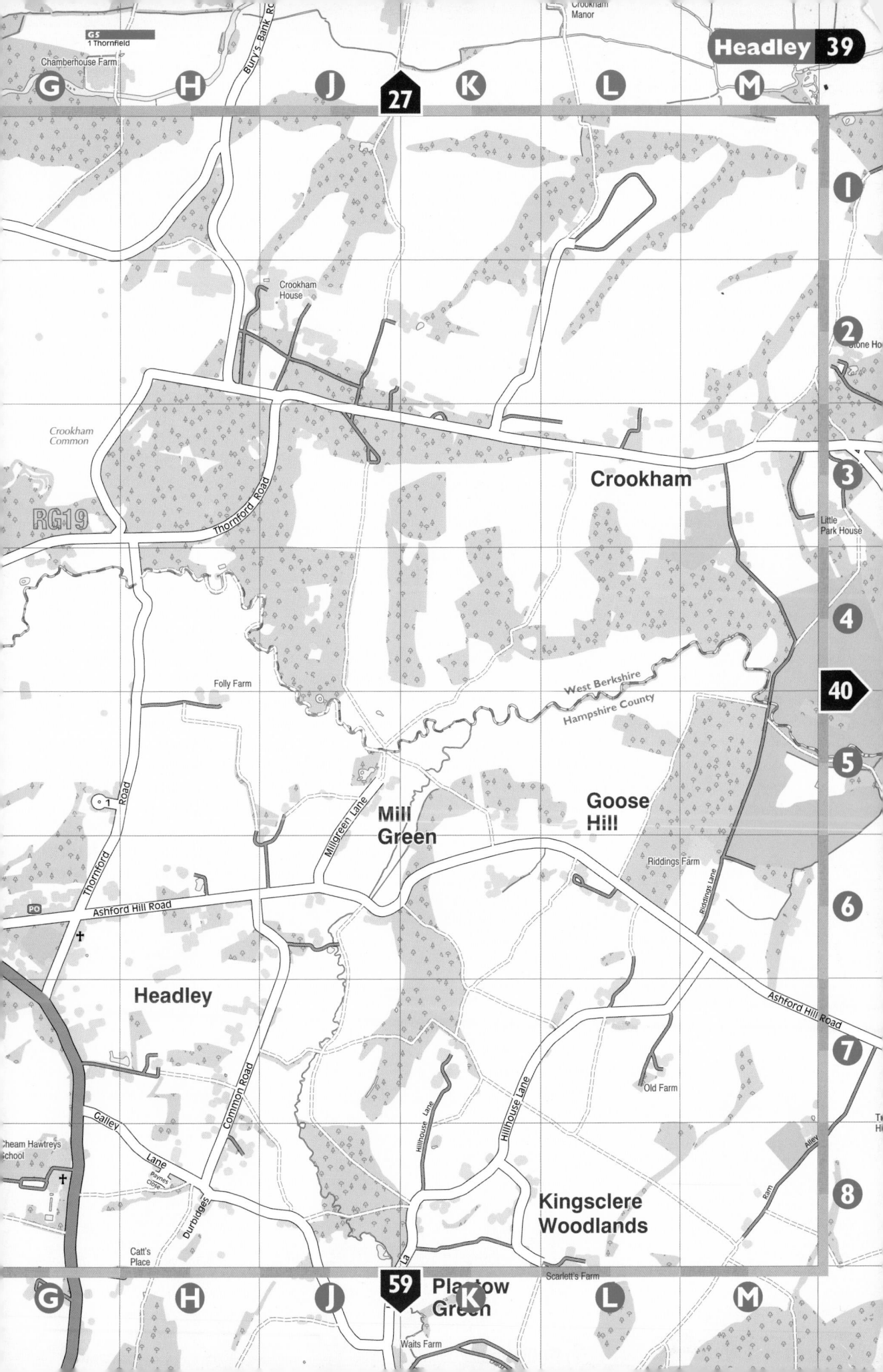

G5
1 Thornfield

Chamberhouse Farm

G H J K L M

27

1

2
Stone Ho

Crookham House

3

Crookham

Little Park House

Crookham Common

RG19

4

Thornford Road

Folly Farm

West Berkshire
Hampshire County

40

5

1

Goose Hill

Mill Green

Millgreen Lane

Riddings Farm

Riddings Lane

Thornford Road

6

PO

Ashford Hill Road

Headley

Ashford Hill Road

7

Common Road

Hillhouse Lane

Hillhouse Lane

Old Farm

Pam Alley

Galley Lane

Cheam Hawtreys School

Durbidges

Paynes Close

Kingsclere Woodlands

8

Catt's Place

G H J K L M

59

Plaistow Green

Scarlett's Farm

Waits Farm

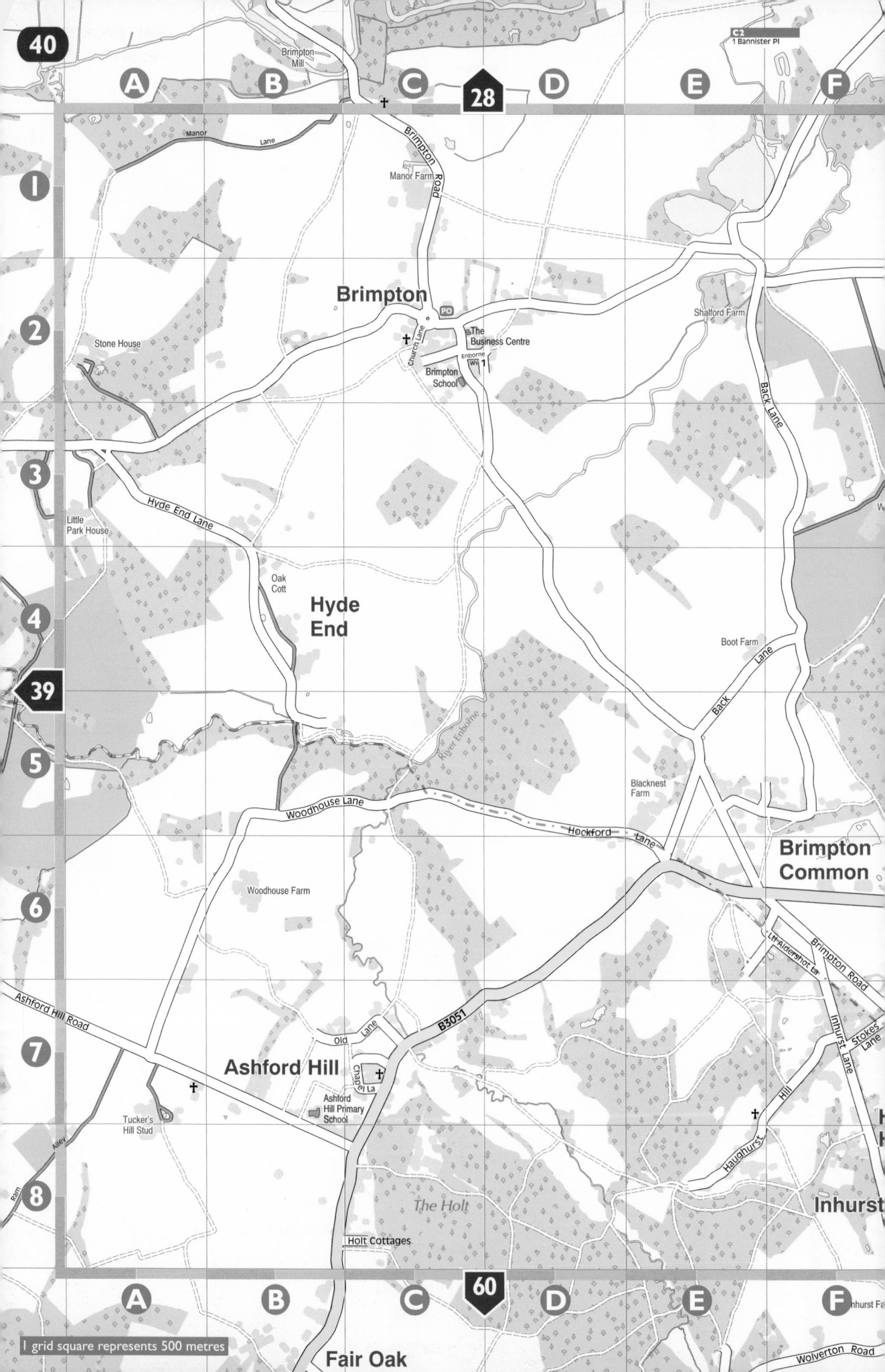
Brimpton Mill
C2
1 Bannister Pl
A
B
C
28
D
E
F
Manor Lane
Brimpton Road
Manor Farm
Brimpton
PO
Church Lane
The Business Centre
Enborne Wy 1
Brimpton School
Stone House
Shalford Farm
Back Lane
Little Park House
Hyde End Lane
Oak Cott
Hyde
End
Boot Farm
Back Lane
39
River Enborne
Blacknest Farm
Woodhouse Lane
Hockford Lane
Brimpton Common
Woodhouse Farm
Ashford Hill Road
B3051
Ltl Aldershot La
Brimpton Road
Old Lane
Ashford Hill
Chapel La
Ashford Hill Primary School
Inhurst Lane
Stokes Lane
Tucker's Hill Stud
Haughurst Hill
Alley
Ram
The Holt
Inhurst
Holt Cottages
1
2
3
4
5
6
7
8
A
B
C
60
D
E
F
1 grid square represents 500 metres
Fair Oak
Wolverton Road

G7
1 Hazel Gn
2 Lakelands
H7
1 Heathlands
H8
1 The Hawthorns
G
H
J
29
K
L
M
Upper
Church Farm
Fisherman's Lane
Aldermaston
C of E School
PH
PO
Wasing Lane
THE ST
Wasing Lower Farm
Aldermaston
Cedars
School
Church Road
Congreve
Close
Church Road
Spring Lane
Portland House
Wasing Lane
A340
Wasing
Red Lane
HILL
Youngs
Industrial
Est
PAICES
42
Wasing Wood
Deco
Pond
A340
Winkworth Lane
Second Avenue
First Avenue
B3051
A340
Plantation Rd
Furze Road
Birch Road
Almswood Road
ALDERMASTON RD
Falcon Fields
Long Gv
Forest Cl
Conifer Cl
Burnham Road
Hanger Rd
Priors Rd
Pinks La
Franklin Av
Silchester Road
The Hurst
Community
School
Woodlands
Fairoak Wy
O'Bee Gardens
Sarum Rd
Holmwood
Health Centre
Silchester Rd
Brick Kiln
Industrial
Est
Brick Kiln
Industrial
Estate
Portway
Shyshack La
Heath End
Franklin Avenue
Meon Close
Tadley Common Road
Pinewood Close
Hepplewhite Close
Adam Cl
Bishopswood Road
Burnham Copse
Junior School
Turbary Gdns
A340
Tadley
Common
Brimpton Road
Mornington Close
Sheridan Crs
Heath End
Newchurch Road
Bishops Cl
Glendale Rd
Honeybottom Rd
Silverdale Rd
Blake's La
Blake's Lane
Broadhalfpenny Lane
Wellington Crs
Ash La
Innhurst Wy
Wigmore Road
Searing Wy
Newtown
Tadley Police Stn
Wickham Cl
Gorselands
hurst
Heathrow Copse
Coppice Cl
Heath La
Bishopswood Road
Hartshill Rd
Huntsmoor
Beavers Cl
Huntsmoor Rd
Sandford Rd
Southdown Road
Stanford Rd
Pleasant Hl
Ambrose Rd
MULFORDS HL
Corselands
Stephens Rd
West St
Poplar Cl
Whitedown Road
Deanswood Rd
The Copse
Newtown Crs
Carrington Cl
Reynards Close
Millers Road
The Lane
Briar Way
Stephens Rd
Giles Road
The Orchard
Sympson Road
Wolverton Road
Baughurst Road
Lane
Mount
Purbrook Rd
Willow Road
Swains Cl
Swains Rd
Maple Gv
Maple Cl
Bowmonts
Brook Green Road
The Oaks
Guttridge
Salisbury Cl
Dammead Rd
Junior School
Tunworth Mews
PO
Rowan
Spiers Cl
The Warren
Infant School
MULFORDS HILL
61
L8
1 Harmsworth Rd
2 Lambdens Wk
L7
1 Oak Tree Cl
2 The Parade
K8
1 Ashurst Cl
2 Greywell Cl
Barlows
Reuben's Crs
New Road
Fullerton Way
Warblington Close
TADLEY HILL
Ropley Cl
Droxford Crs
Pinehurst
Stratfield Av
Herriard Way
Hawkley Drive
Swedish Houses
North View Road
New Road
1
2
3
4
5
6
7
8

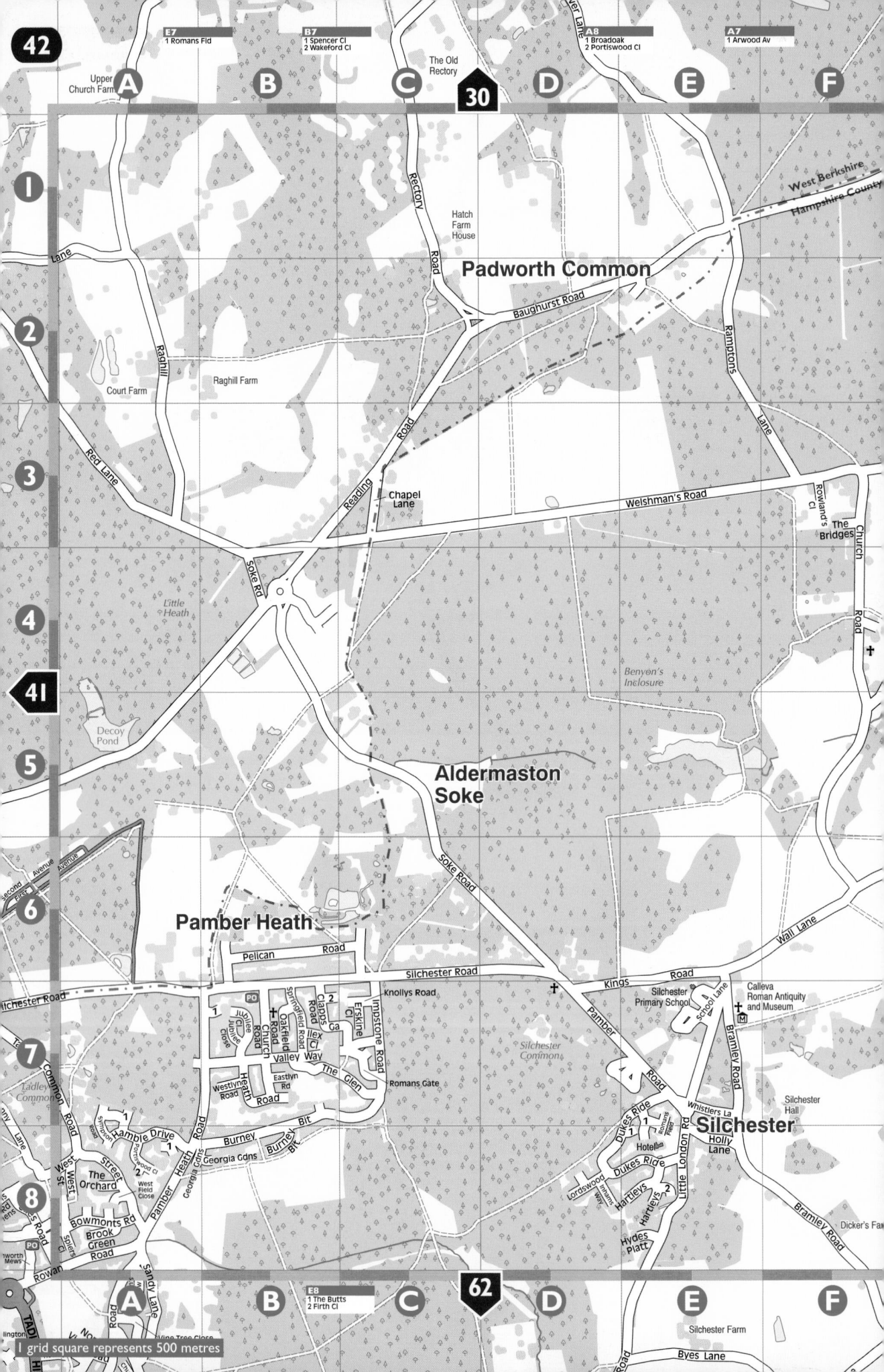
E7
1 Romans Fld
B7
1 Spencer Cl
2 Wakeford Cl
A8
1 Broadoak
2 Portiswood Cl
A7
1 Arwood Av
30
41
62
E8
1 The Butts
2 Firth Cl
Upper Church Farm
The Old Rectory
Rectory Road
Hatch Farm House
Padworth Common
Baughurst Road
West Berkshire
Hampshire County
Ramptons Lane
Raghill
Raghill Farm
Court Farm
Lane
Red Lane
Reading Road
Chapel Lane
Welshman's Road
Rowland's Cl
The Bridges
Church Road
Soke Rd
Little Heath
Benyon's Inclosure
Decoy Pond
Aldermaston Soke
Soke Road
Second Avenue
First Avenue
Pamber Heath
Pelican Road
Silchester Road
Knollys Road
Kings Road
Wall Lane
Silchester Primary School
School Lane
Calleva Roman Antiquity and Museum
Bramley Road
Jubilee Cl
Jubilee Close
Church Road
Oakfield Road
Springfield Road
Clapps Ga
Ilex Cl
Erskine Cl
Impstone Road
Valley Way
The Glen
Romans Gate
Westlyn Road
Heath Road
Eastlyn Rd
Pamber Road
Silchester Common
Silchester Hall
Tadley Common
Common Road
Symonds Road
Hamble Drive
Portiswood Cl
Burney Bit
Georgia Gdns
West Street
West St
The Orchard
West Field Close
Pamber Heath Road
Bowmonts Rd
Brook Green
Spiers Cl
Rowan Road
Sandy Lane
Whistlers La
Silchester
Holly Lane
Dukes Ride
Romans Field
Hotel
Little London Rd
Lordswood
Inhams Way
Hartleys
Hydes Platt
Dicker's Farm
Silchester Farm
Byes Lane
Vine Tree Close
1 grid square represents 500 metres

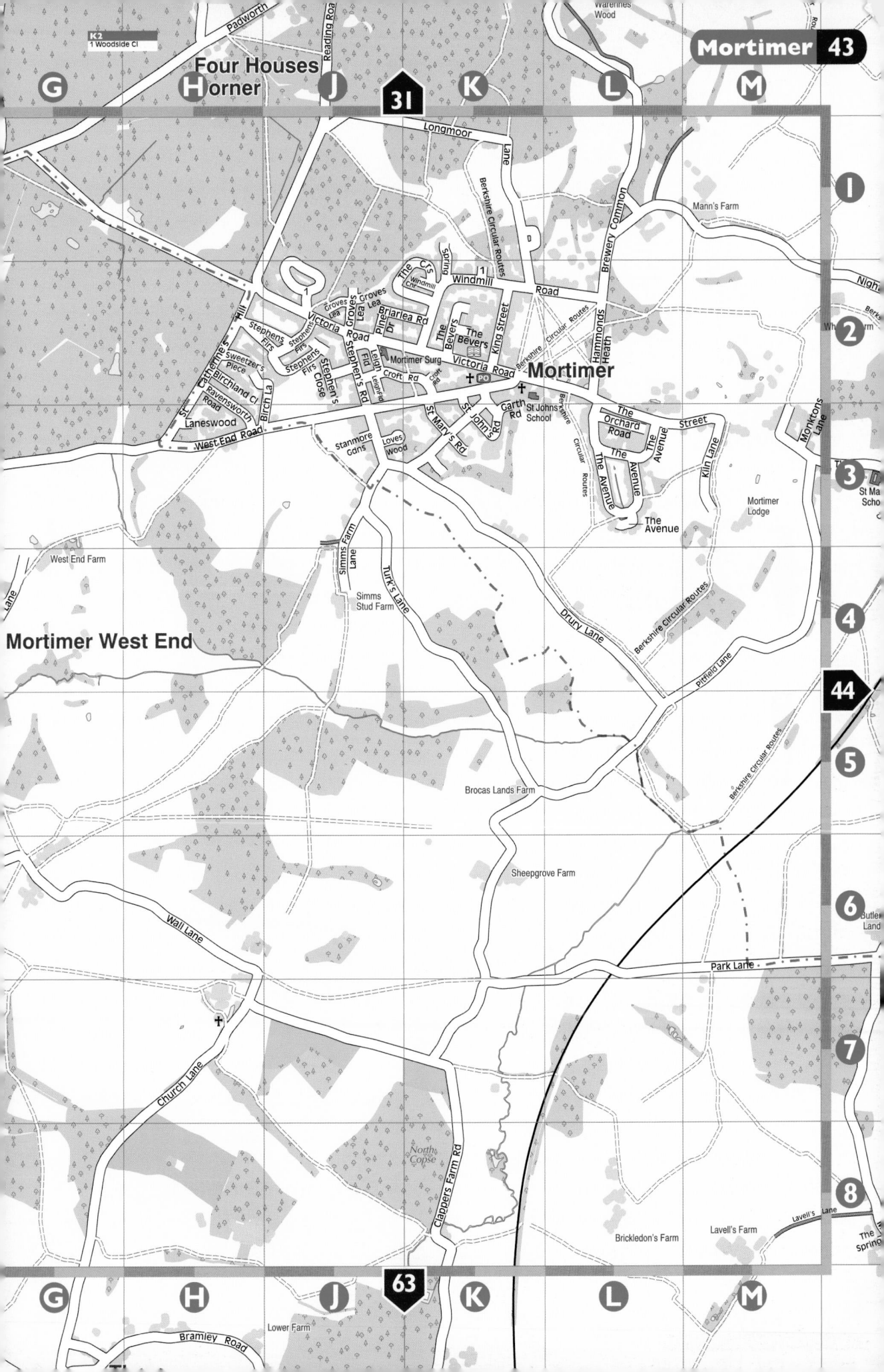

G H J 31 K L M

I
2
3
44
5
6
7
8

1 Woodside Cl
K2

Four Houses Horner

Padworth
Reading Road
Warennes Wood

Longmoor Lane
Berkshire Circular Routes

Mann's Farm

Nigh
Berts
Wh Farm

Spring
The C of E
Windmill Chr
1 Windmill
Road

The Bevers
The Bevers
King Street
Victoria Road

Brewery Common

Hammonds Heath

Groves Lea
Groves Lea
Groves
Pine
Briarlea Rd
Mortimer Surg

Berkshire Circular Routes

Mortimer

Stephens Firs
Stephens Firs
Stephens Firs
Stephens Firs
Stephen's Rd
Stephen's Close
Victoria Road
Leigh Fld
Leigh Fld
Croft Rd
Croft

PO

Garth Rd
St Johns School

The Orchard Road

The Avenue Street
Monktons Lane

St Ma Sch

St Catherine's
Sweetzer's Piece
Birchland Cl
Ravensworth Road
Birch La
Laneswood
West End Road

St Mary's Rd
St John's
py
Berkshire Circular Routes

The Avenue
The Avenue
The Avenue
Kiln Lane

Mortimer Lodge

St Ma Scho

Stanmore Gdns
Loves Wood

West End Farm

Simms Farm
Simms Farm Lane
Simms Stud Farm
Turk's Lane

Drury Lane

Berkshire Circular Routes

Pitfield Lane

Mortimer West End

Lane

Brocas Lands Farm

Berkshire Circular Routes

Butler Land

Sheepgrove Farm

Wall Lane

Park Lane

Church Lane

North Copse

Clappers Farm Rd

Lavell's Farm
Lavell's Lane
The Spring

Bramley Road
Lower Farm
Brickledon's Farm

G H J 63 K L M

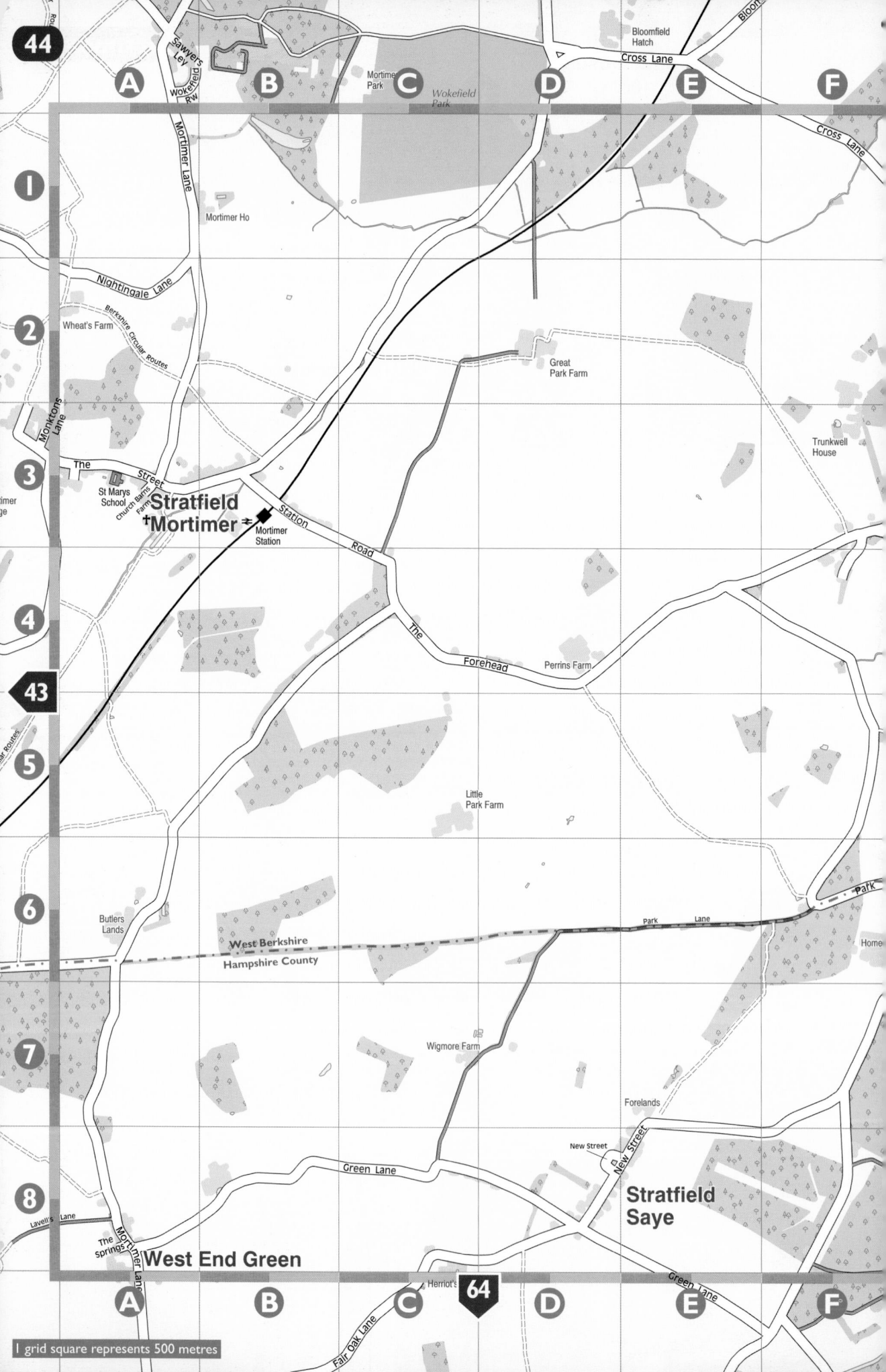

A B C D E F

Bloor

Bloomfield
Hatch

Cross Lane

Cross Lane

I

Nightingale Lane

Mortimer Lane

Mortimer Ho

Sawyer's Ley

Wokefield Rw

Wokefield
Park

Mortimer
Park

2

Wheat's Farm

Berkshire Circular Routes

Great
Park Farm

Trunkwell
House

3

The Street

Monktons Lane

St Marys
School

Church Barns

Church Farms

**Stratfield
†Mortimer**

Station Road

Mortimer
Station

4

The Forehead

Perrins Farm

5

Little
Park Farm

6

Butlers
Lands

West Berkshire
Hampshire County

Park   Lane

Park

Home

7

Wigmore Farm

Forelands

New Street

New Street

8

Lavell's Lane

The springs

Mortimer Lane

West End Green

Green Lane

Herriot's

Fair Oak Lane

**Stratfield
Saye**

Green Lane

A B C D E F

I grid square represents 500 metres

G H J K L M

Heron Industrial Estate

School

Back La

Lambs Farm Business Park

Sheepbridge Court Farm

River Loddon

Brook Farm

Crosslane Farm

Cross Lane

Beech Hill Road

Beech Hill Road

Loddon Court Farm

Loddon Court

Lambs Lane

B3349

Hotel

The Street

Swallowfield Medical Practice

Hornbeams

PO 1

I

Wyvols Court

The Street

Trowe's Lane

The Naylors

2

Beech Hill House

Kingsbridge Hill

Chariton Lane

Trowe's

3

h Hill

Wood Lane

Vale View Drive

The Priory

Barge

Lane

A33

Barge Lane

Spring

Lane

Trowe's

4

West Berkshire
Wokingham

Barge Lane

Lane

BASINGSTOKE ROAD

46

Way

Trowe's Lane

Broad

Bull

Lane

Spring

Riseley

Part Lane

ham La

5

Stanford End

Bull Lane

Lane

Bull Lane

B3349

Norton Rd

Odiham Road

Postway

Chequers

Chequer Lane

Welsh Lane

Bull Lane

Bull Lane

Sun La

B3349

6

air oss

Park Corner

7 AM

Heckfield Heath House

Stratfield Saye Park

Wellington Monument

Heckfield Heath

8

Stratfield Saye

River Loddon

The Causew

G H J 65 K L M

A B C D E F

I

Swallowfield

Swallowfield Medical Practice
PO
Foxborough
The Naylors
Brookside Business Centre
Part Lane
The Street
Hornbeams
Trowe's Lane

Swallow Park

Tanner's Farm

A2
1 Curleys Wy

Kiln Hill
The Chatters
Castle Hill

Swallowfield Road

Swallowfield

Bungler's Hill
Road

PH
Rowe's Farm

2

3
Trowe's Lane
Lane
Part Lane

Cemetery

Nutbean Lane

sandpit
Lane

Farley Court

Riseley Farm

The Broadwater

4

45

Part Lane

School Lane
School Road

Ford Lane

Wokingham
Hampshire County

Benham La
Part Lane

5

Cordery's Farm

Well House Lane
Well
Ho

isey

Wellington Country Park

6
Benham Road
ODIHAM ROAD

Riseley Mill

Bramshill Plantation

Hall's Farm

Ford Lane

7

Springwater Farm

River Whitewater

8
field House

Park Farm

es Lane

A B C D E F

66

1 grid square represents 500 metres

Bramshill

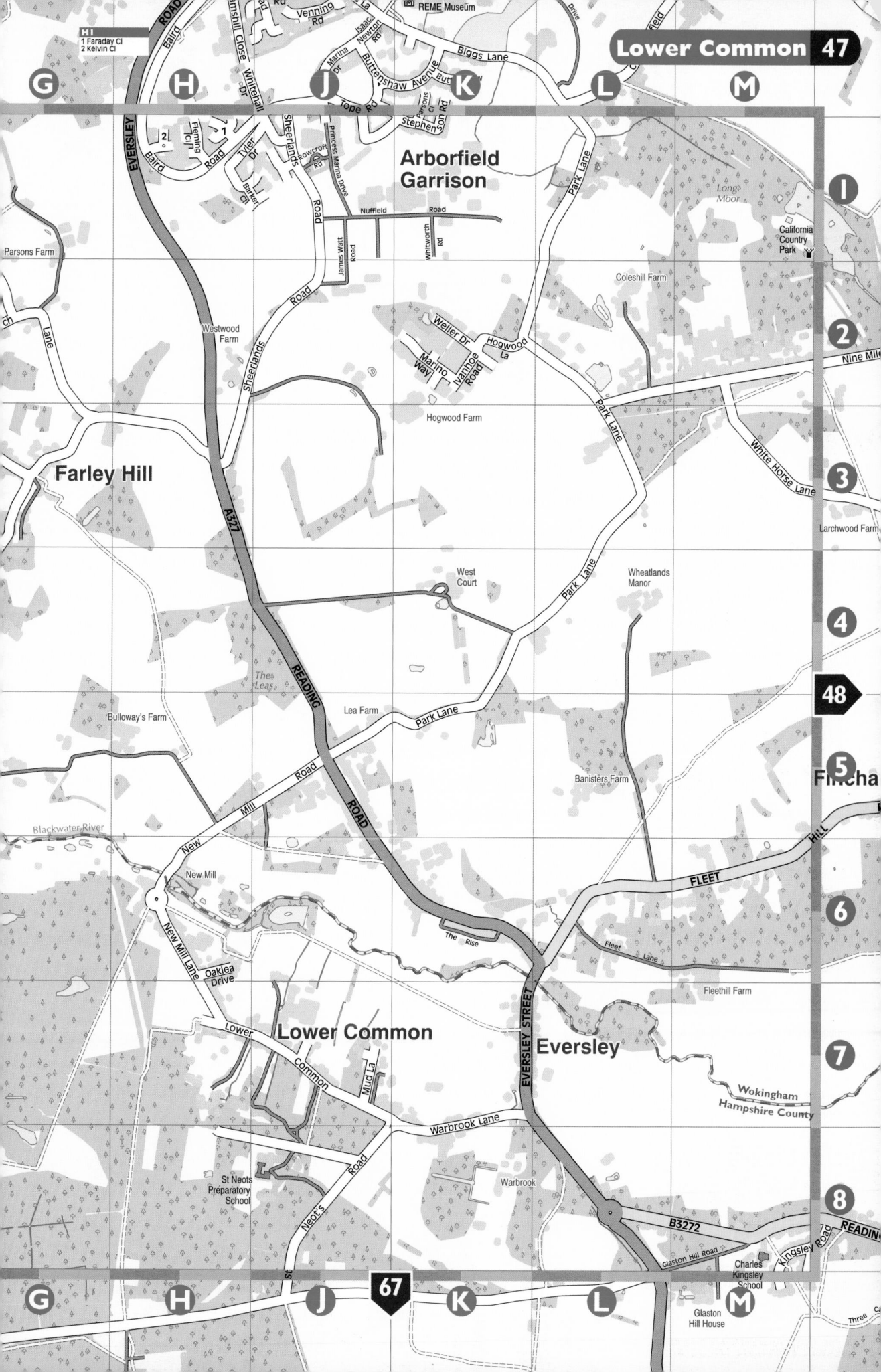

G H J K L M

I
2
3
4
48
5
6
7
8

Arborfield
Garrison

Farley Hill

Parsons Farm

California Country Park

Coleshill Farm

Larchwood Farm

Hogwood Farm

West Court

Wheatlands Manor

The Leas

Lea Farm

Park Lane

Bulloway's Farm

Banisters Farm

Fincha

Blackwater River

New Mill

FLEET HILL

Fleet Lane

The Rise

Fleethill Farm

Lower Common

Eversley

Wokingham
Hampshire County

Oaklea Drive

Warbrook Lane

Warbrook

St Neots Preparatory School

Glaston Hill Road

Charles Kingsley School

Glaston Hill House

B3272

READIN

A   B   C   D   E   F

B2
1 Briarwood Dr
2 Manor Park Dr
3 Redgauntlet

1 Chivers Dr
2 Columbia Ct
3 Copse Wy
4 Heather Cl

A1
1 Manor Park Dr

A1
1 Fernbank
2 Oregon Wk

SAXDHURST

1

California
Country
Park

CYDE

B3016

ROAD

King's
Mere

2

Maryland

Gorse Ride Junior School

Wimbushes

Church Harris

Hazelbank

Kelsey Av

Gibbs Cl

Billing Av

Gorse Ride S

PO

Bank Side

B3430

Wick Hill

Wick Hill La

Heath Ride

Wild Briar

Finchampstead Rd

Birch Rd

Windsor Ride

Foxcote

Kiln Ride

Tomlinson Dr

Johnson Dr

Tintagel Rd

Kiln Ride Extension

Range Road

Hollybush

B3430

Nine Mile Ride

White

Warren   Lane

Warren
Lodge

Lane

3

Larchwood Farm

Ridge Farm

Wick   Hill La

FINCHAMPSTEAD ROAD

Church La

North
Court

JUBILEE ROAD B3016

The Ridges

Wellington
(Arboretum)

4

Church

Church

Lane

JUBILEE ROAD

B3348

WELLINGTONIA   AVEN

47

Rectory Farm

East
Court

Dell

Road

5

Finchampstead

B3348

Finchampstead
Sports Club

PO

THE VILLAGE

Primary
School

Liddell Wy

Longwater

Corfield

Burnmoor
Meadow

Lane

Cricket Hill

Longwater Rd

Wd Moor

Lower Sandhurst Road

Blackwater Vw

Hall Farm

6

Hill

Fleet
Copse

Moor
Green Farm

7

Wokingham
Hampshire County

ROAD

LONGWATER

River Blackwater

Wokingham
Hampshire County

Three   Castles   Path

Millbridge Rd

Blaire Pk

River Mousham

Coombe

8

Eversley
Centre

Kingsley Road

READING   ROAD

Paul's Fld

PO

Mayfield

Staver Cl

The Fielders

Eversley
Cricket
Club

Eversley
Cross

Fox Lan

B3272

Canberra Close

Castles

Crosby
Gdns

Tower Dr

St Ives Cl

Coleridge Cl

A   B   C   D   E   F

B8
1 Bannister Gdns
2 Chapel Mead
3 Grensell Cl
4 Sparvells

C1
1 Challenor Cl

C2
1 The Dittons
2 Vicarage Cl

D1
1 Finch'd Rd
2 Ingle Gln

M8
1 Wellington Ter

C1
1 Coleridge Cl
2 Old Pharmacy Ct

M7
1 Bernersh Cl
2 Braye Cl

READING

Brooklands

Vicarage

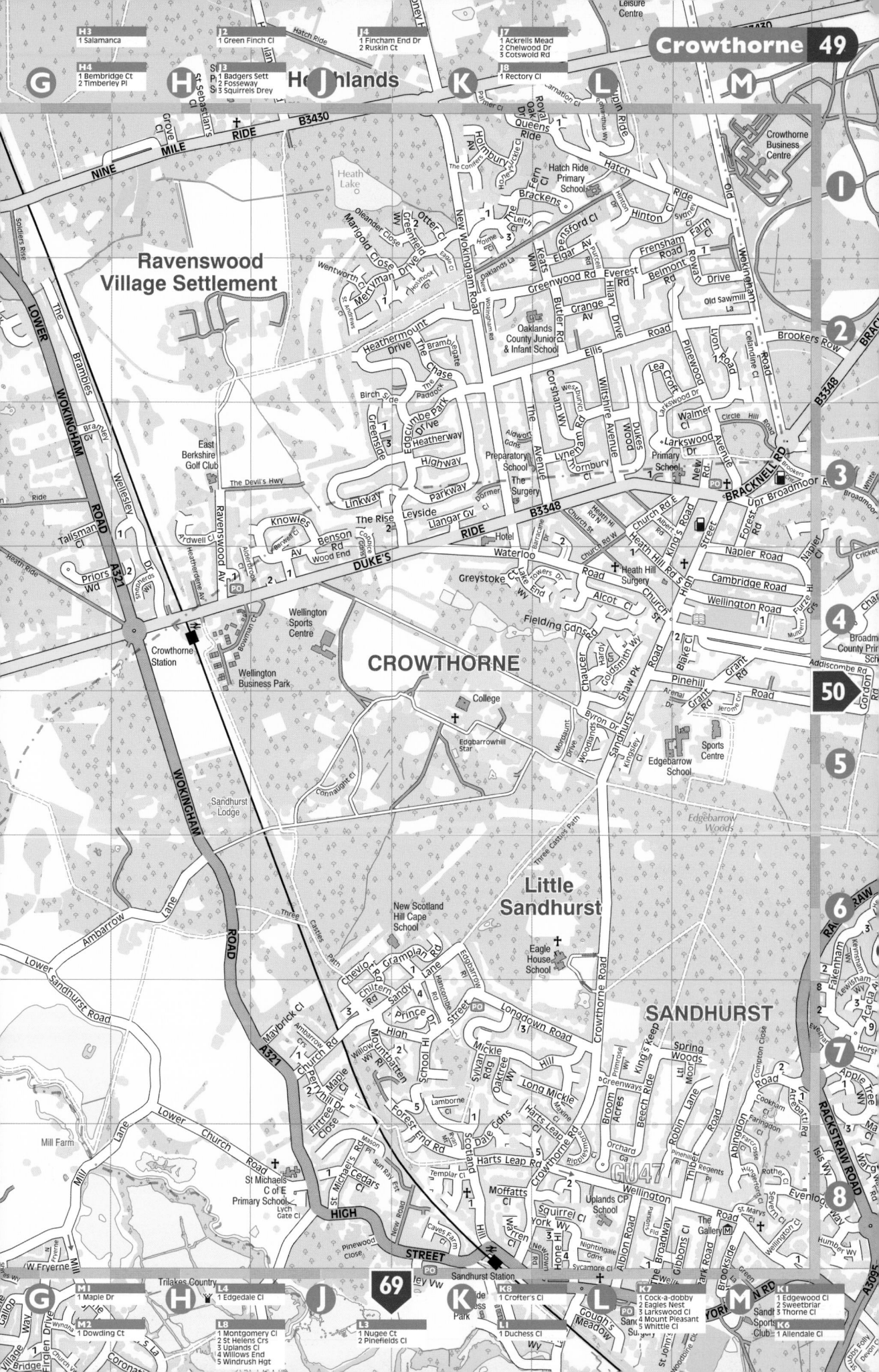
H3
1 Salamanca
H4
1 Bembridge Ct
2 Timberley Pl
J2
1 Green Finch Cl
J3
1 Badgers Sett
2 Fosseway
3 Squirrels Drey
J4
1 Fincham End Dr
2 Ruskin Ct
J7
1 Ackrells Mead
2 Chelwood Dr
3 Cotswold Rd
J8
1 Rectory Cl
Leisure Centre
Hatch Ride
G
H
J
K
L
M
Heathlands
B3430
Nine Mile Ride
Grove Cl
St Sebastian's Cl
Heath Lake
Ravenswood Village Settlement
Soldiers Rise
Lower Wokingham Road
The Brambles
Oleander Close
Marigold Close
Greenfield Wy
Otter Cl
Merryman Drive
Wentworth Cl
St Andrews
New Wokingham Road
Holmbury Av
The Conifers
Honeysuckle Cl
The Brackens
The Leith
Holme Cl
Fern Cl
Queens Ride
Royal Oak Dr
Palmer Cl
Carnation Cl
Lupin Ride
Hatch Ride Primary School
Crowthorne Business Centre
Old Wokingham Road
Hinton Dr
Hinton Cl
Sydney Cl
Ride
Frensham Road
Farm Cl
Rowan Drive
Pensford Cl
Elgar Av
Purcell Rd
Keats Way
Oaklands La
Greenwood Rd
Everest Rd
Hilary Drive
Belmont Rd
Old Sawmill La
Butler Rd
Grange Av
Oaklands County Junior & Infant School
Ellis Road
Brookers Row
Pinewood
Lyon Road
Celandine Cl
B3348
Heathermount Drive
The Chase
Bramblegate
The Paddock
Birch Side
Greenside
Edgcumbe Park Drive
Heatherway
Highway
Linkway
Parkway
Corsham Wy
Westbury Cl
Wiltshire Avenue
Lynenham Rd
Dukes Wood
Lea Croft
Larkswood Dr
Walmer Cl
Larkswood Dr
Circle Hill Road
Avenue
East Berkshire Golf Club
The Devil's Hwy
Ride
Wellesley
Bramley Gv
Talisman Cl
Priors Wd
Shepherds Wy
Ravenswood Av
Ardwell Cl
Heatherdene Av
Alderbrook Cl
Knowles Av
Barwell Cl
Benson Rd
Wood End
Coppice Gdns
The Rise
Leyside
Llangar Gv
Dormer Cl
Preparatory School
The Surgery
Aldworth Gdns
The Avenue
Thornbury Cl
Primary School
New Rd
Bracknell Rd
Brookers Cnr
Upr Broadmoor Rd
Broadmoor
Duke's Ride
Hotel
A321
Crowthorne Station
Bowman Cl
Wellington Sports Centre
Wellington Business Park
Waterloo Road
Greystoke Ct
Lake End Wy
Towers Dr
Barracane Dr
Heath Hill Rd N
Church St
Church Rd W
Church Rd E
Albert Rd
Heath Hill Rd S
King's Road
High Street
Heath Hill Surgery
Forest Rd
Napier Road
Napier Cl
Cambridge Road
Wellington Road
Furze Hill Crs
Mulberry Crs
Cricket
Alcot Cl
Fielding Gdns
Chaucer Rd
Hardy Gn
Goldsmith Wy
Church St
Shaw Pk
Blake Cl
Pinehill Road
Arenal Dr
Grant Rd
Jerome Cnr
Addiscombe Rd
Broadmoor County Primary School
Gordon Rd
50
CROWTHORNE
College
Edgbarrowhill Star
Connaught Cl
Byron Dr
Mordaunt Drive
Woodlands Av
Sandhurst Road
Kingsley Cl
Edgebarrow School
Sports Centre
Edgebarrow Woods
Sandhurst Lodge
Three Castles Path
Little Sandhurst
New Scotland Hill Cape School
Eagle House School
Ambarrow Lane
Lower Sandhurst Road
Wokingham Road
Cheviot Rd
Grampian Rd
Chiltern Rd
Sandy Lane
Hancombe Rd
Edgbarrow Ri
Prince Dr
Maybrick Cl
Ambarrow Crs
Church Rd
High Street
Willow Wy
Mountbatten Ri
School Hl
Longdown Road
Mickle Hill
Sylvan Rdg
Oaktree Wy
Long Mickle
Maxine Cl
Crowthorne Road
SANDHURST
King's Keep
Primrose Wy
Spring Woods
Ltl Moor
Compton Close
Greenways
Broom Acres
Beech Ride
Robin Lane
Road
Lower Church Road
Mill Lane
Mill Farm
Maple Cl
Perryhill Dr
Firtree Close
Lamborne Cl
Forest End Rd
Ryan Mt
Dale Gdns
Harts Leap Cl
Harts Leap Rd
Ripplesmere
Orchard Ca
GU47
Abingdon Road
Cookham Cl
Faringdon Cl
Farcrosse Cl
Attebatti Rd
Hungerford Cl
Rother Cl
Severn Cl
Evenlode Way
Isis Wy
Rackstraw Road
Apple Tree Wy
St Michael's Rd
Mason Pl
Sun Ray Est
Cedars Cl
Templar Cl
Scotland Hill
Moffatts Cl
Wellington Road
Pinehill Rl
Regents Pl
Thibet Road
St Michaels C of E Primary School
Lych Gate Cl
Squirrel Cl
Uplands CP School
York Wy
Hone Hl
Warren Cl
Newtown Rd
Nightingale Gdns
Sycamore Cl
Albion Road
Parsons Fld
The Broadway
Gibbons Cl
Park Road
The Gallery
Brookside
St Marys Rd
Wellington Cl
Humber Wy
W Fryerne
Fryerne
New Road
Pinewood Close
Caves Farm Cl
High Street
Sandhurst Station
69
Trilakes Country
A3095
M1
1 Maple Dr
M2
1 Dowding Ct
L4
1 Edgedale Cl
L8
1 Montgomery Cl
2 St Helens Crs
3 Uplands Cl
4 Willows End
5 Windrush Hgt
L3
1 Nugee Ct
2 Pinefields Cl
K8
1 Crofter's Cl
L1
1 Duchess Cl
K7
1 Cock-a-dobby
2 Eagles Nest
3 Larkswood Cl
4 Mount Pleasant
5 Whittle Cl
K1
1 Edgewood Cl
2 Sweetbriar
3 Thorne Cl
K6
1 Allendale Cl
Gough's Meadow
Yorktown Rd
Sandhurst Sports Club
Fakenham
Keynsham Wy
Lewisham Wy
Acacia Av
Eversley
Horsham
Wargrave
Stubbs Folly
Devon Cl
Gallop
Village Way
Virginia Drive
Wyndham
Bridge
Church Wy
Coronation
2
3
4
5
6
7
8

50
B6
1 Barkis Mead
2 Frodsham Wy
3 Peggotty Pl
4 Steerforth Copse
5 Trotwood Cl
A8
1 Centurion Cl
2 Cornbunting Cl
3 Mulberry Cl
4 Rockfield Wy
5 Shrivenham Cl
6 Sonninge Cl
7 Tarbat Ct
A7
1 Cherry Tree Cl
2 Faversham Rd
3 Hailsham Cl
4 Helksham Cl
5 Hormer Cl
6 Hornbeam Cl
7 Magnolia Cl
8 Okingham Cl
9 Waltham Cl
A6
1 Darleydale Cl
2 Georgeham Rd
3 Kirkham Cl
A
B
C
D
E
F
1
2
3
4
5
6
7
8
Crowthorne Business Centre
BRACKNELL ROAD
B3348
A3095
FORESTERS WAY
Crowthorne Wood
RG45
Three Castles Path
Kentigern Drive
Club La
White City
Upr Broadmoor Rd
Upper Broadmoor Rd
The Terrace
Cricket Fld Gv
Broadmoor Hospital
Napier Cl
Furze Hl Crs
Mulberry Cl
Chaplain's Hill
School Hill
Broadmoor County Primary School
Lower Broadmoor Road
Eastern Lane
Broadmoor Farm
Addiscombe Rd
Gordon Rd
South Meadow
South Road
49
RACKSTRAW ROAD
ROAD A3095
Copperfield Av
Hexham Cl
Dovedale Cl
Way
Wasdale Cl
Magdalene Road
Merton Cl
Keble Wy
Owlsmoor
Durham Rd
Rookwood Av
Oxford Rd
Trinity
Yale Cl
Peterhouse Cl
Fakenham
Keynsham Wy
Lewisham Wy
Acacia Av
Tottenham Wk
Union Cl
Church Road
Cambridge Rd
Owlsmoor Primary School
Nuffield Dr
Woodlands Ct
Wadham
Avenue
Culver Rd
Millins Cl
Evesham Wk
Horsham Rd
Road
Victoria Rd
Moor Cl
Birkbeck Pl
Balliol Way
Harvard Rd
Compton Close
Apple Tree Wy
The Surgery
Yeovil Road
Girton Cl
Linnes
Chariton Ct
Brook Cl
Oak
Owlsmoor
Whitmore Cl
Cookham Cl
Faringdon Cl
Atrebatti Rd
May Cl
Sandhurst School
College Town
Isis Wy
Wargrove Dr
Silver Hl
Hallmark Cl
Cannon Close
Rother Cl
Wantage Rd
Bittern Cl
Blackbird Cl
Blackcap Pl
Range Vw
Windsor Ride
Epsom Close
Goodwood
Road
Dawnay Road
Venlode Way
Wellington Cl
Crane Ct
Crake Pl
Junior School
College Crs
The Close
The Hospital
Humber Wy
Avocet Crs
Richmond Rd
Branksome Hill Road
College Road
The Breech
Range Ride
Woods
Hillside Road
Egerton Rd
Road
70
B7
1 Crown Pl
2 Grantham Cl
3 Rugby Cl
B8
1 Bluethroat Cl
2 Bullfinch Cl
3 Chaffinch Cl
D8
1 Dawnay Rd
F8
1 Overlord Cl
Sandhurst Sports Club
Travis Lane
Dalley Ct
Clarke Crs
Old Green La
1 grid square represents 500 metres

G H J K L M

A322

I

Rapley Farm

A322

2

Rapley
Lake

3

Bracknell Forest
Surrey County

4

Vicarage

BAGSH

Bagshot
Heath

Connaught
Rd

5

Wellesley Cl

Ride

Pinewood
Gdns

Heywood
Dr

Higgs La

College

Yaverland Dr

Hotel

Wishmoor
Bottom

JENKINS HILL LONDON RO

6

Lupin
Cl

7

Olddean
Common

Bracknell

Pineridge
County
First School

Mitcham

Surbiton Rd

Esher Rd

Kingston

Rd

Mitcham

LONDON ROAD

Highview
Crs

Wimbledon

Bracknell

Rd

Kingston Rd

Carshalton Rd

Sutton Rd

Road

Maultway N

Wychwood Dr

B3015 THE
MAULTWAY

Tree Tops Av

Collingwood Grn

Maultway Crs

Foxhill Crs

B3015

8

Queen
Elizabeth
Road

Duke Of
Cornwall Av

Academy Close

Birch Rd

Larch Rd

Saddleback Road

Star Post Road

Wishmoor Rd

Rowan Rd

Highview
Crs

Horseshoe
Crs

Hampshire
Road

Berkshire Road

Middle
School

Kingston

First
School

Collingwood
College

Ballard Road

Ltl Paddock

Seymour
Dr

College
Road

Fossewood Dr

1

Upper

Ride

Highland
Road

Poppyhills
Rd

Deer Rock Hill Rd

Rapley Rd

Turf Hill Rd

Cordwalles
Rd

Paschal Rd

Lorraine Rd

Caesar's Road

PO

Buchan

The

Highbury Crs

ROAD

Collingwood Grn

Waterloo Dr

Sovereign Dr

Oaken
Copse

G H **CAMBERLEY** J K L M

ROAD

Diamond Ridge

Upland Road

Old Dean

Crosby Hill Dr

Frawley Ridge

Diamond

A325

Beaufront

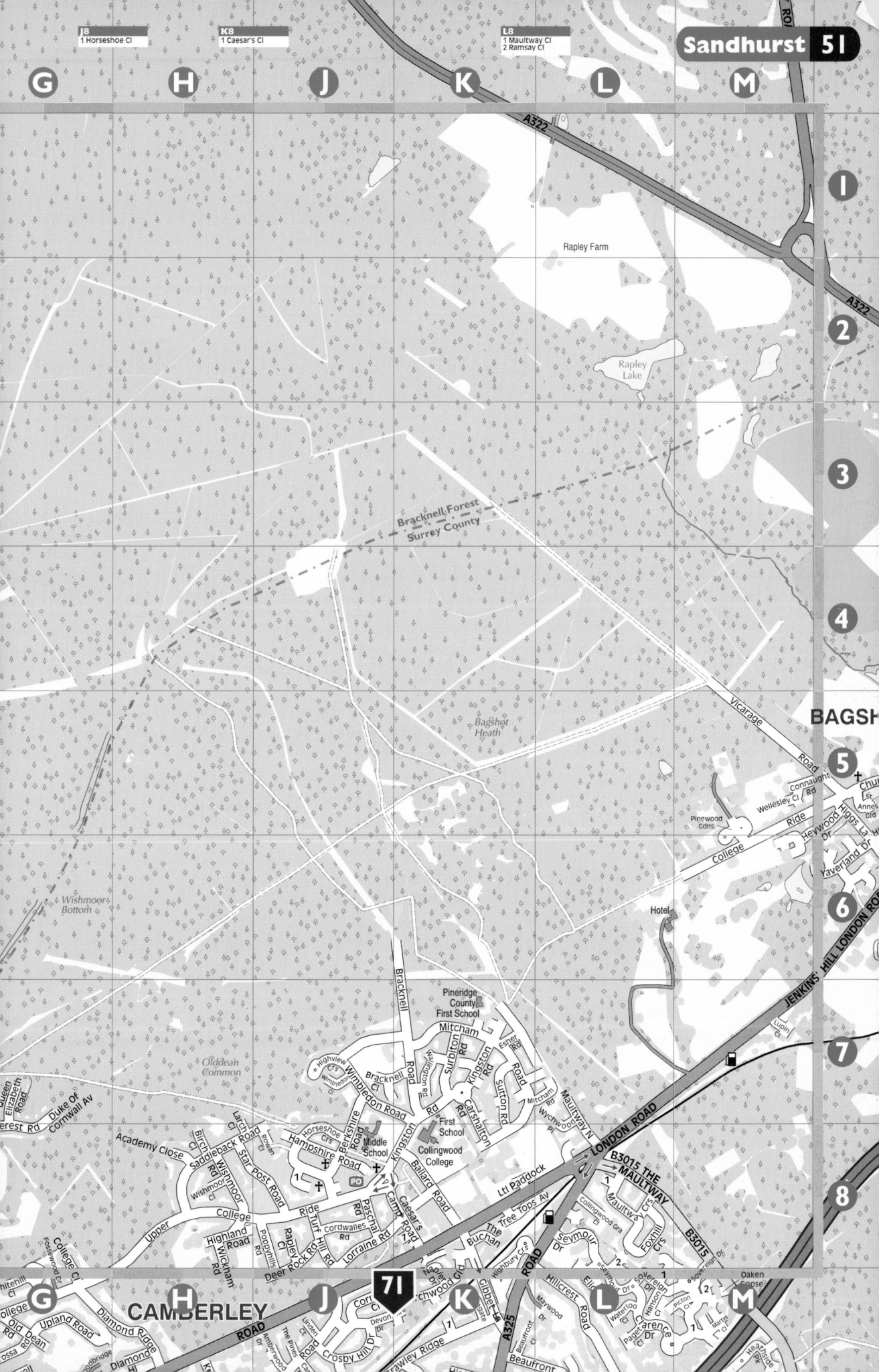

52

Rivar

32

A B C D E F

Wood

1

Rivar Down

2

New Buildings

's Farm

3

Bishop's Barn

Manor Farm

4

Ashley Drove

Moordown Farm

Ashley Drove

Smay Down

5

Smay Down Lane

PO

Oxenwood

Henley

6

Pearce's Farm

Fosbury House

†

Upper Row Farm

Church Farm

Wiltshire County
Hampshire County

7

Beacon Farm

Fosbury

8

Vernham Row

A B C 72 D E F

Tunball Lane

East Down

Bowers Lane

1 grid square represents 500 metres

G H J **33** K L M

Buttermere

Town Farm
Road
Downs Lane
Heath Lane
Grange Farm
Church Lane
Lane
Farm
White
Manor Farm

Buttermere Wood

Ballyack House

Rockmoor Down

Wiltshire County
Hampshire County

Combe Wood

Rockmoor Lane

Winterside Farm

Littledown

Vernham Street

Box Farm
Lane

Wright's Farm

Test Way

Hart Hill Down

Test Way

Manor House

Link

Manor Farm

1
2
3
4
54
5
6
7
8

G H J **73** K L M

54

A   B Walbury   C   34   D   E   F
         Hill

Wright's Farm

Test Way

West
Woodhay
Down

Wayfarer's Walk

1

Lower Farm

Combe

Manor Farm   Hampshire Cou
                                    West Berkshire
2   church Lane

3   Eastwick

4   Hogs
                               Hole

53

West Berkshire
Hampshire County
5

Test Way   Wayfarer's Walk
6

7
                                    Faccombe
nor House

Linkenholt
PO

Manor Farm
8   Netherton

Test Way

A   B   C   74   D   E   F

1 grid square represents 500 metres

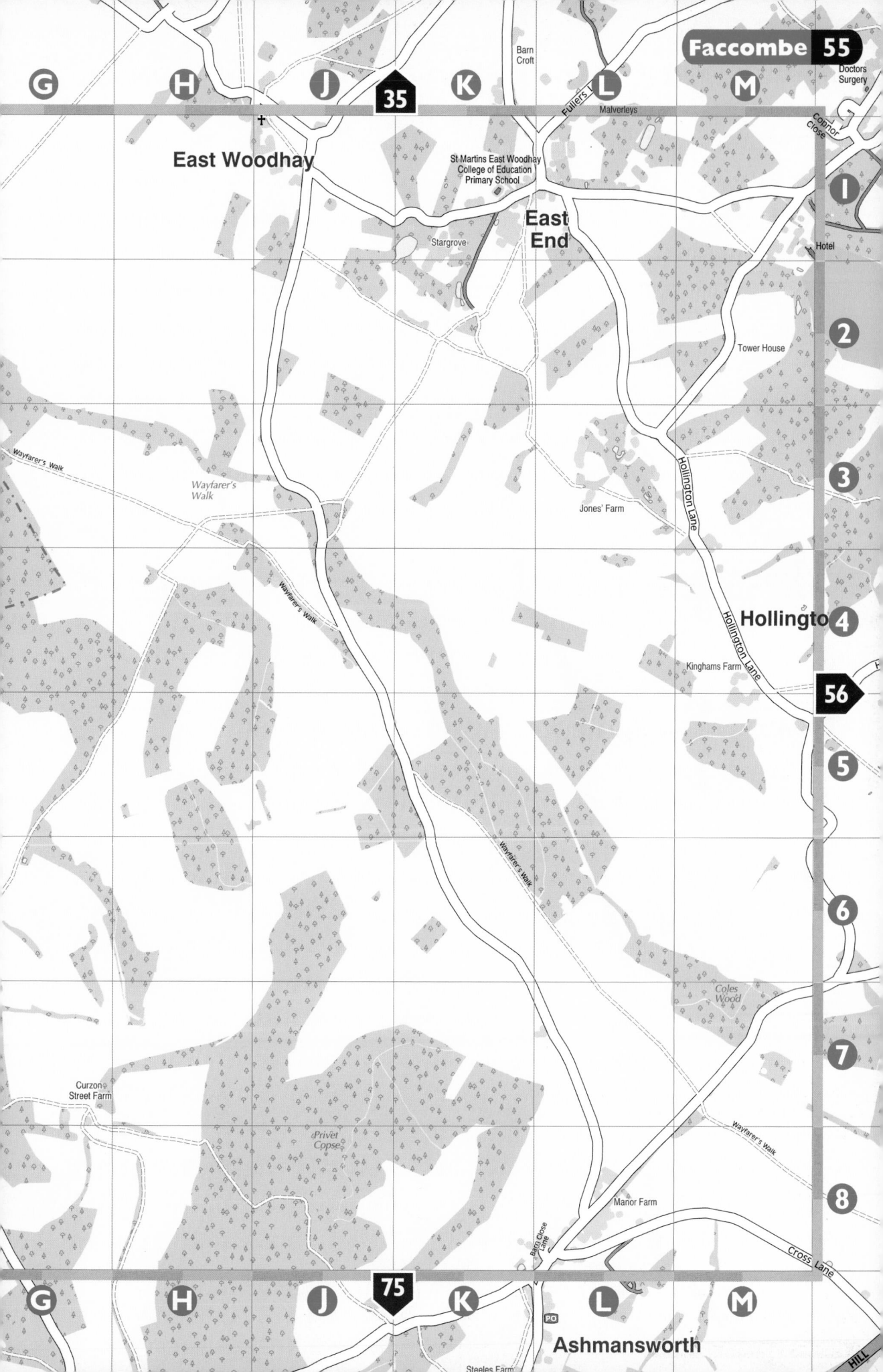

G H J **35** K L M

Barn
Croft

Doctors
Surgery

Fullers
Malverleys

I

East Woodhay

St Martins East Woodhay
College of Education
Primary School

**East
End**

Copnor
Close

Hotel

Stargrove

Tower House

2

Wayfarer's Walk

Wayfarer's
Walk

Jones' Farm

Hollington Lane

3

Hollingto **4**

Hollington Lane

Kinghams Farm

56

Wayfarer's Walk

5

6

Coles
Wood

7

Curzon
Street Farm

Wayfarer's Walk

Privet
Copse

Manor Farm

8

Barn Close Lane

Cross Lane

HILL

G H J **75** K L M

PO

Ashmansworth

Steeles Farm

A

† St Thomas
Infant School

B

C

The
Mount

D

Penwood

E

F

Pound
Street

Doctors
Surgery

Church Lane

Connor Close

Woolton
Hill

Woolton
Hill County
Junior School

Thorngrove
School

Mount Rd

36

Heathlands

Penwood Heights

Woodlands

Farmhouse
Gallery

I

Hotel

Lane

Pantings

Mount Cl

Four
Oaks

Clere
Wood

Milford
Lake

2

ver House

Tubb's

Arkwright
Cl

Byeways

Star
La

Highclere

White
Oak House

3

Crowshott

Westridge

Burfield

†

Flexford
Cl

Du
Me

Westridge

4

Hol gton

Lane

Hollington Lane

Highclere Farm

55

Highclere
Street

Flexford House

†

A343

5

Hollington
Cross

Highclere
Park

6

PH

Maple Farm

Highclere
Castle

Limetree

Zell House
Farm

7

Avenue

Shearer's Walk

8

Cross Lane

A343

Three Legs House

Grotto
Copse

A

B

C

76

D

E

F

Shearer's Walk

Hill

Highclere Stud

1 grid square represents 500 metres

Earlstone Common
37
G
H
J
K
L
M
Burghclere
A34(T)
B4640
Lane
Limes Av
The Clere Secondary School
Palmer's Hill House
Breachfield
Coronation
Cl
Church Lane
Burghclere CP School
Well Street
Pound La
Harts Lane
St Michaels School
Sandham Memorial Chapel (NT)
Norman Farm
Spring Lane
Budd's Farm
Wellhouse Farm
West Street
Earlstone Manor
West Street
Ridgemoor Farm
Well Street
Whitway
58
Duncroft Farm
White Hill
Wergs Farm
Old Burghclere
Sydmonton C
Sydmo
Ivory Farm
77
1
2
3
4
5
6
7
8

A
B
C
38
D
E
F
Brock's Green
Frith Copse
Hyde Farm
1
Whitehouse Farm
Hyde Lane
2
Kisby's Farm
Woodside Farm
3
4
Cowhouse Farm
Mill Lane
Oakfields Close
White Hill
57
Ecchinswell
Frobury Farm
5
Watership Farm
6
Nuthanger Farm
7
Fossicks
Sydmonton Court
Sydmonton
8
A
B
C
78
D
E
F
1 grid square represents 500 metres
Watership

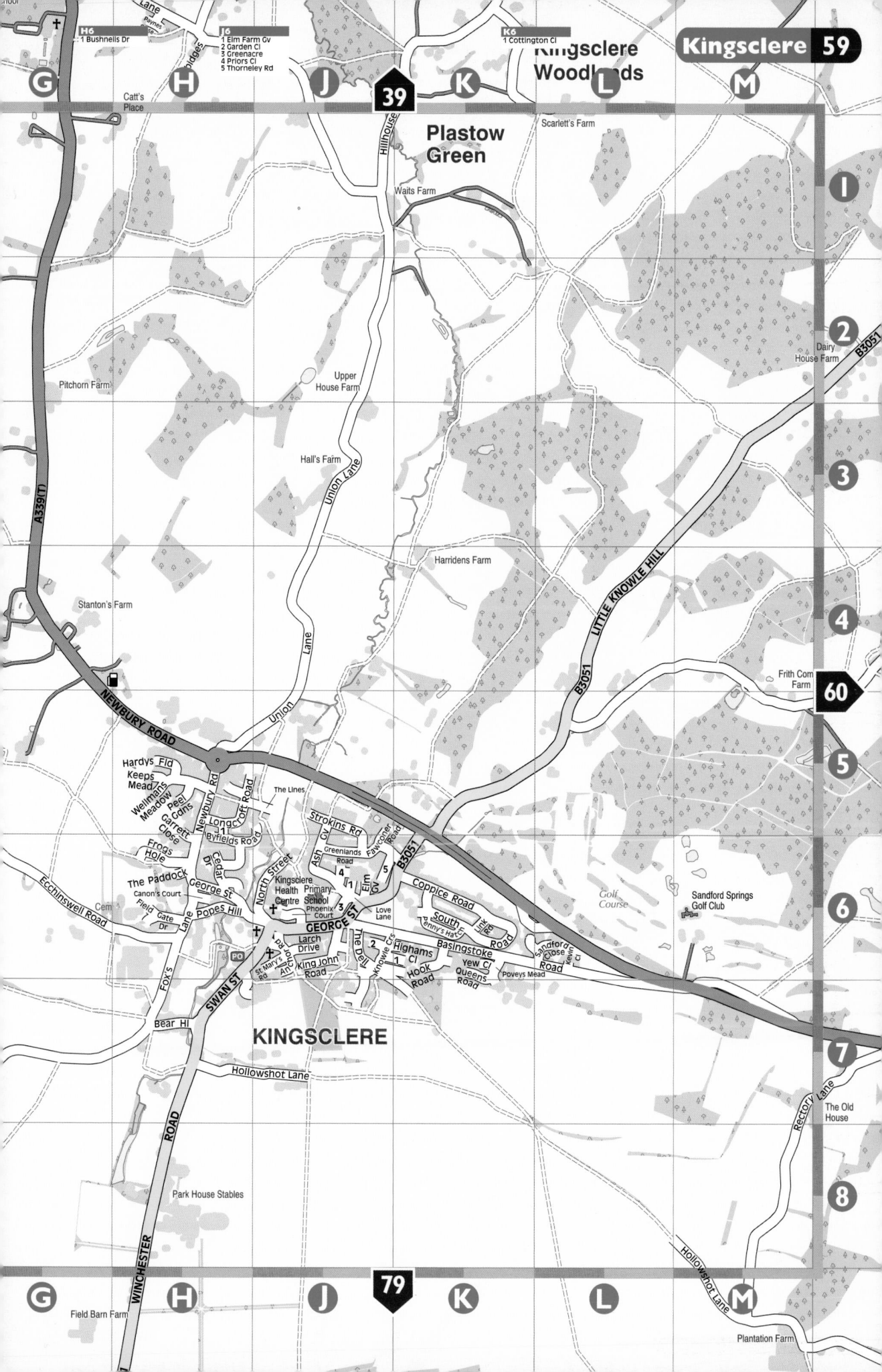

G H J **39** K L M

H6
1 Bushnells Dr

J6
1 Elm Farm Gv
2 Garden Cl
3 Greenacre
4 Priors Cl
5 Thorneley Rd

K6
1 Cottington Cl

Kingsclere
Woodlands

Plastow
Green

Scarlett's Farm

Hillhouse

Waits Farm

1

2
Dairy
House Farm
B3051

Pitchorn Farm

Upper
House Farm

3

Hall's Farm

Union Lane

Harridens Farm

LITTLE KNOWLE HILL

Stanton's Farm

4

B3051

Frith Com
Farm
60

NEWBURY ROAD

Union
Lane

5

Hardys Fld
Keeps
Mead
Wellmans
Meadow
Peel
Garrett
Close
Frogs
Hole
The Paddock
Canon's Court
Field Gate
Dr
Popes Hill

Newbury Rd
Croft Road
Longc
Byfields Road
Cedar Dr
The Lines

Ash Gv
Strokins Rd
Greenlands
Road
4 1
North Street
Kingsclere
Health
Centre
Primary
School
3
Phoenix
Court
George St

Elm Gv
5
Fawcett
Road
B3051

Coppice Road

Love
Lane
South
Link
Road
Basingstoke
Road

Golf
Course

Sandford Springs
Golf Club

Sandford
Close
Kelvin Cl

6

GEORGE ST
Larch
Drive
St Mary's
Rd
King John
Road
PO
Fox's
The Dell
Knowle Crs
1
Hook
Road
Highams
Cl
Yew Cl
Queens
Road
Poveys Mead

Penny's Hat

Road

7
Rectory Lane
The Old
House

SWAN ST

Bear Hl

KINGSCLERE

Hollowshot Lane

8

WINCHESTER ROAD

Ecchinswell Road

Cem

Park House Stables

Field Barn Farm

G H J **79** K L M

Hollowshot Lane

Plantation Farm

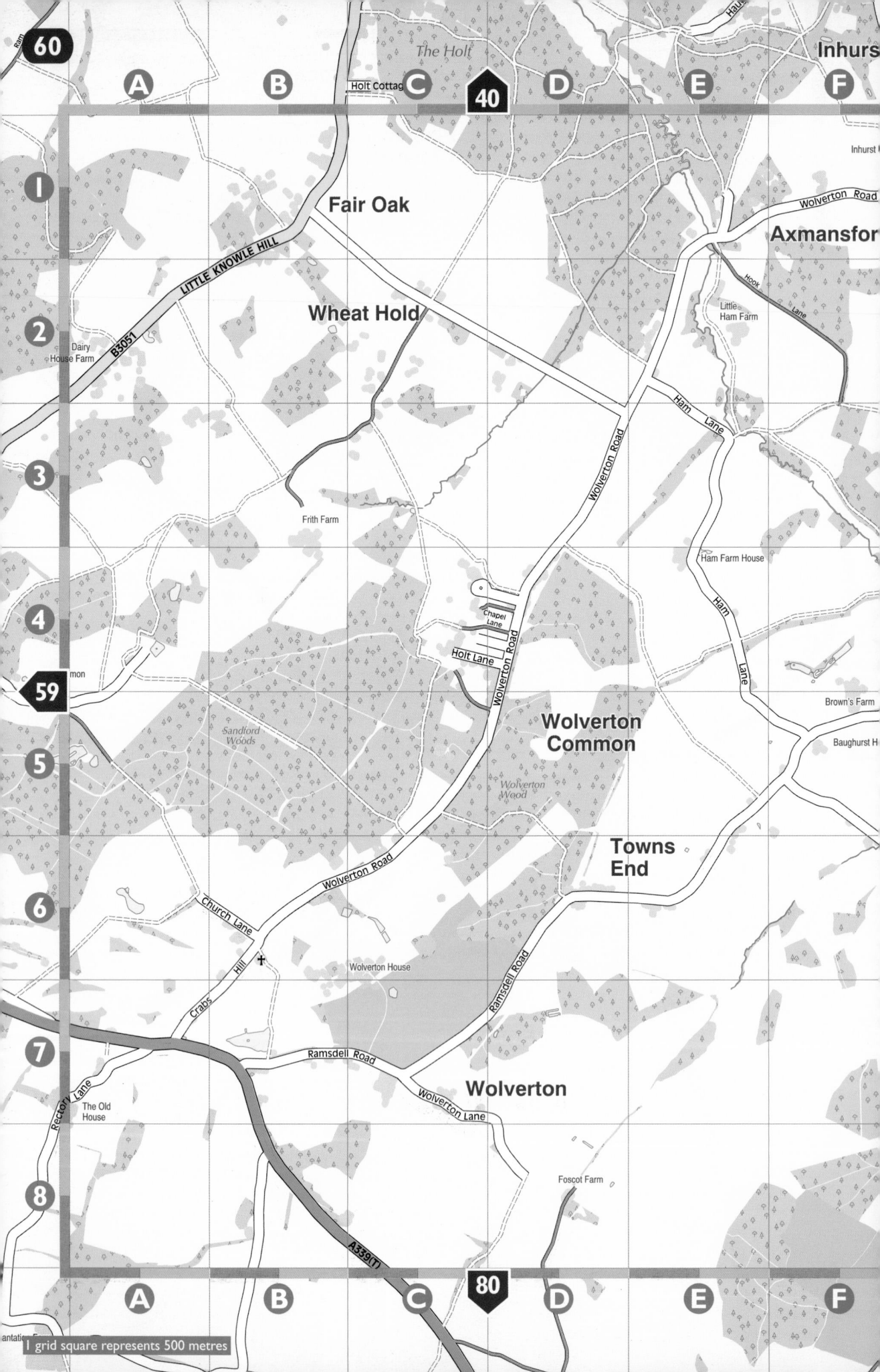

60
40
59
80
A
B
C
D
E
F
1
2
3
4
5
6
7
8
The Holt
Holt Cottag
Inhurs
Inhurst
Fair Oak
Wolverton Road
Axmansfor
LITTLE KNOWLE HILL
B3051
Wheat Hold
Hook Lane
Little Ham Farm
Dairy House Farm
Ham Lane
Wolverton Road
Frith Farm
Ham Farm House
Chapel Lane
Holt Lane
Ham Lane
Brown's Farm
Baughurst H
Sandford Woods
Wolverton Common
Wolverton Wood
Towns End
Wolverton Road
Church Lane
Crabs Hill
Wolverton House
Ramsdell Road
Ramsdell Road
Wolverton
Wolverton Lane
Rectory Lane
The Old House
Foscot Farm
A339(T)
1 grid square represents 500 metres

L1
1 Abbottswood Cl
2 Candover Cl
3 Cheriton Cl
4 Herriard Wy
5 Monks Wood Crs

L2
1 Crookham Cl

M1
1 Christy Ct
2 Finch Cl
3 Titchfield Cl

41

62

Baughurst

Whitedown Road

New Road

Shaw

Rimes's

Lane

Oak
House

Church

Brook

Church

Brook

Church Brook Farm

Hawley House

Church Rd

Church Road

TADLEY

TADLEY HILL

A340

Skates Lane

Skate's Farm

Hollybush Lane

Old Vyne
Lane

Baughurst

Road

Hillside

Pound Green

Browninghill
Green

Stratton Manor

Wyeford Farm

Stony
Heath

Povey's Farm

The Firs

West
Heath

Baughurst

Road

Sherborne

Road

White Hart
Lane

PH

Charter
Alley

Tubb's

Rawlins Farm

Ewnurst

Road

Skyer's Farm

Ramsdell

RG26

Morland
Surgery

Infant School

Junior
School

Tadley CP
School

Rectory
Close

The Green

The Green

62
42
61
82
A
B
C
D
E
F
1
2
3
4
5
6
7
8
Pamber Green
Little London
Court Corner
Pamber End
Salters Heath
Pamber Forest
Gravelpit Copse
Mariner's Copse
Cranes Copse
Silchester Farm
Froglane Farm
Pamber Farm
Hill End Farm
Beaurepaire Farm
Rawlins Farm
Priory Farm
The Priory Primary School
Tadley CP School
Byes Lane
Little London Road
Silchester Road
Frog Lane
Forest Lane
Kimbers La
New Road
Green La
Boar's Bridge
Bramley Road
Ramsdell Road
Morgaston Road
A340
ALDERMASTON RD
ALDERMASTON ROAD
MAIN ROAD
Skates Lane
Sandy Lane
Vine Tree Close
Mariners Close
Manse La
Knapp Lane
Winston Avenue
Malthouse Lane
North View Road
Fairlawn
Cedar Cl
Rampton's Meadow
Bowmonts Rd
Brook Green
Road
Rowan
Tunworth Mews
The Orchard
West Field Close
Pamber Heath
Dukes Ride
Lordswood
Hartleys
Hydes Platt
Beach's Crs
Dicker's
1 grid square represents 500 metres

K5
1 Pheaben's Fld
L5
1 Jibbs Meadow
2 Longbridge Rd
M6
1 Beech Cl
43
83
64
Three Ashes
Bramley Road
Lower Farm
Clappers Farm
Lavell's
Haines Farm
Barefoot House
Holly Cross
Stratfield Saye Road
Bramley Lane
Oliver's Lane
Oliver's Farm
Folly Farm
Minchens Lane
Moat Close
Bramley C of E Primary School
Meltner Cl
Tottenham Cl
Bramley
Clift Surgery
Bromelia Close
Osler Cl
Strawberry Fields
Bramley Station
Sherfield Road
The Street
Ringshall Gdns
Pound Cl
Ellen Gdns
Coopers Lane
Longbridge Rd
Dollis Gn
The Smithy
Farriers Cl
Coopers Ct
Europa Cl
Bramley Corner
Silchester Road
Middle Farm
Beaurepaire Cl
Church Lands
The Street
Locksbridge Lane
The Maltings
Lane End
Bramley Green
Forge Cl
Pigeon Cl
Holly Cl
Green Road
German Road
St John Cl
Taylor Dr
Walls Dr
Officers Row
Bow Brook
Watford Copse
Vyne Road
Baker's Farm
Vyne Lodge Farm
Cufaude
Ragg Copse
mere Green

Green Lane

Stratfield Saye

C8
1 Bow Gdns
2 Goddards Cl

A West End Green B C **44** D E F

Green Lane

Herriot's Farm

Lavell's Lane

The Spring

Fair Oak Lane

Kings Farm

1

2 Fair Oak Green

Ives Farm

Saye Road

Folly Lane

Mill Lane

Southend Farm

River Loddon

3

Heywood's Farm

4

St Tu

iver's Farm

Folly Lane

Folly Farm

63

The Fishery

5

River Loddon

Potters Lane

Spanish Green

Lillymill Farm

Mill Lane

Bramley Green

Newhouse Farm

Forge Cl

Sherfield Road

Green Holly

6 Campbell Rd

Taylor Dr

St John Cl

The Limes

St Barbara's Cl

Woodland Dr

St Mary Av

The Ms

Hartley Lane

erman Road

Wallis Dr

Sims Cl

Sherfield Road

Officers Row

Floods Farm

The Meadow

Northfield Rd

Northfield

Longbridge Cl

7

Willow

Bramley Road

Poplar

WN Gv

Bow Gv

Poplar Cl

Bulls Down Cl

Carpenters

Bow Drive

1

Greenway

Goddards Cl

2

Sherfield on Loddon

PO

River Loddon

Dixon Road

Breach La

Pound Meadow

8

Reading Road

Wildmoor

Ragg Cops

A B C **84** D E F

Wildmoor Lan

Lance Levy Farm

G   H   J   45   K   L   M

1

2

3

4

66

5

6

7

8

Stratfield Saye Park

River

Stratfield Saye

Park Pitham Copse

BASINGSTOKE   ROAD

Lower Pitham

Hotel

PH

A33

Lawn Farm

Daneshill School

Bylands Farm

Hartley House

Chandlers Green

Rotherwick Lane

Rotherwick

ley pall

Mill Farm

Lane

Sheldons Farm

Home Farm

Wellington Monument

Heckfield Heath House

Heckfield

Church Lane

Highfield House

B3349

Hotel

The Causeway

Vicarage   Lane

Thackham's Farm

Blue House Farm

Bottle Lane

Black Wood

Froc

G   H   J   85   K   L   M

66
46
65
86
A
B
C
D
E
F
1
2
3
4
5
6
7
8
ROAD
River Whitewater
Park
Heckfield Place
Bramshill
Copes Lane
B3011
B3349
Laundry Lane
Laundry La
Great Danmoor Copse
Holdshott Farm
Hotel
Highfield House
Plough Lane
Plough
Lane
Hazeley Lea
Hazeley
Hudsons Meadow
Hound Green
Hound Gn Cl
Alder Moor Copse
Hazeley Heath
Red Hill
Hazeley Bottom
Blue House Farm
READING ROAD
Mattingley
Dipley
Stoken Lane
Lane
PH
RG27
1 grid square represents 500 metres

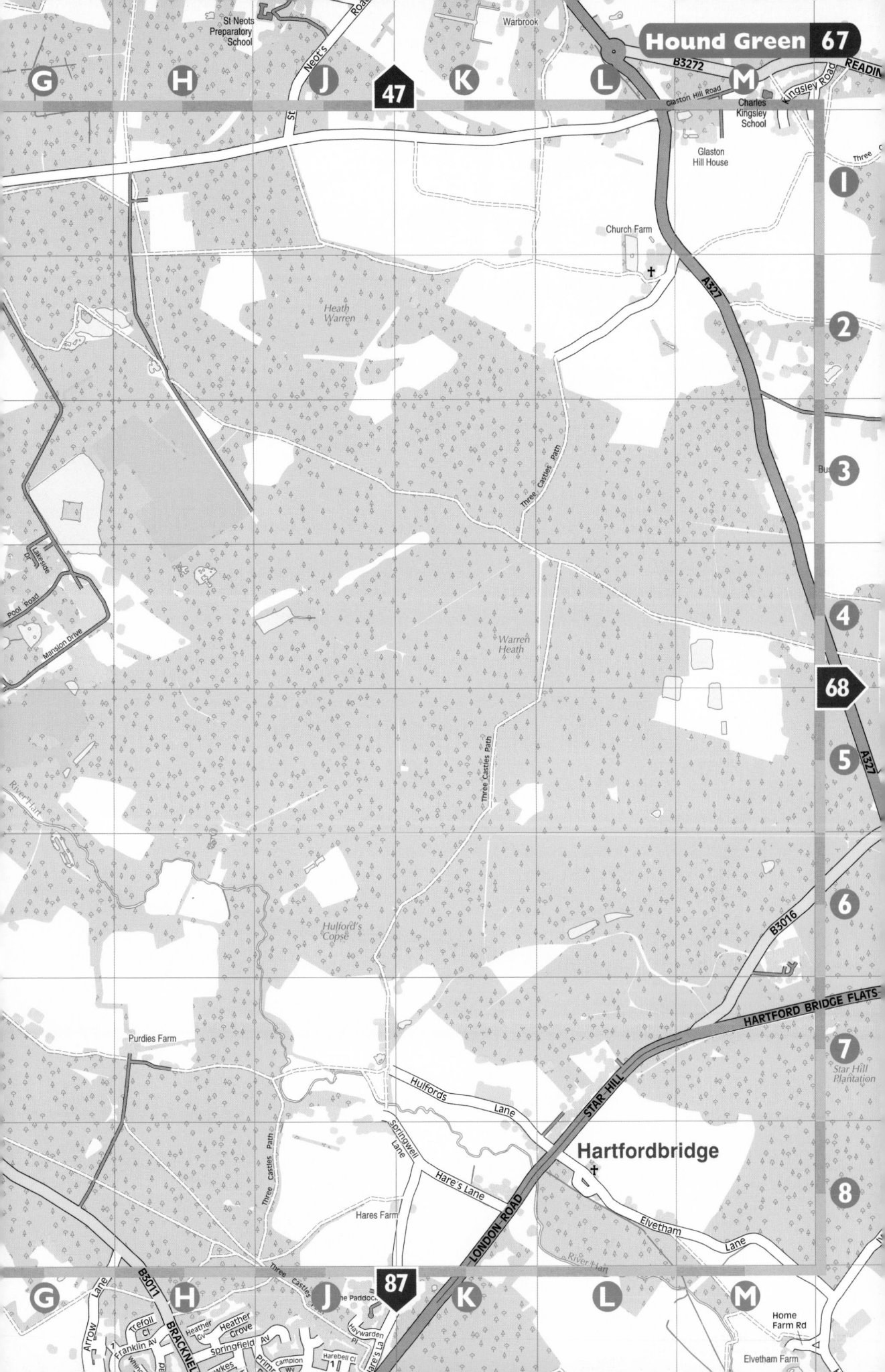
Hound Green
67
47
68
87
G
H
J
K
L
M
I
2
3
4
5
6
7
8
St Neots Preparatory School
St Neot's Road
Warbrook
B3272
Glaston Hill Road
Kingsley Road
READIN
Charles Kingsley School
Glaston Hill House
Three
Church Farm
A327
Heath Warren
Three Castles Path
Lakeside Dr
Pool Road
Mansion Drive
Warren Heath
River Hart
Hulford's Copse
B3016
HARTFORD BRIDGE FLATS
Purdies Farm
Star Hill Plantation
STAR HILL
Hulfords Lane
Springwell Lane
Hartfordbridge
Hare's Lane
LONDON ROAD
Elvetham Lane
Hares Farm
River Hart
B3011
BRACKNEL
Arrow Lane
Trefoil Cl
Franklin Av
Heather Gv
Heather Grove
Springfield Av
Campion Wy
Harebell Cl
Haywarden Pl
Hare's La
Home Farm Rd
Elvetham Farm

E4
1 Brocklands
2 Byron Cl
E3
1 Badgers Holt
E2
1 Falcon Wy
2 Mallard Wy
3 Raven Cl
4 Turnstone End
5 Wren Cl
D2
1 Honeysuckle Cl
2 Tresham Crs
E1
1 Fareham Dr
Eversley Cricket Club
Eversley Cross
Up Green
Brooklands
Firgrove Manor
Kits Croft
Busta Farm
Eversley Common
Blackbushe Airport
Westfield County Junior School
Yateley School
Star Hill Plantation
Yateley Heath Wood
West Minley Farm
Home Farm Rd
F1
1 Elm Bank
2 White Hse Gdns
F2
1 Florence Cl
F3
1 Alder Gv
2 Doyle Gdns
3 Dumas Cl
4 Merron Cl
F4
1 Kipling Cl
2 Silverglades
1 grid square represents 500 metres

48
67
88

G1
1 Green End
2 Harpdon Pde
3 Heathwood Cl
G2
1 Rosary Gdns
2 Woodbourne Cl
G3
1 Barnfield
2 Brockenhurst Dr
3 Lower Moor
4 Tudor Dr
5 Wentworth Cl
G4
1 Dungells Farm Cl
2 Glenavon Gdns
H3
1 Denham Dr
2 Mason Cl
49
70
89
Trilakes Country Park
Sandhurst Station
Lakeside Business Park
Sandhurst Surgery
Sandhurst Sports Club
Uplands CP School
YORKTOWN RD
A321
MARSHALL ROAD
Yateley Manor Preparatory School
St Peters GM C of E School
Health Centre
YATELEY
County Infant School
Bracknell Forest
Hampshire County
Frogmore
Darby Green
Cricket Hill
READING ROAD
B3272
Potley Hill County Primary School
Frogmore Community School
Frogmore Junior School
Frogmore County Infant School
The Surgery
Cemetery
Hill Farm
Yateley Common
A30
GU17
Starve Acre
Hornley Common
Hawley Common
Minley Manor
Minley Wood
MINLEY ROAD
A327
Home Farm
Hawley Lake
Ripon Road
M3
1 Grayshot Dr
2 Salisbury Rd
M2
1 Ringwood Rd
2 Romsey Cl
3 Selborne Cl
4 Southampton Cl
5 Winchester Wy
M1
1 Travis La
L3
1 Acorn Rd
2 Brooksby Cl
J3
1 Bannister Gdns
2 Caswall Ride
3 Hatherwood
Pinewood Infants School

70
50
69
90
A
B
C
D
E
F
1
2
3
4
5
6
7
8
D7
1 Claydon Gdns
E2
1 Willington Cl
C5
1 Campion Cl
C7
1 Cypress
2 Fernhill Wk
3 Recreation Cl
C1
1 Church Rd
B3
1 Chestnut Cl
B4
1 Broom Cl
2 Glenhurst Cl
3 Ryecroft Gdns
B1
1 Rosedene La
B2
1 Hepworth Cft
2 M Brown End
3 Seebys Oak
4 Thorburn Cha
A1
1 Balintore Ct
2 Burghead Cl
3 Castlecraig Ct
4 Findhorn Cl
5 Fortrose Cl
6 Hopeman Cl
7 Waterh'se Mead
A2
1 Bacon Cl
2 Reynolds Gn
A3
1 Clanfield Ride
2 Russell Ct
3 Tichborne Cl
A4
1 Harlech Rd
2 Jays Nest Cl
3 Quebec Gdns
4 Springcross Av
A5
1 Belvedere Ct
2 Clarendon Ct
E3
1 Hatfield Ct
2 Heatherley Cl
3 Hollyfields Cl
4 Montague Cl
5 St Michaels Rd
6 Woodway
E4
1 Burford Rd
2 Butterfield
3 Crondall Ct
4 Donnington Cl
E5
1 Dorcas Ct
E6
1 Bramley Rd
E7
1 Mayfield Rd
E8
1 Prentice Cl
F2
1 St Mary's Rd
F3
1 Albert Rd
2 Bennett Ct
3 Park La
F4
1 Birchfields
1 grid square represents 500 metres
Blackwater
York Town
Hawley
Fox Lane
Royal Military Academy
Sandhurst Sports Club
Staff College
Upper Lake
Lower Lake
Junior School
The Hospital
MARSHALL ROAD
A3095
A321
A30
LONDON RD
B3411
FRIMLEY ROAD
A331
B3272
M3
Junction 4
White Hart Industrial Estate
Blackwater Station
Blackwater & Hawley Leisure Centre
Hawley CP School
Hawley Park
Hawley Place School
Fernhill Primary School
Fernhill Sch Sch
Coliseum Business Cen
Camberley Town Football Club
Sampson Business Park
St Georges Industrial Est
Camberley Health Centre
Camberley Rugby Football Club
Farrell Middle School
France Hill School
First School
Lyndhurst School
Camberley County Infant School
Arena Leisure Centre
West Sussex Co Council
St Catherine's School
Hawley Lane Industrial Estate
Farnborough Town Football Club
Blackwater River
Starve Acre
Hawley Common

G2
1 Lancaster Dr
2 Markham Ct
3 Townside Pl
G3
1 Dennistoun Cl
2 Firlands Av
G4
1 Longford Cl
G5
1 The Pavilions End
2 Watchetts Lake Cl
G7
1 Frimley High St
G8
1 Frimley High St
2 Kenmore Cl
3 Shamrock Cl
H2
1 Branksome Cl
51
CAMBERLEY
LONDON ROAD
PORTSMOUTH ROAD
A325
M3
B3015
B311
UPPER CHOBHAM ROAD
Crawley Hill
Heatherside
Frimley Ridge
Frimley
GU15
Portesbery School
Camberley Magistrates Court
Crawley Ridge First School
Hotel
Clewborough House Preparatory School
Prior Heath School
Camberley Heath Golf Club
Carwarden House School
Camberley Cricket Club
Frimley Park Hospital
A&E
Grove County Primary School
Tomlinscote School
Tomlin's Pond
Primary School
Oaken Copse
Heatherside Surg
Royal Logistic Corps M
M1
1 Consort Dr
2 Curtis Cl
M3
1 Augustus Gdns
M4
1 Pollard Gv
2 Redmayne
M5
1 Edgemoor Rd
2 Haslemere Cl
3 Paterson Cl
CHOBHAM ROAD
B3411 FRIMLEY GREEN ROAD
CHURCH RD
GROVE CROSS RD
Frith Hill Road
Rhododendron Road
Valley Road
DEEPCUT BRIDGE ROAD
91
L1
1 Darracott Cl
L4
1 Amber Hl
2 Bentley Copse
K1
1 Silverwood Dr
K3
1 Ardrossan Av
2 Southcote Dr
J8
1 Oldbury Cl
2 Petworth Cl
J6
1 Mulgrave Rd
J7
1 Broughton Ms
2 Kilmartin Gdns
3 Stamford Av
J1
1 Gainsborough Cl
J3
1 Crawley Wood Cl
H6
1 Lanark Cl
2 Montrose Cl
3 Nairn Cl
4 Stirling Cl
Frimley
The Princess

52
94
Vernham Row
Vernham Bank
Bowers Lane
East Down
Oakhill Wood
Tunball Lane
Fosbury Farm
The Slay
254
Haydown Hill
Hippenscombe
Conholt Hill
Cleves Copse
Little Down
Chute Causeway
Middle Conholt Farm
Conholt House
Hungerford Lane
Conholt Park
Hampshire Gate
Wiltshire County
Hampshire County
Cathanger Wood
Standen House
Chute Standen
Breach La
Dummer Lane
Dudley Lane
Chute Cadley
Lower Chute
Dowlands
A
B
C
D
E
F
1
2
3
4
5
6
7
8
1 grid square represents 500 metres

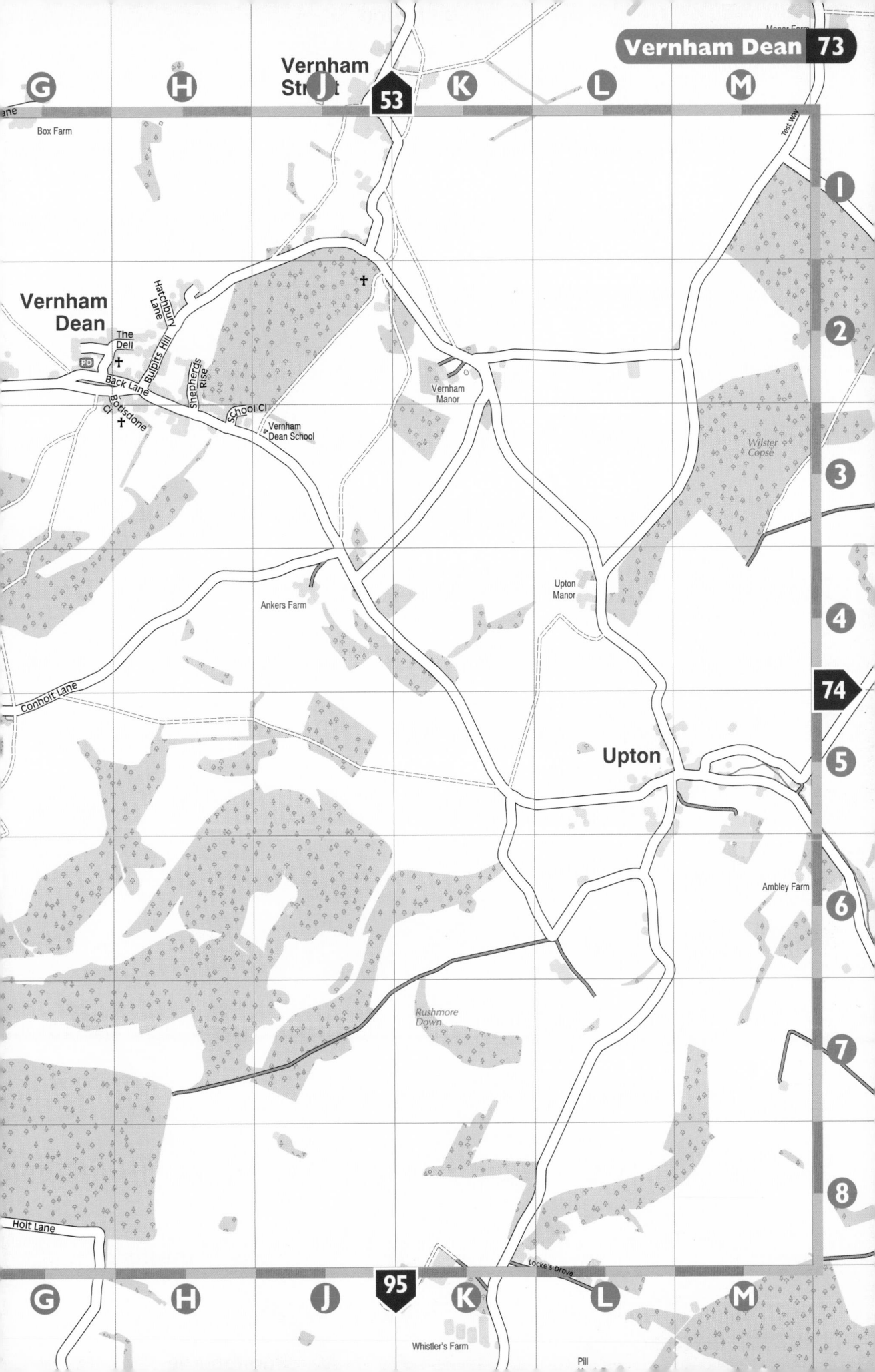

G   H   **Vernham Street** J   53   K   L   M

Vernham Dean

Box Farm

Hatchbury Lane
Bulpits Hill
The Dell
PO
Back Lane
Shepherds Rise
Botsdone Cl
School Cl
Vernham Dean School

Vernham Manor

Wilster Copse

Ankers Farm

Conholt Lane

Upton Manor

74

Upton

Ambley Farm

Rushmore Down

Holt Lane

Locke's Drove

G   H   J   95   K   L   M

Whistler's Farm

Pill

1
2
3
4
5
6
7
8

Netherton

A   B   C   54   D   E   F

1

2

Wilster
Copse

3   Test Way

Clinchorn Farm

4

73

5

Ambley Farm

6   River Swift

7   Dunstan's Drove

Ibthorpe

8   Locke's Drove

A   B   C   96   D   E   F

Faccombe
Wood

Doyley
Manor

Test Way

Horseshoe Lane

Bladon
Gallery

The Dene

PO   The Crescent Dean Rise

River Swift

Hurstbourne

I grid square represents 500 metres

G   H   J   55   K   L   M

Manor Farm

Cross Lane

Barn Close Lane

1

PO

Ashmansworth

HILL

Steeles Farm

RED

2

Alexander Farm

Church Farm

✝

Crux Easton

✝

3

Lower Manor Farm

4

Sidley Wood

76

5

A343

Hotel

Lye Farm

Easton Park Wood

6

43

7

Lower Doiley Farm

Sladen Green

Highfield House

Dolley Bottom

8

Binley

G   H   J   97   K   L   M

Cross Lane

Three Legs House

A   B   C   D   E   F

I

HILL

A343

RED

2

ux Easton

3 †

Wayfarer's Walk

Grotto
Copse

Mopper's Barn

Highclere Stud

Upper
Woodcott
Down

Wayfarer's Walk

4

Beech
Hanger
Copse

Lower
Woodco
Down

Hook
Copse

5

Woodcott

†

Easton
Pa...

6

Lower Woodcott Farm

7

Paul's
Copse

Stubb's
Copse

Woodcott House

8

Buckets Down Farm

Dunley

A   B   C   D   E   F

I grid square represents 500 metres

Sydmo

G H J 57 K L M

I

2

3

78

5

6

7

8

Ivory Farm

262
▲
Beacon
Hill

234
▲
Ladle
Hill

*Great
Litchfield
Down*

Wayfarer's Walk

A34(T)

Down Farm

*Wormley
Copse*

Litchfield

Sydmo

Sydmonton

78

A B C **58** D E F

I

Watership
Down

Wayfarer's Walk

Wayfarer's Walk

2

Cannon Heath Down

3

4

Ashley Warren Farm

77

Cannon Heath Farm

5

Hare Warren
Farm

6

Polhampton
Lodge Stud

Robley Belt

7

8

Caesar's
Belt

A B C **100** D E F

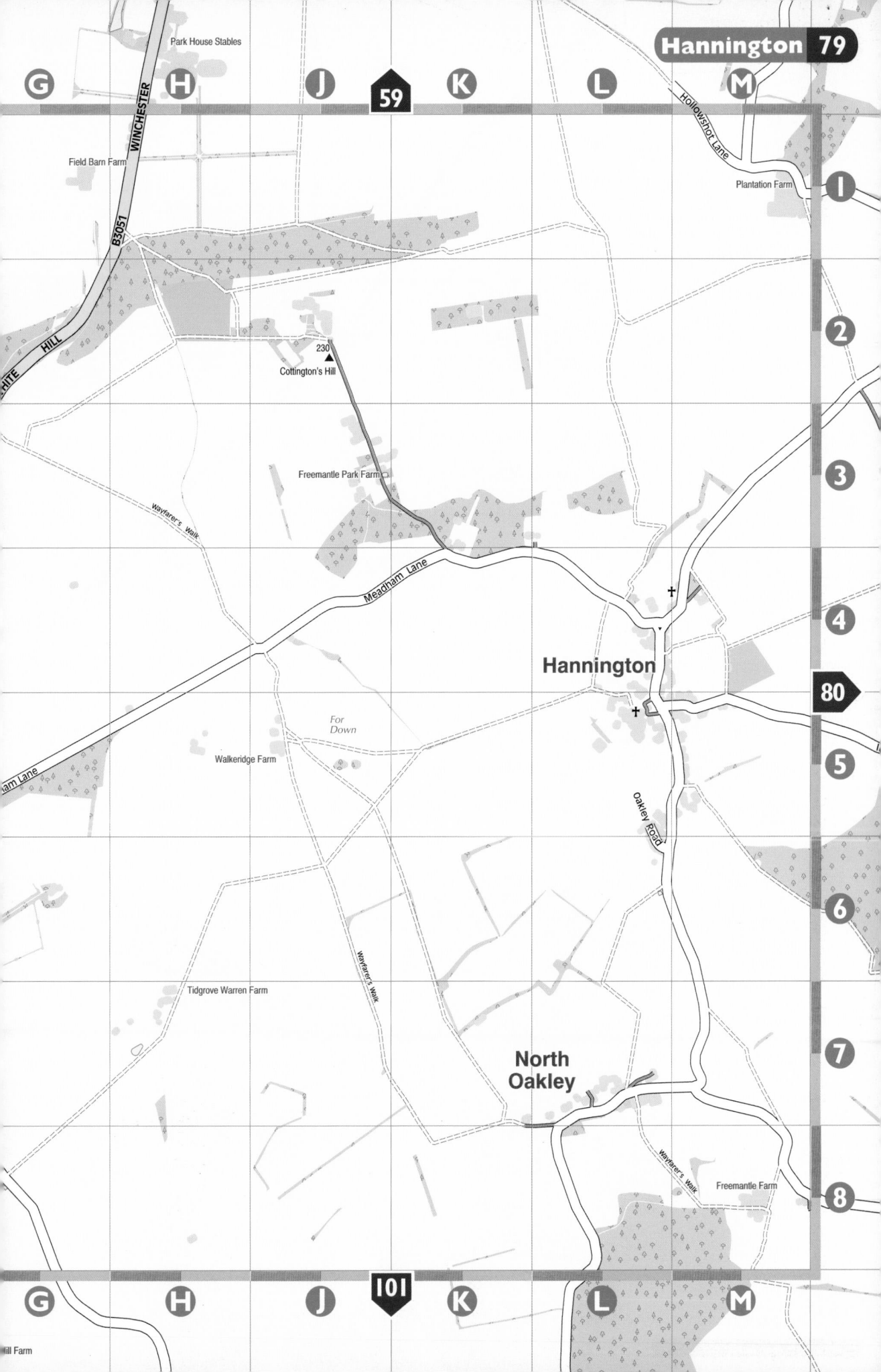

G H J **59** K L M

I

2

3

4

80

5

6

7

8

Park House Stables

Field Barn Farm

WINCHESTER

B3051

WHITE HILL

230
Cottington's Hill

Freemantle Park Farm

Wayfarer's Walk

Meadham Lane

For Down

Walkeridge Farm

ham Lane

Wayfarer's Walk

Tidgrove Warren Farm

Hannington

Oakley Road

North Oakley

Wayfarer's Walk

Plantation Farm

Hollowshot Lane

Freemantle Farm

ill Farm

80

Ⓐ   Ⓑ   A339(T)   Ⓒ   **60**   Ⓓ   Ⓔ   Ⓕ

Foscot Farm

Ⅰ

Plantation

Home Farm

2

Dorrel Wood

Ewhurst House

3

Pitt Hall Fm

Folly Dairy

4

◀ **79**

Ibworth Lane

5

Balstone Farm

Ibworth

6

7

Warren Bottom Copse

Hook Lane

ntle Far

8

Ⓐ   Ⓑ   Ⓒ   **102**   Ⓓ   Ⓔ   Ⓕ

Hay Wood

1 grid square represents 500 metres

G H J **61** K L M

Ramsdell

Monk

White Hart Lane
She— Road
PH

Charter L lley
Beal's Pightie
Rawlins Farm

RG26

I

Ewhurst Road

Skyer's Farm

Sheedwash Lane

Skyer's Wood

Privett Copse

2

The C

Kiln Lane
Kiln Green

3

Lower Farm

4

82

5

Basingstoke Road

Field Barn Farm

6

Woodgarston Farm

Upper Wootton

A339(T) KINGSCLERE ROAD

Basingstoke Road

A339(T)
KINGSCLERE

7

Tangier

Whitedown

8

G H J **103** K L M
PO

Wootton

82
Salters Heath
62
Rawlins Farm
Monk Sherborne
Salters Heath Road
Morgaston Road
Cranes Copse
Morgaston Wood
Kiln Lane
Kiln Green
The Cl
Salters Heath Rd
Weybrook Ct
West End
Manor Farm
Cranes Rd
Cranesfield
Cem
Vyne Meadow
Vyne Road
Sherborne St John Primary School
Sherborne St John
Spring Cl
Cranes Road
Bourne Fld
The Severals
Tyfield
Dark La
Dancers Meadow
Kiln Road
Elm Road
Manor Road
81
ALDERMASTON ROAD
ALDERMASTON ROAD A340
Elm Bottom Cross
Chineham
Sherborne Road
KINGSCLERE ROAD
Rooksdown Lane
Nightingale Gdns
Barron Pl
Gander Dr
Rooksdown Av
Mill Rd
Julius Cl
Vespasian Gdns
Saxonwood School for the Handicapped
Priestley Road
A&E
North Hampshire Hospital
Vickers Business Cen
Hotel
Tintern Cl
Buckfast Cl
Romsey Cl
Merton County Junior School
Abbey Road
A339
RINGWAY NORTH
A339(T)
104
Roman Rd
Augustus Dr
Dunsford Crs
Rose Hodson Pl
Terrace
Napoleon Dr
Hazelwood Dr
Hazelwood Cl
Beech Way
Hamilton Close
Edison Rd
Aldermaston Rd
Tempus Business Cen
Millard Close
Oakridge Road
Oakridge County Junior School
M8
1 Amport Cl
2 Brickfields Cl
3 Cavel Ct
4 Charldon Gn
Houndmills
1 grid square represents 500 metres

Chineham 83
G6
1 Carpenter's Dn
G8
1 Lansley Rd
2 Normanton Rd
3 Stratfield Rd
H6
1 Falkland Rd
2 Montserrat Pl
3 Tasmania Cl
H8
1 Myland Cl
K5
1 Aghemund Cl
2 Southlands
K6
1 Great Oaks Cha
2 Longacre Ri
3 Minden Cl
L4
1 Greenwood Dr
2 Parkwood Cl
3 Renown Wy
63
Cufaude
Upper Cufaude Farm
Cufaude Lane
Vyne (NT)
Vyne Farm
Razor's Farm
Crockford Lane
Lime Tree Way
Mary's Lane
Carpenters Down Wood
Chineham
Whitewood
Hanmore Road
Thornhill Way
Reading Road
Saffron Close
Bowman Road
Petty's Brook Rd
Mongers Piece
Belvedere Gdns
Lovegroves
84
Four Lanes End
Long Lane
Superstore
Onslow Cl
Binfields Cl
Pyotts Court
Pyott's Hill
Bilton Industrial Estate
Great Binfields Road
Daneshill
Basingstoke & Deane Borough Council
Popley
Popley Fields House
Marnel Infant & Junior Schools
John Hunt of Everest Community School
Longfellow Parade Clinic
Doctors Surgery
Primary School
Jersey Cl
Guernsey Cl
Carpenter's Down
Shetland Popley Way
Shakespeare Road
A33
A33 READING ROAD
A339 RINGWAY NORTH
RG24
5
105
M6
1 Merrydown La
M7
1 Beddington Ct
M5
1 Brookfield Cl
2 Gilbard Ct
3 Guinea Ct
4 Nursery Cl
5 Warbleton Rd
M4
1 Belvedere Gdns
2 Copse View Cl
3 Summerfields
4 Woodlands
L8
1 Bracken Bank
2 Clover Fld
3 Crofters Meadow
4 Dragonfly Dr
L6
1 Hazeldene
2 Remember. Gdns
3 St Joseph's Crs
4 Wallins Copse
L5
1 Birchwood
2 Larchwood
3 Martins Wd
4 Thumwood
Daneshill Industrial Estate
Dove House School

on Loddon

Goddards Cl

1 Petersfield Cl
A4

Pound
Meadow

A B C 64 D E F

I

Ragg
Copse

Lance Levy Farm

Wildmoor Lane

North
Foreland Lodge

2

Sherfield
Court

Church End

Wildmoor Lane

3

Wildmoor

Sherfield
Hall

Moulshay Lane

Ellis Farm

Belvedere
Gdns

Foxs Furlong

4

Moulshay Farm

83

Longstock Cl

Whitmarsh Lane

Lovegroves

5

6

Blackland's Farm

Hale Farm

River Loddon

Lodge
Farm

7

Pyott's Hill

Newnham Lane

Newnham Lane

Poors Lane

8

Poors Farm

Gold's Farm

Pot Lane

Riverside Close

Oliver's
Battery

A B C 106 D E F

Water End Lane

Riley Lane

Cem

L7
1 Bowling Green Dr
2 Garden Cl
3 Shaw Pightle
4 Trust Cl
5 Whites Cl

L8
1 Froud Cl
2 Newnham Pk
3 Seton Dr

M6
1 Broad Leaze
2 Chalky Copse
3 Elms Rd
4 Ferndale Gdns
5 Hatchgate Mead
6 John Morgan Cl
7 Nursery Cl
8 Reading Rd
9 Wash Brook

G H J **65** K L M

I
2
3
4
86
5
6
7
8

Lyde Green

Rotherwick

Black Wood

Wedman's Lane

Lampards Cl

Cowfold Lane

Street End Copse

Readon Pond

Whitewater
C of E (Controlled)
Primary School

The Street

Hook Road

Mill Farm

Mill Lane

Summerstead Farm

Lyde River

The Old House

Tylney Park Golf Club

Hotel

Tylney House

Post

Horn Lane

Frog Lane

Coppice

Great Sheldons Coppice

John Morgan Cl
Reading Rd
Asheta
Alder
Oak
Oak Tree La
Hazel Coppice

Birch Gv
Birch Cv

Goose Gn

Goose La

Elms Road
Reading

Middle
Mid
Nightingale Gdns

Painters Pightle

Brown Cft

Ferrell Fld
Scures Rd
Garden Cl
Sheldon's La

Middle
Mead
Dorchester Road

Sheldon's Rd

The Surg

London

Hook

Newnham Lane

Tylney Lane

Ridge Lane

Owen's Farm

Carleton

Hog Gdn
Hog

Raven
New

Bell Meadow
Comiston

PO

Station Road

Hook Station

Rawlings Rd

Manor Farm

Newnham

Newnham Road

Crown Lane

Old School Rd

Morris Street

London Road A30

Memorial Road

Rectory Road

Osborn Way
Industrial Est

Hook Way

Nately
Scures

Hotel

HOOK COMMON

A287

B3349

Hook Road

M7
1 Butts Meadow
2 Harfield Cl
3 Middle Mead

A **B** **C** **D** **E** **F**

66

B6
1 Coltsfoot Pl
2 Four Acre
Coppice
3 Heathview
4 Rose Bay Gdns
5 Squarefield Gdns
6 Whitewater Ri

A7
1 Compass Fld
2 Gower Crs
3 Kerfield Wy
4 Oak Hanger Cl
5 Rookswood Cl
6 St Johns Cl
7 Valmeade Cl

A6
1 Aspen Gdns
2 Beechcrest Vw
3 Hawthorn Ri
4 Hazel Coppice
5 Hornbeam Pl

A5
1 John Morgan Cl

ngley

Ripley

Inholmes
Court

I

RG27

Cowfold Farm

Sherwoods

River Whitewater

West Green Road

Dutch Ho

2

**West
Green**

West Green House
& Gardens (NT)

3

Bunker's
Hill Farm

Murrell Green Road

Thackham's Lane

PH

4

Borough
Court

85

Scutts Farm

A30

Murrell
Green

London Road

5

B3349

Searl's
Lane

LONDON ROAD A30

Hook House
Hotel

PH

Murrell
Green
Business
Park

6

GRIFFIN WAY NORTH

Reading Road

Coppice

John Morgan

Ashlea

Alder Wood

Oak Tree Dr

Oak Drive

Birch Gv

Cherry Cl

Hazel Coppice

Hornbeam

Wagon

Holt Way

Whitewater

Four Acre Coppice

Holt Lane

Holt Lane

7

The Spinney

Nottingale Gdns

Chester Road

Elm Rd

Linwood Gdns

Reading Road

Church Rd

Hook Infant
School
Junior School

B3349

GRIFFIN WAY SOUTH

Ravens

Bow Field

Bow Fld

Bow Fld

Pantile Dr

Smallfield Dr

Wild Herons

Vetch Flds

Driftway Rd

Hook

Quince Tree Way

Second Dress

Compass Way

Holt

Holt Lane

PO

Raven Rd

Bell Meadow

Bramshott Drive

Station Rd

Hook
Station

Bartley Wy

Bartley Wood Business Park

Bartley Way

Rawlings Rd

Osborn Way

Holt Lane

Scotland Farm

8

Rectory Road

Osborn Way
Industrial Est

Osborn Way

Totters La

Potbridge Road

Potbridge

A **B** **C** **D** **E** **F**

108

B7
1 Farm Ground Cl
2 Four Acre
Coppice
3 Hunts Cl
4 Ravens Cft
5 Wild Herons

B3349

ODIHAM

Poland
Mill

I grid square represents 500 metres

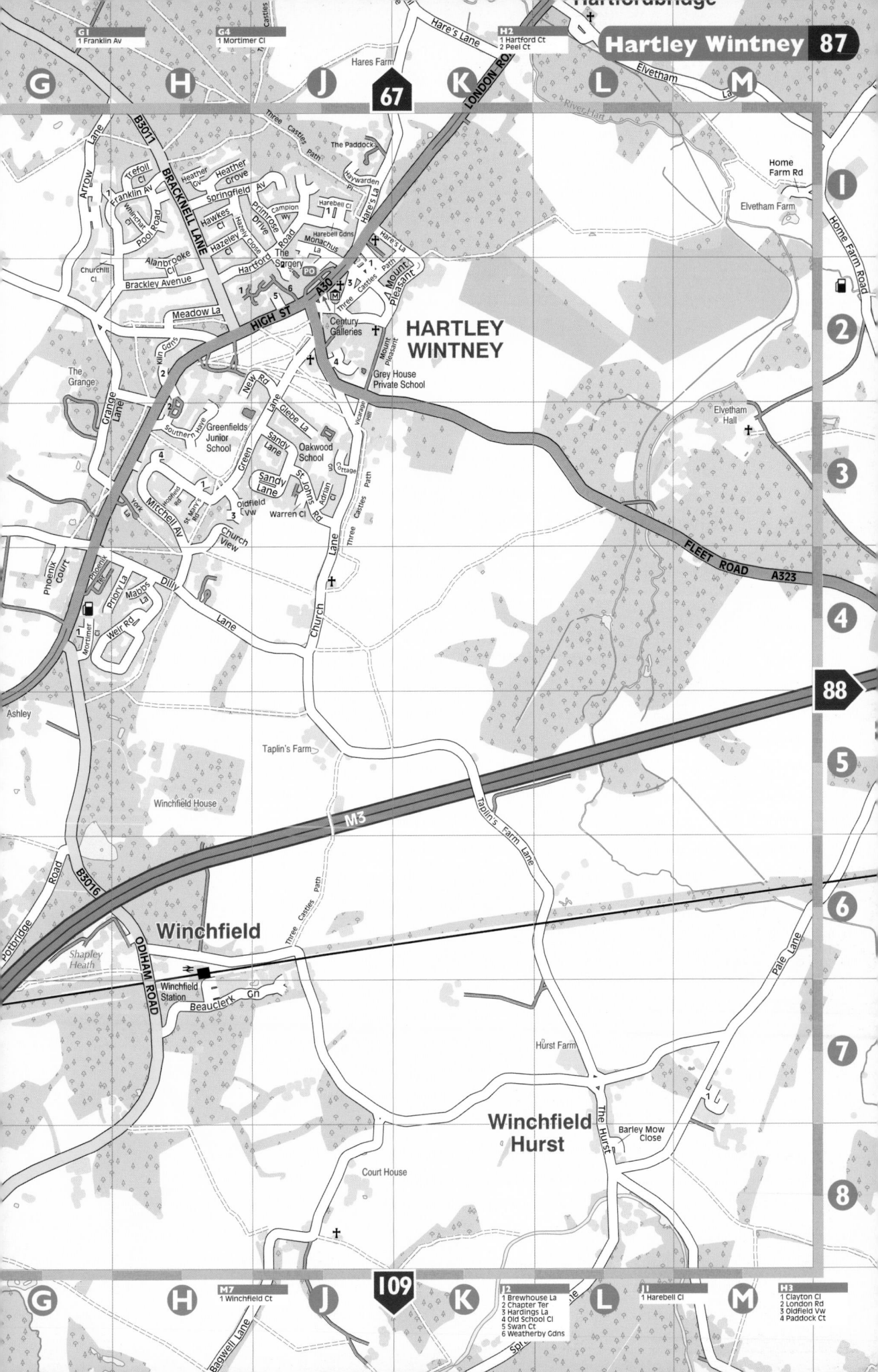
G1
1 Franklin Av
G4
1 Mortimer Cl
H2
1 Hartford Ct
2 Peel Ct
Hartfordbridge
Hares Farm
Hare's Lane
67
G
H
J
K
L
M
LONDON RD
Elvetham
La
River Hart
B3011
Three Castles Path
The Paddock
Arrow Lane
Trefoil Cl
Franklin Av
Heather Gv
Heather Grove
Springfield Av
Haywarden Pl
Hare's La
Home Farm Rd
Elvetham Farm
Home Farm Road
BRACKNELL LANE
Whinchat Cl
Pool Road
Hawkes Cl
Hazeley Cl
Hazely Close
Primrose Drive
Campion Wy
Harebell Cl
Harebell Gdns
Monachus La
Road
Churchill Cl
Alanbrooke Cl
Brackley Avenue
Hartford
The Surgery
PO
Mount Pleasant
A30
HIGH ST
Meadow La
Century Galleries
HARTLEY WINTNEY
Kiln Gdns
The Grange
Grange Lane
New Rd
Mount Pleasant
Grey House Private School
Vicarage Hill
Elvetham Hall
Southern Haye
Greenfields Junior School
Glebe La
Lane
Sandy Lane
Oakwood School
Green
Cottage Gn
Three Castles Path
Sandy Lane
St Johns Rd
Adrian Cl
Hopfield Rd
St Mary's Rd
York La
Mitchell Av
Oldfield Vw
Warren Cl
Church View
FLEET ROAD
A323
Phoenix Court
Phoenix Ter
Priory La
Mabbs La
Dilly Lane
Church Lane
Weir Rd
Mortimer Cl
Ashley
88
Taplin's Farm
Winchfield House
M3
Taplin's Farm Lane
Road
B3016
Potbridge
Three Castles Path
Winchfield
Shapley Heath
ODIHAM ROAD
Winchfield Station
Beauclerk Gn
Pale Lane
Hurst Farm
Winchfield Hurst
The Hurst
Barley Mow Close
Court House
1
2
3
4
5
6
7
8
109
M7
1 Winchfield Ct
J2
1 Brewhouse La
2 Chapter Ter
3 Hardings La
4 Old School Cl
5 Swan Ct
6 Weatherby Gdns
J1
1 Harebell Cl
H3
1 Clayton Cl
2 London Rd
3 Oldfield Vw
4 Paddock Ct
Bagwell Lane

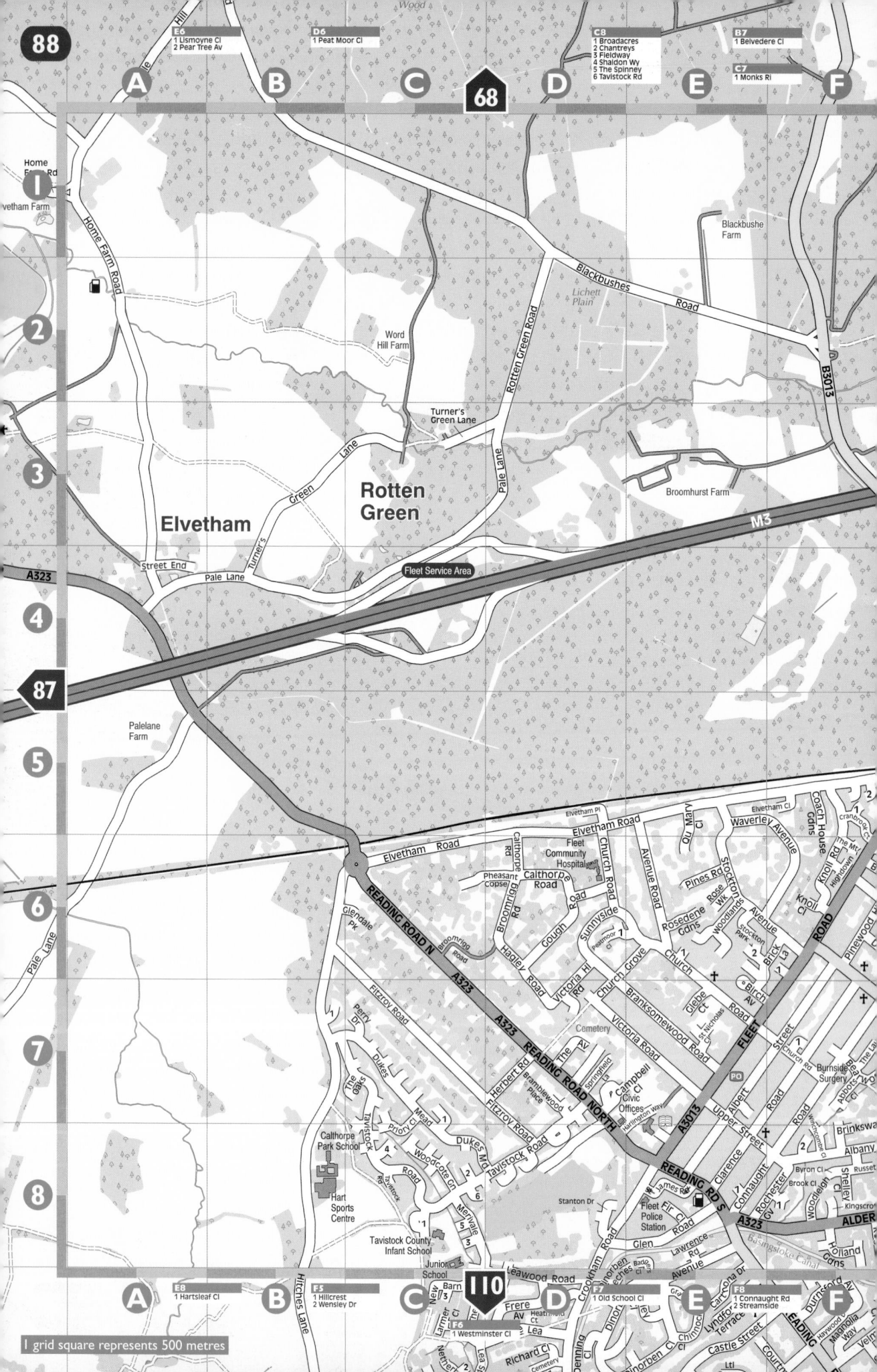
E6
1 Lismoyne Cl
2 Pear Tree Av
D6
1 Peat Moor Cl
C8
1 Broadacres
2 Chantreys
3 Fieldway
4 Shaldon Wy
5 The Spinney
6 Tavistock Rd
B7
1 Belvedere Cl
C7
1 Monks Ri
A
B
C
68
D
E
F
1
2
3
4
5
6
7
8
87
110
Home Farm Rd
Elvetham Farm
Home Farm Road
Blackbushe Farm
Blackbushes Road
Lichett Plain
Word Hill Farm
Rotten Green Road
B3013
Turner's Green Lane
Green Lane
Pale Lane
Rotten Green
Elvetham
Broomhurst Farm
M3
Street End
Pale Lane
Turner's
Fleet Service Area
A323
Palelane Farm
Elvetham Pl
Elvetham Cl
Elvetham Road
Fleet Community Hospital
Church Road
Avenue Road
Waverley Avenue
Coach House Gdns
Knoll Rd
Pheasant Copse
Calthorpe Road
Broomrigg Rd
Pines Rd
Stockton
Rose Wk
Rosedene Gdns
Woodlands
Stockton Park
Avenue
Knoll Cl
Hagley Road
Gough Road
Sunnyside
Peatmoor Cl
Glendale Pk
READING ROAD N
Broomrigg Road
Church Grove
Victoria Hl Rd
Branksomewood Road
Church
Glebe Ct
Birch Av
Brick La
Fitzroy Road
A323
Perry Dr
Cemetery
Victoria Road
St Nicholas Ct
FLEET
ROAD
Pinewood
Dukes
The Oaks
READING ROAD NORTH
The Av
Springfield La
Herbert Rd
Bramblewood Place
Campbell Cl
Civic Offices
Harlington Way
A3013
Albert
Upper Street
Street
Church Rd
Burnside Surgery
Abbots Cl
Brinkswa
Albany
Calthorpe Park School
Tavistock
Priory Cl
Mead
Dukes Md
Woodcote Gn
Fitzroy Road
Tavistock Road
Road
Road
Winchcombe Cl
Clarence
Connaught
Rochester Gv
Woodleigh
Shelley Cl
Byron Cl
Brook Cl
Russet
Kingscro
Hart Sports Centre
Tavistock Rd
Merivale
Stanton Dr
James Rd
Fleet Police Station
Fir Cl
READING RD S
A323
ALDER
Basingstoke Canal
Holland Gdns
Tavistock County Infant School
Glen Road
Lawrence Rd
Crookham Road
Avenue
Junior School
Leawood Road
E8
1 Hartsleaf Cl
Hitches Lane
F5
1 Hillcrest
2 Wensley Dr
New Barn
Frere Av
Heathfield Ct
Lea
F7
1 Old School Cl
F8
1 Connaught Rd
2 Streamside
Durnsford Av
Haywood
Magnolia Way
Larmer Cl
F6
1 Westminster Cl
Richard Cl
Castle Street
Lyndford Terrace
Chinnock Cl
Dinorben
Dennings Cl
1 grid square represents 500 metres

69

G3
1 Kerry Cl

G4
1 Argente Cl
2 Cherberry Cl
3 Dexter Wy
4 Hereford Mead
5 Jersey Cl
6 Lime Dr

G5
1 Minley Gv

G7
1 Berkeley Cl

G8
1 Medonte Cl
2 Moorlands Cl

H3
1 Mill Cnr
2 Ryeland Cl

H4
1 Colbred Cnr
2 Fallowfield
3 Threshers Cnr

G H J K L M I

2
3
4
90
5
6
7
8

MINLEY ROAD A327

Junction 4a

M3

Brook House

Bramshot Lane

Great Bramshott Farm

A327

FLEET ROAD

COVE ROAD A3013

Southwood Lane

B3014 FLEET ROAD

A327

SUMMIT AVE

Southwood

Fleet Station

Fleet Pond

Kennels Lane

Pondtail

Constant Road

Bramshott Road

Armstrong Way

The Fairway

Ively Road

Boundary Road

Norris Bridge

NORRIS ROAD

A323

KINGS ROAD

Kenilworth Road

Woodside Gdns

Williams Way

Marlborough Road

Farnham Road

Westbury Gdns

Pondtail Gdns

St Michaels Cl

Velmead Rd

G H J K L M

M5
1 Ash Tree Cl
2 Grenadiers Wy
3 The Pathfinders
4 Regiment Cl
5 Rifle Wy
6 Stanley Dr
7 Whitbms Gdns
8 Yew Tree Cl

M4
1 Coriander Cl
2 Pyestock Crs

M3
1 Baywood Cl
2 Cherry Tree Cl
3 Kenilworth Rd
4 Nutmeg Ct
5 Pinewood Crs
6 Purmerend Cl

H8
1 Hawkins Wy

H5
1 Foxwood
2 Woodgate

L4
1 Marjoram Cl

H7
1 Kenwith Av

90
D1
1 Appledore Ms
2 Belstone Ms
3 Grace Bennett Cl
4 Heddon Wk
5 Instow Gdns
6 Lydford Cl
7 Spring Gdns
8 Stratton Wk
C4
1 Cottage Gdns
2 Cranleigh Ct
C5
1 Maple Leaf Cl
2 St Christ. Pl
3 Wilson Rd
C1
1 Pegasus Rd
B5
1 Primrose Gdns
2 Windermere Cl
B6
1 Heather Gdns
B1
1 Cairngorm Pl
2 Fintry Pl
3 Snowdon Rd
B4
1 Ferndown Gdns
2 Kendal Cl
3 Langdale Cl
A
B
C
70
D
E
F
1
2
3
4
5
6
7
8
Farnborough Town Football Club
Pinewood Infants School
Guillemont County Junior School
M3
Hawley Lane
The Sixth Form College
Infant School
Oak Farm Community School
Farnborough Rugby Football Club
St Bernadettes RC Primary School
Cove
Infant School
Secondary School
Junior School
West Heath
Farnborough Hill School
Farnborough Main Station
GU14
89
Jenner House Surgery
Cove Cricket Club
FARNBOROUGH
Rafborough
Doctors Surgery
Farnborough Recreation Centre
Police Station
Kingsgrove Industrial Est
Rushmoor Borough Council
Southwood Golf Club
Arrow Industrial Est
Farnborough Business Centre
Royal Aircraft Establishment
Defence Research Agency
Farnborough Airport
Farnborough Aerospace Centre
112
The Surgery
Junior School
A3
1 Shakespeare Gdn
2 Twelve Acre Crs
A4
1 Westgalde
2 Woodcot Gdns
A5
1 Cornelia Cl
2 Lauderdale
3 Lodsworth
4 Nevada Cl
5 Palmerston Cl
6 Rydal Cl
7 Tweedsmuir Cl
D2
1 Combe La
2 Hartland Pl
3 Liskeard Dr
4 Saunton Gdns
E1
1 Cromwell Wy
2 Highgrove
3 Worcester Cl
E4
1 Firgrove Pde
2 Greencroft
3 Helen Ct
4 Pipers Patch
5 Sullivan Cl
E7
1 Raf Gate Rd
E8
1 Queen's Cl
F4
1 Rapallo Cl
F6
1 Belvedere Rd
F7
1 Aircraft Esp
2 Alexandra Ct
3 Belsize Rd
4 Buller Ct
5 Cambridge Rd E
6 St Marks Cl
1 grid square represents 500 metres

Farnborough 91
G4
1 Montacute Cl
2 Old Rectory Gdns
3 Syon Pl
G5
1 Clandon Ct
2 Clevedon Ct
3 Upton Cl
4 Woodend
G6
1 Fairfax Ms
2 Gainsborough Cl
G7
1 Hermitage Cl
H4
1 Coleford Bridge Rd
H5
1 Goodwood Pl
2 Hatfield Gdns
3 Longleat Sq
H6
1 Adlington Pl
2 Andrewartha Rd
3 Broadlands
4 Eldergrove
71
Frimley Green
Frimley C of E First & Middle School
FRIMLEY GREEN RD B3411
GU16
Deepcut
Lakeside Country Club
Frimley Green Medical Centre
Cheswycks School
GUILDFORD B3012 ROAD
Old Guildford Road
Brunswick Road
Lake Road
St Cross Rd
Blackdown Road
Bellew Road
B3015
The Princess Royal Barracks
Royal Logistic Corps Museum
Basingstoke Canal
Deepcut Place
Farnborough North Sta
North Farnborough County Infant School
Street
Farnborough Park
Mytchett
Mytchett County First School
The Jigsaw School
Linsford Business Park
STURT ROAD
MYTCHETT ROAD
Coleford Bridge Road
Mytchett Heath
Mytchett Place
Mytchett Place Road
Keogh Close
Keogh Barracks
Mytchett Lake
Mytchett Lake Road
Grayswood Drive
South Farnborough County Junior School
Salesian College
South Farnborough
South Farnborough Infant School
Salesian View
Holly Lodge CP School
North Camp Station
LYNCHFORD RD
A3011
A331
LYSONS AV
FRIMLEY ROAD
STRATFORD RD B3165
Homeleigh Crescent
Rosemary Avenue
Station Vw
Station Ap
1
2
3
4
5
6
7
8
113
F8
1 Lynchford Rd
2 Tredenham Cl
3 Wetherby Gdns
K5
1 Nightingale Dr
2 Vine House Cl
M1
1 Mainstone Cl
K1
1 Banbury Cl
2 Lydford Cl
3 Membury Cl
J7
1 The Beeches
2 Oak Tree Cl
J8
1 Cordelia Gdns
J4
1 Coleford Paddocks
J5
1 Huntsman's Ms
H7
1 Whitby Cl
J1
1 Elmcroft Cl
Greatbottom Flash

Ducis

A338

LUDGERSHALL RD

TREE Penn HI

Cadley R E6
1 Lady Jane Wk
2 Levell Ct
3 Stoney Cross

D6
1 Crown La

D5
1 Castle Ct

A B C D E F

1

Mount
Orleans Farm

Wick Down

2

A346

3

SHAW HILL

4

Widgerly Down

Blackmore Lane

Blackmore Down

Crawl

A342

Castle Farm

Station Ap

Crawlboys Lane

5

Windmillhill Down

Castle St
Ludgershall Castle

Recreation Rd
Old Common Ws

LUDGERS

Dewews Lane

Byron Cl
Byron Rd

Ludgershall
Health Centre

School

Perham Crs

6

BUTT ST
CASTLE ST HIGH ST

Chapel
Church

Laurence Ct

Central St

Lady
Place

Short
Street

PO

Williamson

2

Fleming Close

Challis

Coronat
Rd

Meade

TIDWORTH RD

Eleanor Ct

Ludgershall
Sports Club

Astor

Clarence Rd

Empress Way

Clover Gdns

Primrose

PO

Camomile
Dr

Mead
Rd

Bren

Crescent

Prs Mary Gdns

Queens Cl

Rd

TIDWORTH ROAD

Roberts
Rd

Lena
Close

Brydes Rd

Teasel Cl

Edelweiss

Orchid
Drive

Cornflower
Way

Castledown
Comprehensive
School

LC

Simonds Road

New Crs

New Drove

7

A3026

Somme Road

8

NORTH TIDWORTH

A B C D E F

Perham
Bwn

Woodham Cl
Somme Road
Hatton Rd
Upnor Close

Kemmel Rd
Lamb

Sheddesden

An

1 grid square represents 500 metres

G H J K L M

I ow

Chute
Down

Honey
Bottom

Coldridge
Wood

Forest House

Jolly's Farm

2

Forest Lane

Hookwood Lane

3

Stert
Copse

4

Coldridge
Down

94

Long
Bottom

Long Bottom

Longbottom Farm

Lodge Lane

5

Biddesden House

6

Biddesden Lane

Crawlboys Lane

Biddesden Lane

Spray Leaze

Abbatt Cl

Gresham Rd

Pretoria Rd

Wiltshire County
Hampshire County

Wiltshire

Hampshire

7

Faberstown

ROAD

A342

ANDOVER ROAD

116

Redenham House

Redenham Drove

New House

8

Tilly Down

G H J K L M

Redenham

Ⓐ   Ⓑ   Ⓒ   **72**   Ⓓ   Ⓔ   Ⓕ

Chute
Standen

Chute
Cadley

Dowlands

Ⓘ

Lower Chute

Tangley
Bottom

Ⓞ2

st House

Jolly's Farm

Clark
Lane

Tangley

Ⓞ3

Limekiln Road

Lodge Lane

Hungerford Lane

Ⓞ4

Coach
Hill

93

Chute
Lodge

Ⓞ5

Lodge Lane

Roundaway Lane

Roundaway Farm

Ⓞ6

Redhouse Farm

Wiltshire County
Hampshire County

Wiltshire County
Hampshire County

Ⓞ7

Flinty
Cott

Wiltshire County
Hampshire County

Ⓞ8

Flint Lane

Nutbane

Lane

House Lane

New

Ⓐ   Ⓑ   Ⓒ   **117**   Ⓓ   Ⓔ   Ⓕ

Redenham

Clanville

1 grid square represents 500 metres

G H J 73 K L M

I

2

3

4

96

5

6

7

8

Locke's Drove

Whistler's Farm

Pill
Heath Farm

Tangley
Farm

Blagden
Copse

Blagden House

Doles Farm

A345 NEWBURY ROAD

The Avenue

Wildhern

Hatherden
Manor

Hungerford Lane

Hatherden
House

Plough Farm

Hungerford Lane

Green

The
Close

Cemetery

Hatherden C of E
Primary School

Hatchet Lane

Hatherden

Goddards Farm

Pigeon
House Farm

Charlton Down
Farm

Cullum
Chione
Close

Court

Newbury
Road

74
C8 1 Ridges Cl
B8 1 Greenfields
Locke's Drove
Horseshoe Lane
Test Way
Bladon Gallery
The Dene
Dines Close
Windmill Lane
The Crescent
Dean Rise
River Swift
Hurstbourne Tarrant
Doctors Drove
CHURCH STREET
B3048
Windmills
Hurstbourne Tarrant School
Bourne Rivulet
Doles Wood
95
Bourne Park
Frenches Farm
A343 NEWBURY ROAD
Rag Copse
Green Drove
Little London
Upper Enham
Road
MacCullum
Weston Court
Amlone Close
Lane
Dunhills
Ridges Copse
Stoke Road
119
Malt House
Newbury Road
Road
Enham Alamein
1 grid square represents 500 metres

G H J 75 K L M

Binley

Prior's Farm

Slade Bottom Farm

Elm Farm

Binley Bottom

B3048

Long Leaze

Chapel La

Stoke

I

2

3

4

98 Cold H.

5

Wakeswood

Gangbridge

Lane

Wadwick Bottom

Swampton

Stoke Hill

Baptist Hill

Spring Hill

Test Way

Oak Tree Farm

Schools

Batsford

Lane

6

PO

PH

Hirst Copse

Egbury

Upper Wyke

Bourne Meadow

Stevens Green

St Mary Bour

B3048

7

Bourne

Derry Down Health Clinic

Test Way

South Vw

8

Test Way

od

Middle W.   rm

G H J 120 K L M

Derrydown Farm

Road

A
B
C
D
E
F
76
Buckets Down Farm
Dunley
1
2
3
4
5
6
7
8
97
Wadwick Bottom
Wadwick
Egbury
Bradley
Downhams Farm
Egbury Castle Farm
Cold Harbour
Egbury Road
Hirst Copse
Jamaica Farm
Hogdigging Copse
Stevens Green
St Mary Bourne
Bourne Court
Test Way
South Vw Ter
B3048
Derrydown Farm
Dirty Corner
Bloswood Lane
Bar
121
Harroway
1 grid square represents 500 metres

Wormle
Copse

Litchfield

G   H   J   **77**   K   L   M

I

2

3

4

100

5

6

7

8

Angledown
Copse

Clap Gate

Twinley Manor

Cole Henley
Manor Farm

**Cole
Henley**

Larks

Barrow

Hill

A34(T)

Newbury
Road

Harroway

RG28

Wooldings Farm

The
Orchards

Watch

Lane

Harroway

Priory Lane

Watch Lane

G   H   J   **122**   K   L   M

Farm

Vw Cottages

Home

A
B
C
78
D
E
F
Caesar's Belt
1
2
3
4
99
5
6
7
8
Ridgeway Farm
Willesley Warren Farm
Whitnal
New Barn
Court Drove
Hill Mead
Primary School
Court
Lordsfield Gdns
Court Drove
Lane
Glebe Meadow
Lynch
Silk Mill
The Lynch
Southington La
Southington Close
White Hart Gallery
Bridge St
HIGH ST
Harveys Fld
King's Meadow
Woodlands
Oak Close
Red Lion La
Lion
Watch Lane
Watch Lane
S Vw Cottages
A
B
C
123
D
B3400
Lane
E
F
Southington
Dellands Lane
Kerchiers Fld
Dellands
Crawts
Charles
1 grid square represents 500 metres

G8
1 Waltham Ct
G
H
J
79
K
L
M
1
2
3
4
102
5
6
7
8
ill Farm
Frith Wood
Ashe Warren Ho
Overton Station
Foxdown
Station Hill
Elm Rd
Beech Cl
Copse Road
Polhampton Farm
Quidhampton
Deane
Ashe
Source of the River Test
Waltham Rd
Station Road
LONDON ROAD B3400
B3400
ANDOVER ROAD
Cheesedown Farm
Two Ga Meadow
The Green
Two Gate Lane
Berrydown Court
Berrydown Lane
Berrydown Farm
124
Ashe Park
OVERTON
Mede Close
Waltham
Pound Road

102
80
101
125
A
B
C
D
E
F
1
2
3
4
5
6
7
8
Hook La
Hay Wood
Shear Down Farm
White Lane
Frith Wood
Malshangar House
Wayfarer's Walk
Great Deane Wood
Summer Down Lane
Summer Down Farm
Little Deane Wood
Ivy Down Lane
Malshanger Lane
Deane Down Farm
Harrow Way
B3400
Clarken Green
Boon Way
Station Road
Barra Cl
Arran Cl
Mull Cl
Oban Cl
Caithness Cl
Lomond
Church Oakley
Rectory Road
ANDOVER ROAD
County Infant School
Oakley C of E Junior School
Deane
OAKLEY
PH
Cheesedown Farm
Beech Tree Cl
1 grid square represents 500 metres

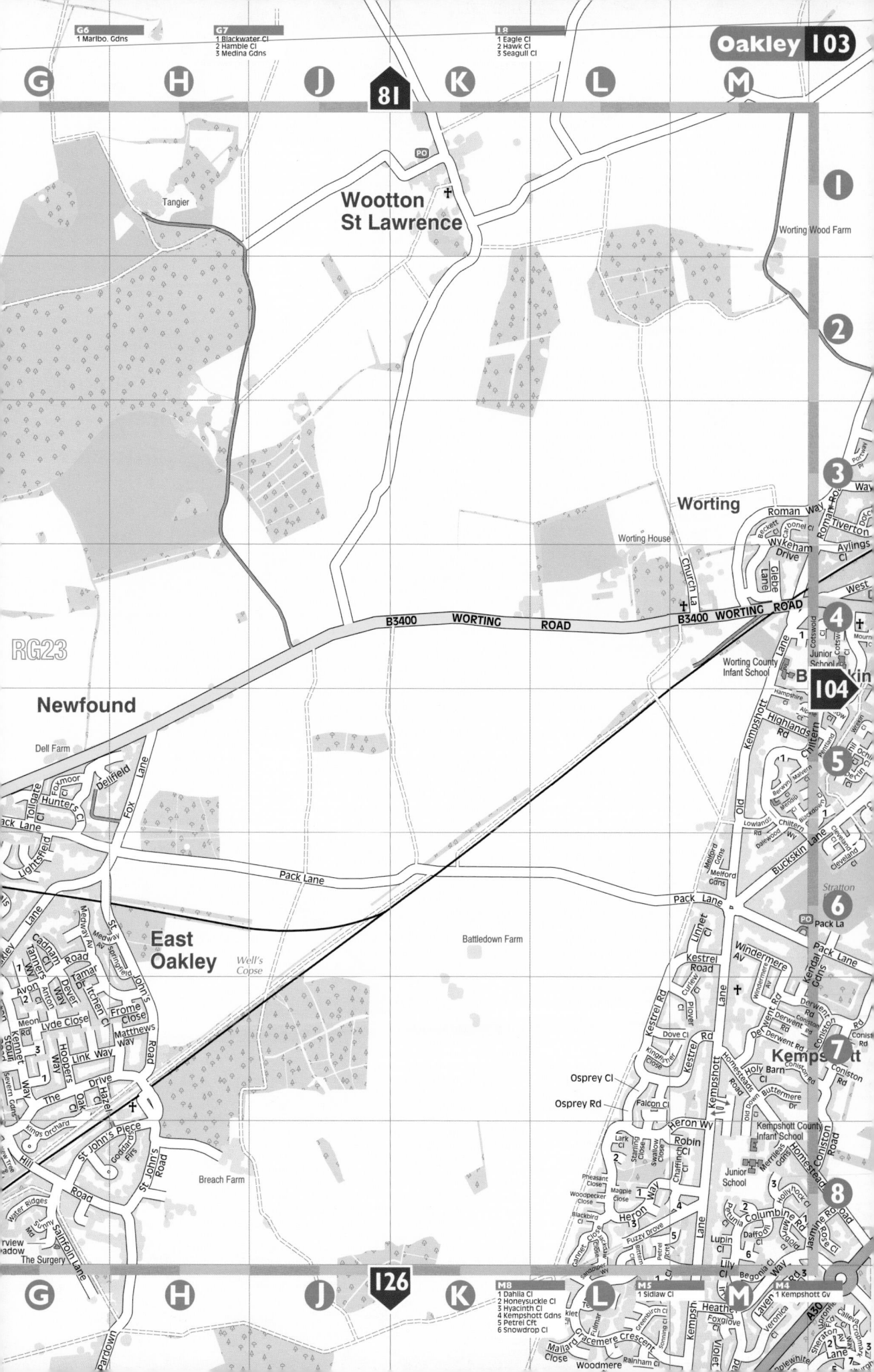
G6
1 Marlbo. Gdns
G7
1 Blackwater Cl
2 Hamble Cl
3 Medina Gdns
L8
1 Eagle Cl
2 Hawk Cl
3 Seagull Cl
81
Wootton St Lawrence
Tangier
Worting Wood Farm
Worting
Worting House
Church La
B3400 WORTING ROAD
Roman Way
Wykeham Drive
Glebe Lane
Beckett Cl
Carbonel Cl
Tiverton
Aylings Cl
West
Worting County Infant School
Junior School
104
Newfound
RG23
Dell Farm
Dellfield
Fox Lane
Foxmoor Cl
Hunters Cl
Tollgate
Pack Lane
Lightsfield
Old Kempshott Lane
Highlands Rd
Chiltern
Hampshire Cl
Alpine Cl
Malvern
Berwyn
Mendip Cl
Lowlands Rd
Dalewood
Chiltern Wy
Buckskin Lane
Cleveland Cl
Melford Gdns
Stratton
Pack La
East Oakley
Well's Copse
Battledown Farm
Medway Av
St John's Road
Springfield
Cadnam Cl
Tanners Way
Road
Tamar Dr
Itchen Cl
Avon Cl
Anton
Dever Way
Frome Close
Lyde Close
Matthews Way
Meon Rd
Kennet
Stour
Link Way
Hoopers Way
The Oak Drive
Hazel Cl
Severn Gdns
Kings Orchard
St John's Piece
Goddards Firs
Hill Road
Water Ridges
Sainfoin Lane
The Surgery
Breach Farm
Linnet Cl
Kestrel Road
Curlew Cl
Plover Cl
Kestrel Rd
Dove Cl
Kingfisher Close
Osprey Cl
Osprey Rd
Falcon Cl
Heron Wy
Robin Cl
Lark Cl
Starling Close
Swallow Close
Chaffinch Cl
Pheasant Close
Woodpecker Close
Magpie Close
Blackbird Cl
Heron Way
Fuzzy Drove
Gannet Close
Jackdaw Close
Bittern
Petrel Cft
Kempshott Lane
Windermere Av
Kendal Gdns
Derwent Rd
Coniston Rd
Kempshott
Holy Barn Cl
Buttermere Dr
Old Down Cl
Homesteads Road
Kempshott County Infant School
Junior School
Merrileas Gdns
Homestead
Coniston Road
Columbine Rd
Hollyhock Cl
Petunia Cl
Daffodil Cl
Lupin Cl
Lily Cl
Begonia Cl
Jasmine Road
Rose Cl
Laven
126
M8
1 Dahlia Cl
2 Honeysuckle Cl
3 Hyacinth Cl
4 Kempshott Gdns
5 Petrel Cft
6 Snowdrop Cl
M5
1 Sidlaw Cl
M4
1 Kempshott Gv
Fulmar
Mallard Close
Gracemere Crescent
Greenbirch Cl
Sonning Cl
Rainham Cl
Woodmere
Heather
Foxglove Cl
Violet
Veronica
A30
Sheraton
Pardown

104
B5
1 Colyer Cl
2 Cornish Cl
3 St Christophers
C5
1 Westside Cl
B1
1 Claudius Dr
2 Hadrians Wy
B3
1 Caernarvon Cl
A8
1 Canterbury Cl
2 Coventry Cl
3 Durham Wy
4 Rochester Cl
A4
1 Cairngorm Cl
2 Charnwood Cl
A5
1 Antrim Cl
A2
1 Hillcrest Ct
2 Kenilworth Rd
A3
1 Pembroke Rd
82
Hampshire Hospital
Vickers Business Cen
Hotel
A339(T)
RINGWAY NORTH
A339
Worting Wood Farm
Wellington Terrace
Napoleon Dr
Roman Rd
Oaklands Way
Beech Way
Elmwood Wy
Hawthorn Wy
Sycamore Wy
Cedar Way
Hazelwood Dr
Hazelwood Cl
Blackthorn Way
Fort Hill School
Infant School
Wimott Junior School
Winklebury Way
Watson Wy
Wilmott Wy
Willoughby Wy
Warwick Rd
Bury Rd
Woolford Wy
Dover Cl
Winklebury
Kenilworth Rd
Forthill Surgery
Winklebury Medical Centre
Caernarvon Close
Forthill Junior School
Ludlow Cl
Ludlow Gdns
Harlech Close
Winklebury Way
Tiverton Rd
Wayside Rd
Roman Way
Pembroke Rd
Hastings Cl
Dorchester Cl
Aylings Cl
Wykeham Drive
Glebe Lane
Houndmills
Houndmills Industrial Estate
Hamilton Close
Edison Rd
Telford Road
Houndmills Road
Brunel Road
Stephenson Rd
Priestley
RINGWAY WEST
A340
Tempus Business Cen
Aldermaston Rd
Hubbard Rd
Joule Rd
Millard Close
Osborne Cl
Hillary Road
Merton Road
Lancaster Rd
Kingsclere Rd
Oakridge Road
Oakridge County Junior School
Sherborne Rd
Upr Sherborne Rd
Pelton Road
BASINGSTO
Town Centre redevelopment due for Completion 2001
The Anvil Concert Ha
VICTORY ROUNDABOU
A3010
CHURCHILL WAY WEST
Milestones Museum
West Ham
Euskirchen Way
Basingstoke Ice Rink
Wessex Bowl
B3400 CHURCHILL WAY WEST
B3400 WORTING ROAD
Grafton Way
Morse Rd
Worting Rd
Lower Brook Street
George St
Superstore
Thorneycroft Industrial Est
Welton Ct
Southend Rd
College
Essex Road
West Ham Lane
Fiske Cl
Mercer Cl
W Ham Cl
Old Worting Road
Worting Road
St Nicholas Ct
Overbridge Surgery
Amazon Cl
Attwood Cl
Knight St
Stukeley Road
Packenham Rd
Packenham Road
Buckskin
103
Kempshott Rd
Highlands Rd
Chiltern Wy
Grampian Wy
Cheviot
Pennine Wy
Edgehill Cl
Cairngorm Cl
Alliston Way
Branton Cl
Claythorpe Rd
Chivers Cl
Cambrian Wy
Buckskin Lane
Park View Junior School
Park View Infant School
Stratton Park
Peter's Rd
Bardwell Cl
Michael's Rd
Bishop Challoner RC Secondary School
Challoner Cl
Limington House School
South Ham
Margaret Rd
Charles St
St Andrew's Rd
Western Way
King's Furlong
King's Rd
Princes' Crs
Bolton Crs
Elizabeth Rd
Diana Cl
Kimberley Rd
St Patrick's Road
Hill View Rd
Kipling Walk
Tennyson Wy
RINGWAY
A340
Cem
Infant School
Junior School
Kings Furlong Dr
Portacre Ri
Winchester St
Hardy La
Cordale Rd
Culver Rd
Culver Road
Wessex Cl
South Ham Medical Centre
Paddock Rd
St Annes Catholic Primary School
Pinkerton Road
Stag Hill
Richard Aldworth Community School
Baird Avenue
Mansfield Rd
Kelvin Hl
Austen Gv
Cobbett Gn
Winchester Road Industrial Est
Cranbourne Secondary School
Cranbourne
A30 RINGWAY
A30
Denham Drive
Hulbert Way
Seymour Rd
Pitman Cl
Brackley Way
Shipton Way
Abbott Cl
Widmore Rd
Phoebe Road
Buckland Avenue
Woodroffe Dr
Basingstoke Town Football Club
Basingstoke Business Cen
Chichester Pl
WINCHESTER RD
Pack La
Pack Lane
Kendal Gdns
Basingstoke Rugby Club
Winchester Road
Hotel
White House
The Harrow Way
Lister Rd
Lennox Rd
Sherrington Way
Horwood Gardens
Cranbourne La
Midlane Cl
Halliday Cl
Chandler Rd
Sheppard Rd
Radford Gdns
Bessemer Rd
Stratton Rd
Loggon Road
Morley Rd
The Harrow Way
Kempshott
Coniston Rd
Derwent Rd
Windermere Av
Kempshott County Infant School
Homesteads Road
The Hawthorns School
RG22
Brighton Hill Community School
WINCHESTER ROAD
A30
Quilter Rd
Brighton Way
Cumberland Avenue
Ravel Cl
Grainger Cl
Porter Rd
Chalkridge School
Hatch Warren Lane
Jays Close
Viables Industrial Estate
Gillies Health Centre
Sullivan Rd
Elgar Cl
Britten Road
Borodin Cl
Brighton Hill
Primary School
Chopin Road
Lehar Close
Verdi Cl
Haydn Road
Brahms Rd
Mozart Cl
Wagner Cl
Rossini Close
Stravinsky Road
Berkeley Dr
Columbine Rd
Jasmine Rd
Worcester Av
Lincoln Cl
Gloucester Dr
Lennon Wy
McCartney Wk
Stanford Rd
Dankworth Rd
Bernstein Road
127
C8
1 Headington Cl
2 Musgrave Cl
D5
1 Tennyson Wy
D7
1 Cumberland Av
E3
1 College Rd
E4
1 Lawrencedale Ct
2 Westdean Ct
E6
1 Cranbourne La
E8
1 Mahler Cl
2 Maw Cl
3 Oldberg Gdns
F3
1 Brookvale Cl
2 Hadleigh Pl
F5
1 Charles Richards Cl
2 Hammond Rd
Hatch Warren County Junior School
Hatch Warren County Infant School
Hatch Warren La
Watling End
M3
1 grid square represents 500 metres

G1
1 Marshall Gdns
2 Middleton Gdns
3 Normanton Rd
4 St Thomas' Cl
G4
1 Anchor Yd
G5
1 Montague Pl
H1
1 Cowdrey Cl
83
Oakridge
Daneshill
Old Basing
Eastrop
Black Dam
Basingstoke Station
Basingstoke & Deane Borough Council
Hassocks Wood Industrial Est
Daneshill Ind Estate
Daneshill Industrial Estate
Daneshill East Industrial Estate
Loddon Business Cen
The Hampshire Clinic
Cowdrey Hts
The AA - Fanum House
Basing House
Old Basing County Infants School
Dove House School
Phoenix Park Terrace
Police Station
Basingstoke County Court
The Malls/The Walks Shopping Cen
Basingstoke Sports Cen
EASTROP ROUNDABOUT
CHURCHILL WAY EAST
A3010
RINGWAY EAST
A339
A30
M3
Surrey Hants Borders NHS Trust
The Business Cen
Haymarket Theatre
Magistrates Court
Harriet Costello School
Hotel
Basingstoke & Deane Borough Council Offices
Civic Offices
War Memorial Park
John Arlott Pavilion
HACKWOOD ROAD ROUNDABOUT
Hampshire County Council
Primary School
Deane's Almshouses
RINGWAY SOUTH
School
Junction 6
106
New Park
Dicken's Lane Plantation
Home Farm
Audleys Wood
Hackwood House
FARLEIGH ROAD
B3046
LONDON
Queen Marys College
RG21
128
F6
1 Aylwin Cl
2 Kathleen Cl
3 Ross Cl
L1
1 Blackberry Wk
2 Whitehead Cl
J3 cont.
5 Hamble Ct
6 Medway Ct
7 Ribble Wy
8 Roding Cl
9 Rothay Ct
10 Severn Wy
11 Thames Ct
12 Trent Wy
13 Weysprings Cl
H5
1 Camrose Wy
2 Chesterfield Rd
3 Howard Rd
J3
1 Buckby La
2 The Butty
3 Colne Wy
4 Duddon Wy
cont.
H2
1 Gordon Cl
H3
1 St Mary's Ct
G H J K L M
1 2 3 4 5 6 7 8

106
84
105
129
A
B
C
D
E
F
1
2
3
4
5
6
7
8
Old Basing
Hatch
Andwell
Mapledurwell
Oliver's Battery
Poors Farm
Hodd's Fm
Priory Farm
Police Station
St Marys C of E Junior School
Basing County Infants School
Old Basing Surgery
Huish House
Moorhams Farm
Gray's Farm
Hungry Lodge
Polecat Corner
Hackwood Farm
Roundtown
Tunworth House
Down Farm
LONDON ROAD
M3
Greywell Road
Tunworth Road
Huish Lane
Frog Lane
Down Lane
Ashmoor Lane
Water End Lane
Andwell Lane
Hatch Lane
Park Lane
Linden Avenue
Park Avenue
Riley Lane
Rainbow Cl
Batchelor Dr
Crabtree Wy
B3
1 Fairthorne Rl
1 grid square represents 500 metres

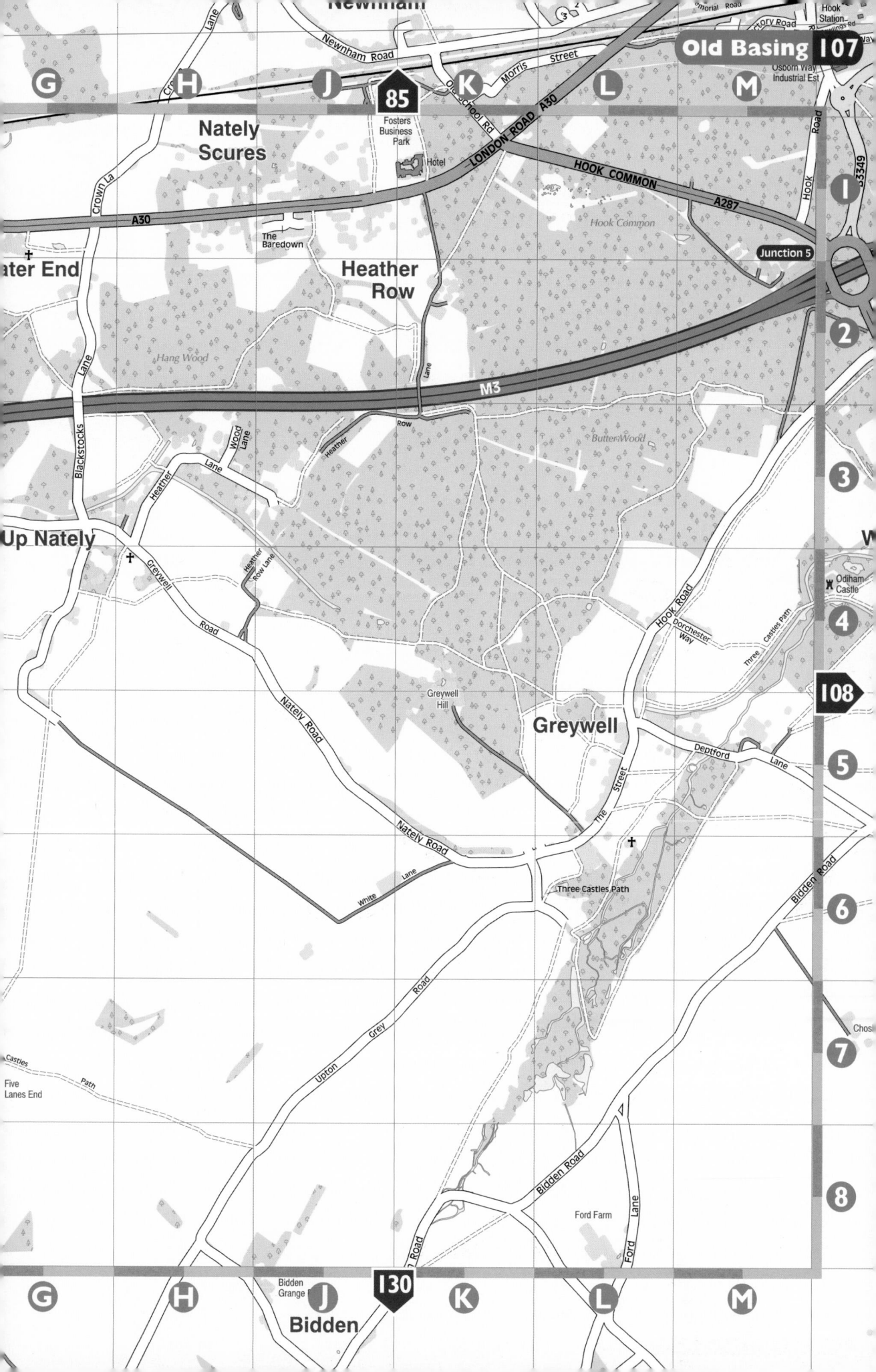

Old Basing 107
85
108
130
Nately Scures
Heather Row
Up Nately
Greywell
Bidden
Hook Common
Hang Wood
Butter Wood
Greywell Hill
Fosters Business Park
Hotel
The Baredown
Junction 5
Odiham Castle
Three Castles Path
Five Lanes End
Ford Farm
Bidden Grange
Newnham Road
Morris Street
London Road A30
Hook Common A287
A30
M3
Crown La
Blackstocks Lane
Heather Lane
Wood Lane
Heather Row Lane
Greywell Road
Nately Road
White Lane
The Street
Deptford Lane
Hook Road
Dorchester Way
Bidden Road
Upton Grey Road
Ford Lane
Osborn Way Industrial Est
Hook Station

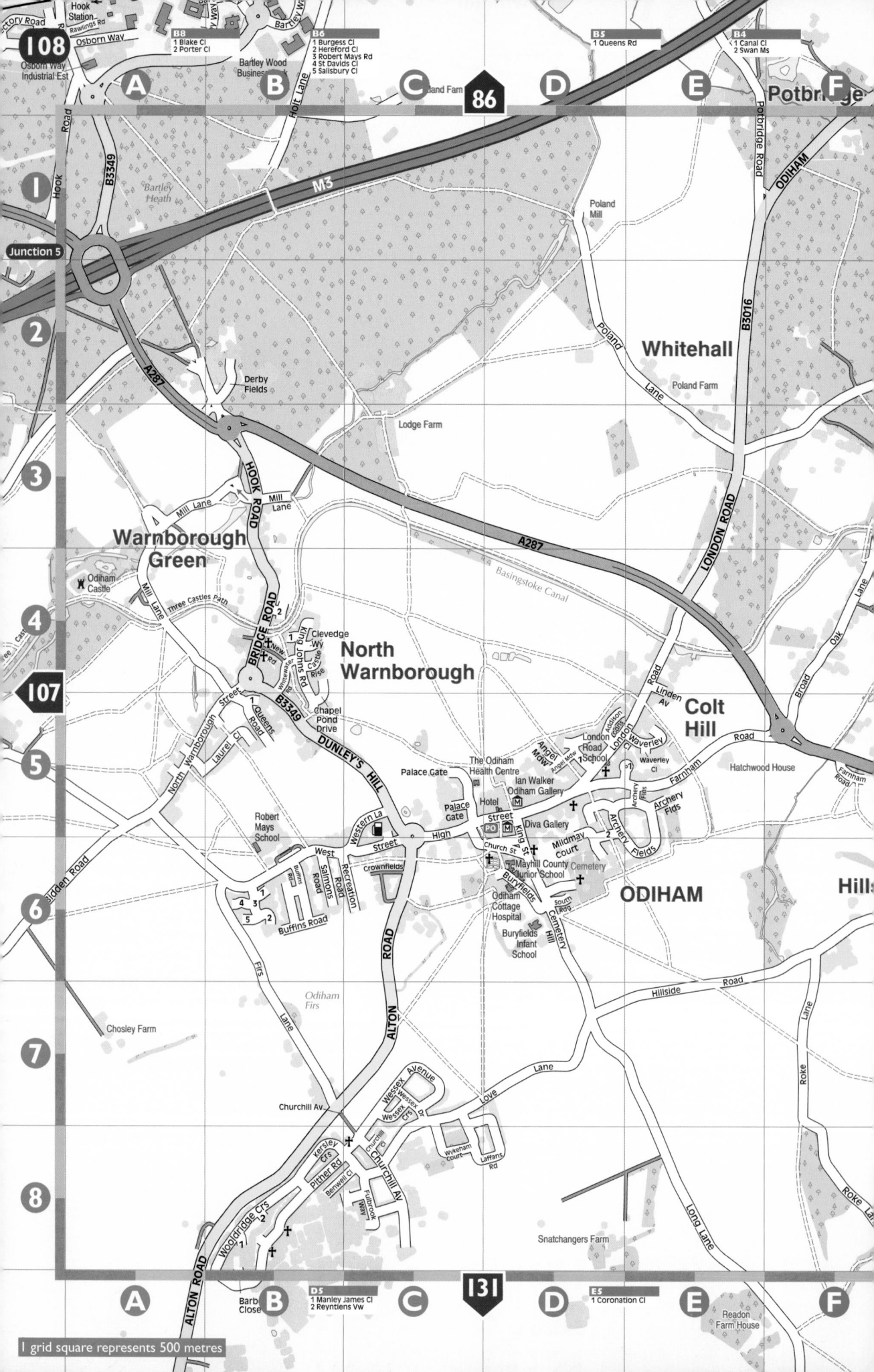

108
86
107
131
B8
1 Blake Cl
2 Porter Cl
B6
1 Burgess Cl
2 Hereford Cl
3 Robert Mays Rd
4 St Davids Cl
5 Salisbury Cl
B5
1 Queens Rd
B4
1 Canal Cl
2 Swan Ms
D5
1 Manley James Cl
2 Reyntiens Vw
E5
1 Coronation Cl
Hook Station
Osborn Way
Osborn Way Industrial Est
Rawlings Rd
Bartley Wood Business Park
Holt Lane
Potbridge
Potbridge Road
M3
Junction 5
Hook Road
B3349
Bartley Heath
Poland Mill
Poland Lane
Whitehall
Poland Farm
B3016
ODIHAM
A287
Derby Fields
Lodge Farm
HOOK ROAD
Mill Lane
Warnborough Green
Odiham Castle
Three Castles Path
Basingstoke Canal
LONDON ROAD
BRIDGE ROAD
New Rd
Clevedge Wy
King Johns Rd
Castle Rise
North Warnborough
Street
Queens Road
Laurel Cl
North Warnborough
Chapel Pond Drive
DUNLEY'S HILL
Colt Hill
Linden Av
Waverley
Waverley Cl
Farnham Road
Hatchwood House
Broad Oak Lane
Angel Mdw
London Road School
Addison Gdns
London Cl
The Odiham Health Centre
Ian Walker Odiham Gallery
Palace Gate
Hotel
Street
High
Diva Gallery
Archery Flds
Archery Fields
Mildmay Court
Church St
King St
Mayhill County Junior School
Cemetery
ODIHAM
Hills
Western La
West
Robert Mays School
Buffins Rd
Salmons Road
Recreation Road
Crownfields
Buffins Road
Bidden Road
Odiham Cottage Hospital
Buryfields
South Rdg
Cemetery Hill
Buryfields Infant School
Firs Lane
Odiham Firs
ALTON ROAD
Hillside Road
Chosley Farm
Roke Lane
Love Lane
Wessex Avenue
Wessex Dr
Wessex Crs
Churchill Av
Churchill Cl
Wykeham Court
Laffans Rd
Kersley Crs
Pither Rd
Benwell Cl
Fulbrook Way
Woolridge Crs
Snatchangers Farm
Long Lane
Barb Close
Readon Farm House
1 grid square represents 500 metres

Court House

G **H** **J** **87** **K** **L** **M**

1

Bagwell Lane

Sprat's Hatch Lane

Dogmersfield C of E
Primary School

Dogmersfield

2

Basingstoke Canal

Swan's Farm

Sprat's Hatch
Farm

Tundry
Pond

Sprat's Hatch
Lane

3

Great Park

Ormersfield Farm

Three Castles Path

iham
mmon

4

Dogmersfield
Lake

110

Dogmersfield
Park

Chalky Lane

Coxmoor
Wood

5

Farnham Rd

6

Coxmoor
Farm Light
Industrial Es

A287

Bullock's Farm

Small
Acres Farm

FARNHAM ROAD

**Mill
Lane**

Rye
Common

7

Buttridge

8

G **H** **J** **132** **K** **L** **M** nel
Home Farm

Roke Lane

Roke Farm

E4
1 Christchurch Cl
D4
1 Annettes Cft
D3
1 Cavendish Rd
2 Eggleton Cl
3 Meadow Vw
4 Thirlmere Crs
C1
1 Leawood Rd
2 Netherhouse Mr
3 New Barn Cl
88
109
133
F4
1 Pipers Cft
Sports Centre
Tavistock Infant School
Junior School
Crookham Village
Grove Farm
Church Crookham
Court Moor School
Richmond Surgery
Conifer Close
Crookham C of E Infants School
Hancock's Farm
Coxmoor Wood
Coxmoor Farm Light Industrial Estate
Finns Industrial Park
Mill Lane
Velmead Farm
Tennis Club
Redfields Industrial Est
Redfields Ind Park
Stillers Farm
Redfields
St Nicholas School
Dares Farm
Downsland House
Marsh Farm Business Centre
Bowling Alley
Hannam's Copse
Eastbridge
Lea Farm
Itchel Home Farm
Warren Corner
Redlands
Pilcot Road
Hitches Lane
Leawood Road
Crookham Road
Reading Rd S
A323
B3013
Basingstoke Canal
Basingbourne Road
Castle Street
Wickham Road
Coxheath Road
Cranford Avenue
The Street
Stroud Lane
Crondall Road
Gally Hl Rd
Aldershot Rd
Ewshot Lane
Watery Lane
Redfields Lane
Dare's Lane
Odiham Road
Hyde Lane
Redlands La
1 grid square represents 500 metres

Crown
Gdns Mont-
dars rose
Cl
The Aloes G2
RO 1 Hamilton Rd
2 Northfield Cl
Albany Cl
Westbury
Westbury Gdns
Road
G3
1 Castor Ct
2 Lingmala Gv
Gdns
G4
1 Polkerris Wy
Fairway

Victor
Way
Magaz

Pondtail

G   H   J   K   L   M

89

NORRIS HILL ROAD   Norris Bridge

Wellington

Firtree Way
Prioe
Keep
Velmead   St Michaels Cl

Crown
Cl   Fairfield   Velmead Close
Road

Pyestock
Wood

A323

FLEET ROAD   Basingstoke Canal   Pavilion   Tra

Eelmoor
Bridge   Laffan

I

2

Velmead
Rose   Road

Beaufort Road   Burns Av
Carlton   Madeley Rd
Barbara   Gordon Av

Lennel Gdns
Cl   Grove   Heron Cl
Annes   Sian   Spencer
Way   Cl   Northfield Rd
Pine   Grove Rd   Cormoor
Weldon   Aldershot Road
Cl   Cl

Aldershot Road

Long Valley

Ravine
Head

Eelmoor

3

PO   Azalea Gardens
PO
compton
Road   Avesgarth
B3013   St
ompton

Redwoods   Foye
Oaken   Lane   Holly   Lion
Copse   Cader Way   Lane   Way
chool   Earlsbourne   Kimberley   cockade
Lane   Weseldown Rd   Hawkwell

Bourley Road

BEACON

Chestnut
Copse

HILL

Fleet
Business
Park   Wakefords
Copse

Leipzig Road

Leipzig Barracks

Outridden
Copse

4

Claycart
Bottom

112

5

B3013   ROAD   Lane

Tadpole

Bourley Road

Bourley Lane   Bourley Road

6

7

B3013

Hampshire County
Surrey County

8

hill   Nightale   2
4   Badger Way   1   5
3   Fox Way

G   H   J   K   L   M

134

Sandy   Eton   Macdonald
Brougham   Pl   Stuart   Swift Rd
Lane   Blackheath   Road   Sandford Rd
Barton   Hale County
First &
Middle School   Cemetery   ALMA   LAN

ALMA
Heath   Yolland   Hill
B3005   Ball   Hill   Rd

G8   1 Magpie Cl
2 Partridge Cl
3 Sparrowhawk Cl
4 Woodpecker Cl

Nel
Chai   Nelson
Crescent   Rd

The
Glade

The   santina
Cl
Crescent
Crs   Hillside
PO   The Glade

Bicksbury
Hill   engnall

Rd

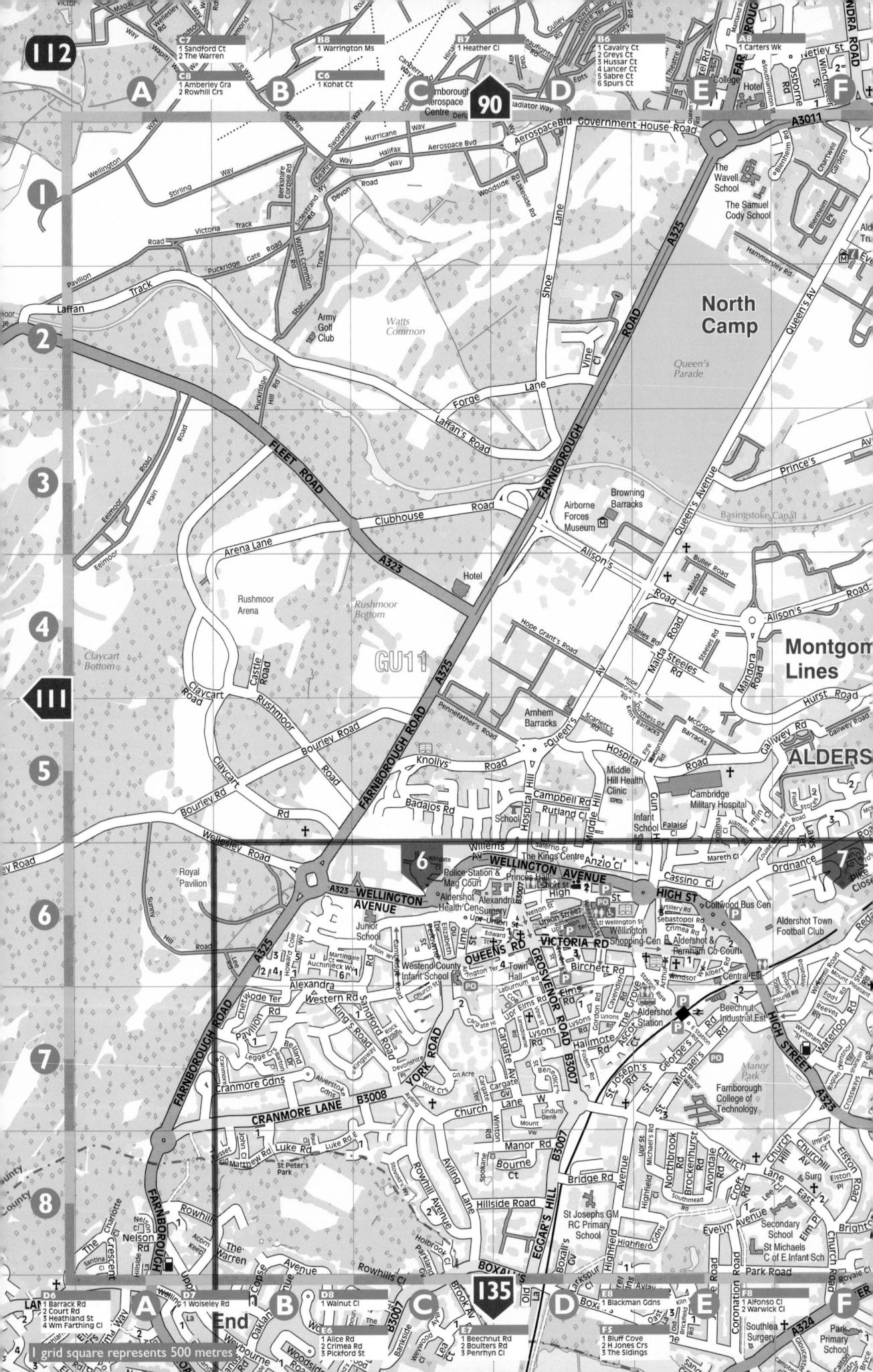

112
90
111
135
A
B
C
D
E
F
1
2
3
4
5
6
7
8
C7
1 Sandford Ct
2 The Warren
C8
1 Amberley Gra
2 Rowhill Crs
B8
1 Warrington Ms
C6
1 Kohat Ct
B7
1 Heather Cl
B6
1 Cavalry Ct
2 Greys Ct
3 Hussar Ct
4 Lancer Ct
5 Sabre Ct
6 Spurs Ct
A8
1 Carters Wk
Farnborough Aerospace Centre
Government House Road
A3011
Aerospace Bvd
Hurricane Way
Halifax Way
Swordfish Way
Spitfire
Wellington Way
Stirling Way
Berkshire Corsey Rd
Sidestrand Wy
Devon Road
Woodside Rd
Lakeside Rd
Victoria Track
Puckridge Gate Road
Watts Common Rd
Pavilion Road
Laffan Track
Army Golf Club
Watts Common
Shoe Lane
Vine Cl
Forge Lane
Laffan's Road
The Wavell School
The Samuel Cody School
Hammersley Rd
Blenheim Rd
Chartwell Gardens
Queen's Av
North Camp
Queen's Parade
Prince's Av
Puckridge Hill Rd
Eelmoor Road
Plain Road
Eelmoor
FLEET ROAD
A323
FARNBOROUGH ROAD
A325
Clubhouse Road
Arena Lane
Hotel
Browning Barracks
Airborne Forces Museum
Basingstoke Canal
Queen's Avenue
Alison's Road
Buller Road
Maida Rd
Rushmoor Arena
Rushmoor Bottom
Claycart Bottom
GU11
Hope Grant's Road
Steeles Rd
Steeles Road
Maida Road
Mandora Road
Montgom
Lines
Hurst Road
Castle Road
Claycart Road
Rushmoor Road
Bourley Road
Pennefather's Road
Arnhem Barracks
Scarlett's Rd
Duchess of Kent Barracks
McGrigor Barracks
Galliwey Rd
Knollys' Road
Hospital Road
Fire Station Rd
ALDERS
Middle Hill Health Clinic
Cambridge Military Hospital
Campbell Rd
Rutland Cl
Badajos Rd
Hospital Hill
Middle Hill
School
Infant School
Gun Hill
Falaise Cl
Bourley Rd
Wellesley Road
Royal Pavilion
Willems Av
WELLINGTON AVENUE
The Kings Centre
Anzio Cl
Police Station & Mag Court
Princes Hall
Aldershot Health Cen
Alexandra Surgery
Mareth Cl
Cassino Cl
Ordnance Rd
HIGH ST
Coltwood Bus Cen
Aldershot Town Football Club
Sebastopol Rd
Crimea Rd
Artillery Rd
Union Street
Upr Union St
Wellington Shopping Cen
Aldershot & Farnham Co Court
VICTORIA RD
QUEENS RD
GROSVENOR ROAD
Birchett Rd
Junior School
Westend County Infant School
Town Hall
Alexandra Rd
Western Rd
Sandford Road
King's Road
Chetwode Ter
Pavilion Rd
Sunny Hill Road
Lee Rd
Auchinleck Wy
Martingale Ct
Howard Cole Wy
Elms Rd
Laburnum Rd
Upr Elms Rd
Lysons Rd
Halimote Rd
Cavendish Rd
Gordon Rd
The Grove
Ascot Ct
Aldershot Station
Central Est
Beechnut Industrial Est
St George's Rd
St Michael's Rd
St Joseph's Rd
Manor Park
Farnborough College of Technology
HIGH STREET
A323
Waterloo Rd
Windmill Rd
Church Lane W
Church Lane East
Cargate Av
YORK ROAD
York Crs
Devonshire Pl
Kingsway
Legge Cr
Cranmore Gdns
Alverstoke Gdns
CRANMORE LANE
B3008
Luke Rd
Matthew Rd
St Peter's Park
Rowhill Avenue
Ayling Lane
Hillside Road
Manor Rd
Bourne Ct
Winton Rd
Bridge Rd
EGGAR'S HILL
B3007
St Josephs GM RC Primary School
Highfield Avenue
Highfield Gdns
Northbrook Rd
Brockenhurst Rd
Avondale Rd
Church Hill
Churchill Av
Elston Road
Evelyn Avenue
Secondary School
St Michaels C of E Infant Sch
Park Road
Coronation Road
Church Road
Brighton
Nelson Rd
The Charlotte Crescent
The Warren
Holbrook Cl
Parkland
Rowhills Cl
Rowhills
FARNBOROUGH
BOXALLS
Boxall's Gv
D6
1 Barrack Rd
2 Court Rd
3 Heathland St
4 Wm Farthing Cl
D7
1 Wolseley Rd
D8
1 Walnut Cl
E6
1 Alice Rd
2 Crimea Rd
3 Pickford St
E7
1 Beechnut Rd
2 Boulters Rd
3 Penrhyn Cl
E8
1 Blackman Gdns
F5
1 Bluff Cove
2 H Jones Crs
3 The Sidings
F8
1 Alfonso Cl
2 Warwick Cl
Southlea Surgery
Park Primary School
A324
End
1 grid square represents 500 metres

G1 1 Gaffney Cl 2 Rimbault Cl
G7 1 Northfield Cl
H1 Holly Lodge Schl 1 Napier Cl
H8 1 Hawthorn Cl 2 Oxenden Ct
G6 1 South Wk 2 Thirsk Ct
G8 1 Tichborne Pl
J3 1 Wyvern Cl

G **H** **J** **91** **K** **L** **M**

1
2
3
4
5
6
7
8

Ash Vale

Ash

North Town

GU12

K3 1 Richards Cl 2 Woodlands Cl
K1 1 Alder Cl
J7 1 Manor Farm Cl 2 Windsor Gdns
K6 1 Deedman Cl
K2 Poyle Farm 1 Waverley Gdns
J8 1 Manorside Cl 2 Moore Cl

114
F1
1 Forest Dr
E4
1 Canons Cl
2 Deans Cl
E2
1 Woodcock Cl
D8
1 Church Mdw
Zouch Primary School
Wavell Rd
Churchill Cl
Circular
Pennings Road
Ludgershall Road
A3026
Manor Br Ct
Lahore Close
Zouch Av
Zouch Close
Daunch Cl
Abbotts Rd
Abbotts Cl
Kohat Cl
Nepaul Road
Zouch Farm Road
Elm House Surg
Plassey Rd
Ebble Cl
Wylye Road
Clarendon County Junior & Infant School
Chestnut Av
Cherry Tree Av
Beech Hill Rd
Hawthorn Rd
Kestrel Cl
Falcon Cl
Lark Cl
Forest Dr
Naini Tal Rd
Margha Rd
St Georges Rd
St Andrews Road
Dr. Gregs Surg
Ordnance Rd
Nadder
Martin Cl
Bourne Road
Napier
Auckland Cl
Dunedin Cl
Kennet Road
Raven Cl
Swallow Cl
Tidworth Health Centre
Ashdown Family & Health Centre
Group Practice
Bazaar Road
Lowa Road
Garrison Theatre
St Patricks Av
St Michaels Av
Lowa Cl
Lowa Rd
Meerut Rd
Lahore Rd
Station Road
Lady Godley Cl
Kirkee Road
Jamrud Road
Avon Rd
Bulford Road
Komat Rd
Kirkee Rd
Ashdown Terrace
Plantation Rd
Furse Hill Road
Church Lane
Bishops Cl
Winton
Park Road
A338
The Mall
Adampur Rd
Agra Rd
Baroda Road
Cabul Road
Dasna Road
Grand Trunk Road
River Bourne
Lane
Club Lane
The Avenue
South Dr
South Tidworth
Humber
Jagdalik Rd
Stables Road
Baroda Rd
Tidworth Garrison Golf Club
SP9
Tidworth House
Arcot Road
Salisbury Road
Hare Warren
Ashdown Copse
Home Farm
Humber Lane
Wiltshire County
Hampshire County
The Belt
Bulford Road
The Cross Belt
Bulford Road
Sarum Close
Sarum Cl
Hedge Cl
High
Primary
Kingfishers
138
F2
1 Gisbourne Cl
2 Pheasant Cl
3 Sycamore Cl
Threadgill Way
Muscott Cl
Parkhouse
Mayfield Cl
Manor Cl
St Peters Cl
Bourne La
Shipton Bellinger
1 grid square represents 500 metres

1 Brisbane Cl
2 Sydney Cl

G **H** **J** **92** **K** **L** **M** **I**

WORTH

Perham Down

Somme

Wouldham Cl

Upnor Close

South Park

Andover Lane

Kemmel Rd

Halton Rd

Adelaide Cl

Perth

Lambdown Terrace

Lambdown Way

Benin Rd

Tobruk Rd

Fyfield Way

Appleshaw Way

Downsview Way

Lamb Down

Great Shod so **2**

Wiltshire County

Hampshire County

Newdown Copse

3

4

Kimpton Down Farm

116

Down Road

5

Kimpton Wood

Ox Drove

6

Ox Drove

7

Old Coach Road

8

G **H** **J** **139** **K** **L** **M**

Snoddington

116

A   B   C 93 D   E   F

Tilly Dow

1

Al Lane

South Park

2 eat Shoddesden

Little Shoddesden

Shoddesden Lane

Redenham House

Privet Lane

ANDOVER ROAD   A342

Redenham Dro

New

R

3

Deacon Road

Littleton Copse

Privet Lane

4

115

Deacon Road

Deacon Rd

Cow La

Privet Lane

5

Fyfield Lane

Lane

Dauntsey Drove

6

Down Road

Kimpton

Deacon Road

Duncan's Close

Grange Cl

Fyfield

Fyfield Road

May Ave Ind

Dauntsey Lane

7

Snoddington Road

Stanbury Road

Kimpton Primary School

8

Thruxton Aerodrome and ● Motor Racing Circuit

Mullenspond

Elm Cl

Stanbury Cl

ambourne Way

Thruxton

Stanbury Road

PO

Beech Close

yon Dr

Pillhill Brook

A   B   C 140 D   E   F

A303(T)

1 grid square represents 500 metres

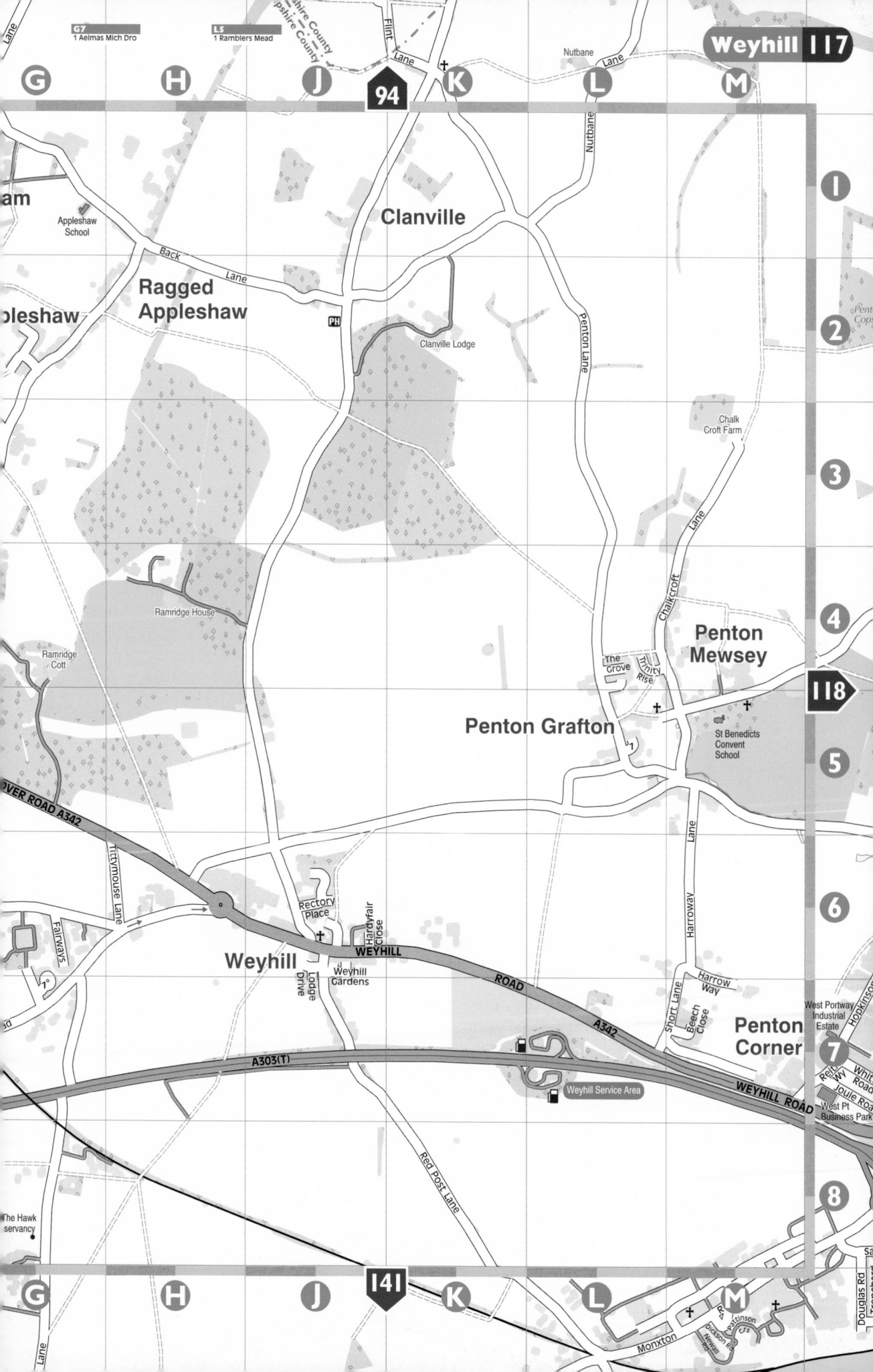

G7 1 Aelmas Mich Dro
L5 1 Ramblers Mead

G
H
J
94
K
L
M

I

1

2
Pent
Cops

3

4
118

5

6

7

8

Nutbane Lane

Nutbane

Clanville

Clanville Lodge

PH

Penton Lane

Chalk Croft Farm

Chalkcroft Lane

Penton Mewsey

The Grove
Trinity Rise

Penton Grafton

St Benedicts Convent School

Ramridge House

Ramridge Cott

OVER ROAD A342

Tittymouse Lane

Fairways

Rectory Place

Hardyfair Close

WEYHILL

Weyhill

Lodge Drive

Weyhill Gardens

ROAD
A342

Short Lane

Harroway

Harrow Way

Beech Close

West Portway Industrial Estate

Penton Corner

Hopkinson

A303(T)

Red Post Lane

Weyhill Service Area

WEYHILL ROAD

Joule Road

West Pt Business Park

Reith Wy
Whit

The Hawk servancy

G
H
J
141
K
L
M

Monxton

Douglas Rd

Flint Lane

shire County
pshire County

Back Lane

Lane

SP11

Penton Copse

Cemetery

New Street Football Club

Knights Enham

Manor Farm

Enha

nedicts nt

Foxcotte

Richborough Drive

Mercia Close

Mercia Avenue

Brayder Way

Avenue

Enham Lane

Saxon Blg

English Rd

Jutland Drive

Burral

Way

Cole Cl

Rune Drive

Saxon Way

Kiel

Burmarsh Drive

Ryon Cl

Melot Rd

Tintagel Close

Arthur's

4

Andras Ct

Holland Dr

Junior School

King M

Launcelot Cl

Porchester

Bede Drive

Tower Cl

Litchfield Cl

Recover Wy

Dere Cl

St Thomas

Aldrin Cl

Armstrong Rd

Collins Wy

Saxon Way

Krum Cl

Altona Gdns

Elbe Way

Cuxhaven

Flensburg Cl

Emden Rd

Lubeck Drive

Calahad Close

PO

Bremen Gdns

Foxcotte Lane

Foxcotte Cl

Lakeside Close

Sunnyside Cl

Carter's Meadow

Wetherby Gdns

Goch Way

Charlton

Goch Way

Andover Football Club

WEST PORTWAY

West Portway

Way

Way

Hopkinson

Smeaton Rd

West Portway Industrial Estate

Macadam Cl

Mitchell Cl

Cogwith Park

Royce Close

CHURCHILL WAY WEST

Parkview Cl

8 A343

Harrow Way Community School

Silchester Cl

Harrow

Way

War Memorial Hospital

Lawrence Cl

Ward Ct

Poynters Close

Artists

Stubbs

Landseer

Artists Wy

Hepworth

Penton Corner

Reith Wy

Whittle Road

Joule Road

West Pt Business Park

Caxton Cl

Sterling Pk

Watt Cl

Portway Drive

Blendon Drive

Milton Av

Chaucer Av

Shakespeare Av

Brackenbury

Apple Tree Grove

Cherry Tree Rd

Tollgate Rd

Charlton Hill Surgery

Charlton Health Centre

2

Dell Rd

Manor Rd

Down Rd

Wellington Rd

Charlton

Redon Way

A343

Constable Ct

nton Dr

Moore

SP10

Stephenson Close

Upper Drove

East Drove

Porters

Eardley Av

Chichester

Orchard Rd

May Tree Road

King George Road

Hanson Road

Ferndale Rd

Beckett Rd

Watson Acre

Mylen Road

Andover Stn

Station Ap

Halfax Rd

Cross Lane

Junction

Wessex Close

Heather Dr

Charlton Rd

Charlton Road

Western Av

Cricklade Coll

WEYHILL ROAD

Monxton Rd

Danehurst Pl

Gallaghers Mead

Portway County Infants and Junior Schools

Ash Tree Road

Cheaviley Close

Ashfield Road

Portway Road

The Amber Gdns

Crescent

Haig Rd

Albany Rd

Mylen Business Cen

P

Glen Rd

Kenions Rd

Roundway

Millway

Whynot Lane

The Avenue

The Pines

Bishop's Way

John Hanson Community School

Winterdyne Mews

Alexandra Road

Warner Ct

Osborne Rd

Queens Av

Windsor Rd

Magistrates Court

Wes Ct

B3402

Salmond Road

Ellington

Portail

Siesson Cl

The Link

The

Meadow

PO

St John the B RC Primary School

1 Agravaine Cl

River

Plantation Rd

Beech Hurst

Test Valley Borough Council

St Hubert Rd

Suffolk

E4 1 Marsum Cl

D6 1 The Green

F4 1 Gawaine Cl

F5 1 Agravaine Cl

G2
1 Chapel La
G3
1 Icknield Wy
2 Lillywhite Crs
G4
1 Corinthian Cl
2 Danegeld Cl
3 Olaf Cl
G6
1 Blackbird Ct
2 Dove Cl
3 Martin Wy
4 Plover Cl
96
Ridges Copse
Hackwood Copse
Stoke Road
Dunhills
Lane
Malt House Lane
NEWBURY ROAD
Landale Cl
Kings Rd
Alamein Rd
Enham Alamein
Tobruk Close
Knightsbridge Rd
Anton Lane
Woodhouse
Smannell & Enham Primary School
Smannell
A343
Finkley House
Finkley Road
Finkley Manor Farm
Smannell Road
East Anton
Icknield Way
Edgar Close
Moot Cl
Witan Cl
Viking Way
Livia Close
Roman
Turin Court
Genoa Court
Venice Court
Florence Court
Caesar Rd
Tiberius Road
Shepherd Spring Medical Centre
Sobers Sq
Swallowfields
Crickleters
Goddard Sq
Grace Sq
Hobbs Sq
Hutton Sq
Laker Sq
Lock Sq
Farm Park
North Wy
Walworth Road
Picket Piece
120
River Way
Kennet Ct
Ouse Ct
Prince Cl
Queensway
North Way
Kingsway
Itchen Court
Ribble Ct
Wye
Icknield School
River Pde
CHURCHILL WAY A3093
Pilgrims Way
Ox Drove
South Way
Central Way
West Way
Focus 303 Business Cen
Focus Wy
South Way
Flinders Cl
Watery Lane
Majorca Av
Toledo Grove
Colenzo Drive
Madrid Road
March Cl
Seville Crs
Granada Pl
Bilbao Court
Main
Valencia Way
Vigo County Infant School
Vigo Road
Junior School
Doughty Way
Livingstone Road
Magellan Cl
Scott Cl
Columbus Wy
CHURCHILL WAY
Admirals Way
LONDON ROAD
Down House
Andover Down
NEW STREET
Corunna
St John's Rd
Batchelors Barn Road
Mark Way School
The Winton School
Winton Play School
Borsberry Cl
Recreation Rd
Andover Mus & the Mus of the Iron Age
The Manse Health Cen
Acre Path
London Road
Stiles Drive
Springfield Close
Pearman Drive
Adelaide Medical Cen
Eastfield Rd
Woodlands Way
Sheep Fair
Sidmouth Road
Winton Chase
Picket Twenty Farm
Grove Ct
C of E Primary Sch
143
J8
1 Charlotte Cl
2 Palmer Dr
J6
1 Thames Ct
2 Tyne Ct
H8
1 Eastfield Cl
H6 cont.
8 Forth Ct
9 Helford Ct
10 Hendren Sq
11 Humber Ct
12 Jardine Sq
13 Larwood Sq
14 Nene Ct
H6
1 Avon Ct
2 Beaulieu Ct
3 Bourne Ct
4 Calder Ct
5 Clyde Ct
6 Dart Ct
7 Derwent Ct
cont.
G7
1 Barcelona Cl
2 Dances Cl
3 Spring Ms
G8
1 Bracher Cl
2 Silkweavers Rd
ANDOVER
Vincent Dr
Wolversdene Road
Leigh
Micheldever
The Grange

120

97

A   B   C   D   E   F

Hackwood
Copse

Middle
Wyke Farm

Derry
Farm

1

Finkley   Road

Test Way

Lower
Wyke Farm

2

Harroway

3

Apsley Farm

4

Walworth Road

Test Way

119

Faulkner's
Down Farm

Ox Drove
Rise

5

✝

Tinker's
Hill

6

Harewood
Peak

Fox
Cottages

Test Way

B3400

7

B3400   LONDON ROAD

ROAD

House

**Andover
Down**

8

The
Middleway

Test Way

A   B   C   D   E   F

144

1 grid square represents 500 metres

G H J **98** K L M

I

Dirty Corner

Bloswood Lane

New Barn Farm

Harroway

2

Chapmansford Farm

Cowdown Copse

skyle Rise

Bloswood Lane

3

nor F

Bourne Rivulet

The Mansion

Hurstbourne Park

4

122

5

The Common

B3048

B3400

6 Ho

Hurstbourne Priors

7

LONGPARISH ROAD

Testbourne

udgett Farm

Drury Ct

8

Tracy's Dell

Paper Mill Farm

East

122
Down Farm
C3
1 Meadow Pound
B4
1 Sheppard Cl
B3
1 Clemence Gdns
2 Jobson Cl
3 Longs Ct
4 The Rookery
A3
1 Bradbury Cl
2 Hartley Meadow
Harroway
99
A
B
C
D
E
F
Priory Lane
Berehill Farm
A34(T)
Newbury Road
Whitchurch Station
Greenwoods
Station Rd
Fairfield
Bere Hill
Dances Lane
Newbury District Council
Freefolk
PH
Skylark Rise
Caesar's Way
Witan Ct
Lapwing Rise
Evingar Industrial Est
Kingsley Pk
Evingar Gdns
Evingar Road
Bloswood Lane
Meadow Vw
Bloswood Drive
Ardglen Road
Lwr Evingar Road
Oakland Rd
Firs Way
Bellevue
Newbury St
Kings Wk
WHITCHURCH
Lynch Hill Park
B3400
LONDON ROAD
Manor Farm
The Lynch
LONDON ST
Town Mill Lane
The Green
The Gables
Bell Street
Lynch Hill
Whitchurch Medical Centre
Fair Cl
CHURCH STREET
PO
Test Road
Silk Mill
Winchester Street
Whitchurch C of E Primary School
Daniel Rd
McFauld Way
River Test
Cemetery
Wells's Lane
Alliston Wy
Neuvic Wy
Wheeler Cl
Brooks Cl
The Knowlings
Micheldever Road
Testbourne Community School
Queens Rd
Southfield Farm
121
The Weir
Winchester Road
Webbs Farm Cl
Charlcot Farm
Charlcot Cl
Micheldever Cl
Tufton
Manor Ho
1
2
3
4
5
6
7
8
146
1 grid square represents 500 metres

Whitchurch 123
100
124
147
Lynch
Southington
Laverstoke
Laverstoke Ho
Home Farm
LONDON ROAD
ROTTEN HILL
B3400
Turrill Hill Farm
Spring Pond Farm
New Barn Cotts
Laverstoke Grange Farm
Laverstoke Lane
Micheldever Road
New Barn Farm
Laverstoke Wood
Upper Whitehill Farm
Lower Whitehill Cottage
Florence Portal Cl
Colne Valley Way
Southington Close
Southington La
Vinns Lane
HIGH ST
Dellands Lane
Dellands
Red Lion Lane
Winchester Street
Alexander Road
Sapley Lane
Pond Close
Poultons Road
Charledown Road
Crawts Road
Oak Close
Silk Mill
The Lynch
1 Marsden Ct

124
101
123
148
A
B
C
D
E
F
1
2
3
4
5
6
7
8
OVERTON
Ashe
Source of the River Test
LONDON ROAD B3400
B3400
Station Road
Winchester Street
Red Lion Lane
Alexander Road
Gate Lane
Nightingale Rise
Waltham Road
Pound Road
Mede Close
Pond Close
Poultons Road
Charledown Road
Berrydown Court
Berrydown Lane
Berrydown Farm
Ashe Park
Burley Wood
Burley Lane
Sapley Farm House
Waltham Lane
Bramdown Copse
Basset's Farm
Lower Whitehill Cottages
Southley Farm
Upper Whitehill Farm
Pilgrim's Farm
Golf Course
Steventon Warren Farm
1 grid square represents 500 metres

K7
1 Old Barn Cl
2 Ramsholt Cl

L7
1 Burydown Cl
2 Meadow Ri

102

G   H   J   K   L   M

I

Parde

Fairview
Meadow
The

Wayfarer's Walk

Bull's
Bushes
Copse

Bull's Bushes F

2

3

Dean
Heath
Copse

Steventon

4

126

Stubb's
Copse

5

West
Wood

Village Farm

6

Mary Lane

North Waltham

No
Bus
Ce

Waltham

Manor Farm

Church

Steventon Rd

Elizabethan Rd

Smiths Md

Longfield

Home Md

Lane

North
Waltham
School

2

Well
Close

2

Cuckoo Cl

Chapel St

7

1

Folly Farm

Cuckoo Cl

St Michael's Close

Church Road

Yew Tree Lane

Up St

Maidenthorn   Lane

7

Coldharbour

PH

Popham   Lane

A30

M3

8

149

G   H   J   K   L   M

126
103
125
150
A
B
C
D
E
F
1
2
3
4
5
6
7
8
Breach Farm
Fairview Meadow
The Surgery
Water Ridges
Sainfoin Lane
St John Road
Pardown
Bushes Farm
South Wood
Dean Heath Copse
Wayfarer's Walk
WINCHESTER ROAD
A30
M3
Junction 7
The Copse
Club House
Golf Course
Industrial Estate
Beggarwood
Hatch Warren Retail Park
North Waltham Business Centre
Chapel House Gallery
Dummer
Down St
Up Street
The Barns
Queensfield
Glebe Close
Porters Cl
Post Office La
Nutley Lane
Clump Farm
Farleigh
Kempshott Lane
Gracemere Crescent
Woodmere Croft
Bunting Close
Mallard Close
Fuzzy Drove
Heron
Heather
Foxglove
Violet Cl
Aster Road
Zinnia Cl
Wallop Dr
Windsor Gdns
Monarch Cl
Junior School
F1
1 Berewyk Cl
2 Bunting Ms
3 Sunflower Cl
E1
1 Brambling Cl
2 Pintail Cl
RG25
1 grid square represents 500 metres

Brighton Hill
G1
1 Chantry Ms
2 Fayrewood Cha
3 Matilda Dr
4 Paxton Cl
5 Sandbanks Dr
6 Westminster Cl
7 Wights Wk
G2
1 Petworth Cl
G3
1 Burrowfields
2 Grosvenor Cl
Viables Industrial
104
Manorfield Infant School
Hatch Warren County Junior School
Hatch Warren County Infant School
St Marks Primary School
M3
Cliddesden
Woods Lane
Church Lane
Hoopersmead
Station
Manor Farm
Cliddesden Primary School
FARLEIGH ROAD B3046
Broadmere
128
Farleigh Wallop
The Avenue
Grammarsham Lane
Bedlam Bottom
Farleigh House School
Manor Farm
Northgate Farm
Inwood Copse
Great Wood
Norton's Wood
Gobley Hole
B3046
Green Lane
Farrier's Field
151
K1
1 Hatchwar. Gdns
J1
1 Arne Cl
H3
1 Tamarisk Cl
2 Tithe Meadow
H2
1 The Brackens
2 Holmes Cl
3 Whitestones
H1
1 Mitchell Gdns
Nutley Wood
Upper Common
Furzen Lane
Hatchwarren Lane
Cliddesden Lane
Beggarwood Lane
Woodbury Road
Danebury Road
Highwood Rdg
Gershwin Road
Brighton Way
Stanford Road
Bach Close
Novello Cl
Beethoven Rd
Sibelius Cl
Lennon Wy
McCartney Wk
Octavian Cl
Centurion Way
Magnus Drive
Lymington Cl
Birches Crest
The Cornfields
The Beeches
The Crofts
Sherwood Cl
Lapin Lane
Cyprus Rd
Primrose Gdns
Heritage Park
Mayfield Ridge
Meadowridge
Belmont Hts
Ridge Cl
Ketelbey Rise
Chopin Road
Haydn Road
G H J K L M
1 2 3 4 5 6 7 8

128
105
127
152
A
B
C
D
E
F
1
2
3
4
5
6
7
8
Audleys Wood
Hackwood House
Hackwood Park
Hoopersmead
Lane
Station Road
Hackwood Lane
A339
ddesden
mary School
Swallick Farm
Winslade
Allwood Copse
Three Castles Path
Northgate Farm
Northgate Lane
Bushywarren Lane
Herriard
Manor Farm
Church Lane
Ellisfield
Ellisfield Manor
Furze Lane
Merritts Farm
Herriard Grange
1 grid square represents 500 metres

Hackwood Farm

G Roundtown

H

J unworth   Down 106

K

L

M

1

Cleves

2

Upton Grey House

Upton Grey

3

Cemetery Lane

Longroden Lane

Tunworth

†

The Dower House

4

Weston Road

130

5

Herriard Park

Weston Corbett

Weston Patrick †

6

Herriard House

Park Farm

7

A339

8

G

H

J 153 Lee Farm

K

L Wood

M New Farm

Nash's Green

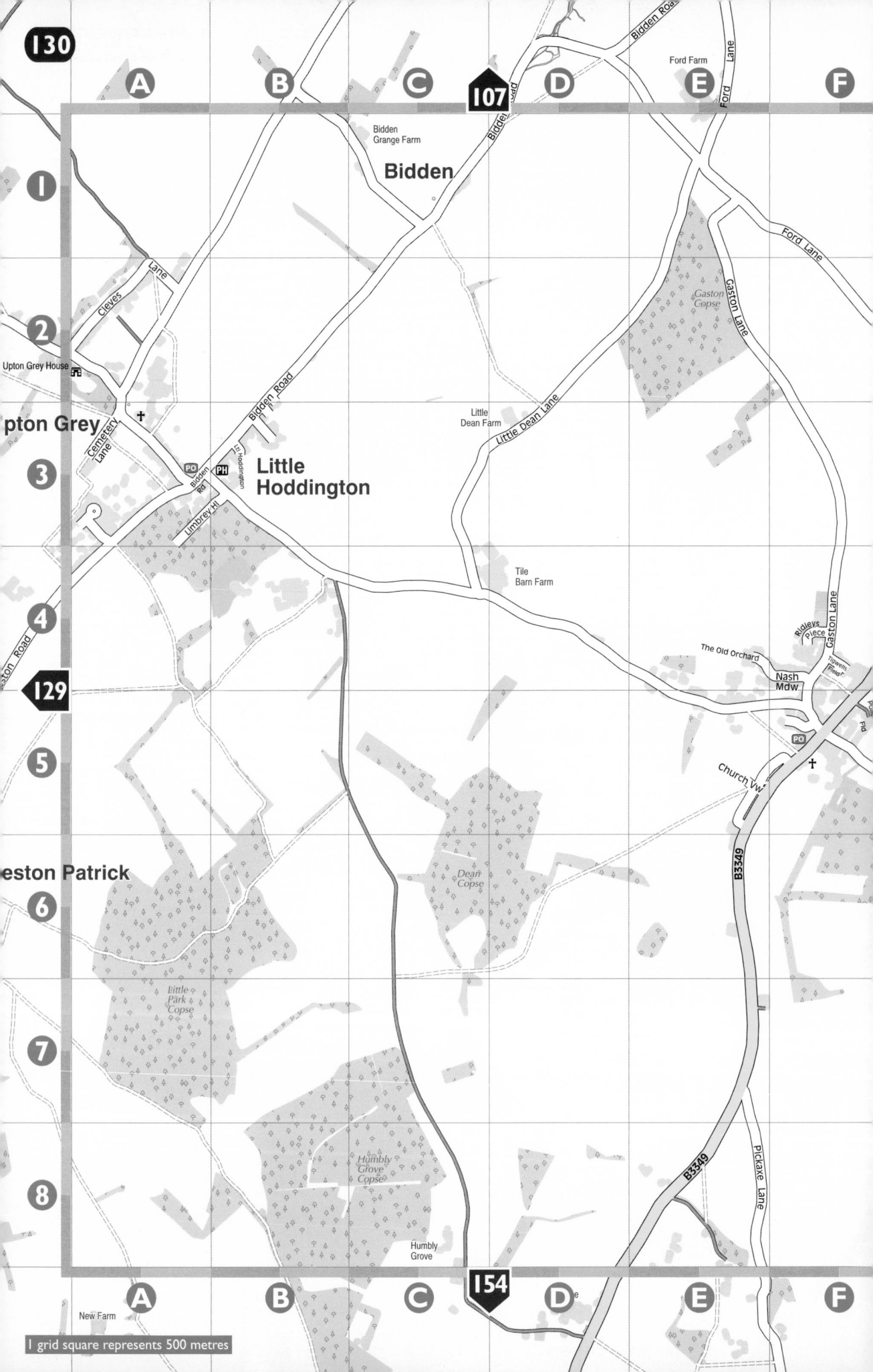

130

A B C **107** D E F

Bidden

Bidden Grange Farm

Ford Farm

Ford Lane

1

Gaston Copse

Cleves Lane

Gaston Lane

2

Upton Grey House

Bidden Road

Little Dean Farm

Little Dean Lane

pton Grey

Cemetery Lane

PO Bidden Rd PH

Lt Hoddington

Little Hoddington

3

Limbrey Hl

Tile Barn Farm

Gaston Road

4

Ridleys Piece

Gaston Lane

The Old Orchard

Tigwells Road

Nash Mdw

129

PO

Post Fld

5

Church Vw.

B3349

eston Patrick

6

Dean Copse

Little Park Copse

7

B3349

Pickaxe Lane

8

Humbly Grove Copse

B3349

Humbly Grove

A B C **154** D E F

New Farm

1 grid square represents 500 metres

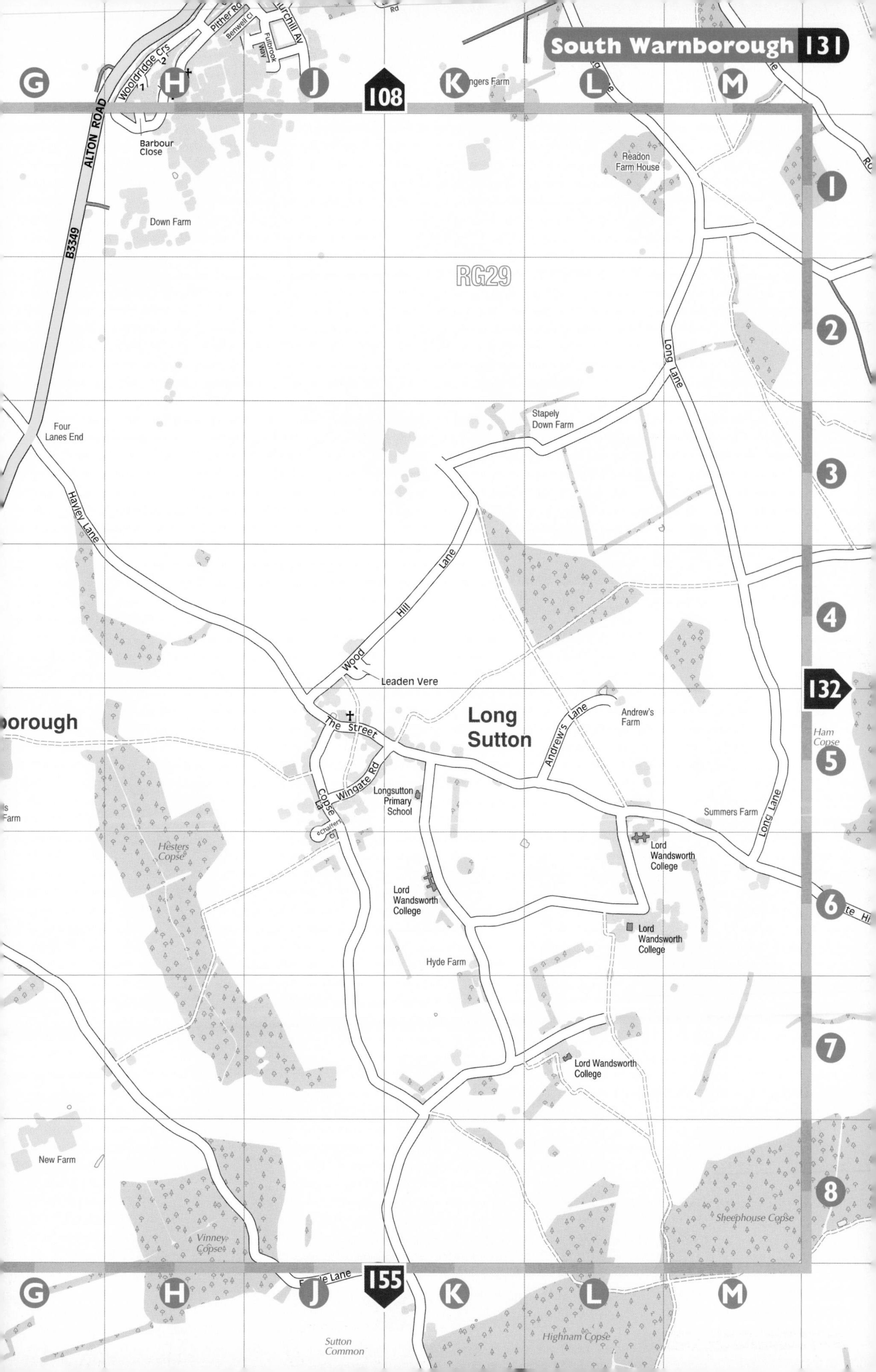

G

J

108

K

L

M

1

2

3

4

132

5

6

7

8

G

H

J

155

K

L

M

ALTON ROAD

B3349

Wooldridge Crs

Pitrher Rd

Benwell Cl

urchill Av

Fulbrook Way

Barbour Close

Down Farm

Four Lanes End

Hayley Lane

RG29

ngers Farm

Reaaon Farm House

Long Lane

Stapely Down Farm

Wood Hill Lane

Leaden Vere

borough

The Street

Wingate Rd

Copse

Chaffers Cl

Longsutton Primary School

Long Sutton

Andrew's Lane

Andrew's Farm

Summers Farm

Long Lane

Ham Copse

te Hi

Lord Wandsworth College

Lord Wandsworth College

Lord Wandsworth College

Hyde Farm

Lord Wandsworth College

Hesters Copse

s Farm

New Farm

Vinney Copse

Eagle Lane

Sutton Common

Sheephouse Copse

Highham Copse

A B C D E F

1

Roke Lane

Roke Farm

Itchel
Home F

2

Penn
Croft Farm

Newlands Farm

Park
Corner Farm

3

*Horsedown
Common*

Swanthorpe Farm

Stapely Farm

4

Thorn's Farm

*Ham
Copse*

5

Long Lane

Travers Farm

6

White Hill

PH

Montgomery's Far

Well

Well Lane

7

Hole Lane

Glade
Farm

8

ephouse Copse

A B C D E F

Isnage Farm

Hill Farm

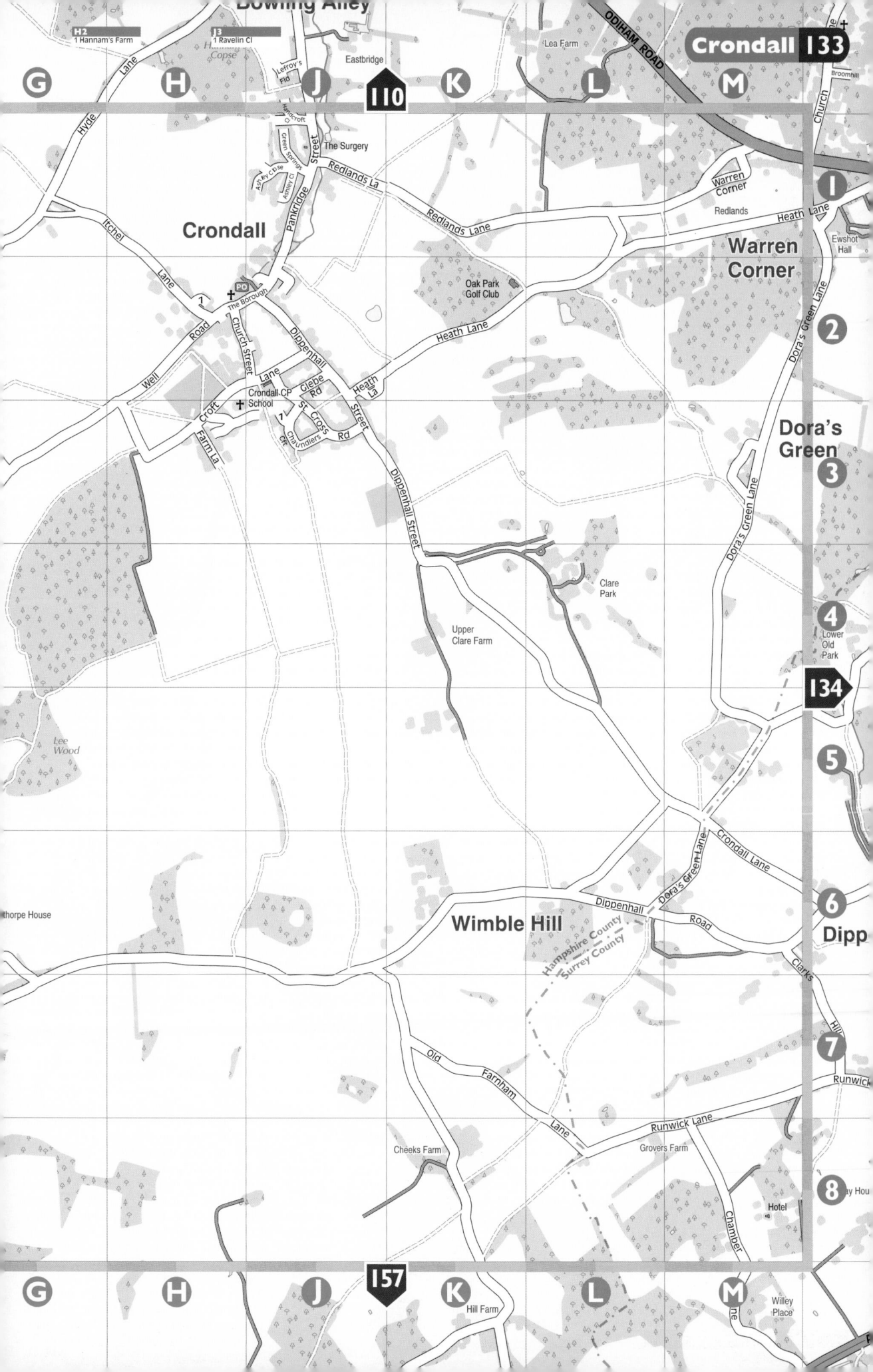

Bowling Alley
H2
1 Hannam's Farm
J3
1 Ravelin Cl
Eastbridge
Lea Farm
ODIHAM ROAD
Broomhill
Church
G
H
J
K
L
M
110
Hyde Lane
Lefroy's Fld
Handcroft Cl
The Surgery
Green Springs
Ashley Close
Ashley Cl
Street
Pankridge
Redlands La
Redlands Lane
Warren Corner
Redlands
Heath Lane
Ewshot Hall
Crondall
Itchel Lane
Oak Park Golf Club
Warren Corner
PO
The Borough
Road
Well
Church Street
Dippenhall
Heath Lane
Dora's Green Lane
Lane
Glebe Rd
Heath La
Crondall CP School
Croft
Farm La
St Cross Rd
Chandlers Cft
Street
Dora's Green
Dippenhall Street
Clare Park
Upper Clare Farm
Lower Old Park
134
Lee Wood
Crondall Lane
Dora's Green Lane
Dippenhall Road
thorpe House
Wimble Hill
Hampshire County
Surrey County
Dipp
Clarks Hill
Runwick
Old Farnham Lane
Runwick Lane
Cheeks Farm
Grovers Farm
Hotel
Chamber
157
Hill Farm
Willey Place
1
2
3
4
5
6
7
8

134
133
111
158
E6
1 College Gdns
2 Fox Yd
3 Long Gdn Wk
4 Long Gdn Wk E
5 Long Gdn Wk W
6 Lower Church La
7 Middle Church La
8 Penns Yd
9 Upper Church La
E1
1 St Marks Pl
E2
1 Balmoral Crs
2 Chatsworth Gv
3 Oaktrees
4 Wings Cl
D6
1 Chantry Cl
D2
1 Ambleside Crs
2 Beck Gdns
3 Dukes Cl
4 Folly La South
5 Trinity Flds
6 Ullswater Cl
D1
1 Lawday Pl
Hampshire County
Surrey County
Warren Corner
Dora's Green
Dippenhall
Hog Hatch
Folly Hill
Upper Hale
Ewshot Hall
Heath Lane
Odiham Road
Upper Hale
B3005
Alma
Hale County First & Middle School
Cemetery
Old Park Lane
Heathyfields Road
Upper Old Park Lane
Upper Old Park
Middle Old Park
Knowle Farm
Lower Old Park
Folly Hill
Farnham Park
Golf Course
The Grange
GU9
Farnham Castle
Castle Hill
Castle St
Three Stiles Rd
Crondall Lane
Beavers Hl
Beavers Close
Beavers Rd
Primary School
Global Adventure Sailing Club
Farnham Museum
New Ashgate Gallery
Health Cen
The Borough
South St
Union Rd
East St
Long Br
Abby St
Firgrove Hill
West Street
Wrecclesham Rd
Farnham By-Pass
A31
Farnham Business Park
Farnham Business Centre
Pilgrims Way Infants School
The Hop Kiln
Weydon Mill La
Red Lion Lane
Cemetery
Runwick Lane
Runwick House
Ridgway House
Clarks Hill
Hotel
Ridgway Road
E7
1 Arthur Cl
2 Whitlet Cl
E8
1 Hillary Cl
2 Weydon Hill Cl
F1
1 Alwin Pl
2 Beam Hollow
3 Heath Cl
4 Old Heath Wy
5 Toplady Pl
6 Trimmers Cl
F2
1 Bshp Sumner D
2 Brookside
3 Levern Dr
4 Queens Rd
F5
1 M Hawthorn Dr
2 St Cross Rd
3 Thorold Rd
4 Weybank Cl
5 Wykeham Rd
F6
1 Brightwells Rd
F7
1 Barncroft
2 Fairholme Gdns
3 Firgrove Ct
4 Merlins Cl
5 Saxon Cft
1 grid square represents 500 metres

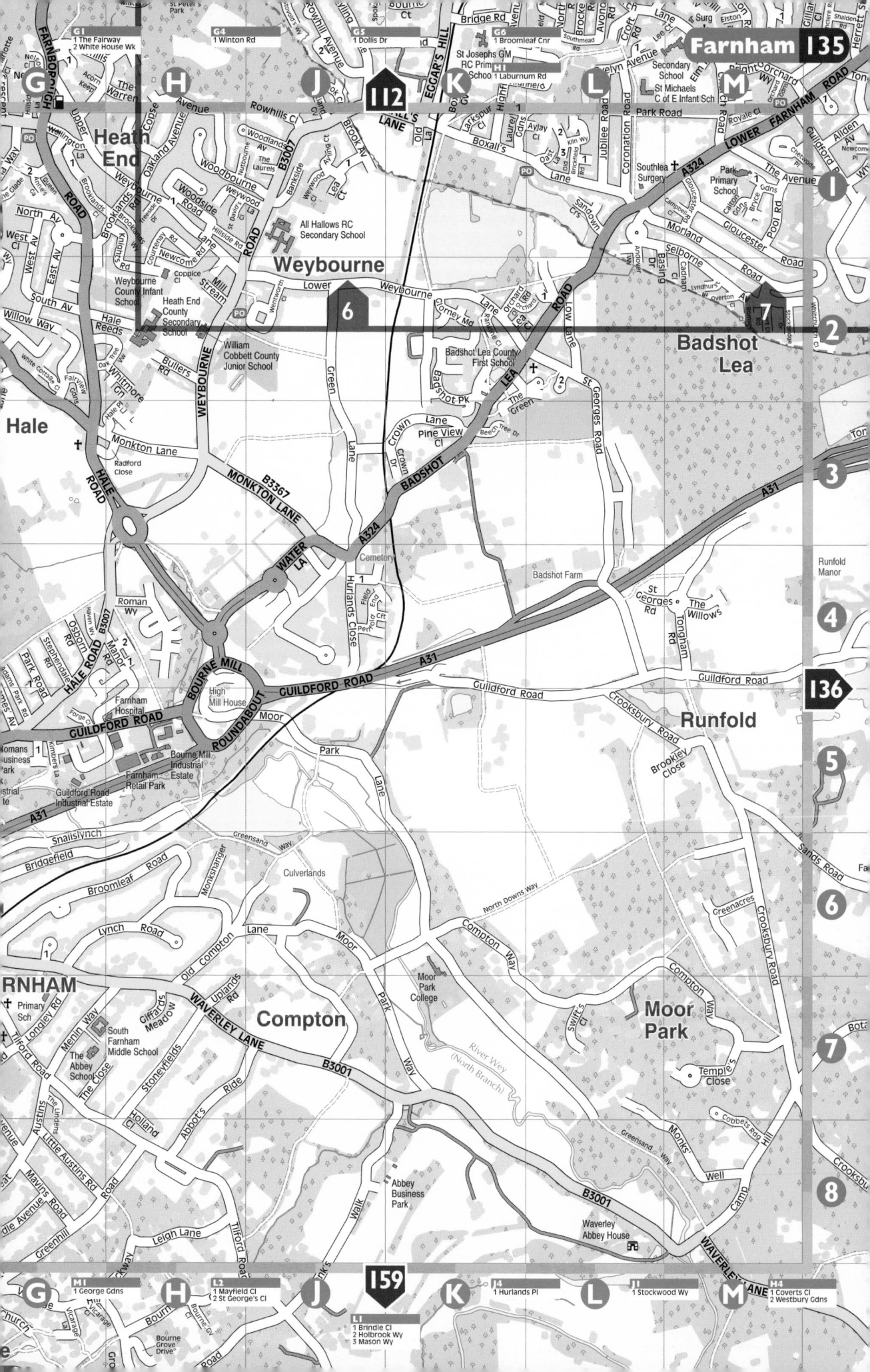
G1
1 The Fairway
2 White House Wk
G4
1 Winton Rd
G5
1 Dollis Dr
G6
1 Broomleaf Cnr
H1
1 Laburnum Rd
112
Heath End
Weybourne
All Hallows RC Secondary School
Weybourne County Infant School
Heath End County Secondary School
William Cobbett County Junior School
Badshot Lea County First School
Badshot Lea
Southlea Surgery
Park Primary School
St Josephs GM RC Prim School
Secondary School
St Michaels C of E Infant Sch
Hale
Radford Close
Monkton Lane
Badshot Farm
Runfold Manor
Cemetery
Hurlands Close
Farnham Hospital
High Mill House
Bourne Mill Industrial Estate
Farnham Retail Park
Guildford Road Industrial Estate
Runfold
Brookley Close
Culverlands
Compton
Moor Park College
Moor Park
Temple's Close
River Wey (North Branch)
Abbey Business Park
Waverley Abbey House
South Farnham Middle School
The Abbey School
136
6
7
159
M1
1 George Gdns
L2
1 Mayfield Cl
2 St George's Cl
J4
1 Hurlands Pl
J1
1 Stockwood Wy
H4
1 Coverts Cl
2 Westbury Gdns
L1
1 Brindle Cl
2 Holbrook Wy
3 Mason Wy

136
113
135
7
A
B
C
D
E
F
1
2
3
4
5
6
7
8
C1
1 The Moors
2 St Pauls Cl
3 Tongham Mdw
B1
1 Blenheim Cl
A1
1 Hampshire Cl
Ash Manor School
Blackwater Trading Estate
Blackwater Way
Farnham Road
Tongham Road
Oakway
Elm La
Ash Green Lane West
Ash Green
Guildford Road
Alden Av
Newcome Pl
Whyte Av
Heron Wood
The Avenue
Pool Rd
The Connaught School
A331
Manor Cl
Field Way
Spoil Lane
The Gardens
Pawley Cl
Lambourne Wy
Ellison Wy
Russet Cl
Garbetts Wy
Chester Wy
Maitlands Cl
Grieve Cl
Newton Wy
St Pauls C of E First School
Poyle Road
Poyle Farm
White Lane
Tongham
The Street
New Rd
Grange Road
Hampshire County
Surrey County
Tongham Rd
Manor Farm
Manor Farm Business Centre
A31
Elstead Road
Wood Lane
Wood La
Seale
Sandy Cross
Thundery Hill
Seale Lane
Puttenham Road
School Hill
Runfold Manor
North Downs Way
Elstead Road
Sands Road
Farnham Golf Club
Blighton Lane
Binton Farm
Binton Lane
The Sands
Sands Cl
The Green
Owlshatch
Botany Hill
Smugglers' Way
Littleworth Road
Long Hill
Crooksbury Road
Seale Road
Littleworth Cross
Crooksbury Common
1 grid square represents 500 metres

Christmaspie
K4
1 M Boro Rd
Green Lane West
Green Lane East
Westwood Lane
Wanborough Wood
Wanborough Manor
Wanborough
Wanborough Hill
Inwood Farm
Hog's Back
B3000
A31(T)
B3000 PUTTENHAM HILL
Puttenham
Puttenham C of E School
School Lane
Dark La
The Street
Munday's Boro
Road
Seale Lane
Shoelands
Totford Lane
Lascombe Lane
Suffield Farm
PUTTENHAM
North Downs Way
Highfield Lane
Lascombe
Hook Lane
Puttenham Common
Church Croft
General's Pond
Puttenham Lane
Lydling Farm
Warren Pond
Suffield Lane
The Tarn
Rodsall Manor
Cutt Mill Ho
Littleworth Road
Aldro School
Rokers La
G H J K L M
1 2 3 4 5 6 7 8

A   B   C   **114**   D   E   F

Bulford   Road

1

Muscott Close

Sarum Cl
Cose
Road
High
Primary
School
Hedges
Street
2
PO
Gardener's
Green
Kingfishers
†
Threadgill
Way
Muscott
Cl
2
Parkhouse
Mayfie Cl
1
Manor Cl
St. Peter's
Bourne
La
**Shipton
Bellinger**
†

2

Hampshire County
Wiltshire County

Snoddington
Manor

3

Althorne

SALISBURY ROAD

A338

4

Park House
A338

Thruxton Farm

5

A303(T)

River Bourne

6

Home Farm

A338

Cholderton House

7

†

Cholderton

mesbury Road

Beech
Hanger
Lud
End
Grateley   Road
Cholderton Road

Cholderton
Lodge

8

Wilbury House

Quarley
Down Farm

A   B   **160**   C   Pit   Bulk   D   E   F

G
H
J
115
K
L
M
1
2
3
4
140
5
6
7
8
G
H
J
161
K
L
M
Snoddington Road
Snoddington Down Farm
Racedown
A303(T)
Lains Farm
Middlecot House
Park Lane
Etwall
Quarley
Cholderton Road
Quarley Manor Farm
Quarley Hill
Grateley Drove
Grateley
High Street
Grateley Junior & Infant School
Portway Farm
CHOLDERTON ROAD
Grateley Business Park
Station Road
Grateley Station
Station Ap
B3084
Campbell

Mullenspond

Thruxton

116

East Cholderton

A303(T)

Bush Farm

A8 1 Hawthorne Cl

A7 1 St Leonards

Lovell Cl

Stanbury Road

Lambourne Cl

Lambourne Way

Beech Close

Pilhill Brook

Wiremead Lane

Hay Down Lane

Furzedown Lane

Amport House

Amport

Amport Pri

Keepers Hill

139

Skew Road

Amport Wood

Fox Farm

Grateley Drove

Georgia Lane

Sarson Wood

Quarley Manor Farm

Monxton Road

Grateley

High Street

The Dell

Hawthorne Lane

Lawrence Houses

PO

Chapel Lane

Grateley Junior & Infant School

Gollard Farm

Georgia Farm

Hurst Copse

162

A B C D E F

G   H   J   **117**   K   L   M

1

2

3

4

142

5

6

7

8

Sarson

Monxton

Little
Ann

Abbotts
Ann

Abbotts Ann
Primary School

Great
Wood

Monxton Farm

Eastover Farm

St John's Cross

Eastover
Copse

Stonehanger
Copse

Little
Park Farm

Sarson Lane

Andover Road

Pillhill Brook

Pillhill Brook

Green Lane

Abbotts Ann Road

Chalkpit Lane

Broad Road

Red Post Lane

Farm Road

Cattle Lane

Hillside

Dunkirt Lane

Bulbery

Warren Drive

Manor Close

Abbotts Close

Hill

Old Salisbury

SALISBURY ROAD

Monxton Road

Red Post Lane

Douglas Rd

The Hawk
Conservation

M4
1 St Mary's Mdw

sunnybank

PO

G   H   J   **163**   K   L   M

142
118
141
164
A
B
C
D
E
F
1
2
3
4
5
6
7
8
D1
1 Chatsworth Dr
2 Durley Cl
3 Goddards Mead
4 Holmes Ct
5 Longstock Cl
6 Newtown Cl
C2
1 Hanover Cl
C1
1 Hackwood Cl
B1
1 Spruce Cl
A4
1 Gilberts Mead Cl
D2
1 Kemmitt Wy
2 Little Copse
E1
1 Victoria Ct
2 Wyndham Rd
E2
1 The Willows
F1
1 Borden Gates
2 Leicester Pl
3 St Ann's Cl
F3
1 Beresford Cl
2 Mornington Cl
WEYHILL ROAD
Portway County Infants and Junior Schools
Ashfield Road
Ash Tree Road
Amber Gdns
Crescent
Salmond Road
Douglas Rd
Trenchard Road
Ellington Cl
Portal Cl
Tedder Cl
Slessor Cl
Cypress Gv
Shaw Close
Larch Dr
A303(T)
St John the Baptist RC Primary School
Balksbury County Infant School
Floral Way
Wisley Rd
Exbury Rd
Magnolia Cl
Millway Road
Millway Close
Jenson Gdns
Plantation Rd
Marchant Rd
St Hubert Rd
Beech Hurst Test Valley Borough Council
John Hanson Community School
Alexandra Road
Queens Av
Osborne Rd
Bingo & Social Club
WEYHILL RD B3402
WESTERN RD
Magistrates Court
Business Cen
Bishop's
The Pines
Suffolk
Mead Cl
Salisbury Rd
Hillbury Av
Clarendon Av
Lansdowne Av
Hedges
Cress Gdns
Redbridge Drive
Anton Mill Road
Anton Trading Estate
Coachways
Pitts La
Anton County Junior School
Anton County Infant School
Anton Road
Wellesley Rd
Rooksbury Rd
Celtic Dr
Stone Cl
Barnfield Rise
Georgia Cl
Hazel Cl
Leyton Way
The Ramparts
Road
Salisbury Road
Anna Valley
Balksbury Road
Balksbury Hill
Balksbury Industrial Estate
Pillhill Brook
Taskers Drive
Foundry Road
Valley Mead
Brook Way
White Oak Wy
Bury Hill Close
Highbury Road
Manor Rise
Valley Rise
Sam Whites Hill
Kingsmead
A343
Water Lane
Norman Court Lane
River Anton
Above Town
The Crescent
Upper Clatford
Bury Hill
Norman Court Farm
Norman Court Lane
Apsley Cl
Barlows La
Chestnut Av
Newcomb Cl
Strathfield Rd
Picton Rd
Cornholt Rd
Anglesey
Old Salisbury Road
Red Rice Road
Home Farm
Stockbridge Road
Red Rice
Farleigh School
Fullerton Road
Barrow Hill
Goodworth Clatford
Clatford Primary School
Yew Tree Cl
The Crs
St Annes Cl
Cottage Grn
Meadow Drive
Green Meadow
1 grid square represents 500 metres

G1
1 Kings Meadow
2 Walled Meadow
3 Winchester St
G2
1 Belmont Cl
H1
1 Greenhaven Cl
2 Wolversdene Cl
Andover Down
ANDOVER
Andover Mus & the Mus of the Iron Age
The Manse
Health Cen
Adelaide Medical Cen
Winton Play School
Way School
Winton School
C of E Primary Sch
Wolverdene School
London Road
Springfield Close
Stiles Drive
Pearman Drive
Winton Chase
Eastfield Rd
Sidmouth Road
Wolversdene Road
Wolversdene Gardens
Micheldever Road
Shepherds Row
Highlands Rd
Leigh Gdns
Leigh Rd
Leigh Cl
Bere Hill Crs
Farrs Av
Love Lane
South View Gdns
Belmont Rd
Belle Vue Rd
Hedge End Rd
Charnwood Cl
S End Rd
Dunmow Rd
End Road
Cornfields
Herons Ri
Winton Road
Vincent Dr
East St
London St
Bere Hill Farm
Picket Twenty Farm
Picket Twenty
A3093
The Grange
Forest Lane
A303(T)
Old Micheldever
Balls Cotta
Cowdown Lane
Cow Down
Cowdown Farmhouse
Augurs Hill Copse
Upping Copse
Hampshire Golf Club
A3057
Test Way
New Barn
New Barn Lane
WINCHESTER ROAD
ROMSEY
LONGPARISH RO
Wherwell School
Old Poun
Test
Park
G H J K L M
1 2 3 4 5 6 7 8
9
119
144
165

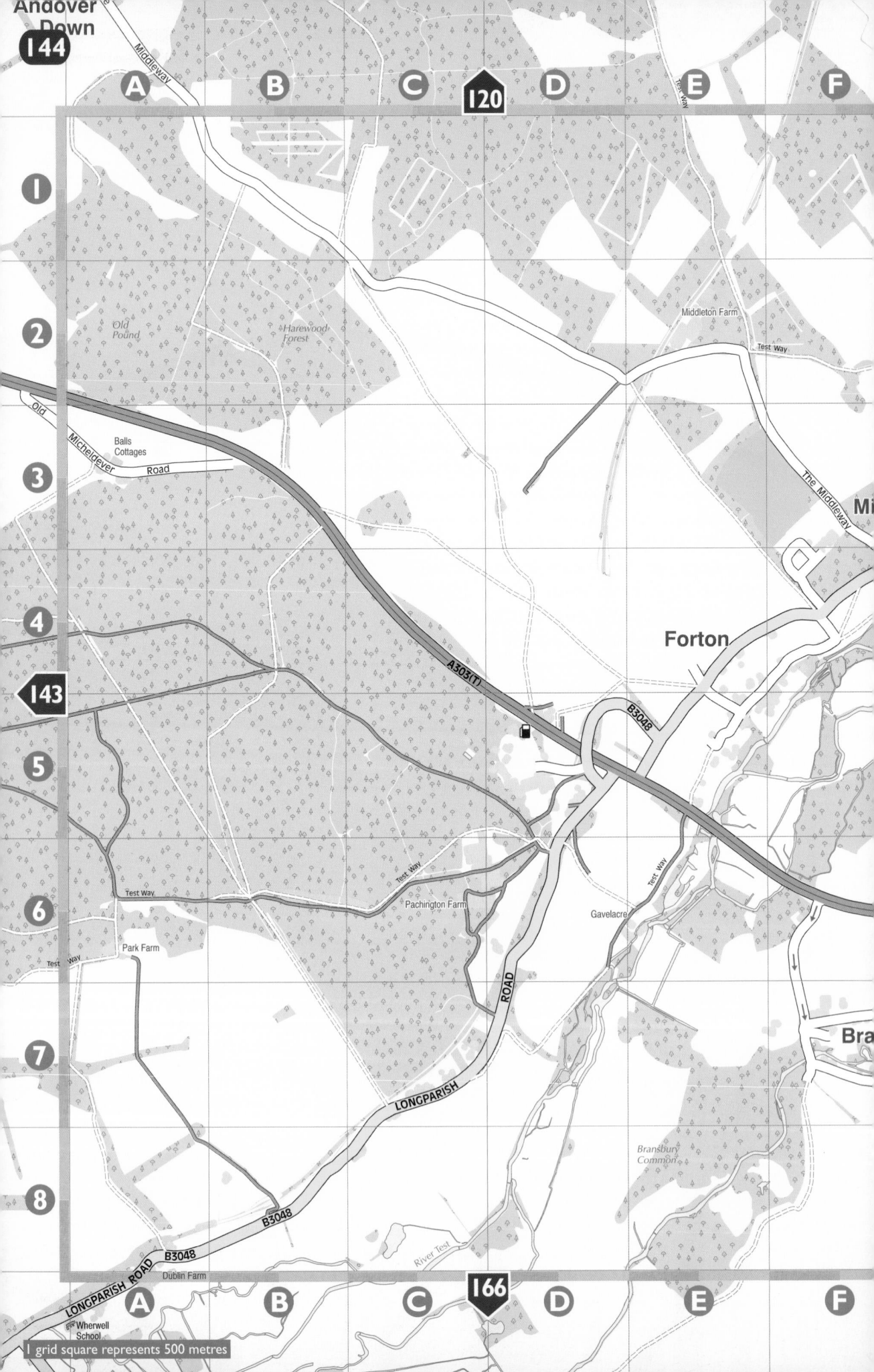

Andover Down
144
120
143
166
A
B
C
D
E
F
1
2
3
4
5
6
7
8
Middleway
Test Way
Old Pound
Harewood Forest
Middleton Farm
Old Micheldever Road
Balls Cottages
The Middleway
Forton
A303(T)
B3048
Pachington Farm
Gavelacre
Park Farm
ROAD
LONGPARISH
Bransbury Common
River Test
LONGPARISH ROAD
Dublin Farm
Wherwell School
1 grid square represents 500 metres

G _Tracy's Dell_   H   J   121   K   Paper Mill Farm   L   M

East Aston

B3048

Longparish Ho

Longparish

River Test

Larkwhistle Farm

Lower Mill

Vale Farm

Mill Lane

Way

PH

Southside

Longparish School

Road

Southside Farm

146

The Avenue

Mortar William Rd

Dawson Rd

Hill Rd

Carpenter Rd

Stevenson Rd

Thuillier Rd

A303(T)

Campbell Road

A303(T)

River Dever

Roberts Road

Tidbury Common

Barton Stacey C of E Primary School

The Green

Roman Way

167

Pheasant Cl

East Rd

West Road

Partridge

Weston Lane

Colne

Lower

G   H   J   K   L   M

1 2 3 4 5 6 7 8

A   B   C   122   D   E   F

1

2   Firgo Farm   Tufton
                           Warren Farm

3

A34(T)

Blind
End
Cops

4

145

5

6   Upper
                                         Norton Farm

Tidbury Farm

7   A30
                    Bullington
                    Cross Inn
                    A303(T)

8   Upper
         Bullington

A   B   C   168   D   E   F

1 grid square represents 500 metres

wer

G H J 123 K L M

I
2
3
4
148
5
6
7
8

Cheldever Road
Barn Farm

Roundwood Farm

Freefolk Wood

A303(T)

Bru...
Andov...

Warren Farm

Upper
Cranbourne Farm

Hunton
Down Farm

G H J 169 K L M

A B C **124** D E F

I

2

Golf Course

Cobley Wood

Bellevue Plantation

Reventon Warren Farm

A303(T)

3

Popham Beacons

4

5

Overton Road

Black Wood

Brunel Close

Andover Road

New Road

Micheldever Station

Micheldever Station

6

Warren Farm

Northbrook Farm

7

Larkwhistle Farm Road

8

A B C **170** D E F

A33

1 grid square represents 500 metres

PH

G H J 125 K L M

Dummer
Down Farm

1

A30

A30

Junction 8

2

3

Waltham
Trinleys

West Farm

A33

Popham
Court Farm

Popham

4

150

5

Bradley Farm

College
Wood

6

M3

Rownest
Wood

Woodmancott

7

8

Lone Farm

150

126

A B C D E F

1

Dummer Down Farm

Dummer Down

Lane

Up St

Bidde Fields

2

Dummer Grange

Wayfarer's Walk

3

Dummer Grange Farm

Flockmoor Cottage

4

The Holt

149

Breach Farm

Wayfarer's Walk

5

6

7

Chilton Wood

8

A B C D E F

172

1 grid square represents 500 metres

G **H**obley Hole J 127 K L M

Nutley Wood

Upper Common

Norton's Wood

Nutley Down

High Wood

Nutley

Berrydown Farm

Axford

152

Damsel Lane

Moundsmere Manor

Fawkners

Southwood Farm

Preston House

B3046

PO Garden

Preston Candover
Preston Candover Primary School

Stenbury Drive

Farrier's Field

Pres. Oak Hill

Bradle

Preston Down

1
2 Low Com
3
4
5
6
7
8

128

151

174

Ⓐ Ⓑ Ⓒ Ⓓ Ⓔ Ⓕ

① ② ③ ④ ⑤ ⑥ ⑦ ⑧

Furzen Lane

Lane

Elisfield Manor

Three Castles Path

Merritts Farm

Herriard Grange

Oxlease Lane

Bell Lane

Hurst Farm

Ba

College Farm

College Lane

Lower Common

Three Castles Path

Bagmore Lane

Berrydown Lane

Herriard Common

Red Lane

Preston Oak Hills

Spain Lane

wood Farm

Three Castles Path

Burkham House

A339

Bradley

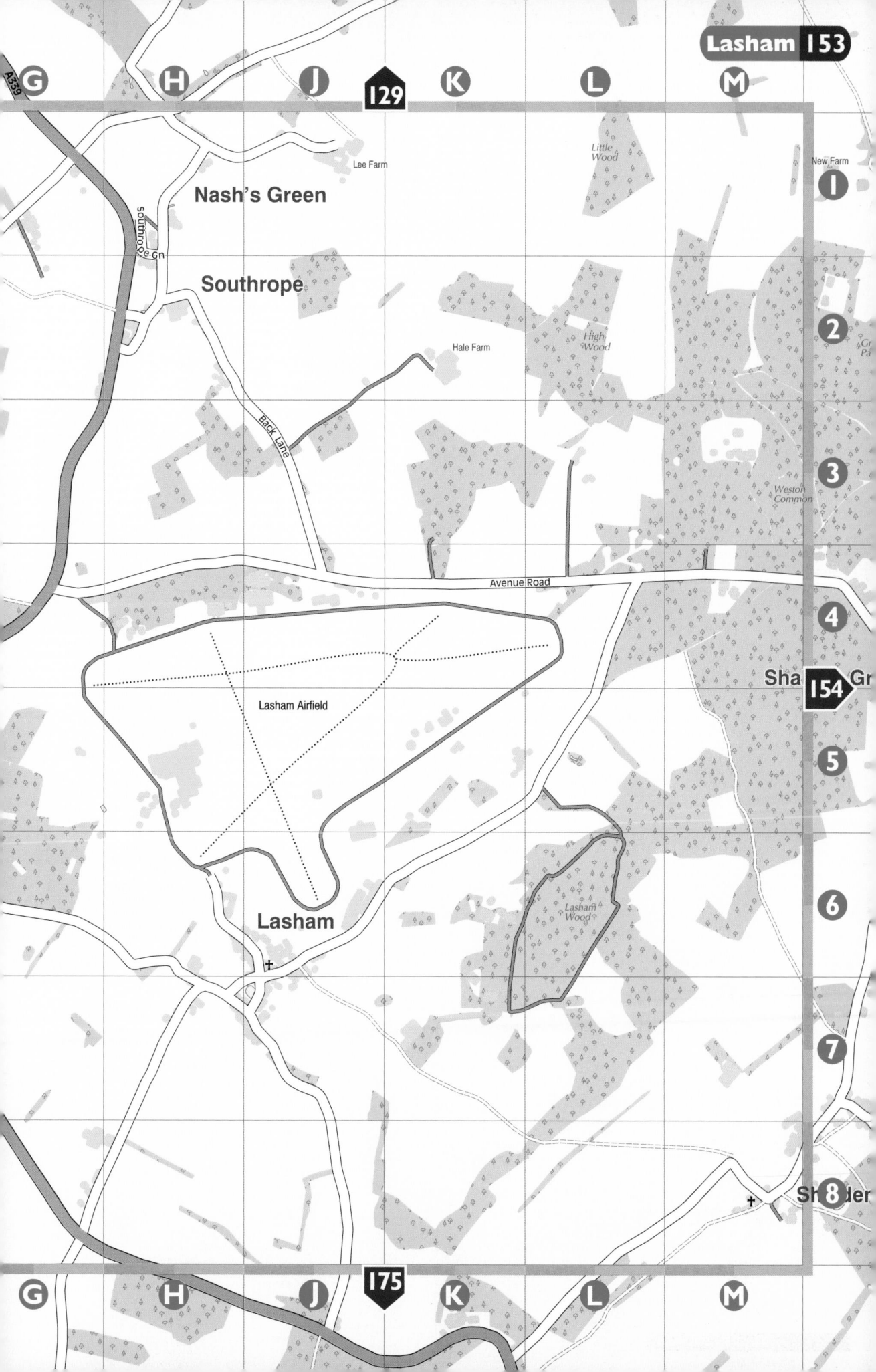

G
H
J
129
K
L
M

New Farm

I

Lee Farm

Nash's Green

Little Wood

Southrope Gn

2

Gr Pa

Southrope

Hale Farm

High Wood

3

Back Lane

Weston Common

Avenue Road

4

Sha
154
Gr

5

Lasham Airfield

Lasham Wood

6

Lasham

†

7

†
Sh **8** der

A339

G
H
J
175
K
L
M

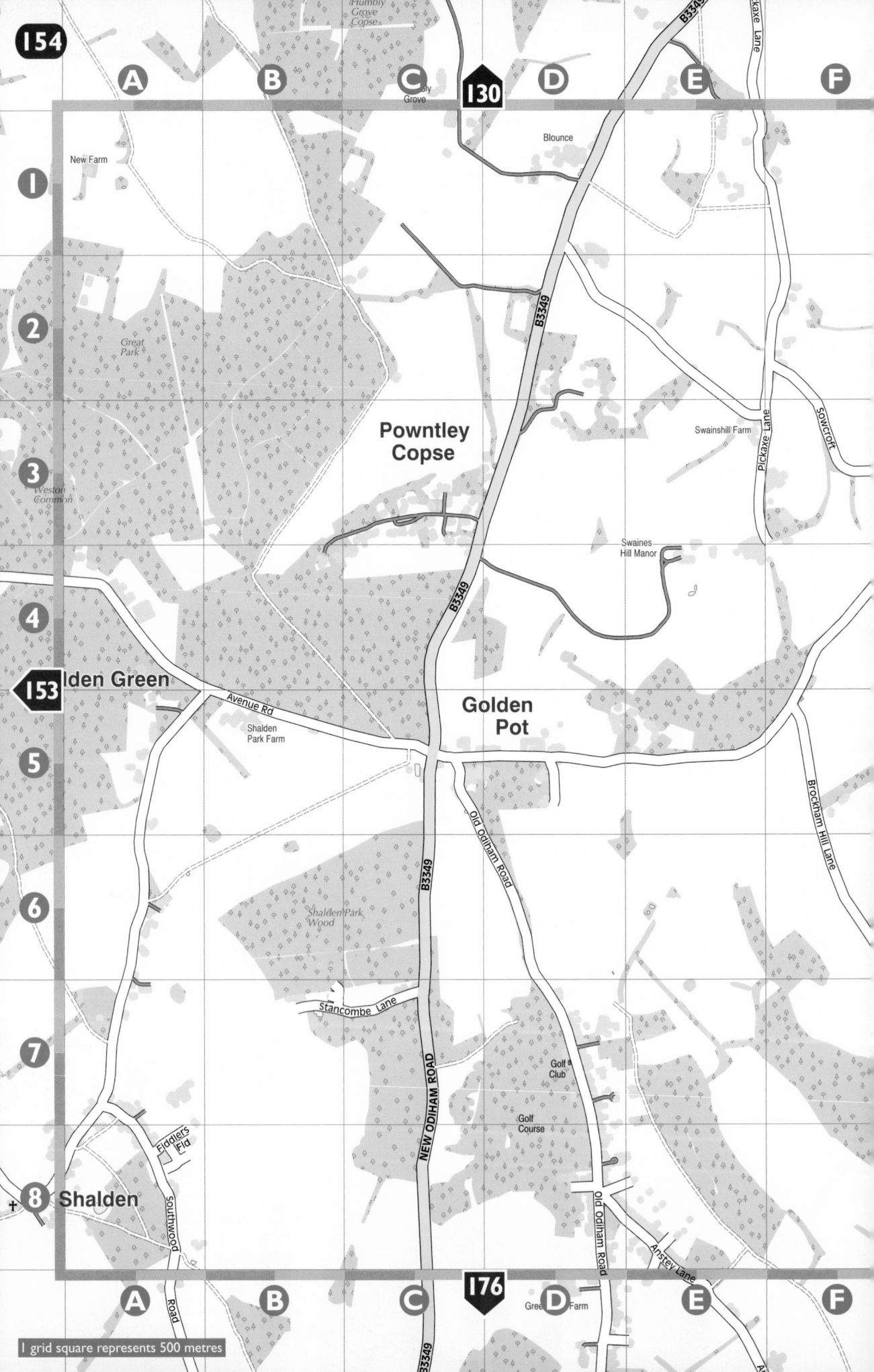

Humbly Grove Copse
130
Holy Grove
Blounce
New Farm
B3349
Great Park
Powntley Copse
Swainshill Farm
Pickaxe Lane
Sowcroft
Weston Common
Swaines Hill Manor
153
Golden Green
Avenue Rd
Shalden Park Farm
Golden Pot
Old Odiham Road
Brockham Hill Lane
Shalden Park Wood
Stancombe Lane
NEW ODIHAM ROAD
Golf Club
Golf Course
Fiddlers Fld
Shalden
Southwood Road
Anstey Lane
176
Green Farm
A
B
C
D
E
F
1
2
3
4
5
6
7
8
1 grid square represents 500 metres

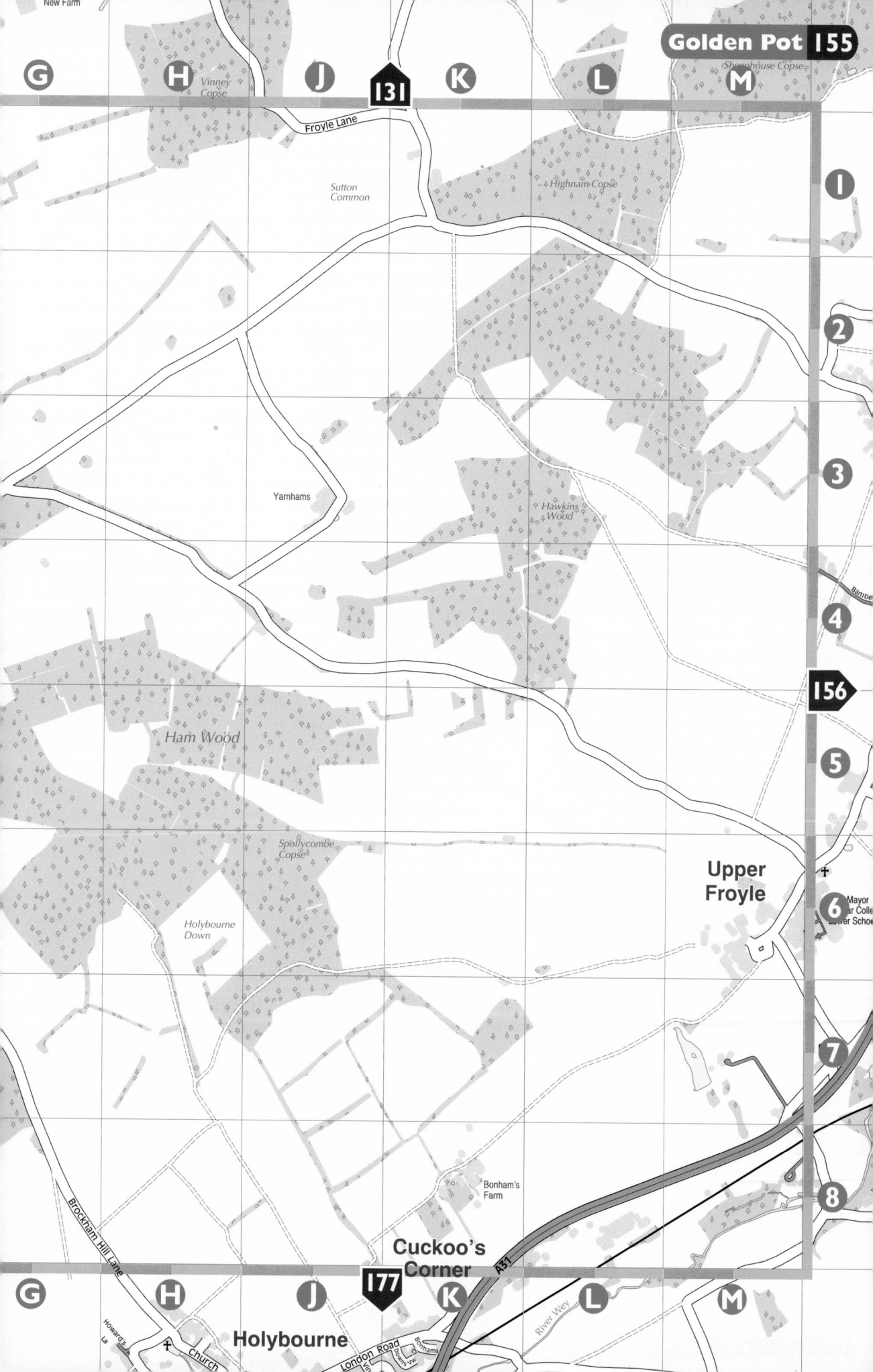

New Farm

G

H
Vinney
Copse

J
131

Froyle Lane

K

L

M
Sheephouse Copse

I

Sutton
Common

Highnam Copse

2

3

Yarnhams

Hawkins
Wood

Bambe

4

156

Ham Wood

5

Spollycombe
Copse

Upper
Froyle

Holybourne
Down

6 Mayor
ar Colle
ower Scho

7

Bonham's
Farm

8

Brockham Hill Lane

Cuckoo's
Corner
177

A31

River Wey

G

H

J

K

L

M

Howard's
La

Church

Holybourne

London Road

156
132
155
178
A
B
C
D
E
F
1
2
3
4
5
6
7
8
B4
1 Barnfield Cl
Isnage Farm
Crest Hill Farm
Well Lane
Lower Froyle
Hussey's Lane
Husseys Farm
Park Lane
Westburn
Bamber Lane
Pax Hill
Jenkyn Place
Hole Lane
Bentley
Oakway
A31
Highway Home
Bentley Green Farm
Old Lane
Isington Lane
Froyle Mill
Lord Mayor Treloar College Lower School
River Wey
Isington Road
Isington
LC
PH
Mill Court
Binstead
Broadview
1 grid square represents 500 metres

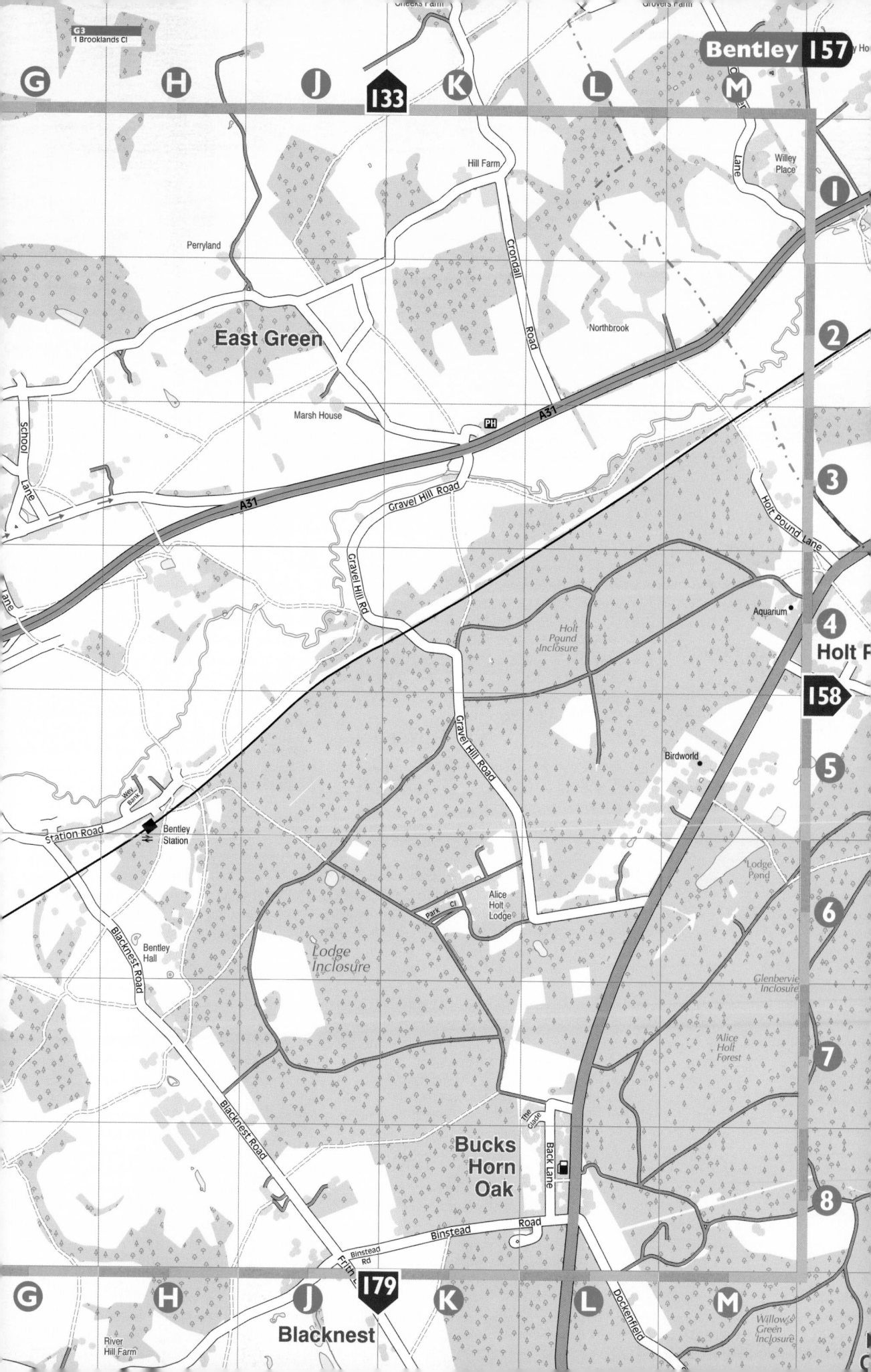

Bentley 157
G3
1 Brooklands Cl
133
158
179
G
H
J
K
L
M
1
2
3
4
5
6
7
8
Hill Farm
Willey Place
Perryland
Crondall Road
East Green
Northbrook
Marsh House
PH
A31
School Lane
Gravel Hill Road
Gravel Hill Rd
Holt Pound Lane
Aquarium
Holt Pound Inclosure
Holt P
Birdworld
Wey Bank
Station Road
Bentley Station
Alice Holt Lodge
Park Cl
Lodge Pond
Bentley Hall
Blacknest Road
Lodge Inclosure
Glenbervie Inclosure
Alice Holt Forest
The Glade
Bucks Horn Oak
Back Lane
Binstead Road
Binstead Rd
Frith L
Dockenfield
Blacknest
River Hill Farm
Willows Green Inclosure

158
Ridgway House
Runwick House
D1
1 Garth Cl
2 Greenhill Cl
3 Selborne Gdns
4 Thurbans Rd
5 Wells Cottages
C4
1 Switchback La
2 Thorn Cl
C3
1 Coleson Hill Rd
C2
1 Heather Cl
2 Hill Crest Dr
3 Pottery La
4 St Peter's Gdns
C1
1 Bryn Rd
2 Church La
3 Weavers Gdns
134
Infants School
Willey Place
Alton Road
River Lane
Wrecclesham Rd
Secondary School
Grovebell Industrial Est
Cemetery
Wrecclesham
The Street
Middle Sch
Shortheath
Shortheath Road
Ridgeway Road
B3384
Middle
The Bourne
Wrecclesham Hill
Echo Barn Lane
Holt Pound Lane
Boundstone
Boundstone Road
Holly Tree Surg
Gardener's Hill Road
Holt Pound
Fullers Road
GU10
Frensham Ct
Rowledge
The Avenue
Switchback La
Edgeborough
Rowledge C of E First School
The Long Road
Pear Tree La
Hawthorn Lane
Lickfolds
Boundary Road
Frensham Road
Frensham Heights
Frensham Heights School
Kennel Farm
Moons Hill
More House School
Lodge Pond
Glenbervie Inclosure
Shortfield Common
Summerfield Lane
Hamlash Lane
Broomfield Lane
Broomfields
Shortfield
West End Lane
West End
Spreakley
Woodhill
157
180
D2
1 Sycamore Dr
D3
1 Rowan Cha
2 Upper Bourne V
D4
1 Pelham Pl
E1
1 Highfield Cl
E3
1 Boundstone Cl
F1
1 Acheulian Cl
F2
1 Winston Wk
Willow's Green Inclosure
Batt's Corner
Pitt Farm
Frensham
1 grid square represents 500 metres

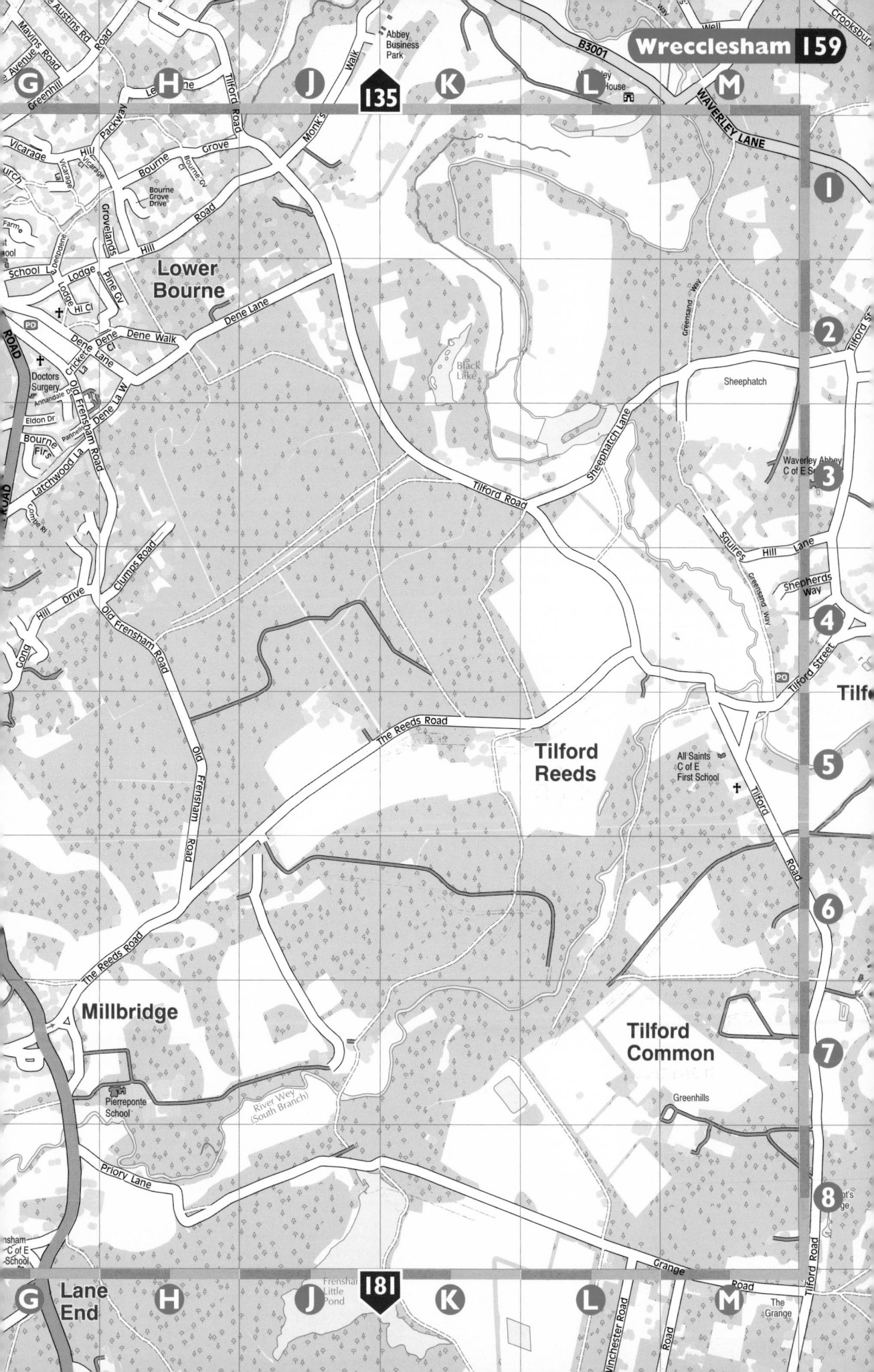

135
Abbey Business Park
B3001
WAVERLEY LANE
Lower Bourne
Bourne Grove Drive
Black Lake
Sheephatch
Sheephatch Lane
Tilford Road
Waverley Abbey C of E School
Squires Hill Lane
Shepherds Way
Greensand Way
Tilford Street
The Reeds Road
Tilford Reeds
All Saints C of E First School
Old Frensham Road
Clumps Road
Hill Drive
Millbridge
Pierreponte School
River Wey (South Branch)
Priory Lane
Tilford Common
Greenhills
Grange Road
Tilford Road
Winchester Road
Lane End
The Grange
181
Dene Lane
Dene Walk
Doctors Surgery
Latchwood La
Pine Gv
Grovelands
Hill Road
Bourne Grove
Packway
Vicarage Hill
Monk's Walk

160

A B C 138 D E F

Quarley
Down Farm

Pit   Walk

Wilbury House

1

Cemetery

River Bourne

Three
Corner Hat

Road

Beechfield

2

PO

Newton Tony

The Croft

Newton
Tony
School

Hampshire County
Wiltshire County

3

St Just Cl.

4

River Bourne

5

6

7

Allington Farm

8

A B C 182 D E F

Boscombe
Down
East

1 grid square represents 500 metres

G   H   J   **OLDER** ◆ **139**   K   L   M

Grateley Junior & Infant School

I

Portway Farm

ROAD

Station Road

Grateley Business Park

▣ Grateley Station

Campbell Cl

Station Ap

B3084

2

Locke Cl

Streetway Road

streetway Road

Ol

Wallop Road

Streetway   Road

Mount Hermon Road

Salisbury Road

Palestine

Palestine Road

Bournemouth Road

Red Lodge Farm

3

Zion Road

Orange Grove

Orange Grove

Olive Grove

Peach Grove

Peach Grove

Mount Carmel Road

4

▶ **162**

Castle Farm

WALLOP ROAD

B3084

5

Martin's Clump

6

Pottery Drove

Croft Farm

7

8

G   H   J   ◆ **183**   K   L   M

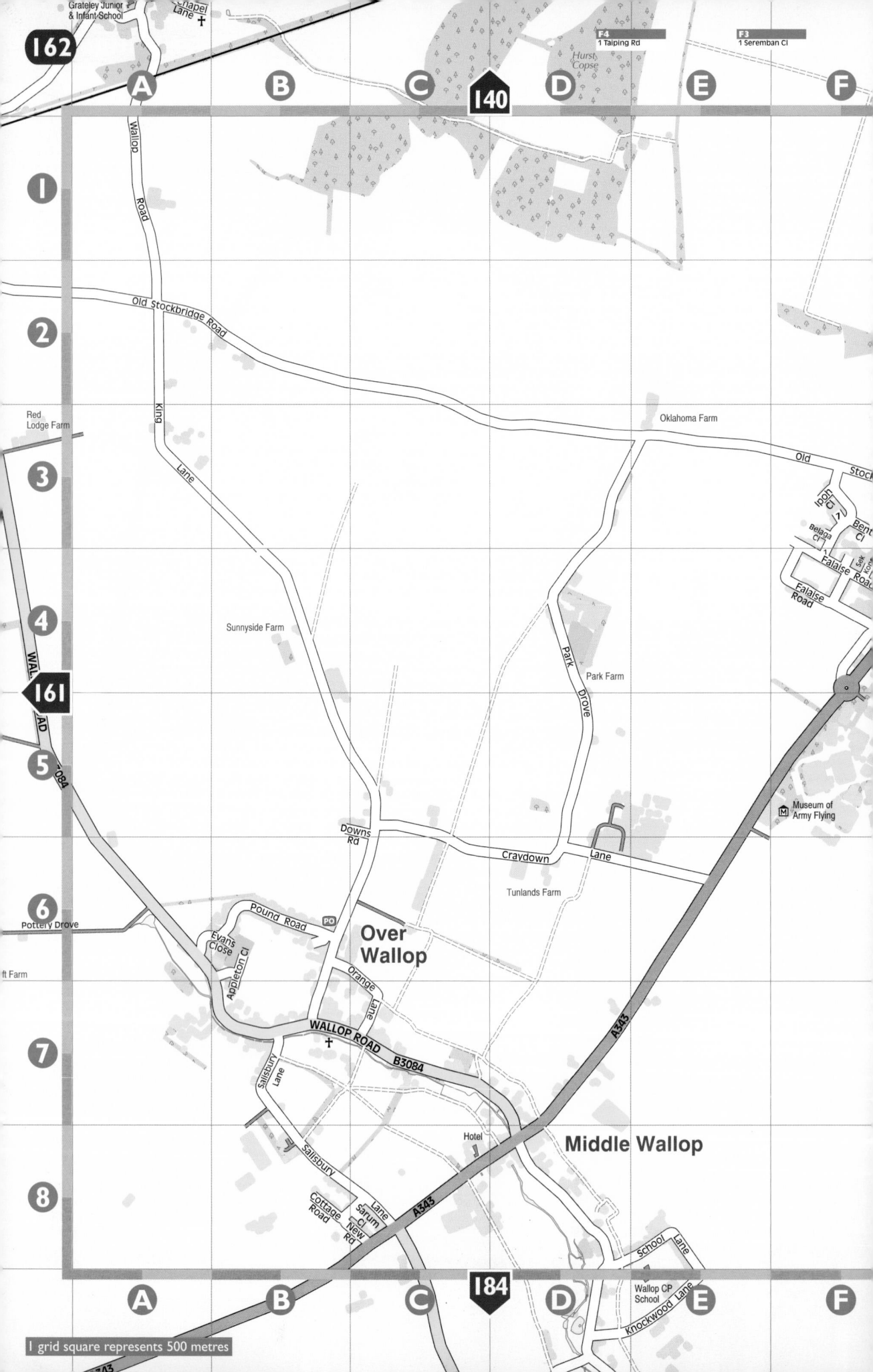
162
Grateley Junior & Infant School
Chapel Lane
140
F4 1 Taiping Rd
F3 1 Seremban Cl
Hurst Copse
A
B
C
D
E
F
1
2
3
4
5
6
7
8
Wallop Road
Old Stockbridge Road
King Lane
Red Lodge Farm
Oklahoma Farm
Old Stock
Ipoh Cl
Bent Cl
Belaga Cl
Falaise Road
Falaise Road
Sunnyside Farm
Park Drove
Park Farm
161
WALLOP ROAD
B3084
Museum of Army Flying
Downs Rd
Craydown Lane
Tunlands Farm
Pottery Drove
Pound Road
PO
Evans Close
Appleton Cl
Over Wallop
Orange Lane
WALLOP ROAD
B3084
A343
Salisbury Lane
Salisbury Lane
Hotel
Middle Wallop
Cottage Road
Sarum Cl
New Rd
A343
School Lane
Wallop CP School
Knockwood Lane
184
1 grid square represents 500 metres

G H J **141** K L M

I
2
3
4
164
5
6
7
8

G H J **185** K L M

Prospect Farm

Stonehanger Copse

Down Farm

A343

Road

Kentsboro

Maple
Birch
Avenue
Willow Way
Pine Cl
Larch Cl
Elm Cl
Chestnut Crescent
Oak Cl
Beech

Dipden Bottom

Saxley Farm

Stockbridge Road

Clatford Oakcuts

Down Farm

143
Danebury Hill

P

The Turret

Danebury Down

Red
Rice

Farleigh
School

Stockbridge Road

Fullerton Road

A **B** **C** 142 **D** **E** **F**

Barrow Hill

Longstock Road

Meadow Drive

I

Dipden
Bottom
2

Flint Farm

3

Rowbury Farm

4

163

Longstock Road

5

Hazel
Down

6

Charity
Down Farm

Hazeldow

7

8

The
Turret

Stockbridge Road

A **B** **C** 186 **D** **E** **F**

Church Road

Cemetery

PH

G H J **143** K L M

L2
1 The Old Hi

M4
1 Lynton Meadow

WINCHESTER

ROMSEY ROAD

A3057

ROAD

B3420

New
Barn

New Barn Way

Lane

LONGPARISH RD

Wherwell
Sch

1

Beech Gr

PO

The Old

Wherwell

Church St

Chant Cl

PH

2

Test Way

Fullerton Road

River Test

Test Way

Winchester

3

Paddock
Field

Joy's Lane

Village Street

PO

7

4

Cottonworth

Coley Lane

River View
Close

Durnford

Chilbolton

166

Fullerton Road

Fullerton Manor

Fullerton

ROMSEY ROAD

River Test

Garston Mede

Branksome

West View

Test Rise

Drove Hill

Eastmar
Field

Station Road

Branksome Avenue

Drove Road

5

Little Drove Road

Testcombe

River Anton

**West
Down**

6

Longstock House

Ivy Farm

A3057

7

8

PO **Leckford**

Leckford Abbas

G H J **187** K L M

LECKFORD LANE

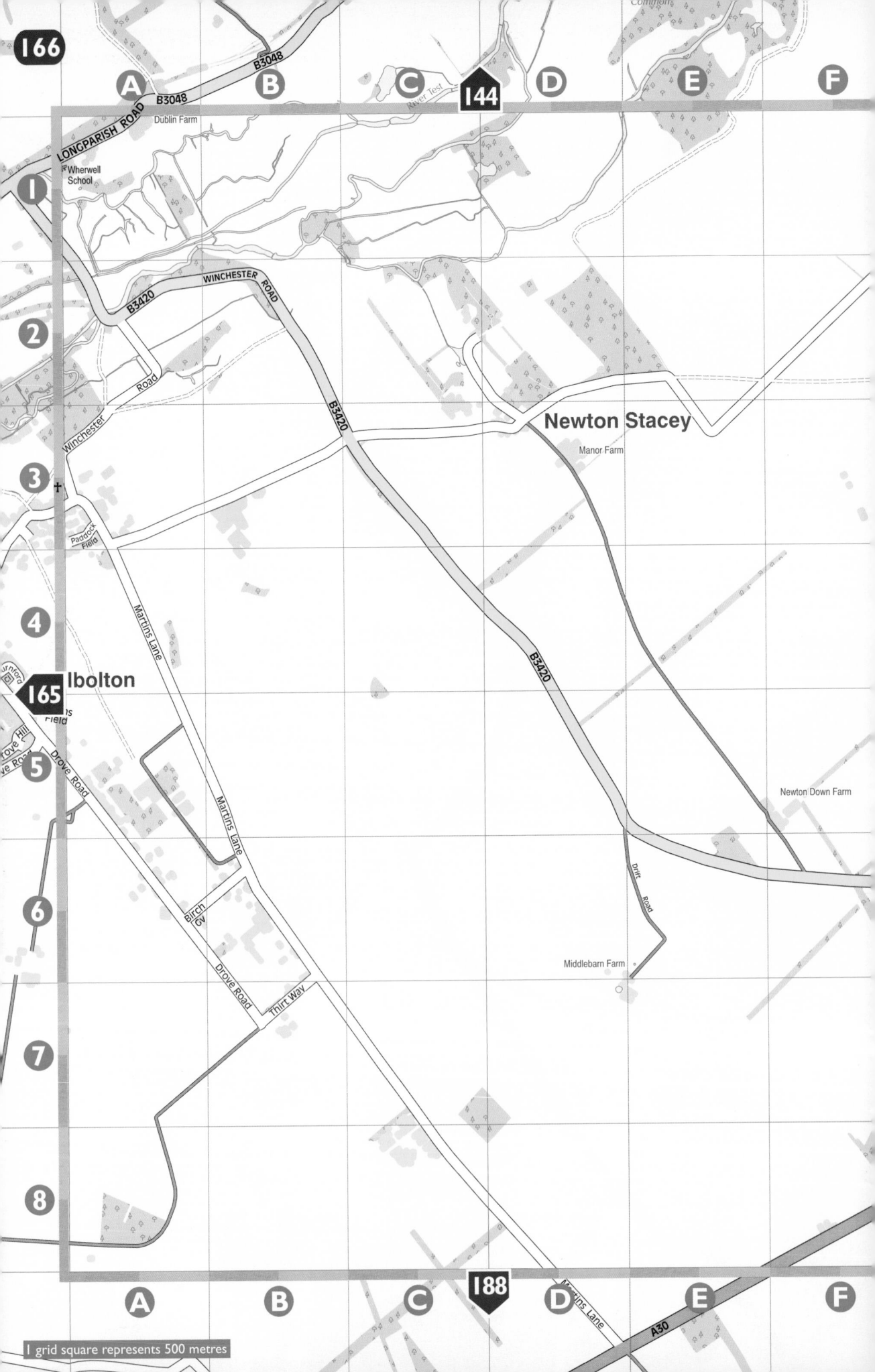

166

A B3048 B **144** C D E F

LONGPARISH ROAD B3048
Dublin Farm

Wherwell School

1

B3420 WINCHESTER ROAD

2

Winchester Road

3 †

Paddock Field

B3420

Newton Stacey

Manor Farm

4

Martins Lane

165 Ibolton

Field

5 Drove Hill Road Drove Road

Martins Lane

Newton Down Farm

6

Birch GV

Drove Road

Drift Road

Middlebarn Farm

7

Thirt Way

8

A B C **188** D Martins Lane E A30 F

G
H
J
K
L
M
145
Roberts
Road
Tidbury Common
Barton Stacey C of E Primary School
The Green
Roman Way
Pheasant Cl
East Rd
West Road
Partridge Cl
Bullington Lane
Lower Bullington
PO
Gravel Lane
King's Elms
Barton Stacey
Ashfields
Greenacres
Barn Hill Lane
Hill Barn
Barton Drove
1
2
3
4
168
5
Cocum Farm
6
Moody's Down Farm
A30
B3420
7
A272
8
Hill Farm
Sutton Down Farm
189

168
Upper
Bullington
A
B
C
146
D
E
F
B4
1 Pigeonhouse Fld
1
wer
Lane
Barn
Hill
Valley
Way
Colne
A34(T)
BULLINGTON
LANE
A30
2
Hill
Barn
Cranbourne
Grange
3
Egypt
Alexandria Rd
Hotel
Services
Barton
Drove
4
BY PASS RD
Saddlers
Cl
Oxford Road
Gratton Surgery
Sutton Scotney
PO
Wonston Grange
Hunton Lane
Hunton Down Lane
River Dever
Stockbridge Road
167
Sutton
Manor
Gratton Cl
Carthagena
Moorcroft Cl
Wonston Close
South Vw Cl
Buddlesgate
Winchester
Hill
Wonston
5
Wonston Lane
Christmas Hill
6
WINCHESTER
BY-PASS
7
Wonston Manor Farm
8
190
West Stoke Farm
1 grid square represents 500 metres

M5
1 Southbrook Pl

G · H · J · 147 · K · L · M

1

Hunton
Down Farm

2

Hunton
Grange Farm

3

Northbrook House

Norsebury
House

4

Northbrook

on Lane

Weston
Colley

170

PO

Micheldever
Primary School

5

Miche

River Dever

PO

Dever Cl

Rook Lane

Church St

River Dever

Duke

6

Old Stoke Road

Borough Farm

PH

7

8

Bazeley
Copse

G · H · J · 191 · K · L · M

A   B   C   148   D   E   F

1

A33

2   Stratton House

Parkhill Farm

West Stratton   M3

3   PO

Church Bank Road   ✝

4   PH   Stratton
                                                        Baring Close

169

Cowdown Farm

5   Micheldever   New Farm
     Micheldever
     Primary School
     Church St   Duke   Street

PH   Hawthorn Close

6   Dodsley Wood

Winchester Road

7

8   Micheldever
                                             Woods

A   B   C   192   D   E   F

1 grid square represents 500 metres

G H J **149** K L M

I

2

3

4

172

5

6

7

8

Lone Farm

Wayfarer's W.

Lone Barn

Gunners Lane

Whiteway Farm

Candover Copse

Thorny Down Wood

Stratton

Foxhill

Copse Lane

Copse Lane

Bryces Lane

Burcot Farm

Totford Farm

Stratton Lane

Totford

Northington Down Farm

Northington

G H **193** J K † L M

172

A B C 150 D E F

1

Lone Barn

2

Chilton Manor

Chilton Candover

B3046

3

Wayfarer's Walk

Gravel Close

4

B3046

171

Candover House

5

Brown Candover

Bryces Lane

Spilers Lane

Oxdrove Way

6

Oxdrove Way

Spybush Lane

7

8

Godsfield Copse

Three Castles Path

A B C 194 D E F

Three Castles Path

1 grid square represents 500 metres

Preston
Candover
Primary School
Stenbury Drive
Preston Candover
Upper Wield 173
Bradle
G
H
J
151
K
L
M
Preston Down
I
Lane
Oxdrove Way
Preston Grange
Down Farm
Three Castles Path
Bentwood
2
3
4
PH
Oxdrove Way
174
5
Three Castles Path
Upper Wield
PO
Home Close
6
Pound Cl
Wield Wood
Three Castles Path
7
Barton Copse
Ferney Lane
Armsworth Hill Farm
Barton Industrial Estate
Newmer Farm
8
Ferney Lane
Armsworth Ho
G
H
J
195
K
L
M
Heath Green Lane
Hoggs Lodge
Lane
Way
Heath

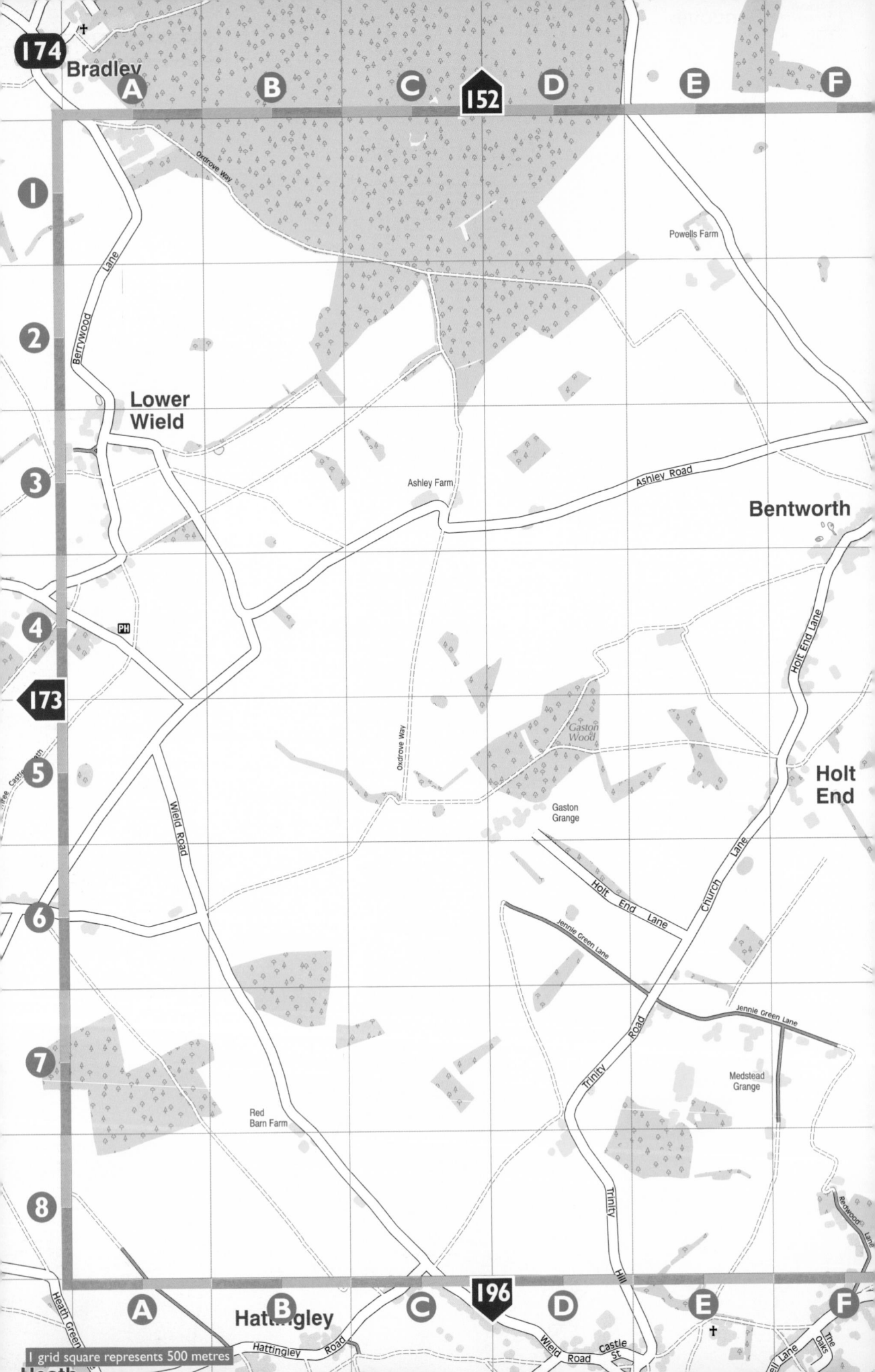

Bradley

A   B   C   152   D   E   F

I

2

Lower
Wield

3   Ashley Farm   Ashley Road   Bentworth

Berrywood Lane

Oxdrove Way

4   PH

173   Holt End Lane

5   Oxdrove Way   Gaston
                                                        Wood   Holt
                                                                    End

Wield Road   Gaston
                                     Grange

6   Holt End Lane   Church Lane

                                     Jennie Green Lane

7   Jennie Green Lane

                                                        Trinity Road   Medstead
                                                                        Grange

Red
Barn Farm

8

                                                        Trinity Hill

A   B   C   196   D   E   F
        Hattingley
            Hattingley Road   Wield Road   Castle
                                                 ST   The Oaks
Heath Green   Redwood Lane

G H J **153** K L M

1

2

3

4

176

5

6

7

8

Wadgett's Copse

Warren Farm

Bentworth Lodge

Thedden Copse

BASINGSTOKE ROAD

Lane

Glebe Cl

Glebe Flds

Summerley

PH

Primary

Street

Childer Hill Farm

Heathcroft Farm

Bentworth Hall

Thedden Grange

Wivelrod Road

Snode Hill

Medstead Road

Wellhouse Road

Cramptons

Beech

Ackender Wood

Wivelrod

Wivelrod Road

King's Hill

Medstead Road

Busby Leaze Wood

The Abbey

Cem

Abbey Road

Jennie Green Lane

Old Park Farm

Chawton Park Farm

Lan

176
Shalden
E3
1 Hillside Cl
2 Maple Cl
3 Vyne Cl
D5
1 The Cooperage
2 Duchess Cl
D3
1 Southview Rl
C6
1 Elmwood Cl
C5
1 Buckingham Cl
2 Sandringham Cl
3 Windsor Cl
154
Greenwood Farm
Southwood Farm
Amery Wood
NEW ODIHAM ROAD
B3349
Anstey Lane
Old Odiham Road
Warren Farm
Brick Kiln Lane
Alton College
Cemetery
Anstey County Junior School
Amery Hill Secondary Sch
St Lawrence C of E (Controlled) Primary Sch
Alton County Infant Sch
Hotel
Curtis Mus
Allen Gallery
ALTON
Wilsc
175
BASINGSTOKE ROAD
A339
Will Hall Farm
Basingstoke Road
Lenten Street
Lower Turk Street
Newtown
Queens Road
The Butts County Primary Sch
Whitedown Special Sch
Borovere Lane
Mount Pleasant Road
The Butts
Wyards Farm
Medstead Road
Whitedown Lane
WHITEDOWN LANE
BASINGSTOKE RD
Beech
Ackender Wood
The Community Hospital
Chawton Park Road
Winchester Road
SELBORNE ROAD
Mounters Lane
Will Hall Cl
A31
Lumbry Farm
Wolf's Lane
Chawton Park Farm
Chawton Pk Road
Northfield Lane
Jane Austen's House
SELBORNE R
198
Chawton
E5
1 Cross & Plry La
E6
1 Calender Cl
2 Churchill Cl
3 Plumpton Wy
F3
1 Pound Ga
2 William Wy
F4
1 Bramley Cl
2 Waterside Ct
F5
1 Blenheim Cl
F6
1 Sandown Cl
1 grid square represents 500 metres

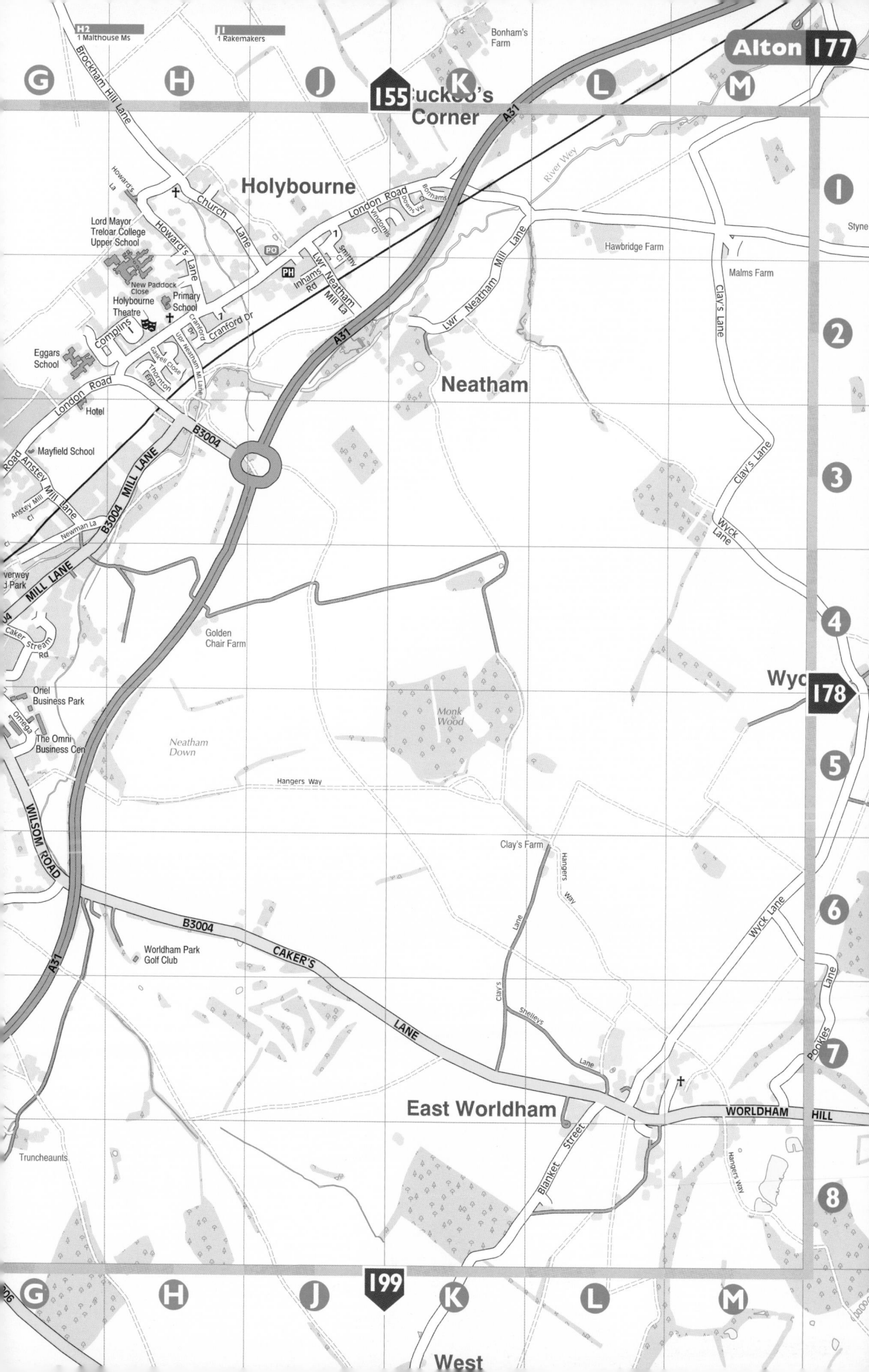
H2
1 Malthouse Ms
J1
1 Rakemakers
G
H
J
155
K
L
M
Cuckoo's Corner
Bonham's Farm
Brockham Hill Lane
Holybourne
Howard's La
Church Lane
Howard's Lane
London Road
Vindomis Cl
Downs Vw
Bonhams
River Wey
Lord Mayor Treloar College Upper School
New Paddock Close
Holybourne Theatre
Primary School
PO
PH
Smithy Cl
Inhams Rd
Lwr Neatham Mill La
Lwr Neatham Mill Lane
Cranford Dr
Upr Neatham Ml Lane
Gaskell Close
Thornton End
Complins
Eggars School
London Road
Hotel
Mayfield School
Anstey Road
Anstey Mill Lane
Anstey Mill Cl
Newman La
B3004
MILL LANE
A31
Neatham
Hawbridge Farm
Malms Farm
Styne
Clay's Lane
Wyck Lane
Golden Chair Farm
Oriel Business Park
Omega
The Omni Business Cen
Caker Stream Rd
WILSOM ROAD
Neatham Down
Monk Wood
Hangers Way
Wyc
178
Clay's Farm
Clay's Lane
Shelleys Lane
Worldham Park Golf Club
CAKER'S LANE
Pookles Lane
East Worldham
WORLDHAM HILL
Blanket Street
Truncheaunts
Hangers Way
1
2
3
4
5
6
7
8
199
West

156

Mill
Court

A   B   C   D   E   F

I

Styne Farm   West Court   Binstead
ms Farm   Binsted C of E
                                          Primary School   The   Street
                                                                                    Thurstons
                                                                            Broadview Cl
                                                                                    Clements
                                                                                    Cl

2   Wyck La   Hay
                                                                     Place

3   Wheatley

ay's Lane

4   Stubbs Farm   South Hay

177 ck

Wyck
Place

5

6   The
                                                                               Strai
Wyc

Pookies Lane

7

ORLDHAM   HILL
                              GREEN
                                       STREET   Lode Farm   FORGE ROAD B3004
                    Oaklands Farm
8
              Kingsley   Stream
ay

A   B   C   D   E   F

200

Rinswood   Rookery Farm

Horn Oak
Kingsley 179
157
Road
G
H
J
K
L
M
Frith End Rd
Dockenfield
Street
Blacknest
River Hill Farm
Willow's Green Inclosure
1
Frith End Road
Goose Green Inclosure
2
Woodlands Farm
A325
Forest Lodge
Abbots Wood Inclosure
3
Straits Inclosure
Frith End Rd
Frithend House
4
180
Frithend
5
Grooms Farm
Sickles
Road
6
Malthouse Farm
Malthouse Farm
Trottsford Farm
River Slea
A325
Picketts Hill
Headley Park
Woodfield
School Flds
PO
Churchfields
Park Cl
Kingsley Business Park
B3004
Forge
Road
7
Sleaford
Kingsley Common
Oxney Stream
8
BROXHEAD FARM
Broxhead Common
Oxney Farm
201
G
H
J
K
L
M

180
158
179
202
End
Spreakley
F4
1 Pond La
Woodhill
Batt's Corner
Boundary Road
Willow's Green
Abbots Wood
Pitt Farm
The Street
Lovers
Peakfield
Mill Lane
Frensham
Bealeswood Lane
Lake Lane
Dockenfield
Dockenfield Street
Green La
The Street
Pitt Lane
Old Lane
Bacon Lane
Hampshire County
Surrey County
High Thicket Road
Manor Farm
Old Lane
Hotel
Heath Hill
Surrey County
Hampshire County
River Wey
Frensham Lane
Wishanger Lodge
Frensham Lane
Wishanger Lane
Stream Farm
Bacon Lane
Mellow Farm
Smithy Lane
Frensham Lane
Smithfield Lane
Headley Park
Headley Park Country Club
Picketts Hill
Pickets Hill Farm
Park View Farm
Smithfield Lane
Tignals
Spats Lane
Churt Road
Headley Wood Farm
Bayfields Farm
Frensham Lane
Hearn
Red Lane
1 grid square represents 500 metres

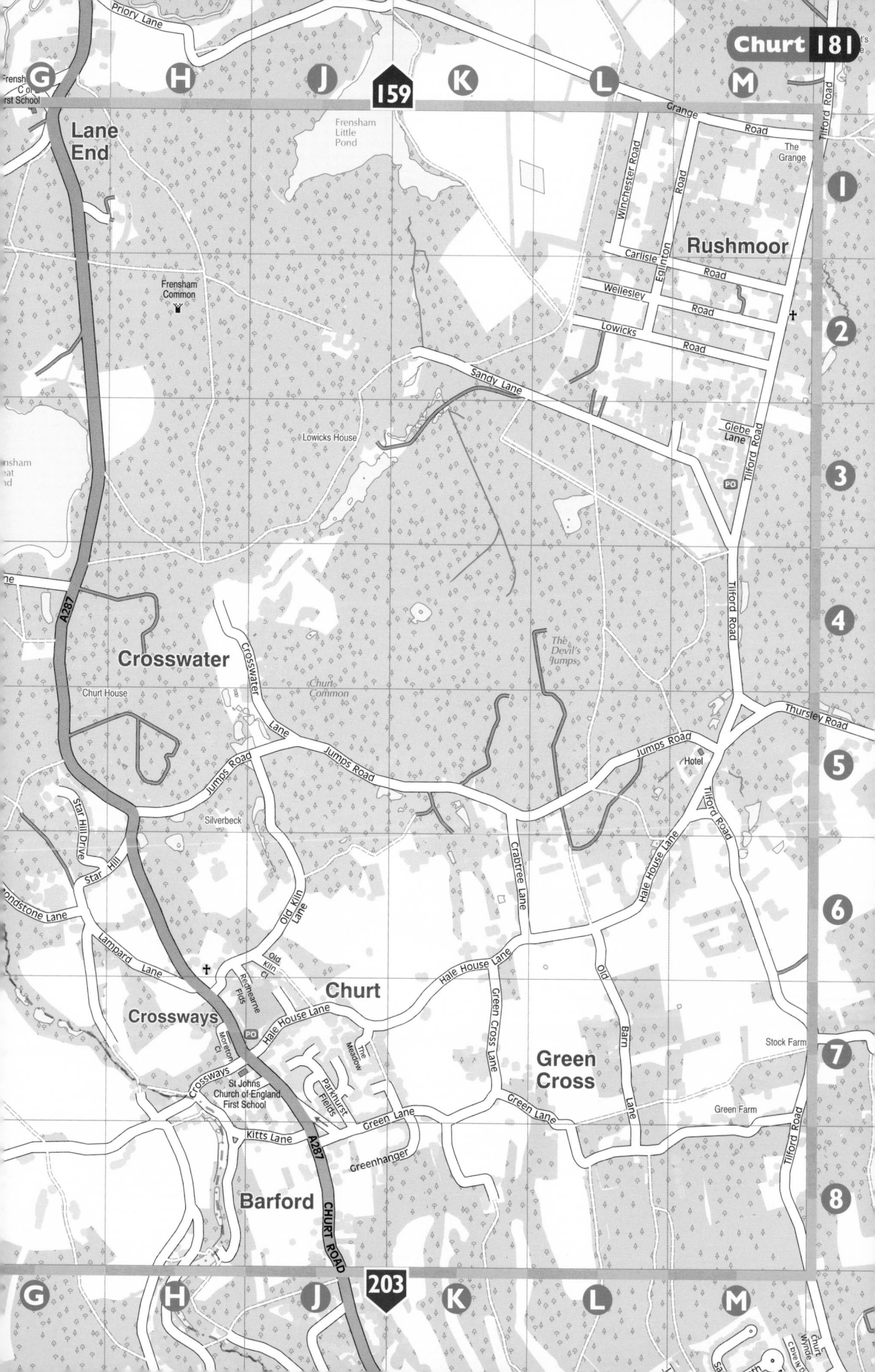

159

Priory Lane

G H J K L M

Fresh
C of
rst School

**Lane
End**

Frensham
Little Pond

Grange Road

Winchester Road

The
Grange

1

Eginton Road

Carlisle Road

Rushmoor

Frensham
Common

Wellesley Road

Tilford Road

2

Lowicks Road

Sandy Lane

Glebe
Lane

PO

†

3

nsham
eat
nd

Lowicks House

A287

Tilford Road

4

Crosswater

The
Devil's
Jumps

Church House

Crosswater Lane

Churt
Common

Thursley Road

Jumps Road

5

Jumps Road

Jumps Road

Hotel

Star Hill Drive

Silverbeck

Tilford Road

Hale House Lane

6

ondstone Lane

Star Hill

Old Kiln Lane

Crabtree Lane

Lampard Lane

Old
Kiln
Ct

†

Churt

Hale House Lane

Old Barn Lane

Stock Farm

7

Crossways

Redhearne
Flds

Moreton Rd

PO

Hale House Lane

Green Cross Lane

**Green
Cross**

Green Farm

Crossways

St Johns
Church of England
First School

The Meadow

Parkhurst Fields

Green Lane

Green Lane

Green Lane

Kitts Lane

A287

Greenhanger

8

Barford

CHURT ROAD

Tilford Road

Churt Wynde

203

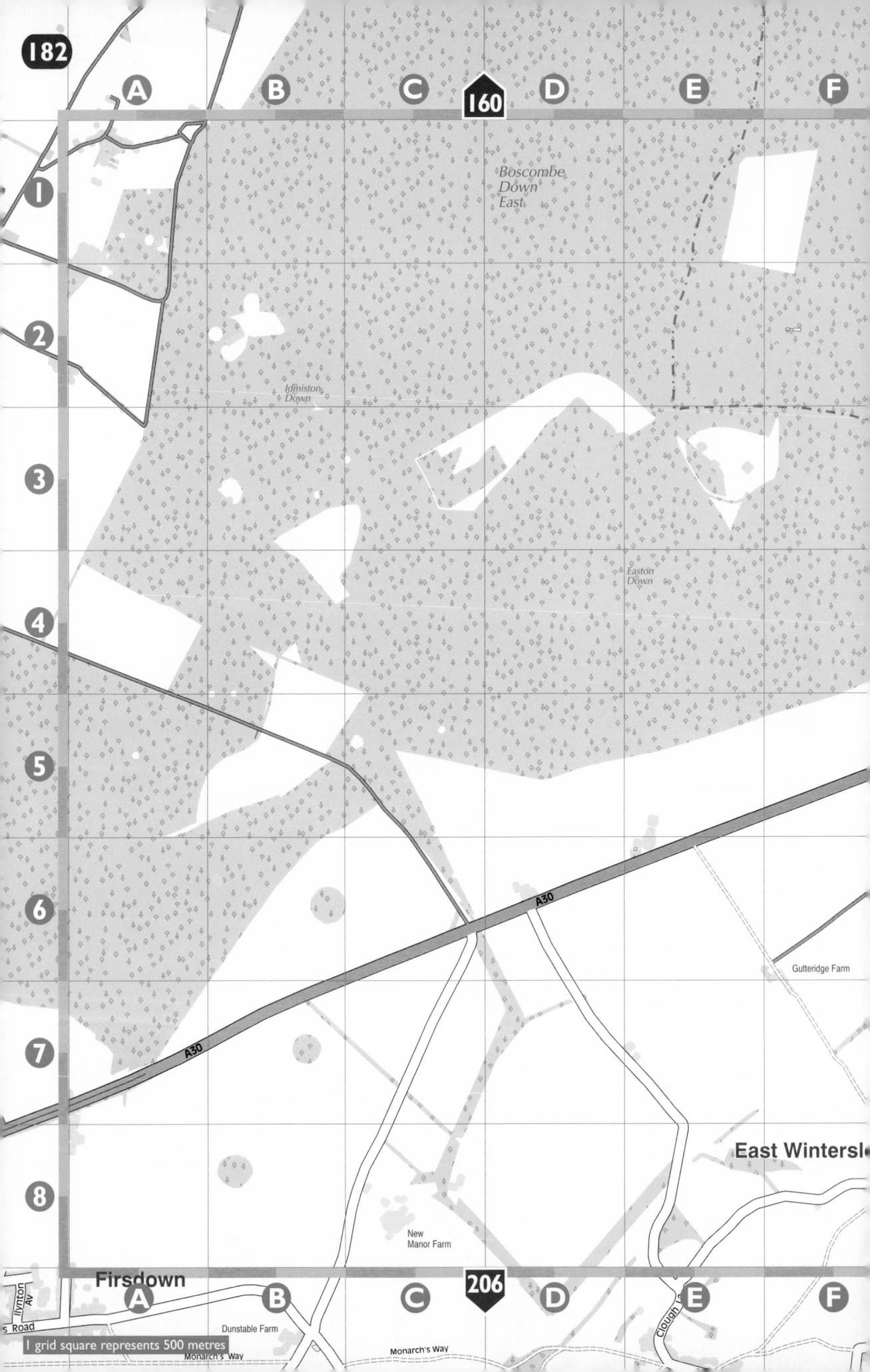

160

Boscombe
Down
East

Idmiston
Down

Easton
Down

A30

A30

Gutteridge Farm

East Wintersl

Firsdown

206

Dunstable Farm

New
Manor Farm

Monarch's Way

Monarch's Way

llynton
Av

s Road

Clough

1 grid square represents 500 metres

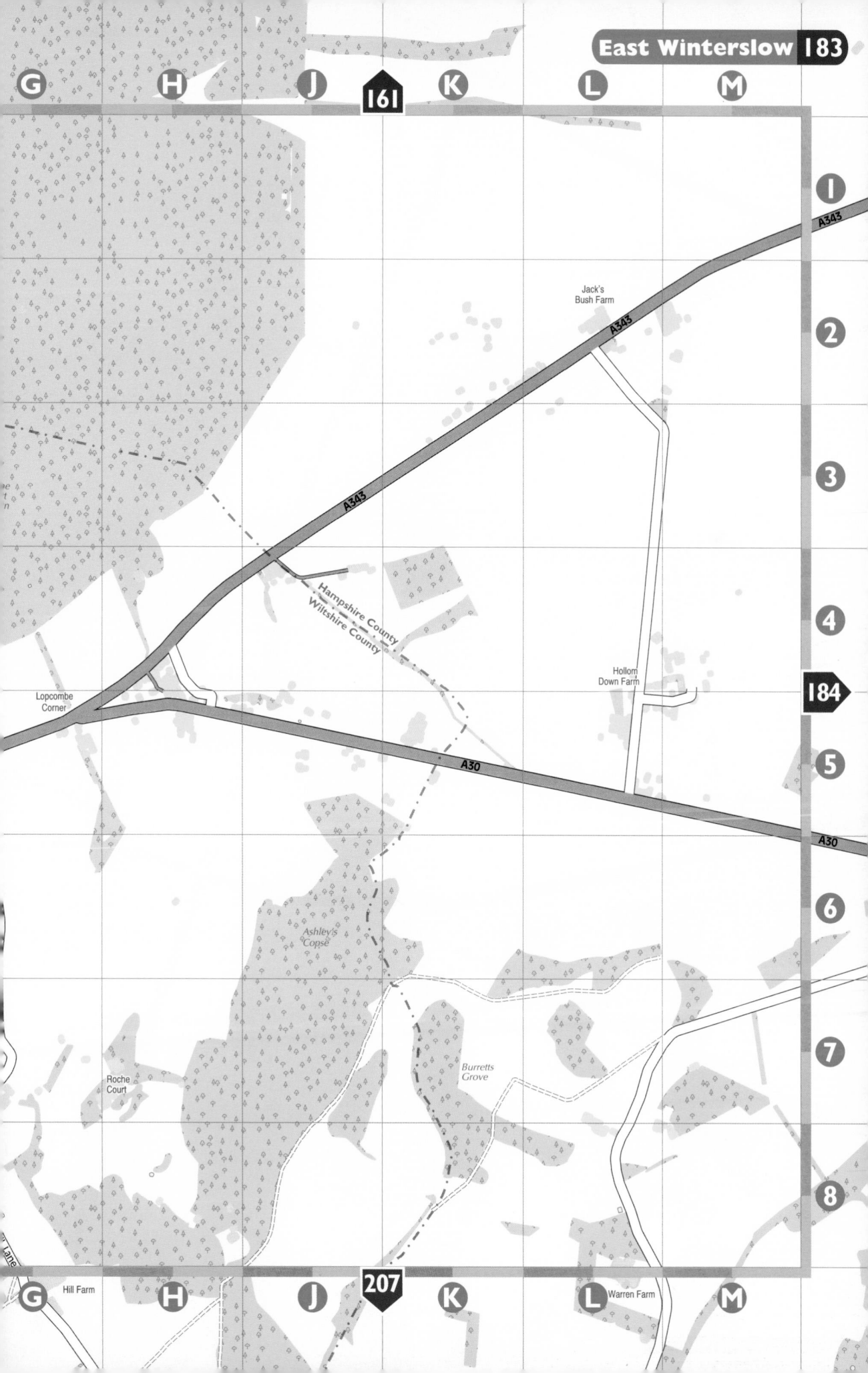

G H J **161** K L M

G H J **207** K L M

1
2
3
4
184
5
6
7
8

A343
A343
A343
A30
A30

Jack's
Bush Farm

Hampshire County
Wiltshire County

Lopcombe
Corner

Hollom
Down Farm

Ashley's
Copse

Burretts
Grove

Roche
Court

Hill Farm

Warren Farm

A   B   C   162   D   E   F

F2
1 The Square

E2
1 The Causeway

Cottage
Road
New
Rd
Sarum
Cl
Lane
lisbury

School Lane

Wallop CP
School

Knockwood Lane

1

A343

ROMSEY

Bent Street

Benham Drove

Farley

Wallop Brook

Wallop House

Street

Wallop Brook
Street

Heathman
1 Church Lane

ROAD

B3084

Hosketts Lane

Ducks Lane

PO

Lane

High Street

Church Hill

Five Bells

Aylwards
Wy

Sheep Drove

Wallop Drove

Berry
Court Farm

183

Beech Farm

A30

A30

A30

SALISBURY ROAD

B3084

Waterloo Farm

Broughton
Down Farm

B3084

Broughton
Down

A   B   C   208   D   E   F

SALISBURY

1 grid square represents 500 metres

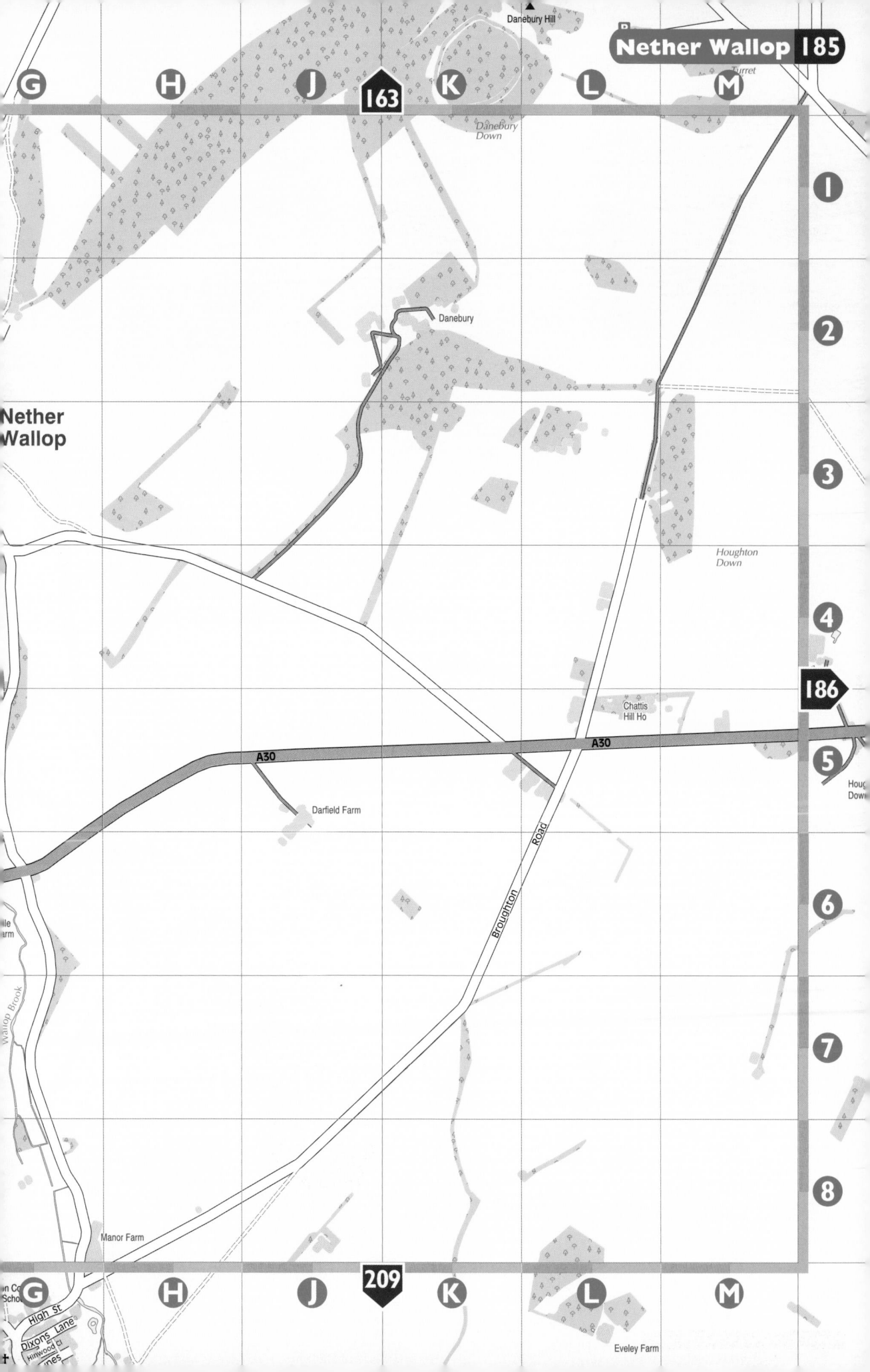

G H J 163 K L M

Danebury Hill

Turret

I

Danebury Down

Danebury

2

Nether
Wallop

3

Houghton
Down

4

186

A30   A30

Chattis
Hill Ho

5

Darfield Farm

Houg
Dow

Broughton Road

6

Wallop Brook

7

8

Manor Farm

G H J 209 K L M

High St
Dixons Lane
Hinwood Cl

n Co
Schoo

Eveley Farm

A   B   164   C   D   E   F

The Turret

1

Church Road

Cemetery

Longstock †

2

PH

3

ghton wn

A3057

4

A30

5

Houghton Down Farm

Roman Rd

HIGH STREET   A30

Stockbridge

Test Valley County Secondary School

†   †

Town Hall

PO

Wykeham Gallery

Nelson Cl

Trafalgar

Stockbridge CP School

Old London Road

Steepleton Home

WINTON

Cemeter

A3057

The Milsons

6

SO20

River Test

Penny Lane

Homestead Farm

7

Common Marsh (NT)

Test Way

North Houghton

Marsh Court

8

A   B   C   210   D   E   F

1 grid square represents 500 metres

G H J K L M

Leckford

PO

165

Leckford Abbas

LECKFORD LANE

A3057

New Farm

A30

A30

Fairview Farm

188

Sandydown Farm

Heath House

Stockbridge Down

Bushy Copse

B3049

B3049

Somborne Park Road

Whitehall Road

North Park Farm

Winter Down Copse

North Park Wood

G H J K L M

211

1 2 3 4 5 6 7 8

A B C 166 D E F

Martins Lane

A30

Brockley Warren

1

Martins Lane

2

Chilbolton Down

A30

3

A30

4

Heath House

Dumper's Oak

5

Crawley Court

6

Long Copse

Bushy Copse

Cemet

7

B3049

Folly Farm

8

B3049

STOCKBRIDGE RD

A B C 212 D E F Kin

I grid square represents 500 metres

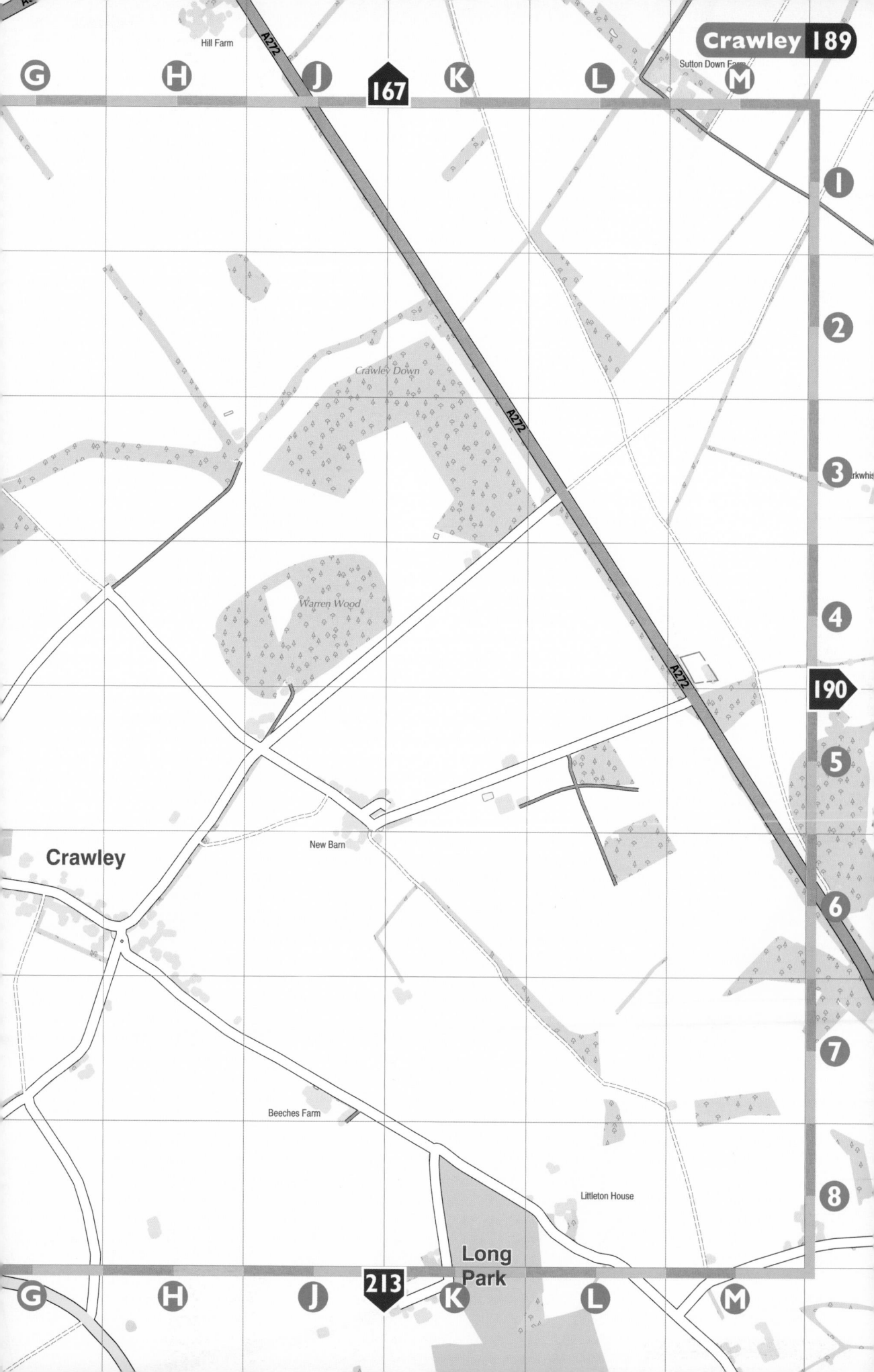

G   H   J   **167**   K   L   M

I
2
3
4
190
5
6
7
8

Hill Farm

A272

Sutton Down Farm

Crawley Down

Warren Wood

Crawley

New Barn

Beeches Farm

Littleton House

Long Park

G   H   J   **213**   K   L   M

168

189

214

D4
1 Hornbeam Cl
2 Paddock Cl

A B C D E F

1
2
3
4
5
6
7
8

West Stoke Farm

SO21

South Wonston Farm

Alresford Drove

Larkwhistle Farm

South Wonston

Stavedown Road
Markson Rd
Wrights Close
Wrights
West Hill Road North
Goldfinch Way
Long Barrow Close
Chaucer Close
Keats Close
Burns Close
Spruce Close
Waverley Drive
Rowan Cl
1
2
Downs Road
Downs Road
Downs Road
Stainers La
Orchard Close
Orchard Road
Blackthorn Cl
Downlands Way
Downlands Way
Walnut Tree Close
Oaklands
Downlands
Way
Cherry Close
South Wonston Primary School
Borman Close
Hunt Close
Anders Rd
Lovell Way
Lovell Close
Armstrong Ct
West Hill Road South
Green Close
Pine Close
Lower Rd
Ox Drove
PO

Christmas Hill

A34(T)

Lower   Road

Worthy Down

Road
Riley
Connaught
Road

Rees Road
Blackwell Rd
Malpass Road
Coate Drive
Coate Drive
Burns Close
Coopers Close
Stanham Close
Cowley Dr
Connaught Road
PO

A272

A34(T)

A272

Down Farm

Down Farm Lane

WINCHESTER   BY-PASS

NDOVER ROAD

Williams Farm

A34(T)

1 grid square represents 500 metres

H8
1 Mountbatten Pl

G   H   J   **169**   K   L   M

Bazeley
Copse

I

Newdown Farm

2

3

BASINGSTOKE ROAD

Burnt
Wood

4

192

Shroner Hill Farm

5

Road

6   M3

Bridgett's Lane

Burntwood Farm

7

A33

Coverbank

Vale
Way

The
Pastures

Kings
Cr

8

Way

Roberts
Close

Bull Farm House

Springvale Road

Edinburgh
Rd

Castle Rise

Churchill
Close

Elizabeth
Cl

Somerville Road

West Fld
Road

Brooke Close

North Road

Fraser Road

Lich
Close

Lane

Sycamore
Dr

Forbes Road

Close

Tudor
Way

Haydn
Close

Boyce

Rise

Harwood
Pl

Stenbroke Av

Loveden

Harwood

Pound Road

Vian
Place

Tower Place

Ramsey

Cedarwood

Bingham Cl

G   H   J   **215**   K   L   M

Springvale Road

Legion Lane

Wesley
Road

Cedarwood

ROAD

Meadowland

Road

Loader Cl

Plympton

170

A B C D E F

1

Newdown Farm

2

3

BASINGSTOKE ROAD

Shroner Wood

4

191

Chillandham Lane

Chillandham Lane

Oxdrove Way

Itchen Wood

Micheldever Wood

M3

5

M3

6

Bridgets Lane

Bridgets Farm

Oxdrove Way

7

Lone Farm

Rectory Lane

8

A B C D E F

216

Old Station

Baring Cl

1 grid square represents 500 metres

G H J **171** K **Northington** L M

I

Swarraton

2

B3046

Swarra

3

4

194

5

6

Abbotstone

7

Fobdown Farm

8

Northington Road

Itchen
Stoke
Down

Three Castles Path

whouse Farm

Northington
Down Farm

The Grange
Farm

The Grange Park

The Grange
Lake

Folly
Hill

Wayfare

A B C **172** D E F

1

Swarraton Farm

2

Spiers Lane

Abbotstone Woods

3

Abbotstone Down

4

Wayfarer's Walk

5

Coombe Farm

Colc

Oxdrove Way

6

Southdowns

Southdowns

7

Old Alresford

Hobdown Farm

Green Cl

Kiln Lane

Colden Lane

Oxdrove Way

8

The Brook

B3046

Alresford House

A B C **218** D E F

SOKE

Old Alresford

Pinglestone Farm

SO24

1 grid square represents 500 metres

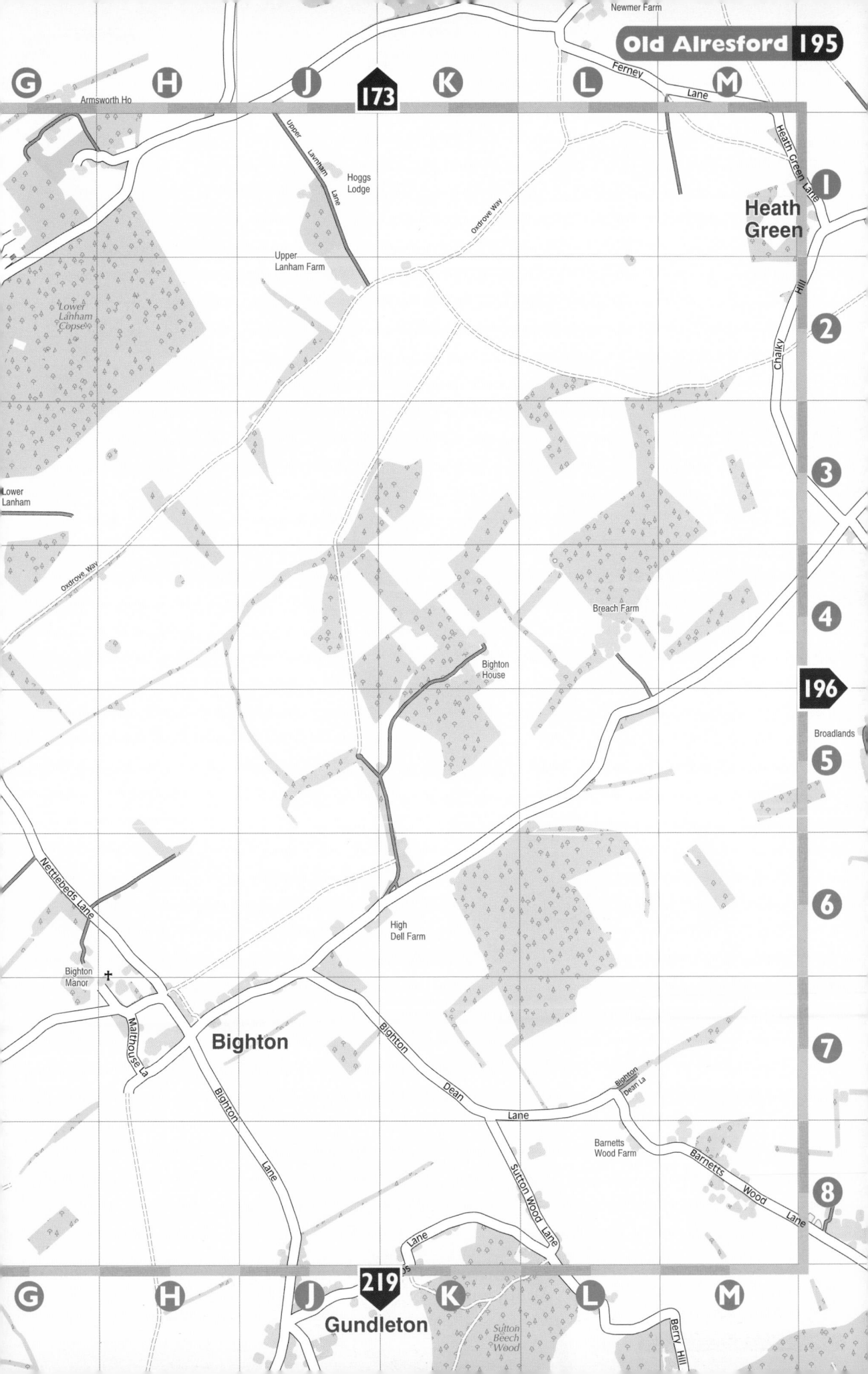

G H J K L M

173

Newmer Farm

Ferney Lane

Armsworth Ho

Heath Green Lane

Upper Lavnham Lane

Hoggs Lodge

Oxdrove Way

Heath
Green

1

Chalky Hill

2

Upper
Lanham Farm

Lower
Lanham
Copse

3

Lower
Lanham

Oxdrove Way

Breach Farm

4

Bighton
House

196

Broadlands

5

High
Dell Farm

Nettlebeds Lane

6

Bighton
Manor †

Malthouse La

Bighton

Bighton

Dean

Lane

Bighton
Dean La

7

Barnetts
Wood Farm

Barnetts

Wood

Lane

8

Sutton Wood Lane

G H J K L M

219

Gundleton

Sutton
Beech
Wood

Berry Hill

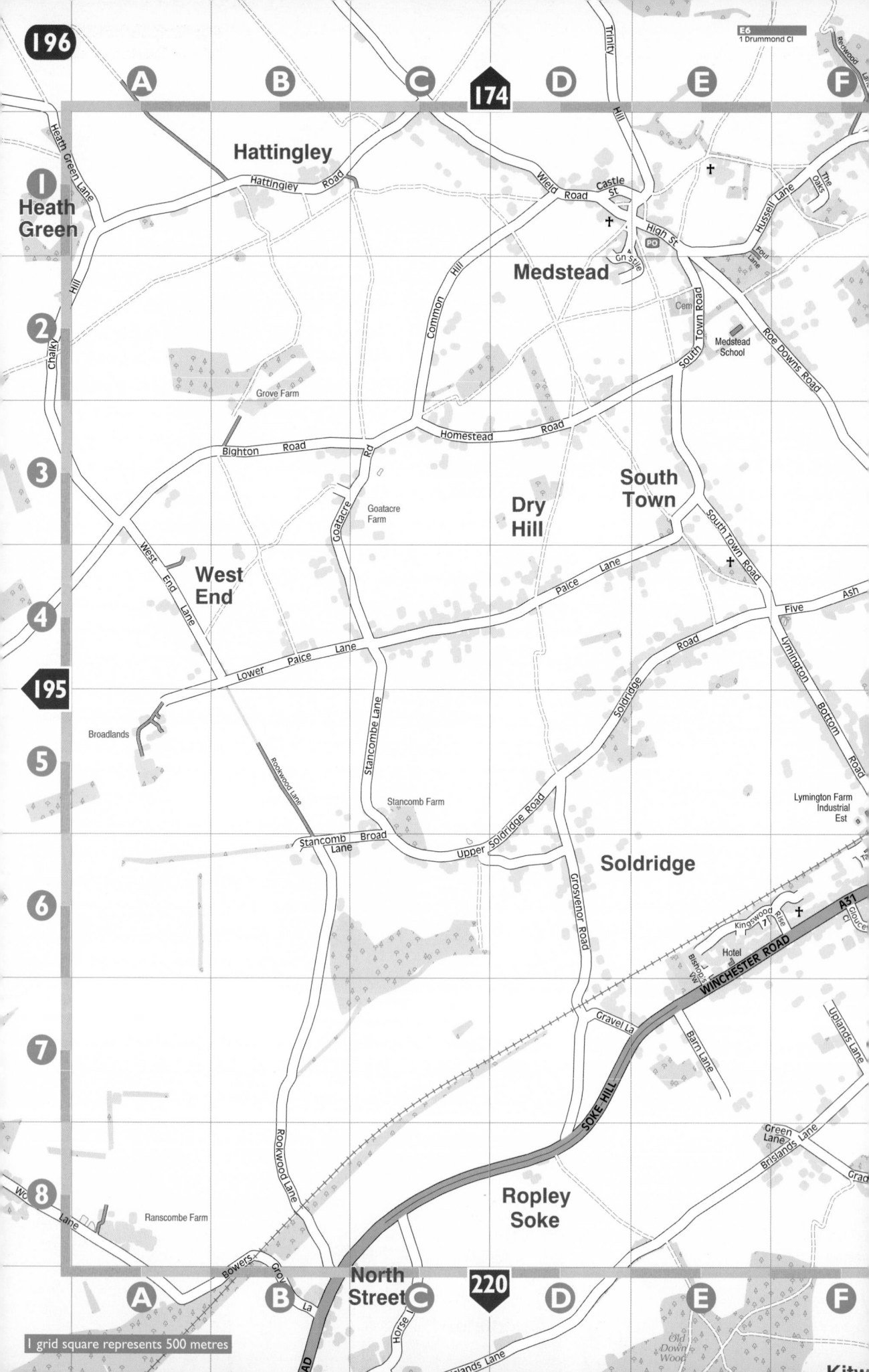

196
174
195
220
A
B
C
D
E
F
1
2
3
4
5
6
7
8
E6
1 Drummond Cl
Hattingley
Heath Green
Heath Green Lane
Hattingley Road
Trinity Hill
Wield Road
Castle St
High St
Gn Stile
Medstead
Hussell Lane
The Oaks
Foul Lane
Roe Downs Road
Cem
South Town Road
Medstead School
Chalky Hill
Grove Farm
Common Hill
Homestead Road
Bighton Road
Goatacre Rd
Goatacre Farm
Dry Hill
South Town
Paice Lane
West End Lane
West End
Lower Paice Lane
Five Ash
Lymington Bottom Road
Soldridge Road
Broadlands
Stancombe Lane
Rookwood Lane
Stancomb Farm
Lymington Farm Industrial Est
Stancomb Broad Lane
Upper Soldridge Road
Soldridge
Grosvenor Road
Kingswood Rise
Hotel
Bishops Vw
WINCHESTER ROAD
A31
Gravel La
Barn Lane
Uplands Lane
SOKE HILL
Green Lane
Brislands Lane
Ropley Soke
Ranscombe Farm
Bowers Grove La
North Street
Horse
Old Down Wood
1 grid square represents 500 metres

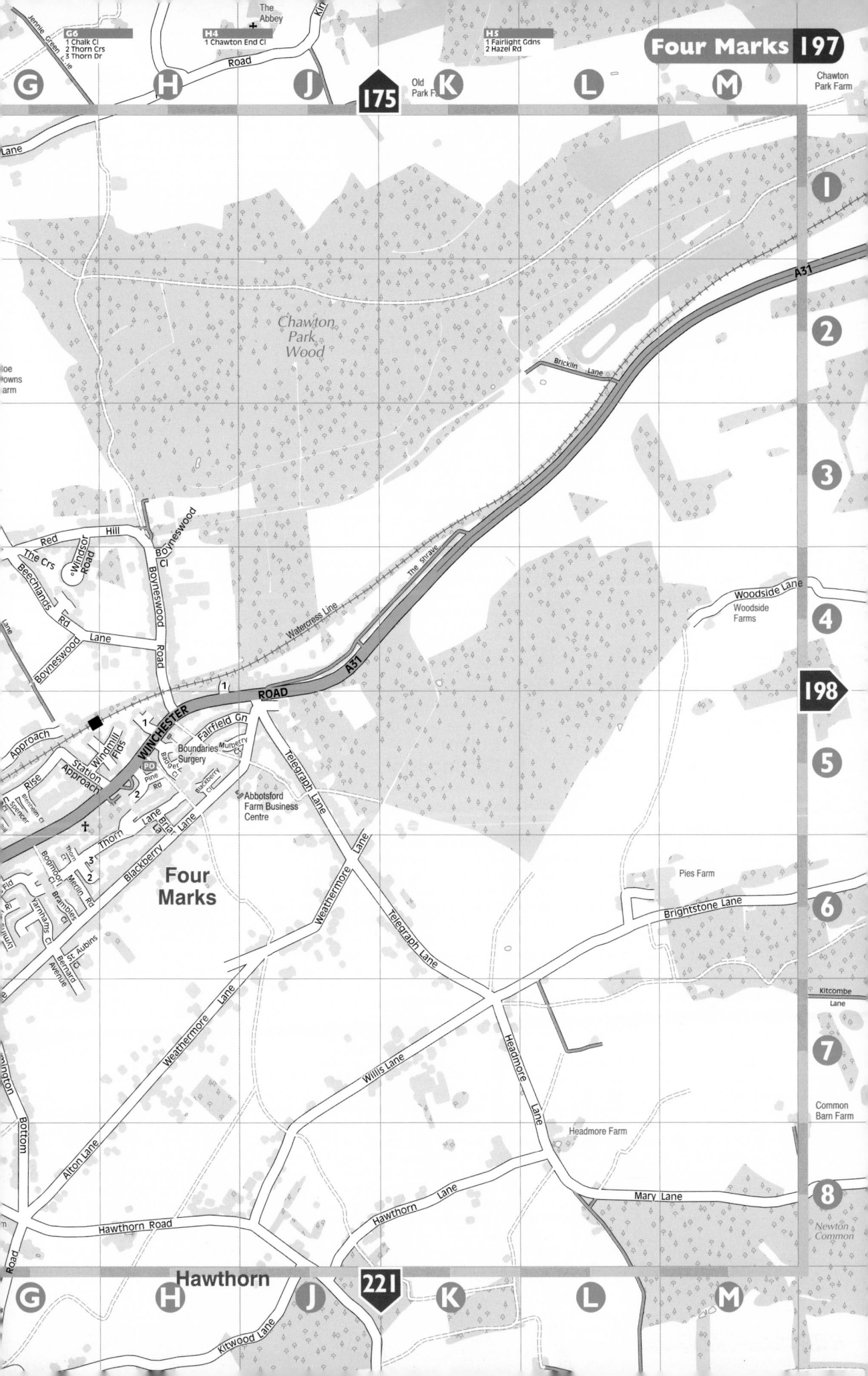

G6
1 Chalk Cl
2 Thorn Crs
3 Thorn Dr

H4
1 Chawton End Cl

H5
1 Fairlight Gdns
2 Hazel Rd

The Abbey

Road

G H J **175** Old Park Fa K L M Chawton Park Farm

1

A31

Chawton Park Wood

2

Bricklin Lane

3

Red Hill
The Crs
Windsor Road
Boyneswood Cl
Boyneswood
Beechlands Rd
Lane

Boyneswood Road

The Shrave

Watercress Line

Woodside Lane
Woodside Farms

4

ROAD
A31

WINCHESTER

198

Approach
Station Approach
Windmill Flds
Rise

Fairfield Gn
Boundaries Surgery
Mulberry Cl
Blackberry Cl
PO Pine Rd
Badger

Abbotsford Farm Business Centre

Telegraph Lane

5

Thorn Lane
Bognor Cl
Merlin Rd
Brambles Cl
Varnams Cl
St Aubins
Bernard Avenue

Blackberry Lane

Four Marks

Pies Farm

Weathermore Lane

Telegraph Lane

Headmore Lane

Brightstone Lane

6

Kitcombe Lane

7

Willis Lane

Common Barn Farm

Alton Lane

ington Bottom

Headmore Farm

Mary Lane

8

Hawthorn Road

Hawthorn Road

Newton Common

Road

Hawthorn

Kitwood Lane

G H J **221** K L M

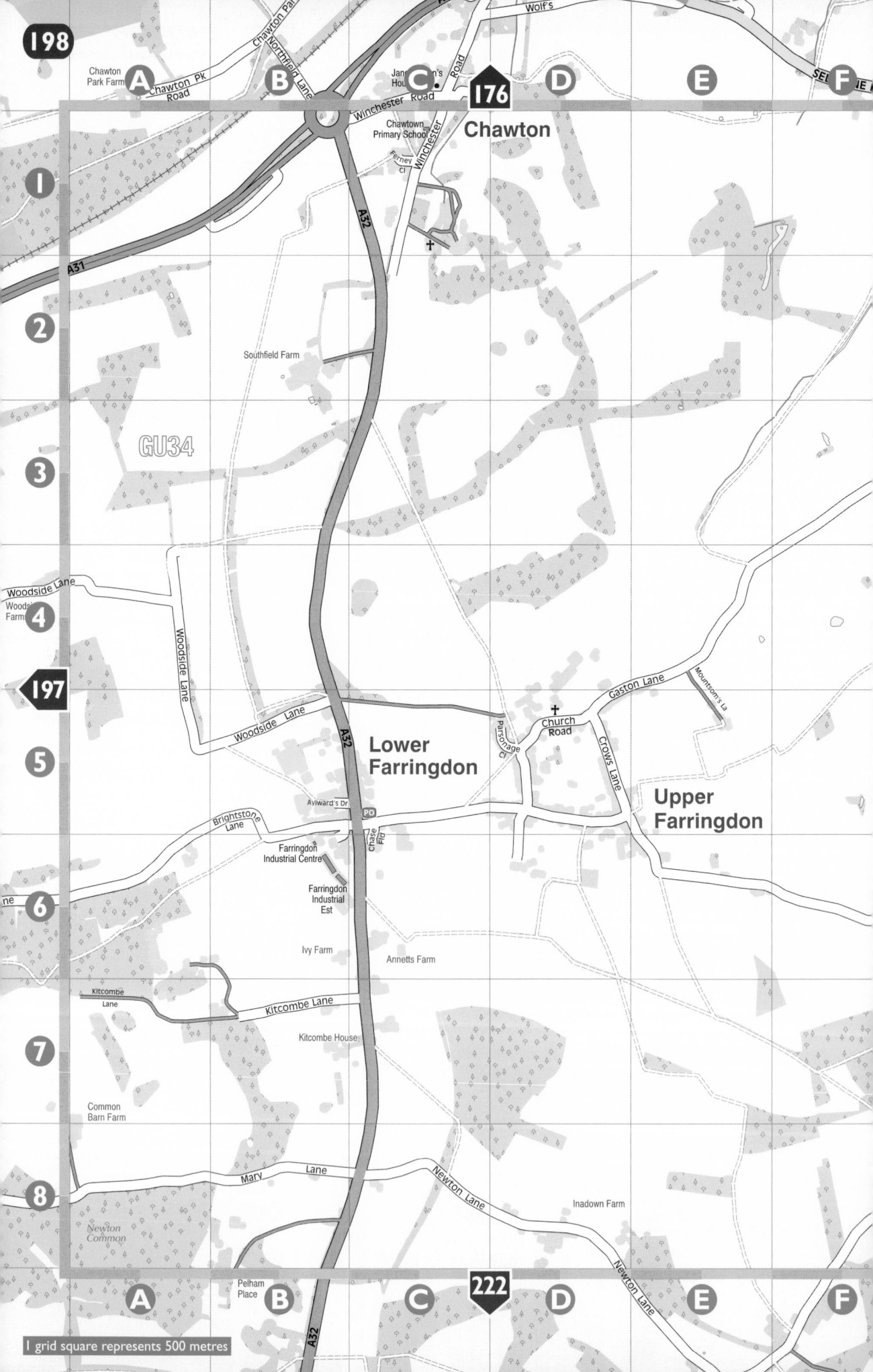

A   B   C   D   E   F

Chawton
Park Farm

Chawton Pk
Road

Chawton Park
Road

Northfield Lane

Janes
House

Winchester Road

Chawtown
Road

176

Chawton

Chawton
Primary School

Ferney
Cl

Winchester

†

A32

A31

Southfield Farm

GU34

Woodside Lane

Woodsi
Farm

197

Woodside Lane

Woodside Lane

A32

Lower
Farringdon

Parsonage Cl

†

Church
Road

Gaston Lane

Mountsom's La

Crows Lane

Upper
Farringdon

Aviward's Dr

PO

Brightstone
Lane

Chase Fld

Farringdon
Industrial Centre

Farringdon
Industrial
Est

Ivy Farm

Annetts Farm

Kitcombe
Lane

Kitcombe Lane

Kitcombe House

Common
Barn Farm

Mary   Lane

Newton Lane

Inadown Farm

Newton
Common

A   B   C   D   E   F

Pelham
Place

222

Newton Lane

A32

1 grid square represents 500 metres

I

2

West Worldham

3

Barleywood Farm

Hartley
Mauditt

Hartley
Park

4

200

5

Hartley
Park Farm
Business Cen

Hartley
Park Farm

Wick
Hill Farm

Norton Farm

6

Fielder's Farm

Hall Lane

SELBORNE ROAD

B3006

Hangers Way

7

Gracious

Gosling's Cft

New
Barn Farm

Selborne
Primary
School

8

Pendulum
Gallery

Selborne

Hastard's Lane

Honey Lane

Maltby's

Selborne
Hanger

Selborne
Common

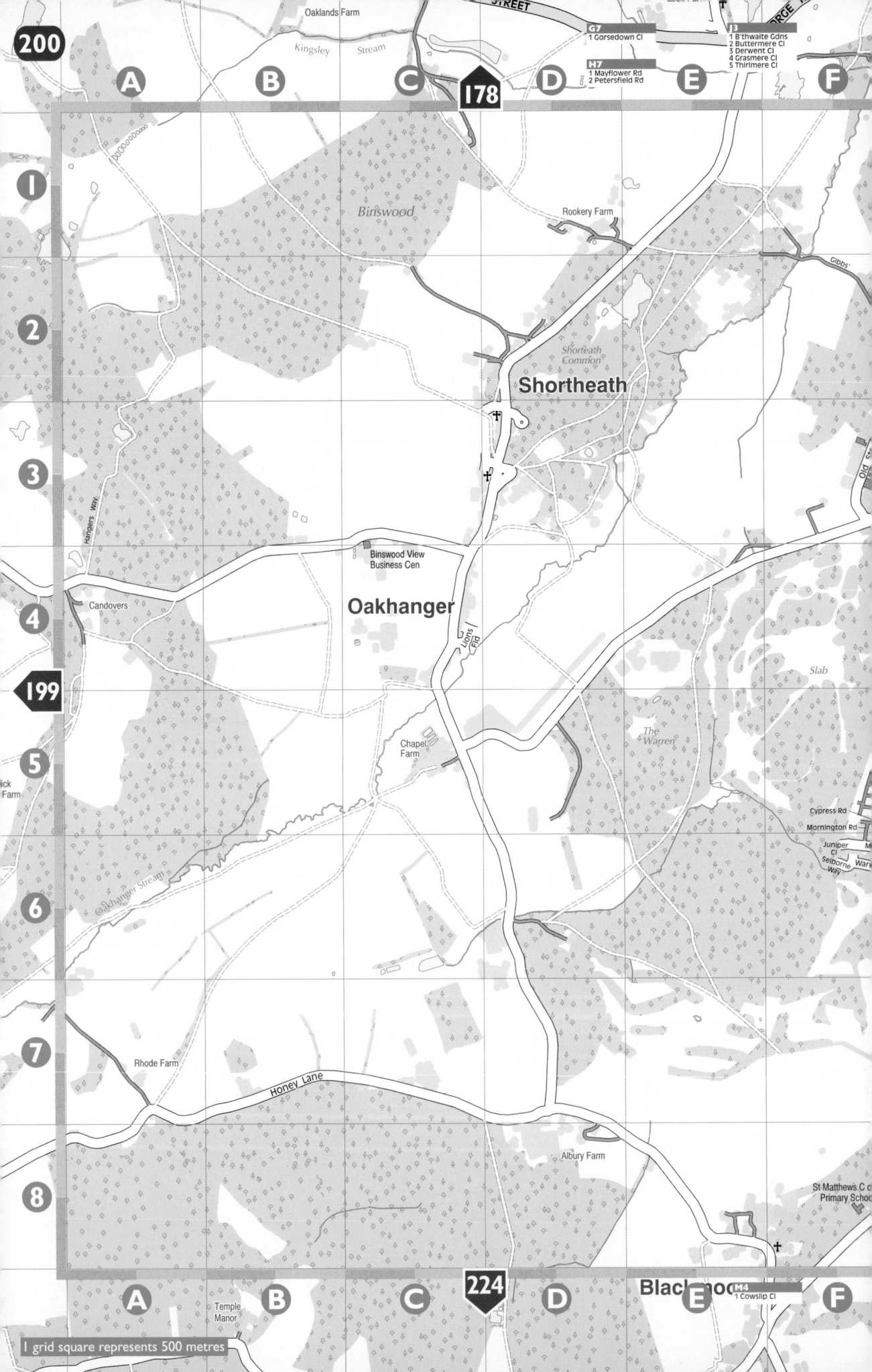

Oaklands Farm
STREET
Kingsley Stream
A
B
C
178
D
E
F
G7
1 Gorsedown Cl
H7
1 Mayflower Rd
2 Petersfield Rd
J3
1 B'thwaite Gdns
2 Buttermere Cl
3 Derwent Cl
4 Grasmere Cl
5 Thirlmere Cl
1
2
3
4
5
6
7
8
Binswood
Rookery Farm
Gibbs'
Shortheath Common
Shortheath
Old St
Hangers Way
Binswood View Business Cen
Candovers
Oakhanger
Lions Fld
199
Slab
The Warren
Chapel Farm
Cypress Rd
Mornington Rd
Juniper Cl
Selborne Way
Oakhanger Stream
Rhode Farm
Honey Lane
Albury Farm
St Matthews C of E Primary School
224
Temple Manor
M4
1 Cowslip Cl
1 grid square represents 500 metres

J5
1 Lavender Gdns
2 Manica Cl
3 Tilbury's Cl
4 Woodside Crs

J6
1 Connaught Cl
2 Dene Cl
3 Melrose Cl
4 Nutley Cl

J7
1 Bedford Cl
2 North'land Rd
3 Richmond Cl

K4
1 Beavers Ms

179

202

225

G | **H** | **J** | **K** | **L** | **M**

M3
1 Buttercup Cl
2 Colts Foot Rd
3 Grayshott Laurels
4 Lynwood Cl
5 Mallow Cl
6 Periwinkle Cl
7 Torrington Cl

L4
1 Greenacres

L5
1 Britannia Cl
2 Mercury Cl

L3
1 Cricket Lea
2 Five Acres Cl

K6 cont.
6 Hibiscus Gv
7 Jasmine Wy
8 Kingfisher Cl
9 Magpie Cl
10 Neptune Rd
11 Nightingale Rd

K6
1 Amber Cl
2 Chestnut Ct
3 Ducklands
4 Foxglove Dr
5 Hendon Rd
cont.

K5
1 Blackthorne Cl
2 Ferncote Rd
3 Norman Cl
4 Primula Rd

D2
1 Kay Crs
B3
1 Pilgrims Wy
2 Yeomans Pl
B2
1 Curtis Cl
A8
1 Arundel Cl
180
Headley Wood Farm
Bayfields Farm
Hearn
Frensham Lane
Spats Lane
Linsted Lane
The Hanger
Red Lane
Hearn Vale
Langton Drive
Churt Road
Land of Nod
Hillside Cl
Alder Road
The Mount
Hollow La
Curtis Lane
Church Lane
Arford
Barley Mow Hill
Arford Common
Beech Hill Road
Arford Common
Claysher's Hill
Birch Rd
Larch Rd
Maple Way
Ling Crs
Pine Vw
Windmill Dr
Long Cross Hill
Arford Rd
Openfields
Farthing Flds
Bowcott Hill
Beech Hill Road
Eddeys La
B3002
Church Fields
High St
Kirk Knoll
Liphook Road
Headley Hill Road
Southview Road
Ludshott Gv
The Boreen
Wilsons Road
GRAYSHOTT
Downsview Rd
Fairview
MILL LANE
B3002
CRABTREE LA
Phillips Crs
FULLERS VALE
BEECH HILL
Honeysuckle La
Kenley Road
Headley
Badgerswood Surgery
Glebe Rd
The Paddock
Crabtree Gdns
Liphook Road
Phillips Cl
Linden Road
Alma Rd
Pound Cl
Hilland
Oak Tree Cl
Rise
Chestnut End
Beech Hl
Oakhill Rd
Furze Vale Rd
West Vw Rd
Headley Flds
Headley Fields
Headley Flds
Verner Cl
May Cl
Churchill Crs
Perry Way
Headley Down
Pond Road
Seymour Rd
Sunnyside Rd
Stonehill Pk
Stonehill Road
Furze Hl Rd
Mill Lane
Headley Mill Farm
Hurland Lane
Gentles Lane
Furze Hill
Stonedene Cl
Rowansich Cl
Birkenholm Cl
201
STANDFORD LANE
Gentles Lane
Gentle's Copse
Liphook Road
Tulls Lane
B3004
Headley Lane
Gentles Lane
Standford Hill
Passfield Mill Business Park
Passfield
Woolmer
Road
Passfield
Ludshott Manor
Passfield Common
B3004
Lynchborough Road
Eleanor Cl
Bramshott Court
Oaklea Farm
Woolmer
226
E2
1 Eddeys Cl
2 Embleton Rd
F3
1 Penryn Dr
F4
1 Gorselands Cl
2 Telconia Cl
3 Withersiack Cl
Burgh Hill Road
Conford
1 grid square represents 500 metres

K4
1 The Paddock
M1
1 Huntingford Cl
M2
1 Caerleon Cl
Bamford
181
G
H
J
K
L
M
1
2
3
4
5
6
7
8
Churt Road
Hammer Lane
Whitmoor Vale Road
Surrey County
Hampshire County
Whitmore Vale
Linkside North
Linkside East
Linkside West
Linkside South
Sandheath Rd
Heath Close
Clovelly Dr
Churt Wynde
Clovelly Road
Glen Rd
Glen Cl
Glen Rd
Grove Road
Hill Road
Beacon Hill
Parsons
Beacon Hill Court
Hindhead Golf Club
Golf Links Av
Fairways
Steepways
Corry Rd
Beacon Hill County Primary School
PO
A287
Road
Firway
Kiln Way
B3002
Headley Road
Grayshott Hall
The Spinney
Waggoners Wy
Waggoners Wy
Saddlers Scarp
Waggoners
Wheelwrights La
Halters End
Bridle Cl
Horseshoe Bend
Whitmore Vale Road
Grayshott Clinic
Beech La
School Rd
Beech Hanger End
Chestnut Cl
Vicarage Gdns
Vale Wood Lane
Church La
204
Headley Road
Grayshott Primary School
Grayshott
Hill Road
The Avenue
Oakl
Stoney Bottom
Kingswood Firs
Kingswood Firs
Ludshott Common
Waggoners Wells Road
Ladygate Drive
Hunters Moon
Mount Alvernia
Kingswood Lane
A3(T)
Summerden
Waggoners Wells
Bramshott Chase
Hammer Lane
Knockhundred Lane
Woolmer Hill Road
Downlands
Bramshott Common
Portsmouth Road
227
Sandy Lane
M5
1 Jubilee La
Rectory Lane
Woolmer Hill

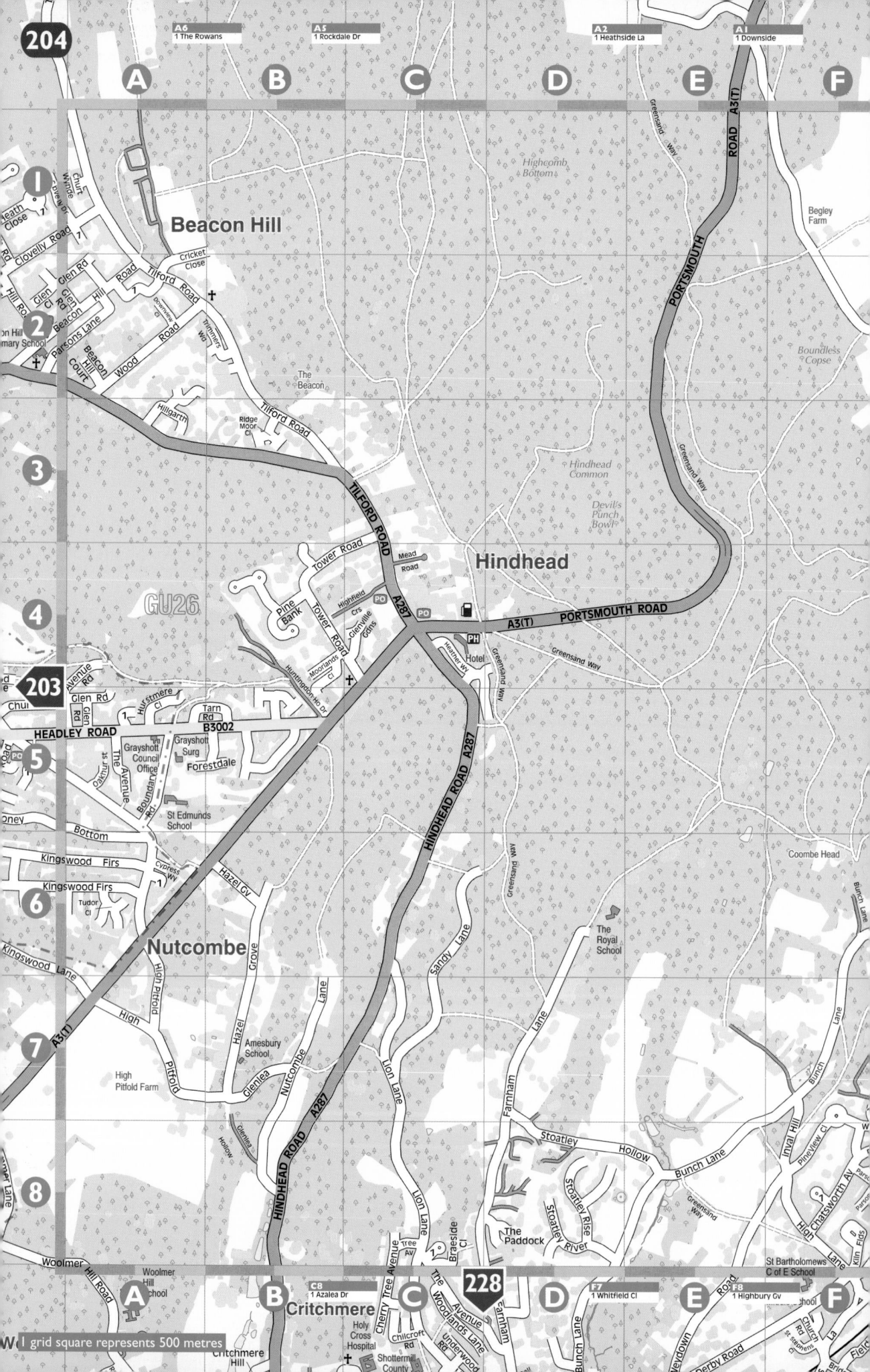

A6 1 The Rowans
A5 1 Rockdale Dr
A2 1 Heathside La
A1 1 Downside
Beacon Hill
Hindhead
Nutcombe
Critchmere
GU26
Highcomb Bottom
Hindhead Common
Devil's Punch Bowl
The Beacon
Begley Farm
Boundless Copse
Coombe Head
The Royal School
Amesbury School
High Pitfold Farm
St Edmunds School
Grayshott Council Office
Grayshott Surg
The Paddock
Woolmer Hill School
Holy Cross Hospital
St Bartholomews C of E School
TILFORD ROAD
HINDHEAD ROAD A287
PORTSMOUTH ROAD A3(T)
HEADLEY ROAD B3002
Greensand Way
C8 1 Azalea Dr
F7 1 Whitfield Cl
F8 1 Highbury Gv
203
228
1 grid square represents 500 metres

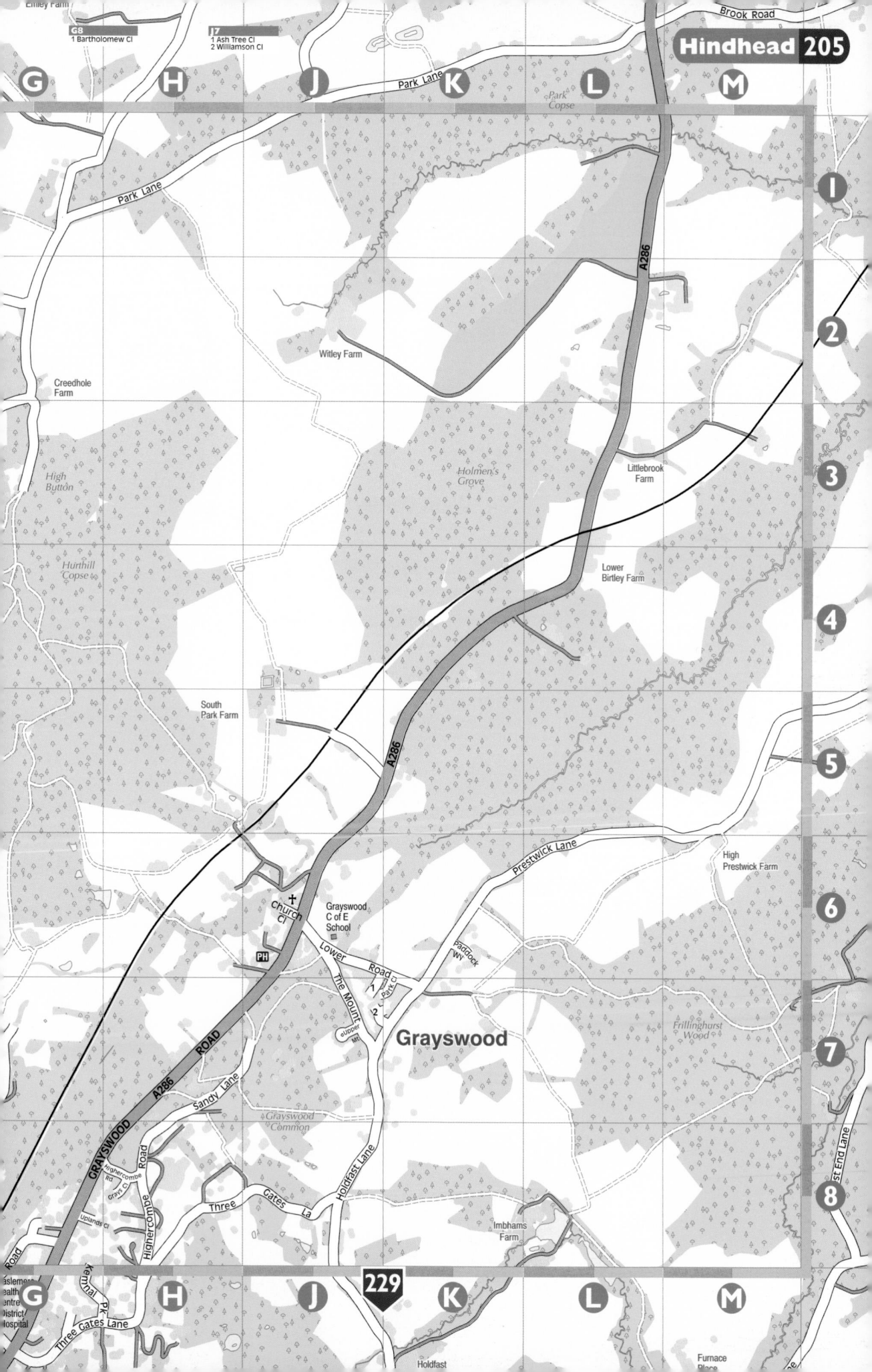
Emley Farm
G8
1 Bartholomew Cl
J7
1 Ash Tree Cl
2 Williamson Cl
Brook Road
Park Lane
Park Copse
Park Lane
A286
Witley Farm
Creedhole Farm
High Button
Holmen's Grove
Littlebrook Farm
Hurthill Copse
Lower Birtley Farm
South Park Farm
A286
High Prestwick Farm
Prestwick Lane
Church Cl
Grayswood C of E School
PH
Lower Road
Paddock Wy
The Mount
Park Cl
Upper Mt
Grayswood
Frillinghurst Wood
GRAYSWOOD A286 ROAD
Sandy Lane
Grayswood Common
Highercombe Road
Highercombe Rd
Grays Cl
Uplands Cl
Three Gates La
Holdfast Lane
Imbhams Farm
Road
Kemnal Pk
Three Gates Lane
Holdfast
Furnace Place
st End Lane

F2
1 Stone Cl
2 Youngs Paddock
E2
1 Yew Tree Cl
E1
1 Woodland Dr
D3
1 Kings Paddock
182
Firsdown
Dunstable Farm
Monarch's Way
Monarch's Way
The Street
Clarendon Way
Clough La
The Flood
Middleton Road
Winterslow Primary School
Highfield Crs
Yarmley Lane
The Surgery
PO
The Plantation
Bentleigh Farm
Clarendon Way
Livery Road
West Winterslow
Weston Lane
Clarendon Way
Woodgate Farmhouse
Glebe Cl
The Gn
Pitton
Livery Road
Hound Wood
Pitton Road
Livery Road
Farleys All Saints Primary School
Farley
Church Road
Park Lane
The Livery
230
Blackmoor Copse
Barnridge Copse
The Street
Oak Cl
Road
A
B
C
D
E
F
1
2
3
4
5
6
7
8
1 grid square represents 500 metres

G2
1 Glenfield Cl

M8
1 The Withies

183

G H J K L M

1

2

3

4

208

5

6

7

8

231

G H J K L M

The
Green

Hill Farm

Warren Farm

low

seway
The Flashett
Gunville Rd
on
Witt
Bentley
Way
Road
Gunville Hill
Easton Common Hl
Tytherley
Road

Clarendon Way
Monarch's Way
Noad's Copse

Hedgemoor
Copse

Picked
Copse

Yew Tree Lane

Bentley
Wood

Norman
Court
School

North

Lane

Park
Lane

Park Lane

Park Lane

Park
Copse

Standing Hill

Home Farm

West Tytherley
Primary School

Rectory Hill

PO

North La

North Lane

Chalk

Pug's Hole

Dean Road

Pug's Hole

The coach

Wes
Tyth

208

A   B   Broughton   C   184   D   E   B3084   F
           Down

Broughton
Down Farm

SALISBURY

I

Church Fa

2   Clarendon Way   Buckholt
                                                     Monarch's Way

                    Clarendon Way
3   Monarch's Way

         Buckholt Farm

4

207

         Yew Tree Lane

5
                                                                                    Queenwood Fa

    North Lane

6

    Red Hill

7 PO
         North Lane   Chalk Pit Lane

Tytherley
ary School
    North La

         West
         Tytherley   Stony Batter

8
                                                 Stride's Farm

                                        Manor Farm
                                                                    Manor
                                                                    Rd
         The Coa   232
The A   ch Road   B   The Coach Road   C   D   E   F
Green
                                                          East
1 grid square represents 500 metres   Tytherley

G H J 185 K L M

Manor Farm

n County School

I

High St

Dixons Lane

Hinwood Cl

Paynes

Chapel Lane

Rectory Lane

Eveley Farm

Broughton

Queenwood Rd

PH PO

High Street

2

Queenwood Rise

Beechcroft Cottages

Coolers Farm

Rookery Lane

Monarch's Way

South Road

3

The Hollow

Roake Farm

Faithfulls Drove

4

Wallop Brook

Horsebridge Road

B3084

210 Bossir

Horsebridge Road

Beech Tree Walk

5

6

Crown Farm

River T

7

8

Bentley Farms

B3084

Pittleworth Farm

G H J 233 K L M

North Houghton

186

F5
1 Nutchers Dro

Marsh
Court

Houghton
Lodge

Church
Lane

River Test

Hoopers Farm

Stevens
Drove

Houghton

Chapel Close

Faithfulls   Drove

Clarendon   Way

Test Way

Cow   Drove   Hill

Cemetery

209

Bossington

Horsebridge Road

King's
Somborne

STOCKBRIDGE ROAD

Old Vicarage

Nutchers Drove

Muss Lane

The
Cross

Church Rd

PO

A3057

Kings Somborne
C of E School

Old Palace Farm

Hayes
Close

Palace Ct

Scott Close

The Gorrings

Eldon
Close
Sopwith
Close

Humbers
View

Horsebridge

ROAD

Horsebridge   Road

River Test

Test Way

ROMSEY

Eldon   Road

ROMSEY ROAD

Compton
Park

234

Humbers
Wood

Eldon Road

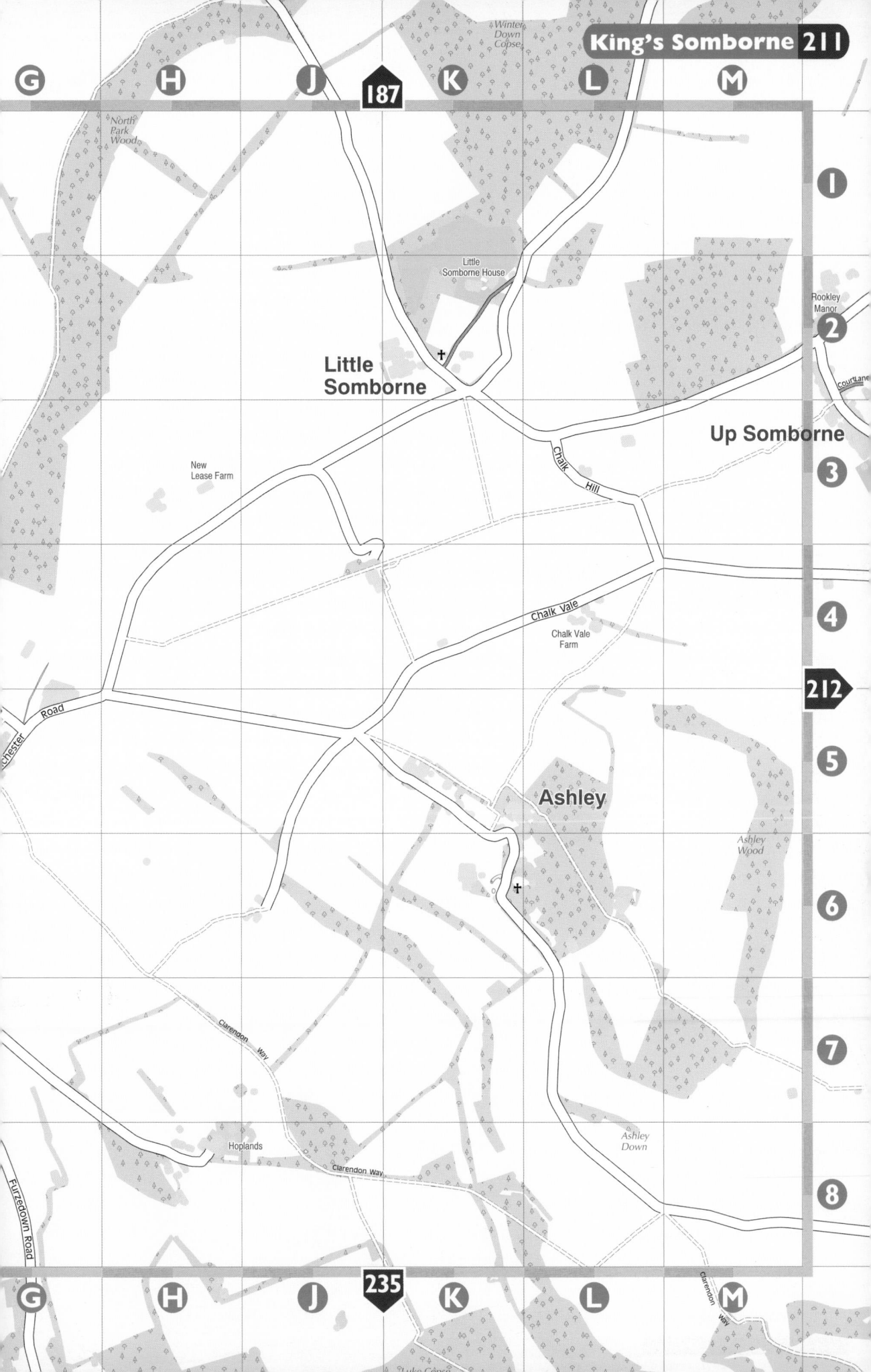
G
H
J
187
K
L
M
Winter Down Copse
North Park Wood
Little Somborne House
Little Somborne
Rookley Manor
Court Lane
Up Somborne
New Lease Farm
Chalk Hill
Chalk Vale
Chalk Vale Farm
212
Road
chester
Ashley
Ashley Wood
Clarendon Way
Hoplands
Ashley Down
Furzedown Road
235
I
2
3
4
5
6
7
8

A   B   C   188   D   E   STOCKBRIDGE RO   F

B3049

Kirt

1

Rookley
Manor

2

Court Lane

Somborne

3

Sparsholt Colle
Hampshire

4

211

5

Ashley
Wood

*Great Up
Somborne Wood*

Well
Copse

6

7

Forest of Bere Farm

*West
Wood*

Farley Mou
Country Pa

Farley
Mount
⚔

8

A   B   C   236   D   E   Clarendon Wa   F

Clarendon Way

G   H   J   **189**   K   **Long Park**   L   M

I

Littleton House

Church Lane

2

New Road

Northwood Park

Rozelle Close   Holm Oak Cl   Fairclose   The Hall

Main Road

Litt

3

Hilden Way   Dale Close   Valley Road   Fyfie

South drive

4

STOCKBRIDGE ROAD B3049

B3049

Westley   Lane

Lainston House Hotel

214

Moor Court Farm   Lock's Lane   Lock's Lane   PH   Woodman Lane   **Dean**   5

Westley   Lane   Home   Lane

Moor Court Lane   Church Lane   Lambourne Close   PO   **Sparsholt**

Watley   Lane

Sparsholt Primary School   Bostock Close   Dean Lane

Littleton Lane   Woodman Close

6

Westview Road

Burrow Road

Lanham Lane   Beec Copse   7

Crab Wood

Lanham Lane   Teg Dow

Crabwood Farm House

8

Clarendon Way

G   H   J   **237**   K   L   M   Royal Winchester Golf Club

Clarendon Way   SARUM ROAD

C8
1 Wordsworth Cl
C6
1 M'sbury Gdns
C4
1 Beaulieu Cl
2 East Woodhay Rd
3 Minstead Cl
4 Southwick Cl
5 Swanmore Cl
B3
1 Lawn Rd
B7
1 Ashmore Rd
2 Sawyer Cl
A
B
C
D
E
F
1
2
3
4
5
6
7
8
190
213
238
10
Down Farm
Down Farm Lane
A272
WINCHESTER BY-PASS
A34(T)
ANDOVER ROAD NORTH B3420
Woodhams Farm
Church Lane
Main Road
New Road
Littleton
Vanguard Hill
Grand Pde
Pembroke Road
Valley Hill
Uphill Road
Westfield Rd
Hilltop
Hillside
Pitter Cl
The Hall Way
Fyfield Way
North Drive
Chestnut Avenue
Valley Road
Dale Close
Bercote Close
South Drive
Kennel Road
Deane Down Drove
Headbourne Worth
Well House Lane
Harestock Road
Harestock Cl
Buriton Road
Grayshott Cl
Priors Dean Rd
Rockbourne Rd
Appleshaw Close
Froxfield Close
Hickory Dr
Larg Drive
Burley Rd
Hambledon
Litchfield Road
Woodgreen Rd
Lyndhurst Cl
Winslade Road
Bradley Road
Rewlands Dr
Abbotts Ann Rd
Amport Cl
Bramshaw Cl
Ashley Cl
Harestock
Henry Beaufort School
Ashurst Cl
Upton Grey Cl
Eling Cl
Harestock Infant School
Halls Farm Cl
Orient Drive
Rowlings Road
Taplings Close
Taplings Road
Devenish Rd
Pemerton Road
Mount Cl
Mountbatten Close
Uplands Road
Bereweeke Road
Barton Farm
Fleming Rd
Great Fld Rd
Trussell Close
Trussell Crs
Westman Road
Ruffield Close
Fromond Road
Burnett Close
Godwin Cl
Salters Acres
B3049
Woodpecker Drive
Stoney Lane
Woodlea Close
Avenue
Lynford Av
Lynford Way
ANDOVER ROAD
Old Park Rd
Park Road
Courtenay Road
Vernham Road
St Matthews Rd
St Stephen's Road
Wessex Drive
High Trees Dr
CP School
Acorn Close
Weeke Manor Close
Weeke
Winchester Lawn Tennis Club
Kynegils Rd
Lynch Close
Bere Cl
Butts Close
Bereweeke Way
Bereweeke Close
Greenacres School
BEREWEEKE ROAD B3041
Winton Close
Lainston Close
Parkside Gdns
Dean Lane
Morninton Dr
Dean Cl
Downside Road
Old Hillside Road
Hillside Close
Croucher's Cft
Sermon Road
Bradley Peak
Goring Field
Groveland Road
Sawyer Cl
Webster Rd
Hillside Road
Meads
Teg Down
Beech Copse
Lanham Lane
S022
Coppice Close
Westley Cl
Stockers Avenue
Hampton Lane
Silwood Cl
Peter Symonds College
Brassey Road
Boscobel Rd
North Hill Close
Andover Road
Lankhills School
Lankhills Road
Hotel
Northlands Dr
Abbey Hill Rd
Denham Cl
Salcot Road
Russell Rd
Knight Cl
Oglander Road
B3047
Edington Rd
Winchester Football Club
Arthur Rd
Lido Sports Club
Saxon Rd
Monks Rd
WORTHY LA
King Alfred Place
Hyde Close
Winchester A
City Business Cen
Hyde Abbey Road
Gordon Road
Swan La
CITY ROAD
NORTH WALLS
B3041
CHILBOLTON AV
STOCKBRIDGE ROAD B3049
Cheriton Close
Cheriton Road
Walnut Grove
Links Road
The Westgate School
Langton Close
Nethercliffe School
Pilgrims Gate
Hatherley Road
Conifer Cl
Fairfield Rd
Cranworth Rd
Andover Road Retail Park
Winchester Station
Fulflood
Fordington Road
Western Road
Elm Road
Coker Close
ST PAUL'S HILL
Station Hill
SUSSEX STREET
Tower Street
Western Primary Sch
Browning Drive
Shelley Close
Byron Avenue
Poets Way
Milverton Road
Middle Road
Clifton Road
St Pauls Hospital
CLIFTON TER
Greenhill Road
West Hill Park
Greenhill Close
West Hill Drive
Greenhill Avenue
West End Close
West End Terrace
Clifton Hill
Hampshire Co Council
HIGH ST
Staple Gardens
JEWRY STREET
St Peter Street
Parchment St
Upper Brook St
ST GEORGE'S ST
Friar
CHILBOLTON AVENUE
Nursery
King Alfred College
B3040
ROMSEY ROAD
Sarum Road
Kerrfield Mws
Sarum Road Hospital
Royal Hampshire Regiment Museum
Cemetery
Archery La
St Swithun St
St Thomas Street
Symonds Street
Dome Alley
Winchester City Museum
Winchester Cathedral
D8
1 Greenhill Ter
2 South Vw
3 Step Ter
E8
1 Gladstone St
2 Newburgh St
3 Tower Rd
4 Upper High St
5 Victoria Rd
F5
1 Manningford Cl
F6
1 Abbey Hill Cl
2 Austen Cl
3 Coram Cl
4 Hussey Cl
F7
1 Gate Hyde
2 King Alfred Ter
3 Rosewarne Ct
F8
1 Cossack La
2 Garden La
3 Merchants Pl
4 Sutton Gdns
1 grid square represents 500 metres

G5
1 Cavendish Gv
G6
1 Green Park Cl
H1
1 Felmer Dr
2 Field End
3 Holdaway Cl
191
216
239
11
KINGS WORTHY
Abbots Worthy
Easton
Winnall
St Giles's Hill
No Man's Land
Kingsworthy Primary School
Princes Mead School
Worthy Park
Hinton House
Lone Barn
Easton Down
Harfield
Larkwhistle Farm
Winnall Down Farm
Wykeham Industrial Estate
Sun Valley Business Park
Easton Lane Business Park
Winnall Fm Industrial Est
Winnall CP School
St Swithuns School
Junction 9
Chesil Theatre
Cemetery
Magdalen Hill Down
M3
A33
A272
B3047
BASINGSTOKE ROAD
WINCHESTER BY-PASS
LONDON ROAD
ALRESFORD ROAD
Itchen Way
Three Castles Path
Long Walk
Easton Lane
Chapel Lane
Fair Lane
Church Lane
Malthouse Cl
Park Lane
King's Way
Loveden Lane
Springvale Road
Nations Hill
Moorside Road
Leicester Way
Longfield Road
Winnall Manor Road
Garbett Road
Imber Road
Shepherds Road
Firmstone Road
Turnpike Down
Northbrook Avenue
Fairdown Cl
Chalk Ridge
Old Station Approach
J8
1 Limetree Wk
2 Spitfire End
J2
1 Old Rectory Gdns
H8
1 Baigent Cl
2 Gatekeeper Cl
3 Longhouse Gn
4 Peacock Pl
5 Ringlet Wy
6 Roundhuts Ri

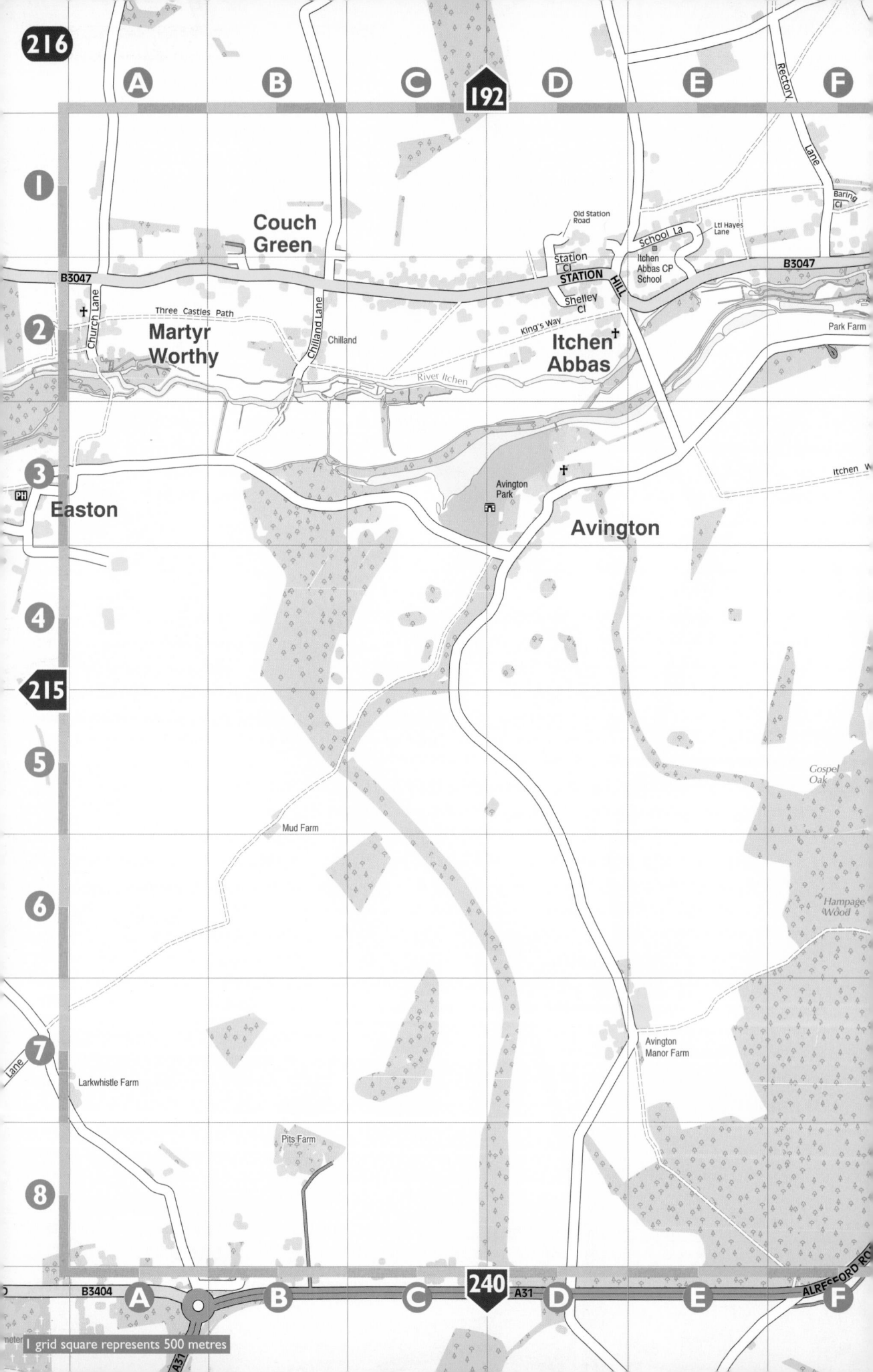

192
A
B
C
D
E
F
1
2
3
4
5
6
7
8
215
240
Couch Green
Martyr Worthy
Easton
PH
Chilland
Chilland Lane
Church Lane
Three Castles Path
B3047
Old Station Road
Station Cl
STATION HILL
Shelley Cl
School La
Ltl Hayes Lane
Itchen Abbas CP School
Itchen Abbas
King's Way
River Itchen
Park Farm
Rectory Lane
Baring Cl
Itchen W
Avington Park
Avington
Mud Farm
Gospel Oak
Hampage Wood
Avington Manor Farm
Larkwhistle Farm
Lane
Pits Farm
B3404
A31
ALRESFORD RO
1 grid square represents 500 metres

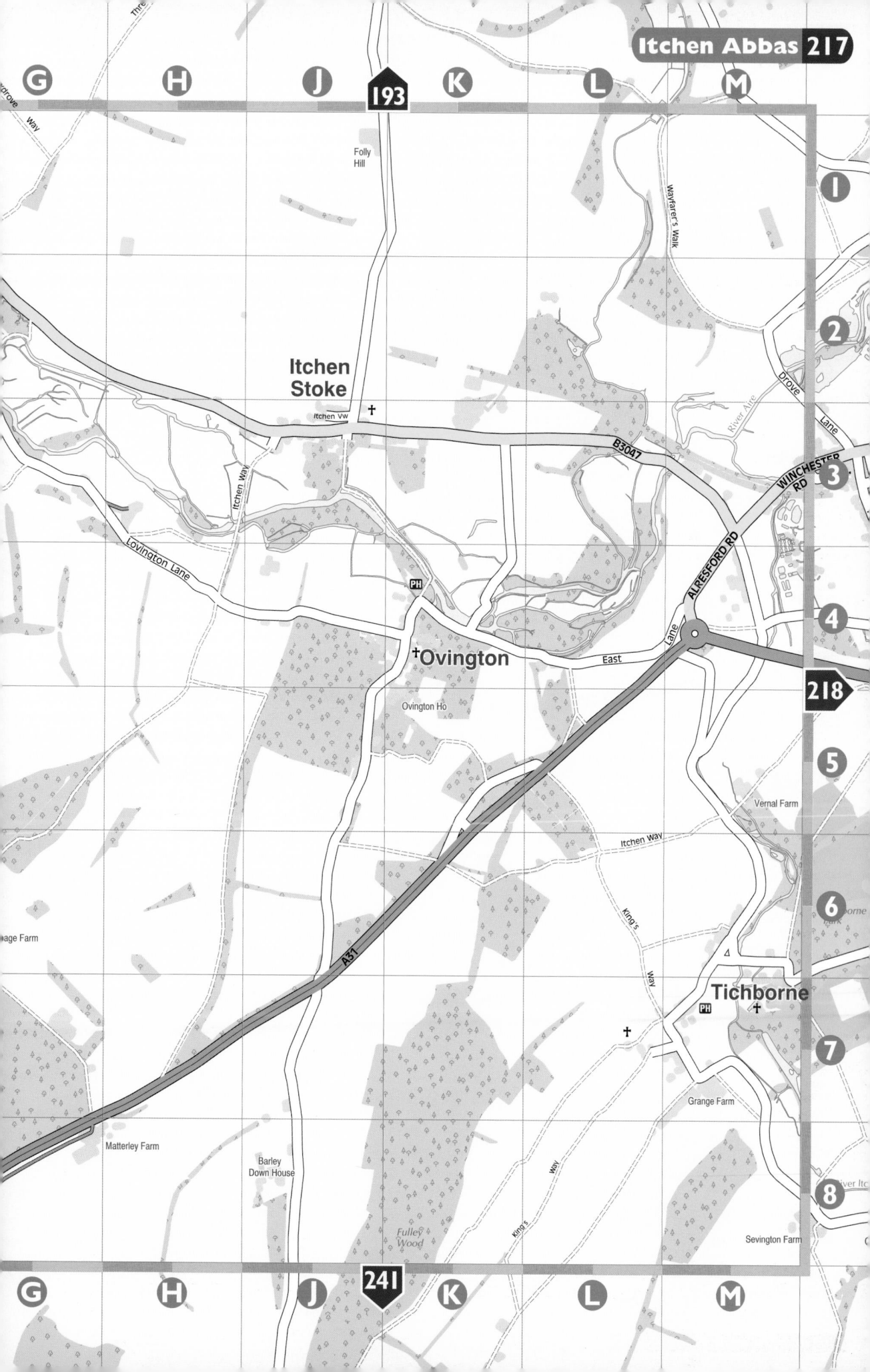
G
H
J
193
K
L
M
Folly Hill
Wayfarer's Walk
Itchen Stoke
Itchen Vw
B3047
Drove Lane
River Aire
WINCHESTER RD
Itchen Way
Lovington Lane
PH
ALRESFORD RD
Lane
Ovington
East
Ovington Ho
218
Vernal Farm
Itchen Way
King's
Way
A31
Tichborne
PH
Grange Farm
Matterley Farm
Barley Down House
King's
Way
Fulley Wood
Sevington Farm
241
1
2
3
4
5
6
7
8

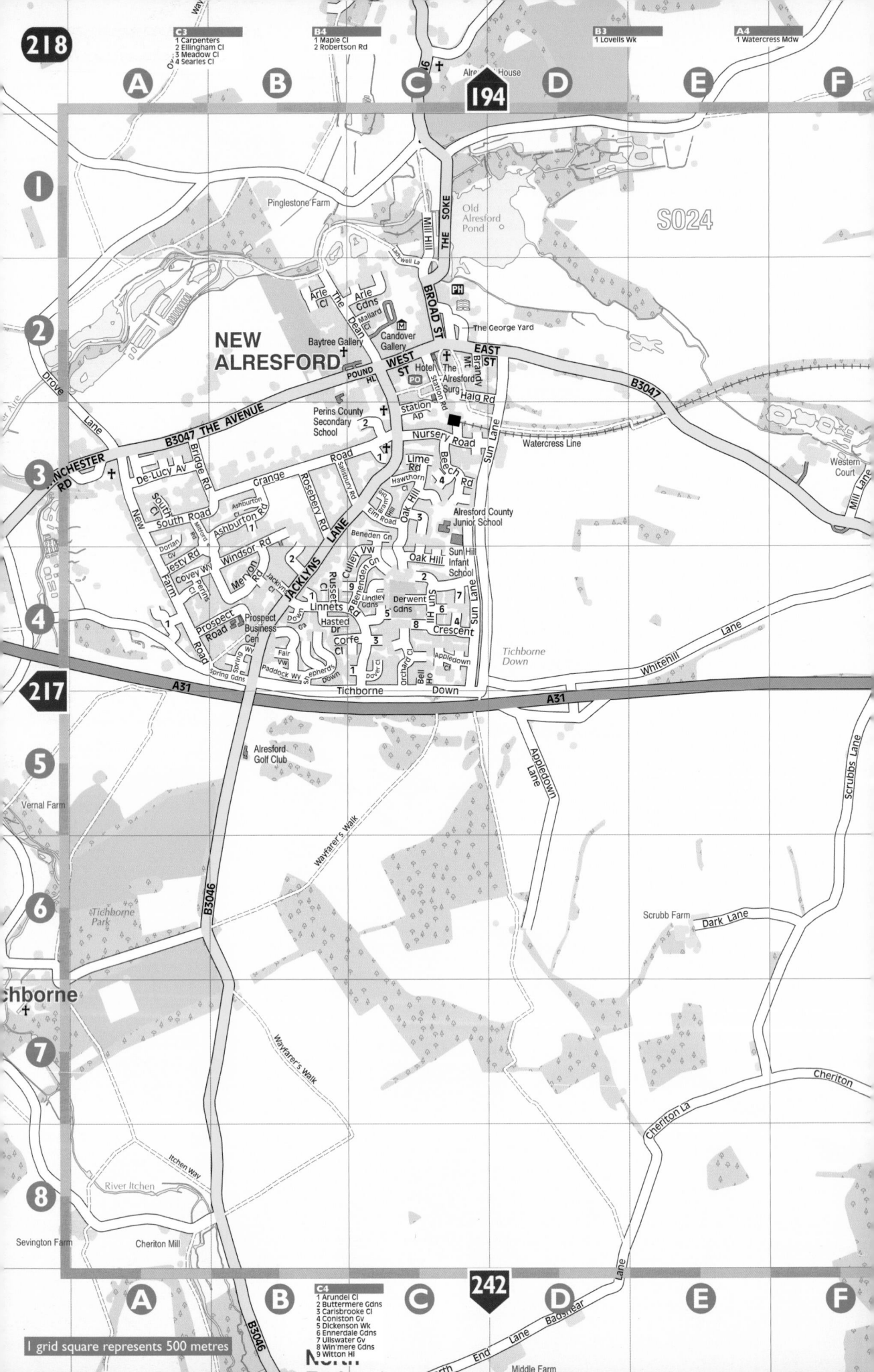

218
C3
1 Carpenters
2 Ellingham Cl
3 Meadow Cl
4 Searles Cl
B4
1 Maple Cl
2 Robertson Rd
B3
1 Lovells Wk
A4
1 Watercress Mdw
194
NEW ALRESFORD
Pinglestone Farm
Old Alresford Pond
SO24
Mill Hill
THE SOKE
BROAD ST
Ladywell La
PH
The George Yard
Arle Cl
The Dean
Arle Gdns
Mallard Cl
Candover Gallery
Baytree Gallery
WEST ST
EAST ST
POUND HL
Hotel
PO
The Alresford Surg
Station Rd
Brandy Mt
Haig Rd
B3047
Station Ap
Perins County Secondary School
Nursery Road
Watercress Line
Sun Lane
B3047 THE AVENUE
Drove Lane
WINCHESTER RD
De-Lucy Av
Bridge Rd
Grange Road
Rosebery Rd
Salisbury Rd
Lime Rd
Beech Rd
Hawthorn Cl
Bramble Hill
Elm Road
Oak Hill
Alresford County Junior School
South Cl
South Road
Ashburton Cl
Ashburton Rd
Mitford Rd
Dorian Gv
Jesty Rd
Windsor Rd
Beneden Gn
Cullev Vw
Sun Hill Infant School
New Farm Road
Covey Wy
Perins Cl
Mervon Rd
Jacklyns Cl
JACKLYNS LANE
Russets Cl
Benenden Gn
Lindley Gdns
Linnets Rd
Derwent Gdns
Sun Hill Crescent
Prospect Road
Prospect Business Cen
Down Ga
Hasted Dr
Corfe Cl
Tichborne Down
Spring Wy
Fair Vw
Paddock Wy
Shepherds Down
Dover Cl
Orchard Cl
Bell Ho
Appledown Cl
Spring Gdns
Tichborne Down
Whitehill Lane
Western Court
Mill Lane
217
A31
Alresford Golf Club
Appledown Lane
Scrubbs Lane
Vernal Farm
Wayfarer's Walk
Tichborne Park
B3046
Scrubb Farm
Dark Lane
Tichborne
Cheriton
Cheriton La
Itchen Way
River Itchen
Sevington Farm
Cheriton Mill
242
C4
1 Arundel Cl
2 Buttermere Gdns
3 Carisbrooke Cl
4 Coniston Gv
5 Dickenson Wk
6 Ennerdale Gdns
7 Ullswater Gv
8 Win'mere Gdns
9 Witton Hl
Badshear Lane
North End Lane
Middle Farm
1 grid square represents 500 metres

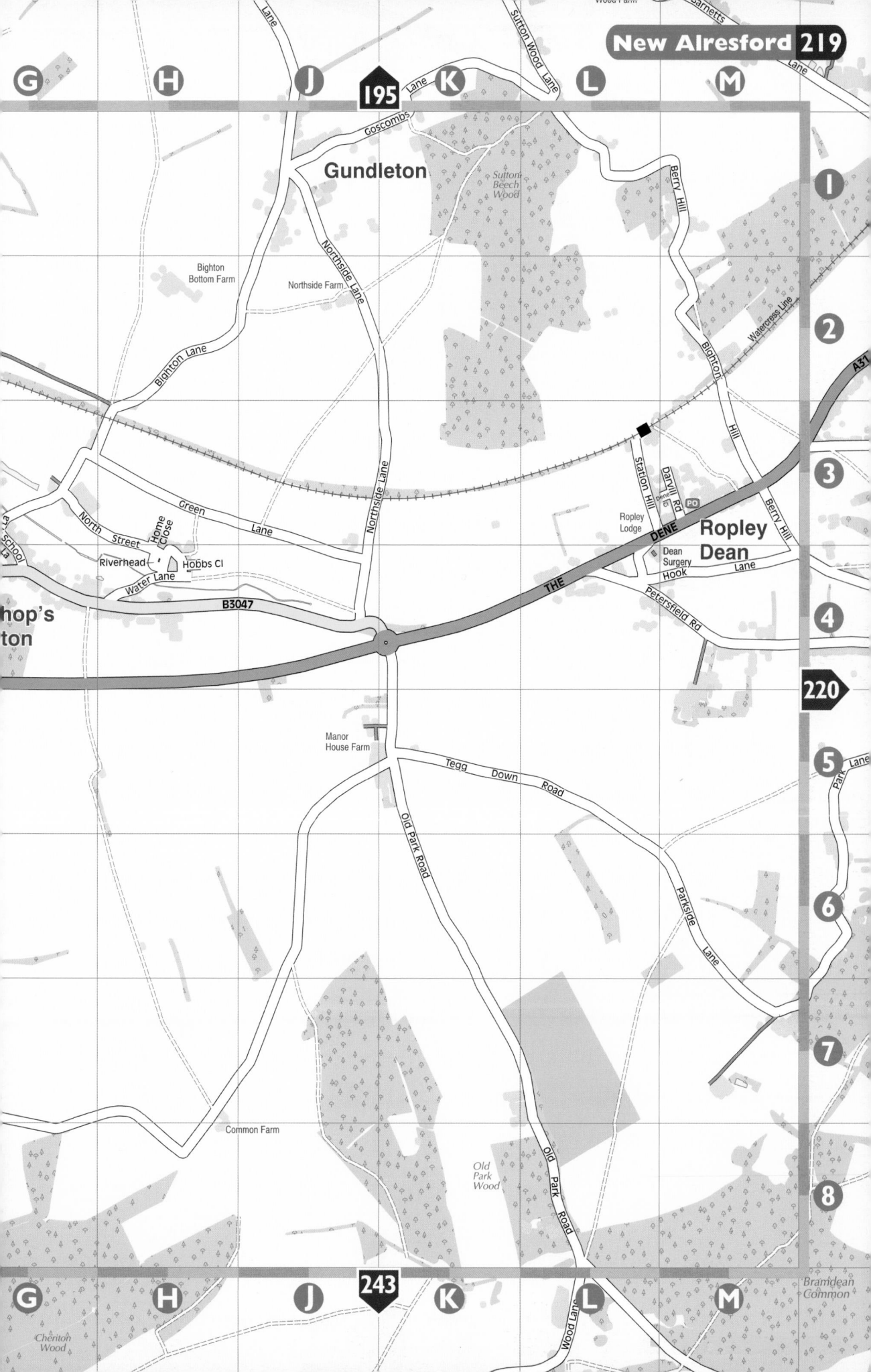

G H J **195** K L M

I

2

A31

Gundleton

Goscombs Lane

Sutton Beech Wood

Berry Hill

Watercress Line

Bighton Bottom Farm

Northside Lane

Northside Farm

Bighton Lane

Bighton Hill

3

Station Hill

Darvill Rd

Dene

PO

Ropley Lodge

Ropley Dean

North Street

School

Home Close

Green Lane

Northside Lane

THE DENE

Dean Surgery

Hook

Lane

Riverhead

Hobbs Cl

Water Lane

hop's ton

B3047

4

Petersfield Rd

220

5

Park Lane

Manor House Farm

Tegg Down Road

Old Park Road

Parkside Lane

6

7

Common Farm

Old Park Wood

Old Park Road

8

Bramdean Common

G H J **243** K L M

Wood Lane

Cheriton Wood

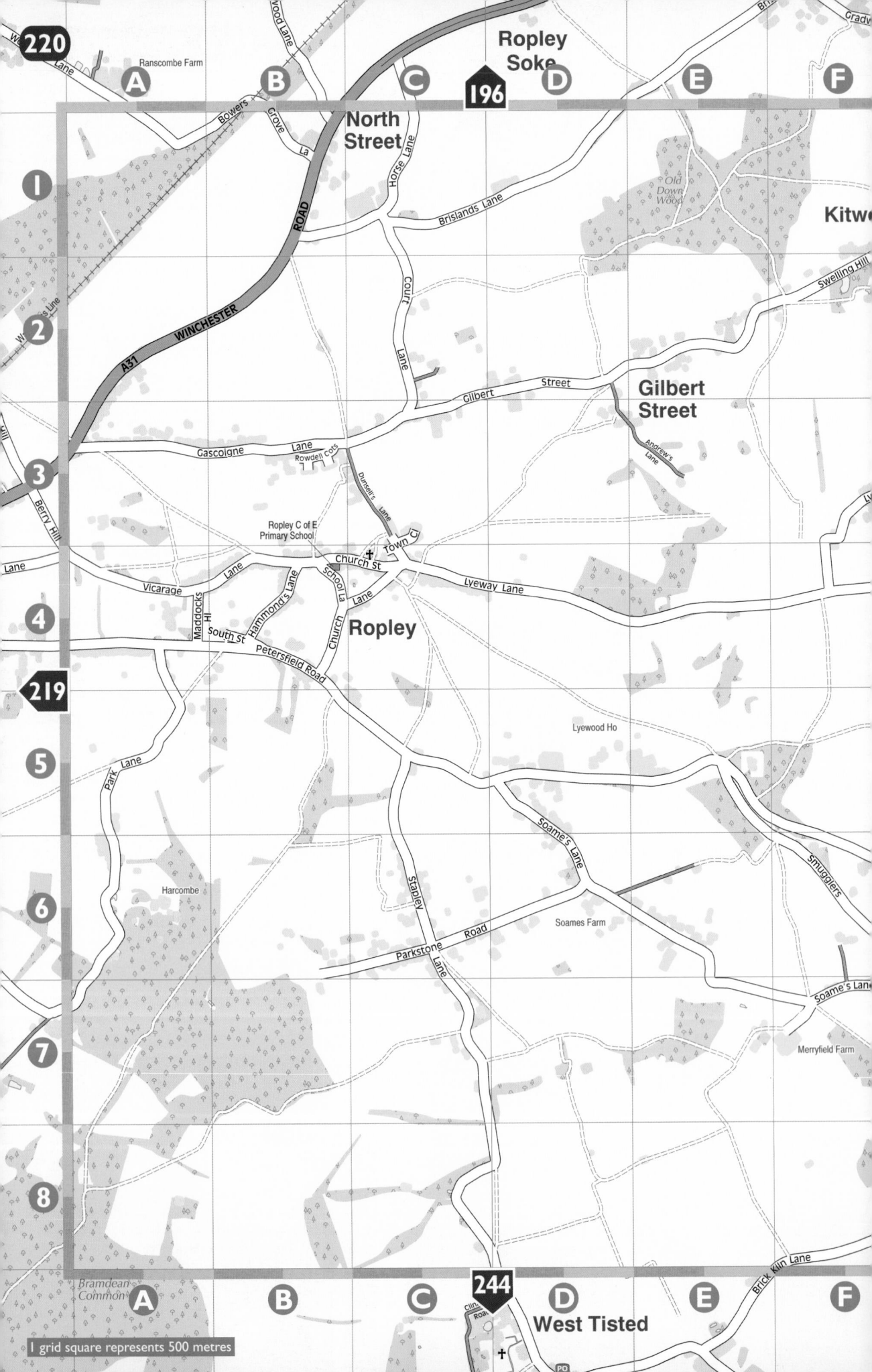
220
196
219
244
Ranscombe Farm
Ropley Soke
North Street
Bowers
Grove La
Horse Lane
Brislands Lane
Old Down Wood
Kitw
Winchester Road
A31
Court Lane
Swelling Hill
Gilbert Street
Gilbert Street
Gascoigne Lane
Rowdell Cots
Andrew's Lane
Dunsell's Lane
Berry Hill
Ropley C of E Primary School
Town Cl
Church St
Vicarage Lane
Lyeway Lane
School La
Hammond's Lane
Maddocks Hl
South St
Church Lane
Ropley
Petersfield Road
Lyewood Ho
Park Lane
Soame's Lane
Smugglers
Stapley Lane
Harcombe
Soames Farm
Parkstone Road
Soame's Lane
Merryfield Farm
Brick Kiln Lane
Bramdean Common
West Tisted
PO
A B C D E F
1 2 3 4 5 6 7 8
1 grid square represents 500 metres

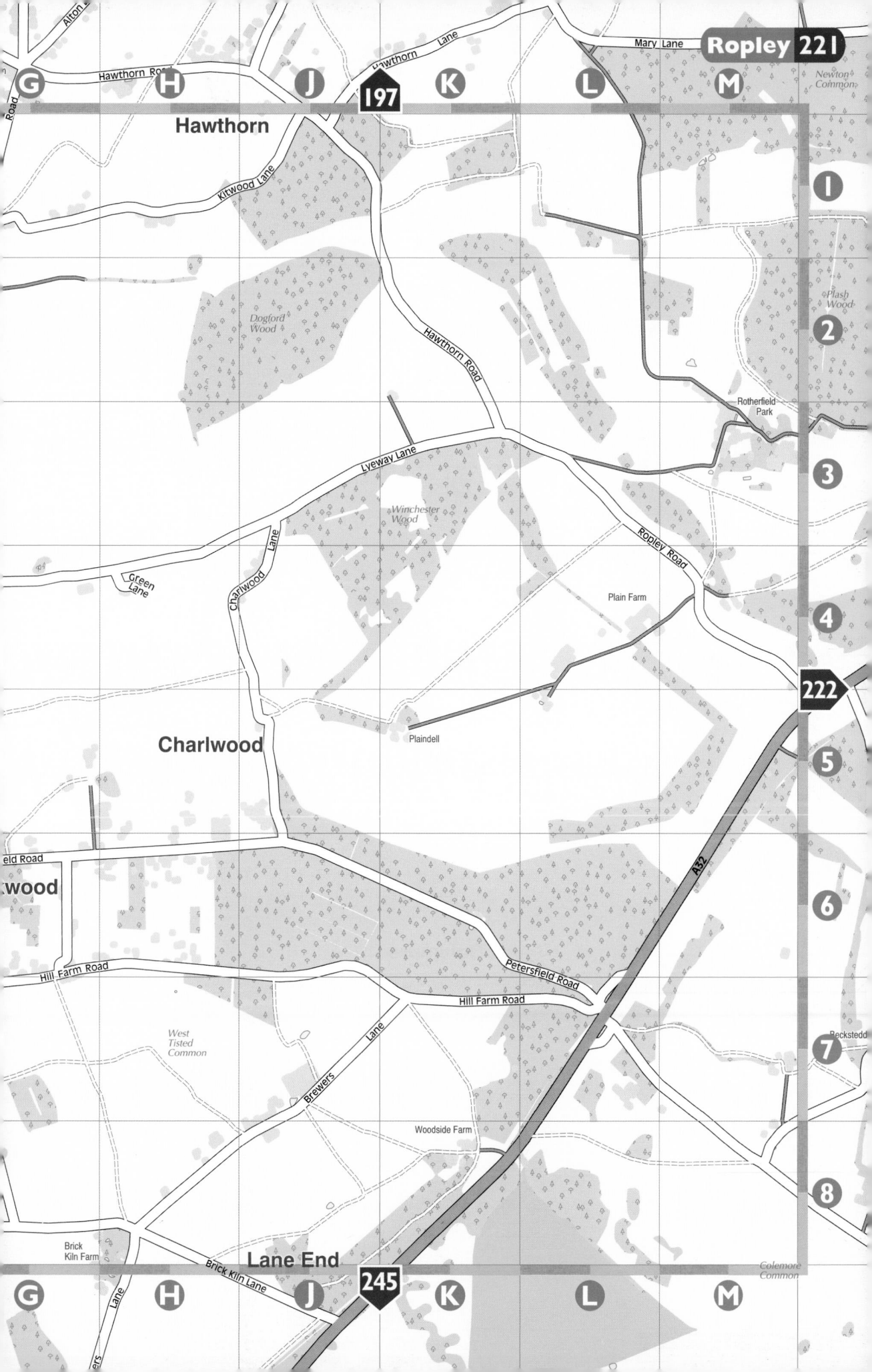

Hawthorn

G H J K L M

197

I

2

3

4

222

5

6

7

8

Newton Common

Plash Wood

Rotherfield Park

Hawthorn Lane

Mary Lane

Hawthorn Road

Kitwood Lane

Dogford Wood

Hawthorn Road

Lyeway Lane

Winchester Wood

Charlwood Lane

Green Lane

Ropley Road

Plain Farm

Charlwood

Plaindell

A32

eld Road

wood

Hill Farm Road

Petersfield Road

Hill Farm Road

Recksteddi

West Tisted Common

Brewers Lane

Woodside Farm

Brick Kiln Farm

Brick Kiln Lane

Lane End

Colemore Common

245

G H J K L M

222

Mary Lane

Newton Lane

Inadown Farm

A **B** **C** 198 **D** **E** **F**

Pelham Place

A32

I

Newton Lane

Shotters Lane

Shotters Farm

Plash Wood

2

Rotherfield Park

Bridle Cl

Old Place Farm

3 A32 East Tisted

PO

Appleton Vw

Heards Farm

4

Goleigh Wood

221

Shell Lane

5

Shell Lane

6

Colemore

Becksteddle Farm

Slade Farm

7

Field Farm

8

Colemore Common

A **B** Herd Farm **C** 246 **D** **E** **F**

I grid square represents 500 metres

G H J K L M

Selborne
Primary
School

Pendulum
Gallery

Selbo **199**

New
Barn Farm

Honey Lane

Cross Lane

Maltby's

PO

Selborne
Hanger

Hangers Way

Ketchers Fld

Sotherington Lane

Burhunt Farm

Longhope

Newton
Valence

Lower Noar
Hill Farm

Hangers Way

Lane

Charity Farm

224

Empshott
Green

Empshott

Churc

Goleigh Farm

Hangers Way

Mill Lane

Lythanger

Button's Lane

Keyham Farm

Vann Farm

Mill Lane

Hawkley
Hurst

Manor House

Eames
Lane

Mill Lane

Lowergreen Farm

Hangers Way

247

Hawkley

Upland
Lane

Hawkley Rd

Scotland Farm

1
2
3
4
5
6
7
8

200

Blackmoor

Temple Manor

Sotherington Lane

Snap Wood

Blackmoor House

Blackmoor Road

St Matthews C Primary Sch

Hunt Farm

Brockbridge Farm

Bradshott Hall

Benhams Lane

Benhams Farm

PO

223

Le Court

Todmore

Hopeswood

Longmoo

Wolm La

Church Lane

Church Lane

Bakers Field

Lythanger

SELBORNE ROAD

Petersfield Road

Greatham Primary School

Greatham

Mill Farm

B3006

Hawkley Hurst

Snailling Lane

Forest Rd

A3(T)

Gre Mo

Goleigh Farm House

B3006

A3(T)

Park Lands Farm

Snailling Lane

248

Forest Road

Forest Corner

GU33

Liss

Scotland Farm

A B C D E F

G   H   J   **201**   K   L   M

I
2
3
4
226
5
6
7
8

Liphook   Road

Hollywater Road

Cranmer
Bottom

Linchborough
Park

Brimstone
Inclosure

Woolmer
Forest

Forkedpond
Inclosure

Woolmer
Pond

Longmoor Road

PORTSMOUTH   ROAD

A3(T)

Queens   Road

Old
& Co

A325

A3(T)

OLMER ROAD

Plumer
Road

Railway Rd

French Rd

Methuen
Rd

Roberts
Rd

Kitchener   Road

Warren
Road

Hunters
Rd

Hamilton
Rd

Longmoor
Camp

Avenue

White

Kimberley Rd

Baden Powell Rd

Union

Paterson
Rd

Pretor
Cl

Jan Smuts Cl

Weaver's
Down

Moor Road

Palmer's
Ball

Longmoor
Inclosure

Sussex Border Path

Fo
M

The
Wylds

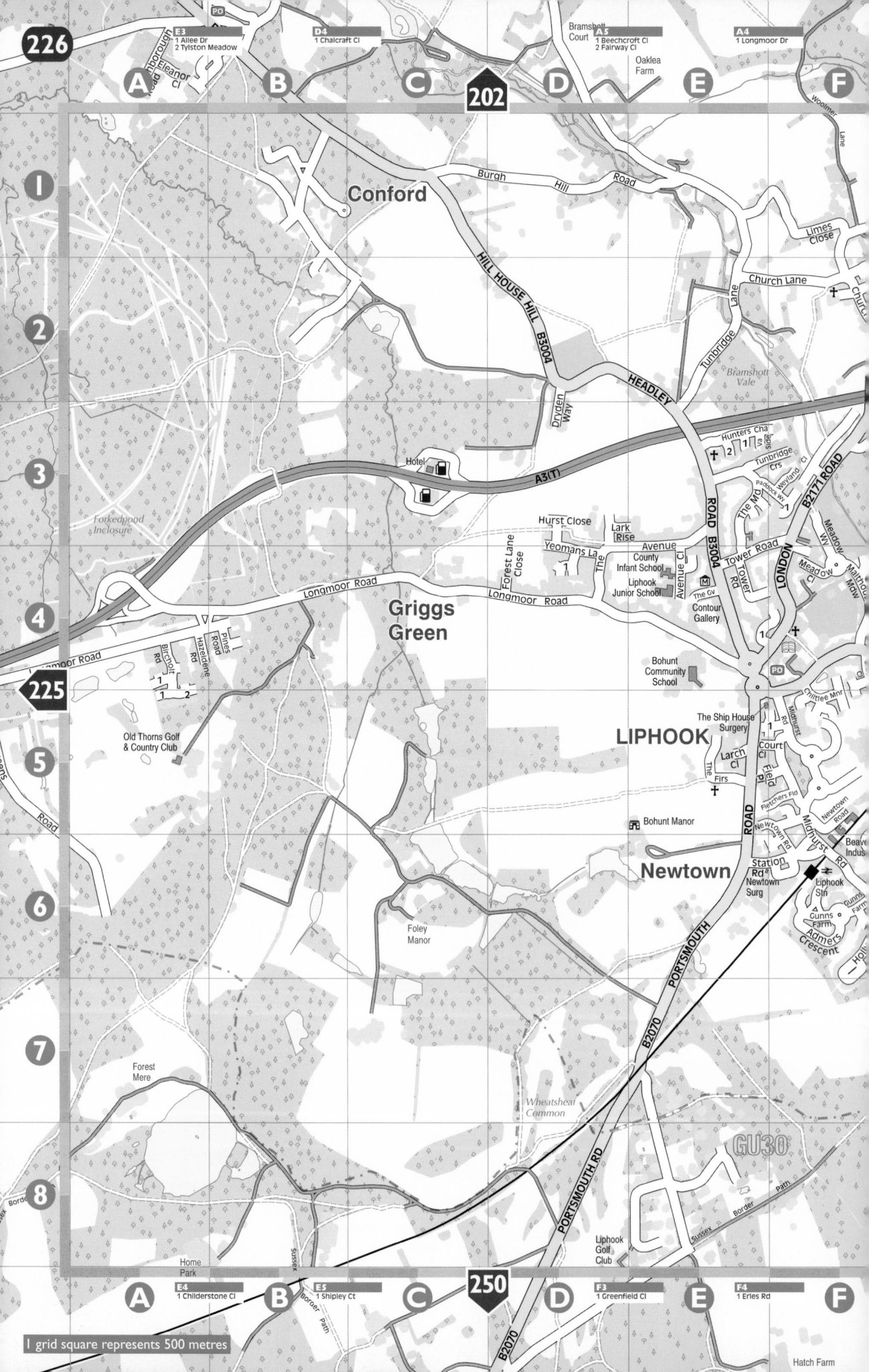
E3
1 Allee Dr
2 Tylston Meadow
D4
1 Chalcraft Cl
A5
1 Beechcroft Cl
2 Fairway Cl
A4
1 Longmoor Dr
202
Bramshott Court
Oaklea Farm
Eleanor Cl
Conford
Burgh Hill Road
Woolmer Lane
Limes Close
Church Lane
Tunbridge Lane
Bramshott Vale
HILL HOUSE HILL B3004
HEADLEY ROAD B3004
Dryden Way
A3(T)
Hotel
Hunters Cha
Tunbridge Crs
Weyland Cl
Paddock Wy
The Md
B2171 ROAD
LONDON
Meadow Wy
Meadow Cl
Forkedpond Inclosure
Hurst Close
Lark Rise
Yeomans La
The Avenue
Forest Lane Close
County Infant School
Liphook Junior School
Avenue Cl
Tower Road
Tower Rd
The Gv
Contour Gallery
Longmoor Road
Griggs Green
Pines Road
Hazeldene Rd
Bircholt Rd
225
Bohunt Community School
Chiltlee Mnr
Old Thorns Golf & Country Club
The Ship House Surgery
LIPHOOK
Larch Cl
Court Cl
Field Pl
The Firs
Midhurst Rd
Fletchers Fld
Newtown Road
Newtown Rd
Bohunt Manor
Station Rd
Newtown
Newtown Surg
Liphook Stn
Gunns Farm
Admers Crescent
Foley Manor
PORTSMOUTH ROAD
B2070
Forest Mere
Wheatsheaf Common
GU30
PORTSMOUTH RD
Sussex Border Path
Liphook Golf Club
Home Park
250
E4
1 Childerstone Cl
E5
1 Shipley Ct
F3
1 Greenfield Cl
F4
1 Erles Rd
Hatch Farm
1 grid square represents 500 metres

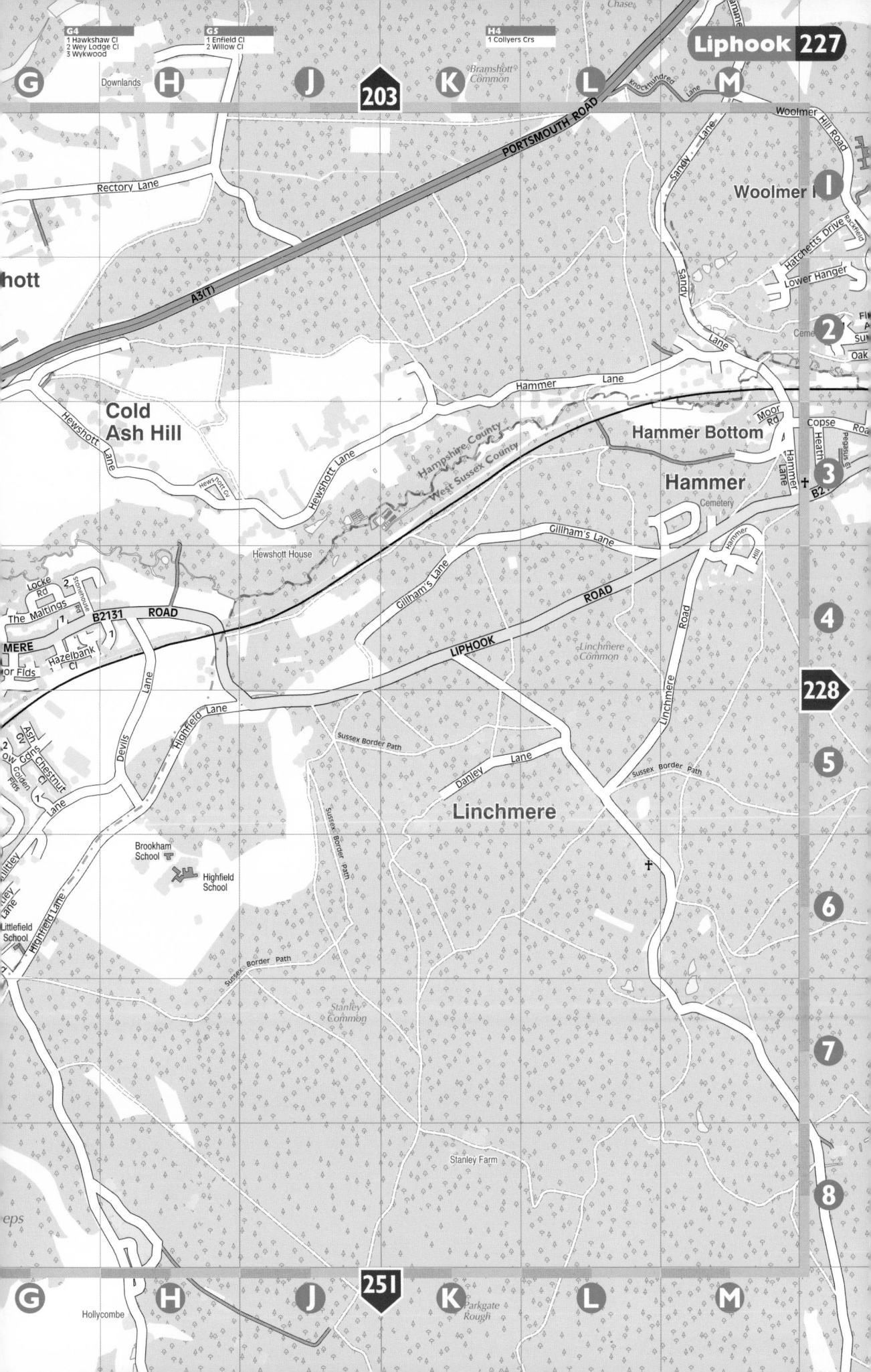
G4
1 Hawkshaw Cl
2 Wey Lodge Cl
3 Wykwood
G5
1 Enfield Cl
2 Willow Cl
H4
1 Collyers Crs
203
Bramshott Common
Downlands
PORTSMOUTH ROAD
A3(T)
Rectory Lane
Woolmer Hill Road
Sandy Lane
Hatchetts Drive
Lower Hanger
Hammer Lane
Cold Ash Hill
Hewshott Lane
Hammer Bottom
Moor Rd
Copse
Heath
Hammer
Cemetery
Hampshire County
West Sussex County
Gillham's Lane
Hewshott House
Locke Rd
Stonehouse Rd
The Maltings
B2131
ROAD
LIPHOOK
Hazelbank Cl
Linchmere Common
Linchmere Road
228
Highfield Lane
Devils Lane
Ash Gv
Chestnut Cl
Sussex Border Path
Danley Lane
Linchmere
Brookham School
Highfield School
Littlefield School
Stanley Common
Stanley Farm
251
Hollycombe
Parkgate Rough

228
C2
1 Cherrimans Orch
2 Timbermill Ct
B2
1 Lucas Fld
2 Mallard Cl
3 Mill Cl
4 Pitfold Cl
A3
1 Hammerwd Cps
2 Puttock Cl
A2
1 Sunvale Cl
204
A
B
C
D
E
F
1
2
3
4
5
6
7
8
227
Woolmer Hill Road
Woolmer Hill School
Woolmer Hill
Hatchetts Drive
Rackfield
Lower Hanger
Woolmer Hill Rd
Critchmere
Critchmere Hill
Holy Cross Hospital
Shottermill County Middle School
Shottermill
Cherry Tree Avenue
Chilcroft Rd
The Woodlands
Avenue
Lion Lane
Underwood Rd
Farnham Lane
Bunch Lane
Dell Close
Weysprings
Weydown Road
Derby Road
St Bartholomews C of E School
Middle School
Church Rd
St Stephens
Tanners La
Bridge Rd
Haslemere Station
Ind Est
Unicorn Trading Est
LOWER ST
B2131
SHEPHERD
Chatsworth Av
High Lane
Bunch Lane
Stoatley Rise
River
The Paddock
Braeside
Greensand Way
Dolphin Cl
Roedeer Copse
Deep Dene
Critchmere Vale
Mnr Cl
Critchmere Lane
Trout Rd
Fox Rd
Buffbeards La
Old Mill Pl
Vicarage La
Priors Wd
Stile Gdns
Vicarage Lane Clinic
HINDHEAD RD
HINDHEAD RD
WEY HILL
Meadow Vale
The Meads
Meadway
Lion Md
PO
Fir Tree Avenue
Sunvale Av
Oak Tree Lane
Border Rd
Pitfold Av
Cemetery
LIPHOOK RD
King's Road
Foundry La
Longdene Road
Courts Mt Rd
Courts Hill Road
Sandrock
Hasle Dr
Hedgehog Lane
Hales
Half Moon Hill
Dene Cl
Park Road
The Herons Swimming and Fitness Centre
Sickle Rd
Sun Brow
The Millstream
Moor Rd
Copse Road
Heath Rd
Pegasus Ct
Hammer Lane
LINCHMERE ROAD
B2131
New Rd
School Rd
Camelsdale County First School
Sturt Av
Moorfield
The Orch
Camelsdale
CAMELSDALE RD
Springfarm Rd
Hillside Rd
Marley Lane
Marley Combe Road
The Old Quarry
Penwith Drive
A287
A286
MIDHURST ROAD
Scotland La
Chiltern Cl
Scotlands Close
Red C
Surrey County
West Sussex County
Bell Vale Lane
Mill Rd
Copse
Green Lane
Green Lane
Sussex Border Path
Valewood Rd
Fernden Lane
Mill Lane
Marley Common
Marley Hanger
BELL ROAD
Marley House
Whitehanger
Cogner Wood
Kingsley Green
Marley Heights
Snipe Lane
Chilcrofts Rd
Chilcroft Lane
HASLEMERE RD
Hatch Lane
Hatch Hill
Hatch La
Square Drive
Hatch Farm Hill
Greenhill Wood
Copyhold
Reeks Wood
Van Common
ROAD
C3
1 Dale Vw
2 Hill Farm Cl
E3
1 Scotlands Dr
F1
1 George Denyer Cl
2 Oaklands
F2
1 Cedar Ct
2 Hollyridge
1 grid square represents 500 metres

205
G
H
J
K
L
M
1
2
3
4
5
6
7
8
1 Cobden La
Highercombe Road
Three Gates Lane
Holdfast Lane
Imbhams Farm
Kemnal Pk
Uplands Cl
HASLEMERE
Holdfast
Furnace Place
Killinghurst Lane
Collards Lane
herd's Hill
Swan Barn Road
PETWORTH ROAD
B2131
Hotel
Ansteadbrook
PETWORTH ROAD
Haste Hill
Haste Hill
Lane
Lythehill House
Tennyson's Lane
Chase Lane
Surrey County
West Sussex County
Home Wood
Sussex Border Path
Tennyson's Lane
Barfold
Jay's Lane
Chase Lane
Tennyson's Lane
Aldworth Ho
Valewood Ho
Sussex Border Path
Roundhurst Farms
Roundhurst Common
Fernden Lane
Black Down
Black Down
Jobson's Lane
Cotchet Farm
280
Blackdown Hill
Abesters
G
H
J
K
L
M

A
B
C
D
E
F
1
2
3
4
5
6
7
8
206
258
Farleys
All Saints
Primary
School
Far
Pitton Road
Parsonage Hill
Church Road
The Street
Oak Cl
Penny's Lane
Lucewood Lane
Ben Lane
Blackmoor Copse
Livery Road
The Livery
Park Lane
Barnridge Copse
Keepers
Grimstead Road
Long Drove
Hawks Grove
East Grimstead
Manor Farm
Road
River Dunn
Dean Road
West Dean Farm
Dean Hill Farm
1 grid square represents 500 metres

207
232
259
G
H
J
K
L
M
1
2
3
4
5
6
7
8
Standing Hill
Home Farm
Dean
Park La
Tyt
The Green
Pug's Hole
Red Lane
Bulls Drove
Howe Copse East
Wiltshire County
Hampshire County
Dean Road
Tytherley Common
Frenchmoor
Drove Farm Ho
Dean Copse
Frenchmoor Lane
Pilgrims Croft
River Dunn
Hill
West Dean
Rectory
Dean Station
Frenchmoor La
Park Farm
Dean Road
Moody's Hill
Hillside Close
Ashmore Lane
East Dean
Glebe Mdw
Deanhill Barn
Gatmore Copse
Mean Wood

Tytherley
232
Stride's Farm
208
Manor Farm
A
B
C
D
E
F
F7
1 Butlers Cl
The Coach Road
The Green
Manor Rd
East Tytherley
Cedars Vw
Pug's Hole
1
2
Drove
Lockerley Hall
Lain Copse
3
Pug's Hole Farm
4
231
Holbury Farm
Holbury
La
Holbury
Lane
5
Holbury Mill
Lockerley Water Farm
River Dunn
River Dun
6
LC
Road
East
Dean
PO
East Dean
Glebe Mdw
Lockerley
7
Lockerley C of E Primary School
Pendle Gn
Lockerley R
Clem's Wy
Cooks Lane
Butlers
Close
Oval Rd
Critchell's Green
Deanhill Barn
8
Cooks Lane
260
Hampshire County
Wiltshire County
Mount
Lane
1 grid square represents 500 metres

G H J K L M

209

Pittleworth

I

2

3

4

234

5

6

7

8

Bentley Farms

B3084

River Test

Back Lane

Spearywell Wood

D

Cadbury Fm

Oakley Fm

Test Way

Spearywell

Oakley Rd

Test Way

Mottisfont Abbey

Mottisfont Abbey Garden House & Estate (NT)

Benger's Lane

Keepers Lane

B3084

Mottisfont Club House

PO

Church Lane

A3057

Hatt Lane

Mottisfont

Church Lane

Hatt Hill

Stonyma

Dunbridge Station

LC

Dunbridge

PH

Russell Dr

Mill Rise

River Dun

Lockerley Road

Canefield

DUNBRIDGE LANE

Kimbridge

Kimbridge Lane

Monarch's Way

Kimbri Lane LC

River Test

Sta

G H J K L M

261

234
210
262
233
A
B
C
D
E
F
1
2
3
4
5
6
7
8
Test Way
ROMSEY ROAD
Compton Park
Compton Manor
Compton
Humbers Wood
Eldon Road
Brook
A3057
Lower Brook
Lower Eldon Fm
Michelmersh Wood
Park Fm
Stubb's Copse
Parnell La
Mesh Road
Church Rd
Monarch's Way
Manor Fm
Stonymarsh
Staff Road
Hackupps Lane
Lane
Michelmersh
Manor Farm
Rudd Lane
PO
Hill View Road
New Road
Chapel La
STOCKBRIDGE ROAD
Mannyngham Way
Timsbury
1 grid square represents 500 metres

G H J K L M

211

I

2

3
Farley Down

Farley F
4

236

5

6

Dore

7
Upper Slackstead

8

Furzedown

Luke Copse

Parnholt Wood

Bailey's Down

Fishponds Fm

Farley Ho

Oakfield

Eldon Road

Hall Place

Furzedown Road

Kings Somborne Road

Pitt Fm

Farley Lane

Monarch's Way

Paynes Hay Road

Braishfield Road

Monarch's Way

Church Lane

Paynes Hay Farm

Ferndon Lane

Lane

Hill

263

G H J K L M **Lower Slackstead**

Braishfield

Dummers

Clarendon Way

Clarendon Way

212

A B C D E F

Farley Mount

Farley Mount
Country Park

Clarendon Way

I

Clarendon Way

Farley Mount Road

2

Mount
Down

3

Farley
Down

4

Farley Fm

Berrydown Farm

South
Lynch

235

✝

Southlynch
Plantn

5

Dores Lane

Dores Lane

6

Gudge
Copse

Merdon Manor Farm

7

ope
ackstead

8

Dores Lane

A B C D E F

264

Home Farm

Claypit

Mon

Hursley

1 grid square represents 500 metres

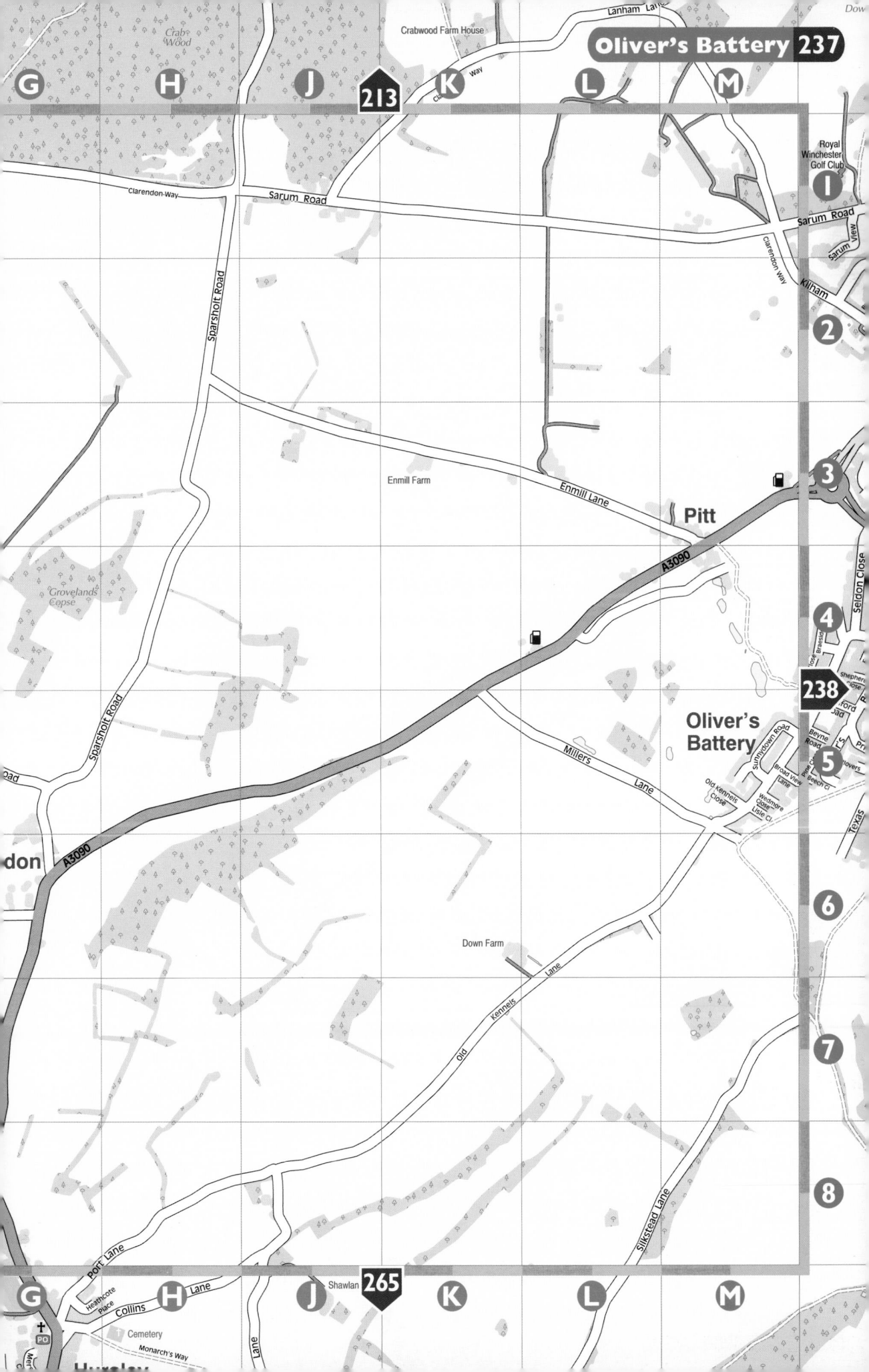
Crab Wood
Crabwood Farm House
Lanham Lane
213
Royal Winchester Golf Club
Clarendon Way
Sarum Road
Sarum Road
Sarum View
Kilham
Sparsholt Road
Enmill Farm
Enmill Lane
Pitt
A3090
Grovelands Copse
Seldon Close
238
Oliver's Battery
Millers Lane
Sunnydown Road
Old Kennels Close
Wedmore Close
Lisle Cl
Broad View Lane
Beyne Road
Texas
Sparsholt Road
A3090
don
Down Farm
Old Kennels Lane
Silkstead Lane
Port Lane
Heathcote Place
Collins Lane
Shawlan
265
Cemetery
Monarch's Way
Lane
G
H
J
K
L
M
1
2
3
4
5
6
7
8

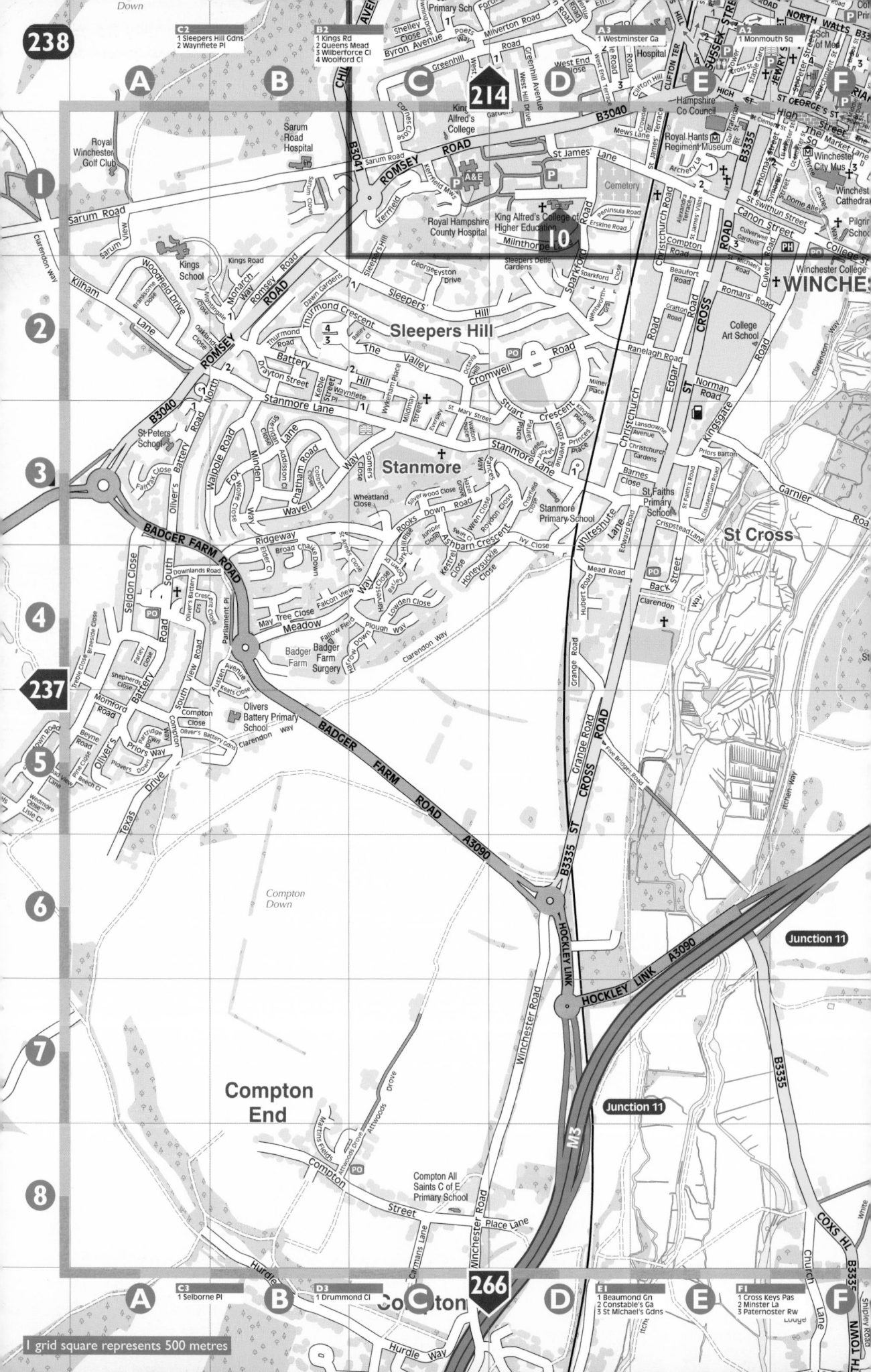
238
C2
1 Sleepers Hill Gdns
2 Waynflete Pl
B2
1 Kings Rd
2 Queens Mead
3 Wilberforce Cl
4 Woolford Cl
A3
1 Westminster Ga
A2
1 Monmouth Sq
A
B
C
D
E
F
214
Royal Winchester Golf Club
Sarum Road Hospital
King Alfred's College
Romsey Road
B3041
B3040
Sarum Road
Royal Hampshire County Hospital
King Alfred's College of Higher Education
St James' Lane
Cemetery
Hampshire Co Council
Royal Hants Regiment Museum
Winchester City Mus
Winchester Cathedral
Winchester College
WINCHESTER
10
Kings School
Kilham Lane
Woodfield Drive
Sleepers Hill
Sleepers' Hill
Thurmond Crescent
The Valley
Battery Hill
Cromwell Road
Stuart Crescent
Stanmore Lane
Stanmore
Stanmore Primary School
Christchurch Road
Edgar Road
St Cross Road
College Art School
Kingsgate
Norman Road
Ranelagh Road
Romans' Road
St Cross
St Faiths Primary School
Garnier Road
St Peters School
Oliver's Battery Road
Badger Farm Road
Ridgeway
Wavell Way
Meadow Way
Badger Farm
Badger Farm Surgery
Olivers Battery Primary School
Clarendon Way
Whiteshute Lane
Grange Road
Back Street
A3090
B3335
Compton Down
Hockley Link
Junction 11
Winchester Road
Compton End
Attwoods Drove
Compton Street
Compton All Saints C of E Primary School
Place Lane
Carmans Lane
Hurdle Way
Itchen Way
Coxs Hl
Church Lane
M3
1
2
3
4
5
6
7
8
237
266
C3
1 Selborne Pl
D3
1 Drummond Cl
E1
1 Beaumond Gn
2 Constable's Ga
3 St Michael's Gdns
F1
1 Cross Keys Pas
2 Minster La
3 Paternoster Rw
Compton
1 grid square represents 500 metres

No Man's Land
St Swithuns School
215
ALRESFORD ROAD B3404
St Giles's Hill
Fairdown Close
Old Station Approach
Chesil Theatre
Northbrook Avenue
Stratton Road
Highmount Cl
Quarry Road
Chalk Ridge
Petersfield Road
Fivefields Road
Gordon Avenue
Primary School
Portal Road
Vale Road
Milland Road
St Catherine's Road
Bar End
BAR END ROAD
CHESIL STREET
MAGDALEN HILL
Winnall CP School
Imber Road
Winnall
Turnpike Down
Shepherds
Firmstone Road
Manor Road
Warren Road
Magdalen Hill Down
Cemetery
PETERSFIELD ROAD
A33
A31
M3
South Downs Way
Chilcomb Lane
Kings Lane
Chilcomb
Junction 10
B3330
Drove
Morestead Road
Twyford Down
240
Fawley Down
Morestead Down
Morestead Farm
ckley Golf Club
New Barn Farm
Hazeley Down
Fawley Lane
Morestead
Hazeley Road
267
G1 1 Bridge St
G2 1 Printstead Cl
H1 1 Palm Hall Cl
G H J K L M
1 2 3 4 5 6 7 8

240

A   B   C   ◆216   D   E   F

D
B3404   A31   ALRESFORD R
Cemetery
I

A31

PETERSFIELD ROAD

Chilcomb
Down

2

A272

King's Way

South Downs Way

3

South Downs Way

Temple
Valley

4

239   King's
                                       Way   A272

5

King's Way

Fawley
Down

6

Longwood
Warren

7

King's Way

Lane

8   Warren

Warren Farm   Old
                                              Down

A   B   C   ◆268   D   E   Honeyman Farm   F
                    Down
1 grid square represents 500 metres   Old

G H J **217** K L M Sevington Farm

1

2

Hill Houses

3

Westfield Farm

4

242

A27

5

Hockley House

6

Rabbit Copse

7

Westfield Drove

Beauworth

8

Barley Down House

Rodfield Lane

Ovington Down Farm

King's Way

South Downs Way

Gander Down

Ganderdown Farm

A272

A272

Holden Lane

Holden Farm

New Warren Farm

South Downs Way

Lane End Down

Hamilton Farm

Lane End

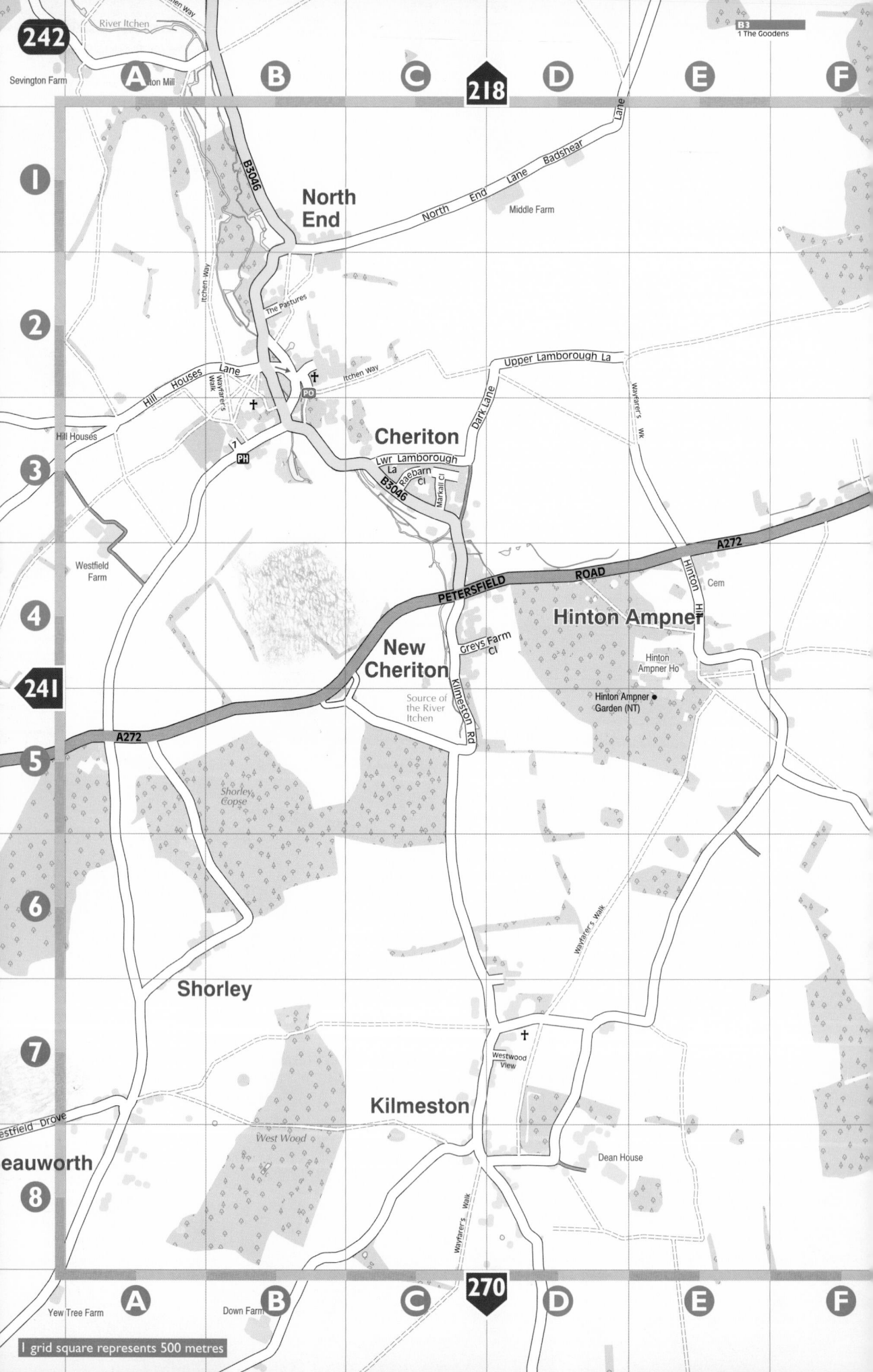

B3
1 The Goodens

A B C **218** D E F

North End

River Itchen

Sevington Farm

Mill

1

B3046

North End Lane

Badshear Lane

Middle Farm

2

The Pastures

Itchen Way

Lane

Hill Houses

Wayfarer's Walk

Itchen Way

PO

Upper Lamborough La

Dark Lane

Wayfarer's Wk

3

Hill Houses

PH

†

Cheriton

Lwr Lamborough La

B3046

Raebarn Cl

Markall Cl

A272

Hinton Hill

Cem

Westfield Farm

PETERSFIELD ROAD

4

Hinton Ampner

New Cheriton

Greys Farm Cl

Hinton Ampner Ho

241

Source of the River Itchen

Kilmeston Rd

Hinton Ampner Garden (NT)

A272

5

Shorley Copse

6

Shorley

Wayfarer's Walk

7

Westwood View

†

Westfield Drove

Kilmeston

Beauworth

8

West Wood

Dean House

Wayfarer's Walk

A B **270** C D E F

Yew Tree Farm Down Farm

1 grid square represents 500 metres

G   H   J   219   K   L   M

1

2

3

Slys Farm

4

244

Hinto Woo

5

The Dean

A272

6

7

8

G   H   J   271   K   L   M

Old Park Wood

Park Road

Bramdean Common

Cheriton Wood

Marriners Farm

Wood Lane

Wood Farm

Bramdean

The Spinney   Wood Lane   Woodlane Close

Church Lane

A272

PH

Woodcote Manor House

Tithelands Lane

Joan's Acre

Brockwood Bottom

Joan's Acre Wood

Brockwood Park

Brockwood Bottom

Black House Farm

Bere Farm

Marldell Farm

244

A　B　C　**220**　D　E　F

I

Bramdean
Common

2

Wolfhanger Farm

3

Slys Farm

243

4

Punsholt Farm

Purser's

Hinton
Woodlands Farm

5

Three Horse
Shoes Farm

6

The
Dean

Kitt's Lane

**West Meon
Woodlands**

Woodlands Farm

7

Shutt's
Copse

West
Meon Hut

8

Highfield

Marlands

A　B　C　**272**　D　E　F

Clinkley
Road

West Tisted

Green La

PO

Punsholt Lane

Brick Kiln Lane

The
Jump

Filmore Hi

Filmorehill Lane

A32

Three Horse Shoes Lane

A272

A272

Vinnells

Hayling
Wood

1 grid square represents 500 metres

G
H
J
K
L
M

Brick Kiln Farm

Lane End

221

Colemore Common

Brick Kiln Lane

I

Brewers Lane

A32

2

Basing Park

Sages Lane

Basing Home Farm

3

Ashen Wood House

Coles

Basing Dean

Fawley Lane

Basing Dean

4

Fawley Farm

Hempland Lane

246

Bailey Green

Farnfield Farm

Hurst Farm

5

rehill Lane

Church Lane

PO

Merepond Lane

Hurst

Stocks Lane

†

6

Privett

Bower Fa

7

A272

8

Pe

G
H
J
K
L
M

273

246
222
245
274
A
B
C
D
E
F
1
2
3
4
5
6
7
8
Field Farm
Colemore Common
Hermitage Farm
PH
Claypitt Lane
Claypit Farm
Barnet Side Lane
Barnet Side
Ragmore Lane
Green Lane
Alexander's Farm
Coles
Basing Dean
King's Lane
Ivyhouse Lane
Blackmore Lane
Ivyhouse Farm
Bensgreen Farm
Hurst Lane
Woolfield Lane
The Slade
High Cross Lane
Week Gree
Privett Road
High Cr
Dellfield
PO
High Cross
Froxfield Endowed Controlled Infant School
Deans Dell
Bower Farm
Bydean Farm
Soalwood Lane
Broadhanger
King Lane
Broad Way
Froxfield Green
Staple Ash Lane
ner's Farm
Ridge Top Lane
1 grid square represents 500 metres

G   H   J   223   K   L   M

I
Scotland Farm

Hawkley
Lowergreen Farm

Eames Lane
Mill Lane

Upland Lane

Pococks Lane

Hawkley Road

2

Cheesecombe Farm Lane

3
Farm

Oakshott Farm

Hangers Way

Oakshott Stream

The Warren

Warren Lane

Cottage Lane

4

Oakshott

Hill Farm

248

Wheatham Farm

5

Lane
Honeycritch

Old Litten Lane

Old Litten Lane

Cold

PH

Cockshott   Lane

6

Hangers   Way

Mill Lane

Bushy Hill

Steep Marsh Farm

Steep Marsh

7

Ashford Chace

Hangers Way

Brickyards Ind Estate

oner Hill

Hangers Way

8

Church Common

Mill Lane

Hangers Way

Steep Farm

Island

Steep

G   H   J   275   K   Church   Steep School   L   M

Stonerwood Park

PH

A3(T)

Farm

F3 1 The Round'bts
F2 1 Beechwood Ct
E4 1 Collard Wy
D3 1 Bishearne Gdns 2 The Green
224
GU33
Scotland Farm
Snailing Lane
Liss Forest
Forest Road
Forest Corner
Briar Wood
Sherwood Close
Newfield Road
Pine
Temple Road
Rotherbank Farm Lane
Forest Rise
Church St
Burgates
B3006
A3(T)
Hawkley Road
FARNHAM ROAD
Kiln Field
Mead Hawks
Barefoots Farm
Lyss Place
West Liss
Liss Business Cen
St Mary's Road
Western Rd
Mainline Business Cen
STATION ROAD
Yorkwood
Riverside Close Surg
Balfour Drive
Riverside Close
Liss Stn
Mill Road
Kelsey Close
Millbrook Cl
Kelseys Doctors Surg
The Oval
Syers Rd
Greenfields
Oak Tree Dr
Middle Meadow
Copse Close
Potters Field
Meadow Wk
Station Rd
Rake Road
Moss Close
Chase Rd
Willow Road
Inwood Rd
Farnham Road
Batt's Brook
Longmead
Linden Dr
Portland Sq
Old School Rd
Rushfield Road
Barnside Way
Road
LISS
Liss County Infant & Junior School
East Hill
East Hill Drive
HILL BROW ROAD
247
Flexcombe
Upper Mt
Nursery Field
Ash
Coldhayes
Andlers
Prince's Marsh
LC
Stodham Lane
Pruetts Lane
Steep Marsh
Steep Marsh Farm
Ind Estate
Bowyer's Common
Stodham Park
Tankerdale Lane
Petersfield Golf Club
Farnham Road
ROAD
276
F4 1 Woodbourne Cl
Upper Adhurst Farm
1 grid square represents 500 metres

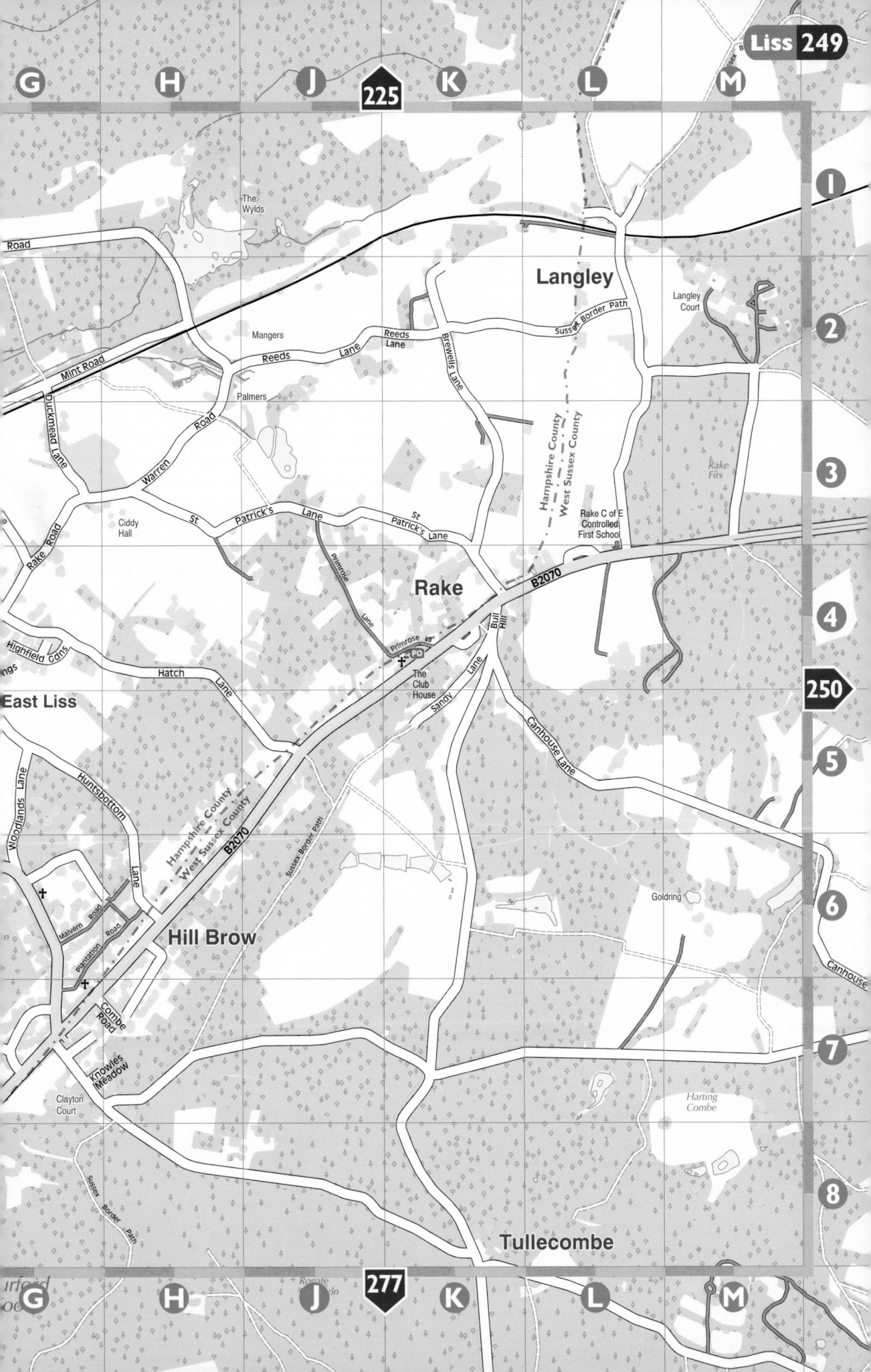

G
H
J
225
K
L
M
1
2
3
4
250
5
6
7
8
277
The Wylds
Road
Langley
Langley Court
Mangers
Reeds Lane
Reeds Lane
Brewells Lane
Sussex Border Path
Mint Road
Palmers
Duckmead Lane
Road
Warren
Hampshire County
West Sussex County
Rake Firs
Ciddy Hall
St Patrick's Lane
St Patrick's Lane
Rake C of E Controlled First School
Rake Road
Primrose Lane
Rake
B2070
Bull Hill
Highfield Gdns
Primrose La
PO
The Club House
Hatch Lane
Sandy Lane
East Liss
Canhouse Lane
Woodlands Lane
Huntsbottom Lane
Hampshire County
West Sussex County
B2070
Sussex Border Path
Goldring
Malvern Road
Plantation Road
Hill Brow
Canhouse
Combe Road
Knowles Meadow
Clayton Court
Harting Combe
Sussex Border Path
Tullecombe
Rogate

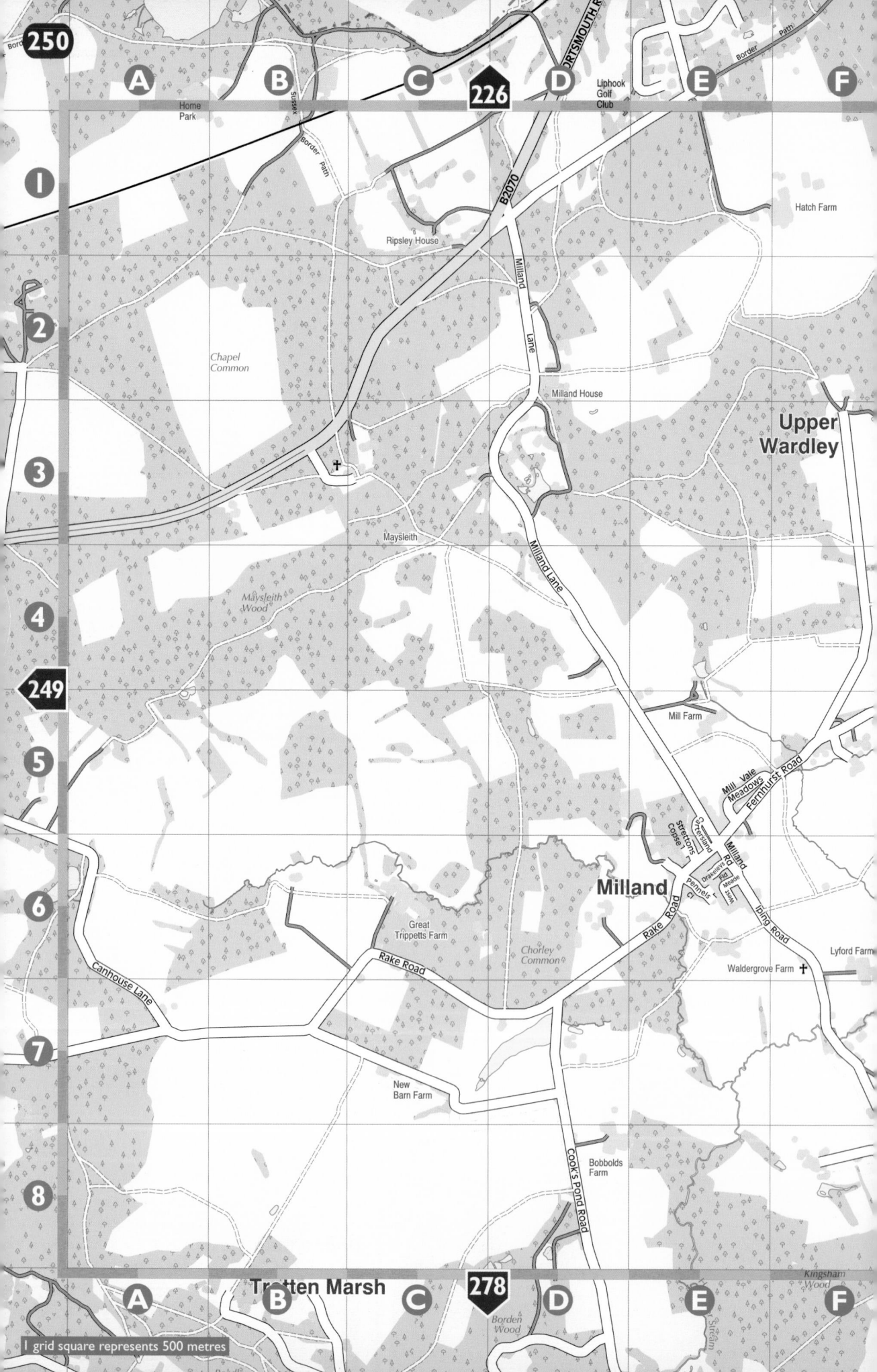

250
226
249
278
A
B
C
D
E
F
1
2
3
4
5
6
7
8
Home Park
Sussex Border Path
B2070
PORTSMOUTH R
Liphook Golf Club
Border Path
Hatch Farm
Ripsley House
Milland Lane
Chapel Common
Milland House
Upper Wardley
Maysleith
Maysleith Wood
Milland Lane
Mill Farm
Mill Vale Meadows
Fernhurst Road
Strettons Copse
Milland Rd
Drakeleys Fld
Meade
Pennels Cl
Milland
Rake Road
Iping Road
Great Trippetts Farm
Chorley Common
Lyford Farm
Waldergrove Farm
Rake Road
Canhouse Lane
New Barn Farm
Bobbolds Farm
Cook's Pond Road
Trotten Marsh
Borden Wood
Kingsham Wood
1 grid square represents 500 metres

G H J 227 K L M

I
2
3
4
5
6
7
8

Stanley Farm

Hollycombe

Parkgate
Rough

Home
Farm

Minepit
Copse

Elmers
Marsh

Elmers
Copse

Northend Farm

Upper North
Park Farm

Woodmansgreen

Lambourne Lane

Inholms
Copse

Redford

Lambourne Lane

PO

Woolbeding
Common

Hurst
Farm

Titty Hill

Queen's
Corner

Linch Road

Linch Road

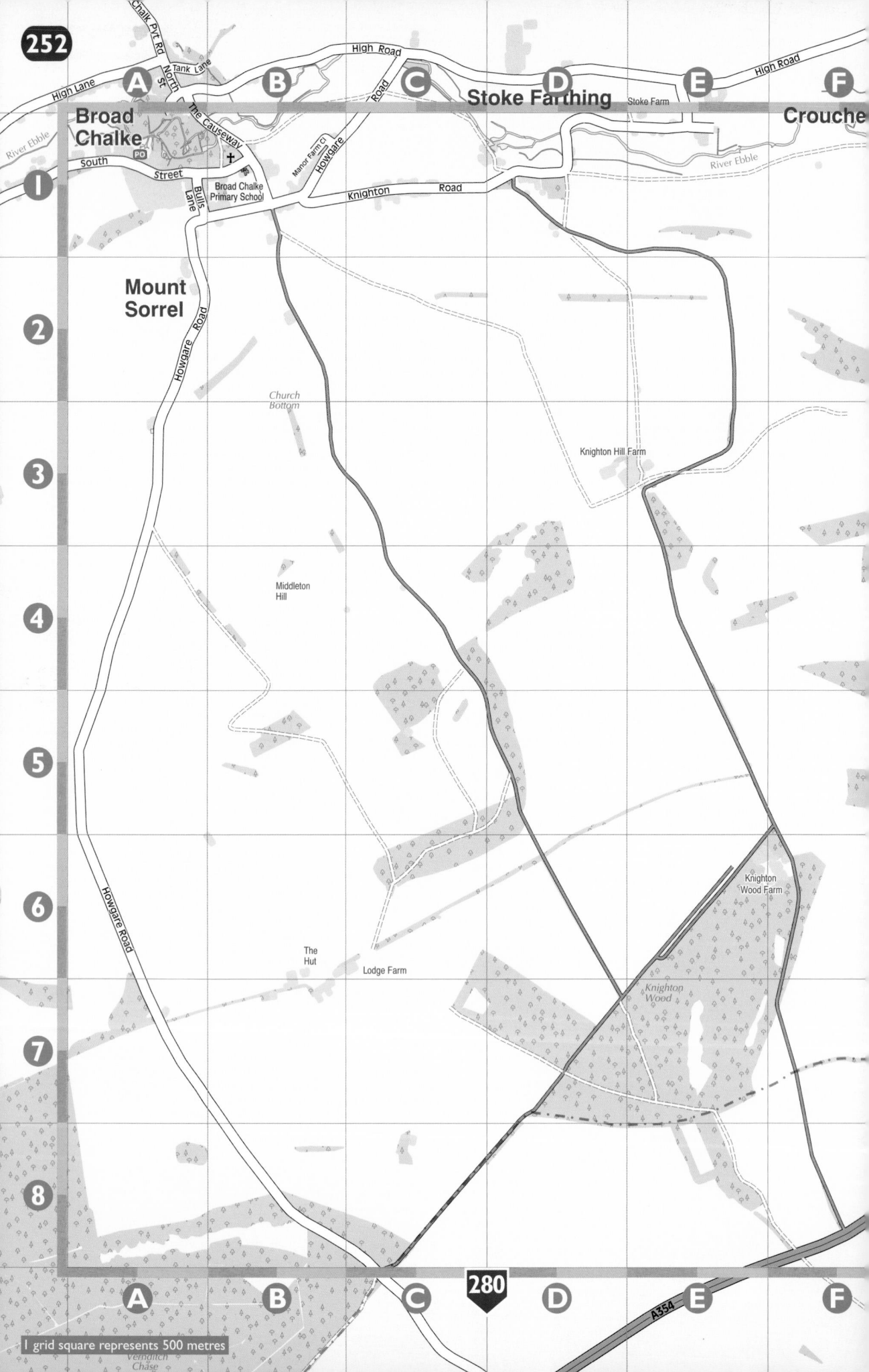

Broad Chalke

Mount
Sorrel

*Church
Bottom*

Knighton Hill Farm

Middleton
Hill

Stoke Farthing

Stoke Farm

Crouche

River Ebble

River Ebble

High Lane

High Road

High Road

High Road

Chalk Pvt Rd

Tank Lane

North St

The Causeway

Manor Farm Cl

Howgare Road

Howgare Road

South Street

Bulls Lane

Broad Chalke Primary School

Knighton Road

PO

Knighton Wood Farm

Knighton Wood

The Hut

Lodge Farm

Howgare Road

A354

Vernditch Chase

1 grid square represents 500 metres

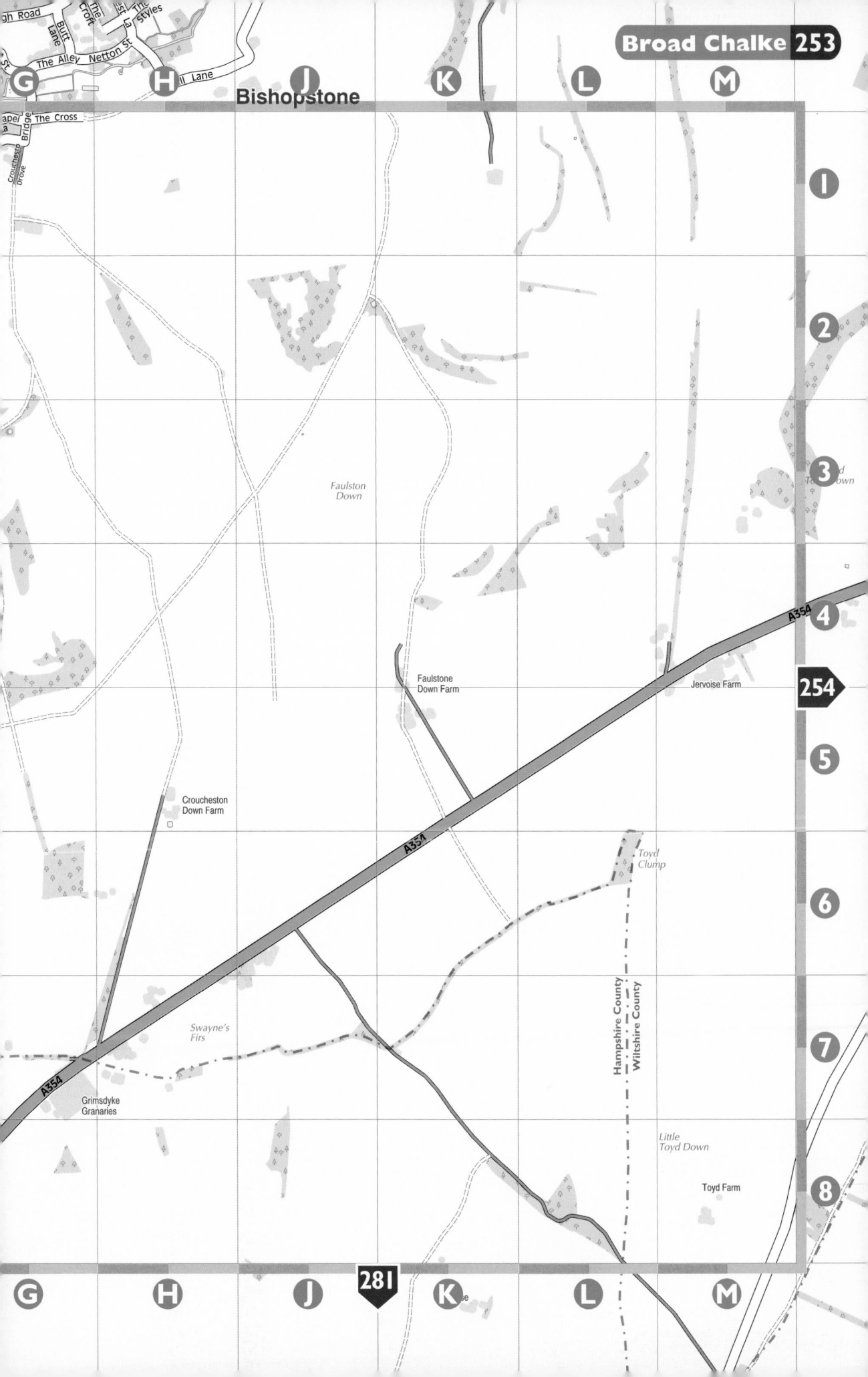

G H Hill Lane J Bishopstone K L M

The Croft
Butt Lane
Netton St
The Alley
High Road
The Styles
Chapel Bridge
The Cross
Croucheston Drove

I

2

3 d
   Down

Faulston
Down

A354 4

Faulstone
Down Farm

Jervoise Farm 254

Croucheston
Down Farm 5

A354

Toyd
Clump

6

A354

Swayne's
Firs 7

A354

Grimsdyke
Granaries

Hampshire County
Wiltshire County

Little
Toyd Down

Toyd Farm 8

A   B   C   D   E   F

BLANDFORD

1

A354

2

Coombe Bissett Down

Homington
Down

3

Stratford
Tony Down

Dow

Southdown Farm

4

A354

Pennings Farm

SP5

Greenacres Farm

Great
Yews

5

Grims
Lodge Farm

Wiltshire County
Hampshire County

6

Black
Hill

Round
Clump

7

8

arm

Tenantry Farm

Whitsbury Down

A   B   C   D   E   F

Rockbourne
Down

1 grid square represents 500 metres

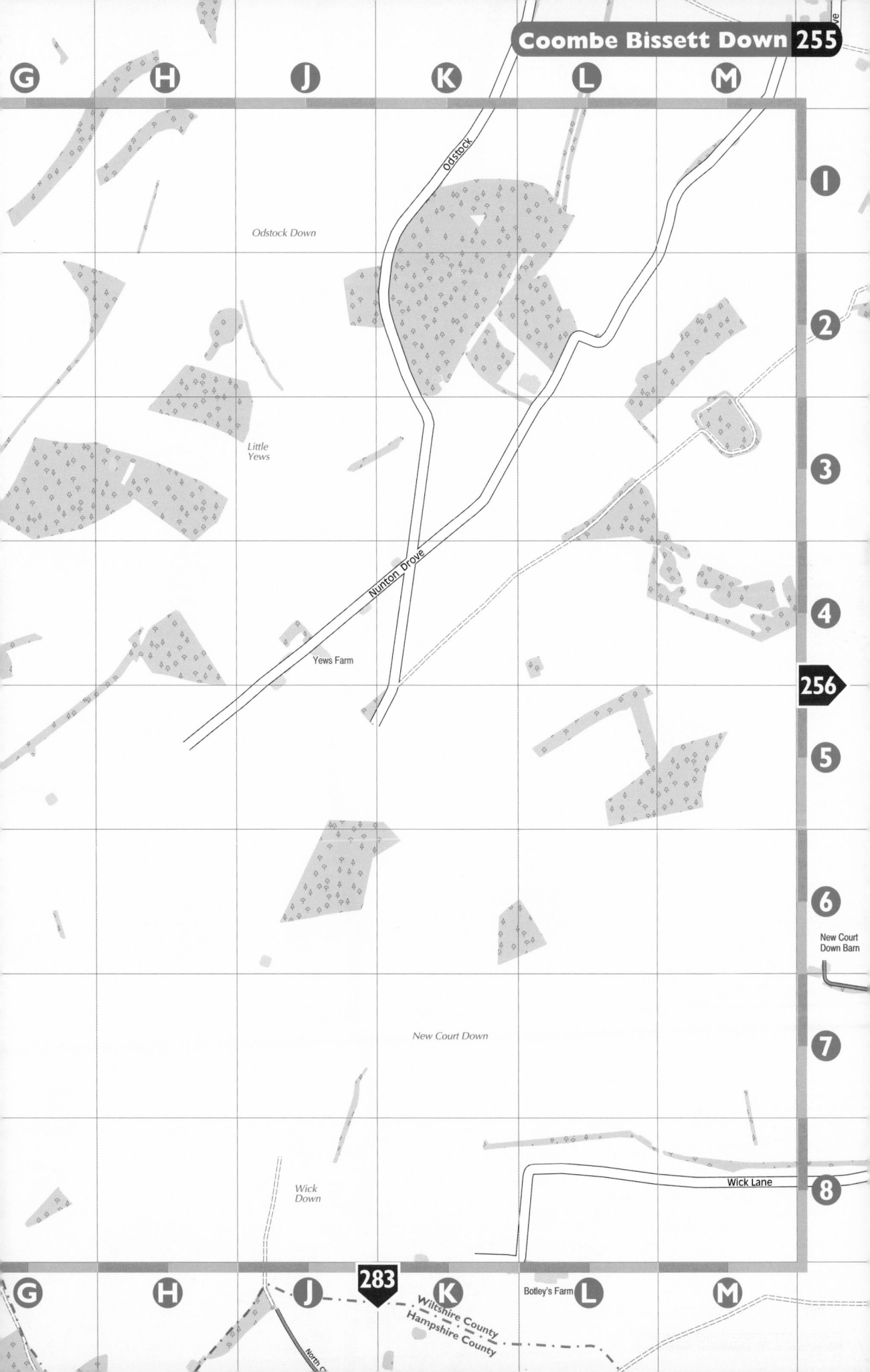

G H J K L M

I

2

3

4

256

5

6

New Court
Down Barn

7

8

Odstock Down

Odstock

Little
Yews

Nunton Drove

Yews Farm

New Court Down

Wick Lane

Wick
Down

283

G H J K L M

Botley's Farm

Wiltshire County
Hampshire County

North C

256
255
284
A
B
C
D
E
F
1
2
3
4
5
6
7
8
F8
1 Church Hatch
Drove
A338
Avon Valley Path
River Avon
Matrimony Farm
Witherington Farm
THE HIGHWAY
Charlton Manor Farm
Church Lane
Chapel La
Lower Rd
Charlton-All-Saints
Warrens Lane
Fish Farm
The Giant's Grave
Barford Park Farm
New Court Down Barn
The Giant's Chair
SALISBURY ROAD
New Court Farm
Downton Industrial Estate
Batten Rd
David Hart Business Centre
Gravel Close
Barford Lane
Wick Lane
Long West Close
Long Cl
Downton C of E Primary School
THE BOROUGH
B3080
Wick
Mesh Pond
Greenacres
Borough
South La
Marie Av
Joanna Cl
Catherine Crescent
Downton County Secondary School
The Surgery
Moot Lane
Saxonhurst
PO
1 grid square represents 500 metres

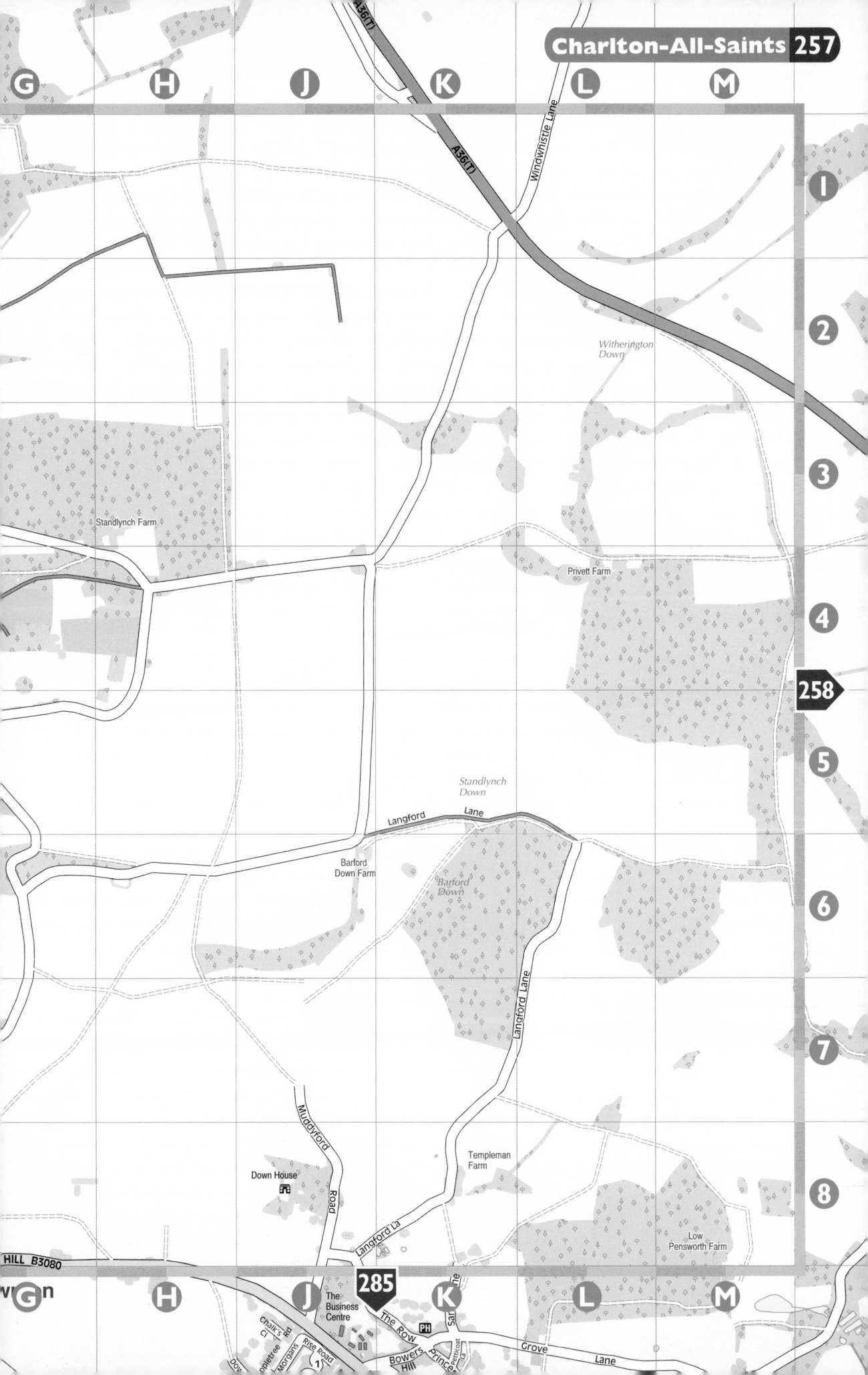
G
H
J
K
L
M
1
2
3
4
5
6
7
8
A36(T)
Windwhistle Lane
Witherington Down
Standlynch Farm
Privett Farm
258
Standlynch Down
Langford Lane
Barford Down Farm
Barford Down
Langford Lane
Muddyford Road
Templeman Farm
Down House
Langford La
Low Pensworth Farm
HILL B3080
285
The Business Centre
The Row
PH
Chalk's Cl
Rise Road
Morgans
Bowers Hill
Grove Lane

258

A   B   C   230   D   E   F

I

2

3   A36(T)   Brickworth La   Brickworth Ho   Whelpley Farm

4   A27   BRICKWORTH   Whit
257   ROAD   A27   TH
   Newton Close   Doves La

5   Newton Lane

6   Lowdens Copse   Newton   Moor Lane   A36(T)

7   Newton Lane   Glazier's Copse

8   Titchborne Farm   East Copse

A   B   C   286   D   E   F

Bagfield Copse

I grid square represents 500 metres

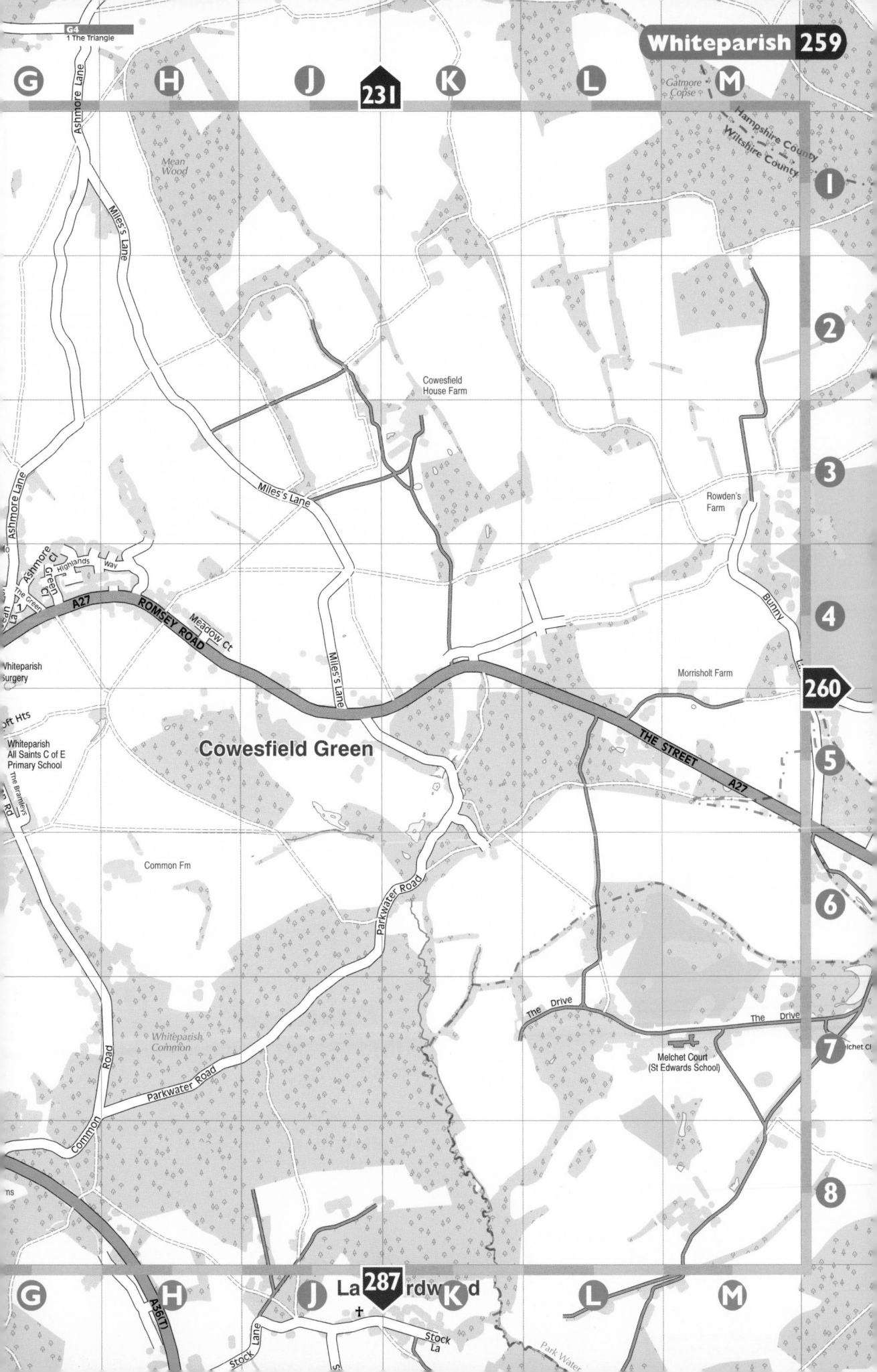

G4
1 The Triangle

G H J **231** K L M

I

2

3

4

260

5

6

7

8

Mean
Wood

Cowesfield
House Farm

Miles's Lane

Ashmore Lane

Gatmore
Copse

Hampshire County
Wiltshire County

Rowden's
Farm

Bunny La

Ashmore Cl
Ashmore
Green Cl
Highlands
Way
The Green

A27
ROMSEY ROAD
Meadow Ct

Miles's Lane

Whiteparish
Surgery

oft Hts

Whiteparish
All Saints C of E
Primary School

The Bramleys

n Rd

Cowesfield Green

Morrisholt Farm

THE STREET
A27

Common Fm

Parkwater Road

Whiteparish
Common

Road

Common

Parkwater Road

The Drive

The Drive

Melchet Court
(St Edwards School)

Melchet Cl

Park Water

ns

G H **287** rdw K d
La

A36(T)

Stock Lane

stock
La

Park Water

J L M

Green
A
B
C
232
D
E
F
Hampshire County
Wiltshire County
Cooks La
Mount
Lane
Painshill Farm
Chapel
Lane
Chapel Farm
Gambledown
Lane
Gambledown Farm
Doctor's Hill
Bryce's Farm
259
Lane
A27
Church La
Pound Lane
Manor Farm
Lane
Branches
Warren Farm
Lane
Graemar
The Drive
PO
Eastwood
THE STREET
A27
PH
The Drive
Melchet Close
Sole Hill Farm
Sherfield English
Graemar
Lane
Ford
Wellow Wood
Mill Lane
Dandy's
Dandy's Ford
Wellow Wood Road
Plaitford Green
Road
Wellow
Drove
Lane
288
Stepl-
English
1
2
3
4
5
6
7
8
I grid square represents 500 metres

G H J K L M

233

Kimbridge

DUNBRI

Monarch's Way

LC

River Test

I

2

Mount Fm

3

Hyde Fm

Awbridge Ho

LANE

Saunders Lane

Test Way

B3084

Canefield

Lockerley Road

Kents Oak

Carter's

Clay Road

Awbridge County School

Danes Road

Awbridge

4

262

STANBRI

Cooks Lane

ewtown

The Square

Upper Ratley

Church Lane

Lower Ratley

Coombe Lane

5

South En

Awbridge Danes

Dunwood Manor Golf Club

6

Dunwood Manor

Danes Road

SALISBURY ROAD

The Frenches

Old Salisbury Lane

Test Way

7

Ro

Frenches Lane

Shootash

Stanbridge Ranvilles Fm

Squabb Wood

8

Tanners Lane

A27

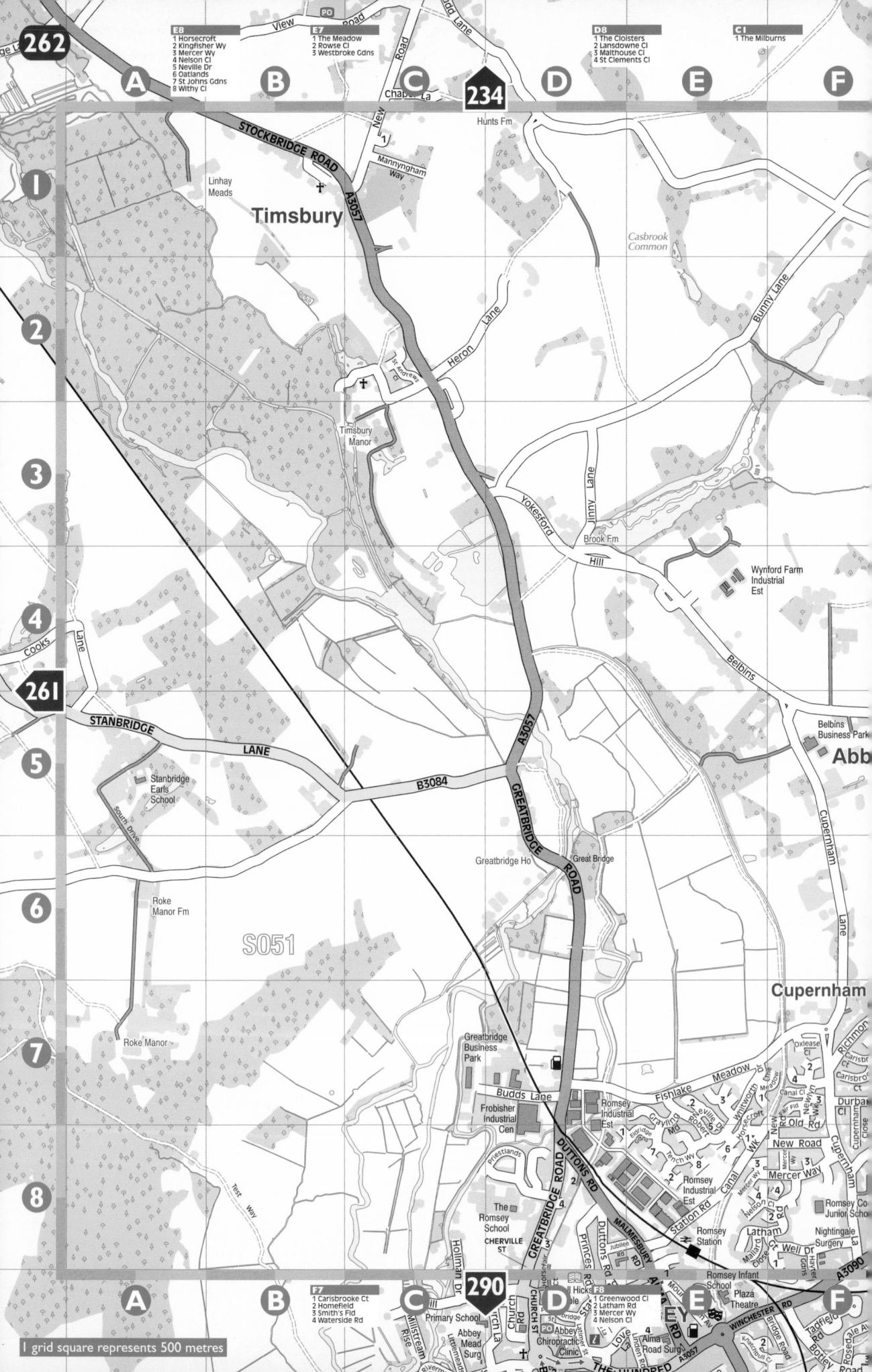

Timsbury

Linhay
Meads

STOCKBRIDGE ROAD

A3057

Mannyngham
Way

New Road

Chapel La

234

Hunts Fm

E8
1 Horsecroft
2 Kingfisher Wy
3 Mercer Wy
4 Nelson Cl
5 Neville Dr
6 Oatlands
7 St Johns Gdns
8 Withy Cl

E7
1 The Meadow
2 Rowse Cl
3 Westbroke Gdns

D8
1 The Cloisters
2 Lansdowne Cl
3 Malthouse Cl
4 St Clements Cl

C1
1 The Milburns

Casbrook
Common

Bunny Lane

Heron Lane

St Andrews Cl

Timsbury
Manor

Yokesford Hill

Jinny Lane

Brook Fm

Wynford Farm
Industrial
Est

Belbins

Cooks Lane

261

STANBRIDGE LANE

B3084

Stanbridge
Earls
School

A3057

GREATBRIDGE ROAD

Belbins
Business Park

Abb

South Drive

S051

Greatbridge Ho

Great Bridge

Cupernham

Roke
Manor Fm

Roke Manor

Test Way

Greatbridge
Business
Park

Budds Lane

Frobisher
Industrial
Cen

DUTTONS RD

Fishlake Meadow

Oxlease

Richmond

Romsey
Industrial
Est

Grayling Rd

Neville Rd

Robert

Whitworth

Horsecroft

New Rd

Carisbt

Carisbro

Durbar
Cl

Priestlands

The
Romsey
School

Tench Wy

New Road

Mercer Way

Romsey Co
Junior School

CHERVILLE
ST

GREATBRIDGE ROAD

DUTTONS RD

MALMESBURY

Duttons Rd

Princes Rd

Jubilee

Romsey
Industrial
Est

Station Rd

Canal

Nelson Rd

Mercer Wy

Latham
Rd

Nightingale
Surgery

Romsey
Station

Well Dr

Romsey Infant
School

F7
1 Carisbrooke Ct
2 Homefield
3 Smith's Fld
4 Waterside Rd

F8
1 Greenwood Cl
2 Latham Rd
3 Mercer Wy
4 Nelson Cl

Primary School

Abbey
Mead
Surg

Millstream Rise

Hollman Dr

Church La

Church St

Abbey
Chiropractic
Clinic

PO

THE HUNDRED

WINCHESTER RD

Plaza
Theatre

Alma
Road Surg

A3090

Botley Road

Tadfield Rd

A3057

1 grid square represents 500 metres

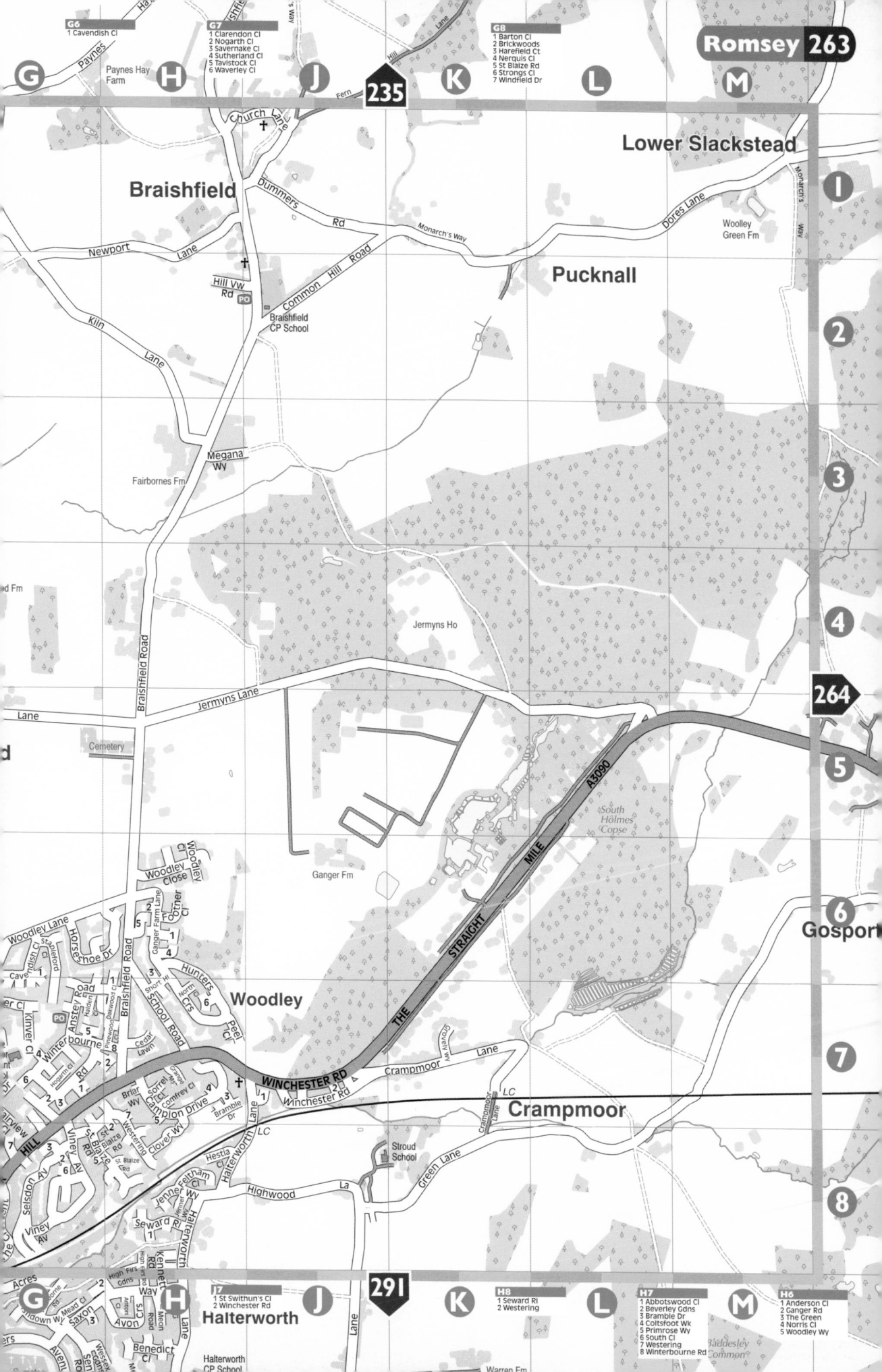

Lower Slackstead

Braishfield

Pucknall

Woolley
Green Fm

Monarch's Way

Dores Lane

Newport   Lane

Monarch's Way

Dummers   Rd

Church Lane

Hill Vw
Rd   PO

Braishfield
CP School

Common Hill Road

Fern

235

264

Kiln

Lane

Megana
Wy

Fairbornes Fm

Jermyns Ho

Braishfield Road

Jermyns Lane

Lane

Cemetery

South
Hölmes
Copse

A3090

MILE

Woodley
Close

THE

STRAIGHT

Woodley Lane

Horseshoe Dr

Ganger Fm

Ganger Farm Lane

Corner
Cl

Hunters
Cl

North
Cls

Woodley Road

Braishfield Road

School Road

Peel
Cl

Woodley

6

Gosport

Crampmoor

WINCHESTER RD

Winchester Rd

LC

Crampmoor Lane

LC

Crampmoor

Green Lane

Briar
Wy

Campion Drive

Sorrel
Cl

Comfrey Cl

Bramble
Dr

Winchester Rd

Stroud
School

HILL

Viney
Rd

St Blaize
Rd

Clover Wy

Westering

Hestia

Feltham Wy

Jenner Wy

Halterworth Lane

LC

Highwood

La

Seward Rl

Selsdon
Av

St Blaize
Rd

Viney
Av

Kennett Rd

High Firs Gdns

Seward Rd

Green Lane

Halterworth

Halterworth
CP School

Warren Fm

Baddesley
Common

G6
1 Cavendish Cl

G7
1 Clarendon Cl
2 Nogarth Cl
3 Savernake Cl
4 Sutherland Cl
5 Tavistock Cl
6 Waverley Cl

G8
1 Barton Cl
2 Brickwoods
3 Harefield Ct
4 Nerquis Cl
5 St Blaize Rd
6 Strongs Cl
7 Windfield Dr

G H J K L M

H
1 St Swithun's Cl
2 Winchester Rd

H8
1 Seward Rl
2 Westering

H7
1 Abbotswood Cl
2 Beverley Gdns
3 Bramble Dr
4 Coltsfoot Wk
5 Primrose Wy
6 South Cl
7 Westering
8 Winterbourne Rd

H6
1 Anderson Cl
2 Ganger Rd
3 The Green
4 Norris Cl
5 Woodley Wy

Paynes Hay
Farm

Paynes

1 2 3 4 5 6 7 8

A　B　C　236　D　E　F

1

2

3

236

Home Farm

Hursley

Monarch's Way

Claypit Road

Ampfield Wood

Monarch's Way

Knapp Lane

Knapp

Monarch's Way

Ratlake Lane

4

263

Ampfield Primary School

Knapp Lane

Ampfield

A3090

Green Pond Lane

Ratlake

Potters Heron Lane

Potters Heron Close

Hotel

Hook Road

Hawstead Farm

Monks Brook

5

Broadgate

Gosport

Pound Lane

Woodlea Way

Hookwood Lane

Hook Close

Hook Crescent

Beechwood Close

6

7

Pound Lane

Flexford Close

Baddesley

Flexford

Merrick Way

Bay Drive

Parry Close

Kielder Close

Crescent

Crummock Road

8

A　B　Bucket Corner　C　292　D　Flexford Road　E　F

Knightwood Road

Merrick Way

Bellflower Way

Glendowan Road

Knightwood Primary School

Bowland Rise

G6
1 Clevelands Cl
2 Rothville Pl
3 Tithewood Cl

G7
1 Albury Pl
2 Apsley Pl
3 Chillington Gdns
4 Lauriston Dr
5 Stratfield Dr
6 The Tanyards
7 Vanburgh Wy

G8
1 Balmoral Cl
2 Barford Cl
3 Drummond Wy
4 Polesden Cl

G H J 237 K L M

1

2

3 Four Dell Farm

4

266

5

6 Otterbourne Primary School

7 Junction 12

8

Hursley

Bunstead

Silkstead

Ladwell

Field House

Hocombe

Hiltingbury

Chandler's Ford

Freemantles Copse

Cranbury House

Home Farm

Cranbury Park

Keble Memorial Primary School

Hiltingbury County Junior & Infant School

Leigh House Hospital

Sherborne House School

Thornden School

Wessex Nuffield Hospital

Pitmore School

Port Lane
Heathcote Place
Collins Lane
Cemetery
Monarch's Way
Poles Lane
Bunstead Lane
Shawlands Farm
Silkstead Lane
Shepherds Lane
Poles Lane

A3090
B3043
HURSLEY ROAD
B3043

M3
A335
A335
ALLBROOK WAY
Otterbourne Hill
Boyatt Lane
Lincolns Rise
Pitmore Close

Hocombe Road
Hocombe Park Close
Ashdown Close
Charnwood Cl
Charnwood Crs
Ashdown Road
Maytree Road
Heathfield Road
Randall Road
Woodlands Close
Hocombe Road
Coultas Road
Hazel Close
Sycamore Avenue
Hiltingbury Road
Nichol Road
Gordon Road
Queen's Road
Lakewood Road
Malcolm Road
Western Road
Sherwood Road
Marlborough Road
Kingsway
Thornbury The Glade
Grosvenor Rd
Hiltingbury Road
Winchester Road
Pine Road
Beech Road
Lake Road
Linden Grove
Cuckoo Bushes Lane
Common Road
Oakwood Road
Lakewood Close
Merdon
Kingsway
Westwood

Millers Dale Surgery

S053

293 Merdon Junior School

Woodhill Prep School

Scantabout Primary School

Brownhill

G H J 293 K L M

H6
1 Charnwood Gdns

238
265
294
A
B
C
D
E
F
1
2
3
4
5
6
7
8
F2 1 St Mary's Ter
F1 1 Franklin Rd 2 Penton Rd
B5 1 Meadowcroft Cl
Compton All Saints C of E Primary School
Compton
Shawford
Shawford Station
Shawford House
Twyford Lodge
Doctors Surgery
Twyford C of E Primary School
South Down
Southdown School
Shepherds Down School
Otterbourne
Otterbourne Primary School
Richmond Park
Twyford Moors
River Itchen
Itchen Way
Brambridge House
The Itchen Navigation
Twyford Surgery
Colden Common Primary School
Brambridge
Highbridge
Hurdle Way
Clease Way
The Spinney
Field Close
Field Way
Cliff Way
Shepherds Lane
Monarch's Way
Otterbourne Road
Tilden Rd
Highways Road
Fairfield Road
Southdown Road
Cross Way
Grove Road
Poles Lane
Copse Close
Sparrowgrove
Waterworks Road
Regent Close
Norlands Drive
Bourne Close
Oakwood Close
Oakwood Avenue
Greenacres Drive
Old Parsonage Ct
Brooklyn
Cranbourne Drive
Coles Mede
Cranbury Close
Main Road
Kiln Lane
Hill
Otterbourne Hill
Boyatt Lane
Chapel Lane
Park Lane
Lincolns Rise
Pitmore Close
Pitmore Road
Boyatt Crescent
A335
ALLBROOK WAY
M3
Berry Lane
Old Rectory Lane
Church Lane
NORTH TOWN
B3335
Shipley Road
SEARLES HILL
Churchfields Road
The Crs
The Av
Finch's Lane
School Road
Hill Rise
Highfield
Highfield Av
Roman Road
HIGH ST
Queen Street
Segars Lane
The Drove
Drove Close
Brewers Lane
Manor Rd
Manor Farm Green
Hare Lane
Woodland
HIGHBRIDGE ROAD
B3354
MAIN ROAD
Fleming Pl
Moors Road
Orchard Close
New Road
Moors Close
Lower Moors
Spring Lane
Frampton Close
Chestnut Avenue
Springfields Close
Spring La
Hill La
Upper Moors Road
St Vigor Way
Ash Close
Hazel Cl
Boyes Lane
Upr Moors Rd
Oak Tree Cl
Pellet Close
Burr Close
Brickmakers Road
Setters Close
Whitebeam Close
Alder Close
Lime Close
Vear's Lane
Aspen
Hawthorn Close
Pennington Close
Grays Close
Piping Road
Piping Close
Hack Drive
Valley Close
Church Lane
Church Lane
Ward
Lordswood
Knowle
Crook
Junction 12
Boyatt Lane
Otterbourne
Farm
1 grid square represents 500 metres

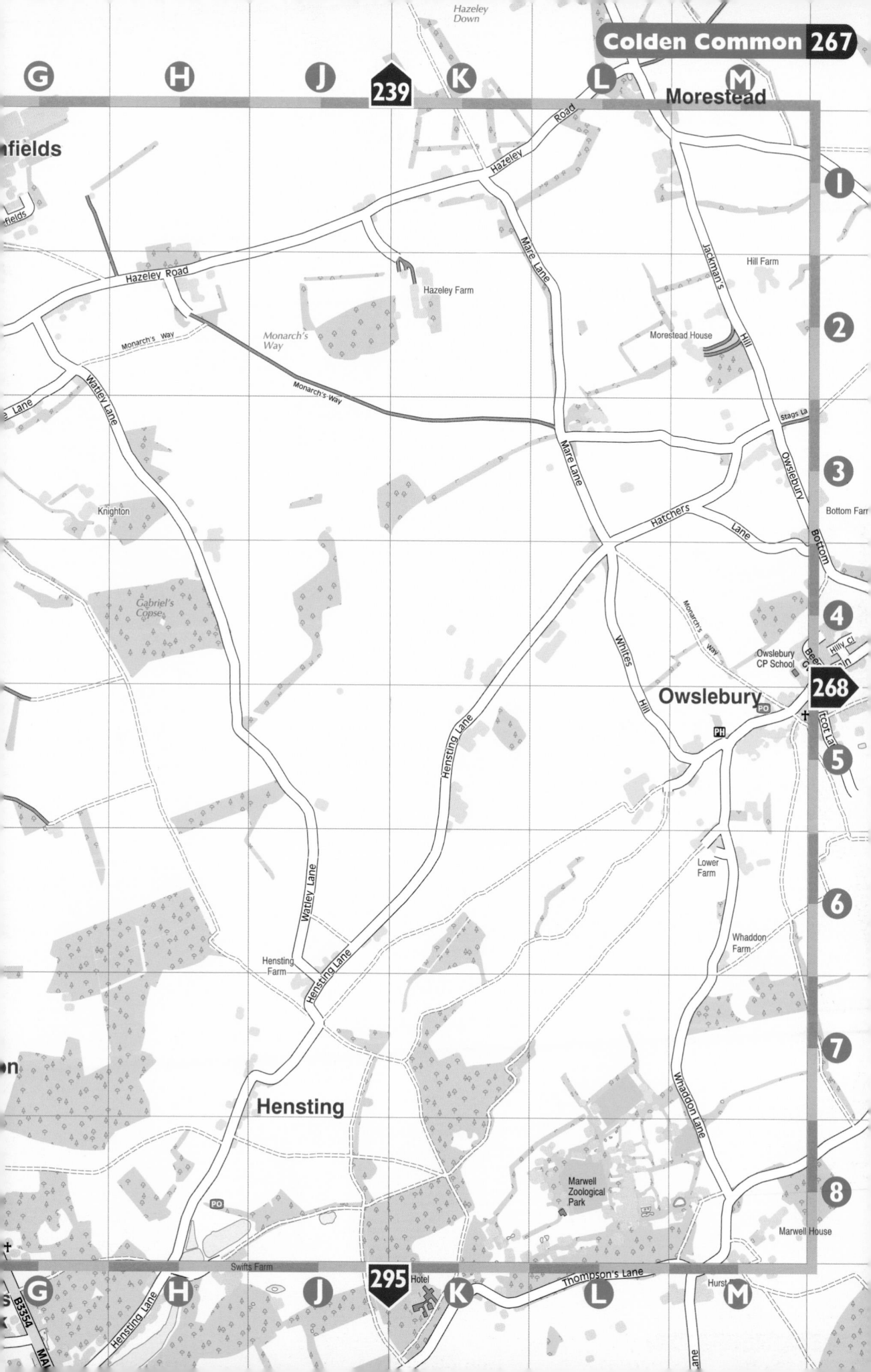

Hazeley Down
G
H
J
239
K
L
M
Morestead
1
2
3
4
5
6
7
8
268
295
Hazeley Road
Mare Lane
Jackman's Hill
Hill Farm
Hazeley Farm
Morestead House
Monarch's Way
Watley Lane
Stags La
Owslebury Bottom
Bottom Farm
Knighton
Hatchers Lane
Gabriel's Copse
Monarch's Way
Whites Hill
Owslebury CP School
Owslebury
PO
PH
Hensting Lane
Lower Farm
Whaddon Farm
Hensting Farm
Hensting
Whaddon Lane
Marwell Zoological Park
Marwell House
Swifts Farm
Hotel
Thompson's Lane
Hurst
B3354

A
B
C
D
E
F
240
Farm
Warren
Old Down
Honeyman Farm
Hill Farm
Longwood House
Stags La
Bottom Farm
Bottom
Longwood Road
Rd
Belmore Lane
King's Way
Baybridge House
Hilly Cl
Main
Beech
Owslebury CP School
267
PO
Pitcot Lane
Baybridge
Blackdown Farm
Baybridge Lane
Lower Baybridge Lane
Rowhay Wood
Woodcote
Woodlock's Down Farm
Marwell House
Lane
Woodcote
296
Monarch's Way
1
2
3
4
5
6
7
8
1 grid square represents 500 metres

Beauworth
Lane End
Hamilton Farm
241
G
H
J
K
L
M
Lane End Farm
Holden Lane
Yew Tree Farm
1
Longwood Dean Lane
2
Greendowns
Lancen Cotts
PH
Salt Lane
South Downs WY
3
Longwood Dean Farm
Dur Wood
4
270
Preshaw House
5
Salt Lane
The Holt
Valley Walk
Stony Hard Farm
6
Monarch's Way
7
Lane
Preshaw
Preshaw
Belmore House
8
Lower
Ower Farm
Stephen's Castle Down
297
G
H
J
K
L
M
Monarch's Way
Stake's Lane

A
B
C
D
E
F
242
269
298
1
2
3
4
5
6
7
8
Dean House
Yew Tree Farm
Down Farm
Wayfarer's Walk
College
Down Farm
Riversdown House
South Downs Wy
Wind Farm
South Downs Way
Rooksgrove Farm
Lomer Farm
Monarch's Way
Love
Lane
Preshaw House
Preshaw
Down
The White Way
Sailor's Lane
Downleaze
Copse
Beacon Hill Lane
Winters
Down
Lone Lane
Corhampton
1 grid square represents 500 metres

Warnford 271
243
272
299
G
H
J
K
L
M
1
2
3
4
5
6
7
8
Black House Farm
Bere Farm
Marldell Farm
Lippen Cotts
Wheely Farm
Wheely Down
Monarch's Way
Warnford
Lippen Lane
A32
Old Winchester Hill Lane
Monarch's Way
Warnford Park
Old Winch
Peake New Road
Peake Farm
Exton
South Downs Way
Monarch
We

272

A B Highfield C **244** D E F

Marlands

A32

1

Vinnells Lane

Hayling Wood

2

Lippen Cotts

3

Long Priors

Knapps Hard

Floud La

Church Lane

Headon Vw

Vinnells Lane

West Meon
Controlled
Primary School

Doctors Lane

The Surgery

East End

Meonwara Crs

West Meon

High Street

PO

Love Lane

Lynch Lane

Station Road

Coombe Lane

Westbury House

River Meon

4

A32

271

Old Winchester Hill Lane

5

6

Monarch's Way

Old Winchester Hill Lane

7

Hen Wood

8

Peake Farm

A B South Downs Way C **300** South Downs Way D E South Downs F

Whitewool Farm

1 grid square represents 500 metres

G   H   J   **245**   K   L   M

Peak Farm

Old
Down Farm

1

Lower
Bordean

2

A272

Tigwell Farm

3

4

274

Bereleigh House

GU32

5

Drayton

Park Farm

6

Pidham Farm

7

East Meon
Controlled
Primary School

Workhouse
Lane

The
Cross

Church
Street

PH
PO

Chapel St

Chidden
Cl

Hill View

Gars

Con Cl

Duncombe
Fldg

Glenthorne
Meadow

High Street

Temple
Lane

Coombe   Road

East Meon

Lower
House Farm

8

Duncombe Farm

G   H   J   **301**   K   L   Oxenbourne House   M

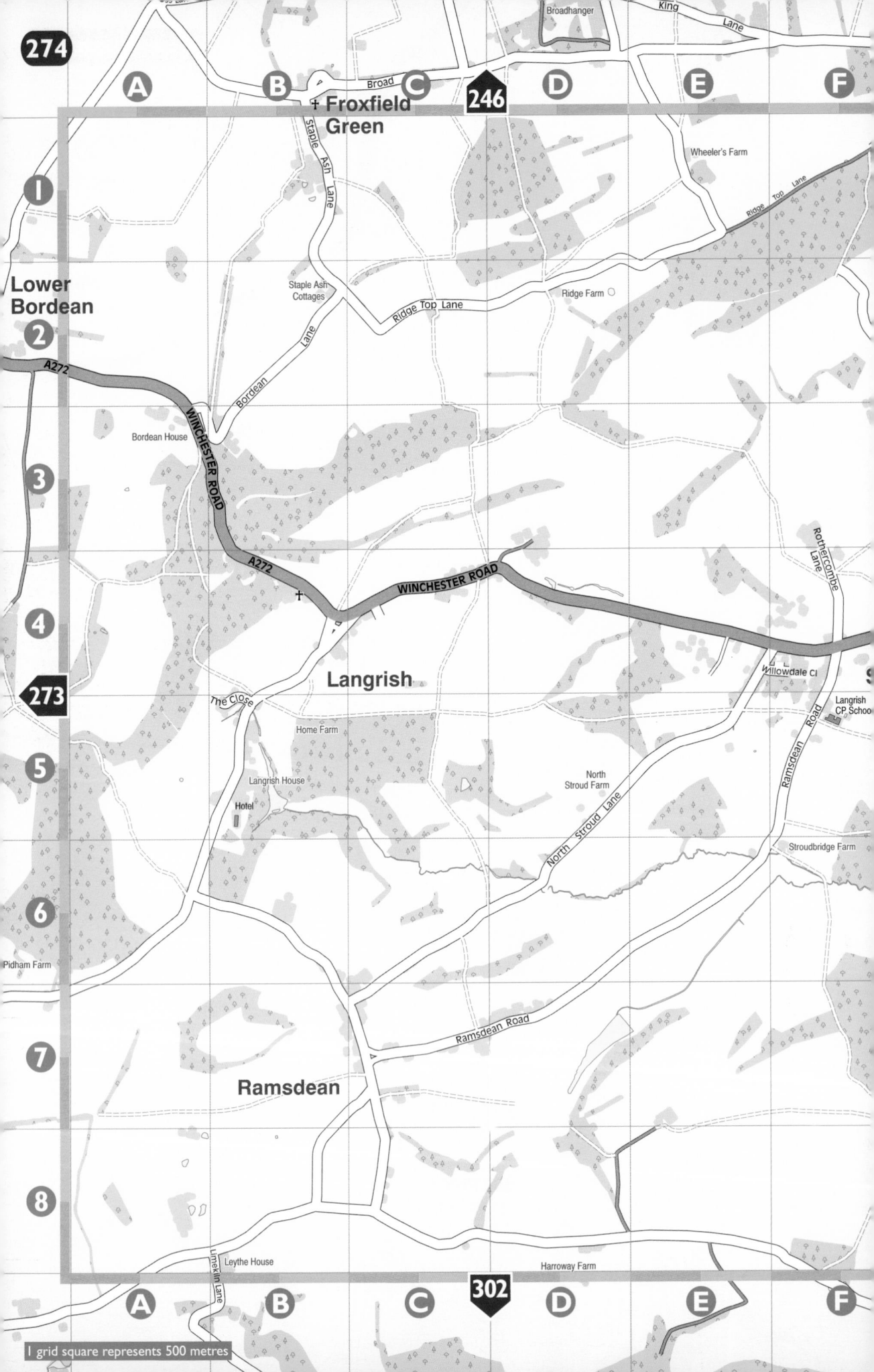

Broadhanger
King Lane
Broad
Froxfield Green
246
Staple Ash Lane
Wheeler's Farm
Ridge Top Lane
Lower Bordean
Staple Ash Cottages
Ridge Top Lane
Ridge Farm
Bordean Lane
A272
WINCHESTER ROAD
Bordean House
A272
WINCHESTER ROAD
Rothercombe Lane
Langrish
Willowdale Cl
273
The Close
Langrish CP School
Home Farm
Ramsdean Road
Langrish House
North Stroud Farm
Hotel
North Stroud Lane
Stroudbridge Farm
Pidham Farm
Ramsdean Road
Ramsdean
Leythe House
Limekiln Lane
Harroway Farm
302
A B C D E F
1 2 3 4 5 6 7 8
1 grid square represents 500 metres

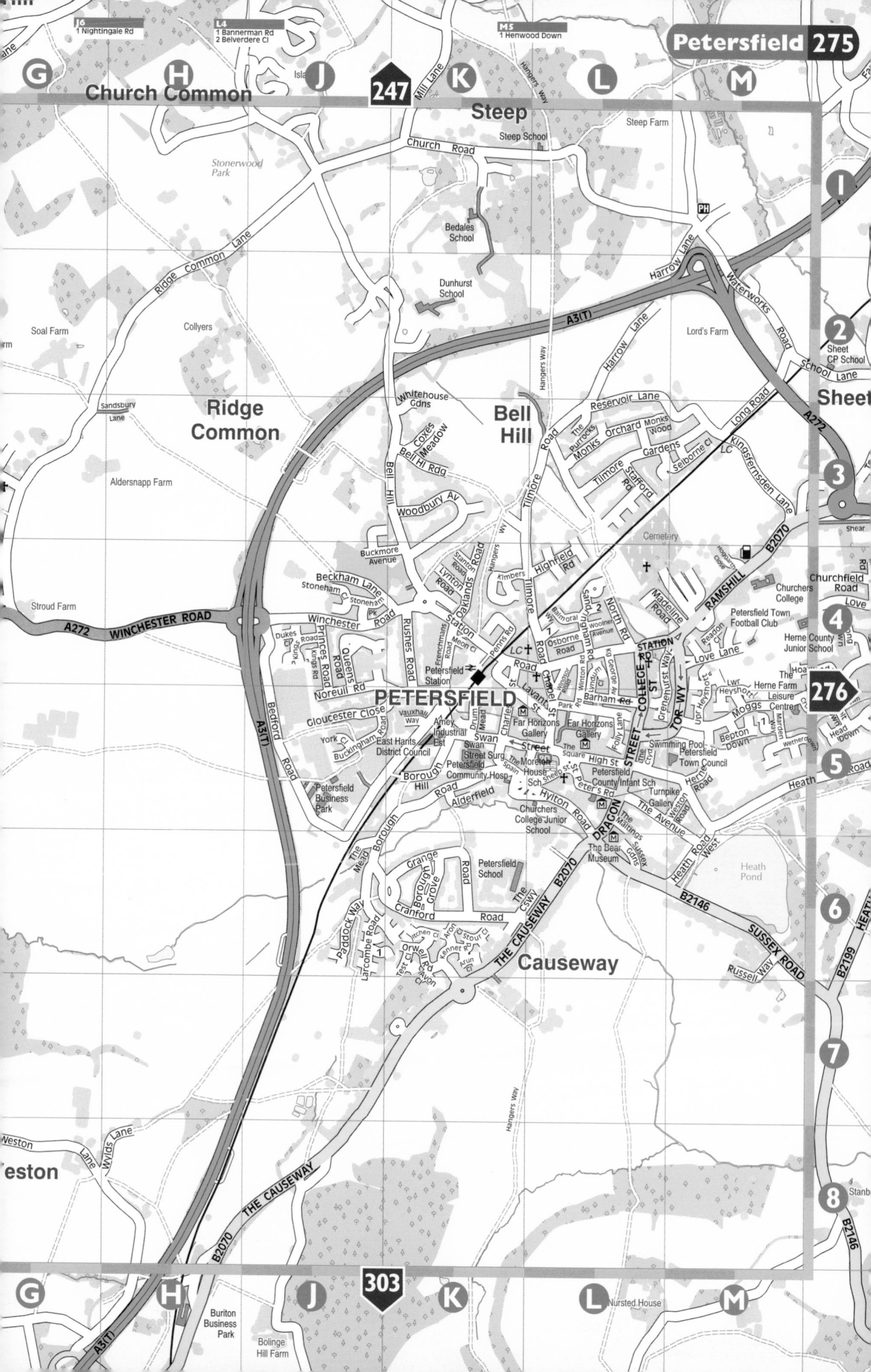
J6
1 Nightingale Rd
L4
1 Bannerman Rd
2 Belverdere Cl
M5
1 Henwood Down
G
H
J
K
L
M
247
Church Common
Mill Lane
Steep
Hangers Way
Steep Farm
Steep School
Church Road
Stonerwood Park
Bedales School
Dunhurst School
PH
Ridge Common Lane
Harrow Lane
Waterworks Road
A3(T)
Soal Farm
Collyers
Lord's Farm
Sheet CP School
School Lane
Sheet
Harrow Lane
Reservoir Lane
Sandsbury Lane
Ridge Common
Whitehouse Gdns
Bell Hill
Coxes Meadow
Bell Hl Rdg
Tilmore Road
The Purrocks
Monks Orchard
Monks Wood
Gardens
Selborne Cl
Long Road
LC
Kingsfernsden Lane
Tilmore
Stafford Rd
Aldersnapp Farm
Woodbury Av
Cemetery
Shear
Churchfield Road
Buckmore Avenue
Stanton Road
Oaklands Road
Lynton Road
Hangers Way
Kimbers
Highfield Rd
Hogarth Close
B2070
Ramshill
Churchers College
Beckham Lane
Stoneham Cl
Stoneham Pk
Stroud Farm
Winchester Road
Rushes Road
Station Road
Penns Rd
Sandringham Rd
North Rd
Madeline Road
Petersfield Town Football Club
Love Lane
Herne County Junior School
A272 Winchester Road
Dukes
Kings Road
Princes Road
Queens Road
Kings Rd
Frenchmans Road
Meon Cl
Petersfield Station
Balmoral Wy
Osborne Road
Woolner Avenue
Station Rd
College St
Grenehurst Way
Tor Wy
Readon Cl
Love Lane
The Hoad
Herne Farm Leisure Centre
276
Noreuil Rd
Petersfield
Road
Chapel St
Winton Rd
Lyndum Cl
George Av
Barham Rd
Upr Heyshott
Lwr Heyshott
Moggs
Marden Way
Bepton Down
Wetherdown
Gloucester Close
Vauxhall Way
Amey Industrial Est
Drum Mead
Charles St
Lavant St
Far Horizons Gallery
Park Rd
Folly Lane
Swimming Pool
Petersfield Town Council
York Cl
Buckingham Road
East Hants District Council
Swan Street
Swan Street Surg
The Square
The Spain
Moreton House Sch
High St
Street
The Clyd
Heath Road
Bedford Road
Borough Hill
Petersfield Community Hosp
Sheep St
St Peter's Rd
Petersfield County Infant Sch
Turnpike Gallery
Herne Road
Petersfield Business Park
Road
Alderfield
Hylton Road
Churchers College Junior School
Dragon
The Maltings
The Avenue
Weston Road
Heath Road West
The Mead
Borough Road
Grange
Borough Grove
Petersfield School
Road
The Bear Museum
Sussex Gdns
Heath Pond
The Cswy
The Causeway
B2070
B2146
Sussex Road
Paddock Way
Larcombe Road
Cranford Road
Itchen Cl
Avon Cl
Stour Cl
Test Cl
Orwell Rd
Kennet Rd
Arun Cl
Avon Cl
Causeway
Russell Way
B2199
Hangers Way
Weston Lane
Wylds Lane
Weston
The Causeway
B2070
Stanb
B2146
303
Buriton Business Park
Bolinge Hill Farm
Nursted House
A3(T)
1
2
3
4
5
6
7
8

276
248
275
304
A
B
C
D
E
F
1
2
3
4
5
6
7
8
B5
1 Heather Rd
2 Wheatear Dr
Petersfield Golf Club
Farnham Road
Stodham Lane
A3(T)
Upper Adhurst Farm
LONDON ROAD
B2070
Adhurst St Mary
Mill Lane
Sheet CP School
School Lane
Sheet
Village Street
A272
Portland's Cl
Town Lane
Parsonage Close
Inmans Lane
LONDON ROAD
Old Mill Lane
Shear Hill
Fernsden Lane
B2070
Westmark Farm
Hampshire County
West Sussex County
River Rother
Churchfield Road
Merryfield Rd
Hazelbank Close
PULENS LANE
Churchers College
Love Lane
Rother Close
Copse Close
Pulens Cr
Geddes Way
Tilmore Brook
Herne County Junior School
Upper Wardown
B2199
Petersfield Rugby Football Club
Council Offices
Durford Abbey Farm
Hanger Way
Great Hanger
Lower Mead
Barnfield Road
Heathfield Road
Marden Way
Wetherdown
Penns Place
Eastlake Cl
Clare Gdns
Heath Road
Durford Road
Fern Close
Sandy Close
Woodlark Gdns
Bramble Road
Rival Moor Road
Ryefield Close
Gorse Road
Harrier Way
Torberry Drive
Thorn Cl
Teazle Cl
Bracken Rd
Broom Rd
Stonechat
Linnet Cl
Rival Moor Road
HEATH ROAD EAST
Heath Pond
Ryefield
Rival Lodge
SUSSEX ROAD
B2199
Harting Pond
Stanbridge Farm
B2146
Hampshire County
West Sussex County
Goose Green
Path
Sussex Border
Quebec
Manor Farm
Collins
Nursted
Westons
1 grid square represents 500 metres

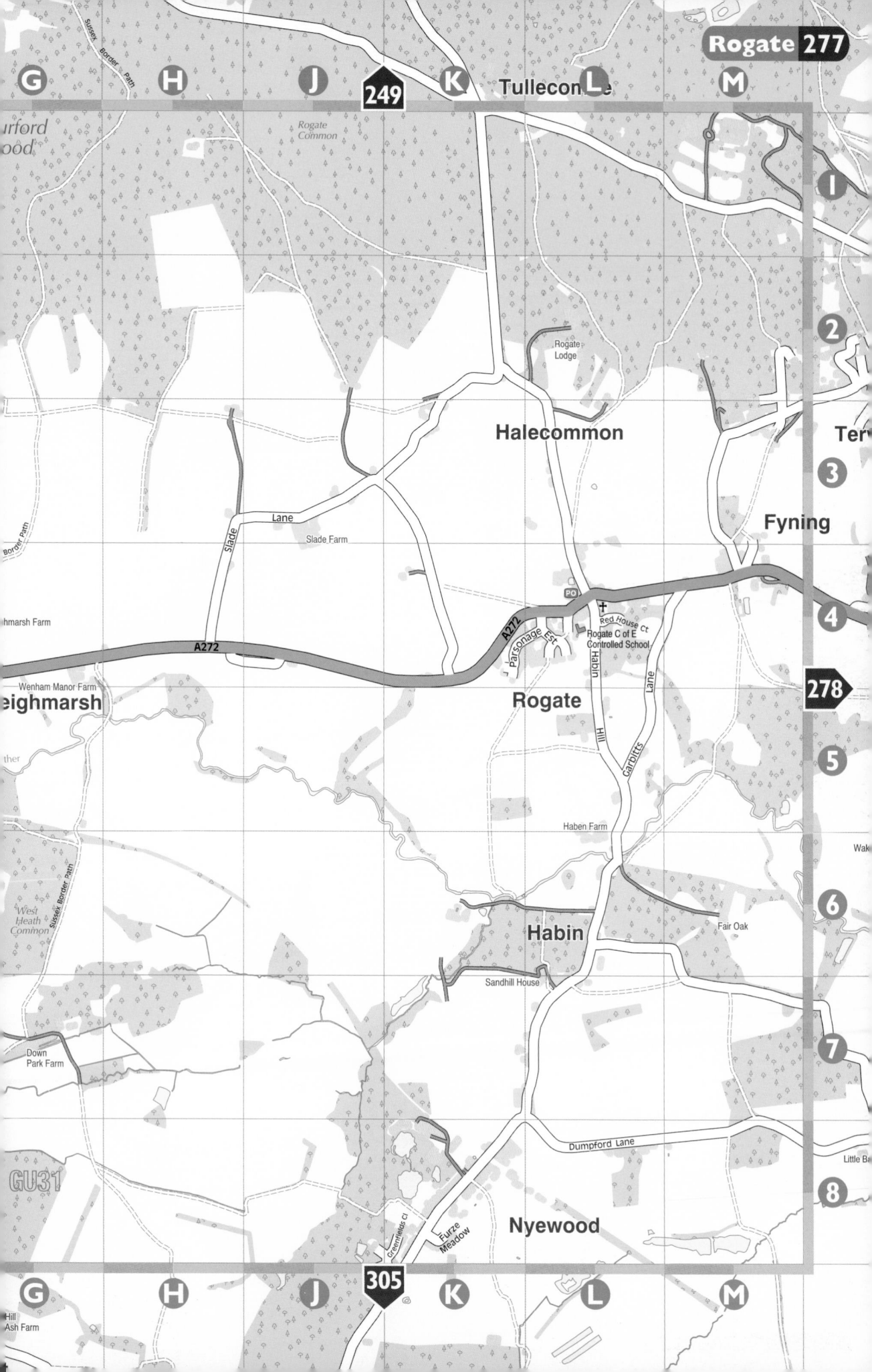

G H J **249** K Tullecon **Le** **M**

1

2

Ter

3

Fyning

4

278

5

6

7

8

G H J **305** K L M

Rogate Common

Rogate Lodge

Halecommon

Lane

Slade Farm

Slade

Border Path

Sussex

shmarsh Farm

PO

Red House Ct

Rogate C of E Controlled School

A272

Parsonage In

A272

Rogate

Wenham Manor Farm

eighmarsh

Habin

Hill

Carbitts Lane

Haben Farm

ther

West Heath Common

Sussex Border Path

Fair Oak

Habin

Sandhill House

Down Park Farm

Dumpford Lane

Little Ba

Wak

GU31

Greenfields Cl

Furze Meadow

Nyewood

Hill Ash Farm

278
250
277
A
B
C
D
E
F
1
2
3
4
5
6
7
8
Bobbolds Farm
Cook's Pond Road
Trotten Marsh
Kingsham Wood
Hammer Stream
Borden Wood
Rondle Wood
Borden Lane
Borden
Chithurst Lane
Dangstein
Gatehouse Lane
Terwick Common
Fyning
Cumber's Farm
Gatehouse Farm
Cemetery
Manor House
Wakeham Farm
A272
Trotton
Rother Lane
River Rother
Trotton Common
Mill Lane
Mill La
Terwick Lane
Hotel
Little Barn
Dumpford
Dumpford Park Farm
Trotton Road
Goldrings Farm
1 grid square represents 500 metres

251

G

Queen's Corner

H

J

K

L

M

I

2

3

4

5

6

7

8

Robins Lane

Bowley Farm

St Cuthmans School

Pound Farm

Pound Common

Eastshaw Farm

Tote Hill

Tentworth

Tote Lane

Linch Road

Eastshaw Lane

Ash House

Woodgate Farm

Iping Lane

Hammer Lane

Stanwater Lane

Stedham Lane

Woolbeding Lane

Brambling Lane

Hollist Lane

Hammerwood House

Crouchhouse Farm

River Rother

Stedham Lane

Woolbeding

Iping

Rotherhill Ho

Mill Lane

Crowshole Farm

Queens St

Common View

PH

School

Stedham CP School

The Street

The Lane

The Alley

Stedham

Iping Common

A272

Stedham Common

Minsted Road

Elsted Road

Severals Road

Sandy Lane

Andrews Lane

Quags Corner

Midhurst Common

G

H

J

K

L

M

8

A B C **252** D E F

A354

Martin Drove End

Martin Drove End

1

2

Vernditch
Chase

Wiltshire County
Hampshire County

A354

3

Mar
End

4

Townsend Lane

5

Martin Down

Sillen Lane

6

Earthpits Lane

Jubilee Trail

Hampshire County
Dorset County

Bokerley
Down

7

gan's
Lane

Whitey
Top

8

Pentridge

A B C **306** D E F

Jubilee Trail

Blagdon Farm

Kites
t Fa

G
H
J
253
K
L
M
Paradise
1
2
St Brides Farm
3
Knap Barrow
Grans Barrow
Toyd Down
4
East Martin
Martin
282
5
Allen River
Tidpit
Knoll Down
6
North Allenford Farm
7
Damerham Knoll
Tidpit Common Down
8
Knoll Fa
Blackheath Down
G
H
J
307
K
L
South Allenford Farm
M

282

A   B   C   254   D   Whitsbury E   F

Tenantry Farm

Rockbourne
Down

1

2

Scotland
Cottage

3

Duck's
Nest

4

Down Farm

281

5

Glebe Farm

6

7

Dâmerham
Knoll

New Rd

Rockbourne

Western Downland
School

8

Knoll Farm

A   B   C   308   Rockbourne Lane   D   E   F

Marsh Farm

West
Park

1 grid square represents 500 metres

G H J K L M

255

I

2

3

4

284

5

6

7

8

G H J K L M

309

Wick Down

Botley's Farm

Wiltshire County
Hampshire County

North Charford Drove

South Charford

Charford Drove

Breamore Down

Giant's Grave

Castle Ditches

Manor House

North Charford Down Farm

South Charford Drove

Down Farm

Breamore Wood

Breamore House

Lower Farm

Lower

Upper Street

Rookery La

Long Steeple Lane

Whitsbury Common

Roundhill Farm

Breamor

Bra
C of E

Rockstead Farm

Green Lane

Radnall Wood

Outwick

Marsh Lane

Flood Street

284
256
283
310
A
B
C
D
E
F
1
2
3
4
5
6
7
8
Wick
Lane
Batten Rd
David Hart Business Centre
F2 1 Eastman Cl
C1 1 Weeke Cl
Barford
Hamilton
Long Cl
Long West Close
Downton C of E Primary School
Close
THE BOROUGH
B3080
The Borough
South La
Mesh Pond
Elizabeth Cl
Joanna Cl
Marie Av
Catherine Crescent
Downton County Secondary School
The Surgery
Saxonhurst
Moot Lane
Moot Close
Moot Gardens
Squarey Close
Twynham Cl
Downlands Cl
Cranbury Cl
A338 BREAMORE ROAD
River Avon
North Charford Drove
North Charford Down Farm
N Charford Crossing
North Charford Manor House
Searchfield Farm
Lod
Breamore House
SALISBURY ROAD
South Charford Farm
North Street
Avon Valley Path
Hale Lane
A338
Rectory La
Breamore
Breamore C of E Primary School
Dodgson Cl
Lwr Densome Wd
Woodgreen
Higherend Farm
Marsh Lane
Grace Lane
Love La
Trimm's Drove
Steels Dro
Drove
Brook
1 grid square represents 500 metres

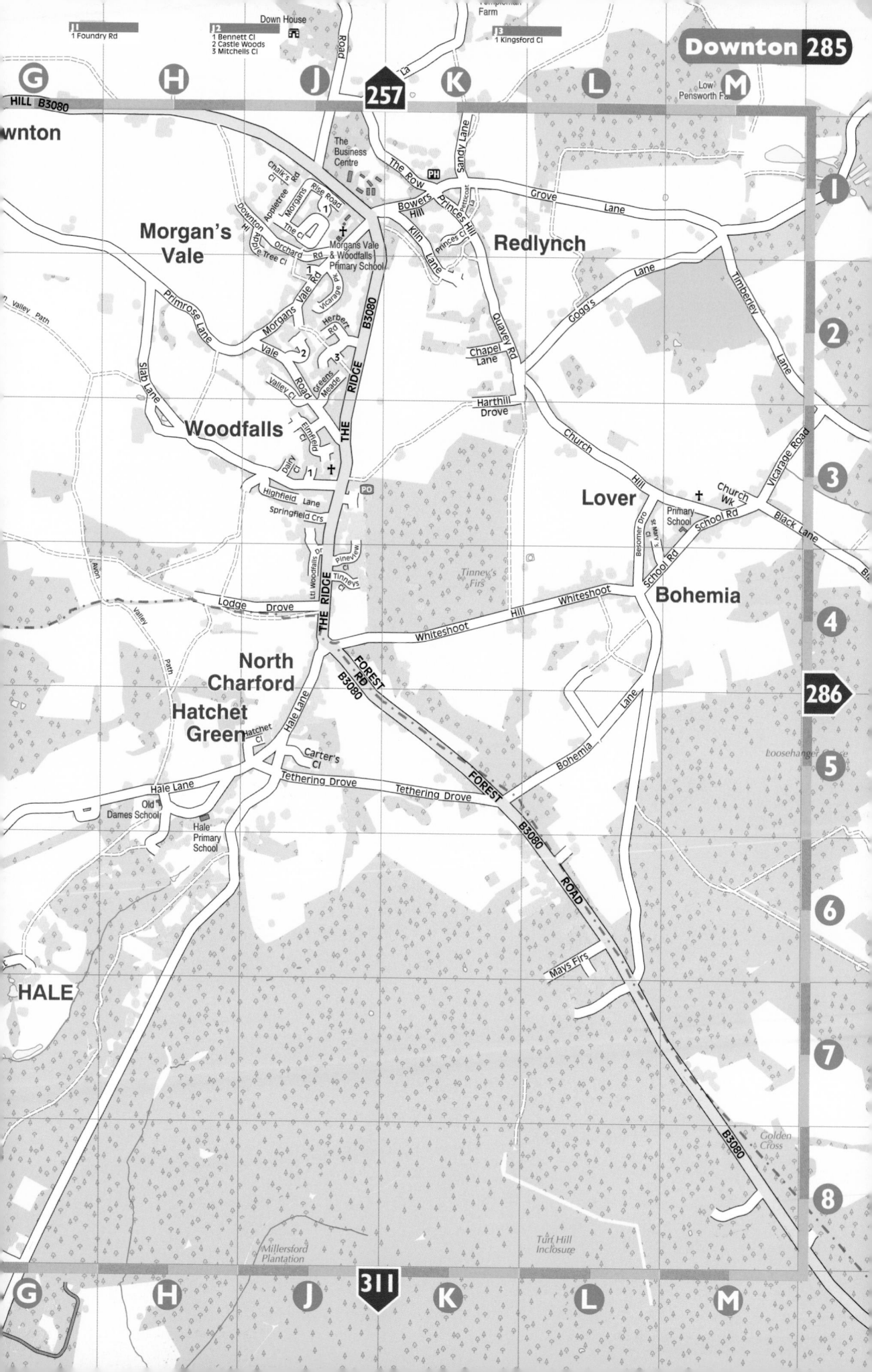

257

G H J K L M

I

1 Foundry Rd
1 Bennett Cl
2 Castle Woods
3 Mitchells Cl
1 Kingsford Cl

Down House

Templeman Farm

Low Pensworth Fa

HILL B3080

wnton

The Business Centre

Morgan's Vale

Chalk's Rd Cl
Appletree
Morgans
Rise Road
The Cl

Downton Hl
Orchard Rd
Maple tree Cl

The Row

Bowers Hill
Princes Hill
Kiln Lane
Princes Cl
Petticoat La

Grove Lane

Redlynch

PH

Sandy Lane

2

Primrose Lane

Morgans Vale & Woodfalls Primary School

Vicarage Rd

Morgans Vale Rd

Herbert Rd

Quavey Rd

Gog's Lane

Timberley Lane

Slab Lane

Vale Road

Greens Meade

Valley Cl

THE RIDGE

B3080

2

3

Chapel Lane

3

Woodfalls

Elmfield Cl

Dairy Cl

Harthill Drove

Church Hill

Lover

Vicarage Road

Black Lane

3

Primary School

Church Wk

Besomer Dro

School Rd

School Rd

Highfield Lane

PO

1

Springfield Crs

Lt. Woodfalls Dr

Pineview

Tinneys Row

Tinney's Firs

Whiteshoot Hill

Whiteshoot

Bohemia

4

Lodge Drove

THE RIDGE

Valley Path

Avon

Whiteshoot Hill

Bohemia Lane

286

North Charford

FOREST RD

B3080

Hale Lane

Hatchet Cl

Carter's Cl

Tethering Drove

FOREST

Bohemia Lane

Loosehanger C

5

Hatchet Green

Tethering Drove

ROAD

Hale Lane

Old Dames School

Hale Primary School

B3080

Mays Firs

6

HALE

Golden Cross

7

B3080

8

Millersford Plantation

Turf Hill Inclosure

311

G H J K L M

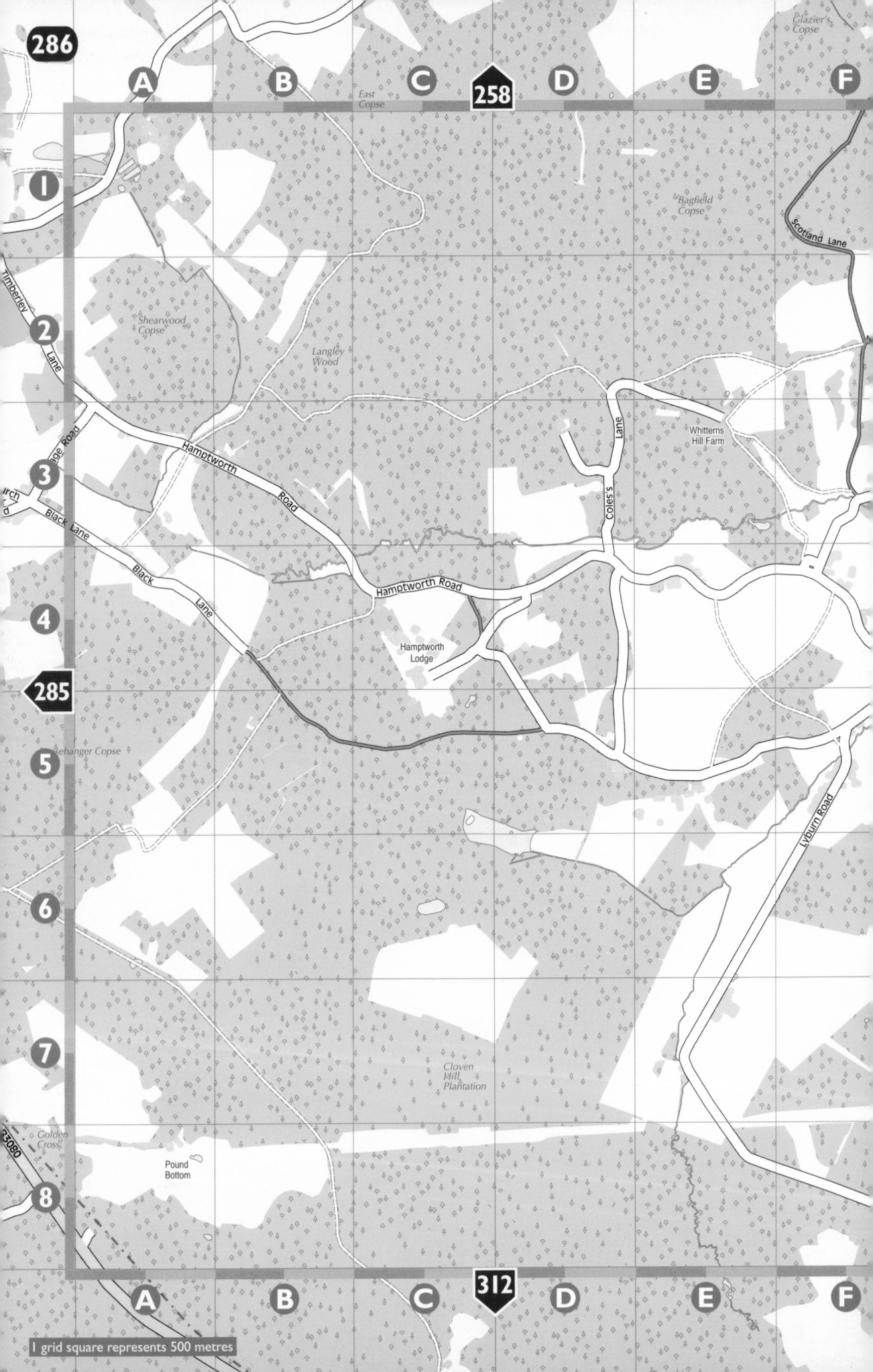

A B East Copse C 258 D E F

1

Bagfield Copse

Scotland Lane

Timberley Lane

2

Shearwood Copse

Langley Wood

age Road

Hamptworth

3

Black Lane

Road

Coles's Lane

Whitterns Hill Farm

Black Lane

Hamptworth Road

4

285

Hamptworth Lodge

Sehanger Copse

5

Lyburn Road

6

7

Cloven Hill Plantation

3080

Golden Cross

Pound Bottom

8

A B C 312 D E F

1 grid square represents 500 metres

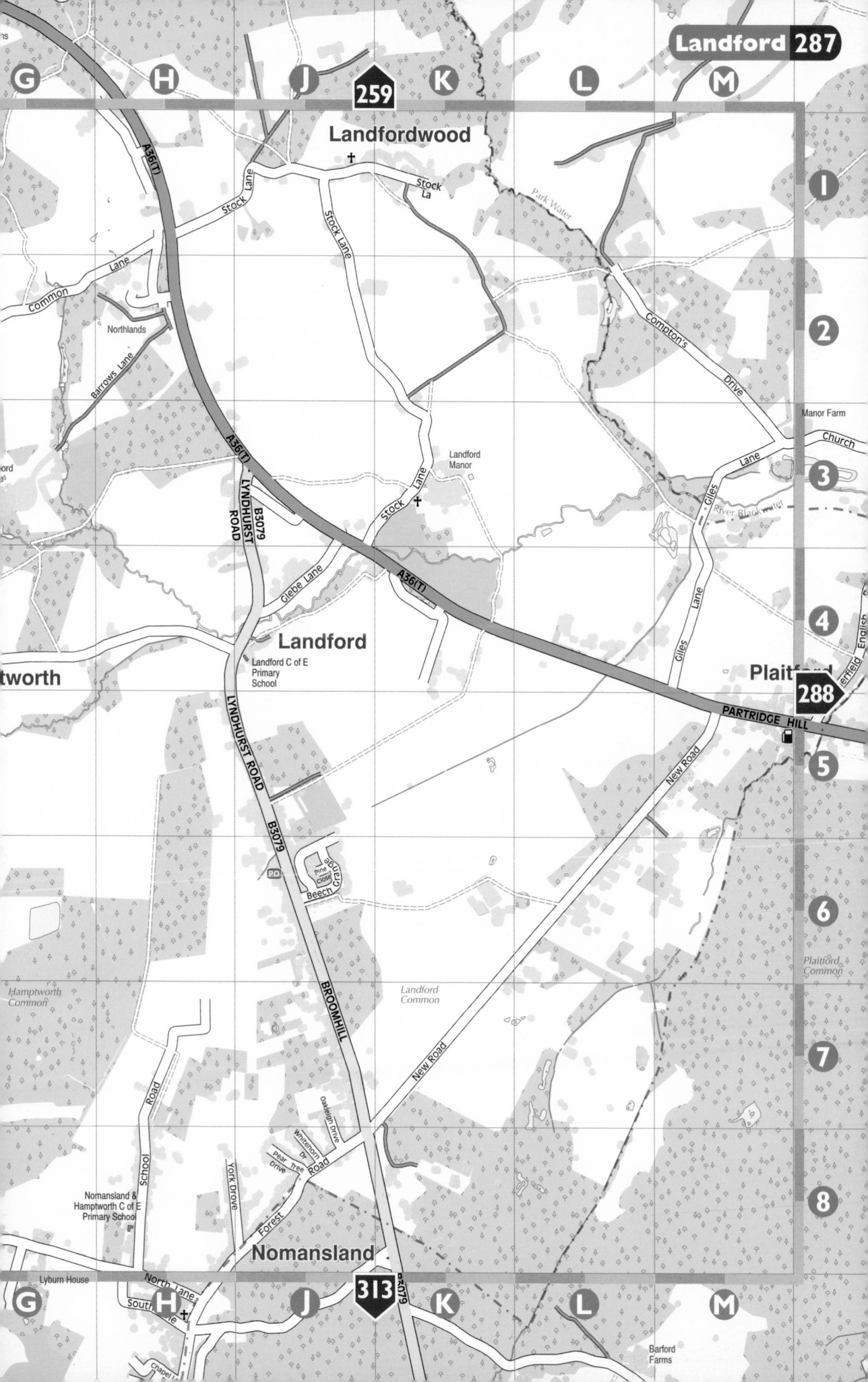

G   H   J   **259**   K   L   M

I

Landfordwood

Stock La

Park Water

Compton's Drive

2

Stock Lane

Barrows Lane

Northlands

Common Lane

Manor Farm

Church

3

A36(T)

LYNDHURST ROAD

B3079

Stock Lane

Landford Manor

Giles Lane

River Blackwater

A36(T)

Glebe Lane

4

tworth

Landford

Landford C of E Primary School

Giles Lane

Plaitford

Enerfield

English

288

PARTRIDGE HILL

New Road

5

LYNDHURST ROAD

B3079

PO

Pine Close

Beech

Landford Common

Plaitford Common

6

BROOMHILL

New Road

Hamptworth Common

7

School Road

Oakleigh Drive

Whitenorth Rd

Pear Tree Drive

York Drive

Nomansland & Hamptworth C of E Primary School

8

Lyburn House

North Lane

south...

Nomansland

Forest

B3079

Barford Farms

G   H   J   **313**   K   L   M

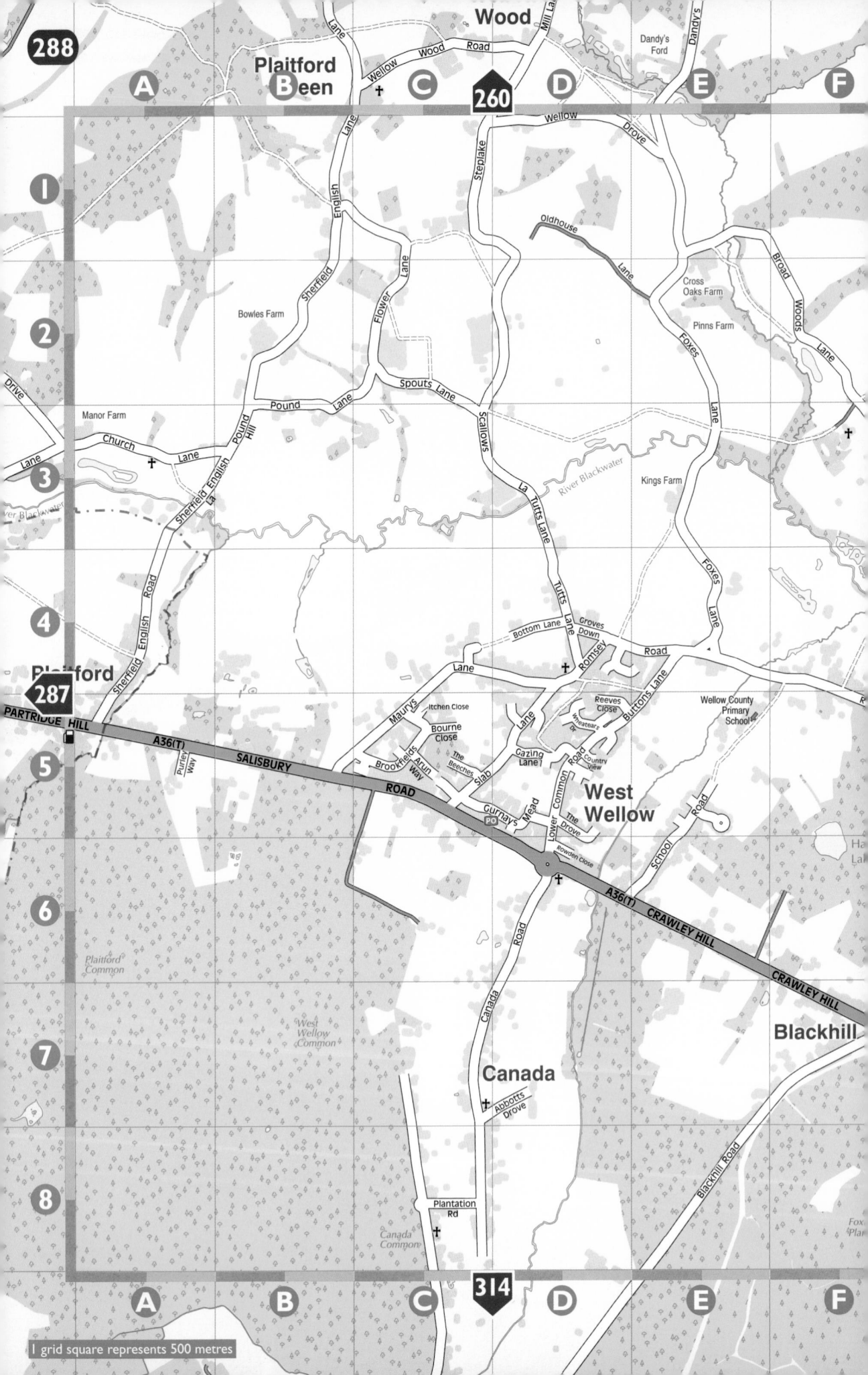

Wood

Plaitford
Been

260

A B C D E F

Wood Road

Wellow

Mill La

Dandy's
Ford

Dandy's

Wellow

Drive

1

English Lane

Sherfield Lane

Flower Lane

Steplake Lane

Oldhouse Lane

Cross Oaks Farm

Broad Woods Lane

2

Bowles Farm

Spouts Lane

Scallows Lane

Pinns Farm

Foxes Lane

Pound Lane

Pound Hill

3

Manor Farm

Church Lane

Sherfield English La

Sherfield English

La Tutts Lane

River Blackwater

Kings Farm

Foxes Lane

River Blackwater

Drive

Lane

4

Sherfield English Road

Bottom Lane

Tutts Lane

Groves Down

Romsey Road

Wellow County Primary School

R

Plaitford

287

PARTRIDGE HILL

Lane

Maurys

Itchen Close

Bourne Close

Reeves Close

Wheatears

Buttons Lane

Country View

5

A36(T) SALISBURY ROAD

Purley Way

Brookfields

Arun Way

The Beeches

Lane

Gazing Lane

Road

Lower Common

the Drove

School Road

Slab

Gurnays PO

Mead

**West
Wellow**

6

Plaitford Common

Rowden Close

A36(T) CRAWLEY HILL

CRAWLEY HILL

Canada Road

Blackhill Road

Blackhill

7

West
Wellow
Common

Canada

Abbotts Drove

Fox
Plan

8

Plantation Rd

Canada Common

314

A B C D E F

1 grid square represents 500 metres

G6
1 Cooper's Cl

G **H** **J** **261** **K** **L** **M**

I

Spursholt Ho

A27

2

Woodington

Embley Lane

Woodington Road

Woodington

Embley Park School

Gardeners Lane

Burnt Grove

3

ow

Hall Copse

Lane

Woodington Rd

Ryedown Lane

Gardeners Lane

4

Warners Fm

290

River Blackwater

Kentford Lake

Whinwhistle Road

5

Hamden

Florence Cl

Cranfield Cl

Crs

Embley Wood

6

Whinwhistle Road

Hammonds Fm

Semple Ho

A3090

7

Shelley Lane

Ridg

8

SALISBURY ROAD

Shelley Fm

G **H** Lake Lane **J** **315** **K** **L** **M**

Bricky

Old Salisbury R

Hotel

F2
1 Petty Cl
2 St Barbe Cl
3 Sydmanton Cl
4 The Tyleshades
F1
1 Jacobs Cl
2 Nursery Gdns
3 Oakleigh Gdns
4 Tadburn Cl
E1
1 Fleming Pl
2 Knatchbull Cl
3 Palmerston St
4 Pembroke Cl
D1
1 Abbey Water
2 Corn Market
3 Narrow La
4 Palmerston St
5 Spring Pl
262
289
316
ROMSEY
Romsey Industrial Est
Station Rd
Canal
Mercer Way
Greatbridge Road
Princes Rd
Station Rd
Alma Rd
Hollman Dr
Mill Lane
Primary School
Millstream Rise
Littlemeads
Abbey Mead Surg
Church La
Church Rd
Church St
Russell Hicks & Temple
Abbey Chiropractic Clinic
Alma Road Surg
The Hundred
Winchester Rd
A3057
Rivermead Cl
The Meads
Bell St
Newton La
The Bus Station
Cressey Rd
The Harrage
Romsey Infant School
Plaza Theatre
Tadfield Rd
Botley Road
Rosedale Av
Bridge Road
Broadwater Rd
Banning St
Middlebridge St
Riverside Gdns
By-Pass Road
A27
A27 Southampton Road
A3090
Romsey Town Football Club
Romsey Sports Centre
Romsey Rugby Football Club
Romsey Cricket Club
Spursholt Ho
Test Way
River Test
Broadlands House
Burnt Grove
Pauncefoot Hill – Mainstone
Pauncefoot Ho
Cutters Barn
Lee Ho
Spaniard's Lane
Yewtree Copse
Ranvilles Fm
Ridge Lane
Ridge
Lee Park Fm
Lee Lane
Lee Church Lane
Lee
Moorcourt Copse
Moorcourt
1 grid square represents 500 metres

G H J **263** K L M

263

G1
1 Eight Acres
2 Halterworth Cl
3 Hereward Cl
4 Nightingale Cl
5 The Vikings

H1
1 Montfort Heights

H2
1 The Thicket

I

2

S052

3

4

292

5

6

7

8

Halterworth

Halterworth
CP School

Warren Fm

Whitenap

Cemetery

Sycamore

Northlands
Rd

Pine
Rd

Chestnut
Cl

Mountbatten
Secondary
School

Premier

LUZBOROUGH LANE

A27

LUZBOROUGH
LANE

Ashfield

Botley Road

BOTLEY ROAD A27

BOTLEY ROAD A27

West Lane

Broad La

Andrews
Cl

Dunnings

Ringwood

Hillcrest

The
Birches

Amberley
Cl

Cerne Cl

Ringwood Drive

Queen's Ride

Copse

Hoe Fm

Willow
Gdns

Cedar
Cl

Juniper

Ash

Crescent

Spring
Gdns

Seymour La

Firgrove
Close

Linden Wk

Emer Cl

Whitenash

Firgrove
Road

Middle Rd

Camellia

Laburnum

Rownhams

North
Baddesley

Rossiyn

The
Vineyards

Church
Cl

Brownhill
Road

Fleming

Norton Welch

Willis
Av

Sylvan
Drive

Launcelyn
Cl

Lavington
Gdns

Mortimer
Way

Proctor
Dr

Dibble
Dr

Christophers

Ennel
Copse

Brook
Cl

Heath
Road

Bracken Road

Meadow

Tanner's Brook

Hoe Lane

Telegraph
Wood

Toothill   Road

Toothill

Packridge
Lane

Rownhams Lane

A3057

Nightingale
Wood

Upper

Toothill

Road

Greenhill Lane

Rownhams Service Area

M27

Rownhams Service Area

G H **317** J K L M

317

M3
1 Emer Cl

L4
1 Heatherb. Gdns
2 Northerwood Cl
3 Tutland Rd
4 Woodside Rd

L3
1 Heatherview Cl
2 Pine Cl

L2
1 Stragwyne Cl

K3
1 Broad La
2 Highlands Cl
3 Overbrook Wy

Upton

E3 1 Celandine Cl
E2 1 Collins Cl 2 Sir Galahad Rd 3 Tolefrey Gdns
C6 1 Woodside Crs
A3 1 Sandy La
Flexford
264
Bucket Corner
Flexford Road
Manor Farm
Knightwood Primary School
Knightwood Farm
Skys Wood Road
Crusaders Way
Harvest Road
Hornbeam Road
Littlefield Crescent
Zionshill Farm
Goodacre Drive
Pilgrims Close
Blencowe Drive
Perryvale Road
St Francis Primary School
The Surgery
Knightwood Road
S052
Nutburn Road
Sandy La
Nutburn
Baddesley Park Industrial Est
Castle Lane
Great Covert
County Infants School
North Baddesley Junior School
Health Centre
291
A27 BOTLEY ROAD
Misslebrook Lane
Sandringham Cl
Blenheim Close
Templars Way
Velmore Farm
Chilworth Old Village
Fowler's Wk
Woodside
Hut Wood
Chilworth
CHILWORTH ROAD
Parkway
Manor Rd
University Pkwy
Enterprise Road
Venture Road
Chilworth Drove
Southampton University
Roman Road
Green Lane
M27
Junction 4
Heatherlands Road
Pinelands Rd
Birch Road
Hutwood Rd
Bournemouth Road
Chilworth Common
Tanner's Brook
318
E4 1 Primrose Cl 2 Tansy Meadow
F1 1 Thetford Gdns
F2 1 Poppyfields 2 Wellowbrook Cl 3 Wild Cherry Wy
F4 1 Caernarvon Gdns 2 Danebury Gdns 3 Newport Cl 4 Warwick Cl 5 Wolvesey Pl
1 grid square represents 500 metres

Eastleigh 293
265
294
319
G2
1 Chepstow Cl
G3
1 Hodder Cl
2 Wansbeck Cl
G4
1 Reliant Cl
2 Thirlstane Firs
G5
1 Brecon Cl
2 Netley Cl
3 Warblington Cl
H2
1 Prospect Pl
2 Sutherlands Ct
H4
1 Keble Cl
H5
1 The Croft
2 Dorset Rd
3 The Oaklands
J2
1 Beechcroft Wy
2 Hardwick Rd
3 Hillcrest Dr
Thornden School
Pitmore School
Sherborne House School
Woodhill Preparatory School
Merdon Junior School
The Fryern Surg
The Brownhill Surg
Scantabout Primary School
Infant School
Fryern Hill
Fryern Junior & Infant School
St Swithun Wells RC Primary School
The Toynbee School
Commercial Business Centre
Rex Industrial Est
Anchor Business Centre
Monks Brook Ind Park
Brickfield Trading Estate
Allbrook
Boyatt Wood
Boyatt Wood Surgery
Peacock Trading Estate
Peacock Trading Est
Boyatt Shopping Cen
St Catherines Road Junior Sch
City Grove Trading Est
Junction 13
Junction 14
Civic Offices
Hotel
Fleming Park Leisure Centre
Eastleigh Borough Council
Brookwood Industrial Estate
Cemetery
Primary School
Hampshire County Council
Eastleigh Health Centre
Norwood CP School
Eastleigh Museum
Eastleigh College of Further Education
St Andrews Surgery
Nightingale County Junior & Infant School
Barton Peveril College
Alderman Quilley Secondary School
Eastleigh Football Club
S053
M3
A335
LEIGH ROAD
ROMSEY ROAD
SOUTHAMPTON ROAD
HURSLEY ROAD
BOURNEMOUTH ROAD B3043
TWYFORD RD
Winchester Road
Kingsway
Woodside Avenue
Chestnut Avenue
Passfield Avenue
Stoneham Lane
Monks Brook Close
Monks Way
Falcon Square
Magpie Lane
Chalvington Road
Shakespeare Road
Parham Dr
Woodside Road
Dew Lane
Factory Rd
Derby Road
Grantham Rd
Mansbridge Rd
Doncaster Road
Lakeside
Mitchell Way
G1
1 Swanton Gdns
L5
1 Browning Cl
2 Masefield Cl
L6
1 Grasmere
2 Thirlmere
L7
1 Jubilee Cl
M1
1 Chilham Cl
M2
1 Breamore Cl
2 Claremont Cl
M3
1 Leander Cl
2 Mountbatten Rd
3 Petworth Gdns
4 Thorn Cl
M4
1 Beaulieu Rd
2 The Quadrangle
M5
1 Laburnum Gv
2 Northlands Rd
3 Smithe Cl
L2
1 Constantine Cl
L3
1 Launceston Dr
2 Lyme Cl
K7
1 The Hawthorns
2 Maple Sq
L1
1 Claudius Cl
2 Solona Cl
K6
1 Passfield Cl
K2
1 Greendale Cl
K3
1 Beresford Cl
2 Beresford Gdns
3 Medina Cl
J6
1 Raven Sq
2 Starling Sq
3 Swallow Sq
J7
1 Chestnut Ri
2 Greenfinch Cl
3 Jackdaw Ri
J3
1 Hamble Ct
J4
1 Rosendale Rd
2 Trevose Cl
Trojans
North

A B C 266 ambDge D E F

D4
1 Colchester Av

D5
1 St Austell Cl

C4
1 Henry Rd
2 Windsor Ct

C5
1 Mainstream Ct

C3
1 Avington Cl
2 Kensington Cl
3 Mintern Cl

A4
1 Salisbury Cl
2 Stratford Pl

A5
1 Leigh Rd

A2
1 The Paddock
2 Rookwood Cl

A3
1 Addison Rd
2 Bramble Cl
3 Milton Rd

Highbridge

Stoke Common

Allbrook

EASTLEIGH

Bishopstoke

Stoke Park Farm

Stoke Park Wood

SO50

West Horton Farm

Lake Farm

Allington Manor Farm

D6
1 Devine Gdns
2 Griffen Cl
3 Lofting Cl
4 Manor Farm Gv

E6
1 Cowdray Cl
2 Rhinefield Cl
3 Squirrel Cl
4 Sunningdale Cl

F5
1 Olympic Wy

F6
1 Cosford Cl
2 Heather Cha

F7
1 Winsford Cl
2 Winsford Gdns

A B C 320 D E F

1 grid square represents 500 metres

G5
1 Brunswick Cl
2 Olympic Wy
3 Wooderson Cl

G6
1 Grangewd Gdns
2 Newbury Cl
3 Stoke Wood Cl
4 Torch Cl

G7
1 Goodison Cl

H5
1 Ridgeway Cl
2 Winifred Cl

Marwell Zoological Park

Marwell House

G   H   J   **267**   K   L   M

I

Swifts Farm

Hotel

Thompson's Lane   Hurst Farm

B3354

MAIN ROAD

B2177   PORTSMOUTH   ROAD

Marwell Manor

PORTSMOUTH   ROAD   B2177

Hurst Lane

2

ther's Pond

B3354

Low Hill Farm

3

Crowdhill

Hill

Park Hills Wood

Stroudwood Lane

4

B3354 WINCHESTER ROAD

Pylehill

Upr Barn Copse
Upr Barn

296

Stroudwood Dairy Farm

Harding La
Harding La
Stoke Hts
Stoke
Pilchards Av
Yew Tree Lane
Mitchell Drive
Brackley

Hall Lands House

5

Brunswick Rd
nd Cl
Latham
Alton
Road
Victena Rd
Witt
Sandy
Campbell Way
Brookfield Rd
Orchard Rd
Spring
Clifford
Glebe Ct

Fair Oak

Hall Lands Lane

Camelia Gv
Glenwood Court
Cedar Wd Close
Mimosa Gv
Magnolia Gv
High Trees

MORTIMERS   LANE

Mortimers Farm

Alma Rd

6

IROAK ROAD
ndy La
Shorts Road
Fairoak Road
PO
B3037
MORTIMERS LANE
Kimberley
Ashlea
Rustan
Mears
Michaels Way
Scotland Cl
Pembers Cl
Osborne Gardens

EASTLEIGH RD
Fratton
White Hart Rd
Noyce Dr
Farley
Heath Cl

Knowle Lane

7

Selhurst Way
Trafford
Dell Cl
Highbury
Elland
Cotsalls
Fair Oak Cem
Pavilion Cl

East Horton Farm

Greenwood Lane

Allington Lane
Dean
Ninian
Anfield
The Wyvern Community Secondary School
Fair Oak Junior & Infant School
B3354
Kings School
Pavilion Close

Greenwood Farm

8

BOTLEY

Knowle Lane

The Cockpit Farm

Durley

Greenwood

K6
1 Bradshaw Cl

J7
1 The Beeches
2 Carroll Cl
3 The Martins
4 Osborne Gdns

J6
1 F Routh Gdns
2 Mortimers Dr
3 Palmers Cl
4 Upper Mead Cl
5 Walkers Cl

H7
1 Eastville Rd
2 Stamford Wy

H6
1 Hawthorn Cl
2 Malmesbury Cl

Fir Tree Lane

Chapel
Angelica Gdns
Burnetts
York
Scot Road
Durley

Marwell House
A
B
C
268
Woodlock's Down Farm
D
E
F8
1 Cunningham Av
2 Hermitage Cl
Woodcote
F
1
Monarch's Way
Roughay Farm
Hatchley Lane
Woodcote
2
Upham
Shoe Lane
Cem
Church Street
Widlers La
Elm Crs
Oak Cl
West Hall
Upham School
Peak
B2177
Lane
Rowhay
3
Upham Street
King's Way
Stakes Lane
Upham Farm
Popes Lane
Stroudwood Farm
King's Way
PORTSMOUTH ROAD
4
Street
Upham
Lower Upham
295
B3037
PO
B2177
Stakes Farm
5
King's Way
Stakes Lane
WINCHESTER ROAD
Cross Lane
Woolstreet Farm
Stakes La
The Crescent
Sciviers's Lane
6
Alma Lane
7
Durley Hall Lane
Wintershill Hall
Wintershill
Ashton Close
Churchill
Marlow Rd
Durley Hall Farm
Sciviers's Lane
Winters Hill
Albany Court
Albany Drive
Albany Road
Durley Street
Newtown
8
Siskin Close
King's Way
The Drove
Durley Street
A
B
PO
C
322
D
E
F
Road
Tangier Lane

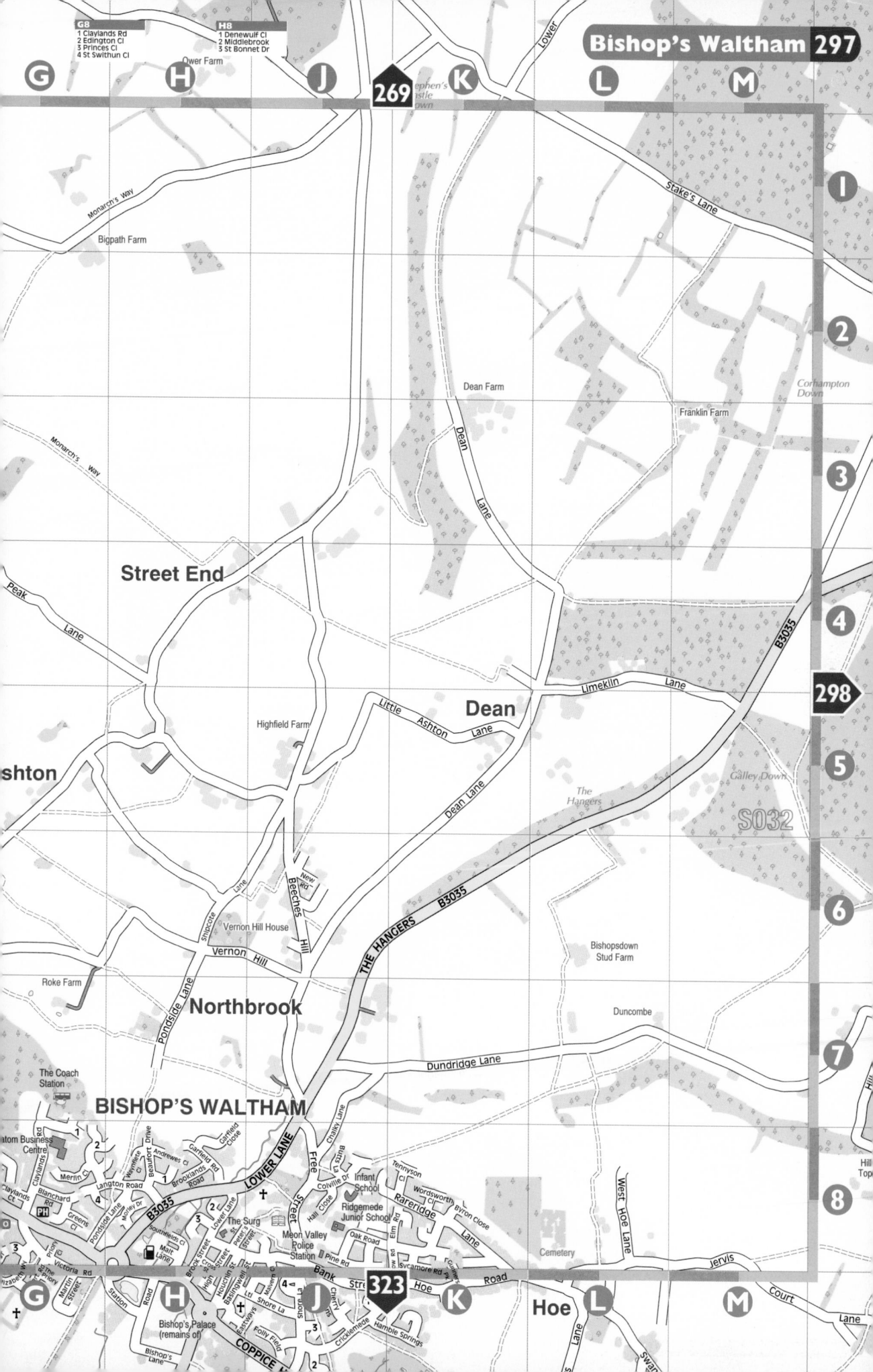
G8
1 Claylands Rd
2 Edington Cl
3 Princes Cl
4 St Swithun Cl
H8
1 Denewulf Cl
2 Middlebrook
3 St Bonnet Dr
Ower Farm
269
K
L
M
Stake's Lane
Monarch's Way
Bigpath Farm
Dean Farm
Franklin Farm
Corhampton Down
Dean Lane
Street End
Peak Lane
Limekiln Lane
B3035
298
Dean
Little Ashton Lane
Highfield Farm
shton
Dean Lane
The Hangers
Galley Down
SO32
New Rd
Beeches Hill
Shipcote Lane
Vernon Hill House
THE HANGERS B3035
Vernon Hill
Bishopsdown Stud Farm
Roke Farm
Northbrook
Pondside Lane
Duncombe
Dundridge Lane
The Coach Station
BISHOP'S WALTHAM
Chalky Lane
LOWER LANE
Free Street
Tennyson Cl
Wordsworth Cl
Byron Close
Rareridge Lane
Infant School
Ridgemede Junior School
West Hoe Lane
Cemetery
Meon Valley Police Station
Oak Road
Pine Rd
Sycamore Rd
Bank Street
Hoe Road
Jervis Court Lane
323
Hoe
Victoria Rd
Station Road
Bishop's Palace (remains of)
Shore La
Folly Field
Crickle mede
Hamble Springs
COPPICE
Bishop's Lane
Blanchard Rd
Greens Cl
Merlin Cl
Langton Road
Brooklands Road
Andrewes Cl
Garfield Rd
Garfield Close
Beaufort Drive
Claylands Rd
Claylands Ct
Malt Lane
Brook Street
Houchin St
Basingwell St
The Surg
Hall Close
Colville Dr
Butts La
Elm Rd
Priory
Martin Street
Eastways
Hill Top
G
H
J
K
L
M

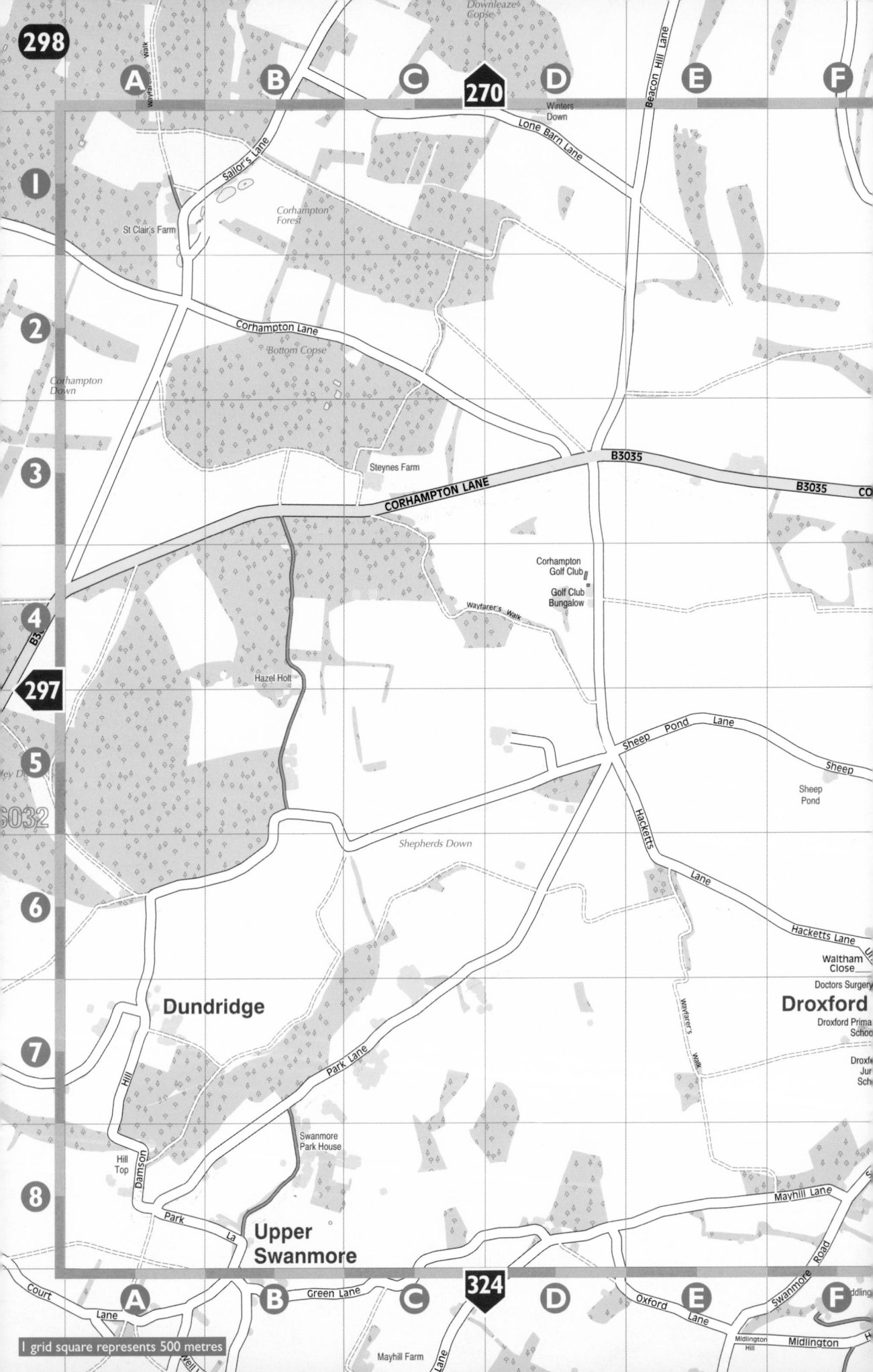
A
B
C
270
D
E
F
Downleaze Copse
Wayfarer's Walk
Winters Down
Beacon Hill Lane
Lone Barn Lane
Sailor's Lane
1
St Clair's Farm
Corhampton Forest
2
Corhampton Lane
Bottom Copse
Corhampton Down
3
Steynes Farm
B3035
CORHAMPTON LANE
Corhampton Golf Club
Golf Club Bungalow
Wayfarer's Walk
4
297
Hazel Holt
5
Sheep Pond Lane
Sheep
Sheep Pond
SO32
Hacketts
Shepherds Down
6
Lane
Hacketts Lane
Waltham Close
Doctors Surgery
Dundridge
Droxford
Wayfarer's Walk
7
Park Lane
Hill
Swanmore Park House
Hill Top
Damson
8
Mayhill Lane
Park
La
Upper Swanmore
Swanmore Road
Court
Lane
Green Lane
324
Oxford
Lane
Midlington Hill
Midlington
Mayhill Farm
1 grid square represents 500 metres

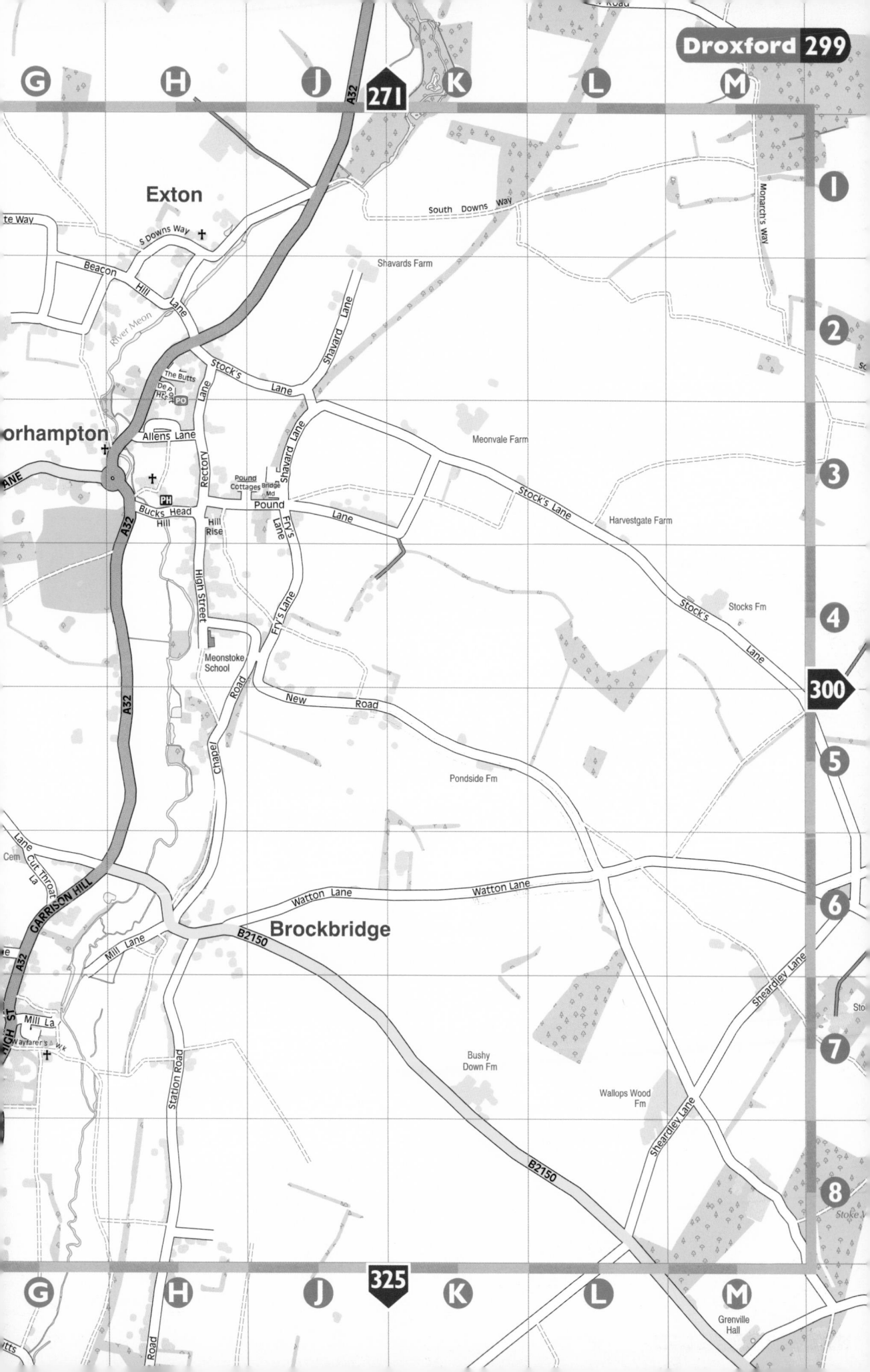

G H J K L M

271 A32

I
2
3
4
300
5
6
7
8

Exton

South Downs Way

Shavards Farm

S Downs Way

Beacon Hill

River Meon

Stock's Lane

Shavard Lane

Monarch's Way

Meonvale Farm

The Butts

...orhampton

Allens Lane

Rectory Lane

Pound Cottages

Bridge Md

Pound Lane

Fry's Lane

Stock's Lane

Harvestgate Farm

Bucks Head Hill

Hill Rise

Stock's Lane

Stocks Fm

PH

High Street

Fry's Lane

Chapel Road

Meonstoke School

New Road

Pondside Fm

A32

Cem

Cut Throat La

Lane

GARRISON HILL

Watton Lane

Watton Lane

Mill Lane

B2150

Brockbridge

Sheardley Lane

HIGH ST

Mill La

Wayfarer's Wk

Station Road

Bushy Down Fm

Wallops Wood Fm

Sheardley Lane

B2150

Stoke...

G H J K L M

325

Grenville Hall

A B C 272 D E F

South Downs Way

South Downs Way

Whitewool Farm

1

Monarch's Way

2

South Downs Way

Coombe

South Downs Way

Monarch's Way

South

Monarch's Way

3

199
Old Winchester Hill

Monarch's Way

Teglease
Down

ks Fm

4

Lane

Little West End
Fm

5

Westend
Down

6

Teglease Fm

Sneardley Lane

Stoke Wood

Whiteleaf Lane

7

Big West
End Fm

Green Lane

Chidden

8

Stoke Wood

Whiteleaf Lane

Green Lane

A B C 326 D E F

Hermitage

Green Lane

Chidden 301
East Meon
Coombe Road
Lower House Farm
Duncombe Farm
273
G H J K L M
Oxenbourne House
Coombe Cross
Harvesting Lane
South Farm
South Downs Way
Stonylands Farm
233
Salt Hill
302
1 2 3 4 5 6 7 8
Old Hambledonians Cricket Club
Hyden Farm Lane
Hyden Wood
Coombe Wood
Hyden Farm
Little Hyden Lane
327
North Fm

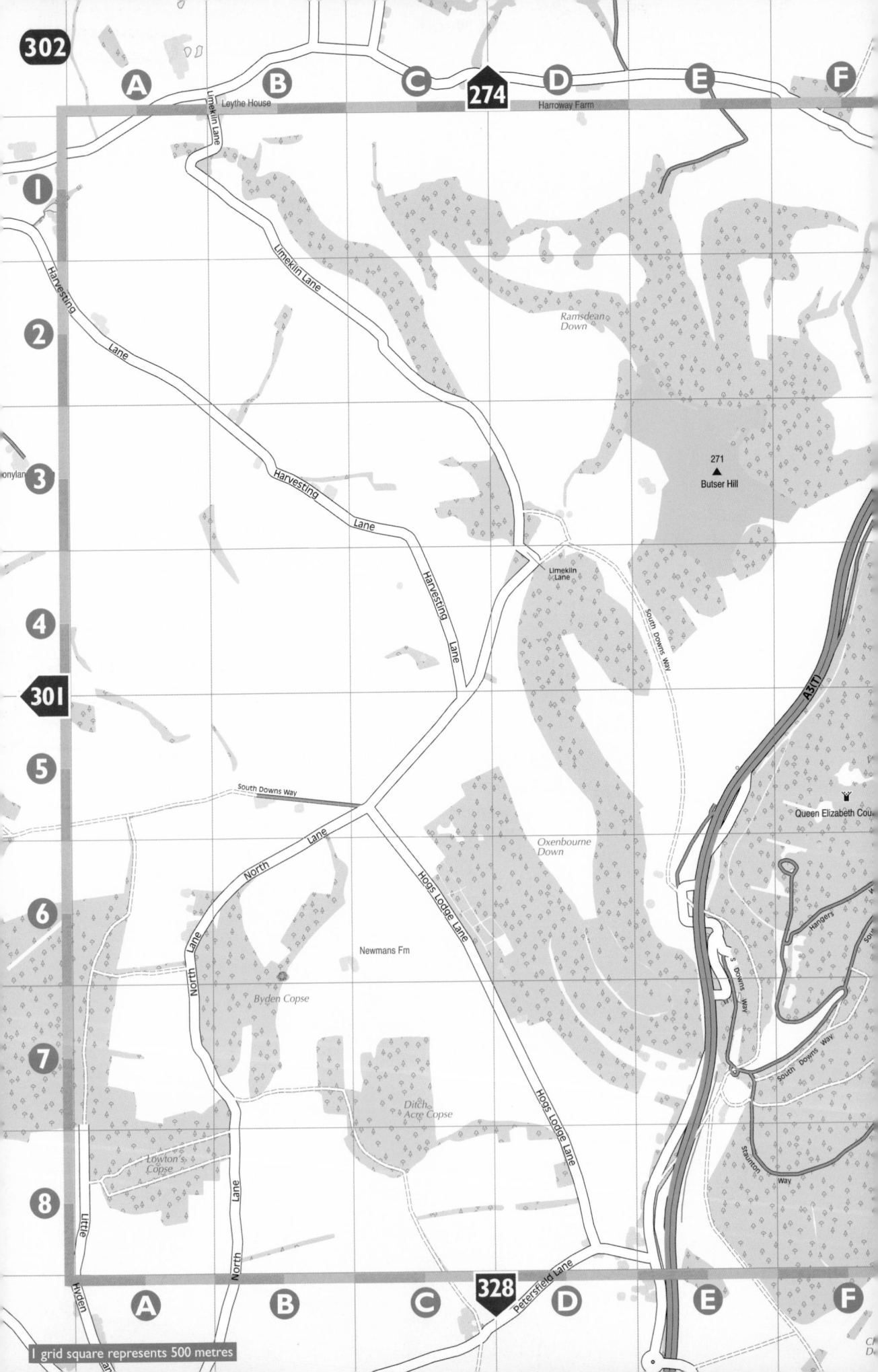

A   **B**   **C**   274   **D**   **E**   **F**

Leythe House

Harroway Farm

1

Limekiln Lane

Harvesting Lane

Limekiln Lane

Ramsdean Down

2

Harvesting Lane

3

eonyland

271 ▲
Butser Hill

Limekiln Lane

4

Harvesting Lane

South Downs Way

301

A3(T)

South Downs Way

5

Queen Elizabeth Cou

Oxenbourne Down

North Lane

Hogs Lodge Lane

S Downs Way

6

Newmans Fm

Hangers

Byden Copse

So

7

South Downs Way

Ditch Acre Copse

North Lane

Staunton Way

Lowton's Copse

8

Little

Hyden

North Lane

Hogs Lodge Lane

Petersfield Lane

A   **B**   **C**   328   **D**   **E**   **F**

Ch
D

Weston
THE CAUSEWAY
B2070
B2146
A3(T)
275
304
329
Buriton Business Park
Bolinge Hill Farm
Nursted House
Greenway
Lane
Hangers Way
Glebe Road
Sumner Rd
Petersfield Rd
Bones Lane
Heatherfield
PH
High Street
Kiln Lane
Kiln La
Buriton CP School
PO
South La
Buriton
North Lane
Pitcroft Lane
Cowhouse Farm
Hangers Way
South Downs Way
Coulters Dean Fm
Newbarn Road
Head Down Plantation
Staunton Way
Oakham Bottom
Downley
Ditcham Park Sch
Hampshire County
West Sussex County
G
H
J
K
L
M
1
2
3
4
5
6
7
8

304

B2146

A

Stanbridge Farm

B

Hampshire County
West Sussex County

C

Goose
Green

276

D

E

F

Manor Farm

Sussex Border Path

Quebec

Collins Lane

I

SUSSEX ROAD

Nursted

Westons

Putmans Lane

2

Hurst
Farm

3

Old
Ditcham

B2146

Sussex Border Path

4

B2146

Cow Lane

303

South L

Leith
Copse

Forty Acre
Lane

Sunwood Fm

South Downs Way

5

Foxcombe Fm

South Downs Way

Sussex Border Pth

6

Hampshire County
West Sussex County

7

West
Harting
Down

Round
Down

8

NT Uppark

Sussex Border Path

A

B

C

330

D

B2146

E

F

I grid square represents 500 metres

GU31

J4 1 Hollist La

K1 1 Greenfields

G H J K L M

277

Nyewood

1 Hill
Ash Farm

Upperton

Woodhouse Farm

Manor House

North Lane

North Lane

Harting

The Square

Mill Lane

Culvers

Tipper
Warren
Side

's Acre
Lane

New Lane

Hill Lane

Down Place

Hollist Lane

Turkey Island

East Harting

East

Harting Street

Street

Lane

East Harting St

1

Orchard Cl

Eastfield Lane

Telegraph Lane

Elsted

Orchard Cl

South Downs Way

B2141

South Downs Way

South Downs Way

South Downs Way

Round Down

South Do

Telegraph House

G H J K L M

331

B2141

Up Park

I 1
2
3
4
5
6
7
8

280

A   B   C   D   E   F

1

2

3

4

5

6

7

8

Kites
Nest Far

Blagdon Farm

West
Blagdon

Penbury
Knoll

Jubilee Trail

Jubilee Trail

Blackbush
Down

Toby's
Bottom

Bowldish
Pond

River Crane

Jubilee Trail

Cranborne Farm

Bo

Burwood

Nine Yews

Manor Farm

Cranborne

The Surgery

A   B   C   D   E   F

Creech
Hill House

Jubilee Trail

Grugs La

The
Square

Salisbury St

Swan
crane
St

Church
St

School

Penny's Md

Water St

Water St

CASTLE STRE

Hibbe

Common
Down

G   H   J   281   K   L   M

Blackheath
Down

South
Allenford Farm

Allen River

I

Martin
Wood

2

Boulsbury Farm

3

Brow

Stony

Hampshire County
Dorset County

4

308

Stapleton Farm

Ashley Park Farm

5

Boulsbury
Wood

6

Boveridge
House
School

7

Biddlesgate
Farm

Hyde Farm

Bratch
Copse

Bellows
Cross

Lopshill

8

Ashes Farm

308
Knoll Farm
A
B
C
282
D
E
F
1
2
3
4
5
6
7
8
307
333
Rockbourne Lane
Marsh Farm
West Park
Roman Villa
Allen River
Allen River
Littlemill La
High Street
Pound Lane
North End
West Park Lane
West Park Drive
Damerham
Browns Lane
Browns Lane
Court Farm
Court Hill
West Park Farm
Church Lane
Steels La
Western Downland Primary School
Stony Lane
Mill End
Lower Court Wood
Cornpits
Ashley Park Farm
South End
Lane
Tanners Lane
Lower Court Wood
Sandleheath
Ashridge Copse
Hampshire County
Dorset County
Road
Alderholt
Hawkhill Ditch
Ashford Water
Alderholt Mill Farm
Bull Hill Farm
Sandleheath Road
Home Farm
Alderholt Park
Hart's Farm
High Wood
Sandleheath Road
1 grid square represents 500 metres

H6
1 Marbrean Cl
J7
1 The Old Vineries
2 The Pantiles
K6
1 Allen Water Dr
2 Avon Meade
3 Cottage Ms
4 Garendon Ct
5 Meadow Cl
6 Oaklands Cl
7 Pealsham Gdns
8 S Martin Gdns
K7
1 Mill Ct
2 Vimoutiers Ct
3 Westgrove
283
Rockstead Farm
Green Lane
Radnall Wood
Flood Street
Brookheath
Peasash Farm
SP6
Upper Burgate
Green La
Fryern Court Road
Fryern Court
Allen's Farm
Wilkins's Coomb
Avon Valley Path
Lower Burgate
310
Lane
Sweatsfords Water
Sandle Dairy Farm
Puddleslosh
Fordingbridge Junior & Infant School
The Burgate School
Arch Farm Industrial Est
Hertford Cl
Dudley Av
Penny's Cl
Penny's Crescent
Burgate Flds
Sandleheath Industrial Est
Marl Lane
Whitsbury Road
Pennys La
Waverley Road
Langley Gdn
Pembridge Rd
Sharpley Cl
Beacon Ct
Charnwood Dr
Parsonage Park Dr
Waverley Cl
Player Ct
St Georges Rd
Orchard Cl
Sandle Manor School
Willow Av
Riverdale
Albion Road
Queens Gdns
Lyster Rd
Salisbury Road
Sandle Manor
Station Road
Normandy Way
Alexandra Rd
Picket Cl
Elmwood Av
Downwood Cl
Park Rd
Bruyn Rd
Sandle Copse
Mayfield Rd
Brympton Cl
Manor Farm Road
Station Road
Ashford Close
Green La
Lwr Bartons
Manor Cl
Jubilee Rd
Ashford
A338
FORDINGBRIDGE
Manor Farm Rd
Fordingbridge Hospital
Bartons Rd
Salisbury St
Victoria Rd
Bridge St
B3078
Station Road
High St
Victoria Gdns
Beechwood
Hotel
End
Flexfields
Shaftesbury St
Council Office
Town Hall
West St
Provost St
Ashford Road
Ringwood Road
Stuckton Road
Cemetery
Road
Mulberry Gdns
Church St
Church Farm
Bowerwood Road
Padstow Pl
Frog Lane
334
L8
1 Brook Ter
L7
1 The Bartons
2 Highbank Gdns
3 Moxhams
4 Orchard Gdns
5 Round Hl
L6
1 Mayfly Cl
2 St Georges Crs
L5
1 Bedford Cl
2 Burnham Rd
3 Merton Cl
K8
1 Bushells Farm
2 Diamond Cl
Fordingbridge Rd
Dorset County
Hampshire County
Ditchend Brook
G
H
J
K
L
M
1
2
3
4
5
6
7
8

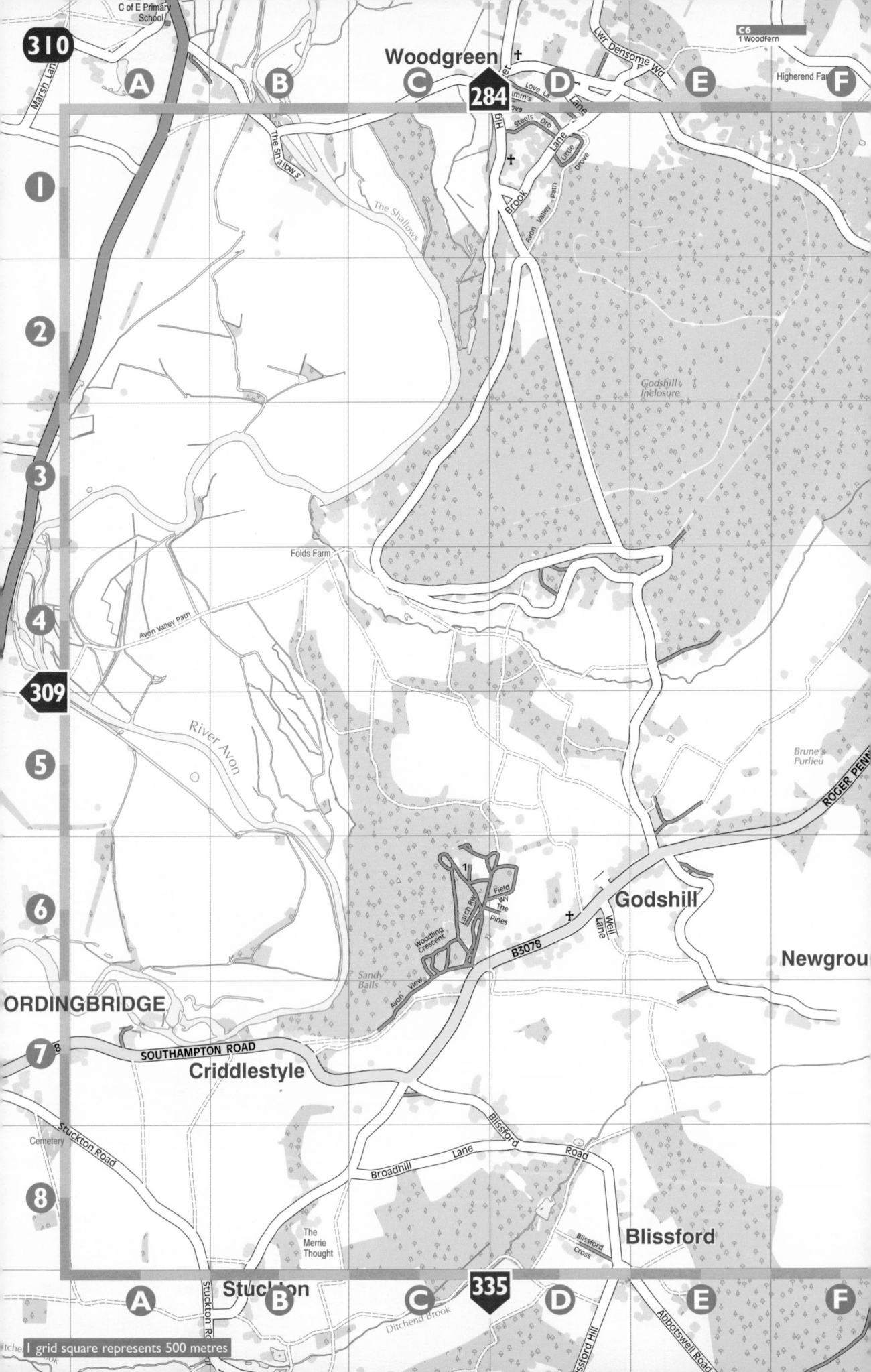

A   **B**   **C**   **D**   **E**   **F**

Marsh Lane

C of E Primary School

1

The Shallows

The Shallows

Woodgreen

284

Lwr Densome Wd

Higherend Farm

C6
1 Woodfern

Love La

Timm's Grove

High

Steels Dro

Lane

Little Drove

Brook

Avon Valley Path

2

Godshill Inclosure

3

Folds Farm

4

Avon Valley Path

309

River Avon

5

Brune's Purlieu

ROGER PENN

6

Larch Rw

Field Wy

The Pines

Godshill

Well Lane

Newgrou

Woodling Crescent

B3078

Sandy Balls

Avon View

ORDINGBRIDGE

7 8

SOUTHAMPTON ROAD

Criddlestyle

Stuckton Rd

Cemetery

Stuckton Road

Broadhill Lane

Blissford Road

Blissford Cross

Blissford

8

The Merrie Thought

Stuckton

335

Ditchend Brook

cksford Hill

Abbotswell Road

Brook

A   **B**   **C**   **D**   **E**   **F**

G H J 285 K Turf Hill L M

I

Millersford
Plantation

2

Millersford
Bottom

ROGER PENNY WAY

B3078 ROGER PENNY WAY

B3078

3

ROGER PENNY WAY

Stone
Quarry
Bottom

Black
Gutter
Bottom

New Forest

4

312

Ditchend Brook

5

Coopers
Hill

6

Pitts
Wood
Inclosure

7

Amberwood
Inclosure

Hampton
Ridge

Alderhill
Inclosure

8

G H J 336 K L M

Sloden

286

A   B   C   D   E   F

1

Pound
Bottom

*Franchises
Wood*

B3080

B3078

Hope
Cottage

2

Picket
Corner

3

Wiltshire County
Hampshire County

*Crow's
Nest
Bottom*

B3078

New

4

*The
Butts*

Forest

311

*Eyeworth
Wood*

5

*Islands
Thorns
Inclosure*

*Longcross
Plain*

Latchmore Brook

6

*Irons
Well*

*Eyeworth
Lodge*

*Fritham
Lodge*

7

*Fritham
House*

Fritham

8

*Hiscocks
Hill*

A   B   C   D   E   F

*Fritham
Plain*

337

*North
Bentley
Inclosure*

I grid square represents 500 metres

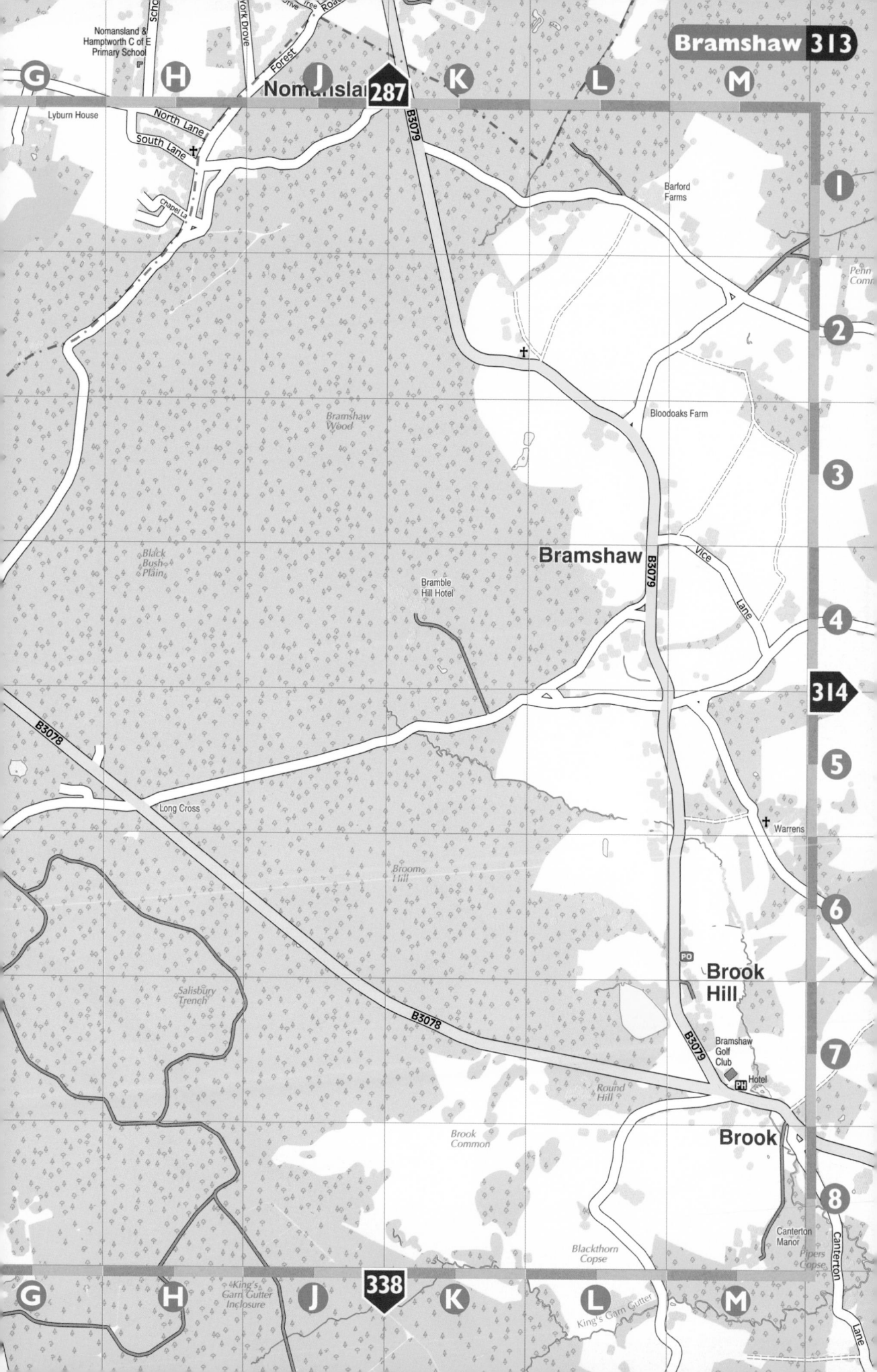

G H J K L M

Nomansland & Hamptworth C of E Primary School

Lyburn House

North Lane

South Lane

Chapel La

Nomanslan **287**

B3079

Barford Farms

Penn Comm

I

2

Bloodoaks Farm

3

Bramshaw Wood

Bramshaw

Vice Lane

B3079

4

Black Bush Plain

Bramble Hill Hotel

314

B3078

5

Long Cross

Warrens

Broom Hill

6

Salisbury Trench

B3078

PO

Brook Hill

Round Hill

Bramshaw Golf Club

Hotel

PH

B3079

7

Brook Common

Brook

Canterton Manor

8

King's Garn Gutter Inclosure

338

Blackthorn Copse

King's Garn Gutter

Pipers Copse

Canterton Lane

G H J K L M

314
288
313
339
A
B
C
D
E
F
1
2
3
4
5
6
7
8
Plantation Rd
Canada Common
Blackhill Rd
Penn Common
Furzley Lane
Furzley
Furzley Common
Furzley Road
Stagbury Hill
Half Moon Common
Cadnam Common
Cadnam River
Blenman's Farm
NEWBRIDGE
Newbridge Road
Cadnam Lane
Warrens
Bunk
Newbridge Rd
Kewlake Lane
Manor Farm
Lane
Cadnam Green
Wittensford Lane
Cadnam Lane
M27
A31
Hotel
rook
B3079
Wittensford
Romsey Road
ROMSEY ROAD
Old Lyndhurst Road
Canterton Manor
Pipers Copse
Canterton
Old Romsey Road
Southampton Road
White Hart Lane
Cadnam
PO
PH
Junction 1
A336
SOUTHAMPTON ROAD
Fir Tree Rd
Rockram Wood
Bignell Wood
Bartley
1 grid square represents 500 metres

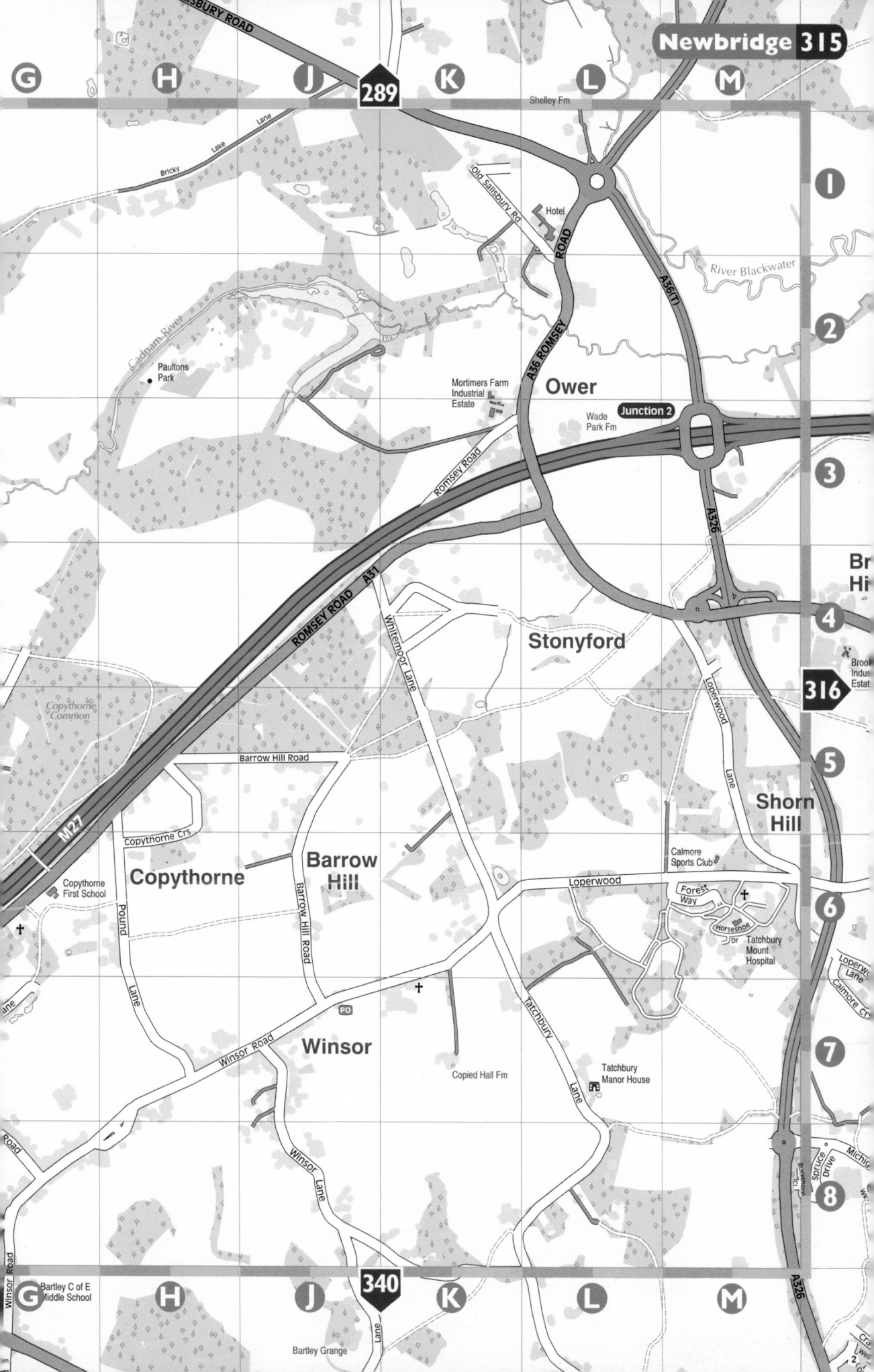

289
340
316
G
H
J
K
L
M
1
2
3
4
5
6
7
8
Shelley Fm
Bricky Lake Lane
Old Salisbury Rd
Hotel
A36 ROMSEY ROAD
A36(T)
River Blackwater
Cadnam River
Paultons Park
Mortimers Farm Industrial Estate
Ower
Junction 2
Wade Park Fm
Romsey Road
A326
ROMSEY ROAD A31
Whitemoor Lane
Stonyford
Copythorne Common
Loperwood Lane
Barrow Hill Road
Shorn Hill
M27
Copythorne Crs
Barrow Hill
Copythorne
Copythorne First School
Calmore Sports Club
Loperwood
Forest Way
Horseshoe Dr
Tatchbury Mount Hospital
Pound Lane
Barrow Hill Road
PO
Tatchbury Lane
Winsor Road
Winsor
Copied Hall Fm
Tatchbury Manor House
Winsor Lane
Spruce Drive
Bartley C of E Middle School
Bartley Grange
Winsor Road
Lane

B8
1 Alfred Cl
2 The Bramblings
3 Cedar Wood Cl
4 Chaffinch Cl
5 Chepstow Cl
6 The Linnets
7 Redwing Gdns
8 Sandlewood Cl
B7
1 Gregory Gdns
2 Treagore Rd
B6
1 Snellgrove Pl
A8
1 Clydesdale Dr
2 Enderwood Cl
3 Perrywood Gdns
290
Lee Church Lane
Moorcourt
Test Way
Wade Hill Fm
Hill Street
River Test
Church Lane
Nursling Ho
Hillstreet
Colbury Ho
Broadlands Lake
Brooke's Hill
Nursling Mill
Mill Lane
Station Road
Manor Ho Fm
Brookes Hill Industrial Estate
315
Salisbury Road
Testwood Ho
Testwood Lakes
Little Testwood Fm
Pauletts Lane
Shorn Hill
Brunel Road
Eddystone Road
Stephenson Rd
Westwood Business Park
Calmore Industrial Estate
Trinity Business Centre
Lulworth Business Centre
Nutwood Way
Tatchbury Mount Hospital
Cooks Lane
Testwood
Calmore
Junior & Infant School
Tennyson Road
Shakespeare Drive
Ewell Way
Testwood School
Testwood Lane
Oakfield Primary School
St. Michaels Road
Michigan Way
Spruce Drive
Calmore Road
Hammond's Green
Totton Recreation Centre
Totton College
Water Lane
Associated Football Club
Dr Munroe & Partners
Test Vale Surg
Civic Cen
Police Station
A326
C8
1 Boniface Cl
2 Selbourne Rd
D7
1 Hamtun Crs
341
D8
1 Meacher Cl
E8
1 Warwick Rd
Abbotswood Junior School
Forest Edge School
Lydlynch County First School
Ringwood Road
Maynard Road
First School
Forest Gate
1 grid square represents 500 metres

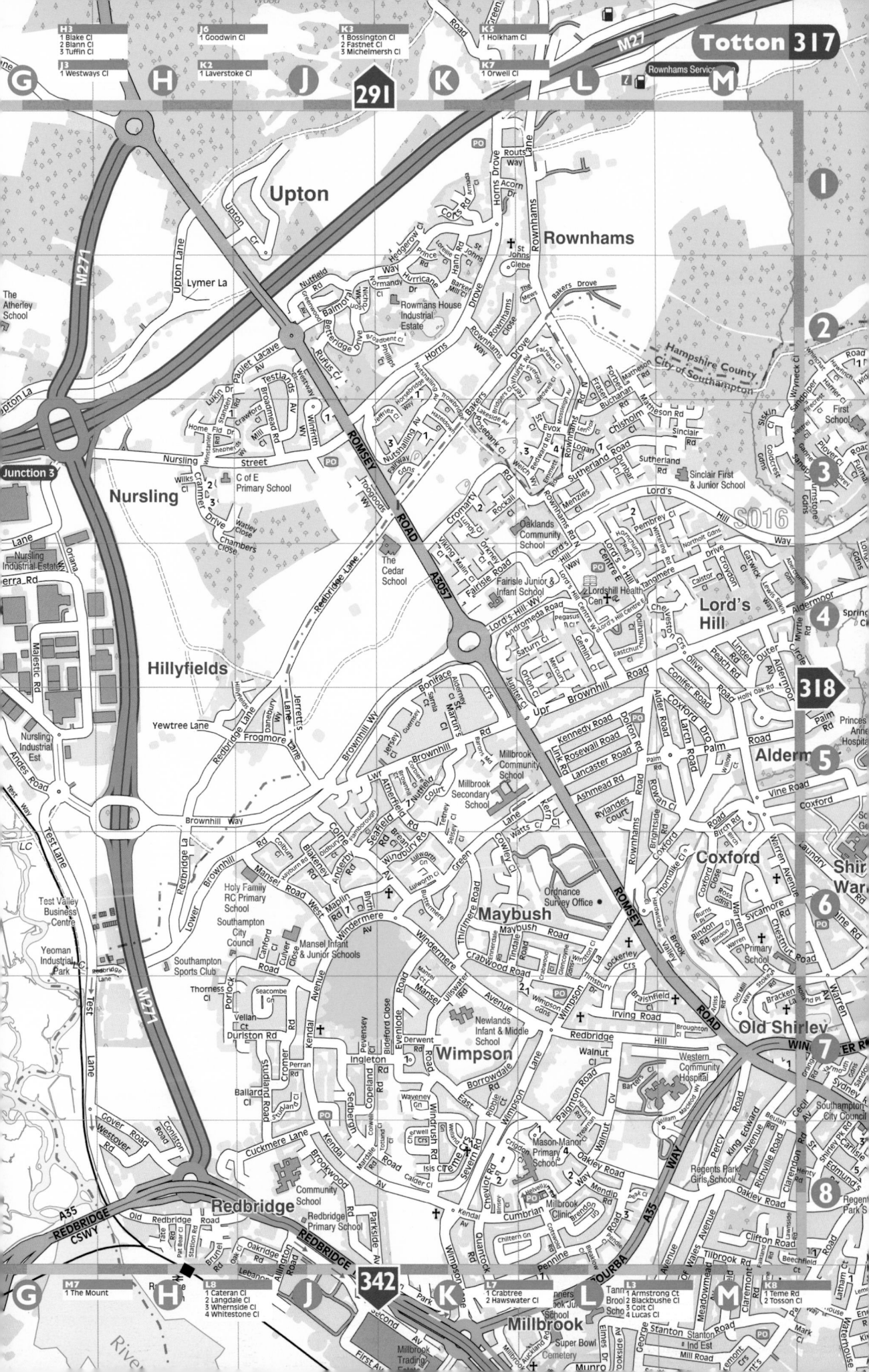

Totton 317
291
318
342
H3 1 Blake Cl 2 Blann Cl 3 Tuffin Cl
J3 1 Westways Cl
J6 1 Goodwin Cl
K2 1 Laverstoke Cl
K3 1 Bossington Cl 2 Fastnet Cl 3 Michelmersh Cl
K5 1 Holkham Cl
K7 1 Orwell Cl
M7 1 The Mount
L8 1 Cateran Cl 2 Langdale Cl 3 Whernside Cl 4 Whitestone Cl
L7 1 Crabtree 2 Haswater Cl
L3 1 Armstrong Ct 2 Blackbushe Cl 3 Colt Cl 4 Lucas Cl
K8 1 Teme Rd 2 Tosson Cl
Rownhams Services
M27
M271
Junction 3
Upton
Rownhams
Nursling
Hillyfields
Lord's Hill
Coxford
Maybush
Wimpson
Redbridge
Old Shirley
Millbrook
Hampshire County
City of Southampton
SO16
ROMSEY ROAD
A3057
A35
REDBRIDGE CSWY
REDBRIDGE
TOURBA WAY
The Atherley School
Rownhams House Industrial Estate
C of E Primary School
The Cedar School
Oaklands Community School
Fairisle Junior & Infant School
Lordshill Health Cen
Sinclair First & Junior School
Millbrook Community School
Millbrook Secondary School
Holy Family RC Primary School
Southampton City Council
Mansel Infant & Junior Schools
Southampton Sports Club
Ordnance Survey Office
Newlands Infant & Middle School
Western Community Hospital
Mason Manor Primary School
Millbrook Clinic
Community School
Redbridge Primary School
Regents Park Girls School
Nursling Industrial Estate
Nursling Industrial Est
Test Valley Business Centre
Yeoman Industrial Park
Millbrook Trading
Super Bowl
Cemetery
Romsey Road
Brownhill Way
Redbridge Lane
Lord's Hill Way
Redbridge Hill
Windermere Av
Coxford Road
Wimpson Lane
Test Lane
Nursling Street
Upton Lane
Horns Drove
Bakers Drove
Aldermoor
Warren Avenue
Oakley Road
Tilbrook Rd
Cumbrian Way
Kendal Avenue
Mansel Road West

318
292
317
343
Junction 4
M27
C6
1 Fushsia Gdns
2 Lincoln Ct
C7
1 Cranbourne Cl
B8
1 Mayflower Rd
2 Victor St
3 Vincent's Gv
C5
1 Lordswood Cl
2 Wolverley Ct
B7
1 Didcot Rd
2 Newbury Rd
3 Vaudrey Cl
B4
1 Bransbury Cl
2 Lyburn Cl
3 Purbrook Cl
B6
1 Vinery Rd
A8
1 Ashdene
2 Church St
3 Newman St
4 Regent's Gv
5 Settle Cl
D5
1 Abingdon Gdns
2 Ashwood Gdns
3 Beaumont Cl
4 Burgess Gdns
5 Fernlea Gdns
6 Sherwood Cl
A2
1 Brambling Cl
F3
1 Hurlingham Gdns
F4
1 Dahlia Rd
F5
1 Oakhurst Rd
F6
1 Highfield Cl
F7
1 Crofton Cl
2 Woodstock Dr
F8
1 C Dibben Ms
2 Highcliff Av
D4
1 Shawford Cl
2 Underwood Cl
3 Wykeham Cl
D8
1 Atherley Ct
2 Buckingham Ga
E1
1 Lingwood Wk
2 Pinehurst Rd
E3
1 Gables Ct
E4
1 The Mount
2 Tudor Wood Cl
E5
1 Meadowhead Rd
E8
1 Ashridge Cl
2 Court Royal Ms
3 Woodlands Wy
F2
1 Northwood Cl
Chilworth Common
Lord's Wood
S016
Lordswood
Bassett
Upper Shirley
Shirley Warren
Shirley
Old Shirley
Southampton Common
Southampton Sports Centre
Southampton City Council
Aldermoor Health Centre
Vermont School
Red Lodge School
The Winchester Gallery
Middle School
Hollybrook Cemetery
Princess Anne Hospital
Southampton General Hosp
Northbrook Industrial Est
Malvern Business Centre
Bellemoor Secondary School
Oatlands House Health Clinic
Doctors Surgery
Taunton's College
King Edward VI School
Cemetery
Hampshire County Cricket Club
University of Southampton
University
Greggs School
Alma Road Surgery
Regents Park Surg
Police Stn
Infant School
Victor Street Surg
Primary School
First School
Junior School
Nuffield Theatre
WINCHESTER ROAD
BASSETT AVENUE
BASSETT AV
HIGHFIELD AVENUE
THE AVENUE
SHIRLEY HIGH ST
A35
A33
A27
Golf Course Road
Bassett Row
Bassett Heath Av
Bassett Wood Rd
Hill Lane
Dale Valley Road
Lordswood Road
Coxford Road
Winchester Road
1 grid square represents 500 metres

G3
1 Evesham Cl
2 Grendon Cl
G8
1 Portswood Pk
2 Thomas Lewis Wy
H3
1 Bembridge Cl
2 Bonchurch Cl
3 Brighstone Cl
4 Field Cl
H5
1 Woodcote Rd
H6
1 Grosvenor Gdns
H8
1 Collier Cl
H4
1 Tulip Rd
L2
1 George Curl Wy
M6
1 Atlantic Park Vw
2 Benhams Rd
3 Camelia Gdns
4 Carpathia Cl
5 Catcombe Gdns
6 Hallet Cl
M7
1 Benhams Farm Cl
2 Longmead Rd
3 Grasdean Cl
4 Hazelwood Rd
5 Wakefield Ct
M8
1 Bramble Ms
2 Hood Rd
3 Macarthur Crs
4 Vanguard Rd
Fred Woolley House (Hospl)
293
North Stoneham
Trojans Sports Club
Wellington Sports Club
Eastleigh Football Club
Stoneham Lane
Southampton Airport Parkway Station
Southampton International Airport
Spitfire Loop
Mitchell Way
Tinker Aly
Wide Lane
A335
M27
Junction 5
St Georges Catholic Boys School
Hampshire County
City of Southampton
Bassett Green Road
A27
Stoneham Way
Orion Business Centre
Stoneham Cemetery Road
Cemetery
Itchen Way
Mansbridge Road
Mans Bridge
320
Burgess Road
A35
Swaythling Station
Swaythling
Hampton Park
Swaythling Primary School
Woodmill Lane
Woodmill
Riverside Park
River Itchen
Townhill Park
The Gregg School
Bitterne Park Secondary School
Bitterne Park Junior & Infant School
Townhill Middle Sch
Townhill Infant Sch
Townhill Park Health Clinic
Portswood
Bitterne Park
SOUTHAMPTON
SO18
Midanbury
St Denys Station
ST DENYS
Thomas Lewis Wy
St Denys' Rd
A3035
Cobden Av
Bitterne Park Clinic
Bitterne Park Surgery
St Christophers School
St Marys College
Moorlands Infant School
Tides Reach
344
L8
1 Dalmally Gdns
M5
1 Creedy Gdns
2 Rostron Cl
3 Webburn Gdns
L6
1 Lingfield Gdns
2 Longmead Rd
L7
1 Trent Cl
L5
1 Hillgrove Rd
K4
1 Alfred Rose Ct
2 Gilbury Cl
3 Grange Cl
4 Howard Cl
5 Ld Mountbtn Cl
6 Meadowside Cl
7 Pilgrim Pl
8 Westbrook Wy
J7
1 St Aug. Gdns
2 Saltmead
J8
1 Pettinger Gdns
2 Riverdene Pl
J3
1 Stoneham Cl
2 Summerfld Gdns
J4
1 Havenstone Wy
2 Rayners Gdns
Centurion Industrial Park
Mount Pleasant Industrial Estate
Bitterne Road West
A3024

320
C7
1 Caversham Cl
2 Glenlea Dr
3 Orchards Wy
4 Runnymede
5 Severn Wy
6 Warden Cl
A8
1 Aberdour Cl
2 The Birches
C6
1 Hornbeam Gdns
A7
1 Ennerdale Gdns
2 Grasmere Cl
3 Hedgerow Dr
4 Nomad Cl
5 Wheatcroft Dr
A5
1 Torridge Gdns
A6
1 Helford Gdns
2 Tresillian Gdns
3 Waldon Gdns
Lake Farm
A
B
C
294
D
E
F
1
2
3
4
5
6
7
8
319
345
Allington Manor Business Centre
Allington Manor Farm
River Itchen
Itchen Way
Decoy Covert
Itchen Valley Country Park
Hogwood Lane
Allington Lane
Oaklands House
Winslowe House
Moorgreen Farm
Quob Lane
M27
A27
Romill Cl
Oak Vale
Cemetery
Lime Gdns
Moorgreen
The Dro
Golden Ct
Raymond Close
Moorgreen Road
Primary School
Quob Farm Cl
Brookside Way
Hornbeam Gdns
Elm Gdns
Holly Gdns
Larch Cl
Hickory Gdns
Redwood Cl
Baker
Catherine Cl
Long Dr
Lt Quob La
Megan Rd
Glenn Rd
Chapel
Hope Road
Princess Close
St James Primary School
Monarch Way
Hatch Bottom
West End Surgery
Moorgreen Hospital
B3035
High Street
Botley Road
Swaythling Road
Barnsland
The Dr
Sharon Road
Charmwen Crs
Barbe
Hatch Md
Midlands Est
Tyne Wy
Avon Wy
St James Road
Lwr New Rd
Upper New Rd
Tower Pl
Woodlea Gdns
Baltic Rd
Hilldene Wy
Crabwood Dr
Kenilworth Gdns
Western Road
Eastern Rd
Southern Rd
Telegraph Road
Beacon
Grosvenor Gdns
West End Road
West End
Hickley Farm
A27 Church Hill
Beechwood Ri
Wilderness Hts
Chalk Hill
Coopers Cl
Manns Cl
Clifton Gdns
Ullswater Av
Barle Cl
Ivy La
Old Ivy La
Harbourne Gdns
Townhill Way
Townhill Surg
Townhill Middle Sch
Townhill Sch
Townhill Park Health Clinic
Arun Road
Eden Rd
Hayle Rd
Thames
Kennet Cl
Tresillian Gdns
Kenwyn Cl
Okement Cl
Welland Gdns
Torridge Gdns
Dart Rd
Frome Rd
Cutbush
Lambourne Rd
Shaw Cl
Monnow Gdns
Windermere Road
Derwent Cl
Edelvale Road
Gorselands Rd
Alpine Cl
Vine Bank
St Francis Av
Moorlands Infant School
Kesteven Wy
Cerne Wy
Duddon Cl
Culver Gdns
Middleton Cl
West End Road
Westend Road
Harefield Junior & Infant School
Wynter Road
Hatley Road
Yeovil Chase
Doctors Surgery
Selborne Av
Tytherley Rd
Exford Drive
Denmead Rd
Chilcomb Rd
Beaulieu Rd
Melchet Rd
Frithan Road
Minstead Av
Meon Ct
Woodlands Community School
Moorhill Road
Somerton Av
Balaclava Rd
Wellington Avenue
Burnham Cha
Harefield Clinic
Dean Rd
Yew Rd
Brook Rd
Pound Street
C8
1 Chawton Cl
2 Leckford Cl
3 Roselands
Cheriton
Blendworth Lane
Thornhill Park
Pine Drive
Kootenay
D5
1 Brookside Wy
D6
1 Monarch Wy
2 Oakwood Ct
3 Willow Cl
D7
1 High St
2 Hilldene Wy
Junction 7
A334
1 grid square represents 500 metres

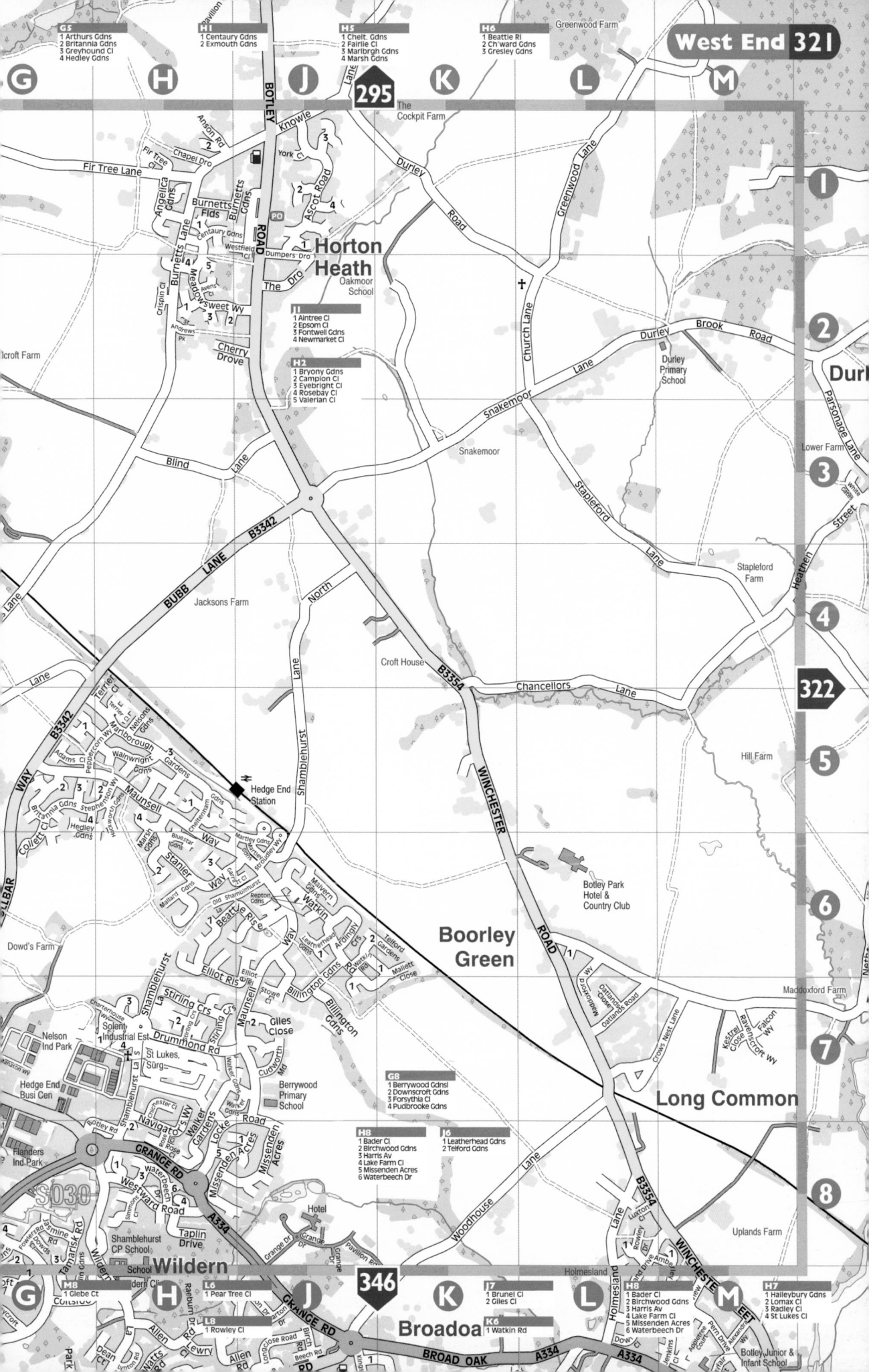

G5
1 Arthurs Gdns
2 Britannia Gdns
3 Greyhound Cl
4 Hedley Gdns

H1
1 Centaury Gdns
2 Exmouth Gdns

H5
1 Chelt. Gdns
2 Fairlie Cl
3 Marlbrgh Gdns
4 Marsh Gdns

H6
1 Beattie Rl
2 Ch'ward Gdns
3 Gresley Gdns

Greenwood Farm

G   H   J   K   L   M

Fir Tree Lane

BOTLEY ROAD

Knowle

295

The Cockpit Farm

Anson Rd

Chapel Dro

Fir Tree

Durley Road

York Cl

Ascot Road

Greenwood Lane

Angelica Gdns

Burnetts Flds

Burnetts Lane

Burnetts Gdns

Westfield Cl

Centaury Gdns

Dumpers Dro

PO

Horton Heath

Oakmoor School

Church Lane

Durley

Brook Road

2

Dur

The Dro

Crispin Cl

Meadowsweet Wy

Andrews Pk

Cherry Drove

I1
1 Aintree Cl
2 Epsom Cl
3 Fontwell Gdns
4 Newmarket Cl

Durley Primary School

Parsonage Lane

Lower Farm

3

Vanille Street

H2
1 Bryony Gdns
2 Campion Cl
3 Eyebright Cl
4 Rosebay Cl
5 Valerian Cl

Snakemoor Lane

Snakemoor

Durley Lane

Stapleford Lane

Heathen

Blind Lane

North Lane

B3342

BUBB LANE

Jacksons Farm

Stapleford Farm

4

Croft House

B3354

Chancellors Lane

Hill Farm

322

5

Icroft Farm

B3342

WAY

Terrier Cl

Nelson Gdns

Marlborough Gardens

Adams Rd

Peppercorn Wy

Walnwright Gdns

Britannia Gdns

Collett Cl

Stephenson Wy

Hedley Gdns

Maunsell Way

March Gdns

Stanier Way

Bluestar Gdns

Mallard Gdns

La Shamblehurst

Hedge End Station

Shamblehurst Lane

WINCHESTER ROAD

Botley Park Hotel & Country Club

Maddoxford Wy

Oatlands Close

Oatlands Road

Maddoxford Farm

6

Dowd's Farm

Beattie Rise

Elliot Rise

Repton Gdns

Stroudley Wy

Martley Gdns

Malvern Gdns

Watkin Way

Leatherhead Gdns

Arlingly Crs

Telford Gdns

Mallett Close

Boorley Green

Kestrel Close

Ravenscroft Wy

Falcon Wy

7

Shamblehurst La

Stirling Crs

Chartered House

Drummond Rd

Stiring Crs

Maunsell Rd

Stowe Cl

Billington Gdns

Giles Close

Billington Gdns

Crows Nest Lane

Uplands Farm

Nelson Ind Park

Solent Industrial Est

St Lukes. Surg

Walker Gdns

Berrywood Primary School

G8
1 Berrywood Gdnsl
2 Downscroft Gdns
3 Forsythia Cl
4 Pudbrooke Gdns

Long Common

8

Hedge End Busi Cen

Manchester Cl

Navigators Wy

Water Gardens

Locke Road

Missenden Acres

H8
1 Bader Cl
2 Birchwood Gdns
3 Harris Av
4 Lake Farm Cl
5 Missenden Acres
6 Waterbeech Dr

I6
1 Leatherhead Gdns
2 Telford Gdns

Woodhouse Lane

Luxton Cl

Flanders Ind Park

S030

Westward Road

Waterbeech Dr

Simmons Wy

Tannarisk Rd

Jasmine Cl

Dowds

Wildern

GRANGE RD

A334

Taplin Drive

Shamblehurst CP School

Wildern

Hotel

Grange Dr

Pavilion Rd

B3354

Holmesland Lane

Winchester Street

Holmesland

Rowley

G   **H**   **J**   **K**   **L**   **M**

M8
1 Glebe Ct

L6
1 Pear Tree Cl

346

J7
1 Brunel Cl
2 Giles Cl

H8
1 Bader Cl
2 Birchwood Gdns
3 Harris Av
4 Lake Farm Cl
5 Missenden Acres
6 Waterbeech Dr

H7
1 Haileybury Gdns
2 Lornax Cl
3 Radley Cl
4 St Lukes Cl

Raeburn Dr

Coltsft

L8
1 Rowley Cl

Allen Rd

Watts Rd

Dean Rd

Broadoa

K6
1 Watkin Rd

Birch Cl

Beech Rd

BROAD OAK

A334

A334

Botley Junior & Infant School

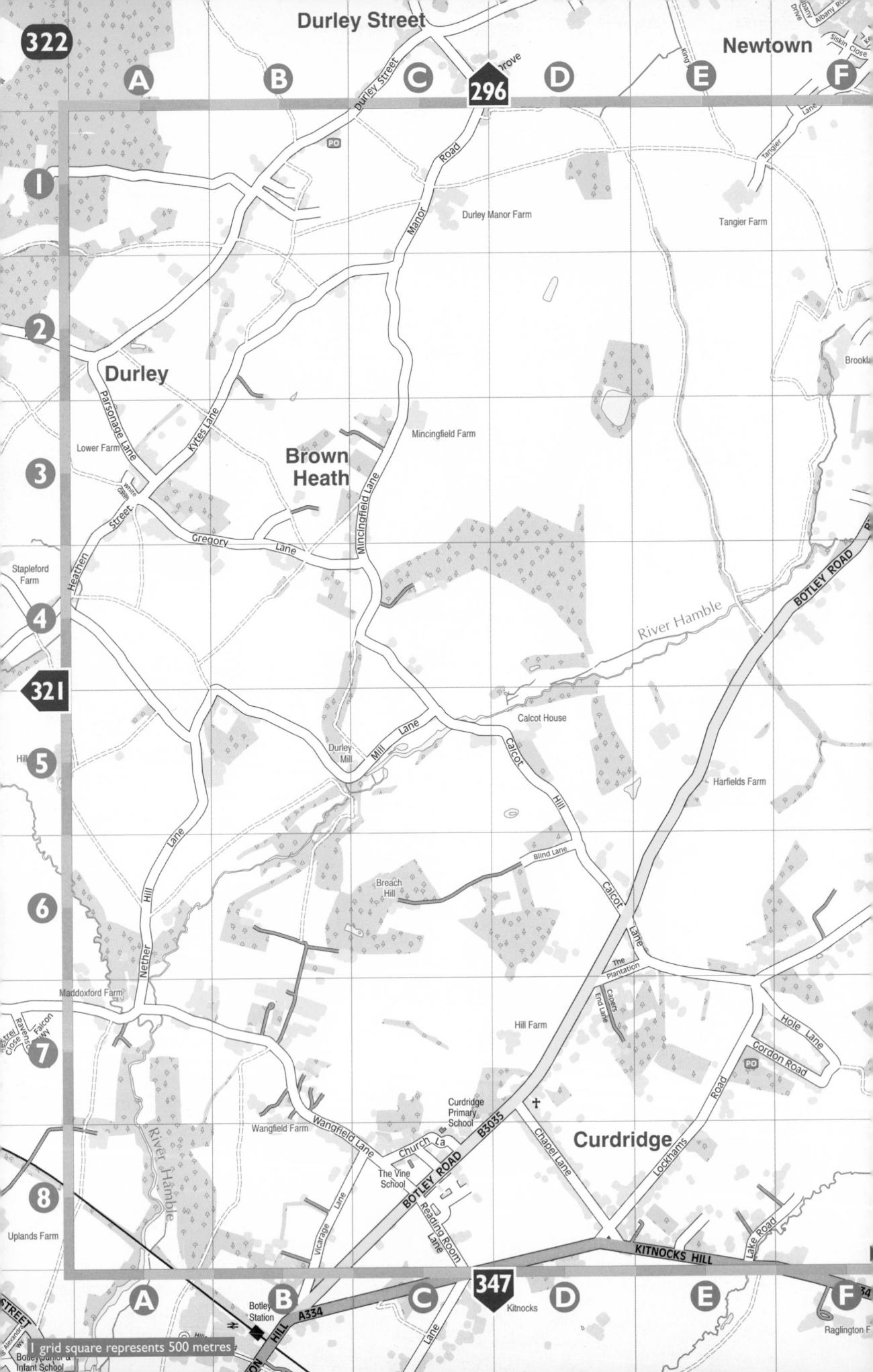
322
296
321
347
A
B
C
D
E
F
1
2
3
4
5
6
7
8
Durley Street
Newtown
Durley
Brown Heath
Curdridge
Durley Manor Farm
Tangier Farm
Mincingfield Farm
Lower Farm
Stapleford Farm
Calcot House
Harfields Farm
Durley Mill
Breach Hill
Hill Farm
Maddoxford Farm
Wangfield Farm
Curdridge Primary School
The Vine School
Uplands Farm
Botley Station
Kitnocks
Raglington F
Brookla
River Hamble
Durley Street
Manor Road
Parsonage Lane
Kytes Lane
Mincingfield Lane
Gregory Lane
Heathen Street
White Gates
Mill Lane
Calcot Hill
Calcot Lane
Blind Lane
Nether Hill Lane
The Plantation
Capers End Lane
Hole Lane
Gordon Road
Lockhams Road
Chapel Lane
Botley Road B3035
BOTLEY ROAD
Wangfield Lane
Church La
Reading Room Lane
Vicarage Lane
Kitnocks Hill
Lake Road
Tangier Lane
King's
Albany Drive
Albany Road
Siskin Close
Falcon Way
Ravens Close
A334
HILL
Lane
PO
1 grid square represents 500 metres

J1
1 Cricklewood Cl
2 Godfrey Pink Wy
3 Penfords Pdk
4 Shore Crs
J4
1 Clayhill Cl
K4
1 Meadow Cl
297
Hoe
Bishop's Palace (remains of)
COPPICE HILL B2177
Thickets House
Locks Farm
Paradise Lane
Swanmore Business Park
Swanmore County Secondary School
Lower Chase Road
Moorlands Road
Swanmore Road
Suetts Lane
Glebe
Curdridge Lane
Sandy Lane
Waltham Chase
Waltham Business Park
Brickyard Road
Forest Road
Forest Farm
Nation's Farm
St John the Baptist School
Solomons Lane
Black Horse Lane
Shirrell Heath
High Street
Winters Road
Twynhams
Hospital Road
Shedfield Grange
Grange Farm Business Park
Hotel
Meon Valley Golf & Country Club
Shedfield House
WINCHESTER ROAD
B2177
324
348
Shedfield
Turkey Island
Upper Church Rd
K5
1 Forest Gdns
Frith Lane

B5 1 Hunters Cha
A4 1 Rowan Cl 2 Russett Cl
A3 1 Beverley Gdns 2 Coronation Rd
298
Upper Swanmore
Park La
Green Lane
Court Lane
Oxford Lane
Swanmore Road
Midlington Hill
Midlington
Mayhill Farm
Mayhill Lane
Well Lane
Hampton Hill
Lane
Cut Throat Lane
Swanmore Road
Vicarage Lane
Church Lane
Hill Place
Swanmore Church of England School
Bucketts Farm Cl
Foxcombe Close
Church Road
Swanmore
Broad Lane
The Drove
Chapel Road
Greenways
Larkspur Cl
Myers Cl
New Road
Spring Vale
Spring Lane
Leacock Cl
Dodds Lane
Droxford Road
Green Lane
King's
Cott Street Lane
Cott Street La
Cott Street Farm
Cott Street
Hillpound
Martin Cl
Medlicott Wy
Glendale
Lakes
323
Orchardlea
Dirty Copse
Mislingford Road
Gravel Hill
Holywell House
Meon Valley
A32
Bishop's Wood Road
Bishopsmore
Westfield Drive
Hawk's Nest
Soberton Heath
Bere Fm
Mislingford
Shirrell Heath
Bishops Lane
Hospital Road
Winters Road
Hill
Newmans Hill
River Meon
Budden's Lane
Heath Road
Liberty Rd
Woodend
Kingsmead
349
Close Wood
1 grid square represents 500 metres

G   H   J   299   K   L   M

1

B2150

Stoke W

2   B2150

Grenville
Hall

Soberton
Towers

Arch

Station Road

†

School Hill

Long   Road

East Hoe Road

Home
Down

3

Soberton

West Street

West
St

Hill

Chalk

Wayfarer's Wak

4

East
Ma

326

Cole   Hill

Wayfarer's Wak

Wayfarer's Wak

King's

Way

High St

High Street

Peststead

Lane

Fm

Webbs Green
Fm

Selworth   Lane

Webbs

Green

Taplands

Hambledon   Lane

Broom Fm

Hambledon Lane

East Hoe Road

5

Hill

Hurs

Plough Lane

Roy's Lane

Hoe Cross
Fm

6

†   Chapel Road

Lane

Goldfield
Gallery   Ⓜ

Armsworth   Lane

Russell's Fm

Hoe Street

King's Way

7

May

Bush

Lane

Ingoldfield Lane

Armsworth Lane

Hill View
Farm

Hole Farm

King's Way

Kiln Hill

southend Lane

Southend

Mensands
Lane

Hoe   Lane

8

Dradfield Lane

G   H   Ingoldfield Lane   J   350   K   L   M

PO   Church Road   Huntbou   King's Way

Hoe Gate

326
300
325
351
A
B
C
D
E
F
1
2
3
4
5
6
7
8
Chidden
Stoke Wood
Big West End Fm
Green Lane
Whiteleaf Lane
Hermitage Fm
B2150
East Hoe Road
Green Lane
Chidden Holt
Brook Lane
Home Down
Hambledon Cricket Club
Brook Lane
Windmill Down
Park Ho
B2150 GREEN LANE
East Hoe Manor
Wayfarer's Walk
Vinyard and Winepress
Dogkennel Lane
Whitedale Ho
Church Lane
Hambledon Infant School
East Street
Glidden Lane
Dogkennel Lane
Lashly Meadow
Stewarts Green
Wayfarer's Walk
Wak
High St
Vicarage La
The Gdns
St
PO
Monarch's Way
Hambledon
West St
Speltham Hill
Old Barn Crs
Cams
Rushmore
WEST STREET
Cams Hill
King's Way
Pitt Hill Lane
Menslands Lane
Wayfarer's Walk
Rushmere Lane
Bury Lodge
B2150
Monarch's Way
Pitt Hill Lane
Pithill Fm
Lane
Harrowgate Lane
Hill
Bittles Fm
HAMBLEDON ROAD
B2150
Pitt
Rushmere Lane
Rookwood Fm
1 grid square represents 500 metres

G
H
J
K
L
M
301
Hyden Farm
North Fm
Monarch's Way
Hyden Farm Lane
Stoneridge Fm
Clanfield
Hambledon Road
Old Mill Lane
Broadhalfpenny Down
Hinton Manor Lane
Downhouse Road
328
Hinton Manor
Harrowgate Lane
Hinton Manor Lane
Catherington Down
Catherington C of E Controll Infant School
Denmead Mill
Hinton Daubnay
Broadway Lane
Old Mill Lane
Roads Hill
Five
Hamb Lane
Lovedean Lane
Tagdell Lane
Monarch's Way
352
Day Lane
Crouch
Lychgate
Drive
Heath Close
Walden Gdns
1
2
3
4
5
6
7
8

328
B8
1 Durlands Rd
B7
1 Comfrey Cl
2 Coombs Cl
3 Down Farm Pl
4 Holdenhurst Cl
5 Juniper Rd
6 Mundays Rw
B6
1 Ennerdale Cl
A6
1 Wrexham Gv
A
B
C
302
D
E
F
1
2
3
4
5
6
7
8
327
353
Copse
Little Hyden Lane
North Lane
Petersfield Lane
Bramble La
Clanfield Junior School
Clanfield
Church
Chalton La
Chalton Lane
Pond La
Nickleby Rd
Homefield Wy
Wilkins Close
Hambledon Road
Peak Rd
Pipers Md
South Lane
Sword Cl
Sunderton Lane
Windmill Cl
Rosewood Gdns
Sandlewood Close
New Road
Maple Crs
Beech Rd
White Beam Ri
Oak Rd
Hazel Rd
Sycamore Cl
Green Lane
Hazelgrove
Aldridge Cl
Jacobs Cl
St David's Rd
Ridge Cl
Jasmine Way
Redwing Rd
Redwing Cl
Fieldfare Cl
Kestrel Cl
Slindon Close
Storrington Rd
Amberley Rd
Duncton Rd
Goring Av
Harting Cl
St James Cl
Petersgate Infant School
Singleton Gdns
Black Berry Cl
London Rd
A3(T)
Elderberry Cl
Meon Cl
Arle Cl
Drift Road
Farm Vw Av
Clanfield Surgery
PO
Godwin Crs
Saxon Cl
First Av
Chalk Rdg
Valley Pk Dr
Hilltop Gdns
Dirt Lane
White Dirt La
Glamorgan Road
Draycote Rd
Viking Wy
Wessex Road
Viking Way
Wode Cl
Southdown Road
Francis Rd
Hawthorn Road
Belmont Close
Romsey Rd
Derwent Cl
Northfield Close
Hilda Av
St Giles Wy
Tarn Rise
Eskdale Cl
St Michaels Way
St Andrew Cl
North Road
Wasdale Cl
Claire Gdns
London Road
St Hubert Road
Southdown Rd
South Road
Well Copse Close
The Vale
Down Rd
Chervil Cl
Downwood Wy
Lovage Way
Lith Lane
Down Rd
LONDON RD
Junction 1
Catherington Lane
Catherington C of E Controlled Infant School
Catherington
Five Heads Road
Hillside Industrial Est
Lith Avenue
Enterprise Industrial Est
Enterprise Rd
Highcroft Industrial Est
Highcroft Lane
Bentley Cl
Lychgate Drive
Horndean Football Club
Princess Gdns
St Ann's Rd
Crescent
C4
1 Chilworth Gdns
2 Lodsworth Cl
3 Middleton Rl
4 Tillington Gdns
Horndean Health Centre
Blendworth
Blendworth
Horndean Down
New Barn Fm
PO8
Crabden Lane
Horndean Road
Castle Road
Woodhouse Road
Maynard Pl
Wentworth Dr
Walden Gdns
Horndean
Junior School
Jodrell Cl
Infant
Cheriton
1 grid square represents 500 metres

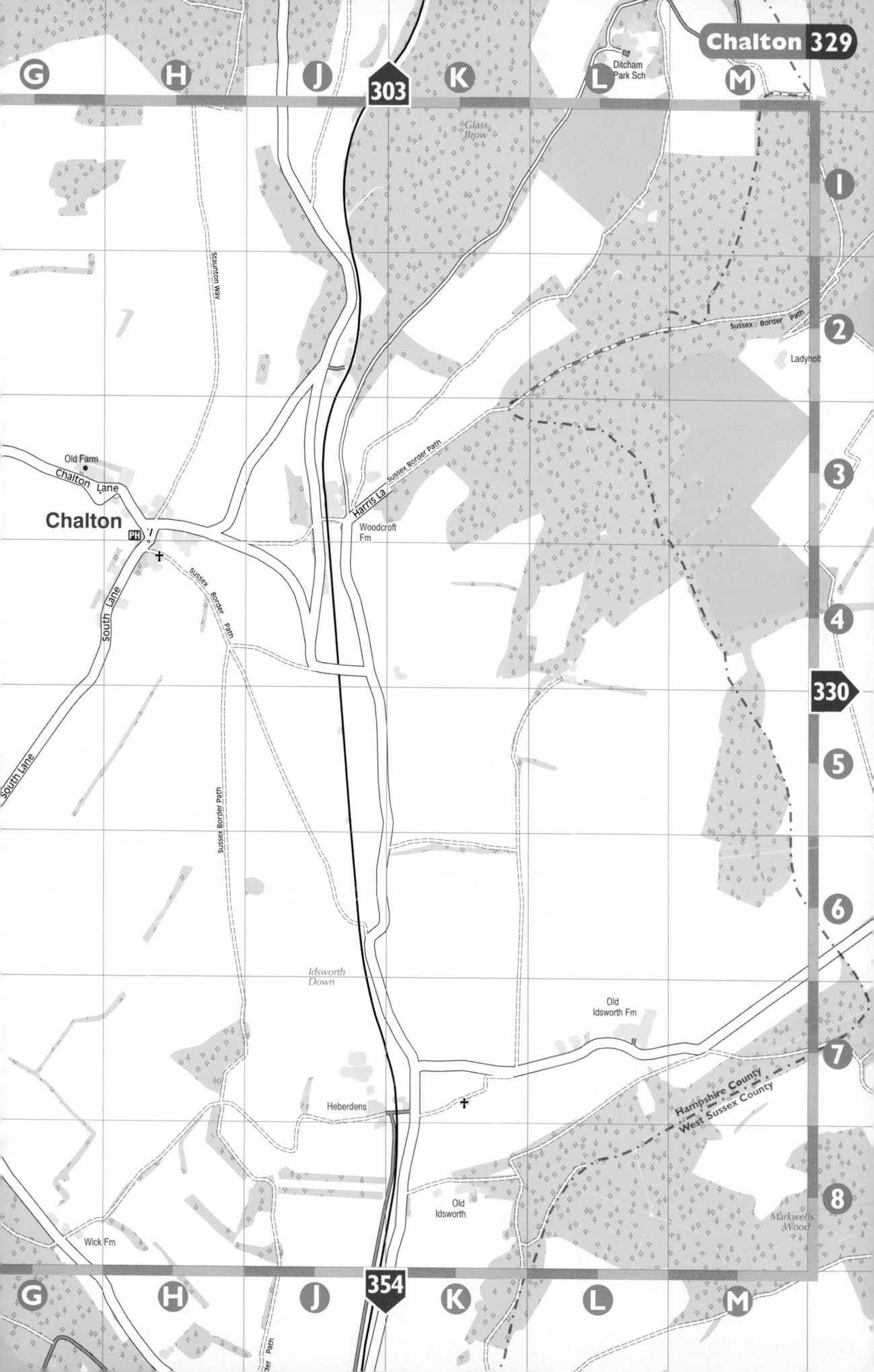

G H J K L M

303

Ditcham
Park Sch

1

2
Sussex Border Path
Ladyholt

Staunton Way

3

Old Farm
Chalton Lane

4

Chalton
PH
Harris La.
Sussex Border Path
Woodcroft
Fm

330

Sussex Border Path

5

South Lane

South Lane

6

Idsworth
Down

Old
Idsworth Fm

7

Hampshire County
West Sussex County

8

Heberdens

Old
Idsworth

Markwells
Wood

Wick Fm

354

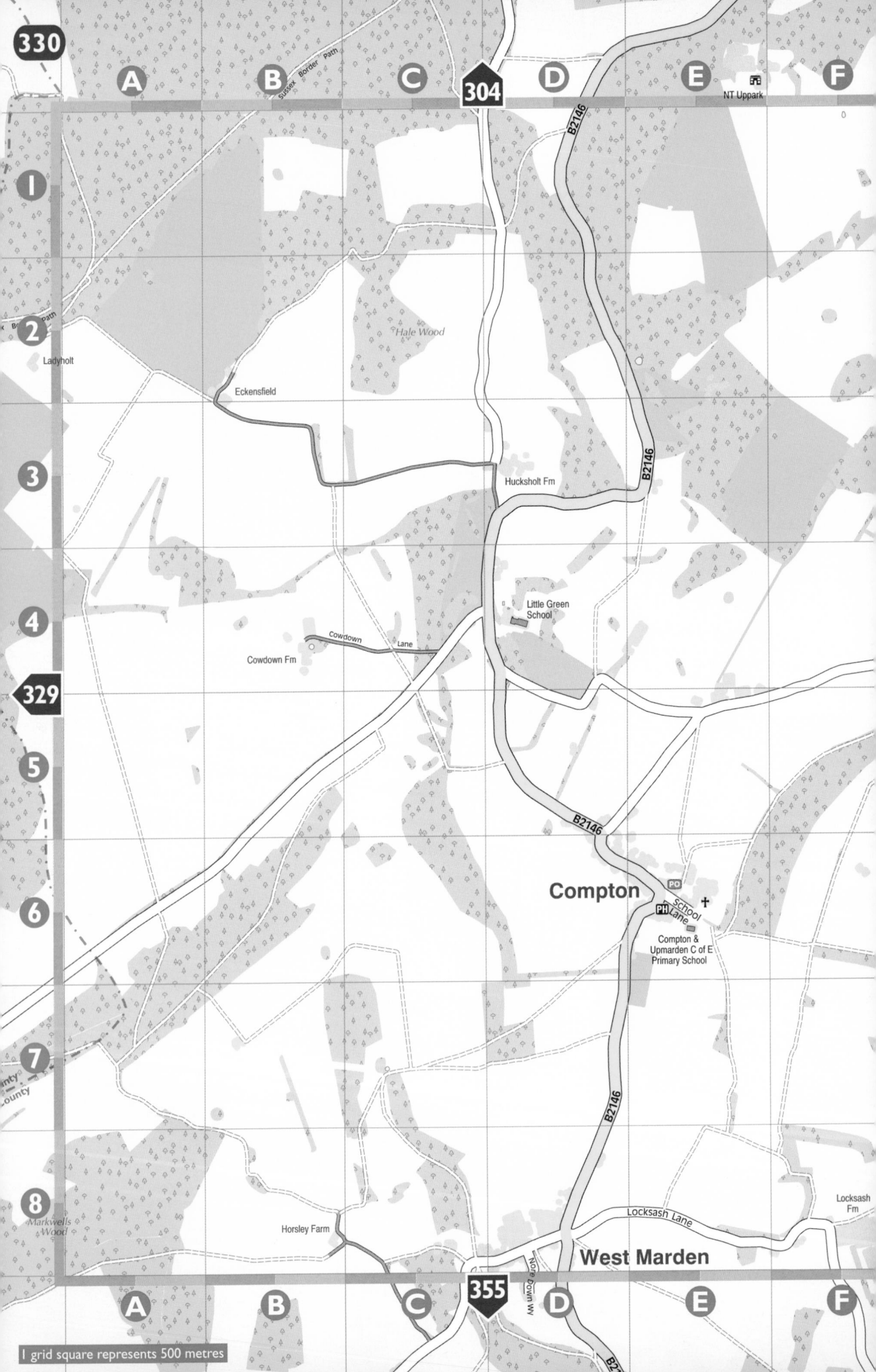

A   B   C   304   D   E   F

🏛 NT Uppark

0

1

2
Ladyholt

Hale Wood

Eckensfield

3
Hucksholt Fm

B2146

Little Green
School

4
Cowdown   Lane
Cowdown Fm

329

5

B2146

6
Compton
PO
PH   School
Lane   ✝
Compton &
Upmarden C of E
Primary School

7
County
County

8
Markwells
Wood
Horsley Farm

Locksash Lane
Locksash
Fm

Nore Down Wa

West Marden

A   B   C   355   D   E   F

B2146

B2146

Sussex   Border   Path

B Border Path

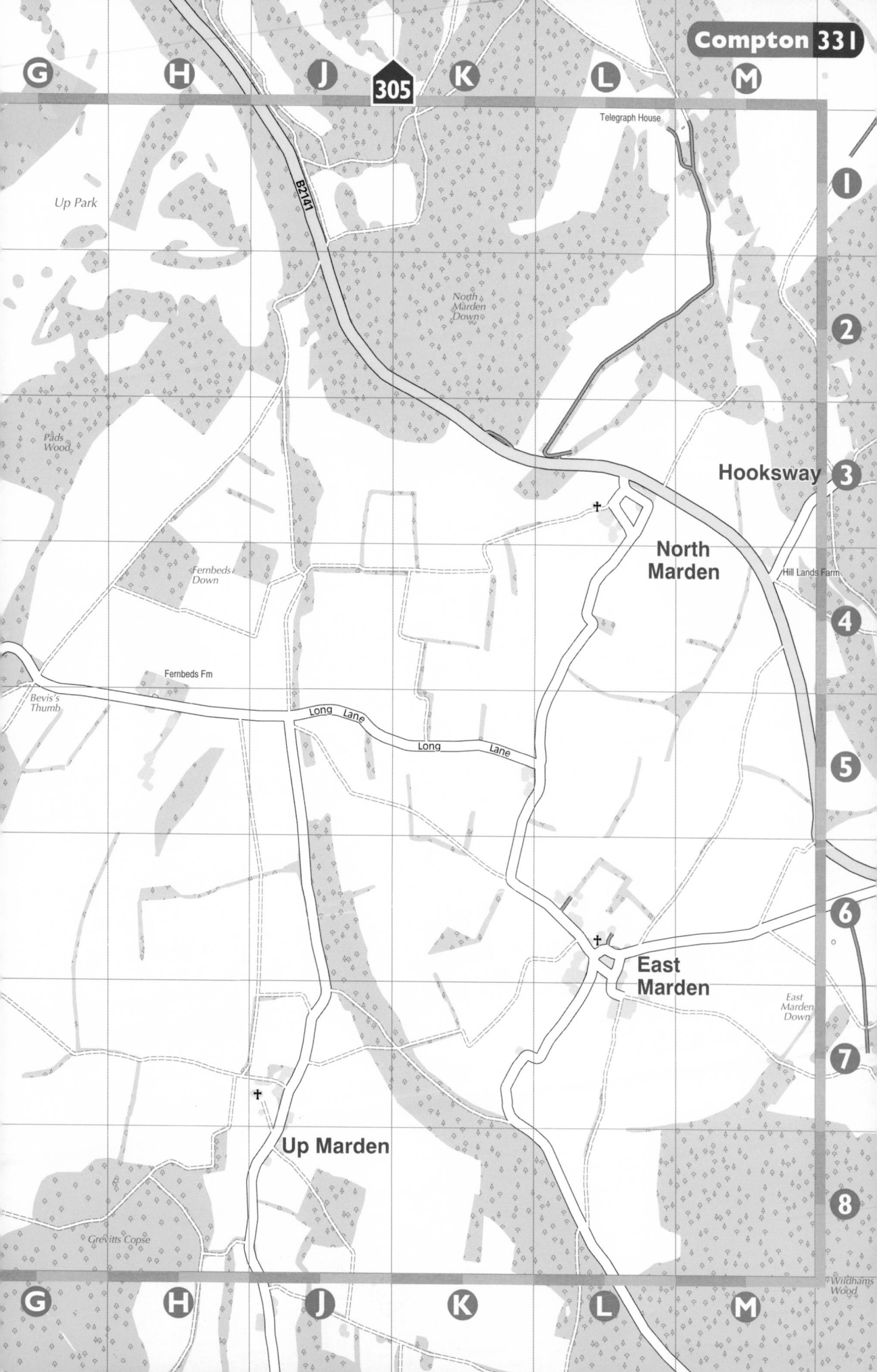

G H J K L M

305
B2141

Up Park

Telegraph House

1

2

Hooksway 3

Pads Wood

North Marden Down

North Marden

Hill Lands Farm

4

Fernbeds Down

Fernbeds Fm

Bevis's Thumb

Long Lane

Long Lane

5

6

East Marden

East Marden Down

7

Up Marden

8

Grevitts Copse

Wildhams Wood

G H J K L M

332
307
356
A
B
C
D
E
F
1
2
3
4
5
6
7
8
Ashes Farm
Lopshill
Lower Daggons
Crendell
Pye Lane
Rushmore Farm
Lower Holwell
B3078
HARE LANE
Hare Lane Farm
CRANBORNE ROAD
King Barrow
Cripplestyle
Batterley Drove
Vale Acre Farm
Gotham
r Farm
Smallbridge Farm
Dorset Heavy Horse Centre
Telegraph Plantation
Pistle Down
River Crane
Westworth Farm
Burrows Farm
Burrows Lane
Stephen's Castle
Eastworth Road
Edmonds
Coopers Lane
Moorlands Rd
Wild Church Bottom
B3081
Romford
STATION ROAD
Station Rd
The Oaks
Park Dr
Coronation Road
Berkeley Cl
Moorlands Road
B3081
DEWLANDS RD
Dewlands Rd
Hillside County First School
Police
BH31
1 grid square represents 500 metres

G H J 308 K L M

I

2

3

4

334

5

6

7

8

H2
1 Highwood Cl

K2
1 Lime Tree Cl

L2
1 Camel Green Rd
2 Down Lodge Cl
3 Fir Tree Hl
4 Silverdale Crs

Home Farm

Alderholt Park

High Wood

Sandleheath Road

FORDINGBRIDGE ROAD

Dorset County
Hampshire County

✝

Camel Green

Windsor Wy

STATION ROAD

Alderholt

Station Rd Yd

Station Road
B3078

DAGGONS ROAD

Daggons

1

Coppers Cl

Hayters

Camel Anteus Wy

Green Road

South Hill

Hilbury Road

Pear Tree Cl

Park Lane

St James Ce (VC) First Sch

✝

Wren Cl

Churchill

Blackwater Gv

Attwood Cl

Charing Cross

Apple Tree Rd

Alder Dr

Earlswood Dr

Oak Road

Birchwood

Broomfield Dr

Fern Cl

Tudor Cl

Pine Rd

Ringwood Road

Drive

Hilbury Road

Drove End Farm

Warren Park Farm

Ringwood Road

Alderholt Common

Drove

Whitefield Bottom

Sleep Brook

Cranborne Common

Dorset County
Hampshire County

Sleep Brook

North Plumley Farm

Hamer Brook

Boveridges Heath

Plumley Wood

M3
1 Kestrel Dale

M2
1 Camel Green Rd
2 Gilbert Cl

L3
1 Ash Cl
2 Beech Cl
3 Bramble Cl
4 Hazel Cl
5 Saxon Wy

Harefield

BOWERWOOD ROAD
Padstow Pl
Church Farm
Frog Lane
309
A B C D E F
1 2 3 4 5 6 7 8
DGE ROAD
Dorset County
Hampshire County
Redbrook
Ditchend Brook
Avon Valley Path
Midgham Farm
Bickton
RINGWOOD ROAD
Hern Lane
A338
Hillbury Road
Drove End Farm
North End Lane
Lawrence
North End Farm
North C
333
Harbridge Drove
Lomer Lane
Bleak Hill
River Avon
Harbridge Green
Churchfield Lane
Huckles Brook
Sou
Avon Va Path
SALISBURY ROAD
Kent Lane
Harbridge
Ibsley Drove
Harbridge School
Turmer
Avon Valley Path
358
Ibs
Mockbeggar Lane
1 grid square represents 500 metres

G   H   J   310   ssfc   K   L   M

The Merrie Thought
Broadhill
ckton
Ditchend Brook
Blissford Cross
I
Frogham Hill
Pentons Lane
Blissford Hill
Frogham
Abbotswell Road
Abbots Well
Latchmore Bottom
2
Hyde
Abbotswell Road
The Paddock
Hyde Common
Abbot's Well Road
Ogdens Farm
Hyde Hill
Gorley Lynch
Hyde (C of E Controlled) Primary School
3
Hungerford Hill
Hungerford
Gorley Lynch
Ogdens
Buddle Hill
4
336
New
5
Huckles Brook
Ogden's Purlieu
Furze Hill
Forest
Brookside
6
Black Barrow
7
Newtown Lane
Ibsley Common
Linwood
Toms Lane
Dockens Water
Toms Lane
8
Avon Valley Path
Whitefield Plantn
Linwood Farm

Avon Valley Path
Dockens

336

A B C D E F

Hampton
Ridge

311

I

Àlderhill
Inclosure

Sloden
Inclosure

2

New

Latchmoor Brook

Forest

3

Hasley
Inclosure

Holly Hatch
Cottage

Holly
Hatch
Inclosure

4

New

335

Forest

Broomy
Inclosure

Broomy
Lodge

5

6

Black
Barrow

High
Corner Inn

Broomy
Plain

7

Toms Lane

8

Linwood

Milkham Inclosure

Linwood Farm

A B C D E F

360

G   H   J   **312**   K   L   M

I

2

3

4

338

5

6

7

8

The Butt

Fritham Plain

North Bentley Inclosure

Janesmoor Plain

South Bentley Inclosure

Anses Wood

Cadman's Pool

Ocknell Inclosure

Ocknell Plain

A31(T)

Slufters Inclosure

Fritham Cross

A31(T)

Highland Water

Bratley Water

A31(T)

Bratley A

G   H   J   **361**   K   L   M

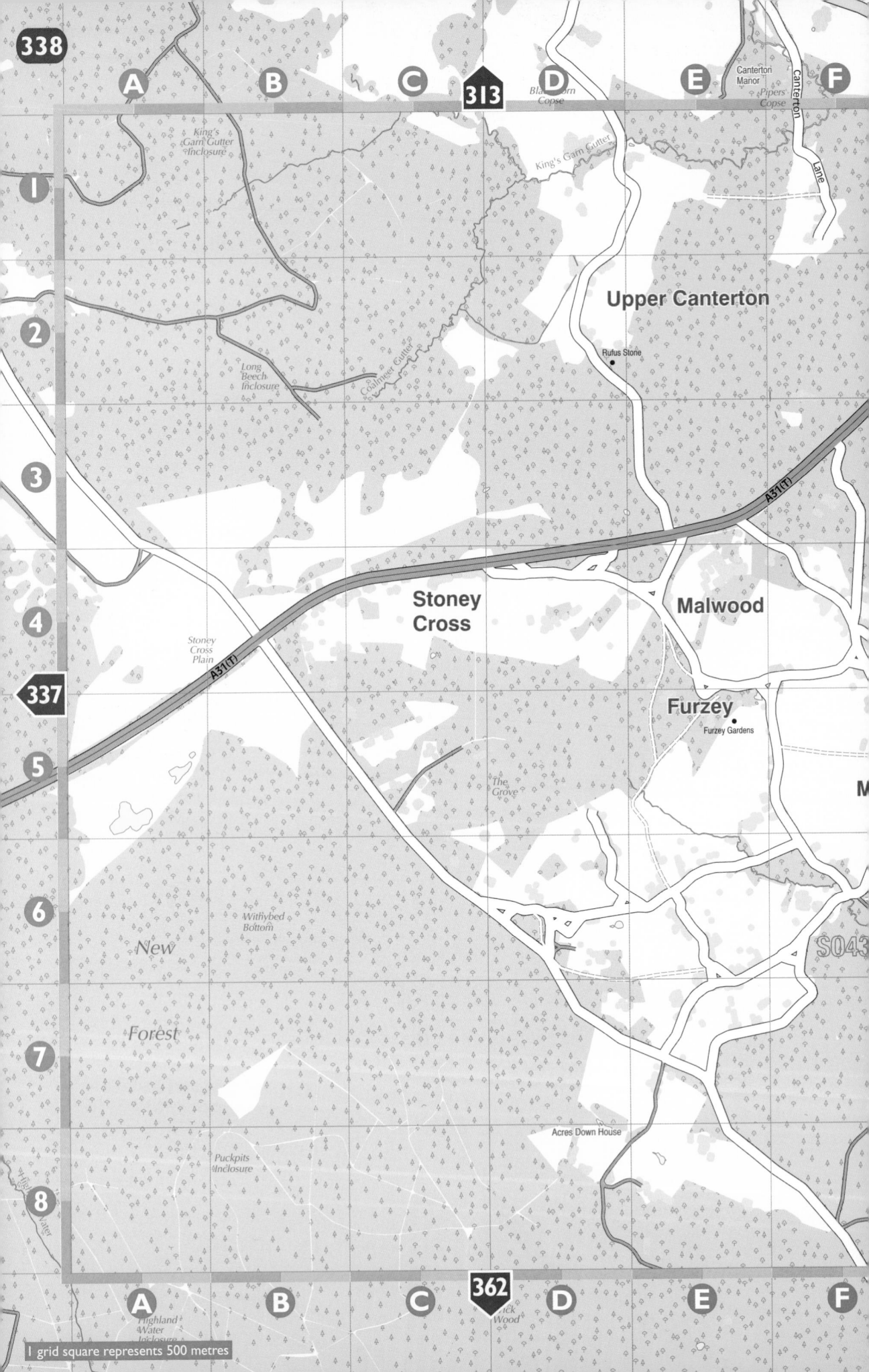

338

A　B　C **313** D　E　F

I

2

3

4

337

5

6

7

8

A B **362** C D E F

King's Garn Gutter
Inclosure

Long Beech
Inclosure

Coalmeer Gutter

King's Garn Gutter

Blackthorn
Copse

Canterton
Manor

Pipers'
Copse

Canterton Lane

Upper Canterton

Rufus Stone

A31(T)

Stoney
Cross

Malwood

Stoney
Cross
Plain

A31(T)

Furzey

Furzey Gardens

The
Grove

M

Withybed
Bottom

New

Forest

S043

Puckpits
Inclosure

Acres Down House

Highland
Water
Inclosure

Black
Wood

Whitley Water

1 grid square represents 500 metres

B3079
Wittensford
M27
Junction 1
A31
A31(T)
Romsey Road
ROMSEY ROAD
Lyndhurst Road
White Hart Lane
Cadnam
PH
PO
314
336
The Brickyard
SOUTHAMPTON ROAD
SOUTHAMPTON ROAD A336
Fir Tree Rd
Cadnam Surgery
Barneyhayes La
Kennington La
Winsor Road
Bartley C of E Middle School
Rockram Wood
LYNDHURST ROAD
A337
Bignell Wood
Bartley Lodge
Bartley
Rockram
Oakfield Rd
New Inn Road
New Inn La
Abbotsford
Chinham
Shepherds Road
Shepherds Cl
Shave Green Inclosure
Shave Wood
Beechwood Road
Brockishill Road
Bartley Manor
Goldenhayes
London Minstead
Brockis Hill
Brockishill Inclosure
340
Minstead Lodge
Bull Lane
Congleton Close
Football Green
Mill Lane
Furzy Lawn Inclosure
Bartley Water
The Kennels
The Mill House
Manor Park
Rushpole Wood
G
H
J
K
L
M
1
2
3
4
5
6
7
8

315

A326

FI
1 Nickleby Gdns
2 Shawford Cl

GI
1 Alfred Cl
2 Bullfinch Cl
3 Cherrywd Gdns
4 Crabapple Cl
5 Cypress Gdns
6 Milkwood Ct
7 Teal Cl
8 Watson Wk
9 Winchester Wy

A   B   C   D   E   F

I

Bartley C of E
Middle School

Bartley Grange

RINGWOOD   ROAD   A336

Netley Marsh C of E
Controlled
Infant School

Carlton Ho

Priestlands Cl

Chinham   Road

Shepherds

Riverside Cl

2

Paradise Lane

Bourne

Bourne Lane

NETLEY
MARSH

Woodlands Road

Willswood Fm

3

Purkiss Cl

Bartley   Road

Lanesbridge Cl

Green Cl
Minvna Cl

PH

Golⁿhayes

4

339

Great Fletchwood Fm

Woodlands Road

5

Foyers

Bartley   Road

Hotel

Woodlands

Busketts
Wood

Woodlands Road

Alpine Road

The Crs

Hazel Gv

Woodlands Drive

Fletchwood Copse

Bartley

6

Busketts
Lawn
Inclosure

Fletchwood Rd

Busketts
Wy

Fir Road

Holly Rd

Princess Rd

Elm
Tre

LYNDHU

Peterscroft Av

PO

7

Ironshill
Lodge

A35

Ashurst Hospital

Ashurst (New Forest) Station

8

Rushpole
Wood

Ironshill
Inclosure

Lodgehill
Cottage

A35

364

shurst
Wood

A   B   C   D   E   F

1 grid square represents 500 metres

Totton 341
316
342
365
G2
1 Ashwood Gdns
2 Chillenden Ct
3 Copinger Cl
4 Driftwood Gdns
5 Maple Gdns
6 Peregrine Cl
7 Timson Cl
G5
1 Wingrove Rd
G6
1 Boakes Pl
H1
1 Drayton Pl
2 Goldsmith Cl
3 Lydgate
4 Priestley Cl
5 Shaw Cl
6 Wilde Cl
H2
1 Chillenden Ct
2 Hudson Ct
3 Thomas Cl
H3
1 Chiltern Cl
2 Highgrove Cl
M1
1 Station Rd South
L2
1 Boothby Cl
K1
1 Sunny Wy
L1
1 Rumbridge Gdns
2 Station Rd North
J3
1 Elldene Ct
2 Falstaff Wy
3 Hambert Wy
4 Trevone Cl
J1
1 Briardene Ct
2 Whitcombe Cl
J2
1 Springfield Dr
Totton Recreation Centre
Associated Football Club
Test Vale Surg.
Police Station
Salterns School
Forest Edge School
Abbotswood Junior School
Lydlynch County First School
Forest Gate Surg
First School
RINGWOOD ROAD
COMMERCIAL ROAD
REDBRIDGE CSWY
Totton Station
HIGH STREET
BY-PASS
RUMBRIDGE STREET
TOTTON
Eling County Infant School
Rushington
The Heritage Centre & Museum
Tide Mill
Eling
Cemetery
Totton Coll
Rushington Business Park
Hampshire Co Council
Hounsdown School
Hounsdown
SPICER'S HILL
MAIN ROAD
MARCHWOOD BY-PASS
A326
A35
HUNTERS HILL
Foxhills County First School
Foxhills
SO40
Ashurst Bridge
Colbury
Colbury Fm
Hunters Inn Hill
Durley Fm
Pound Lane
Longdown Dairy Fm
Ashurst
Deerleap Lane
Deerleap Fm
Churchplace Inclosure
Longdown Estates
Langley Wood
Langley Lodge
Bury Lane
Trotts Lane
Cutter Lane
Jacob's Gutter Lane
Kneller's Lane
Cocklydown Lane
Bartley Water
River Test

342
Redbridge
Community School
Redbridge Primary School
Old Redbridge Road
REDBRIDGE CSWY
D6
1 Pebble Ct
D2
1 Marianne Cl
D1
1 Castleshaw Cl
2 Hameldon Cl
C7
1 Lakeland Gdns
2 Lloyd Av
Regents Park Girls School
Regents Park Surg
Millbrook Clinic
Cumbrian
317
Oakley Road
Mendip
Cheviot Rd
Kendal Av
Quantock Rd
Parkside Av
Pennine
Clifton Road
Tilbrook Rd
Beechfield
Middle & Primary School
Station Rd
Brunel Rd
Oakridge Rd
Lebanon Rd
Allington Road
BRIDGE RD
Green Park Rd
Wimpson Lane
TEBOURBA
Redbridge Station
Tanners Brook Junior School
Tanners Brook Infant School
Millbrook
Super Bowl
Cemetery
Second Av
First Avenue
Millbrook Trading Estate
Trinity Ind Est
Munro Crs
Boundary Cl
Brookside Av
Eimes Dr
George's Avenue
Prince Of Wales Avenue
Meadowmead Av
Westfield
Claremont
Stanton Road
Stanton Ind Est
Mill Road
South Mill Road
Westbury Road
Creighton Road
Vulcan Rd
King
Regent's
Claremont Crs
Langley Rd
Castle Ct
Fawley Rd
Solent Business Cen
Waterhouse Way
English Road
Kingsley Road
Ampthill
Freshfield
Victoria
Testwood Rd
Millbrook Rd W
Manor House Av
Tanner's Brook Wy
MILLBROOK ROAD WEST
Third Avenue
Millbrook Point Rd
Western Avenue
Western Av
Herbert Walker Av
SO15
River Test
Eling
Bury Lane
Marchwood Road
Trotts Lane
341
City of Southampton
Hampshire County
River Test
Bury Fm
Bury Road
Quayside Wk
Maritime Av
Ordnance Way
Magazine La
Admiralty Wy
Cork La
Normandy Way
Trotts
Bury Rd
Cork La
Shorefield Rd
The Gulls
Tide's Way
Old Magazine Cl
Gage Cl
Gardiner Cl
Main Road
Drake Cl
Old Cracknore Cl
Cracknore Hard
LC
MARCHWOOD
Marchwood
Pooksgreen
The Rushes
The Tussocks
Moss Dr
Bilberry Dr
Reed Dr
Alder Cl
Melick Cl
Pond Cl
Lichen Wy
Aaron Cl
The Rowans
Evergreen Cl
Frome Cl
Elder Cl
The Hawthorns
Rosewood Gdns
Kingswood
Dapple Pl
Normandy Way
Marchwood Junior School
The Surg.
Park Lane
Pooksgreen
Bohinton Av
Park Cl
Marshfield Cl
Tavell's Lane
Woodpecker Drive
Kingfisher Wy
Kestrel Cl
Sandpiper
Osprey
Poplar Dr
Woodside Cl
The Crs
Staplewood Lane
Long Lane
BY-PASS
Staplewood La
Langley Lodge
Vicarage Rd
St Johns Ct
Main Road
Mulberry Rd
Oakland Dr
Malthouse Gdns
Philpott Dr
Adams Wd Dr
Burma Wy
Africa Dr
Plantation Dr
Larkspur Dr
Willow Dr
Spindlewood Wy
Hythe Road
Pumpfield Farm
Marchwood C of E Infant School
Lane
MARCHWOOD
366
D7
1 Crooked Hays Cl
2 St Johns Ct
E2
1 Mottisfont Cl
E7
1 Acorn Cl
2 The Limes
3 Malcroft Ms
4 Ripplewood
5 Tanglewood
6 Woodmoor Cl
F1
1 Endeavour Cl
2 Regent's Park Gdns
F2
1 Victory Crs
2 Victory Sq
3 Waterhouse La
BY-PASS
Marchwood
1 grid square represents 500 metres
A
B
C
D
E
F
1
2
3
4
5
6
7
8

Shirley

G   H   I   J   318   K   L   M

G1
1 Beatrice Rd
2 May Rd

G6
1 Crackn. Hd La

H1
1 W District Cut

H2
1 Princes Rd
2 Queenstown Rd

H3
1 Bridgwater Ct
2 Dymott Ci
3 Edith Haisman Ci

L1
1 Central Station
2 Tintern Gv
3 Wyndham Pl

G2
1 Lakelands Dr

Fremantle

I

Mount Pleasant
Industrial Estate

Centurion
Industrial
Estate

The Alpha
Business Park

Meridian TV
Studios

Southampton
Central
Mosque

2

Hindu
Temple

3

S014

344

4

5

6

12   ISLE OF WIGHT   13   7

HYTHE

8

K2
1 Handford Pl
2 Henry St
3 Kenilworth Rd
4 Southampton St
5 Upper Banister St

M2
1 Augustine Rd
2 N'umberland Rd

M3
1 Clifford St
2 Guildford St
3 Nichols Rd
4 St Alban's Rd
5 Wolverton Wy

M5
1 Paget St
2 Richmond St
3 Royal Crescent Rd
4 St Lawrence Rd
5 Saltmarsh Rd

M4
1 Maryfield

M6
1 Atlantic Ci
2 Mermaid Wy

G   H   J   367   K   L   M

M1
1 Ancasta Rd
2 Blackberry Ter
3 Kingsbury Rd
4 Verulam Rd

L4
1 Johnson St
2 St Georges St
3 York Buildings

L1
1 Middle St

K4
1 Albion Pl
2 Scullards La

K6
1 Fitzhugh St
2 Gibbs Rd
3 Havelock Rd
4 West Marlands Rd

L5
1 Charles St
2 Gloucester Sq
3 Market Pl
4 Russell St

L3
1 Broad Gn
2 Compton Wk
3 Craven St
4 North Front
5 Winton St

L2
1 Brinton's Ter
2 Charlotte St
3 Fanshawe St

K5
1 Vyse La

344
319
343
13
368
A
B
C
D
E
F
1
2
3
4
5
6
7
8
ST DENYS
Bitterne
Northam
Merry Oak
Peartree Green
Itchen
Sholing Common
Woolston
Ocean Village
Weston
Newtown
River Itchen
Itchen
BITTERNE ROAD WEST A3024
A3024
A3025
A3035
MAYBRAY KING WY
BURSLEDON ROAD
PORTSMOUTH ROAD
PORTSMOUTH
BRITANNIA ROAD
MARINE PDE
NORTHAM ROAD
THOMAS LEWIS WY
A335
Bitterne Station
Woolston Stn
Sholing Station
Centurion Industrial Park
Mount Pleasant Industrial Estate
The Alpha Business Park
Meridian TV Studios
Northam Business Cen
Northam Bridge
Marina
Willments Industrial Est
Millhouse Business Centre
Central Trading Est
Southampton Technical College
The Itchen Bridge
Longbridge Ind Park
Spitfire Court Surgery
Calshot Spit Lightship
Oceanographic Centre
Itchen College
Sholing Middle School
Sholing Infants School
Girls School
St Monica Middle School
Infant School
Woolston School
Weston Park Junior School
Weston Park First School
Weston Shore First School
The Canute Surg
The Old Fire Station Surgery
Glenfield Infant School
Beechwood Middle School
Bitterne Leisure Centre
Harefield Clinic
Bitterne Health Cen
AMF Bowling
Police Station
Doctors Surgery
Cemetery
Solent Way
Itchen Way
Weston Lane
Portsmouth Rd
C3
1 Braeside Crs
B6
1 Longmore Crs
B4
1 Peartree Cl
A6
1 Ocean Wy
B3
1 Ashburnham Cl
A2
1 Campbell St
2 Charliejoy Gdns
3 Princes Ct
A5
1 Asturias Wy
B5
1 Condor Cl
2 Cooper's La
3 Jackmans Cl
4 Shamrock Rd
B7
1 Dundonald Cl
2 Swift Hollow
3 Victoria Rd
4 Waldegrave Cl
E2
1 Bitterne Crs
2 Somerford Cl
E4
1 Rothbury Cl
2 Torrington Cl
E8
1 Longstock Cl
2 Ropley Cl
3 Winchfield Cl
E5
1 Applewood Gdns
2 Lynden Ga
F1
1 Redcote Cl
2 St Philip's Wy
3 Sunningdale Gdns
F4
1 Cunningham Crs
2 Gort Crs
3 Millbridge Gdns
D7
1 Bramshott Rd
2 Deeping Cl
3 Kingsclere Cl
4 Kipling Ct
5 Wallace Rd
E6
1 Gordon Ter
F3
1 Firtree Wy
F7
1 Wentworth Gdns
C4
1 Elstree Rd
2 Osterly Rd
C5
1 Cheddar Cl
C6
1 Florence Rd
2 Lyndock Cl
3 Torcross Cl
C7
1 Cozens Cl
D3
1 Blackthorn Cl
2 Freemantle Cl
3 Lavender Cl
4 Merryoak Gn
D6
1 Fern Rd
2 Temple Gdns
D8
1 Burghclere Rd
2 Crookham Rd
3 Foxcott Cl
E1
1 Mersham Gdns
1 grid square represents 500 metres

Southampton 345
G1
1 Holmsley Cl
2 Mountain Ash Cl
G4
1 Butt's Crs
2 Imber Cl
G5
1 Grainger Gdns
2 Heathfield Cl
3 Orpen Rd
G6
1 Dawson Rd
2 Stubbs Rd
H2
1 Masefield Gn
H4
1 Butt's Cl
2 Butt's Rd
3 Lydgate Rd
4 Quilter Cl
5 Walton Rd
J1
1 Haselfoot Gdns
Hickley Farm
320
Harefield
Thornhill Park
Woodlands Community School
Junction 7
CHARLES WATTS WAY A334
THORNHILL PK RD
A334
Hedge End Retail Park
HEDGE END
Shamblehurst CP School
Kanes Hill Primary School
Thornhill Park Surgery
Thornhill Clinic
Thornhill First School
Thornhill
KANES HILL
A27
M27
UPPER NORTHAM ROAD B3036
B3033
Police Station
Netley Hill
South West Health Authority
Hightown Primary School
Hightown
Common
Surrey House Health Cen
Surrey House First School
Heathfield Infant & Middle School
346
BURSLEDON ROAD A3024
WEST END ROAD
Junction 8
Windmill Lane
Bursledon Windmill Museum
City of Southampton
Hampshire County
A3025
HAMBLE LANE
PROVIDENCE HILL
OAKHILL BRIDGE ROAD
Old Netley
Lowford
Bursledon C of E Junior & Infant School
Cemetery
Bursledon
Bursledon Station
Bursledon Heath
369
L6
1 Ashley Ct
2 Cambrian Cl
3 Devonshire Gdns
L7
1 Estridge Cl
2 Humber Gdns
3 Lancaster Cl
4 Phoenix Cl
5 Sunnyfield Ri
L8
1 Batchelor Gn
M1
1 Downscroft Gdns
M2
1 Chalice Ct
2 Little Park Cl
3 Oak Tree Gdns
4 Rustan Cl
5 Wheatsheaf Ct
6 Yew Tree Cl
M3
1 New Cliffe Gdns
M4
1 Foord Rd
L2
1 Buttercup Cl
2 Clover Wy
3 St Catherines Vw
L3
1 Norman Gdns
K8
1 Ash Cl
2 Chamberlayne Rd
3 Pilands Wood Rd
L1
1 Goodlands V
K4
1 Mosaic Cl
2 Tumulus Cl
K6
1 Devonshire Gdns
J5
1 Adela Verne Cl
2 Botley Gdns
3 Killarney Cl
K2
1 Kinsbourne Cl
J2
1 Fairfax Ct
2 Kinsbourne Wy
J4
1 Warburton Cl

346
321
345
370
A
B
C
D
E
F
1
2
3
4
5
6
7
8
B2
1 Bedford Cl
2 Hawthorn Cl
3 Hornbeam Cl
4 Mapleton Rd
5 Marls Rd
6 Medlar Cl
7 Sengana Cl
8 Verbena Wy
B1
1 Marvin Wy
2 Poplar Wy
3 Stockton Cl
A3
1 Morgan Rd
2 Primrose Cl
3 Stockholm Dr
A2
1 Freegrounds Av
2 Frensham Cl
3 Larkspur Gdns
Wildern
Westward Road
Shamblehurst CP School
School
Wildern Clinic
Coltsfoot Cl
GRANGE RD
Hotel
Grange Dr
Pavilion Rd
Broadoak
BROAD OAK
A334
HIGH STREET
MILL HILL
WINCHESTER STREET
Holmesland
Botley Junior & Infant School
Botley
Woodhills School
Cobbett Way
Blossom Close
LWR NORTHAM RD
B3033
Lwr Northam Rd
Ratcliffe
Allen Rd
Sherborne Way
Coulsdon Rd
Freegrounds
Police Station
Freeground Junior & Infant School
Kings Copse Av
Sovereign Drive
Precosa Road
Mapleton Rd
Valerian Rd
Hobb Lane
Berry Cl
Crusader Rd
Duke Road
Havendale
Tickner Close
Kings Copse Avenue
Kings Copse Primary School
Kings Copse Rd
Tanhouse Cl
Lwr St. Helens Rd
Upr St. Helens Road
Stockholm Drive
Heathhouse Lane
Sherwood Avenue
Tanhouse Lane
Brook Lane
Church Lane
Steeple Court
Manor Farm
Pyland's Lane
Manor Farm Country Park
River Hamble
Burridge Farm
Burridge Road
Green Lane
Burridge Social Sports Club
S031
Brixedone Farm
Blundell Lane
M27
Coal Pk La
Coal Park Lane
Lower Swanwick
Northview Gallery
Swanwick Lane
Bye Road
Sopwith Way
New Road
Swanwick La
Manor Fm
Glen Ho
BOTLEY ROAD A3051
Lipizzaner Fields
The Whiteley Surgery
Swanwick
Bursledon Station
Swanwick Business Park
Station Hill
Lands End Road
B3
1 Ferndale
2 The Foxgloves
3 Havendale
4 Paxton Cl
5 Tickner Cl
6 Woodstock Cl
B8
1 Lawson Cl
2 L Swanwick Rd
3 Querida Cl
C2
1 Montrose Cl
A3051
1 grid square represents 500 metres

G8
1 Barrie Cl
2 Bronte Gdns
3 Chesterton Pl
4 Fitzgerald Cl
5 John Bunyan Cl

G **H** **J** 322 **K** **L** **M**

OCKS HILL

Lake Road

Row Ash

A334

The Vine School

BOTLEY ROAD

Reading Room

Vicara

Lane

Kitnocks

Raglington Farm

otley
ation

A334

HILL

Hall
Court

1

Outlands

A3051

2

3

ne Manor

Mansfield

Lane

4

Barn Farm

Curbridge

348

5

Ridge La

Bury Farm

6

Ridge Farm

Dimmock's
Moor

Whiteley

Lane

Botley
Wood

7

Browning Close

Whiteley La

Whiteley

Austen
Gdns
Andersen Cl
Christie
Av
Rattigan
Conrad
Gdns
Buchan
Av
ibsen
einbeck
Steinbeck
Way

Thyme Avenue

Coriander Way

Rosemary Gdns

Angelica Way

Flagpond
Copse

8

Fyfield Close

Saffron Way

Marjoram

Lovage
Road

Oakaway

Way

ningway
Way

Hyssop
Close

G **H** **J** 371 **K** **L** **M**

Drive
Drive
erian
Way

DRIVE

sorrel
Drive

Whiteley

Parkway

Whiteley County Primary

Hotel

Titchfi

Lee Ground

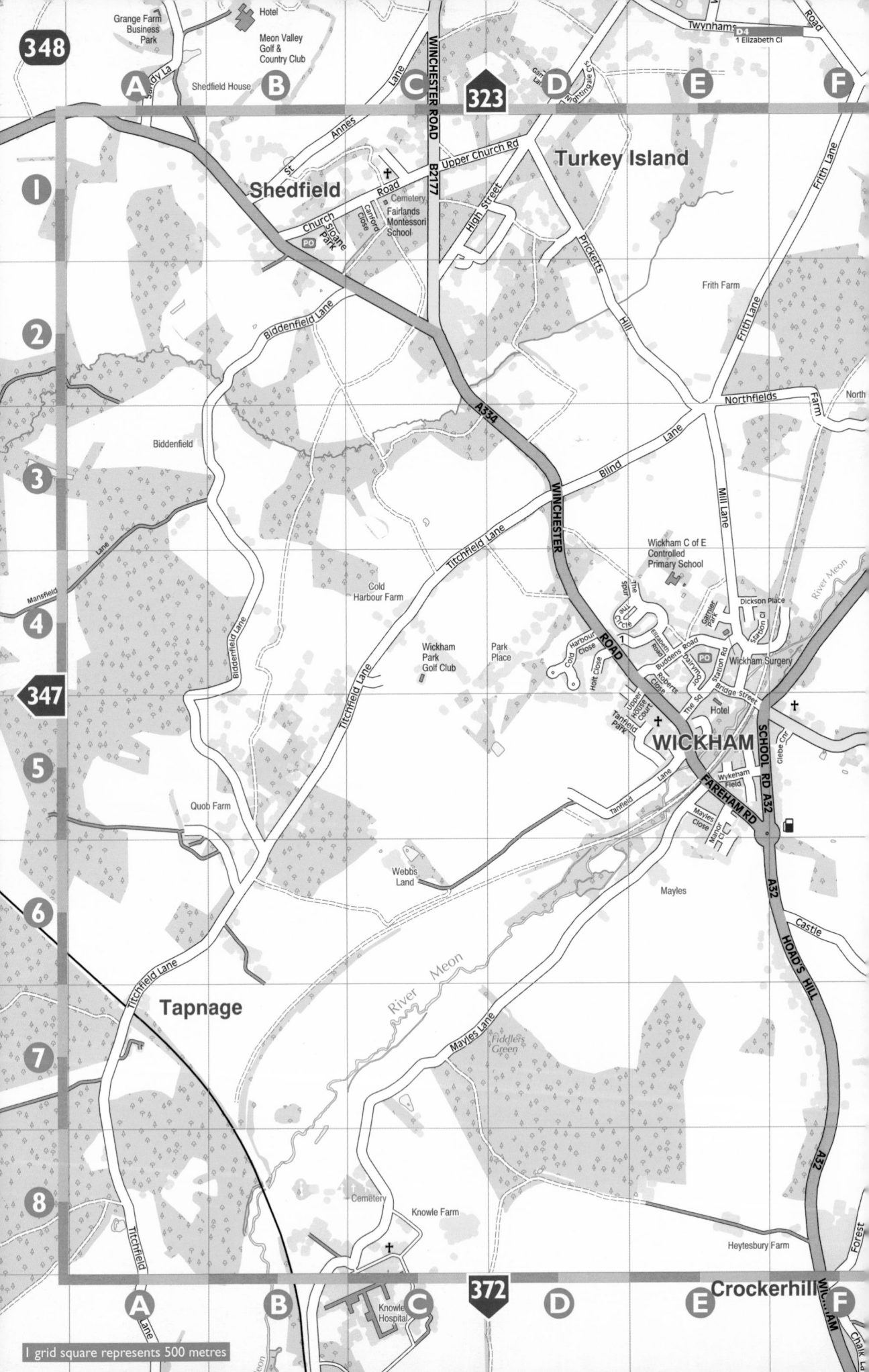

A   B   C   D   E   F

Grange Farm
Business
Park

Hotel

Meon Valley
Golf &
Country Club

Shedfield House

WINCHESTER ROAD

323

Twynhams
Road

1 Elizabeth Cl

Upper Church Rd

Turkey Island

Shedfield

Cemetery
Fairlands
Montessori
School

High Street

Pricketts
Hill

Frith Farm

Frith Lane

1   Church
     Sloane
     Park
     PO

Camford Close
Annes St
Road

Biddenfield Lane

A334

WINCHESTER

Blind Lane

Northfields

North
Farm

Mill Lane

River Meon

2

Biddenfield

3

Mansfield Lane

Biddenfield Lane

Titchfield Lane

Cold
Harbour Farm

Wickham C of E
Controlled
Primary School

Dickson Place

4

Titchfield Lane

Wickham
Park
Golf Club

Park
Place

The Spur
Circle

Cedar Park

Station Rd
Union Cl

ROAD
Cold Harbour Close
Holt Close

Buddens Road
Roberts
Dairymead
PO

Wickham Surgery
Bridge Street

5

Quob Farm

Upper House Court

The Sq
Hotel

WICKHAM

Glebe Ctr

Tanfield Park

Tanfield Lane

Wykenam Field

FAREHAM RD

SCHOOL RD A32

Webbs
Land

Mayles
Close

Manor Cl

Mayles

A32

Castle

6

Titchfield Lane

River Meon

HOAD'S HILL

Tapnage

Mayles Lane

Fiddlers
Green

7

8

Cemetery

Knowle Farm

Forest

Heytesbury Farm

A   B   C   372   D   E   Crockerhill   F

Titchfield Lane

Knowle
Hospital

WILLIAM

Chalk La

G
H
J
K
L
M
324
smead
Lane
Heath
Road
Liberty Rd
Liberty
Road
Woodend
Dradfield Lane
Kingsmead
PO
Church Road
Ne
Road
Acres
Hundred
Newtown Soberton County Primary School
Church Road
West Lodge
Hundred Acres Road
Trampers Lane
Goathouse Fm
Rookesbury Park School
Hundred Acres
350
Little Forest
Hundred Acres Road
WICK
ROAD
B2177
North Boarhunt
Firgrove La
Wickham Common
Wickham Riding School
Trampers Lane
PO
Orchard Copse
South Hants Country Club
Blackhouse Lane
B2177
Bonhams
PO17
Lane
Blackhouse
Staple Cross
La
Farm
Bere
373
re Farm
King's Way
1
2
3
4
5
6
7
8

350
325
349
374
A
B
C
D
E
F
1
2
3
4
5
6
7
8
Southend Lane
Southend
Mensands Lane
Dradfield Lane
King's Way
Ingoldfield Lane
Church Road
Huntbourn
Hoe Gate
Bent Fm
Newtown
Road
Hoe Street
Great Ervills Fm
Rudley Mill
Broad
Upla
St Martin's Corner
Worlds End
Hoe Moor Farm
Bunns Lane
Forest Fm
Crabbick Farm
Trampers Lane
Lower
Forest Road
Goathouse
Kiln Lane
Hipley
Apless Lane
Shoot Hill
Hipley Copse
Beckford Lane
Lower Beckford
Quagg Fm
Ashlands
Lovelocks
Common Lane
Creec
Staple Cross
B2177
Mitchelland
Lodge Farm
Walton Heath
Place Wood
Lane
1 grid square represents 500 metres

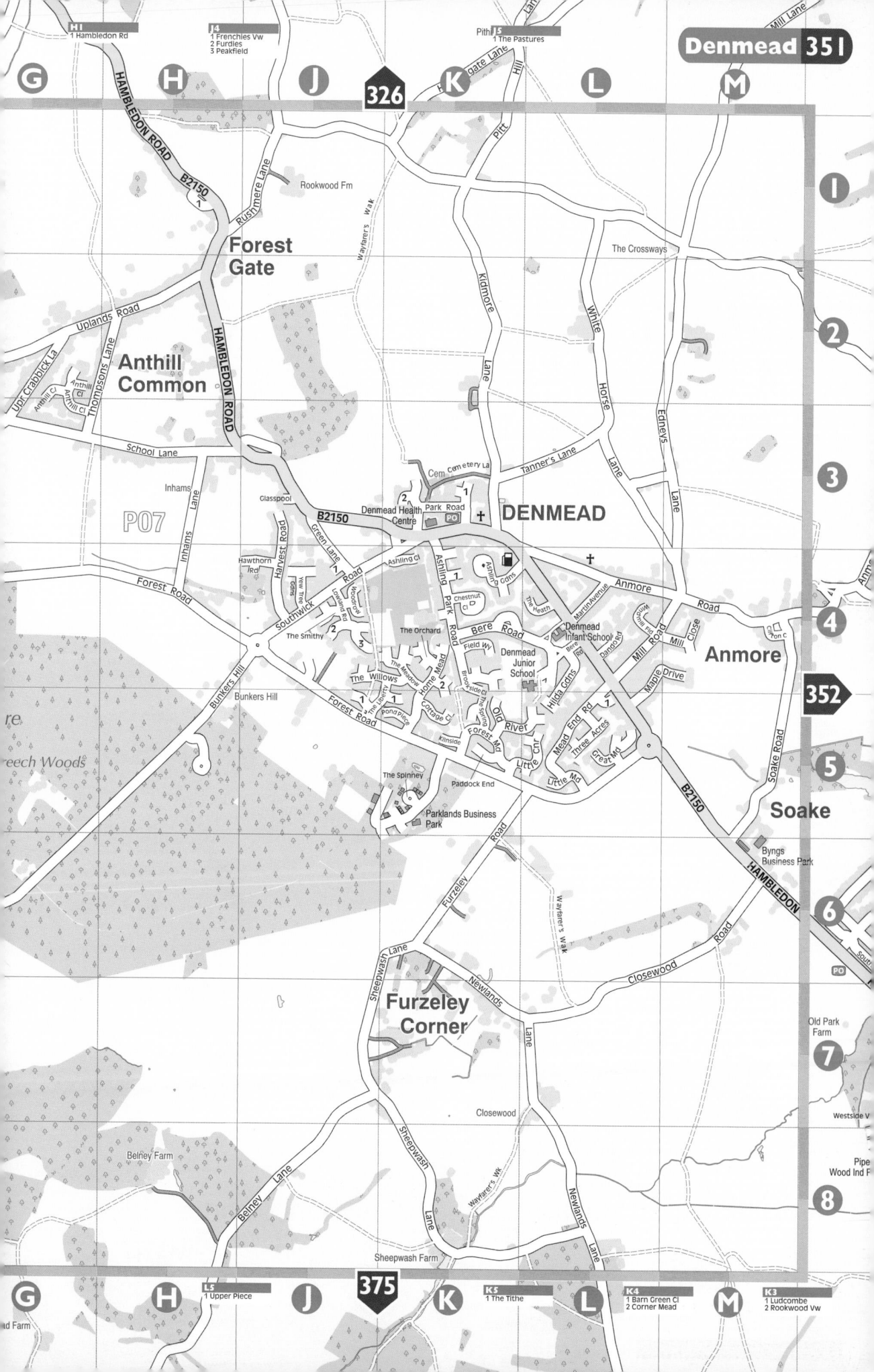

G   H   J   ◆326   K   L   M

H1
1 Hambledon Rd

J4
1 Frenchies Vw
2 Furdies
3 Peakfield

Pith J5
1 The Pastures

Kidmore Lane

Gate Lane

Pitt Hill

HAMBLEDON ROAD B2150

Rushmere Lane

Warfarer's Wak

Rookwood Fm

Forest Gate

The Crossways

White Horse Lane

Edneys Lane

HAMBLEDON ROAD

Uplands Road

Anthill Common

Anthill Cl
Upr Crabbick La
Anthill Cl
Anthill Cl

Thompsons Lane

School Lane

Inhams Lane

Glasspool

Cem Cemetery La

Tanner's Lane

PO7

Forest Road

Harvest Road

Green Lane

B2150

Denmead Health Centre

Park Road

PO

DENMEAD

Anmore Road

Anmore

352

Hawthorn Rd

Yew Tree Gdns

Southwick Road

Woodrow

Upland Rd

Ashling Cl

Ashling Park Road

Ashling Gdns

Chestnut Cl

The Heath

Martin Avenue

Denmead Infant School

Mill Pd

Dangoor Rd

Mill Road

Mill Close

Amore

The Smithy

The Orchard

Bere Road

Field Rd

Denmead Junior School

Brookside Cl

Hilda Gdns

Maple Drive

Bunkers Hill

Bunkers Hill

The Willows

The Liberty

The Meadow

Home Mead

Cottage Cl

Brook Spring

Old River

Mead End Rd

Three Acres

Great Md

Soake

Forest Road

Pond Piece

Kilnside

Forest Md

Little Cnr

Little River

Little Md

5

The Spinney

Paddock End

B2150

HAMBLEDON

Byngs Business Park

Parklands Business Park

6

Furzeley Road

Wayfarer's Wak

Closewood Road

South

PO

Sheepwash Lane

Newlands Lane

Furzeley Corner

Old Park Farm

7

Wayfarer's Wk

Closewood

Belney Farm

Westside V

Belney Lane

Sheepwash Lane

Newlands Lane

Pipe Wood Ind

8

Sheepwash Farm

G   H   J   ◆375   K   L   M

L5
1 Upper Piece

K5
1 The Tithe

K4
1 Barn Green Cl
2 Corner Mead

K3
1 Ludcombe
2 Rookwood Vw

352
327
351
376
A
B
C
D
E
F
1
2
3
4
5
6
7
8
D2 1 Welchwood Cl
D3 1 Renown Gdns
C6 1 Fairbourne Cl 2 Homer Cl 3 Wedgewood Wy
C8 1 Beaconsfield Rd
C4 1 Kingfisher Cl 2 Thrush Wk
B7 1 Armstrong Cl 2 Charlesworth Dr 3 The Hundred 4 Petersham Cl
A6 1 Bernina Cl
B5 1 Sutton Cl
D4 1 Crombie Cl 2 Swinburn Gdns
D5 1 Downham Cl 2 Glenwood Gdns
D6 1 Beech Cl 2 Lawnswood Cl
D8 1 Brooklyn Dr 2 Cavendish Cl 3 Hannah Gdns
E2 1 Churchill Ct 2 Plovers Rd
E3 1 Aspen Wy 2 Cricket Dr 3 Cross La 4 Farmhouse Wy
E4 1 Bowers Cl 2 Ivydene Gdns
E5 1 Ashington Cl
Eastland Gate
Lovedean
Wecock
Cowplain
Soake
Causeway
WATERLOOVILLE
The Queen's Inclosure
Broadway Fm
Shrover
Old Park Farm
Byngs Business Park
Pipers Wood Ind Park
Meadowlands Junior School
Meadowlands Infant School
Rachel Madocks School
Cowplain School
Hart Plain Infant School
Hart Plain Junior School
Waterlooville Health Centre
Churchill Yard Industrial Est
Jubilee Business Cen
Waterlooville Football Club
Padnell Junior School
Padnell Infant School
Queens Inclosure Primary School
Horndean Community School
Doctors Surgery
Police Station
The Waterloo School
Cemetery
Broadway Lane
Anmore Lane
Day Lane
Coldhill Lane
Crouch Lane
New Road
Lovedean Lane
Woodcroft Lane
Milton Road
Hart Plain Avenue
Sunnymead Drive
Hambledon Road
HAMBLEDON ROAD
Silvester Road
Padnell Avenue
Park Lane
LONDON ROAD
A3(T) PORTSMOUTH ROAD
Jubilee Road
Wallis Road
Rowlands Av
Highfield Avenue
Inhurst Av
MAUREPAS WAY
B2150
Victory Avenue
Catherington Lane
Monarch's Way
1 grid square represents 500 metres

Blendworth

HORNDEAN

Cadlington Ho

Horndean Health Centre

Junction 2

Dell Piece East

Holly Bank Cl

Blendworth Common

The Holt

Havant Thicket

Bell's Copse

Woodhouse

Pyle Fm

Monarch's Way

Red Hill

Holt Gdns

Greatfield Way

Durrants

St Johns C of E Primary School

G1
1 Cunningham Rd
2 Nelson Crs
3 Stagshorn Rd

G3
1 Whitebeam Cl

G7
1 Thresher Cl

C5
1 Chatburn Av
2 Chesterton Gdns
3 Maytree Rd
4 Newbolt Cl
5 Shakespeare Gdns

E6
1 Conifer Cl

E7
1 Dorcas Cl
2 The Link
3 Olivia Cl

E8
1 Fabian Cl
2 Florentine Wy
3 Juliet Ct
4 Sebastian Gv
5 Valentine Ct

E1
1 Crossbill Cl
2 Goldcrest Cl
3 Sandpiper Cl
4 Swift Cl
5 Warbler Cl

F1
1 Chantry Rd

F2
1 Crisspyn Cl
2 Kefford Cl
3 Peper Harow
4 Roland Cl

F3
1 Causeway Farm

F4
1 Furze Way

F5
1 Greenfield Ri

F6
1 Stephen Cl

F7
1 Barn Fold
2 Bracken Heath
3 Chepstow Ct
4 Fontwell Ms
5 Hathaway Gdns
6 Haydock Ms
7 Hitherwood Cl
8 Jessica Cl
9 Kempton Pk
10 Moor Pk
11 Octavius Ct
12 Plumpton Gv
13 Ripon Gdns
14 Salet Wy

F8
1 Sonnet Wy

329

Wick Fm

A **B** **C** **D** **E** **F**

Old
Idsworth

Markwells
Wood

1

Idsworth Ho

South
Holt Fm

2

Ashcroft
La

Finchdean

Northwood
Fm

Forests

Road

Maple Road
Lane

Dean
Lane

Woodhouse

3

**Deanlane
End**

Finchdean Rd

Warren
Down

4

Drews Fm

353

Wellsworth

Finchdean Rd

Lane

Wellsworth La

Bowes

Wellwood Gdns

Meadowlands Broad Cft

Border Path

Sussex Border Path

5

Holt Gdns

Stansted Forest

Greatfield
Way

Hill

The The Peak Peak

Uplands Road

Rowlands/
Castle Station

Hare's
Warren

6

Links

The Fairway

Doctors Surgery

PH PO PH

M

Finchdean Rd

Lane

English
Gallery

**Rowland's
Castle**

Sussex Border Path

Monarch's Way

Monarch's Wy

**Red
Hill**

Redhill

Road

College

Glen DI

Woodberry La

Horsepasture Fm

Sussex

Border

Path

7

The

The Drift

rrants

St Johns C of E
Primary School

Sussex   Border   Path

Holme Farm

8

WHICHERS GATE ROAD B2148

LC

Stubbermere

A **B** **C** **D** **E** **F**

378

Hampshire County

Woodberry Lane

1 grid square represents 500 metres

Horsley Farm

G

H

Locksash Lane

J

We330arden

K

L

M

Grevitts Copse

I

Nore Down Wy

B2146

Locksash Lane

2

Oldhouse Lane

Nore Down

Lodge Fm

Lodge Lane

3

Watergate

Watergate Hanger

4

Broadreed Fm

B2146

5

Lumley Seat

Monarch's Way

Monarch's Way

Cooks

Monarch's Wy

Monarch's Way

Monarch's WY

Walde

6

Woodlands Lane

Woodlands Cotts

Monarch's Wy

Woodlands

Cooks Lane

stead House

B2146

7

Newbarn Lane

B2146

Park Lane

8

Sindle's Fm

Monument La

G

H

J

379

K

L

M

B2146

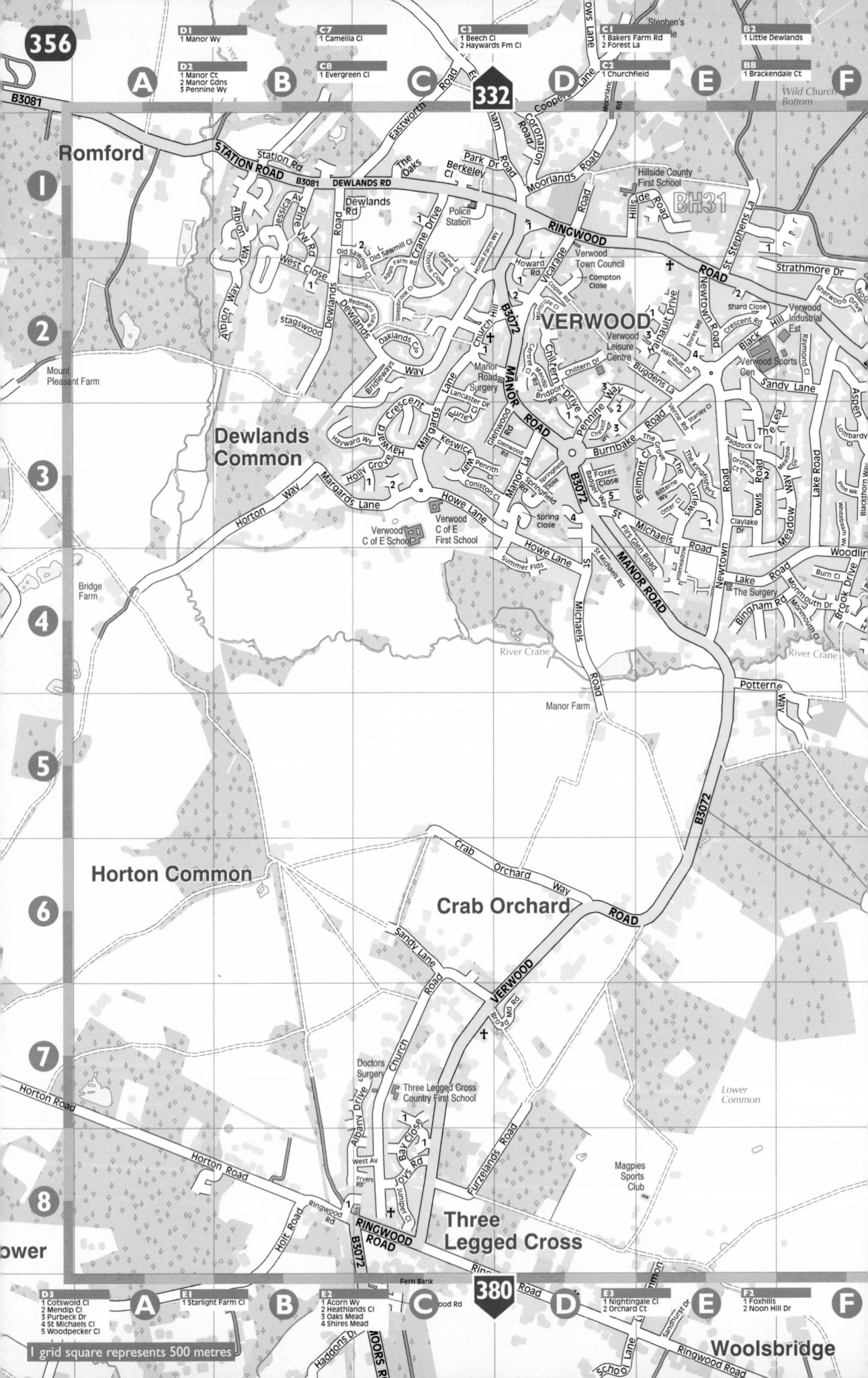

356

B3081

D1
1 Manor Wy

D2
1 Manor Ct
2 Manor Gdns
3 Pennine Wy

C7
1 Camellia Cl

C8
1 Evergreen Cl

C3
1 Beech Cl
2 Haywards Fm Cl

C1
1 Bakers Farm Rd
2 Forest La

C2
1 Churchfield

B2
1 Little Dewlands

B8
1 Brackendale Ct

A B C D E F

332

Romford

Dewlands Common

Horton Common

Crab Orchard

Three Legged Cross

VERWOOD

BH31

Woolsbridge

380

D3
1 Cotswold Cl
2 Mendip Cl
3 Purbeck Dr
4 St Michaels Cl
5 Woodpecker Cl

E1
1 Starlight Farm Cl

E2
1 Acorn Wy
2 Heathlands Cl
3 Oaks Mead
4 Shires Mead

E3
1 Nightingale Cl
2 Orchard Ct

F2
1 Foxhills
2 Noon Hill Dr

A B C D E F

1 grid square represents 500 metres

G1
1 Lavender Cl

Heath

Plumley
Wood

G H J 333 K L M

Plumley Farm

I

Harefield
Plantation

Shepherds Lane

2

Home Farm

Chestnut

Nea Drive

3

Ringwood Forest

Chase

Hunters Cl

Barberry Wy

Ringwood Rd

RINGWOOD ROAD

The Forestside

Rosebery
Close

Black

Moor Rd

Nea Drive

Some Pa

4

Ebblake

Parkland

Cemetery

Brunel Cl

Forest Ci

358

Bessemer
Close

Ebblake Industrial
Est

B3081

5

Duncombe Drive

6

Hampshire County
Dorset County

7

Moors Valley
Country Park

VERWOOD ROAD B3081

Baker's
Hanging

Moors River

8

ath
Est

Watchmoor
Wood

F8 1 Lumby Drive Pk
E8 1 Somerley Vw
D8 1 Manor Gdns
Harbridge
Turmer
334
Avon Val
A338
Ibsley
Mockbeggar Lane
SALISBURY ROAD
River Avon
Lower Turmer
Turmer Brook
Shepherds Hill
Chestnut Avenue
Ellingham Drive
Ellingham Dr
Ellingham Drove
Ellingham
Somerley Park
Nea Drive
Somerley
Ashley Drive
Ivy Lane
357
Avon Va Pth
Snail's Lane
Blashford Farm
Blashford
Woolmer Lane
Headlands Business Park
Avon Valley Path
Waterside Close
North
Morant Road
Ashley Farm
Gouldings Farm
River Avon
Hurst Rd
Northfield Road
Baker's Hanging
Salisbury Road
Gravel Lane
Highfield Drive
Broadshard Lane
Meadow Cl
Hampton Dr
Seymour Rd
Meadow Road
Preparatory School
Gypsy La
Highfield Avenue
Highfield Rd
Pound Cl
Orchard Cl
Middleton Rd
Fieldway
Beechcroft La
Oak La
Manor Ct
Kestrel Ct
Southampton Rd
Lilac Cl
Winston
Kings Stream
RINGWOOD
Linden Gdns
Parsonage
Barn La
382
Watchmoor Wood
Stallards
Gravel La
Carvers Trad Est
Ringwood School
Green La
Ringwood Recreation Centre
Cadogan Rd
Manor Rd
Clough
West St
Strides La
Market Pl
MANSFIELD RD
Dr Hughes & Partners
Collins La
Carvers La
Top La
College Road
Redwood Cl
East View
1 grid square represents 500 metres

G7
1 Frobisher Cl
2 Hawkins Cl
3 Padget Rd
G8
1 Cunningham Cl
2 Hudson Cl
3 Pilgrim Pk
4 Pipers Ash
5 Raleigh Cl
6 Whitehart Flds
Whitefield Plantn
Toms Lane
Linwood Farm
335
Mockbeggar
Digden Bottom
Dockens Water
Avon Valley Path
Appleslade Inclosure
Red Shoot Wood
Rockford Common
Great Linford Inclosure
Highwood
Highwood Lane
360
Little Linford Inclosure
Lin Brook
Linford
Cowpitts Lane
North Poulner
Gorley Road
Old Farm Close
Lin Brook Dr
Junior & Infant School
Shaw Rd
Ross Rd
Lawrence Rd
Hangersley
St Aubyns Lane
Forestside Gdns
Dene Cl
Croft Rd
Holm Cl
Denholm Cl
Butlers La
Linford Road
Drake Cl
Grenville Cl
Chester Rd
Narrow La
Shobley
BH24
Poulner
Anson Cl
Beatty Cl
Somerville Rd
The Mount
Eastfield La
Southampton Road
Audemer Ct
Chaffey Cl
A31(T)
POULNER HILL
Picket Hill
383
Foulford
Nouale
Hill

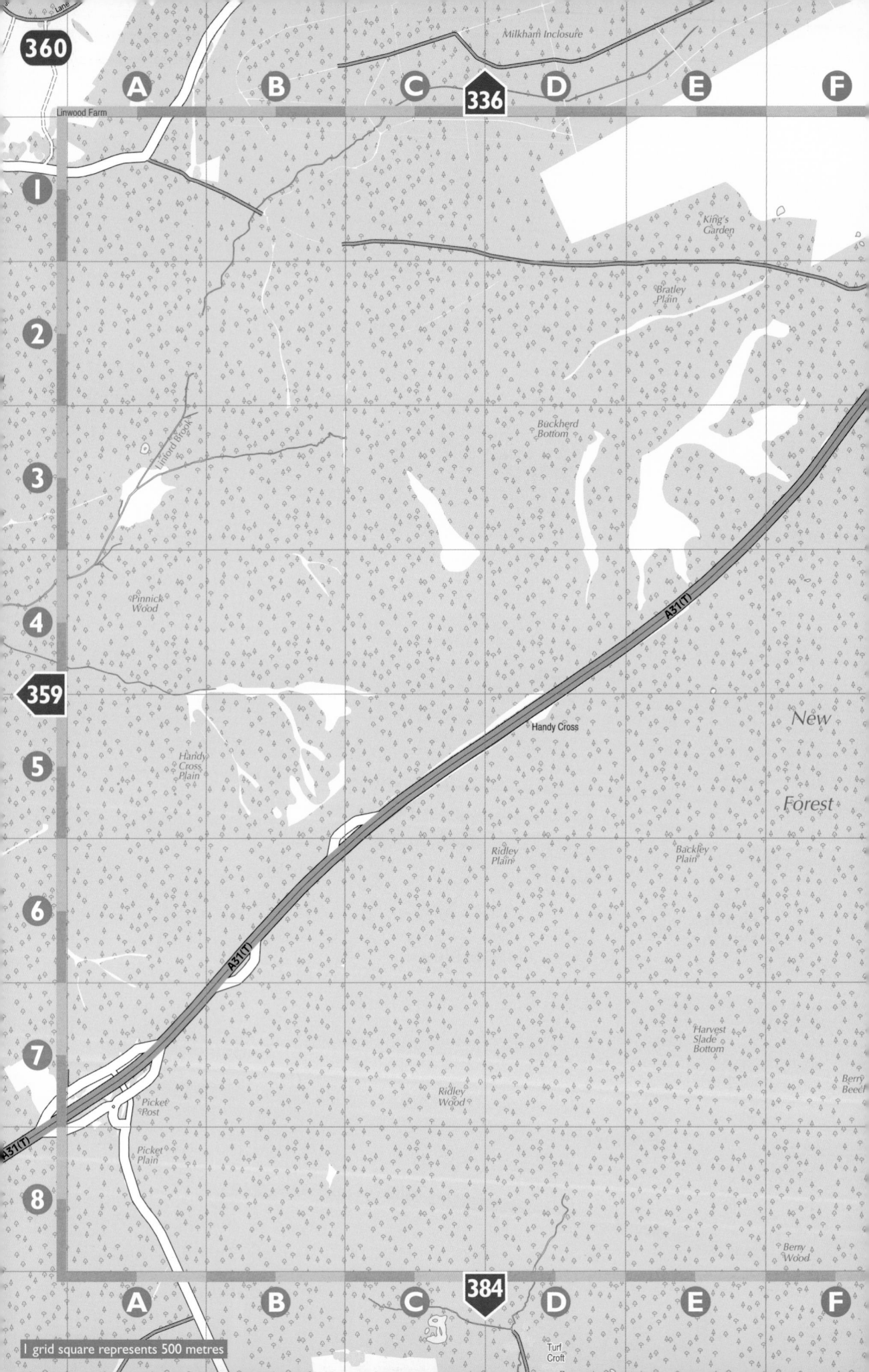

360

A   B   C   336   D   E   F

Linwood Farm

Milkham Inclosure

1

King's
Garden

2

Bratley
Plain

Linford Brook

3

Buckherd
Bottom

Pinnick
Wood

4

A31(T)

359

Handy Cross

New

Handy
Cross
Plain

5

Ridley
Plain

Backley
Plain

Forest

6

A31(T)

Harvest
Slade
Bottom

7

Berry
Beech

Picket
Post

Ridley
Wood

Picket
Plain

A31(T)

8

Berry
Wood

A   B   C   384   D   E   F

Turf
Croft

1 grid square represents 500 metres

G H J 337 K L M

I
2
3
4
362
5
6
7
8

Bratley Water

A31(T)

Bratley Arch

Bratley Inclosure

Bratley Wood

Bolderwood Farm

Bolderwood Cottage

Bolderwood Grounds

Backley Bottom

Backley Inclosure

Bratley Water

Mark Ash Wood

arrow Moor

North Oakley Inclosure

Church Moor

Soarley Beeches

Beech Bed Inclosure

Windin Sheet

Anderwood Inclosure

Old House

Burley Outer Rails Inclosure

Bolderwood Arboretum Ornamental Drive

Burley Lodge

G H J 385 K L M

South Oakley Inclosure

Danes Slough

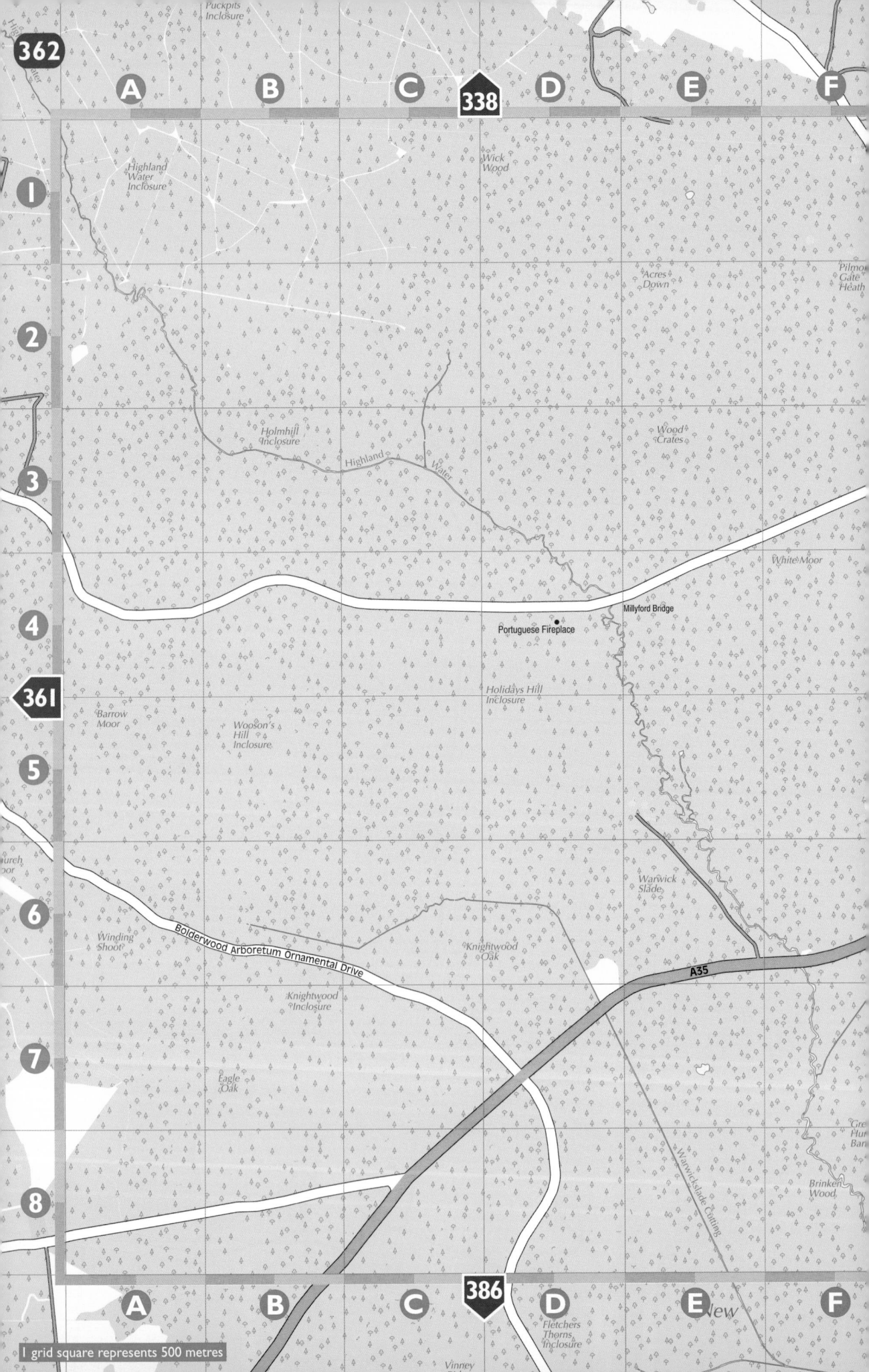

A   B   C   **338**   D   E   F

Puckpits
Inclosure

Wick
Wood

1

Highland
Water
Inclosure

Acres
Down

Pilmo
Gate
Heath

2

Holmhill
Inclosure

Highland   Water

Wood
Crates

3

White Moor

4

Millyford Bridge

Portuguese Fireplace

Barrow
Moor

Holidays Hill
Inclosure

Wooson's
Hill
Inclosure

5

Warwick
Slade

Church
Moor

6

Winding
Shoot

Bolderwood Arboretum Ornamental Drive

Knightwood
Oak

A35

Knightwood
Inclosure

7

Eagle
Oak

Gre
Hur
Bar

Brinken
Wood

8

Warwickslade Cutting

A   B   C   **386**   D   E   F

View

Fletchers
Thorns
Inclosure

Vinney

1 grid square represents 500 metres

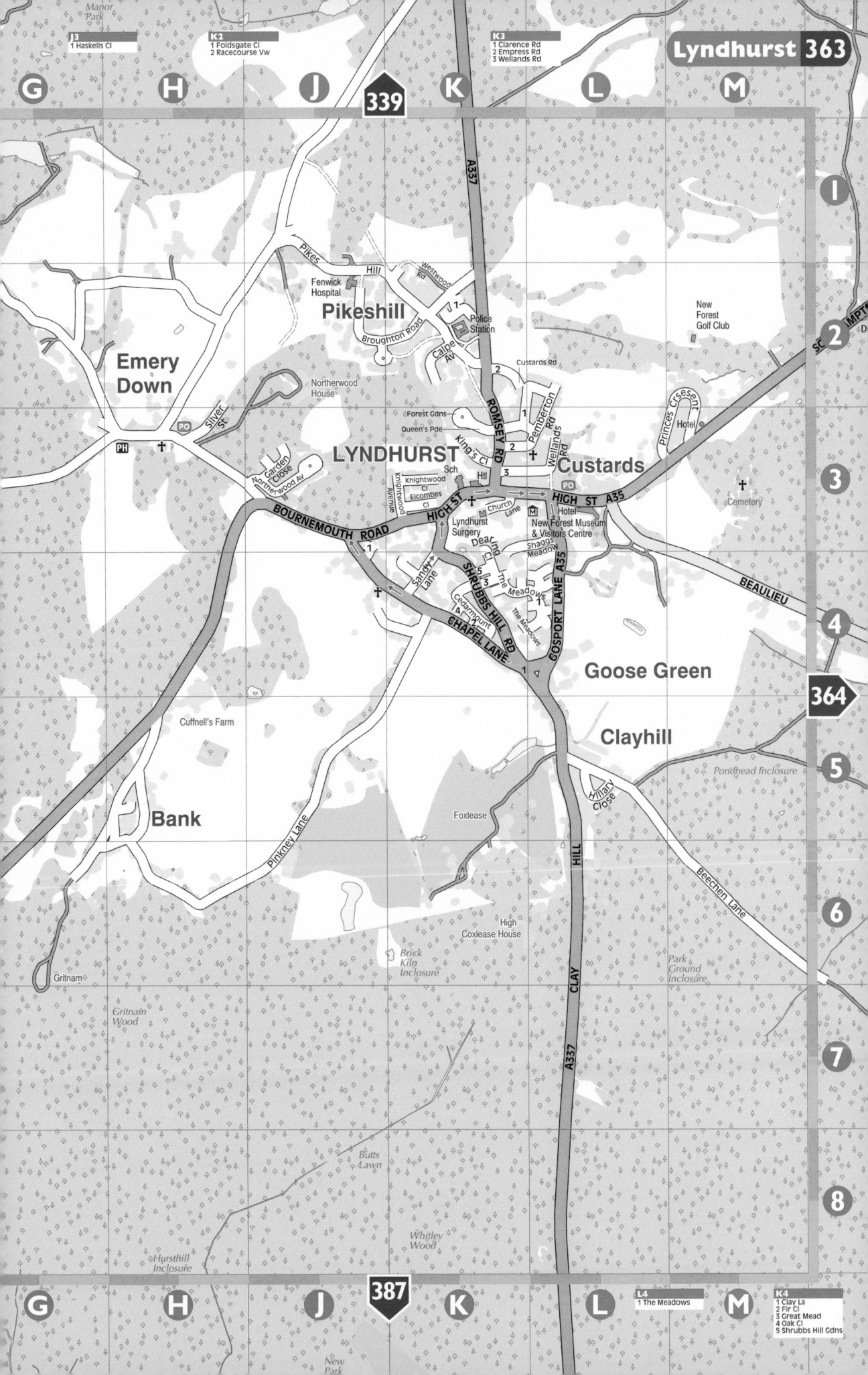

339

364

387

J3
1 Haskells Cl

K2
1 Foldsgate Cl
2 Racecourse Vw

K3
1 Clarence Rd
2 Empress Rd
3 Wellands Rd

G H J K L M

I

2

3

4

5

6

7

8

Manor Park

Emery Down

Pikeshill

Pikes Hill

Westwood Rd

Fenwick Hospital

Broughton Road

Police Station

Calpe Av

Custards Rd

New Forest Golf Club

Princes Crsesent

Hotel

SC IMPT D

Northerwood House

Forest Gdns

Queen's Pde

LYNDHURST

Romsey Rd

King's Cl

Pemberton Rd

Wellands Rd

Custards

Cemetery

Silver St

Garden Close

Northerwood Av

Knightwood Avenue

Knightwood Cl

Elcombes Cl

Sch

Htl

Church Lane

High St A35

PO

Hotel

New Forest Museum & Visitors Centre

Shaggs Meadow

BOURNEMOUTH ROAD

HIGH ST

Lyndhurst Surgery

Dea ing

The Meadows

The Meadows

Gosport Lane A35

BEAULIEU

Sandy Lane

Shrubbs Hill Rd

Cedarmount

Chapel Lane

Goose Green

Clayhill

Willay Close

Pondhead Inclosure

Park Ground Inclosure

Cuffnell's Farm

Pinkney Lane

Foxlease

Bank

Clay Hill

A337

Beechen Lane

Gritnam

Gritnam Wood

Brick Kiln Inclosure

High Coxlease House

Butts Lawn

Whitley Wood

Hurshill Inclosure

New Park

PO

PH

L4
1 The Meadows

K4
1 Clay La
2 Fir Cl
3 Great Mead
4 Oak Cl
5 Shrubbs Hill Gdns

340

A   B   C   D   E   F

Ironshill
Inclosure

shpole
Wood

Lodgehill
Cottage

A35

Ashurst
Wood

1

SOUTHAMPTON   ROAD

Mallard
Wood

Ashurst Lodge

2

Dunces Arch

White
Moor

Beaulieu River

3

etery

BEAULIEU

Matley
Wood

4

ROAD

Matley
Heath

B3056

5

Hotel

Matley
Passage

ad

6

Little
Holmhill
Inclosure

Denny's
Inclosure

7

Park Hill

Denny
Wood

8

Denny
Lodge

A   B   C   388   D   E   F

1 grid square represents 500 metres

Churchplace
Inclosure

Deerleap
Lane

Longdown
Estates

Langley
Wood

G **H** **J** **341** **K** **L** **M**

Deerleap Inclosure

Staplewood
Lane

1

Arters

2

Longdown
Inclosure

Twiggs

3 Farm

Inclosure

4

366

5

Decoy
Pond Farm

Yew
Trees
Heath

Black
Down

6

7

Beaulieu
Road Station

Hotel

Ferny
Crofts

8

New
Forest

G **H** **J** **389** **K** **L** **M**

BEAULIEU ROAD B3056

366
342
365
390
A
B
C
D
E
F
1
2
3
4
5
6
7
8
Marchwood C of E Infant School
Willow Dr
Spindlewood Wy
Hythe Road
LC
Pumpfield Farm
MARCHWOOD
BY-PASS
Main Road
Marchwood Priory Hospital
Veal's
Church Farm Close
Gdn City
Church Farm
A326
Arters Lawn
Twiggs Lane
Twiggs Lane End
Beaulieu Road
Birchlands Farm
Carter's Lane
Foxhill Farm
The Old Manor
Manor Road
HYTHE BY-PASS
Applemore
Marchwood Inclosure
Ipley Inclosure
Ipley Manor
Beaulieu River
King's Hat Inclosure
Fern Crofts
Crabhat Inclosure
1 grid square represents 500 metres

Hythe 367
343
368
391
G4
1 Broomy Cl
2 Eyeworth Wk
3 Magnolia Cl
4 Vaughan Rd
G6
1 Downwood Cl
H7
1 Roman Gdns
J6
1 Marlborough Ct
J7
1 Haynes Wy
2 Woodlands Ct
G5
1 Ridgewood Cl
2 Rockram Gdns
3 Rooksbridge
4 Roundcopse
H6
1 Blackdown Cl
2 Brendon Cl
3 Mendip Gdns
4 Pentland Cl
5 The Quantocks
H5
1 Ashburton Cl
2 The Brackens
3 Capella Gdns
4 Cotswold Cl
5 Moorland Cl
6 The Sylvans
K6
1 Badger Wk
2 Byeways
3 Drakes Cl
4 Forest Hill Wy
5 Heathfield
6 Noads Cl
K8
1 Corbould Rd
L4
1 Alexandra Cl
2 Carpenter Cl
3 Court House Cl
4 Drummond Rd
5 Fairfield Cl
6 Green Cl
7 Mariners Ms
8 Pylewell Rd
L6
1 Frayslea
2 Greatwood Cl
3 Knightstone Gra
4 Langdown Lwn Cl
5 Rose Cl
L7
1 Andrew Cl
2 Buttercup Cl
3 Butts Ash La
4 Chaloner Crs
5 Hartley Cl
6 Ingle Gln
7 Northbourne Cl
8 Silvers End
M5
1 Tates Rd
M6
1 Pinewood Crs
2 Spinney Gdns
3 Tates Rd
M7
1 Furzedown Ms
2 Hamilton Ms
M8
1 Laburnum Crs
2 Maple Rd
L8
1 Devonshire Gdns
2 Stokesay Cl
M4
1 Sir Christopher Cl
L5
1 Abbey Cl
2 Coat Gdns
3 Freedom Ct
L3
1 Mount House Cl
K7
1 Chaveney Cl
2 Hartley Wk
3 Lambourne Cl
4 Ratcliffe Rd
5 Windmill Copse
K5
1 Boundstone
2 Conifer Cl
3 Hawthorn Rd
4 Midway
5 Tormead
Dibden
Lock's Farm
HYTHE
Langdown
Buttsash
Dibden Purlieu
Dibden Inclosure
Marina
Clayfields Sports Centre
Depedene
Orchard County Infant & Junior School
Applemore College
Oak Lodge School
Langdown County Junior School
Langdown County Infants School
Hythe Medical Cen
The Waterside Health Cen
Wildground County Infant School
Junior School
Forestside Medical Practice
Police Station
Waterfront Garden Surgery
School
Forest Lodge
HYTHE BY-PASS
A326
Main Road
Southampton Road
Shore Road
Roman Road
Noads Way
Water Lane
Fawley Road
Butts Ash Lane
Buttsash Avenue
Langdown Lawn
Frost Lane
Hart Hill
Solent Way

A
B
C
D
E
F
1
2
3
4
5
6
7
8
344
367
392
Weston Shore First School
Kingsclere
Fullerton Cl
Drayton
Lambernurst
Sparsholt Rd
International Wy
Abbey Hill
Solent Way
1 Sedgemead
City of Southampton
Hampshire County
Grange Road
Grange Ct
Priory Road
Castle Rd
Queens Vw
Wykeham Road
Mortimer Cl
Monks Rd
New Road
Victoria Road
Garfield Rd
Grange Rd
Chamberlayne Rd
Netley Court School
PO
St Edwards Rd
Langdown
Harvey Gdns
Road
Guillemot Cl
Gannet Cl
Cormorant Dr
Fulmar Drive
Frost Lane
Spinney Dl
Hardy Dr
Lane
Hart Hill
Frostlane
West Road
East Road
Charleston Road
First Street
Second St
Av D
Av C
Avenue E
New Road
Hardley La
Fawley Road
Cadland Rd
Cadland Creek
Southam
Itchen
1 grid square represents 500 metres

Bursledon

Butlocks Heath

Hound

HAMBLE-LE-RICE

G1
1 Calbourne
2 Carisbrooke
3 Culver
4 Kingston
5 Nettlestone
6 Shorewell
7 Whitwell
8 Wootton

G2
1 Arreton
2 The Badgers
3 Newbridge
4 Oakhurst Cl

G3
1 Latelie Cl
2 Waverley Ct

H1
1 Old School Cl

H6
1 Westfield Common

L1
1 Coronation Pde
2 Hardwicke Wy

G
L6
1 Hamble H Gdns

H
L5
1 Oakwood Wy

J

K
L4
1 Kingfisher Cl
2 St Agatha's Rd

L
K6
1 College Cl
2 Pegasus Cl

M
K5
1 Acorn Ct

370
369
346
394
Swanwick
D7
1 Galleon Cl
F3
1 Dove Gdns
2 Northmore Cl
D5
1 Rowe Ashe Wy
2 Wildern Cl
C5
1 Littlewood Gdns
B8
1 Beechwood Cl
2 Birchdale Cl
3 Cheviot Gn
4 Glenda Cl
5 Larchdale Cl
6 Shellcroft
7 Spenser Cl
B1
1 Swanwick Shore Rd
Bursledon Station
Swanwick Business Park
Marina
Brooklands
River Hamble
Swanwick Lane
The Whiteley Surgery
Swanwick
BOTLEY ROAD
A3051
M27
Glen Ho
Lands End Road
Oslands Dr
Glen Road
Spring Road
Chapel Rd
The Green
A27
BRIDGE ROAD
Addison Road
Woodlands Close
Allotment Road
Sarisbury
Sarisbury Green C of E Primary School
Regents Gate
Crableck Lane
Holly Hill Lane
Hawthorn La
Bramble La
Barnes La
Beacon Mt
Park Gate Business Cen
Talisman Business Cen
Beacon Bottom
Beacon Wy
Station Rd
Pine Walk
Coldeast Wy
Brook Lane
Park Gate Jun School
Northmore Road
Sarisbury Infant School
Brookfield Secondary School
Brookfield Gardens
Sherwood Gdns
Barnbrook Road
Headland Dr
Moorland Cl
Highnam Gdns
Battle Road
Locks Road
Home Rule Road
Chancel Rd
Church Rd
Hill La
Holly Hill
Winnards Pk
Dormy Cl
Vine Cl
Barnes Lane
Brook Lane
Brook Avenue
Peters Road
Holland Park
Heath Rd N
Strawberry Hl
Lockswood Rd
Centre Way
Lockswood Surgery
Maytree Close
Heath Rd
Woodpecker Copse
Cem
Upr Brook Dr
Upper Brook Dr
Peters Rd
Crescent Road
Lydney Road
Locks Road Surgery
The Chestnuts
Monterey Dr
Coltsfoot Drive
Greenaway Lane
Greenaway La
Herb Yarrow Wy
Raley Road
Warsash Road
Lawn Dr
Glendale
Locksheath
Thornton Avenue
Crofton Way
Mariners Wy
Passage Lane
Warsash
Whiteways Ms
Corvette Av
Schooner Wy
Shorewood Cl
Locksheath County Infants & Primary School
Victoria Rd
Sovereign Crescent
Titchfield Common
Havelock Road
Garden Ms
Foy Gdns
Dibles Road
Fleet End Road
Green Lane
Fleetend
Sixpenny Close
The Florins
Osborne Road
Bevis Cl
Church Rd
Elmdale Close
Spruce Cl
Hook with Warsash Primary School
New Rd
Oakwood Cl
Meadcroft
C7
1 Albacore Av
2 Enterprise Cl
3 Knights Cl
4 Trimaran Rd
5 Westerley Cl
Abshot
Abshot Rd
D6
1 Bryony Cl
2 Burgundy Cl
3 Elder Cl
4 Larkspur Cl
5 Shepherds P Cl
6 Snapdragon Cl
7 Speedwell Cl
Newtown Road
Queen's Rd
Pitchponds Rd
Hornby Road
Howerts Cl
Rossan Av
Lower Spinney
Fleet End Bottom
Fleet End Road
Hook La
Newtown
Hook Park Rd
F4
1 Laurel Cl
2 St Cuthberts Cl
F5
1 Conference Dr
2 St Simon Cl
F6
1 CoombeDl
2 Glendale
Gilchrist
1 grid square represents 500 metres
A B C D E F
1 2 3 4 5 6 7 8

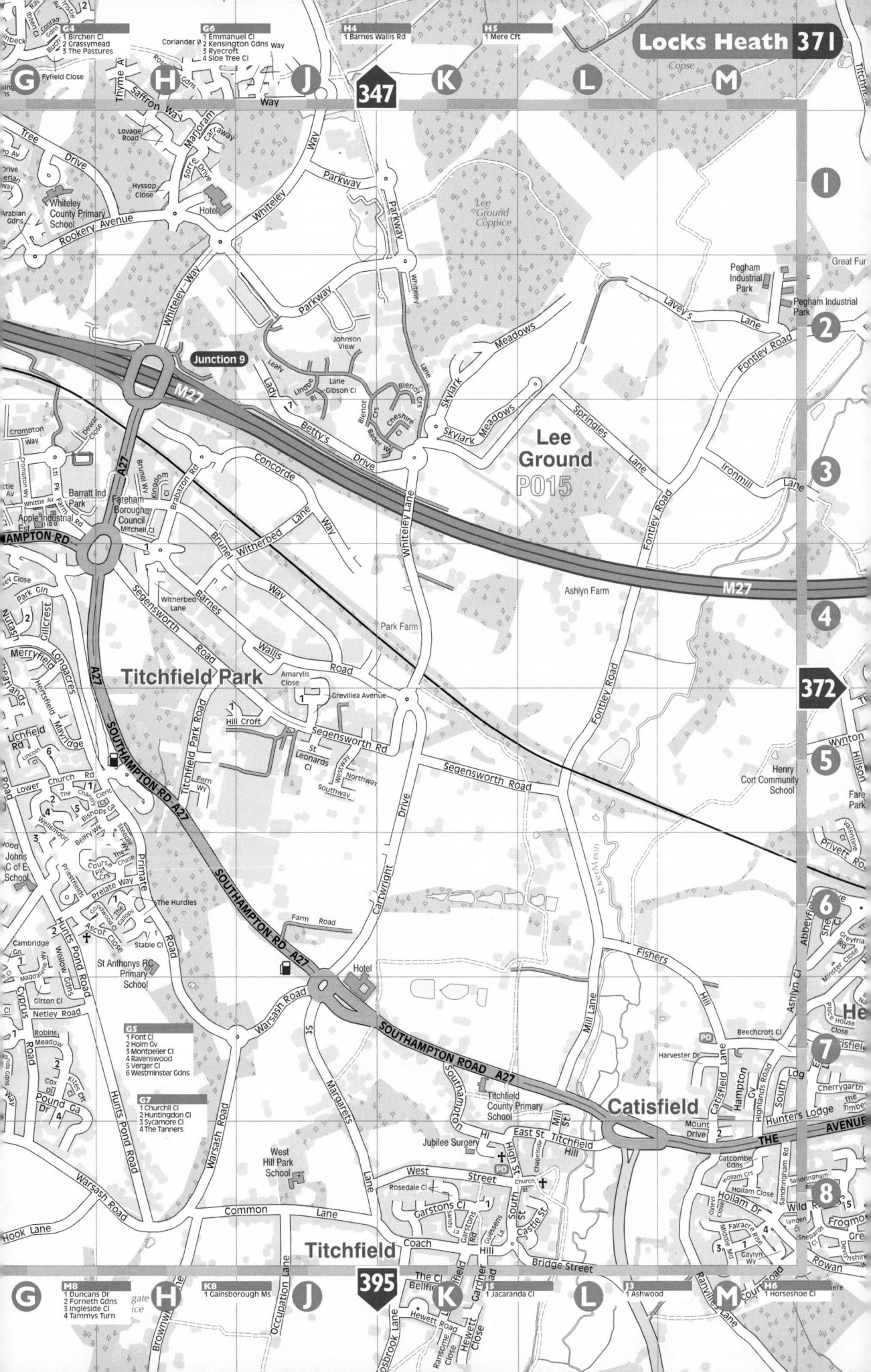

G4
1 Birchen Cl
2 Grassymead
3 The Pastures

G6
1 Emmanuel Cl
2 Kensington Gdns
3 Ryecroft
4 Sloe Tree Cl

H4
1 Barnes Wallis Rd

H5
1 Mere Cft

G **H** **J** **347** **K** **L** **M**

I

2

Pegham Industrial Park

Lee Ground Coppice

Great Fur

3

Lee Ground
P015

4

M27

372

Ashlyn Farm

Henry Cort Community School

5

Junction 9

M27

A27

Fareham Borough Council

Barratt Ind Park

Apple Industrial Est

HAMPTON RD

Titchfield Park

Segensworth Road

Segensworth Rd

Segensworth Road

6

7

SOUTHAMPTON RD - A27

St Anthonys RC Primary School

Warsash Road

Hotel

SOUTHAMPTON ROAD A27

Catisfield

G5
1 Font Cl
2 Holm Gv
3 Montpelier Cl
4 Ravenswood
5 Verger Cl
6 Westminster Gdns

G7
1 Churchill Cl
2 Huntingdon Cl
3 Sycamore Cl
4 The Tanners

West Hill Park School

Titchfield County Primary School

Jubilee Surgery

West Street

East St Titchfield Hill

8

Titchfield

G **M8** **H** **K8** **J** **395** **K** **L** **M** **H6**

M8
1 Duncans Dr
2 Forneth Gdns
3 Ingleside Cl
4 Tammys Turn

K8
1 Gainsborough Ms

G5
1 Jacaranda Cl

J3
1 Ashwood

H6
1 Horseshoe Cl

B8
1 Cherry Tree Av
2 Hayling Cl
3 Sibland Cl
4 Thorney Cl
5 Tortworth Cl
B6
1 Badger Cl
2 Barfleur Cl
3 Pelican Cl
4 Shannon Cl
5 Triumph Cl
B5
1 Beaumont Cl
B3
1 Deer Leap
A7
1 Friars Pond Rd
B4
1 Beaumont Ri
A8
1 Cromhall Cl
2 Pilning Cl
3 Sandisplatt
4 Sharpness Cl
5 Thornbury Cl
B7
1 Appleton Rd
2 Wood Barn Rd
C5
1 Craven Ct
2 Dundee Cl
3 Mary Rose Cl
348
371
Knowle Farm
Heytesbury Farm
Knowle Hospital
Crockerhill
Great Funtley Farm
Pegham Industrial Park
Charity Farm
River Lane
Fontley Road
Funtley Road
Honey Lane
Lakeside
Funtley
The Waters
Dean Farm
Dean Farm Estate
Kneller Court
Junction 10
M27
A32
Hill Park
Fareham Park Infant School
Junior School
Henry Cort Community School
Orchard Lea Junior & Infant Schools
Hill Park Clinic
Highlands Medical Centre
Gudge Heath Surgery
Uplands County Primary School
Fareham Leisure Centre
Heathfield
Blackbrook Business Park
FAREHAM
Fareham Station
The Practice Doctors Surgery
Magistrates Court
St Francis School
Heathfield School
Ranvilles Junior & Infant School
St Judes Catholic Primary Sch
Fareham College
Wallisdean County Infant School
Wallisdean County Junior School
Neville Lovett Community School
West End
The Boatyard Industrial Est
THE AVENUE A27
A27 WESTERN WAY
396
C6
1 Marigold Cl
C8
1 Whitebeam Cl
D6
1 Lawrence Rd
2 Rowland Rd
D7
1 Brook Farm Av
E6
1 Tennyson Gdns
E7
1 The Gillies
2 Maytree Rd
E8
1 Alexander Gv
F5
1 Hanover Gdns
2 The Potteries
3 Swallow Wd
1 grid square represents 500 metres

G6
1 Archery La
2 Wallington Hl

H6
1 The Maltings

H7
1 Waterside Gdns

J8
1 Goldcrest Cl
2 Partridge Cl

G   **H**   **J**   349   **K**   **L**   **M**

Bere Farm

King's Way

1

Portchester

2

Whitedell Farm

Manor Farm

✝ **Boarhunt**

Ashley
Down Fa

3

Whitedell Lane

North Fareham Farm

Spurlings Road

Nine Elms Lane

Boarhunt Road

Monument Lane

4

Down
Barn Farm

Boarhunt Road

King's Way

374 ◄

Fort Nelson

Swivelton Lane

Nelson Lane

5

M27

Junction 11

National Museum
of Artillery

Portsdown Hill Road

6

M27

Standard Way

Wallington

Ft Wallington
Industrial
Estate

Military Rd

Military
Road

King's Way

Downend Road

King's Way

allington

WALLINGTON WAY

Pinks Hill

A27

Paradise Lane

King's Way

Downend Road

Danes Rd

Dore Aven
High

Lancaster Cl

Merlin
Gdns

Jute Cl

Camelot
Vw

Solent

Junior &
Infant
School

7

EASTERN WAY

Wykeham
House School

15

Cams Hill

The Ridgeway

St Catherines Way

Alum Way

The
Causeway

The Thicket

The Spinney

The Pines

Tamar Cl

Winnham Drive

Rockingham Wy

Redwood Dr

Hawthorn Cl

Red Barn County
Primary School

Linden

Simpson

The Dell

Cams Hill
School

Paradise Lane

CAMS HILL A27

PO16

Shearwater

Rookswway Grove

Birdwood Grove

Crew Dr

Chaffinch Wy

Teal Cl

Swancote

Wagtail

The Peregrines

Kingfishers

Flamingo Ct

Condor Avenue

A27 PORTCHESTER RD

Beaulieu

Ashtead Cl

Romsey Avenue

Quintrell Av

Dore Avenue

Redwood
Dr

Red Barn County
Primary School

The
Kingsway

8

PORTCHEST

Cams
Hall

Peacock Close

Cams Hall Estate
Golf Club

Wicor County
Primary School

White Hart

G   **H**   **J**   397   **K**   **L**   **M**

M8
1 Hatherley Dr
2 Rudgwick Cl
3 Stoneleigh Cl

M7
1 Boxwood Cl
2 Tudor Cl

L8
1 Severn Cl

Fareham
Borough
Council

K8
1 Cormorant Cl
2 Cygnet Ct
3 Eagle Cl
4 Falcon Cl
5 Grebe Cl
6 Lapwing Gv
7 The Linnets
8 Wren Wy

K7
1 Cams Bay Cl
2 East Cams Cl

Westland
Medical
Centre

Cranleigh Rd

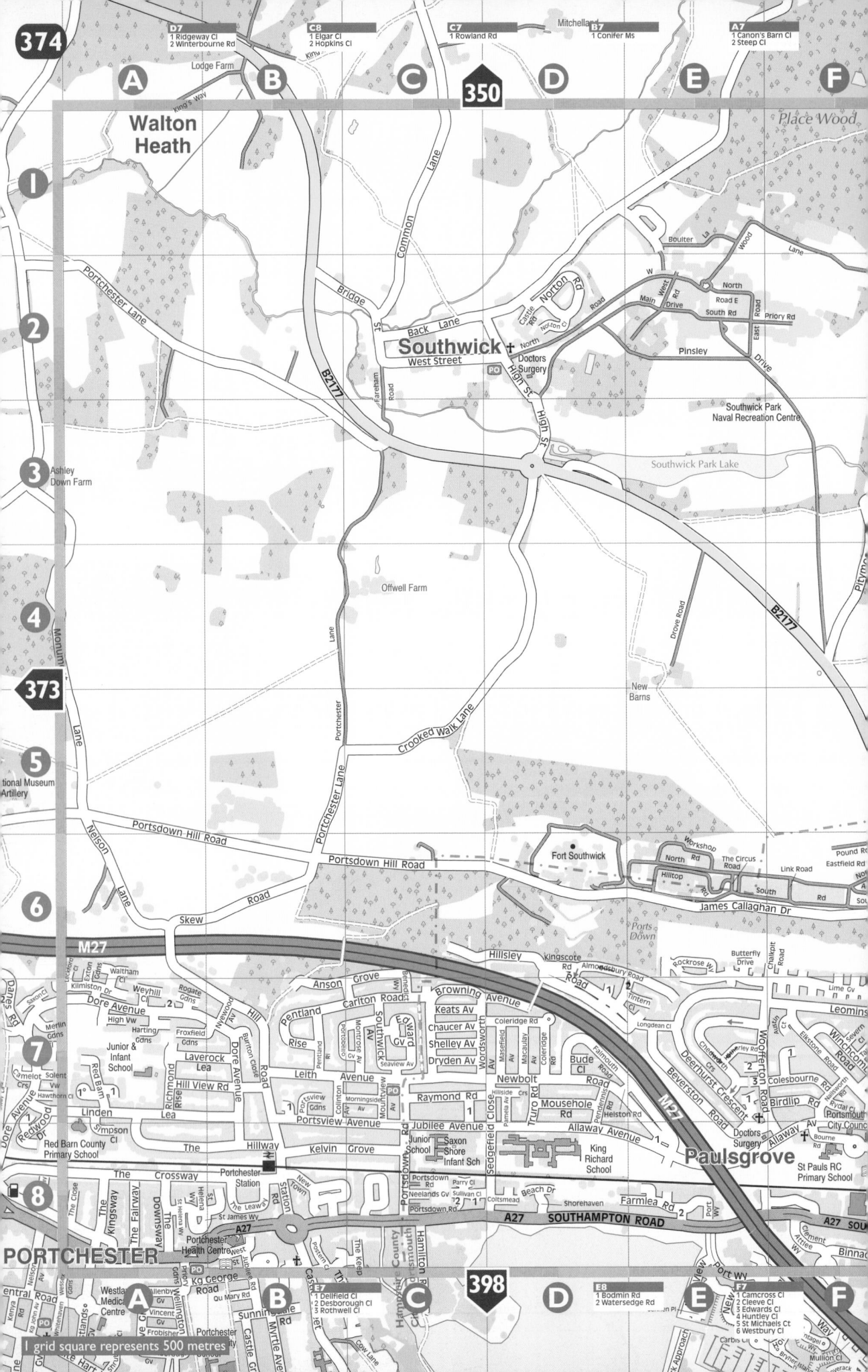

374
D7
1 Ridgeway Cl
2 Winterbourne Rd
C8
1 Elgar Cl
2 Hopkins Cl
C7
1 Rowland Rd
Mitchelland
B7
1 Conifer Ms
A7
1 Canon's Barn Cl
2 Steep Cl
Lodge Farm
King's Way
350
Walton Heath
Place Wood
Common Lane
Portchester Lane
Bridge St
Back Lane
Southwick
West Street
North
Doctors Surgery
PO
High St
Fareham Road
B2177
Castle Rd
Norton Rd
Norton Cl
Road
Main
West Rd
Drive
Boulter La
Wood Lane
North Road E
South Rd
East Road
Priory Rd
Pinsley
Drive
Southwick Park Naval Recreation Centre
Southwick Park Lake
Ashley Down Farm
Offwell Farm
Drove Road
Monument Lane
373
New Barns
Portchester Lane
Crooked Walk Lane
tional Museum Artillery
Portsdown Hill Road
Nelson Lane
Fort Southwick
Workshop
North Rd
Hilltop Rd
The Circus Road
Link Road
South Rd
Pound Rd
Eastfield Rd
James Callaghan Dr
Skew Road
Ports Down
M27
Hillsley
Kingscote Rd
Almondsbury Road
Tintern Cl
Rockrose Wy
Butterfly Drive
Chalkpit Road
Lime Gv
Leominster
Anson Grove
Benedict Wy
Browning Avenue
Carlton Road
Pentland Rise
Southwick Av
Edward Gv
Keats Av
Chaucer Av
Shelley Av
Dryden Av
Wordsworth Av
Coleridge Rd
Masefield Av
Macaulay Av
Longdean Cl
Dore Avenue
High Vw
Weyhill Cl
Rogate Gdns
Waltham Cl
Nyewood Av
Froxfield Gdns
Laverock Lea
Hill View Rd
Richmond Rise
Burrill Road
Junior & Infant School
Red Barn Av
Linden Lea
Simpson Cl
The Hillway
Leith Avenue
Portsview Avenue
Raymond Rd
Jubilee Avenue
Kelvin Grove
Junior School
Saxon Shore Infant Sch
Sedgefield Close
Newbolt Rd
Truro Rd
Mousehole Rd
Bude Cl
Falmouth Road
Helston Rd
Allaway Avenue
King Richard School
Beverston Road
Deerhurst Crescent
Woofferton Road
Colesbourne Rd
Birdlip Rd
Winchcombe Road
Doctors Surgery
Paulsgrove
St Pauls RC Primary School
Portsmouth City Council
Red Barn County Primary School
The Crossway
Portchester Station
New Town Rd
Station
Portsdown Rd
Neelands Gv
Parry Cl
Sullivan Cl
Coltsmead
Beach Dr
Shorehaven
Farmlea Rd
Port Wy
A27 SOUTHAMPTON ROAD
The Close
The Kingsway
The Fairway
Downsway
PORTCHESTER
Portchester Health Centre
Kg George Road
Qu Mary Rd
Sunningdale Rd
Myrtle Av
Castle Gr
Hampshire County
Hamilton Rd
The Keep
398
E7
1 Dellfield Cl
2 Desborough Cl
3 Rothwell Cl
E8
1 Bodmin Rd
2 Watersedge Rd
F7
1 Camcross Cl
2 Cleeve Cl
3 Edwards Cl
4 Huntley Cl
5 St Michaels Ct
6 Westbury Cl
Westlands Medical Centre
Central Road
Portchester Community School
Clement Attlee Wy
Binnacle
1 grid square represents 500 metres

G7
1 Cinderford Cl
2 Dorstone Rd

H7
1 Fitzpatrick Ct
2 Sheringham Rd
3 Walsingham Cl

H8
1 Blackwater Cl
2 Bryson Rd
3 Hadleigh Rd
4 Hockley Cl
5 Maldon Rd
6 Mellor Cl
7 Parr Rd
8 Pebmarsh Rd

G   H   J   K   L   M

351   376

I
2
3
4
5
6
7
8

Wood Ind

Wood Ind

Belney Farm

Wayfarer's Walk

Newlands Farm

Southwick House

Pitymoor Lane

Farm

Hookheath Farm

Purbrook Heath Road

Purbrook Heath Road

Purbrook Cricket Club

Broomfield House

Mill Lane

Widley Walk

Potwell

Pigeon House Lane

Pigeon House Farm

Widley Farm

Widley Walk

New Down La

Meadow Edge

Wayfarer's Walk

Highbank Av

Victoria Av

Geoffrey Avenue

Lansdowne Av

Lily Av

Hillside Av

Greenlea Cl

Cranborne Av

Oakhurst Gdns

Boundary Way

Hilltop Crs

The Crest

Bushy

Applewood Gv

Parke Garde

The

The

Hampshire County
City of Portsmouth

SOUTHWICK ROAD B2177

Callaghan Dr

B2177

B2177 SOUTHWICK HILL ROAD

Fort Widley

PORTSDOWN HILL ROAD

B2177

Drayton

Down End

Down

Augustine Rd

Blakemere Crescent

Bredenbury Crs

Willersley Cl

Meadowsweet Way

Harleston Rd

Lowestoft Rd

Mablethorpe Road

Norwich Rd

Cromer Rd

Peterborough Rd

Ashfoe

Cavell Dr

Kintyre Rd

Shetland Cl

Jura

Chalkridge Road

Carmarthen Avenue

Brecon Avenue

Merthyr Avenue

Aberdare Av

ington Rd

low

Road

Rapson Cl

Credenhill Rd

Abbeydore Rd

Allaway Avenue

Washbrook Road

Harwich Rd

Turretfield

Colchester Road

Maidstone Crs

Deal

Fairfield

Orkney Rd

Islay Gdns

Cosham
London Road

Courtmount Gv

Colville Rd

Courtmount Gv

Lampeter Av

Penarth Av

Painswick Cl

Stratton Cl

Cl

Braintree Road

Sudbury Rd

Clacton Rd

Rochford Rd

Cheltenham

Sevenoaks Road

Whitstable

Westerham Cl

Queen Alexandra
A&E Hosp

Wymering

Portsmouth
City Council

Hythe Road

St John's
Road

St Matthew's

Southdown Rd

Padwick Avenue

Burrill Av

Lodge Av

East Cosham

Bernard Av

School

Dursley Crs

Sydney

Trewesbury Cl

Stanford

SOUTHAMPTON   ROAD

A3

Halstead Rd

Bell Rd

Medina

Old Wymering La

Greenwood Av

Sixth Av

Fifth Av

Ashurst Rd

Third Av

Second Av

First Av

Spur Rd

NORTHERN RD

LONDON RD

St George's

Regal Cl

Havant Road

Havant Road

Havant Road

PO

Aidsworth Rd

Manor Ms

Chilgrove

Acorn
Business
Cen

Northarbou

Medina Rd

Freshwater

Portsmouth City

Scotland

Wayte St

Doctors Surgery

Pervin Rd

Albert Rd

Dean Rd

Cosham
Health
Cen

Cosham

Magd

Mulberry

Wollner

Cashalton Av

Racton

Me

WESTERN ROAD

Junction 12

A27

M27

Lordington Cl

M8

Brid

Gurnard

Down Road

399

Dorking Crs

Health
Cen

Vectis

Cosham Pk
Av

Park
Gv

M6
1 Christ. Gdns
2 Thornton Cl

K8
1 Mallow Cl

Hilary Av

School

Mansvid
Av

Beaconsfield Avenue

Gofton Av

Braemar
Av

Lonsdale Avenue

Invergordon

Kirton

Court

Springf

Centra

L8
1 Glebefield Gdns
2 Tankerton Cl
3 Wymering Mr Cl

G   H   J   K   L   M

WATERLOOVILLE

352

I grid square represents 500 metres

Havant 377
353
378
401
G4
1 Boldre Cl
2 Crookham Cl
3 Dibden Cl
4 Dockenfield Cl
5 Rhinefield Cl
6 Rockbourne Cl
G6
1 Belmont Gv
H1
1 Crabwood Ct
2 Hannington Rd
H2
1 Durford Ct
2 Hurstbourne Cl
3 Locksheath Ct
H3
1 Farleigh Cl
2 Monkwood Cl
3 Testwood Rd
4 Tichborne Gv
5 Weyhill Cl
6 Winslade Rd
H4
1 Cheriton Cl
H5
1 Milford Ct
2 Wellow Cl
J4
1 Adsdean Cl
2 Alresford Rd
3 Park Pde
M2
1 Blissford Cl
2 Burley Cl
3 Chilbolton Ct
4 Houghton Cl
5 Iford Ct
6 Kimpton Ct
7 Scotney Ct
8 Shaldon Rd
9 Soldridge Cl
10 Sopley Ct
11 Sydmonton Ct
12 Verwood Rd
13 Wonston Ct
14 Wyeford Cl
15 Yaldhurst Ct
M3
1 Ashe Rd
2 Bentley Ct
3 Bramshaw Ct
4 Deane Ct
5 Fawley Ct
6 Fullerton Cl
7 Heckfield Cl
8 Holbury Ct
9 Meadend Cl
10 Muscliffe Ct
11 Newnham Ct
12 Oakfield Ct
13 Stanford Ct
14 Stockbridge Cl
15 Sway Ct
16 Tisted Ct
17 Tunworth Ct
18 Warbrook Ct
19 Wherwell Ct
20 Woolmer Ct
21 Worthy Ct
M4
1 Redlynch Cl
M7
1 Castleway
2 Green Pond Cnr
3 Nightingale Pk
4 Ryecroft
5 Woodpecker Cl
L4
1 Douglas Gdns
2 Muccleshell Cl
L5
1 Anderson Cl
2 Flexford Gdns
3 Hodges Cl
L7
1 White Ladies Cl
St Johns C of E Primary School
PO9
Staunton Park Community School
Leigh Park
West Leigh
Stockheath
HAVANT
Brockhampton
Warblington
Park Community School
Riders Junior & Infant School
Front Lawn GM Junior School
Front Lawn Infant School
Sharps Copse Junior & Infant School
Havant Town Football Club
Portsmouth City Council
Middle Park Medical Centre
Barncroft Junior School
Barncroft Infant School
St Albans C of E Primary School
Hayward Business Cen
St Thomas Mores RC Primary School
Havant Rugby Football Club
Havant College
Havant Leisure Centre
Civic Offices
Magistrates Court
Havant Station
Bedhampton Station
Warblington Station
Havant War Memorial Hospital
Havant Sports Club
Catherine Corbett Clinic
Fairfield Infant School
Glenhurst School
Havant Mus
Hampshire Co Council
Warblington School
Bosmere Junior School
Bidbury Junior & Infant School
Havant Business Center
Cemetery
Middle Park Way
Petersfield Road B2149
New Road B2149
Bedhampton Rd B2149
Park Road North B2149
Havant Road A27(T)
A27(T)
B2150
B2148
L3
1 Curdridge Cl
2 Hiltingbury Av
3 Rooksbury Cft
4 Witchampton Cl
K7
1 The Parchment
L2
1 Broxhead Rd
2 Langrish Cl
3 Woodington Cl
K5
1 Compton Cl
2 Havant Farm Cl
3 Linden Wy
J7
1 Clarendon Rd
2 Selbourne Rd
K4
1 Colemore Sq
2 Woodlands Wy
J5
1 Winkton Cl
J6
1 Brookfield Cl
2 Chidham Sq
J2
1 Cotswold Cl
2 Danebury Cl
3 Fleetend Cl
4 Hawkley Cl
5 Marvic Ct
6 Warsash Cl
7 Winterslow Dr

378
354
377
17
402
A
B
C
D
E
F
1
2
3
4
5
6
7
8
D6
1 Emsbrook Dr
D4
1 Winfield Wy
C5
1 Barwell Gv
2 Panton Cl
A5
1 Bladon Cl
2 Bramble Cl
3 Marlborough Pk
4 Spindle Warren
Stubbermere
Southleigh Forest
Southleigh Park
Denvilles
New Brighton
Lumley
Hermitage
Warblington
EMSWORTH
Emsworth Common Road
Woodberry Lane
Horndean Road
Comley Hill
Havant Road
Westbourne Road
New Brighton Road
North St
Long Copse Lane
West Sussex County
Hampshire County
D8
1 Frobisher Gdns
2 King's Ter
3 Orange Rw
E6
1 Westbourne Cl
E8
1 The Fishermans
2 Frankland Ter
3 Harbour Wy
4 Marina Cl
5 Pelham Ter
F3
1 Byerley Cl
F5
1 Church Vw
2 Old Rectory Cl
3 The Square
1 grid square represents 500 metres

G   H   J   **355**   K   L   M

I

2

Staines Fm

Sindle's Fm

Park Lane

Monument La

B2146

Racton Park Fm

B2146   HARES

Aldsworth

B2147

3

Common Road

Ractonparks Wood

Common Road

Marlpit Lane

Hambrook Business Cen

4

FOXBURY LANE

B2147

Woodmancote Lane

Woodmancote

Marlpit Lane

Woodmancote Lane

W Ashling Rd

Cheesemans

Cemetery

Cemetery Lane

Duffield Lane

Walnut Tree DF

South La

Woodmancote Lane

Hambrook HI (North)

Nightingale Lane

5

Devils Copse

A27(T)

A27(T)

W

Lane

A27(T)

Hambrook HI (South)

Broad Road

6

Farm

A27(T)

Stein Rd

South Lane

Lane

Hither Gn

Fraser Gdns

Lauder Cl

Cheshire Wy

Breach Avenue

East Fld Cl

Hambrook

Scant Road (West)

Conifer Dr

PO

The Avenue

7

Bourne Vw Cl

Haslemere Road

Clovelly Road

Mountwood Road

Smallcutts Av

Park Road

Kelsey Av

Glenwood Rd

Bramfield

Furnston Gv

Priors Leaze Lane

Priors Leaze

Oak Tree Farm

Yeomans Fld

The Bourne Community College

St John's Rd

Breach

Hartland Ct   PO

Manor Road

Manor Gdns

Manor Way

Priors Cl

Cooks Lane

Priors Leaze Lane

Broad Rd

LC

LC

Guildford Cl

Hurstwood Av

Inlands Road

LC

Nutbourne Station

LC

8

First Av

Lazy Acre

The Drive

Southbourne Station

Lodgebury Close

Southbourne County Junior & Infant School

Goodwood Court

Alfrey Cl

Longlands Road

Garsons Road

New Rd

Mosdell Rd

Southbourne

Flatt Rd

Pottery La

Flatt Rd

Flatt Rd

N ROAD   A259

The Crescent

Prinsted Lane

Frarydene

Church Rd

Surgery

MAIN RD   PO   A259

MAIN

G **Prinsted**   H   Ham La   J   School   **403**   Farm   K **Nutbourne**   L   A259   M

A259

Maybush Drive

Ivydene Crescent

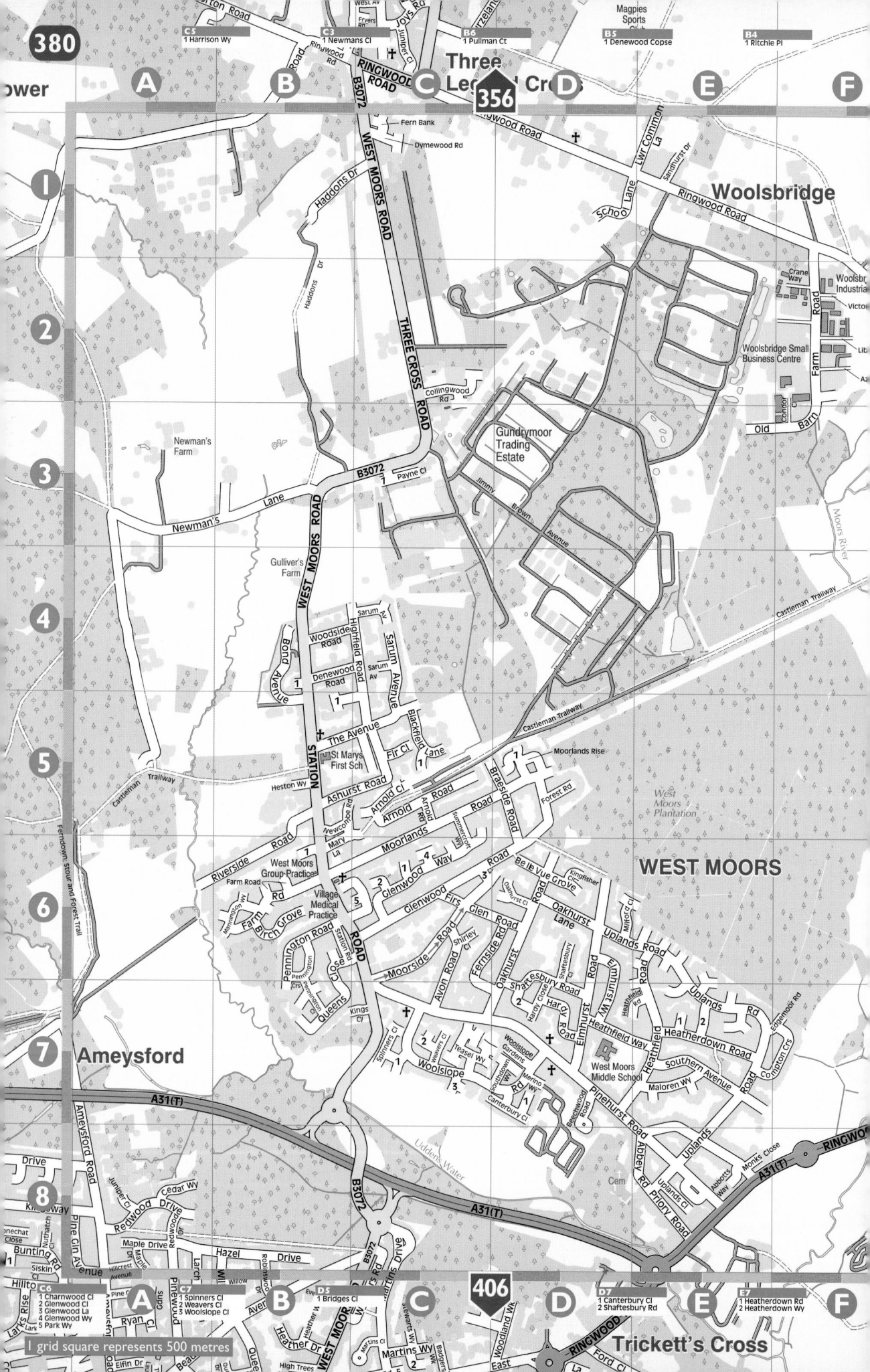
C5
1 Harrison Wy
C3
1 Newmans Cl
B6
1 Pullman Ct
B5
1 Denewood Copse
B4
1 Ritchie Pl
Magpies Sports
Three Legged Cross
356
Woolsbridge
Ringwood Road
School Lane
Lwr Common La
Sandhurst Dr
Fern Bank
Dymewood Rd
WEST MOORS ROAD
THREE CROSS ROAD
Haddons Dr
Crane Way
Woolsbridge Industrial
Farm Road
Woolsbridge Small Business Centre
Collingwood Rd
Gundrymoor Trading Estate
Jimmy Brown Avenue
Old Barn Farm Road
Condor Cl
Newman's Farm
Newman's Lane
B3072
Payne Cl
Gulliver's Farm
Moors River
Castleman Trailway
WEST MOORS
West Moors Plantation
Moorlands Rise
Forest Rd
Braeside Road
Sarum Av
Woodside Road
Highfield Road
Sarum Avenue
Bond Avenue
Denewood Road
The Avenue
Blackfield Lane
St Marys First Sch
Fir Cl
Heston Wy
STATION ROAD
Ashurst Road
Arnold Cl
Arnold Road
Newcombe Rd
Mary La
Moorlands Road
Summercroft Way
Riverside Road
West Moors Group Practice
Village Medical Practice
Farm Road
Mannington Wy
Farm Rd
Birch Grove
Glenwood Way
Glenwood Road
Belle Vue Grove
Kingfisher Cl
Oakhurst Cl
Oakhurst Road
Oakhurst Lane
Milford Cl
Uplands Road
Firs Glen Road
Pennington Road
Station Rd
Pennington Crs
Close
Queens
Kings Cl
Moorside Road
Shirley Cl
Avon Road
Fernside Rd
Shaftesbury Road
Shaftesbury Cl
Hardy Close
Hardy Road
Elmhurst Road
Elmhurst Wy
Heathfield Rd
Heathfield Way
Heathfield Road
Heatherdown Road
Uplands Rd
Edgemoor Rd
Compton Crs
Spinners Cl
Weavers Cl
Teasel Wy
Woolslope Gardens
Woolslope
Southdown Wy
Merino Wy
Canterbury Cl
West Moors Middle School
Southern Avenue
Maloren Wy
Beechwood Road
Pinehurst Road
Abbey Rd
Priory Road
Uplands Cl
Uplands
Abbotts Way
Monks Close
Cem
Ameysford
A31(T)
Uddens Water
RINGWOOD
Ferndown, Stour and Forest Trail
Ameysford Road
Juniper Cl
Cedar Wy
Redwood Drive
Kingsway
Nuthatch Cl
Bunting Rd
Siskin Cl
Pine Glen Avenue
Hillcrest Avenue
Maple Drive
Maple Dr
Redwood Dr
Larch
Hazel Drive
Robinswood Dr
Willow
Pinewood Gdns
Ryan Cl
Larks Rise
Martins Drive
B3072
C6
1 Charnwood Cl
2 Glenwood Cl
3 Glenwood La
4 Glenwood Wy
5 Park Wy
C7
1 Spinners Cl
2 Weavers Cl
3 Woolslope Cl
D5
1 Bridges Cl
406
D7
1 Canterbury Cl
2 Shaftesbury Rd
E7
1 Heatherdown Rd
2 Heatherdown Wy
Heather Dr
WEST MOORS
Stewarts Wy
Martins Wy
Woodland Wk
Trickett's Cross
Ford Cl
High Trees
Elfin Dr
A B C D E F
1 2 3 4 5 6 7 8
1 grid square represents 500 metres

West Moors 381
H3
1 Forest Edge Cl
J5
1 Cedar Av
2 Garden-La
K2
1 High St
357
382
407
G
H
J
K
L
M
1
2
3
4
5
6
7
8
Watchmoor Wood
Moors River
Castleman Trailway
Wools Bridge
Horton Road
Horton Rd
Peveril Cl
Forest Edge Dr
Webbs Cl
Pine Mnr Rd
Burton Cl
Lions Lane
Evans Cl
Elmore Dr
Evergreens
Ashley Drive W
Ashley Dr N
Ashley Heath
The Spinney
Struan Gardens
Struan Dr
Struan Court
Ashley Park
Whitfield Pk
Strode Gdns
St Ives CP School
St Ives Park
St Ives Wood
Hesketh Cl
Sandy Lane
Fernwood Cl
Pineholt Cl
Post Office La
St Ives
Langley Chase
Baggers Cl
Ashley Dr S
Grosvenor Cl
Dryden Cl
Shelley Cl
Lions Lane
St Leonards Way
Bushmead Drive
The Glade
Woolsbridge Road
Monkworthy Dr
Hill Wy
Gainsborough Road
Norris Cl
Fernlea Cl
Bracken Close
Windsor Cl
Paddock Cl
Sandy Lane
Coppice
Greenwood Way
St Ives End La
School Lane
Larch Cl
Azalea Cl
Glenives Cl
Lions Hill Way
Willow Cl
Lions Lane
Sylvan Cl
Cragside
Holly Cl
Garth Cl
Heath
Conifer Cl
Spinney Cl
Gorse Cl
Ivy Cl
Rd
Rowan Cl
St Leonards
Braeside Road
Lions Wd
Cornerways Surg
Woodlands Wy
Pine Drive
Knoll Gdns
Hobbs Park
Pinewood Rd
King Cl
Laurel Close
Laurel Lane
Laurel Dr
Hazlemere
Drive
Acorn Cl
Heather Cl
Malmesbury Rd
Oaks
Birch Close
Cedar Avenue
Cherry Tree Cl
Oaks
Drive
Fir Tree Cl
RINGWOOD ROAD A31(T)
Birch Road
Brocks Pine
Avon Heath Country Park
Beech Lane
Grange Road
Eucalyptus Av
Barnsfield Road
Barnsfield Rd
East Moors Farm
Boundary Lane
Boundary La
Boundary Lane
St Leonards Hospital
Wayside Road
Grange Estate
Foxbury Road
Ringwood Waldorf School
Plant Park Road
Alpine Road
Matcham's House
Hurn Road
M3
1 Russell Gdns
L4
1 The Close
2 Greenwd Cps
L3
1 Cptn Beeches

RINGWOOD

358

D1
1 Centre Pl
2 The Close
3 Cottage Ms
4 High St
5 Kings Arms Rw
6 Meeting Hse La
7 The Sweep

A   B   C   D   E   F

I

2

3

4

381

5

6

7

8

Ashley

Moortown

Kingston

A   B   **E2 cont.**   C   408   D   **F2**   E   F
7 Victoria Gdns   1 Coniston Rd
8 Waterloo Wy
9 Woodstock La

Ringwood 383
G2
1 The Cloisters
2 Greenfinch Wk
3 Linnet Cl
4 Lych Gate Ct
5 Old Stacks Gdns
6 Sanderlings
7 Wren Cl
H2
1 Forest Court Hills
A31(T)
POULNER HILL
Beatty Cl
Picket Hill
359
Foulford
Noualle Lane
Hightown
Hightown Road
Hightown Hill
Forest Lane
Holmwood Garth
Ashburn Garth
Lakeside
Lakeview Dr
Forestlake Av
Ashley Cl
Merlin Cl
Pelican Md
Swan Md
Hurn Farm
Wood End Rd
Forest Edge Rd
Knaves Ash
Vales Moor
Crow
Crow Hill Top
Barrack Lane
Strodgemoor Bottom
384
Charles's Lane
Cranes Moor
Kingston Great Common
Bagnum Farm
Sandford
409
Bisterne Common

E5
1 Doveys Cl
2 Howard Cl
3 The Mall
D5
1 Esdalle La
A
B
C
360
D
E
F
Berry Wood
1
2
3
4
383
5
6
7
8
Turf Croft
Vereley
Coach Hill La
Coach Hill Lane
Ringwood Rd
Randalls Lane
PO
Forest Road
Burley Moor
Vales Moor
Burley Street
Tyrells Lane
Longmead Road
Black Bush
Castle Hill Lane
Ringwood Road
Hotel
Chapel Lane
Castle Hill
Burle
The Wishing Well Gallery
Lyndhurst Rd
Church Lane
Clouch Lane 1
Garden Rd
PH
The Cross
Burley CP School
Burley Golf Club
Honey Lane
Copse Road
Cranes Moor
Burnt Axon
Lane
Warnes Lane
Burley Beacon
Meadow Cl
Shappen Hill Lane
Moorhill
Road
Hotel
Pound Lane
New
Forest
410
1 grid square represents 500 metres
Dur Hill

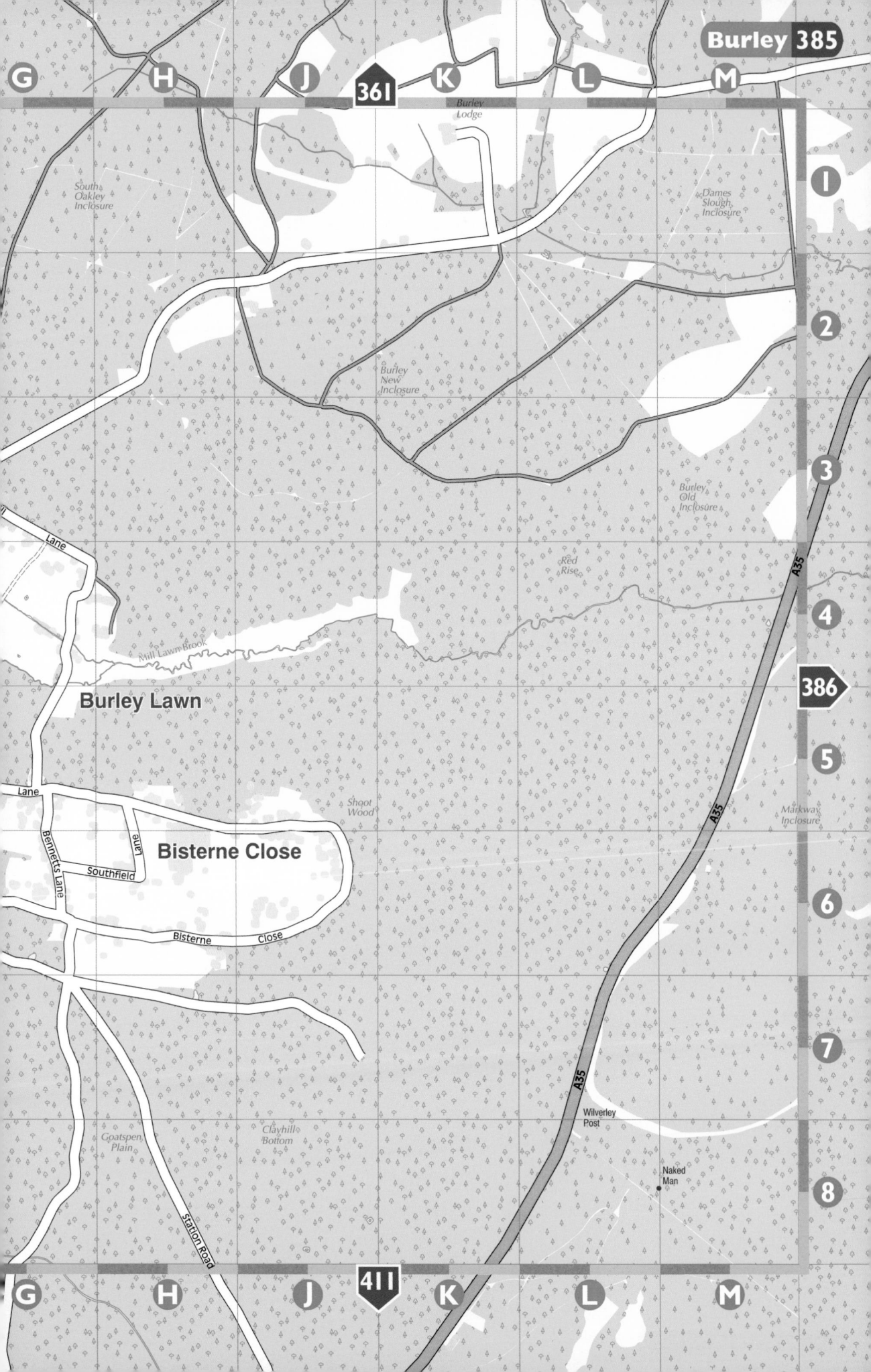

G   H   J   361   K   L   M

I

2

3

4

386

5

6

7

8

South
Oakley
Inclosure

Burley
Lodge

Dames
Slough
Inclosure

Burley
New
Inclosure

Burley
Old
Inclosure

Red
Rise

A35

Markway
Inclosure

Lane

Mill Lawn Brook

Burley Lawn

Lane

Shoot
Wood

Bennetts Lane

Southfield

Lane

Bisterne Close

Bisterne   Close

Goatspen
Plain

Clayhill
Bottom

Station Road

Wilverley
Post

Naked
Man

386

A   B   C   362   D   E   F

1

New

Fletchers
Thorns
Inclosure

Vinney
Ridge
Inclosure

Forest

2

Poundhill
Inclosure

3

Rhinefield
Sandy's
Inclosure

Rhinefield Ornamental Drive

A35

4

385

Hotel

Aldridgehill
Inclosure

5

Markway
Inclosure

Ober Water

6

Crab
Tree
Earth

Duck
Hole

7

White
Moor

Five
Thorns Hill

8

Wilverley
Plain

Hinchelsea
Moor

A   B   C   412   D   E   F

Burley Road

1 grid square represents 500 metres

K7
1 Culverley Cl
2 The Paddock
3 Wide Lane Cl

L6
1 Horlock Rd
2 Waters Gn
3 Waters Green Ct

L7
1 Auckland Pl
2 Forest Hall
3 Greenways Rd
4 Sutton Pl

G H J K L M

363

1
2
3
4
388
5
6
7
8

Whitley Wood
New Park Plantation
Poundhill Heath
ck Water
Ober Heath
Bolderford Bridge
Ober Water
Highland Water
Black Knowl
New Park
Hotel
Hotel
Hollands Wood
Ramnor Inclosure
Balmer Lawn
Hotel

Balmerlawn
BALMER LAWN Rd

Beacheern Wood
Ober House
The Coppice
Oberfield Rd
Whitemoor Road
Moorlands Cl
New Forest Drive
Broadlands Rd
Forest Park Road
Knowle Rd
Rhinefield Close
Ober Rd

BROCKENHURST
Meerut Rd
Butts Lawn
Butts Paddock
Brookside Road
Careys Cottages
Martin's Rd
Meerut Rd
Waters Gn
Park Cl
Burford La
Hth
Fathersfield
Butts Lawn Road

GRIGG LANE
Chestnut Rd
Noel Cl
North Rd
North Rd
Hotel
Brockenhurst College

LYNDHURST ROAD A337

MILL LANE

New Forest Dr
Forest Glade
New Forest Drive
Forest Vw
Armstrong Lane
Armstrong Road
Armstrong Cl
Wilverley Road
Broadlands Rd
The Rise
Flibbards
Brookley Road
Brookley Rd
Hotel

North Weirs
orth Weirs
North Weirs

Brockenhurst Primary School
Avenue Rd
Partridge Rd
Highwood Road
The Surgery
Tattenham Rd
Addison Road
Collvers Rd

Auckland
E Bank Rd
Brockenhurst Station
LC

Church Lane

Brockenhurst Park

South Weirs
Burley Road
South Weirs

SWAY ROAD

Tilebarn Lane

413

G H J K L M

A   B   C   364   D   E   F

Denny
Lodge

1

Parkhill
Inclosure

2

Ramnor
Inclosure

3

Pignal
Inclosure

Stubby
Copse
Inclosure

Balmer
Lawn

4

Perrywood
Haseley
Inclosure

5

Balmerlawn

S042

BALMER

LAWN

Hotel

New Copse
Inclosure

ROAD

6

B3055

Ladycross
Lodge

B3055

B3055

7

Perrywood
Ironshill
Inclosure

Brockenhurst
Park

Round Hill

Lymington River

8

A   B   C   414   D   Dilton   E   F

1 grid square represents 500 metres

G   H   J   365   K   L   M

ILIEU ROAD B3056

New Forest

I

Pig Bush

2

Culverley Farm

Shepton Bridge

3

Rowbarrow

Tantany Wood

4

390

Stubbs Wood

Frame Heath Inclosure

LC

Frame Wood

5

Moon Hill

6

Hawkhill Inclosure

Furzey Lodge

7

Stockley Inclosure

Hatch Gate

8

Furzey Lane

B3055

G   H   J   415   K   L   M

Masseys La

East

B3054

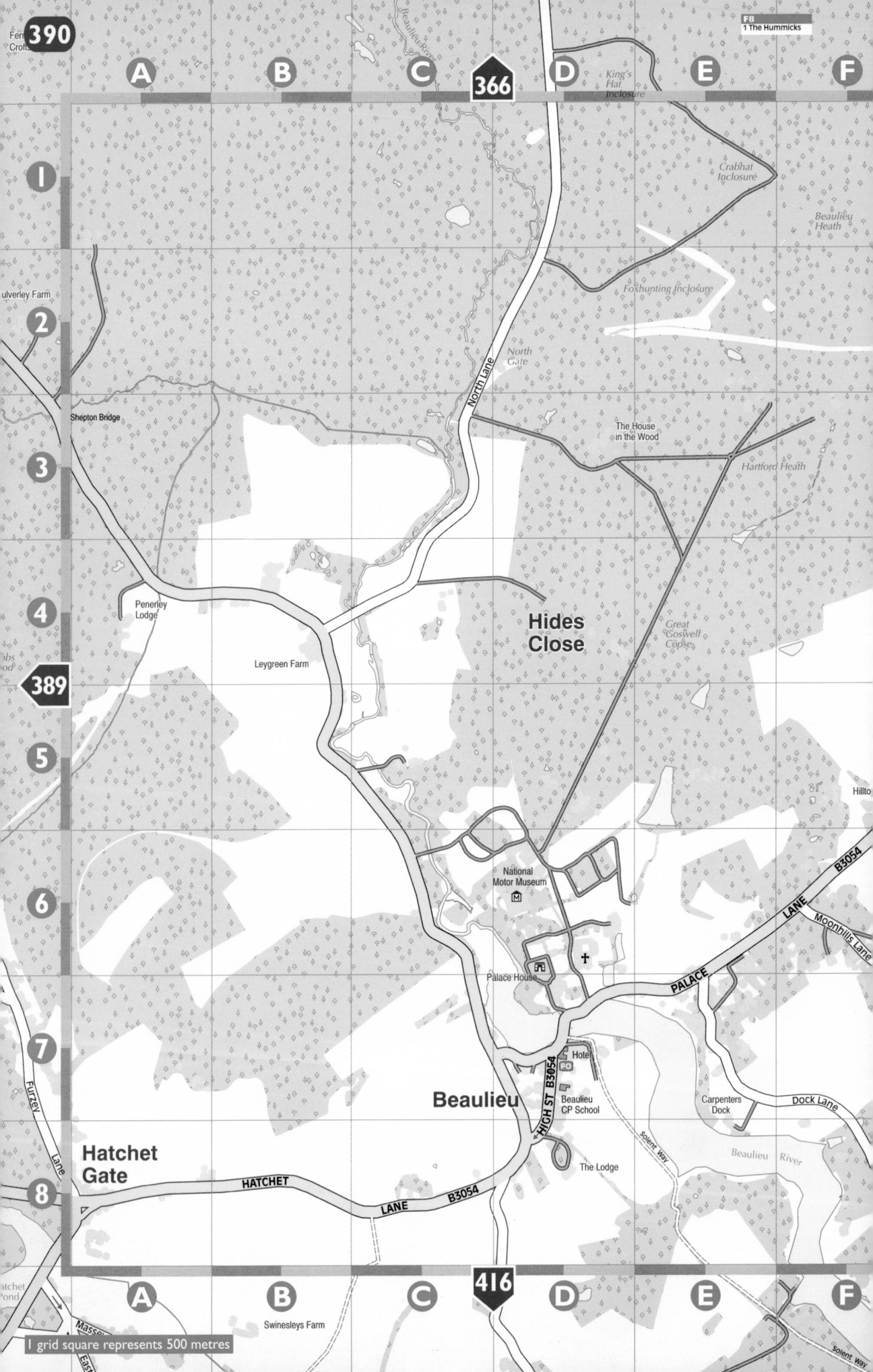
390
366
416
389
F8
1 The Hummicks
A
B
C
D
E
F
1
2
3
4
5
6
7
8
Beaulieu River
King's Hat Inclosure
Crabhat Inclosure
Beaulieu Heath
Foxhunting Inclosure
North Gate
North Lane
ulverley Farm
Shepton Bridge
The House in the Wood
Hartford Heath
Penerley Lodge
Hides Close
Great Goswell Copse
Leygreen Farm
Hillto
National Motor Museum
B3054
Moonhills Lane
LANE
PALACE
Palace House
Hotel
PO
HIGH ST B3054
Beaulieu
Beaulieu CP School
Carpenters Dock
Dock Lane
Solent Way
The Lodge
Beaulieu River
Furzey Lane
Hatchet Gate
HATCHET
LANE
B3054
Swinesleys Farm
Solent Way
1 grid square represents 500 metres

M2
1 Forest La
2 Henry Cl
3 Hunter Cl

M3
1 Hadley Fld
2 Tennyson Cl

M4
1 Shapton Cl
2 Teachers Wy

Dibden Inclosure

Roman Road

Monks Wk

Beverley Road

Warry's Ashleigh

Beech Crs

G   H   J   367   Butts   K   L   M

HYTHE   BY-PASS   A326

Holly Close

Elm Crs

Laburnum Crs

Cedar

Hamilton Rd

Fawley Rd

Hardley La

New

Fawley Inclosure

Solent Way

B3054

Solent Wy

BEAULIEU ROAD

Solent Way

Fawley Road

I

New Rd

A326

Old School Cl

Roman Rd

2

Hard

Main R

Chevron Business Park

Lime Mill Pond

Harrier Wy

Falconer Ct

Larch Av

3

Sycamore Dr

Lime Kiln Lane

2

Little Holb

Stonyford Pond

Holbury Purlieu

The Warren

Larkspur Gdns

Manor Infant School

Wedgewood Cl

Southb

4

Manor

Lime Kiln La

Holbury

Park Lane

Lime Kiln

1

2

Dedi

Oaks Close

392

2

Studwell Av

Broadoak

School

Redr

Cl

5

Moat Cl

Foxcroft Dr

Whyte Cl

1   3

Easte

Cr Cl

Fenwey

3

Stonymoor

Whit

Eims

Rollestone Road

Rollston

6

Roughd

Otterwood Gate

7

Row Down

Summer Lane

Cowleys Lane

Stock Water

The Hummicks

Otterwood

Kings Copse Inclosure

8

Spearbed Copse

G   H   J   417   K   L   M

Summer Lane

Steerleys Copse

B6
1 Wentworth Gdns
B5
1 Ashleycross Cl
2 Hobson Wy
B4
1 Sloane Av
2 Sloane Ct
A5
1 Pondhead Cl
2 Roewood Cl
3 Stockley Cl
A4
1 Broadley Cl
2 Hayward Ct
3 Ridley Cl
A
B
C
368
D
E
F
1
2
3
4
5
6
7
8
391
Hardley
Little Holbury
Holbury
Oil Refinery
Fawley
Blackfield
Langley
Cadland Creek
Hardley School
Manor Infant School
Blackfield Health Centre
Blackfield Junior & Infant School
Fawley County First School
Fawley Business Centre
Rollstone Farm
Row Down
Blackwell Common
Tom's Down
Mopley Pond
Fields Heath
Badminston Common
Cem
PO
SO45
A326
B3053
New Road
Hardley La
Fawley Road
New Rd
Main Rd
Cadland Road
Cadlands Pk Est
LONG LANE
Long Lane
Larch Av
Sycamore Dr
The Warren
Larkspur Gdns
Wedgewood Cl
Southbourne Avenue
Ivor Close
Manor Road
Westbourne
Drove
Renda Road
Waltons Avenue
Stanley Rd
Springfield Gv
Springfield Cl
The Close
Ruxley Cl
Watton Rd
Watton Road
Oakley Close
Nelson
Holbury
Bower Cl
Studley Av
Broadoak Cl
Redrise Cl
Eastcot Cl
Gt Elms Cl
Whitefield
Beechwood Rd
William Cl
Winters Cl
Hobson Way
Raymond Cl
May Crs
May Close
Alum Cl
Long Lane Close
Fairfcross Cl
Roewood Rd
Bramble Cl
Myvern Cl
Crawte Avenue
Went Worth Gv
Long Copse
Rollestone Road
Rollestone Rd
Newlands Road
Page Cl
D Avenue
13th Street
12th Street
11th Street
10th Street
9th Street
8th Street
7th Street
6th Street
5th Street
4th Street
3rd Street
2nd St
1st Street
6th St
14th Street
A Avenue
B Avenue
C Avenue
D Av
E Avenue
H Avenue
J Av
South Avenue
FAWLEY ROAD
Ashdown
Ashdown Road
Slades Hill
Blackfield Rd
The Pentagon
Chapel La
Foreshore
P.L.P.H. Rd
Burman Road
Cadland Road
Marsh Lane
Marsh Ln
Saltern
Church Lane
Orchard Cl
Woodville Rd
Forest Edge
Colesville Av
School Rd
Falcon Flds
Fry Cl
Toomer Cl
Thornhill Rd
Smith Cl
Milliken Cl
Glyn Jones Cl
Heather Cl
Heather
Foresters Rd
Furzey Cl
Hedley Cl
Blackfield Road
Dark Lane
Priest Cft Dr
The Fowey
Hampton Lane
Wilverley Pl
The Drove
Hugh's Cl
New Rd
St Michaels Cl
Newlands Copse
Exbury Rd
Hartsgrove Close
Newlands Cl
Walkers Lane N
Wheelers Walk
Saxon Rd
Dane Cl
Wessex Cl
Cedric
Viking Cl
Norman Rd
Janes Cl
Hampton Gdns
Hampton Cl
Northampton La
Holly Rd
Thornbury Avenue
Walker's Lane South
Green Lane
Chapel Lane
King's Copse Road
Roughdown Lane
C6
1 The Greenwich
2 Harvey Ct
C7
1 Edward Cl
2 Fields Cl
3 Pendleton Gdns
D6
1 Fourshells Cl
2 Thornhill Cl
418
D7
1 Valley Cl
F5
1 Admirals Cl
2 Churchfields
3 Denny Cl
4 The Lane
5 Linda Rd
cont.
Lea Road
Charnwood Way
Chalewood Road
Clare Gdns
Foxhayes La
Forest
1 grid square represents 500 metres

G H J K **369** L **M**

Hamble Spit

Solent Way

ISLE OF WIGHT

I
2
3
4
394
5
6
7
8

Road

Burnah Road N

South Trestle Road

Old Agwi Road

Road

Agitor Road

Flume Rd

ne Lane

Ashlett Creek

Ashlett

Ashlett Road

Stonehills

Stonehills

BYPASS B3053

Northern Access Road

Norther Access Rd

Badminston Farm

Badminston Lane

Calshot Castle

Ower

B3053

Calshot

PO

Calshot Cl

Badminston Drove

Badminston

Stanswood Road

419

Castle Lane

B3053

Hillhead

G H J K L M

Abshot
Hook
Newtown
Hook Park
Hook with Warsash Primary School
Queen's Rd
Meadcroft Cl
Pitchponds Rd
Lower Spinney
Jumar Close
Rossan Av
Romford Rd
Hornby Cl
New Rd
Oakwood Cl
Gilchrist Gdns
Hook Park Rd
Hook Park Road
Hook Lane
Hook La
Solent Drive
Cowes Lane
Workman's Lane
Workman's La
Chilling Lane
Chilling
Solent Court
Solent Way
End Bottom
Fleet
Calshot Castle
370
393
A
B
C
D
E
F
1
2
3
4
5
6
7
8
1 grid square represents 500 metres

L6
1 Fitzwilliam Av
M3
1 Hazelwood
M4
1 Dolphin Ct
2 Forties Cl
3 Shannon Rd
4 Tawny Owl Cl
Hill Park School
West Street
Common Lane
Rosedale Cl
Garstons Cl
Coach
Titch 371
Bridge Street
Hookgate Coppice
Brownwich Lane
Occupation Lane
Posbrook Lane
The Cl
Bellfield
Lwr Bellfield
Gardner Road
Hewett Road
Ransome Close
Hewett Close
TITCHFIELD ROAD
Ranvilles Lane
Harcourt Road
Templemere
Rowan
Catcombe Gdns
Cemetery
Singledge
Little Posbrook
Triangle Lane
P014
Lychgate Gn
Cuckoo Lane
Country Vw
Carnett Close
Tawny Owl Cl
Puffin Crs
The Oakes
Turtle Close
Kestrel Cl
Finisterre Cl
Old St
Anker Lane
Upr Old St
396
Cromarty Close
Old Street
Shannon Road
Mallin Cl
Vicar
Cutlers
River Meon
Meon View Farm
Meon
Old Street
Fair Isle Cl
Dover Cl
Fury Way
Drive
Viking Cl
Robins Close
The Gannets
Berry Lane
Plover Cl
Vixen Cl
Plymouth
Hawk Cl
Anne Dale County Junior & Infant School
Bells
The Grove
Andrew Place
Cowdray Park
Pytchley Close
Barlow Close
Whaddon Chase
Fernie Cl
Violet Av
Harriet Cl
Carisbrooke
Avenue
Denham Close
Mancroft Avenue
Hammond C
Pembroke Crescent
Corfe Close
Berkeley Close
Walnut Drive
Bank Road
Ltl Gays
Gt Gays
Old Street
Short Road
Solent Road
Elsfred Rd
Sanross Cl
Way
Lane
Knights Haven Crs
Cliff Road
Hill Head
Bramble Cl
Cottes
Cottesway East
Crofton
Bell Davies Road
Robinson Road
Caspar John Close
Moody
Old Farm Lane
Midways
Farm Edge Road
Beverley Road
Springfield Way
Titchfield Haven
Solent Way
Osborne Vw Rd
Hurst Close
Ellerslie Close
Valsheba Drive
Pilgrims Way
Hill Head Road
Seafield Park Road
Monks Way
Salterns
Solent Way
Road
Brownwich Lane
Solent Way
The Solent

396
372
14
395
420
West End
STUBBINGTON
Woodcot
Peel Common
Gosport Airfield
HMS Collingwood
HMS Daedalus
Chark Common
PO14
B6 1 Orion Cl
B7 1 Tonnant Cl
B4 1 Derwent Cl 2 Pinewood Cl 3 Thirlmere Cl
B5 1 Belmont Cl 2 Peartree Cl
B3 1 Summerleigh Wk
A6 1 Wedgewood Cl
A3 1 Discovery Cl
A4 1 The Paddock
A7 1 Dallington Cl 2 Ferncroft Cl 3 Mayflower Cl 4 Tamarisk Cl
D1 1 Elizabeth Ct 2 Tudor Ct
D2 1 Wallington Ct
E2 1 Southwick Ct
E6 1 Keyhaven Cl
F1 1 The Moorings
F2 1 Farrier Wy
F5 1 Honeysuckle Cl 2 The Mead 3 Myrtle Cl 4 Nesbitt Cl 5 Puffin Gdns
F6 1 Dandelion Cl 2 Mallard Gdns
F7 1 Ankerwyke 2 Calshot Wy
Rowan Way
Longfield Avenue
Peak Lane
Ranvilles Lane
Oakcroft Lane
Stroud Green Lane
Tanners Lane
Newlands Farm
Newgate Lane
B3385
Titchfield Road
B3334
Gosport Road
Rowner Road
Broom Way
Brune Lane
Shoot Lane
Chark La
Woodcote Lane
Albert Road
Cemetery
Meoncross School
Crofton School
Baycroft School
Hammond County Junior & Infant School
Anne Dale County Junior & Infant School
Hammond Industrial Est
Redlands County Primary School
Palmerston Business Park
Fort Fareham
Collingwood Business Park
Fareham Megabowl
Jubilee Court
Park Lane
Stubbington Lane
Stubbington Green
Crofton Avenue
Sea La
Burnt House Lane
May's Lane
Marks Rd
Mary's Road
Cuckoo Lane
Anker Lane
Vicarage La
Bells Lane
Eric Road
Martin Av
Moody Road
Old Farm Lane
Westways
Southways
Queens Rd
Oakdown Rd
Beresford Rd
Alfred Rd
Crescent
Harold Road
Tukes Avenue
Heron Way
Brookers Lane
Dell Quay Close
Avocet Walk
Gosport Road A32
Elms Road
Alders Road
Geoffrey Crescent
Fairfield Avenue
St Michael's Grove
Tanners La
Sumar Close
Spartan Cl
Windermere Av
Pembury Rd
Tangyes Close
Grasmere Way
Spencer Court
Mark's Road
1 grid square represents 500 metres

Stubbington 397
G3
1 Bridgemary Wy
G5
1 Cameron Cl
G6
1 Beaulieu Pl
2 Birchmore Cl
3 Clover Cl
4 Nicholl Pl
5 Niton Cl
6 Ramsay Pl
7 Warsash Gv
G7
1 Hoylake Cl
2 The Fairway
3 Sunningdale Cl
G8
1 Davis Cl
2 Snape Cl
373
15
398
421
Cams Hall Estate Golf Club
Wicor County Primary School
PORTCHESTER
Condor Avenue
Quintrell Av
A27 PORTCHESTER
Fareham Borough Council
Westland Medical Centre
G4
1 Harwood Cl
2 Mountbatten Cl
J7
1 The Chine
2 The Glen
3 The Hoe
4 The Mount
5 Sycamore Cl
6 The Thicket
7 Yewside
H6
1 The Coppice
2 Holland Pl
3 Jacomb Pl
4 Kielder Gv
5 Savernake Cl
6 Stocker Pl
H8
1 Gilbert Cl
2 Tudor Cl
Central Road
Orchard Grove
White Hart Lane
Cranleigh Rd
King's Way
Wicor Mill Lane
Seafield Road
Foxbury Gv
Windmill Grove
Kilwich Way
Foxbury Point
Fleetlands
Pewit Island
FAREHAM ROAD
Lederle Lane
Main Road
Foxbury Lane
Foxbury La
Aerodrome Road
Bedenham Lane
Venture Ind Park
Bedenham County Junior & Infant School
Bridgemary Community School
Bridgemary Avenue
Montgomery Rd
Keyes Road
Perth Rd
Balmoral Close
Camp Rd
Tedder Rd
Wavell Rd
Braemar Road
Brewers Lane
Beauchamp Av
Rowner Close
Tichborne Way
Downside
FAREHAM ROAD A32
Aspengrove
Vineside
The Nook
Holbrook Recreation Centre
Gosport Ice Rink
Rowner County Infant School
Junior School
Green Crescent
Rowner Lane
Rowner Health Centre
ROWNER ROAD B3334
Gorselands Way
Charden Rd
Landon Rd
Turner Av
Doctors Surg
Shackleton Road
Brune Park Community School
Fort Brockhurst
Wingate Road
Gunners Rd
Elson Rd
Brighton Av
Worthing Avenue
Selsey Avenue
Elson Lane
Elson County Infant School
Elson County Junior School
Goodway Sea School
Elson
Eastbourne Av
Weymouth Av
Beryl Av
Battery Close
Frater Lane
Richard Gv
Chestnut Wk
Quay Lane
St Thomas's Road
Bucklers Road
Amberley Rd
Palmyra Rd
Reeds Rd
Hardway
Rowner
M8
1 Moraunt Cl
& Infant School
M1
1 Sissinghurst Rd
J8
1 Madison Cl
2 Newbroke Rd
K8
1 Eastbrook Cl
2 Jason Wy
3 Tynedale Cl
L8
1 Beaumont Ct
1 Lombardy Cl
H7
1 Lawn Cl
2 Orange Gv
3 The Spinney
4 Walker Pl
Samson Close
Cornwell Close
Carless Close
Brockhurst Medical Cen
G H J K L M
1 2 3 4 5 6 7 8

398
PORTCHESTER
374
Paulsgrove
St Pauls RC Primary School
A27 SOUTHAMPTON ROAD
Portchester Station
Portchester Health Centre
Westlands Medical Centre
Portchester Community School
Castle County Primary School
White Hart Lane
Castle Street
Castle St
Hospital Lane
Church Rd
Portchester Castle
Cemetery
Wicor Pth
Waterside La
King's Way
Marina Keep
Lock Approach
Port Wy
Sennen Pl
Carbis Cl
Mullion Cl
Portsmouth Harbour
Whale Island
N Battery Rd
Whaley Rd
Wardroom Road
Quarterdeck Av
Guardroom Rd
W Battery Rd
Chatfield Av
Pier Head
397
422
Hardway
Bucklers Road
Godwit Cl
Pipit Cl
Merganser Cl
Widgeon Cl
1 grid square represents 500 metres
A
B
C
D
E
F
1
2
3
4
5
6
7
8

G5 1 Tipner Gn
G6 1 Victory Gn
H6 1 Connaught Rd 2 Kg Edwd's Crs 3 Penrose Cl
H7 1 Bucklers Ct 2 Croft Rd 3 St Mark's Rd
J3 1 Midway Rd 2 Portswood Rd
J4 1 Eastwood Rd 2 Falklands Rd 3 St Francis Ct
H8 1 Chapel St 2 Dumbarton Cl 3 Hercules St 4 Kilpatrick Cl 5 Silverlock Cl 6 Spenlow Cl
K4 1 Balderton Cl 2 Benham Dr 3 Breech Cl 4 Escur Cl 5 Newey Cl 6 Oldgate Gdns 7 Padbury Cl 8 St Barbara Wy 9 Thorncliffe Cl
M4 1 Hartwell Rd
M5 1 Latimer Ct 2 Plumpton Gdns
L8 1 Eastbourne Rd 2 Moneyfield La 3 Stapleton Rd
M1 1 Court Mead
L2 1 Wembley Gv
K8 1 Northcote Av
L1 1 The Close
K1 1 Aldroke St 2 Glenleigh Av 3 Roebuck Cl
J5 1 Kearsney Av 2 Templeton Cl
J8 1 Pink Rd 2 St Stephen's Rd
375
400
423
Portsmouth City Council
Cosham
Highbury
Hilsea
North End
Copnor
Portsea Island
M27
A27
A3
A397
A288
A2047
M275
Junction 12
Western Road
Northern Road
London Rd
Copnor Road
Northern Parade
Cosham Station
Hilsea Station
Highbury College
Redwood Park School
The City of Portsmouth Boys School
Portsmouth Rugby Football Club
Civil Service Sports Ground
City of Portsmouth Sports Club
Shawcross Ind Park
Highgrove Ind Park
O Jays Industrial Park
Victory Trading Est
Admiral Lord Nelson School
Burrfields Retail Park
Fairway Business Cen
Acorn Business Cen
Medina Primary School
Stamshaw Junior School
Cliffdale Primary School
Odeon Cinema
Buckland Medical Cen
Copnor Infant School
PO2
PO3
PO6

400
Drayton
Farlington
376
Anchorage Park
399
424
Baffins
Farlington Marshes
RSPB Reserve
North Binness Island
Baker's Island
South Binness Island
Broom Channel
Langstone Harbour
Russell's Lake
Langstone Channel
Hampshire County
City of Portsmouth
Solent Way
A27
A27(T)
A2030
EASTERN RD
HAVANT ROAD
Eastern Industrial Cen
Warrior Business Centre
Springfield School
Solent Junior School
Admiral Lord Nelson School
Burrfields Retail Park
Portsmouth Sixth Form College
Fairway Business Cen
C1
1 Watermead Rd
A4
1 Adstone La
2 Broughton Ct
3 Everdon La
4 Maidford Gv
1 grid square represents 500 metres

Brockhampton
Brookside Rd
Havant Business Center
Farm Way
Southmoor Lane
Penner Road
Southbrook Road
Longmead Gdns
Langstone Av
The Mallards
Regents Ct
Rectory Rd
Woodbury
Hamilton
Wade Lane
South Cl
Norris Gdns
Warblingt
Solent Way
Cemetery
377
16
17
Langstone
Mill Lane
Harbourside
Langstone High St
PH
Towers Gdns
The Saltings
Solent Way
LANGSTONE ROAD
Langstone Bridge
A3023
Broad Lake
Long Island
Northney Road
Hotel
Northney Road
St Peter's
402
Clover Rd
Pycroft Close
New Cut
Island Cl
Kingsway
Queensway
Avenue Road
HAVANT ROAD
Meadow Cl
Rogers Md
Victoria Road
Mill Close
HAYLING ISLAND
St Peter's Road
Stoke
Croft Lane
Northwood Lane
Castlemans Lane
West Lane
Copse Lane
PO
Fleet
Yew Tree Rd
Daw Lane
HAVANT ROAD
425
A3023
Mill Rythe
G
H
J
K
L
M
1
2
3
4
5
6
7
8

402
Warblington

A

B

C

378

D

E

F

I

Cemetery

17

Conigar Point

2

Fowley Island

3

Sweare Deep

Wickor Point

EMSWORTH

Solent Way

Western Parade

Creek End

Wayfarer's Walk

Solent Way

West Rd

Brent Ct

Maisemor Gdns

Meadow

Far Meadow

Brook Garden

Beach Road

Kingsey Av

Clovelly Road

Valetta Park

Beacon Sq

Warblington Road

Curfew Cl

Lane End Drive

Waters Edge Gdns

The Promenade

B Road

South St

St Peter's Sq

Bridgefoot Path

Swan Cl

Nile St

Tower St

King St

Emsworth Surg

West St

School La

Queen St

Spring Gdns

Stanley Rd

Slipper Road

Mill Quay

Roundhouse Meadow

Heron Quay

Osprey Quay

Avocet Quay

Thorney Road

Sussex Border Path

Pagham Cl

PK Rd

Bramley

Apple Grove

PH

PO

Sussex Border Path

Cordes Road

Great Deep

Thorney Road

Emsworth Road

4

401

Northney

Spinnaker Grange

Northney La

St Peter's Rd

North Rd Road

Clovelly Rd

5

Church Lane

North Hayling

Pycroft Close

St Peter's Av

Sussex Border Path

Hampshire County

West Sussex County

Hunter Rd

Swift Road

Startan Cl

Sabre Rd

N Bay

S Bay

Meteor Road

Canberra Rd

Hornet Road

Ullswater Road

Emsworth Rd

Thorney County Primary School

6

St Peter's Road

7

Tye

Chichester Road

Gutner Lane

Woodgason Lane

Marker Point

Emsworth Channel

8

A

B

C

426

D

E

F

1 grid square represents 500 metres

Southbourne

Prinsted

Nutbourne

`379`

MAIN RD

A259

Maybush Drive

Cot Lane

Chidham Point

Prinsted Point

Marsh Lane

Marsh La

PH

Stanbury Point

Cobnor Fm

New Barn

orney Island

Thorney Island Airfield

West Thorney

Smith Lane

Church

Victor Rd

Vulcan Road

Road

Valiant Road

Varsity Road

Valetta Road

Pleasant Lane

Thorney Channel

Cobnor Ho

`427`

G H J K L M

G H J K L M

1 2 3 4 5 6 7 8

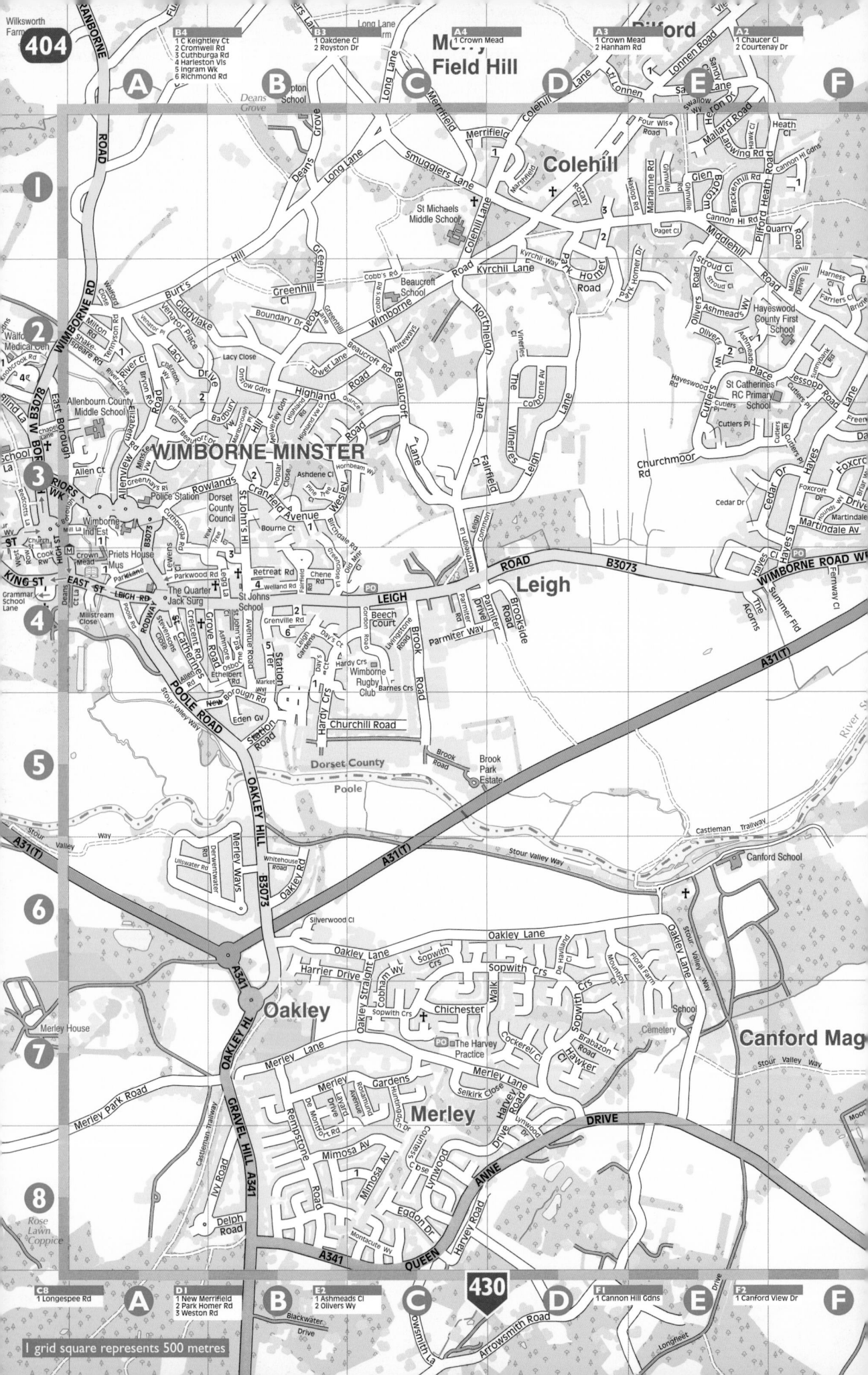

404
B4
1 C Keightley Ct
2 Cromwell Rd
3 Cuthburga Rd
4 Harleston Vls
5 Ingram Wk
6 Richmond Rd
B3
1 Oakdene Cl
2 Royston Dr
A4
1 Crown Mead
A3
1 Crown Mead
2 Hanham Rd
A2
1 Chaucer Cl
2 Courtenay Dr
Field Hill
Colehill
WIMBORNE MINSTER
Leigh
Oakley
Merley
Canford Mag
Dorset County
Poole
St Michaels Middle School
Beaucroft School
Hayeswood County First School
St Catherines RC Primary School
Allenbourn County Middle School
Police Station
Dorset County Council
Wimborne Ind Est
Priests House Mus
The Quarter Jack Surg
St Johns School
Wimborne Rugby Club
Brook Park Estate
Canford School
The Harvey Practice
Merley House
Cemetery
School
Wilksworth Farm
Deans Grove
Rose Lawn Coppice
WIMBORNE RD
WIMBORNE ROAD
LEIGH ROAD
B3073
A31(T)
A341
POOLE ROAD
OAKLEY HILL
GRAVEL HILL
OAKLEY HL
QUEEN ANNE DRIVE
Merley Park Road
Merley Lane
Oakley Lane
Colehill Lane
Smugglers Lane
Long Lane
Burt's Hill
Kyrchil Lane
Northleigh Lane
Leigh Lane
Brook Road
Stour Valley Way
Castleman Trailway
C8
1 Longespee Rd
D1
1 New Merrifield
2 Park Homer Rd
3 Weston Rd
E2
1 Ashmeads Cl
2 Olivers Wy
430
F1
1 Cannon Hill Gdns
F2
1 Canford View Dr
1 grid square represents 500 metres

G2
1 Hunter Cl
2 Saddle Cl
3 Spur Cl
4 Suffolk Cl
L2
1 Barrow Vw
Bedborough Farm
A31(T)
Uddens Drive
Cannon Hill Plantation
Ferndown,Stour and Forest Trail
Castleman Trailway
Maple Business Park
Fernside Business Park
Lancaster Rd
Lindbergh Rd
Mitchell Rd
Johnson Rd
Cobham Road
Haviland Road
Whittle Rd
Nimrod Way
Dorset County Council
Old Forge Rd
Brickyard Lane
Telford Rd
Bunting Rd
Hilltop Road
Kestrel Cl
Curlew Cl
Bracken Rd
Bracken Road
Larks Rise
Clayford Av
Coppice Av
Laburnum Cl
Red Oaks Cl
Barrow Vw
Pine Glen Avenue
Ameysford Road
Hill Vw Rd
Ferndown Upper School
Ferndown Sports Centre
Cherry Grove
Ferndown Town Council
Ferndown Middle School
Ferndown First School
FERNDOWN
Wimborne Road East
Wimborne Road West
Forest View Drive
St James Road
Paddock Cl
Forest Wy
Award Road
Stapehill
Stapehill Road
Stapehill Abbey
Keepers Lane
Chestnut Grove
Abbey Gdns
Fox La
Wyelands Avenue
HAM LANE
Fox Lane
Ham La
Little Canford
Old Ham Lane
Stour Close
B3073
Pompeys Lane
Dunedin Cl
Dunedin Dr
Dunedin Gdns
Angel Lane
Coneygar La
RINGWOOD
A348
406
Holmwood
Hampreston Primary School
Stapehill Road
Hampreston
Gillsons
High Md
High Mead Lane
HAM LA B3073
CHRISTCHURCH ROAD
Longham
Green Lane
River Stour
Dorset County
Poole
Stour Valley Way
Ferndown, Stour and Forest Trail
Knighton
Knighton Lane
ROAD
431
Longham Bridge

406
C3
1 Pringles Cl
C1
1 Amberwood
2 Garden Wk
B5
1 Brune Wy
2 Glenmoor Rd
3 Wincombe Cl
B2
1 Bramley Rd
A3
1 Old School Cl
A5
1 Heath Farm Cl
380
Trickett's Cross
FERNDOWN
BH22
405
Parley Common
Gibbet Firs
Dudsbury
West Parley
Parley Cross
432
C8
1 Elm Tree Wk
2 Longfield Dr
D1
1 Ameys La
D2
1 Dugdell Cl
E1
1 Emberley Cl
E2
1 Severn Rd
1 grid square represents 500 metres

G   H   J   **381**   K   L   M

Matcham's House

Hurn Road

Grange Estate

Matcham's Park

I

Foxbury Road

2

A338

Foxbury Road

3

Hill

Road

Heath Road West

Barnsfield Heath

Matchams

4

Fir Grove Farm

Watermain Road

Plantation Road

Christch Ski & Le Centre

408

Heath Road West

Matchams Lane

5

Moors River

Moors River

d-Hurn Forest

6

Avon Common

7

Chapel Lane

Bournemouth International Airport

8

Matchams Lane

Parley Lane

East Parley

B3073

McIntyre Rd

Brackley Cl

Theobald Rd

Dorset County Police

G   H   J   **433**   K   L   M

Merritown La

Pusey

Lane

Hurn

Avon Causeway

Merritown

Parley Lane

Matcham's House

A B C 382 D E F

I

2

3

4

407

5

6

7

8

H 1 grid square represents 500 metres

A B C 434 D E F

Hurn Road

A338

Matchams Lane

A338

Matcham Lane

Church Leisure
Centre

Avon Common

Matchams Lane

Avon Causeway

Sopley

River Avon

Week Farm

Week Common

Pithouse Farm

Pithouse Lane

River Avon

Avon Valley Path

Avon Valley Path

Dragon Lane

Upper Bisterne Fa

Bisterne
Manor

Bisterne

B3347

Lower
Bisterne Farm

Avon Valley Ptn

Anna Lane

Hotel

Avon Tyrrell Farm

London Lane

Avon

B3347

London Lane

Avon Valley Path

Court Farm

B3347

RINGWOOD

Avon Valley Path

Meadow Cl

F Lane

ROAD

Sandford

L7 1 Brookside Cl
L8 1 Woodlands Cl

M7 1 Bramble Wy
2 Rosehill Cl
3 Shackleton Sq
4 Shears Brook Cl

G H J 383 K L M

1

2

Bisterne
Common

3

Avon
Tyrrell

Shirley
Common

4

410

North
Ripley

Anna Lane

Martin's
Copse

Purlieu

5

Thatchers Lane

6

Ripley

Shirley

Sopley
CP School

Thatchers Lane

Lane

Stibbs Wy

7

House

Burnt

Cedar

Pl

Tyrrells court

Bransgore Gdns

Rosehill
Drive

Shirley Dr

Betsy Lane

The New
Medical Cen

Canute
Drive

Cuckoo
Way

Ringwood

Hungerfield
Close

The Wishing
Well Gallery

Poplar Lane

Clare
Cl

Road

St Georges

St Mary's
Close

Road

Chapel Lane

Brookside

Pear Tree Cl

Twin Oaks
Medical Cen

Ringwood Road

Derritt Lane

Wiltshire
Gdns

Merryfield
Close

West
Road

West
Stands

Colbourne
Close

8

BRANSGORE

Wiltshire Rd

Hill Lane

Bransgore
Primary
School

G H J 435 K L M

Derritt Lane

Hampshire County
Dorset County

Burley Road

Westbury Cl

Meyrick Close

M8 1 Halton Cl

A8
1 The Orchard
A7
1 Mnt Pleas. Dr
2 Wedgewd Gdns
384
Forest
Dur Hill Down
Holmsley Ridge
Whitten Bottom
Thorney Hill Holms
Shirley Common
Burley Rd
Forest Rd
School Lane
School Road
Forest Road
Brick Lane
Valley Lane
Brick Lane
Whitelands
Thorney Hill
Willow Lane
Burley Road
Hill Farm
Plain Heath
Purlieu
409
Poors Common
Dial Cl
Lane
Stibbs Way
House
Burley Road
Bransgore
Forest Lodge
A35
The Ne
Medical
Canute Drive
Whistlers Cl
Cuckoo Hill Way
Bransgore Ho
Heathfield
Blackbird Way
Poplar Lane
St Georges Cl
St Mary's Close
Lyndhurst Road
Ringwood Road
Poplar Cl
Beech House
North Hinton Farm
Bransgore Primary School
436
Harrow Road
1 grid square represents 500 metres

G   H   J   385   K   L   M

I
2
3
4
412
5
6
7
8

Naked

Wilverley
Inclosure

Holmsley
Inclosure

Station Road

A35

A35

Brownhill
Inclosure

Wootton Coppice
Inclosure

Wootton
Old Farm

Brownhill   Road

Wootton Farm Road

Rhinefield Road

Wilverly Road

HOLMSLEY

ROAD

Eastley
Wootton

Wootton

Manor Farm

B3058

North Drive

Ossemsley

Ossemsley

South Drive

North Drive

BASHLEY COMMON ROAD

B3058

Marlpit Lane

Wootton

Rough

Tipto

Road

St Johns

G   H   J   437   K   L   M

Bashley

Five
Thorns Hill
F6
1 Highfield Gdns
A
B
C
D
E
F
386
Wilverley
Plain
Hinchesl
Moor
Burley Road
1
2
3
4
5
6
7
8
Hinchesl
Wood
Long
Slade
Bottom
Setthorns Cottage
Avon Water
411
Set
Thorns
Inclosure
Broadley
Inclosure
Cemetery
Manchester
Brighton
Road
Adlam's
Lane
Oakenbrow
The Close
Normandy
Close
Gilpin
Kitchers Hill
Rhiners Close
Bond Close
Durrant W
Buldowne walk
Stanford
Hawthorn Drive
Middle
Anderwo
Cruse
Station
Mead End Road
Hotel
Heron Cl
Sway
Sway
Station
The Gallery
Road
Rowan
Sway Park
Industrial Estate
Hotel
Hollies Cl
Boundway
Mead
End
Mead End Road
Marley Mount
Fairlight Lane
Tiptoe Road
Rough
Tiptoe
CP School
Danehurst New
Road
Middle Road
Tiptoe
Crabbswood
Broadley House
Lower
Mead
End
Road
Avon Water
Arnewood
Manor
438
Northover Lane
ARNEWOOD
BRIDGE
ROAD
1 grid square represents 500 metres

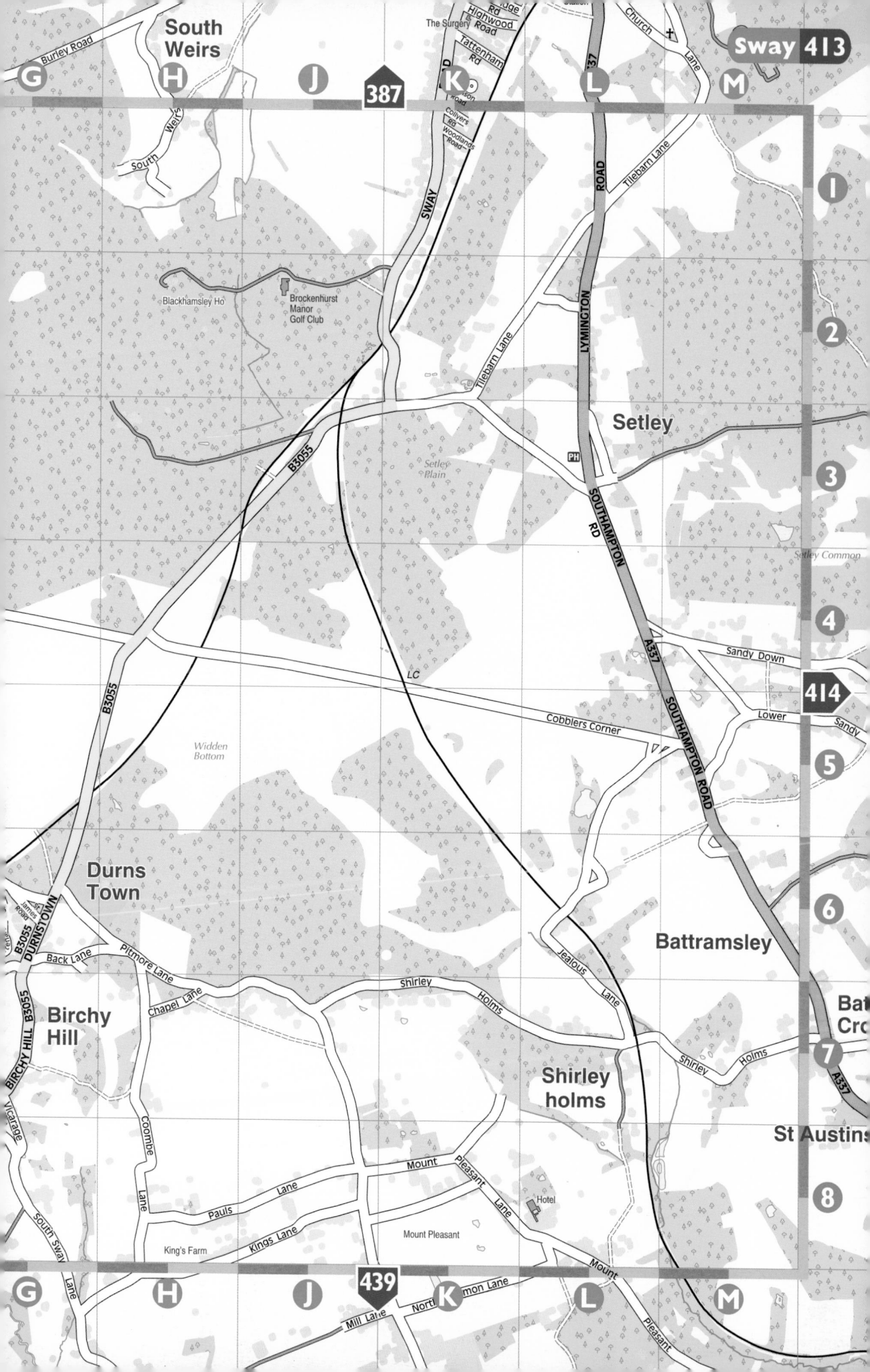

Sway 413
387
414
439
G
H
J
K
L
M
1
2
3
4
5
6
7
8
South Weirs
Burley Road
South Weirs
The Surgery
Highwood Road
Tattenham Rd
Collyers Rd
Woodlands Road
Church Lane
Tilebarn Lane
SWAY
LYMINGTON ROAD
A337
Blackhamsley Ho
Brockenhurst Manor Golf Club
Tilebarn Lane
Setley
PH
Setley Plain
B3055
SOUTHAMPTON RD
Setley Common
Sandy Down
A337
SOUTHAMPTON ROAD
LC
Lower Sandy
Cobblers Corner
B3055
Widden Bottom
Durns Town
St James Road
B3055
DURNSTOWN
Back Lane
Pitmore Lane
Jealous Lane
Battramsley
Chapel Lane
Shirley Holms
Birchy Hill
BIRCHY HILL B3055
Shirley Holms
Shirley holms
A337
St Austins
Vicarage
Coombe Lane
Mount Pleasant Lane
Pauls Lane
Hotel
Kings Lane
Mount Pleasant
King's Farm
South Sway Lane
Mount Pleasant
Mill Lane
North
mon Lane

414
388
413
440
A
B
C
D
E
F
1
2
3
4
5
6
7
8
Dilton
Lymington River
Newlands Copse
Dilton Farm
Roydon Manor
Dilton Gardens
Setley Common
Greenmoor
Sandy Down
Haywards Farm
Lower
Sandy
Down
Lane
Royden Lane
Church Lane
Boldre Grange
Rodlease Lane
Rodlease House
Slade
Pilley
Pilley Bailey
Pilley St
Wooden House La
Battramsley Cross
Hill House School
Rope Hill
Boldre
William Gilpin C of E Primary School
Gilpin Close
Pilley
Hill
May La
PO
Lucky La
Jordans
Lane
Burnt
House Lane
Hudson Davies Cl
A337
SOUTHAMPTON ROAD
Tweed Lane
Boldre Lane
Shallow Lane
Garden
St Austins
School
Warborne
Warborne Lane
Hundred
Portmore
Vicars Hill
1 grid square represents 500 metres

B3055
Pilley 415
389
G
H
J
K
L
M
Hatchet Pond
Hatchet Moor
B3054
HATCHET
LANE
East
Boldre
Heath
2
3
4
416
5
6
7
8
Beaulieu Heath
B3054
Crockford Bridge
Crockford Stream
Norley Inclosure
Norley Farm
Norleywood
Norleywood Road
Joys La
Thatchers Lane
Norleywood
Road
Main
Road
St Leonards Rd
441
G
H
J
K
L
M
Broom Hill
Rowes
Lane
Road
Brook

Hatchet
Gate

HATCHET   LANE   B3054

A   B   C   **390**   D   E   F

1 Masseys La

East
Heath La
Whithers La
Boldre
Pages Lane
Caza Av
Matthews Lane
Swerns Lease

Swinesleys Farm

Beufre Farm

Keeping
Copse

Solent Way

2 PO
Wallace La
Chapel
Watton Cl
Lane

Lodge
Lane

Knights
Copse

Ashen
Wood

3 New Inn La
Cripple   Gate   Lane
East Boldre
Church La

Little Purnel

4

415
Newhouse
Copse

Lodge Farm

Tylers
Copse

5

6 Newlands

Coopers
Wood

7 Horsemoor
Copse
Newlands
Plantation

Bergerie

8 Main Road
St Leonards Rd
St Leonards Road
Beck Farm
Solent Way

A   B   C   **442**   D   E   F

Sowley Lane   Thorns Lane

G H J **391** K L M

Summer Lane

Steerleys Copse

Spearbed Copse

Kings Copse

1

Beaulieu River

Yard Wood

2

Main Drive

Keeping

Gilbury Hard

3

Bucklers Hard

Exbury House

Exbury

PH

Hotel

Maritime Museum

4

418

Salternshill Copse

5

Clobb

6

Salternshill

Lower Exbury

Drokes

Gins

7

St Leonards Grange

Gins Lane

Beaulieu River

Gins House

Warren Lane

8

The Log House

Nec Ore Point

G H J **443** K L M

Warren Lane

Warren Farm

418
392
417
Blackfield
Blackwell Common
Langley
West Common
Exbury
Lepe
Tom's Down
D1
1 Foxglade
2 Foxlands
3 Fox's Wk
4 Foxy Paddock
5 Langley L Gdns
6 The Mews
C1
1 Bowland Wy
2 St Francis Cl
Whitefield Farm
East Hill Farm
Lepe Farm
Inchmery House
Haxland Pits
Needs Ore Point
The Solent
Dark Water
Lepe Road
Stanswood Road
Mopley
Chapel Lane
Lea Road
Charnwood Way
Kings Ride
Chalewood Road
St Francis Rd
Nicholas Rd
Forge Road
Homer Farm Lane
West Common
W Common Dr
Wychwood
Northampton La
Holly Rd
Thornbury Avenue
Mopley Cl
Clare Gdns
Foxhayes La
Forest Ga
Cem
1 grid square represents 500 metres

Calshot

G H J K L M

Badminston

Sprat's Down

393

Stanswood Road

Tristan Close

PO K

Castle Close

B3053

Castle Lane

Hillhead

Eaglehurst

1

The Solent

2

Stanswood Road

Stanswood Road

Nelson's Place

Stanswood Bay

3

Stanswood Farm

4

Cadland House

5

6

Stansore Point

7

8

G H J K L M

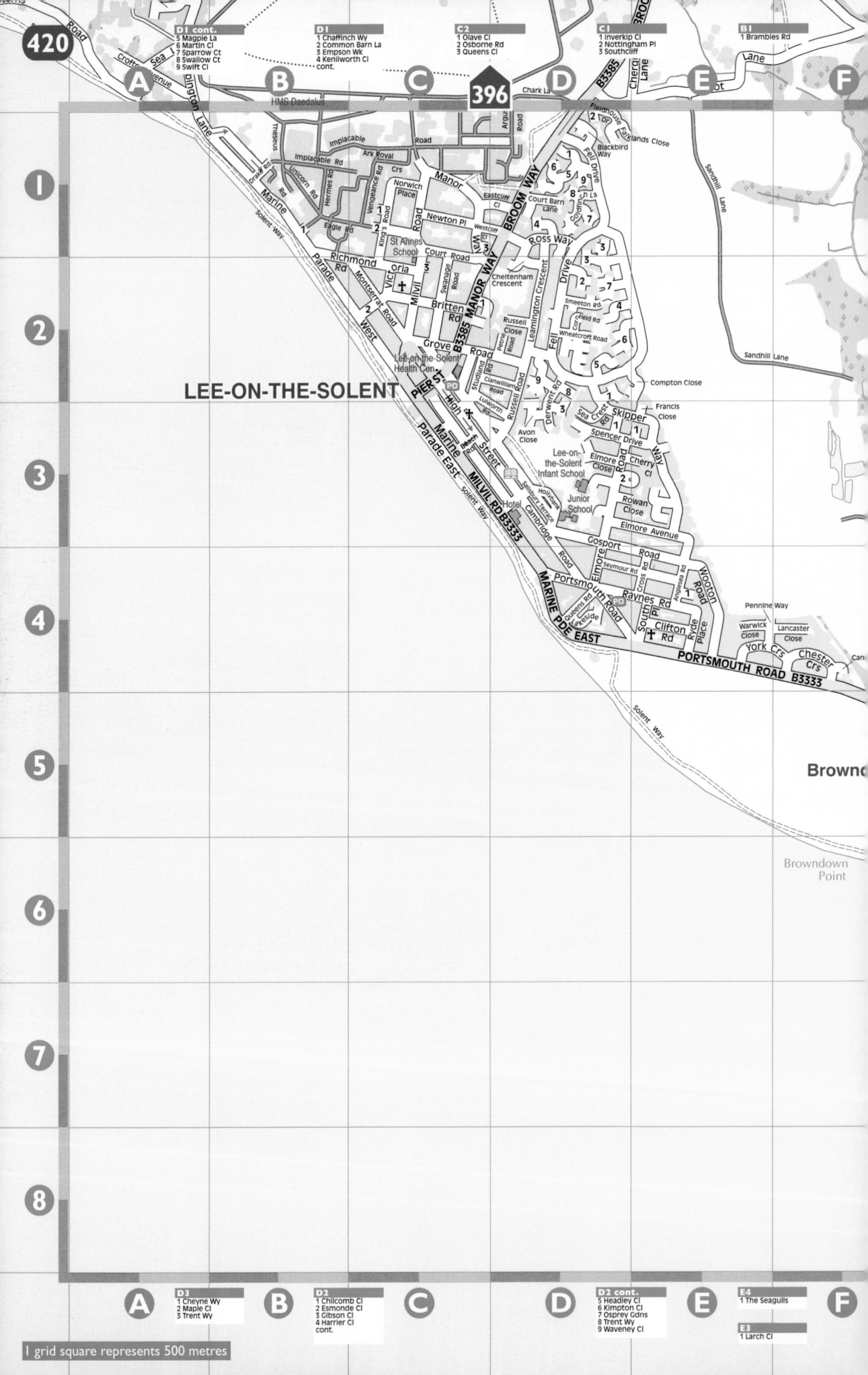

420
D1 cont.
5 Magpie La
6 Martin Cl
7 Sparrow Ct
8 Swallow Ct
9 Swift Cl
D1
1 Chaffinch Wy
2 Common Barn La
3 Empson Wk
4 Kenilworth Cl
cont.
C2
1 Olave Cl
2 Osborne Rd
3 Queens Cl
C1
1 Inverkip Cl
2 Nottingham Pl
3 Southcliff
B1
1 Brambles Rd
396
A
B
C
D
E
F
HMS Daedalus
Chark La
B3385
Lane
Sandhill Lane
Implacable Road
Implacable Rd
Ark Royal Crs
Theseus
Drake Rd
Unicorn Rd
Hermes Rd
Vengeance Rd
Eagle Rd
Marine Parade West
Solent Way
Norwich Place
King's Road
Manor Way
Eastcliff Cl
Westcliff Cl
Newton Pl
St Annes School
Court Road
Richmond Rd
Victoria Rd
Montserrat Road
Milvil Road
Swanage Road
Britten Rd
B3385 MANOR WAY
BROOM WAY
Cheltenham Crescent
Court Barn Lane
Ross Way
Fieldhouse Dr
Fairlands Close
Blackbird Way
Fell Drive
Goldfinch La
Leamington Crescent
Smeeton Rd
Field Rd
Wheatcroft Road
Russell Close
Petrie Road
Grove Road
Lee-on-the-Solent Health Cen
LEE-ON-THE-SOLENT
PIER ST
High Street
Studland Rd
Clanwilliam Road
Lulworth Rd
Russell Road
Derwent Rd
Sea Crest Rd
Skipper Way
Compton Close
Francis Close
Avon Close
Spencer Drive
Lee-on-the-Solent Infant School
Junior School
Elmore Close
Elmore Road
Cherry Cl
Rowan Close
Elmore Avenue
Marine Parade East
MILVIL RD B3333
Hotel
Cambridge Road
Salisbury Terrace
Hollybank
Gosport Road
Seymour Rd
Cross Rd
Anglesea Rd
Wooton Road
Portsmouth Road
Raynes Rd
South Pl
Clifton Rd
Ryde Place
Queens Rd
MARINE PDE EAST
PORTSMOUTH ROAD B3333
Pennine Way
Warwick Close
Lancaster Close
York Crs
Chester Crs
Brownd
Browndown Point
1
2
3
4
5
6
7
8
D3
1 Cheyne Wy
2 Maple Cl
3 Trent Wy
D2
1 Chilcomb Cl
2 Esmonde Cl
3 Gibson Cl
4 Harrier Cl
cont.
D2 cont.
5 Headley Cl
6 Kimpton Ct
7 Osprey Gdns
8 Trent Wy
9 Waveney Cl
E4
1 The Seagulls
E3
1 Larch Cl
1 grid square represents 500 metres

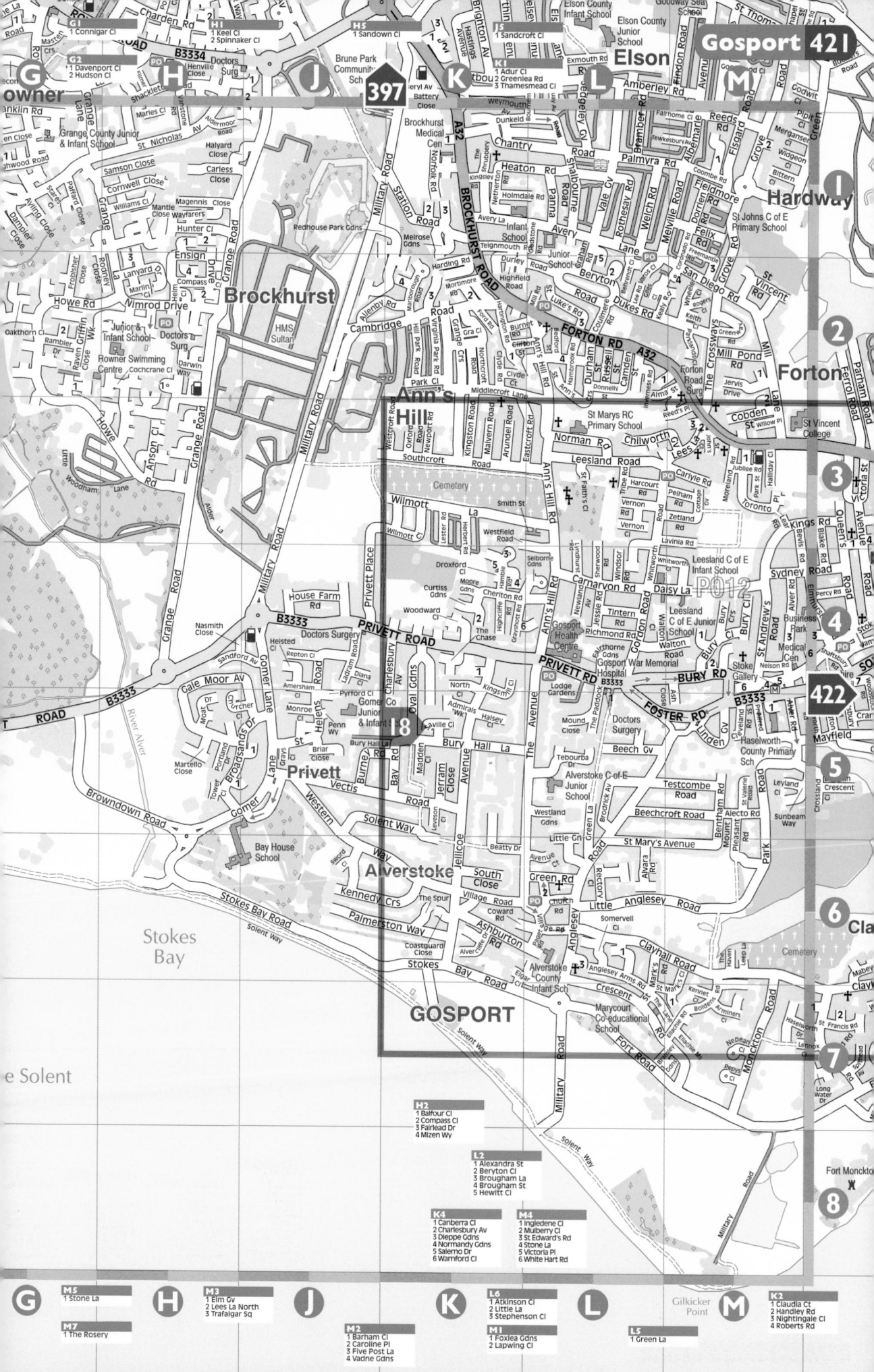

Gosport 421
G1
1 Connigar Cl
G2
1 Davenport Cl
2 Hudson Cl
H1
1 Keel Cl
2 Spinnaker Cl
H5
1 Sandown Cl
J5
1 Sandcroft Cl
K1
1 Adur Cl
2 Greenlea Rd
3 Thamesmead Cl
397
Elson
Hardway
Forton
Brockhurst
HMS Sultan
Ann's Hill
Privett
Alverstoke
GOSPORT
Stokes Bay
Solent
PO12
422
18
B3334
B3333
A32
BROCKHURST ROAD
FORTON RD
PRIVETT ROAD
PRIVETT RD
BURY RD
FOSTER RD
Military Road
Grange Road
Stokes Bay Road
Browndown Road
Cemetery
Gosport War Memorial Hospital
Haselworth County Primary Sch
Alverstoke County Infant Sch
Marycourt Co-educational School
Bay House School
Leesland C of E Infant School
St Vincent College
Fort Monckton
Gilkicker Point
H2
1 Balfour Cl
2 Compass Cl
3 Fairlead Dr
4 Mizen Wy
L2
1 Alexandra St
2 Beryton Cl
3 Brougham La
4 Brougham St
5 Hewitt Cl
K4
1 Canberra Cl
2 Charlesbury Av
3 Dieppe Gdns
4 Normandy Gdns
5 Salerno Dr
6 Wamford Cl
M4
1 Ingledene Cl
2 Mulberry Cl
3 St Edward's Rd
4 Stone La
5 Victoria Pl
6 White Hart Rd
G
H
J
K
L
M
M5
1 Stone La
M3
1 Elm Gv
2 Lees La North
3 Trafalgar Sq
L6
1 Atkinson Cl
2 Little La
3 Stephenson Cl
K2
1 Claudia Ct
2 Handley Rd
3 Nightingale Cl
4 Roberts Rd
M7
1 The Rosery
M2
1 Barham Cl
2 Caroline Pl
3 Five Post La
4 Vadne Gdns
M1
1 Foxlea Gdns
2 Lapwing Cl
L5
1 Green La

422
E4
1 Beehive Wk
2 Grays Ct
3 King Charles St
D5
1 Seager's Ct
B4
1 Thorngate Wy
A5
1 Thornbrake Rd
A7
1 Constable Cl
2 Wilberforce Rd
A3
1 Battenburg Rd
2 Carlton Rd
3 Carlton Wy
4 Fey Rd
5 Pearce Ct
A
B
C
398
D
E
F
1
Hardway
Johns C of E
Primary School
2
Forton
3
Newtown
4
5
6
Clayhall
7
8
City of Portsmouth
Hampshire County
Burrow Island
Yacht Marina
Portsmouth Harbour
HM Naval Base
Mary Rose Ship Hall
HMS Victory
HMS Nelson
Royal Naval Museum
Dockyard Apprentice Exhibition
Mary Rose Exhibition
HMS Warrior
Portsmouth Harbour Station
Portsea
19
20
St Vincent College
Gosport Museum
Town Hall
Bus Station
Richard Martin Gallery & Bookshop
Hampshire Co Council
Haselworth County Primary Sch
St Georges Beneficial C of E Prim Sch
University
Victoria Park
Treadgold Mus
United Services Cricket Grnd
United Services Rugby Club
University of Portsmouth
St Georges Business Cen
Isle of Wight Car Ferry Terminal
Fish Market
HMS Temeraire
Portsmouth City Council
City Mus & Art Gallery
Goldfield Gallery
Portsmouth Cathedral Church of St Thomas of Canterbury
Clarence Pier and Amusement Centre
Hovercraft Terminal
Royal Navy Submarine Museum Offices
HMS Dolphin
Royal Hospital Haslar
Cemetery
Golf Club
Fort Monckton
ISLE OF WIGHT
JERSEY; ST MALO; CHERBOURG; CAEN; LE HAVRE; BILBAO
A32
MUMBY ROAD
SOUTH STREET
SOUTH ST
Haslar Road
BROAD STREET
HIGH ST
A3
B2154
ST GEORGE'S RD
CAMBRIDGE RD
MUSEUM RD
PIER ROAD
A288
Queen St
421
A4
1 Henery St
2 Joseph St
3 Leventhorpe Ct
4 Molesworth Rd
5 Prince of Wales Rd
6 Stoke Gdns
7 Woodley Rd
E3
1 Aylward St
2 Beneficial St
3 Britain St
4 Clock St
5 College St
6 Havant St
7 Margery's Ct
8 Old Star
9 Ordnance Rw
10 Rosemary La
11 St Georges Sq
12 Ship Leopard St
13 Three Tun Cl
E5
1 Battery Rw
2 Camber Pl
3 French St
4 Grand Pde
5 Halfpenny La
6 Oyster Ms
7 Peacock La
8 Pembroke Cl
9 Poynings Pl
10 Wyndham Ms
F4
1 Colpoy St
2 King Richard 1 Rd
3 Landport St
4 Landsdowne St
5 Lord Monty Wy
6 Melbourne Pl
7 Meriden Rd
8 St Paul's Rd
9 St Vincent St
10 Waltham St
11 Wiltshire St
F5
1 Cecil Gv
2 Cecil Pl
3 Chadderton Ct
4 Chapel St
5 Copper St
6 Diamond St
7 Elm St
8 Gold St
9 Gordon Rd
10 L Hambrook
11 L Hambrook
12 Meadow St
13 Nickel St
14 Regent Pl
15 Silver St
16 Slingsby Cl
F3
1 Beck St
2 Lion St
3 Purbeck St
4 St James's St
5 Spring Gdns
1 grid square represents 500 metres

Portsmouth 423
399
424
21
G
H
J
K
L
M
1
2
3
4
5
6
7
8
Baffins
Kingston
Fratton
Somers Town
PO4
PO5
THSEA
Cemetery
Fratton Station
Fratton Park Portsmouth FC
Natural Sciences Museum
D Day Museum
Southsea Castle and Museum
The Pyramid Leisure Centre
South Parade Pier
Royal Marines Museum
St James Hospital
University of Portsmouth
Kings Theatre
Carnegie Library
Cumberland Business Cen
Cluster Industrial Est
St Georges Ind Est
Warren Avenue Industrial Est
Terminus Industrial Est
WINSTON CHURCHILL AV A2030
GOLDSMITH AVENUE
MILTON ROAD
BAFFINS ROAD
FRATTON RD A2047
KINGSTON RD A2047
A2030 VELDER AV
EASTNEY RD A288
HIGHLAND ROAD B2154
EASTERN PARADE A288
CLARENCE PARADE
SOUTH PDE
CLARENDON RD
ALBERT RD
VICTORIA RD NORTH
LAKE RD
MILE END RD
ELM GV B2154
Esplanade
Clarence Esplanade
Solent Way
G1
1 Church St
2 Fitzherbert St
3 Old Commer. Rd
G6
1 Auckland Rd W
2 Lennox Rd N
3 Netley Rd
4 Richmond Pl
5 Serpentine Rd
6 The Vale
L1
1 Dudley Rd
L4
1 Carisbrooke Rd
L5
1 Blenheim Ct
2 Carpenter Cl
3 Pedam Cl
L6
1 Nettlestone Rd
2 Worsley St
M3
1 Blendworth Rd
2 CheveningCt
3 Oxted Ct
4 Plover Reach
M4
1 Hester Rd
2 Melrose Cl
3 Milton Park Av
4 Old Canal
M5
1 Billing Cl
2 Tranmere Rd
M6
1 Drysdale Ms
2 Eastney St
3 Mountbatten Sq
4 Pitcairn Ms
5 Saunders Ms
H2
1 Clarendon Pl
2 Common St
3 Drummond Rd
4 King Albert St
5 P Chandler St
6 Settlers Cl
J1
1 Arthur St
2 Buckland St
3 Cowper Rd
4 Ewart Rd
5 Little Arthur St
6 Little George St
G5
1 Belmont Pl
2 Bush St West
3 Chivers Cl
4 Gloucester Ter
5 Hyde St
6 Ormsby Rd
7 Queen's Pl
8 Queen's Wy
9 South St
10 Sussex Pl
11 The Thicket
12 Wilberforce Rd
13 Worsley Rd
H4
1 Aldwell St
2 Blackfriars Cl
3 Cross St
4 Forbury Rd
5 Froddington Rd
6 L Forbury Rd
7 Quinton Cl
8 Sedgley Cl
J4
1 Shanklin Rd
2 Ventnor Rd
J7
1 Craneswater Ga
2 Kirkstall Rd
G4
1 Bedford St
2 Brunswick St
3 Crabbe Ct
4 Dunsmore Cl
5 Earlsdon St
6 Gloucester Vw
7 Ockendon Cl
8 Peel Pl
9 Plymouth St
10 Waterloo St
11 Wellington St
12 Yorke St
G3
1 Buckingham St
2 C Dickens St
3 D Dymond St
4 D Drummond St
5 Durham St
6 East Surrey St
7 I Brunel Rd
8 Lwr Church Pth
9 The M Rose Street
G2
1 Andrew Bell St
2 Brewer St
3 Charlotte St
4 Church Pth N
5 Commercial Pl
6 Commercial Rd
7 Eden St
8 Lake Rd
9 Landport Vw
10 Toby St
H1
1 Baythorn Cl
2 Brownlow Cl
3 Dickens Cl
4 Havisham Rd
5 Northbrook Cl
H6
1 The Circle
2 Freestone Rd
3 Maple Rd
4 Marmion Av
5 Taswell Rd
6 Theatre Ms
7 Wimbldn Pk Rd
8 Yves Ms
K1
1 Victor Rd
K4
1 Chestnut Av
K5
1 White Cloud Park
J5
1 Grenville Rd
2 Norland Rd
J6
1 Herbert Rd
2 Waverley Gv
J3
1 Ariel Rd
2 Claremont Rd
3 Cumberland Rd
4 Kingsdown Pl
5 Lucknow St
6 Sandringham La
7 Sheffield Rd
8 Sydenham Ter
J2
1 Forton Rd
2 Power Rd
3 Trafalgar Pl
H7
1 Beaufort Rd
2 Eastern Villas Rd
3 Furness Rd
4 Jack Cockerill Wy
5 Kenilworth Rd
6 Onslow Rd
7 Villiers Rd
H5
1 Cavendish Rd
2 Hereford Rd
3 Hillborough Crs
4 St Bart's Gdns
5 The Thicket
H3
1 Boarhunt Cl
2 Claxton St
3 Cottage Vw
4 Glidden Cl
5 Maxstoke Cl
6 Murefield Rd
7 Northam Ms
8 Port Royal St

A5
1 Eastney Farm Rd

A4
1 Towpath Mead

A3
1 Brasted Ct
2 Longfield Cl
3 Redwing Ct
4 Wayfarer Cl

A2
1 Godwit Rd
2 Revenge Cl
3 Seagull Cl

A   B   C   400   D   E   F

Baffins

Stanley Avenue

Stanley's Rd

Tangier Road

Portsmouth Sixth Form College

1

Avenue
Jenkins Grove
Cedar Gv
Avenue

Ebery Grove

EASTERN   ROAD A2030

Sword Sands Rd

Langstone Channel

Sinah Lake

2

Eastern Av

Salterns

Eastern Av

School
East Shore School

The Hvn

Moorings Way Infant School

Moorings Way

Moorings

Schooner Way

Way

3

Avenue

Industrial Est

Mariner's Wk

Fenbridge Rd

Milebush Rd

Godwit

Atalanta Cl

Whimbrel Ct

Sanderling Rd

Dunlin Ct

Rd

Way

Solent Way

St James Hospital

Shelford Rd
Mayles Rd

Junior School

Milton

Furze Lane

Lane

Furze

Broom Sq

Waterlock Gdns

Longshore Way

Solent Way

Hampshire County
City of Portsmouth

University of Portsmouth

4

Shelford Rd
Mayles Rd

Rd
Rosetta

Morgan Rd

Trevis Rd

Ironbridge

Berney Rd
Shirley Av

Redlands Gv
Redlands Gdns

Amyas Ct

Lockway Road

Seaway

Crescent

Ferry Road

Ferry Road

423

P04

Dunb

Maurice
Road

Yeo Ct

Torrida Ct

Leoric Ct

Horse Sands Ck

Fort Cumberland

Solent Way

5

Fordingbridge Rd

Minster

Henderson

Bransbury Rd

Cadnam Rd

Tamarisk Cl

Road

Haslar Rd

Wood Rd

Holne Court

Cocklesheli Gdns

Halliday Crescent

Ferry Road

Finch Rd

Gibraltar Rd

Lumsden Rd

Fort Cumberland   Road

Eastney

Road

Sinah Common

Glasgow

Row

Royal Marines Museum

Esplanade Gdns

Melville

Driftwood Gdns

Gdns

Eastney Swimming Baths

6

Esplanade

West Winner

East Winner

7

8

A   B   C   D   E   F

B3
1 Sovereign Dr

I grid square represents 500 metres

J4
1 Aubrey Cl
2 Grayland Cl
3 Lexden Gdns
4 Newtown La
5 Spinnaker Cl

K5
1 Walnut Tree Cl

L5
1 Spencer Cl
2 Willow Wood Rd

G   H   J   401   K   L   M

401

I

PO11

Manor Ho

A3023

A3023

Mill Rythe La

1

2

3

4

426

5

6

7

8

Woodlands La

Denhill

Saltmarsh La

West Lane

Brights La

Higworth La

Lulworth Cl

Kings Road

Rest-A-Wyle Av

Pound Lea

Dover Court

Globe Cl

Atherley Road

Wardens Cl

Katrina Gdns

Church Road

PO11

Tournerbury Lane

Dundonald

Burwood Grove

Eastwood Cl

Laburnum Grove

North Shore Road

Warren Cl

Warren Close

Park Road

Hayling Billy Business Cen

Station Theatre

Charles ... on Cl

Dacres W...

West Lane

Hamfield Drive

Gilbert Mead

Sycamore Dr

Fathoms Reach

Southleigh Gv

St Mary's Road

Mengham Infant School

Palmerston Rd

Mengham Junior School

Hawthorne Cl

Poplar Grove

Beech Grove

Legion Rd

St Thomas Av

Richmond Dr

Richmond Cl

James Cl

Old Court

Cherrywood Gdns

Linden Cl

Fir Tree Gv

St Leonard's Av

East Margarets Rd

West Town

St Catherine's

St Aubin's Park

St Helen's Road

St George's Road

St Thomas Av

Staunton Avenue

Thomas Av

Fermhurst Close

Stamford Av

Bathurst Cl

Garden Cl

Garden Cl

Hollow Lane

Elwell Gn

Brattwood

Oakwood Rd

1

2

Hayling Island Health Centre

Elm Gv

St Leonard's Av

Mengham Rd

Selsmore

Mengham Lane

Mengham Road

Mengham

Salterns Lane

Blackthorn

Blackthorn Rd

Ilex Walk

Fishery Lane

Lime Gv

Sinah Ct

Links Lane

Ferry Road

St Hermans Rd

Bacon Lane

Westmead

Winston Cl

Magdala Rd

Green Lane

Sea Front

Westfield

Beach Road

Westfield Avenue

Old Timbers

Hollow Lane

South Road

Victoria Av

Alexandra Avenue

Chichester Avenue

Wyndhurst Cl

Tudor Cl

Manor Wy

Bea Grove Av

Ramsey Rd

Webb La

Grand Pde

Webb Cl

1

Orchard Rd

Wyborn Cl

St Andrew's Road

Old School Dr

Norman Rd

Silversand Gdns

Harold Road

Old School Dr

North Crs

Rails

Osprey Gv

Teal Cl

Coburg Cl

Stead Close

My Lords Gdns

Beach Rd

Westfield

SOUTH HAYLING

Sea Front

Sea Front

St Hermans

Southwo...

The Clade

Bembridge D...

Hayling Bay

G   H   J   K   M6   L   M5   M   L6

M6
1 Pebble Cl
2 Sunshine Av

M5
1 Whitethorn Rd

L6
1 The Sanderlings

A   B   C   **402**   D   E   F

I

2

3

4

425

5

Mill Rithe

Pils
San

Stocker's La

Mengham
Salterns

Black Point

Bracklesham
Rd

Simmons
Ct

Salterns Cl

Salterns

Lane

Marine

Walk

Seaview
Rd

Seaview

Road

ngham

orth Crs

Blackthorn Dr

Blackthorn Dr

Selsmore Avenue

Kingfisher

Arcadia

Selsmore

Witterina

Road

Earnley

Selsey Cl

Norman Rd

Blackthorn

Ilex Walk

Rd

Fishery

Fishery

Marshall Rd

Lane

Earnley

Haslemere Gdns

Itchenor Rd

Sidlesham

Cl

Pagham

Gdns

Bracklesham

Silversands Av

Road

Fishermans

Wk

Eastoke

Avenue

Bosmere Rd

6

2

Old School Dr

Old School Dr

PO

Foreland
Ct

St Hermans Rd

Eastoke

Rowin Close

Avenue

Eastoke

Creek

Rd

Birdham

Haven Road

Haven

Road

Point

Road

Road

Sea
Front

Southwood

The Clade

Bembridge Drive

Meath Cl

Road

The Strand

Eastoke
Creek

Burgess Cl

West Haye
Road

Sandy

Nutbourne Road

Coronation

Treloar

Treloar
Rd

7

Winsor Cl

Wheatlands

Avenue

1

Rd

Southwood Road

Eastoke Point

West Sussex County

Hampshire County

8

A   B   C   D   E   F

403

G H J K L M

I

2

3

4

5

6

7

8

Longmere
Point

Pilsey
Island

Chichester Harbour

East Head

Rookwood
Lane

Rookwood
Lane

Sheepwash Lane

ROOKWOOD RD

Rookwood
Road

Ellanore Lane

Roman Landing

Roman Landing

Roman
Landing

Roman
Landing

Coastguard Lane

West Wittering
Parochial School

Pound Rd

The Wad

B2179

Summerfield Road

Summerfield
Rd

Locksash C

PO

Elmstead
Gdns

Elmstead Pk Rd

Cunliffe
Close

Elmstead
Park Road

Meadow
La

Elms
Wy

Elms Lane

Elms Lane

Nunnington Farm

Royce Way

Royce
Close

Elms
Ride

Elms
Ride

The Byeway

West Wittering

Middlefield

Seaward
Dr.

Wellsfield

West
Strand

Berrybarn Lane

East
Strand

CAKEHAM

ROAD

B2179

**East
Wittering**

Howard Avenue

Jolliffe Road

Southcote

Marine Dr W

Border
Path

F8
1 Bell Heather Cl
E8
1 Gurjun Cl
2 Hickory Cl
A
B
C
D
E
F
1
2
3
4
5
6
7
8
A350
Sandy Lane
Old Market Road
Henbury Plantation
Castle Court School
Knoll Lane
Castle Farm Road
Crumpet's Farm
Slony Down Plantation
Crumpets Dr
Drove
Rushall Lane
Barrow Hill
Wimborne Road
Poor Common
Dairy Cl
Lytchett Matravers
Wareham
Huntick Road
Foxhills Dr
BLANDFORD ROAD
NORTH
Maylyn Rd
Old Wareham Road
Beacon Hill
Beacon Hl La
Lytchett Heath
Race Farm
BH16
Foxhills Lane
Huntick Road
Randalls Hill
Blandford Rd N
Cemetery
Post Green Road
Post Green
Lytchett Minster Upper School
Redwood
Ash Road
Beacon
Marsh La
Policemans La
Pinewood Rd
Upton Infant
1 grid square represents 500 metres

G3
1 Thornton Cl

G4
1 Froud Wy

G8
1 Meadows Cl
2 Turbary Ct

H1
1 Central Av
2 Towers Farm

H2
1 Birch Cl
2 Henbury View Rd
3 Rushcombe Wy

H3
1 Highmoor Cl

H4
1 Dalkeith Rd

Rushcombe Bottom

Corfe Hills School

HIGHER BLANDFORD ROAD B3074

Rushcombe County First Sch

Corfe View First School

Hill View

BH18

Broadstone

Broadstone Middle School

First School

The Harvey Practice

430

Hilbourne

Hilbourne Middle School

Hilbourne First School

DARBY'S CORNER

Upton Heath

Dogwood Road

Waterloo

Parkstone Grammar School for Girls

BH17

Creekmoor

Brownsea Open Air Theatre

Birchwood Medical Cen

444

G6
1 Allenby Cl
2 Clyde Rd
3 Hastings Rd

M7
1 Underwood Cl

H5
1 L Blandford Rd

L4
1 L Blandford Rd

L6
1 Stoborough Dr
2 York Cl

L3
1 Springdale Rd

K7
1 Bullfinch Cl
2 Greenfinch Cl
3 Hyacinth Cl
4 Redshank Cl
5 Sandpiper Cl

K6
1 Cowslip Rd
2 Stonecrop Cl

L5
1 Buckthorn Cl
2 Chaffinch Cl

J2
1 Heather Cl
2 Wayman Rd

FLE CORNER

1 Gladelands Cl
2 Gladelands Wy

UPTON ROAD

C5
1 Harcombe Cl
2 Willwood Cl
B7
1 Bredy Cl
2 Waterston Cl
3 Woodlake Cl
A8
1 Hatch Pond Rd
A7
1 Terence Av
A2
1 Merriefield Av
404
429
445
Arrowsmith Road
Blackwater Drive
GRAVEL HILL A349
Portmore Close
Merriefield Close
Merriefield Dr
Cemetery
Broadstone Middle School
Dunyeats Road
Laurel Drive
Ashwood Drive
Westcroft Pk
Whitchurch Av
Barn Road
Loders Cl
Tollerford Road
Edgarton Road
Holywell Cl
Whitecross Close
Portesham Way
Pilsdon Dr
Poole Grammar School
Canford Heath
CANFORD HEATH ROAD
B3074
Cogdeane Road
Bere Close
Sandhills Cl
Halstock Crs
Culliford Crs
Doctors Surgery
Canford Hth Group Practice
Hasler Road
Clayford Cl
Redhoave Road
Thorncombe Cl
Police Station
DARBY'S CORNER
Hilary Rd
Denison Rd
Sopers Lane
Parkstone Grammar School for Girls
WATERLOO ROAD
Plantation
West Canford Heath Medical Cen
Stinsford Road
Witney Road
Ad Astra County First School
Ashdown School
Haymoor Middle School
Canford Heath
Sherborn Crs
Bovington Close
Chetnole Close
Adastral Road
Verity Crescent
Warburton Road
Beamish Rd
Kellaway Road
Megabowl
Acorn Business Centre
DORSET WAY
A3049
Fancy Road
Cuckoo Road
Old Wareham Road
New Fields Business Park
Cowley Road
Abingdon Road
Hatch Pond Rd
Kennington Rd
Morris Rd
Darby's La
Dundas Rd
Mitchell Road
The Surgery
Newtown
C6
1 Corscombe Cl
C8
1 Burbridge Cl
2 Nicholson Cl
3 Warburton Rd
4 Wykeham Cl
D8
1 Samples Wy
E6
1 Carsworth Wy
2 Henbury Cl
F6
1 Stockbridge Cl
FLEET'S CORNER
Kingsmill Road
Middle School
First School
Industrial Estate
1 grid square represents 500 metres

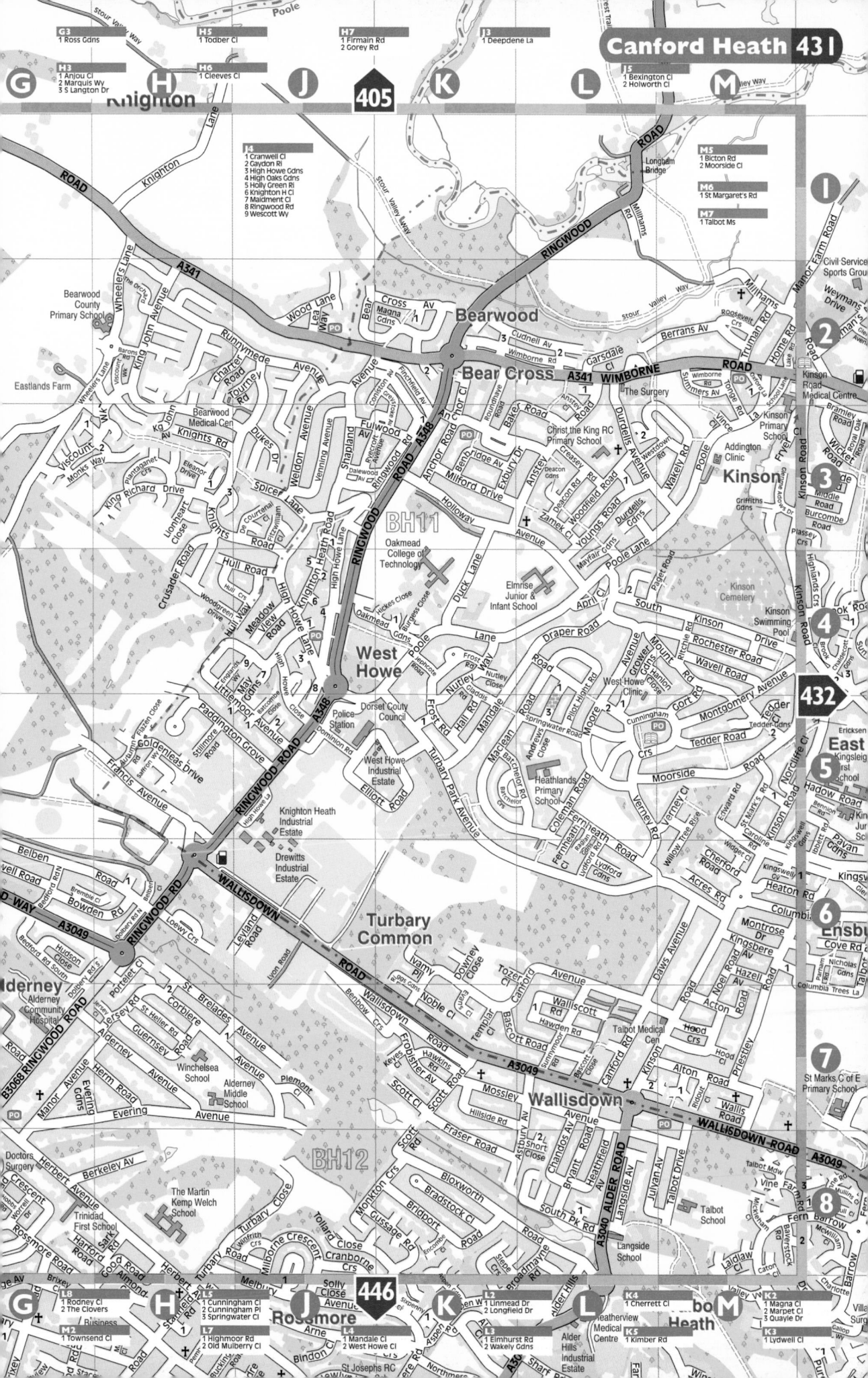
G3
1 Ross Gdns
H5
1 Todber Cl
H7
1 Firmain Rd
2 Gorey Rd
J3
1 Deepdene La
H3
1 Anjou Cl
2 Marquis Wy
3 S Langton Dr
H6
1 Cleeves Cl
J5
1 Bexington Cl
2 Holworth Cl
405
J4
1 Cranwell Cl
2 Gaydon Ri
3 High Howe Gdns
4 High Oaks Gdns
5 Holly Green Ri
6 Knighton H Cl
7 Maidment Cl
8 Ringwood Rd
9 Wescott Wy
M5
1 Bicton Rd
2 Moorside Cl
M6
1 St Margaret's Rd
M7
1 Talbot Ms
Knighton
Longham Bridge
Bearwood County Primary School
Eastlands Farm
Bearwood
Bear Cross
A341 WIMBORNE ROAD
RINGWOOD ROAD
Civil Service Sports Group
Kinson Road Medical Centre
The Surgery
Bearwood Medical Cen
Christ the King RC Primary School
Kinson Primary School
Addington Clinic
Kinson
BH11
Oakmead College of Technology
Elmrise Junior & Infant School
Kinson Cemetery
Kinson Swimming Pool
West Howe
Police Station
Dorset County Council
West Howe Industrial Estate
West Howe Clinic
Heathlands Primary School
432
East
Knighton Heath Industrial Estate
Drewitts Industrial Estate
WALLISDOWN ROAD
Turbary Common
Alderney
Alderney Community Hospital
Winchelsea School
Alderney Middle School
Talbot Medical Cen
Wallisdown
St Marks C of E Primary School
BH12
Doctors Surgery
The Martin Kemp Welch School
Trinidad First School
Talbot School
Langside School
A3040 ALDER ROAD
A3049
A348
B3068 RINGWOOD ROAD
446
L8
1 Rodney Cl
2 The Clovers
M2
1 Townsend Cl
L5
1 Cunningham Cl
2 Cunningham Pl
3 Springwater Cl
L7
1 Highmoor Rd
2 Old Mulberry Cl
L4
1 Mandale Cl
2 West Howe Cl
L2
1 Linmead Dr
2 Longfield Dr
L3
1 Elmhurst Rd
2 Wakely Gdns
K4
1 Cherrett Cl
K5
1 Kimber Rd
K2
1 Magna Cl
2 Marpet Cl
3 Quayle Dr
K3
1 Lydwell Cl
Rossmore
Heatherview Medical Centre
Alder Hills Industrial Estate
St Josephs RC

432
406
431
447
West
B5 1 Fletcher Cl
B6 1 Kingswell Cl 2 St Thomas's Cl
B3 1 Ashridge Gdns 2 Dudley Gdns 3 Northbourne Pl 4 Pinewood Cl
B1 1 Markham Cl
A6 1 Adamsfield Gdns 2 Columbian Wy 3 Glenville Gdns
A8 1 Georgina Cl 2 Smithson Cl 3 Vine Farm Cl
A3 1 Howton Cl
A4 1 Cartwright Cl 2 Merryfield La 3 St Merrin's Cl
B4 1 Dowlands Cl
D7 1 Kilmarnock Rd 2 Lampton Gdns 3 Morden Rd 4 Smithfield Pl 5 St John's Gdns
D8 1 Junction Rd
E4 1 Castle La West 2 Portswood Dr 3 Redhill Ct 4 The Circle
E5 1 Franklin Rd 2 Malvern Cl 3 Redbreast Rd N 4 Webster Rd
E6 1 Derwent Cl 2 Forest View Cl 3 Mcwilliam Rd 4 Minterne Rd 5 Rosebud Av
E7 1 Garth Rd
F4 1 Bosworth Ms 2 Cerne Cl 3 Iwerne Cl 4 Sturminster Rd
F5 1 Charnwood Av 2 Chickerell Cl 3 Knowlton Gdns 4 Shillingstone Dr
F6 1 Charminster Cl 2 Luckham Cl 3 Luckham Pl 4 Luckham Rd East 5 Oakwood Cl
F7 1 Camden Cl 2 West Way Cl
F8 1 Cecil Hl
B7 1 Ashburton Gdns 2 Ensbury Cl 3 Glenmoor Cl 4 Newbury Dr
C2 1 Austen Av 2 Old Vicarage Cl
C3 1 Heads Farm Cl 2 Saxonhurst Cl
C4 1 Headswell Gdns 2 Saxonhurst Gdns
C5 1 Broughton Cl 2 Romney Cl
C6 1 Parkside Gdns
D4 1 Georgian Wy
D5 1 Old St John's Ms
Ensbury
Northbourne
Red Hill
Muscliff
East Howe
Ensbury Park
Talbot Village
Moordown
Winton
BH10
BH9
WIMBORNE ROAD A341
WHITELEGG WAY A347
CASTLE LANE WEST A3060
REDHILL AVENUE A347
BOUNDARY ROAD A347
WALLISDOWN ROAD A3049
TALBOT ROAD
ALMA A3049
Bournemouth University
Ensbury Bridge
Stour Valley Way
River Stour
Dorset County
Bournemouth
1 grid square represents 500 metres

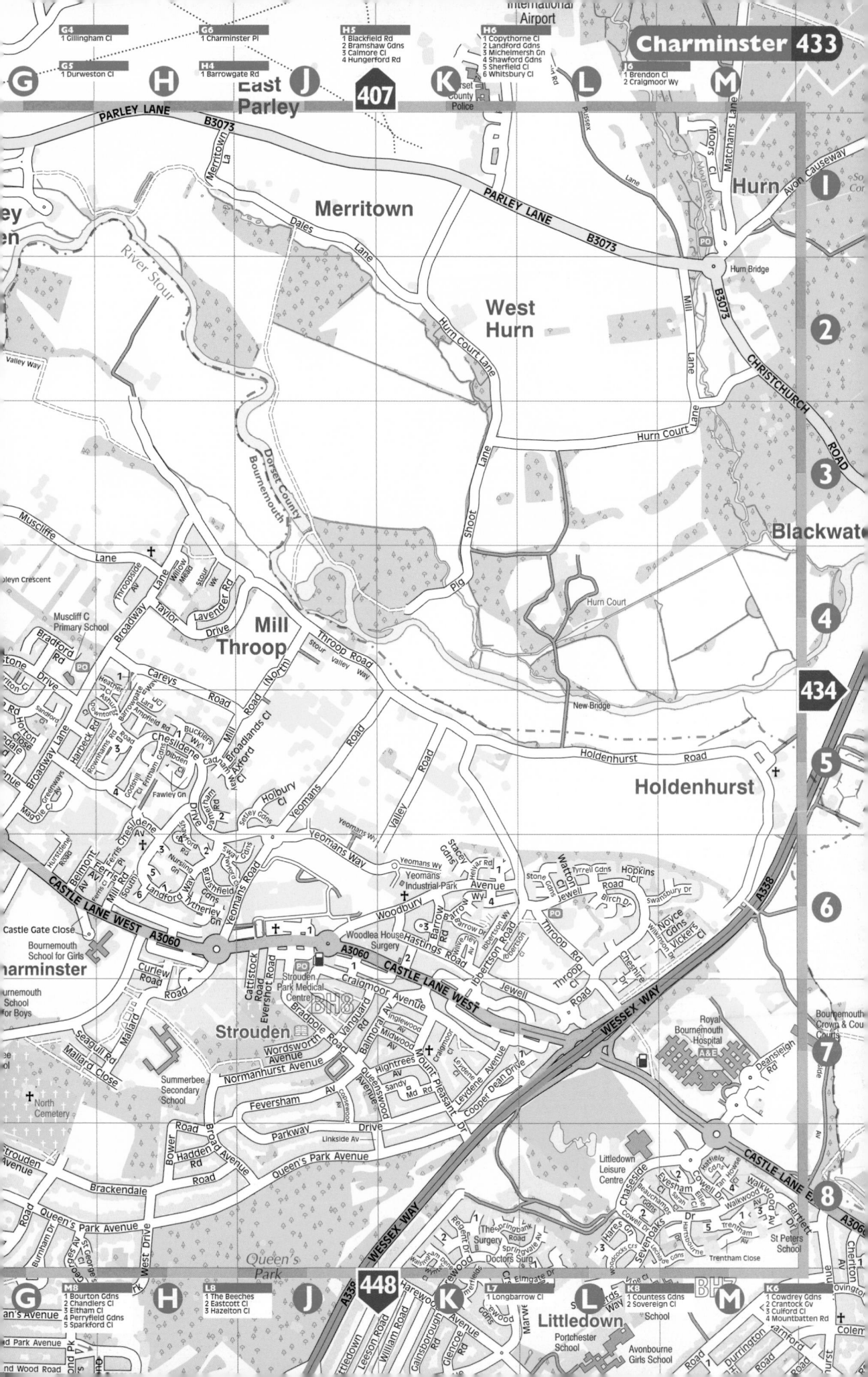
G4
1 Gillingham Cl
G5
1 Durweston Cl
G6
1 Charminster Pl
H4
1 Barrowgate Rd
H5
1 Blackfield Rd
2 Bramshaw Gdns
3 Calmore Cl
4 Hungerford Rd
H6
1 Copythorne Cl
2 Landford Gdns
3 Michelmersh Gn
4 Shawford Gdns
5 Sherfield Cl
6 Whitsbury Cl
J6
1 Brendon Cl
2 Craigmoor Wy
Airport
East Parley
407
434
448
PARLEY LANE
B3073
Merritown
Merritown La
Dales Lane
West Hurn
Hurn Court Lane
Hurn Court Road
Hurn
Hurn Bridge
Avon Causeway
Matchams Lane
Moors Cl
Moors River
Mill Lane
CHRISTCHURCH ROAD
River Stour
Dorset County
Bournemouth
Shoot Lane
Pig
Blackwater
Hurn Court
New Bridge
Holdenhurst Road
Holdenhurst
Muscliffe Lane
Valley Way
Muscliff C Primary School
Mill Throop
Throop Road
Stour Valley Way
Broadway Lane
Taylor Drive
Lavender Rd
Careys Road
Mill Road (North)
Broadlands Cl
Yeomans Road
Yeomans Way
Valley Road
Holbury Cl
Chesildene Av
Yeomans Industrial Park
Woodbury Avenue
Watton Cl
Jewell Road
Hopkins Cl
Throop Rd
Cheshire Dr
Castle Gate Close
Bournemouth School for Girls
CASTLE LANE WEST
A3060
Woodlea House Surgery
Hastings Road
Ibbertson Road
Craigmoor Avenue
Strouden
Strouden Park Medical Centre
BH8
Cattistock Road
Evershot Road
Bradpole Road
Vanguard Rd
Curlew Road
Mallard Road
Seagull Rd
Mallard Close
Summerbee Secondary School
North Cemetery
Wordsworth Avenue
Normanhurst Avenue
Feversham Av
Queenswood Avenue
Mount Pleasant Dr
Cooper Dean Drive
Levdene Avenue
Parkway Drive
Linkside Av
Broad Avenue
Bower Road
Hadden Rd
Queen's Park Avenue
Brackendale Road
Queen's Park
WESSEX WAY
A338
Royal Bournemouth Hospital
A&E
Deansleigh Rd
Littledown Leisure Centre
Chaseside
Evesham Cl
Sevenoaks Dr
Walkwood Av
Trentham Av
Trentham Close
St Peters School
The Surgery
Doctors Surg
Springbank Road
Elmgate Dr
CASTLE LANE EAST
M8
1 Bourton Gdns
2 Chandlers Cl
3 Eltham Cl
4 Perryfield Gdns
5 Sparkford Cl
L8
1 The Beeches
2 Eastcott Cl
3 Hazelton Cl
L7
1 Longbarrow Cl
K8
1 Countess Gdns
2 Sovereign Cl
K6
1 Cowdrey Gdns
2 Crantock Gv
3 Culford Cl
4 Mountbatten Rd
Littledown
Portchester School
Avonbourne Girls School
BH7
Harewood Avenue
Leeson Road
William Road
G
H
J
K
L
M
1
2
3
4
5
6
7
8

B8
1 Sycamore Cl
B6
1 Old Barn Cl
2 Squirrels Cl
B4
1 Valencia Cl
2 Whitby Cl
A8
1 Hursley Cl
408
433
449
Blackwater
St Catherine's Hill
Fairmile
Jumpers Common
Town Common
Sopley Common
Winkton Common
Dudmoor Farm
Hurn Bridge
Bournemouth Crown & County Courts
St Peters School
Christchurch Hospital
Cemetery
Christchurch Stn
Briar Park Business Centre
River Stour
River Avon
C8
1 Bernards Cl
2 Eleanor Gdns
3 The Hurdles
D6
1 Lincoln Av
D8
1 Adelaide Cl
2 Endfield Rd
3 Kimberley Cl
4 Regency Crs
E7
1 Emily Cl
2 Queensmead
E8
1 Latch Farm Av
1 grid square represents 500 metres

G5
1 Avon View Rd
2 Harrison Cl
3 Heathlands Cl
4 K Chance Cl
5 Kirkham Av
6 Pittmore Rd

G6
1 Barlands Cl
2 Summerfield Cl

G7
1 Burton Cl

H5
1 Burton Hall Pl

H6
1 Woodstock Rd

H7
1 Martins Hill La

H8
1 Sarah Sands Cl

Twin Oaks Medical Cen

RAMSGORE

409

Bransg Prima School

Westbury Cl

Meyrick Close

Hampshire County
Dorset County

Burley Road

Harrow Road

North Bockhampton

Neacroft

Lr Clockhouse Farm

BH23

Chisels Croft La
Croft Road

Lyndhurst Road

Godsw

Winkton

Burley Road

Middle Bockhampton

Bockhampton Road

Waterditch

Homefield School

Avon Valley path

Hawthorn Road

Lyndhurst Road

Waterditch Road

South Bockhampton

Waterditch Farm

Waterditch Road

436

Hill Lane

Salisbury Road

Primary School

Campbell Park

Farwell Cl

Winkton Burns Cl

The Lindens

Preston Lane

Moorcroft Av

Vinneys Cl

Vicarage Way

Hawthorn Road

Hill Lane

Hampshire County

Dorset County

Priory Vw Rd

Meadow La

Crabtree Cl

Footners La

Whitehayes Cl

Bodowen Rd

Bodowen

Treebys

Burton

Holly Gdns

Summers Lane

Whitehayes Road

Medlar Cl

Hill

Alder Cl

Gordon

Martins Hill short

Sandy Plot

Salisbury Road

Lyndhurst

Lyndhurst

Westfield Gdns

Buttercup

Snowdrop Gdns

Clover Dr

Harrow Cl

Vetch Cl

Blue bell Cl

Celandine Cl

B3347

sur Hill

Watery Lane

Ambury

BY-PASS

A35

St Josephs RC School

Dorset Road

Mallory Cl

Somerford Av

Saffron Wy

Saffron

Sorrell Wy

Sea Vixen Industrial Est

HIGHCLIFFE ROAD A337

Hoburne

CHRISTCHURCH

Irvine Wy

Everest Road

Hunt

Edward Road

Edward Rd

Kingsley House Surg

Amethyst Road

Somerford Rd

B3059

Christchurch Business

M8
1 Bellflower Cl
2 Honeysuckle Wy
6 Speedwell Dr

M7
1 Columbine Cl
2 Monkshood Cl

L7
1 Meadow La

K8
1 Charles Rd
2 Coleridge Gn

J8
1 Bonington Cl
2 Hillary Rd

B3059

PUREWELL CROS

Somerford

Grange Comprehensive School

Junior School

Infant Sch

Somerford Rd

Somerford Business Park

Hughes Business Cen

Silver Business

Orange Road Business Cen

Delta Est

Halifax Wy

Hunter

Newlands

The Runway

Brabazon

Wessex

Orchid

C7
1 Birchwood Cl
2 Milverton Cl
C8
1 Knightwood Cl
B8
1 Burnside
2 Farmdene Cl
3 Harriers Cl
4 Saulfland Pl
B7
1 Fir Tree La
2 Winsford Cl
A8
1 Clematis Cl
2 Foxglove Cl
Beech House
410
North Farm
Harrow Road
Harrow Lodge
Lyndhurst Road
Ringwood Road
Godswinscroft
Hinton Park
Hinton
Dark Lane
Burton Common
435
A35
LYNDHURST RD
Station Road
Hintonwood La
Hinton Admiral Station
ROAD
The Meadway
Havelock Wy
Clive Road
Woodhayes Av
Forest Rise
Smugglers La North
Hinton Wd Av
Hurstbourne Avenue
Terrington Av
Thursby
Talbot Drive
Amberwood Dr
Amberwood Gdns
Dunbar Crescent
Pinewood
Glenavon Road
Holmhurst Avenue
Shepherd Close
Braemar
Denham Drive
St Marks C of E County Infant Sch
School
Highcliffe
Haslemere Place
Haslemere Av
Chewton Common
Southwood Av
Heath Road
Jacobean Close
Chewton Way
Plantation Dr
Glenville Road
Highcliffe GM Comprehensive School
Smugglers Wd Rd
Hoburne Lane
Cornflower Dr
Primrose Way
Balfour Cl
Ridgefield Gdns
Nea Close
North
Rowan Dr
Saulfland Dr
Cornford Wy
Woodland Way
Curzon Way
Copse Wy
Nea Road
Pine Crs
Silver Way
Castle
Kilmington Way
Lyme Crs
Jesmond Av
Highcliffe Medical Centre
Bucehayes Cl
Stanley Road
Gordon Rd
Police Station
Stuart Road
Waterford
Montagu
Sundew Close
Saffron
Yarrow Cl
Vetch Cl
A337
D8
1 Angeline Cl
2 Norleywood
E6
1 Beckley Copse
F6
1 Clinton Cl
2 Nicholas Cl
3 Wyndham Cl
451
LYMINGTON RD
Castle Golf Club
Rothesay Drive
Maple Cl
Beacon Dr
F7
1 Gordon Mt
2 Walkford Wy
Elmwood Way
Wharncliffe Road
F8
1 Jay's Ct
Wellington
1 grid square represents 500 metres

H8
1 Rockb. Gdns
2 Sellwood Wy
3 Studley Ct
J3
1 Cherry Tree Dr
J4
1 The Hyde
J8
1 Christchurch Rd
2 Dunford Cl
K4
1 Deer Park Cl
2 Rosecrae Cl
G
H
J
K
L
M
411
438
452
Marlpit Lane
North Drive
South Drive
St Johns Road
Bashley
Bashley Park
Bashley Drive
BASHLEY ROAD
Mark's Lane
New Lane
Smithy Lane
Ossemsley Manor
SWAY ROAD
CROSS ROAD B3055
BASHLEY
Beckley
Birch Av
Forest View
Robin Cl
Lawn View
Vintage Motorcycle Museum
Bashley Manor Farm
Stem Lane
FERNHILL LA
B3058
BH25
Cull Lane
Holland Wy
Keswick Rd
Gainsborough Av
Brook Avenue
Marston Rd
Charles Crs
Hilton Rd
Ferndale Road
Oakwood
Winchester Road
Violet Lane
Palmer Pl
Linford Close
Ballard Lake Preparatory School
Barrs Avenue
North Avenue
Wood Road
Velvet Lawn Road
Doe Copse Way
Hazelwood Avenue
Beechwood Av
Rosewood Gardens
Kennard Road
New Milton
Lake Grove Road
Fernhill Road
Leigh Road
Ballard College
Brook Avenue
Manor Road
Walkford Lane
Walkford Brook
Chatsworth Way
Arundel Cl
Queensway
Marryat Road
Drake Close
Nelson Close
Pond Cl
Avenue Road
New Milton Station
The Arnewood Practice
Osborne Road
Herbert Road
York Av
Lyon Avenue
Warwick Av
Wick 1 Industrial Est
Wick 2 Industrial Est
Nova Business Park
Chaffinch Close
Fawcett Road
Gore Road
Whitefield Road
Vincent Rd
Peckham Avenue
New Forest District Council
New Milton Town Council
Spencer Road
Old Milton Rd
Copse Road
Hale Av
Fir Avenue
South Av
Mendip Cl
Caird Avenue
New Milton Recreation Centre
Milton Md
Culver Rd
Cemetery
Hobart Road
Compton Road
Police Station
STATION ROAD B3058
Waverley Road
Milton Gv
Haven Gdns
Eastlands
New Milton Junior School
Infant School
Barton Court Road
Mount Avenue
Cowper Av
Grove
Arnewood School
Old Milton
OLD MILTON GN
Church La
A337
LYMINGTON ROAD
CHRISTCHURCH ROAD
Southlawns Walk
Bouverie Cl
Barton Surgery
Moat Lane
Albany Cl
Hotel
Dorset County
Hampshire County
Holly Lane
J5
1 Breamore Cl
2 Hatfield Ct
3 Stratfield Pl
4 Thoresby Ct
K5
1 Balmoral Wk
2 Brooklyn Ct
3 Foxcote Gdns
4 Linnet Ct
5 Wilton Gdns
K7
1 Manor Farm Cl
2 Moore Cl
3 Prestwood Cl
4 Wendover Cl
Chiltern Drive
Parkland Drive
Three Acre Dr
Eldon Av
Moorland Av
Wavendon Avenue
Hengistbury Road
Seafield Road
Barton Way
Arnolds Close
Barton Dr
Court
Highlands Rd
Farm Lane N
Farm Lane South
Uplands Av
Chestnut
Westbury Close
Ashmore Av
Green La
Greenacre
Barton Cft
Durlston Court School
Newton Rd
Barton Common Lane
B3058
Glen Cl
East Cl
Western
Barton
Byron Road
Sea Road
Knight Park
Seacroft Av
Pine Cl
Carlton Av
Field Place
The Crescent
Bartonside Rd
Cul-De-Sac
Glendrive
The Dell
Drive
Homeopathic
Seaward
Keysworth Avenue
Fairfield
Barton Wd
Beach Avenue
Marine
Cliffe Rd
Purbeck Rd
Meadow Wy
Barton
Mirway
Silverdale
The Martells
MILFORD
M7
1 Baden Cl
2 Greenwoods
M8
1 Arlington Ct
2 Hedgerley
3 Seaway
M3
1 Marston Cl
M6
1 Arden Wk
2 Rothbury Pk
3 Stannington Cl
M2
1 Kamptee Copse
L6
1 Derrybrian Gdns
L7
1 Spindlewood Cl
L4
1 Forest Pines
K6
1 Goldfinch Cl
2 Magpie Gv
3 Wagtail Dr
4 Wren Cl
2
3
4
5
6
7
8

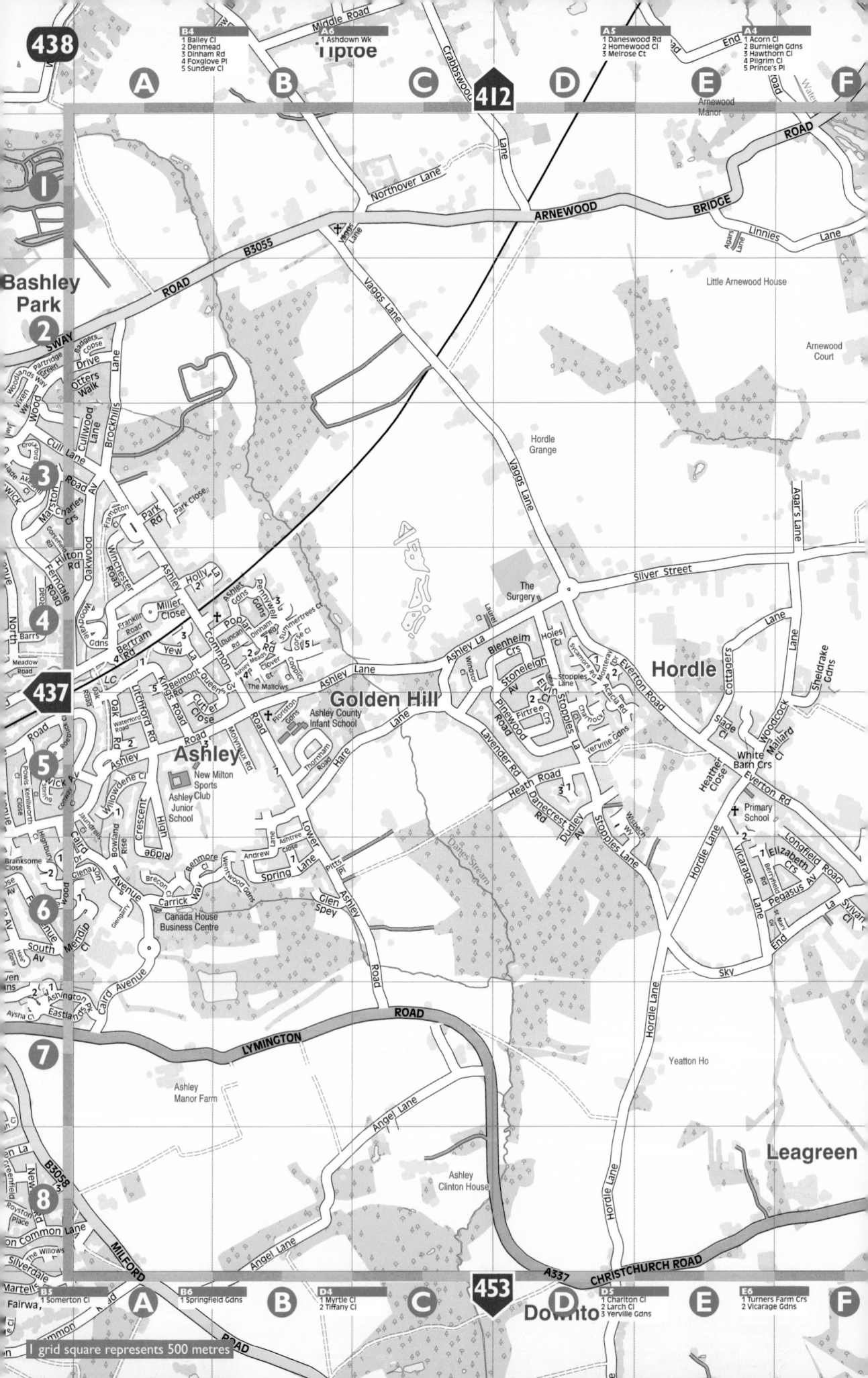

438
B4
1 Bailey Cl
2 Denmead
3 Dinham Rd
4 Foxglove Pl
5 Sundew Cl
A6
1 Ashdown Wk
Tiptoe
412
A5
1 Daneswood Rd
2 Homewood Cl
3 Melrose Ct
A4
1 Acorn Cl
2 Burnleigh Gdns
3 Hawthorn Cl
4 Pilgrim Cl
5 Prince's Pl
Arnewood Manor
Bashley Park
B3055
ARNEWOOD
BRIDGE
ROAD
Northover Lane
Vaggs Lane
Linnies
Little Arnewood House
Arnewood Court
Hordle Grange
Silver Street
The Surgery
Golden Hill
Hordle
Ashley
Ashley County Infant School
New Milton Sports Club
Ashley Junior School
Canada House Business Centre
Primary School
LYMINGTON
ROAD
Ashley Manor Farm
Yeatton Ho
Leagreen
Ashley Clinton House
Angel Lane
Hordle Lane
A337
CHRISTCHURCH ROAD
MILFORD
437
453
B5
1 Somerton Cl
B6
1 Springfield Gdns
D4
1 Myrtle Cl
2 Tiffany Cl
D5
1 Charlton Cl
2 Larch Cl
3 Yerville Gdns
E6
1 Turners Farm Crs
2 Vicarage Gdns
Downton
1 grid square represents 500 metres

G H J **413** K L M

H8
1 Beech Cl
2 Cedar Dr
3 Cherry Tree Cl
4 Oak Gdns

J7
1 Branwood Cl
2 West La

J8
1 Laburnum Dr
2 Wainsford Pltn

Mount Pleasant

Lane

Pauls

Kings Lane

King's Farm

Mount Pl

North Common Lane

Mill Lane

Mount

Pleasant

Lane

I

Flexford

Hazelhurst
Farm

South Sway Lane

Sway Road

2

Sway Road

**Bowling
Green**

Gordleton Industrial Estate

Ramley

Road

3

Gordleton
Farm

Hotel

Silver Street

Ramley

Avon Water

Ramley Road

Northover
Rd

Brownings Cl

Yaldhurst

4

440

Hazel
Road

Pinetops
Cl

St. Marks
Rd

Yaldhurst Lane

Ramley Road

Lodge Road

Cemetery

Arnewood Ho

Batchley Fm

Upr Common Rd

Middle
Common Rd

**Upper
Pennington**

Lawn
Rd

Oliver Rd

PO

Priestlands

5

Wainsford

Road

Wainsford Cl

West Cl

South

Pound Rd

6

Wainsford Ho

Wainsford Road

Pennington
Ov

Conifer
Crs

Howards
Mead

Corbin Road

Efford Way

Broomhill Cl

Broadly

Efford Wy

Haglane Copse

Deneside
Gdns

Harford
Cl

Wainsford Road

Efford Ho

Avon Water

ROAD

7

MILFORD

Greenmead
Avenue

Buckstone

Everton

Everlea
Lane

Frys

Manor Ho

Everton Rd

Golden
Crs

Beacon
Cl

Fox
Fld

Centre Lane

East La

Firmount
Cl

Yeovilton
Cl

Roberts Cl

Elkhams Close

Old Christchurch Rd

Crossways

Farmers
Walk

A337

CHURCH RD

Ash
Grove

Lime
Grove

The Gra

Grange
Close

MILFORD ROAD

Experimental
Horticulture Station

8

G H J **454** K L M

Newlands
Manor

LYMING

Lymore Lan

Barnes

B4
1 Qn Elizab. Av
B5
1 Melbury Cl
B2
1 Bankside
2 Hives Wy
3 Sarum Wk
B3
1 Carpenter Cl
2 Marlborough Pl
A6
1 Kingston Pk
2 Pennington Cl
A7
1 Saracen Cl
A4
1 Bramble Wk
A5
1 Brookland Cl
414
439
455
Portmore
Buckland
Lower Buckland
Walhampton
LYMINGTON
Pennington
Woodside
Waterford
Lower Pennington
SO41
Lymington Town Station
Lymington Pier Station
Ferry Terminal
B6
1 De Mowbray Wy
C3
1 Campion Cl
2 Fromond Cl
3 Seaton Cl
4 William Rd
C4
1 Jasmine Ct
C6
1 Bramley Cl
2 Gold Mead Cl
3 Peartree
4 Peartree Ct
D4
1 Mill La
D5
1 Winton Cl
D6
1 Brackens Wy
2 Conference Pl
3 Worcester Pl
E6
1 Kingsfield
1 grid square represents 500 metres

G   H   J   415   K   L   M

Joys La
Thatchers Lane
Norleywood   Road
St Leonards Rd

1

East End

Brook   Hill

2

Newtown Park

† **South Baddesley**

South Baddesley
C of E Primary
School

Lymington Road

PH

Broom Hill

Rowes Lane

†

Solent Way

3

Solent Way

arm

Road

Sowley Lane

Mill   Lane

Pitts

Deep   Lane

4

442

Sports   Lane

Tanners   Lane

Lisle Court

5

Road

Lisle Court

6

The Solent

7

8

YARMOUTH

G   H   J   K   L   M

St Leonards Rd

St Leonards Road

Beck Farm

Bergerie

Solent Way

A   B   C   D   E   F

East
End

Sowley Lane

Thorns Lane

Thorns Farm

Solent Way

Thorns Beach

Sowley
Pond

Thorns Lane

Thorns Lane

Sowley Lane

Browns Lane

Sandpit Lane

Pitts Deep Lane

Sandpit Lane

Colgrims

Pitts
Deep

A   B   C   D   E   F

1 grid square represents 500 metres

G H J K L M

Ore Point

The Log
House

417

I

Warren Lane

Warren Farm

2

3

Park
Shore

4

rsh

5

6

7

8

G H J K L M

444
429
C6
1 Kangaw Pl
2 Salerno Pl
D4
1 Inglesham Wy
2 Symes Rd
C1
1 Palmerston Cl
C5
1 Freshwater Dr
2 Hercules Rd
3 Nathen Gdns
B4
1 Redhorn Cl
A4
1 Peverell Rd
A1
1 Coronation Av
2 Egdon Ct
3 Foxgloves
4 Purbeck Cl
5 Richard Cl
Creekmoor
Cemetery
A35
A350
UPTON ROAD
POOLE RD
BLANDFORD RD N
BLANDFORD ROAD
B3068
DORCHESTER ROAD
Upton
Upton Infant School
Upton Junior School
Yarrells Preparatory School
Upton Health Centre
Sandy Lane
Upton House
Upton Country Park
Pergins Island
Lytchett Bay
Dorset County
Poole
Turlin Moor
Turlin Moor First School
Turlin Moor Middle School
Hamworthy Station
Hamworthy
Dawkins Business Cen
Hamworthy Community Clinic
BH15
Holes Bay
Rockley Sands
Carter Community School
Hamworthy First Sch
Hamworthy Middle Sch
The Old Rope Wk
Lake
Lower Hamworthy
Wareham Channel
Gold Point
A2
1 Heatherdell
2 Lytchett Wy
3 Shore Gdns
B1
1 Briarswood Rd
2 Davenport Cl
3 Meadows Dr
4 Preston Cl
5 Upton Ct
D5
1 Aldis Gdns
2 Beckhampton Rd
3 Carisbrooke Crs cont.
D5 cont.
4 Inglesham Wy
5 Manton Rd
6 Ridgemount Gdns
7 St Michaels Cl
D6
1 Hamilton Cl
2 Joshua Cl
C4
1 Rice Gdns
E6
1 Hinchliffe Cl
E7
1 Tuckers La
F1
1 Littlemead Cl
2 Oakmead Rd
3 Pilgrims Wy
1 grid square represents 500 metres

G6
1 Bay Hog La
2 Levet's La
3 Marston Rd
4 St Aubyns Ct
5 West Butts St
H6
1 Carter's La
2 Chapel La
3 Emerson Cl
4 Malthouse
5 Vanguard Rd
J2
1 Brampton Rd
J3
1 Simmonds Cl
430
G
H
J
K
L
M
BH17
BH15
Stanley Green
Oakdale
Longfleet
Sterte
POOLE
Fleetsbridge Business Park
FLEET'S CORNER
Sovereign Business Park
Stanley Green Industrial Est
Chalwyn Industrial Estate
Newtown Business Park
St Edward Comprehensive School
Longspee School
Middle School
First School
The Surgery
Oakdale South Road Middle School
Poole Technical High School
Poole Stadium (Speedway Track & Football Stadium)
Poole Town Football Club
Poole Station
Poole Borough Council
Dorset Magistrates Court
Longfleet House Surg
Poole Hospital NHS Trust
A&E
St Marys RC School
Jellicoe Theatre
College
Eagle House School
Bournemouth & Poole College of Further Education
Evergreen Oak Surgery
Poole Co Court Offices
Poole Borough Council
Police Station
Civic Centre Annexe
Buckholme School
Wessex Road Surgery
John Neame
Baden Powell & St Peters C of E (VC) School
Parkstone Cemetery
Poole Park
Poole Arts Centre
Poole Sports Centre
Dolphin Swimming Pool
Dolphin Shopping Centre; Sports Centre and Library
National Slimming & Medical Centres
Aquarium
Poole Pottery
Purbeck Pottery
Poole Harbour
Parkstone Bay
WIMBORNE ROAD
A35
FERNSIDE ROAD
DORSET WAY
A3049
RINGWOOD
SEA VIEW RD
B3061
B3068
B3093
LONGFLEET RD
PARKSTONE ROAD
A350
COMMERCIAL RD
SANDBANKS ROAD
WEST QUAY RD
WEST STREET
TOWNCATE BR
KINGLAND RD
HIGH ST N
446
G7
1 Barbers Piles
2 Cinnamon La
3 New St
4 Paradise St
5 St James Cl
6 Sarum St
7 Thames Ms
H7
1 Drake Rd
2 Fishermans Rd
3 Gray's Yd
4 Propsperous St
5 Taylor's Buildings
J5
1 Cranes Ms
2 Elizabeth Rd
3 Seldown
4 Shaftesbury Rd
456
M5
1 Mentone Rd
M3
1 Woolven Cl
K3
1 Kingsbere Rd
K1
1 Adastral Rd
J6
1 Taverner Cl
M6
1 Daylesford Cl
2 Waterford Cl
3 Woodstock Rd
M4
1 Conways Dr
M1
1 White Cl
L3
1 Pound Cl
K2
1 Stenhurst Rd
J7
1 Balter Gdns
2 Ballard Cl
3 Colborne Cl
4 Green Cl

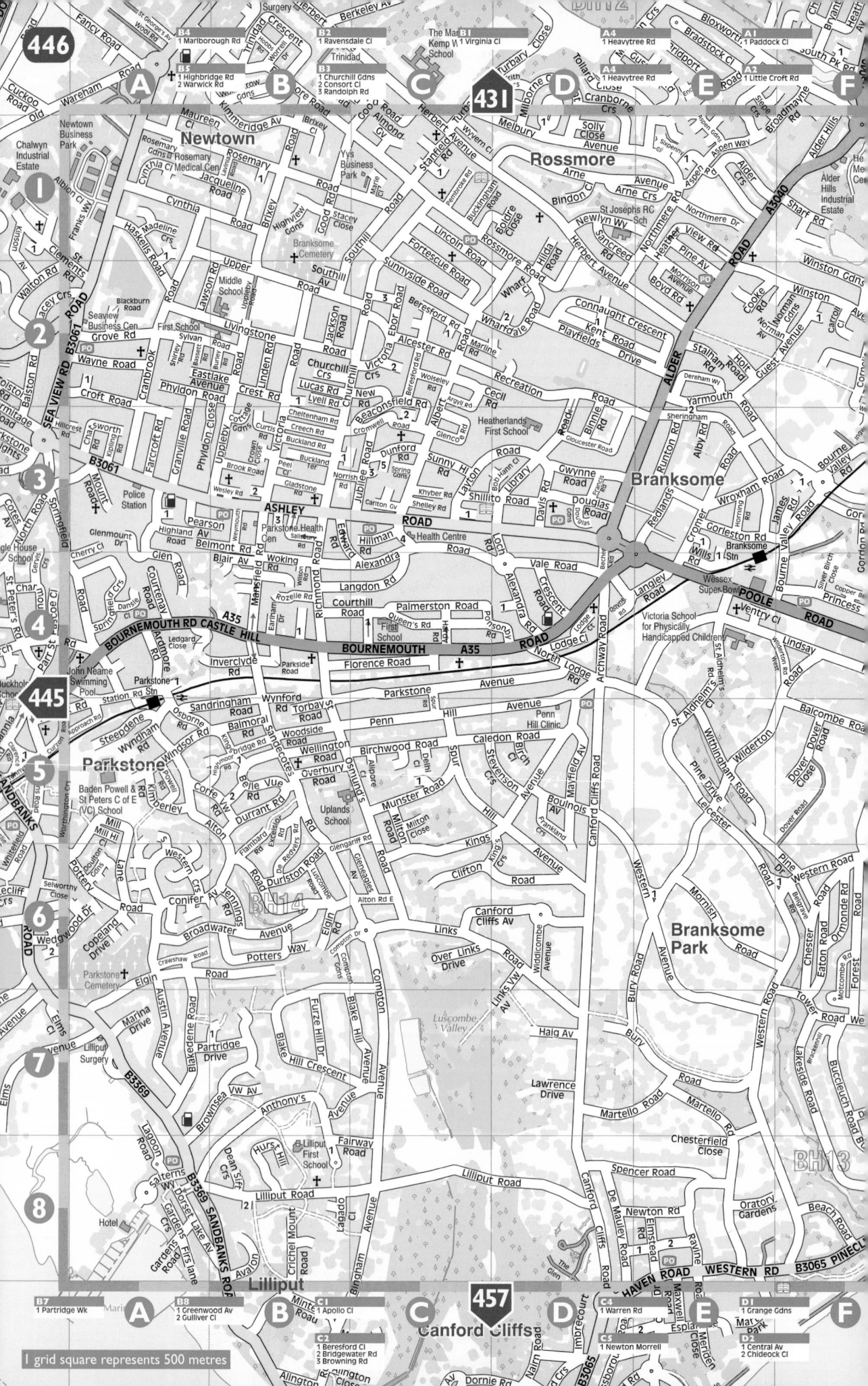
B4
1 Marlborough Rd
B5
1 Highbridge Rd
2 Warwick Rd
B2
1 Ravensdale Cl
B3
1 Churchill Gdns
2 Consort Cl
3 Randolph Rd
B1
1 Virginia Cl
A4
1 Heavytree Rd
A4
1 Heavytree Rd
A1
1 Paddock Cl
A2
1 Little Croft Rd
431
445
457
Newtown
Newtown Business Park
Chalwyn Industrial Estate
Rossmore
Alder Hills Industrial Estate
Branksome
Branksome Park
Parkstone
Lilliput
Canford Cliffs
Ashley Road
Bournemouth Rd
Castle Hill
Bournemouth Road
A35
A3040
Alder Road
Poole Road
Seaview Rd
B3061
B3369
Sandbanks Road
B3065
Pinecliff
Haven Road
Western Rd
Wareham Road
Old Wareham Road
Cuckoo Road
Fancy Road
Kimmeridge Av
Rosemary Road
Jacqueline Road
Cynthia Road
Upper Road
Livingstone Road
Churchill Rd
Victoria Road
Jubilee Road
Richmond Road
Mansfield Rd
Alexandra Rd
Palmerston Road
Courthill Road
Florence Road
Parkstone Avenue
Penn Hill Avenue
Caledon Road
Birchwood Road
Munster Road
Uplands School
Canford Cliffs Road
Western Avenue
Bury Road
Martello Road
Chesterfield Close
Spencer Road
Lilliput Road
Compton Avenue
Luscombe Valley
Haig Av
Lawrence Drive
Links Road
Canford Cliffs Av
Kings Avenue
Clifton Road
Durrant Rd
Broadwater Avenue
Potters Way
Elgin Road
Parkstone Cemetery
Branksome Cemetery
Middle School
Heatherlands First School
Parkstone Health Cen
Health Centre
Police Station
John Neame Swimming Pool
Parkstone Stn
Branksome Stn
Wessex Super Bowl
Victoria School for Physically Handicapped Children
St Josephs RC Sch
Baden Powell & St Peters C of E (VC) School
Lilliput First School
Penn Hill Clinic
Yys Business Park
Seaview Business Cen
Lilliput Surgery
Hotel
Recreation Road
Sunnyside Road
Rossmore Road
Herbert Avenue
Connaught Crescent
Playfields Drive
Wharfdale Road
Yarmouth Road
Wroxham Road
Bourne Valley Rd
Gorleston Rd
Princess Road
Lindsay Road
Balcombe Road
Western Road
Mornish Road
Tower Road
Lakeside Road
Buccleuch Road
Beach Road
Oratory Gardens
Newton Rd
BH14
BH13
B7
1 Partridge Wk
B8
1 Greenwood Av
2 Gulliver Cl
C1
1 Apollo Cl
C2
1 Beresford Cl
2 Bridgewater Rd
3 Browning Rd
C4
1 Warren Rd
C5
1 Newton Morrell
D1
1 Grange Gdns
D2
1 Central Av
2 Chideock Cl
1 grid square represents 500 metres

Bournemouth 447
Talbot Village
G5 1 Eldon Pl 2 Seamoor La
G6 1 Drury Rd 2 Groveley Rd
H1 1 Bishop Cl
H5 1 Heatherbank Rd 2 Landseer Rd
H7 1 Crosby Rd
J4 1 Kensington Dr
J5 1 Suffolk Rd S
K4 1 Durrant Rd
432
Winton
Talbot Woods
Talbot Avenue A347
Alma Road A3049
Charminster Road
Meyrick Park
Meyrick Park Golf Course
22
23
Lansdowne Road
Wimborne Road
Dean Park Cricket Ground
BH3
BH2
BH4
Wessex Way A338
Richmond Hill Roundabout
448
Westbourne
West Cliff
Bournemouth
Poole Bay
Pier Theatre
Oceanarium
International Centre & Leisure Pool
Russell-Cotes Art Gallery & Museum
Alum Chine
West Undercliff Promenade
E6 1 Bury Rd
F6 1 Leicester Rd
C3 1 Carnegie Cl 2 Heatherlands Ri 3 Jubilee Crs 4 Madeira Rd 5 The Drive
E1 1 Cashmoor Cl
E8 1 Chaucer Rd 2 Moorfields Rd
E3 1 Cromer Gdns 2 Thetford Rd
F2 1 Guest Cl
K6 1 Durley Rd South 2 Durley Rbt 3 Hahnemann Rd 4 Kerley Rd 5 South View Pl 6 West Cliff Gdns
D4 1 Highwood Rd
E4 1 Cardigan Rd
F3 1 Yarmouth Cl
458
M5 1 Cumnor Rd 2 St Peters Rbt
M6 1 Bath Hill Rbt
M3 1 Coach House Pl
M4 1 The Firs 2 Lansdowne Gdns 3 Park Rd 4 St Pauls Rbt
L6 1 B. Int Cen Rbt 2 Exeter Park Rd 3 South Cliff Rd
L4 1 St Stephen's Wy
L5 1 Albert Rd 2 Post Office Rd 3 Verulam Pl
L1 1 Bonham Rd 2 Crimea Rd
L2 1 Rushton Crs
K5 1 Mannington Pl 2 Orchard St 3 The Triangle 4 West Hill Pl

448
433
447
23
A
B
C
D
E
F
1
2
3
4
5
6
7
8
C4
1 Hengist Rd
D3
1 Palmerstone Ms
2 Shelley Cl
C2
1 Avon Cl
2 Bethia Cl
3 Egerton Gdns
4 Richmond Pk Cl
5 Richmond Pk Rd
6 St Ledger's Pl
A5
1 The Lan. Rbt
2 Meyrick Rd
3 Weston Dr
A3
1 Ascham Rd
A4
1 B. Stn Rbt
2 Oxford Rd
3 St Paul's Pl
B2
1 Lawrence Ct
2 Malmesbury Ct
3 Melbourne Rd
4 Nortoft Rd
5 Shelbourne Cl
B3
1 Corporation Rd
2 Elwyn Rd
3 Henville Rd
4 Lowther Gdns
5 Mlmsbry Pk Pl
6 Methuen Cl
7 Methuen Rd
8 Stewart Cl
C3
1 Austin Cl
Queen's Park
Littledown
Portchester School
Springbourne
Boscombe
BOURNEMOUTH
Dean Court (Bournemouth FC)
King's Park
Kings Park Primary School
Kings Park Community Hosp
East Cemetery
Bournemouth & East Dorset Hosp Management Committee
The Bournemouth Nuffield Hospital
Lansdowne Clinic
Parkway Retail Park
Bournemouth Station
Superstore
Central Business Park
Bournemouth College
Bournemouth Court
Bournemouth Business Cen
University
College
Shelley Museum
Boscombe Manor Medical Centre
Boscombe Dental Health Centre
Malmesbury Park School
Linwood School
Cemetery
Richmond Court Business Cen
St Clements
Bethany C of E Junior School
Russell-Cotes Art Gallery Museum
WESSEX WAY
HOLDENHURST RD
ASHLEY ROAD
CHRISTCHURCH ROAD
RICHMOND PARK ROAD
ST PAULS RD
ST SWITHUN'S RD S
A35
A338
A3049
B3063
B3064
B3059
BH1
BH5
Overcliff Drive
Undercliff Drive
Boscombe Cliff Road
D4
1 Carnarvon Rd
2 Palmerston Rd
3 Randolph Rd
4 Salisbury Rd
D5
1 Michelgro. Rd
E3
1 Ashley Rd
2 Haviland Rd West
3 Tamworth Rd
E4
1 Grantley Rd
E5
1 Woll'craft Rd
F1
1 Henley Gdns
1 grid square represents 500 metres

G
- **G1**
  1 Petersfield Pl
  2 Swanmore Cl
- **G2**
  1 Durrington Pl
  2 Harewood Pl

G5
1 Rotherfield Rd

G4
1 Seabourne Rd

H
- **H1**
  1 Southwick Pl
- **H2**
  1 Amesbury Rd

L
1 Appletree Cl
2 Douglas Ms

434

450

G3
1 Ashbourne Rd
2 Chilcombe Rd
3 Connaught Rd
4 Cromwell Pl
5 Hampden La
6 Seabourne Pl
7 Southville Rd
8 Stedman Rd
9 Stourvale Pl

M1
1 Addiscombe Rd
2 Arthur La

M2
1 Turnberry Cl

M3
1 Magnolia Cl
2 Wickmeads Rd
3 Willow Wy

M4
1 Kingsley Av

M5
1 Stevenson Rd

F3
1 Colonnade Rd
2 Morley Rd
3 Pauncefote Rd
4 Rosebery Rd
5 St James's Sq
6 West Rd

G
- **G4**
  1 Twynham Rd
- **G5**
  1 Admiralty Rd
  2 Shires Copse
  3 Warren Edge Cl

H
- **L2**
  1 Galton Av
  2 Wentworth Dr
- **L3**
  1 Riverside Rd

J

L1
1 Hussar Cl

K
- **K2**
  1 Kingfisher Cl
- **K5**
  1 Avoncliffe Rd
  2 Bolton Rd

L

J3
1 Heytesbury Rd

M
- **J1**
  1 Shakespeare Rd
- **J2**
  1 Kittiwake Cl

450

435

449

D2
1 Alexander Cl
2 Buccaneers Cl
3 Groveley Rd
4 Johnstone Rd
5 Rosedale Cl
6 Stroud Gdns

D1
1 Bingham Cl
2 Court Cl
3 Wolfe Cl

C2
1 Addington Pl
2 Asquith Cl
3 Grafton Cl

A5
1 Selfridge Cl

C1
1 Amsterdam Sq
2 Cameron Rd
3 Chant Cl
4 Delft Ms
5 Haking Rd
6 Livingstone Rd
7 Utrecht Ct

CHURCH

Purewell

Somerford

Stanpit

CHRISTCHURCH

Wick

Christchurch
Harbour

Dorset County
Bournemouth

Hengistbury
Head

D3
1 Harbour Crs

E1
1 Amethyst Rd
2 Marmion Gn
3 Southey Rd

E2
1 Drake Cl
2 Frobisher Cl
3 The Hawthorns

E3
1 Mudeford Gn Cl

E4
1 Hamilton Cl

F2
1 Ambassador Cl
2 Cunningham Cl
3 Grebe Cl
4 Lark Rd

F3
1 Anchor Cl
2 Mountbatten Cl
3 Partridge Cl

1 grid square represents 500 metres

A2
1 Regent Wy
2 Silver St
3 Wickfield Cl
A4
1 Roscrea Cl
G1
1 Beaufort Cl
2 Britannia Wy
3 Caledonian Cl
4 Sunderland Dr
5 Swordfish Dr
G2
1 B Homage Gdns
2 Sopwith Cl
3 The Coppice
H1
1 Auckland Rd
2 Saxonford Rd
L1
1 Abbots Cl
436
452
LYMINGTON RD
SHELLEY HL
A337
Highcliffe Castle Golf Club
Friars Cliff
Highcliffe Medical Centre
Wellington Av
Rothesay Drive
Wharncliffe Road
Waterford Gardens
Waterford Road
Stuart Road
Seafield Road
Hynesbury Road
Southcliffe Road
Friars Road
Avon Run Road
Bure Lane
Seaway Avenue
East Cliff Way
Capesthorne
Hotel
Business

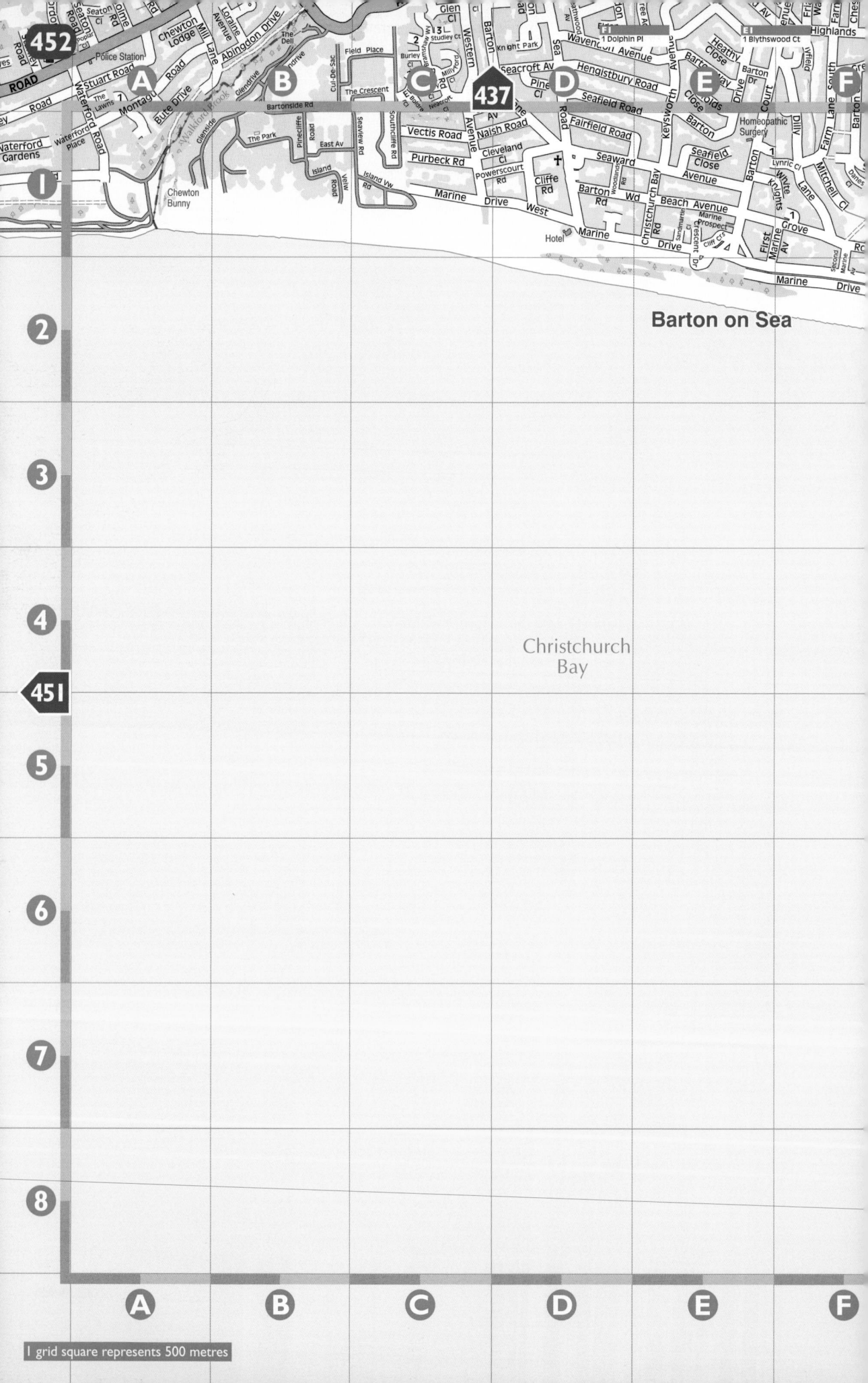

ROAD

Waterford
Gardens

Police Station

Stuart Road

Chewton Lodge

Mill Lane

Abingdon Drive

Glendrive

The Dell

Field Place

Glen Cl

3 L Studley Ct

Burley

Western

Barton

Knight Park

Wavendon Av

1 Dolphin Pl

Dolphin Avenue

F1

Heathy Close

1 Blythswood Ct

E1

Highlands

A **B** **C** 437 **D** **E** **F**

The Lawns 7

Montagu

Bute Drive

Walkford Brook

Glenside

The Park

Pinecliffe Road

East Av

Island Road

Seaview Rd

Southcliffe Rd

Bartonside Rd

The Crescent

Vectis Road

Purbeck Rd

Cleveland Cl

Powerscourt Rd

Naish Road

Avenue

Seacroft Av

Hengistbury Road

Pine Cl

Seafield Road

Fairfield Road

Keysworth Avenue

Barton Close

Homeopathic Surgery

Seafield Close

Barton Court

Lynric Cl

Barton Dr

White Knights

Dilly Lane

Farm Lane

Mitchell Cl

Chewton Bunny

Island Vw Rd

View Road

Island Vw

Marine Drive West

Cliffe Rd

Hotel

Marine

Christchurch Rd

Barton Rd

Wd

Woodland Rd

Seaward

Beach Avenue

Marine Prospect

Crescent

Marine Dr

Cliff Cts

First Marine Av

Grove

Second Marine Av

Marine Drive

Barton on Sea

**Christchurch
Bay**

451

1

2

3

4

5

6

7

8

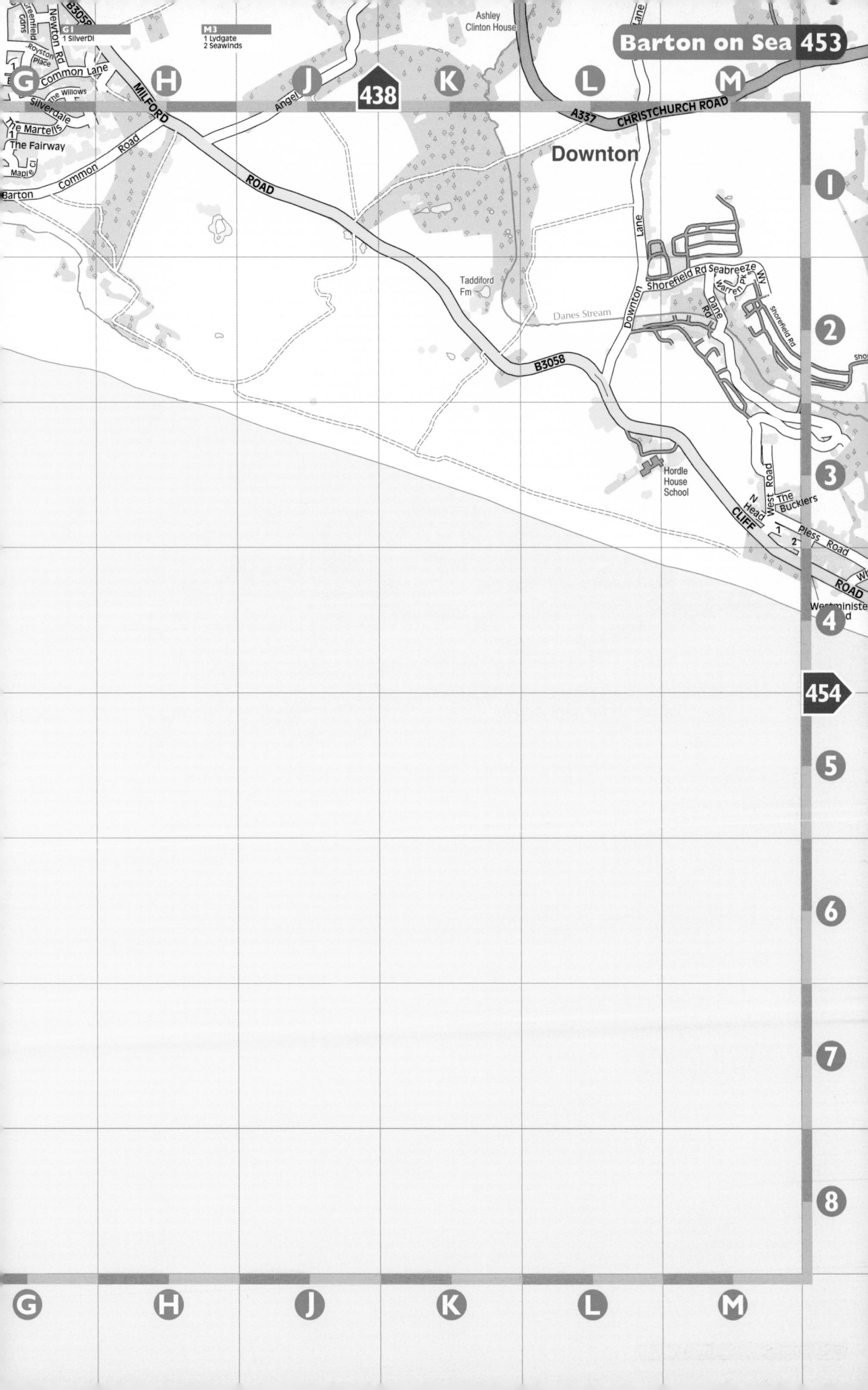

G H J 438 K L M

CHRISTCHURCH ROAD
A337

Downton

Taddiford Fm

Danes Stream

B3058

Hordle House School

Ashley Clinton House

MILFORD

Common ROAD

Angel Lane

Barton

The Fairway
The Martells
Silverdale
The Willows
Newton Rd
B3058
Royston Place
Common Lane
G1
1 SilverDl
M3
1 Lydgate
2 Seawinds
Mapl

Downton Lane
Shorefield Rd
Seabreeze Rd
Warren Pk
Ivy
Dane Rd
Shorefield Rd
sho

West Road
The Bucklers
N Head
CLIFF
Pless Road
1
2
ROAD
Wr
Westminster Rd

I
2
3
4
454
5
6
7
8

G H J K L M

C4
1 Danestream Cl
C3
1 GlebeFlds
B4
1 Woodland Wy
Experimental Horticulture Stati
Ash Grove
Lime Grove
439
453
Newlands Manor
Barnes Lane
Barnes La
LYMING
Lymore Lane
Lymore Va
Lymore
Agarton Lane
Hotel
Milford C of E School
School Lane
B3058
Manor Rd
Manor Close
Kitwalls Lane
Knowland Dr
Lymefields
Greenways
Shorefield Way
Shorefield Wy
George Rd
Shorefield Road
Blackbush Road
Shorefield Crs
Sycamore Cl
Wayside
Broadfields Close
Deans Ct
Sharvells Road
Studland Dr
Vinegar Hl
Windmill Cl
Chaucer Dr
Keats Av
Dryden Pl
Wolsey Wy
Lyndale Cl
Carrington Lane
Carrington Cl
Church Hl
Greenbanks Cl
Danes Stream
West
N Head
The Bucklers
CLIFF
Pless Road
Holly Gdns
New Valley Road
Mill Meadow
Wood La
The Orchard
Milford Ct
MILFORD CRS
Park Cl
Park Road
Northfields Rd
Lawn Cl
Lawn Rd
Whitby Rd
ROAD
Maryland Gdns
Cornwallis Rd
St Georges Hospital
Victoria Road
De La Warr Rd
Hamilton Ct
Kivernell Road
Kensington Park
Rookcliff Wy
HIGH STREET
High St
Solent Wy
Champion Cl
Eastern Wy
Aubrey Cl
Westminister Road
B3058
PARK LANE
Lucerne Rd
River Gdns
Sea Road
Keyhaven Road
Keyhaven
Laundry La
Swallow Dr
Plover Dr
Grebe Cl
Shingle Bank Dr
Westover Rd
Ravens Wy
Needles Point
Gillingham Rd
War Memorial Hosp
Overstand Crs
Manderley
Sea Rd
Island View Close
Castle Cl
Aubrey House
Keyh
MILFORD ON SEA
Hurst Road
New Lane
Sturt Pond
Solent Way
Solent Wy
Lymore
Lane
Lane
1
2
A
B
C
D
E
F
1
2
3
4
5
6
7
8
1 grid square represents 500 metres

Lower
Pennington

440

The Salterns

Woodside

PH

Platoff

Woodside

Lwr Pennington Lane

Iley Lane

Pennington House

Pennington
Marshes

Solent Way

Solent Way

Avon Water

Keyhaven
Marshes

Solent Way

Solent Way

Solent Way

G H J K L M

G H J K L M

I 2 3 4 5 6 7 8

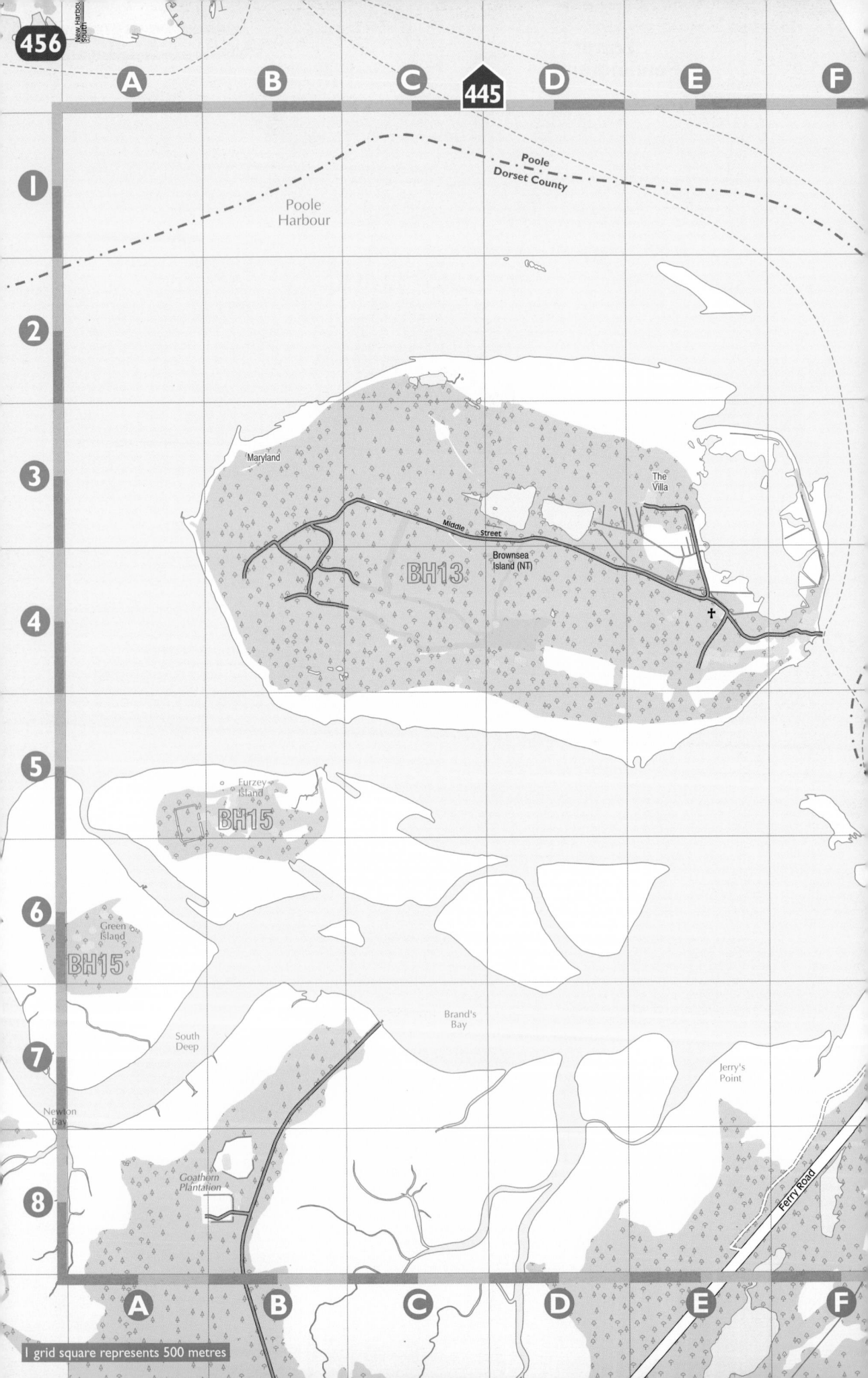

New Harbour South

A   B   C   445   D   E   F

1

Poole
Dorset County

Poole
Harbour

2

3   Maryland

The
Villa

Middle   Street

BH13   Brownsea
Island (NT)

†

4

5   Furzey
Island

BH15

6   Green
Island

BH15

Brand's
Bay

South
Deep

7

Jerry's
Point

Newton
Bay

Ferry Road

8   Goathorn
Plantation

A   B   C   D   E   F

I grid square represents 500 metres

G H J K L M

1 Harbour Cl
1 Chad. Wood Rd

1 Beaumont Rd
2 Bodley Rd
3 Macandrew Rd

Lilliput

Canford Cliffs

Mount Grace Drive

Alington
Alington Close

Minterne Road

Dornie Rd

Brudenell Av

Brudenell Road

Canford Crs

Nairn Road

SHORE ROAD

HAVEN ROAD

Chaddesley

B3369

Hotel

St Anns Hospital

Glen

Flaghead Chine Rd

Cliff Drive

St Clair Rd

Bessborough Road

Flaghead Rd

Imbrecourt

Esplanade

Maxwell Road

Meriden Close

Martello Park

HAVEN ROAD

WESTERN RD **B3065**

Canford Cliffs Chine

Flag Head Chine

Shore Road

Hotel

Poole Head

BANKS ROAD

B3369

PO

Coastguard Road

PANORAMA ROAD

Grasmere

Seacombe Road

Brownsea Road

Salter Rd

BANKS ROAD

B3369

Sandbanks

Hotel

FERRY WY

Ferry Wy

Shell Bay

South West Coast Path

CHERBOURG

GUERNSEY AND JERSEY
SUMMER ONLY

SANTANDER
VIA JERSEY
WINTER ONLY

446

Branksome

1 2 3 4 5 6 7 8

G H J K L M

Studland Bay

Abbotstone 193 L6
Abbotswood 262 F5
Abbots Worthy 215 J2
Abbotts Ann 141 K5
Abshot 370 E8
Alderholt 333 K2
Aldermaston 41 J1
Aldermaston Soke 42 C5
Aldermaston Wharf 29 M5
Aldermoor 317 M5
Alderney 431 G7
Aldershot 6 F1
Allbrook 293 M2
Alton 176 D5
Alverstoke 18 B7
Ameysford 380 A7
Ampfield 264 B5
Amport 140 F3
Anchorage Park 400 A5
Andover 9 J5
Andover Down 119 M8
Andwell 106 F3
Anmore 351 M4
Anna Valley 142 C3
Ann's Hill 18 A1
Ansteadbrook 229 M3
Anthill Common 351 H2
Applemore 366 E4
Appleshaw 117 G2
Arborfield Garrison 47 K1
Arford 202 B2
Ash 113 K5
Ashe 101 K8
Ashfield 291 G4
Ashford 309 J7
Ashford Hill 40 B7
Ashlett 393 G5
Ashley 211 L5
Ashley 382 A3
Ashley 438 A5
Ashley Heath 381 K2
Ashmansworth 75 L1
Ashton 297 G5
Ashurst 341 G6
Ashurst Bridge 341 G3
Ash Vale 113 K2
Avington 216 D3
Avon 408 D6
Awbridge 261 K4
Axford 151 H5
Axmansford 60 F1
Badshot Lea 135 M2
Baffins 423 M1
Bagmore 152 F2
Bagshot 32 C1
Bagshot 51 M5
Bailey Green 245 H5
Ball Hill 35 M5
Balmerlawn 387 M5
Bank 363 H5
Bar End 239 G2
Barford 181 H8
Barrow Hill 315 J6
Barrow Hill 428 B4
Bartley 339 L1
Barton on Sea 452 E2
Barton Stacey 167 J2
Bashley 437 L1
Bashley Park 437 M2
Basingstoke 4 C6
Bassett 318 F3
Bassett Green 318 F3
Battramsley 413 L6
Battramsley Cross 414 A7
Batt's Corner 180 A1
Baughurst 61 G1
Baybridge 268 B5
Beacon Hill 204 A1
Beacon Hill 428 E6
Bear Cross 431 K2
Bearwood 431 K2
Beaulieu 390 C7
Beauworth 241 M8
Beckley 437 G3
Bedhampton 377 G7
Beech 175 M7
Beech Hill 44 F3
Beenham 29 J2
Beenham Stocks 29 L2
Bell Hill 275 K3
Bentley 156 E3
Bentworth 174 E3
Bickton 334 D2
Bidden 130 C1
Bighton 195 H7
Binley 75 L8
Binstead 178 D1
Birchy Hill 413 G7
Bishop's Green 38 D5
Bishop's Sutton 219 G4
Bishopstoke 294 B6
Bishop's Waltham 297 G7
Bisterne 408 D2
Bisterne Close 385 H6
Bitterne 344 C1
Bitterne Park 319 J7
Black Dam 105 J5
Blackfield 392 E8
Blackhill 288 F7
Blackmoor 224 E1
Blacknest 179 J1
Blackwater 70 A4
Blackwater 433 M3
Blashford 358 D5
Bleak Hill 334 A5
Blendworth 353 J1
Blissford 310 D8
Boarhunt 373 M3
Bohemia 285 L4
Boldre 414 B7
Boorley Green 321 K6
Borden 278 C2
Bordon 201 H5
Boscombe 448 D4
Bossington 210 A5
Botley 346 F2
Boundstone 158 E4
Bournemouth 23 G6
The Bourne 158 F2
Bourne Valley 446 F2
Boveridge 306 F6
Bowling Alley 110 B8
Bowling Green 439 K2
Boyatt Wood 293 L3
Bradley 152 A8
Braishfield 263 H1
Brambridge 266 C8
Bramdean 243 H3
Bramley 63 K4
Bramley Corner 63 G5
Bramley Green 63 M6
Bramshaw 313 L4
Bramshill 66 E1
Bramshott 226 F2
Branksome 446 D3
Branksome Park 446 E6
Bransbury 144 F7
Bransgore 409 M8
Breach 379 H7
Breamore 283 M7
Bridgemary 396 F5
Brighton Hill 104 C8
Brimpton 40 B2
Brimpton Common 40 F6
Broad Chalke 252 A1
Broadgate 264 D6
Broad Layings 36 B7
Broadmere 127 J4
Broad Oak 108 F4
Broadoak 346 C1
Broadstone 429 M4
Brockbridge 299 J6
Brockenhurst 387 J7
Brockhampton 16 A7
Brockhurst 421 H2
Brock's Green 58 D1
Brook 234 B2
Brook 313 M8
Brooke's Hill 316 A4
Brook Hill 313 M6
Broughton 209 H2
Brown Candover 172 A5
Browndown 420 F5
Brown Heath 322 B3
Browninghill Green 61 J5
Bucket Corner 292 B1
Buckland 440 A3
Bucklers Hard 417 G3
Bucks Horn Oak 157 K8
Buckskin 103 M4
Bull Hill 414 F7
Bunker's Hill 314 F6
Bunstead 265 H2
Burgates 248 D2
Burghclere 57 J1
Burghclere Common 37 K7
Burghfield 31 M3
Burghfield Common 31 K6
Burghfield Hill 31 M5
Buriton 303 K3
Burley 384 F5
Burley Beacon 384 C6
Burley Lawn 385 G5
Burley Street 384 C3
Burridge 346 F7
Bursledon 345 L8
Burton 435 G7
Bury's Bank 38 B1
Butlocks Heath 369 H1
Buttermere 53 H1
Buttsash 367 M8
Butt's Green 232 F7
The Butts 176 D6
Cadnam 314 E8
Calmore 316 B7
Calshot 393 K8
Camberley 71 H1
Camel Green 333 M2
Camelsdale 228 D3
Canada 288 C7
Canford Cliffs 457 J1
Canford Heath 430 C7
Canford Magna 404 E7
Carter's Clay 260 F2
Catherington 327 M7
Catisfield 371 L7
Causeway 275 K6
Causeway 352 F3
Chalton 329 G3
Chandlers Green 65 J6
Charlton 118 D6
Chandler's Ford 265 J8
Charlton-All-Saints 256 E4
Charlwood 221 H5
Charminster 433 G7
Charter Alley 61 L8
Chawton 198 C1
Cheriton 242 C3
Chidden 300 E8
Chilbolton 165 M4
Chilbolton Down 188 D2
Chilcomb 239 L3
Chilton Candover 172 D3
Chilworth 292 C7
Chilworth Old Village 292 B6
Chineham 83 L5
Chithurst 278 F5
Cholderton 138 B7
Christchurch 450 A3
Church Common 247 G8
Church Crookham 110 E3
Church End 84 B2
Church Oakley 102 D6
Churt 181 J7
Chute Cadley 94 C1
Chute Standen 72 A8
Clanfield 327 M2
Clanville 117 J1
Clarken Green 102 C6
Clatford Oakcuts 163 M4
Clayhall 19 G8
Clayhill 363 L5
Cliddesden 127 L1
Colbury 341 H6
Cold Ash 26 F1
Cold Ash Hill 227 H3
Colden Common 266 F7
Cole Henley 99 J5
Colehill 404 D1
Colemore 222 C6
College Town 50 B8
Colt Hill 108 E5
Colthrop 27 L5
Combe 54 A2
The Common 206 F2
Compton 135 J7
Compton 234 B1
Compton 266 C1
Compton 330 D6
Compton End 238 B7
Conford 226 C1
Coombe 300 E2
Copnor 399 L7
Copythorne 315 H6
Corfe Mullen 429 G2
Corhampton 299 G3
Cosham 375 L8
Cottonworth 165 K4
Couch Green 216 B1
Court Corner 62 A5
Cove 90 B2
Cowesfield Green 259 H5
Cowplain 352 D5
Coxford 317 M6
Crab Orchard 356 C6
Crampmoor 263 K7
Cranborne 306 C8
Cranbourne 104 E6
Crawley 189 G6
Crawley Hill 71 H3
Creekmoor 429 L8
Crendell 332 D1
Cricket Hill 69 H3
Criddlestyle 310 A7
Cripplestyle 332 E3
Critchell's Green 232 E8
Critchmere 228 B1
Crockerhill 372 E1
Crockham Heath 36 C2
Crondall 133 H1
Crookham 39 L3
Crookham Village 110 B2
Crosswater 181 H4
Crossways 181 H7
Croucheston 252 F1
Crow 383 G4
Crowdhill 295 H3
Crowthorne 49 J4
Crux Easton 75 M3
Cuckoo's Corner 155 K8
Cufaude 83 K1
Cupernham 262 F7
Curbridge 347 H4
Curdridge 322 D8
Custards 363 L3
Daggons 333 G3
Damerham 308 C3
Daneshill 5 M2
Darby Green 69 K2
Deadwater 201 L5
Dean 213 K5
Dean 297 K5
Deane 101 M7
Deanlane End 354 B3
Deepcut 91 M2
The Dene 74 E8
Denmead 351 K3
Denvilles 17 L2
Dewlands Common 356 B3
Dibden 367 H3
Dibden Purlieu 367 G7
Dilton 414 D1
Dipley 66 D8
Dippenhall 134 A6
Dockenfield 180 C2
Dogmersfield 109 M2
Donnington 25 G2
Dora's Green 133 M3
Downton 285 C1
Downton 453 L1
Drayton 376 A8
Droxford 298 F7
Dry Hill 196 D3
Dudsbury 406 A7
Dummer 126 C7
Dumpford 278 D8
Dunbridge 233 H7
Dundridge 298 A7
Dunley 76 F8
Durleighmarsh 276 F5
Durley 322 A2
Durley Street 296 B8
Durns Town 413 G6
Durrants 353 M8
Earlstone Common 37 J8
East Anton 119 H4
East Aston 145 J1
East Boldre 416 B3
East Cholderton 140 E2
East Dean 231 M6
East End 55 K1
East End 272 C3
East End 441 M1
East Fields 3 G6
East Green 157 H2
East Grimstead 230 B4
East Harting 305 J5
East Howe 432 A5
Eastland Gate 352 B3
Eastleigh 294 A5
East Liss 249 G5
East Marden 331 L6
East Martin 281 H4
East Meon 273 J8
Eastney 424 A5
East Oakley 103 H6
Eastoke 426 A6
Easton 215 M3
East Parley 407 J8
Eastrop 5 J9
East Stratton 170 F4
East Tisted 222 B3
East Tytherley 232 E1
East Wellow 288 F3
East Winterslow 182 E8
East Woodhay 55 H1
East Worldham 177 K7
Ebblake 357 H4
Ecchinswell 58 D5
Egbury 98 B2
Egypt 168 C3
Eling 341 M3
Ellingham 358 C3
Ellisfield 128 A8
Elmers Marsh 251 K3
Elson 397 L8
Elsted 305 M4
Elvetham 88 A3
Emery Down 363 H2
Empshott 223 M5
Empshott Green 223 L5
Emsworth 402 C1
Enborne 24 C8
Enborne Row 36 E4
Enham Alamein 119 H1
Ensbury 432 C2
Ensbury Park 432 A6
Eversley 47 L7
Eversley Centre 48 A8
Eversley Cross 48 C8
Everton 439 J7
Ewshot 110 F8
Exbury 417 M3
Exton 299 H1
Faberstown 93 G7
Faccombe 54 E7
Fairmile 434 D7
Fair Oak 60 B1
Fair Oak 295 H6
Fair Oak Green 64 A2
Fareham 14 F5
Farleigh Wallop 127 K6
Farley 206 C8
Farley Hill 47 G3
Farlington 376 B8
Farnborough 90 D5
Farnborough Green 90 F3
Farnborough Park 91 G5
Farnborough Street 90 F3
Farnham 135 G7
Fawley 392 F6
Ferndown 405 M3
Filmore Hill 244 F4
Finchampstead 48 A5
Finchdean 354 B2
Firsdown 206 A1
Fisher's Pond 295 G2
Fleet 88 F7
Fleet 401 K8
Fleetend 370 D7
Fleetlands 397 G3
Flexford 264 E8
Flood Street 309 L1
Folly Hill 134 D3
Fordingbridge 309 M7
Forest Gate 351 H1
Forestside 354 F2
Forton 144 E4
Forton 421 M2
Fosbury 52 C7
Foulford 383 L1
Four Houses Corner 31 H8
Four Marks 197 H6
Foxdown 101 H6
Foxhills 341 H5
Fox Lane 70 C7
Foyers 340 A5
Fratton 423 J2
Freefolk 122 E2
Freemantle 343 G2
The Frenches 261 G6
Frenchmoor 231 L2
Frensham 180 E1
Friars Cliff 451 H2
Frimley 71 K6
Frimley Green 91 J1
Frimley Ridge 71 K5
Fritham 312 E7
Frithend 179 M5
Frogham 335 J2
Frogmore 69 L2
Frostlane 368 A6
Froxfield Green 246 B8
Fryern Hill 293 J2
Fulflood 10 B6
Fullerton 165 H5
Funtley 372 C3
Furzedown 235 G1
Furze Hill 335 J5
Furzeley Corner 351 K7
Furzey 338 E5
Furzey Lodge 389 M7
Furzley 314 C3
Fyfield 116 D6
Fyning 277 M3
Gilbert Street 220 E2
Glebe 323 H5
Gobley Hole 127 H8
Godshill 310 D6
Godswinscroft 435 M3
Goldenhayes 339 M4
Golden Hill 438 B5
Golden Pot 154 C5
Goldfinch Bottom 38 F3
Goodworth Clatford 142 E7
Goose Green 363 L4
Goose Hill 39 L5
Gore End 35 L4
Gosport 19 H2
Gosport 263 M6
Gotham 332 C5
Grange Estate 381 K8
Grateley 139 M7
Grayshott 203 L5
Grayswood 205 K7
Greatham 224 E7
Great Shoddesden 115 M2
Green Cross 181 L7
Greenham 25 M8
The Green 232 A1
Greywell 107 K5
Griggs Green 226 C4
Gundleton
Habin
Hale
Hale
Halecommon
Halterworth
Ham
Hambledon
Hamble-le-Rice
Hambrook
Hammer
Hammer Bottom
Hampreston
Hampton Park
Hamptworth
Hamstead Marshall
Hamworthy
Hangersley
Hannington
Harbridge
Harbridge Green
Hardley
Hardway
Harefield
Harestock
Hartfordbridge
Hartley Mauditt
Hartley Wespall
Hartley Wintney
Haslemere
Hatch
Hatch Bottom
Hatchet Gate
Hatchet Green
Hatch Farm Hill
Hatch Warren
Hatherden
Hatt Hill
Hattingley
Haughurst Hill
Havant
Hawkley
Hawley
Hawley Lane
Hawthorn
Hayling Island
Hazeley
Hazeley Bottom
Hazeley Lea
Headbourne Worthy
Headley
Headley
Headley Down
Hearn
Heath End
Heath End
Heath End
Heather Row
Heatherside
Heathfield
Heath Green
Heckfield
Hedge End
Hell Corner
Henley
Hensting
Hermitage
Herriard
Hides Close
Highbridge
Highbury
Highclere
Highclere Street
Highcliffe
High Cross
Highfield
Hightown
Hightown
Highwood
Hillbourne
Hill Brow
Hill Head
Hill Park
Hillpound
Hillside
Hill Side
Hillstreet
Hill Top
Hill View
Hillyfields
Hilsea
Hiltingbury
Hindhead
Hinton
Hinton Ampner
Hocombe
Hoe
Hoe Gate
Hog Hatch
Holbury
Holdenhurst
Hollington
Hollington Cross
Hollywater
Holt
Holt End
Holt Pound
Holybourne
Hook
Hook
Hook Park
Hooksway
Hordle
Horndean
Horsebridge
Horton Common
Horton Heath
Houghton
Hound
Hound Green
Houndmills
Hounsdown
Hungerford
Hunton
Hurn
Hursley
Hurstbourne Priors
Hurstbourne Tarrant

11 H5
335 G2
End 40 B4
367 M4
358 E1
'pe 74 B8
th 80 E6
449 J1
st 40 F8
n 33 M3
n Common 34 C3
279 H6
on 156 D7
344 C5
Abbas 216 D2
Stoke 217 J2
ers Common 434 C8
shott 103 M7
Oak 261 K3
ven 454 F5
reen 28 E2
ston 242 C7
ridge 233 K8
ton 116 A6
clere 59 H7
clere Woodlands 39 K8
Furlong 104 D4
ley 178 F7
ley Green 228 C6
mead 324 B8
Somborne 210 E5
ton 382 C7
ton 423 K1
Worthy 215 H2
n 431 M3
od 220 F1
p 264 C4
ton 405 H8
ts Enham 118 F3
ell 265 G4
444 C7
ord 287 J4
ordwood 287 J1
End 181 G1
End 241 H8
End 245 J1
own 367 M5
ey 249 L2
ey 418 B1
rish 274 B4
stone 401 J2
m 153 J6
mere Green 62 F3
stoke 123 H3
een 438 E8
ord 165 J8
290 F8
round 371 L3
n-the-Solent 420 A2
404 D4
Park 377 H4
418 E6
t 457 H1
mere 227 K5
ord 201 L4
rd 359 L6
nholt 54 A7
ood 335 M8
ok 226 D5
248 F5
orest 248 E1
field 77 H8
Ann 141 M4
Canford 405 G4
down 53 J8
down 448 F1
Hoddington 130 B3
Holbury 391 M3
London 62 C5
London 96 C8
Posbrook 395 J3
Sandhurst 49 K6
Shoddesden 116 B2
Somborne 211 J2
ton 214 A3
erley 232 D7
Heath 370 F4
on Minstead 339 G4
Common 321 L7
fleet 445 H4
ham 405 M7
parish 145 G2
Park 189 K8
stock 186 D1
Sutton 131 K5
s Hill 317 M4
swood 318 C4
dean 352 C3
285 L3
r Bordean 273 M2
r Bourne 159 H2
r Brook 234 A4
r Buckland 440 C3
r Bullington 167 M1
r Burgate 309 L4
r Chute 94 A1
r Common 47 J7
r Common 152 A2
r Daggons 332 E1
r Farringdon 198 C5
r Froyle 156 B3
r Green 33 L3
r Hamworthy 444 F7
r Holwell 332 B2
r Padworth 30 A3
r Pennington 440 A8
r Ratley 261 L5
r Slackstead 263 L1
r Swanwick 346 A8
r Turmer 358 B1
r Upham 296 C4
r Wield 174 A2
ord 345 L7
ershall 92 F5
ey 378 E7
Green 85 J1
ngton 440 B4
re 454 E2

Lynch 100 D8
Lynch Hill 122 C3
Lyndhurst 363 J3
Malwood 338 E4
Mapledurwell 106 D5
Marchwood 342 C6
Marley Heights 228 C7
Marsh Benham 24 A5
Martin 281 H5
Martin Drove End 280 B1
Martyr Worthy 216 A2
Mattingley 66 A8
Maybush 317 K6
Mead End 412 C7
Medstead 196 D2
Mengham 425 M5
Meon 395 J5
Merley 404 C7
Merritown 433 J1
Merry Oak 344 C3
Meyrick Park 22 C1
Micheldever 170 A5
Micheldever Station 148 A6
Michelmersh 234 B7
Midanbury 319 L8
Middle Bockhampton 435 K2
Middle Bourne 158 F1
Middleton 144 F3
Middle Wallop 162 D8
Middle Winterslow 206 F1
Midgham 28 B5
Midgham Green 28 E3
Miles's Green 27 M1
Milford on Sea 454 A5
Milland 250 D6
Millbridge 159 G7
Millbrook 342 C1
Mill Green 39 J5
Mill Lane 109 M7
Mill Throop 433 J4
Milton 424 A4
Minstead 338 F5
The Mint 248 F3
Mockbeggar 359 H1
Monk Sherborne 82 A2
Monkwood 220 F6
Montgomery Lines 112 F4
Monxton 141 H3
Moorcourt 316 B1
Moordown 432 E7
Moorgreen 320 E5
Moor Park 135 L7
Moortown 382 E3
Morestead 239 L8
Morgan's Vale 285 H1
Mortimer 43 K2
Mortimer West End 43 G4
Mottisfont 233 K6
Mount Sorrel 252 A2
The Mount 56 C1
Mudeford 450 F3
Mullenspond 116 D8
Murrell Green 86 D5
Muscliff 432 F3
Mytchett 91 H5
Mytchett Place 91 K6
Nash's Green 153 H1
Nately Scures 107 H1
Neacroft 435 M2
Neatham 177 K2
Netherton 54 C8
Nether Wallop 185 G3
Netley 368 F2
Netley Hill 345 L4
Netley Marsh 340 E2
New Alresford 218 B2
Newbridge 314 D5
New Brighton 378 E5
Newbury 2 C4
New Cheriton 242 C4
Newfound 103 G5
Newgrounds 310 F6
New Milton 437 J4
Newnham 85 J8
Newton 258 E6
Newton Stacey 166 D3
Newton Tony 160 A3
Newton Valence 223 G2
Newtown 37 L4
Newtown 176 C6
Newtown 226 E6
Newtown 261 G4
Newtown 296 E8
Newtown 338 F6
New Town 344 E7
Newtown 350 A1
Newtown 394 B1
Newtown 446 A1
Nob's Crook 294 F1
No Man's Land 215 L8
Nomansland 287 J8
Norleywood 415 K8
North Baddesley 291 M4
North Boarhunt 349 L6
North Bockhampton 435 J1
Northbourne 432 B4
Northbrook 169 L4
Northbrook 297 H7
North Camp 112 E2
North Charford 285 H4
North End 35 J6
North End 242 B1
North End 308 B3
North End 399 K6
Northfields 266 F1
North Gorley 334 F5
North Hayling 402 A5
North Houghton 186 C8
Northington 171 L8
North Kingston 383 G6
North Marden 331 L4
Northney 402 A4
North Oakley 79 K7
North Poulner 359 H6
North Ripley 409 H4
North Stoneham 319 J1
North Street 220 C1
North Street 284 A6

North Tidworth 114 F1
North Town 113 H6
North Waltham 125 K6
North Warnborough 108 B4
North Weirs 387 G7
Nursling 317 H3
Nursted 304 B1
Nutbourne 403 K1
Nutburn 292 A3
Nutcombe 204 A6
Nutley 151 H3
Nyewood 277 K8
Oakdale 445 K2
Oakhanger 200 C4
Oakley 102 F7
Oakley 404 B7
Oakridge 4 E3
Oakshott 247 J4
Ocean Village 13 K7
Odiham 108 D6
Ogdens 335 K3
Old Alresford 194 B7
Old Basing 105 M2
Old Burghclere 57 H8
Old Milton 437 J7
Old Netley 345 J7
Old Portsmouth 20 C3
Old Shirley 317 M7
Oliver's Battery 237 M5
Ossemsley 411 J7
Otterbourne 266 A4
Otterwood 391 H8
Outwick 283 K8
Overton 124 A1
Over Wallop 162 C6
Ovington 217 K4
Ower 315 L2
Owlsmoor 50 A6
Owslebury 267 L5
Oxenwood 52 A5
Padworth 30 B7
Padworth Common 42 C2
Palestine 161 K2
Pamber End 62 A7
Pamber Green 62 B4
Pamber Heath 42 A6
Pardown 126 A2
Park Gate 370 F3
Parkstone 446 A5
Parley Green 433 G1
Passfield 202 C7
Paulsgrove 374 E8
Peartree Green 344 B4
Peel Common 396 D6
Pennington 440 A6
Penton Corner 117 M7
Penton Grafton 117 K5
Penton Mewsey 117 M4
Pentridge 280 A8
Penwood 56 C1
Perham Down 115 H1
Petersfield 275 J5
Pheonix Green 86 F4
Picket Hill 359 L8
Picket Piece 119 M6
Pikeshill 363 J2
Pilley 414 F6
Pilley Bailey 414 D6
Pitt 237 M3
Plaitford 287 M4
Plaitford Green 260 B8
Plastow Green 59 K1
Pokesdown 448 F3
Pondtail 89 J8
Pooksgreen 342 B6
Poole 445 G6
Popham 149 K4
Popley 83 G7
Portchester 373 M8
Portmore 440 E1
Portsea 20 E1
Portsea Island 399 M8
Portswood 319 G7
Post Green 428 B8
Potbridge 86 F8
Poulner 359 H8
Pound Green 61 G5
Pound Street 56 F1
Powntley Copse 154 C3
Preston Candover 151 H8
Prince's Marsh 248 E6
Prinsted 403 G1
Privett 245 H6
Privett 421 J5
Pucknall 263 L2
Purbrook 376 B3
Purewell 450 B1
Puttenham 137 L3
Pylehill 295 H5
Pyott's Hill 83 M7
Quarley 139 M4
Queen's Corner 251 H8
Quidhampton 101 G7
Racedown 139 K2
Rafborough 90 B5
Ragged Appleshaw 117 H2
Rake 249 K4
Ramsdean 274 B7
Ramsdell 81 K1
Ratlake 264 D5
Ravenswood Village Settlement 49 H2
Redbridge 317 H8
Redenham 116 F1
Redford 251 K7
Red Hill 353 M7
Red Hill 432 D4
Redlynch 285 K1
Red Rice 142 B8
Ridge 290 B7
Ridge Common 275 H3
The Ridges 48 E4
Ringwood 358 C8
Ripley 409 G6
Riseley 45 M5
Rivar 32 C8
Robins 278 F1
Rockbourne 282 D7

Rockford 359 G3
Rogate 277 K5
Romsey 290 D1
Ropley 220 C4
Ropley Dean 219 M3
Ropley Soke 196 D8
Rossmore 446 D1
Rotherwick 85 K3
Rotten Green 88 C3
Round Hill 388 D8
Row Ash 322 F8
Rowland's Castle 354 B6
Rowledge 158 C5
Rowner 397 G8
Rownhams 317 L1
Runfold 135 M5
Rushcombe Bottom 429 J1
Rushington 341 K2
Rushmoor 181 M1
Rushmore 326 D6
St Austins 413 M8
St Catherine's Hill 434 C5
St Cross 238 E3
St Denys 319 H8
St Giles's Hill 11 K8
St Ives 381 L3
St Leonards 381 J4
St Mary Bourne 97 M7
Salters Heath 62 C8
Sandbanks 457 H5
Sandford 383 G8
Sandhurst 49 L7
Sandleheath 308 E6
The Sands 136 B6
Sandy Cross 136 C4
Sandy Down 414 A4
Sarisbury 370 C3
Sarson 141 G2
Seale 136 E4
Selborne 199 J8
Selsmore 426 B6
Setley 413 L3
Shalbourne 32 C5
Shalden 153 M8
Shalden Green 153 M4
Shaw 25 L3
Shawford 266 D1
Shedfield 348 B1
Sheet 276 A3
Shepherd's Hill 228 F2
Sherborne St John 82 C5
Sherfield English 260 C7
Sherfield on Loddon 64 D8
Shipton Bellinger 138 C1
Shirley 318 C8
Shirley 409 L6
Shirley Holms 413 L7
Shirley Warren 318 A6
Shirrell Heath 323 M7
Shobley 359 L7
Sholing 344 F4
Sholing Common 344 E3
Shootash 261 J7
Shorley 242 A7
Shorn Hill 315 M5
Shortfield Common 158 E6
Shortheath 158 E2
Shortheath 200 D2
Shottermill 228 B2
Silchester 42 E8
Silkstead 265 K3
Skinners Green 24 E8
Sladen Green 75 L7
Sleaford 179 K7
Sleepers Hill 238 C2
Smannell 119 K2
Soake 351 M5
Soberton 325 H2
Soberton Heath 324 F7
Soldridge 196 D6
Somerford 450 E1
Sopley 434 F1
Southampton 12 F7
South Baddesley 441 J2
South Bockhampton 435 H4
Southbourne 379 J8
Southbourne 449 K5
South Down 266 C3
South End 308 B5
South Farnborough 91 G7
South Gorley 334 F6
South Ham 104 C5
South Harting 304 F4
South Hayling 425 J6
Southington 123 L1
Southrope 153 H2
South Tidworth 114 E4
South Town 196 D3
South View 4 E4
South Warnborough 130 F5
South Weirs 387 H8
Southwick 374 C2
South Wonston 190 B3
Southwood 89 L5
Spanish Green 64 E5
Sparsholt 213 H5
Spearywell 233 J5
Speen 24 F3
Spreakley 158 E8
Springbourne 23 M1
Stamshaw 398 F7
Standford 201 M6
Standon 236 F6
Stanford End 45 H5
Stanley Green 445 G2
Stanmore 238 C3
Stanpit 450 D2
Stapehill 405 J3
Stedham 279 K7
Steep 275 K1
Steep Marsh 247 M7
Sterte 445 G4
Steventon 125 G4
Stockbridge 186 E5
Stockcross 24 C3
Stockheath 377 J5
Stoke 97 H4
Stoke 401 L6

Stoke Charity 168 F5
Stoke Common 294 B3
Stonehills 393 G6
Stoner Hill 247 G8
Stoney Cross 338 C4
Stony Batter 208 B8
Stonyford 315 L4
Stony Heath 61 G7
Stonymarsh 233 M7
The Straits 178 F6
Stratfield Mortimer 44 A3
Stratfield Saye 44 E8
Stratfield Turgis 64 F4
Street End 297 H4
Stroud 274 F4
Strouden 433 H7
Stroud Green 3 G7
Stubbermere 354 E8
Stubbington 396 B5
Stuckton 335 G1
Sulhampstead Abbots 31 J4
Sulhampstead Bannister Upper End 31 G3
Sulhamstead 30 E2
Sutton Scotney 168 C4
Swallowfield 46 A2
Swampton 97 L5
Swanmore 324 A3
Swanwick 370 E1
Swarraton 193 L1
Sway 412 E7
Swaythling 319 K5
Sydmonton 58 A8
Tadley 61 M1
Talbot Heath 447 G1
Talbot Village 432 A8
Talbot Woods 447 J1
Tangley 94 D2
Tapnage 348 A7
Terwick Common 278 A3
Testwood 316 D6
Thatcham 26 F4
Thorney Hill 410 C4
Thorney Island 403 G5
Thornhill 345 J3
Thornhill Park 345 H1
Thorns Beach 442 F2
Three Ashes 63 G1
Three Legged Cross 356 C8
Thruxton 116 C8
Tichborne 217 M7
Tidpit 281 J6
Tilford Common 159 L7
Tilford Reeds 159 L5
Tilly Down 116 F1
Timsbury 262 B1
Tipner 398 F5
Tiptoe 412 B8
Titchfield 371 J8
Titchfield Common 370 E7
Titchfield Park 371 H5
Titcomb 34 B1
Titty Hill 251 H8
Tongham 136 C2
Toothill 291 K7
Tote Hill 279 K3
Totford 171 M8
Tot Hill 37 H7
Totton 316 F8
Townhill Park 319 L6
Towns End 60 D6
Trapshill 34 B4
Trash Green 31 K1
Trickett's Cross 406 D1
Trotten Marsh 278 B1
Trotton 278 D7
Trotts 342 A5
Tuckton 449 L3
Tufton 122 A6
Tullecombe 249 K8
Tunworth 129 H2
Turbary Common 431 J6
Turgis Green 64 F5
Turkey Island 348 D1
Turlin Moor 444 A4
Turmer 334 B8
Turner's Green 27 L1
Twyford 266 F2
Tye 402 A7
Ufton Green 30 E3
Ufton Nervet 31 G4
Up Green 68 B2
Upham 296 E2
Up Marden 331 J8
Up Nately 107 G4
Upper Bucklebury 27 M2
Upper Bullington 146 B8
Upper Burgate 309 M2
Upper Canterton 338 D2
Upper Clatford 142 D4
Upper Common 151 L1
Upper Enham 96 A8
Upper Farringdon 198 E5
Upper Froyle 155 M6
Upper Green 34 A5
Upper Hale 134 E2
Upper Pennington 439 L5
Upper Ratley 261 L4
Upper Shirley 318 C6
Upper Slackstead 235 M7
Upper Street 283 L6
Upper Swanmore 298 B8
Upper Wardley 250 F3
Upper Wield 173 L6
Upper Woolhampton 28 E4
Upper Wootton 81 H6
Up Somborne 211 M3
Upton 73 L5
Upton 317 J1
Upton 444 A1
Upton Grey 129 M3
Vernham Bank 72 F2
Vernham Dean 73 G2
Vernham Row 52 E8
Vernham Street 53 J8
Verwood 356 D2
Wadwick 98 B2
Walhampton 440 E3

Walkford	436 F7	
Wallington	15 M4	
Wallisdown	431 L7	
Waltham Chase	323 K5	
Walton Heath	374 A1	
Wanborough	137 L2	
Warblington	17 K6	
Wardley	250 F4	
Warnborough Green	108 A4	
Warnford	271 K4	
Warren Corner	133 M1	
Warren Corner	246 F5	
Warsash	370 B7	
Wash Common	37 G3	
Wash Water	36 E5	
Wasing	41 G3	
Waterditch	435 L3	
Water End	107 G2	
Waterford	440 E6	
Waterloo	429 M8	
Waterlooville	352 D8	
Wecock	352 C4	
Weeke	10 B4	
Well	132 B6	
Wellow Wood	260 C8	
Westbourne	378 F4	
Westbourne	447 G6	
West Cliff	22 B8	
West Common	418 C2	
West Dean	231 J5	
West Down	165 L6	
West End	14 E8	
West End	158 C8	
West End	196 A4	
West End	320 D8	
West End Green	44 A8	
Westfield	425 J6	
West Fields	2 B5	
West Green	86 E3	
West Ham	104 C3	
West Harting	304 F1	
West Heath	61 K7	
West Heath	90 B3	
West Howe	431 J4	
West Hurn	433 K2	
West Leigh	377 L3	
West Liss	248 E3	
West Marden	330 D8	
West Meon	272 A4	
West Meon Woodlands	244 B6	
West Moors	380 E6	
Weston	275 G8	
Weston	344 C7	
Weston Colley	169 K4	
Weston Common	344 F4	
Weston Corbett	129 L6	
Weston Patrick	129 M6	
West Parley	406 D8	
West Southbourne	449 J3	
West Stratton	170 D3	
West Thorney	403 H6	
West Tisted	244 D1	
West Town	425 J5	
West Tytherley	208 A8	
West Wellow	288 D5	
West Winterslow	206 C3	
West Wittering	427 L7	
West Woodhay	34 F5	
West Worldham	199 K1	
Weybourne	6 C8	
Weyhill	117 H6	
Wheat Hold	60 B2	
Wheatley	178 F5	
Wherwell	165 K2	
Whitchurch	122 B3	
Whitehall	108 E2	
Whitehill	201 H6	
Whitehouse Green	31 K2	
Whitenap	291 H1	
Whiteparish	258 F4	
Whitsbury	282 F5	
Whitway	57 G4	
Wick	284 B1	
Wick	450 A4	
Wickham	348 E5	
Wick Hill	48 D2	
Widley	376 A6	
Wildern	346 A1	
Wildhern	95 K6	
Wildmoor	84 D3	
Wilsom	176 F4	
Wimble Hill	133 K6	
Wimborne Minster	404 A3	
Simpson	317 K7	
Winchester	11 G9	
Winchfield	87 H6	
Winchfield Hurst	87 K8	
Winklebury	104 A2	
Winkton	435 G3	
Winnall	11 L6	
Winslade	128 E3	
Winsor	315 J7	
Wintershill	296 C7	
Winton	447 L1	
Wittensford	314 C8	
Wivelrod	175 H7	
Wolverton	60 C7	
Wolverton Common	60 D5	
Wonston	168 E5	
Woodcot	396 E5	
Woodcott	76 C6	
Woodfalls	285 H3	
Woodgreen	2	
Woodhouse	1	
Woodington	2	
Woodlands	3	
Woodley	2	
Woodmancote	3	
Woodmancott	1	
Woodmansgreen	2	
Woodside	4	
Woodspeen		
Woolbeding	2	
Woolhampton		
Woolmer Hill	2	
Woolsbridge	3	
Woolston	3	
Woolton Hill		
Wootton	4	
Wootton St Lawrence	1	
Worlds End	1	
Worting	1	
Wrecclesham	1	
Wyck	1	
Wymering	3	
Yateley		
York Town		

USING THE STREET INDEX

Street names are listed alphabetically. Each street name is followed by its postal town or area locality, the Postcode District, the page number, and the reference to the square in which the nar is found.

Example: **Abbey Cl** *FAWY* SO45   367 L5 ⓵

Some entries are followed by a number in a blue box. This number indicates the location of the street within the referenced grid square. The full street name is listed at the side of the map pa

GENERAL ABBREVIATIONS

ACC	ACCESS	CUTT	CUTTINGS	HOL	HOLLOW	NW	NORTH WEST	SKWY	SK
ALY	ALLEY	CV	COVE	HOSP	HOSPITAL	O/P	OVERPASS	SMT	SU
AP	APPROACH	CYN	CANYON	HRB	HARBOUR	OFF	OFFICE	SOC	SO
AR	ARCADE	DEPT	DEPARTMENT	HTH	HEATH	ORCH	ORCHARD	SP	
ASS	ASSOCIATION	DL	DALE	HTS	HEIGHTS	OV	OVAL	SPR	SF
AV	AVENUE	DM	DAM	HVN	HAVEN	PAL	PALACE	SQ	SQ
BCH	BEACH	DR	DRIVE	HWY	HIGHWAY	PAS	PASSAGE	ST	
BLDS	BUILDINGS	DRO	DROVE	IMP	IMPERIAL	PAV	PAVILION	STN	STA
BND	BEND	DRY	DRIVEWAY	IN	INLET	PDE	PARADE	STR	STI
BNK	BANK	DWGS	DWELLINGS	IND EST	INDUSTRIAL ESTATE	PH	PUBLIC HOUSE	STRD	STI
BR	BRIDGE	E	EAST	INF	INFIRMARY	PK	PARK	SW	SOUTH
BRK	BROOK	EMB	EMBANKMENT	INFO	INFORMATION	PKWY	PARKWAY	TDG	TRA
BTM	BOTTOM	EMBY	EMBASSY	INT	INTERCHANGE	PL	PLACE	TER	TER
BUS	BUSINESS	ESP	ESPLANADE	IS	ISLAND	PLN	PLAIN	THWY	THROUGH
BVD	BOULEVARD	EST	ESTATE	JCT	JUNCTION	PLNS	PLAINS	TNL	TU
BY	BYPASS	EX	EXCHANGE	JTY	JETTY	PLZ	PLAZA	TOLL	TOL
CATH	CATHEDRAL	EXPY	EXPRESSWAY	KG	KING	POL	POLICE STATION	TPK	TURN
CEM	CEMETERY	EXT	EXTENSION	KNL	KNOLL	PR	PRINCE	TR	T
CEN	CENTRE	F/O	FLYOVER	L	LAKE	PREC	PRECINCT	TRL	
CFT	CROFT	FC	FOOTBALL CLUB	LA	LANE	PREP	PREPARATORY	TWR	TC
CH	CHURCH	FK	FORK	LDG	LODGE	PRIM	PRIMARY	U/P	UNDER
CHA	CHASE	FLD	FIELD	LGT	LIGHT	PROM	PROMENADE	UNI	UNIVE
CHYD	CHURCHYARD	FLDS	FIELDS	LK	LOCK	PRS	PRINCESS	UPR	U
CIR	CIRCLE	FLS	FALLS	LKS	LAKES	PRT	PORT	V	
CIRC	CIRCUS	FLS	FLATS	LNDG	LANDING	PT	POINT	VA	VA
CL	CLOSE	FM	FARM	LTL	LITTLE	PTH	PATH	VIAD	VIA
CLFS	CLIFFS	FT	FORT	LWR	LOWER	PZ	PIAZZA	VIL	
CMP	CAMP	FWY	FREEWAY	MAG	MAGISTRATE	QD	QUADRANT	VIS	
CNR	CORNER	FY	FERRY	MAN	MANSIONS	QU	QUEEN	VLG	VIL
CO	COUNTY	GA	GATE	MD	MEAD	QY	QUAY	VLS	
COLL	COLLEGE	GAL	GALLERY	MDW	MEADOWS	R	RIVER	VW	
COM	COMMON	GDN	GARDEN	MEM	MEMORIAL	RBT	ROUNDABOUT	W	
COMM	COMMISSION	GDNS	GARDENS	MKT	MARKET	RD	ROAD	WD	
CON	CONVENT	GLD	GLADE	MKTS	MARKETS	RDG	RIDGE	WHF	W
COT	COTTAGE	GLN	GLEN	ML	MALL	REP	REPUBLIC	WK	
COTS	COTTAGES	GN	GREEN	ML	MILL	RES	RESERVOIR	WKS	W
CP	CAPE	GND	GROUND	MNR	MANOR	RFC	RUGBY FOOTBALL CLUB	WLS	V
CPS	COPSE	GRA	GRANGE	MS	MEWS	RI	RISE	WY	
CR	CREEK	GRG	GARAGE	MSN	MISSION	RP	RAMP	YD	
CREM	CREMATORIUM	GT	GREAT	MT	MOUNT	RW	ROW	YHA	YOUTH HC
CRS	CRESCENT	GTWY	GATEWAY	MTN	MOUNTAIN	S	SOUTH		
CSWY	CAUSEWAY	GV	GROVE	MTS	MOUNTAINS	SCH	SCHOOL		
CT	COURT	HGR	HIGHER	MUS	MUSEUM	SE	SOUTH EAST		
CTRL	CENTRAL	HL	HILL	MWY	MOTORWAY	SER	SERVICE AREA		
CTS	COURTS	HLS	HILLS	N	NORTH	SH	SHORE		
CTYD	COURTYARD	HO	HOUSE	NE	NORTH EAST	SHOP	SHOPPING		

POSTCODE TOWNS AND AREA ABBREVIATIONS

ALDT	Aldershot	CHIN	Chineham	HLER	Hamble-le-Rice	NTHA	Thatcham north	STHA	Thatcham sc
ALTN	Alton	CHOB/PIR	Chobham/Pirbright	HORN	Horndean	NTID	North Tidworth	STOK	Stockbr
AMSY	Amesbury	CWTH	Crowthorne	HSEA	Hilsea	NWBY	Newbury	SWGE	Swar
AND	Andover	DEAN	Deane/Oakley	HTWY	Hartley Wintney	ODIM	Odiham	TADY	Tady
ASC	Ascot	ELGH	Eastleigh	HUNG	Hungerford/Lambourn	OVTN	Overton/Rural Basingstoke	THLE	Theale/Rural Rea
ASHV	Ash Vale	EMRTH	Emsworth/Southbourne	ITCH	Itchen	PLE	Poole	TOTT	To
BAGS	Bagshot	ENEY	Eastney	KEMP	Kempshott	PSEA	Portsea	TWDS	Talbot Wc
BDST	Broadstone	EPSF	Petersfield east	KSCL	Kingsclere/Rural Newbury	PSF	Petersfield	UPTN	U
BFOR	Bracknell Forest/Windlesham	EWKG	Wokingham east	LIPH	Liphook	PSTN	Parkstone	VWD	Verv
BKME/WDN	Branksome/Wallisdown	FARN	Farnborough	LISS	Liss	PTSW	Portswood	WBNE	Westbo
BLKW	Blackwater	FAWY	Fawley/Hythe	LSOL/BMARY	Lee-on-the-Solent/	RAND	Rural Andover	WCLF	West
BMTH	Bournemouth	FBDG	Fordingbridge		Bridgemary	RCCH	Rural Chichester	WEND	West
BOR	Bordon	FERN	Ferndown/West Moors	LTDN	Littledown	RDGW	Reading west	WHAM	Wick
BOSC	Boscombe	FHAM	Fareham	LTWR	Lightwater	RFNM	Rural Farnham	WHCH	Whitch
BPWT	Bishop's Waltham	FHAM/PORC	Fareham/Portchester	LYMN	Lymington	RGUW	Rural Guildford west	WHIT	Whitley/Arbor
BROC	Brockenhurst	FHAM/STUB	Fareham/Stubbington	LYND	Lyndhurst	RGWD	Ringwood	WIMB	Wimborne Mir
BSTK	Basingstoke	FLET	Fleet	MARL	Marlborough	ROMY	Romsey	WINC	Winche
BWD	Bearwood	FNM	Farnham	MFD/CHID	Milford/Chiddingfold	ROWN	Rownhams	WINW	Winchester v
CBLY	Camberley	FRIM	Frimley	MIDH	Midhurst	RSAL	Rural Salisbury	WSHM	Southampton v
CCLF	Canford Cliffs	GPORT	Gosport	MOOR/WNTN	Moordown/Winton	RWIN	Rural Winchester	WVILLE	Waterlooville/Denn
CFDH	Canford Heath	GSHT	Grayshott	NALR	New Alresford	SBNE	Southbourne	YTLY	Yat
CHAM	Cosham	HASM	Haslemere	NBAD	North Baddesley	SELS	Selsey		
CHAR	Charminster	HAV	Havant	NBNE	Northbourne	SHAM	Southampton		
CHCH/BSGR	Christchurch/Bransgore	HEND	Hedge End	NEND	North End	SHST	Sandhurst		
CHFD	Chandler's Ford	HISD	Hayling Island	NMIL/BTOS	New Milton/Barton on Sea	SSEA	Southsea		

: FAWY SO45 392 B4
: FAWY SO45 392 B3
: FAWY SO45 392 B3
: FAWY SO45 392 B2
: FAWY SO45 392 A3
-AWY SO45 392 E5
FAWY SO45 392 E3
FAWY SO45 392 D4
FAWY SO45 392 D4
FAWY SO45 392 D3
FAWY SO45 392 D2
FAWY SO45 392 C3
FAWY SO45 392 C4
FAWY SO45 392 B4

A

Cl CFDH BH17 445 L1
Ct TOTT SO40 342 D6
WY SO45 392 B3
: Cl RAND SP11 93 G6
's La CBLY GU15 70 E5
Cl FAWY SO45 367 L5
Y RG14 2 F9
dore Rd CHAM PO6 375 G7
field Dr FHAM PO15 372 A6
fields Cl HLER SO31 369 H2
Gdns WIMB BH21 405 H3
Hl ITCH SO19 344 C8
Hill Cl WINC SO23 11 G3
Hill Rd WINC SO23 10 F3
Pk THLE RG7 31 J5
Rd ALTN GU34 175 H8
RG24 4 C2
BH22 380 E8
PO15 14 B4
St FNM GU9 134 F7
Water ROMY SO51 290 D1
Wy FARN GU14 90 F4
sbury Rd BDST BH18 429 J3
SO50 294 E6
s Cl CHCH/BSGR BH23 451 L1
GU13 88 F7
LE PO7 376 A4
sfield TOTT SO40 341 J1
sfield Cl ROWN SO16 318 B3
sford TOTT SO40 339 M2
s Ride FNM GU9 135 H8
s Rd NWBY RG14 2 F7
RG7 31 J5
stone Av HAV PO9 377 L4
s Wy FHAM PO15 14 A5
SO31 369 H2
s Well Rd FBDG SP6 335 K1
swood Cl ROMY SO51 263 H7
Cl KEMP RG22 104 B6
Rd MOOR/WNTN BH9 432 E8
s Ann Rd WINW SO22 214 C5
SP11 141 H3
s Cl NTID SP9 114 D1
SP11 141 M4
SO23 11 H2
s Dro ROMY SO51 288 D7
s Hl RAND SP11 141 M5
s Rd ELGH SO50 293 K7
SP9 114 D1
SO23 11 G2
s Wy FERN BH22 380 E8
SO17 319 G7
swood Cl TADY RG26 61 L1
ombie Gdns
SO16 317 M4
re Av CHAM PO6 375 M7
re Rd NBNE BH10 432 C5
en Cl FHAM PO15 14 D2
en Rd PTSW SO17 319 H7
our Cl WEND SO18 320 A8
d NWBY RG14 3 K4
lon Dr
/BSGR BH23 437 G8
lon Gdns ROWN SO16 318 D5
lon Rd CFDH BH17 430 B7
GU47 49 M8
r Rd LTDN BH7 448 F2
Rd NBNE BH10 432 B5
Bar St SHAM SO14 12 F1
Town RAND SP11 142 D4
m Cl HEND SO30 346 B3
Cl FHAM/STUB PO14 370 F7
Rd FHAM/STUB PO14 370 F7
Av SHST GU47 50 A7
BH31 357 G4
Gdns HORN PO8 352 F3
Rd ITCH SO19 344 D3
SO41 438 D4
ny Cl CBLY GU15 51 H8
ors Cl ALTN GU34 176 E2
y HAV PO9 377 M4
ian Cl FNM GU9 158 F1
s Cl CHAM RG24 83 L4
der Rd ALTN GU34 176 D5
s Md SHST GU47 49 J7
rth Rd HSEA PO3 399 L3
Rd MOOR/WNTN BH9 432 F8
Cl CHAM PO6 376 C8
/BSGR BH23 434 D8
SO22 10 A3
/BMARY PO13 397 H7
/BTOS BH25 438 A4
BH24 381 J5
SO40 342 E7
Ct HLER SO31 369 K5
Dr NTHA RG18 27 G3
SO16 317 K1
Gv NBAD SO52 292 E4
Keep FNM GU9 112 A8
Rd BLKW GU17 69 L3
orns HLER SO31 345 K8
BH21 404 E4
Wy VWD BH31 356 E2
HORN PO8 353 G7
th AND SP10 9 K5
d BWD BH11 431 M6
Rd NBNE BH10 431 M7
d ENEY PO4 423 L6
Cl TADY RG26 41 H7

Adames Rd PSEA PO1 423 J2
Adampur Rd NTID SP9 114 B4
Adams Cl HEND SO30 321 G5
Adams Dr FLET GU13 89 G7
Adamson Cl CHFD SO53 265 J8
Adams Park Rd FNM GU9 135 G4
Adams Rd FAWY SO45 367 L6
Adams Wy ALTN GU34 176 F4
Adams Wood Dr TOTT SO40 342 D7
Adastral Rd CFDH BH17 430 C8
Adderbury Av EMRTH PO10 378 D4
Addiscombe Rd CWTH RG45 49 M4
Addison Gdns ODIM RG29 108 D5
Addison Rd BROC SO42 387 K8
ELGH SO50 294 A3
ENEY PO4 21 L5
FRIM GU16 71 H8
HLER SO31 370 D2
Addison Sq RGWD BH24 382 F1
Addisson Cl WINW SO22 238 B3
Adelaide Cl RAND SP11 115 J1
Adelaide Rd AND SP10 9 J5
PTSW SO17 319 H8
Adela Verne Cl ITCH SO19 345 J5
Adeline Rd BMTH BH1 448 D4
Adey Cl ITCH SO19 344 F6
Adey's Cl NWBY RG14 3 G7
Adhurst Rd HAV PO9 377 L4
Adlam's La LYMN SO41 412 D5
Adlington Pl FARN GU14 91 H6
Admers Crs LIPH GU30 226 F6
Admirals Cl FAWY SO45 392 F5
Admirals Rd HLER SO31 370 F4
Admirals Wk GPORT PO12 18 A4
Admirals Wy AND SP10 119 J8
Admiralty Rd PSEA PO1 20 C1
Admiralty Wy CBLY GU15 70 C4
TOTT SO40 342 D5
Adrian Cl HTWY RG27 87 J3
Adsdean Cl HAV PO9 377 J4
Adstone La HSEA PO3 400 A4
Adur Cl GPORT PO12 421 K1
WEND SO18 320 A7
Adwood Ct STHA RG19 27 H5
Aelmas Mich Dro RAND SP11 117 G7
Aerial Rd CHAM PO6 374 F6
Aerodrome Rd
LSOL/BMARY PO13 397 H4
Aerospace Bvd ALDT GU11 112 D1
FARN GU14 112 C1
Africa Dr TOTT SO40 342 D7
Agars La LYMN SO41 438 E1
LYMN SO41 438 F3
Agarton La LYMN SO41 454 E2
Aggis Farm Rd VWD BH31 356 C2
Aghemund Cl CHAM RG24 83 K5
Agincourt Rd NEND PO2 423 H1
Agitor Rd FAWY SO45 393 G3
Agnew Rd LSOL/BMARY PO13 397 G5
Agra Rd NTID SP9 114 B4
Agravaine Cl AND SP10 118 F5
Agricola Wy STHA RG19 27 J6
Aikman La TOTT SO40 340 F1
Ailsa La ITCH SO19 344 B4
Ainsdale Rd CHAM PO6 376 B7
Ainsley Gdns ELGH SO50 293 M3
Aintree Cl ELGH SO50 321 J1
NWBY RG14 3 J8
Aintree Dr WVILLE PO7 352 F7
Aintree Rd TOTT SO40 316 B7
Aircraft Esp FARN GU14 90 F7
Aird Cl KSCL RG20 36 B8
Airetons Cl BDST BH18 430 A5
Airfield Rd CHCH/BSGR BH23 450 E1
Airfield Wy CHCH/BSGR BH23 450 E1
Airport Service Rd HSEA PO3 399 M5
Ajax Cl CHAM RG24 83 L4
FHAM/STUB PO14 396 B7
Akeshill Cl NMIL/BTOS BH25 437 M3
Alameda Rd WVILLE PO7 376 B4
Alameda Wy WVILLE PO7 376 B4
Alamein Rd ALDT GU11 7 G1
RAND SP11 119 G1
Alanbrooke Cl HTWY RG27 87 H2
Alanbrooke Rd ALDT GU11 113 G2
Alandale Rd ITCH SO19 345 H4
Alan Drayton Wy ELGH SO50 294 D6
Alan Gv FHAM PO15 14 C4
Albacore Av HLER SO31 370 C7
Albany Cl FLET GU13 89 G8
NMIL/BTOS BH25 437 K7
Albany Ct BPWT SO32 296 F8
Albany Dr BPWT SO32 296 F8
WIMB BH21 356 C8
Albany Gdns PLE BH15 444 E6
Albany Pk FRIM GU16 70 F7
Albany Rd AND SP10 8 C4
BPWT SO32 296 F8
FAWY SO45 392 A4
FLET GU13 88 F8
ROMY SO51 290 D1
SSEA PO5 21 J6
WSHM SO15 343 G2
Albatross Wk
LSOL/BMARY PO13 396 F6
Albemarle Av GPORT PO12 421 M1
Albemarle Rd TWDS BH3 447 L1
Albert Cl HLER SO31 369 G3
Albert Gv SSEA PO5 21 K6
Albert Rd ALDT GU11 7 H2
ALTN GU34 176 D6
BKME/WDN BH12 446 C3
BMTH BH1 22 E5
BPWT SO32 323 G1
CBLY GU15 70 F3
CHAM PO6 399 K1
CWTH RG45 49 L3
ELGH SO50 294 A3
FARN GU14 90 F6
FERN BH22 406 B3
FHAM/STUB PO14 396 D6
HEND SO30 345 M3
NMIL/BTOS BH25 437 K6
NWBY RG14 2 D3
SSEA PO5 21 K7
WIMB BH21 429 H3
Albert Rd North SHAM SO14 13 K5
Albert Rd South SHAM SO14 13 K6

Albert St FLET GU13 88 E7
GPORT PO12 19 G2
Albion Cl FHAM/PORC PO16 397 M2
Albion Pl SHAM SO14 12 F4
Albion Rd CHCH/BSGR BH23 434 D7
FBDG SP6 309 L6
SHST GU47 69 L1
Albion Wy VWD BH31 356 B2
Albretia Av HORN PO8 352 B5
Albury Pl CHFD SO53 265 G7
Alby Rd BKME/WDN BH12 446 E3
Alcantara Crs SHAM SO14 13 K6
Alcester Rd BKME/WDN BH12 446 C2
Alcot Cl CWTH RG45 49 L4
Alderbrook Cl CWTH RG45 49 H4
Alder Cl ALTN GU34 176 D3
ASHV GU12 113 K1
CHCH/BSGR BH23 435 H7
FAWY SO45 367 G5
ROMY SO51 291 J2
RWIN SO21 266 F8
TOTT SO40 342 D6
Alder Crs BKME/WDN BH12 446 E1
Alder Dr FBDG SP6 333 K3
Alderfield PSF GU32 275 K5
Alder Gld THLE RG7 31 J5
Alder Gv YTLY GU46 68 F3
Alder Hill Dr TOTT SO40 316 A8
Alder Hills BKME/WDN BH12 446 F1
Alderholt Rd FBDG SP6 308 F7
Alder La LSOL/BMARY PO13 421 H3
Alderley Rd NBNE BH10 432 B4
Aldermaston Rd TADY RG26 62 A3
Aldermaston Rd South
BSTK RG21 4 A4
Aldermoor Av ROWN SO16 317 M4
Aldermoor Cl ROWN SO16 318 B4
Aldermoor Rd
LSOL/BMARY PO13 421 H1
ROWN SO16 317 M4
WVILLE PO7 376 B4
Aldermoor Rd East
WVILLE PO7 376 B3
Alderney Av BKME/WDN BH12 431 H7
KEMP RG22 127 G1
Alderney Cl ROWN SO16 317 K4
Alder Rd BKME/WDN BH12 431 L8
BOR GU35 202 E2
ROWN SO16 317 L5
Aldershot Rd ASHV GU12 113 J7
FLET GU13 88 F8
FLET GU13 110 E4
Alders Rd FHAM/PORC PO16 396 F1
The Alders NTHA RG18 27 G4
Alderwood CHAM RG24 83 L5
Alderwood Av CHFD SO53 292 F2
Alderwood Cl HAV PO9 376 E5
Alder Wood Dr HTWY RG27 86 A6
Aldis Gdns PLE BH15 444 D5
Aldrich Rd PSEA PO1 422 E2
Aldridge Cl HORN PO8 328 B3
Aldridge Rd FERN BH22 406 C5
NBNE BH10 432 A3
Aldrin Cl AND SP10 118 D5
Aldrin Pl FARN GU14 90 A4
Aldroke St CHAM PO6 399 K1
Aldsworth Cl CHAM PO6 376 A8
Aldsworth Gdns CHAM PO6 376 A8
Aldwell St SSEA PO5 21 J3
Aldwick Cl FARN GU14 90 D2
Aldworth Crs KEMP RG22 104 D4
Aldworth Gdns CWTH RG45 49 K3
Alec Rose La PSEA PO1 21 G2
Alecto Rd GPORT PO12 18 E6
Alencon Cl GPORT PO12 398 A8
Alencon Link BSTK RG21 4 D7
Alexander Cl TOTT SO40 316 C8
WVILLE PO7 376 B3
Alexander Gv
FHAM/PORC PO16 15 H8
Alexander Rd OVTN RG25 123 M1
STHA RG19 27 H6
Alexandra Av CBLY GU15 70 D3
HISD PO11 425 K6
Alexandra Cl FAWY SO45 367 L4
Alexandra Ct FARN GU14 90 F7
BOR GU35 201 J5
Alexandra Rd ALDT GU11 6 B3
ALTN GU34 176 E3
AND SP10 8 F5
ASHV GU12 113 J7
BSTK RG21 4 B8
CHFD SO53 265 L8
FARN GU14 90 F6
FAWY SO45 367 L4
FBDG SP6 309 L6
HEND SO30 345 M3
LYMN SO41 440 A3
PSEA PO1 423 H2
PSTN BH14 446 D4
SBNE BH6 449 G3
WSHM SO15 343 H2
Alexandra St GPORT PO12 421 L2
Alexandra Ter WINC SO23 10 E9
Alexandra Wy HEND SO30 346 E1
Alexandria Rd RWIN SO21 168 C3
Alfonso Cl ASHV GU12 7 K5
Alford Rd TWDS BH3 447 J1
Alfred Cl TOTT SO40 316 B8
TOTT SO40 341 G1
Alfred Rd FHAM/STUB PO14 396 B5
FNM GU9 134 F7
PSEA PO1 20 F1
Alfred Rose Ct WEND SO18 319 K4
Alfred St SHAM SO14 343 M2
Alfrey Cl EMRTH PO10 379 G8
Alfriston Gdns ITCH SO19 344 F5
Alfriston Rd FRIM GU16 91 M1
Algiers Rd HSEA PO3 399 M8
Alhambra Rd ENEY PO4 21 L9
Alice Rd ALDT GU11 7 G2
Alington Cl PSTN BH14 457 H1
Alington Rd PSTN BH14 457 H1
TWDS BH3 447 M2
Alipore Cl PSTN BH14 446 C5
Alison Cl FARN GU14 90 C5
THLE RG7 31 J7
Alison Dr CBLY GU15 71 J3

Alison's Rd ALDT GU11 112 D3
Alison Wy ALDT GU11 6 C2
Allan Gv ROMY SO51 291 G1
Allaway Av CHAM PO6 374 D8
Allbrook Cl HAV PO9 377 H2
Allbrook Hl ELGH SO50 294 A1
Allbrook Knoll ELGH SO50 293 M1
Allbrook Wy ELGH SO50 265 M8
Allcot Rd HSEA PO3 399 K6
Allden Av ASHV GU12 7 L7
Allee Dr LIPH GU30 226 E3
Allenby Gv FHAM/PORC PO16 398 A1
Allenby Rd CBLY GU15 70 D2
CFDH BH17 429 M7
GPORT PO12 421 J2
Allen Cl ALTN GU34 176 F3
BSTK RG21 104 E5
Allen Ct WIMB BH21 404 A3
Allendale Av EMRTH PO10 378 C5
Allendale Cl SHST GU47 49 K6
Allen Rd HEND SO30 346 A1
WIMB BH21 404 A4
Allens La BPWT SO32 299 H3
UPTN BH16 444 C3
Allen's Rd SSEA PO5 21 L7
UPTN BH16 444 B2
Allenview Rd WIMB BH21 404 A3
Allen Water Dr FBDG SP6 309 K6
Allerton Cl TOTT SO40 316 C7
The Alley MIDH GU29 279 K7
Alliance Cl LSOL/BMARY PO13 397 H8
Allington La HEND SO30 320 D3
Allington Rd WSHM SO15 342 B1
Alliston Wy KEMP RG22 104 B5
WHCH RG28 122 C4
Allmara Dr WVILLE PO7 376 C3
Allnutt Av BSTK RG21 5 H8
Allotment Rd HLER SO31 370 C3
All Saints Crs FARN GU14 70 B7
All Saints Rd LYMN SO41 440 C6
PSEA PO1 423 H1
Alma Cl ASHV GU12 113 G5
Alma La BPWT SO32 296 A6
FNM GU9 134 F1
Alma Rd BOR GU35 201 K5
BOR GU35 202 F3
MOOR/WNTN BH9 447 M1
ROMY SO51 290 E1
SHAM SO14 318 F8
Alma St GPORT PO12 421 L2
Almatade Rd WEND SO18 344 E1
Alma Ter ENEY PO4 423 L5
Alma Wy FNM GU9 135 G1
Almer Rd PLE BH15 444 D5
Almond Av NWBY RG14 25 K3
Almond Cl CHAM RG24 105 M2
CHAM PO6 376 D8
FARN GU14 90 D1
HORN PO8 353 G4
Almond Dr NTHA RG18 27 G4
Almond Gv BKME/WDN BH12 446 C1
Almond Rd WSHM SO15 343 G3
Almondsbury Rd CHAM PO6 374 D6
Almondside
LSOL/BMARY PO13 397 J7
Almswood Rd TADY RG26 41 K6
The Aloes FLET GU13 89 G8
Alphington Av FRIM GU16 71 J7
Alphington Gn FRIM GU16 71 H7
Alpine Cl FARN GU14 90 A5
WEND SO18 320 A8
Alpine Ct KEMP RG22 103 M5
Alpine Rd BOR GU35 201 J7
RGWD BH24 382 A6
TOTT SO40 340 D5
Alresford Dro RWIN SO21 190 E3
Alresford Rd HAV PO9 377 J4
NALR SO24 217 M4
RWIN SO21 239 L1
WINC SO23 11 L8
Alsford Rd WVILLE PO7 376 B3
Alston Ms STHA RG19 26 F6
Alten Rd WVILLE PO7 352 A6
Althorpe Dr HSEA PO3 400 A4
Altona Gdns AND SP10 118 E5
Alton Cl ELGH SO50 295 G6
Alton Gv FHAM/PORC PO16 398 A2
Alton La ALTN GU34 197 G8
Alton Ride BLKW GU17 69 M2
Alton Rd FLET GU13 89 H7
NBNE BH10 431 M7
RFNM GU10 158 A1
ODIM RG29 131 G4
PSTN BH14 446 A5
Alton Rd East PSTN BH14 446 C6
Alum Chine Rd WBNE BH4 447 G5
Alum Cl FAWY SO45 392 B5
Alumdale Rd WBNE BH4 447 G6
Alumhurst Rd WBNE BH4 447 G6
Alum Wy FHAM/PORC PO16 373 J7
WEND SO18 344 F1
Alvara Rd GPORT PO12 18 D7
Alvercliffe Dr GPORT PO12 18 B8
Alver Rd GPORT PO12 18 F5
PSEA PO1 423 J2
Alverstoke Gdns ALDT GU11 6 B4
Alverstone Rd ENEY PO4 423 L4
Alverton Av PLE BH15 445 L5
Alveston Av FHAM/STUB PO14 372 A8
Alwin Pl FNM GU9 134 F1
Alyth Rd TWDS BH3 447 H2
Amarylis Cl FHAM PO15 371 J4
Amazon Cl BSTK RG21 4 A9
Ambarrow Crs SHST GU47 49 J7
Ambarrow La CWTH RG45 49 G6
Amber Cl BOR GU35 201 K6
Amber Gdns AND SP10 8 B5
Amber Hl CBLY GU15 71 L4
Amberley Cl CHCH/BSGR BH23 436 C8
HEND SO30 321 L8
NBAD SO52 291 K3
NWBY RG14 2 C1
Amberley Ct TOTT SO40 341 J2
Amberley Gra ALDT GU11 6 C5
Amberley Rd GPORT PO12 397 L8
HORN PO8 328 C3
NEND PO2 399 K5
Amber Rd WIMB BH21 429 G4

Amberslade Wk FAWY SO45 367 K7
Amberwood FERN BH22 406 C1
Amberwood Cl TOTT SO40 316 B6
Amberwood Dr CBLY GU15 71 J1
CHCH/BSGR BH23 436 E6
Amberwood Gdns
CHCH/BSGR BH23 436 E6
Ambledale HLER SO31 370 C4
Ambleside CHCH/BSGR BH23 434 B5
HEND SO30 346 B3
Ambleside Cl FARN GU14 90 B4
FRIM GU16 91 K6
Ambleside Crs FNM GU9 134 D2
Ambleside Gdns ITCH SO19 344 E5
Ambleside Rd LYMN SO41 440 C6
Ambrose Rd TADY RG26 41 L8
Ambury La CHCH/BSGR BH23 435 K8
Amersham Cl GPORT PO12 421 J4
Amery Hl ALTN GU34 176 E4
Amery St ALTN GU34 176 E5
Amesbury Rd RAND SP11 116 F7
Amethyst Gv WVILLE PO7 352 F8
Amethyst Rd
CHCH/BSGR BH23 450 E1
Ameysford Rd FERN BH22 380 A7
Ameys La FERN BH22 406 D1
Amherst Rd BOR GU35 201 H2
Amoy St WSHM SO15 343 K2
Ampere Rd NWBY RG14 3 G3
Ampfield Cl HAV PO9 376 F4
Ampfield Rd CHAR BH8 433 H5
Amport Cl CHAM RG24 83 M8
WINW SO22 214 B5
Amport Ct HAV PO9 377 H2
Ampthill Rd WSHM SO15 342 F1
Amyas Ct ENEY PO4 424 A4
Ancasta Rd SHAM SO14 343 M1
Ancells Rd FARN GU14 89 G3
Anchorage Rd HSEA PO3 399 M5
The Anchorage GPORT PO12 19 H4
Anchor Cl BWD BH11 431 K3
Anchor Ga PSEA PO1 422 E2
Anchor La PSEA PO1 422 E2
Anchor Meadow FARN GU14 90 C4
Anchor Ms LYMN SO41 440 C4
Anchor Rd BWD BH11 431 K3
KSCL RG20 59 J6
Anchor Yd BSTK RG21 4 F9
Andalusian Gdns HLER SO31 346 F8
Andeferas Rd AND SP10 118 E5
Anderby Rd ROWN SO16 317 J6
Andersen Cl HLER SO31 347 G8
Anderson Cl HAV PO9 17 G1
ROMY SO51 263 H6
Anderson's Rd SHAM SO14 13 K5
Anders Rd RWIN SO21 190 D4
Anderwood Dr LYMN SO41 412 F6
Andes Cl SHAM SO14 13 L6
Andes Rd ROWN SO16 317 G5
Andlers Ash Rd LISS GU33 248 D6
Andover Cl CHCH/BSGR BH23 451 G1
Andover Dro KSCL RG20 36 E4
Andover La RAND SP11 115 M1
Andover Rd BLKW GU17 69 M2
DEAN RG23 102 C7
ENEY PO4 423 K6
WINW SO22 10 F3
KSCL RG20 36 E6
NWBY RG14 37 H1
OVTN RG25 101 M8
RAND SP11 92 F6
RAND SP11 141 K2
RWIN SO21 148 A6
WSHM SO15 343 H2
Andover Rd North WINW SO22 214 B1
Andover Wy ALDT GU11 7 H8
FNM GU9 7 H8
Andrewartha Rd FARN GU14 91 H6
Andrew Bell St PSEA PO1 423 G2
Andrew Cl FAWY SO45 367 L7
PSEA PO1 423 K2
TOTT SO40 341 H1
Andrew Crs WVILLE PO7 352 B7
Andrewes Cl BPWT SO32 297 H8
Andrew La NMIL/BTOS BH25 438 B6
Andrew Pl FHAM/STUB PO14 395 M6
Andrews Cl BWD BH11 431 L5
FLET GU13 110 F2
Andrew's La NALR SO24 220 E3
ODIM RG29 131 L5
Andrews Rd FARN GU14 90 B3
Andromeda Rd ROWN SO16 317 K4
Andwell La HTWY RG27 106 F2
Anfield Cl ELGH SO50 295 H7
Angel Ct NWBY RG14 2 E2
Angel Crs ITCH SO19 344 D2
Angelica Gdns ELGH SO50 321 H1
Angelica Wy FHAM PO15 347 J8
Angeline Cl
CHCH/BSGR BH23 436 D8
Angel La FERN BH22 405 M5
NMIL/BTOS BH25 438 B8
Angel Md THLE RG7 28 F6
Angel Mdw ODIM RG29 108 D5
Angelo Cl WVILLE PO7 352 E8
Angelus Cl FHAM/STUB PO14 396 A6
Angerstein Rd NEND PO2 399 H7
Anglers Wy HLER SO31 346 B8
Anglesea Rd
LSOL/BMARY PO13 420 E4
PSEA PO1 20 F2
WSHM SO15 318 A7
Anglesea Ter SHAM SO14 13 K5
Anglesey Arms Rd GPORT PO12 18 C8
Anglesey Av FARN GU14 90 C1
Anglesey Cl AND SP10 142 F3
CHAM RG24 83 H6
Anglesey Rd ASHV GU12 7 L3
GPORT PO12 18 C8
Angora Wy FARN GU14 89 G4
Angus Cl FHAM PO15 14 C2
Anjou Crs FHAM PO15 14 B4
Anker La FHAM/STUB PO14 396 A4
Ankerwyke
LSOL/BMARY PO13 396 F7
Anmore Dr WVILLE PO7 352 B6
Anmore La WVILLE PO7 352 A4
Anmore Rd WVILLE PO7 351 L4

Anna La CHCH/BSGR BH23 408 E4
Annandale Dr RFNM GU10 159 G3
Anne Armstrong Cl ALDT GU11 113 G3
Anne Cl CHCH/BSGR BH23 434 E7
Anne Crs WVILLE PO7 376 C2
Annerley Rd BMTH BH1 23 L4
Annes Wy FLET GU13 111 G2
Annet Cl PLE BH15 444 D6
Annettes Cft FLET GU13 110 D4
Annett's La HUNG RG17 32 C1
Ann's Hill Rd GPORT PO12 18 C4
Ansell Rd FRIM GU16 71 H8
Anson Cl CHCH/BSGR BH23 450 E2
LSOL/BMARY PO13 421 H3
RGWD BH24 359 G8
Anson Dr ITCH SO19 345 G3
Anson Gv FHAM/PORC PO16 374 B7
Anson Rd ELGH SO50 321 H1
ENEY PO4 423 K3
Anstey Cl BSTK RG21 104 F6
BWD BH11 431 L2
Anstey La ALTN GU34 154 E8
Anstey Mill Cl ALTN GU34 177 G3
Anstey Mill La ALTN GU34 177 G3
Anstey Pl THLE RG7 31 K5
Anstey Rd ALTN GU34 176 F4
BWD BH11 431 L3
ROMY SO51 263 G7
Antar Cl BSTK RG21 4 A9
Antell's Wy FBDG SP6 333 L2
Anthill Cl WVILLE PO7 351 G2
Anthony Gv GPORT PO12 397 K7
LSOL/BMARY PO13 397 K7
Anthony's Av PSTN BH14 446 B7
Antler Dr NMIL/BTOS BH25 437 J4
Anton Cl DEAN RG23 103 G7
ROMY SO51 291 H1
Anton La RAND SP11 119 G2
Anton Mill Rd AND SP10 8 F8
Anton Rd AND SP10 9 G8
Antrim Cl KEMP RG22 104 A5
Anvil Cl HORN PO8 353 G7
Anvil Crs BDST BH18 429 J3
Anzac Cl FHAM/STUB PO14 396 A4
Anzio Cl ALDT GU11 6 F1
Apex Dr FRIM GU16 71 G7
Apless La WVILLE PO7 350 D4
Apollo Dr BOR GU35 201 K6
WVILLE PO7 376 D5
Apollo Ri FARN GU14 90 A4
Apollo Rd CHFD SO53 293 L1
Appelford Cl STHA RG19 27 G6
Apple Cl BKME/WDN BH12 446 F4
Appledore Ms FARN GU14 90 D1
Appledown Cl NALR SO24 218 C4
Appledown La NALR SO24 218 D5
Applegarth Cl BSTK RG21 105 H5
Apple Gv CHCH/BSGR BH23 434 C6
EMRTH PO10 378 F8
Applelands Cl RFNM GU10 158 D4
Appleshaw Cl WINW SO22 214 C4
Appleshaw Wy RAND SP11 115 J2
Appleslade Wy
NMIL/BTOS BH25 437 M3
Appleton Cl STOK SO20 162 B7
Appleton Rd FHAM PO15 372 A7
WEND SO18 319 K7
Appleton Vw ALTN GU34 222 C3
Apple Tree Cl NWBY RG14 37 H1
RSAL SP5 285 J1
Appletree Cl DEAN RG23 103 G8
NMIL/BTOS BH25 437 L7
TOTT SO40 316 B8
Appletree Ct HEND SO30 346 E1
Apple Tree Gv AND SP10 8 B2
FERN BH22 406 C3
Apple Tree Rd FBDG SP6 333 K3
Appletree Rd RSAL SP5 285 J1
Apple Tree Wy SHST GU47 50 A7
Apple Wy CHAM RG24 106 A3
Applewood Gdns ITCH SO19 344 E5
Applewood Gv WVILLE PO7 376 A6
Applewood Pl TOTT SO40 341 G2
Applewood Rd HAV PO9 377 G5
Appley Dr CBLY GU15 70 E3
Approach Rd FNM GU9 134 F7
PSTN BH14 446 A5
April Cl BWD BH11 431 L4
CBLY GU15 70 F6
WEND SO18 344 F1
April Gv HLER SO31 370 C5
April Sq PSEA PO1 423 H2
Apsley Cl AND SP10 142 E3
Apsley Crs CFDH BH17 430 A7
Apsley Pl CHFD SO53 265 G7
Apsley Rd ENEY PO4 423 L4
Aquila Wy HLER SO31 369 K6
Arabian Gdns FHAM PO15 371 G1
Aragon Wy MOOR/WNTN BH9 432 F3
Arcadia Av CHAR BH8 448 A1
Arcadia Cl ROWN SO16 318 A5
Arcadia Rd CHCH/BSGR BH23 434 D7
Archangel Wy NTHA RG18 27 J4
Archdale Cl NBNE BH10 432 B6
Archers Cl TOTT SO40 316 B6
Archers Rd ELGH SO50 293 M4
WSHM SO15 343 J2
Archery Flds ODIM RG29 108 E5
Archery Gdns ITCH SO19 344 D6
Archery Gv ITCH SO19 344 C6
Archery La FHAM/PORC PO16 15 L4
WINC SO23 10 E8
Archery Ri ALTN GU34 176 D6
Archery Rd ITCH SO19 344 C7
Archway Rd CCLF BH13 446 D4
Arcot Rd NTID SP9 114 C5
Arden Cl WEND SO18 320 A7
Arden Rd MOOR/WNTN BH9 432 D5
Arden Wk NMIL/BTOS BH25 437 M6
Ardglen Rd WHCH RG28 122 A3
Ardingly Crs HEND SO30 321 J6
Ardington Ri WVILLE PO7 376 C5
Ardmore Rd PSTN BH14 446 A4
Ardrossan Av CBLY GU15 71 K3
Ardwell Cl CWTH RG45 49 H3
Arena La ALDT GU11 112 B4
Arenal Dr CWTH RG45 49 L5
Arford Common BOR GU35 202 C2
Arford Rd BOR GU35 202 C2
Argente Cl FARN GU14 89 G4
Argosy Cl HLER SO31 370 D7
Argus Rd LSOL/BMARY PO13 420 D2
Argyle Cl BOR GU35 201 J6
Argyle Crs FHAM PO15 14 D3
Argyle Rd CHCH/BSGR BH23 450 D3
NWBY RG14 2 D6
SHAM SO14 13 H1
Argyll Rd BKME/WDN BH12 446 C2
BOSC BH5 448 D4
Ariel Cl SBNE BH6 450 A3
Ariel Dr SBNE BH6 450 A4
Ariel Rd FARN GU14 90 D6
PSEA PO1 21 L1
Arkle Av STHA RG19 26 C5
Ark Royal Crs
LSOL/BMARY PO13 420 C1
Arkwright Cl KSCL RG20 56 C2
Arle Cl HORN PO8 328 B4
NALR SO24 218 B2
Arle Gdns NALR SO24 218 C2
Arley Rd PSTN BH14 445 M6
Arlington Ct
NMIL/BTOS BH25 437 M8
Arlington Ter ALDT GU11 6 D2
Arliss Rd ROWN SO16 317 M7
Arlott Ct WSHM SO15 343 J1
Arlott Dr BSTK RG21 4 F4
Armada Cl ROWN SO16 317 K1
Armada Dr FAWY SO45 367 K6
Arminers Cl GPORT PO12 18 E9
Armitage Av FAWY SO45 367 K7
Armitage Dr FRIM GU16 71 J7
Armory La PSEA PO1 20 D4
Armstrong Cl BROC SO42 387 J7
RWIN SO21 190 D4
WVILLE PO7 352 B7
Armstrong Ct ROWN SO16 317 L3
Armstrong La BROC SO42 387 J7
Armstrong Ml FARN GU14 90 A4
Armstrong Ri AND SP10 118 D5
Armstrong Rd BROC SO42 387 J7
CHAM RG24 5 L4
Armstrong Wy FARN GU14 89 L7
Armsworth La BPWT SO32 325 J6
Arnaud Cl NEND PO2 423 H1
Arne Av BKME/WDN BH12 446 D1
Arne Cl KEMP RG22 127 J1
Arne Crs BKME/WDN BH12 446 D1
Arnett Av EWKG RG40 48 B1
Arnewood Bridge Rd
LYMN SO41 438 D1
Arnewood Rd SBNE BH6 449 H3
Arnheim Cl ROWN SO16 318 B4
Arnheim Rd ROWN SO16 318 C4
Arnhem Cl ALDT GU11 7 H1
Arnhem Rd NWBY RG14 3 H4
Arnold Cl FERN BH22 380 C5
Arnold Rd ELGH SO50 293 M8
FERN BH22 380 C5
PTSW SO17 319 H6
Arnolds Cl NMIL/BTOS BH25 437 K8
Arnside Rd WVILLE PO7 352 C8
Arnwood Av FAWY SO45 367 K8
Aron Cl PSF GU32 275 K6
Arragon Ct WVILLE PO7 352 E8
Arran Cl CHAM PO6 375 K7
DEAN RG23 102 F6
Arran Wy CHCH/BSGR BH23 436 F7
Arreton HLER SO31 369 G2
Arrow Cl ELGH SO50 293 M4
ITCH SO19 344 B7
Arrow La HTWY RG27 87 G1
Arrow Rd FARN GU14 90 C6
Arrowsmith La WIMB BH21 430 C1
Arrowsmith Rd WIMB BH21 430 B2
Arrow Smith Wy STHA RG19 27 J6
Arters Lawn TOTT SO40 365 M2
Arthur Cl FNM GU9 134 E7
WCLF BH2 22 F2
Arthur Rd CHCH/BSGR BH23 449 M1
ELGH SO50 293 M4
FNM GU9 134 F7
NWBY RG14 2 B6
WINC SO23 11 G4
WSHM SO15 343 H1
Arthurs Gdns HEND SO30 321 G5
Arthur St ALDT GU11 7 G3
NEND PO2 423 J1
Artillery Cl CHAM PO6 375 G8
Artillery Rd ALDT GU11 7 G1
Artists Wy AND SP10 8 E1
Arun Cl EPSF GU31 275 K6
Arundel Cl FLET GU13 89 G8
LIPH GU30 202 A8
NALR SO24 218 C4
NMIL/BTOS BH25 437 J5
Arundel Dr FHAM/PORC PO16 15 G4
Arundel Gdns DEAN RG23 104 A1
Arundel Rd CBLY GU15 71 M4
ELGH SO50 293 M2
GPORT PO12 18 B1
TOTT SO40 316 F8
Arundel St PSEA PO1 21 K1
Arundel Wy CHCH/BSGR BH23 451 L1
Arun Rd WEND SO18 320 A6
Arun Wy ROMY SO51 288 C5
Arwood Av TADY RG26 42 A7
Ascension Cl CHAM RG24 83 H7
Ascham Rd CHAR BH8 23 J2
Ascot Cl ALTN GU34 176 F6
FHAM/STUB PO14 371 G6
NWBY RG14 3 J9
Ascot Ct ALDT GU11 6 F3
Ascot Rd BDST BH18 429 L4
ELGH SO50 321 J1
HSEA PO3 423 L1
Ascupart St SHAM SO14 13 J3
Asford Gv ELGH SO50 294 C4
Ashbarn Crs WINW SO22 238 C3
Ashbourne Cl ASHV GU12 113 M5
Ashbourne Wy STHA RG19 26 E5
Ashbridge Ri CHFD SO53 264 F7
Ashburn Garth RGWD BH24 383 H2
Ashburnham Cl ITCH SO19 344 B3
Ashburton Cl FAWY SO45 367 H5
NALR SO24 218 B3
Ashburton Rd GPORT PO12 18 B8
NALR SO24 218 B3
SSEA PO5 21 G7
Ashbury Dr FARN GU14 70 D7
Ashbury Rd BOR GU35 201 J6
Ashby Pl SSEA PO5 21 H8
Ashby Rd ITCH SO19 344 F5
TOTT SO40 341 H1
Ash Church Rd ASHV GU12 113 L6
Ash Cl ASHV GU12 113 L5
BLKW GU17 69 M3
FAWY SO45 367 L8
FBDG SP6 333 L3
FHAM/STUB PO14 14 C7
GPORT PO12 18 E4
HLER SO31 345 K8
HORN PO8 352 C5
ITCH SO19 345 G2
NBAD SO52 291 L3
NTID SP9 114 F1
ROMY SO51 291 H2
RWIN SO21 266 E8
UPTN BH16 428 F8
Ash Copse HORN PO8 352 D3
Ashcroft La HORN PO8 354 B2
Ashdale Pk EWKG RG40 48 F1
Ashdell Rd ALTN GU34 176 F5
Ashdene WSHM SO15 318 A8
Ashdene Cl WIMB BH21 404 B3
Ashdene Crs ASHV GU12 113 K5
Ashdene Rd ASHV GU12 113 K5
TOTT SO40 340 F6
Ashdown FAWY SO45 392 D5
LSOL/BMARY PO13 397 H7
Ashdown Av FARN GU14 91 H6
Ashdown Cl CHFD SO53 265 H6
Ashdown Dr CHFD SO53 265 H6
Ashdown Rd CHFD SO53 265 H7
FAWY SO45 392 D6
Ashdown Ter NTID SP9 114 E3
Ashdown Wk
NMIL/BTOS BH25 438 A6
Ashdown Wy ROMY SO51 291 G1
Ashen Cl CHFD SO53 265 H8
Ashe Rd HAV PO9 377 M3
Ashfield CHAM RG24 83 L5
Ashfield Gn YTLY GU46 69 J3
Ashfield Rd AND SP10 8 A4
Ashfields RWIN SO21 167 J2
Ashford Cl CHAM PO6 375 J7
FBDG SP6 309 J7
Ashford Crs FAWY SO45 367 M5
Ashford Hill Rd STHA RG19 39 G6
Ashford Rd FBDG SP6 309 H8
SBNE BH6 449 J1
Ash Ga NTHA RG18 27 J4
Ash Green La East ASHV GU12 113 M8
Ash Green La West ASHV GU12 113 J8
Ash Green Rd ASHV GU12 113 M7
Ash Gv CHAM RG24 106 B2
KSCL RG20 59 J6
LIPH GU30 227 G5
LYMN SO41 439 H8
RGWD BH24 383 G1
TOTT SO40 341 G6
Ash Hill Rd ASHV GU12 113 L5
Ashington Cl HORN PO8 352 E5
Ashington Pk
NMIL/BTOS BH25 437 M7
Ash La TADY RG26 41 H7
TADY RG26 63 G3
THLE RG7 31 K4
Ashlawn Gdns AND SP10 9 J8
Ashlea HTWY RG27 86 A6
Ashlea Cl ELGH SO50 295 J6
Ashleigh Cl FAWY SO45 367 L8
Ashlet Gdns NMIL/BTOS BH25 438 B4
Ashlett Cl FAWY SO45 393 G5
Ashlett Rd FAWY SO45 393 G5
Ashley Cl BMTH BH1 448 C2
FRIM GU16 91 K2
WINW SO22 214 B5
HAV PO9 377 H4
HLER SO31 370 F1
HORN PO8 352 D3
RFNM GU10 133 J1
RGWD BH24 383 H2
Ashley Common Rd
NMIL/BTOS BH25 438 A4
Ashley Ct HLER SO31 345 L6
Ashley Crs ITCH SO19 345 G6
Ashleycross Cl FAWY SO45 392 B5
Ashley Dr BLKW GU17 69 M4
RGWD BH24 358 A8
Ashley Dr North RGWD BH24 381 K3
Ashley Dr South RGWD BH24 381 K3
Ashley Dr West RGWD BH24 381 K3
Ashley Dro MARL SN8 52 C4
Ashley Gdns BPWT SO32 323 K5
CHFD SO53 293 K3
Ashley La LYMN SO41 440 C4
NMIL/BTOS BH25 438 B4
Ashley Mdw ROMY SO51 262 F8
Ashley Meads
NMIL/BTOS BH25 438 B4
Ashley Pk RGWD BH24 381 L2
Ashley Rd ALTN GU34 174 E3
BMTH BH1 448 D2
FARN GU14 91 G4
NMIL/BTOS BH25 437 L6
PSTN BH14 446 B3
Ashling Cl CHAR BH8 433 G8
WVILLE PO7 351 K4
Ashling Gdns WVILLE PO7 351 K4
Ashling La NEND PO2 399 H8
Ashling Park Rd WVILLE PO7 351 K4
Ash Lodge Cl ASHV GU12 113 K7
Ash Lodge Dr ASHV GU12 113 K7
Ashlyn Cl FHAM PO15 371 M7
Ashman Rd STHA RG19 27 J5
Ashmead BOR GU35 201 J5
Ashmead Rd ROWN SO16 317 L5
Ashmeads Cl WIMB BH21 404 E2
Ashmeads Wy WIMB BH21 404 E2
Ashmoor La CHAM RG24 106 D2
Ashmore WIMB BH21 404 B4
Ashmore Av NMIL/BTOS BH25 437 M8
PLE BH15 444 E7
Ashmore Cl RSAL SP5 259 G4
Ashmore Green Rd NTHA RG18 26 D1
Ashmore Gv CHCH/BSGR BH23 436 C7
Ashmore La RSAL SP5 259 G3
Ashmore Rd WINW SO22 216 B7
Ashridge FARN GU14 90 C1
Ashridge Av NBNE BH10 432 B3
Ashridge Cl WSHM SO15 318 E8
Ash Rd ASHV GU12 7 L5
KSCL RG20 38 C5
TOTT SO40 340 F6
Ash St ASHV GU12 113 K7
Ashtead Cl FHAM/PORC PO16 373 L8
Ashton Cl BPWT SO32 296 F7
Ashton Cross ROMY SO51 288 F6
Ashton La BPWT SO32 296 F6
Ashton Rd MOOR/WNTN BH9 432 D6
Ashton Wy FHAM/STUB PO14 396 B8
Ash Tree Cl DEAN RG23 102 F8
FARN GU14 89 M5
HASM GU27 205 J7
Ashtree Cl NMIL/BTOS BH25 438 B6
Ash Tree Gv KSCL RG20 35 L1
Ash Tree Rd AND SP10 118 B8
WEND SO18 319 K7
Ashurst Bridge Rd TOTT SO40 341 G2
Ashurst Cl WINW SO22 214 C5
ITCH SO19 344 E7
TADY RG26 41 K8
TOTT SO40 340 F6
Ashurst Rd ASHV GU12 113 J4
CHAM PO6 375 J8
CHAR BH8 433 H5
FERN BH22 380 B5
Ashwell Av CBLY GU15 71 J2
Ashwood FHAM PO15 371 J3
HLER SO31 371 G6
Ashwood Cl HAV PO9 376 F5
HISD PO11 425 L5
Ashwood Dr BDST BH18 430 A4
NWBY RG14 3 M2
Ashwood Gdns ROWN SO16 318 D5
TOTT SO40 341 G2
Ashwood Wy DEAN RG23 104 C1
Ashworth Dr STHA RG19 26 F6
Aspen Av HLER SO31 370 B8
Aspen Cl HEND SO30 346 B1
BOR GU35 201 J7
RWIN SO21 266 F8
Aspen Dr VWD BH31 356 F2
Aspen Gdns BKME/WDN BH12 446 E1
HTWY RG27 86 A6
Aspengrove
LSOL/BMARY PO13 397 J7
Aspen Holt ROWN SO16 318 F3
Aspen Pl NMIL/BTOS BH25 437 M7
Aspen Rd BKME/WDN BH12 446 E1
Aspen Wk TOTT SO40 316 A8
Aspen Wy BKME/WDN BH12 446 E1
HORN PO8 352 E3
Aspin Wy BLKW GU17 69 L3
Astbury Av BKME/WDN BH12 431 L8
Aster Rd KEMP RG22 126 F1
ROWN SO16 319 H4
Astley St SSEA PO5 21 G4
Aston Md CHCH/BSGR BH23 434 C4
Aston Rd WVILLE PO7 352 B7
Astor Crs RAND SP11 92 D6
Astra Ct FAWY SO45 367 L3
Astral Gdns HLER SO31 369 K5
Astrid Cl HISD PO11 426 A5
Asturias Wy SHAM SO14 13 L6
Asylum Rd WSHM SO15 343 L2
Atalanta Cl ENEY PO4 424 A3
Atbara Rd FLET GU13 110 F4
Atheling Rd FAWY SO45 367 L4
Athelstan Rd ITCH SO19 344 C1
SBNE BH6 449 K3
Athena Av WVILLE PO7 376 D5
Athena Cl ELGH SO50 294 F5
Atherfield Rd ROWN SO16 317 K5
Atherley Ct WSHM SO15 318 D8
Atherley Rd HISD PO11 425 J3
WSHM SO15 343 H2
Athlone Cl RAND SP11 96 A8
Atholl Ct AND SP10 118 F5
Atholl Rd BOR GU35 201 J7
Atkinson Cl GPORT PO12 18 D8
Atkins Pl FHAM PO15 372 A5
Atlantic Cl SHAM SO14 13 K8
Atlantic Park Vw
WEND SO18 319 M6
Atlantis Av WVILLE PO7 376 D6
Atrebatti Rd SHST GU47 49 M7
Attenborough Cl FARN GU14 89 G5
Attfield Cl ASHV GU12 113 J7
Attlee Gdns FLET GU13 110 E4
Attwood Cl BSTK RG21 4 A9
BSTK RG21 104 E4
FBDG SP6 333 K3
Attwoods Dro RWIN SO21 238 C8
Aubrey Cl HISD PO11 425 J4
LYMN SO41 454 E4
Auchinleck Wy ALDT GU11 6 B2
Auckland Cl NTID SP9 114 F2
Auckland Pl BROC SO42 387 L7
Auckland Rd WSHM SO15 342 D1
Auckland Rd East SSEA PO5 21 H8
Auckland Rd West SSEA PO5 21 G8
Auclum Cl THLE RG7 31 L6
Auclum La THLE RG7 31 L6
Audemer Ct RGWD BH24 359 G8
Audley Cl NWBY RG14 26 A3
Audret Cl FHAM/PORC PO16 397 M2
Augustine Rd CHAM PO6 376 A7
SHAM SO14 343 M2
Augustine Wy AND SP10 118 C5
Augustus Dr DEAN RG23 104 B1
Augustus Gdns CBLY GU15 71 M3
Augustus Wy CHFD SO53 293 K1
Aukland Av BROC SO42 387 L7
Auklet Cl KEMP RG22 126 E1
Auriol Dr CHAM PO6 376 E8
Austen Av WINW SO22 238 B5
Austen Cl TOTT SO40 341 H2
WINC SO23 11 H2
Austen Gdns HLER SO31 347 G8
Austen Gv KEMP RG22 104 D6
Austen Rd FARN GU14
Austerberry Wy
LSOL/BMARY PO13
Auster Cl CHCH/BSGR BH23
Austin Av PSTN BH14
Austin Ct CHAM PO6
Australia Cl PSEA PO1
Aust Rd FHAM/STUB PO14
Autumn Cl FERN BH22
Autumn Rd BWD BH11
TOTT SO40
Avalon PSTN BH14
Avebury Av NBNE BH10
Avebury Gdns CHFD SO53
Aveley La FNM GU9
Avenger Cl CHFD SO53
Avens Cl ELGH SO50
Avenue C FAWY SO45
Avenue Cl AND SP10
LIPH GU30
Avenue Ct GPORT PO12
Avenue D FAWY SO45
Avenue De Caen SSEA PO5
Avenue E FAWY SO45
Avenue La WCLF BH2
Avenue Rd ALTN GU34
BROC SO42
CHCH/BSGR BH23
CHCH/BSGR BH23
FARN GU14
FHAM/STUB PO14
FLET GU13
WINW SO22
GPORT PO12
GSHT GU26
HISD PO11
LYMN SO41
NMIL/BTOS BH25
SHAM SO14
WCLF BH2
WIMB BH21
Avenue Sucy CBLY GU15
The Avenue ALDT GU11
AND SP10
BPWT SO32
CBLY GU15
CCLF BH13
CWTH RG45
EPSF GU31
FERN BH22
FHAM PO15
FHAM/STUB PO14
FLET GU13
GPORT PO12
GSHT GU26
HASM GU27
LIPH GU30
MOOR/WNTN BH9
NALR SO24
RFNM GU10
NTID SP9
OVTN RG25
PTSW SO17
RAND SP11
RCCH PO18
RWIN SO21
RWIN SO21
THLE RG7
Avery Cl EWKG RG40
Avery La GPORT PO12
Avington Cl ELGH SO50
Avington Ct ROWN SO16
Avocet Crs SHST GU47
Avocet Quay EMRTH PO10
Avocet Wk LSOL/BMARY PO13
Avon Av RGWD BH24
Avonborne Wy CHFD SO53
Avon Buildings
CHCH/BSGR BH23
Avon Castle Dr RGWD BH24
Avon Cswy CHCH/BSGR BH23
Avon Cl ASHV GU12
FARN GU14
LSOL/BMARY PO13
LYMN SO41
PSF GU32
Avon Crs ROMY SO51
Avondale ASHV GU12
Avondale Rd ALDT GU11
FLET GU13
PSEA PO1
WVILLE PO7
Avon Gdns CHCH/BSGR BH23
Avon Gn CHFD SO53
Avon Meade FBDG SP6
Avon Pk RGWD BH24
Avon Rd CHAR BH8
DEAN RG23
FERN BH22
FNM GU9
NTID SP9
WEND SO18
Avon Rd East
CHCH/BSGR BH23
Avon Rd West
CHCH/BSGR BH23
Avon Run Cl CHCH/BSGR BH23
Avon Run Rd
CHCH/BSGR BH23
Avon Valley Pth RGWD BH24
RSAL SP5
Avon Vw FBDG SP6
Avon Wy HEND SO30
Avonway NWBY RG14
Avon Wy THLE RG7
Award Rd FLET GU13
WIMB BH21
Awbridge Rd HAV PO9
Axford Cl CHAR BH8
Ayesgarth FLET GU13
Ayjay Cl ALDT GU11
Aylen Rd HSEA PO3
Aylesbury Rd BMTH BH1
NEND PO2
Aylesford Wy STHA RG19
Aylesham Wy YTLY GU46
Ayling Cl LSOL/BMARY PO13
Ayling Ct FNM GU9

Hl ALDT GU11 6 C4
La ALDT GU11 6 D5
Cl DEAN RG23 104 A4
d's Dr ALTN GU34 198 B5
d St PSEA PO1 20 D1
ds Wy STOK SO20 184 E3
Cl BSTK RG21 104 F6
a KSCL RG20 37 J8
e Gdns FARN GU14 89 G4
th Rd WVILLE PO7 352 C8
Cl NMIL/BTOS BH25 437 M7
Av BOR GU35 201 M3
Cl HAV PO9 378 A4
) BH24 381 L3
Dr HASM GU27 204 C8
Gdns FLET GU13 111 G3
Wy CBLY GU15 71 L2

B

Md FNM GU9 134 D6
ds RFNM GU10 156 F3
KEMP RG22 127 J1
HUNG RG17 34 C1
SO41 413 G6
GU10 157 L8
RG25 153 J3
SP11 73 C2
SP11 117 H1
SO51 233 J3
RG7 29 K2
RG7 40 E5
RG7 42 F4
M PO17 374 C2
f the Walls SHAM SO14 13 C5
t WINC SO23 238 E4
Cl ITCH SO19 344 D7
GU47 70 A2
La HISD PO11 425 H5
GU10 180 F4
y Cl BDST BH18 430 A5
y Vw WIMB BH21 404 B3
sley Cl NBAD SO52 291 L3
sley Rd CHFD SO53 264 F7
Cl NMIL/BTOS BH25 437 M7
Powell Rd LISS GU33 225 H6
Cl HEND SO30 321 H8
Rd CFDH BH17 430 C8
Wy FHAM PO15 371 J3
Brow WVILLE PO7 376 E2
Cl ALTN GU34 197 H5
SO50 294 E6
PO15 14 A3
Farm Rd WINW SO22 238 A3
's Bank CHAM RG24 83 L8
's Cl FLET GU13 88 E8
SO41 413 G6
) BH24 381 K3
's Copse CBLY GU15 71 H5
/BTOS BH25 438 A2
's Gld THLE RG7 31 K6
's Holt YTLY GU46 68 E3
's Run HLER SO31 370 C2
's Sett CWTH RG45 49 J3
dgers HLER SO31 369 G2
's Wk FAWY SO45 367 K6
BH22 406 C1
Wy RFNM GU10 111 G8
BH31 356 D3
wood Dr FRIM GU16 71 G6
nston Dro FAWY SO45 393 G8
nston La FAWY SO45 393 C7
ar La NALR SO24 242 D1
ot Lea Rd FNM GU9 135 K3
ot Pk FNM GU9 135 K2
Rd HSEA PO3 423 L2
Rd TOTT SO40 341 K1
re La OVTN RG25 152 D3
s Wy NWBY RG14 2 A6
ll La ODIM RG29 109 H1
t Cl WINC SO23 11 L7
Cl FRIM GU16 71 G8
SO22 238 C2
) SO30 346 D2
/BTOS BH25 438 B4
Crs PLE BH15 445 H1
Dr CHCH/BSGR BH23 449 L1
Cl BLKW GU17 69 L4
s Rd SSEA PO5 21 J3
NTHA RG18 26 E4
CBLY GU15 70 E7
v KEMP RG22 104 D6
d FARN GU14 90 F2
Rd BWD BH11 431 K3
Dro ROWN SO16 317 K3
Farm Rd VWD BH31 356 C1
Fld LISS GU33 224 E6
St NEND PO2 423 H1
va Rd WEND SO18 344 E1
be Rd CCLF BH13 446 F5
ton Cl NEND PO2 399 K4
s FNM GU9 134 D8
n Cl CHCH/BSGR BH23 450 C2
Cl CHCH/BSGR BH23 436 B8
/BMARY PO13 421 H2
Crs NWBY RG14 36 F3
Dr LISS GU33 248 D4
Rd ITCH SO19 344 F3
R/WNTN BH9 432 D7
PO2 399 J7
re Ct SHST GU47 70 A1
ury Hl RAND SP11 142 C3
ury Rd RAND SP11 142 D3
Cl UPTN BH16 444 B1
Wicket La FNM GU9 134 F1
yne Rd FARN GU14 90 D2
Cl KEMP RG22 104 B5
/BTOS BH25 437 M4
V SO16 317 H7
Rd CBLY GU15 51 K8
H15 445 J7
Cl FHAM/STUB PO14 371 G7
Rd NEND PO2 423 J1
Wy SHST GU47 50 B7
n Rd FARN GU14 90 E6
Lawn Rd BROC SO42 387 M5
Balmoral Av CHAR BH8 433 J7
Balmoral Cl ALTN GU34 176 C5
CHFD SO53 265 G8
LSOL/BMARY PO13 397 H5
ROWN SO16 318 B3
Balmoral Crs FNM GU9 134 E2
Balmoral Dr FRIM GU16 71 H8
WVILLE PO7 376 A4
Balmoral Rd AND SP10 9 G5
ASHV GU12 113 K4
FHAM PO15 14 D2
PSTN BH14 446 B5
Balmoral Wk
NMIL/BTOS BH25 437 K5
Balmoral Wy KEMP RG22 126 F1
PSF GU32 275 L4
ROWN SO16 317 J2
Balston Rd PSTN BH14 445 M3
Baltic Rd HEND SO30 320 D6
Bamber La ALTN GU34 156 A4
Banbury Av ITCH SO19 345 G4
Banbury Cl FRIM GU16 91 K1
Bangor Rd WSHM SO15 342 F2
Banister Gdns WSHM SO15 343 K1
Banister Rd WSHM SO15 343 K1
Bankhill Dr LYMN SO41 440 B3
Bank Rd ALDT GU11 113 G3
Bank Side EWKG RG40 48 C2
Bankside FNM GU9 6 C8
LYMN SO41 440 B2
Bank Side WEND SO18 319 J4
Bankside Rd
MOOR/WNTN BH9 432 E5
Banks Rd CCLF BH13 457 G5
The Banks ROMY SO51 260 F3
Bank St BPWT SO32 323 J1
Bankview LYMN SO41 440 B2
Bannerman Rd PSF GU32 275 L4
Banning St ROMY SO51 290 D2
Bannister Gdns HTWY RG27 48 B8
YTLY GU46 69 J3
Bannister Pl THLE RG7 40 C2
Bannister Rd THLE RG7 31 J6
Banstead Rd WIMB BH21 429 L3
Bapaume Rd HSEA PO3 399 K3
Baptist Hl RAND SP11 97 L6
Barbara Cl FLET GU13 111 G2
Barbe Baker Av HEND SO30 320 B6
Barbel Av BSTK RG21 5 K7
Barberry Cl FLET GU13 110 F2
Barberry Wy BLKW GU17 70 C5
VWD BH31 357 G3
Barbour Cl ODIM RG29 131 H1
Barcelona Cl AND SP10 9 K3
Bardon Wy FHAM/STUB PO14 14 B8
Bardsley Dr FNM GU9 134 D8
Bardwell Cl KEMP RG22 104 B4
The Baredown HTWY RG27 107 J1
Bar End Rd WINC SO23 239 G3
Barfield Cl WINC SO23 239 G2
Barfield Rd NTHA RG18 26 D4
Barfields LYMN SO41 440 C4
Barfleur Cl FHAM PO15 14 A3
Barfleur Rd FHAM/STUB PO14 396 E3
Barford Cl CHFD SO53 265 G8
FLET GU13 89 J8
Barford La RSAL SP5 256 F8
Bargates CHCH/BSGR BH23 449 M1
Bargate St SHAM SO14 12 F4
Barge Cl ALDT GU11 113 H3
Barge La THLE RG7 45 K3
Barham Cl GPORT PO12 421 M2
Barham Rd PSF GU32 275 L5
Barham Wy NEND PO2 399 H4
Baring Cl RWIN SO21 170 F4
RWIN SO21 216 F1
Baring Rd SBNE BH6 449 M4
WINC SO23 11 K9
Barker Cl WHIT RG2 47 H1
Barker Mill Cl ROWN SO16 317 K2
Barkis Md SHST GU47 50 B6
Barle Cl WEND SO18 320 A7
Barley Down Dr WINW SO22 238 C4
Barley Mow Cl HTWY RG27 87 L8
Barley Mow Hl BOR GU35 202 C2
Barley Wy FARN GU14 89 G3
Barlow Cl FHAM/STUB PO14 395 M6
Barlows La AND SP10 142 E3
Barlows Rd TADY RG26 61 L1
Barnard Cl FRIM GU16 71 J8
Barnbrook Rd HLER SO31 370 C4
Barn Cl CBLY GU15 71 H2
EMRTH PO10 378 B8
Barn Close La KSCL RG20 55 L8
Barn Crs NWBY RG14 37 G1
Barncroft FNM GU9 134 F7
RAND SP11 116 F3
Barncroft Wy HAV PO9 377 H5
Barnes Cl FARN GU14 91 G4
HLER SO31 370 B4
ITCH SO19 345 G2
NBNE BH10 432 B5
WINC SO23 238 D3
Barnes Crs NBNE BH10 432 B5
WIMB BH21 404 C4
Barnes La HLER SO31 370 C3
LYMN SO41 439 G8
Barnes Rd FRIM GU16 71 H8
ITCH SO19 345 G2
NBNE BH10 432 B5
PSEA PO1 423 J2
Barnes Wallis Rd
FHAM PO15 371 H4
Barnes Wy HAV PO9 377 G5
Barnet Side La PSF GU32 246 C3
Barnetts Wood La NALR SO24 195 M8
Barney Evans Crs HORN PO8 352 B5
Barneyhayes La TOTT SO40 314 F8
Barnfield CHCH/BSGR BH23 436 B8
YTLY GU46 69 G3
Barnfield Cl ALTN GU34 156 B4
EMRTH PO10 379 J6
ITCH SO19 344 C7
Barnfield Ct FHAM/STUB PO14 14 D8
ITCH SO19 344 D7
Barnfield Ri AND SP10 8 C9
Barnfield Rd EPSF GU31 276 B5
ITCH SO19 344 C7
Barnfield Wy ITCH SO19 344 D7
Barn Fold HORN PO8 352 F7
Barn Green Cl WVILLE PO7 351 K4
Barn La ALTN GU34 196 E7
DEAN RG23 102 F8
Barn Meadow Cl FLET GU13 110 E5
Barn Owl Wy THLE RG7 31 L5
Barn Piece NBAD SO52 292 E2
Barn Rd BDST BH18 429 M5
Barnsfield Crs TOTT SO40 341 G1
Barnsfield Rd RGWD BH24 381 L7
Barnside Wy LISS GU33 248 E5
Barnsland HEND SO30 320 B6
Barnsley Cl FRIM GU16 91 L7
Barns Rd FERN BH22 406 E2
The Barns OVTN RG25 126 C8
Baroda Rd NTID SP9 114 B4
Baron Rd HLER SO31 369 K5
Barons Md ROWN SO16 317 K5
Barons Rd BWD BH11 431 H2
Barossa Rd CBLY GU15 71 G1
Barracane Dr CWTH RG45 49 L4
Barrack La RGWD BH24 383 H4
Barrack Rd ALDT GU11 6 E2
CHCH/BSGR BH23 434 C8
FERN BH22 406 E6
Barracks Rd STHA RG19 38 C4
Barra Cl DEAN RG23 102 F6
Barrie Cl HLER SO31 347 G8
Barrie Rd FNM GU9 134 D1
MOOR/WNTN BH9 432 D5
Barrington Cl ELGH SO50 293 L3
Barron Pl CHAM RG24 82 A8
Barrow Down Gdns ITCH SO19 345 J5
Barrow Dr CHAR BH8 433 K6
Barrowgate Wy CHAR BH8 433 H5
Barrow Hl RAND SP11 142 D8
Barrow Hill Rd TOTT SO40 315 J5
Barrow Rd CHAR BH8 433 K6
Barrows La LYMN SO41 438 F1
RSAL SP5 287 G2
Barrow Vw FERN BH22 405 L2
Barrow Wy CHAR BH8 433 K6
Barrs Av NMIL/BTOS BH25 437 L4
Barrs Wood Dr
NMIL/BTOS BH25 437 M4
Barrs Wood Rd
NMIL/BTOS BH25 437 M4
Barry Gdns BDST BH18 429 K3
Barry Rd ITCH SO19 344 F3
Barry Wy KEMP RG22 127 J1
Barters Cl ROWN SO16 317 L7
Barters La BDST BH18 429 K4
Bartholomew Cl HASM GU27 205 G8
Bartholomew St NWBY RG14 2 D6
Bartlemy Cl NWBY RG14 2 A9
Bartlemy Rd NWBY RG14 2 A9
Bartlett Cl FHAM PO15 14 C2
Bartlett Dr LTDN BH7 433 M8
The Bartletts HLER SO31 369 L6
Bartley Av TOTT SO40 341 J2
Bartley Rd TOTT SO40 340 A5
Bartley Wy HTWY RG27 86 B8
Bartok Cl KEMP RG22 104 D7
Barton Cl ALDT GU11 6 A3
AND SP10 118 C5
ROMY SO51 263 G8
Barton Common La
NMIL/BTOS BH25 437 M8
Barton Common Rd
NMIL/BTOS BH25 453 G1
Barton Court Av
NMIL/BTOS BH25 452 E1
Barton Court Rd
NMIL/BTOS BH25 437 L7
Barton Crs WEND SO18 319 L7
Barton Cft NMIL/BTOS BH25 452 F1
Barton Cross HORN PO8 352 F1
Barton Dr HEND SO30 346 B1
HLER SO31 369 K5
NMIL/BTOS BH25 437 K8
Barton Dro RWIN SO21 167 M4
Barton Gn NMIL/BTOS BH25 452 F2
Barton La NMIL/BTOS BH25 437 H8
Barton Rd ELGH SO50 294 B5
Barton's Dr YTLY GU46 69 G4
Bartonside Rd
NMIL/BTOS BH25 437 G8
Bartons La CHAM RG24 83 M8
Bartons Rd FBDG SP6 309 L7
HAV PO9 377 L3
The Bartons FBDG SP6 309 L7
Bartons Wy FARN GU14 89 M1
Barton Wy NMIL/BTOS BH25 437 K8
Barton Wood Rd
NMIL/BTOS BH25 452 D1
Bartram Rd TOTT SO40 341 L2
Barwell Cl CWTH RG45 49 J4
Barwell Gv EMRTH PO10 378 C5
Bascott Cl BWD BH11 431 L7
Bascott Rd BWD BH11 431 K7
Bashley Common Rd
NMIL/BTOS BH25 411 L8
Bashley Cross Rd
CHCH/BSGR BH23 437 H3
Bashley Dr NMIL/BTOS BH25 437 M2
Bashley Rd NMIL/BTOS BH25 437 L1
Basingbourne Cl FLET GU13 110 F2
Basingbourne Rd FLET GU13 110 E3
Basing Dean ALTN GU34 245 K3
Basing Dr ALDT GU11 7 H8
Basing Rd CHAM RG24 5 M6
HAV PO9 377 J3
Basingstoke Rd ALTN GU34 176 A5
HTWY RG27 65 J2
KSCL RG20 59 K6
RWIN SO21 191 M4
TADY RG26 81 K3
THLE RG7 29 K7
WINC SO23 215 J2
Basing Vw BSTK RG21 5 H6
Basing Wy CHFD SO53 292 F4
Basingwell St BPWT SO32 323 H1
Basin St NEND PO2 399 H8
Bassenthwaite Gdns
BOR GU35 201 J3
Bassett Av ROWN SO16 318 E3
Bassett Cl FRIM GU16 71 H8
ROWN SO16 318 E4
Bassett Crs East ROWN SO16 318 E4
Bassett Crs West ROWN SO16 318 E5
Bassett Dl ROWN SO16 318 E2
Bassett Gdns ROWN SO16 318 D4
Bassett Gn ROWN SO16 319 G3
Bassett Green Cl ROWN SO16 318 F3
Bassett Green Dr ROWN SO16 318 F3
Bassett Green Rd ROWN SO16 318 F2
Bassett Heath Av ROWN SO16 318 E1
Bassett Meadow ROWN SO16 318 E5
Bassett Ms ROWN SO16 318 E3
Bassett Rd BKME/WDN BH12 446 A2
Bassett Rw ROWN SO16 318 E2
Bassett Wood Dr ROWN SO16 318 E2
Bassett Wood Rd ROWN SO16 318 E2
Bat & Ball La FNM GU9 158 D2
RFNM GU10 158 D3
Batchelor Crs BWD BH11 431 K5
Batchelor Dr CHAM RG24 106 B3
Batchelor Gn HLER SO31 345 L8
Batchelor Rd BWD BH11 431 K5
Batchelors Barn Rd AND SP10 9 L4
Batcombe Cl BWD BH11 431 J5
Bath Cl ITCH SO19 344 F2
Bath Hill Rbt BMTH BH1 22 F7
Bathing La PSEA PO1 20 B4
Bath La FHAM/PORC PO16 15 M6
Bath Lane (Lower)
FHAM/PORC PO16 15 M7
Bath Rd BMTH BH1 22 F7
CBLY GU15 70 F2
EMRTH PO10 378 D8
ENEY PO4 423 K5
ITCH SO19 344 F2
LYMN SO41 440 D5
NTHA RG18 26 C4
NWBY RG14 25 G3
THLE RG7 28 C6
Bath Sq PSEA PO1 20 B4
Bath St SHAM SO14 343 L1
Bathurst Cl HISD PO11 425 J5
Batsford RAND SP11 97 L6
Battenburg Av NEND PO2 399 K6
Battenburg Rd GPORT PO12 19 G2
Batten Cl CHCH/BSGR BH23 435 H8
Batten Rd RSAL SP5 256 D8
Battens Av OVTN RG25 101 G8
Battens Wy HAV PO9 377 K4
Batterley Dro WIMB BH21 332 D4
Battery Cl GPORT PO12 397 K8
Battery End NWBY RG14 37 G2
Battery Hl BPWT SO32 297 G8
WINW SO22 238 B2
Battery Rw PSEA PO1 20 C6
Battle Cl HLER SO31 370 D4
NWBY RG14 25 G4
Battle Rd NWBY RG14 36 F2
Baughurst Rd TADY RG26 41 H8
THLE RG7 42 D2
B Av FAWY SO45 392 B3
Baverstock Rd
BKME/WDN BH12 431 M8
Baverstocks ALTN GU34 176 F2
The Baxendales NWBY RG14 3 J8
Baxter Rd ITCH SO19 345 J4
Baybridge La BPWT SO32 268 D6
Baybridge Rd HAV PO9 377 M3
Bay Cl ITCH SO19 344 E5
UPTN BH16 444 A2
WIMB BH21 356 C8
Bayfield Av FRIM GU16 71 H6
Bayford Cl FARN GU14 70 D7
Bayly Av FHAM/PORC PO16 398 B2
Baynard Cl BSTK RG21 5 G4
Bay Rd GPORT PO12 18 A6
ITCH SO19 344 E5
Bays Rd LYMN SO41 440 A5
Baythorn Cl NEND PO2 423 H1
Bay Trees ITCH SO19 345 J2
Bay Tree Wy CHCH/BSGR BH23 436 B7
Baywood Cl FARN GU14 89 M3
Bazaar Rd NTID SP9 114 B3
Beach Av NMIL/BTOS BH25 452 E1
Beach Dr CHAM PO6 374 D8
Beach Rd CCLF BH13 446 F8
EMRTH PO10 378 C8
HISD PO11 425 J5
LSOL/BMARY PO13 420 C3
SSEA PO5 21 K9
Beach's Crs TADY RG26 62 D5
Beachway FHAM/PORC PO16 398 B2
Beacon Bottom HLER SO31 370 E2
Beacon Cl HLER SO31 370 E2
LYMN SO41 439 H7
RFNM GU10 158 D3
Beacon Ct FBDG SP6 309 K5
Beacon Dr CHCH/BSGR BH23 451 L1
Beacon Gdns BDST BH18 429 J5
Beacon Hill Ct GSHT GU26 204 A2
Beacon Hill La BPWT SO32 270 E8
BPWT SO32 299 G2
UPTN BH16 428 F5
Beacon Hill Rd FLET GU13 111 G4
GSHT GU26 203 M2
Beacon Mt HLER SO31 370 E2
Beacon Park Crs UPTN BH16 428 E8
Beacon Park Rd UPTN BH16 428 E8
Beacon Rd BDST BH18 429 H5
FARN GU14 90 E8
HEND SO30 320 C8
UPTN BH16 444 A1
WCLF BH2 22 D7
Beaconsfield Av CHAM PO6 399 L1
Beaconsfield Rd
BKME/WDN BH12 446 C3
BSTK RG21 105 G4
CHCH/BSGR BH23 450 A1
FHAM/PORC PO16 15 J8
WVILLE PO7 352 C8
Beacon Sq EMRTH PO10 402 C1
Beacon Wy BDST BH18 429 J5
HLER SO31 370 E2
Beale's Cl AND SP10 9 K5
Beales La RFNM GU10 158 C1
Bealeswood La RFNM GU10 180 B2
Bealing Cl ROWN SO16 319 G4
Beal's Pightle TADY RG26 81 L1
Beam Hollow FNM GU9 134 F1
Beamish Rd CFDH BH17 430 D8
Beancroft Rd STHA RG19 27 G6
Bear Cross Av BWD BH11 431 J2
Bear Hl KSCL RG20 59 H7
Bear La FNM GU9 134 E5
NWBY RG14 2 E4
Bearslane Cl TOTT SO40 316 C7
Bearwood FLET GU13 88 F7
Beatrice Rd ENEY PO4 21 M7
WSHM SO15 343 G1
Beattie Ri HEND SO30 321 H6
Beatty Cl HLER SO31 370 F4
RGWD BH24 359 G8
Beatty Dr GPORT PO12 18 B7
Beatty Rd MOOR/WNTN BH9 432 F7
Beauchamp Av
LSOL/BMARY PO13 397 G6
Beauchamps Gdns LTDN BH7 433 L8
Beauclerk Gn HTWY RG27 87 H7
Beaucroft La WIMB BH21 404 C2
Beaucroft Rd BPWT SO32 323 K5
WIMB BH21 404 B2
Beaufighter Rd FARN GU14 90 D8
Beaufort Av FHAM/PORC PO16 14 E2
Beaufort Dr BPWT SO32 297 H8
WIMB BH21 404 A3
Beaufort Rd FLET GU13 111 G1
FNM GU9 134 F5
HAV PO9 16 A3
BOR GU35 201 J3
SBNE BH6 449 H3
SSEA PO5 21 K9
WINC SO23 238 E2
Beaufoys Av FERN BH22 406 A1
Beaufoys Cl FERN BH22 406 A1
Beaufront Cl CBLY GU15 71 K1
Beaufront Rd CBLY GU15 71 K1
Beaulieu Av CHCH/BSGR BH23 449 K1
FHAM/PORC PO16 373 L8
HAV PO9 377 H2
Beaulieu Cl WINW SO22 214 C4
ROWN SO16 318 A3
Beaulieu Ct AND SP10 119 H6
Beaulieu Gdns BLKW GU17 69 M3
Beaulieu Pl
LSOL/BMARY PO13 397 G6
Beaulieu Rd BROC SO42 365 K8
BROC SO42 391 G4
CHCH/BSGR BH23 449 K1
ELGH SO50 293 M4
FAWY SO45 367 J7
LYND SO43 363 M4
NEND PO2 399 J7
TOTT SO40 366 B3
WBNE BH4 447 G7
Beaumaris Cl AND SP10 8 D9
Beaumaris Gdns FAWY SO45 367 K4
Beaumaris Pde FRIM GU16 71 J8
Beaumond Gn WINC SO23 10 F8
Beaumont Cl FHAM PO15 14 B1
ROWN SO16 318 D5
Beaumont Ct GPORT PO12 397 L8
Beaumont Gv ALDT GU11 6 B2
Beaumont Ri FHAM PO15 372 B4
Beaumont Rd CCLF BH13 457 L1
TOTT SO40 341 L1
Beaurepaire Cl TADY RG26 63 J5
Beauworth Av WEND SO18 320 B8
Beaver Dr ELGH SO50 294 F6
Beaver La YTLY GU46 69 H3
Beavers Cl ALTN GU34 176 D4
FNM GU9 134 D6
TADY RG26 41 J7
Beavers Hl FNM GU9 134 C6
Beavers Ms BOR GU35 201 K4
Beavers Rd FNM GU9 134 D6
Beccles Cl PLE BH15 444 E6
Becher Rd PSTN BH14 446 D4
Beck Cl HLER SO31 370 C5
Beckett Cl DEAN RG23 103 M3
Beckett Rd AND SP10 8 D4
Beckford La WHAM PO17 350 C7
Beck Gdns FNM GU9 134 D2
Beckham La PSF GU32 275 J4
Beckhampton Rd PLE BH15 444 D5
Beckley Copse
CHCH/BSGR BH23 436 E6
Beck St PSEA PO1 20 E1
Becton La NMIL/BTOS BH25 453 G1
Becton Md NMIL/BTOS BH25 437 M7
Bedale Wy PLE BH15 445 L3
Beddington Ct CHAM RG24 83 M7
Bede Dr AND SP10 118 C5
Bedenham La
LSOL/BMARY PO13 397 J5
Bedfield La WINC SO23 215 G3
Bedford Av FRIM GU16 91 J3
ITCH SO19 344 C6
Bedford Cl FBDG SP6 309 L5
HAV PO9 17 J6
HEND SO30 346 B2
BOR GU35 201 J7
NWBY RG14 36 F3
Bedford Crs FRIM GU16 91 H2
LTDN BH7 449 H1
Bedford La FRIM GU16 91 J2
Bedford Pl WSHM SO15 343 K2
Bedford Rd PSF GU32 275 J5
Bedford Rd North
BKME/WDN BH12 431 G6
Bedford Rd South
BKME/WDN BH12 431 G6
Bedford St GPORT PO12 421 L2
SSEA PO5 21 G3
Bedhampton Hl CHAM PO6 376 E7
Bedhampton Hill Rd
HAV PO9 376 F7
Bedhampton Rd HAV PO9 377 G6
NEND PO2 399 K7
Bedhampton Wy HAV PO9 377 K4
Bedwell Cl ROWN SO16 317 L3
Beecham Berry KEMP RG22 127 J1
Beecham Rd PSEA PO1 423 J1
Beech Av CBLY GU15 71 G4
CHCH/BSGR BH23 434 B8
RFNM GU10 158 F3
SBNE BH6 449 H4

WEND SO18 344 C1
Beechbrook Av YTLY GU46 69 G3
Beech Cl BDST BH18 429 H4
CHFD SO53 265 J8
FBDG SP6 333 L3
WINW SO22 238 A5
HLER SO31 369 J6
HORN PO8 352 D6
LYMN SO41 439 H8
OVTN RG25 101 G6
RAND SP11 116 D8
ROMY SO51 291 H2
STOK SO20 163 G4
TADY RG26 63 M6
TLHT RG30 31 L4
VWD BH31 356 C3
Beech Copse WINW SO22 214 A7
Beech Ct WIMB BH21 404 C4
Beech Crs FAWY SO45 367 L8
Beechcrest Vw HTWY RG27 86 A6
Beechcroft Cl CHFD SO53 293 J3
FHAM PO15 371 M7
LIPH GU30 226 A5
Beechcroft Cottages
STOK SO20 209 G2
Beechcroft La RGWD BH24 358 F8
Beechcroft Rd GPORT PO12 18 D6
Beechcroft Wy CHFD SO53 293 J2
Beechdale Cl TOTT SO40 316 B6
Beech Dr BLKW GU17 70 A4
Beechen La LYND SO43 363 M6
Beeches Hl BPWT SO32 297 J6
The Beeches ASHV GU12 91 J7
ELGH SO50 295 J7
KEMP RG22 127 J2
ROMY SO51 288 C5
Beechey Rd BMTH BH1 23 H2
CHAR BH8 23 H1
Beechfield AMSY SP4 160 A2
Beechfield Ct WSHM SO15 317 M8
Beech Gdns HLER SO31 369 J6
Beech Gra RSAL SP5 287 J6
Beech Gv GPORT PO12 18 D5
HISD PO11 425 M4
RAND SP11 165 L2
RWIN SO21 267 M4
Beech Hanger AMSY SP4 138 C7
Beech Hanger End GSHT GU26 203 L5
Beech Hl BOR GU35 202 E4
Beech Hill Rd BOR GU35 202 C2
NTID SP9 114 F1
THLE RG7 45 H2
Beeching Cl ASHV GU12 113 L5
Beechlands Rd ALTN GU34 197 G4
Beech La GSHT GU26 203 L4
RGWD BH24 381 J6
Beechmount Rd ROWN SO16 318 E3
Beechnut Dr BLKW GU17 69 L2
Beechnut Rd ASHV GU12 7 H3
Beech Ride FLET GU13 110 E1
SHST GU47 49 L8
Beech Rd CHFD SO53 265 J8
FARN GU14 90 E1
FHAM PO15 14 D4
FRIM GU16 91 J2
HASM GU27 229 G1
HEND SO30 346 B1
HORN PO8 328 C3
KSCL RG20 38 D6
NALR SO24 218 C3
TOTT SO40 340 F6
WSHM SO15 342 F2
Beech Tree Cl DEAN RG23 102 F8
Beech Tree Dr FNM GU9 135 K3
Beech Tree Wk ROMY SO51 209 H5
Beech Wk STHA RG19 27 H6
Beech Wy DEAN RG23 104 B1
HORN PO8 352 F3
Beechwood FBDG SP6 309 J7
Beechwood Av BOSC BH5 448 E4
NMIL/BTOS BH25 437 J4
WVILLE PO7 376 C2
Beech Wood Cl BDST BH18 429 L5
Beechwood Cl CHFD SO53 264 F7
FLET GU13 110 D2
HLER SO31 370 B8
KEMP RG22 127 H2
Beechwood Ct LISS GU33 248 F2
Beechwood Crs CHFD SO53 264 F6
Beechwood Gdns BOSC BH5 448 F4
WEND SO18 319 K8
Beechwood La RGWD BH24 384 F5
Beechwood Ri WEND SO18 320 B7
Beechwood Rd ALTN GU34 176 C6
FAWY SO45 392 A5
FERN BH22 380 D8
NEND PO2 399 J4
TOTT SO40 339 K3
Beechwood Wy FAWY SO45 367 G6
Beechworth Rd HAV PO9 17 G4
Beehive Wk PSEA PO1 20 D4
Beethoven Rd KEMP RG22 104 D8
Beeton's Av ASHV GU12 113 K4
Beggar's La WINC SO23 11 J7
Beggarwood La DEAN RG23 126 F3
KEMP RG22 127 J2
Begonia Cl KEMP RG22 126 F1
Begonia Rd ROWN SO16 319 G4
Behrendt Cl GPORT PO12 421 L2
Belaga Cl STOK SO20 162 F3
Belben Cl BKME/WDN BH12 431 H6
Belben Rd BKME/WDN BH12 431 G6
Belbins ROMY SO51 262 E4
Beldham Rd RFNM GU10 158 C1
Belfield Rd SBNE BH6 449 M4
Belfry Wk FHAM/STUB PO14 371 G6
Belgrave Ct BLKW GU17 70 A5
Belgrave Rd CCLF BH13 446 F6
PTSW SO17 319 H6
Belgravia Rd NEND PO2 399 K7
Bellair Rd HAV PO9 17 G5
Belland Dr ALDT GU11 6 B3
Bell Cl FARN GU14 90 F2
Bell Crs WVILLE PO7 376 C2
Bell Davies Rd
FHAM/STUB PO14 395 M7
Bellemoor Rd WSHM SO15 318 C7
Bellever Hl CBLY GU15 71 H3
Bellevue WHCH RG28 122 B3
Belle Vue Cl ASHV GU12 7 M2
SBNE BH6 449 J4
Belle Vue Crs SBNE BH6 449 L4
Belle Vue Gv FERN BH22 380 D6
Bellevue La EMRTH PO10 378 D6
Belle Vue Rd AND SP10 9 J8
PSTN BH14 446 B5
SBNE BH6 449 J5
ASHV GU12 7 L2
CHAM RG24 106 A2
Bellevue Rd ELGH SO50 293 M5
WSHM SO15 343 L2
Bellevue Ter SSEA PO5 20 E6
Belle Vue Wk FERN BH22 406 C6
Bellew Rd FRIM GU16 91 L2
Bellflower Wy NBAD SO52 292 E1
Bell Heather Cl UPTN BH16 428 F8
Bell Hl PSF GU32 275 J3
Bell Hill Rdg PSF GU32 275 K3
Bell Holt NWBY RG14 36 F3
Bell House NALR SO24 218 C4
Bellingham Cl CBLY GU15 71 M4
Bell La BLKW GU17 69 M3
HUNG RG17 34 A5
RFNM GU10 158 B5
OVTN RG25 152 C2
Bell Meadow Rd HTWY RG27 86 A7
Bell Rd AND SP10 9 L6
CHAM RG24 5 L5
CHAM PO6 375 H8
HASM GU27 228 D5
Bells La FHAM/STUB PO14 396 A6
Bell St RAND SP11 92 F6
ROMY SO51 290 D1
SHAM SO14 13 H5
WHCH RG28 122 B3
Bell Vale La HASM GU27 228 E4
Belmont Av CHAR BH8 433 G6
Belmont Cl AND SP10 9 K8
FARN GU14 90 C1
FAWY SO45 367 L6
FHAM/STUB PO14 396 B5
HORN PO8 328 B6
VWD BH31 356 E3
Belmont Gv HAV PO9 377 G6
Belmont Hts KEMP RG22 127 H3
Belmont Ms CBLY GU15 70 F5
Belmont Pl SSEA PO5 21 H5
Belmont Rd AND SP10 9 J8
CBLY GU15 70 F4
CHFD SO53 293 J5
CWTH RG45 49 L2
NMIL/BTOS BH25 438 A4
PSTN BH14 446 A3
PTSW SO17 319 G8
Belmont St SSEA PO5 21 H5
Belmore Cl PSEA PO1 423 J1
Belmore La LYMN SO41 440 C5
RWIN SO21 268 C3
Belmore Rd LYMN SO41 440 B5
Belney La WHAM PO17 351 J8
Belsize Rd FARN GU14 90 F7
Belstone Ms FARN GU14 90 D1
Belstone Rd TOTT SO40 341 J1
Belton Rd CBLY GU15 71 H3
ITCH SO19 344 F5
Belvedere Cl FLET GU13 88 B7
Belvedere Ct BLKW GU17 70 A5
Belvedere Dr NWBY RG14 2 E9
Belvedere Gdns CHAM RG24 83 M4
Belvedere Rd
CHCH/BSGR BH23 449 M1
FARN GU14 90 F6
FAWY SO45 367 L6
TWDS BH3 447 M2
Belverdere Cl PSF GU32 275 L4
Belvidere Rd SHAM SO14 13 L2
Belvidere Ter SHAM SO14 13 L1
Belvoir Cl FHAM/PORC PO16 15 J7
FRIM GU16 71 J7
Bembridge HLER SO31 369 G2
Bembridge Cl ROWN SO16 319 H3
Bembridge Ct CWTH RG45 49 H4
Bembridge Crs ENEY PO4 21 L9
Bembridge Dr HISD PO11 426 A7
Bemister Rd
MOOR/WNTN BH9 432 E8
Benbow Cl HORN PO8 353 G1
Benbow Crs BKME/WDN BH12 431 J7
Benbow Pl PSEA PO1 20 C1
Benbridge Av BWD BH11 431 K3
Bendigo Rd CHCH/BSGR BH23 434 C8
Beneden Gn NALR SO24 218 C3
Benedict Cl ROMY SO51 291 H1
Benedict Wy
FHAM/PORC PO16 374 C6
RWIN SO21 266 F1
Beneficial St PSEA PO1 20 C2
Benellen Av WBNE BH4 447 H4
Benellen Gdns WBNE BH4 447 H4
Benellen Rd WBNE BH4 447 H3
Benenden Gn NALR SO24 218 C4
Benett Cl NWBY RG14 25 J3
Benett Gdns NWBY RG14 25 J3
Bengal Rd MOOR/WNTN BH9 432 C7
Benger's La ROMY SO51 233 J6
Benham Cha KSCL RG20 24 B3
Benham Dr HSEA PO3 399 K4
Benham Dro STOK SO20 184 C2
Benham Gv FHAM/PORC PO16 398 B2
Benham Hl NTHA RG18 26 D4
Benham La THLE RG7 46 A5
Benhams Farm Cl
WEND SO18 319 M7
Benhams La LISS GU33 224 E4
Benhams Rd WEND SO18 319 M6
Benin Rd RAND SP11 115 J2
Benjamin Rd PLE BH15 444 D6
Ben La RSAL SP5 230 C1
Benmoor Rd CFDH BH17 429 L8
Benmore Cl NMIL/BTOS BH25 438 A6
Benmore Gdns CHFD SO53 265 G8
Benmore Rd
MOOR/WNTN BH9 432 E7
Bennet Cl ALTN GU34 176 D4
BSTK RG21 5 H4
Bennett Cl RSAL SP5 285 J2
Bennett Ct CBLY GU15 70 F3
Bennett Rd CHAR BH8 448 B2
Bennett's Hl TLHT RG30 31 L1
Bennetts La RGWD BH24 385 G6
Bennion Rd NBNE BH10 432 A5
Benridge Cl BDST BH18 429 L5
Benson Cl CHCH/BSGR BH23 409 M7
Benson Rd CWTH RG45 49 J3
WSHM SO15 318 A8
Benta Cl STOK SO20 162 F3
Bentham Rd GPORT PO12 18 E6
Bentham Wy HLER SO31 346 B8
Bentley Cl HORN PO8 328 B8
WINC SO23 215 G2
Bentley Copse CBLY GU15 71 L4
Bentley Ct HAV PO9 377 M3
Bentley Crs FHAM/PORC PO16 14 F3
Bentley Gn WEND SO18 320 B8
Bentley Rd MOOR/WNTN BH9 432 D5
Bentley Wy RSAL SP5 207 G3
Bent St STOK SO20 184 D2
Benwell Cl ODIM RG29 108 B8
Bepton Down EPSF GU31 275 M5
Berber Cl FHAM PO15 371 G1
Bercote Cl WINW SO22 214 A3
Bere Cl CFDH BH17 430 B6
CHFD SO53 264 F8
WINW SO22 10 A3
Bere Farm La WHAM PO17 349 K8
Bere Hl WHCH RG28 122 B2
Bere Hill Cl WHCH RG28 122 C2
Bere Hill Crs AND SP10 9 L7
Berehurst ALTN GU34 176 D6
Bere Rd WVILLE PO7 351 L4
Beresford Cl AND SP10 142 F3
CHFD SO53 293 K3
FRIM GU16 91 J2
WVILLE PO7 376 C2
Beresford Gdns
CHCH/BSGR BH23 450 D2
CHFD SO53 293 K3
Beresford Rd
BKME/WDN BH12 446 C2
CHFD SO53 293 K3
FHAM/STUB PO14 396 B5
LYMN SO41 440 A4
NEND PO2 399 J6
SBNE BH6 449 G4
Bereweeke Av WINW SO22 10 C1
Bereweeke Cl WINW SO22 10 C4
Bereweeke Rd WINW SO22 10 C4
Bereweeke Wy WINW SO22 10 D3
Berewyk Cl KEMP RG22 126 F1
Bergen Crs HEND SO30 346 A3
Berkeley Av BKME/WDN BH12 431 G8
Berkeley Cl FHAM/STUB PO14 395 M6
FLET GU13 89 G7
VWD BH31 356 C1
WSHM SO15 343 J1
Berkeley Crs FRIM GU16 71 K8
Berkeley Dr KEMP RG22 104 E8
Berkeley Gdns HEND SO30 346 A3
Berkeley Rd NWBY RG14 2 C5
TWDS BH3 447 K1
Berkeley Sq HAV PO9 17 J4
Berkley Av FERN BH22 406 B6
Berkshire Circular Routes
HUNG RG17 33 H3
KSCL RG20 24 D8
THLE RG7 30 B2
THLE RG7 43 L4
Berkshire Cl PSEA PO1 21 K2
Berkshire Corpse Rd
ALDT GU11 112 B1
Berkshire Dr STHA RG19 27 K6
Berkshire Rd CBLY GU15 51 J8
Bermuda Cl CHAM RG24 83 H7
Bernard Av ALTN GU34 197 G6
CHAM PO6 375 L8
Bernard St SHAM SO14 13 G5
Bernersh Cl SHST GU47 49 M7
Berney Rd ENEY PO4 424 A4
Bernina Av WVILLE PO7 352 A6
Bernina Cl WVILLE PO7 352 A6
Bernstein Rd KEMP RG22 104 B8
Bernwood Gv FAWY SO45 418 C1
Berrans Av BWD BH11 431 M2
Berrybank SHST GU47 70 B2
Berrybarn La SELS PO20 427 K8
Berry Cl HEND SO30 346 B2
Berrydown La OVTN RG25 124 B1
OVTN RG25 152 B4
Berrydown Rd HAV PO9 377 G1
Berryfield Rd LYMN SO41 438 E6
Berry Hl NALR SO24 219 M3
Berrylands LISS GU33 248 F1
Berry La FHAM/STUB PO14 395 L6
RWIN SO21 266 F1
Berrywood Gdns
HEND SO30 321 G8
HEND SO30 345 M1
Berrywood La NALR SO24 174 A2
Bertie Rd ENEY PO4 423 M4
Bertram Rd NMIL/BTOS BH25 438 A4
Berwick Rd TWDS BH3 447 K2
Berwyn Cl KEMP RG22 103 M5
Beryl Av GPORT PO12 397 K8
Beryton Cl GPORT PO12 421 L2
Beryton Rd GPORT PO12 421 L2
Besomer Dro RSAL SP5 285 L4
Bessborough Rd CCLF BH13 457 K1
Bessemer Rd BSTK RG21 104 E6
Beswick Av NBNE BH10 432 B6
Beta Rd FARN GU14 90 C3
Bethel Cl FNM GU9 135 G2
Bethel La FNM GU9 135 G2
Bethia Rd CHAR BH8 448 C2
Betjeman Wk YTLY GU46 68 E4
Betsy Cl CHCH/BSGR BH23 409 M7
Betsy La CHCH/BSGR BH23 409 M7
Betteridge Dr ROWN SO16 317 J2
Betteridge Rd STHA RG19 27 J6
Bettesworth Rd PSEA PO1 423 J1
Bettiscombe Cl CFDH BH17 430 B6
Betula Cl WVILLE PO7 376 E2
Beulah Rd ROWN SO16 317 M7
Bevan Cl ITCH SO19 344 C7
Bevan Rd HORN PO8 352 D3
Beveren Cl FARN GU14 89 G4
Beverley Cl ASHV GU12 113 J7
BSTK RG21 105 G7
CBLY GU15 71 M2
HLER SO31 371 G4
NTHA RG18 26 F4
Beverley Crs FARN GU14 90 C5
Beverley Gdns BPWT SO32 324 A3
HLER SO31 345 J7
NBNE BH10 432 B5
ROMY SO51 263 H7
Beverley Hts WEND SO18 319 L5
Beverley Rd FAWY SO45 367 K8
FHAM/STUB PO14 396 A7
Beverly Cl LSOL/BMARY PO13 397 H6
The Bevers THLE RG7 43 K2
Beverston Rd CHAM PO6 374 E7
Bevis Cl FAWY SO45 392 D6
HLER SO31 370 B8
Bevis Rd GPORT PO12 18 F2
NEND PO2 399 H7
Bevois Gdns SHAM SO14 343 L1
Bevois Hl PTSW SO17 319 G8
Bevois Valley Rd SHAM SO14 343 M1
Bexmoor CHAM RG24 105 M2
Bexmoor Wy CHAM RG24 105 M2
Beyne Rd WINW SO22 238 A5
Bible Flds OVTN RG25 126 B8
Bicester Cl WHCH RG28 122 B3
Bickerley Gdns RGWD BH24 382 D2
Bickerley Rd RGWD BH24 382 D2
Bicknell Rd FRIM GU16 71 H6
Bidbury La HAV PO9 377 G7
Biddenfield La WHAM PO17 348 B4
Bidden Rd ODIM RG29 107 M6
OVTN RG25 130 A3
Biddesden La RAND SP11 93 G6
Biddlecombe Cl
LSOL/BMARY PO13 397 G8
Bideford Cl FARN GU14 90 D1
ROWN SO16 317 K7
Bighton Dean La NALR SO24 195 J7
Bighton Hl NALR SO24 219 M2
Bighton La NALR SO24 219 H2
Bighton Rd ALTN GU34 196 B3
Bilbao Ct AND SP10 119 J7
Bilberry Cl HLER SO31 370 D6
Bilberry Dr TOTT SO40 342 C6
Billett Av WVILLE PO7 352 D7
Billing Av EWKG RG40 48 B2
Billing Cl ENEY PO4 423 M5
Billington Gdns HEND SO30 321 J7
Billington Wy NTHA RG18 26 F2
Billy Lawn Av HAV PO9 377 K4
Bilton Wy HSEA PO3 400 A6
Bindon Cl BKME/WDN BH12 446 D1
ROWN SO16 317 M6
Bindon Rd ROWN SO16 317 M6
Binfields Cl CHAM RG24 83 L7
Bingham Av PSTN BH14 457 J1
Bingham Dr LYMN SO41 440 C5
Bingham Rd CHCH/BSGR BH23 450 D1
MOOR/WNTN BH9 432 E8
VWD BH31 356 E4
Bingley Cl ALTN GU34 176 D4
Binley Bottom RAND SP11 97 K3
Binnacle Wy CHAM PO6 374 F8
Binness Wy CHAM PO6 400 C1
Binnie Rd BKME/WDN BH12 446 D3
Binsey Cl ROWN SO16 317 K8
Binstead Cl ROWN SO16 319 H3
Binstead Rd ALTN GU34 157 J8
RFNM GU10 157 K8
Binsted Dr BLKW GU17 70 A3
Binsteed Rd NEND PO2 399 J8
Binton La RFNM GU10 136 B6
Birch Av CHCH/BSGR BH23 435 G5
FERN BH22 406 D7
FLET GU13 88 E7
NMIL/BTOS BH25 437 H2
STOK SO20 163 G4
Birch Cl CBLY GU15 51 H8
HORN PO8 352 C5
BOR GU35 201 K6
LISS GU33 248 F4
RFNM GU10 158 D4
PSTN BH14 446 D5
RGWD BH24 381 H5
ROMY SO51 291 H2
ROWN SO16 317 M6
WIMB BH21 429 H2
Birch Dl FAWY SO45 367 M6
Birchdale Cl HLER SO31 370 B8
Birchdale Rd WIMB BH21 404 B3
Birch Dr BLKW GU17 70 A5
CHAR BH8 433 L6
LSOL/BMARY PO13 397 G4
Birchen Cl HLER SO31 371 G4
The Birches Cl NBAD SO52 291 L3
Birches Crest KEMP RG22 127 J2
The Birches BLKW GU17 69 L3
FARN GU14 90 A4
WEND SO18 320 A8
Birchett Rd ALDT GU11 6 E2
FARN GU14 90 B3
Birchfields CBLY GU15 70 F4
Birch Gv ELGH SO50 293 L2
FERN BH22 380 B6
HTWY RG27 86 A6
BOR GU35 201 J7
STOK SO20 166 A6
Birchland Cl THLE RG7 43 H2
Birchlands TOTT SO40 341 H3
Birch La THLE RG7 43 J3
Birchmore Cl
LSOL/BMARY PO13 397 G6
Bircholt Rd LIPH GU30 226 A4
Birch Rd EWKG RG40 48 D1
HEND SO30 346 B1
BOR GU35 202 E2
RGWD BH24 381 M4
ROWN SO16 292 F8
ROWN SO16 317 M6
TADY RG26 41 H6
THLE RG7 31 J5
Birch Side CWTH RG45 49 J2
Birch Tree Cl EMRTH PO10 378 D4
Birch Tree Dr EMRTH PO10 378 D4
Birchview Cl YTLY GU46 68 F4
Birch Wy ASHV GU12
Birchwood CHAM RG24
Birch Wd ITCH SO19
Birchwood Cl
CHCH/BSGR BH23 43
Birchwood Dr FBDG SP6
Birchwood Gdns HEND SO30 32
Birchwood Rd NWBY RG14
PSTN BH14
UPTN BH16
Birchy Hl LYMN SO41
Birdham Rd HISD PO11
Birdhaven RFNM GU10
Birdlip Cl HORN PO8
Birdlip Rd CHAM PO6
Bird's Hill Rd PLE BH15
Birds La THLE RG7
Birdwood Gv
FHAM/PORC PO16
Birdwood Rd CBLY GU15
Birinus Rd WINC SO23
Birkbeck Pl SHST GU47
Birkdale Av CHAM PO6
Birkdale Ct WIMB BH21
Birkdale Rd WIMB BH21
Birkenholme Cl BOR GU35
Biscay Cl FHAM/STUB PO14 39
Bishearne Gdns LISS GU33 24
Bishop Ct RGWD BH24 38
Bishop Rd MOOR/WNTN BH9
Bishops Cl FLET GU13
LTDN BH7
NTID SP9
TADY RG26
TOTT SO40
Bishops Ct ELGH SO50
Bishops Crs ITCH SO19
Bishopsfield Rd
FHAM/STUB PO14
Bishops Ga FHAM/STUB PO14
Bishop's La BPWT SO32
BPWT SO32
Bishop's Md FNM GU9
Bishops Rd FNM GU9
ITCH SO19
Bishopstoke La ELGH SO50
Bishopstoke Rd ELGH SO50
HAV PO9
Bishop St PSEA PO1
Bishop Sumner Dr FNM GU9 13
Bishop's Vw ALTN GU34
Bishop's Wy AND SP10
Bishopswood La TADY RG26
Bishop's Wood Rd BPWT SO32
Bishopswood Rd TADY RG26
Bisterne Cl RGWD BH24
Bitham La HUNG RG17
Bittern Cl GPORT PO12
KEMP RG22
SHST GU47
Bitterne Cl HAV PO9
Bitterne Crs ITCH SO19 34
Bitterne Rd East WEND SO18
Bitterne Rd West WEND SO18
Bitterne Wy ITCH SO19
LYMN SO41
VWD BH31
Blackberry Cl ALTN GU34
Black Berry Cl HORN PO8
Blackberry La ALTN GU34
CHCH/BSGR BH23
Blackberry Ter SHAM SO14 34
Blackberry Wk CHAM RG24
Blackbird Cl CFDH BH17
HORN PO8
KEMP RG22
SHST GU47
THLE RG7
Blackbird Ct AND SP10 11
Blackbird Rd ELGH SO50
Blackbird Wy
CHCH/BSGR BH23
LSOL/BMARY PO13
Blackbrook House Dr
FHAM PO15
Blackbrook Park Av
FHAM PO15
Blackbrook Rd FHAM PO15
Blackburn Rd
BKME/WDN BH12
Blackbushe Cl ROWN SO16 31
Blackbushes Rd HTWY RG27
Blackbush Rd LYMN SO41
Blackcap Cl HAV PO9
Blackcap Pl SHST GU47
Blackdown Cl FAWY SO45 36
KEMP RG22
Blackdown Crs HAV PO9
Blackdown Rd FRIM GU16
Blackdown Wy STHA RG19
Blackfield La FERN BH22
Blackfield Rd FAWY SO45
Blackfriars Cl SSEA PO5
Blackfriars Rd SSEA PO5
Blackheath Rd FNM GU9
Black Hl VWD BH31
Blackhill Rd ROMY SO51
Black Horse La BPWT SO32
Blackhouse La WHAM PO17
Blacklands Rd THLE RG7
Black La RSAL SP5
Blackman Gdns ALDT GU11
Blackmoor Rd LISS GU33
Blackmore La MARL SN8
PSF GU32
Blacknest Rd ALTN GU34
Black Pond La RFNM GU10
Blacksmith Cl WIMB BH21
Blackstocks La HTWY RG27
Blackstone Cl FARN GU14
Blackthorn Cl ITCH SO19 34
LYMN SO41
RWIN SO21
Blackthorn Crs FARN GU14
Blackthorn Dr GPORT PO12
HISD PO11
NTHA RG18
Blackthorne Cl BOR GU35 20

iorn Gn RWIN SO21 266 F8
iorn Rd HISD PO11 426 A5
SO19 344 D3
iorn Wy DEAN RG23 104 B2
BH31 356 F3
ater Cl ASHV GU12 113 K7 1
RG21 5 H8
PO6 375 H8 1
RG23 103 G7 1
ater Dr TOTT SO40 316 C7
BH21 430 B1
ater Gv FBDG SP6 333 J3
ater Ms TOTT SO40 316 C7
ater Vw EWKG RG40 48 D6
ater Wy ASHV GU12 7 M6
ell Rd RWIN SO21 190 B6
Cl HAV PO9 17 L1
Rd ROWN SO16 318 B6
n Cl STHA RG19 26 A8 1
PSTN BH14 446 B4
NMIL/BTOS BH25 437 J5
k YTLY GU46 48 E8
BSTK RG21 104 F5
FARN GU14 91 G5
CWTH RG45 49 M4
RG29 108 B8 1
SO16 317 H3 1
ene Rd PSTN BH14 446 A7
ill Av PSTN BH14 446 B7
ill Crs PSTN BH14 446 B7
ere Crs CHAM PO6 375 G7
ey Rd ROWN SO16 317 J6
d CHAM PO6 376 B7
T PO12 19 G2
La TADY RG26 41 L7
ey La HSEA PO3 400 A4
Ride YTLY GU46 68 E2
ard Rd BPWT SO32 297 G8
ord Cl PLE BH15 444 E6
ord Rd PLE BH15 444 F7
SP5 254 C1
BH16 444 B2
ord Rd North
BH16 428 D5
Cl THLE RG7 31 J6
Wy WIMB BH21 429 G2
St ALTN GU34 177 L8
ey Cl
/STUB PO14 395 M6 1
ROWN SO16 317 H3 2
w Cl ROWN SO16 317 L8
nden Ter WSHM SO15 12 D2
v Cl NWBY RG14 37 G3 1
we Dr NBAD SO52 292 D3
n Dr AND SP10 8 A3
orth Crs HAV PO9 377 J5
orth La HORN PO8 353 H1
SO18 345 G1
orth Rd ENEY PO4 423 M3 1
m Av PTSW SO17 318 F7
m Cl ALTN GU34 176 F5 1
GU34 197 G5
SO52 292 E4
GU10 136 B1 1
SO40 341 H2
m Ct ENEY PO4 423 L5 1
GU14 91 G6
m Crs FNM GU9 134 D2
SO41 438 C4
m Dr CHCH/BSGR BH23 451 G1
m Gdns FAWY SO45 367 H6
T PO12 397 M8
O9 17 L2
SO17 319 G6
m Pk ALDT GU11 112 F1
m Rd ALDT GU11 112 F1
RG24 106 B3
SO50 293 M6
PO8 352 E3
RG14 2 C4
Crs FHAM PO15 371 K2
ont Crs WSHM SO15 342 F2
n La RFNM GU10 136 A6
BPWT SO32 321 H3
SP6 335 G7
PO17 348 D3
KEMP RG22 104 D7
E PO7 376 C3
d Cl HAV PO9 377 M2 1
rd Cross FBDG SP6 310 D8
rd Hl FBDG SP6 335 J2
rd Rd FBDG SP6 310 C7
ield Av
/WNTN BH9 432 D6
sbury Wy BLKW GU17 69 M5
n Cl HEND SO30 346 C2
od Dr WHCH RG28 122 A3
od La WHCH RG28 98 E8
Rd PSEA PO1 20 E5
orth Rd
/WDN BH12 431 K8
all Hl WINC SO23 11 J7
ll Cl CHCH/BSGR BH23 435 M8
E PO7 376 D2
ll Copse HLER SO31 370 D6
ll Dr THLE RG7 31 J5
ll La CFDH BH17 429 J7
ll Rd BOR GU35 201 M3
SO16 319 G4
ll Wy NTHA RG18 27 G3
ats NTHA RG18 27 G4
ar Gdns HEND SO30 321 H6
roat Cl SHST GU47 50 B8 1
ove ALDT GU11 112 F5 1
ll La HLER SO31 346 A6
en Cl BSTK RG21 104 E7
en Rd FARN GU14 90 C3
STHA RG19 27 H6
CHCH/BSGR BH23 434 B4
SO16 317 J6
Rd WIMB BH21 429 H2
wood Ct
/BTOS BH25 452 E1 1
ood Dr FRIM GU16 71 G6
s Pl TOTT SO40 341 G6 1
s La KSCL RG20 36 C3
unt Cl PSEA PO1 21 J1 1
unt Rd WHAM PO17 373 L4
Boar's Br TADY RG26 62 D6
Bob Hann Cl BKME/WDN BH12 446 D3
Bockhampton Rd
CHCH/BSGR BH23 435 J3
Bodin Gdns NWBY RG14 25 K8
Bodley Rd CCLF BH13 457 L1 2
Bodmin Cl KEMP RG22 104 A5
STHA RG19 26 F6
Bodmin Rd CHAM PO6 374 E8 1
ELGH SO50 294 D5
Bodorgan Rd WCLF BH2 22 E4
Bodowen Cl CHCH/BSGR BH23 435 H6
Bodowen Rd
CHCH/BSGR BH23 435 H6
Bodycoats Rd CHFD SO53 293 J2
Bofors Rd FARN GU14 90 D8
Bogmoor Cl ALTN GU34 197 G6
Bognor Rd BDST BH18 429 K4
Bohemia La RSAL SP5 285 L5
Boiler Rd PSEA PO1 422 D2
Bolde Cl HSEA PO3 399 M5
Boldens Rd GPORT PO12 18 E9
Bolderford Br BROC SO42 387 J3
Bolderwood
Arboretum Ornamental Dr
LYND SO43 361 L4
RGWD BH24 362 A6
Bolderwood Cl ELGH SO50 294 E5
Boldre Cl BKME/WDN BH12 446 D1
HAV PO9 377 G4 1
NMIL/BTOS BH25 437 H8
Boldre La LYMN SO41 440 B1
Boldrewood THLE RG7 31 J6 1
Boldrewood Rd ROWN SO16 318 D4
Boleyn Crs MOOR/WNTN BH9 433 G4
Bolhinton Av TOTT SO40 342 B7
Bolingbroke Wy STHA RG19 27 J5
Bolle Rd ALTN GU34 176 C6
Bolley Av BOR GU35 201 G3
Bolton Crs FERN BH22 406 E2
KEMP RG22 104 D5
The Boltons WVILLE PO7 376 C5 1
Bonchurch Cl ROWN SO16 319 H3 2
Bonchurch Rd ENEY PO4 423 L3
Bond Av FERN BH22 380 B4
Bond Cl CHAM RG24 5 M1
LYMN SO41 412 F5
Bondfields Crs HAV PO9 377 K2
Bond Rd PLE BH15 445 L3
WEND SO18 319 K7
Bond St SHAM SO14 344 A2
Bone La NWBY RG14 3 H4
Bonemill La KSCL RG20 25 G6
Bones La EPSF GU31 303 J3
Bonfire Cnr PSEA PO1 422 E2
Bonhams Cl ALTN GU34 177 K1
Boniface Cl TOTT SO40 316 C8 1
Boniface Crs ROWN SO16 317 K5
Bonners Fld RFNM GU10 156 F3
Boon Wy DEAN RG23 102 F6
Boothby Cl TOTT SO40 341 L2 1
Bordean La PSF GU32 274 A3
Borden Gates AND SP10 9 H7
Borden La LIPH GU30 278 C2
Border Dr UPTN BH16 444 B3
Border Rd HASM GU27 228 A2
UPTN BH16 444 B3
Borderside YTLY GU46 68 D2
Bordon Cl TADY RG26 41 K8
Bordon Rd HAV PO9 377 K3
The Boreen BOR GU35 202 E3
Boreham Rd SBNE BH6 449 J3
Borkum Cl AND SP10 118 E5
Borley Rd CFDH BH17 429 L8
Borman Wy RWIN SO21 190 D4
Borodin Cl KEMP RG22 104 E8
Borough Gv PSF GU32 275 K6
Borough Hl PSF GU32 275 K5
Borough Rd PSF GU32 275 J6
The Borough FNM GU9 134 E6
RFNM GU10 133 H2
RSAL SP5 284 D1
Borovere Cl ALTN GU34 176 D6
Borovere Gdns ALTN GU34 176 D6
Borovere La ALTN GU34 176 D6
Borrowdale Rd ROWN SO16 317 K7
Borsberry Cl AND SP10 9 K4
Borthwick Rd BMTH BH1 448 D3
Boscawen Wy STHA RG19 27 K5 1
Boscobel Rd WINW SO22 10 E4
Boscombe Cliff Rd BOSC BH5 448 D5
Boscombe Grove Rd
BMTH BH1 448 C3
Boscombe Overcliff Dr
BOSC BH5 448 E5
Boscombe Spa Rd BOSC BH5 448 C4
Bosham Rd NEND PO2 399 K8
Bosham Wk
LSOL/BMARY PO13 396 F6
Bosley Cl CHCH/BSGR BH23 434 C6
Bosley Wy CHCH/BSGR BH23 434 C6
Bosmere Gdns EMRTH PO10 378 C7
Bosmere Rd HISD PO11 426 C6
Bossington Cl ROWN SO16 317 K3 1
Bostock Cl RWIN SO21 213 J5
Boston Rd CHAM PO6 375 J7
Bosuns Cl FHAM/PORC PO16 396 F2
Bosville ELGH SO50 293 M2
Boswell Cl HEND SO30 346 D1
ITCH SO19 345 G2
Botany Bay Rd ITCH SO19 344 E6
Botany Cl STHA RG19 27 J5 1
Botany Hl RFNM GU10 136 A7
Botisdone Cl RAND SP11 73 G2
Botley Dr HAV PO9 377 H3
Botley Gdns ITCH SO19 345 J5 2
Botley Rd BPWT SO32 322 C8
ELGH SO50 295 J8
HEND SO30 320 E7
HEND SO30 347 H2
HLER SO31 346 E8
ITCH SO19 345 H5 1
NBAD SO52 291 L3
Bottle La HTWY RG27 65 M8
Bottom La ROMY SO51 288 D4
Boulnois Av PSTN BH14 446 D5
Boulter La WHAM PO17 374 E1
Boulters Rd ASHV GU12 7 H3
Boulton Rd SSEA PO5 21 L6
Boundary Cl WSHM SO15 342 D2
Boundary Dr WIMB BH21 404 B2
Boundary La RGWD BH24 381 H7
Boundary Rd FARN GU14 89 M7
GSHT GU26 204 A5
HLER SO31 345 K8
MOOR/WNTN BH9 432 B8
NBNE BH10 432 B7
RFNM GU10 180 A2
NWBY RG14 3 H5
Boundary Wy CHAM PO6 375 M6
HAV PO9 16 D4
Bound La HISD PO11 425 L6
Boundstone FAWY SO45 367 K5 1
Boundstone Cl RFNM GU10 158 E3 1
Boundstone Rd RFNM GU10 158 C4
Boundway LYMN SO41 412 B7
Bounty Ri BSTK RG21 104 F4
Bounty Rd BSTK RG21 104 F4
Bourley La RFNM GU10 111 J6
Bourley Rd FLET GU13 111 H4
Bourne Arch NTHA RG18 26 E4
Bourne Av WCLF BH2 22 C5
WSHM SO15 318 B7
Bourne Cl HORN PO8 352 F2
ROMY SO51 288 C5
RWIN SO21 266 A4
WBNE BH4 22 A5
Bourne Ct ALDT GU11 6 E5
AND SP10 9 L1
WIMB BH21 404 B3
Bourne Dene RFNM GU10 158 D3
Bourne Fld CHAM RG24 82 D4
Bournefields RWIN SO21 267 G1
Bourne Firs RFNM GU10 159 G3
Bourne Gv RFNM GU10 159 H1
Bourne Grove Cl FNM GU9 159 H1
Bourne Grove Dr RFNM GU10 159 H1
Bourne La NTID SP9 138 E1
RWIN SO21 266 F1
TOTT SO40 340 B3
Bourne Meadow RAND SP11 97 M7
Bourne Mill Rbt FNM GU9 135 H5
Bournemouth Av GPORT PO12 421 L1
Bournemouth
International Centre Rbt
WCLF BH2 22 E7
Bournemouth Rd CHFD SO53 293 G5
LYND SO43 363 J3
PSTN BH14 446 B4
RAND SP11 161 K3
ROWN SO16 292 F8
Bournemouth Road Castle Hl
PSTN BH14 446 A4
Bournemouth Station Rbt
BMTH BH1 23 J4
Bourne Rd CHAM PO6 374 F8
NTID SP9 114 E2
STHA RG19 26 E4
TOTT SO40 340 A3
WSHM SO15 12 B1
The Bourne FLET GU13 110 F2
Bourne Valley Rd
BKME/WDN BH12 446 F3
Bourne View Cl EMRTH PO10 379 H6
Bournewood Dr WBNE BH4 447 H4
Bouverie Cl NMIL/BTOS BH25 437 K7
Boveridge Gdns
MOOR/WNTN BH9 432 F4
Bovington Cl CFDH BH17 430 D7
Bowater Cl TOTT SO40 316 B7
Bowater Wy TOTT SO40 316 B7
Bowcombe HLER SO31 369 G1
Bowcott Hl BOR GU35 202 C3
Bowden La PTSW SO17 319 H6
Bowden Rd BKME/WDN BH12 431 G6
Bow Dr HTWY RG27 64 C8
Bowenhurst Gdns FLET GU13 110 F4
Bowenhurst Rd FLET GU13 110 F3
Bowenhust La RFNM GU10 110 B5
Bower Cl FAWY SO45 392 A5
ITCH SO19 344 D7
Bower Rd CHAR BH8 433 H8
RFNM GU10 158 D3
Bowers Cl HORN PO8 352 E4
Bowers Grove La ALTN GU34 220 B1
Bowers Hl RSAL SP5 285 K1
Bowers La RAND SP11 72 F1
Bowerwood Rd FBDG SP6 309 H8
Bowes Hl HAV PO9 354 A5
Bowes Rd STHA RG19 27 G6
Bow Fld HTWY RG27 86 B7
Bow Gdns HTWY RG27 64 C8 1
Bow Gv HTWY RG27 64 C7
Bowland Ri CHFD SO53 292 F1
NMIL/BTOS BH25 438 A6
Bowland Wy FAWY SO45 418 C1 1
Bowler Av PSEA PO1 423 K2
Bowler Ct HSEA PO3 423 K2
Bowling Court Gn FRIM GU16 91 H1
Bowling Green Dr HTWY RG27 85 L7 1
Bowling Green Rd NTHA RG18 26 D3
Bowman Ct CWTH RG45 49 H4
Bowman Rd CHAM RG24 83 L4
Bowmonts Rd TADY RG26 42 A8
Bow St ALTN GU34 176 D6
Boxall's Gv ALDT GU11 6 E6
Boxall's La ALDT GU11 6 F7
FNM GU9 6 D6
Box Cl CFDH BH17 445 G1
Boxwood Cl
FHAM/PORC PO16 373 M7 1
WVILLE PO7 376 C2
Boyatt Crs ELGH SO50 265 M8
Boyatt La CHFD SO53 265 M7
ELGH SO50 266 A7
Boyce Cl KEMP RG22 104 B8
Boyd Cl FHAM/STUB PO14 395 M7 1
Boyd Rd BKME/WDN BH12 446 E2
LSOL/BMARY PO13 396 F5
Boyes La RWIN SO21 266 F7
Boyle Crs WVILLE PO7 376 B3
Boyne Mead Rd WINC SO23 215 G1
Boyne Ri WINC SO23 191 G8
Boyneswood Cl ALTN GU34 197 H4
Boyneswood La ALTN GU34 197 G4
Boyneswood Rd ALTN GU34 197 H4
Boynton Cl CHFD SO53 265 G8
Brabant Cl HLER SO31 370 F1
Brabazon Dr CHCH/BSGR BH23 451 G1
Brabazon Rd FHAM PO15 371 H3
WIMB BH21 404 D7
Brabon Rd FARN GU14 90 C3
Brabourne Av FERN BH22 406 A4
Bracebridge CBLY GU15 70 D3
Bracher Cl AND SP10 9 J4
Bracken Bank CHAM RG24 83 L8 1
Brackenbury AND SP10 8 A3
Bracken Cl NBAD SO52 291 M5
RGWD BH24 381 H4
Bracken Crs ELGH SO50 294 E6
Brackendale Cl FRIM GU16 71 H5
Brackendale Ct WIMB BH21 356 B8 1
Brackendale Rd CBLY GU15 71 G4
CHAR BH8 433 G8
Brackendene ASHV GU12 113 M5
Bracken Gln PLE BH15 445 K4
Bracken Heath HORN PO8 352 F7
Brackenhill CCLF BH13 446 F7
Brackenhill Rd WIMB BH21 404 E1
Bracken La BOR GU35 200 F8
ROWN SO16 317 M7
YTLY GU46 68 D2
Bracken Pl ELGH SO50 318 F1
Bracken Rd EPSF GU31 276 B6
FERN BH22 405 M1
NBAD SO52 291 M5
SBNE BH6 449 H4
The Brackens CWTH RG45 49 K1
FAWY SO45 367 H5 2
HLER SO31 370 F6
KEMP RG22 127 H2 1
Brackens Wy LYMN SO41 440 D6 1
Bracken Wy CHCH/BSGR BH23 436 F7
THLE RG7 31 K6 1
Brackenway Rd CHFD SO53 265 H8
Bracklesham Cl FARN GU14 90 D1
ITCH SO19 344 D5
Bracklesham Rd HISD PO11 426 D7
LSOL/BMARY PO13 397 H8
Brackley Av ELGH SO50 295 G6
HTWY RG27 87 H2
Brackley Cl CHCH/BSGR BH23 407 L8
Brackley Wy KEMP RG22 104 B7
TOTT SO40 316 C8
Bracknell Cl CBLY GU15 51 J7
Bracknell La HTWY RG27 87 H1
Bracknell Rd CBLY GU15 51 K6
CWTH RG45 49 M3
Bradburne Rd WCLF BH2 22 C5
Bradbury Cl WHCH RG28 122 A3 1
Bradford Rd
MOOR/WNTN BH9 433 G4
SSEA PO5 21 K3
Brading Av ENEY PO4 423 L6
LSOL/BMARY PO13 397 G6
Brading Cl ROWN SO16 319 H3
Bradley Ct HAV PO9 377 M3
Bradley Gn ROWN SO16 318 A4
Bradley-Moore Sq NTHA RG18 27 H3
Bradley Peak WINW SO22 214 B7
Bradley Rd WINW SO22 214 B5
Bradly Rd FHAM PO15 372 A7
Bradpole Rd CHAR BH8 433 J7
Bradshaw Cl ELGH SO50 295 K6 1
Bradstock Cl BKME/WDN BH12 431 K8
Bradwell Cl AND SP10 118 C5
Braehead FAWY SO45 367 K6
Braemar Av CHAM PO6 399 M1
SBNE BH6 449 M4
Braemar Cl FHAM PO15 14 D1
FRIM GU16 71 J7
LSOL/BMARY PO13 397 H6
SBNE BH6 449 M4
Braemar Dr CHCH/BSGR BH23 436 D7
DEAN RG23 102 F6
Braemar Rd
LSOL/BMARY PO13 397 H5
Braemore Cl STHA RG19 27 G7
Braeside Cl WINW SO22 238 A4
HASM GU27 204 C8
Braeside Crs ITCH SO19 344 C3 1
Braeside Rd FERN BH22 380 C5
ITCH SO19 344 C3
RGWD BH24 381 J4
Brahms Rd KEMP RG22 104 D8
Braidley Rd WCLF BH2 22 D3
Brailswood Rd PLE BH15 445 J4
Braintree Rd CHAM PO6 375 H7
Brairwood Gdns HISD PO11 425 K5
Braishfield Cl ROWN SO16 317 L7
Braishfield Gdns CHAR BH8 433 H6
Braishfield Rd HAV PO9 377 L4
ROMY SO51 263 H7
Brake Rd FARN GU14 90 B7
Bramber Rd GPORT PO12 421 L1
Bramble Bank FRIM GU16 91 K2
Bramble Cl ELGH SO50 294 A3 2
FAWY SO45 392 A5
FBDG SP6 333 L3 3
FHAM/STUB PO14 395 L7
Bramble Dr ROMY SO51 263 H7 3
Bramblegate CWTH RG45 49 K2
Bramble Hl CHFD SO53 293 G2
NALR SO24 218 C3
Bramble La CHCH/BSGR BH23 436 F7
HLER SO31 370 C3
HORN PO8 328 A1
Bramble Ms WEND SO18 319 M8 1
Bramble Rd ENEY PO4 21 L4
EPSF GU31 276 B5
Brambles Cl ALTN GU34 197 G6
ASHV GU12 113 L7
RWIN SO21 266 F8
Brambles Rd
LSOL/BMARY PO13 420 B1 1
The Brambles CWTH RG45 49 G2
NWBY RG14 25 H8
Brambleton Av FNM GU9 158 E1
Bramble Wk LYMN SO41 440 A4 1
Bramble Wy CHAM RG24 106 B2
LSOL/BMARY PO13 396 E6
Bramblewood Pl FLET GU13 88 D7
Brambling Cl KEMP RG22 126 E1 1
ROWN SO16 318 A2 1
Brambling La MIDH GU29 279 L5
Brambling Rd HAV PO9 353 M7
The Bramblings TOTT SO40 316 B8 2
Bramblys Cl BSTK RG21 4 D9
Bramblys Dr BSTK RG21 4 C9
Bramcote CBLY GU15 71 M3
Bramdean Dr HAV PO9 377 H3
Bramdean Rd WEND SO18 345 H1
Bramdown Hts KEMP RG22 127 G2
Bramham Moor
FHAM/STUB PO14 395 M6 2
Bramley Cl ALTN GU34 176 F4 1
LYMN SO41 440 C6 1
WVILLE PO7 352 D8
Bramley Crs ITCH SO19 344 F6
Bramley Gdns EMRTH PO10 378 F8
GPORT PO12 421 L7
Bramley Green Rd TADY RG26 63 M6
Bramley Gv CWTH RG45 49 G3
Bramley La BLKW GU17 69 L3
TADY RG26 63 L4
Bramley Rd CBLY GU15 70 E6 1
FERN BH22 406 B2 1
HTWY RG27 64 C7
NBNE BH10 432 A3
TADY RG26 62 C7
THLE RG7 42 E7
The Bramleys RSAL SP5 259 G5
Bramley Wk BOR GU35 201 G6
Bramling Av YTLY GU46 68 E2
Brammpton Gdns KEMP RG22 127 G3
Brampton La HSEA PO3 400 A4
Brampton Rd PLE BH15 445 J2
Bramshaw Cl WINW SO22 214 B5
Bramshaw Ct HAV PO9 377 M3 3
Bramshaw Wy
NMIL/BTOS BH25 437 H8
Bramshot Dr FLET GU13 88 F6
Bramshot La FARN GU14 89 K3
Bramshott Dr HTWY RG27 86 A7
Bramshott Rd ENEY PO4 423 K4
FARN GU14 89 K7
ITCH SO19 344 D7 1
Bramston Rd WSHM SO15 318 B8
Bramwell Cl STHA RG19 27 J6 2
Brancaster Av AND SP10 118 C5 3
Branches La ROMY SO51 260 E6
Branders Cl SBNE BH6 449 M4
Branders La SBNE BH6 449 M3
Brandon Cl ALTN GU34 176 C4
Brandon Rd FLET GU13 110 D3
SSEA PO5 21 J8
Brandy Mt NALR SO24 218 C2
Branksea Av PLE BH15 444 C7
Branksea Cl PLE BH15 444 D7
Branksome Av STOK SO20 165 M5
WSHM SO15 318 B7
Branksome Cl CBLY GU15 71 H2 1
WINW SO22 238 A2
NMIL/BTOS BH25 437 M6
STOK SO20 165 L5
Branksome Dene Rd
WBNE BH4 447 G6
Branksome Hill Rd SHST GU47 70 B1
WBNE BH4 447 G3
Branksome Park Rd CBLY GU15 71 H2
Branksome Towers CCLF BH13 447 G8
Branksome Wood Gdns
WCLF BH2 22 B3
Branksomewood Rd FLET GU13 88 D7
Branksome Wood Rd
WBNE BH4 447 H3
Bransbury Cl ROWN SO16 318 B4 1
Bransbury Rd ENEY PO4 423 M5
Bransgore Av HAV PO9 377 G4
Bransgore Gdns
CHCH/BSGR BH23 409 M7
Bransley Cl ROMY SO51 263 G7
Branson Rd BOR GU35 201 K5
Branton Cl KEMP RG22 104 B5
Branwell Cl CHCH/BSGR BH23 434 E7
Branwood Cl LYMN SO41 439 J7 1
Brasenose Cl
FHAM/STUB PO14 371 G7
Brasher Cl ELGH SO50 294 F6
Brassey Cl MOOR/WNTN BH9 432 E7
Brassey Rd WINW SO22 10 E4
MOOR/WNTN BH9 432 D7
Brasted Ct ENEY PO4 424 A3 1
Braunfels Wk KSCL RG20 2 A6
NWBY RG14 2 A5
Braye Cl SHST GU47 49 M7 2
Brazil Rd SHAM SO14 13 J8
Breach Av EMRTH PO10 379 H6
Breachfield KSCL RG20 57 J1
Breach La HTWY RG27 64 D8
RAND SP11 72 A8
Breamore Cl ELGH SO50 293 M2 1
NMIL/BTOS BH25 437 J5 1
Breamore Rd RSAL SP5 284 C2
WEND SO18 345 H1
Brean Cl ROWN SO16 317 K5
Brecon Av CHAM PO6 375 M7
Brecon Cl CHFD SO53 293 G5 1
FARN GU14 90 A1
FAWY SO45 367 J5
FHAM/STUB PO14 14 B7
NBNE BH10 432 C2
NMIL/BTOS BH25 438 A6
Brecon Rd ITCH SO19 345 G3
Bredenbury Crs CHAM PO6 375 G7
Breech Cl HSEA PO3 399 K4 3
The Breech CBLY GU15 70 B1
Bremble Cl BKME/WDN BH12 431 G6
Bremen Gdns AND SP10 118 E6
Brenchley Cl
FHAM/PORC PO16 397 L1
Brendon Cl FAWY SO45 367 H6 2
Brendon Gn ROWN SO16 317 L8
Brendon Rd FARN GU14 90 A1
FHAM/STUB PO14 14 B8
Brent Cl STHA RG19 27 G6
Brent Ct EMRTH PO10 378 C8
Brentwood Crs WEND SO18 319 M7
Bret Harte Rd FRIM GU16 71 H7
Breton Cl FHAM PO15 370 F1
Brewells La LISS GU33 249 K2
Brewer Cl HLER SO31 370 F4

KEMP RG22 104 B5
Brewers Cl FARN GU14 90 D3
Brewers La LSOL/BMARY PO13 397 G6
NALR SO24 221 J7
RWIN SO21 266 E3
Brewer St PSEA PO1 423 G2
Brewery Common THLE RG7 43 L2
Brewhouse La HTWY RG27 87 J2
Brewhouse Sq GPORT PO12 19 J1
Brewster Cl HORN PO8 352 E5
Briar Cl CHCH/BSGR BH23 450 E2
GPORT PO12 421 J5
HORN PO8 352 F3
PLE BH15 445 K3
Briardene Ct TOTT SO40 341 J1
Briarfield Gdns HORN PO8 352 F2
Briar La ALTN GU34 197 H5
Briarlea Rd THLE RG7 43 J2
Briars Cl FARN GU14 90 A5
The Briars ASHV GU12 113 L7
Briarswood ROWN SO16 318 A7
Briarswood Ri FAWY SO45 367 H6
Briarswood Rd UPTN BH16 444 B1
Briar Wy ROMY SO51 263 H7
TADY RG26 41 M8
WIMB BH21 404 F3
Briar Wd LISS GU33 248 F1
Briarwood Cl FHAM/PORC PO16 15 J7
Briarwood Dr EWKG RG40 48 B2
Briarwood Rd TOTT SO40 341 G2
Brickfield La CHFD SO53 293 G3
LYMN SO41 440 D3
Brickfield Rd PTSW SO17 319 H6
Brickfields Cl CHAM RG24 83 M8
Brickiln La ALTN GU34 197 L2
Brick Kiln La ALTN GU34 176 B4
NALR SO24 244 E1
Brick La CHCH/BSGR BH23 410 C4
FLET GU13 88 F6
Brickmakers Rd RWIN SO21 266 E8
Bricksbury Hl FNM GU9 134 F1
Brickwoods ROMY SO51 263 G8
Brickworth La RSAL SP5 258 B4
Brickworth Rd RSAL SP5 258 D4
Brickyard La WIMB BH21 405 L2
Brickyard Rd BPWT SO32 323 L5
The Brickyard TOTT SO40 315 G8
Bricky Lake La ROMY SO51 315 H1
Bridefield Cl HORN PO8 352 B5
Bridefield Crs HORN PO8 352 B5
Bridge Ap PLE BH15 445 G7
Bridge Cl HLER SO31 345 M7
Bridge End CBLY GU15 70 E4
Bridgefield FNM GU9 135 G6
Bridgefoot Dr
FHAM/PORC PO16 15 M5
Bridgefoot Pth EMRTH PO10 378 D8
Bridgemary Av
LSOL/BMARY PO13 397 H5
Bridgemary Gv
LSOL/BMARY PO13 397 G4
Bridgemary Rd
LSOL/BMARY PO13 397 G3
Bridgemary Wy
LSOL/BMARY PO13 397 G3
Bridge Md BPWT SO32 299 J3
Bridgemead FRIM GU16 71 G8
Bridge Mdw LISS GU33 248 E4
Bridge Pl NBNE BH10 432 B1
Bridge Rd ALDT GU11 6 F5
CBLY GU15 70 E5
EMRTH PO10 378 D7
FARN GU14 90 C4
HASM GU27 228 F1
HLER SO31 345 M7
HLER SO31 370 C2
ITCH SO19 344 B5
LYMN SO41 440 D4
NALR SO24 218 A3
ODIM RG29 108 B4
ROMY SO51 290 E1
RSAL SP5 253 G1
Bridgers Cl ROWN SO16 317 K3
Bridges Cl ELGH SO50 293 L5
FERN BH22 380 D5
Bridgeside Cl PSEA PO1 21 K1
The Bridges RGWD BH24 382 C1
THLE RG7 42 F3
Bridge St AND SP10 9 H6
CHCH/BSGR BH23 450 B2
FBDG SP6 309 L7
FHAM/STUB PO14 371 L8
NWBY RG14 2 E4
OVTN RG25 100 F8
WHAM PO17 348 E4
WHAM PO17 374 B2
WINC SO23 11 J8
Bridget Cl HORN PO8 353 G1
Bridgetts La RWIN SO21 192 A6
Bridge Wk YTLY GU46 69 G1
Bridgwater Ct WSHM SO15 12 A1
Bridle Cl ALTN GU34 222 C3
GSHT GU26 203 K5
UPTN BH16 444 C1
Bridle Ct ALDT GU11 6 B2
Bridle Crs LTDN BH7 434 A8
Bridle Wy WIMB BH21 404 F2
Bridleways VWD BH31 356 C2
Bridlington Av WSHM SO15 318 C8
Bridport Rd BKME/WDN BH12 431 K8
VWD BH31 356 D2
Bridport St PSEA PO1 21 H1
Brierley Av FERN BH22 406 C7
Brierley Cl NBNE BH10 432 C3
Brierley Rd NBNE BH10 432 C4
Briff La THLE RG7 27 L2
Brigantine Rd HLER SO31 370 C7
Brighstone Cl ROWN SO16 319 H3
Brightlands Av SBNE BH6 449 L4
Brighton Av GPORT PO12 397 K8
Brighton Rd ALDT GU11 7 K6
LYMN SO41 412 E5
WSHM SO15 343 K1
Brighton Wy KEMP RG22 104 C7
Bright Rd PLE BH15 445 J2
Brightside WVILLE PO7 376 B2
Brightside Rd ROWN SO16 317 L6
Brights La HISD PO11 425 K3
Brightstone La ALTN GU34 197 M6
Brightstone Rd CHAM PO6 399 J1
Brightwells Rd FNM GU9 134 F6
Brimpton Rd THLE RG7 28 B7
THLE RG7 40 F6
Brindle Cl ALDT GU11 7 G7
ROWN SO16 318 F3
Brinksway FLET GU13 88 F8
Brinn's La BLKW GU17 69 M3
Brinsons Cl CHCH/BSGR BH23 435 G5
Brinton La FAWY SO45 367 L3
Brinton's Rd SHAM SO14 13 H1
Brinton's Ter SHAM SO14 343 L2
Brisbane Cl RAND SP11 115 J1
Brisbane Rd CHCH/BSGR BH23 434 C7
Brislands La ALTN GU34 220 C1
Bristol Rd ENEY PO4 423 K6
Bristow Rd CBLY GU15 70 E5
Britain St PSEA PO1 20 D2
Britannia Cl BOR GU35 201 L5
Britannia Gdns HEND SO30 321 G5
Britannia Rd PSTN BH14 445 M5
SHAM SO14 13 K1
SSEA PO5 21 K4
Britannia Rd North SSEA PO5 21 K4
Briton St SHAM SO14 12 F6
Britten Cl ASHV GU12 113 L6
Britten Rd LSOL/BMARY PO13 420 C2
Britten Wy WVILLE PO7 376 C4
Brixey Cl BKME/WDN BH12 446 B1
Brixey Rd BKME/WDN BH12 446 B1
Broadacres FLET GU13 88 C8
Broad Av CHAR BH8 433 H8
Broadbent Cl ROWN SO16 317 J2
Broad Chalke Down
WINW SO22 238 B4
Broad Cft HAV PO9 354 A6
Broadcut FHAM/PORC PO16 15 M3
Broadfields Cl LYMN SO41 454 C3
Broad Gdns CHAM PO6 378 B8
Broad Gn SHAM SO14 13 H2
Broadhalfpenny La TADY RG26 41 M7
Broad Ha'penny RFNM GU10 158 D3
Broadhill La FBDG SP6 310 C8
Broadhurst FARN GU14 89 M4
Broadhurst Av NBNE BH10 432 C4
Broadhurst Gv CHAM RG24 105 L1
Broadlands FARN GU14 91 H6
FRIM GU16 71 J8
Broadlands Av ELGH SO50 293 M3
SBNE BH6 449 L4
WVILLE PO7 376 C2
Broadlands Cl CHAR BH8 433 H5
CHCH/BSGR BH23 436 F6
Broadlands Rd BROC SO42 387 J6
PTSW SO17 319 G5
Broad La BPWT SO32 323 M3
LYMN SO41 440 D5
NBAD SO52 291 K3
THLE RG7 27 L2
WVILLE PO7 350 F2
Broad Leaze HTWY RG27 85 M6
Broadley Cl FAWY SO45 392 A4
Broadly Cl LYMN SO41 439 M6
Broadmayne Rd
BKME/WDN BH12 446 E1
Broadmead FARN GU14 90 A5
Broadmeadow Cl TOTT SO40 341 J1
Broadmeadow End NTHA RG18 27 J5
Broadmeadows La
WVILLE PO7 376 E1
Broadmead Rd ROWN SO16 317 J2
Broad Mead Rd WIMB BH21 356 C7
Broadmere Av HAV PO9 377 K3
Broadmoor Rd WIMB BH21 429 G2
Broad Oak HEND SO30 346 C1
Broadoak TADY RG26 42 A8
Broadoak Cl FAWY SO45 392 A5
Broad Oak La ODIM RG29 108 F5
Broad Rd RAND SP11 141 G5
RCCH PO18 379 M8
Broadsands Dr GPORT PO12 421 H5
Broadshard La RGWD BH24 358 E7
Broadstone Wy BDST BH18 429 K7
Broad St NALR SO24 218 C2
PSEA PO1 20 B5
Broadview Cl ALTN GU34 178 D1
Broad View La WINW SO22 237 M5
Broad Wk FRIM GU16 71 H6
Broadwater Av PSTN BH14 446 A6
Broadwater Rd ROMY SO51 290 D2
WEND SO18 319 L5
Broad Wy HLER SO31 369 J3
FARN GU14 90 D8
PSF GU32 246 C8
THLE RG7 42 G5
Broadway SBNE BH6 449 M4
STHA RG19 27 G5
WHCH RG28 122 C4
Broadway La CHAR BH8 433 G5
HORN PO8 352 B2
The Broadway NBNE BH10 432 B2
SHST GU47 69 L1
WINC SO23 11 H8
Broadwell Rd RFNM GU10 158 C2
Broad Woods La ROMY SO51 288 F1
Brocas Dr BSTK RG21 5 H4
Brocas Rd THLE RG7 31 J7
Brockenhurst Av HAV PO9 377 H2
Brockenhurst Dr YTLY GU46 69 G3
Brockenhurst Rd ALDT GU11 7 G5
MOOR/WNTN BH9 432 F6
Brockham Hill La ALTN GU34 154 F5
Brockhampton La HAV PO9 16 D5
Brockhampton Rd HAV PO9 16 B5
Brockhills La NMIL/BTOS BH25 438 A3
Brockhurst Ldg FNM GU9 158 E1
Brockhurst Rd GPORT PO12 421 H2
Brockishill Rd LYND SO43 339 K4
TOTT SO40 339 L3
Brocklands HAV PO9 16 B4
YTLY GU46 68 E4
Brockley Rd NBNE BH10 432 B4
Brocks Cl FAWY SO45 367 H6
Brocks Pine RGWD BH24 381 K5
Brockwood Bottom
NALR SO24 243 K7
Brodrick Av GPORT PO12 18 D6
Brokenford Av TOTT SO40 341 L1
Brokenford La TOTT SO40 341 K1
Broken Wy KSCL RG20 37 L6
Bromelia Cl TADY RG26 63 L4
Bromley Rd WEND SO18 319 L7
Brompton Rd ENEY PO4 423 K6
Bromyard Crs CHAM PO6 375 G8
Bronte Av CHCH/BSGR BH23 434 F7
Bronte Cl TOTT SO40 341 H2
Bronte Gdns FHAM PO15 347 G8
Bronte Wy ITCH SO19 344 C2
Brook Av FNM GU9 6 D7
HLER SO31 370 A5
NMIL/BTOS BH25 437 M4
Brook Av North
NMIL/BTOS BH25 437 M3
Brook Cl FLET GU13 88 F8
HLER SO31 370 B5
NBAD SO52 291 M5
NBNE BH10 432 A4
SHST GU47 50 B7
Brookdale Cl WIMB BH21 429 L4
WVILLE PO7 352 C8
Brook Dr VWD BH31 356 F4
Brooke Cl WINC SO23 191 G8
Brookers Cnr CWTH RG45 49 M3
Brookers La
LSOL/BMARY PO13 396 E5
Brookers Rw CWTH RG45 49 M2
Brook Farm Av FHAM PO15 14 E5
Brookfield Cl CHAM RG24 83 M5
HAV PO9 16 D2
Brookfield Gdns HLER SO31 370 D4
Brookfield Rd ASHV GU12 113 H6
ELGH SO50 295 G6
PSEA PO1 423 J2
Brookfields ROMY SO51 288 C5
Brook Gdns EMRTH PO10 378 B8
FARN GU14 90 C6
Brook Gn TADY RG26 42 A8
Brook Hl LYMN SO41 441 J1
Brookhouse Rd FARN GU14 90 C5
Brookland Cl LYMN SO41 440 A5
Brooklands ALDT GU11 6 B3
Brooklands Cl FNM GU9 135 G1
RFNM GU10 157 G3
Brooklands Rd BPWT SO32 297 H8
HAV PO9 376 F6
Brooklands Wy FNM GU9 6 A8
Brook La CHCH/BSGR BH23 435 L1
FBDG SP6 310 D1
HEND SO30 346 D2
HLER SO31 370 A7
WIMB BH21 429 G2
WVILLE PO7 326 A2
Brookley Cl RFNM GU10 135 L5
Brookley Rd BROC SO42 387 K7
Brookly Gdns FLET GU13 89 G6
Brooklyn Cl RWIN SO21 266 B5
Brooklyn Ct
NMIL/BTOS BH25 437 K5
Brooklyn Dr WVILLE PO7 352 D8
Brooklynn Cl BPWT SO32 323 K6
Brookmeadow FHAM PO15 14 E5
Brookmead Wy HAV PO9 16 E8
Brook Rd BKME/WDN BH12 446 B3
CBLY GU15 70 E4
ELGH SO50 295 H6
LYMN SO41 440 D6
NBNE BH10 432 A4
WEND SO18 344 E1
WIMB BH21 404 C4
Brooksby Cl BLKW GU17 69 L3
Brooks Cl RGWD BH24 382 F2
WHCH RG28 122 C4
Brookside FBDG SP6 335 G6
FNM GU9 134 F2
LSOL/BMARY PO13 396 F3
SHST GU47 69 M1
TOTT SO40 341 K3
Brookside Av WSHM SO15 342 D1
Brookside Cl WVILLE PO7 351 K4
Brookside Rd BROC SO42 387 K6
CHCH/BSGR BH23 409 L8
HAV PO9 16 B6
HAV PO9 377 G6
WIMB BH21 404 D4
Brookside Wy
CHCH/BSGR BH23 436 C7
HEND SO30 320 D5
WEND SO18 319 K4
Brooks Rd NTHA RG18 27 H4
Brook St BPWT SO32 323 H1
Brook Ter FBDG SP6 309 L8
The Brook NALR SO24 194 C8
Brookvale Cl BSTK RG21 4 C8
Brookvale Rd PTSW SO17 318 F7
Brook Va ROWN SO16 317 M6
Brook Wy CHCH/BSGR BH23 451 H1
Brookway NWBY RG14 26 B5
RAND SP11 142 B4
Brook Wy ROMY SO51 262 F7
Brookwood Av ELGH SO50 293 L5
Brookwood Rd FARN GU14 91 G4
ROWN SO16 317 J8
Broom Acres FLET GU13 110 E2
SHST GU47 49 L8
Broom Cl BLKW GU17 70 B4
ENEY PO4 424 B4
WVILLE PO7 376 E3
Broome Cl YTLY GU46 68 F1
Broomfield Crs
LSOL/BMARY PO13 420 F1
Broomfield Dr FBDG SP6 333 L3
Broomfield La LYMN SO41 440 C4
RFNM GU10 158 D7
Broomfield Rd BOR GU35 201 G6
Broom Hl LYMN SO41 441 M1
Broomhill RFNM GU10 111 G8
RSAL SP5 287 J7
Broomhill Rd FARN GU14 90 A3
Broom Hill Wy ELGH SO50 293 L1
Broomleaf Cnr FNM GU9 135 G6
Broomleaf Rd FNM GU9 135 G6
Broomrigg Rd FLET GU13 88 C6
Broom Rd BKME/WDN BH12 431 G7
EPSF GU31 276 B6
Brooms Gv ITCH SO19 345 H5
Broom Sq ENEY PO4 424 B4
Broom Wy LSOL/BMARY PO13 420 D1
Broomwood Wy RFNM GU10 158 F2
Broomy Cl FAWY SO45 367 G4
Brougham La GPORT PO12 421 L2
Brougham Pl FNM GU9 134 E6
Brougham Rd SSEA PO5 21 G4
Brougham St GPORT PO12 421 L2
Broughton Av NBNE BH10 432 C4
Broughton Cl ROWN SO16 317 M7
Broughton Ct HSEA PO3 400 A4
Broughton Ms FRIM GU16 71 J7
Broughton Rd LYND SO43 363 J2
STOK SO20 185 K6
Brown Cft HTWY RG27 85 L7
Browndown Rd
LSOL/BMARY PO13 421 G5
Brownen Rd
MOOR/WNTN BH9 432 F8
Brownhill Cl CHFD SO53 293 H1
Brownhill Ct ROWN SO16 317 K5
Brownhill Rd CHFD SO53 293 H1
NBAD SO52 292 A4
NMIL/BTOS BH25 411 H5
Brownhill Wy ROWN SO16 317 H5
Browning Av BOSC BH5 448 E4
CHAM PO6 374 C7
ITCH SO19 345 H2
Browning Cl CBLY GU15 71 M4
CHAM RG24 5 G1
ELGH SO50 293 L5
HLER SO31 347 G8
NTHA RG18 26 F4
TOTT SO40 341 H1
Browning Dr WINW SO22 10 B6
Browning Rd FLET GU13 110 D5
Brownings Cl LYMN SO41 439 L4
Brownlow Av ITCH SO19 344 E2
Brownlow Cl PSEA PO1 423 H1
Brownlow Gdns ITCH SO19 344 E2
Browns Cl TADY RG26 63 K4
Brownsea Av WIMB BH21 429 H2
Brownsea Cl NMIL/BTOS BH25 437 J5
Brownsea Rd CCLF BH13 457 G5
Brownsea View Av PSTN BH14 446 A7
Brownsfield Rd NTHA RG18 26 F5
Browns La FBDG SP6 308 A3
LYMN SO41 442 A3
Brownsover Rd FARN GU14 89 M4
Browns Wk RFNM GU10 158 C3
Brownwich La
FHAM/STUB PO14 395 H3
The Brow WVILLE PO7 376 A6
Broxburn Cl CHFD SO53 265 K7
Broxhead Farm Rd BOR GU35 179 K8
Broxhead Rd HAV PO9 377 L2
Brtten Rd KEMP RG22 104 D8
Bruan Rd NWBY RG14 25 J8
Bruce Cl FHAM/PORC PO16 15 H2
Bruce Rd ENEY PO4 423 K6
Brudenell Av CCLF BH13 457 J1
Brudenell Rd CCLF BH13 457 J1
Brue Cl CHFD SO53 293 G1
Brummell Rd NWBY RG14 2 A1
Brune La LSOL/BMARY PO13 396 E7
Brunel Cl HEND SO30 321 J7
RWIN SO21 148 A6
Brunel Rd BSTK RG21 104 D2
NEND PO2 399 J5
TOTT SO40 316 C5
WSHM SO15 342 A1
Brunel Wy FHAM PO15 371 H3
Brunstead Pl
BKME/WDN BH12 447 G4
Brunstead Rd
BKME/WDN BH12 446 F4
Brunswick Cl ELGH SO50 295 G5
Brunswick Gdns HAV PO9 16 A3
Brunswick Pl LYMN SO41 440 C4
WSHM SO15 343 K2
Brunswick Rd ELGH SO50 295 G5
FRIM GU16 91 M2
Brunswick Sq SHAM SO14 13 G6
Brunswick St SSEA PO5 21 G4
Bruntile Cl FARN GU14 91 G7
Bruyn Rd FBDG SP6 309 M7
Bryanstone Cl FLET GU13 110 F2
Bryanstone Rd TWDS BH3 447 K1
Bryanston Rd ITCH SO19 344 B4
Bryant Rd BKME/WDN BH12 431 L8
Bryce Gdns ALDT GU11 7 K8
Bryces La NALR SO24 171 M5
Brydes Rd RAND SP11 92 E6
Bryher Island CHAM PO6 398 F1
Brympton Cl FBDG SP6 309 H6
Bryn Rd RFNM GU10 158 C1
Bryon Rd WIMB BH21 404 A2
Bryony Cl BDST BH18 429 K5
HLER SO31 370 D6
Bryony Gdns ELGH SO50 321 H2
Bryony Wy WVILLE PO7 376 E2
Bryson Rd CHAM PO6 375 H8
Bubb La BPWT SO32 321 H4
HEND SO30 321 G5
Bub La CHCH/BSGR BH23 450 D2
Buccleuch Rd CCLF BH13 446 F7
Bucehayes Cl
CHCH/BSGR BH23 436 E8
Buchanan Av LTDN BH7 448 D2
Buchanan Dr EWKG RG40 48 B1
Buchanan Rd ROWN SO16 317 L3
Buchanan Sq STHA RG19 27 H7
Buchan Av FHAM PO15 347 G8
Buchan Ct FAWY SO45 367 G6
The Buchan CBLY GU15 51 K8
Buckby La BSTK RG21 5 K7
HSEA PO3 400 A4
Bucketts Farm Cl BPWT SO32 324 A3
Buckfast Cl CHAM RG24 82 F7
Buckholt Rd STOK SO20 208 F2
Buckhurst Rd FRIM GU16 91 J2
Buckingham Cl ALTN GU34 176 C5
Buckingham Ga WSHM SO15 318 D8
Buckingham Rd
BKME/WDN BH12 446 C1
NWBY RG14 2 B7
PSF GU32 275 J5
Buckland Av KEMP RG22 104 C7
Buckland Cl ELGH SO50
FARN GU14
WVILLE PO7
Buckland Dene LYMN SO41
Buckland Gdns TOTT SO40
Buckland Gv CHCH/BSGR BH23
Buckland Rd BKME/WDN BH12
Buckland St NEND PO2
Buckland Ter
BKME/WDN BH12
Bucklers Ct HAV PO9
NEND PO2
Bucklers Rd GPORT PO12
The Bucklers LYMN SO41
Bucklers Wy CHAR BH8
Buckmore Av PSF GU32
Bucksey Rd
LSOL/BMARY PO13
Bucks Head Hl BPWT SO32
Buckskin La KEMP RG22
Buckstone Cl LYMN SO41
Buckthorn Cl TOTT SO40
WIMB BH21
Budden's La WHAM PO17
Buddens Rd WHAM PO17
Buddle Hl FBDG SP6
Buddlesgate RWIN SO21
Budd's Cl BSTK RG21
Budds La BOR GU35
ROMY SO51
Bude Cl CHAM PO6
Buffbeards La HASM GU27
Buffins Rd ODIM RG29
Bugdens La VWD BH31
Bugkingham Wy FRIM GU16
Bugle St SHAM SO14
Bulbeck Rd HAV PO9
Bulbery RAND SP11
Buldowne Wk LYMN SO41
Bulford Rd NTID SP9
NTID SP9
Bullar Rd WEND SO18
Bullar St SHAM SO14
Bull Dro WINC SO23
Buller Ct FARN GU14
Buller Rd ALDT GU11
Bullers Rd FNM GU9
Bullfinch Cl CFDH BH17
SHST GU47
TOTT SO40
Bull Hl LISS GU33
LYMN SO41
Bullington La RWIN SO21
Bull La BPWT SO32
LYND SO43
THLE RG7
Bullrush Cl FAWY SO45
Bulls Copse La HORN PO8
Bulls Down Cl HTWY RG27
Bulls Dro RSAL SP5
Bulls La RSAL SP5
Bulpits Hl RAND SP11
Bunces La THLE RG7
Bunch La HASM GU27
Bunch Wy HASM GU27
Bungalow Rd FARN GU14
Bungler's Hl THLE RG7
Bunkers Hl NWBY RG14
WVILLE PO7
Bunnian Pl BSTK RG21
Bunns La WVILLE PO7
Bunny La ROMY SO51
RSAL SP5
Bunstead La RWIN SO21
Bunting Cl KEMP RG22
Bunting Gdns HORN PO8
Bunting Ms KEMP RG22
Buntings ALTN GU34
Burbidge Gv ENEY PO4
Burbush Cl FAWY SO45
Burchell Rd NWBY RG14
Burcombe Rd NBNE BH10
Burcote Dr HSEA PO3
Burdale Dr HISD PO11
Burdens Heath NTHA RG18
Burdock Cl CHCH/BSGR BH23
RAND SP11
THLE RG7
Bure Cl CHCH/BSGR BH23
Bure Haven Dr
CHCH/BSGR BH23
Bure Homage La
CHCH/BSGR BH23
Bure La CHCH/BSGR BH23
Bure Pk CHCH/BSGR BH23
Bure Rd CHCH/BSGR BH23
Burfield KSCL RG20
Burford Cl CHCH/BSGR BH23
Burford La BROC SO42
Burford Rd CBLY GU15
Burgate Cl HAV PO9
Burgate Flds FBDG SP6
Burgess Cl BWD BH11
HISD PO11
ODIM RG29
Burgess Gdns ROWN SO16
Burgess La KSCL RG20
Burgess Rd BSTK RG21
PTSW SO17
WSHM SO15
Burghclere Rd HAV PO9
ITCH SO19
Burghead Cl SHST GU47
Burgh Hill Rd LIPH GU30
Burgoyne Rd CBLY GU15
ITCH SO19
SSEA PO5
Burgundy Cl HLER SO31
Buriton Cl FHAM/PORC PO16
Buriton Rd WINW SO22
Buriton St PSEA PO1
Burkal Dr AND SP10
Burke Dr ITCH SO19
Burleigh Rd FRIM GU16
NEND PO2
SBNE BH6
Burley Cl CHFD SO53
HAV PO9

/BTOS BH25 437 H8
BH31 356 C3
Down CHFD SO53 293 G4
La OVTN RG25 124 C7
Lawn RGWD BH24 384 F4
Rd BKME/WDN BH12 446 B2
SO42 412 E1
/BSGR BH23 410 B3
/BSGR BH23 435 G3
/ SO22 214 C4
Wy BLKW GU17 69 M2
ton Ct BLKW GU17 69 M5
ton Rd NEND PO2 399 J7
M SO15 343 J2
Rd North FAWY SO45 393 G2
Rd South FAWY SO45 392 F3
Wy TOTT SO40 342 D8
se Cl FHAM PO15 371 G1
y Cl KEMP RG22 104 B5
y Rd PSEA PO1 20 E2
BH4 447 H7
ke Rd VWD BH31 356 D3
nk Gdns TOTT SO40 341 J1
ae Rd FERN BH22 406 B7
VWD BH31 356 F4
Cl RWIN SO21 190 C6
Jones Dr SHST GU47 70 A2
t Av CHCH/BSGR BH23 449 K1
t Cl FAWY SO45 367 M6
/ SO22 214 B6
SO18 319 K7
t Rd CHCH/BSGR BH23 449 L1
T PO12 421 K2
ts Flds ELGH SO50 321 H1
ts Gdns ELGH SO50 321 J1
ts La HEND SO30 321 G4
Bit TADY RG26 42 B8
Rd GPORT PO12 421 J5
ate Rd PLE BH15 444 D6
am Beeches CHFD SO53 293 G2
am Cha WEND SO18 344 F1
am Dr CHAR BH8 448 B1
am Rd CHAM PO6 376 B7
/BSGR BH23 435 G6
SP6 309 L5 2
RG26 41 J6
ams Cl AND SP10 118 F5
am Wd
/PORC PO16 15 G1
gh Gdns
/BTOS BH25 438 A4 2
y Cl TADY RG26 61 L1
oor Meadow
G RG40 48 B6
ll Cl FARN GU14 90 E2
Av FLET GU13 111 G2
Cl CHAM RG24 5 H2
SO50 293 K7
GU14 90 C2
/ SO21 190 D4
de LSOL/BMARY PO13 396 F3
LE PO7 352 E7
Pl ROWN SO16 317 M6
Rd ELGH SO50 293 L7
SO19 345 H3
BH6 449 J1
Hill Rd RFNM GU10 158 F2
Hill Wy RFNM GU10 158 E3
House La
/BSGR BH23 409 M7
/STUB PO14 396 B5
/ SO41 414 D7
d Gv LYMN SO41 440 D6
RWIN SO21 266 E8
Rd FRIM GU16 70 F8
lds Rd HSEA PO3 399 M7
ge Rd HLER SO31 346 E6
Av CHAM PO6 375 L8
MARL SN8 32 B6
vfields KEMP RG22 127 G3 1
v Rd RWIN SO21 213 H7
vs Cl HAV PO9 17 H1
vs La VWD BH31 332 D8
ood Gdns ASHV GU12 113 K4
don Hts HLER SO31 345 M7
don Pl WVILLE PO7 376 B3
don Rd HEND SO30 345 M3
SO19 344 E2
LE PO7 376 B3
Rd SBNE BH6 449 K5
Cl RGWD BH24 381 H3
croft CHCH/BSGR BH23 435 G5
Rd CCLF BH13 446 F5
/BSGR BH23 450 D1
M SO15 343 J1
's Gdns CHAM RG24 106 A1
Hl WIMB BH21 404 A2
od Gv HISD PO11 425 L4
GPORT PO12 18 F4
rs GPORT PO12 18 E4
own Cl OVTN RG25 125 L7 1
elds ODIM RG29 108 D6
all La GPORT PO12 18 A5
ill Cl RAND SP11 142 C4
TOTT SO40 341 M3
d CCLF BH13 446 E7
V RG23 104 C2
RT PO12 18 E4
SO40 342 C6
Bank Rd STHA RG19 27 H8
RG19 38 A1
l Rd PLE BH15 445 H1
ls Farm FBDG SP6 309 K8 1
Rd CHAR BH8 433 G7
ead Dr RGWD BH24 381 J3
ells Dr KSCL RG20 59 H6 1
aint West SSEA PO5 21 G5 1
East SSEA PO5 21 G5
Md WVILLE PO7 376 A5
warren La OVTN RG25 128 E7
rs FARN GU14 90 C5
La WINC SO23 11 H8
tts Wy TOTT SO40 340 E6
er St PSEA PO1 20 C2
r CHCH/BSGR BH23 452 A1
Cl KEMP RG22 104 B4
Rd CWTH RG45 49 L2
s Cl ROMY SO51 232 F7 1

Butlers La RGWD BH24 359 G7
Butson Cl NWBY RG14 2 A4
Butt Cl RAND SP11 92 D5
Buttercup Cl FAWY SO45 367 L7 2
HEND SO30 317 K8
BOR GU35 201 M3 1
Buttercup Dr
CHCH/BSGR BH23 435 M7
Buttercup Pl NTHA RG18 27 G4
Buttercup Wy HLER SO31 370 C5
Butterfield CBLY GU15 70 E4 2
Butterfield Rd ROWN SO16 318 D4
Butterfly Dr CHAM PO6 374 E6
Buttermer Cl RFNM GU10 158 B1
Buttermere Cl FARN GU14 90 B4
BOR GU35 201 J3 2
ROWN SO16 317 K6
Buttermere Dr KEMP RG22 103 M7
Buttermere Gdns
NALR SO24 218 C4 2
The Buttery CHCH/BSGR BH23 450 C1
Button's La ALTN GU34 223 G6
ROMY SO51 288 D5
Buttsash Av FAWY SO45 367 L8
Butts Ash Gdns FAWY SO45 367 L7
Butts Ash La FAWY SO45 367 L7 3
Butts Bridge Hl FAWY SO45 367 L6
Buttsbridge Rd FAWY SO45 367 L7
Butts Cl WINW SO22 10 B4
ITCH SO19 345 H4 1
Butt's Crs ITCH SO19 345 G4 1
Butts La BPWT SO32 297 J8
Butts Lawn BROC SO42 387 K6
Butts Meadow HTWY RG27 85 M7 1
Butts Ms ALTN GU34 176 D6
Butts Paddock BROC SO42 387 K6
Butts Rd ALTN GU34 176 D7
ITCH SO19 344 F5
ITCH SO19 345 H4 1
Butt's Sq ITCH SO19 345 G4
The Butts BPWT SO32 299 H2
THLE RG7 42 E8 1
Butt St RAND SP11 92 D6
The Butty BSTK RG21 5 K7
Byerley Cl EMRTH PO10 378 F3 1
Byerley Rd PSEA PO1 423 K2
Byes La THLE RG7 62 E1
Byeways FAWY SO45 367 K6 2
KSCL RG20 56 B3
The Byeway SELS PO20 427 L7
Byfields Rd KSCL RG20 59 H6
Byfleet Av CHAM RG24 106 A3
By-pass Rd ROMY SO51 290 D2
By Pass Rd RWIN SO21 168 A4
Byrd Cl WVILLE PO7 376 C3
Byrd Gdns KEMP RG22 127 H1
Byron Av FRIM GU16 71 L5
WINW SO22 10 A7
Byron Cl BPWT SO32 297 K8
CHAM RG24 83 H7
FHAM/PORC PO16 15 G3
FLET GU13 88 F8
NWBY RG14 37 J1
RAND SP11 92 E6
YTLY GU46 68 E4 2
Byron Dr CWTH RG45 49 L5
Byron Rd BOSC BH5 448 E4
ELGH SO50 294 A4
ITCH SO19 345 H2
NEND PO2 399 K8
NMIL/BTOS BH25 437 J8
Byways YTLY GU46 68 E3
Byworth Cl FNM GU9 134 C6
Byworth Rd FNM GU9 134 C6

C

Cable St SHAM SO14 13 L1
Cabot Dr FAWY SO45 367 G5
Cabot La CFDH BH17 429 L8
Cabot Wy NMIL/BTOS BH25 437 K5
Cabrol Rd FARN GU14 90 D3
Cabul Rd NTID SP9 114 C3
Cadet Wy FLET GU13 111 G4
Cadgwith Pl CHAM PO6 398 F1
Cadhay Cl NMIL/BTOS BH25 437 J5
Cadland Rd FAWY SO45 392 B1
Cadlands Park Est FAWY SO45 392 A2
Cadnam Cl ALDT GU11 7 J8
DEAN RG23 103 G6
Cadnam La TOTT SO40 314 E5
Cadnam Rd ENEY PO4 423 M5
Cadnam Wy CHAR BH8 433 H5
Cadogan Rd RGWD BH24 382 F1
Cadogen Rd ALDT GU11 113 G1
Cador Dr FHAM/PORC PO16 397 M2
Caerleon Av ITCH SO19 345 G2
Caerleon Cl GSHT GU26 203 M2 1
Caerleon Dr AND SP10 118 F4
ITCH SO19 344 F2
Caernarvon FRIM GU16 71 J8
Caernarvon Cl DEAN RG23 104 B3 1
Caernarvon Gdns
CHFD SO53 292 F4 1
Caesar Ct ALDT GU11 6 B2
Caesar Rd AND SP10 119 G5
Caesar's Camp Rd CBLY GU15 51 K8
Caesar's Cl CBLY GU15 51 K8 1
Caesar's Wy WHCH RG28 122 A2
WIMB BH21 429 J4
Cains Cl FHAM/STUB PO14 396 A5
Caird Av NMIL/BTOS BH25 437 M5
Cairn Cl FRIM GU16 71 L5
Cairngorm Cl KEMP RG22 104 A4 1
Cairngorm Pl FARN GU14 90 B1 1
Cairngorm Rd STHA RG19 27 G6 1
Cairns Cl CHCH/BSGR BH23 434 D8
Cairo Ter NEND PO2 423 H1
Caister Cl FERN BH22 406 A2
Caistor Cl ROWN SO16 317 M4
Caithness Cl DEAN RG23 102 F6
Cakeham Rd SELS PO20 427 L8
Caker's La ALTN GU34 177 J6
Caker Stream Rd ALTN GU34 177 G4
Calabrese HLER SO31 370 F1
Calard Dr NTHA RG18 26 D3
Calbourne HLER SO31 369 G1 1
Calcot Hl BPWT SO32 322 D5
Calcot La BPWT SO32 322 D6
Calcott Pk YTLY GU46 68 F2
Calder Cl ROWN SO16 317 K8
Calder Ct AND SP10 119 H6 1
Calder Rd CFDH BH17 430 D8
Calderwood Dr ITCH SO19 344 E4
Caledonia Dr FAWY SO45 367 H5
Caledon Rd PSTN BH14 446 C5
Calender Cl ALTN GU34 176 E6 1
Calkin Cl CHCH/BSGR BH23 434 E7
Calleva Cl KEMP RG22 127 G1
Calluna Rd BKME/WDN BH12 430 F7
Calmore Crs TOTT SO40 316 A7
Calmore Dr TOTT SO40 316 B6
Calmore Gdns TOTT SO40 341 G1
Calmore Rd TOTT SO40 316 A7
Calpe Av LYND SO43 363 K2
Calshot Cl FAWY SO45 393 K8
Calshot Dr CHFD SO53 292 F4
Calshot Rd FAWY SO45 392 F5
HAV PO9 377 G1
Calshot Wy FRIM GU16 91 K1
LSOL/BMARY PO13 396 F7 2
Calthorpe Rd FLET GU13 88 D6
HTWY RG27 88 D5
Calton Gdns ALDT GU11 7 J8
Calvecroft LIPH GU30 226 F4
Calvert Cl ASHV GU12 7 M4
Calvin Cl CBLY GU15 71 L4
Calvin Rd MOOR/WNTN BH9 432 D8
Camargue Cl HLER SO31 346 F8
Camber Pl PSEA PO1 20 B5
Camberry Cl BSTK RG21 105 H5
Cambria Dr FAWY SO45 367 H5
Cambrian Cl CBLY GU15 70 E3
HLER SO31 345 L6 2
Cambrian Rd FARN GU14 90 A1
Cambrian Wy KEMP RG22 104 A5
Cambridge Dr CHFD SO53 293 H5
Cambridge Gdns
CHCH/BSGR BH23 434 D6
Cambridge Gn
FHAM/STUB PO14 371 G6
Cambridge Rd ALDT GU11 6 C2
CWTH RG45 49 M4
GPORT PO12 421 J2
LSOL/BMARY PO13 420 D4
PSEA PO1 20 E4
SHAM SO14 318 F8
SHST GU47 50 B7
WCLF BH2 22 B5
Cambridge Rd East
FARN GU14 90 F7 1
Cambridge Rd West FARN GU14 90 F7
Camcross Cl CHAM PO6 374 F7 1
Camden St GPORT PO12 421 L2
Camden Wk FLET GU13 89 H7
Camel Green Rd FBDG SP6 333 L2 1
FBDG SP6 333 M2 1
Camelia Cl HAV PO9 377 M5
NBAD SO52 291 M3
Camelia Gdns WEND SO18 319 M6 1
Camelia Gv ELGH SO50 295 K6
Camellia Cl WIMB BH21 356 C7 1
Camellia Gdns
NMIL/BTOS BH25 437 M6
Camelot Cl AND SP10 118 F6
Camelot Crs FHAM/PORC PO16 373 M7
Camelsdale Rd HASM GU27 228 C3
Camel Wy FARN GU14 90 D8
Cameron Cl
LSOL/BMARY PO13 397 G5 1
Cameron Rd ALDT GU11 113 G1
Camfield Cl BSTK RG21 105 H5
Camlea Cl BSTK RG21 105 H5
Camley Cl ITCH SO19 344 C7
Cammel Rd FERN BH22 406 B6
Camomile Dr RAND SP11 92 E6
Campbell Cl ALDT GU11 7 H8
FLET GU13 88 D7
RAND SP11 161 K1
YTLY GU46 69 J2
Campbell Pl FRIM GU16 71 J5
Campbell Rd ALDT GU11 112 D5
BMTH BH1 448 D3
CHCH/BSGR BH23 435 G5
ELGH SO50 294 A7
RWIN SO21 145 H6
SSEA PO5 21 K5
TADY RG26 64 A6
Campbell St SHAM SO14 344 A2 1
Campbell Wy ELGH SO50 295 H6
Camp Farm Rd ALDT GU11 113 G3
Camp Hl RFNM GU10 135 M8
Campion Cl BLKW GU17 70 C5 1
ELGH SO50 321 H2 1
HLER SO31 370 C7
BOR GU35 201 M4
LYMN SO41 440 C3 1
WVILLE PO7 376 E2 2
Campion Dr ROMY SO51 263 H7
Campion Gv CHCH/BSGR BH23 450 E2
Campion Rd ITCH SO19 345 H3
Campion Wy HTWY RG27 87 J1
LYMN SO41 440 C3
WINC SO23 215 H2
Camp Rd FARN GU14 90 F8
BOR GU35 201 J3
LSOL/BMARY PO13 397 H5
THLE RG7 30 F5
Campsie Cl KEMP RG22 104 A4
Camrose Wy BSTK RG21 105 H5 1
Cams Bay Cl
FHAM/PORC PO16 373 K7 1
Cams Hl FHAM/PORC PO16 373 J7
WVILLE PO7 326 A7
Camus Cl FLET GU13 110 C3
Camwood Cl BSTK RG21 105 H5
Canada Rd ITCH SO19 344 C6
ROMY SO51 288 C7
Canada Wy BOR GU35 201 J4
Canal Cl ALDT GU11 113 G3
ODIM RG29 108 B4 1
ROMY SO51 262 F7
Canal View Rd NWBY RG14 3 M4
Canal Wk ROMY SO51 262 E8
SHAM SO14 13 G5
SSEA PO5 21 J2
Canberra Cl GPORT PO12 18 B4
HTWY RG27 68 D1
Canberra Rd CHCH/BSGR BH23 434 C7
EMRTH PO10 402 E5
ROWN SO16 317 G4
Canberra Wy FARN GU14 90 C8
Candover Cl TADY RG26 61 L1 2
Candy La WEND SO18 345 J1
Canes La BOR GU35 201 L3
Canford Av BWD BH11 431 K7
Canford Bottom WIMB BH21 405 G2
Canford Cliffs Av PSTN BH14 446 C6
Canford Cliffs Rd CCLF BH13 446 D6
Canford Cl BPWT SO32 348 C1
ROWN SO16 317 J6
Canford Crs CCLF BH13 457 K1
Canford Heath Rd CFDH BH17 430 B7
Canford Rd BWD BH11 431 L7
PLE BH15 445 J4
Canford View Dr
WIMB BH21 404 F2 1
Canford Wy BKME/WDN BH12 431 G6
Canhouse La LISS GU33 249 L5
Canning Rd ASHV GU12 7 L2
Cannon Cl BDST BH18 429 K7
SHST GU47 50 C8
Cannon Hill Gdns
WIMB BH21 404 F1 1
Cannon Hill Rd WIMB BH21 404 E1
Cannon St LYMN SO41 440 C4
WSHM SO15 318 B8
Canoe Cl HLER SO31 370 D7
Canon's Barn Cl
FHAM/PORC PO16 374 A7 1
Canons Cl NTID SP9 114 E4 1
Canon's Ct KSCL RG20 59 H6
Canon St WINC SO23 10 F9
Cansfield End NWBY RG14 2 D3
Canterbury Av ITCH SO19 345 G5
Canterbury Cl FERN BH22 380 D7 1
KEMP RG22 104 A8 1
LSOL/BMARY PO13 420 F4
Canterbury Dr FAWY SO45 367 G5
Canterbury Rd ASHV GU12 113 K5
ENEY PO4 423 K5
FARN GU14 91 G6
FHAM/STUB PO14 396 A5
Canterton La LYND SO43 314 A8
Canton St WSHM SO15 343 K2
Canute Dr CHCH/BSGR BH23 409 M7
Canute Rd SHAM SO14 13 K6
WINC SO23 239 G2
Capella Gdns FAWY SO45 367 H5 3
Capel Ley WVILLE PO7 376 C4
Capers End La BPWT SO32 322 D7
Capesthorne
CHCH/BSGR BH23 451 G3
Capper Rd CBLY GU15 70 D1
Capstone Pl CHAR BH8 448 C2
Capstone Rd CHAR BH8 448 B2
Captains Pl SHAM SO14 13 J6
Captain's Rw LYMN SO41 440 D4
PSEA PO1 20 B5
Carberry Dr FHAM/PORC PO16 397 M1
Carbery Av SBNE BH6 449 J4
Carbery Ct HAV PO9 377 H1
Carbery Gdns SBNE BH6 449 K3
Carbinswood La THLE RG7 29 G4
Carbis Cl CHAM PO6 398 E1
Carbonel Cl DEAN RG23 103 M3
Cardew Rd LISS GU33 248 F5
Cardiff Rd NEND PO2 399 H6
Cardigan Rd
MOOR/WNTN BH9 432 D8
Cardinal Dr WVILLE PO7 352 F7
Cardinal Wy HLER SO31 370 F5
Carey Rd ITCH SO19 345 G3
Careys Cottages BROC SO42 387 K6
Careys Rd CHAR BH8 433 H4
Carfax Av RFNM GU10 113 J8
Cargate Av ALDT GU11 6 E3
Cargate Gv ALDT GU11 6 D4
Cargate Hl ALDT GU11 6 D3
Cargate Ter ALDT GU11 6 D4
Carisbrooke FRIM GU16 71 J8
HLER SO31 369 G1 2
Carisbrooke Av
FHAM/STUB PO14 395 L6
Carisbrooke Cl DEAN RG23 104 B2
HAV PO9 17 J3
NALR SO24 218 C4 1
Carisbrooke Ct
NMIL/BTOS BH25 437 K5
ROMY SO51 262 F7 1
Carisbrooke Crs CHFD SO53 293 K3
PLE BH15 444 D5 1
Carisbrooke Dr ITCH SO19 344 D2
Carisbrooke Rd ENEY PO4 423 L4 1
LSOL/BMARY PO13 396 F5
Carisbrooke Wy
CHCH/BSGR BH23 436 C7
Carless Cl LSOL/BMARY PO13 421 H1
Carleton Cl HTWY RG27 85 L7
Carlinwark Dr CBLY GU15 71 J1
Carlisle Cl DEAN RG23 104 B2
Carlisle Rd RFNM GU10 181 L1
ROWN SO16 318 A8
SSEA PO5 21 K2
Carlton Av NMIL/BTOS BH25 452 C1
Carlton Cl FRIM GU16 71 L5
Carlton Crs FLET GU13 111 G2
WSHM SO15 343 K2
Carlton Gv PSTN BH14 446 C3
Carlton Pl WSHM SO15 343 K2
Carlton Rd BMTH BH1 23 M3
FHAM/PORC PO16 374 B7
GPORT PO12 19 H3
BOR GU35 202 F4
WSHM SO15 343 K1
Carlton Wy GPORT PO12 19 H2
Carlyle Rd GPORT PO12 18 E1
SBNE BH6 449 J2
Carlyn Dr CHFD SO53 293 J1
Carlyon Cl FARN GU14 90 F4
FRIM GU16 91 J4
Carmans La RWIN SO21 266 C1
Carmarthen Av CHAM PO6 375 M7
Carmarthen Cl FARN GU14 90 C1
Carmichael Wy KEMP RG22 104 B8
Carnarvon Rd GPORT PO12 18 C3
NEND PO2 399 K8
Carnation Rd ROWN SO16 319 H4
Carne Cl CHFD SO53 265 H8
Carnegie Rd NWBY RG14 2 F5
Carolina Pl EWKG RG40 48 B1
Caroline Av CHCH/BSGR BH23 450 D3
Caroline Rd BWD BH11 431 M5
Caroline Wy FRIM GU16 71 J7
Carolyn Cl ITCH SO19 344 C6
Carpathia Cl WEND SO18 319 M6 4
Carpenter Cl ENEY PO4 423 L5 2
FAWY SO45 367 L4 2
LYMN SO41 440 B3 1
Carpenter Rd RWIN SO21 145 H6
Carpenters NALR SO24 218 C3 1
Carpenters Cl HTWY RG27 64 C7
Carpenter's Down
CHAM RG24 83 G6 1
Carraway FHAM PO15 371 H1
Carrbridge Cl TWDS BH3 447 J1
Carrbridge Rd TWDS BH3 447 J1
Carrick La YTLY GU46 69 H2
Carrick Wy NMIL/BTOS BH25 438 A6
Carrington Cl LYMN SO41 454 D4
Carrington Crs TADY RG26 41 L8
Carrington La LYMN SO41 454 D3
Carrinton La ASHV GU12 91 J8
Carroll Av FERN BH22 406 B3
Carroll Cl BKME/WDN BH12 446 F2
ELGH SO50 295 J7 2
Carronade Wk HSEA PO3 399 K3
Carshalton Av CHAM PO6 375 M8
Carshalton Rd CBLY GU15 51 K7
Carters Av PLE BH15 444 C4
Carter's Clay Rd ROMY SO51 261 G3
Carter's Cl FBDG SP6 285 J5
Cartersland LIPH GU30 250 E5
Carter's La TOTT SO40 366 C3
Carter's Meadow AND SP10 118 C6
Carters Wk FNM GU9 112 A8 1
Carthage Cl CHFD SO53 293 L1
Carthagena RWIN SO21 168 C4
Carthona Dr FLET GU13 110 E1
Cartref Cl VWD BH31 356 D2
Cartwright Dr FHAM PO15 371 K6
Carvers Hl MARL SN8 32 A6
Carvers La RGWD BH24 382 E1
Cary Cl NWBY RG14 37 G2
Carysfort Rd BMTH BH1 448 C4
Cask St PSEA PO1 423 G2
Caslake Cl NMIL/BTOS BH25 437 K7
Caspar John Cl
FHAM/STUB PO14 395 M7
Caspian Cl HLER SO31 370 F1
Cassel Av WBNE BH4 447 G7
Cassino Cl ALDT GU11 7 G1
Castle Av CHCH/BSGR BH23 436 C8
HAV PO9 17 K5
Castle Cl CBLY GU15 71 J4
LYMN SO41 454 D5
SSEA PO5 21 G5
Castle Ct RAND SP11 92 D5 1
WSHM SO15 342 E2
Castlecraig Ct SHST GU47 70 A1 3
Castledene Crs PSTN BH14 445 M6
Castle Farm La WHAM PO17 348 F6
Castle Gate Cl CHAR BH8 433 G6
Castle Gv FHAM/PORC PO16 398 B1
NWBY RG14 25 J3
Castle Hl FNM GU9 134 E5
THLE RG7 46 F1
Castle Hill La RGWD BH24 384 B4
Castle La CHFD SO53 292 F4
FAWY SO45 419 K1
NBAD SO52 292 A4
NWBY RG14 25 H2
SHAM SO14 12 F4
Castle Lane East LTDN BH7 433 M8
Castle La West CHAR BH8 433 K6
MOOR/WNTN BH9 432 E4
Castlemain Av SBNE BH6 449 H3
Castlemans La HISD PO11 401 L7
Castleman Trailway
CFDH BH17 429 J8
FERN BH22 380 A5
RGWD BH24 381 H3
WIMB BH21 404 E5
Castleman Wy RGWD BH24 382 E2
Castlemews RGWD BH24 382 A3
Castle Ri ODIM RG29 108 B4
WINC SO23 191 H7
Castle Rd ALDT GU11 112 B4
BSTK RG21 105 G5
CBLY GU15 71 H4
HAV PO9 353 L6
HLER SO31 368 F2
MOOR/WNTN BH9 432 D7
SSEA PO5 20 F6
WEND SO18 319 K6
WHAM PO17 374 D2
Castleshaw Cl ROWN SO16 342 D1 1
Castle Sq SHAM SO14 12 F5
Castle St ALTN GU34 196 D1
CHCH/BSGR BH23 450 A2
FHAM/PORC PO16 398 B1
FHAM/STUB PO14 371 K8
FLET GU13 110 E1
FNM GU9 134 E5
PLE BH15 445 H7
RAND SP11 92 D5
SHAM SO14 343 L1
Castleton Av NBNE BH10 432 B2
Castle Vw GPORT PO12 397 M8
Castle View Rd
FHAM/PORC PO16 398 B2
Castleway HAV PO9 17 K5
Castle Wy SHAM SO14 12 F4
Castlewood RGWD BH24 382 B3
Castle Woods RSAL SP5 285 J2 2
Castor Ct FLET GU13 111 G3 1
YTLY GU46 68 E1
Caswall Ride YTLY GU46 69 J3 2
Caswell Cl FARN GU14 90 C2

Catalina Cl *CHCH/BSGR* BH23 450 F2
Catalina Dr *PLE* BH15 445 K7
Catamaran Cl *HLER* SO31 370 D7
Cateran Cl *ROWN* SO16 317 L8 1
Catesby Gdns *YTLY* GU46 68 D3
Cathay Gdns *FAWY* SO45 367 G5
Cathedral Vw *WINC* SO23 239 G2
Catherine Cl *HEND* SO30 320 D6
Catherine Crs *RSAL* SP5 284 C1
Catherine Gdns *HEND* SO30 320 D6
Catherine Rd *NWBY* RG14 2 E6
Catherington La *HORN* PO8 352 F1
Catherington Wy *HAV* PO9 377 K4
Catisfield La *FHAM* PO15 371 M7
Catisfield Rd *ENEY* PO4 423 M3
FHAM PO15 372 A7
Catkin Cl *CHAM* RG24 83 L5
Caton Cl *BKME/WDN* BH12 431 M8
Cattistock Rd *CHAR* BH8 433 J7
Cattle La *RAND* SP11 141 M4
Caunter Rd *NWBY* RG14 25 G4 1
Causeway Crs *TOTT* SO40 316 F8
Causeway Farm *HORN* PO8 352 F3
The Causeway *EPSF* GU31 275 K6
FHAM/PORC PO16 373 J7
HTWY RG27 65 M1
RSAL SP5 206 F2
STOK SO20 184 E2 1
Cavalier Cl *CHAM* RG24 106 B2
FAWY SO45 367 G5
NWBY RG14 25 M3
Cavalier Rd *CHAM* RG24 106 B2
Cavalier Wy *ALTN* GU34 176 C6
Cavalry Ct *ALDT* GU11 6 B2
Cavan Crs *CFDH* BH17 429 M7
Cavanna Cl *LSOL/BMARY* PO13 396 F5
Cavan's Rd *ALDT* GU11 112 F2
Cavel Ct *CHAM* RG24 83 M8 1
Cavell Dr *CHAM* PO6 375 J7
Cavendish Cl *ROMY* SO51 263 G6 1
WVILLE PO7 352 D8 2
Cavendish Ct *BLKW* GU17 70 A5
NWBY RG14 26 B3
Cavendish Dr *WVILLE* PO7 376 D1
Cavendish Gv *WINC* SO23 11 J1
WSHM SO15 318 E8
Cavendish Ms *WSHM* SO15 318 E8
Cavendish Pl *BMTH* BH1 23 G2
Cavendish Rd *ALDT* GU11 6 F3
BMTH BH1 23 G2
FLET GU13 110 D3 1
SSEA PO5 21 J6
WCLF BH2 22 F2
C Av *FAWY* SO45 392 B3
Caversham Cl *HEND* SO30 320 C7 1
ITCH SO19 344 E4
PLE BH15 444 D5
Caves Farm Cl *SHST* GU47 49 K8
Cawdor Rd *TWDS* BH3 447 J1
Cawte Rd *WSHM* SO15 343 G2
Caxton Av *ITCH* SO19 344 F2
Caxton Cl *AND* SP10 118 B7
CHCH/BSGR BH23 450 E1
Cayman Cl *CHAM* RG24 83 H7
Cecil Av *CHAR* BH8 433 G8
ROWN SO16 318 A7
TOTT SO40 341 G6
Cecil Cl *WIMB* BH21 429 J2
Cecil Gv *SSEA* PO5 20 F6
Cecil Pl *SSEA* PO5 20 F6 1
Cecil Rd *BKME/WDN* BH12 446 C2
BOSC BH5 448 D4
ITCH SO19 344 D5
Cedar Av *BLKW* GU17 70 A3
CHCH/BSGR BH23 434 B8
NBNE BH10 432 B2
RGWD BH24 381 J5 1
WSHM SO15 318 C8
Cedar Cl *ASHV* GU12 113 H8
GPORT PO12 397 L7
HEND SO30 346 A1
HLER SO31 345 K8
TADY RG26 62 A2
UPTN BH16 428 F8
WINC SO23 191 G8
WVILLE PO7 376 C2
Cedar Ct *HASM* GU27 228 F2 1
Cedar Crs *HORN* PO8 353 G3
NBAD SO52 291 L3
Cedar Dr *FLET* GU13 89 H7
KSCL RG20 59 H6
LYMN SO41 439 H8 2
WIMB BH21 404 F3
Cedar Gdns *HAV* PO9 17 G2
Cedar Gv *HSEA* PO3 423 M1
STHA RG19 26 F5
Cedar Lawn *ROMY* SO51 263 H7
Cedarmount *LYND* SO43 363 K4
Cedar Mt *NWBY* RG14 25 J8
Cedar Pl *CHCH/BSGR* BH23 409 M7
Cedar Rd *ELGH* SO50 293 K7
FARN GU14 90 F5
FAWY SO45 391 L1
SHAM SO14 318 F8
Cedars Cl *SHST* GU47 49 J8
The Cedars *FLET* GU13 89 G8
Cedars Vw *RSAL* SP5 232 D1
Cedar Tree Cl *DEAN* RG23 102 F8
Cedar Wy *DEAN* RG23 104 C1
FERN BH22 380 A8
Cedarways *FNM* GU9 158 E1
Cedarwood *WINC* SO23 215 H1
Cedar Wood Cl *ELGH* SO50 295 K6
TOTT SO40 316 B8 3
Cedric Cl *FAWY* SO45 392 D8
Celandine Av *HLER* SO31 370 D6
HORN PO8 353 G5
Celandine Cl *CHCH/BSGR* BH23 435 M8
CWTH RG45 49 M2
NBAD SO52 292 E3 1
Celandine Ct *YTLY* GU46 68 D1
Celandine Gv *NTHA* RG18 27 J5
Celia Cl *WVILLE* PO7 352 F8
Cellars Farm Rd *SBNE* BH6 449 M5
Celtic Dr *AND* SP10 8 C8
Cement Ter *SHAM* SO14 12 F5 1
Cemetery Av *PLE* BH15 445 L2
Cemetery Hl *ODIM* RG29 108 D6
Cemetery La *EMRTH* PO10 379 G5
OVTN RG25 130 A3
WVILLE PO7 351 K3
Cemetery Rd *FLET* GU13 110 D1
WSHM SO15 318 D8
Centaur St *NEND* PO2 399 H8
Centaury Gdns *ELGH* SO50 321 H1 1
Centenary Cl *LYMN* SO41 413 G6
Centenary Wy *BMTH* BH1 448 D3
Central Av *WIMB* BH21 429 H1 1
Central Br *SHAM* SO14 13 J5
Central Dr *WCLF* BH2 22 D1
Central Rd *CHAM* PO6 400 A1
FHAM/PORC PO16 397 M1
BOR GU35 201 J2
SHAM SO14 13 H7
Central Station Br *WSHM* SO15 12 C2
Central St *PSEA* PO1 423 H2
RAND SP11 92 E6
Centre Dr *CHAM* RG24 83 L7
Centre La *LYMN* SO41 439 J7
Centre Pl *RGWD* BH24 382 D1 1
Centre Terrace Rd *FARN* GU14 90 D8
Centre Wy *HLER* SO31 370 E5
Centurion Cl *SHST* GU47 50 A8 1
Centurion Wy *KEMP* RG22 127 G2
Cerdic Ms *HLER* SO31 369 L4
Cerne Cl *NBAD* SO52 291 K4
WEND SO18 320 A7
Chadderton Gdns *PSEA* PO1 20 E5
Chaddesley Gln *CCLF* BH13 457 J2
Chaddesley Wood Rd
CCLF BH13 457 K3 1
Chadwell Av *ITCH* SO19 344 F4
Chadwick Rd *ELGH* SO50 293 K6
Chafen Rd *WEND* SO18 319 J8
Chaffers Cl *ODIM* RG29 131 J6
Chaffey Cl *RGWD* BH24 359 G8
Chaffinch Cl *CFDH* BH17 429 K6 2
KEMP RG22 103 M8
NMIL/BTOS BH25 437 K6
SHST GU47 50 B8 3
TOTT SO40 316 B8 2
Chaffinch Gn *HORN* PO8 352 C4
Chaffinch Wy
FHAM/PORC PO16 373 K8
LSOL/BMARY PO13 420 D1 1
Chalbury Cl *CFDH* BH17 430 E6
Chalcraft Cl *LIPH* GU30 226 D4 1
Chalcrafts *ALTN* GU34 176 F3
Chaldecott Gdns *NBNE* BH10 432 A4
Chaldon Rd *CFDH* BH17 430 D6
Chale Cl *LSOL/BMARY* PO13 397 G6
Chalet Hl *BOR* GU35 201 K5
Chalewood Rd *FAWY* SO45 418 C1
Chalfont Av *CHCH/BSGR* BH23 434 B5
Chalfont Dr *FARN* GU14 90 F6
Chalford Rd *NWBY* RG14 2 A5
Chalice Ct *HEND* SO30 345 M2 1
Chalk Cl *ALTN* GU34 197 G6 1
Chalkcroft La *RAND* SP11 117 L4
Chalk Hl *BPWT* SO32 325 H3
STOK SO20 211 L3
WEND SO18 320 B7
Chalk La *WHAM* PO17 372 F1
Chalkpit La *RAND* SP11 141 J3
Chalk Pit La *RSAL* SP5 208 A7
Chalkpit Rd *CHAM* PO6 374 F6
Chalk Rdg *HORN* PO8 328 C5
WINC SO23 11 M9
Chalkridge Rd *CHAM* PO6 375 L7
Chalk's Cl *RSAL* SP5 285 J1
Chalk V *CHAM* RG24 106 B3
STOK SO20 211 L4
Chalky Copse *HTWY* RG27 85 M6 2
Chalky Hl *ALTN* GU34 195 M2
Chalky La *BPWT* SO32 297 J8
HTWY RG27 109 L5
Challenger Wy *FAWY* SO45 367 H4
Challenor Cl *EWKG* RG40 48 C1 1
Challis Cl *KEMP* RG22 104 B6
Challis Ct *RAND* SP11 92 F6
SHAM SO14 13 H5
Challoner Cl *KEMP* RG22 104 B5
Chalmers Wy *HLER* SO31 369 J5
Chaloner Crs *FAWY* SO45 367 L7 1
Chalton Crs *HAV* PO9 377 H3
Chalton La *HORN* PO8 328 E2
Chalvington Rd *CHFD* SO53 293 H3
Chalybeate Cl *ROWN* SO16 318 A6
Chamberlain Gv
FHAM/STUB PO14 15 G8
Chamberlain Rd *PTSW* SO17 318 F5
Chamber La *RFNM* GU10 133 M8
Chamberlayne Rd *ELGH* SO50 293 M7
HLER SO31 345 K8 2
Chambers Av *ROMY* SO51 291 G1
Chambers Cl *ROWN* SO16 317 H3
Chambers Rd *ASHV* GU12 113 L2
Chamomile Gdns *FARN* GU14 89 M3
Champion Cl *LYMN* SO41 454 D4
Champion Wy *FLET* GU13 110 F3
Champney Cl *BOR* GU35 201 H7
Chancellors La *BPWT* SO32 321 K5
Chancel Rd *HLER* SO31 370 F5
Chander Cl *FERN* BH22 406 C4
Chandler Rd *BSTK* RG21 104 F6
Chandlers Cl *HISD* PO11 426 A6 1
Chandlers La *YTLY* GU46 68 F1
Chandlers Rd *ASHV* GU12 113 L4
Chandlers Wy *HLER* SO31 370 F2
Chandos Av *BKME/WDN* BH12 431 L8
Chandos Rd *NWBY* RG14 25 J8
Chandos St *SHAM* SO14 13 H5
Channels Farm Rd
ROWN SO16 319 J3
Channel Wy *SHAM* SO14 13 K6
Chant Cl *RAND* SP11 165 L2
Chantreys *FLET* GU13 88 C8 2
Chantry Cl *CHCH/BSGR* BH23 436 D7
FNM GU9 134 D6 1
Chantry Ms *KEMP* RG22 127 G1 1
Chantry Rd *GPORT* PO12 421 L1
HORN PO8 352 F1
SHAM SO14 13 K5
The Chantrys *FNM* GU9 134 C6
Chantry St *AND* SP10 9 H5
The Chantry *FHAM/STUB* PO14 371 G5
Chapel Cl *OVTN* RG25 126 C7
RAND SP11 141 G2
STOK SO20 210 B3
WIMB BH21 429 G2
Chapel Ct *NTHA* RG18 27 H4
Chapel Crs *ITCH* SO19 344 E4
Chapel Dro *ELGH* SO50 321 H1
HEND SO30 345 M2
Chapel Gdns *BOR* GU35 201 L3
Chapel Hl *BSTK* RG21 4 D6
Chapel La *BPWT* SO32 322 D8
BROC SO42 416 A2
CHCH/BSGR BH23 407 G5
CHCH/BSGR BH23 409 L8
ELGH SO50 266 A7
FARN GU14 70 C8
FAWY SO45 392 C8
FAWY SO45 392 E5
LYMN SO41 413 H7
LYND SO43 363 K4
RAND SP11 92 D6
RAND SP11 97 H4
RAND SP11 119 G2 1
RAND SP11 140 A8
RGWD BH24 384 F5
ROMY SO51 234 C8
ROMY SO51 260 D2
RSAL SP5 253 G1
RSAL SP5 256 E3
RSAL SP5 285 K2
RSAL SP5 313 H1
RWIN SO21 215 M6
STHA RG19 40 C7
STOK SO20 209 G1
TADY RG26 60 C4
THLE RG7 42 C3
TOTT SO40 341 J3
WIMB BH21 429 G3
Chapel Md *HTWY* RG27 48 B8 2
Chapel Pond Dr *ODIM* RG29 108 B5
Chapel Ri *RGWD* BH24 382 B6
Chapel River Cl *AND* SP10 8 B6
Chapel Rd *BPWT* SO32 299 H5
BPWT SO32 324 A3
BPWT SO32 325 G6
CBLY GU15 70 E3
HEND SO30 320 D6
HLER SO31 370 C2
KSCL RG20 24 B2
RFNM GU10 158 B5
PSTN BH14 445 M4
SHAM SO14 13 J4
Chapelside *FHAM/STUB* PO14 371 L8
Chapel Sq *CBLY* GU15 70 C2
Chapel St *FARN* GU14 91 G2
GPORT PO12 397 M8
NEND PO2 399 H8 1
NTHA RG18 27 H5
OVTN RG25 125 K7
PSF GU32 273 J8
PSF GU32 275 L4
SSEA PO5 20 F5 1
Chaplains Av *HORN* PO8 352 B5
Chaplains Cl *HORN* PO8 352 B4
Chaplain's Hl *CWTH* RG45 50 A4
Chapman Wk *NTHA* RG18 26 E4
Chappell Cl *LIPH* GU30 226 F4
Chapter Ter *HTWY* RG27 87 J2 2
Charborough Rd *BDST* BH18 429 M5
Charden Rd *ELGH* SO50 294 F7
LSOL/BMARY PO13 397 H8
Charfield Cl *FHAM/STUB* PO14 14 A7
WINW SO22 238 D3
Charing Cl *RGWD* BH24 382 E2 1
Chark La *LSOL/BMARY* PO13 396 D8
Charlcot Cl *WHCH* RG28 122 B5
Charlcot Farm *WHCH* RG28 122 B5
Charldon Gn *CHAM* RG24 83 M8 1
Charlecote Cl *FARN* GU14 91 G5
Charlecote Dr *CHFD* SO53 264 F8
Charledown Cl *OVTN* RG25 123 M1
Charledown Rd *OVTN* RG25 123 M1
Charlesbury Av *GPORT* PO12 18 A4
Charles Cl *HTWY* RG27 85 M7
WINC SO23 11 H2
WVILLE PO7 376 B2
Charles Crs *NMIL/BTOS* BH25 437 M3
Charles Dickens St *PSEA* PO1 21 G2 1
Charles Gdns *NBNE* BH10 432 A6
Charles Knott Gdns
WSHM SO15 343 K1
Charles Richards Cl
BSTK RG21 104 F5 1
Charles Rd *PLE* BH15 445 J5
Charles's La *RGWD* BH24 383 H6
Charles St *CBLY* GU15 70 F3
KEMP RG22 104 C4
NWBY RG14 37 G2
PSEA PO1 423 H2
PSF GU32 275 K5
SHAM SO14 13 H5 1
Charleston Cl *HISD* PO11 425 J4
Charleston Rd *FAWY* SO45 368 B8
Charles Watts Wy
HEND SO30 345 J1
Charlesworth Dr
WVILLE PO7 352 B7 2
Charlesworth Gdns
WVILLE PO7 352 B7
Charliejoy Gdns *SHAM* SO14 344 A2 2
Charlock Cl *NTHA* RG18 27 H3
Charlotte Cl *AND* SP10 119 J8 1
BKME/WDN BH12 447 H1
CHCH/BSGR BH23 450 F2
FNM GU9 112 A8
Charlotte Pl *SHAM* SO14 343 L2 2
Charlotte St *PSEA* PO1 423 G2 1
Charlton Cl *LYMN* SO41 438 D5 1
MOOR/WNTN BH9 433 G4
Charlton Ct *SHST* GU47 50 A7
Charlton La *THLE* RG7 45 M3
Charlton Pl *NWBY* RG14 2 F2
Charlton Rd *AND* SP10 8 D2
WSHM SO15 343 H1
Charlwood La *ALTN* GU34 221 H4
Charminster Av
MOOR/WNTN BH9 432 F7
Charminster Cl *WVILLE* PO7 352 C8
Charminster Rd *CHAR* BH8 432 F7
Charmouth Gv *PSTN* BH14 445 M4
Charmus Rd *TOTT* SO40 316 A6
Charmwen Crs *HEND* SO30 320 B6
Charmwood Cl *NWBY* RG14 25 J3 1
Charnock Cl *LYMN* SO41 438 D5
Charnwood
LSOL/BMARY PO13 397 H6
Charnwood Cl *AND* SP10 9 K8
CHFD SO53 265 H6
FERN BH22 380 C6 1
KEMP RG22 104 A4 2
TOTT SO40 316 C7
Charnwood Crs *CHFD* SO53 265 H6
Charnwood Dr *FBDG* SP6 309 K6
Charnwood Gdns
CHFD SO53 265 H6 1
Charnwood Wy *FAWY* SO45 418 B1
Charterhouse Wy *HEND* SO30 321 G7
Charter Rd *BWD* BH11 431 H2
NWBY RG14 25 J8
Chart House Rd *ASHV* GU12 113 K1
Chartwell *FNM* GU9 158 C2
FRIM GU16 91 H3
Chartwell Cl *ELGH* SO50 294 A2
FHAM/STUB PO14 371 G7
Chartwell Dr *HAV* PO9 17 L1
Chartwell Gdns *ALDT* GU11 112 F1
Chase Cl *LISS* GU33 248 F4
Chase Farm Cl *BPWT* SO32 323 K5
Chase Fld *ALTN* GU34 198 C6
Chase Gv *BPWT* SO32 323 K5
Chase La *HASM* GU27 229 H4
Chase Rd *BOR* GU35 201 L3
LISS GU33 248 F4
Chaseside *LTDN* BH7 433 L8
The Chase *CWTH* RG45 49 K2
FARN GU14 91 G2
FHAM/STUB PO14 371 H6
GPORT PO12 18 A4
NWBY RG14 25 J1 1
RGWD BH24 382 B3
VWD BH31 356 F2
Chasewater Av *HSEA* PO3 423 L1
Chatburn Av *HORN* PO8 352 C5
Chatfield Av *NEND* PO2 398 E7
Chatfield Cl *FARN* GU14 90 F6
Chatfield Rd
LSOL/BMARY PO13 397 G4
Chatham Dr *PSEA* PO1 20 E5
Chatham Rd *WINW* SO22 238 B3
Chatsworth Av *CHAM* PO6 399 L2
HASM GU27 204 F8
Chatsworth Cl *FHAM* PO15 372 A7
Chatsworth Dr *AND* SP10 8 B7
Chatsworth Gn *KEMP* RG22 127 H2
Chatsworth Gv *FNM* GU9 134 E2 2
Chatsworth Hts *CBLY* GU15 71 K1
Chatsworth Rd *CHAR* BH8 448 A2
ELGH SO50 294 A2
FARN GU14 91 H5
ITCH SO19 344 E3
PSTN BH14 446 A3
Chatsworth Wy
NMIL/BTOS BH25 437 J5
The Chatters *THLE* RG7 46 F1
Chaucer Av *AND* SP10 8 A2
CHAM PO6 374 C7
Chaucer Cl *CHAM* RG24 83 H7
FHAM/PORC PO16 14 F4
RWIN SO21 190 D3
WIMB BH21 404 A2 1
WVILLE PO7 352 C6
Chaucer Crs *NWBY* RG14 25 H3
Chaucer Dr *LYMN* SO41 454 C3
Chaucer Gv *CBLY* GU15 71 G3
Chaucer Rd *CCLF* BH13 446 E8 1
CWTH RG45 49 L4
FARN GU14 90 C2
ITCH SO19 345 H2
Chaundler Rd *WINC* SO23 11 H3
Chaundlers Cft *RFNM* GU10 133 J3
Chauntsingers Rd *ALTN* GU34 176 E4
Chaveney Cl *FAWY* SO45 367 K7 1
Chawton Cl *WINW* SO22 214 C4
WEND SO18 320 C8 1
Chawton End Cl *ALTN* GU34 197 H4 1
Chawton Park Rd *ALTN* GU34 176 A8
Cheam Rd *BDST* BH18 429 K4
Cheam Wy *TOTT* SO40 316 C7
Cheap St *NWBY* RG14 2 E4
Cheavley Cl *AND* SP10 118 B8
Cheddar Cl *ITCH* SO19 344 C5 1
Cheddington Rd
MOOR/WNTN BH9 432 E4
Chedington Cl *CFDH* BH17 430 C6
Chedworth Crs *CHAM* PO6 374 E7
Cheesecombe Farm La
LISS GU33 247 L2
Cheetah Rd *FARN* GU14 90 E6
Chelmsford Rd *NEND* PO2 399 K6
UPTN BH16 444 A1
Chelsea Rd *SSEA* PO5 21 K6
Cheltenham Crs
LSOL/BMARY PO13 420 D2
Cheltenham Gdns
HEND SO30 321 H5 1
Cheltenham Rd
BKME/WDN BH12 446 B3
CHAM PO6 375 G8
Chelveston Crs *ROWN* SO16 317 L4
Chelwood Dr *SHST* GU47 49 J7 2
Chene Rd *WIMB* BH21 404 B4
Cheping Gdns *HEND* SO30 346 E2
Chepstow Cl *CHFD* SO53 293 G2 1
TOTT SO40 316 B8 3
Chepstow Ct *WVILLE* PO7 352 F7
Chequer La *THLE* RG7 45 H6
Chequers La *HTWY* RG27 68 B1
Chequers Rd *BSTK* RG21 4 F8
Cherberry Cl *FARN* GU14 89 G4 2
Cherbourg Rd *ELGH* SO50 293 L7
Cherford Rd *BWD* BH11 431 M6
Cherita Ct *PLE* BH15 445 L2
Cheriton Av *LTDN* BH7 434 A8
WEND SO18 345 G1
Cheriton Cl *WINW* SO22 10 B5
HAV PO9 377 H4 1
HORN PO8
NWBY RG14
TADY RG26
Cheriton La *NALR* SO24
Cheriton Rd *ELGH* SO50
WINW SO22
GPORT PO12
Cheriton Wy *BLKW* GU17
WIMB BH21
Cherque La *LSOL/BMARY* PO13
Cherries Dr *MOOR/WNTN* BH9
Cherrimans Orch
HASM GU27 22
Cherry Cl *HTWY* RG27
LSOL/BMARY PO13
NWBY RG14
PSTN BH14
RWIN SO21
Cherry Dro *ELGH* SO50
Cherry Gdns *BPWT* SO32
Cherrygarth Rd *FHAM* PO15
Cherry Gv *FERN* BH22
Cherryhill Gv *ALDT* GU11
Cherry Hill Gv *UPTN* BH16
Cherryton Gdns *FAWY* SO45 39
Cherry Tree Av
FHAM/STUB PO14
HASM GU27
HORN PO8
NTID SP9
Cherry Tree Cl *FARN* GU14 8
LYMN SO41 43
RGWD BH24
SHST GU47 5
Cherry Tree Dr
NMIL/BTOS BH25 4
Cherry Tree Rd *AND* SP10
RFNM GU10
Cherry Wk *WSHM* SO15
Cherryway *ALTN* GU34
Cherrywood *HEND* SO30
Cherrywood Gdns
TOTT SO40 34
HISD PO11
Cherrywood Rd *FARN* GU14
Chervil Cl *HORN* PO8
Cherville St *ROMY* SO51
Chervil Wy *THLE* RG7
Cherwell Crs *ROWN* SO16
Cherwell Gdns *CHFD* SO53
Cheshire Cl *FHAM* PO15
Cheshire Dr *CHAR* BH8
Cheshire Wy *EMRTH* PO10
Chesildene Av *CHAR* BH8
Chesildene Dr *CHAR* BH8
Chesil St *WINC* SO23
Chesilton Crs *FLET* GU13
Cheslyn Rd *HSEA* PO3
Chessel Av *BOSC* BH5
ITCH SO19
Chessel Crs *ITCH* SO19
Chester Cl *ASHV* GU12
NWBY RG14
Chester Crs *LSOL/BMARY* PO13
Chesterfield Cl *CCLF* BH13
Chesterfield Rd *BSTK* RG21 10
HSEA PO3
NWBY RG14
Chester Pl *BSTK* RG21
SSEA PO5
Chester Rd *ASHV* GU12
CCLF BH13
WEND SO18
WINC SO23
Chesters Rd *CBLY* GU15
Chesterton Gdns *HORN* PO8
Chesterton Pl *FHAM* PO15 34
Chesterton Rd *NTHA* RG18
Chester Wy *RFNM* GU10
Chestnut Av *AND* SP10
ASHV GU12
CBLY GU15
CHCH/BSGR BH23
CHFD SO53
ELGH SO50
ENEY PO4 42
FNM GU9
WINW SO22
HASM GU27
HAV PO9
HORN PO8
NMIL/BTOS BH25
NTID SP9
RGWD BH24
RWIN SO21
SBNE BH6
TOTT SO40
Chestnut Cl *ALTN* GU34
BLKW GU17
CHFD SO53
FARN GU14
GSHT GU26
LIPH GU30
ROMY SO51
WVILLE PO7
Chestnut Ct *ASHV* GU12
BOR GU35 2
Chestnut Crs *NWBY* RG14
STOK SO20
Chestnut Dr *TLHT* RG30
Chestnut End *BOR* GU35
Chestnut Gv *FLET* GU13
WIMB BH21
Chestnut Ri *BPWT* SO32
ELGH SO50 2
Chestnut Rd *BROC* SO42
FARN GU14
ROWN SO16
The Chestnuts *HLER* SO31
Chestnut Wk *GPORT* PO12
Chestnut Wy
CHCH/BSGR BH23
FHAM/STUB PO14
Cheswell Gdns *FLET* GU13
Chetnole Cl *CFDH* BH17
Chettle Rd *ITCH* SO19
Chetwode Pl *ALDT* GU11
Chetwode Ter *ALDT* GU11

'ode Wy CFDH BH17 429 M6
'ynd Dr ROWN SO16 318 E4
'ynd Rd ENEY PO4 21 L5
'N SO16 318 E4
ning Ct ENEY PO4 423 M3 2
ot Cl CBLY GU15 71 M4
V GU14 90 B1
'P RG22 104 A5
'Y RG14 36 F3
ot Dr FARN GU14 89 G4
V SO45 367 H5
ot Gn HLER SO31 370 B8 3
ot Rd ROWN SO16 317 K8
GU47 49 J7
ot Wy VWD BH31 356 D3
ter Cl SSEA PO5 21 L9
ton Common Rd
H/BSGR BH23 436 E7
ton Farm Rd
H/BSGR BH23 437 G7
ton Ldg
H/BSGR BH23 436 F8
ton Wy
H/BSGR BH23 436 F7
e Gdns WBNE BH4 447 H6
e Wy FARN GU14 90 C1
/BMARY PO13 420 D3 1
ester Av HISD PO11 425 K6
ester Cl AND SP10 8 A4
D SO30 321 H7
R SO31 370 C5
/BMARY PO13 396 F6
Y SO51 289 G6
ester Pl KEMP RG22 104 D6
ester Rd ASHV GU12 113 K5
PO11 402 A7
D PO2 399 J8
D BH24 359 G8
D SO18 344 E1
ester Wk WIMB BH21 404 C7
enhall La ELGH SO50 294 B6
en Cl PSF GU32 273 J7
en Holt CHFD SO53 292 F3
am Cl HAV PO9 16 D2
am Dr HAV PO9 16 C2
am Rd CHAM PO6 375 L7
am Sq HAV PO9 16 C3
ell Rd CHAR BH8 433 G7
ilton Av WINW SO22 10 A6
ilton Ct HAV PO9 377 M2 3
mb Cl
/BMARY PO13 420 D2 1
mbe Cl HAV PO9 377 J5
mb La RWIN SO21 239 K3
C SO23 239 G3
mb Rd WEND SO18 320 B8
te Rd HSEA PO3 423 L1
oft La HASM GU27 228 E7
oft Rd HASM GU27 228 C1
ofts Rd HASM GU27 228 D7
rstone Cl LIPH GU30 226 E4 1
e Sq NEND PO2 399 G6
ome Cl CFDH BH17 430 A7
ove Rd CHAM PO6 376 A8
am Cl ELGH SO50 293 M1 1
M GU16 71 J8
ndham La RWIN SO21 192 B5
nd La RWIN SO21 216 B2
nden Ct TOTT SO40 341 H2 2
ton HLER SO31 369 G2
gham Wy CBLY GU15 70 F4
g La HLER SO31 394 C3
gton Gdns CHFD SO53 265 G7 3
own Wy WVILLE PO7 376 C3
rn Av FARN GU14 90 A4
rn Cl FARN GU14 89 M4
GU13 111 G3
M GU27 228 E3
L/BTOS BH25 437 K7
BY RG14 36 F3
T SO40 341 H3 1
VE BH4 447 G3
rn Dr NMIL/BTOS BH25 437 J8
D BH31 356 D2
rn Gn ROWN SO16 317 K6
rn Rd SHST GU47 49 J7
rn Wy KEMP RG22 103 M5
ee Cl LIPH GU30 226 F5
ee Mnr LIPH GU30 226 F4
ey La LIPH GU30 227 G6
ey Wy LIPH GU30 226 F6
n Rdg KEMP RG22 127 G3
orth Cl ROWN SO16 292 C7
orth Dro ROWN SO16 292 B8
orth Gdns HORN PO8 328 C4 1
orth Gv GPORT PO12 18 D1
orth Rd ROWN SO16 292 D7
Av ITCH SO19 344 C2
Cl HLER SO31 370 E4
Crs WCLF BH2 22 B7
Crescent Rd WBNE BH4 22 B7
ham La CHAM RG24 5 H2
M RG24 82 F6
ham Park Ct CHAM RG24 5 J1
nine LSOL/BMARY PO13 397 J7 1
M GU10 158 C3
Wk FERN BH22 406 C7
ford Av FARN GU14 90 F3
am Rd TOTT SO40 339 M2
ock Cl FLET GU13 110 E1
ead Rd CHAM PO6 375 K8
s La CHCH/BSGR BH23 435 M2
olm Cl ROWN SO16 317 L3
ell Rd CFDH BH17 430 B7
urst La LIPH GU30 278 E2
Rd ENEY PO4 423 L6
rs Cl KEMP RG22 104 A5
PO5 21 H5 1
's Dr EWKG RG40 48 B1 1
ham Rd FRIM GU16 71 H6
erton Rd AMSY SP4 138 D7
D SP11 139 J5
ey Cl STHA RG19 27 J5
n Rd KEMP RG22 104 C8
ey Cl PLE BH15 445 H2
nas Av ASHV GU12 7 K4
nas Pl ASHV GU12 7 K4
Christchurch Bay Rd
NMIL/BTOS BH25 452 E1
Christchurch By-pass
CHCH/BSGR BH23 435 J8
Christchurch Cl FLET GU13 110 E4 1
Christchurch Dr BLKW GU17 69 M2
Christchurch Gdns
CHAM PO6 375 M6 1
WINC SO23 238 D3
Christchurch Rd BMTH BH1 23 M5
BOSC BH5 448 F3
CHCH/BSGR BH23 433 M2
FERN BH22 405 M6
LYMN SO41 453 L1
NMIL/BTOS BH25 437 J8 1
RGWD BH24 382 D1
WINC SO23 238 E2
Christie Av HLER SO31 347 G8
Christie Hts NWBY RG14 25 L8
Christie Wk YTLY GU46 68 F4
Christine Cl ASHV GU12 113 J7
Christmas Hl RWIN SO21 168 B6
Christopher Ct NWBY RG14 3 H6
Christopher Crs PLE BH15 445 H2
Christopher Wy EMRTH PO10 378 D6
Christy Ct TADY RG26 61 M1 1
Church Av FARN GU14 90 F6
Church Bank Rd RWIN SO21 170 E3
Church Barns Farm THLE RG7 44 A3
Church Brook TADY RG26 61 K2
Church Cir FARN GU14 90 F7
Church Cl AND SP10 9 J5
ELGH SO50 294 B4
HASM GU27 205 J6
HLER SO31 370 F5
HORN PO8 328 A2
KSCL RG20 36 B2
NBAD SO52 291 M4
Churcher Cl GPORT PO12 421 H5
Churcher Rd EMRTH PO10 378 F4
Church Farm FBDG SP6 309 L8
Church Farm Cl FAWY SO45 366 F2
OVTN RG25 125 K6
Churchfield VWD BH31 356 C2 1
Churchfield Crs PLE BH15 445 K4
Churchfield La RGWD BH24 334 C6
Churchfield Rd EPSF GU31 276 A4
PLE BH15 445 K5
Churchfields FAWY SO45 392 F5 2
BOR GU35 179 G7
Church Flds BOR GU35 202 B3
Churchfields Rd RWIN SO21 266 E2
Church Ga STHA RG19 27 G5
Church Gv FLET GU13 88 D7
Church Hams EWKG RG40 48 A2
Church Hatch RSAL SP5 256 F8 1
Church Hl ALDT GU11 7 J5
ASHV GU12 7 J4
CBLY GU15 71 H3
HEND SO30 320 B7
LYMN SO41 454 D3
RSAL SP5 285 L3
STOK SO20 184 F3
VWD BH31 356 C2
Churchill Av ASHV GU12 7 J5
BPWT SO32 296 F7
ODIM RG29 108 B7
Churchill Cl ALTN GU34 176 E6 2
ALTN GU34 197 G5
FBDG SP6 333 J3
FHAM/STUB PO14 371 G7 1
HTWY RG27 87 G2
ODIM RG29 108 C8
TADY RG26 62 A1
WINC SO23 191 G7
Churchill Ct HORN PO8 352 E2 1
Churchill Crs BKME/WDN BH12 446 B2
FARN GU14 70 E8
BOR GU35 202 C4
Churchill Dr EMRTH PO10 378 D4
Churchill Rd BKME/WDN BH12 446 B3
BMTH BH1 448 C3
WIMB BH21 404 B5
Churchill Wy AND SP10 9 L2
BSTK RG21 4 E7
Churchill Wy East BSTK RG21 5 H7
Churchill Wy West AND SP10 8 A3
BSTK RG21 4 A8
KEMP RG22 104 C3
Church Lands TADY RG26 63 J5
Church La ALTN GU34 174 E6
ALTN GU34 177 H1
ALTN GU34 245 H5
ASHV GU12 113 L6
BPWT SO32 321 L2
BPWT SO32 322 C8
BPWT SO32 324 B2
BROC SO42 387 L8
BROC SO42 416 B3
CHAM RG24 106 A2
CHCH/BSGR BH23 450 A2
DEAN RG23 103 M4
ELGH SO50 266 D8
EWKG RG40 48 B4
FARN GU14 90 B4
FAWY SO45 392 E5
FBDG SP6 308 C4
FERN BH22 432 D1
WINW SO22 213 M2
GSHT GU26 203 M5
HASM GU27 228 F1
HAV PO9 17 K7
HEND SO30 345 M3
HEND SO30 346 E3
HISD PO11 402 A5
HLER SO31 345 M8
HTWY RG27 65 M2
HTWY RG27 87 J4
HUNG RG17 54 A2
KSCL RG20 36 A8
KSCL RG20 57 K1
BOR GU35 202 A2
LIPH GU30 226 E2
LISS GU33 224 A5
LISS GU33 224 C6
LYMN SO41 412 F7
LYMN SO41 414 B5
LYMN SO41 440 C5
LYND SO43 363 K3
MARL SN8 53 H2
NALR SO24 219 G4
NALR SO24 220 B4
NALR SO24 243 H4
RFNM GU10 134 A1
RFNM GU10 156 F2
RFNM GU10 158 B5
RFNM GU10 158 C1 2
NMIL/BTOS BH25 437 K7
NTID SP9 114 E4
NWBY RG14 25 G4
OVTN RG25 127 M1
OVTN RG25 128 A7
PSF GU32 272 A3
PTSW SO17 319 G6
RAND SP11 52 F8
RAND SP11 92 D6
RAND SP11 142 F7
RGWD BH24 384 E5
ROMY SO51 233 L6
ROMY SO51 260 C5
ROMY SO51 261 K4
ROMY SO51 263 H1
ROMY SO51 288 A3
ROMY SO51 290 D1
ROWN SO16 316 E3
RSAL SP5 256 D3
RWIN SO21 213 H5
RWIN SO21 215 L3
RWIN SO21 216 A2
RWIN SO21 238 F8
RWIN SO21 266 E8
STHA RG19 27 G5
STOK SO20 184 F3
STOK SO20 210 B2
TADY RG26 60 A6
THLE RG7 30 E4
THLE RG7 40 C2
THLE RG7 43 H7
THLE RG7 47 G2
WINC SO23 215 H2
WVILLE PO7 326 C5
Church La East ALDT GU11 6 F4
Church La West ALDT GU11 6 D4
Church Md LYMN SO41 440 C6
Church Mdw NTID SP9 114 D8 1
Churchmoor Rd WIMB BH21 404 E3
Church Pth ASHV GU12 113 K5
EMRTH PO10 378 D8
FHAM/PORC PO16 15 L5
GPORT PO12 19 K4
HORN PO8 353 H2
Church Pth North PSEA PO1 423 G2 4
Church Rd ALDT GU11 7 J6
ALTN GU34 198 D5
BPWT SO32 324 A2
BPWT SO32 348 B1
CBLY GU15 70 C1 1
ELGH SO50 294 C3
EMRTH PO10 378 F5
EMRTH PO10 403 H1
EMRTH PO10 403 H7
FERN BH22 406 A2
FHAM/PORC PO16 398 C2
FLET GU13 88 D6
FRIM GU16 71 G8
GPORT PO12 18 C7
HASM GU27 228 F1
HISD PO11 425 L3
HLER SO31 370 B8
HLER SO31 370 F5
ITCH SO19 344 B7
KSCL RG20 24 B3
LIPH GU30 226 F2
MARL SN8 32 E6
NWBY RG14 25 K3
OVTN RG25 100 F8
OVTN RG25 125 K7
PSF GU32 275 K1
PSTN BH14 445 M4
ROMY SO51 234 C6
ROMY SO51 290 D1
RSAL SP5 230 B1
SBNE BH6 449 L5
SHST GU47 49 J7
SHST GU47 50 A7
STOK SO20 186 C1
STOK SO20 210 F5
TADY RG26 42 B7
TADY RG26 61 L2
THLE RG7 41 K1
THLE RG7 41 M2
WHAM PO17 349 M1
WIMB BH21 356 C7
Church Rd East CWTH RG45 49 L3
FARN GU14 91 G7
Church Rd West CWTH RG45 49 L4
FARN GU14 90 F7
Church Sq BSTK RG21 4 E8
Church St ALDT GU11 6 C3
ALTN GU34 174 F3
ALTN GU34 176 E4
BPWT SO32 296 E2
BSTK RG21 4 E8
CHCH/BSGR BH23 450 A2
CWTH RG45 49 L3
FBDG SP6 309 K8
FHAM/STUB PO14 371 K6
LISS GU33 248 D2
NALR SO24 220 B4
RFNM GU10 133 H2
ODIM RG29 108 C6
PLE BH15 445 G7
PSEA PO1 423 G1 1
PSF GU32 273 J7
RAND SP11 96 D1
RAND SP11 165 M2
ROMY SO51 290 D1
RWIN SO21 169 M5
WHCH RG28 122 B4
WSHM SO15 318 A8 2
Church Street Rbt PSEA PO1 423 G1
Church Vw ASHV GU12 113 K6
EMRTH PO10 378 F5 1
ENEY PO4 423 L4
HTWY RG27 86 A7
HTWY RG27 87 H3
ODIM RG29 130 E5
THLE RG7 29 K2
YTLY GU46 69 G1
Church View Cl ITCH SO19 344 E5
Church Wk RSAL SP5 285 M3
Churchward Gdns
HEND SO30 321 H6 2
Churn Cl CHAM RG24 106 A1
Churt Rd BOR GU35 202 D1
RFNM GU10 181 J8
Churt Wynde GSHT GU26 204 A1
Chute Cswy RAND SP11 72 A5
Cibbons Rd CHAM RG24 83 L5
Cinderford Cl CHAM PO6 375 G7 1
Circle Hill Rd CWTH RG45 49 M3
The Circle SSEA PO5 21 J8
WHAM PO17 348 D4
Circular Rd PSEA PO1 422 F2
The Circus WVILLE PO7 374 E6
Cirrus Gdns HLER SO31 369 K6
City Rd WINC SO23 10 F6
Civic Centre Rd HAV PO9 16 E2
SHAM SO14 12 F2
Civic Wy FHAM/PORC PO16 15 L5
Clack La FBDG SP6 308 F2
Clacton Rd CHAM PO6 375 H8
Claire Gdns HORN PO8 328 B6
Clandon Ct FARN GU14 91 G5 1
Clandon Dr ELGH SO50 293 L2
Clanfield Cl CHFD SO53 293 J2
Clanfield Dr CHFD SO53 293 J2
Clanfield Ride BLKW GU17 70 A3 1
Clanfield Rd WEND SO18 345 G1
Clanfield Wy CHFD SO53 293 J2
Clanwilliam Rd
LSOL/BMARY PO13 420 C2
Clappers Farm Rd THLE RG7 43 K8
Clapps Gate Rd TADY RG26 42 B7
Clare Cl FHAM/STUB PO14 371 G7
Clare Gdns EPSF GU31 276 B5
FAWY SO45 418 D1
Clare Lodge Cl
CHCH/BSGR BH23 409 L8
Clare Md RFNM GU10 158 C5
Claremont Av CBLY GU15 71 J3
MOOR/WNTN BH9 432 F6
Claremont Cl ELGH SO50 293 M2 2
Claremont Crs WSHM SO15 342 E1
Claremont Gdns WVILLE PO7 376 C4
Claremont Rd
MOOR/WNTN BH9 432 F6
PSEA PO1 21 L2
WSHM SO15 342 E1
Clarence Cl ASHV GU12 7 K2
RAND SP11 92 D6
Clarence Dr CBLY GU15 71 L1
Clarence Esp SSEA PO5 20 E7
Clarence Pde SSEA PO5 20 F7
Clarence Park Rd LTDN BH7 448 F2
Clarence Rd FLET GU13 88 E8
GPORT PO12 19 K2
LYND SO43 363 K3 1
PSTN BH14 445 M5
SSEA PO5 21 J9
Clarence St PSEA PO1 423 G2
Clarendon Av AND SP10 8 D8
Clarendon Cl BDST BH18 429 L4
ROMY SO51 263 G7 1
Clarendon Ct BLKW GU17 70 A5 2
Clarendon Crs
FHAM/STUB PO14 370 F7
Clarendon Gdns NWBY RG14 2 F2
Clarendon Pk LYMN SO41 440 B6
Clarendon Pl PSEA PO1 21 H1 1
PSEA PO1 423 H2 5
Clarendon Rd BDST BH18 429 J5
CHCH/BSGR BH23 449 M1
HAV PO9 16 D5
ROWN SO16 317 M8
SSEA PO5 21 H7
WBNE BH4 22 A7
Clarendon St PSEA PO1 423 H2
Clarendon Wy RSAL SP5 207 K2
STOK SO20 208 E2
STOK SO20 210 B4
STOK SO20 236 B1
Clarewood Dr CBLY GU15 71 H2
Clarke Crs CBLY GU15 70 B1
Clarke's La RAND SP11 94 E2
Clarkes Rd PSEA PO1 423 K2
Clark's Cl RGWD BH24 382 E1 2
Clarks Hl RFNM GU10 133 M6
Claude Ashby Cl WEND SO18 319 K4
Claudeen Cl WEND SO18 319 K3
Claudia Ct GPORT PO12 421 K2 1
Claudius Cl AND SP10 119 G4
CHFD SO53 293 L1 1
Claudius Dr DEAN RG23 104 B1 1
Claudius Gdns CHFD SO53 293 L2
Clausentum Cl CHFD SO53 293 K1
Clausentum Rd SHAM SO14 343 L1
WINC SO23 238 E3
Clausen Wy LYMN SO41 440 A7
Claxton St PSEA PO1 21 J1
Claybank Sp HSEA PO3 399 L7
Claycart Rd ALDT GU11 112 A5
Claydon Av ENEY PO4 423 L4
Claydon Gdns FARN GU14 70 D7 1
Clayford Av FERN BH22 405 M1
Clayford Cl CFDH BH17 430 B6
Clayhall Rd GPORT PO12 18 D8
Clay Hl BROC SO42 363 L7
Clayhill Cl BPWT SO32 323 J4 1
Clay Hill Crs NWBY RG14 26 A3 1
Clayhill Rd THLE RG7 31 J5
Claylake Dr VWD BH31 356 E3
Claylands Ct BPWT SO32 297 G8
Claylands Rd BPWT SO32 297 G8 1
Clay La LYND SO43 363 K4 1
THLE RG7 29 J2
Claypit Rd ROMY SO51 264 A1
Claypits La FAWY SO45 367 G4
Claypitt La ALTN GU34 246 B2
Clay's La ALTN GU34 177 K7
Clay St RSAL SP5 258 F5
Claythorpe Rd KEMP RG22 104 A5
Clayton Barracks ALDT GU11 113 G4
Clayton Cl HTWY RG27 87 H3 1
Clayton Rd FARN GU14 70 C7
Cleasby Cl ROWN SO16 342 C1
Clease Wy RWIN SO21 266 B1
Clee Av FHAM/STUB PO14 14 A7
Cleethorpes Rd ITCH SO19 344 F4
Cleeve Cl CHAM PO6 374 F7 2
The Cleeves TOTT SO40 341 G2
Clegg Rd ENEY PO4 423 L5
Clemence Gdns WHCH RG28 122 B3 1
Clement Attlee Wy CHAM PO6 374 F8
Clements Cl ALTN GU34 178 D1
Clem's Wy ROMY SO51 232 F7
Clere Gdns CHAM RG24 83 L6
Clerewater Pl STHA RG19 26 D5 1
Cleric Ct FHAM/STUB PO14 371 H5
Clevedge Wy ODIM RG29 108 B4
Clevedon Ct FARN GU14 91 G5 2
FRIM GU16 71 K8
Cleveland Cl KEMP RG22 104 A5
NMIL/BTOS BH25 452 C1
Cleveland Dr FAWY SO45 367 H6
FHAM/STUB PO14 14 B7
Cleveland Gdns BMTH BH1 23 M1
Cleveland Gv NWBY RG14 2 D3
Cleveland Rd BMTH BH1 448 C3
GPORT PO12 18 F5 1
SSEA PO5 21 L4
WEND SO18 319 L6
Clevelands Cl CHFD SO53 265 G6 1
Cleves La OVTN RG25 130 A2
Clewborough Dr CBLY GU15 71 L2
Clewers Hl BPWT SO32 323 J4
Clewers La BPWT SO32 323 J4
Cliddesden Ct BSTK RG21 105 G6
Cliddesden La KEMP RG22 127 G3
Cliddesden Rd BSTK RG21 105 G5
Cliff Crs NMIL/BTOS BH25 452 E1
Cliff Dr CCLF BH13 457 K2
CHCH/BSGR BH23 451 H2
Cliffe Av HLER SO31 369 J5
Cliffe Rd NMIL/BTOS BH25 452 D1
Clifford Dibben Ms
SHAM SO14 318 F8 1
Clifford Pl ELGH SO50 295 H6
Clifford Rd MOOR/WNTN BH9 432 E7
Clifford St SHAM SO14 13 J2
Cliff Rd FHAM/STUB PO14 395 K7
LYMN SO41 453 M3
WSHM SO15 12 A1
Cliff Wy RWIN SO21 266 C2
Clifton Cl RFNM GU10 158 D4
Clifton Crs WVILLE PO7 351 M4
Clifton Gdns FERN BH22 406 A4
FRIM GU16 91 J2
WEND SO18 320 B7
Clifton Hl WINW SO22 10 E7
Clifton Rd WINW SO22 10 D6
LSOL/BMARY PO13 420 E4
NWBY RG14 2 A5
PSTN BH14 446 C6
SBNE BH6 449 J5
SSEA PO5 21 G8
WSHM SO15 317 M8
Clifton St GPORT PO12 421 K2
PSEA PO1 423 J2
Clifton Ter BSTK RG21 4 F6
WINW SO22 10 E7
Clingan Rd SBNE BH6 449 J2
Clinkley Rd NALR SO24 244 C1
Clinton Cl CHCH/BSGR BH23 436 F6 1
Clinton Rd LYMN SO41 440 C3
WVILLE PO7 352 A5
Clipper Cl HLER SO31 370 C7
Clitheroe Rd FARN GU14 69 J7
Cliveden Cl FERN BH22 406 A1
Clive Gv FHAM/PORC PO16 398 A1
Clive Rd ASHV GU12 7 L4
CHCH/BSGR BH23 436 C6
MOOR/WNTN BH9 432 D7
PSEA PO1 423 J2
Clockhouse Rd FARN GU14 90 E4
Clock St PSEA PO1 20 C2
Clocktower Dr ENEY PO4 423 M6
The Cloisters FHAM PO15 372 A6
FRIM GU16 71 G7
RGWD BH24 383 G2 1
ROMY SO51 262 D8 1
ROWN SO16 318 F4
The Close Bellfield
FHAM/STUB PO14 395 K1
The Close BDST BH18 429 J5
CHAM PO6 399 L1 1
FAWY SO45 392 B5
FHAM/PORC PO16 374 A8
FNM GU9 135 G7
FRIM GU16 70 F8
HEND SO30 345 M2
LYMN SO41 412 E6
NMIL/BTOS BH25 437 L8
NTHA RG18 26 E4
PSF GU32 274 B5
RAND SP11 95 H6
RGWD BH24 381 L4 1
RGWD BH24 382 D1 2
RSAL SP5 285 J1
SHST GU47 50 B8
TADY RG26 82 A2
THLE RG7 31 K5
WEND SO18 345 H1
Closewood Rd WVILLE PO7 351 L7
Closeworth Rd FARN GU14 91 H8
Clouch La RGWD BH24 384 D5
Clough La RSAL SP5 206 E1
Clough's Rd RGWD BH24 382 F1
Clouston Rd FARN GU14 90 C3
Clovelly Dr GSHT GU26 203 M1
Clovelly Rd EMRTH PO10 378 C8
EMRTH PO10 379 H7
ENEY PO4 423 L4
GSHT GU26 203 M2
HISD PO11 402 A4
SHAM SO14 343 L2
Cloverbank WINC SO23 191 G6
Clover Cl CHCH/BSGR BH23 435 M8
HLER SO31 370 C6
BOR GU35 201 M3
LSOL/BMARY PO13 397 G6 3
Clover Ct NMIL/BTOS BH25 438 B4

Clover Dr CFDH BH17 429 K7
Clover Fld CHAM RG24 5 M3
Clover Gdns RAND SP11 92 E6
Clover La YTLY GU46 68 D2
Clover Wy HEND SO30 345 L2 2
ROMY SO51 263 H8
Clowes Av SBNE BH6 450 A5
Club House La BPWT SO32 323 J5
Clubhouse Rd ALDT GU11 112 C3
Club La CWTH RG45 50 A3
NTID SP9 114 D4
Clumps Rd RFNM GU10 159 H4
Clydebank Rd NEND PO2 399 H8
Clyde Ct GPORT PO12 421 K2
Clyde Rd GPORT PO12 421 K2
Clydesdale Dr TOTT SO40 316 A8 1
Clydesdale Rd HLER SO31 370 F1
Clydesdale Wy TOTT SO40 316 A8
Coach Hl FHAM/STUB PO14 371 K8
RAND SP11 94 A4
Coach Hill Cl CHFD SO53 293 G1
Coach Hill La RGWD BH24 384 B2
Coach House Cl FRIM GU16 71 H5
Coach House Gdns FLET GU13 88 F5
Coach House Pl BMTH BH1 23 H2
Coachmans Copse
WEND SO18 319 M6
Coachman's Ct NWBY RG14 25 L3 1
Coach Rd HLER SO31 369 J6
The Coach Rd RSAL SP5 208 A8
Coachways AND SP10 9 G8 1
Coal Park La HLER SO31 346 B7
Coalville Rd ITCH SO19 344 F4
Coastguard Cl GPORT PO12 18 A8
Coastguard La SELS PO20 427 J7
Coastguard Wy
CHCH/BSGR BH23 450 E4
Coate Dr RWIN SO21 190 C6
Coates Cl KEMP RG22 104 E7
Coates Rd ITCH SO19 345 H4
Coates Wy WVILLE PO7 376 C3
Coat Gdns FAWY SO45 367 L5 2
Cobbets Rdg RFNM GU10 135 M7
Cobbett Cl WINW SO22 238 B3
Cobbett Gn KEMP RG22 104 D6
Cobbett Rd WEND SO18 344 C1
Cobbett's La BLKW GU17 69 J4
YTLY GU46 69 J3
Cobbetts Wy FNM GU9 158 C2
Cobbett Wy HEND SO30 346 C1
Cobblers Cnr LYMN SO41 413 L5
Cobblewood EMRTH PO10 378 D5
Cobbs La PLE BH15 445 K2
Cobb's Rd WIMB BH21 404 C2
Cobden Av HSEA PO3 399 L8
WEND SO18 319 J8
Cobden Crs WEND SO18 319 L8
Cobden Gdns WEND SO18 319 K7
Cobden La HASM GU27 229 G1 1
Cobden St GPORT PO12 18 E1
Cobham Rd MOOR/WNTN BH9 432 E5
WIMB BH21 405 K1
Cobham Wy WIMB BH21 404 C7
Coblands Av TOTT SO40 341 H1
Coburg St PSEA PO1 21 K1
SHAM SO14 344 A2
Cochrane Cl
LSOL/BMARY PO13 421 H2
Cochrane Cl STHA RG19 27 H5 1
Cock-a-dobby SHST GU47 49 K7 1
Cockerell Cl WIMB BH21 404 D7
Cockleshell Gdns ENEY PO4 424 A5
Cocklydown La TOTT SO40 341 J3
Cockshott La PSF GU32 247 H6
Cody Cl ASHV GU12 113 J3
Cody Rd FARN GU14 90 C5
Coe Cl ALDT GU11 6 E3
Cogdeane Rd CFDH BH17 430 B6
Coghlan Cl FHAM/PORC PO16 15 J3
Cokenor Wd RFNM GU10 158 C2
Coker Cl WINW SO22 10 D6
Colbeck FLET GU13 111 G4
Colborne Av WIMB BH21 404 D3
Colborne Cl LYMN SO41 440 C3
Colbourne Cl
CHCH/BSGR BH23 409 L8
Colbred Cnr FARN GU14 89 H4 1
Colburn Cl ROWN SO16 317 J6
Colbury Gv HAV PO9 377 G4
Colchester Av ELGH SO50 294 D4
Colchester Rd CHAM PO6 375 H7
Cold East Cl HLER SO31 370 C3
Coldeast Wy HLER SO31 370 D3
Colden La NALR SO24 194 D7
Coldharbour OVTN RG25 125 K7
Cold Harbour Cl WHAM PO17 348 D4
Coldharbour Farm Rd
EMRTH PO10 378 D7
Cold Harbour La FARN GU14 70 C8
Coldharbour La ROWN SO16 290 F8
Coldhill La HORN PO8 352 C1
Colebrook Av HSEA PO3 423 M1
WSHM SO15 318 B7
Colebrook Pl WINC SO23 11 J9
Colebrook St WINC SO23 11 H9
Colebrook Wy AND SP10 8 B6
Cole Cl AND SP10 118 F4
Coleford Bridge Rd
FRIM GU16 91 H4 1
Coleford Cl FRIM GU16 91 J5
Coleford Paddocks
FRIM GU16 91 J4 1
Cole Hl BPWT SO32 325 G3
Colehill Crs MOOR/WNTN BH9 432 F2
Colehill La WIMB BH21 404 C1
Coleman Cl BSTK RG21 5 H3
Coleman Rd ASHV GU12 7 L4
BWD BH11 431 L5
Coleman St SHAM SO14 13 J3
Colemere Gdns
CHCH/BSGR BH23 436 D7
Colemore Rd LTDN BH7 449 H1
Colemore Sq HAV PO9 377 K4 1
Colenso Rd FHAM/PORC PO16 15 H4
Colenzo Dr AND SP10 9 K2
Coleridge Av YTLY GU46 69 H3
Coleridge Cl CWTH RG45 49 M4 1
HLER SO31 370 B7
Coleridge Gdns HORN PO8 352 D4
Coleridge Rd CHAM PO6 374 D7
Coles Av PLE BH15 444 D6
Colesbourne Rd CHAM PO6 374 F7
Coles Cl RWIN SO21 266 F1
Coles Gdns PLE BH15 444 D6
Coles Mede RWIN SO21 266 A5
Coleson Hill Rd RFNM GU10 158 C3 1
Coleson Rd WEND SO18 319 K8
Coles's La RSAL SP5 286 D3
Coleville Av FAWY SO45 392 F5
Coleville Rd FARN GU14 90 C3
Coley La STOK SO20 165 L4
Colin Cl WIMB BH21 429 H3
Colinton Av
FHAM/PORC PO16 374 B7
Collards La HASM GU27 229 G2
Collard Wy LISS GU33 248 E4 1
Collaroy Rd NTHA RG18 26 F1
College Cl CBLY GU15 51 G8
HAV PO9 354 A7
HLER SO31 369 K6 1
College Crs SHST GU47 50 B8
College Gdns FNM GU9 134 E6 1
College Hl HASM GU27 228 F2
College Hill Ter HASM GU27 228 F2
College La OVTN RG25 152 A2
PSEA PO1 20 C2 2
College Piece THLE RG7 43 J2
College Ride BAGS GU19 51 M6
CBLY GU15 71 G1
College Rd ASHV GU12 113 K5
BOSC BH5 448 F4
BSTK RG21 4 B7
ITCH SO19 344 C6
PSEA PO1 20 C1
RGWD BH24 382 E1
SHST GU47 70 B1
WVILLE PO7 376 C6
College St EPSF GU31 275 L5
PSEA PO1 20 C2
SHAM SO14 13 H5
WINC SO23 11 G9
College Wk WINC SO23 238 F2
Collett Cl HEND SO30 321 G6
Collier Cl FARN GU14 90 A3
PTSW SO17 319 H8 1
Collingbourne Av SBNE BH6 449 J2
Collingbourne Dr CHFD SO53 292 F2
Collington Crs CHAM PO6 374 F7
Collingwood FARN GU14 91 H6
Collingwood Grange Cl
CBLY GU15 51 L8
Collingwood Ri CBLY GU15 71 K1
Collingwood Rd SSEA PO5 21 K7
WIMB BH21 380 C2
Collingworth Cl HLER SO31 370 F2
Collins Cl AND SP10 118 D5
NBAD SO52 292 E2 1
NWBY RG14 3 J1
Collins Gdns ASHV GU12 113 L6
Collins La EPSF GU31 304 E1
RGWD BH24 382 E1
RWIN SO21 265 H1
Collins Rd ENEY PO4 423 L6
Collis Rd HSEA PO3 399 L8
Collwood Cl PLE BH15 445 H1
Collyers Crs LIPH GU30 227 H4 1
Collyers Rd BROC SO42 387 K8
Colne Av ROWN SO16 317 J5
Colne Valley Wy WHCH RG28 123 G3
Colne Wy ASHV GU12 113 K7
BSTK RG21 5 J8
Colpoy St SSEA PO5 20 F4
Colson Rd WINC SO23 11 K6
Colt Cl ROWN SO16 317 L3 3
WIMB BH21 404 F2
Colthrop La STHA RG19 27 L6
Coltsfoot Cl HEND SO30 345 M1
THLE RG7 31 L5
Coltsfoot Dr HLER SO31 370 C6
WVILLE PO7 376 D3
Coltsfoot Pl HTWY RG27 86 B6 1
Colts Foot Rd BOR GU35 201 M3 2
Coltsfoot Wk ROMY SO51 263 H7 1
Coltsmead CHAM PO6 374 D8
Colts Rd ROWN SO16 317 K1
Columbia Ct EWKG RG40 48 B1 2
Columbia Rd NBNE BH10 431 M6
Columbia Trees La NBNE BH10 432 A7
Columbine Rd KEMP RG22 103 M8
Columbus Dr FARN GU14 89 M5
Columbus Wy AND SP10 119 K8
Colville Cl BOSC BH5 448 F3
Colville Dr BPWT SO32 297 J8
Colville Rd BOSC BH5 448 F3
CHAM PO6 375 L8
Colwell Cl ROWN SO16 317 J8
Colwell Rd CHAM PO6 399 K1
Colwyn Cl YTLY GU46 68 E2
Colyer Cl KEMP RG22 104 B5 1
Combe La FARN GU14 90 D2 1
Combe Ri RFNM GU10 159 G3
Combe Rd LISS GU33 249 G7
Comber Rd MOOR/WNTN BH9 432 D5
Comet Wy CHCH/BSGR BH23 450 F2
Comfrey Cl FARN GU14 89 M3
HORN PO8 328 B7 1
ROMY SO51 263 H7
Comines Wy HEND SO30 345 J2
Comley Hl HAV PO9 378 A1
Comley Rd MOOR/WNTN BH9 432 D6
Commercial Pl PSEA PO1 423 G2 6
Commercial Rd ASHV GU12 7 K5
PLE BH15 445 L4
PSEA PO1 21 G1
PSEA PO1 423 G2 8
TOTT SO40 341 L1
WCLF BH2 22 C6
WSHM SO15 12 F1
Commercial St WEND SO18 344 F1
Common Barn La
LSOL/BMARY PO13 420 D1 2
Common Cl CHFD SO53 265 H8
Common Gdns CHFD SO53 265 H8
Common Hl ALTN GU34 196 C2
Common Hill Rd ROMY SO51 263 J2
Common La FHAM/STUB PO14 371 H8
WHAM PO17 350 C7
Common Rd CHFD SO53 265 H8
EMRTH PO10 379 K3
RSAL SP5 259 G5
STHA RG19 39 H8
Commonside EMRTH PO10 378 F3
Common St PSEA PO1 423 H2 1
The Common RSAL SP5 207 G2
Common Vw MIDH GU29 279 J7
Compass Cl
LSOL/BMARY PO13 421 H2 2
Compass Fld HTWY RG27 86 A7 1
Compass Rd CHAM PO6 374 F8
Complins ALTN GU34 177 G2
Compound Rd FARN GU14 90 D6
Compton Av PSTN BH14 446 C6
Compton Beeches
RGWD BH24 381 L3 1
Compton Cl ELGH SO50 293 L2
FLET GU13 111 G3
WINW SO22 238 A5
HAV PO9 16 E1
HTWY RG27 86 A8
LSOL/BMARY PO13 420 E2
SHST GU47 49 M7
VWD BH31 356 D2
Compton Crs FERN BH22 380 E7
Compton Dr PSTN BH14 446 B6
Compton Gdns PSTN BH14 446 B6
Compton Rd FLET GU13 111 G3
NEND PO2 399 K5
NMIL/BTOS BH25 437 L6
TOTT SO40 316 F8
WINC SO23 10 E9
Compton's Dr ROMY SO51 287 L2
Compton St RWIN SO21 238 B8
Compton Wk SHAM SO14 13 G1
Compton Wy WINW SO22 238 A5
RFNM GU10 135 K6
Conan Rd NEND PO2 399 J4
Concorde Wy FHAM PO15 371 J3
Conde Wy BOR GU35 201 J6
Condor Av FHAM/PORC PO16 373 K8
Condor Cl ITCH SO19 344 B5 1
Condor Rd FARN GU14 90 E6
Coneygar La FERN BH22 405 L5
Conference Dr HLER SO31 370 F5 1
Conference Pl LYMN SO41 440 D6 2
Conford Ct HAV PO9 377 H2
Congleton Cl LYND SO43 339 G5
Congreve Cl THLE RG7 41 J1
Conholt Hl RAND SP11 72 E3
Conholt La RAND SP11 73 G5
Conholt Rd AND SP10 142 F3
Conifer Av PSTN BH14 446 A6
Conifer Cl CHCH/BSGR BH23 434 B5
FAWY SO45 367 K5 2
FERN BH22 406 D7
FLET GU13 110 E3
WINW SO22 10 D5
HORN PO8 352 E6
BOR GU35 201 H7
RGWD BH24 381 H4
TADY RG26 41 H7
Conifer Crs LYMN SO41 439 M5
Conifer Crest NWBY RG14 36 F4
Conifer Dr CBLY GU15 71 K2
Conifer Gv LSOL/BMARY PO13 397 G4
Conifer Ms
FHAM/PORC PO16 374 B7 1
Conifer Rd ROWN SO16 317 M4
The Conifers CWTH RG45 49 K1
Conigar Rd EMRTH PO10 378 D5
Coniston Av BWD BH11 431 J5
HSEA PO3 399 L8
Coniston Cl CBLY GU15 71 M5
FARN GU14 90 B5
STHA RG19 26 D5
VWD BH31 356 C3
Coniston Dr FNM GU9 134 D2
Coniston Gdns HEND SO30 345 M3
Coniston Gv NALR SO24 218 C4 1
Coniston Rd ELGH SO50 293 L6
KEMP RG22 104 A7
BOR GU35 201 H3
RGWD BH24 382 F2 1
ROWN SO16 317 H8
Coniston Wy FLET GU13 110 D3
Connaught Barracks
ALDT GU11 113 G2
Connaught Cl BOR GU35 201 J6 1
NMIL/BTOS BH25 437 J8
YTLY GU46 68 E2
Connaught Crs
BKME/WDN BH12 446 D2
Connaught Rd ASHV GU12 7 K2
BAGS GU19 51 M5
CBLY GU15 71 J3
FLET GU13 88 F8 1
HAV PO9 17 G4
NEND PO2 399 H6 1
NWBY RG14 3 G4
RWIN SO21 190 B6
Connell Rd PLE BH15 445 H3
Connemara Crs HLER SO31 370 F1
Connigar Cl
LSOL/BMARY PO13 421 G1 1
Connop Wy FRIM GU16 71 J5
Conqueror Wy
FHAM/STUB PO14 396 B6
Conrad Gdns FHAM PO15 347 G8
Consort Dr CBLY GU15 71 M1 1
Consort Rd ELGH SO50 294 A3
Constable Cl BSTK RG21 105 J5
GPORT PO12 18 F9
ITCH SO19 345 G6
Constable Ct AND SP10 9 G3
Constable's Ga WINC SO23 10 E8
Constable Wy SHST GU47 70 B2
Constantine Av CHFD SO53 293 K2
Constantine Cl CHFD SO53 293 L2 1
Constantine Wy KEMP RG22 126 F2
Constant Rd FARN GU14 89 K6
Constitution Hill Rd
PSTN BH14 445 L4
Convent La EMRTH PO10 378 D8
Conway Cl CHFD SO53 293 G5
NMIL/BTOS BH25 437 M5
Conway Dr FARN GU14 90 A3
NTHA RG18 26 E3
Cook Cl RGWD BH24 359 G8
Cooke Rd BKME/WDN BH12 446 E2
Cookham Cl SHST GU47 49 M7
Cooks La EMRTH PO10 379 J7
RCCH PO18 355 M6
ROMY SO51 260 C1
ROMY SO51 261 M4
TOTT SO40 316 B6
Cook's Pond Rd LIPH GU30 250 D8
Cook St SHAM SO14 13 H4
Coolarne Ri CBLY GU15 71 K2
Coolers Farm STOK SO20 209 H2
Coombe Av NBNE BH10 432 C6
Coombe Cl FRIM GU16 71 G8
Coombe Ct NTHA RG18 27 H5
Coombedale HLER SO31 370 F6 1
Coombe Dr FLET GU13 89 H7
Coombe Farm Av
FHAM/PORC PO16 15 H8
Coombe Gdns NBNE BH10 432 B6
Coombehurst Dr BSTK RG21 105 G6
Coombe La LYMN SO41 413 H7
PSF GU32 272 D4
ROMY SO51 261 L5
Coombe Rd GPORT PO12 421 M1
PSF GU32 273 H8
YTLY GU46 68 E1
Coombe Sq STHA RG19 27 H5
Coombs Cl HORN PO8 328 B7 2
The Cooperage ALTN GU34 176 D5 1
Cooper Dean Dr CHAR BH8 433 K7
Cooper Gv FHAM/PORC PO16 398 B2
Cooper Rd HSEA PO3 423 M1
TOTT SO40 341 G5
Cooper's Cl ROMY SO51 289 G6 1
RWIN SO21 190 C6
WEND SO18 320 B7
Coopers Ct TADY RG26 63 L5
Coopers Crs NTHA RG18 26 F4
Cooper's Hl HTWY RG27 68 A5
Cooper's La ITCH SO19 344 B5 2
TADY RG26 63 K5
VWD BH31 356 D1
Cope Hall La NWBY RG14 36 E1
Copeland Dr PSTN BH14 446 A6
Copeland Rd ROWN SO16 317 J7
Copes La HTWY RG27 66 D1
Copinger Cl TOTT SO40 341 G2 3
Copland Cl KEMP RG22 104 B8
Copnor Cl KSCL RG20 35 M8
Copnor Rd NEND PO2 399 K4
Copped Hall Dr CBLY GU15 71 M2
Copped Hall Wy CBLY GU15 71 M2
Copper Beech Cl
BKME/WDN BH12 446 F4
Copper Beech Dr CHAM PO6 376 C8 2
Copper Beech Gdns
NBNE BH10 432 B6
Copperfield Av SHST GU47 50 B6
Copperfield Rd ROWN SO16 318 F3
Copperfields TOTT SO40 340 F1
Coppers Cl FBDG SP6 333 L2
Copper St SSEA PO5 20 F5
Coppice Av FERN BH22 405 M2
Coppice Cl FNM GU9 6 B9
WINW SO22 214 B7
NMIL/BTOS BH25 438 B4
NWBY RG14 3 G9
RGWD BH24 381 K4
TADY RG26 41 G8
Coppice Gdns CWTH RG45 49 J3
YTLY GU46 68 F3
Coppice Hl BPWT SO32 323 H1
Coppice Ms DEAN RG23 104 B2
Coppice Rd KSCL RG20 59 K6
TOTT SO40 316 B6
The Coppice BROC SO42 387 H6
HORN PO8 352 E2
LSOL/BMARY PO13 397 H6 1
Coppice Vw NBNE BH10 432 C5
Coppice Wy FHAM PO15 14 A2
Coppins Gv FHAM/PORC PO16 398 A2
Copse Av FNM GU9 6 A7
NMIL/BTOS BH25 437 M6
Copse Cl CBLY GU15 71 K3
EPSF GU31 276 B4
LISS GU33 248 F4
NBAD SO52 291 L4
PLE BH15 445 L5
RWIN SO21 266 B4
TOTT SO40 341 K2
WVILLE PO7 376 B6
Copse End CBLY GU15 71 J2
Copse La HISD PO11 401 L8
HLER SO31 369 K6
LSOL/BMARY PO13 397 H7
NALR SO24 171 K5
ODIM RG29 131 J5
ROWN SO16 292 E7
Copse Rd HASM GU27 228 A3
NMIL/BTOS BH25 437 M6
OVTN RG25 101 G6
RGWD BH24 384 D6
VWD BH31 356 D2
WEND SO18 319 L6
The Copse CHFD SO53 293 K3
DEAN RG23 126 C5
FARN GU14 90 A5
FHAM PO15 372 B4
RFNM GU10 158 C4
TADY RG26 41 K8
Copse Vw ITCH SO19 345 J3
Copse View Cl CHAM RG24 83 M4 2
Copse Wy CHCH/BSGR BH23 436 C8
EWKG RG40 48 B1 3
RFNM GU10 158 C2
Copsewood Av CHAR BH8 433 J7
Copsewood Rd FAWY SO45 367 K5
TOTT SO40 341 G5
WEND SO18 319 K6
Copsey Cl CHAM PO6 376 B8
Copsey Gv CHAM PO6 376 B8
Copthorne La FAWY SO45 392 F5
Copyhold Hl HASM GU27 228 F8
Copythorne Crs TOTT SO40 315 H6
Copythorn Rd NEND PO2 399 K7
Coracle Cl HLER SO31
Coral Cl FHAM/PORC PO16
Coralin Gv WVILLE PO7
Coram Cl WINC SO23
Corbar Rd CHCH/BSGR BH23
Corbett Rd WVILLE PO7
Corbiere Av BKME/WDN BH12
Corbiere Cl ROWN SO16
Corbin Av FERN BH22
Corbin Rd LYMN SO41
Corbould Rd FAWY SO45
Corby Crs HSEA PO3
Cordale Rd BSTK RG21
Cordelia Cl FAWY SO45
Cordelia Gdns ASHV GU12
Corderoy Cl STHA RG19
Cordwalles Rd CBLY GU15
Corfe Cl FHAM/STUB PO14
NALR SO24
Corfe Gdns FRIM GU16
Corfe Lodge Rd WIMB BH21
Corfe View Rd PSTN BH14
WIMB BH21
Corfe Wy BDST BH18
FARN GU14
Corfield Cl EWKG RG40
Corhampton Crs HAV PO9
Corhampton La BPWT SO32
Corhampton Rd SBNE BH6
Coriander Cl FARN GU14
Coriander Dr TOTT SO40
Coriander Wy FHAM PO15
Corinna Gdns FAWY SO45
Corinthian Cl AND SP10
KEMP RG22
Corinthian Rd CHFD SO53
Cork La TOTT SO40
Cormorant Cl
FHAM/PORC PO16
Cormorant Dr FAWY SO45
Cormorant Pl SHST GU47
Cornaway La
FHAM/PORC PO16
Cornbrook Gv HORN PO8
Cornbunting Cl SHST GU47
Cornelia Cl FARN GU14
Cornelia Crs BKME/WDN BH12
Cornelius Dr WVILLE PO7
Cornel Rd ITCH SO19
Corner Md WVILLE PO7
Cornes Cl WINW SO22
Cornfield FHAM/PORC PO16
Cornfield Cl NBAD SO52
Cornfield Rd
LSOL/BMARY PO13
Cornfields AND SP10
YTLY GU46
The Cornfields KEMP RG22
Cornflower Cl HLER SO31
Cornflower Dr
CHCH/BSGR BH23
Cornflower Wy RAND SP11
Cornford Wy
CHCH/BSGR BH23
Cornforth Rd TOTT SO40
Cornish Cl KEMP RG22
Cornish Gdns NBNE BH10
Corn Market ROMY SO51
Cornpits La FBDG SP6
Cornwall Cl CBLY GU15
Cornwall Crs WEND SO18
Cornwallis Crs PSEA PO1
Cornwallis Rd LYMN SO41
Cornwall Rd CHFD SO53
BOR GU35
PSEA PO1
WEND SO18
Cornwell Cl LSOL/BMARY PO13
NEND PO2
Coronado Rd GPORT PO12
Coronation Av
MOOR/WNTN BH9
UPTN BH16
Coronation Cl KSCL RG20
ODIM RG29
Coronation Pde HLER SO31
Coronation Rd ALDT GU11
BPWT SO32
BSTK RG21
HISD PO11
RAND SP11
VWD BH31
YTLY GU46
Corporation Rd BMTH BH1
Correlli Rd KEMP RG22
Corringway FLET GU13
Corry Rd GSHT GU26
Corsair Dr FAWY SO45
Corsham Wy CWTH RG45
Cortina Wy HEND SO30
Cort Wy FHAM PO15
Corunna Main AND SP10
Corvette Av HLER SO31
Cosford Cl ELGH SO50
Cosham Park Av CHAM PO6
Cossack Gn SHAM SO14
Cossack La WINC SO23
Coster Cl NWBY RG14
Cosworth Dr FAWY SO45
Cotes Av PSTN BH14
Cotlands Rd BMTH BH1
Cot La RCCH PO18
Cotsalls ELGH SO50
Cotswold Cl FARN GU14
FAWY SO45
HAV PO9
KEMP RG22
VWD BH31
Cotswold Rd ROWN SO16
SHST GU47
Cottage Cl WVILLE PO7
Cottage Gdns
BKME/WDN BH12
FARN GU14
Cottage Gn HTWY RG27
RAND SP11
Cottage Gv GPORT PO12
SSEA PO5

e La LISS GU33 247 L4
e Ms FBDG SP6 309 K6 3
'D BH24 382 D1 3
e Rd STOK SO20 162 B8
ers La LYMN SO41 438 E5
e Vw PSEA PO1 21 J1
Wy FHAM/STUB PO14 395 L7
way East
M/STUB PO14 395 L7
gton Cl KSCL RG20 59 K6 1
a RGWD BH24 384 F6
Cl BSTK RG21 104 F6
Cl BDST BH18 429 K3
SO50 294 D5
Dr EMRTH PO10 378 C5
BPWT SO32 324 F4
treet La BPWT SO32 324 F4
ll Av HORN PO8 352 F4
ere Rd GPORT PO12 421 L2
don Rd HEND SO30 346 A2
s Rd CHFD SO53 265 K6
il Rd BSTK RG21 105 G4
ess Cl WIMB BH21 404 C7
y Vw FHAM/STUB PO14 395 M4
Y SO51 288 D5
y Gdns
M/STUB PO14 372 A8
e Park Crs
M/STUB PO14 371 G6
Barn La
/BMARY PO13 420 D1
Cl CHAM PO6 399 M1
GU30 226 E5
N SO41 440 B6
SO40 316 B6
Dro OVTN RG25 100 F8
enay Dr WIMB BH21 404 A2 2
enay Pl LYMN SO41 440 C6
enay Rd FNM GU9 6 A9
BH14 446 A4
SO23 11 G2
Gdns CBLY GU15 71 G3
Hl FBDG SP6 308 D4
hill Rd PSTN BH14 446 B4
House Cl FAWY SO45 367 L4 3
land Gdns ROWN SO16 319 G3
ands Rd NWBY RG14 3 G8
La ALTN GU34 220 C2
M PO6 399 M1
SO20 212 A2
Md CHAM PO6 399 M1 1
moor Av FLET GU13 110 E1
mount Gv CHAM PO6 375 L8
Rd ALDT GU11 6 F1
/BMARY PO13 420 C1
R/WNTN BH9 432 F7
C SO23 215 H3
M SO15 343 K1
Royal Ms WSHM SO15 318 E8 2
Hill Rd HASM GU27 228 E2
Mount Rd HASM GU27 228 E2
ourtyard EPSF GU31 275 L5
ns Gv ENEY PO4 423 L6
a Rd SBNE BH6 449 J2
try Cl KEMP RG22 104 A8 2
B BH21 429 G4
try Crs CFDH BH17 429 L7
try Rd WSHM SO15 343 K2
ack Wy CHAM PO6 398 F1
Rd FARN GU14 89 G5
E BH10 432 A6
Gv WVILLE PO7 376 E3
ts Cl FNM GU9 135 H4 1
overt FARN GU14 70 B8
Y SO51 291 G2
Cl FARN GU14 70 D8
Wy NALR SO24 218 A4
gton Rd EMRTH PO10 378 F3
Rd WVILLE PO7 376 B3
rd Rd GPORT PO12 18 B8
own La RAND SP11 143 J5
PO18 330 B4
ray Cl ELGH SO50 294 E6 1
N SO16 318 A4
ray Pk ALTN GU34 176 E6
M/STUB PO14 395 L6
rey Cl BSTK RG21 5 H3
rey Hts CHAM RG24 5 L6
rove Hl STOK SO20 210 E4
Dr LTDN BH7 433 L8
La HLER SO31 394 B2
old La HTWY RG27 85 M2
a CHAM PO6 399 H1
GU31 304 F4
M/PORC PO16 398 C1
D SP11 116 A5
y Cl ROWN SO16 317 K6
y Dr RWIN SO21 190 C6
y Rd LYMN SO41 440 A4
ys La BROC SO42 391 J8
ys Rd CHCH/BSGR BH23 435 G6
er Av NMIL/BTOS BH25 437 L7
er Rd ITCH SO19 345 H2
R/WNTN BH9 432 D6
PO1 423 J1 3
tts La RGWD BH24 359 H6
ade NWBY RG14 25 G3 2
ip Bank CHAM RG24 105 L1
ip Cl HLER SO31 370 C7
GU35 201 M4 1
/BMARY PO13 397 G6
ip Crs NTHA RG18 27 G4
ip Rd WIMB BH21 429 J6 1
MOOR/WNTN BH9 432 F5
idge FNM GU9 134 C7
idge Mdw FNM GU9 134 C7
MOOR/WNTN BH9 432 F4
FHAM/STUB PO14 371 G7
Meadow PSF GU32 275 K3
er Rd NWBY RG14 2 A1
rd Cl ROWN SO16 317 M6
rd Dro ROWN SO16 317 M5
rd Rd ROWN SO16 317 L6
een SHST GU47 70 A2
ath Rd FLET GU13 110 D2
oor Cl FLET GU13 111 H3
CHFD SO53 293 J5
Dr ITCH SO19 344 F6
Coxs Hl RWIN SO21 238 F8
Cox's La MARL SN8 32 C5
THLE RG7 28 A5
Coxstone La RGWD BH24 382 E2
Coy Pond Rd
BKME/WDN BH12 446 F3
Cozens Cl ITCH SO19 344 C7 1
Crabapple Cl TOTT SO40 341 G1 4
Crabbe Ct SSEA PO5 21 H4 1
Crabbs Wy TOTT SO40 340 F1
Crabbswood La LYMN SO41 412 C8
Crabden La HORN PO8 328 D8
Crableck La HLER SO31 370 A3
Crab Orchard Wy WIMB BH21 356 C6
Crabs Hl TADY RG26 60 A7
Crabthorne Farm La
FHAM/STUB PO14 395 M5 2
Crabton Close Rd BOSC BH5 448 E3
Crabtree ROWN SO16 317 L7 1
Crabtree Cl CHCH/BSGR BH23 435 G6
Crabtree Gdns BOR GU35 202 B3
Crabtree La BOR GU35 202 B3
RFNM GU10 181 K6
Crabtree Rd CBLY GU15 70 E6
Crabtree Wy CHAM RG24 106 A4
Crabwood Cl ROWN SO16 317 L7
Crabwood Ct HAV PO9 377 H1 1
Crabwood Dr HEND SO30 320 D7
Crabwood Rd ROWN SO16 317 K6
Cracknore Hard TOTT SO40 343 G6
Cracknore Hard La TOTT SO40 342 F7
TOTT SO40 343 G6 1
Cracknore Rd WSHM SO15 12 A2
Craigmoor Av CHAR BH8 433 J7
Craigmoor Cl CHAR BH8 433 K7
Craigside Rd RGWD BH24 381 H4
Craigwell Rd WVILLE PO7 376 B4
Craigwood Dr FERN BH22 406 C4
Crake Pl SHST GU47 50 A8
Crampmoor La ROMY SO51 263 J7
Cramptons ALTN GU34 175 M6
Cranberry Cl TOTT SO40 342 D7
Cranborne Crs
BKME/WDN BH12 431 J8
Cranborne Gdns CHFD SO53 265 G7
Cranborne Rd CHAM PO6 375 L7
FBDG SP6 332 E3
WCLF BH2 22 D7
Cranbourne Cl WSHM SO15 318 C7 1
Cranbourne Dr RWIN SO21 266 A5
Cranbourne La BSTK RG21 104 E6 1
Cranbourne Rd GPORT PO12 19 G5
Cranbrook Ct FLET GU13 88 F5
Cranbrook Rd
BKME/WDN BH12 446 A2
Cranbury Av SHAM SO14 343 M2
Cranbury Cl RSAL SP5 284 E2
RWIN SO21 266 A5
Cranbury Gdns HLER SO31 345 K7
Cranbury Pl SHAM SO14 343 L2
Cranbury Rd ELGH SO50 293 M6
ITCH SO19 344 D5
Crane Cl VWD BH31 356 C1
Crane Ct SHST GU47 50 A8
Crane Dr VWD BH31 356 C2
Cranemoor Av
CHCH/BSGR BH23 436 C6
Cranemoor Cl
CHCH/BSGR BH23 436 C6
Cranemoor Gdns
CHCH/BSGR BH23 436 D6
Cranesfield CHAM RG24 82 D4
Cranes Rd CHAM RG24 82 D4
Craneswater Av ENEY PO4 21 M8
Craneswater Ga ENEY PO4 21 M9 1
Craneswater Pk ENEY PO4 21 M9
Cranfield Av WIMB BH21 404 B3
Cranford Av FLET GU13 110 D3
Cranford Dr ALTN GU34 177 H2
Cranford Gdns CHFD SO53 265 G8
Cranford Park Dr YTLY GU46 69 G2
Cranford Rd PSF GU32 275 K6
Cranford Wy PTSW SO17 318 F6
Cranleigh Av PSEA PO1 423 J2
Cranleigh Cl SBNE BH6 449 K3
Cranleigh Ct FARN GU14 90 C4 2
Cranleigh Gdns SBNE BH6 449 K3
Cranleigh Rd
FHAM/PORC PO16 397 L1
HEND SO30 346 A2
PSEA PO1 423 J2
SBNE BH6 449 J2
Cranmer Dr ROWN SO16 317 H3
Cranmer Rd MOOR/WNTN BH9 432 D8
Cranmore HLER SO31 369 G1
Cranmore Cl ALDT GU11 6 A4
Cranmore Gdns ALDT GU11 6 B4
Cranmore La ALDT GU11 6 A4
Cranmore Rd FRIM GU16 91 J4
Cranwell Cl CHCH/BSGR BH23 409 M7
Cranworth Rd WINW SO22 10 E5
Crasswell St PSEA PO1 423 G2
Craven Cl RFNM GU10 158 F2
Craven Ct FHAM PO15 14 B2
Craven Dene NWBY RG14 3 H2
Craven Rd CHFD SO53 293 J2
HUNG RG17 33 L2
NWBY RG14 2 A5
Craven St SHAM SO14 13 H2 1
Crawford Cl ROWN SO16 317 J3
Crawford Dr FHAM/PORC PO16 14 E1
Crawford Gdns CBLY GU15 70 E3
Crawford Pl NWBY RG14 2 D3
Crawlboys La RAND SP11 92 E5
Crawley Av HAV PO9 377 L2
Crawley Dr CBLY GU15 71 J2
Crawley Hl CBLY GU15 71 J3
ROMY SO51 288 E6
Crawley Rdg CBLY GU15 71 J2
Crawley Wood Cl CBLY GU15 71 J3 1
Crawshaw Rd PSTN BH14 446 A6
Crawte Av FAWY SO45 392 B6
Crawts Rd OVTN RG25 123 M1
Craydown La STOK SO20 162 D6
Creasey Rd BWD BH11 431 L3
Credenhill Rd CHAM PO6 375 G7
Credon Cl FARN GU14 90 B3
Creech Rd BKME/WDN BH12 446 B3
Creedy Gdns WEND SO18 319 M5 1
Creek End EMRTH PO10 402 D1
Creekmoor La CFDH BH17 429 K7
Creek Rd GPORT PO12 19 J3
HISD PO11 426 B6
Creighton Rd WSHM SO15 342 D2
Cremyll Cl FHAM/STUB PO14 396 A6
Crerar Cl FARN GU14 90 A5
Crescent Cl WINW SO22 238 A4
Crescent Dr NMIL/BTOS BH25 452 E1
Crescent La ASHV GU12 113 L3
Crescent Rd FHAM/PORC PO16 15 H6
GPORT PO12 18 C9
HLER SO31 370 D5
NBAD SO52 291 L3
PSTN BH14 446 D4
VWD BH31 356 E2
WCLF BH2 22 C5
WIMB BH21 404 A4
The Crescent ALTN GU34 197 G4
BMTH BH1 448 D4
BPWT SO32 296 B6
ELGH SO50 293 M4
EMRTH PO10 379 H8
FARN GU14 90 F5
FLET GU13 110 B2
FNM GU9 112 A8
HLER SO31 368 F2
ITCH SO19 344 E6
NMIL/BTOS BH25 437 G8
RAND SP11 96 D1
RAND SP11 142 D4
RAND SP11 142 E7
ROMY SO51 263 G8
RWIN SO21 266 F2
THLE RG7 29 M4
THLE RG7 43 K2
TOTT SO40 340 C5
WVILLE PO7 376 A4 2
Crescent Wk FERN BH22 406 C6
Cressey Rd ROMY SO51 290 E1
Cress Gdns AND SP10 8 E8
Cresswell Rd NWBY RG14 3 M1
Cressy Rd NEND PO2 423 H1
Cresta Gdns FERN BH22 406 C6
Crest Cl FHAM/PORC PO16 373 H7
Crestland Cl HORN PO8 352 E5
Crest Rd BKME/WDN BH12 446 B2
The Crest WVILLE PO7 376 A6
Crest Wy ITCH SO19 345 G4
Crete La FAWY SO45 367 K7
Crete Rd FAWY SO45 367 K8
Cribb Cl CFDH BH17 445 K1
Crichel Mount Rd PSTN BH14 446 B8
Crichel Rd MOOR/WNTN BH9 432 E8
Cricket Cl CHCH/BSGR BH23 450 E3
RWIN SO21 189 G6
Cricket Dr HORN PO8 352 E3
Cricketers KSCL RG20 24 B2
Cricketers Wy AND SP10 119 G5
Cricket Field Gv CWTH RG45 50 A4
Cricket Hl EWKG RG40 48 C6
Cricket Hill La BLKW GU17 69 G5
YTLY GU46 69 H3
Cricket La RFNM GU10 159 G2
Cricket Lea BOR GU35 201 L3 1
Cricklemede BPWT SO32 323 J1
Cricklewood Cl BPWT SO32 323 J1 1
Crigdon Cl ROWN SO16 317 K8
Crimea Rd ALDT GU11 7 G2
Cringle Av SBNE BH6 449 M4
Crinoline Gdns ENEY PO4 423 L6
Cripley Rd FARN GU14 90 B3
Cripple Gate La BROC SO42 416 B3
Crispin Cl CHCH/BSGR BH23 436 D8
ELGH SO50 321 H2
HLER SO31 370 F4
Crispstead La WINC SO23 238 E3
Crisspyn Cl HORN PO8 352 F2
Critchmere Hl HASM GU27 228 B1
Critchmere La HASM GU27 228 B2
Critchmere V HASM GU27 228 A2
Crittall Cl LYMN SO41 413 G6
Cricket Cl GSHT GU26 204 A2
Crockford Br LYMN SO41 415 H6
Crockford Cl NMIL/BTOS BH25 437 M3
Crockford La CHAM RG24 83 K4
Crockford Rd EMRTH PO10 378 F4
Crocus Md NTHA RG18 27 H4
Croft Av AND SP10 9 H8
Croft Cl WIMB BH21 429 H1
Crofter's Cl SHST GU47 49 K8 1
Crofters Meadow CHAM RG24 83 L8 3
Croft Gdns AND SP10 9 H9
Croft Hts RSAL SP5 259 G5
Croftlands Av
FHAM/STUB PO14 396 A5
Croft La HISD PO11 401 L7
RFNM GU10 133 H3
NWBY RG14 2 B2
YTLY GU46 68 F1
Crofton Av LSOL/BMARY PO13 396 A8
Crofton Cl CHCH/BSGR BH23 434 C8
PTSW SO17 318 F7 1
WVILLE PO7 376 A3
Crofton La FHAM/STUB PO14 395 M7
Crofton Rd ENEY PO4 423 M3
NEND PO2 399 J6
Crofton Wy BPWT SO32 323 M3
HLER SO31 370 A7
Croft Rd ALDT GU11 7 H6
BKME/WDN BH12 446 A2
CHCH/BSGR BH23 435 M2
CHCH/BSGR BH23 450 E1
DEAN RG23 102 F6
MOOR/WNTN BH9 432 D6
NEND PO2 399 H7 2
NWBY RG14 2 D9
RGWD BH24 359 G7
THLE RG7 43 J2
The Crofts KEMP RG22 127 H2
The Croft AMSY SP4 160 A2
CHFD SO53 293 H5 1
FHAM/STUB PO14 396 A4
TOTT SO40 316 B6
Croft Wy FRIM GU16 71 J7
Cromarty Av ENEY PO4 423 M4
Cromarty Cl FHAM/STUB PO14 395 M5
Cromarty Rd ROWN SO16 317 K3
Crombie Cl HORN PO8 352 D4
Cromer Rd BKME/WDN BH12 446 E3
CHAM PO6 375 H7
CHAR BH8 448 C1
ROWN SO16 317 J7
Cromhall Cl
FHAM/STUB PO14 372 A8 1
Crompton Wy FHAM PO15 371 G3
Cromwell Cl CHAM RG24 106 A2
Cromwell Rd
BKME/WDN BH12 446 C3
BOSC BH5 449 G3
BSTK RG21 4 D5
CBLY GU15 71 G1
ENEY PO4 423 M6
WINW SO22 238 C2
NWBY RG14 25 M3
WSHM SO15 343 K1
Cromwell Wy FARN GU14 90 E1 1
Crondall Av HAV PO9 377 J2
Crondall Ct CBLY GU15 70 E4 3
Crondall End YTLY GU46 68 F1
Crondall La RFNM GU10 133 M6
Crondall Rd RFNM GU10 110 B5
RFNM GU10 157 K1
Crooked Hays Cl TOTT SO40 342 D7 1
Crooked Walk La WHAM PO17 374 C5
Crookham Cl HAV PO9 377 G4 2
TADY RG26 61 L2 1
Crookham Reach FLET GU13 110 D3
Crookham Rd FLET GU13 110 D2
ITCH SO19 344 D8 2
Crookhorn La WVILLE PO7 376 C7
Crooksbury Rd RFNM GU10 135 L5
Cropmark Wy KEMP RG22 127 G1
Cropper Cl STHA RG19 27 K5
Crosby Gdns YTLY GU46 68 D1
Crosby Hill Dr CBLY GU15 71 J1
Crosby Wy FNM GU9 134 D7
Crosfield Cl ROMY SO51 289 G6
Cross & Pillory La ALTN GU34 176 E5 1
Crossbill Cl HORN PO8 352 E1
Crossborough Hl BSTK RG21 105 H4
Cross Gdns FRIM GU16 91 J2
Crosshouse Rd SHAM SO14 13 L6
Cross Keys Pas WINC SO23 11 H8 1
Crossland Cl GPORT PO12 19 G6
Crossland Dr HAV PO9 17 G1
Cross La AND SP10 8 E4
BPWT SO32 296 F5
FRIM GU16 91 J2
HORN PO8 352 E3
KSCL RG20 55 M8
THLE RG7 45 G1
Crossmead Av
NMIL/BTOS BH25 437 L6
Cross Rd ASHV GU12 113 L5
FARN GU14 90 B7
ITCH SO19 344 C1
LSOL/BMARY PO13 420 E4
Cross St ALDT GU11 6 E2
BPWT SO32 297 H8
BSTK RG21 4 E9
FARN GU14 90 F8
PSEA PO1 20 D1
SSEA PO5 21 J3 3
WINC SO23 10 F7
The Cross PSF GU32 273 J7
RGWD BH24 384 E5
RSAL SP5 253 G1
STOK SO20 210 F5
Crosswater La RFNM GU10 181 H4
Cross Wy CHCH/BSGR BH23 434 B7
HAV PO9 16 C3
RWIN SO21 266 C3
Crossways ASHV GU12 7 K4
LYMN SO41 439 H7
RFNM GU10 181 H7
The Crossways AND SP10 8 F4
GPORT PO12 421 M2
UPTN BH16 444 B1
The Crossway
FHAM/PORC PO16 374 A8
Crosswell Cl ITCH SO19 345 G3
Croucher's Cft WINW SO22 214 A7
Croucheston Dro RSAL SP5 253 G1
Crouch La HORN PO8 352 E1
Crow Arch La RGWD BH24 382 F2
Crowder Ter WINW SO22 10 E8
Crowfield Dr STHA RG19 26 E5
Crow La RGWD BH24 383 G2
Crowley Dr ALTN GU34 176 F5
Crown Acre Cl STHA RG19 26 F5 1
Crown Cl BKME/WDN BH12 446 B3
WVILLE PO7 376 C5
Crown Dr FNM GU9 135 K3
Crownfields ODIM RG29 108 C6
Crown Gdns FLET GU13 89 G8
Crown La CHAM RG24 105 M2
FNM GU9 135 K3
HTWY RG27 85 H8
RAND SP11 92 D6 1
Crown Md WIMB BH21 404 A3 1
Crown Pl SHST GU47 50 B7 1
Crown St PSEA PO1 423 H2
WSHM SO15 318 A8
Crowsbury Cl EMRTH PO10 378 C5
Crows La ALTN GU34 198 D5
Crows Nest La BPWT SO32 321 L7
Crowsport HLER SO31 369 L5
Crowther Cl ITCH SO19 345 G4
Crowthorne Rd SHST GU47 49 L8
Croyde Cl FARN GU14 90 D2
Croydon Cl ROWN SO16 317 M4
Croye Cl AND SP10 8 E5
Cruikshank Lea SHST GU47 70 B2
Crummock Rd CHFD SO53 292 F1
Crumpets Dr UPTN BH16 428 B3
Crundles EPSF GU31 275 M5
Crusader Rd HEND SO30 346 B3
WIMB BH21 431 H4
Crusaders Wy NBAD SO52 292 E2
Cruse Cl LYMN SO41 412 F6
Crystal Wy WVILLE PO7 352 F8
Cucklington Gdns
MOOR/WNTN BH9 432 F5
Cuckmere La ROWN SO16 317 J8
Cuckoo Bushes La CHFD SO53 265 G8
Cuckoo Cl OVTN RG25 125 K7
Cuckoo Hill Wy
CHCH/BSGR BH23 410 A7
Cuckoo La FHAM/STUB PO14 395 M4
Cuckoo Rd BKME/WDN BH12 430 E8
Cudnell Av BWD BH11 431 K2
Cudworth Md HEND SO30 321 J7
Cufaude La TADY RG26 83 L2
Cuffelle Cl CHAM RG24 83 M5
Cuffnells Cl RGWD BH24 334 F8
Cul-de-sac NMIL/BTOS BH25 437 G8
Culford Av TOTT SO40 341 K2
Culford Wy TOTT SO40 341 K2
Cull Cl BKME/WDN BH12 432 A8
Cullen Cl YTLY GU46 68 F3
Culley Vw NALR SO24 218 C4
Culliford Crs CFDH BH17 430 C6
Cull La NMIL/BTOS BH25 437 M3
Culloden Cl FHAM PO15 14 D3
Culloden Rd FHAM/STUB PO14 396 D2
Cullwood La NMIL/BTOS BH25 438 A3
Culver HLER SO31 369 G1 3
Culver Cl ROWN SO16 317 J6
Culver Dr HISD PO11 426 A7
Culverlands Crs ASHV GU12 113 J5
Culverley Cl BROC SO42 387 K7 1
Culver Rd BSTK RG21 104 F5
ENEY PO4 423 L6
NMIL/BTOS BH25 437 K6
NWBY RG14 25 J8 1
SHST GU47 50 A7
WINC SO23 238 E2
Culvers EPSF GU31 305 G5
Culverwell Gdns WINC SO23 10 F9
Culvery Gdns WEND SO18 319 M6
Cumberland Av CHFD SO53 293 K3
EMRTH PO10 378 C4
KEMP RG22 104 D7 1
Cumberland Pl WSHM SO15 12 E1
Cumberland Rd CBLY GU15 71 M4
SSEA PO5 21 L2 1
Cumberland St PSEA PO1 422 E2
SHAM SO14 13 J3 1
Cumberland Wy FAWY SO45 367 H5
Cumber Rd HLER SO31 370 C5
Cumbria Ct FARN GU14 91 H7
Cumbrian Wy ROWN SO16 317 K8
Cumnor Rd BMTH BH1 23 G5
Cunard Av WSHM SO15 318 B8
Cunard Rd SHAM SO14 13 H8
Cundell Wy WINC SO23 191 G7
Cunliffe Cl SELS PO20 427 L6
Cunningham Av BPWT SO32 296 F8 1
Cunningham Cl RGWD BH24 359 G8 1
Cunningham Crs BWD BH11 431 L5
ITCH SO19 344 F4 1
Cunningham Dr HLER SO31 370 E4
LSOL/BMARY PO13 397 H5
Cunningham Rd HORN PO8 353 G1 1
WVILLE PO7 376 B3
Cunnington Rd FARN GU14 91 H7
Cupernham Cl ROMY SO51 262 F8
Cupernham La ROMY SO51 262 F5
Curdridge Cl HAV PO9 377 L3 1
Curdridge La BPWT SO32 322 F6
Curlew Cl EMRTH PO10 378 C8
FERN BH22 405 M1
KEMP RG22 103 M7
ROWN SO16 318 A3
STHA RG19 26 F5 2
Curlew Dr FAWY SO45 367 M6
FHAM/PORC PO16 373 K8
Curlew Gdns HORN PO8 352 D4
Curlew Rd CHAR BH8 433 H6
CHCH/BSGR BH23 450 F2
Curlews ALTN GU34 176 E2
The Curlews VWD BH31 356 E3
Curleys Wy THLE RG7 46 A2 1
Curlieu Rd PLE BH15 445 K2
Curling Wy NWBY RG14 3 K1
Curly Bridge Cl FARN GU14 70 C8
Curtis Cl CBLY GU15 71 M1 2
BOR GU35 202 B2 1
Curtis La BOR GU35 202 B2
Curtis Md NEND PO2 399 K4
Curtis Rd ALTN GU34 176 F6
BKME/WDN BH12 446 B3
Curtiss Gdns GPORT PO12 18 A3
The Curve HORN PO8 352 D2
LSOL/BMARY PO13 396 F6
Curzon Dr FLET GU13 110 F3
Curzon Howe Rd PSEA PO1 20 D1
Curzon Pl LYMN SO41 440 B6
Curzon Rd CHAR BH8 448 C2
PSTN BH14 445 M5
WVILLE PO7 376 C1
Curzon Wy CHCH/BSGR BH23 436 B8
Cusden Dr AND SP10 9 G1
Custards Rd LYND SO43 363 K2
Cutbush La WEND SO18 319 M5
WEND SO18 320 A8
Cuthbert Rd ASHV GU12 113 L2
PSEA PO1 423 K2
Cuthburga Rd WIMB BH21 404 A3
Cutler Cl BKME/WDN BH12 447 H1
NMIL/BTOS BH25 438 A5
Cutlers La FHAM/STUB PO14 396 A5
Cutlers Pl WIMB BH21 404 E3
Cutter Av HLER SO31 370 C7
Cut Throat La BPWT SO32 299 G6
BPWT SO32 324 B2
Cutting Hl HUNG RG17 32 D4
Cutts Arch BPWT SO32 325 G1
Cutts Rd ALDT GU11 113 G1
Cuxhaven Wy AND SP10 118 E5
Cygnet Cl STHA RG19 26 E5
Cygnet Ct FHAM/PORC PO16 373 K8 2
Cygnet Rd CHAM PO6 400 D1
Cygnus Gdns FAWY SO45 367 G5
Cynthia Cl BKME/WDN BH12 446 A1
Cynthia Rd BKME/WDN BH12 446 A1
Cypress FARN GU14 70 C7 1
Cypress Av ITCH SO19 344 D3
Cypress Crs HORN PO8 352 E3
Cypress Dr FLET GU13 89 H7
Cypress Gdns HEND SO30 346 E1
TOTT SO40 341 G1 5

Cypress Gv ASHV GU12 113 J1
RAND SP11 142 B1
Cypress Rd BOR GU35 200 F5
Cypress Wy GSHT GU26 204 A6
Cyprus Rd FHAM/STUB PO14 371 G7
KEMP RG22 127 H3
NEND PO2 399 J8
Cyril Rd CHAR BH8 448 B2
Cyril Vokins Rd NWBY RG14 26 B6

D

Dacombe Cl UPTN BH16 444 B1
Dacombe Dr UPTN BH16 444 B1
Dacre Cl AND SP10 118 C5
Daffodil Cl KEMP RG22 103 M8
Daffodil Cl ROWN SO16 319 H4
Daggons Rd FBDG SP6 333 G2
Dahlia Cl KEMP RG22 103 M8 1
Dahlia Rd ROWN SO16 318 F4 1
Daintree Cl ITCH SO19 345 H5
Dairy Cl CHCH/BSGR BH23 450 C1
RSAL SP5 285 J3
WIMB BH21 428 F4
Dairy Gate Rd FARN GU14 90 E8
Dairy La ROWN SO16 316 F4
Dairymoor WHAM PO17 348 E4
Daisy La GPORT PO12 18 D3
HLER SO31 370 F5
Daisy Md WVILLE PO7 376 E2
Daisy Rd ROWN SO16 319 H4
Dalby Crs NWBY RG14 3 H9
Dale Cl WINW SO22 213 M3
RFNM GU10 158 C1
PLE BH15 445 L2
Dale Dr LSOL/BMARY PO13 396 F3
Dale Gdns SHST GU47 49 K8
Dale Rd FAWY SO45 367 K5
FHAM/STUB PO14 396 B5
PLE BH15 445 L2
ROWN SO16 318 B6
Dales Cl WIMB BH21 405 G2
Dales Dr WIMB BH21 404 F3
Dales La CHCH/BSGR BH23 433 J1
Dales Wy TOTT SO40 316 A8
The Dale WVILLE PO7 376 A6
Dale Valley Cl ROWN SO16 318 B6
Dale Valley Gdns ROWN SO16 318 B6
Dale Valley Rd PLE BH15 445 K1
ROWN SO16 318 B5
Dale Vw HASM GU27 228 C3 1
Dalewood KEMP RG22 103 M6
Dalewood Av BWD BH11 431 J3
Dalewood Rd FHAM PO15 14 B5
Dalkeith Rd CCLF BH13 446 F7
WIMB BH21 429 H4 1
Dalley Ct SHST GU47 70 A1
Dalling Rd BKME/WDN BH12 446 F3
Dallington Cl
FHAM/STUB PO14 396 A7 1
Dalmally Gdns WEND SO18 319 L8 1
Dalmeny Rd SBNE BH6 449 M5
Damask Gdns WVILLE PO7 352 F7
Damen Cl HEND SO30 345 M3
Damerham Rd CHAR BH8 449 H5
Dampier Cl LSOL/BMARY PO13 421 G1
Damsel La OVTN RG25 151 J5
Damsel Pth BSTK RG21 5 K8
Damson Hl BPWT SO32 298 A8
Danbury Ct EMRTH PO10 378 E6
Dancers Meadow CHAM RG24 82 E5
Dances Cl AND SP10 9 J3
Dances La WHCH RG28 122 B2
Dances Wy HISD PO11 425 J4
Dandelion Cl
LSOL/BMARY PO13 396 F6 1
Dando Rd WVILLE PO7 351 L4
Dandy's Ford La ROMY SO51 260 E8
Danebury Cl HAV PO9 377 J2 2
Danebury Gdns CHFD SO53 292 F4 2
Danebury Rd KEMP RG22 127 G2
Danebury Wy ROWN SO16 317 J5
Dane Cl FAWY SO45 392 D7
Danecourt Cl PSTN BH14 445 L4
Danecourt Rd PSTN BH14 445 L4
Danecrest Rd LYMN SO41 438 D5
Dane Dr FERN BH22 406 C5
Danegeld Cl AND SP10 119 G4 2
Danehurst New Rd
LYMN SO41 412 A8
Danehurst Pl AND SP10 118 B8
Dane Rd LYMN SO41 453 M2
Danesbrook La WVILLE PO7 376 E1 2
Danesbury Av SBNE BH6 449 L4
Danes Cl NMIL/BTOS BH25 452 F1
Daneshill Dr CHAM RG24 83 L8
Danes Rd FHAM/PORC PO16 373 M7
ROMY SO51 261 J4
WINC SO23 11 G4
Danestream Cl LYMN SO41 454 C4 1
Daneswood Rd
NMIL/BTOS BH25 438 A5 1
Daniell's Cl LYMN SO41 440 C5
Daniell's Wk LYMN SO41 440 C6
Daniel Rd WHCH RG28 122 C4
Dankworth Rd KEMP RG22 104 B8
Danley La HASM GU27 227 K5
Dansie Cl PSTN BH14 446 A4
Danvers Cl STHA RG19 27 G6 2
Danvers Dr FLET GU13 110 C4
Daphne Dr FLET GU13 110 D5
Dapple Pl TOTT SO40 342 E7
Darby Green La BLKW GU17 69 L3
Darby Green Rd BLKW GU17 69 K3
Darby's Cl PLE BH15 445 J2
Darby's La PLE BH15 445 J2
Dare's La RFNM GU10 110 D7
Dark La CHAM RG24 82 D5
CHCH/BSGR BH23 436 E4
FAWY SO45 392 D7
NALR SO24 218 E6
NALR SO24 242 C3
RGUW GU3 137 L4
Darleydale Cl SHST GU47 50 A6 1
Darley Rd FERN BH22 406 A5
Darlington Gdns WSHM SO15 318 C8
Darlington Rd BSTK RG21 4 D4
ENEY PO4 21 L5
Darracott Cl CBLY GU15 71 L1 1
Darracott Rd BOSC BH5 448 F4
Darren Cl FHAM/STUB PO14 396 B4
Darset Av FLET GU13 88 F6
Dart Cl EWKG RG40 48 C1
NTHA RG18 26 E3
Dart Ct AND SP10 119 H6 3
Dartington Rd ELGH SO50 294 C3
Dartmouth Rd HSEA PO3 399 L6
Dart Rd FARN GU14 90 A2
WEND SO18 320 A5
Darvill Rd NALR SO24 219 M3
Darvills La FNM GU9 134 F6
Darwin Av CHCH/BSGR BH23 434 C7
Darwin Gv ALDT GU11 112 F5
Darwin Rd ELGH SO50 294 A4
WSHM SO15 343 H1
Darwin Wy LSOL/BMARY PO13 421 H2
Dashwood Cl ALTN GU34 176 C6
Dasna Rd NTID SP9 114 C3
Daulston Rd PSEA PO1 423 J1
Daunch Cl NTID SP9 114 C1
Dauntless Rd THLE RG7 31 L5
Dauntsey Dro RAND SP11 116 F6
Dauntsey La RAND SP11 116 F7
Davenport Cl
LSOL/BMARY PO13 421 G2 1
UPTN BH16 444 B1 2
Daventry La HSEA PO3 400 A4
D Av FAWY SO45 392 B2
David's La RGWD BH24 382 A3
David Wy PLE BH15 444 C6
Davis Cl LSOL/BMARY PO13 397 G8 1
Davis Fld NMIL/BTOS BH25 437 K6
Davis Gdns SHST GU47 70 B1
Davis Rd PSTN BH14 446 D3
Davy Cl KEMP RG22 104 D3
Dawkins Rd PLE BH15 444 C4
Dawkins Wy NMIL/BTOS BH25 437 L6
Daw La HISD PO11 401 K8
Dawlish Av WSHM SO15 318 C8
Dawnay Cl ROWN SO16 319 J3
Dawnay Rd CBLY GU15 50 D8 1
Dawn Cl NBNE BH10 432 A6
Dawn Gdns WINW SO22 238 B2
Daws Av BWD BH11 431 M6
Dawsmere Cl CBLY GU15 71 M3
Dawson Rd ITCH SO19 345 G6 1
RWIN SO21 145 H5
Day La HORN PO8 352 B1
Dayrell Cl TOTT SO40 316 A7
Day's Ct WIMB BH21 404 B4
Dayshes Cl LSOL/BMARY PO13 396 F5
Dayslondon Rd WVILLE PO7 376 B3
Deacon Cl ITCH SO19 344 E3
Deacon Crs ITCH SO19 344 E2
Deacon Gdns BWD BH11 431 L3
Deacon Rd BWD BH11 431 L3
HLER SO31 370 F5
ITCH SO19 344 E3
RAND SP11 116 B6
Deadbrook La ASHV GU12 113 H5
Deadmans La STHA RG19 37 L2
Deadmoor La KSCL RG20 37 H6
Deal Cl FHAM/STUB PO14 396 A4
Deal Rd CHAM PO6 375 J7
Dean Cl WINW SO22 214 B6
PLE BH15 444 D5
Dean Ct HEND SO30 345 M1
Deane Ct HAV PO9 377 M3 1
Deane Down Dro WINW SO22 214 A4
The Deanery CHFD SO53 265 G8
Deane's Cl BSTK RG21 5 G5
Deane's Park Rd
FHAM/PORC PO16 373 H7
Deanfield Cl HLER SO31 369 K6
Dean La BPWT SO32 297 K5
HORN PO8 354 B3
RSAL SP5 259 G4
RWIN SO21 213 K5
Dean Park Crs BMTH BH1 22 E4
WCLF BH2 22 E4
Dean Park Rd BMTH BH1 22 F4
WCLF BH2 22 F3
Dean Ri RAND SP11 96 E1
Dean Rd CHAM PO6 399 K1
ELGH SO50 295 G7
RSAL SP5 230 C5
WEND SO18 344 E1
Deans Cl NTID SP9 114 E4 2
Deans Ct LYMN SO41 454 C3
Deanscroft Rd NBNE BH10 432 C4
Deans Dell PSF GU32 246 D7
Deans Ga FHAM/STUB PO14 396 A7
Deans Gv WIMB BH21 404 B1
Deansleigh Rd LTDN BH7 433 M7
Dean's Rd BOSC BH5 449 G3
The Deans BMTH BH1 22 F3
Dean St PSEA PO1 20 D2 1
Dean Swift Crs PSTN BH14 446 B8
Deanswood Dr WVILLE PO7 352 C7
Deanswood Rd TADY RG26 41 K8
The Dean NALR SO24 218 B2
Dear Hay La PLE BH15 445 H6
Dearing Cl LYND SO43 363 K3
De Courtenai Cl BWD BH11 431 J3
Decouttere Cl FLET GU13 110 D3
Dee Cl CHFD SO53 292 F3
Deedman Cl ASHV GU12 113 K6 1
Deep Dene HASM GU27 228 B2
Deepdene RFNM GU10 159 G2
Deeping Cl ITCH SO19 344 D7 2
Deeping Ga WVILLE PO7 376 E1
Deep La BSTK RG21 4 A8
Deep Well Dr CBLY GU15 71 H3
Deerhurst Cl TOTT SO40 341 H2
Deerhurst Crs CHAM PO6 374 E7
Deer Leap FHAM PO15 372 B3 1
Deerleap La TOTT SO40 341 J8
Deerleap Wy FAWY SO45 367 L5
NMIL/BTOS BH25 437 M2
Deer Park Cl
NMIL/BTOS BH25 437 K4 1
Deer Rock Rd CBLY GU15 71 J1
Dee Wy PLE BH15 445 G6
Defender Rd ITCH SO19 344 B5
Defiant Rd FARN GU14 90 C8
De Grouchy La PTSW SO17 318 F7
De Havilland Cl WIMB BH21 404 D6
De Havilland Wy
CHCH/BSGR BH23 450 F3
Delamere Gdns NBNE BH10 432 C5
Delamere Rd ENEY PO4 21 M5
De La Warr Rd LYMN SO41 454 B4
Delft Cl HLER SO31 370 D5
Delft Gdns WVILLE PO7 352 B6
Delhi Cl PSTN BH14 446 C5
Delhi Rd NBNE BH10 432 C6
Delibes Rd KEMP RG22 104 E8
Delilah Rd PLE BH15 444 C6
De Lisle Cl NEND PO2 399 K4
De Lisle Rd TWDS BH3 447 L1
Delius Av ITCH SO19 345 H5
Delius Cl KEMP RG22 104 D7
Dellands OVTN RG25 123 M1
Dellands La OVTN RG25 100 E8
Dell Cl BDST BH18 429 J4
CHAM PO6 375 M6
ELGH SO50 295 H7
HASM GU27 228 D1
Dellcrest Pth CHAM PO6 375 M7
Dellfield DEAN RG23 103 G5
PSF GU32 246 D6
Dellfield Cl CHAM PO6 374 E7 1
Dell Gv FRIM GU16 71 J6
Dell Piece East HORN PO8 353 H3
Dell Piece West HORN PO8 353 G3
Dell Quay Cl FHAM/STUB PO14 396 E6
Dell Rd AND SP10 8 E2
EWKG RG40 48 D5
WEND SO18 319 L6
WINC SO23 239 G2
The Dell FHAM/PORC PO16 373 H7
FNM GU9 134 F1
HAV PO9 376 F6
KSCL RG20 59 J6
NMIL/BTOS BH25 437 G8
RAND SP11 73 H2
RAND SP11 140 A7
YTLY GU46 68 F3
Delme Dr FHAM/PORC PO16 373 H6
Delphi Wy WVILLE PO7 376 D6
Delph Rd WIMB BH21 404 B8
Delta Cl CHCH/BSGR BH23 450 F1
De-Lucy Av NALR SO24 218 A3
Delville Cl FARN GU14 90 A5
De Mauley Rd CCLF BH13 446 D8
De Montfort Rd NWBY RG14 25 G3
WIMB BH21 404 B7
De Mowbray Wy LYMN SO41 440 B6 1
Dempsey Cl ITCH SO19 344 F4
Denbigh Cl ELGH SO50 293 L3
TOTT SO40 341 H3
Denbigh Dr FHAM/PORC PO16 14 F3
Denbigh Gdns ROWN SO16 318 E4
Denbigh Rd HASM GU27 229 G3
Denby Rd PLE BH15 445 J4
Dene Cl HASM GU27 228 F2
HLER SO31 370 C4
BOR GU35 201 J6 2
NALR SO24 219 L3
RFNM GU10 159 G2
RGWD BH24 359 G7
ROWN SO16 318 E1
Dene Ct AND SP10 9 J7
Dene Hollow CHAM PO6 376 B8
Dene La RFNM GU10 159 G2
Dene La West RFNM GU10 159 G3
Dene Rd AND SP10 9 J7
FARN GU14 90 C5
TOTT SO40 341 G6
Deneside Copse LYMN SO41 439 M7
Deneside Gdns LYMN SO41 439 M6
The Dene NALR SO24 219 L4
Deneve Av CFDH BH17 430 A7
Dene Wk FERN BH22 406 C7
RFNM GU10 159 H2
Dene Wy NWBY RG14 25 J3
TOTT SO40 341 G5
Denewood Copse
FERN BH22 380 B5 1
Denewood Rd FERN BH22 380 B4
WBNE BH4 447 G6
Denewulf Cl BPWT SO32 297 H8 1
Denham Cl CFDH BH17 430 C5
FHAM/STUB PO14 395 M6
WINC SO23 10 F3
Denham Ct WINC SO23 11 G2
Denham Dr CHCH/BSGR BH23 436 D7
KEMP RG22 104 B6
YTLY GU46 69 H3 1
Denham Gdns HLER SO31 368 F3
Denhill Cl HISD PO11 425 J3
Denholm Cl RGWD BH24 359 H7
Denison Rd CFDH BH17 430 A7
Denman Cl FLET GU13 89 H7
Denmark La PLE BH15 445 J5
Denmark Rd
MOOR/WNTN BH9 432 D7
NWBY RG14 3 G4
PLE BH15 445 J5
Denmark Sq ASHV GU12 7 M1
Denmark St ASHV GU12 7 M1
Denmead NMIL/BTOS BH25 438 B4 2
Denmead Rd SBNE BH6 449 J1
TADY RG26 41 L8
WEND SO18 320 B8
Denning Cl FLET GU13 110 D1
Dennis Rd WIMB BH21 429 H3
Dennistoun Av
CHCH/BSGR BH23 450 E1
Dennistoun Cl CBLY GU15 71 G3 1
Dennis Wy LISS GU33 248 F5
Denny Cl FAWY SO45 392 F5 1
Denton Cl STHA RG19 26 F6
Denton Wy FRIM GU16 71 G6
Denville Av FHAM/PORC PO16 398 B2
Denville Cl CHAM PO6 376 D8
Denvilles Cl HAV PO9 17 J2
Denzil Av HLER SO31 369 G2
Depedene Cl FAWY SO45 391 M4
De Port Hts BPWT SO32 299 H2
Deptford La ODIM RG29 107 M5
Derby Flds ODIM RG29 108 B2
Derby Rd BMTH BH1 23 M4
ELGH SO50 293 L6
HASM GU27 228 E1
NEND PO2 399 H7
NWBY RG14 2 D7
SHAM SO14 13 J1
De Redvers Rd PSTN BH14 446 B6
Dereham Wy
BKME/WDN BH12 446 E2
Deridene Ct TOTT SO40 341 H2
Derlyn Rd FHAM/PORC PO16 15 H5
Derritt La CHCH/BSGR BH23 435 G1
Derrybrian Gdns
NMIL/BTOS BH25 437 L6 1
Derry Cl ASHV GU12 113 J3
Derry Rd FARN GU14 70 C7
Derwent Av ASHV GU12 113 J4
Derwent Cl FARN GU14 90 A4
FERN BH22 406 E2
FHAM/STUB PO14 396 B4 1
FNM GU9 134 D2
HORN PO8 328 B6
BOR GU35 201 J3 3
WEND SO18 320 A7
Derwent Dr TOTT SO40 316 A8
Derwent Gdns NALR SO24 218 C4
Derwent Rd KEMP RG22 103 M7
LSOL/BMARY PO13 420 D3
NMIL/BTOS BH25 437 M3
ROWN SO16 317 K7
STHA RG19 26 D5
Derwentwater Rd WIMB BH21 404 B6
Desborough Cl CHAM PO6 374 E7 2
Desborough Rd ELGH SO50 293 M6
Devenish Rd WINW SO22 10 B1
Dever Cl RWIN SO21 169 M5
Deverel Cl CHCH/BSGR BH23 434 E8
Deverell Pl WVILLE PO7 376 A5
Dever Wy DEAN RG23 103 G7
The Devil's Hwy CWTH RG45 49 H3
Devils La LIPH GU30 227 H5
Devine Gdns ELGH SO50 294 D6 1
Devon Cl FARN GU14 89 G4
SHST GU47 70 A1
Devon Dr CHFD SO53 293 H5
Devon Rd ALDT GU11 112 B1
CHCH/BSGR BH23 434 C8
HSEA PO3 399 L5
BOR GU35 201 J5
PLE BH15 445 K3
Devonshire Av ENEY PO4 423 L5
Devonshire Dr CBLY GU15 71 J1
Devonshire Gdns FAWY SO45 367 L8 1
HLER SO31 345 K6 1
HLER SO31 345 L6 3
Devonshire Pl ALDT GU11 6 C4
BSTK RG21 104 F4
Devonshire Rd WSHM SO15 343 K2
Devonshire Sq ENEY PO4 423 K4
Devonshire Wy
FHAM/STUB PO14 372 A8
Deweys La RAND SP11 92 E6
Dewlands Rd VWD BH31 356 B1
Dewlands Wy VWD BH31 356 B2
Dew La ELGH SO50 293 L5
Dewlish Cl CFDH BH17 430 E6
Dewpond Wk CHAM RG24 83 L8
Dexter Wy FARN GU14 89 G4 1
Dial Cl CHCH/BSGR BH23 410 A6
Diamond Cl FBDG SP6 309 K8 2
Diamond Hl CBLY GU15 71 G1
Diamond Rdg CBLY GU15 71 G1
Diamond St SSEA PO5 20 F5 2
Diamond Wy FARN GU14 90 B8
Diana Cl EMRTH PO10 378 C4
GPORT PO12 421 J4
KEMP RG22 104 D5
Diana Wy WIMB BH21 429 J1
Dibble Dr NBAD SO52 291 L5
Dibden Cl CHAR BH8 433 H5
HAV PO9 377 G4 1
Dibden Lodge Cl FAWY SO45 367 K3
Dibles Rd HLER SO31 370 B7
Dibley Cl KEMP RG22 104 B5
Dickens Cl NEND PO2 423 H1 1
Dickens Dell TOTT SO40 340 F1
Dickens Dr HLER SO31 347 G8
Dickens La CHAM RG24 105 M4
OVTN RG25 105 L6
Dickenson Wk NALR SO24 218 C4 1
Dickens Rd SBNE BH6 449 J1
Dickens Wy YTLY GU46 68 F4
Dicker's La ALTN GU34 176 F4
Dickson Pl WHAM PO17 348 E4
Dickson Rd RAND SP11 141 M1
Didcot Rd WSHM SO15 318 B7 1
Dieppe Crs NEND PO2 399 J4
Dieppe Gdns GPORT PO12 18 B3
Digby Rd NWBY RG14 2 B1
Diligence Cl HLER SO31 345 L7
Dilly La HTWY RG27 87 H4
NMIL/BTOS BH25 452 F1
Dimond Cl WEND SO18 319 K7
Dimond Hl WEND SO18 319 K7
Dimond Rd WEND SO18 319 K6
Dines Cl RAND SP11 96 C1
Dingle Rd BOSC BH5 449 G4
Dingle Wy HLER SO31 370 E4
Dingley Rd PLE BH15 445 J2
Dingley Wy FARN GU14 90 D8
Dinham Rd NMIL/BTOS BH25 438 B4 3
Dinorben Av FLET GU13 110 D1
Dinorben Beeches FLET GU13 110 D1
Dinorben Cl FLET GU13 110 E1
Dippenhall Rd RFNM GU10 133 L6
Dippenhall St RFNM GU10 133 J2
Diprose Rd WIMB BH21 429 J1
Discovery Cl
FHAM/STUB PO14 396 A3 1
Disraeli Rd CHCH/BSGR BH23 450 C2
Ditcham Crs HAV PO9 377 J4
Ditchbury LYMN SO41 440 B2
Ditton Cl FHAM/STUB PO14 396 A5
The Dittons EWKG RG40 48 C2 1
Divers Cl ALTN GU34 176 E2
Dixon Rd HTWY RG27 64 A8
Dixons La STOK SO20 209 G1
Dockenfield Cl HAV PO9 377 G4 1
Dockenfield St RFNM GU10
Dock La BROC SO42
Dock Rd GPORT PO12
Doctors Dro RAND SP11
Doctor's Hl ROMY SO51
Doctors La PSF GU32
Dodds La BPWT SO32
Dodgson Cl FBDG SP6
Dodwell La HLER SO31
Doe Copse Wy
NMIL/BTOS BH25
Dogflud Wy FNM GU9
Dogkennel La WVILLE PO7
Dogwood Dell WVILLE PO7 37
Dogwood Rd WIMB BH21
Doiley Bottom RAND SP11
Dolbery Rd North
BKME/WDN BH12
Dolbery Rd South
BKME/WDN BH12
Dollis Dr FNM GU9 13
Dollis Gn TADY RG26
Dolman Rd GPORT PO12
NWBY RG14
Dolomans La RAND SP11
Dolphin Av NBNE BH10
Dolphin Cl ELGH SO50
HASM GU27
Dolphin Ct
FHAM/STUB PO14 39
Dolphin Crs GPORT PO12
Dolphin Hl RWIN SO21
Dolphin Pl NMIL/BTOS BH25 45
Dolphin Wy GPORT PO12
Dolton Rd ROWN SO16
Doman Rd CBLY GU15
Dome Aly WINC SO23
Dominica Cl CHAM RG24
Dominion Rd BWD BH11
Domum Rd NEND PO2
WINC SO23
Domvilles Ap NEND PO2
Donaldson Rd CHAM PO6
Doncaster Rd ELGH SO50
Donigers Dell BPWT SO32
Donlan Dr FARN GU14
Donnelly Rd SBNE BH6
Donnelly St GPORT PO12
Donnington Cl CBLY GU15
Donnington Dr
CHCH/BSGR BH23
CHFD SO53
Donnington Gv PTSW SO17
Donnington Pk NWBY RG14
Donnington Sq NWBY RG14
Donoughmore Rd BMTH BH1
Dora's Green La RFNM GU10
Dorcas Cl WVILLE PO7 35
Dorcas Ct CBLY GU15
Dorchester Cl DEAN RG23
Dorchester Gdns PLE BH15
Dorchester Rd HTWY RG27
PLE BH15
Dorchester Wy ODIM RG29
Dore Av FHAM/PORC PO16
Doreen Cl FARN GU14
Dores La ROMY SO51
RWIN SO21
Dorian Gv NALR SO24
Doric Cl CHFD SO53
Dorking Crs CHAM PO6
Dorland Gdns TOTT SO40
Dormer Cl CWTH RG45
NWBY RG14
Dormington Rd CHAM PO6
Dormy Cl HLER SO31
Dormy Wy LSOL/BMARY PO13
Dornie Rd CCLF BH13
Dornmere La WVILLE PO7 37
Dorothy Dymond St
PSEA PO1
Dorrel Cl KEMP RG22
Dorrien Rd GPORT PO12
Dorrita Av HORN PO8
Dorrita Cl ENEY PO4
The Dorrits TOTT SO40
Dorset Av FERN BH22
Dorset Cl HORN PO8
Dorset Lake Av PSTN BH14
Dorset Rd ASHV GU12
CHCH/BSGR BH23
CHFD SO53 29
WBNE BH4
Dorset St PTSW SO17
Dorset Wy BKME/WDN BH12
PLE BH15
Dorstone Rd CHAM PO6 37
Doswell Wy BSTK RG21
Douai Cl FARN GU14
Doublet Cl STHA RG19
Doughty Wy AND SP10
Douglas Av CHCH/BSGR BH23
Douglas Cl UPTN BH16
Douglas Crs ITCH SO19
Douglas Gdns
BKME/WDN BH12
HAV PO9 37
Douglas Gv RFNM GU10
Douglas Ride KSCL RG20
Douglas Rd BKME/WDN BH12
PSEA PO1
RAND SP11
SBNE BH6
Douglas Wy FAWY SO45
Doulton Gdns PSTN BH14
Doussie Cl UPTN BH16
Dove Cl AND SP10 11
HORN PO8
KEMP RG22
Dove Dl ELGH SO50
Dovedale Cl SHST GU47
Dove Gdns HLER SO31 37
Dover Cl CCLF BH13
DEAN RG23
FHAM/STUB PO14
NALR SO24
Dover Ct HISD PO11
Dovercourt Rd CHAM PO6

d CCLF BH13 446 F5
PO3 399 L8
t SHAM SO14 343 L1
ill Crs NBNE BH10 432 B5
ill Gdns NBNE BH10 432 B5
a RSAL SP5 258 F5
n Wy NWBY RG14 3 H1
Cl RGWD BH24 384 E5 1
n Gv ALTN GU34 176 E3
g Ct CWTH RG45 49 M2 1
Cl HEND SO30 321 G8
ds Rd NBNE BH10 432 A4
nd CHAM PO6 376 A7
nd Rd CHAM PO6 376 A7
nd Rd
/PORC PO16 373 L6
Cl BWD BH11 431 K6
arm La WINW SO22 190 B8
arm Pl HORN PO8 328 B7 3
a NALR SO24 218 B4
am Cl HORN PO8 352 D5
ouse Rd HORN PO8 327 M4
g St FNM GU9 134 E6
nd Cl HEND SO30 346 D1
SO31 370 E4
nd Pl HEND SO30 345 M4
nds Cl RSAL SP5 284 E2
nds Rd WINW SO22 238 A4
nds Wy RWIN SO21 190 C4
a OVTN RG25 106 F6
y Rd HAV PO9 377 M4
odge Cl FBDG SP6 333 L2 2
d HORN PO8 328 A7
SP11 115 L5
Cl WVILLE PO7 376 D5
roft Gdns
SO30 321 G8 2
SO30 345 M1 1
de GSHT GU26 204 A1 1
BMARY PO13 397 H6
de Av ITCH SO19 344 E2
de Rd WINW SO22 214 A6
E PO7 376 A5 1
and Rd BSTK RG21 4 B9
La MARL SN8 53 G1
Park Av TOTT SO40 341 L2
Park Crs TOTT SO40 341 L2
Park Rd TOTT SO40 341 L2
Rd RWIN SO21 190 B4
SO20 162 B5
t OVTN RG25 126 C7
Vw ALTN GU34 177 K1
view Rd BOR GU35 202 F3
view Wy RAND SP11 115 J2
Wy ALTN GU34 176 C6
wnsway
/PORC PO16 374 A8
on Cl CHAR BH8 433 G5
on Hl RSAL SP5 285 H1
on La LYMN SO41 453 L2
on Rd WEND SO18 319 L6
iew Cl GSHT GU26 204 A2
iew Rd FBDG SP6 280 F4
ood Cl FAWY SO45 367 G6 1
SP6 309 J6
ood Wy HORN PO8 328 B7
v NEND PO2 399 J4
l NEND PO2 399 J4
t ITCH SO19 344 D7
dns YTLY GU46 68 F3 2
Rd PSTN BH14 446 D4
ld La BPWT SO32 325 H8
fly Dr CHAM RG24 83 L8 4
La RGWD BH24 382 E8
St EPSF GU31 275 L6
n Cl ITCH SO19 345 G4
n Ct ALDT GU11 6 B2 2
n Wy CHCH/BSGR BH23 449 L1
v FRIM GU16 91 K7
l EWKG RG40 48 B1
SO31 370 F3
BTOS BH25 437 K5
BH24 359 G7
SO40 342 D6
ys Fld LIPH GU30 250 E6
d ELGH SO50 294 D4
BMARY PO13 420 B1
Cl FAWY SO45 367 K6 3
Cl STHA RG19 27 G6
Rd BWD BH11 431 L4
/BSGR BH23 450 D1
e Rd HORN PO8 328 B5
t Rd NBNE BH10 432 B6
n's Wy ALTN GU34 176 E5
n Cl ITCH SO19 344 D8
n La CHAM PO6 375 M7
n Pl TOTT SO40 341 H1 1
n Rd NEND PO2 399 J7
n St WINW SO22 238 B2
ought Rd
/STUB PO14 396 C3
n Dr HORN PO8 352 B6
ck Cl CHCH/BSGR BH23 434 B4
BKME/WDN BH12 447 H1
FHAM/PORC PO16 15 M3
PO8 328 A3
U35 201 G8
SO20 166 E6
t HAV PO9 353 M7
y Rd HTWY RG27 86 B7
od Gdns ENEY PO4 424 A6
SO40 341 G2 4
ed Rd NEND PO2 398 F7
ater Cl ELGH SO50 293 L5
ve DEAN RG23 103 G7
H PO10 379 H8
/PORC PO16 15 G5
GU9 158 E1
O9 16 E1
SO30 320 A5
BMARY PO13 396 E6
RG14 2 B9
SO51 259 L7
SO51 288 F6
SO40 341 K3
l RWIN SO21 266 E3
Hl STOK SO20 165 M5
a NALR SO24 217 M2

Drove Rd ITCH SO19 344 F4
STOK SO20 165 M5
WHAM PO17 374 E4
Drovers End FARN GU14 89 H4
Drovers Wy ASHV GU12 113 M7
FNM GU9 134 D2
The Drove AND SP10 8 B4
BPWT SO32 296 C8
BPWT SO32 324 A3
ELGH SO50 321 J2
FAWY SO45 392 C7
HEND SO30 320 E5
ROMY SO51 288 D5
RWIN SO21 266 E3
TOTT SO40 316 A7
WEND SO18 344 E1
Droxford Cl GPORT PO12 18 B3 1
Droxford Crs TADY RG26 61 K1
Droxford Rd BPWT SO32 324 B4
LTDN BH7 449 G2
Druce Wy STHA RG19 27 G5
Druids Cl FERN BH22 406 B6
Druitt Rd CHCH/BSGR BH23 435 K8
Drum Md PSF GU32 275 K5
Drummond Cl ALTN GU34 196 E6 1
WINW SO22 238 D3 1
Drummond Rd BMTH BH1 448 C4
FAWY SO45 367 L4 4
HEND SO30 321 H7
PSEA PO1 423 H2 2
Drummond Wy CHFD SO53 265 G8 3
Drury Cl WHCH RG28 121 J8
Drury La ALTN GU34 174 F3
THLE RG7 43 L4
Dryden Av CHAM PO6 374 C7
Dryden Cl FHAM/PORC PO16 14 F4
NTHA RG18 26 F3
RGWD BH24 381 J3
WVILLE PO7 352 B6
Dryden Pl LYMN SO41 454 C3
Dryden Rd FARN GU14 90 C2
ITCH SO19 345 J3
Dryden Wy LIPH GU30 226 D3
Drysdale Ms ENEY PO4 423 M6 1
Duchess Cl ALTN GU34 176 D5 2
CWTH RG45 49 L1 1
Duchess of Kent Barracks
ALDT GU11 112 E5
Ducking Stool La
CHCH/BSGR BH23 450 A2
Duck Island La RGWD BH24 382 E2 2
Ducklands BOR GU35 201 K6 3
Duck La BWD BH11 431 K4
Duckmead La LISS GU33 249 G2
Ducks La STOK SO20 184 E2
Duddon Cl WEND SO18 320 A7
Duddon Wy BSTK RG21 5 K8
Dudleston Heath Dr
HORN PO8 352 F6
Dudley Av FBDG SP6 309 L5
LYMN SO41 438 D6
Dudley Cl DEAN RG23 104 A3
BOR GU35 201 H7
Dudley Rd HSEA PO3 423 L1 1
NBNE BH10 432 B3
Dudmoor Farm Rd
CHCH/BSGR BH23 434 D5
Dudmoor La CHCH/BSGR BH23 434 D4
Dudsbury Av FERN BH22 406 B4
Dudsbury Crs FERN BH22 406 B4
Dudsbury Gdns FERN BH22 406 C8
Dudsbury Rd FERN BH22 406 B6
Duffield La EMRTH PO10 379 H5
Dugald Drummond St
PSEA PO1 21 G2 3
Dugdell Cl FERN BH22 406 D2 1
Duisburg Wy SSEA PO5 20 E6
Duke Crs PSEA PO1 423 H1
Duke of Cornwall Av
CBLY GU15 51 G7
Duke Rd HEND SO30 346 B3
Dukes Cl ALTN GU34 176 C6
FNM GU9 134 D2 3
PSF GU32 275 J4
Dukes Dr BWD BH11 431 J3
Dukesfield CHCH/BSGR BH23 434 B6
Dukes Md FLET GU13 88 C7
Dukes Pk ALDT GU11 113 G2
Duke's Ride CWTH RG45 49 J4
THLE RG7 42 E8
Dukes Rd GPORT PO12 421 L2
SHAM SO14 319 G8
Duke St RWIN SO21 170 A5
SHAM SO14 13 J5
Dukes Wd CWTH RG45 49 L3
Dukeswood Dr FAWY SO45 367 K7
Dulsie Rd TWDS BH3 447 H1
Dumas Cl YTLY GU46 68 F3 3
Du Maurier Cl FLET GU13 110 D5
Dumbarton Cl NEND PO2 399 H8 2
Dumbleton Cl ITCH SO19 345 K4
Dummer Ct HAV PO9 377 H2
Dummer Down La OVTN RG25 150 A1
Dummer La RAND SP11 72 A8
Dummers Rd ROMY SO51 263 J1
Dumpers Dro ELGH SO50 321 J2
Dumpford La EPSF GU31 277 L8
Dump Rd FARN GU14 90 B7
Dunbar Cl ROWN SO16 317 L3
Dunbar Crs CHCH/BSGR BH23 436 D6
Dunbar Rd ENEY PO4 423 M4
FRIM GU16 91 J1
TWDS BH3 447 K2
Dunbridge La ROMY SO51 233 K8
Duncan Cl ITCH SO19 344 C8
Duncan Rd HLER SO31 370 F3
NMIL/BTOS BH25 438 B4
SSEA PO5 21 K7
Duncan's Cl RAND SP11 116 D6
Duncans Dr
FHAM/STUB PO14 371 M8 1
Duncliff Rd SBNE BH6 449 M4
Duncombe Dr RGWD BH24 357 M6
Duncombe Rd PSF GU32 273 J8
Duncton Rd HORN PO8 328 C3
Dundaff Cl CBLY GU15 71 K3
Dundas Cl HSEA PO3 399 M6
Dundas La HSEA PO3 399 M7

Dundas Rd CFDH BH17 430 C8
Dundas Sp HSEA PO3 399 M6
Dundee Cl FHAM PO15 14 D2
Dundee Rd PTSW SO17 319 H7
Dundonald Cl HISD PO11 425 L3
ITCH SO19 344 B7 1
Dundridge La BPWT SO32 297 K7
Dundry Wy HEND SO30 346 A1
Dunedin Cl FERN BH22 405 M5
NTID SP9 114 F2
Dunedin Dr FERN BH22 405 M5
Dunedin Gdns FERN BH22 405 M5
Dunedin Gv CHCH/BSGR BH23 451 H1
Dunford Cl NMIL/BTOS BH25 437 J8 2
Dunford Rd BKME/WDN BH12 446 C3
Dungells Farm Cl YTLY GU46 69 G4 1
Dungells La YTLY GU46 68 F4
Dunhills La RAND SP11 96 B8
Dunhurst Cl HAV PO9 377 L5
Dunkeld Rd GPORT PO12 421 L1
TWDS BH3 447 J2
Dunkirk Cl ROWN SO16 318 C4
Dunkirk Rd ROWN SO16 318 C4
Dunkirt La RAND SP11 141 K5
Dunley's Hl ODIM RG29 108 B5
Dunlin Cl CHCH/BSGR BH23 451 G3
ENEY PO4 424 B3
Dunmow Hl FLET GU13 88 F6
Dunmow Rd AND SP10 9 K8
Dunn Cl ENEY PO4 423 M5
Dunnings La NBAD SO52 291 K3
Dunnock Cl HAV PO9 353 M7
Dunsbury Wy HAV PO9 377 J3
Dunsell's La NALR SO24 220 C3
Dunsford Crs DEAN RG23 104 B1
Dunsmore Cl SSEA PO5 21 H4 2
Dunsmore Gdns YTLY GU46 68 D3
Dunstall Pk FARN GU14 90 D1
Dunstan Rd NTHA RG18 27 H4
Dunstan's Dro RAND SP11 74 B7
Dunstans La PSTN BH14 445 L2
Dunster Cl ROWN SO16 318 B3
Dunvegan Dr ROWN SO16 318 B3
Dunyeats Rd BDST BH18 429 M4
Durban Cl ROMY SO51 262 F7
Durban Rd PSEA PO1 423 K1
Durbidges STHA RG19 39 H8
Durdells Av BWD BH11 431 L3
Durdells Gdns BWD BH11 431 L3
Durford Ct HAV PO9 377 H2 1
Durford Rd EPSF GU31 276 B5
Durham Gdns WVILLE PO7 376 D3
Durham Rd SHST GU47 50 B6
Durham St GPORT PO12 421 L2
PSEA PO1 21 H1
Durham Wy KEMP RG22 104 A8 3
Durland Cl NMIL/BTOS BH25 437 L7
Durlands Rd HORN PO8 328 B8 1
Durley Av HORN PO8 352 D5
Durley Brook Rd BPWT SO32 321 L2
Durley Chine Rd WCLF BH2 22 B6
Durley Chine Rd South
WCLF BH2 22 B8
Durley Cl AND SP10 8 C7
Durley Crs TOTT SO40 341 H3
Durley Gdns WCLF BH2 22 B8
Durley Hall La BPWT SO32 296 A7
Durley Rd ELGH SO50 321 K1
GPORT PO12 421 L2
WCLF BH2 22 C7
Durley Rd South WCLF BH2 22 C7
Durley Rbt WCLF BH2 22 B7
Durley St BPWT SO32 322 C1
Durlston Crs CHCH/BSGR BH23 434 B4
Durlston Rd PSTN BH14 446 B6
ROWN SO16 317 H7
Durnford Cl STOK SO20 165 M4
Durnford Rd SHAM SO14 343 M2
Durngate Pl WINC SO23 11 J7
Durngate Ter WINC SO23 11 J7
Durnsford Av FLET GU13 110 F1
Durnstown LYMN SO41 413 G6
Durrant Rd PSTN BH14 446 B5
WCLF BH2 22 D4
Durrants Gdns HAV PO9 353 M8
Durrants Rd HAV PO9 377 M1
Durrant Wy LYMN SO41 412 F6
Durrington Rd LTDN BH7 449 G1
Dursley Crs CHAM PO6 375 G8
Dutton La ELGH SO50 294 A5
Duttons Rd ROMY SO51 262 D8
Dyer Rd WSHM SO15 343 G1
Dymewood Rd WIMB BH21 380 C1
Dymoke St EMRTH PO10 378 C4
Dymott Cl WSHM SO15 12 A1
Dyram Cl ELGH SO50 293 L3
Dysart Av CHAM PO6 399 M1
Dyserth Cl ITCH SO19 344 F7
Dyson Dr WINC SO23 11 H2
Dysons Cl NWBY RG14 2 B4

E

Eadens La TOTT SO40 340 B1
Eagle Av HORN PO8 352 B4
Eagle Cl ALTN GU34 176 E2
CHFD SO53 293 G4
CWTH RG45 49 K1
FHAM/PORC PO16 373 K8 3
KEMP RG22 103 L8 1
Eagle Rd BKME/WDN BH12 446 F4
FARN GU14 90 E6
KSCL RG20 38 D6
LSOL/BMARY PO13 420 B1
Eagles Nest SHST GU47 49 K7 2
Eames La LISS GU33 223 L8
Eardley Av AND SP10 8 A3
Earle Rd WBNE BH4 447 H7
Earlham Dr PSTN BH14 446 B4
Earlsbourne FLET GU13 111 G4
Earls Cl ELGH SO50 294 F6
Earlsdon St SSEA PO5 21 G4 2
Earlsdon Wy CHCH/BSGR BH23 436 D8
Earls Gv CBLY GU15 71 H2
Earls Rd FHAM/PORC PO16 15 J9
SHAM SO14 318 F8

Earlswood Dr FBDG SP6 333 K3
Earnley Rd HISD PO11 426 D6
Earthpits La RSAL SP5 280 A6
East Av FNM GU9 135 G2
NMIL/BTOS BH25 452 B1
TWDS BH3 447 H2
East Bank Rd BROC SO42 387 L8
East Boldre Rd BROC SO42 416 A1
Eastbourne Av GPORT PO12 397 L8
WSHM SO15 318 C8
Eastbourne Rd HSEA PO3 399 L8 1
Eastbrook Cl GPORT PO12 397 K8 1
HLER SO31 370 E3
Eastbrooke Rd ALTN GU34 176 F4
East Cams Cl
FHAM/PORC PO16 373 K7 2
Eastchurch Cl ROWN SO16 317 L4
Eastcliff Cl LSOL/BMARY PO13 420 C1
East Cliff Wy
CHCH/BSGR BH23 451 H1
East Cl NMIL/BTOS BH25 437 H8
East Cosham Rd CHAM PO6 375 M8
Eastcot Cl FAWY SO45 391 M5
East Ct CHAM PO6 375 M8
Eastcroft Rd GPORT PO12 18 C1
East Dean Rd ROMY SO51 232 C6
East Dr ELGH SO50 294 C4
Eastern Av AND SP10 9 J7
HSEA PO3 423 M2
Eastern La CWTH RG45 50 C4
Eastern Pde ENEY PO4 423 K7
FHAM/PORC PO16 15 K9
Eastern Rd ASHV GU12 7 M2
CHAM PO6 400 B2
ENEY PO4 423 M3
HAV PO9 17 G3
HEND SO30 320 C7
HSEA PO3 400 A4
BOR GU35 201 J2
LYMN SO41 440 B4
NEND PO2 398 F6
Eastern Villas Rd ENEY PO4 423 H7 2
Eastern Wy FHAM/PORC PO16 15 L6
LYMN SO41 454 E4
Easter Rd MOOR/WNTN BH9 432 E6
Eastfield Av BSTK RG21 5 G8
FHAM/STUB PO14 396 D2
Eastfield Cl AND SP10 9 L5
East Field Cl EMRTH PO10 379 J6
Eastfield Cl RGWD BH24 383 G1
Eastfield La EPSF GU31 305 K5
RGWD BH24 359 G8
Eastfield Rd AND SP10 9 J5
CHAM PO6 374 F6
ENEY PO4 423 L5
Eastgate St SHAM SO14 13 G5
WINC SO23 11 J8
East Gn BLKW GU17 69 M4
East Harting St EPSF GU31 305 J5
East Hl LYMN SO41 440 C4
WINC SO23 239 G2
East Hill Cl FHAM/PORC PO16 373 H6
East Hill Dr LISS GU33 248 F5
East Hoe Rd WVILLE PO7 325 M5
East House Av
FHAM/STUB PO14 396 B6
East Howe La NBNE BH10 432 A4
Eastlake Av BKME/WDN BH12 446 A2
Eastlake Cl EPSF GU31 276 B5
Eastlands NMIL/BTOS BH25 437 M7
East La LYMN SO41 439 J7
NALR SO24 217 L4
Eastleigh Rd ELGH SO50 295 H7
East Leigh Rd HAV PO9 378 A5
East Ldg FHAM PO15 372 A7
East Lodge Pk CHAM PO6 376 D8
Eastlyn Rd TADY RG26 42 B7
Eastman Cl RSAL SP5 284 F2 1
Eastmans Fld STOK SO20 165 M5
Eastmead FARN GU14 90 E4
Eastmeare Ct TOTT SO40 341 G2
Eastney Farm Rd ENEY PO4 424 A5 1
Eastney Rd ENEY PO4 423 M5
Eastney St ENEY PO4 423 M6 2
Eastoke Av HISD PO11 426 B7
Easton Common Hl RSAL SP5 207 H2
Easton La RWIN SO21 215 J6
WINC SO23 11 L6
East Overcliff Dr BMTH BH1 23 H7
Eastover Ct HAV PO9 377 H2
East Park Ter SHAM SO14 13 G1
East Portway AND SP10 118 B8
East Quay Rd PLE BH15 445 H7
East Rd FAWY SO45 368 B8
RWIN SO21 167 K1
WHAM PO17 374 E2
Eastrop La BSTK RG21 5 G8
Eastrop Rbt BSTK RG21 5 G7
Eastrop Wy BSTK RG21 5 G7
Eastshaw La MIDH GU29 279 M4
East Station Rd ASHV GU12 7 G3
East Strd SELS PO20 427 K8
East St AND SP10 9 J6
EMRTH PO10 378 F5
FHAM/PORC PO16 15 M6
FHAM/STUB PO14 371 K8
FNM GU9 134 F6
HAV PO9 16 F5
NALR SO24 218 C2
PLE BH15 445 H6
PSEA PO1 20 B4
SHAM SO14 13 G4
WVILLE PO7 326 C5
East Surrey St PSEA PO1 21 H1 2
East View Rd RGWD BH24 382 F1
Eastville Rd ELGH SO50 295 H7 1
East Wy CHAR BH8 432 F7
WIMB BH21 429 H3
Eastways BPWT SO32 323 H1
Eastwood ROMY SO51 260 B7
Eastwood Av FERN BH22 406 C2
Eastwood Cl HISD PO11 425 M4
East Woodhay Rd
WINW SO22 214 C4 2
Eastwood Rd NEND PO2 399 J4 1
Eastworth Rd VWD BH31 356 C1
Eaton Rd CBLY GU15 70 E4
CCLF BH13 446 F6

E Av FAWY SO45 392 C3
Ebble Cl NTID SP9 114 E1
Ebden Rd WINC SO23 11 K6
Ebery Gv HSEA PO3 423 M2
Ebor Cl FERN BH22 406 C6
Ebor Rd BKME/WDN BH12 446 C2
Ecchinswell Rd KSCL RG20 59 G6
Eccles Rd PLE BH15 444 F6
Echo Barn La RFNM GU10 158 B3
Ecton La HSEA PO3 400 A5
Eddeys Cl BOR GU35 202 E2 1
Eddeys La BOR GU35 202 E3
Eddy Rd ASHV GU12 7 J3
Edelvale Rd WEND SO18 320 A7
Edelweiss Cl RAND SP11 92 E7
Edenbridge Rd ENEY PO4 423 M3
Eden Gv WIMB BH21 404 B5
Eden Ri FHAM/PORC PO16 15 J8
Eden Rd WEND SO18 320 A6
Eden St PSEA PO1 423 G2 2
Eden Wk CHFD SO53 292 F3
Edgar Cl AND SP10 119 G4
Edgar Crs FHAM/PORC PO16 398 B2
Edgar Rd WINC SO23 238 E2
Edgarton Rd CFDH BH17 430 B5
Edgbarrowhill Star CWTH RG45 49 K5
Edgbarrow Ri SHST GU47 49 K6
Edgcumbe Park Dr CWTH RG45 49 K3
Edgecombe Crs
LSOL/BMARY PO13 397 G8
Edgecombe La NWBY RG14 25 M3
Edgedale Cl CWTH RG45 49 L4 1
Edgefield Gv HORN PO8 353 G7
Edgehill Cl KEMP RG22 104 A5
Edgehill Rd MOOR/WNTN BH9 432 C8
WEND SO18 319 L7
Edgell Rd EMRTH PO10 378 F4
Edgemoor Rd FERN BH22 380 F7
FRIM GU16 71 M5 1
Edgerly Gdns CHAM PO6 399 K2
Edgeware Rd ENEY PO4 423 L3
Edgewood Cl CWTH RG45 49 K1 1
Edifred Rd MOOR/WNTN BH9 432 E4
Edinburgh Rd PSEA PO1 20 F1
PSEA PO1 21 G1 1
WINC SO23 191 G7
Edington Cl BPWT SO32 297 G8 2
Edington Rd WINC SO23 11 G3
Edith Haisman Cl WSHM SO15 12 B1
Edmondsham Rd VWD BH31 332 C8
Edmund Rd ENEY PO4 21 M5
Edmunds Cl HEND SO30 346 B3
NMIL/BTOS BH25 437 L7
Edney Cl FLET GU13 111 G2
Edneys La WVILLE PO7 351 L3
Edric's Gn AMSY SP4 138 C7
Edward Av CBLY GU15 70 D3
ELGH SO50 294 C4
Edward Cl FAWY SO45 392 C7 1
Edward Gdns HAV PO9 377 G7
Edward Gv FHAM/PORC PO16 374 C7
Edward Rd ALTN GU34 176 F3
BWD BH11 431 M5
CHCH/BSGR BH23 435 K8
FAWY SO45 367 L4
FNM GU9 158 F1
PSTN BH14 446 B3
WINC SO23 238 D4
WSHM SO15 342 F1
Edwards Cl CHAM PO6 374 F7 3
WVILLE PO7 352 D6
Edward St ALDT GU11 6 D2
Edwina Cl ITCH SO19 344 D2
NBAD SO52 291 M4
RGWD BH24 359 G7
Edwina Dr CFDH BH17 429 M6
Edwin Cl STHA RG19 27 J5
Eeklo Pl NWBY RG14 2 F8
Eelmoor Br ALDT GU11 111 M2
Eelmoor Plain Rd ALDT GU11 112 A4
Eelmoor Rd ALDT GU11 112 A3
FARN GU14 90 C6
Effingham Gdns ITCH SO19 345 G4
Efford Wy LYMN SO41 439 M6
Egan Cl NEND PO2 399 K5
Egbert Rd WINC SO23 11 G4
Egbury Rd RAND SP11 97 M6
Egdon Ct UPTN BH16 444 A1 2
Egdon Dr WIMB BH21 404 C8
Egerton Rd CBLY GU15 70 C2
CHAR BH8 448 C2
SHST GU47 70 B2
Eggars Cl ALTN GU34 177 G4
Eggars Fld RFNM GU10 157 G3
Eggar's Hl ALDT GU11 6 E6
Eggleton Cl FLET GU13 110 D3 2
Eglantine Cl HORN PO8 352 F4
Eglantine Wk HORN PO8 352 F4
Eglinton Rd RFNM GU10 181 L2
Egmont Cl RGWD BH24 382 A6
Egmont Dr RGWD BH24 382 B6
Egmont Gdns RGWD BH24 382 B6
Egmont Rd UPTN BH16 444 A4
Eight Acres ROMY SO51 291 G1 1
Elaine Gdns HORN PO8 352 D3
Elan Cl WEND SO18 320 A7
Eland Rd ASHV GU12 7 L4
Elbe Wy AND SP10 118 E5
Elbow Cnr BSTK RG21 4 E8
Elcombes Cl LYND SO43 363 K3
Elderberry Bank CHAM RG24 83 L8
Elderberry Cl HORN PO8 328 C4
Elderberry La
CHCH/BSGR BH23 450 E2
Elderberry Rd BOR GU35 201 M3
Elderberry Wy HORN PO8 352 F4
Elder Cl WINW SO22 238 B4
HLER SO31 370 D6 3
TOTT SO40 342 E7
Elderfield Cl EMRTH PO10 378 E5
Elderfield Rd HAV PO9 377 H1
Elder Gn RWIN SO21 266 F8
Eldergrove FARN GU14 91 H6 4
Elder Rd HAV PO9 17 K1
Eldon Av NMIL/BTOS BH25 437 J8
Eldon Cl NMIL/BTOS BH25 437 J8
STOK SO20 210 F6
Eldon Dr RFNM GU10 159 G3

Eldon Rd MOOR/WNTN BH9 432 C7
STOK SO20 210 F7
Eldon St SSEA PO5 21 G4
Eldridge Gdns ROMY SO51 262 E8
Eleanor Cl LIPH GU30 202 A8
Eleanor Ct RAND SP11 92 D6
Eleanor Dr BWD BH11 431 H3
Electron Wy CHFD SO53 293 H2
Elettra Av WVILLE PO7 352 B8
Elfin Dr FERN BH22 406 A1
Elgar Av CWTH RG45 49 L2
Elgar Cl CHAM PO6 374 C8 1
GPORT PO12 18 B8
KEMP RG22 104 D8
Elgar Rd ITCH SO19 345 G5
NBNE BH10 432 B4
Elgar Wk WVILLE PO7 376 D4 1
Elgin Cl FAWY SO45 367 L5
FHAM PO15 14 E3
Elgin Rd BLKW GU17 69 H7
CHAM PO6 399 K2
PSTN BH14 446 A6
WBNE BH4 22 A1
WSHM SO15 12 A1
Elgin Wy FRIM GU16 91 J1
Eling Cl WINW SO22 214 C5
Eling Ct HAV PO9 377 H2
Eling Hl TOTT SO40 341 M3
Eling La TOTT SO40 341 L2
Eliot Cl CBLY GU15 71 L1
NTHA RG18 26 F3
Eliot Dr HASM GU27 228 B2
Elise Cl LTDN BH7 433 M8
Elizabethan Ri OVTN RG25 125 K6
Elizabeth Av CHCH/BSGR BH23 434 D8
NWBY RG14 37 G1
Elizabeth Cl HEND SO30 320 C7
RSAL SP5 284 C1
WHAM PO17 348 D4 1
WINC SO23 191 G7
Elizabeth Ct
FHAM/STUB PO14 396 D1 1
Elizabeth Crs LYMN SO41 438 E6
Elizabeth Dr FLET GU13 110 F3
Elizabeth Gdns ENEY PO4 423 K6
FAWY SO45 367 L7
Elizabeth Rd
FHAM/STUB PO14 396 B6
KEMP RG22 104 D4
PLE BH15 445 J5
WHAM PO17 348 E4
WIMB BH21 404 A3
WVILLE PO7 376 D2
Elizabeth Wy BPWT SO32 323 G1
Elkhams Cl LYMN SO41 439 H7
Elkstone Rd CHAM PO6 374 F7
Ellachie Gdns GPORT PO12 18 E9
Ellachie Ms GPORT PO12 18 E9
Ellachie Rd GPORT PO12 18 E9
Elland Cl ELGH SO50 295 H7
Ellanore La SELS PO20 427 K5
Elldene Ct TOTT SO40 341 J3 1
Ellen Dr FARN GU14 89 H4
Ellen Gdns CHFD SO53 292 F3
TADY RG26 63 K5
Elleray Ct ASHV GU12 113 K3
Ellerslie Cl FHAM/STUB PO14 395 L7
Ellery Gv LYMN SO41 440 C3
Elles Cl FARN GU14 90 E5
Ellesfield Dr FERN BH22 406 B5
Ellesmere Orch EMRTH PO10 378 F4
Elles Rd FARN GU14 90 B6
Ellingham Cl NALR SO24 218 C3 2
Ellingham Dr RGWD BH24 358 C3
Ellingham Dro RGWD BH24 358 D3
Ellingham Rd
NMIL/BTOS BH25 437 H8
Ellington Cl RAND SP11 142 A1
Ellington Dr KEMP RG22 127 H1
Elliot Cl TOTT SO40 341 H2
Elliot Ri HEND SO30 321 H6
Elliott Rd BWD BH11 431 J5
Ellisfield Rd HAV PO9 377 J4
Ellison Wy RFNM GU10 136 C1
Ellis Rd CWTH RG45 49 L2
ITCH SO19 345 J3
Ellwood Av ITCH SO19 345 J3
Ellwood Cl ITCH SO19 345 J2
Elm Av CHCH/BSGR BH23 434 C7
LYMN SO41 440 A7
NMIL/BTOS BH25 437 L6
Elm Bank YTLY GU46 68 F1 1
Elm Bank Rd AND SP10 9 H7
Elm Cl HISD PO11 425 L5
BOR GU35 201 K5
RAND SP11 93 G6
RAND SP11 116 C8
STOK SO20 163 G4
Elm Crs BPWT SO32 296 D2
FAWY SO45 391 L1
FNM GU9 135 G1
Elmcroft Cl FRIM GU16 91 J1 1
Elmdale Cl HLER SO31 370 B8
Elmdale Gv ROMY SO51 288 F7
Elm Dr TLHT RG30 31 L3
Elmers Wy CHCH/BSGR BH23 409 M7
Elmes Dr WSHM SO15 342 D1
Elmes Rd MOOR/WNTN BH9 432 C6
Elmeswelle Rd HORN PO8 352 E2
Elm Farm Gv KSCL RG20 59 J6 1
Elmfield Cl RSAL SP5 285 J3
Elm Gdns HEND SO30 320 C6
WBNE BH4 447 H3
Elmgate Dr LTDN BH7 448 E1
Elm Gv ELGH SO50 293 L6
FNM GU9 134 F1
GPORT PO12 18 F1
HISD PO11 425 L5
KSCL RG20 59 J6
NTHA RG18 26 E3
SSEA PO5 21 H5
Elm Grove Rd FARN GU14 90 E4
Elmhurst TADY RG26 61 L1
Elmhurst Rd FERN BH22 380 D7
FHAM/PORC PO16 15 J7
GPORT PO12 19 G3
NTHA RG18 26 D3
Elmhurst Wy FERN BH22 380 D6
Elm La HAV PO9 16 E4
RFNM GU10 113 J8
Elmleigh Rd HAV PO9 16 E2
Elmore Av LSOL/BMARY PO13 420 D3
Elmore Cl LSOL/BMARY PO13 420 D3
Elmore Dr RGWD BH24 381 J2
Elmore Rd LSOL/BMARY PO13 420 D3
Elm Park Rd HAV PO9 16 F3
Elm Pl ALDT GU11 7 J6
Elm Rd BPWT SO32 297 K8
CHAM RG24 82 C6
FNM GU9 135 G1
WINW SO22 10 D6
HAV PO9 17 H6
NALR SO24 218 C3
OVTN RG25 101 G6
Elms Av PSTN BH14 445 M7
STHA RG19 27 H5
Elms Cl FBDG SP6 308 F6
PSTN BH14 445 M7
Elms La SELS PO20 427 L7
Elmsleigh Gdns ROWN SO16 318 F4
Elmsleigh Rd FARN GU14 90 D4
Elmslie Gdns HLER SO31 345 K7
Elms Ride SELS PO20 427 L7
Elms Rd ALDT GU11 6 F3
FHAM/PORC PO16 15 J9
FLET GU13 89 H7
HTWY RG27 85 M6 3
Elmstead Gdns SELS PO20 427 L6
Elmstead Park Rd SELS PO20 427 L6
Elmstead Rd CCLF BH13 446 E8
The Elms AND SP10 8 F6
RFNM GU10 136 C1
Elm St SHAM SO14 13 K4
SSEA PO5 20 F5 3
Elms Wy SBNE BH6 449 K4
SELS PO20 427 L6
Elm Ter SHAM SO14 13 K5
Elm Tree Cl TOTT SO40 340 F6
Elmtree Gdns ROMY SO51 291 H2
Elmtree Rd CHAM PO6 376 C8 3
Elm Vw ASHV GU12 113 L5
Elmwood Av FBDG SP6 309 H6
WVILLE PO7 376 C2
Elmwood Cl ALTN GU34 176 C6 1
Elmwood Rd NEND PO2 399 J4
Elmwood Wy
CHCH/BSGR BH23 451 L1
DEAN RG23 104 B1
Elphinstone Rd
CHCH/BSGR BH23 436 F8
SSEA PO5 21 G7
Elsenwood Crs CBLY GU15 71 K2
Elsenwood Dr CBLY GU15 71 K1
Elsfred Rd FHAM/STUB PO14 395 L7
Elsley Cl FRIM GU16 91 J2
Elson La GPORT PO12 397 L8
Elson Rd GPORT PO12 397 L8
Elstead Gdns WVILLE PO7 376 A4
Elstead Rd RFNM GU10 136 D3
Elston Pl ASHV GU12 7 J5
Elston Rd ASHV GU12 7 J5
Elstree Rd ITCH SO19 344 C4 1
Elvetham Cl FLET GU13 88 E5
Elvetham La HTWY RG27 67 L8
Elvetham Pl HTWY RG27 88 D5
Elvetham Rd FLET GU13 88 C6
Elvin Cl LYMN SO41 438 D4
Elwell Gn HISD PO11 425 K5
Elwyn Rd BMTH BH1 23 L2
Ely Cl FRIM GU16 91 K1
Emanuel St NEND PO2 423 H1
Embankment Wy RGWD BH24 382 F2
Emberley Cl FERN BH22 406 E1 1
Embleton Rd BOR GU35 202 E2 2
Embley Cl TOTT SO40 316 C6
Embley La ROMY SO51 289 J2
Embsay Rd HLER SO31 346 B8
Emden Rd AND SP10 118 E5
Emerald Cl ITCH SO19 344 E2
Emer Cl NBAD SO52 291 M3 1
Emerson Rd PLE BH15 445 H6
Emmanuel Cl
FHAM/STUB PO14 371 G6 1
Emmett Rd ROWN SO16 317 L3
Emmons Cl HLER SO31 369 K7
Empress Av FARN GU14 90 E3
Empress Rd LYND SO43 363 K3 2
SHAM SO14 13 J9
SHAM SO14 343 M1
Empress Wy RAND SP11 92 E6
Empshott Rd ENEY PO4 423 K4
Empson Wk
LSOL/BMARY PO13 420 D1 3
Emsbrook Dr EMRTH PO10 378 D6 1
Emsworth Common Rd
EMRTH PO10 378 B3
Emsworth House Cl
EMRTH PO10 378 C7
Emsworth Rd HAV PO9 17 K5
EMRTH PO10 402 F4
HAV PO9 17 G5
LYMN SO41 440 C4
NEND PO2 399 J7
WSHM SO15 318 A8
Enborne Gv NWBY RG14 2 B6
Enborne Pl NWBY RG14 2 B6
Enborne Rd KSCL RG20 24 F7
NWBY RG14 2 B6
Enborne St KSCL RG20 36 D4
Enborne Wy THLE RG7 40 C2
Encombe Cl BKME/WDN BH12 431 K8
Endeavour Cl GPORT PO12 19 J4
WSHM SO15 342 F1 1
Endeavour Wy FAWY SO45 367 K3
Enderwood Cl TOTT SO40 316 A8 2
Endfield Cl CHCH/BSGR BH23 434 D7
Endfield Rd CHCH/BSGR BH23 434 C7
MOOR/WNTN BH9 432 E6
Endle St SHAM SO14 13 K5
Endofield Cl FHAM/STUB PO14 396 D2
Enfield Av PLE BH15 445 K2
Enfield Cl LIPH GU30 227 G5 1
Enfield Crs PLE BH15 445 K2
Enfield Gv ITCH SO19 344 C6
Enfield Rd ASHV GU12 113 L3
PLE BH15 445 K2
Englands Wy BWD BH11 431 H4
Englefield Rd WEND SO18 344 B1
English Rd WSHM SO15 342 F1
Enham La AND SP10 118 D5
Enmill La WINW SO22 237 L3
Ennel Copse NBAD SO52 291 M4
Ennerdale Cl HORN PO8 328 B6 1
KEMP RG22 104 A6
Ennerdale Gdns NALR SO24 218 C4 3
WEND SO18 320 A7 1
Ennerdale Gv FNM GU9 134 D2
Ennerdale Rd
FHAM/STUB PO14 396 B4
BOR GU35 201 J3
ROWN SO16 317 K6
Ennerdale Wy STHA RG19 26 D5 2
Ensbury Av NBNE BH10 432 B7
Ensbury Park Rd
MOOR/WNTN BH9 432 C6
Ensign Dr LSOL/BMARY PO13 421 H2
Ensign Wy HLER SO31 369 J6
Enterprise Cl HLER SO31 370 C7 2
Enterprise Rd ROWN SO16 292 B7
Enterprise Wy SHAM SO14 13 J7
STHA RG19 27 K6
Epping Cl WEND SO18 320 A7
Epsom Cl CBLY GU15 50 F8
ELGH SO50 321 J1 2
Epsom Crs NWBY RG14 3 H8
Epsom Down ALTN GU34 176 E6
Epts Rd FARN GU14 90 D8
Epworth Rd NEND PO2 399 K7
Equine Wy NWBY RG14 37 L1
Equinne Wy NWBY RG14 37 L1
Erica Cl HLER SO31 370 D5
HORN PO8 352 F5
Erica Dr WIMB BH21 429 H2
Erica Wy HORN PO8 352 F4
Ericksen Rd NBNE BH10 432 A5
Eric Rd FHAM/STUB PO14 396 A6
Erleigh Dene NWBY RG14 2 C8
Erles Rd LIPH GU30 226 F4 1
Ernest Cl EMRTH PO10 378 D7
RFNM GU10 158 E2
Ernest Rd HAV PO9 377 G4
PSEA PO1 423 J1
Erpingham Rd
BKME/WDN BH12 446 F3
Erskine Cl TADY RG26 42 C7
Erskine Rd WINW SO22 10 D9
Escombe Rd ELGH SO50 294 C5
Escur Cl NEND PO2 399 K4 1
Esdaile La RGWD BH24 384 D5 1
Esher Cl KEMP RG22 104 C7
Esher Gv WVILLE PO7 352 A6
Esher Rd CBLY GU15 51 K7
Eskdale Cl HORN PO8 328 B6
Eskdale Wy CBLY GU15 71 M4
Esmond Cl EMRTH PO10 378 D8
Esmonde Cl
LSOL/BMARY PO13 420 D2 2
Esmonde Wy CFDH BH17 430 D8
Esplanade CCLF BH13 457 L1
ENEY PO4 423 J7
PLE BH15 445 H5
Esplanade Gdns ENEY PO4 424 A6
The Esplanade GPORT PO12 19 M4
Essex Av CHCH/BSGR BH23 434 D6
Essex Cl FRIM GU16 91 K1
Essex Rd BSTK RG21 4 D8
ENEY PO4 423 L4
BOR GU35 201 J4
Essex St NWBY RG14 37 G1
Estella Rd NEND PO2 399 H8
Estridge Cl HLER SO31 345 L7 1
Ethelbert Dr AND SP10 118 C5 1
Ethelbert Rd WIMB BH21 404 B4
Ethelburt Av ROWN SO16 319 H3
Ethelred Gdns TOTT SO40 341 G2
Ethel Rd PSEA PO1 423 J2
Eton Cl KEMP RG22 126 F2
Eton Gdns WBNE BH4 447 G4
Eton Pl FNM GU9 134 E1
Eton Rd SSEA PO5 21 L3
Etps Rd FARN GU14 90 E8
Ettrick Rd CCLF BH13 446 F7
Etwall RAND SP11 139 M4
Eucalyptus Av RGWD BH24 381 L6
Europa Cl TADY RG26 63 L5
European Wy SHAM SO14 13 J8
Euryalus Rd FHAM/STUB PO14 396 D2
Euskirchen Wy KEMP RG22 104 B3
Euston Gv RGWD BH24 382 F2
Euston Rd ENEY PO4 423 M3
Evans Cl BWD BH11 431 K7
NEND PO2 398 F6
RGWD BH24 381 J2
STOK SO20 162 A6
Evans Rd ENEY PO4 423 L4
Evans St SHAM SO14 13 H4
Evelegh Rd CHAM PO6 376 B8
Eveley Cl BOR GU35 201 G8
Evelyn Av ALDT GU11 7 H6
Evelyn Cl BPWT SO32 323 K4
Evelyn Crs WSHM SO15 318 C8
Evelyn Rd MOOR/WNTN BH9 432 E7
Evelyn Woods Rd ALDT GU11 112 F1
Evening Gld FERN BH22 406 C5
Evenlode Rd ROWN SO16 317 K7
Evenlode Wy SHST GU47 49 M8
Everdon La HSEA PO3 400 A4 3
Everest Rd CBLY GU15 51 G8
CHCH/BSGR BH23 435 J8
CWTH RG45 49 L2
Everglades Av HORN PO8 352 D5
Everglades Cl FERN BH22 406 B1
Evergreen Cl TOTT SO40 342 D7
WIMB BH21 356 C8 1
WVILLE PO7 376 B1 1
Evergreen Rd FRIM GU16 71 J6
Evergreens RGWD BH24 381 J3
Evering Av BKME/WDN BH12 431 H7
Evering Gdns
BKME/WDN BH12 431 G7
Everlea Cl LYMN SO41 439 H7
Everon Gdns NMIL/BTOS BH25 437 M7
Eversfield Cl AND SP10 8 E5
Evershot Rd CHAR BH8 433 J7
Eversley Crs HAV PO9 377 H4
Eversley Pl WINW SO22 238 C3
Eversley St HTWY RG27 47 K7
Everton Rd LYMN SO41 438 D4
Evesham Cl LTDN BH7 433 L8
ROWN SO16 319 G3 1
Evesham Wk SHST GU47 49 M7
Evingar Gdns WHCH RG28 122 B2
Evingar Rd WHCH RG28 122 B2
Evreux Cl STHA RG19 27 J6 1
Ewart Ct FAWY SO45 367 L3
Ewart Rd PSEA PO1 423 J1 1
Ewell Wy TOTT SO40 316 C7
Ewhurst Cl HAV PO9 377 H4
Ewhurst Rd TADY RG26 81 H1
Ewins Cl ASHV GU12 113 K6
Ewshot La FLET GU13 110 E5
Exbury Cl ELGH SO50 294 E6
Exbury Dr BWD BH11 431 K3
Exbury Rd FAWY SO45 392 C8
HAV PO9 377 L3
Exbury Wy AND SP10 8 C7
Excellent Rd
FHAM/STUB PO14 396 D3
Excelsior Rd PSTN BH14 446 B6
Exchange Rd PSEA PO1 20 F2 1
Exeter Cl ELGH SO50 293 L3
EMRTH PO10 378 D5
HLER SO31 370 D5
KEMP RG22 127 G1
WEND SO18 319 M7
Exeter Crs WCLF BH2 22 E7
Exeter Gdns YTLY GU46 68 E1
Exeter Park Rd WCLF BH2 22 E7
Exeter Rd ASHV GU12 113 K5
ENEY PO4 423 K6
WCLF BH2 22 E6
WEND SO18 319 M8
Exford Av WEND SO18 320 B8
Exford Dr WEND SO18 320 B8
Exhibition Rd FARN GU14 90 D8
Exleigh Cl ITCH SO19 344 F2
Exmoor Cl KEMP RG22 104 A5
Exmoor Rd STHA RG19 26 F5
Exmouth Gdns ELGH SO50 321 H1 2
Exmouth Rd GPORT PO12 397 L8
SSEA PO5 21 K7
Express Wy NWBY RG14 26 B6
Exton Gdns FHAM/PORC PO16 374 A7
Exton Rd HAV PO9 377 M3
SBNE BH6 449 J1
Eyebright Cl ELGH SO50 321 H2 3
Eyeworth Wk FAWY SO45 367 G4 2
Eynham Av ITCH SO19 345 G2
Eynham Cl ITCH SO19 344 F2
Eyre Cl TOTT SO40 341 H2

F

Faber Cl HAV PO9 377 L4
Fabian Cl WVILLE PO7 352 E8 1
Factory Rd ELGH SO50 293 M6
UPTN BH16 444 B2
Fairacre KSCL RG20 36 C8
Fairacre Ri FHAM/STUB PO14 371 M8
Fairbairn Wk NBAD SO52 292 E2
Fairbourne Cl HORN PO8 352 C6
Fair Cl WHCH RG28 122 B4
Fairclose Dr WINW SO22 214 A3
Faircross Cl FAWY SO45 392 A5
Fairdown Cl WINC SO23 11 M8
Fairfax Cl WINW SO22 238 A3
Fairfax Ct ITCH SO19 345 J3 1
Fairfax Ms FARN GU14 91 G6 1
ITCH SO19 345 J2
Fairfax Pl NWBY RG14 26 B3 1
Fairfax Rd FARN GU14 90 E1
Fairfield CHCH/BSGR BH23 450 A1
Fair Fld ROMY SO51 262 F7
Fairfield WHCH RG28 122 B2
Fairfield Av FHAM/STUB PO14 14 D9
Fairfield Cl EMRTH PO10 378 D6
FAWY SO45 367 L4 3
LYMN SO41 440 C5
WIMB BH21 404 C3
Fairfield Dr FRIM GU16 71 H5
Fairfield Gn ALTN GU34 197 H5
Fairfield Rd WINW SO22 10 D5
HAV PO9 16 F4
NMIL/BTOS BH25 452 D1
RWIN SO21 266 C3
WIMB BH21 404 B4
Fairfield Sq CHAM PO6 375 J8
Fairfields Rd BSTK RG21 105 G5
The Fairfield FNM GU9 134 F6
Fair Gn ITCH SO19 344 F3
Fairholme Gdns FNM GU9 134 F7 2
Fairhome Cl GPORT PO12 421 L1
Fair Isle Cl FHAM/STUB PO14 395 M5
Fairisle Rd ROWN SO16 317 K4
Fairland Cl FLET GU13 89 G8
Fair La RWIN SO21 215 M7
Fairlawn Cl ROWN SO16 317 L2
Fairlawn Rd TADY RG26 62 A1
Fairlead Dr
LSOL/BMARY PO13 421 H2 3
Fairlea Rd EMRTH PO10 378 D5
LYMN SO41 440 C4
Fairlie RGWD BH24 359 G7
Fairlie Cl HEND SO30 321 H5 2
Fairlie Pk RGWD BH24 358 F7
Fairlight Gdns ALTN GU34 197 H5 1
Fairlight La LYMN SO41 412 B7
Fairmead Cl SHST GU47 70 B1
Fairmead Wk HORN PO8 352 F5
Fairmead Wy TOTT SO40 341 J3
Fairmile FLET GU13 110 F2
Fairmile Rd CHCH/BSGR BH23 434 E8
Fair Oak HAV PO9 16 E1
Fair Oak La THLE RG7 64 B1
Fairoak Rd ELGH SO50 294 C6
Fairoak Wy TADY RG26 41 G7
Fairthorne Gdns GPORT PO12 18 D4
Fairthorne Ri CHAM RG24 106 B3 1
Fair Vw NALR SO24 218 B4
Fairview Cl FAWY SO45
ROMY SO51
Fairview Crs WIMB BH21
Fairview Dr FAWY SO45
ROMY SO51
WIMB BH21
Fairview Gdns FNM GU9
Fairview Meadow DEAN RG23
Fairview Pde FAWY SO45
Fairview Rd ASHV GU12
BOR GU35
WIMB BH21
Fairwater Cl
LSOL/BMARY PO13
Fairway Cl LIPH GU30
Fairway Dr CHCH/BSGR BH23
Fairway Gdns ROWN SO16
Fairway Hts CBLY GU15
Fairway Rd FAWY SO45
PSTN BH14
Fairways FERN BH22
GSHT GU26
RAND SP11
The Fairway FARN GU14
FHAM/PORC PO16
FNM GU9
FRIM GU16
HAV PO9
BOR GU35
LSOL/BMARY PO13
NMIL/BTOS BH25
Fairwood Rd VWD BH31
Fairy Crossway HORN PO8
Faithfulls Dro STOK SO20
Fakenham Wy SHST GU47
Falaise Cl ALDT GU11
ROWN SO16
Falaise Rd STOK SO20
Falcon Cl FHAM/PORC PO16
KEMP RG22
NTID SP9
Falcon Coppice KSCL RG20
Falcon Dr CHCH/BSGR BH23
Falconer Ct FAWY SO45
Falconer Dr PLE BH15
Falcon Flds FAWY SO45
TADY RG26
Falcon House Gdns KSCL RG20
Falcon Rd HORN PO8
Falcon Sq ELGH SO50
Falcon Vw WINW SO22
Falcon Wy BPWT SO32
YTLY GU46
Falkland Dr NWBY RG14
Falkland Garth NWBY RG14
Falkland Rd CHAM RG24
CHFD SO53
NWBY RG14
WSHM SO15
Falklands Cl
LSOL/BMARY PO13
Falklands Rd NEND PO2
Falkner Rd FNM GU9
Falkners Cl FARN GU14
Fallowfield FARN GU14
Fallow Fld WINW SO22
Fallowfield YTLY GU46
Falmouth Cl CBLY GU15
Falmouth Rd CHAM PO6
Falmouth Wy STHA RG19
Falstaff Wy TOTT SO40
Fancy Rd BKME/WDN BH12
Fannys La THLE RG7
Fanshawe St SHAM SO14
Fantails ALTN GU34
Faraday Cl WHIT RG2
Faraday Rd CHAM RG24
FARN GU14
NWBY RG14
Farcroft Rd PSTN BH14
Farcrosse Cl SHST GU47
Fareham Dr YTLY GU46
Fareham Park Rd FHAM PO15
Fareham Rd
LSOL/BMARY PO13
WHAM PO17
WHAM PO17
Faringdon Cl SHST GU47
Faringdon Rd WEND SO18
Farleigh Cl HAV PO9
Farleigh La OVTN RG25
Farleigh Ri BSTK RG21
Farleigh Rd OVTN RG25
Farley Cl ELGH SO50
WINW SO22
Farley La ROMY SO51
Farley Mount Rd RWIN SO21
Farley St STOK SO20
Farlington Av CHAM PO6
Farlington Rd NEND PO2
Farm Cl CWTH RG45
RGWD BH24
YTLY GU46
Farm Dr FARN GU14
Far Meadow Wy EMRTH PO10
Farm Edge Rd
FHAM/STUB PO14
Farmers Wk LYMN SO41
Farmery Cl ELGH SO50
Farm Gdns HSEA PO3
Farm Ground Cl HTWY RG27
Farmhouse Wy FLET GU13
HORN PO8
Farm La CHCH/BSGR BH23
RFNM GU10
RCCH PO18
Farm La North
NMIL/BTOS BH25
Farm La South
NMIL/BTOS BH25
Farmlea Rd CHAM PO6
Farm Rd ASHV GU12
FERN BH22
FHAM/STUB PO14
FRIM GU16
RAND SP11
Farmside Gdns HSEA PO3
Farm Vw EMRTH PO10

GU46 69 G3
iew Av HORN PO8 328 A3
iew Dr CHAM RG24 83 M5
'k ASHV GU12 113 M8
rough Rd ALDT GU11 112 A7
GU14 90 E8
GU9 112 A8
rough St FARN GU14 91 G3
m By-pass FNM GU9 134 C8
m La HASM GU27 204 D7
m Park Cl FNM GU9 134 E2
m Rd BKME/WDN BH12 446 F1
GU13 89 J7
GU35 201 J2
U33 248 D4
RG29 108 F5
U32 248 A8
s Md LYMN SO41 440 C6
l CHAM RG24 83 J7
Cl FHAM/STUB PO14 395 M5
Cl CBLY GU15 70 F5
s Cl TADY RG26 63 L5
BH21 404 F2
s Fld OVTN RG25 127 M8
s Wy HORN PO8 353 G7
Wy
/PORC PO16 396 F2
don Rd HAV PO9 377 L4
don Wy TADY RG26 61 L1
ford Rd ITCH SO19 345 H2
/ AND SP10 9 K8
g Flds BOR GU35 202 B3
gs Ga WVILLE PO7 376 C5
Cl CHCH/BSGR BH23 435 G5
Rd BKME/WDN BH12 431 G6
Cl ROWN SO16 317 K3
Wy
/STUB PO14 395 M5
sfield BROC SO42 387 K7
's Reach HISD PO11 425 J4
WY SO45 392 D2
am Rd SHST GU47 50 A7
Rd ENEY PO4 21 L3
'BTOS BH25 437 K6
er Rd KSCL RG20 59 J6
By-pass FAWY SO45 392 F5
Ct HAV PO9 377 M3
Gn CHAR BH8 433 H5
La ALTN GU34 245 G4
SO21 239 L8
Rd FAWY SO45 367 M8
SO45 392 C5
PO2 399 J3
/I SO15 342 E2
dns NMIL/BTOS BH25 437 K4
'HAM/STUB PO14 396 A6
d FHAM/PORC PO16 15 H9
ood Cha KEMP RG22 127 G1
Rd NEND PO2 399 J6
's La BSTK RG21 4 F9
ge Cl FRIM GU16 71 J6
CHAM RG24 105 M1
GPORT PO12 421 M1
LER SO31 370 E4
LSOL/BMARY PO13 420 D1
Rd FARN GU14 91 G7
Dr WINC SO23 215 H1
n Cl ROMY SO51 263 H8
Crs CHCH/BSGR BH23 436 D8
Rd PSTN BH14 445 L3
Pl HSEA PO3 399 K3
FHAM/PORC PO16 396 F1
n Cl NMIL/BTOS BH25 437 M8
Cl CHAM RG24 83 M3
GU14 89 L4
RG14 26 A3
Gdns LYMN SO41 440 B3
Cl WVILLE PO7 352 B7
Rd SBNE BH6 449 H2
FLET GU13 110 F2
on Cl BSTK RG21 104 F6
nk EWKG RG40 48 A1
nk WIMB BH21 380 C1
rrow
/WDN BH12 431 M8
e Cl RFNM GU10 158 E6
CHCH/BSGR BH23 435 G6
RG45 49 L1
GU31 276 B5
SP6 333 L3
GU16 71 M5
e Rd BOR GU35 201 K5
ft Cl
/STUB PO14 396 A7
ft Gdns NBNE BH10 432 B3
ft Rd NBNE BH10 432 B3
e HEND SO30 346 B3
E PO7 376 D1
e Ct STHA RG19 27 G5
e Gdns HTWY RG27 85 M6
e Ms
BMARY PO13 396 F4
e Rd AND SP10 8 C3
GU13 110 E3
'BTOS BH25 437 M4
SO40 342 D7
ne Wy WEND SO18 319 L8
n La HASM GU27 228 E5
wn Gdns FARN GU14 90 B4
wn, Stour &
Trail FERN BH22 405 M2
BH21 405 G1
FLET GU13 110 D2
O9 17 G2
am Rd FHAM PO15 372 A6
Cl ALTN GU34 198 C1
La ALTN GU34 173 L8
de NMIL/BTOS BH25 437 L5
ath Cl BWD BH11 431 L6
ath Rd BWD BH11 431 L5
Cl CFDH BH17 430 E6
GU14 70 B7
GU9 134 E2
Dr FNM GU9 134 E2
La FARN GU14 70 C7
GU9 134 E1
'BTOS BH25 437 L2
l La ROMY SO51 235 J8

Fernhill Rd BLKW GU17 70 B6
FARN GU14 90 B1
NMIL/BTOS BH25 437 L4
Fernhills Rd FAWY SO45 367 M7
Fernhill Wk FARN GU14 70 C7
Fernhurst Cl HISD PO11 425 J5
Fernhurst Rd ENEY PO4 423 K4
LIPH GU30 250 E5
Fernie Cl FHAM/STUB PO14 395 M6
Ferniehurst CBLY GU15 71 J4
Fernlea BOR GU35 201 G7
Fernlea Av FERN BH22 406 B4
Fernlea Cl FERN BH22 406 B4
RGWD BH24 381 J4
Fernlea Gdns FERN BH22 406 B4
ROWN SO16 318 D5
Fernlea Wy FAWY SO45 367 H5
Fernleigh Ri FRIM GU16 91 M1
Fern Rd FAWY SO45 367 K5
ITCH SO19 344 D6
Fernside Av PSTN BH14 445 L4
Fernside Rd FERN BH22 380 C6
MOOR/WNTN BH9 432 B8
PLE BH15 445 K4
Fern Wy FHAM PO15 371 H5
Fernway Cl WIMB BH21 404 F4
Fernwood Cl RGWD BH24 381 M3
Fernyhurst Av ROWN SO16 317 L2
Ferrell Fld HTWY RG27 85 L7
Ferris Av CHAR BH8 433 G6
Ferris Cl CHAR BH8 433 G6
Ferris Pl CHAR BH8 433 H6
Ferrol Rd GPORT PO12 422 A2
Ferry Rd ENEY PO4 424 B5
FAWY SO45 367 K5
HISD PO11 424 E4
PLE BH15 445 G7
SBNE BH6 449 L5
Ferry Wy CCLF BH13 457 G5
Festing Gv ENEY PO4 423 K6
Festing Rd ENEY PO4 423 K6
Feversham Av CHAR BH8 433 J7
Fey Rd GPORT PO12 19 G2
Fibbards Rd BROC SO42 387 K7
Fiddlers Fld ALTN GU34 154 A8
Field Cl HLER SO31 370 F6
LSOL/BMARY PO13 396 F3
ROMY SO51 290 F1
ROWN SO16 319 H3
RWIN SO21 266 B2
THLE RG7 31 L6
Fielden Cl NBAD SO52 291 L4
Field End FNM GU9 135 J4
WINC SO23 215 H1
Fielders Ct ALTN GU34 176 E5
The Fielders HTWY RG27 48 B8
Fielders Wy ROMY SO51 289 G6
Fieldfare Av YTLY GU46 68 D2
Fieldfare Cl HORN PO8 328 B4
Fieldfare Ct TOTT SO40 316 B8
Field Gate Dr KSCL RG20 59 H6
Fieldhouse Dr
LSOL/BMARY PO13 396 D8
Fielding Gdns CWTH RG45 49 K4
Fielding Rd SHST GU47 70 B2
Field La FRIM GU16 71 H7
Fieldmore Rd GPORT PO12 421 M1
Field Pl LIPH GU30 226 E5
NMIL/BTOS BH25 437 G8
Fieldridge NWBY RG14 25 M3
Field Rd FARN GU14 70 C7
Fields Cl FAWY SO45 392 C7
Field Stores Ap ALDT GU11 112 F5
Field Vw NBAD SO52 292 E2
Field Wk LYMN SO41 440 B3
Field Wy ASHV GU12 113 H6
CHCH/BSGR BH23 436 B7
FBDG SP6 310 D6
RFNM GU10 136 C1
RWIN SO21 266 B2
WVILLE PO7 351 K4
Fieldway FLET GU13 88 C8
HASM GU27 228 F1
RGWD BH24 358 F8
Fie Yard Rd FARN GU14 90 D6
Fifield La RFNM GU10 158 F6
Fifth Av CHAM PO6 375 J8
HAV PO9 17 K2
Fifth Rd NWBY RG14 2 A8
Fifth St PSEA PO1 423 K1
STHA RG19 38 C3
Filmer Cl LSOL/BMARY PO13 397 H8
Filmorehill La ALTN GU34 244 E5
Filton Cl TOTT SO40 316 B8
Filton Rd LYMN SO41 440 B4
Fincham End Dr CWTH RG45 49 J4
Finchampstead Rd
EWKG RG40 48 D1
Finch Cl TADY RG26 61 M1
Finchdean Rd HAV PO9 354 A6
HAV PO9 377 H4
Finches Gn ALTN GU34 176 E2
Finchfield Av BWD BH11 431 K2
Finchmead La PSF GU32 275 G4
Finch Rd ENEY PO4 424 B5
Finch's La RWIN SO21 266 E2
Finch Wy THLE RG7 31 L5
Findhorn Cl SHST GU47 70 A1
The Findings FARN GU14 70 B8
Findon Rd GPORT PO12 397 M8
Fingle Dr AND SP10 8 D5
Finisterre St FHAM/STUB PO14 395 M4
Finkley Rd RAND SP11 119 L3
Fintry Pl FARN GU14 90 B1
Finzi Cl ITCH SO19 345 G5
Fiona Cl WINC SO23 11 L6
Fir Acre Rd ASHV GU12 113 K2
Fir Av NMIL/BTOS BH25 437 M6
Firbank Rd MOOR/WNTN BH9 432 F8
Fir Cl FERN BH22 380 C5
FLET GU13 88 E8
LYND SO43 363 K4
Fir Copse Rd WVILLE PO7 376 B5
Fir Croft Dr CHFD SO53 293 J3
Fir Dr BLKW GU17 70 A5
Firecrest Cl ROWN SO16 318 A3
Firecrest Rd KEMP RG22 126 E2
Fire Station Rd ALDT GU11 112 E5

Fire Thorn Cl FLET GU13 110 E2
Firfield Rd FNM GU9 158 D1
Firglen Dr YTLY GU46 69 G1
Fir Gv BOR GU35 201 G7
Firgrove Cl NBAD SO52 291 L4
Firgrove Ct FNM GU9 134 F7
Firgrove Crs HSEA PO3 399 K3
Firgrove Hl FNM GU9 134 F7
Firgrove La WHAM PO17 349 K6
Firgrove Pde FARN GU14 90 E4
Firgrove Rd FARN GU14 90 E4
HTWY RG27 68 B2
BOR GU35 201 G7
NBAD SO52 291 M3
WSHM SO15 343 G1
YTLY GU46 68 E2
Firlands Av CBLY GU15 71 G3
Firlands Ri CHAM PO6 376 E7
Firmount Cl LYMN SO41 439 J7
Firmstone Rd WINC SO23 11 L7
Fir Rd TOTT SO40 340 F6
Firs Av WVILLE PO7 352 D6
Firs Cl EWKG RG40 48 C1
FARN GU14 90 F6
Firs Crs WINC SO23 190 F8
Firs Dr HEND SO30 345 L2
Fir's End THLE RG7 31 K6
Firs Glen Rd FERN BH22 380 C6
MOOR/WNTN BH9 432 B8
VWD BH31 356 D3
Firshill CHCH/BSGR BH23 436 C7
Firside Rd WIMB BH21 429 G4
Firs La ODIM RG29 108 B6
PSTN BH14 446 A8
First Av CHAM PO6 375 K8
CHAM PO6 376 C8
EMRTH PO10 379 H8
HAV PO9 17 J3
HORN PO8 328 B5
THLE RG7 41 M6
WSHM SO15 342 B1
The Firs BMTH BH1 23 H4
LIPH GU30 226 E5
LSOL/BMARY PO13 397 H7
NTHA RG18 26 E4
ROWN SO16 318 E4
First Marine Av
NMIL/BTOS BH25 452 E1
First St FAWY SO45 368 C8
STHA RG19 38 D3
Firs Wy DEAN RG23 104 A1
WHCH RG28 122 B3
Firth Cl THLE RG7 42 E8
Fir Tree Av HASM GU27 228 A2
Fir Tree Cl ELGH SO50 321 H1
RGWD BH24 381 H6
Firtree Cl SHST GU47 49 J8
Firtree Crs LYMN SO41 438 D5
Firtree Gdns HORN PO8 353 G3
Fir Tree Hl FBDG SP6 333 L2
Fir Tree La ELGH SO50 321 G1
NWBY RG14 26 B4
Fir Tree Rd HISD PO11 425 L5
TOTT SO40 339 L1
Firtree Wy FLET GU13 89 G8
ITCH SO19 344 F3
Fir Vale Rd BMTH BH1 22 F5
Firway GSHT GU26 203 H3
Firwood Cl CHFD SO53 265 H8
Firwood Dr CBLY GU15 70 F3
Fisgard Rd GPORT PO12 421 M1
Fisher Cl FHAM/STUB PO14 395 M5
Fisherman's Av SBNE BH6 449 G4
Fisherman's La THLE RG7 41 K1
The Fishermans
EMRTH PO10 378 E8
Fishermans Wk HISD PO11 426 C6
Fishermen's Cl ALDT GU11 113 H3
Fisher Rd LSOL/BMARY PO13 397 G5
Fishers Gv CHAM PO6 400 C1
Fishers Hl FHAM PO15 371 L6
Fisher's Rd TOTT SO40 341 L2
Fishery La HISD PO11 426 A6
Fishlake Mdw ROMY SO51 262 E7
Fiske Cl KEMP RG22 104 B4
Fitzgerald Cl HLER SO31 347 G8
Fitzharris Av
MOOR/WNTN BH9 447 M1
Fitzherbert Rd CHAM PO6 400 B1
Fitzherbert Sp CHAM PO6 400 C1
Fitzherbert St PSEA PO1 423 G1
Fitzhugh Pl WSHM SO15 343 K1
Fitzhugh St SHAM SO14 12 E2
Fitzmaurice Rd
CHCH/BSGR BH23 434 C8
Fitzpain Cl FERN BH22 406 B6
Fitzpain Rd FERN BH22 406 B6
Fitzpatrick Ct CHAM PO6 375 H7
Fitzroy Cl ROWN SO16 318 E1
Fitzroy Rd FLET GU13 88 C7
Fitzwilliam Av
FHAM/STUB PO14 395 L6
Fitzwilliam Cl BWD BH11 431 J3
Fitzworth Av UPTN BH16 444 B4
Fitzwygram Crs HAV PO9 16 E1
Five Acres Cl BOR GU35 201 L3
Five Ash Rd ALTN GU34 196 F4
Five Bells La STOK SO20 184 D3
Five Bridges Rd WINC SO23 238 D5
Five Elms Dr ROMY SO51 291 G2
Fivefields Cl WINC SO23 11 L9
Fivefields Rd WINC SO23 11 M9
Five Heads Rd HORN PO8 327 M8
Five Post La GPORT PO12 421 M2
Flaghead Chine Rd CCLF BH13 457 K2
Flaghead Rd CCLF BH13 457 K1
Flag Staff Gn GPORT PO12 422 B2
Flag Staff Sq STHA RG19 27 H7
Flag Wk HORN PO8 352 D3
Flambard Av
CHCH/BSGR BH23 434 D7
Flambard Rd PSTN BH14 446 B6
Flamborough Cl ROWN SO16 317 J6
Flamingo Ct
FHAM/PORC PO16 373 K8
Flanders Rd HEND SO30 321 G8
The Flashett RSAL SP5 207 G2
Flathouse Rd PSEA PO1 423 G1

The Flats BLKW GU17 69 L4
Flatt Rd RCCH PO18 379 M8
Flaxfield Ct BSTK RG21 4 D8
Flaxfield Rd BSTK RG21 4 D8
Flaxfields End FBDG SP6 309 K7
Flazen Cl BWD BH11 431 H5
Flecker Cl NTHA RG18 26 F3
Fleet Cl LSOL/BMARY PO13 397 H7
Fleet End Bottom HLER SO31 370 D8
Fleetend Cl HAV PO9 377 J2
Fleet End Rd HLER SO31 370 D8
Fleet Hl EWKG RG40 47 M6
Fleet La EWKG RG40 47 L6
Fleet Rd ALDT GU11 111 L2
FARN GU14 89 M4
FLET GU13 88 E7
HTWY RG27 87 M3
Fleets La PLE BH15 445 H2
Fleetwood Cl NWBY RG14 26 A3
Fleming Av NBAD SO52 291 M4
Fleming Cl FARN GU14 91 G2
RAND SP11 92 E6
WHIT RG2 47 H1
Fleming Pl ROMY SO51 290 E1
RWIN SO21 266 E7
Fleming Rd WINW SO22 214 B5
NWBY RG14 3 G3
ROWN SO16 319 J4
Flensburg Cl AND SP10 118 E5
Fletcher Cl BSTK RG21 104 E4
FAWY SO45 367 H5
Fletcher Rd NBNE BH10 432 B5
Fletchers Fld LIPH GU30 226 E5
Fletchwood La TOTT SO40 340 F2
Fletchwood Rd TOTT SO40 340 F2
Fleuret Cl FAWY SO45 367 L8
Flexford Cl CHFD SO53 264 F7
KSCL RG20 56 C3
Flexford Gdns LYMN SO41 439 G2
Flexford Rd NBAD SO52 292 B2
Flint Cl AND SP10 8 B9
ITCH SO19 345 J4
Flint La RAND SP11 94 C8
Flint St SSEA PO5 20 F5
Floating Bridge Rd SHAM SO14 13 L6
The Flood RSAL SP5 206 E1
Floral Farm WIMB BH21 404 E6
Floral Wy AND SP10 8 C8
NTHA RG18 27 G3
RAND SP11 8 A9
Floreat Gdns NWBY RG14 2 A7
Florence Cl ROMY SO51 289 G6
YTLY GU46 68 F2
Florence Ct AND SP10 119 G5
Florence Portal Cl WHCH RG28 123 G3
Florence Rd BOSC BH5 448 D4
FLET GU13 111 G2
ITCH SO19 344 C6
PSTN BH14 446 B4
SHST GU47 70 B1
SSEA PO5 21 K9
Florence Wy CHAM RG24 82 B8
Florentine Wy WVILLE PO7 352 E8
The Florins HLER SO31 370 E7
WVILLE PO7 376 C5
Floriston Gdns
NMIL/BTOS BH25 438 B5
Floud La PSF GU32 272 A3
Flowerdown Cl TOTT SO40 316 B8
Flower La ROMY SO51 288 C2
Flowers Cl HLER SO31 369 J5
Flume Rd FAWY SO45 393 G4
Flushards LYMN SO41 440 D5
Focus Wy AND SP10 119 J7
Foden Rd ALDT GU11 6 F3
Fokerham Rd STHA RG19 27 J6
Foldsgate Cl LYND SO43 363 K2
Folkestone Rd HSEA PO3 423 L1
Folly Cl FLET GU13 110 F1
Folly Farm La RGWD BH24 382 A2
Folly Fld BPWT SO32 323 J1
Folly Hl FNM GU9 134 D3
Folly La EPSF GU31 275 L5
TADY RG26 64 A4
THLE RG7 31 J3
Folly La North FNM GU9 134 E1
Folly La South FNM GU9 134 D2
Folly Rd HUNG RG17 33 M2
The Folly NWBY RG14 3 G8
Font Cl FHAM/STUB PO14 371 G5
Fontley Rd FHAM PO15 371 L5
Fontmell Rd BDST BH18 430 A6
Fontwell Cl TOTT SO40 316 B7
Fontwell Dr ALTN GU34 176 E6
Fontwell Gdns ELGH SO50 321 J1
Fontwell Ms HORN PO8 352 F7
Fontwell Rd NWBY RG14 3 H8
SSEA PO5 21 J7
SSEA PO5 21 J7
Foord Rd HEND SO30 345 M4
Football Gn LYND SO43 339 G5
Footner Cl ROMY SO51 263 H6
Footners La CHCH/BSGR BH23 435 G6
Forbes Cha SHST GU47 70 A1
Forbes Cl ROWN SO16 317 L2
Forbes Rd WINC SO23 191 G8
Forbury La HUNG RG17 34 E1
Forbury Rd SSEA PO5 21 J3
Ford Av CHFD SO53 293 J4
Ford Cl FERN BH22 406 D1
Fordingbridge Rd ENEY PO4 423 M5
FBDG SP6 333 M1
Fordington Av WINW SO22 10 B6
Fordington Rd WINW SO22 10 C6
Ford La FERN BH22 406 E1
RFNM GU10 158 E2
ODIM RG29 130 F1
THLE RG7 46 D4
Ford Rd GPORT PO12 421 K2
The Forehead THLE RG7 44 C4
Foreland Cl CHCH/BSGR BH23 434 B4
Foreland Ct HISD PO11 426 A6
Foreland Rd UPTN BH16 444 A4
Foreman Pk ASHV GU12 113 L6
Foreman Rd ASHV GU12 113 L7
Foreshore North FAWY SO45 392 F2
Foreshore South FAWY SO45 392 F2
Forest Av HORN PO8 352 D5

Forest Cl BPWT SO32 323 K5
CHCH/BSGR BH23 436 B7
CHFD SO53 265 H8
HORN PO8 352 D5
NBAD SO52 291 K3
TADY RG26 41 H7
VWD BH31 357 H4
Forest Cnr LISS GU33 248 F1
Forest Court Hills
RGWD BH24 383 H2
Forestdale GSHT GU26 204 A5
Forest Dean FARN GU14 89 H4
Forest Dr CHAM RG24 83 L4
RFNM GU10 158 F4
NTID SP9 114 F1
Forest Edge FAWY SO45 392 E5
Forest Edge Cl RGWD BH24 381 H3
Forest Edge Dr RGWD BH24 381 H3
Forest Edge Rd RGWD BH24 383 J3
Forest End FLET GU13 110 E2
WVILLE PO7 376 B1
Forest End Rd SHST GU47 49 J7
Forester Rd BPWT SO32 324 F7
Foresters Ga FAWY SO45 418 C1
Foresters Rd FAWY SO45 392 D6
Foresters Wy CWTH RG45 50 C1
Forest Front FAWY SO45 367 K8
Forest Gdns BPWT SO32 323 K5
LYND SO43 363 K3
Forest Ga FAWY SO45 418 D1
Forest Gate Gdns LYMN SO41 440 B7
Forest Gld RFNM GU10 158 A5
Forest Glade Cl BROC SO42 387 H7
Forest Hall BROC SO42 387 L7
Forest Hills CBLY GU15 70 E4
Forest Hills Dr WEND SO18 319 K5
Forest Hill Wy FAWY SO45 367 K6
Forestlake Av RGWD BH24 383 H2
Forest La FAWY SO45 391 M2
BOR GU35 201 M2
RAND SP11 143 L2
RGWD BH24 383 J2
TADY RG26 62 A2
VWD BH31 356 C1
WHAM PO17 348 F8
Forest Lane Cl LIPH GU30 226 D4
Forest Md WVILLE PO7 351 K5
Forest Meadow FAWY SO45 367 L8
Forest Oak Dr
NMIL/BTOS BH25 437 L3
Forest Park Rd BROC SO42 387 J6
Forest Pines
NMIL/BTOS BH25 437 L4
Forest Ri CHCH/BSGR BH23 436 B6
LISS GU33 248 F2
Forest Rd BPWT SO32 323 L5
CCLF BH13 446 F6
CHCH/BSGR BH23 410 C3
CHFD SO53 265 J8
CWTH RG45 49 M3
FBDG SP6 285 J4
FERN BH22 380 D5
BOR GU35 201 J7
LISS GU33 248 E1
RGWD BH24 384 D3
RSAL SP5 287 J8
WVILLE PO7 350 E4
Forestside Av HAV PO9 377 L3
Forestside Gdns RGWD BH24 359 G7
The Forestside VWD BH31 357 H3
Forest Vw BROC SO42 387 H7
NMIL/BTOS BH25 437 H3
SHAM SO14 12 F5
Forest View Dr WIMB BH21 405 L2
Forest View Rd
MOOR/WNTN BH9 432 E5
Forest Wy CHCH/BSGR BH23 436 B7
LSOL/BMARY PO13 397 H6
LYMN SO41 439 H7
TOTT SO40 315 M6
WIMB BH21 405 L3
Forge Cl FNM GU9 135 G5
HLER SO31 345 L7
TADY RG26 63 M6
Forge La ALDT GU11 112 C2
Forge Rd FAWY SO45 418 D1
BOR GU35 178 F8
Forneth Gdns FHAM PO15 371 M8
Forster Rd SHAM SO14 343 L1
Forsyth Gdns NBNE BH10 432 A7
Forsythia Cl HAV PO9 377 M4
HEND SO30 321 G8
Fort Cumberland Rd
ENEY PO4 424 B5
Fortescue Rd
BKME/WDN BH12 446 C1
TWDS BH3 447 M2
Fort Fareham Rd
FHAM/STUB PO14 396 D2
Forth Cl CHFD SO53 293 G3
FARN GU14 90 A2
FHAM/STUB PO14 395 M5
Forties Cl FHAM/STUB PO14 395 M4
Forton Rd GPORT PO12 18 E1
PSEA PO1 423 J2
Fort Rd GPORT PO12 18 C9
ITCH SO19 344 C5
Fortrose Cl SHST GU47 70 A1
Fortunes Wy CHAM PO6 376 D7
Forty Acre La EPSF GU31 304 A5
Forward Dr LYMN SO41 440 A6
Fosseway CWTH RG45 49 J3
Fossewood Dr CBLY GU15 51 G8
Foster Cl FHAM/STUB PO14 396 A4
Foster Rd GPORT PO12 18 D5
PSEA PO1 423 H2
Foul La ALTN GU34 196 E1
Founders Wy
LSOL/BMARY PO13 397 H6
Foundry La HASM GU27 228 D2
WSHM SO15 318 A8
Foundry Rd RAND SP11 142 B4
RSAL SP5 285 J1
Fountains Cl CHAM RG24 82 F7
Fountain St PSEA PO1 21 G1
Fountain Wy
CHCH/BSGR BH23 450 A2
Four Acre HEND SO30 346 E2

Four Acre Coppice
HTWY RG27 86 B6 2
HTWY RG27 86 B7 2
Four Lanes Cl CHAM RG24 83 M5
Four Oaks KSCL RG20 56 C2
Four Posts Hl WSHM SO15 12 C1
Fourshells Cl FAWY SO45 392 D6 1
Fourth Av CHAM PO6 375 J8
HAV PO9 17 J3
Fourth St PSEA PO1 423 K2
Four Wells Rd WIMB BH21 404 E1
Fowey Cl CHFD SO53 293 G1
The Fowey FAWY SO45 392 C6
Fowler Av FARN GU14 90 E6
Fowler Rd FARN GU14 90 C6
Fowler's Rd ALDT GU11 112 F3
HEND SO30 321 G8
Fowler's Wk NBAD SO52 292 C6
Foxborough THLE RG7 46 A2
Foxbury Cl FAWY SO45 367 L6
Foxbury Gv FHAM/PORC PO16 397 M1
Foxbury La EMRTH PO10 379 G4
LSOL/BMARY PO13 397 H4
Foxbury Rd RGWD BH24 381 K7
Fox Cl ELGH SO50 294 E6
THLE RG7 31 K5
Foxcombe Cl BPWT SO32 323 M2
Foxcote EWKG RG40 48 D1
Foxcote Gdns
NMIL/BTOS BH25 437 K5 3
Foxcott Cl ITCH SO19 344 D8 3
Foxcotte Cl AND SP10 118 C6
Foxcotte La RAND SP11 118 A6
Foxcott Gv HAV PO9 377 K3
Fox Cft FLET GU13 110 F3
Foxcroft Dr FAWY SO45 391 M5
WIMB BH21 404 F3
Foxdown OVTN RG25 100 F6
Foxdown Cl CBLY GU15 70 F3
Fox Dr YTLY GU46 69 G1
Foxes Cl VWD BH31 356 D3
WVILLE PO7 376 C2
Foxes La ROMY SO51 288 E4
Fox Fld LYMN SO41 439 H7
Foxglade FAWY SO45 418 D1 1
Foxglove Cl KEMP RG22 126 F1
Foxglove Dr BOR GU35 201 K6 1
Foxglove Pl
NMIL/BTOS BH25 438 B4 1
Foxgloves FHAM/PORC PO16 15 L1
UPTN BH16 444 A1 3
The Foxgloves HEND SO30 346 B3 2
Foxglove Wy NTHA RG18 27 H3
Foxhayes La FAWY SO45 418 D1
Fox Heath FARN GU14 89 M5
Foxhill Crs CBLY GU15 51 L8
Foxhills TOTT SO40 341 G4
VWD BH31 356 F2 1
Foxhills Cl TOTT SO40 341 G5
Fox Hills La ASHV GU12 113 M5
Foxholes Rd PLE BH15 445 L2
SBNE BH6 449 L4
Foxhunter Wy STHA RG19 26 C5 1
Foxhurst Rd ASHV GU12 113 K3
Foxlands FAWY SO45 418 D1 2
Fox La DEAN RG23 103 H5
WINW SO22 238 B3
HTWY RG27 48 C8
WIMB BH21 405 G3
Foxlea Gdns GPORT PO12 421 M1 1
Foxley Cl BLKW GU17 69 M3
Foxley Dr HSEA PO3 399 M4
Foxmoor Cl DEAN RG23 103 G5
Fox Pond La LYMN SO41 440 A6
Fox Rd HASM GU27 228 B2
RFNM GU10 158 F2
Foxs Furlong CHAM RG24 84 A4
Fox's La KSCL RG20 59 H7
Fox's Wk FAWY SO45 418 D1 3
Foxtail Dr FAWY SO45 367 K7
Fox Wy RFNM GU10 111 G8
Foxwood FARN GU14 89 H5 1
Foxwood Av
CHCH/BSGR BH23 450 E3
Fox Yd FNM GU9 134 E6 2
Foxy Paddock FAWY SO45 418 D1 4
Foye La FLET GU13 111 G3
Foy Gdns HLER SO31 370 A7
Foyle Pk BSTK RG21 105 G6
Foyle Rd CHFD SO53 293 G2
Frampton Cl NMIL/BTOS BH25 438 A3
RWIN SO21 266 E7
Frampton Pl RGWD BH24 382 E1 3
Frampton Rd
MOOR/WNTN BH9 432 E8
Frampton Wy TOTT SO40 341 K2
WINC SO23 215 H1
France Hill Dr CBLY GU15 70 F3
Frances Rd BMTH BH1 23 K4
BSTK RG21 104 F4
WVILLE PO7 376 B5
The Frances NTHA RG18 27 G4
Francis Av BWD BH11 431 H5
ENEY PO4 423 K5
Francis Cl LSOL/BMARY PO13 420 E3
Francis Gdns WINC SO23 11 J2
Francis Pl FHAM/STUB PO14 396 B6
Francis Rd BKME/WDN BH12 446 D3
HORN PO8 328 B5
Frankland Crs PSTN BH14 446 D5
Frankland Ter EMRTH PO10 378 E8 2
Franklin Av HTWY RG27 87 G1 1
TADY RG26 41 K7
Franklin Rd LSOL/BMARY PO13 421 G1
NMIL/BTOS BH25 438 A4
RWIN SO21 266 F1 1
Franklyn Av ITCH SO19 344 E4
Franklyn Cl UPTN BH16 444 A1
Frankston Rd SBNE BH6 449 H4
Fraydene EMRTH PO10 379 H8
Fraser Cl CHAM RG24 106 B2
ROWN SO16 317 L2
Fraser Gdns EMRTH PO10 379 J6
Fraser Md SHST GU47 70 B2
Fraser Rd BKME/WDN BH12 431 K7
HAV PO9 16 B2
LSOL/BMARY PO13 397 G4
NEND PO2 398 F6 1
SSEA PO5 21 J3
WINC SO23 191 G8
Frater La GPORT PO12 397 L7
Fratton Rd PSEA PO1 423 J2
Fratton Wy ELGH SO50 295 H7
Frayslea FAWY SO45 367 L6 1
Freda Rd CHCH/BSGR BH23 449 L2
Freda Routh Gdns
ELGH SO50 295 J6 1
Frederica Rd
MOOR/WNTN BH9 432 C8
Frederick St ALDT GU11 6 E2
SHAM SO14 343 M2
Freedom Ct FAWY SO45 367 L5 3
Freegrounds Av HEND SO30 346 A2 1
Freegrounds Cl HEND SO30 346 A2
Freegrounds Rd HEND SO30 346 A2
Freelands Dr FLET GU13 110 D3
Freemans Cl WIMB BH21 404 F2
Freemans La WIMB BH21 404 F3
Freemantle Cl BSTK RG21 5 J3
ITCH SO19 344 D3 2
Freemantle Common Rd
ITCH SO19 344 D3
Freemantle Rd GPORT PO12 421 M1
Freestone Rd SSEA PO5 21 J8 1
Free St BPWT SO32 297 J8
Frenches La ROMY SO51 261 G7
French Gdns BLKW GU17 70 A4
Frenchies Vw WVILLE PO7 351 J4 1
Frenchmans Rd PSF GU32 275 K4
Frenchmoor La RSAL SP5 231 L5
French Rd CFDH BH17 429 M7
LISS GU33 225 J5
French St PSEA PO1 20 C5 1
SHAM SO14 12 F6 1
Frendstaple Rd WVILLE PO7 376 E3
Frensham Av FLET GU13 89 H7
Frensham Cl HEND SO30 346 A2 2
NBNE BH10 432 C5
YTLY GU46 68 E2
Frensham Ct RFNM GU10 158 E4
Frensham Heights Rd
RFNM GU10 158 D6
Frensham La BOR GU35 201 M2
Frensham Rd CWTH RG45 49 L1
ENEY PO4 423 K4
FNM GU9 159 G1
RFNM GU10 159 G4
Frensham V RFNM GU10 158 F4
Frere Av FLET GU13 110 D1
Frescade Crs BSTK RG21 104 F5
Freshfield Gdns WVILLE PO7 352 C8
Freshfield Rd WSHM SO15 342 F1
Freshfield Sq WSHM SO15 342 F1
Freshwater Dr PLE BH15 444 C5 1
Freshwater Rd CHAM PO6 399 J1
CHCH/BSGR BH23 451 H2
Freshwood Dr YTLY GU46 68 F4
Friarscroft HLER SO31 368 F1
Friars Cft TOTT SO40 316 A6
Friarsgate WINC SO23 11 H7
Friars Pond Rd FHAM PO15 372 A7 1
Friars Rd CHCH/BSGR BH23 451 G2
ELGH SO50 293 L7
NWBY RG14 2 E9
Friars Wk NMIL/BTOS BH25 437 L8
Friars Wy WEND SO18 319 J4
Friend Av ASHV GU12 7 M4
Friesian Cl FARN GU14 89 G4
Frimley Green Rd FRIM GU16 71 H8
Frimley Grove Gdns FRIM GU16 71 G7
Frimley Hall Dr CBLY GU15 71 J2
Frimley High St FRIM GU16 71 G7 1
FRIM GU16 71 G8 1
Frimley Rd ASHV GU12 91 K8
CBLY GU15 70 E4
FRIM GU16 70 F7
Fritham Cl TOTT SO40 341 G1
Fritham Gdns CHAR BH8 433 H5
Fritham Rd WEND SO18 320 B8
Frith End Rd ALTN GU34 157 J8
BOR GU35 179 L4
Frith Hill Rd FRIM GU16 71 M7
Frith La WHAM PO17 348 E2
Frithmead Cl BSTK RG21 104 F6
Frobisher Av
BKME/WDN BH12 431 K7
Frobisher Cl
LSOL/BMARY PO13 421 G2
RGWD BH24 359 G7 1
Frobisher Gdns
EMRTH PO10 378 D8 1
ITCH SO19 345 G4
Frobisher Gv
FHAM/PORC PO16 398 A1
Froddington Rd SSEA PO5 21 K3 1
Frodsham Wy SHST GU47 50 B6 2
Froghall FAWY SO45 367 K7
Frogham Hl FBDG SP6 335 G1
Frog La FBDG SP6 334 C1
HTWY RG27 85 J1
OVTN RG25 106 E3
TADY RG26 62 E3
Frogmore FHAM/STUB PO14 372 A8
Frogmore Gv BLKW GU17 69 M4
Frogmore La HORN PO8 352 E2
ROWN SO16 317 J5
Frogmore Park Dr BLKW GU17 70 A4
Frogmore Rd BLKW GU17 69 M4
ENEY PO4 423 K4
Frogs Hole KSCL RG20 59 H6
Frome Cl BSTK RG21 5 J7
DEAN RG23 103 H7
FARN GU14 90 A2
TOTT SO40 342 E6
Frome Rd WEND SO18 319 M5
Fromond Cl LYMN SO41 440 C3 2
Fromond Rd WINW SO22 214 B5
Fromont Dr STHA RG19 27 G5
Frosthole Cl FHAM PO15 14 D1
Frosthole Crs FHAM PO15 14 C1
Frost La FAWY SO45 368 A6
Frost Rd BWD BH11 431 K4
Froud Cl HTWY RG27 85 L8 1
Frouds La THLE RG7 29 J6
Froud Wy WIMB BH21 429 G4 1
Froxfield Cl WINW SO22 214 C4
Froxfield Gdns
FHAM/PORC PO16 374 A7
Froxfield Rd HAV PO9 377 M3
Froyle Ct HAV PO9 377 M3
Froyle La ODIM RG29 130 F5
Fry Cl FAWY SO45 392 D6
HLER SO31 369 L4
Fryer Cl BWD BH11 431 M3
Fryern Cl CHFD SO53 293 K2
Fryern Court Rd FBDG SP6 309 K4
Fryer's Copse WIMB BH21 405 G2
Fryers Rd WIMB BH21 356 C8
Fry's La BPWT SO32 299 J4
LYMN SO41 439 H7
YTLY GU46 69 H1
Fugelmere Rd FLET GU13 89 H6
Fulbrook Wy ODIM RG29 108 C8
Fulflood Rd HAV PO9 377 J3
Fuller Cl STHA RG19 27 J6
Fullers La KSCL RG20 55 L1
Fullers Rd RFNM GU10 158 A4
Fullers V BOR GU35 202 C3
Fullerton Cl HAV PO9 377 M3 3
ITCH SO19 344 D8
Fullerton Rd LYMN SO41 440 A4
RAND SP11 142 B8
Fullerton Wy TADY RG26 61 M1
Fulmar Cl KEMP RG22 126 E1
ROWN SO16 318 A3
Fulmar Dr FAWY SO45 367 M6
Fulmar Rd CHCH/BSGR BH23 450 F3
Fulmer Wk HORN PO8 352 C4
HORN PO8 352 C4
Fulwood Av BWD BH11 431 J3
Funtington Rd NEND PO2 399 K8
Funtley Hl FHAM/PORC PO16 372 C4
Funtley Rd FHAM PO15 372 B3
Furdies WVILLE PO7 351 J4 2
Furley Cl WINC SO23 11 K7
The Furlong RGWD BH24 382 D1
Furneaux Gdns
FHAM/PORC PO16 15 J1
Furnell Rd PLE BH15 445 J7
Furness Rd SSEA PO5 423 H7 2
Furniss Wy HISD PO11 425 H4
Furnston Gv EMRTH PO10 379 J7
Furse Cl CBLY GU15 71 L4
Furse Hill Rd NTID SP9 114 E3
Further Vell-Mead FLET GU13 110 D4
Fury Wy FHAM/STUB PO14 395 M5
Furzebrook Cl CFDH BH17 430 C6
Furze Cl ASHV GU12 113 K1
Furze Cft NMIL/BTOS BH25 437 L7
Furzedale Gdns FAWY SO45 367 M7
Furzedale Pk FAWY SO45 367 M7
Furzedown Crs HAV PO9 377 L3
Furzedown La RAND SP11 140 D3
Furzedown Ms FAWY SO45 367 M7 1
Furzedown Rd PTSW SO17 318 F6
STOK SO20 210 F7
Furze Dr RAND SP11 115 J2
Furzehall Av FHAM/PORC PO16 15 J1
Furze Hill Crs CWTH RG45 49 M4
Furze Hill Dr PSTN BH14 446 B7
Furze Hill Rd BOR GU35 202 F4
Furzelands Rd WIMB BH21 356 C8
Furze La ENEY PO4 424 B3
Furzeley Rd WVILLE PO7 351 K6
Furze Meadow EPSF GU31 277 K8
Furze Pk La OVTN RG25 152 A1
Furze Rd ITCH SO19 344 E3
TADY RG26 41 J6
Furze Vale Rd BOR GU35 202 E4
Furze Wy HORN PO8 352 F4
Furzey Cl FAWY SO45 392 D7
Furzey La BROC SO42 389 M7
Furzey Rd UPTN BH16 444 A2
Furzley Ct HAV PO9 377 G2
Furzley La ROMY SO51 314 C3
Furzley Rd ROMY SO51 314 C3
Fushia Cl HAV PO9 378 A4
Fushsia Gdns ROWN SO16 318 C6 1
Fuzzy Dro KEMP RG22 103 L8
Fyeford Cl ROWN SO16 317 L2
Fyfield Cl BLKW GU17 70 A3
FHAM PO15 347 G8
Fyfield La RAND SP11 116 F6
Fyfield Rd RAND SP11 116 F6
STHA RG19 27 G6
Fyfield Wy WINW SO22 214 A3
RAND SP11 115 J2
Fylingdales STHA RG19 26 F6
Fylingdales Cl KEMP RG22 103 M5
Fyning St PSEA PO1 423 H2

G

Gables Cl ASHV GU12 113 K3
FARN GU14 90 D4
Gables Ct ROWN SO16 318 E3 1
Gables Rd FLET GU13 110 E4
Gables Wy STHA RG19 27 L6
Gabriel Dr CBLY GU15 71 L4
The Gabriels NWBY RG14 37 G2
Gaffney Cl ALDT GU11 113 G1 1
Gage Cl CHAM RG24 105 L1
TOTT SO40 342 E6
Gainsborough Av
NMIL/BTOS BH25 437 M3
Gainsborough Cl CBLY GU15 71 J1 1
FARN GU14 91 G6 2
Gainsborough Ms
FHAM/STUB PO14 371 K8 1
Gainsborough Rd BSTK RG21 105 H6
LTDN BH7 448 E1
RGWD BH24 381 J3
Gainsford Rd ITCH SO19 344 C3
Gain's Rd ENEY PO4 21 L7
Galahad Cl AND SP10 118 F6
Galaxie Rd HORN PO8 352 F4
Gale Moor Av GPORT PO12 421 H5
Gallaghers Md AND SP10 118 A8
Galleon Cl HLER SO31 370 D7 1
Galley La STHA RG19 39 G7
The Gallops FHAM/STUB PO14 371 H6
The Gallop YTLY GU46 69 G1
Gallop Wy BKME/WDN BH12 447 H1
Galloway Cl FARN GU14 89 H4
KEMP RG22 104 A5
Galloway Rd PLE BH15 444 C4
Gallows Dr FERN BH22 406 B7
Gallwey Rd ALDT GU11 112 E5
Gally Hill Rd FLET GU13 110 E4
Galsworthy Rd TOTT SO40 341 H1
Galt Rd CHAM PO6 376 B8
Gamble Cl ITCH SO19 344 D4
Gambledown La ROMY SO51 260 D3
Gamblins La BPWT SO32 323 L8
Gander Dr CHAM RG24 82 B8
Gangbridge La RAND SP11 97 J5
Ganger Farm La ROMY SO51 263 H6
Ganger Rd ROMY SO51 263 H6 2
Gannet Cl FAWY SO45 367 M6
KEMP RG22 126 E1
ROWN SO16 318 A3
The Gannets
FHAM/STUB PO14 395 M6
Garbett Rd WINC SO23 11 L7
Garbetts Wy RFNM GU10 136 B2
Garbitts La EPSF GU31 277 L5
Garden City FAWY SO45 366 E2
Garden Cl FARN GU14 90 B6
HISD PO11 425 K5
HTWY RG27 85 L7 2
KSCL RG20 59 J6 2
LYND SO43 363 J3
NMIL/BTOS BH25 437 L7
OVTN RG25 151 G7
Garden Close La NWBY RG14 37 G4
Gardeners Gn NTID SP9 138 C1
Gardener's Hill Rd RFNM GU10 158 E4
Gardeners La ROMY SO51 289 L2
Garden-lane RGWD BH24 381 J5 2
Garden La SSEA PO5 21 G6
WINC SO23 11 H7
Garden Ms HLER SO31 370 A7
Garden Rd RGWD BH24 384 D6
Gardens Crs PSTN BH14 446 A8
Gardens Rd PSTN BH14 446 A8
The Gardens HAV PO9 17 K6
RFNM GU10 136 C1
WVILLE PO7 326 C5
Garden Wk FERN BH22 406 C1 2
Gardiner Cl TOTT SO40 342 E6
Gardner Rd CHCH/BSGR BH23 434 C8
FHAM/STUB PO14 395 K1
RGWD BH24 382 F2
Garendon Ct FBDG SP6 309 K6 4
Garfield Av BMTH BH1 448 C3
Garfield Cl BPWT SO32 297 H8
Garfield Rd BPWT SO32 297 H8
CBLY GU15 70 F3
HLER SO31 368 E2
ITCH SO19 344 C1
NEND PO2 399 H8
Garford Crs NWBY RG14 25 G8
Garland Av EMRTH PO10 378 D5
Garland Rd PLE BH15 445 J4
Garlands Cl THLE RG7 31 K6
Garnet Fld YTLY GU46 68 D3
Garnet Rd BOR GU35 201 K6
Garnett Cl FHAM/STUB PO14 396 A4
Garnier Pk WHAM PO17 348 E4
Garnier Rd WINC SO23 238 F3
Garnier St PSEA PO1 21 K1
Garnock Rd ITCH SO19 344 B6
Garratt Cl HEND SO30 321 H6
Garrett Cl ITCH SO19 344 E7
KSCL RG20 59 H5
Garrick Gdns ITCH SO19 344 E6
Garrick Wy FRIM GU16 91 H2
Garrison Hl BPWT SO32 299 G6
Garrow Dr LYMN SO41 440 C3
Garsdale Cl BWD BH11 431 L2
Garsons Rd EMRTH PO10 379 H8
Garston Cl PSF GU32 273 J8
Garston Mede STOK SO20 165 M4
Garstons Cl FHAM/STUB PO14 371 K8
Garstons Rd FHAM/STUB PO14 371 K8
Gar St WINC SO23 10 F8
Garth Cl FNM GU9 158 D1 1
RGWD BH24 381 H4
Garth Rd THLE RG7 43 K3
The Garth ASHV GU12 113 J7
FARN GU14 91 G4
Garton Rd ITCH SO19 344 B5
Gascoigne La NALR SO24 220 A3
Gaskell Cl ALTN GU34 177 H2
Gaston La ALTN GU34 198 D5
ODIM RG29 130 E2
Gatcombe HLER SO31 369 G1
Gatcombe Av HSEA PO3 399 K6
Gatcombe Dr NEND PO2 399 K5
Gatcombe Gdns
FHAM/STUB PO14 371 M8
WEND SO18 319 M6 3
Gatehouse La EPSF GU31 278 C2
Gate House Rd
FHAM/PORC PO16 397 L1
Gate Hyde WINC SO23 11 G5 1
Gatekeeper Cl WINC SO23 11 M7
The Gates FARN GU14 89 H4
Gatwick Cl ROWN SO16 317 M4
Gaulter Cl HAV PO9 17 G1
Gauvain Cl ALTN GU34 176 F6
Gavan St ITCH SO19 345 H3
G Av FAWY SO45 392 D2
Gawaine Cl AND SP10 118 F4 1
Gaylyn Wy FHAM/STUB PO14 371 M8
Gaywood Dr NWBY RG14 3 L1
Gaza Av BROC SO42 416 A2
Gazing La ROMY SO51 288 D5
Geale's Crs ALTN GU34 176 F3
Geddes Wy EPSF GU31 276 B4
Gemini Cl ROWN SO16 317 L4
Geneva Av SBNE BH6 449 J3
Genoa Cl LYMN SO41 440 A7
Genoa Ct AND SP10 119 G5
Gentles La LIPH GU30 202 D7
Gento Cl HEND SO30 346 C2
Geoffrey Av WVILLE PO7 375 M6
Geoffrey Crs
FHAM/PORC PO16 396 F2
George Byng Wy NEND PO2 399 G8
George Curl Wy ELGH SO50
George Denyer Cl
HASM GU27
George Eyston Dr WINW SO22
George Gdns ALDT GU11
Georgeham Rd SHST GU47
George Rd FLET GU13
LYMN SO41
George St BSTK RG21
ELGH SO50
GPORT PO12
KSCL RG20
PSEA PO1
George Yd AND SP10
The George Yd NALR SO24
Georgia Cl AND SP10
Georgia Gdns TADY RG26
Georgia La RAND SP11
Georgian Cl CBLY GU15
RGWD BH24
Gerald Rd TWDS BH3
Gerald Sq ALTN GU34
Gerard Crs ITCH SO19
Germaine Cl CHCH/BSGR BH23
German Rd TADY RG26
Gershwin Rd KEMP RG22
Gervis Crs PSTN BH14
Gervis Pl BMTH BH1
Gervis Rd BMTH BH1
Gibbet La CBLY GU15
Gibbons Cl SHST GU47
Gibbs Cl EWKG RG40
Gibbs' La BOR GU35
Gibbs Rd SHAM SO14
Gibbs Wy YTLY GU46
Gibraltar Cl FHAM PO15
Gibraltar Rd ENEY PO4
FHAM/STUB PO14
Gibson Cl FHAM PO15
LSOL/BMARY PO13
Gibson Rd CFDH BH17
Giddylake WIMB BH21
Gid La ALTN GU34
Giffard Dr FARN GU14
Giffards Meadow FNM GU9
Gifford Cl FHAM PO15
Gilbard Ct CHAM RG24
Gilbert Cl FBDG SP6
LSOL/BMARY PO13
LYMN SO41
Gilbert Md HISD PO11
Gilbert Rd CHAR BH8
FRIM GU16
Gilbert's Gn NTID SP9
Gilberts Mead Cl RAND SP11
Gilbert St NALR SO24
Gilbert Wy WVILLE PO7
Gilbert White Wy ALTN GU34
Gilbury Cl WEND SO18
Gilchrist Gdns HLER SO31
Giles Cl FHAM/PORC PO16
GPORT PO12
HEND SO30
Giles La ROMY SO51
RSAL SP5
Giles Rd TADY RG26
Gilkicker Rd GPORT PO12
Gillam Rd NBNE BH10
Gillcrest FHAM PO15
Gillett Rd BKME/WDN BH12
Gillham's La HASM GU27
Gillian Av ASHV GU12
Gillian Cl ASHV GU12
Gillies Dr CHAM RG24
The Gillies FHAM/PORC PO16
Gillingham Cl WINC SO23
Gillingham Rd LYMN SO41
Gillman Rd CHAM PO6
Gilpin Cl ITCH SO19
LYMN SO41
Gilpin Hl LYMN SO41
Gilroy Cl NWBY RG14
Gins La BROC SO42
Girton Cl FHAM/STUB PO14
SHST GU47
Gisbourne Cl NTID SP9
Gitsham Gdns WVILLE PO7
Gladdis Rd BWD BH11
Glade Cl CHAM RG24
Gladelands Cl BDST BH18
Gladelands Wy BDST BH18
The Glades HLER SO31
The Glade CHFD SO53
FAWY SO45
FHAM PO15
FNM GU9
FRIM GU16
HISD PO11
RFNM GU10
NWBY RG14
RGWD BH24
WVILLE PO7
Gladiator Wy FARN GU14
Gladstone Cl CHCH/BSGR BH23
Gladstone Gdns
FHAM/PORC PO16
Gladstone Rd
BKME/WDN BH12
GPORT PO12
ITCH SO19
LTDN BH7
Gladstone Rd East LTDN BH7
Gladstone Rd West BMTH BH1
Gladstone St WINC SO23
Gladys Av HORN PO8
NEND PO2
Glaisdale STHA RG19
Glamis Av NBNE BH10
Glamis Cl DEAN RG23
FRIM GU16
WVILLE PO7
Glamorgan Rd HORN PO8
Glasgow Rd ENEY PO4
Glasslaw Rd WEND SO18
Glasspool WVILLE PO7
Glastonbury Cl CHAM RG24
Glaston Hill Rd HTWY RG27
Glayshers Hl BOR GU35

we Av
/BSGR BH23 449 L2
Cl ALTN GU34 175 G2
PO11 425 J3
RG25 126 C7
RG26 61 M1
Cnr WHAM PO17 348 F5
Ct ELGH SO50 295 J6
GU13 88 E7
SO30 321 M8 1
SO17 318 F6
Dr LSOL/BMARY PO13 397 G7
ield Gdns CHAM PO6 375 J8 1
Flds ALTN GU34 175 G2
ields LYMN SO41 454 C3 1
Y RG14 25 L3 2
and Rd CBLY GU15 70 C4
ands RAND SP11 143 G6
RG19 26 F5
La DEAN RG23 103 M4
Y RG27 87 J3
RG20 24 B3
M GU10 181 M3
SP5 287 J4
Meadow OVTN RG25 100 F8
SP5 231 M6
Park Av CHAM PO6 376 E7
Rd EPSF GU31 303 J3
GU14 90 C3
GU35 202 B3
M GU10 133 J2
be BLKW GU17 70 B4
M/STUB PO14 396 A7
Av PSTN BH14 445 M5
Rd PSTN BH14 445 M5
on NMIL/BTOS BH25 437 M6
on Gdns YTLY GU46 69 G4 2
on Rd
/BSGR BH23 436 D7
ook Wk
M/STUB PO14 372 A8
rron Wy ROWN SO16 318 D5
AND SP10 8 C5
GU26 203 M2
/BTOS BH25 437 H8
e Cl FRIM GU16 71 J8
e Rd BKME/WDN BH12 446 C3
BH7 448 E1
PO1 423 K1
yne Gdns ROWN SO16 317 L6
Cl HLER SO31 370 B8 4
le BPWT SO32 324 A4
HAV PO9 354 B7
le HLER SO31 370 F6 2
le Av FERN BH22 406 B2
Y RG14 36 F3
le Cl CHCH/BSGR BH23 434 B5
B BH21 404 A3
le Pk FLET GU13 88 B6
le Rd SBNE BH6 449 M4
RG26 41 K7
n Av NBNE BH10 432 A2
wan Rd CHFD SO53 292 F1
ive NMIL/BTOS BH25 437 G8
gles Av PSTN BH14 446 C6
gles Cl FERN BH22 406 D2
gles Dr FARN GU14 89 M5
V PO8 352 F6
g FHAM PO15 14 E3
ha Gdns FHAM PO15 14 B3
yre Dr ROWN SO16 318 F3
yre Rd ROWN SO16 318 E3
yre Wy ROWN SO16 318 F4
rness Av TWDS BH3 447 J2
ern Rd BMTH BH1 23 G5
eld Av WEND SO18 344 D1
eld Cl RSAL SP5 207 G2 1
eld Crs WEND SO18 344 D1
eld Wy WEND SO18 344 D1
riff Rd PSTN BH14 446 B6
rry NMIL/BTOS BH25 438 A6
rry Wy
/BSGR BH23 451 H2
rst Cl BLKW GU17 70 B4 2
nes SHST GU47 50 C7
es Cl RGWD BH24 381 K4
GSHT GU26 204 B7
Cl HEND SO30 320 C7
Dr HEND SO30 320 C7 2
Hollow GSHT GU26 204 B8
gh Av CHAM PO6 399 K1 2
gh Pk HAV PO9 17 K3
e Adows Dr BWD BH11 431 M3
oor Rd FERN BH22 406 A5
R/WNTN BH9 432 B8
ore Cl STHA RG19 27 G6 3
ount Dr PSTN BH14 446 A3
ount Rd FRIM GU16 91 K6
Rd HEND SO30 320 C6
SO31 370 C2
BOSC BH5 448 D4
GU13 88 E8
GU26 203 M2
SO31 370 C1
SO19 344 B7
BH14 446 A4
yd Gdns SBNE BH6 449 J4
le FAWY SO45 367 K5
/BTOS BH25 452 A1
le Av ITCH SO19 345 H4
ey NMIL/BTOS BH25 438 B6
en CCLF BH13 446 D8
/BMARY PO13 397 J7 2
RG26 42 B7
orne Cl
M/STUB PO14 396 B7
orne Meadow
U32 273 K8
orne Rd HSEA PO3 399 L7
e Cl CHCH/BSGR BH23 436 F6
le Gdns GSHT GU26 204 C4
le Rd CHCH/BSGR BH23 436 F6
E BH10 432 A6
ood Av ROWN SO16 318 F3
ood Cl FERN BH22 380 C6 2
ood Ct ELGH SO50 295 K6
ood Gdns HORN PO8 352 D5
ood La FERN BH22 380 C6 3
Glenwood Rd EMRTH PO10 379 H7
FERN BH22 380 C6
VWD BH31 356 C3
Glenwood Wy FERN BH22 380 C6 4
Glidden Cl PSEA PO1 21 J1
Glidden La WVILLE PO7 326 D5
Glissons FERN BH22 405 L6
Globe Farm La BLKW GU17 69 L3
Glorney Md FNM GU9 6 E9
Gloucester Cl ALTN GU34 196 F6
FRIM GU16 91 H2
PSF GU32 275 J5
Gloucester Dr KEMP RG22 127 G1
Gloucester Rd ALDT GU11 7 J7
BKME/WDN BH12 446 D3
LTDN BH7 448 E3
NWBY RG14 2 B5
PSEA PO1 422 E2
WVILLE PO7 376 D2
Gloucester Sq SHAM SO14 13 G6
Gloucester Ter SSEA PO5 21 G5 2
Gloucester Vw SSEA PO5 21 G5 3
Glyn Dr FHAM/STUB PO14 396 A6
Glyn Jones Cl FAWY SO45 392 D6
Glynswood CBLY GU15 71 J5
RFNM GU10 158 D4
Glynville Cl WIMB BH21 404 E1
Glynville Rd WIMB BH21 404 E1
Glyn Wy FHAM/STUB PO14 396 A6
Goatacre Rd ALTN GU34 196 B3
Goathorn Cl UPTN BH16 444 C4
Goat La BSTK RG21 5 G8
Goch Wy AND SP10 118 D6
Goddard Dr THLE RG7 28 C5
Goddards Cl HTWY RG27 64 C8 2
Goddards Firs DEAN RG23 103 H8
Goddards La CBLY GU15 70 E5
Goddards Md AND SP10 8 D7
Goddard Sq AND SP10 119 G6
Godfrey Pink Wy BPWT SO32 323 J1 2
Godmanston Cl CFDH BH17 430 E7
Godshill Cl CHAR BH8 433 H5
Godwin Cl EMRTH PO10 378 C5
WINW SO22 214 B5
Godwin Crs HORN PO8 328 B4
Godwit Cl GPORT PO12 397 M8
Godwit Rd ENEY PO4 424 A2 1
Gofton Av CHAM PO6 399 M1
Gogg's La RSAL SP5 285 L2
Goldcrest Cl
FHAM/PORC PO16 373 J8 1
HORN PO8 352 E1
YTLY GU46 68 E2
Goldcrest Gdns ROWN SO16 317 M3
Goldcrest La TOTT SO40 316 B8
Golden Ct HEND SO30 320 E6
Golden Crs LYMN SO41 439 H7
Golden Flds LIPH GU30 227 G5
Golden Gv SHAM SO14 13 J2
Golden Hind Pk FAWY SO45 367 K6
Goldenleas Dr BWD BH11 431 H5
Goldfinch Cl
NMIL/BTOS BH25 437 K6 1
Goldfinch La
LSOL/BMARY PO13 420 D1
Goldfinch Rd CFDH BH17 429 J8
Goldfinch Wy RWIN SO21 190 D3
Goldhill RFNM GU10 158 F2
Golding Cl STHA RG19 27 J5 2
Gold La ALDT GU11 113 H4
Gold Mead Cl LYMN SO41 440 C6 2
Goldney Rd CBLY GU15 71 L4
Goldring Cl HISD PO11 425 L5
Goldsmith Av ENEY PO4 21 M2
Goldsmith Cl NTHA RG18 26 F3
TOTT SO40 341 H1 2
Goldsmith Rd ELGH SO50 293 L7
Goldsmith Wy CWTH RG45 49 L4
Gold St SSEA PO5 20 F5 4
Goldwell Dr NWBY RG14 2 C2
Golf Course Rd ROWN SO16 318 D2
Golf Dr CBLY GU15 71 J4
Golf La BOR GU35 201 G7
Golf Links Av GSHT GU26 203 L2
Golf Links Rd BDST BH18 429 M3
FERN BH22 406 C3
Goliath Rd PLE BH15 444 C6
Gomer La GPORT PO12 421 J4
Gondreville Gdns FLET GU13 110 D4
Gong Hl RFNM GU10 159 G5
Gong Hill Dr RFNM GU10 159 G4
Goodacre Dr NBAD SO52 292 E3
Goodden Crs FARN GU14 90 C6
The Goodens NALR SO24 242 B3 1
Goodison Cl ELGH SO50 295 G7 1
Goodlands V HEND SO30 345 L1 1
Goodman Cl BSTK RG21 104 E4
Good Rd BKME/WDN BH12 446 B1
Goodsell Cl
FHAM/STUB PO14 395 M6 3
Goodwin Cl ROWN SO16 317 J6 1
Goodwood Cl ALTN GU34 176 E6
CBLY GU15 50 F8
FHAM/STUB PO14 371 G6
GPORT PO12 397 M8
THLE RG7 31 J6
WVILLE PO7 352 F7
Goodwood Ct EMRTH PO10 379 J8
Goodwood Gdns TOTT SO40 316 B8
Goodwood Pl FARN GU14 91 H5 1
Goodwood Rd ELGH SO50 293 K3
SSEA PO5 21 L6
Goodwood Wy NWBY RG14 3 K8
Goodwyns Cl NTID SP9 138 C1 1
Goodyers ALTN GU34 176 F5
Goose Gn HTWY RG27 85 L6
Goose Green Wy STHA RG19 27 H5 2
Goose La HTWY RG27 85 M6
Gordon Av CBLY GU15 70 E4
FLET GU13 111 G2
SHAM SO14 318 F8
WINC SO23 239 H2
Gordon Cl BSTK RG21 5 H5
Gordon Crs CBLY GU15 70 F4
Gordon Mt CHCH/BSGR BH23 436 F7 1
Gordon Rd ALDT GU11 6 F3
BKME/WDN BH12 446 F3
BMTH BH1 448 C4
BPWT SO32 322 E7
CBLY GU15 70 F4
CHCH/BSGR BH23 436 E8
CHFD SO53 265 J7
CWTH RG45 50 A5
EMRTH PO10 402 F1
FARN GU14 91 G8
FHAM/PORC PO16 15 G5
GPORT PO12 18 D4
LYMN SO41 440 A5
NTHA RG18 26 D3
NWBY RG14 3 G5
PSEA PO1 20 E6
WIMB BH21 404 C4
WINC SO23 11 H5
WVILLE PO7 376 B2
Gordon Rd South
BKME/WDN BH12 446 F4
Gordon Ter ITCH SO19 344 E6 1
Gordon Wk YTLY GU46 69 H3
Gordon Wy CHCH/BSGR BH23 435 G7
Gore End Rd KSCL RG20 35 L5
Gore Rd NMIL/BTOS BH25 437 J6
Goring Av HORN PO8 328 B4
Goring Fld WINW SO22 214 B7
Goring La THLE RG7 31 J7
Gorleston Rd
BKME/WDN BH12 446 E3
Gorley Ct HAV PO9 377 G2
Gorley Lynch FBDG SP6 335 H4
Gorley Rd RGWD BH24 359 G8
Gorran Av LSOL/BMARY PO13 397 G7
The Gorrings STOK SO20 210 F6
Gorsecliff Rd NBNE BH10 432 B7
Gorse Cl FNM GU9 158 D2
HLER SO31 370 D6
NMIL/BTOS BH25 438 B4
RGWD BH24 381 H4
Gorsedown Cl BOR GU35 201 G7 1
Gorsefield Rd
NMIL/BTOS BH25 437 M3
Gorse Hill Cl PLE BH15 445 K3
Gorse Hill Crs PLE BH15 445 K3
Gorse Hill Rd PLE BH15 445 K3
Gorseland Ct FERN BH22 406 C5
Gorselands NWBY RG14 37 G3
TADY RG26 41 M8
YTLY GU46 68 F4
Gorselands Cl ASHV GU12 113 K3
BOR GU35 202 F4 1
Gorselands Rd WEND SO18 320 A7
Gorselands Wy
LSOL/BMARY PO13 397 H8
Gorse La RFNM GU10 158 D2
UPTN BH16 444 B1
Gorse Ride North EWKG RG40 48 B1
Gorse Ride South EWKG RG40 48 B1
Gorse Rd EPSF GU31 276 B5
FRIM GU16 71 H6
WIMB BH21 429 G3
Gorseway FLET GU13 110 F1
Gort Cl ALDT GU11 113 H1
Gort Crs ITCH SO19 344 F4 2
Gort Rd BWD BH11 431 M5
CFDH BH17 429 L7
Goscombs La NALR SO24 219 J1
Gosling Cl CFDH BH17 445 L1
Goslings Cft ALTN GU34 199 K7
Gosport La LYND SO43 363 L4
Gosport Rd FHAM/PORC PO16 15 K7
FHAM/STUB PO14 396 B6
LSOL/BMARY PO13 420 D3
Gosport St LYMN SO41 440 D4
Gough Crs CFDH BH17 429 M6
Gough Rd FLET GU13 88 D6
Gough's Meadow SHST GU47 69 L1
Gould Cl RAND SP11 92 D6
Government House Rd
ALDT GU11 112 D1
Government Rd ALDT GU11 113 H4
Governor's Rd CBLY GU15 70 C2
Gover Rd ROWN SO16 317 H7
Gower Cl BSTK RG21 4 E4
Gower Crs HTWY RG27 86 A7 2
Gower Pk SHST GU47 70 A1
Grace Bennett Cl FARN GU14 90 D1 3
Grace Dieu Gdns HLER SO31 345 K7 1
Grace La FBDG SP6 284 D8
Gracemere Crs KEMP RG22 126 E1
Grace Sq AND SP10 119 H6
Gracious St ALTN GU34 199 J8
Graddidge Wy TOTT SO40 341 H1
Gradwell La ALTN GU34 196 F8
Graemar La ROMY SO51 260 B7
Grafton Cl BOR GU35 201 K6
TWDS BH3 447 M1
Grafton Gdns LYMN SO41 440 A7
ROWN SO16 318 B3
Grafton Rd TWDS BH3 447 M2
WINC SO23 238 E2
Grafton St NEND PO2 423 G1
Grafton Wy KEMP RG22 104 C4
Graham Rd ENEY PO4 21 M6
GPORT PO12 421 L2
SHAM SO14 343 M2
Graham St SHAM SO14 344 A2
Grainger Cl KEMP RG22 104 D7
Grainger Gdns ITCH SO19 345 G5 1
Grammarsham La OVTN RG25 127 L6
Grampian Rd SHST GU47 49 J6
Grampian Wy KEMP RG22 104 A5
Granada Cl HORN PO8 352 E5
Granada Pl AND SP10 9 M3
Granada Rd ENEY PO4 21 L9
HEND SO30 345 L3
Granby End THLE RG7 31 L5 2
Granby Gv PTSW SO17 319 G5
Granby Rd MOOR/WNTN BH9 432 E4
Grand Av CBLY GU15 70 F2
SBNE BH6 449 H4
Grand Pde WINW SO22 214 B3
HISD PO11 425 L6
PSEA PO1 20 C6
Grand Trunk Rd NTID SP9 114 B4
Grange Av CWTH RG45 49 L2
Grange Cl GPORT PO12 421 K2
HAV PO9 17 J3
LYMN SO41 439 J8
RAND SP11 116 D6
WEND SO18 319 K4 3
Grange Crs GPORT PO12 421 K2
Grange Dr HEND SO30 321 J8
Grange Farm Rd ASHV GU12 113 K5
Grange La HTWY RG27 87 G3
LSOL/BMARY PO13 397 G8
Grange Ms ROMY SO51 263 H7
Grange Rd ASHV GU12 113 L7
BDST BH18 429 L4
CBLY GU15 71 H3
CHCH/BSGR BH23 451 G1
FARN GU14 90 E1
FLET GU13 110 E3
HEND SO30 321 H8
HLER SO31 368 E2
LSOL/BMARY PO13 421 H4
NALR SO24 218 B3
NEND PO2 399 H7
RFNM GU10 136 B2
RFNM GU10 159 L8
PSF GU32 275 K6
RGWD BH24 381 H6
ROWN SO16 318 A7
SBNE BH6 449 J5
WINC SO23 238 D4
The Grange LYMN SO41 439 J8
NWBY RG14 36 F3
Grangewood Gdns
ELGH SO50 295 G6 1
Grantham Av HLER SO31 369 J5
Grantham Cl SHST GU47 50 B7 2
Grantham Rd BMTH BH1 448 D3
ELGH SO50 293 L6
ITCH SO19 344 D2
Grantley Dr FLET GU13 110 E1
Grant Rd CHAM PO6 376 B8
CWTH RG45 49 M5
Grant's Av BMTH BH1 448 C2
Grants Cl BMTH BH1 448 C2
Granville Cl HAV PO9 17 H5
Granville Rd BOSC BH5 448 F3
PSTN BH14 446 A3
Granville St SHAM SO14 13 K4
Grasdean Cl WEND SO18 319 M7 3
Grasmere ELGH SO50 293 L6 1
Grasmere Cl CHCH/BSGR BH23 434 B5
BOR GU35 201 J3 4
WEND SO18 320 A7 2
Grasmere Gdns
NMIL/BTOS BH25 437 M3
Grasmere Rd BOSC BH5 448 F4
CCLF BH13 457 G5
FARN GU14 90 B5
FNM GU9 134 D2
Grasmere Wy
FHAM/STUB PO14 396 B4
Graspan Rd RAND SP11 93 G7
Grassington Pl STHA RG19 27 G5
Grassmead STHA RG19 27 J6
Grassmere Wy HORN PO8 352 F7
Grassymead FHAM PO15 371 G4 2
Grateley Crs HAV PO9 377 G4
Grateley Dro RAND SP11 139 L7
RAND SP11 140 C6
Grateley Rd AMSY SP4 138 C7
Gratton Cl RWIN SO21 168 C4
Gravel Cl NALR SO24 172 B4
RSAL SP5 256 D8
Gravel Hl BPWT SO32 324 A5
KSCL RG20 24 B3
WIMB BH21 404 B7
Gravel Hill Rd RFNM GU10 157 J4
Gravel La ALTN GU34 196 D7
RGWD BH24 358 E8
RWIN SO21 167 J2
Gravelly Cl KSCL RG20 35 K5
TADY RG26 61 M2
Gravel Rd FARN GU14 91 G8
FLET GU13 111 G2
FNM GU9 134 E1
Gray Cl CFDH BH17 430 D8
HLER SO31 370 D6
Graycot Cl NBNE BH10 432 A3
Grayland Cl HISD PO11 425 J4 2
Grayling Md ROMY SO51 262 E7
Grays Av FAWY SO45 367 M5
Grays Cl ELGH SO50 266 E8
GPORT PO12 421 J5
HASM GU27 205 H8
ROMY SO51 290 F1
Grays Ct PSEA PO1 20 D4
Grayshot Dr BLKW GU17 69 M3 1
Grayshott Cl WINW SO22 214 C4
Grayshott Laurels
BOR GU35 201 M3 3
Grayshott Rd ENEY PO4 423 K4
GPORT PO12 18 B4
BOR GU35 202 F3
Grayswood Dr FRIM GU16 91 K7
Grayswood Rd HASM GU27 205 G8
Great Austins FNM GU9 135 G8
Great Binfields Crs CHAM RG24 83 L8
Great Binfields Rd CHAM RG24 105 L1
Great Br ROMY SO51 262 D6
Greatbridge Rd ROMY SO51 262 D5
Great Copse Dr HAV PO9 377 K3
Great Elms Cl FAWY SO45 391 M5
Greatfield Cl FARN GU14 70 E8
Greatfield Rd FARN GU14 70 D8
Great Field Rd WINW SO22 10 B1
Greatfield Wy HAV PO9 353 M6
Great Gays FHAM/STUB PO14 395 L7
Great Hanger EPSF GU31 276 A5
Great La WHCH RG28 122 B3
Great Md LYND SO43 363 K4 3
WVILLE PO7 351 L5
Great Minster St WINC SO23 11 G8
Great Oaks Cha CHAM RG24 83 K6 1
Great Sheldons Coppice
HTWY RG27 85 M6
Great Southsea St SSEA PO5 21 G5
Great Well Dr ROMY SO51 262 E8
Greatwood Cl FAWY SO45 367 L6 2
Greaves Cl NBNE BH10 432 A5
Grebe Cl ALTN GU34 176 D2
CFDH BH17 429 J8
FHAM/PORC PO16 373 K8 5
HORN PO8 352 C4
KEMP RG22 126 E1
LYMN SO41 454 D4
Green Acre ALDT GU11 6 D4
Greenacre KSCL RG20 59 J6 3
NMIL/BTOS BH25 437 L8
Greenacre Cl UPTN BH16 444 B2
Greenacre Gdns WVILLE PO7 376 B4
Greenacres KSCL RG20 36 B8
BOR GU35 201 L4 1
RFNM GU10 135 M6
RSAL SP5 284 C1
RWIN SO21 167 H2
Greenacres Cl NBNE BH10 432 C1
Green Acres Cl RGWD BH24 382 B3
Greenacres Dr RWIN SO21 266 B5
Greenaway La HLER SO31 370 B6
Greenbank Crs ROWN SO16 318 E3
Greenbanks Cl LYMN SO41 454 C3
Greenbanks Gdns
FHAM/PORC PO16 373 H6
Greenbirch Cl KEMP RG22 126 E1
Green Bottom WIMB BH21 404 E1
Greenbury Cl DEAN RG23 104 B3
Green Cl FAWY SO45 367 L4 6
RSAL SP5 259 G4
TOTT SO40 340 D4
NALR SO24 194 C7
RWIN SO21 190 D4
Greenclose La WIMB BH21 404 B4
Green Crs LSOL/BMARY PO13 397 G7
Greencroft FARN GU14 90 E4 2
Green Cross La RFNM GU10 181 K7
Greendale Cl CHFD SO53 293 K2 1
The Greendale FHAM PO15 372 B4
Green Dro RAND SP11 96 A6
Green End YTLY GU46 69 G1 1
Greenfield Cl LIPH GU30 226 F3 1
Greenfield Crs HORN PO8 352 F5
Greenfield Gdns
NMIL/BTOS BH25 437 M8
Greenfield Ri HORN PO8 352 F5
Greenfield Rd FNM GU9 158 C1
PLE BH15 445 K2
Greenfields EPSF GU31 305 K1 1
LISS GU33 248 F4
RAND SP11 96 B8 1
Greenfields Av ALTN GU34 176 D4
TOTT SO40 316 D7
Greenfields Cl EPSF GU31 277 K8
Greenfield Wy CWTH RG45 49 K1
Greenfinch Cl CFDH BH17 429 K7
Green Finch Cl CWTH RG45 49 J2 1
Greenfinch Cl ELGH SO50 293 J7 2
Greenfinch Wk RGWD BH24 383 G2 2
Green Glades FLET GU13 110 E3
Greenham Rd NWBY RG14 2 F6
Greenhanger RFNM GU10 181 J8
Greenhaven YTLY GU46 68 E3
Greenhaven Cl AND SP10 9 L6 1
Greenhayes BDST BH18 430 A6
Greenhays Ri WIMB BH21 404 A3
Greenhill Av WINW SO22 10 C7
Green Hill Cl CBLY GU15 71 M2
Greenhill Cl FNM GU9 158 D1 2
WINW SO22 10 C7
WIMB BH21 404 B2
Greenhill La ROWN SO16 291 K8
WIMB BH21 404 B2
Green Hill Rd CBLY GU15 71 M2
Greenhill Rd FNM GU9 135 G8
WINW SO22 10 B7
WIMB BH21 404 B1
Greenhill Ter WINW SO22 10 C7
Greenhill Wy FNM GU9 158 D1
Green Hollow Cl
FHAM/PORC PO16 14 D1
Green Jacket Cl WINW SO22 238 D3
Greenlands KSCL RG20 36 B7
Greenlands Rd CBLY GU15 70 E7
KSCL RG20 59 J6
NWBY RG14 3 G9
Green La ALTN GU34 196 E8
ALTN GU34 221 H4
BLKW GU17 69 L4
BLKW GU17 70 B4
BPWT SO32 324 B1
FAWY SO45 392 D8
FBDG SP6 283 H8
FERN BH22 405 L7
FNM GU9 6 D9
FNM GU9 134 D8
GPORT PO12 18 C7
HASM GU27 228 E4
HISD PO11 425 J6
HLER SO31 345 J7
HLER SO31 346 B8
HLER SO31 346 E7
HLER SO31 369 L6
HLER SO31 370 D7
HORN PO8 328 C3
HSEA PO3 399 L5
HTWY RG27 87 H3
NALR SO24 219 H3
NALR SO24 244 C2
NBNE BH10 432 A5
RFNM GU10 180 B2
RFNM GU10 181 J8
NMIL/BTOS BH25 437 M8
NWBY RG14 2 B5
OVTN RG25 127 M8
PSF GU32 246 E3
RAND SP11 141 H3
RGWD BH24 382 E1
RGWD BH24 382 F5
ROMY SO51 263 K8
ROWN SO16 292 E7
ROWN SO16 317 K6
RSAL SP5 256 E8
SHST GU47 69 M1
STHA RG19 26 F5
TADY RG26 62 B4
THLE RG7 30 F6
THLE RG7 44 C8
TOTT SO40 316 A4
WVILLE PO7 325 L8
WVILLE PO7 351 J3
YTLY GU46 68 E1

Green Lane Cl CBLY GU15 70 F1
Greenlea Cl CHAM PO6 375 M6
Greenlea Crs ROWN SO16 319 J3
Greenlea Rd GPORT PO12 421 K1 2
Greenleas FRIM GU16 71 H6
Greenleas Cl YTLY GU46 68 F1
Green Leys FLET GU13 110 E4
Greenmead Av LYMN SO41 439 H7
Green Meadows La
RAND SP11 142 F6
Green Park Cl WINC SO23 11 J2
Green Park Rd ROWN SO16 342 C1
Green Pond Cnr HAV PO9 17 J5
Green Pond La ROMY SO51 264 B5
Green Rd FHAM/STUB PO14 396 A4
GPORT PO12 18 C7
MOOR/WNTN BH9 432 E8
PLE BH15 445 H6
SSEA PO5 21 G5
Greensand Wy FNM GU9 135 H6
GSHT GU26 204 D6
HASM GU27 228 F1
Greens Cl BPWT SO32 297 G8
ELGH SO50 294 F7
Greenside CWTH RG45 49 J3
Greensleeves Av BDST BH18 429 M2
Greens Meade RSAL SP5 285 J2
Greensome Dr FERN BH22 406 D2
Green Springs RFNM GU10 133 J1
Green Stile ALTN GU34 196 D2
Green St BOR GU35 178 C8
The Green AND SP10 118 D6 1
FNM GU9 134 F2
FNM GU9 135 K3
FRIM GU16 91 J2
HLER SO31 370 B2
LISS GU33 248 D3 2
RFNM GU10 136 B7
OVTN RG25 101 G8
ROMY SO51 263 H6 3
RSAL SP5 259 G4
TADY RG26 61 M2
WHCH RG28 122 C3
Green Wy ASHV GU12 113 H5
Greenway HTWY RG27 64 C8
Greenway Cl LYMN SO41 440 A4
Greenway La EPSF GU31 303 H2
Greenway Rd GPORT PO12 421 M2
Greenways BPWT SO32 324 A3
CHCH/BSGR BH23 436 D8
CHFD SO53 293 J2
FLET GU13 110 E2
KSCL RG20 36 B7
LYMN SO41 454 B3
ROWN SO16 319 J3
SHST GU47 49 L7
Greenways Av CHAR BH8 433 G5
Greenways Rd BROC SO42 387 L7 3
The Greenwich FAWY SO45 392 C6 1
Greenwich Wy AND SP10 118 F6
Greenwood Av CHAM PO6 375 H8
FERN BH22 406 B2
PSTN BH14 446 B8 1
ROWN SO16 317 J2
Greenwood Cl
FHAM/PORC PO16 372 E4
ROMY SO51 262 F8 1
Greenwood Copse
RGWD BH24 381 L4 2
Greenwood Dr CHAM RG24 83 L4 1
Greenwood La BPWT SO32 295 M8
Greenwood Rd CWTH RG45 49 K2
MOOR/WNTN BH9 432 C7
Greenwoods
NMIL/BTOS BH25 437 M7 2
WHCH RG28 122 B2
Greenwood Wy RGWD BH24 381 K4
Greetham St SSEA PO5 21 H2
Gregory Cl BSTK RG21 5 H3
Gregory Gdns TOTT SO40 316 B7 1
Gregory La BPWT SO32 322 A3
Gregson Cl LSOL/BMARY PO13 397 G5
Greig Rd KEMP RG22 104 D7
Grenadier Cl HLER SO31 370 F6
Grenadier Rd ASHV GU12 113 L4
Grenadiers Wy FARN GU14 89 M5 2
Grendon Cl ROWN SO16 319 G3 2
Grenehurst Wy EPSF GU31 275 L5
Grenfell Rd MOOR/WNTN BH9 432 D5
Grensell Cl HTWY RG27 48 B8 2
Grenville Cl LIPH GU30 226 F4
RGWD BH24 359 G7
Grenville Dr FLET GU13 110 D1
Grenville Gdns FAWY SO45 367 L7
FRIM GU16 91 H2
Grenville Rd ENEY PO4 21 L5 1
WIMB BH21 404 B4
Gresham Rd MOOR/WNTN BH9 432 E7
Gresham Wy FRIM GU16 91 H2
Gresley Gdns HEND SO30 321 H6 3
Gresley Rd BSTK RG21 5 K5
CHAM RG24 5 K4
Grevillea Av FHAM PO15 371 J5
Greville Gn EMRTH PO10 378 C5
Greville Rd WSHM SO15 343 H1
Greyberry Copse Rd STHA RG19 26 A8
Greyfriars Rd FHAM PO15 372 A6
Greyhound Cl ASHV GU12 113 J7
HEND SO30 321 G5 3
Greyhound La OVTN RG25 123 M1
Greys Ct ALDT GU11 6 A2 1
Greys Farm Cl NALR SO24 242 C4
Greyshott Av
FHAM/STUB PO14 372 A8
Greystead Pk RFNM GU10 158 B2
Greystoke Av BWD BH11 431 K2
Greystoke Ct CWTH RG45 49 K4
Greywell Av ROWN SO16 318 A4
Greywell Cl TADY RG26 41 K8 2
Greywell Rd CHAM RG24 106 C3
HTWY RG27 107 H4
Grieve Cl RFNM GU10 136 B1
Griffen Cl ELGH SO50 294 D6 2
Griffin Ct PTSW SO17 319 H8
Griffin Wk LSOL/BMARY PO13 421 G2
Griffin Wy South HTWY RG27 86 A5
Griffiths Cl STHA RG19 27 J6
Griffiths Gdns BWD BH11 431 M3
Griffon Cl FARN GU14 90 A5
HLER SO31 345 L7
Grigg La BROC SO42 387 L7
Grimstead Rd RSAL SP5 230 B2
Grindle Cl NTHA RG18 26 F3
Gritanwood Rd ENEY PO4 423 M5
Grosvenor Cl KEMP RG22 127 G3 2
PTSW SO17 319 H6
RGWD BH24 381 H3
Grosvenor Ct BLKW GU17 70 A5
Grosvenor Dr WINC SO23 11 J2
Grosvenor Gdns BMTH BH1 448 D4
HEND SO30 320 C7
PTSW SO17 319 H6 1
Grosvenor Rd ALDT GU11 6 E2
ALTN GU34 196 D6
CHFD SO53 265 K7
PTSW SO17 319 H6
WBNE BH4 447 H5
Grosvenor Sq WSHM SO15 343 K2
Grosvenor St SSEA PO5 21 H3
Grove Av FHAM/PORC PO16 398 A2
GPORT PO12 19 G2
Grove Cl BSTK RG21 105 H5
EWKG RG40 49 H1
Grove Cross Rd FRIM GU16 71 G7
Grove End Rd FNM GU9 158 E1
Grovefields Av FRIM GU16 71 G7
Grove Gdns ITCH SO19 344 F7
Groveland Rd NWBY RG14 25 G3
Grovelands RFNM GU10 159 H1
Grovelands Rd WINW SO22 214 A7
Grove La RSAL SP5 285 L1
Grovely Av BOSC BH5 448 E4
Grovely Wy ROMY SO51 263 K7
Grove Pastures LYMN SO41 440 C5
Grove Pl ITCH SO19 344 F6
LYMN SO41 440 C5
Grove Rd ALTN GU34 176 E6
ASHV GU12 113 K4
BKME/WDN BH12 446 A2
BMTH BH1 23 H6
BSTK RG21 105 H6
CBLY GU15 71 H3
CHAM PO6 400 A1
FHAM/PORC PO16 15 G6
FLET GU13 111 G3
GPORT PO12 421 M1
GSHT GU26 203 M2
HAV PO9 16 F5
LSOL/BMARY PO13 420 C2
LYMN SO41 440 D5
NMIL/BTOS BH25 452 F1
NWBY RG14 25 G3
RWIN SO21 266 C3
WIMB BH21 404 A4
WSHM SO15 343 G1
Grove Rd East
CHCH/BSGR BH23 434 E8
Grove Rd North SSEA PO5 21 H5
Grove Rd South SSEA PO5 21 H6
Grove Rd West
CHCH/BSGR BH23 434 D8
Groves Cl RWIN SO21 190 B4
Groves Down ROMY SO51 288 D4
Groves Lea THLE RG7 43 J2
The Grove ALDT GU11 6 F3
CHCH/BSGR BH23 434 C7
EMRTH PO10 378 F5
FARN GU14 91 G7
FERN BH22 406 A4
FHAM/STUB PO14 395 M6
FRIM GU16 71 G7
HLER SO31 345 L7
HLER SO31 369 H1
ITCH SO19 344 F7
LIPH GU30 226 E4
MOOR/WNTN BH9 432 D5
NTHA RG18 27 G4
RAND SP11 117 L4
VWD BH31 356 E3
Grower Gdns BWD BH11 431 L4
Gruneisen Rd NEND PO2 399 G6
Guardhouse Rd PSEA PO1 422 F1
Guardroom Rd NEND PO2 398 F7
Gudge Heath La FHAM PO15 14 B2
Guernsey Cl CHAM RG24 83 H6
ROWN SO16 317 K5
Guernsey Dr FARN GU14 89 G4
Guernsey Rd
BKME/WDN BH12 431 H7
Guessens La FHAM/STUB PO14 371 K8
Guest Av BKME/WDN BH12 446 E2
Guest Rd ELGH SO50 294 C5
UPTN BH16 444 A1
Guildford Cl EMRTH PO10 379 H7
Guildford Dr CHFD SO53 293 G5
Guildford Rd ALDT GU11 7 L7
FLET GU13 89 H7
FNM GU9 135 G5
FRIM GU16 91 K3
RFNM GU10 135 K4
PSEA PO1 21 M1
Guildford Rd East FARN GU14 90 F7
Guildford Rd West FARN GU14 90 F7
Guildford St SHAM SO14 13 K1 1
Guildhall Wk PSEA PO1 20 F3
Guildhill Rd SBNE BH6 449 K4
Guillemont Flds FARN GU14 89 M3
Guillemot Cl FAWY SO45 367 M5
Guillemot Gdns
LSOL/BMARY PO13 396 F5
Guinea Ct CHAM RG24 83 M5 3
Gull Cl LSOL/BMARY PO13 396 F6
Gulley Rd FARN GU14 90 D8
Gulliver Cl PSTN BH14 446 B8 2
The Gulls TOTT SO40 342 D6
Gullycroft Md HEND SO30 345 M1
Gun Hl ALDT GU11 112 E5
Gunners La RWIN SO21 171 M2
Gunners Pk BPWT SO32 297 K8
Gunners Rw ENEY PO4 423 M6
Gunners Wy GPORT PO12 397 K8
LSOL/BMARY PO13 397 L7
Gunns Farm LIPH GU30 226 F6
Gunville Crs MOOR/WNTN BH9 432 F5
Gunville Hl RSAL SP5 207 H2
Gunville Rd RSAL SP5 207 G2
Gunwharf Rd PSEA PO1 20 C4
Gurdons ALTN GU34 176 C7
Gurjun Cl UPTN BH16 428 E8 1
Gurnard Rd CHAM PO6 399 J1
Gurnays Md ROMY SO51 288 C5
Gurney Rd ENEY PO4 423 M4
WIMB BH21 429 J2
WSHM SO15 318 B8
Gussage Rd BKME/WDN BH12 431 J8
Gutner La HISD PO11 402 A7
Guttridge La TADY RG26 41 K8
Gwatkin Cl HAV PO9 377 G5 1
Gwenlyn Rd UPTN BH16 444 B2
Gwyn Cl NWBY RG14 25 J8
Gwynne Rd BKME/WDN BH12 446 D3
Gypsy La HORN PO8 352 D3
RGWD BH24 358 F8

H

Haarlem Ms CHCH/BSGR BH23 450 C1
Habin Hl EPSF GU31 277 L4
Hack Dr RWIN SO21 266 E8
Hacketts La BPWT SO32 298 F6
Hackleys La ROMY SO51 289 G3
Hacks La RWIN SO21 189 G5
Hackupps La ROMY SO51 234 B7
Hackwood Cl AND SP10 8 B7
Hackwood La OVTN RG25 128 A2
Hackwood Rd BSTK RG21 105 H5
Hackwood Road Rbt
BSTK RG21 105 H5
Hackworth Gdns HEND SO30 321 H6
Hadden Rd CHAR BH8 433 H8
Haddon Cl FHAM PO15 14 D6
Haddon Dr ELGH SO50 293 M3
Haddons Dr WIMB BH21 380 B1
Hadleigh Gdns ELGH SO50 293 M3
Hadleigh Pl BSTK RG21 4 D8
Hadleigh Rd CHAM PO6 375 H8 3
Hadley Fld FAWY SO45 391 M3 1
Hadleys RFNM GU10 158 B5
Hadley Wy BDST BH18 429 J5
Hadow Rd BWD BH11 432 A5
Hadrian Cl FERN BH22 406 B6
Hadrian Rd AND SP10 119 G5
Hadrians Cl CHFD SO53 293 K1
Hadrians Wy DEAN RG23 104 B1 2
Hadrian Wy ROWN SO16 318 D1
Haflinger Dr HLER SO31 346 F8
Haglane Copse LYMN SO41 439 M6
Hagley Rd FLET GU13 88 D6
Hahnemann Rd WCLF BH2 22 C7
Haig Av PSTN BH14 446 D7
Haig La FLET GU13 111 G3
Haig Rd AND SP10 8 C4
ASHV GU12 7 K3
CBLY GU15 70 C2
ELGH SO50 294 F6
NALR SO24 218 C2
Haileybury Gdns HEND SO30 321 H7 1
Hailsham Cl SHST GU47 50 A7 3
Hailstone Rd BSTK RG21 4 E2
Hainault Dr VWD BH31 356 E2
Haining Gdns FRIM GU16 91 K5
Halcyon Dr RAND SP11 116 D8
Halden Cl ROMY SO51 263 G7
Hale Av NMIL/BTOS BH25 437 M6
Hale Gdns NMIL/BTOS BH25 437 M6
Hale House La RFNM GU10 181 K7
Hale La FBDG SP6 284 E7
Hale Pl FNM GU9 135 H3
Hale Reeds FNM GU9 135 G2
Hale Rd FNM GU9 135 G5
Hales Dr HEND SO30 345 L3
Hales Fld HASM GU27 228 F2
Hale St North PSEA PO1 423 H2
Hale St South PSEA PO1 423 H2
Hale Wy FRIM GU16 71 G7
Halewood Wy
CHCH/BSGR BH23 434 D8
Half Moon Hl HASM GU27 228 F2
Halfpenny La PSEA PO1 20 D5 1
Halifax Cl AND SP10 8 E3
FARN GU14 90 C5
Halifax Pl NTHA RG18 26 F4 1
Halifax Ri WVILLE PO7 376 D1
Halifax Wy CHCH/BSGR BH23 451 G1
FARN GU14 112 C1
Halimote Rd ALDT GU11 6 F3
Hall Cl BPWT SO32 297 J8
CBLY GU15 71 H2
Hallet Cl WEND SO18 319 M6 5
Hallett Rd HAV PO9 17 K3
Halletts Cl FHAM/STUB PO14 396 A5
Hall Farm Crs YTLY GU46 68 F3
The Halliards
FHAM/PORC PO16 396 F1
Halliday Cl BSTK RG21 104 F6
GPORT PO12 18 F2
Halliday Crs ENEY PO4 424 A5
Hall Lands La ELGH SO50 295 J6
Hall La ALTN GU34 199 H6
YTLY GU46 68 F3
Hallmark Cl SHST GU47 50 B8
Hall Rd ALTN GU34 176 F2
BWD BH11 431 K5
FARN GU14 90 E6
Halls Farm Cl WINW SO22 214 D5
The Hall Wy WINW SO22 214 A3
Halsey Cl GPORT PO12 18 B5
Halstead Rd CHAM PO6 375 H8
WEND SO18 319 L6
Halstock Crs CFDH BH17 430 B6
Halter Pth PLE BH15 444 D5
Halter Ri WIMB BH21 405 G2
Halters End GSHT GU26 203 K5
The Halters NWBY RG14 37 L1 1
Halterworth Cl ROMY SO51 291 G1 2
Halterworth La ROMY SO51 263 H8
Haltons Cl TOTT SO40 316 C7
Halyard Cl LSOL/BMARY PO13 421 H1
Hambert Wy TOTT SO40 341 J3 3
Hamble Av BLKW GU17 70 A3
Hamble Cl DEAN RG23 103 G7 2
HLER SO31 370 A7
Hamble Ct BSTK RG21 5 K8
CHFD SO53 293 J3 1
Hambledon Cl WINW SO22 214 C4
Hambledon Gdns SBNE BH6 449 H2
Hambledon La BPWT SO32 325 H6
Hambledon Rd HORN PO8 327 M3
LTDN BH7 449 G1
SBNE BH6 449 H2
WVILLE PO7 326 C8
WVILLE PO7 351 H1 1
Hamble Dr TADY RG26 42 A8
Hamble House Gdns
HLER SO31 369 L6 1
Hamble La HLER SO31 345 K6
WVILLE PO7 376 C3
Hamble Rd GPORT PO12 18 B3
PLE BH15 445 L1
Hamble Springs BPWT SO32 323 J1
Hambleton Cl CBLY GU15 71 L5
Hamblewood HEND SO30 346 E2
Hamborne Ga NWBY RG14 25 G7
Ham Br STHA RG19 26 B5
Hambridge La NWBY RG14 26 B6
Hambridge Rd NWBY RG14 3 J5
Hambrook Hl (North)
RCCH PO18 379 M5
Hambrook Hl (South)
RCCH PO18 379 M6
Hambrook Rd GPORT PO12 421 L2
Hambrook St SSEA PO5 20 F6
Hamburg Cl AND SP10 118 E5 1
Hamdens NWBY RG14 36 F2
Hamdown Crs ROMY SO51 289 G5
Hameldon Cl ROWN SO16 342 D1 2
Hamelyn Rd BSTK RG21 104 F4
Hamesmoor Rd FRIM GU16 91 H4
Hamesmoor Wy FRIM GU16 91 J4
Hamfield Dr HISD PO11 425 J4
Hamilton Cl BMTH BH1 448 C3
HAV PO9 16 F7
BOR GU35 201 L4
NWBY RG14 2 F9
PLE BH15 444 D6 1
Hamilton Ct LYMN SO41 454 B4
Hamilton Crs PLE BH15 444 D6
Hamilton Gv
LSOL/BMARY PO13 396 F7
Hamilton Ms FAWY SO45 367 M7 2
Hamilton Pk RSAL SP5 256 F8
Hamilton Rd BMTH BH1 448 C4
CHAM PO6 374 C8
ELGH SO50 294 C5
FAWY SO45 367 M8
FLET GU13 111 G2 1
LISS GU33 225 J6
PLE BH15 444 D6
SSEA PO5 21 J7
WIMB BH21 429 J3
Ham La EMRTH PO10 403 H1
GPORT PO12 397 L7
HORN PO8 327 L8
TADY RG26 60 E4
WIMB BH21 404 F4
Hamlash La RFNM GU10 158 F7
Hamlet Wy GPORT PO12 397 L7
LSOL/BMARY PO13 397 K7
Hammer Hl HASM GU27 227 M4
Hammer La GSHT GU26 203 M8
HASM GU27 227 M3
LIPH GU30 227 K2
MIDH GU29 279 G4
Hammersley Rd ALDT GU11 112 E1
Hammerwood Copse
HASM GU27 228 A3 1
Hammond Cl FHAM PO15 14 B3
STHA RG19 27 H6
Hammond Rd BSTK RG21 104 F5 2
FHAM PO15 14 C3
Hammonds Cl TOTT SO40 316 D8
Hammond's Gn TOTT SO40 316 C8
Hammonds Heath THLE RG7 43 L2
Hammond's La NALR SO24 220 B4
TOTT SO40 316 D8
Hammonds Wy TOTT SO40 316 D8
Hampshire Cl ASHV GU12 7 M7
CHCH/BSGR BH23 434 D6
KEMP RG22 103 M5
Hampshire Hatches La
RGWD BH24 382 E4
Hampshire Rd CBLY GU15 51 J8
BOR GU35 201 J4
Hampshire St PSEA PO1 423 J1
Hampshire Ter PSEA PO1 20 F4
Hampton Cl FAWY SO45 392 C8
FLET GU13 110 F4
WVILLE PO7 376 E1 1
Hampton Dr RGWD BH24 358 F7
Hampton Gdns FAWY SO45 392 C8
Hampton Gv FHAM PO15 371 M7
Hampton Hl BPWT SO32 324 A2
Hampton La FAWY SO45 392 C6
WINW SO22 214 B7
Hampton Rd FNM GU9 134 D3
NWBY RG14 2 D7
Hamptworth Rd RSAL SP5 286 C4
Ham Rd HUNG RG17 32 D5
Hamtun Crs TOTT SO40 316 D7 1
Hamtun Gdns TOTT SO40 316 D7
Hamtun Rd ITCH SO19 345 G6
Hamtun St SHAM SO14 12 F5
Hanbidge Crs
LSOL/BMARY PO13 397 H4
Hanbury Wy CBLY GU15 70 F5
Hancombe Rd SHST GU47 49 K6
Handcroft Cl RFNM GU10 110 C8
Handel Cl KEMP RG22 104 D7
Handel Rd WSHM SO15 12 E1
Handel Ter WSHM SO15 12 D1
Handford La YTLY GU46 69 G4
Handford Pl WSHM SO15 343 K2 1
Handley Rd GPORT PO12 421 K2 2
Hangerfield Cl YTLY GU46 68 F3
Hanger Rd TADY RG26 41 J7
The Hangers BPWT SO32 297 M4
Hangers Wy ALTN GU34 176 F4
EPSF GU31 303 H4
HORN PO8 302 F6
The Hanger BOR GU35
Hanger Wy EPSF GU31
Hanham Rd WIMB BH21 4
WIMB BH21
Hankinson Rd
MOOR/WNTN BH9
Hanley Rd WSHM SO15
Hanlon Cl BWD BH11
Hanmore Rd CHAM RG24
Hannah Gdns WVILLE PO7 3
Hannam's Farm RFNM GU10 1
Hannay Ri ITCH SO19
Hannington Rd HAV PO9 3
LTDN BH7
Hanningtons Wy THLE RG7
Hann Rd ROWN SO16
Hanns Wy ELGH SO50
Hanover Buildings SHAM SO14
Hanover Cl AND SP10
FRIM GU16
Hanover Dr FARN GU14
Hanover Gdns BSTK RG21
FARN GU14
FHAM/PORC PO16
Hanoverian Wy FHAM PO15
Hanover St PSEA PO1
Hanson Cl CBLY GU15
Hanson Rd AND SP10
Hanway Rd NEND PO2
Ha'penny Dell WVILLE PO7 3
Harbeck Rd CHAR BH8
Harbour Cl CCLF BH13 4
FARN GU14
Harbour Hill Crs PLE BH15
Harbour Hill Rd PLE BH15
Harbourne Gdns WEND SO18
Harbour Pde SHAM SO14
WSHM SO15
Harbour Rd GPORT PO12
HISD PO11
SBNE BH6
Harbourside HAV PO9
Harbour Vw
FHAM/PORC PO16
Harbour View Cl PSTN BH14
Harbour View Rd PSTN BH14
Harbour Wy EMRTH PO10 3
NEND PO2
Harbridge Ct HAV PO9
Harbridge Dro FBDG SP6
Harcourt Cl HORN PO8
Harcourt Rd BOSC BH5
CBLY GU15
FHAM/STUB PO14
GPORT PO12
PSEA PO1
WEND SO18
Harding La ELGH SO50
Harding Rd GPORT PO12
Hardings La HTWY RG27
Hardley La FAWY SO45
The Hard PSEA PO1
Hardwicke Cl ROWN SO16
Hardwicke Wy HLER SO31 3
Hardwick Rd CHFD SO53 2
Hardy Av YTLY GU46
Hardy Cl FERN BH22
HLER SO31
NMIL/BTOS BH25
NTHA RG18
WSHM SO15
Hardy Crs WIMB BH21
Hardy Dr FAWY SO45
Hardyfair Cl RAND SP11
Hardy Gn CWTH RG45
Hardy La BSTK RG21
Hardy Rd CHAM PO6
ELGH SO50
FERN BH22
PSTN BH14
Hardys Fld KSCL RG20
Harebell Cl FHAM/PORC PO16
HTWY RG27
Harebell Dr NTHA RG18
Harebell Gdns HTWY RG27
Harefield Ct ROMY SO51 2
Harefield Rd PTSW SO17
Hare La NMIL/BTOS BH25
RWIN SO21
WIMB BH21
Hares Gn LTDN BH7
Hare's La HTWY RG27
RCCH PO18
Harestock Cl WINW SO22
Harestock Rd WINW SO22
HAV PO9
Harewood Av LTDN BH7
Harewood Cl ELGH SO50
Harewood Crs LTDN BH7
Harewood Gdns LTDN BH7
Harewood Gn LYMN SO41
Harfield Cl HTWY RG27
Harford Cl LYMN SO41
Harford Rd BKME/WDN BH12
Harkness Dr WVILLE PO7
Harkwood Dr PLE BH15
Harland Crs WSHM SO15
Harland Rd SBNE BH6
Harlaxton Cl ELGH SO50
Harlech Cl DEAN RG23
Harlech Dr CHFD SO53
Harlech Rd BLKW GU17
Harlequin Gv FHAM PO15
Harleston Rd CHAM PO6
Harlington Wy FLET GU13
Harlyn Rd ROWN SO16
Harmsworth Rd TADY RG26
Harness Cl WIMB BH21
Harold Cl TOTT SO40
Harold Gdns ALTN GU34
Harold Rd EMRTH PO10
ENEY PO4
FHAM/STUB PO14
HISD PO11
WSHM SO15
Harpdon Pde YTLY GU46
Harper's Rd ASHV GU12
Harpton Cl YTLY GU46

ay La CHCH/BSGR BH23 .. 435 G2
rage ROMY SO51 290 E1
Cl HORN PO8 352 E1
/BMARY PO13 420 D2 4
V SO16 318 A2
Dr WIMB BH21 404 B6
Wy EPSF GU31 276 B6
SO45 391 M2
Cl FHAM/STUB PO14 395 M6
gton Cl NWBY RG14 26 A3
Av HEND SO30 321 H8 3
Hl KEMP RG22 127 G1
La HORN PO8 329 J3
n Av BMTH BH1 448 C2
n Rd FHAM/PORC PO16 15 J3
SO17 319 H5
n Wy FERN BH22 380 C5 1
Rd LSOL/BMARY PO13 397 G5
vay RAND SP11 120 F3
H RG28 99 G7
vay La RAND SP11 117 M6
v Cl CHCH/BSGR BH23 435 M1
v Down WINW SO22 238 C4
vgate La WVILLE PO7 326 E8
v La PSF GU32 275 L2
v Rd CHCH/BSGR BH23 435 L1
PO5 21 L3
v Wy AND SP10 8 A2
RG25 102 A5
SP11 117 M6
rrow Wy KEMP RG22 104 D7
Barrow Cl RGWD BH24 .. 382 E2 3
FARN GU14 70 B8
/BTOS BH25 437 K4
rd Bridge Flats
Y RG27 67 M7
rd Ct HTWY RG27 87 H2 1
rd Ri CBLY GU15 71 G2
rd Rd HTWY RG27 87 H2
FAWY SO45 368 A7
ll Dro RSAL SP5 285 K3
g Cl HORN PO8 328 C4
g Down EPSF GU31 276 A5
g Gdns
M/PORC PO16 374 A7
g Rd SBNE BH6 449 J1
gton Rd GPORT PO12 421 K2
M SO14 13 K1
nd Ct EMRTH PO10 379 H7
nd Pl FARN GU14 90 D2 2
nd's Rd
M/PORC PO16 15 K6
y Av PTSW SO17 319 G6
y Cl BLKW GU17 69 L3
H SO50 294 F7
Y SO45 367 L7 5
y Ct ROWN SO16 318 F4
y Gdns TADY RG26 61 L1
y La HTWY RG27 64 E6
y Meadow
CH RG28 122 A3 2
y Rd ELGH SO50 294 F6
D PO2 399 H5
ys THLE RG7 42 D8
y Wk FAWY SO45 367 K7 2
ead Rd STHA RG19 27 H5
lain Av HORN PO8 352 C6
bourne Dr LTDN BH7 433 M8
Farm Wy HAV PO9 377 G8
grove Cl FAWY SO45 392 C8
Hill Rd NTHA RG18 27 H4
ill Rd TADY RG26 41 J8
La KSCL RG20 57 H2
E RG7 30 E3
eaf Cl FLET GU13 88 E8 1
Leap Cl SHST GU47 49 K7
Leap Rd SHST GU47 49 K8
Wy LYMN SO41 439 H7
wood CHAM RG24 83 K6
art FNM GU9 134 E6
vell Rd HSEA PO3 399 M5 1
vood Gdns HORN PO8 352 C6
rd Rd SHST GU47 50 C7
st Cl WINW SO22 238 C4
GU46 68 E4
st Crs FARN GU14 89 G3
ster Dr FHAM PO15 371 M7
ster Wy LYMN SO41 440 B2
st Gn NWBY RG14 2 B8
sting La PSF GU32 301 M2
st Rd NBAD SO52 292 E2
LLE PO7 351 J4
st Wy CHAM RG24 83 L8
y Ct FAWY SO45 392 C6 2
y Crs HLER SO31 370 D6
y Gdns FAWY SO45 367 M5
y Rd BOSC BH5 448 F3
H SO50 294 D5
N GU14 89 M3
B BH21 404 C8
eys Fld OVTN RG25 100 F8
ch Rd CHAM PO6 375 H7
ood Cl
L/BMARY PO13 397 G4 1
T SO40 316 C8
ood Pl WINC SO23 191 H8
ood Ri KSCL RG20 36 C7
ood Rd
L/BMARY PO13 397 G5
bury Rd TOTT SO40 341 K1
Foot Gdns WEND SO18 .... 345 J1 1
worth Dr GPORT PO12 18 F9
lls Cl LYND SO43 363 J3 1
lls Rd BKME/WDN BH12 446 A1
r Crs WVILLE PO7 352 A6
r Rd GPORT PO12 19 J7
Dr HASM GU27 228 E3
mere Av
H/BSGR BH23 436 D8
mere Cl FRIM GU16 71 M5 2
mere Gdns HISD PO11 426 D6
mere Pl
H/BSGR BH23 436 E8
mere Rd EMRTH PO10 379 H6
Y PO4 423 K6
M GU27 228 E6
H GU30 227 G4
r Rd CFDH BH17 430 A6
Haslop Rd WIMB BH21 404 D1
The Hassocks WVILLE PO7 376 E1
Hastards La ALTN GU34 199 K8
Hasted Dr NALR SO24 218 B4
Haste Hl HASM GU27 229 G3
Hastings Av GPORT PO12 397 K8
Hastings Cl DEAN RG23 104 A3
FRIM GU16 91 K1
Hastings Rd CHAR BH8 433 K6
Hatchbury La RAND SP11 73 H2
Hatch Cl THLE RG7 28 F1
Hatch Ct HAV PO9 377 G1
Hatchers La RWIN SO21 267 L3
The Hatches FNM GU9 134 C8
FRIM GU16 91 J2
Hatchet Cl FBDG SP6 285 J5
Hatchet La BROC SO42 390 B8
RAND SP11 95 H7
Hatchetts Dr HASM GU27 227 M2
Hatchgate Cl NTHA RG18 26 F2
Hatchgate Md HTWY RG27 85 M6 5
Hatch Hl HASM GU27 228 E7
Hatch La CHAM RG24 106 A3
HASM GU27 228 E6
LISS GU33 249 H4
THLE RG7 28 F2
Hatchley La RWIN SO21 296 A2
Hatch Md HEND SO30 320 B6
Hatch Ride CWTH RG45 49 L1
Hatchwarren Gdns
KEMP RG22 127 K1 1
Hatch Warren La KEMP RG22 .... 104 E7
Hatchwarren La KEMP RG22 127 H1
Hatfield Ct CBLY GU15 70 E3 1
NMIL/BTOS BH25 437 J5 2
Hatfield Gdns FARN GU14 91 H5 2
LTDN BH7 433 M8
Hatfield Rd ENEY PO4 423 L5
Hathaway Cl ELGH SO50 294 A4
Hathaway Gdns CHAM RG24 5 H1
WVILLE PO7 352 F7
Hathaway Rd SBNE BH6 449 J4
Hatherden Av PSTN BH14 445 L3
Hatherell Cl HEND SO30 320 C7
Hatherley Crs
FHAM/PORC PO16 397 M1
Hatherley Dr
FHAM/PORC PO16 373 M8 1
Hatherley Rd CHAM PO6 374 E7
WINW SO22 10 D5
Hatherwood YTLY GU46 69 J3 3
Hatley Rd WEND SO18 320 A8
Hattem Pl AND SP10 118 E6 1
Hattingley Rd ALTN GU34 196 B1
Hatt La ROMY SO51 233 K6
Haughurst Hl STHA RG19 40 E8
Havant Farm Cl HAV PO9 16 F1
Havant Rd CHAM PO6 375 K8
EMRTH PO10 17 M5
HAV PO9 17 J6
HISD PO11 401 K5
HORN PO8 353 H2
NEND PO2 399 H7
Havant St PSEA PO1 20 C2 3
Havelock Rd BKME/WDN BH12.. 446 F3
HLER SO31 370 A7
SHAM SO14 12 E1
SSEA PO5 21 K4
WSHM SO15 12 E1
Havelock Wy
CHCH/BSGR BH23 436 B6
Haven Crs FHAM/STUB PO14 395 K7
Havendale HEND SO30 346 B3 3
Haven Gdns NMIL/BTOS BH25 437 M6
Haven Rd CCLF BH13 457 K2
HISD PO11 426 C7
WIMB BH21 429 G2
Havenstone Wy WEND SO18 ... 319 J4 1
The Haven ELGH SO50 294 A3
ENEY PO4 423 M3
GPORT PO12 18 E8
H Av FAWY SO45 392 D2
Haven Wy FNM GU9 135 G4
Haverstock Rd
MOOR/WNTN BH9 432 F6
Haviland Rd BMTH BH1 448 E3
WIMB BH21 405 L1
Haviland Rd East LTDN BH7 448 E3
Havisham Rd NEND PO2 423 H1 4
Hawden Rd BWD BH11 431 L7
Haweswater Cl BOR GU35 201 J3
Hawfinch Cl ROWN SO16 318 A2
Hawkchurch Gdns CFDH BH17 .. 430 C6
Hawk Cl FHAM/STUB PO14 395 M6
KEMP RG22 103 L8 2
WIMB BH21 404 E1
Hawker Cl WIMB BH21 404 D7
Hawker Rd ASHV GU12 113 J3
Hawkes Cl HTWY RG27 87 H1
Hawke St PSEA PO1 20 C1
Hawkeswood Rd WEND SO18 344 A1
Hawkewood Av WVILLE PO7 352 B6
Hawkfield La BSTK RG21 104 F5
Hawkhill FAWY SO45 367 G4
Hawkhurst Cl ITCH SO19 344 E7
Hawkins Cl RGWD BH24 359 G7 2
Hawkins Gv FLET GU13 110 C2
Hawkins Rd BKME/WDN BH12 .. 431 K7
LSOL/BMARY PO13 397 H6
Hawkins Wy FLET GU13 89 H8 1
Hawkley Cl HAV PO9 377 J2 4
Hawkley Dr TADY RG26 61 M1
Hawkley Gn ITCH SO19 344 D8
Hawkley Rd LISS GU33 247 L1
Hawkshaw Cl LIPH GU30 227 G4 1
Hawkswood Av FRIM GU16 71 J6
Hawksworth Rd THLE RG7 31 L5
Hawkwell FHAM/PORC PO16 .... 373 K8
FLET GU13 111 G4
Hawkwood Rd BOSC BH5 448 D4
Hawley Gn BLKW GU17 70 B5
Hawley La FARN GU14 70 E8
Hawley Rd BLKW GU17 70 B5
Haworth Cl CHCH/BSGR BH23 .... 434 E7
Hawswater Cl ROWN SO16 317 L7 2
Hawthorn Cl ASHV GU12 113 H8 1
ELGH SO50 295 H6 1
FHAM/PORC PO16 373 M7
HEND SO30 346 B2 2
NALR SO24 218 C3
NMIL/BTOS BH25 438 A4 3
RWIN SO21 170 A6
RWIN SO21 266 F8
Hawthorn Crs CHAM PO6 399 L2
Hawthorn Dr CFDH BH17 429 K7
LYMN SO41 412 F6
Hawthorne Cl RAND SP11 140 A8 1
Hawthorne Crs BLKW GU17 70 B4
Hawthorne Gv HISD PO11 425 L4
Hawthorne Rd TOTT SO40 316 C8
Hawthorn La ALTN GU34 197 J8
HLER SO31 370 C3
RFNM GU10 158 C5
Hawthorn Ri HTWY RG27 86 A6 3
Hawthorn Rd ALTN GU34 197 G8
CHCH/BSGR BH23 435 J6
FAWY SO45 367 K5 3
FRIM GU16 71 J6
HORN PO8 328 B6
MOOR/WNTN BH9 432 D8
NTID SP9 114 E1
NWBY RG14 2 E1
PTSW SO17 318 F6
WVILLE PO7 351 H4
Hawthorns ALTN GU34 176 D3
The Hawthorns ELGH SO50 293 K7 1
TADY RG26 41 H8 1
TOTT SO40 342 E7
Hawthorn Wy DEAN RG23 104 B2
Hayburn Rd ROWN SO16 317 J6
Haydn Cl WINC SO23 191 G8
Haydn Rd KEMP RG22 104 C8
Haydock Cl ALTN GU34 176 E6
TOTT SO40 316 B8
Haydock Ms WVILLE PO7 352 F7
Haydon Rd CCLF BH13 447 G7
Hay Down La RAND SP11 140 D3
Hayes Av LTDN BH7 448 D2
Hayes Cl STOK SO20 210 E6
WIMB BH21 404 E4
Hayes La WIMB BH21 404 F4
Hayes Md FAWY SO45 391 M3
Hayeswood Rd WIMB BH21 404 E2
Hayle Rd WEND SO18 320 A6
Hayley Cl FAWY SO45 367 K8
Hayley La ODIM RG29 131 G3
Hayling Av HSEA PO3 423 M1
Hayling Cl FHAM/STUB PO14 14 A8
Haymoor Rd PLE BH15 445 M1
Haynes Av PLE BH15 445 J4
Haynes Wy FAWY SO45 367 J7 1
Haysoms Cl NMIL/BTOS BH25 .... 437 M7
Hay St PSEA PO1 20 E2
Hayter Gdns ROMY SO51 262 F8
Hayters Wy FBDG SP6 333 L2
Hayward Cl TOTT SO40 341 H1
Hayward Ct FAWY SO45 392 A4 2
Hayward Crs VWD BH31 356 C3
Haywarden Pl HTWY RG27 87 J1
Haywards Farm Cl
VWD BH31 356 C3 2
The Haywards NTHA RG18 27 G4
Hayward Wy VWD BH31 356 B3
Haywood Dr FLET GU13 110 F1
Hazel Av FARN GU14 90 C6
Hazelbank EWKG RG40 48 A2
Hazelbank Cl EPSF GU31 276 A4
LIPH GU30 227 G4
Hazel Cl CHCH/BSGR BH23 436 A7
CHFD SO53 265 H6
DEAN RG23 103 G7
FBDG SP6 333 L3 4
RAND SP11 8 B9
RWIN SO21 266 F7
TLHT RG30 31 L3
Hazel Coppice HTWY RG27 86 A6 4
Hazeldean Dr HAV PO9 353 M7
Hazeldene CHAM RG24 83 L6 1
Hazeldene Rd LIPH GU30 226 A4
Hazeldown Cl ROWN SO16 317 K3
Hazel Dr FERN BH22 380 B8
Hazeleigh Av ITCH SO19 344 C6
Hazeley Cl HTWY RG27 87 H1
Hazeley Rd RWIN SO21 266 F2
Hazel Farm Rd TOTT SO40 341 G1
Hazel Gv HLER SO31 370 F6
TOTT SO40 340 D5
Hazel Gn TADY RG26 41 G7 1
Hazel Gv WINW SO22 238 C3
GSHT GU26 204 B7
Hazelgrove HORN PO8 328 B3
Hazel Gv NTHA RG18 27 G3
Hazelholt Dr HAV PO9 16 A1
Hazell Av NBNE BH10 431 M6
Hazell Rd FNM GU9 134 C6
Hazel Rd ALTN GU34 197 H5 2
ASHV GU12 136 F1
FRIM GU16 91 K6
HORN PO8 328 B3
ITCH SO19 344 B5
LYMN SO41 439 L4
Hazelwood
FHAM/STUB PO14 395 M3 1
Hazelwood Av HAV PO9 376 F5
NMIL/BTOS BH25 437 J4
Hazelwood Cl DEAN RG23 104 C1
Hazelwood Dr DEAN RG23 104 C1
VWD BH31 356 F4
Hazelwood Rd WEND SO18 .... 319 M7 4
Hazely Cl HTWY RG27 87 H1
Hazlebury Rd CFDH BH17 445 G1
Hazlemere Dr RGWD BH24 381 J5
Hazleton Wy HORN PO8 352 F5
Head Down EPSF GU31 276 A5
Headington Cl KEMP RG22 104 C8 1
Headland Dr HLER SO31 370 E4
Headley Cl
LSOL/BMARY PO13 420 D2 5
Headley Flds BOR GU35 202 B4
Headley Hill Rd BOR GU35 202 C3
Headley La LIPH GU30 202 B6
Headley Rd GSHT GU26 203 J4
BOR GU35 201 M3
LIPH GU30 226 D2
Headmore La ALTN GU34 197 K7
Headon Vw PSF GU32 272 B3
Heads La HUNG RG17 34 D3
NBNE BH10 432 C3
Headswell Av NBNE BH10 432 C4
Headswell Crs NBNE BH10 432 C4
Heanor Cl NBNE BH10 432 A6
Heardman Cl STHA RG19 27 J6
Hearmon Cl YTLY GU46 69 G2
Hearne Gdns BPWT SO32 323 M7
Hearn V BOR GU35 202 D1
Hearsey Gdns BLKW GU17 69 L2
Heath Av PLE BH15 445 J2
Heath Cl ELGH SO50 295 J7
FNM GU9 134 F1 3
GSHT GU26 203 M1
HORN PO8 352 F1
WIMB BH21 404 F1
Heathcote Pl RWIN SO21 265 G1
Heathcote Rd ASHV GU12 113 L5
BMTH BH1 448 E4
BOSC BH5 448 E4
CBLY GU15 71 G3
CHFD SO53 293 J2
BOR GU35 201 K5
NEND PO2 399 K7
Heath End Rd TADY RG26 41 H7
Heathen St BPWT SO32 322 A4
Heatherbrae Gdns
NBAD SO52 291 L4 1
Heatherbrae La UPTN BH16 444 A2
Heather Cha ELGH SO50 294 F6 2
Heather Cl ALDT GU11 6 A3
ASHV GU12 113 L3 1
CHAR BH8 433 H4
CHCH/BSGR BH23 436 E7
EWKG RG40 48 B1 4
FNM GU9 158 C2 1
BOR GU35 201 G7
LSOL/BMARY PO13 396 F6
LYMN SO41 438 E5
RGWD BH24 381 J5
TOTT SO40 341 J1
WIMB BH21 429 J2 1
WVILLE PO7 376 D2
Heather Ct WEND SO18 345 G1
Heatherdale Rd CBLY GU15 70 F4
Heatherdeane Rd PTSW SO17 .... 318 F6
Heatherdell UPTN BH16 444 A2 1
Heatherdene Av CWTH RG45 49 H4
Heatherdene Rd CHFD SO53 265 K7
Heatherdown Rd
FERN BH22 380 E7 1
Heatherdown Wy
FERN BH22 380 E7 2
Heather Dr AND SP10 8 F3
FERN BH22 406 B1
FLET GU13 110 E3
BOR GU35 201 L3
NTHA RG18 27 G3
TADY RG26 41 J6
Heatherfield EPSF GU31 303 J3
Heather Gdns FARN GU14 90 B6 1
FHAM PO15 14 B2
Heather Gv HTWY RG27 87 H1
Heatherlands Rd ROWN SO16 .... 292 E8
Heather La HTWY RG27 107 H3
Heatherlea Rd SBNE BH6 449 J4
Heatherley Cl CBLY GU15 70 E3 2
Heatherley Rd CBLY GU15 70 E3
Heather Md FRIM GU16 71 J6
Heathermount Dr CWTH RG45 .... 49 J2
Heather Rd EPSF GU31 276 B5 1
FAWY SO45 392 D6
NBNE BH10 432 B5
Heather Row La HTWY RG27 107 J3
Heatherstone Av FAWY SO45 .... 367 K8
Heatherton Ms EMRTH PO10 .... 378 D5
Heatherview Cl NBAD SO52 291 L3 1
Heather View Rd
BKME/WDN BH12 446 E1
Heatherway CWTH RG45 49 K3
Heather Wy FERN BH22 406 B1
GSHT GU26 204 C4
KEMP RG22 126 F1
Heath Farm Rd FERN BH22 406 A5
Heath Farm Wy FERN BH22 406 A5
Heathfield FAWY SO45 367 K6 5
Heathfield Av
BKME/WDN BH12 431 L8
FHAM PO15 14 A6
Heathfield Cl ITCH SO19 345 G5 2
Heathfield Ct FLET GU13 110 D1
Heathfield Rd CHFD SO53 265 H6
EPSF GU31 276 B5
FERN BH22 380 E7
ITCH SO19 344 F5
KEMP RG22 127 J1
NEND PO2 399 H8
Heathfield Wy FERN BH22 380 D7
Heath Gdns HLER SO31 369 H1
Heath Green La ALTN GU34 195 M1
Heath Hl RFNM GU10 180 B5
Heath Hill Rd North CWTH RG45.. 49 L3
Heath Hill Rd South CWTH RG45.. 49 L3
Heath House Cl HEND SO30 345 M4
Heath House Gdns HEND SO30.. 345 M4
Heathhouse La HEND SO30 345 M4
Heathlands KSCL RG20 36 D8
TADY RG26 41 H7 1
Heathlands Av FERN BH22 406 B6
Heathlands Cl CHFD SO53 265 H8
VWD BH31 356 E2 2
Heathlands Rd CHFD SO53 265 H8
Heathland St ALDT GU11 6 F2
Heath La BROC SO42 416 A1
FNM GU9 134 F1
MARL SN8 53 H1
RFNM GU10 133 J2
NTHA RG18 26 F3
Heath Lawns FHAM PO15 14 B6
Heathman St STOK SO20 184 F2
Heath Ride CWTH RG45 49 G4
EWKG RG40 48 E2
Heath Ri CBLY GU15 71 G3
Heath Rd BPWT SO32 324 F7
CHCH/BSGR BH23 436 F7
EPSF GU31 275 M5
HASM GU27 228 A3
HLER SO31 370 D5
ITCH SO19 344 E3
LYMN SO41 438 D5
NBAD SO52 291 M5
RGWD BH24 381 H4
TADY RG26 42 B7
WHAM PO17 324 E8
Heath Rd East EPSF GU31 276 A6
Heath Rd North HLER SO31 370 D5
Heath Rd South HLER SO31 370 D5
Heath Rd West
CHCH/BSGR BH23 407 J2
EPSF GU31 275 M6
Heathrow Copse TADY RG26 41 G8
Heathside La GSHT GU26 204 A2 1
Heathside Pk CBLY GU15 71 M1
The Heath WVILLE PO7 351 L4
Heath V AND SP10 9 J7
Heathvale Bridge Rd
ASHV GU12 113 K2
Heathview HTWY RG27 86 B6 3
Heathway CBLY GU15 71 G3
Heathway Cl CBLY GU15 71 G3
Heathwood Av
NMIL/BTOS BH25 437 J8
Heathwood Cl YTLY GU46 69 G1 3
Heathwood Rd
MOOR/WNTN BH9 432 C8
Heathy Cl NMIL/BTOS BH25 437 K8
Heathyfields Rd FNM GU9 134 C2
Heaton Rd GPORT PO12 421 L1
NBNE BH10 431 M6
Hebden Cl STHA RG19 26 F7
Hebrides Cl
FHAM/STUB PO14 395 M5 7
Heckfield Cl HAV PO9 377 M3 7
Heckford La PLE BH15 445 J4
Heckford Rd PLE BH15 445 J4
WIMB BH21 429 G3
Hector Cl WVILLE PO7 376 C6
Hector Rd FHAM/STUB PO14 396 E3
Heddon Wk FARN GU14 90 D1 4
Hedera Rd HLER SO31 370 D5
Hedge End Rd AND SP10 9 K8
Hedgehog La HASM GU27 228 E3
Hedgerley NMIL/BTOS BH25 .. 437 M8 2
Hedgerow Cl ROWN SO16 317 K2
Hedgerow Dr WEND SO18 320 A7 3
Hedgerow Gdns EMRTH PO10 .. 378 D5
The Hedgerows CHAM RG24 83 M8
Hedges Cl NTID SP9 138 C1
Hedges Md AND SP10 8 E8
Hedgeway NWBY RG14 3 K1
Hedley Cl FAWY SO45 392 D7
Hedley Gdns HEND SO30 321 G5 4
Heenan Cl FRIM GU16 91 H1
Heidelberg Rd ENEY PO4 423 K4
Heights Ap UPTN BH16 444 B1
Heights Rd UPTN BH16 429 G8
The Heights FHAM/PORC PO16.. 373 H6
HEND SO30 345 L2
Hei-Lin Wy RAND SP11 92 D6
Hele Cl BSTK RG21 104 F6
Helena Rd ENEY PO4 423 K6
Helen Ct FARN GU14 90 E4 3
Helford Ct AND SP10 119 H6 9
Helford Gdns WEND SO18 320 A6 1
Helksham Cl SHST GU47 50 A7 4
Hellyer Rd ENEY PO4 423 L5
Helm Cl LSOL/BMARY PO13 421 H2
Helsted Cl GPORT PO12 421 J4
Helston Dr EMRTH PO10 378 C5
Helston Rd CHAM PO6 374 D7
Helvellyn Rd ROWN SO16 317 L8
Helyar Rd CHAR BH8 433 K6
Hemdean Gdns HEND SO30 320 C7
Hemlock Rd HORN PO8 352 C4
Hemlock Wy NBAD SO52 292 E3
Hemming Cl TOTT SO40 341 J2
Hemmingway Gdns
FHAM PO15 347 G8
Hempland La ALTN GU34 245 H4
Hempsted Rd CHAM PO6 374 F7
Hemsley Wk HORN PO8 352 E4
Henbury Cl WIMB BH21 429 H2
Henbury Ri WIMB BH21 429 H2
Henbury View Rd
WIMB BH21 429 H2 2
Henderson Rd ENEY PO4 423 M5
Hendford Rd NBNE BH10 432 B6
Hendon Rd BOR GU35 201 K6 5
Hendren Sq AND SP10 119 H6 10
Hendy Cl SSEA PO5 21 J5 1
Henery St GPORT PO12 19 H3 1
Hengest Cl AND SP10 118 C5 5
Hengistbury Rd
NMIL/BTOS BH25 437 J8
SBNE BH6 449 L5
Henley Cl FARN GU14 70 B8
Henley Dr FRIM GU16 91 H1
Henley Gdns FHAM PO15 372 B4
YTLY GU46 69 G3
Henley Rd ENEY PO4 423 K5
Henning's Park Rd PLE BH15 .... 445 J3
Henry Cl FAWY SO45 391 M2 2
Henry Rd ELGH SO50 294 C4 1
WSHM SO15 342 F1
The Henrys NTHA RG18 27 G4
Henry St WSHM SO15 343 K2 2
Henshaw Crs NWBY RG14 25 G8
Henstead Rd WSHM SO15 343 K2
Hensting La RWIN SO21 267 K5
Henty Rd ROWN SO16 317 M8
Henville Cl LSOL/BMARY PO13.... 397 H8
Henville Rd CHAR BH8 23 L1
Henwick Cl NTHA RG18 26 D2
Henwick La NTHA RG18 26 D3
Henwood Down EPSF GU31 .. 275 M5 1
Hepplewhite Cl TADY RG26 41 H7
Hepplewhite Dr KEMP RG22 126 F1
Hepworth Cl AND SP10 9 H2
ITCH SO19 345 G6
Hepworth Cft SHST GU47 70 B2 1
Herbert Av BKME/WDN BH12 .... 431 G8
Herberton Rd SBNE BH6 449 H3
Herbert Rd ENEY PO4 21 L8
FLET GU13 88 D7
GPORT PO12 18 B2
NMIL/BTOS BH25 437 M5

RSAL SP5 285 J2
WBNE BH4 447 G6
Herbert St PSEA PO1 423 G1
Herbert Walker Av WSHM SO15 12 E5
Herbs End FARN GU14 89 M3
Hercules Rd PLE BH15 444 C5 2
Hercules St NEND PO2 399 H8 3
Hereford Cl ODIM RG29 108 B6 2
Hereford La FNM GU9 134 E2
Hereford Md FARN GU14 89 G4 4
Hereford Rd DEAN RG23 104 B3
SSEA PO5 21 J6
Hereward Cl ROMY SO51 291 G1 3
Herewood Cl NWBY RG14 2 C1
Heritage Pk DEAN RG23 127 G3
Hermes Cl FLET GU13 89 H7
Hermes Rd LSOL/BMARY PO13 420 B1
Hermitage Cl BPWT SO32 296 F8 2
FARN GU14 91 G7 1
FRIM GU16 71 J7
HAV PO9 377 J4
Hermitage Rd PSTN BH14 445 M2
Hermits Cl THLE RG7 31 L5
Herm Rd BKME/WDN BH12 431 G7
Herne Rd CHAM PO6 375 J8
EPSF GU31 275 M5
Hern La FBDG SP6 334 F2
Heron Cl ALTN GU34 176 E2
ENEY PO4 423 M3
FLET GU13 111 H3
FRIM GU16 91 J4
LYMN SO41 412 F6
Heron Court Rd
MOOR/WNTN BH9 447 M1
TWDS BH3 447 M2
Herondale HASM GU27 228 B2
Heron Dr WIMB BH21 404 E1
Heron La ROMY SO51 262 C2
Heron Pk CHAM RG24 83 L7
Heron Quay EMRTH PO10 402 E1
Herons Cl FHAM/STUB PO14 396 A4
Herons Sq ELGH SO50 293 K7
Herons Ri AND SP10 9 K9
Heron Wy KEMP RG22 103 L8
LSOL/BMARY PO13 396 E5
STHA RG19 26 E5
THLE RG7 29 L5
Heron Wood Rd ASHV GU12 7 M6
Herretts Gdns ASHV GU12 7 M4
Herrett St ASHV GU12 7 L5
Herriard Wy TADY RG26 61 L1 4
Herrick Cl FRIM GU16 71 M5
ITCH SO19 345 H4
Herriot Ct YTLY GU46 68 F4
Herriott Cl HORN PO8 352 E3
Herstone Cl CFDH BH17 430 D7
Hertford Cl FBDG SP6 309 L5
Hertford Pl PSEA PO1 423 H1
Hertsfield FHAM/STUB PO14 371 G4
Hesketh Cl RGWD BH24 381 L3
Hester Rd ENEY PO4 423 M4 1
Hestia Cl ROMY SO51 263 H8
Heston Cl CHCH/BSGR BH23 434 B4
Heston Wy FERN BH22 380 B5
Hewett Cl FHAM/STUB PO14 395 K1
Hewett Rd FHAM/STUB PO14 395 K1
NEND PO2 399 J6
Hewetts Ri HLER SO31 370 A8
Hewitt Cl GPORT PO12 421 L2 5
Hewitt Rd PLE BH15 444 D4
Hewitt's Rd WSHM SO15 12 B2
Hewshott Gv LIPH GU30 227 H3
Hewshott La LIPH GU30 227 G3
Hexham Cl SHST GU47 50 A6
Heyes Dr ITCH SO19 345 G5
Heysham Rd BDST BH18 429 L5
WSHM SO15 318 A8
Heyshott Rd ENEY PO4 423 K4
Heyward Rd ENEY PO4 21 L4
Heywood Dr BAGS GU19 51 M6
Heywood Gn ITCH SO19 345 J3
Hibberd Wy NBNE BH10 432 B7
Hibbs Cl UPTN BH16 444 B1
Hibiscus Gv BOR GU35 201 K6 5
Hickes Cl BWD BH11 431 K4
Hickory Cl UPTN BH16 428 E8 2
Hickory Dr WINW SO22 214 B4
Hickory Gdns HEND SO30 320 C5
Hicks La BLKW GU17 69 L3
Hides Cl WHCH RG28 122 B4
Highams Cl KSCL RG20 59 J6
Highbank Av WVILLE PO7 375 M5
Highbank Gdns FBDG SP6 309 L7 2
High Beeches FRIM GU16 71 G6
Highbridge Rd ELGH SO50 294 C1
Highbury Cl ELGH SO50 295 H7
NMIL/BTOS BH25 437 M5
Highbury Crs CBLY GU15 71 K1
Highbury Gv CHAM PO6 399 L2
HASM GU27 204 F8 1
Highbury Rd RAND SP11 142 C4
Highbury St PSEA PO1 20 D4
Highbury Wy CHAM PO6 399 K2
Highclere Av HAV PO9 377 H4
Highclere Dr CBLY GU15 71 K1
Highclere Rd ASHV GU12 7 L5
ROWN SO16 318 C5
Highclere Wy CHFD SO53 292 F5
Highcliff Av SHAM SO14 318 F8 2
Highcliffe Dr ELGH SO50 293 M1
Highcliffe Rd
CHCH/BSGR BH23 435 L8
GPORT PO12 18 B4
WINC SO23 239 G2
Highcroft La HORN PO8 328 B8
High Cross PSF GU32 246 D6
High Cross La PSF GU32 246 A8
Highcrown St PTSW SO17 318 F6
Highdown FLET GU13 88 F6
Highdowns KEMP RG22 127 H2
High Dr KEMP RG22 104 B6
LSOL/BMARY PO13 397 G7
Higher Blandford Rd
BDST BH18 429 L3
WIMB BH21 429 K2
Highercombe Rd HASM GU27 205 H8
Higher Md CHAM RG24 83 L8
Highfield LYMN SO41 440 B5
RWIN SO21 266 F3
Highfield Av ALDT GU11 6 F6
FHAM/STUB PO14 14 E8
LYMN SO41 440 A5
NWBY RG14 2 E5
PTSW SO17 318 E5
RGWD BH24 358 E8
RWIN SO21 266 F3
WVILLE PO7 352 E8
Highfield Cha BSTK RG21 4 B8
Highfield Cl ALDT GU11 7 G6
CHFD SO53 293 J2
FARN GU14 90 C4
FNM GU9 158 E1 1
LYMN SO41 412 F6
PTSW SO17 318 F6 1
WIMB BH21 429 J3
WVILLE PO7 352 D7
Highfield Crs GSHT GU26 204 B4
PTSW SO17 319 G6
RSAL SP5 206 E2
Highfield Dr RGWD BH24 358 E7
Highfield Gdns ALDT GU11 6 F6
LISS GU33 249 G4
LYMN SO41 412 F6 1
Highfield La LIPH GU30 227 G6
PTSW SO17 318 F6
RGUW GU3 137 K5
RSAL SP5 285 J3
Highfield Pth FARN GU14 90 C4
Highfield Rd CHFD SO53 293 K2
FARN GU14 90 C4
FERN BH22 380 B4
GPORT PO12 421 K2
LYMN SO41 440 A4
MOOR/WNTN BH9 432 C6
NWBY RG14 2 D9
PSEA PO1 21 K1
PSF GU32 275 L4
PTSW SO17 318 E7
RGWD BH24 358 E8
WIMB BH21 429 J3
High Firs Gdns ROMY SO51 291 H1
High Firs Rd ITCH SO19 344 F3
ROMY SO51 263 H8
Highgate La FARN GU14 90 F3
Highgate Rd HSEA PO3 399 L7
Highgrove FARN GU14 90 E1 2
Highgrove Cl TOTT SO40 341 H3 2
Highgrove Rd HSEA PO3 399 M8
High Howe Cl BWD BH11 431 J4
High Howe La BWD BH11 431 J4
Highland Av CHCH/BSGR BH23 436 F7
Highland Cl EMRTH PO10 378 C8
Highland Dr DEAN RG23 102 F6
FARN GU14 89 G5
Highland Rd ASHV GU12 7 L2
CBLY GU15 51 H8
EMRTH PO10 378 C7
ENEY PO4 423 K5
PSTN BH14 446 A3
WIMB BH21 404 B3
Highlands Cl FAWY SO45 367 L6
FNM GU9 158 E1
NBAD SO52 291 K3 2
Highlands Crs NBNE BH10 432 A4
Highlands Rd AND SP10 9 M6
CHAM PO6 376 B8
FHAM PO15 14 A2
FNM GU9 134 F1
KEMP RG22 103 M5
NMIL/BTOS BH25 437 L8
Highland St ENEY PO4 423 L6
Highlands Wy FAWY SO45 367 K6
RSAL SP5 259 G4
Highland View Cl WIMB BH21 404 B3
High La HASM GU27 204 F8
High Lawn Wy HAV PO9 377 J3
High Md FERN BH22 405 L6
FHAM PO15 14 C1
High Mead La FERN BH22 405 L7
High Meadow ITCH SO19 345 G2
Highmoor Cl WIMB BH21 429 H3 1
Highmoor Rd PSTN BH14 446 B5
WIMB BH21 429 H3
Highmoors CHAM RG24 83 K5
Highmount Cl WINC SO23 11 K9
Highnam Gdns HLER SO31 370 D4
High Oaks Cl HLER SO31 370 E5
High Park Rd BDST BH18 429 J4
FNM GU9 134 E5
High Pitfold GSHT GU26 204 A7
Highridge ALTN GU34 176 C5
High Ridge Crs
NMIL/BTOS BH25 438 A5
High Rd ELGH SO50 319 J3
ROWN SO16 319 J5
High St ALDT GU11 6 E5
ALTN GU34 176 E5
ALTN GU34 196 E1
AND SP10 9 H5
ASHV GU12 7 H3
BPWT SO32 299 G7
BPWT SO32 323 H1
BPWT SO32 325 G5
BPWT SO32 348 C1
BROC SO42 390 D8
CBLY GU15 71 G2
CHAM PO6 399 K1
CHCH/BSGR BH23 450 A2
CWTH RG45 49 M4
ELGH SO50 293 M7
EMRTH PO10 378 D8
EPSF GU31 275 L5
EPSF GU31 303 J3
FARN GU14 90 F8
FAWY SO45 367 L3
FBDG SP6 308 B2
FBDG SP6 309 L7
FBDG SP6 310 D1
FHAM/PORC PO16 15 L4
FHAM/STUB PO14 371 K8
GPORT PO12 19 K3
HASM GU27 229 G2
HEND SO30 320 D7 2
HEND SO30 346 E1
HLER SO31 369 M1
HTWY RG27 87 J2
BOR GU35 201 J5
BOR GU35 202 B3
LSOL/BMARY PO13 420 C2
LYMN SO41 440 C5
LYMN SO41 454 C4
LYND SO43 363 K3
RFNM GU10 158 B5
NTID SP9 114 D8
ODIM RG29 108 C6
OVTN RG25 100 F8
PLE BH15 445 G7
PSEA PO1 20 C5
PSF GU32 272 B3
PSF GU32 273 K7
RAND SP11 92 D6
RAND SP11 140 A7
RGWD BH24 381 J2 1
RGWD BH24 382 D1 2
RWIN SO21 266 F3
SHAM SO14 13 G6
SHST GU47 49 J8
STHA RG19 27 G5
STOK SO20 184 F3
STOK SO20 186 D5
STOK SO20 209 G1
TOTT SO40 341 L1
WHAM PO17 374 D3
WINC SO23 10 F7
WVILLE PO7 326 C5
High St North PLE BH15 445 J5
High Thicket Rd RFNM GU10 180 A4
Hightown Gdns RGWD BH24 382 F2
Hightown Hl RGWD BH24 383 K1
Hightown Rd RGWD BH24 382 E2
Hightrees Av CHAR BH8 433 J7
High Trees Dr WINW SO22 10 C3
High Trees ELGH SO50 295 K6
WVILLE PO7 352 D8
High Trees Wk FERN BH22 406 B1
High Vw FHAM/PORC PO16 374 A7
Highview Cl CHCH/BSGR BH23 434 C5
High View Cl FARN GU14 90 D4
Highview Crs CBLY GU15 51 J7
Highview Gdns
BKME/WDN BH12 446 B1
High View Rd FARN GU14 90 D4
High View Wy WEND SO18 319 L8
High Wy BDST BH18 429 K5
Highway CWTH RG45 49 K3
Highways Rd RWIN SO21 266 B3
The Highway RSAL SP5 256 C2
Highwood Cl FBDG SP6 333 H2 1
NWBY RG14 25 L2
YTLY GU46 68 F4
Highwood La RGWD BH24 359 G6
ROMY SO51 263 J8
Highwood Rdg KEMP RG22 127 G2
Highwood Rd BROC SO42 387 K8
LSOL/BMARY PO13 421 G1
Higworth La HISD PO11 425 K3
Hilary Av CHAM PO6 399 L1
Hilary Dr CWTH RG45 49 L2
Hilary Rd CFDH BH17 430 A7
Hilda Gdns WVILLE PO7 351 L4
Hilda Rd BKME/WDN BH12 446 D2
Hilden Wy WINW SO22 213 M3
Hilder Gdns FARN GU14 91 G5
Hiley Rd PLE BH15 445 H2
Hilfield BLKW GU17 69 J3
Hilland Ri BOR GU35 202 C4
Hillary Cl FHAM/PORC PO16 14 E3
FNM GU9 134 E8 1
LYND SO43 363 L5
Hillary Rd BSTK RG21 4 B4
FNM GU9 158 E1
Hill Barn La RWIN SO21 167 M2
Hillborough Crs SSEA PO5 21 J6 2
Hillbourne Rd CFDH BH17 429 L6
Hillbrook Ri FNM GU9 134 D2
Hillbrow Cl FHAM PO15 14 B1
Hill Brow Cl HAV PO9 353 M7
Hill Brow Rd LISS GU33 248 E5
Hillbrow Rd SBNE BH6 449 G2
Hillbury Av AND SP10 8 D8
Hillbury Rd FBDG SP6 333 L2
Hill Cl CHCH/BSGR BH23 435 L1
ELGH SO50 295 H3
NWBY RG14 37 G1
Hill Ct FARN GU14 70 C7
Hillcrest FLET GU13 88 F5 1
Hillcrest Av CHFD SO53 293 J2
FERN BH22 406 A1
Hillcrest Cl MOOR/WNTN BH9 432 E5
NBAD SO52 291 L3
Hillcrest Ct DEAN RG23 104 A2 1
Hillcrest Dr CHFD SO53 293 J2 2
Hill Crest Dr RFNM GU10 158 C2 2
Hill Crest Gdns BPWT SO32 323 J4
Hillcrest Rd BKME/WDN BH12 445 M3
CBLY GU15 71 L1
MOOR/WNTN BH9 432 E5
WIMB BH21 429 G3
Hill Cft FHAM PO15 371 H5
Hilldene Wy HEND SO30 320 D7 2
Hillditch LYMN SO41 440 B2
Hilldown Rd PTSW SO17 318 F5
Hilldowns Av NEND PO2 399 G6
Hill Farm Cl HASM GU27 228 C3 2
Hill Farm Rd NALR SO24 221 G7
WSHM SO15 343 J2
Hillgarth GSHT GU26 204 A3
Hillgrove Rd WEND SO18 319 L5 1
Hill Head Rd FHAM/STUB PO14 395 L7
Hill House Hl LIPH GU30 226 C1
Hillhouse La STHA RG19 39 K7
Hill Houses La NALR SO24 242 A3
Hillier Wy WINC SO23 11 H3
Hill La CHCH/BSGR BH23 409 L8
CHCH/BSGR BH23 435 K6
EPSF GU31 305 H6
ROWN SO16 318 C5
RWIN SO21 266 E7
WSHM SO15 318 D7
Hillman Rd PSTN BH14 446 C3
Hillmead Gdns HAV PO9 376 F6
Hill Meadow OVTN RG25 100 F6
Hillmeadow VWD BH31 356 E4
Hill Park Rd FHAM PO15 372 B4
GPORT PO12 421 K2
Hill Pl HLER SO31 345 M8
Hill Ri BPWT SO32 299 H3
RWIN SO21 266 F2
Hill Rd DEAN RG23 102 F7
FHAM/PORC PO16 374 B7
FNM GU9 135 G1
GSHT GU26 203 M2
GSHT GU26 203 M5
HASM GU27 228 F2
NWBY RG14 2 A2
RGWD BH24 407 L2
RWIN SO21 145 G6
Hillsborough Ct FARN GU14 70 B8
Hillsborough Pk CBLY GU15 71 M3
Hill School RFNM GU10 158 C1
Hillside CBLY GU15 70 C1
WINW SO22 214 B3
RAND SP11 141 L4
TADY RG26 61 G4
THLE RG7 31 M5
Hillside Av ROMY SO51 290 F1
WEND SO18 319 K7
WVILLE PO7 375 M6
Hillside Cl ALTN GU34 176 E3 1
CHFD SO53 293 J2
FLET GU13 110 B2
WINW SO22 214 B6
BOR GU35 202 D2
RSAL SP5 231 J6
Hillside Ct AND SP10 8 E6 1
Hillside Crs CHAM PO6 374 D7
FRIM GU16 91 J1
Hillside Dr CHCH/BSGR BH23 434 B4
Hillside Gdns WIMB BH21 429 G4
Hillside La FNM GU9 135 G1
Hillside Rd ALDT GU11 6 D6
ASHV GU12 113 L5
BKME/WDN BH12 431 K7
FNM GU9 6 B8
WINW SO22 214 B7
HASM GU27 228 C3
LYMN SO41 440 A5
RFNM GU10 158 E5
ODIM RG29 108 E7
VWD BH31 356 E1
WIMB BH21 429 G3
Hillsley Rd CHAM PO6 374 D6
Hillson Dr FHAM PO15 372 A5
Hill St PLE BH15 445 H6
ROMY SO51 316 B2
Hilltop WINW SO22 214 B3
Hilltop Cl FERN BH22 405 M1
Hilltop Crs CHAM PO6 375 M6
Hilltop Dr ITCH SO19 345 G4
Hilltop Gdns HORN PO8 328 C5
Hilltop Rd FERN BH22 405 M1
OVTN RG25 101 G6
WIMB BH21 429 J3
WVILLE PO7 374 E6
Hilltop Vw YTLY GU46 68 E3
Hillview HORN PO8 353 G3
Hill Vw PSF GU32 273 J7
Hill View Rd FERN BH22 406 A2
FHAM/PORC PO16 374 A7
FNM GU9 134 C6
KEMP RG22 104 D5
ROMY SO51 234 B8
ROMY SO51 263 H2
Hillview Rd FAWY SO45 367 K5
NBNE BH10 432 C5
Hill Wy RGWD BH24 381 J3
The Hillway CHFD SO53 293 J1
FHAM/PORC PO16 374 A8
Hilly Cl RWIN SO21 268 A4
Hillyfields ROWN SO16 317 H4
Hilsea Crs NEND PO2 399 J3
Hiltingbury Av HAV PO9 377 L3 2
Hiltingbury Cl CHFD SO53 265 J7
Hiltingbury Rd CHFD SO53 265 G7
Hiltom Rd RGWD BH24 382 F1
Hilton Cl PLE BH15 445 M2
Hilton Rd GPORT PO12 19 H6
NMIL/BTOS BH25 437 M4
Hinaidi Wy FARN GU14 90 C8
Hinchcliffe Cl PLE BH15 444 E6 1
Hinchcliffe Rd PLE BH15 444 E6
Hindell Cl FARN GU14 70 D8
Hindhead Rd HASM GU27 204 B8
Hinkler Rd ITCH SO19 345 G3
Hinstock Cl FARN GU14 90 D5
Hinton Cl CWTH RG45 49 L1
HAV PO9 377 G4
TADY RG26 61 L1
Hinton Crs ITCH SO19 345 J3
Hinton Dr CWTH RG45 49 L1
Hinton Flds WINC SO23 215 H2
Hinton Hl NALR SO24 242 E4
Hinton Manor La HORN PO8 327 K7
Hinton Rd BMTH BH1 22 F6
Hinton Wood Av
CHCH/BSGR BH23 436 C7
Hintonwood La
CHCH/BSGR BH23 436 C6
Hinwood Cl STOK SO20 209 G1
Hipley Rd HAV PO9 377 L5
Hirst Copse RAND SP11 97 M6
Hirst Rd FAWY SO45 367 M5
Hispano Av FHAM PO15 371 G1
Hitches La FLET GU13 110 B1
Hither Gn EMRTH PO10 379 J6
Hitherwood Cl HORN PO8 352 F7
Hives Wy LYMN SO41 440 B2 2
H Jones Crs ALDT GU11 112 F5 2
Hoadlands EPSF GU31 275 M4
Hoad's Hl WHAM PO17 348 F6
Hobart Dr FAWY SO45 367 M5
Hobart Rd NMIL/BTOS BH25 437 K6
Hobb La HEND SO30 346 B2
Hobbs Cl NALR SO24 219 H4
Hobbs Pk RGWD BH24 381 K4
Hobbs Rd BKME/WDN BH12 431 G8
Hobbs Sq AND SP10 119 H6
Hobby Cl HSEA PO3 399 L4
Hobson Wy FAWY SO45 392 B5 2
Hoburne Gdns
CHCH/BSGR BH23 436 A7
Hoburne La CHCH/BSGR BH23 435 M8
Hockford La THLE RG7
Hockham Ct HAV PO9
Hockley Cl CHAM PO6
Hockley Link RWIN SO21
Hocombe Dr CHFD SO53
Hocombe Park Cl CHFD SO53
Hocombe Rd CHFD SO53
Hocombe Wood Rd
CHFD SO53
Hodder Cl CHFD SO53
Hodges Cl CFDH BH17
HAV PO9
Hoeford Cl FHAM/PORC PO16
Hoe La ROMY SO51
Hoe Rd BPWT SO32
Hoe St WVILLE PO7
The Hoe LSOL/BMARY PO13
Hogarth Cl BSTK RG21
ROMY SO51
SHST GU47
Hogarth Ct AND SP10
Hoggarth Cl EPSF GU31
Hoghatch La FNM GU9
Hogmoor Rd BOR GU35
Hogs Lodge La HORN PO8
Hogue Av NBNE BH10
Hogwood La EWKG RG40
HEND SO30
Holbeche Cl YTLY GU46
Holbein Cl BSTK RG21
Holborne Cl NWBY RG14
Holbrook Cl FNM GU9
Holbrook Rd FHAM/PORC PO16
PSEA PO1
Holbrook Wy ALDT GU11
Holbury Cl CHAR BH8
Holbury Ct HAV PO9
Holbury Dro FAWY SO45
Holbury La RSAL SP5
Holcombe Rd UPTN BH16
Holcot La HSEA PO3
Holcroft Rd ITCH SO19
Holdaway Cl WINC SO23
Holdenbury Ct HSEA PO3
Holdenhurst Av LTDN BH7
Holdenhurst Cl HORN PO8
Holdenhurst Rd BMTH BH1
CHAR BH8
CHAR BH8
Holden La RWIN SO21
Holder Rd ASHV GU12
Holdfast La HASM GU27
Holding La NALR SO24
Hole La BPWT SO32
RFNM GU10
WVILLE PO7
Holes Bay Rd PLE BH15
Holes Cl LYMN SO41
Holkham Cl ROWN SO16
Hollam Cl FHAM/STUB PO14
Hollam Crs FHAM/STUB PO14
Hollam Dr FHAM/STUB PO14
Hollam Rd ENEY PO4
Holland Cl FNM GU9
Holland Dr AND SP10
Holland Gdns FLET GU13
Holland Pk HLER SO31
Holland Pl
LSOL/BMARY PO13
ROWN SO16
Holland Rd ENEY PO4
ITCH SO19
TOTT SO40
The Hollands STHA RG19
Hollands Wood Dr
NMIL/BTOS BH25
Holland Wy BDST BH18
Hollies Cl LYMN SO41
The Hollies NWBY RG14
Hollingbourne Cl WEND SO18
Hollington La KSCL RG20
Hollist La EPSF GU31
Hollis Wood Dr RFNM GU10
Hollman Dr ROMY SO51
Holloway Av BWD BH11
Hollow La HISD PO11
BOR GU35
Hollowshot La KSCL RG20
TADY RG26
The Hollow STOK SO20
Holly Av FRIM GU16
Hollybank LSOL/BMARY PO13
Holly Bank Cl HORN PO8
Hollybank Crs FAWY SO45
Hollybank La EMRTH PO10
Hollybank Rd FAWY SO45
Hollybrook Av ROWN SO16
Hollybrook Cl ROWN SO16
Hollybrook Gdns HLER SO31
Hollybrook Pk BOR GU35
Hollybrook Rd ROWN SO16
Hollybush La ALDT GU11
HTWY RG27
TADY RG26
THLE RG7
Hollybush Ride EWKG RG40
Holly Cl ASHV GU12
FARN GU14
FAWY SO45
HLER SO31
BOR GU35
RGWD BH24
TADY RG26
Hollycombe Cl LIPH GU30
Holly Dell ROWN SO16
Holly Dr CHAM RG24
WVILLE PO7
Hollyfields Cl CBLY GU15
Holly Gdns CHCH/BSGR BH23
HEND SO30
LYMN SO41
Holly Gv FHAM/PORC PO16
VWD BH31
Holly Hatch Rd TOTT SO40
Holly Hedge Cl FRIM GU16
Holly Hedge La CFDH BH17
Holly Hedge Rd FRIM GU16
Holly Hl ROWN SO16

ill Cl ROWN SO16 318 D3
ill La HLER SO31 370 A4
ock Cl KEMP RG22 103 M8
1 CHCH/BSGR BH23 437 G6
SO41 414 F7
/BTOS BH25 438 A4
RG7 42 E8
ak Rd ROWN SO16 317 M5
dge HASM GU27 228 F2
d ASHV GU12 7 K2
GU14 90 C4
SO45 392 C8
SO40 340 F6
: GPORT PO12 19 H3
ee Gdns FRIM GU16 71 G8
ees FLET GU13 110 D2
ater Rd LIPH GU30 201 L8
y BLKW GU17 70 A4
ell Dr CHAM PO6 398 F1
ood Cl NBAD SO52 291 L4
ood La LYMN SO41 440 B3
n Cl HORN PO8 352 E6
rook Cl FARN GU14 89 M4
ury Av CWTH RG45 49 K1
l RGWD BH24 359 G7
ale Rd GPORT PO12 421 K1
ene THLE RG7 31 L5
Cl CWTH RG45 49 K1
ield Av
/STUB PO14 396 D2
Rd CHCH/BSGR BH23 436 F8
Cl KEMP RG22 127 H2
Ct AND SP10 8 C6
sland Dr HEND SO30 346 D1
sland La HEND SO30 346 D1
eld Av LTDN BH7 449 H1
rove
/STUB PO14 371 G5
ill La CHCH/BSGR BH23 436 F1
urst Av
/BSGR BH23 436 D7
ak Cl WINW SO22 213 M3
ey Cl LYMN SO41 439 M6
SO18 345 G1
ey Rd NMIL/BTOS BH25 411 H6
ood Garth RGWD BH24 383 H2
t ENEY PO4 424 A5
Rd CFDH BH17 430 B7
KEMP RG22 127 K1
y WVILLE PO7 376 D3
FARN GU14 90 F1
PO17 348 D4
ttages STHA RG19 40 C8
ITCH SO19 344 C8
wn EPSF GU31 276 A5
d La ALTN GU34 174 D6
GU34 174 F4
ns HAV PO9 353 M5
HTWY RG27 108 B1
SP11 73 G8
RG26 60 C4
und La RFNM GU10 157 M3
BKME/WDN BH12 446 E2
BH21 356 B8
SO15 343 K1
HTWY RG27 86 B6
od Rd KSCL RG20 35 L2
rn Cl KEMP RG22 103 M7
rne Rd ROMY SO51 291 G1
urne Rd HAV PO9 16 E1
ok Cl CWTH RG45 49 K2
od Av PTSW SO17 319 G6
od Cl WVILLE PO7 376 E1
ll Cl CFDH BH17 430 B5
GU14 90 D1
ll Ct STHA RG19 27 G5
Cl NALR SO24 173 M6
SO24 219 H3
arm Cl FARN GU14 91 G2
SO45 367 M6
arm Gdns AND SP10 118 C5
arm Rd HTWY RG27 88 A1
arm Wy VWD BH31 356 C2
eld ROMY SO51 262 F7
ield Dr ROWN SO16 317 H3
eld Rd CHAM PO6 400 A1
H PO10 378 F4
eld Wy HORN PO8 328 A2
a RWIN SO21 213 H5
a Cl FARN GU14 70 E8
igh Crs ASHV GU12 91 K8
ld OVTN RG25 125 L7
E PO7 351 K5
lead Cl NWBY RG14 25 H8
ark Rd YTLY GU46 68 F2
Cl HORN PO8 352 C6
BMARY PO13 396 F8
Farm La FAWY SO45 418 C2
d BWD BH11 431 M2
ule Rd HLER SO31 370 E4
de Rd
R/WNTN BH9 432 E6
ead Rd ALTN GU34 196 C3
eads Rd KEMP RG22 103 M7
Vy EPSF GU31 276 B5
vell HAV PO9 16 E5
ood Cl
BTOS BH25 438 A5
SHST GU47 69 L1
ottom Rd TADY RG26 41 L7
ourne Crs SBNE BH6 449 M4
ritch La PSF GU32 247 G5
La ALTN GU34 223 L1
PO15 372 B3
BH24 384 C6
uckle Cl CWTH RG45 49 K1
SO22 238 C4
SO31 370 E3
RG22 103 M8
BMARY PO13 396 F5
GU46 68 D2
uckle Ct WVILLE PO7 376 D3
uckle La CFDH BH17 429 K7
U35 202 E3
uckle Rd ROWN SO16 319 G4
uckle Wy NBAD SO52 292 F2
vood Cl HSEA PO3 399 K4
SO40 316 C7
Honister Gdns FLET GU13 89 H6
Hood Cl HLER SO31 370 F4
NBNE BH10 431 M7
Hood Crs NBNE BH10 431 M7
Hood Rd WEND SO18 319 M8
Hook Cl CHFD SO53 264 F6
Hook Crs CHFD SO53 264 F6
Hooke Cl CFDH BH17 430 E6
Hook La HLER SO31 394 E1
NALR SO24 219 M4
TADY RG26 60 E2
TADY RG26 80 F8
Hook Park Rd HLER SO31 394 A1
Hookpit Farm La WINC SO23 191 G8
Hook Rd HTWY RG27 85 M3
HTWY RG27 107 M1
KSCL RG20 59 K6
ODIM RG29 107 L4
ODIM RG29 108 B3
ROMY SO51 264 D5
Hook's Farm Wy HAV PO9 16 A1
Hook's La HAV PO9 16 B2
Hookstile La FNM GU9 134 F7
Hook Water Rd CHFD SO53 264 F6
Hookwood La RAND SP11 93 M1
ROMY SO51 264 E6
Hoopersmead OVTN RG25 127 M1
Hoopers Wy DEAN RG23 103 G7
Hope Fountain CBLY GU15 71 J4
Hope Grant's Rd ALDT GU11 112 D4
Hope La FNM GU9 134 E2
Hopeman Cl SHST GU47 70 A1
Hope Rd HEND SO30 320 D6
Hope St PSEA PO1 423 G2
Hopeswood LISS GU33 224 E5
Hopfield Cl WVILLE PO7 376 C2
Hopfield Ms WVILLE PO7 376 C2
Hopfield Rd HTWY RG27 87 H3
Hop Gdn FLET GU13 110 D4
Hop Garden Rd HTWY RG27 85 L7
The Hop Gdn EPSF GU31 304 F5
Hopkins Cl CHAM PO6 374 C8
CHAR BH8 433 L6
Hopkinson Wy AND SP10 118 A7
Hopton Garth CHAM RG24 83 M7
Hopwood Cl NWBY RG14 3 L1
Horace Rd BOSC BH5 448 D4
Hordle La LYMN SO41 438 D8
Hordle Rd HAV PO9 377 G4
Horlock Rd BROC SO42 387 L6
Hormer Cl SHST GU47 50 A7
Hornbeam Cl FARN GU14 89 M3
HEND SO30 346 B2
RWIN SO21 190 D4
SHST GU47 50 A7
Hornbeam Gdns HEND SO30 320 C6
Hornbeam Pl HTWY RG27 86 A6
Hornbeam Rd HAV PO9 17 K1
NBAD SO52 292 D3
Hornbeams THLE RG7 45 M1
Hornbeam Wy WIMB BH21 404 B3
Hornby Cl HLER SO31 370 B8
Hornchurch Rd ROWN SO16 317 L3
Horndean Rd EMRTH PO10 378 B4
HORN PO8 328 D8
Horne Rd STHA RG19 27 G6
Hornet Cl FHAM PO15 14 A3
GPORT PO12 19 H6
Hornet Rd EMRTH PO10 402 E5
FHAM/STUB PO14 396 D3
Horning Rd BKME/WDN BH12 446 E3
Horn Rd FARN GU14 90 B3
Horns Dro ROWN SO16 317 K2
Horns Hl BPWT SO32 325 G6
Horsa Cl SBNE BH6 449 K4
Horsa Ct SBNE BH6 449 K4
Horsa Rd SBNE BH6 449 K4
Horsea La NEND PO2 399 H4
Horsea Rd NEND PO2 399 J3
Horsebridge Rd HAV PO9 377 L4
STOK SO20 209 K4
Horsebridge Wy ROWN SO16 317 K3
Horsecroft ROMY SO51 262 E8
Horsefair Ct ROMY SO51 290 D1
Horse La ALTN GU34 220 C1
Horsepost La WVILLE PO7 327 G6
Horse Sands Cl ENEY PO4 424 B5
Horseshoe Bend GSHT GU26 203 K5
Horseshoe Cl CBLY GU15 51 J8
FHAM/STUB PO14 371 H6
WIMB BH21 404 F2
Horseshoe Crs CBLY GU15 51 J8
BOR GU35 201 K5
THLE RG7 31 K5
Horseshoe Dr ROMY SO51 263 H6
Horseshoe End NWBY RG14 37 L1
Horseshoe La ASHV GU12 113 K2
RAND SP11 74 C8
Horseshoe Ldg HLER SO31 370 C7
Horsham Av NBNE BH10 432 A2
Horsham Rd SHST GU47 50 A7
Horton Cl MOOR/WNTN BH9 433 G5
Horton Rd LSOL/BMARY PO13 397 G4
RGWD BH24 381 G2
Horton Wy ELGH SO50 294 E7
VWD BH31 356 B3
Horwood Gdns BSTK RG21 104 E6
Hose Hl THLE RG7 31 K1
Hosker Rd BOSC BH5 449 G3
Hosketts La STOK SO20 184 D3
Hospital Hl ALDT GU11 6 E1
Hospital La FHAM/PORC PO16 398 C2
Hospital Rd ALDT GU11 112 D5
BPWT SO32 323 M7
Hostel Rd FARN GU14 90 E8
Hotspur Cl FAWY SO45 367 K3
Houchin St BPWT SO32 323 H1
Houghton Cl HAV PO9 377 M2
Houlton Rd PLE BH15 445 K4
Hound Cl HLER SO31 369 H3
Hound Green Cl HTWY RG27 66 A5
Houndmills Rd BSTK RG21 104 D2
Hound Rd HLER SO31 369 H2
Hound Road Gdns HLER SO31 369 H3
Hounds Wy WIMB BH21 404 F3
Hound Wy HLER SO31 369 H2
Houndwell Pl SHAM SO14 13 H4
Hounsdown Av TOTT SO40 341 K3
Hounsdown Cl TOTT SO40 341 K3
Hounslow Cl PLE BH15 444 D6
House Cl RWIN SO21 266 F7
House Farm Rd GPORT PO12 421 J4
Houseman Rd FARN GU14 90 C2
Hoveton Gv CHFD SO53 265 G8
Howard Cl CHCH/BSGR BH23 450 E2
CHFD SO53 293 J4
ELGH SO50 295 H6
FLET GU13 89 H7
RGWD BH24 384 E5
WEND SO18 319 K4
Howard Cole Wy ALDT GU11 6 A2
Howard Dr FARN GU14 89 L4
Howard Rd BSTK RG21 105 H5
CHAR BH8 448 B1
NEND PO2 399 J4
NWBY RG14 2 E7
VWD BH31 356 D2
WSHM SO15 343 H2
Howard's Gv WSHM SO15 318 B8
Howard's La ALTN GU34 177 H1
Howards Md LYMN SO41 439 M6
Howe Cl CHCH/BSGR BH23 450 E3
NMIL/BTOS BH25 437 K5
Howe La VWD BH31 356 C3
Howe Rd LSOL/BMARY PO13 421 G2
Howerts Cl HLER SO31 394 B1
Howes Gdns FLET GU13 110 D2
Howeth Cl NBNE BH10 432 B5
The Howe FARN GU14 89 L7
Howeth Rd NBNE BH10 432 A4
Howgare Rd RSAL SP5 252 A6
Howlett Cl LYMN SO41 440 A4
Howton Rd NBNE BH10 432 A3
Hoxley Rd NBNE BH10 432 B4
Hoyal Rd PLE BH15 444 C5
Hoylake Cl
LSOL/BMARY PO13 397 G7
Hoylake Rd CHAM PO6 376 A7
Hoylecroft Cl FHAM PO15 14 C1
Hubbard Rd BSTK RG21 4 A4
Hubert Rd WINC SO23 238 D4
Huddington Gld HTWY RG27 68 D3
Hudson Cl BKME/WDN BH12 431 G6
LSOL/BMARY PO13 421 G2
RGWD BH24 359 G8
Hudson Ct TOTT SO40 341 H2
Hudson Davies Cl LYMN SO41 414 D7
Hudson Rd SSEA PO5 21 J4
Hudsons Meadow HTWY RG27 66 A5
Hugh's Cl FAWY SO45 392 C7
Huish La OVTN RG25 106 A6
Hulbert Rd HAV PO9 376 F3
WVILLE PO7 376 E1
Hulbert Wy KEMP RG22 104 B6
Hulfords La HTWY RG27 67 K7
Hullam La ALTN GU34 223 G3
Hull Crs BWD BH11 431 H4
Hulles Wy NBAD SO52 291 L4
Hull Rd BWD BH11 431 H4
Hull Wy BWD BH11 431 H4
Hulse Rd WSHM SO15 318 E8
Hulton Cl ITCH SO19 344 B7
Humber Cl
FHAM/STUB PO14 395 M5
NTHA RG18 26 E3
Humber Gdns HLER SO31 345 L7
Humber La NTID SP9 114 C4
Humber Rd FERN BH22 406 E2
Humberstone Rd AND SP10 9 H8
Humbers Vw STOK SO20 210 F7
Humber Wy SHST GU47 50 A8
The Hummicks BROC SO42 390 F8
Hundred Acres Rd
WHAM PO17 349 L3
Hundred La LYMN SO41 440 D1
The Hundred ROMY SO51 290 D1
WVILLE PO7 352 B7
Hungerfield Cl
CHCH/BSGR BH23 409 L7
Hungerford HLER SO31 369 K1
Hungerford Cl SHST GU47 49 M8
Hungerford Hl FBDG SP6 335 G3
Hungerford La AND SP10 118 F2
RAND SP11 72 D6
Hungerford Rd MARL SN8 52 F2
Hunnels Cl FLET GU13 110 D5
Hunt Av HLER SO31 369 G2
Hunt Cl RWIN SO21 190 D4
Hunter Cl CHCH/BSGR BH23 450 F1
FAWY SO45 391 M2
LSOL/BMARY PO13 421 H1
WIMB BH21 405 G2
Hunter Rd EMRTH PO10 402 E4
ENEY PO4 423 K5
FARN GU14 90 C5
Hunters Cha BPWT SO32 324 B5
LIPH GU30 226 E3
Hunters Cl DEAN RG23 103 G5
VWD BH31 357 G3
Hunters Crs ROMY SO51 263 H6
TOTT SO40 340 F2
Hunter's Hl THLE RG7 31 J5
TOTT SO40 341 H5
Hunters Ldg FHAM PO15 371 M8
Hunters Ride WVILLE PO7 376 C1
Hunters Rd LISS GU33 225 J6
Hunters Wy ELGH SO50 294 F6
Huntfield Rd
MOOR/WNTN BH9 432 F5
Huntick Rd UPTN BH16 428 A5
Huntingdon Cl
FHAM/STUB PO14 371 G7
TOTT SO40 316 D7
Huntingdon Dr WIMB BH21 404 C7
Huntingdon Gdns
CHCH/BSGR BH23 434 D6
Huntingdon House Dr
GSHT GU26 204 B4
Huntingford Cl GSHT GU26 203 M1
Huntley Cl CHAM PO6 374 F7
Huntly Rd TWDS BH3 447 J2
Huntly Wy WEND SO18 344 D1
Hunton Cl ROWN SO16 318 C5
Hunton Down La RWIN SO21 168 F4
Hunton La RWIN SO21 168 E4
Hunt Rd CHCH/BSGR BH23 435 K8
PLE BH15 445 K4
Huntsbottom La LISS GU33 249 G5
Hunts Cl HTWY RG27 86 B7
Huntsman's Ms FRIM GU16 91 J5
Huntsmead ALTN GU34 176 F5
Huntsmoor Rd TADY RG26 41 J8
Hunts Pond Rd HLER SO31 370 F4
Huntvale Rd
MOOR/WNTN BH9 432 F5
The Hurdles FHAM/STUB PO14 371 H6
Hurdle Wy RWIN SO21 238 B8
Hurland La BOR GU35 202 C4
Hurlands Cl FNM GU9 135 J4
Hurlands Pl FNM GU9 135 J4
Hurlingham Gdns
ROWN SO16 318 F3
Hurn Cl RGWD BH24 382 B2
Hurn Ct HAV PO9 377 M2
Hurn Court La
CHCH/BSGR BH23 433 K2
Hurn La RGWD BH24 382 B2
Hurn Rd CHCH/BSGR BH23 434 C5
RGWD BH24 382 A8
Hurn Wy CHCH/BSGR BH23 434 B7
Hurricane Dr ROWN SO16 317 K2
Hurricane Wy FARN GU14 112 C1
Hursley Dr FAWY SO45 418 C1
Hursley Rd CHFD SO53 293 C1
HAV PO9 377 H3
RWIN SO21 265 G4
Hurstbourne Av
CHCH/BSGR BH23 436 C7
Hurstbourne Cl HAV PO9 377 H2
Hurst Cl CHCH/BSGR BH23 437 G6
CHFD SO53 292 F4
FHAM/STUB PO14 395 L7
LIPH GU30 226 D3
TOTT SO40 316 E8
Hurstdene Rd CHAR BH8 433 G6
Hurst Gn LSOL/BMARY PO13 396 F6
Hurst Green Cl HORN PO8 352 F6
ITCH SO19 344 E7
Hurst Hl PSTN BH14 446 B8
Hurst La ALTN GU34 246 A5
RWIN SO21 295 M2
Hurstmere Cl GSHT GU26 204 A5
Hurst Rd ALDT GU11 112 F5
FARN GU14 70 E8
LYMN SO41 454 D5
RGWD BH24 358 E7
The Hurst HTWY RG27 87 L7
Hurstville Dr WVILLE PO7 376 D1
Hurstwood Av EMRTH PO10 379 J8
Hussar Ct ALDT GU11 6 A2
Hussell La ALTN GU34 196 E1
Hussey Cl WINC SO23 11 H2
Hussey's La ALTN GU34 156 B3
Hutton Cl NWBY RG14 3 G1
Hutton Rd ASHV GU12 113 K2
Hutton Sq AND SP10 119 H6
Hutwood Rd ROWN SO16 292 F8
Huxley Cl HLER SO31 370 F6
Huxley Ct FAWY SO45 367 G6
Hyacinth Cl CFDH BH17 429 K7
KEMP RG22 103 M8
Hyde Abbey Rd WINC SO23 11 G6
Hyde Church La WINC SO23 11 G5
Hyde Cl LYMN SO41 412 F6
TOTT SO40 340 F1
WINC SO23 10 F5
WSHM SO15 318 B7
Hyde End La STHA RG19 40 A3
Hyde La FBDG SP6 335 G3
KSCL RG20 58 D2
RFNM GU10 133 G1
Hyden Farm La HORN PO8 327 J2
Hyde Park Rd SSEA PO5 21 H3
Hyde Rd NBNE BH10 432 A3
Hydes Platt THLE RG7 42 E8
Hyde St SSEA PO5 21 G5
WINC SO23 11 G5
The Hyde NMIL/BTOS BH25 437 J4
Hylton Rd PSF GU32 275 L5
Hymans Wy TOTT SO40 341 J1
Hynesbury Rd
CHCH/BSGR BH23 451 H2
Hyson Crs RAND SP11 93 G6
Hyssop Cl FHAM PO15 371 H1
Hythe By-pass FAWY SO45 366 F4
Hythe Rd CHAM PO6 375 J8
PLE BH15 445 M1
TOTT SO40 342 D8

I

Ibbertson Cl CHAR BH8 433 K6
Ibbertson Rd CHAR BH8 433 K7
Ibbertson Wy CHAR BH8 433 K6
Ibbett Rd NBNE BH10 432 A6
Ibbotson Wy TOTT SO40 341 H3
Iberian Wy CBLY GU15 71 K2
Ibsen Cl HLER SO31 347 G8
Ibsley Cl CHAR BH8 448 B2
Ibsley Dro RGWD BH24 334 E7
Ibsley Gv HAV PO9 16 A1
Ibworth La TADY RG26 80 A5
Icarus Pl WVILLE PO7 376 D6
Icknield Wy AND SP10 119 G3
Iddesleigh Rd TWDS BH3 447 L2
Idsworth Cl HORN PO8 353 H2
Idsworth Rd HORN PO8 352 F6
HSEA PO3 399 L8
Iford Ct HAV PO9 377 M2
Iford Gdns LTDN BH7 449 H1
Iford La SBNE BH6 449 K1
Ilex Cl TADY RG26 42 B7
WINC SO23 191 G8
YTLY GU46 68 E2
Ilex Crs HLER SO31 370 D5
Ilex Wk HISD PO11 426 A5
Iley La LYMN SO41 455 H1
Ilford Cl SBNE BH6 449 L2
Ilkley Wy STHA RG19 26 F6
Imadene Crs BOR GU35 201 L4
Imber Cl ITCH SO19 345 G4
Imber Dr CHCH/BSGR BH23 436 D8
Imber Rd WINC SO23 11 L6
Imber Wy ITCH SO19 345 G4
Imbrecourt CCLF BH13 457 K1
Imjin Cl ALDT GU11 112 E5
Imperial Av WSHM SO15 342 F1
Imperial Rd SHAM SO14 343 M1
Implacable Rd
LSOL/BMARY PO13 420 B1
Impstone Rd TADY RG26 42 C7
Imran Ct ASHV GU12 7 J5
Ingersley Ri HEND SO30 320 C7
Ingle Dell CBLY GU15 71 G4
Ingledene Cl GPORT PO12 18 E4
HAV PO9 16 A3
Ingle Gln EWKG RG40 48 D1
FAWY SO45 367 L7
Ingle Gn TOTT SO40 316 A7
Ingles Edge HUNG RG17 34 A4
Inglesham Wy PLE BH15 444 D4
PLE BH15 444 D5
Ingleside HLER SO31 369 G1
Ingleside Cl
FHAM/STUB PO14 371 M8
Ingleton Rd ROWN SO16 317 J7
Inglewood Av CBLY GU15 71 M4
CHAR BH8 433 K7
Inglewood Dr KEMP RG22 127 G2
NMIL/BTOS BH25 437 M6
Inglis Rd SSEA PO5 21 L5
Ingoldfield La WHAM PO17 350 A1
Ingworth Rd
BKME/WDN BH12 446 F3
Inhams La WVILLE PO7 351 H4
Inhams Rd ALTN GU34 177 J2
Inhams Wy THLE RG7 42 D8
Inhurst Av WVILLE PO7 352 E8
Inhurst La STHA RG19 40 F7
Inhurst Rd NEND PO2 399 J6
Inhurst Wy TADY RG26 41 J7
Inkerman Rd ITCH SO19 344 B5
Inkpen Gdns CHAM RG24 83 M8
Inlands Rd RCCH PO18 379 K7
Inmans La PSF GU32 276 A3
Innisfail Gdns ALDT GU11 6 C5
Insley Crs WIMB BH21 429 J3
Institute Rd ASHV GU12 7 L5
Instow Gdns FARN GU14 90 D1
International Wy ITCH SO19 344 C8
Inval Hl HASM GU27 204 F8
Inveravon CHCH/BSGR BH23 450 E4
Inverclyde Rd PSTN BH14 446 B4
Invergordon Av CHAM PO6 399 M1
Inverkip Cl
LSOL/BMARY PO13 420 C1
Inverleigh Rd SBNE BH6 449 H2
Inverness Av FHAM PO15 14 C2
Inverness Rd NEND PO2 423 J1
Inverness Wy SHST GU47 70 A1
Invincible Rd FARN GU14 90 D6
Inwood Rd LISS GU33 248 F5
Ionic Cl CHFD SO53 293 L1
Iping Av HAV PO9 377 H3
Iping La MIDH GU29 279 H5
Iping Rd LIPH GU30 250 E6
Ipley Wy FAWY SO45 367 L6
Ipoh Cl STOK SO20 162 F3
Ipswich Rd WBNE BH4 447 G4
Ireland Wy WVILLE PO7 376 C3
Iris Cl KEMP RG22 126 F1
Iris Rd MOOR/WNTN BH9 432 D7
ROWN SO16 319 G4
Ironbridge Crs HLER SO31 370 E2
Ironbridge La ENEY PO4 424 A4
Iron Mill Cl FHAM PO15 14 A1
Ironmill La FHAM PO15 371 M3
Irvine Cl FHAM/PORC PO16 15 G2
Irvine Dr FARN GU14 70 B8
Irvine Wy CHCH/BSGR BH23 435 J8
Irving Rd ROWN SO16 317 L7
SBNE BH6 449 J3
Irwell Cl BSTK RG21 5 J8
CHFD SO53 292 F3
Isaacs Cl BKME/WDN BH12 447 G1
Isambard Brunel Rd PSEA PO1 21 G2
Isington La ALTN GU34 156 D5
Isington Rd ALTN GU34 156 C8
Isis Cl ROWN SO16 317 K8
Isis Wy SHST GU47 50 A8
Island Cl HISD PO11 401 L5
Island Farm Rd THLE RG7 31 H7
Island View Av
CHCH/BSGR BH23 451 G2
Island View Cl LYMN SO41 454 D5
Island View Rd
NMIL/BTOS BH25 452 C1
Island View Ter NEND PO2 399 G7
Islay Gdns CHAM PO6 375 K7
Itchel La RFNM GU10 133 G1
Itchen Av ELGH SO50 294 E6
Itchen Cl DEAN RG23 103 G7
PSF GU32 275 K6
ROMY SO51 288 C5
Itchen Ct AND SP10 9 M1
Itchenor Rd HISD PO11 426 D6
Itchen Rd HAV PO9 377 M2
Itchenside Cl WEND SO18 319 L4
Itchen Vw NALR SO24 217 J3
Itchen Wy ELGH SO50 294 A2
ITCH SO19 344 B5
NALR SO24 218 A8
RWIN SO21 215 J3
RWIN SO21 216 F3
WINC SO23 11 M1
Itchin Cl TOTT SO40 341 H2
Ithica Cl HISD PO11 425 L4
Ivamy Pl BWD BH11 431 K6
Ivanhoe Rd EWKG RG40 42 K2
WSHM SO15 318 C7
Ivar Gdns CHAM RG24 83 M8
Ively Rd FARN GU14 89 M7
Ives Cl YTLY GU46 68 E1
Ivor Cl FAWY SO45 392 A4
Ivor Rd PLE BH15 444 F7
WIMB BH21 429 H4
Ivy Cl WINW SO22 238 D3
RGWD BH24 381 H4
TOTT SO40 316 D6
Ivy Ct WVILLE PO7 376 B4

Ivy Dene ITCH SO19 345 H4
Ivydene Crs RCCH PO18 403 M1
Ivydene Gdns HORN PO8 352 E4
Ivy Down La DEAN RG23 102 D5
Ivyhole Hl HTWY RG27 68 A8
Ivyhouse La PSF GU32 246 D5
Ivy La FNM GU9 134 E6
HEND SO30 320 A6
RGWD BH24 358 E5
Ivy Rd ASHV GU12 113 H6
PTSW SO17 319 H8
WIMB BH21 404 B8

J

Jacaranda Cl FHAM PO15 371 J5 1
Jacaranda Rd BOR GU35 201 J6
Jack Cockerill Wy SSEA PO5 423 H7 2
Jackdaw Cl HORN PO8 352 C4
KEMP RG22 103 L8
Jackdaw Ri ELGH SO50 293 J7 3
Jackie Wigg Gdns TOTT SO40 341 K1
Jacklyns Cl NALR SO24 218 B4
Jacklyns La NALR SO24 218 B4
Jackmans Cl ITCH SO19 344 B5 3
Jackman's Hl RWIN SO21 267 M1
Jackson Cl CHAM PO6 400 A2
Jackson Rd BKME/WDN BH12 446 B2
Jacobean Cl CHCH/BSGR BH23 436 F7
Jacob Rd CBLY GU15 70 D1
Jacobs Cl HORN PO8 328 B3
ROMY SO51 290 F1 1
Jacob's Gutter La TOTT SO40 341 K3
Jacobs Rd PLE BH15 444 D6
Jacob's St PSEA PO1 423 G2
Jacobs Wk TOTT SO40 341 J4
Jacomb Pl
LSOL/BMARY PO13 397 H6 3
Jacqueline Av WVILLE PO7 376 B4
Jacqueline Rd
BKME/WDN BH12 446 A1
Jagdalik Rd NTID SP9 114 D4
Jago Rd PSEA PO1 422 D2
Jaguar Rd FARN GU14 90 E6
Jamacia Pl GPORT PO12 19 G4
Jamaica Pl GPORT PO12 19 G4
Jamaica Rd GPORT PO12 19 K1
James Callaghan Dr
CHAM PO6 374 E6
James Cl BSTK RG21 5 G3
HISD PO11 425 J5
LSOL/BMARY PO13 397 G4
James Copse Rd HORN PO8 352 D3
James Grieve Av HLER SO31 370 E6
Jameson Rd MOOR/WNTN BH9 432 C7
James Rd ALDT GU11 113 G1
BKME/WDN BH12 446 F3
CBLY GU15 70 E6
HAV PO9 16 B2
LSOL/BMARY PO13 397 G4
James St SHAM SO14 13 J3
James Wy CBLY GU15 70 E6
Jamrud Rd NTID SP9 114 C3
Janaway Gdns PTSW SO17 319 H8
Janes Cl FAWY SO45 392 C8
Jan Smuts Cl LISS GU33 225 J7
Janson Rd WSHM SO15 343 G1
Japonica Wy HAV PO9 378 A4
Jaques's La THLE RG7 31 J2
Jardine Sq AND SP10 119 H6 12
Jarvis Cl HTWY RG27 48 B8
Jarvis Flds HLER SO31 345 M8
Jasmine Ct LYMN SO41 440 C4 1
Jasmine Gv WVILLE PO7 376 E2
Jasmine Rd HEND SO30 321 G8
KEMP RG22 104 A8
Jasmine Wy HORN PO8 328 B3
BOR GU35 201 K6 2
Jasmond Rd CHAM PO6 399 K2
Jason Pl WVILLE PO7 376 C6
Jason Wy GPORT PO12 397 K8 2
Jaundrells Cl NMIL/BTOS BH25 438 A5
Java Dr FHAM PO15 371 G1
Java Rd SHAM SO14 13 K9
Javelin Rd EMRTH PO10 402 E5
J Av FAWY SO45 392 D2
Jay Cl FHAM/STUB PO14 395 M4
HORN PO8 352 E1
KEMP RG22 104 F7
Jay's Ct CHCH/BSGR BH23 436 F8 1
Jay's La HASM GU27 229 L5
Jays Nest Cl BLKW GU17 70 A4 2
Jealous La LYMN SO41 413 L6
Jedburgh Cl STHA RG19 27 J5
Jefferson Av CHAR BH8 448 C2
Jefferson Rd BSTK RG21 4 F3
Jeffries Cl ROWN SO16 317 K3
Jellicoe Av GPORT PO12 18 B7
Jellicoe Cl PSTN BH14 445 L3
Jellicoe Dr CHCH/BSGR BH23 450 E2
Jenkins Cl HEND SO30 346 E1
Jenkins Gv HSEA PO3 423 M1
Jenkins' Hill London Rd
BAGS GU19 51 M7
Jenner Wy ALTN GU34 176 F2
ROMY SO51 263 H8
Jennie Green La ALTN GU34 174 D6
Jennings Rd PSTN BH14 446 B6
TOTT SO40 316 F8
Jenny's Wk YTLY GU46 69 H2
Jenson Gdns AND SP10 8 C6
Jephcote Rd BWD BH11 431 K4
Jermyns La ROMY SO51 263 H5
Jerome Cnr CWTH RG45 49 M5
Jerome Ct ITCH SO19 345 H2
Jerram Cl GPORT PO12 18 A6
Jerrett's La ROWN SO16 317 J5
Jersey Brow Rd FARN GU14 90 D6
Jersey Cl BKME/WDN BH12 431 G7
CHAM RG24 83 H6
FARN GU14 89 G4 5
FHAM/STUB PO14 396 B7
ROWN SO16 317 K5
Jersey Rd BKME/WDN BH12 431 H7
NEND PO2 399 J8
Jervis Court La BPWT SO32 297 M8
Jervis Dr GPORT PO12 421 M2
Jervis Rd NEND PO2 399 G6
Jesmond Av CHCH/BSGR BH23 436 D8
Jesmond Dene NWBY RG14 2 C2
Jesmond Gv HLER SO31 370 E7
Jessamine Rd ROWN SO16 318 A6
Jesse Cl BLKW GU17 69 J3
Jessett Dr FLET GU13 110 D4
Jessica Av VWD BH31 356 B1
Jessica Cl WVILLE PO7 352 F7
Jessie Rd ENEY PO4 21 M4
GPORT PO12 18 D4
HAV PO9 377 G5
Jessop Cl FAWY SO45 367 K3
Jessopp Cl NBNE BH10 432 D4
Jessopp Rd WIMB BH21 404 F2
Jesty Rd NALR SO24 218 A4
Jetty Rd FAWY SO45 392 F3
Jewell Rd CHAR BH8 433 K7
Jewry St WINC SO23 11 G7
Jex Blake Cl ROWN SO16 318 A4
Jibbs Meadow TADY RG26 63 L5 1
Jimmy Brown Av WIMB BH21 380 C3
Jinny La ROMY SO51 262 D3
Joanna Cl RSAL SP5 284 C1
Jobson Cl WHCH RG28 122 B3 2
Jobson's La HASM GU27 229 M8
Jockey La ELGH SO50 294 D3
Jodrell Cl HORN PO8 353 G1
John Bunyan Cl FHAM PO15 347 G8 5
John Cl ALDT GU11 6 A5
John Hunt Cl STHA RG19 27 J6 3
John Morgan Cl HTWY RG27 85 M6 5
HTWY RG27 86 A5 1
Johnson Dr EWKG RG40 48 E1
Johnson Rd WIMB BH21 405 L1
Johnson St SHAM SO14 13 H3 1
Johnson Vw FHAM PO15 371 J2
Johnson Wy FLET GU13 110 E2
Johns Rd FHAM/PORC PO16 15 J9
ITCH SO19 344 B5
Johnston Rd PLE BH15 445 J1
John St SHAM SO14 13 H6
Jolliffe Av PLE BH15 445 J4
Jolliffe Rd PLE BH15 445 J4
Jonathan Cl LYMN SO41 440 C3
Jonathan Hl KSCL RG20 37 L5
Jonathan Rd FHAM PO15 14 C5
Jones La FAWY SO45 367 K4
Jopps Cnr CHCH/BSGR BH23 435 G4
Jordans La LYMN SO41 413 G5
THLE RG7 31 J6
Joseph St GPORT PO12 19 H3 2
Joshua Cl PLE BH15 444 D6 2
Jouldings La HTWY RG27 47 G4
Joule Rd AND SP10 118 A7
BSTK RG21 4 B4
Jowitt Dr NMIL/BTOS BH25 437 K6
Joyce Dickson Cl RGWD BH24 382 F2
Joys La LYMN SO41 415 J8
STOK SO20 165 M4
Joys Rd WIMB BH21 356 C8
Jubilee Av CHAM PO6 374 C8
Jubilee Cl ELGH SO50 293 L7 1
FARN GU14 89 M4
RGWD BH24 359 G8
TADY RG26 42 B7
WIMB BH21 429 J1
Jubilee Ct FHAM/STUB PO14 396 E1
LYMN SO41 412 F7
Jubilee Dr ASHV GU12 113 K2
Jubilee Gdns NBNE BH10 432 B6
WEND SO18 344 E1
Jubilee Hall Rd FARN GU14 90 F4
Jubilee La GSHT GU26 203 M5 1
RFNM GU10 158 D3
Jubilee Pth HAV PO9 377 G7
Jubilee Rd ALDT GU11 7 H7
BSTK RG21 105 G4
ENEY PO4 423 K5
EWKG RG40 48 C5
FBDG SP6 309 H7
FHAM/PORC PO16 374 B8
FRIM GU16 91 K6
GPORT PO12 18 E2
NWBY RG14 3 G6
PSTN BH14 446 C3
ROMY SO51 262 D8
WIMB BH21 429 J2
WVILLE PO7 352 C8
Jubilee Ter SSEA PO5 20 F5 1
Jubilee Trail WIMB BH21 306 B6
Julia Cl CHCH/BSGR BH23 436 D8
Julian Cl ROWN SO16 318 A4
Julian Rd ITCH SO19 344 F5
Julie Av FHAM PO15 14 C5
Juliet Ct WVILLE PO7 352 E8 3
Julius Cl CHAM RG24 82 B8
CHFD SO53 293 K2
Julyan Av BKME/WDN BH12 431 L8
Jumar Cl HLER SO31 394 B1
Jumpers Av CHCH/BSGR BH23 434 C8
Jumpers Rd CHCH/BSGR BH23 434 D8
Jumps Rd RFNM GU10 181 H5
Junction Rd AND SP10 8 E3
TOTT SO40 341 L1
UPTN BH16 444 C4
Junction Ter NWBY RG14 3 J5
June Dr DEAN RG23 104 A3
Juniper Cl CHAM RG24 83 M4
FERN BH22 380 A8
WINW SO22 238 C3
BOR GU35 200 F6
LYMN SO41 439 M6
NBAD SO52 291 L3
WIMB BH21 356 C8
Juniper Rd FARN GU14 89 M3
HORN PO8 328 B7 3
WEND SO18 344 D1
Juniper Sq HAV PO9 16 F5
Jupiter Cl ROWN SO16 317 K4
Jura Cl CHAM PO6 375 K7
Jurds Lake Wy ITCH SO19 344 B7
Jurd Wy HLER SO31 345 K7
Justice Cl STHA RG19 27 J6
Justin Cl FHAM/STUB PO14 14 C6
Justin Gdns NBNE BH10 432 C4
Justinian Cl CHFD SO53 293 L1
Jute Cl FHAM/PORC PO16 373 M7
Jutland Cl FHAM PO15 370 F1
Jutland Crs AND SP10 118 E4

K

Kamptee Copse
NMIL/BTOS BH25 437 M2 1
Kanes Hl ITCH SO19 345 K2
Kangaw Pl PLE BH15 444 C6 1
Karachi Cl NTID SP9 114 D1
Karen Av CHAM PO6 400 A2
Kassassin St ENEY PO4 423 L6
Kassel Cl WVILLE PO7 352 F7
Kathleen Cl BSTK RG21 104 F6 2
Kathleen Rd ITCH SO19 344 F5
Katrina Gdns HISD PO11 425 L3
Katrine Crs CHFD SO53 292 F1
Katterns Cl CHCH/BSGR BH23 434 C6
Kayak Cl HLER SO31 370 C7
Kay Crs BOR GU35 202 D2 1
Kayleigh Cl TOTT SO40 341 H2
Keable Rd RFNM GU10 158 C1
Kealy Rd GPORT PO12 421 L2
Kearsney Av NEND PO2 399 J5 1
Keats Av CHAM PO6 374 C7
LYMN SO41 454 C3
Keats Cl CHAM RG24 83 H7
WINW SO22 238 B4
HORN PO8 352 D4
RWIN SO21 190 C4
Keats Rd WEND SO18 345 G2
Keats Wy CWTH RG45 49 L1
YTLY GU46 68 E4
Keble Cl CHFD SO53 293 H4 1
Keble Rd CHFD SO53 293 H4
Keble St WINW SO22 238 B2
Keble Wy SHST GU47 50 B6
Keeble Cl NBNE BH10 432 B2
Keeble Crs NBNE BH10 432 B2
Keeble Rd NBNE BH10 432 B2
Keel Cl HSEA PO3 400 A5
LSOL/BMARY PO13 421 H1 1
Keepers Cl CHFD SO53 293 G2
Keeper's Hl RAND SP11 140 F3
Keepers La ROMY SO51 233 H6
WIMB BH21 405 J3
Keeps Md KSCL RG20 59 H5
The Keep FHAM/PORC PO16 374 C8
FHAM/PORC PO16 398 B1
Kefford Cl HORN PO8 352 F2
Keighley Av BDST BH18 429 K6
Keighley Cl STHA RG19 26 F6
Keith Cl GPORT PO12 421 M2
Keith Lucas Rd FARN GU14 90 C6
Keith Rd TWDS BH3 447 H2
Kelburn Cl CHFD SO53 293 G1
Kellaway Rd CFDH BH17 430 D8
Kellett Rd WSHM SO15 318 C8
Kelly Cl CFDH BH17 430 D8
Kellynch Cl ALTN GU34 176 D4
Kelly Rd WVILLE PO7 376 C3
Kellys Wk AND SP10 8 C6
Kelmscott Gdns CHFD SO53 264 F7
Kelsall Gdns NMIL/BTOS BH25 437 L5
Kelsey Av EMRTH PO10 379 J7
EWKG RG40 48 B2
Kelsey Cl FHAM/STUB PO14 370 F7
LISS GU33 248 F3
Kelsey Gv YTLY GU46 69 H3
Kelvin Cl FAWY SO45 367 L5
WHIT RG2 47 H1 2
Kelvin Gv FHAM/PORC PO16 374 B8
HLER SO31 369 G2
Kelvin Hl KEMP RG22 104 D6
Kelvin Rd ELGH SO50 293 L6
NWBY RG14 3 G2
Kemmel Rd RAND SP11 115 H1
Kemmitt Wy AND SP10 8 C9
Kemnal Pk HASM GU27 205 G8
Kemp Rd MOOR/WNTN BH9 432 D8
Kempshott Gdns
KEMP RG22 103 M8 4
Kempshott Gv KEMP RG22 103 M4 1
Kempshott La KEMP RG22 103 M7
Kempton Cl ALTN GU34 176 E6
NWBY RG14 3 K8
Kempton Ct FARN GU14 90 C6
Kempton Pk WVILLE PO7 352 F7
Kemshott Ct HAV PO9 377 H2
Ken Berry Ct HAV PO9 377 M2
Kendal Av HSEA PO3 399 L7
ROWN SO16 317 J7
Kendal Cl CHFD SO53 293 K1
FARN GU14 90 B4 2
HORN PO8 352 F4
NTHA RG18 26 F4
Kendal Gdns KEMP RG22 104 A7
Kendrick Rd NWBY RG14 37 G3
Kenilworth Cl
LSOL/BMARY PO13 420 D1 4
NMIL/BTOS BH25 437 M5
Kenilworth Crs FLET GU13 89 H6
Kenilworth Dr ELGH SO50 293 M2
Kenilworth Gdns HEND SO30 320 D7
Kenilworth Rd DEAN RG23 104 A2 2
FARN GU14 89 M3 3
FLET GU13 89 G7
SSEA PO5 21 K9
WSHM SO15 343 K2 3
Kenley Rd BOR GU35 202 E3
Kenmore Cl FLET GU13 111 G3
FRIM GU16 71 G8 2
TOTT SO40 341 H3
Kennard Ct NMIL/BTOS BH25 437 K5
Kennard Rd NMIL/BTOS BH25 437 K4
Kennart Rd CFDH BH17 444 F1
Kennedy Av FHAM PO15 372 C4
Kennedy Cl NWBY RG14 37 G2
WVILLE PO7 376 C4
Kennedy Crs GPORT PO12 421 J6
Kennedy Rd ROWN SO16 317 L5
Kennel La RFNM GU10 158 F6
Kennel Rd WINW SO22 214 A4
Kennels La FARN GU14 89 L5
Kennet Cl ASHV GU12 113 K7
BSTK RG21 5 J8
FARN GU14 90 A2
GPORT PO12 18 E9
STHA RG19 27 H5
WEND SO18 320 A5
Kennet Pl THLE RG7 31 L5
Kennet Rd NTID SP9 114 F2
NWBY RG14 2 D5
PSF GU32 275 K6
Kennet Side NWBY RG14 3 J4
Kennett Rd ROMY SO51 263 H8
Kennet Wy DEAN RG23 103 G7
Kennington La TOTT SO40 339 M1
Ken Rd SBNE BH6 449 K4
Kensington Cl ELGH SO50 294 C3 2
Kensington Dr WCLF BH2 22 B4
Kensington Flds FAWY SO45 367 H6
Kensington Gdns
FHAM/STUB PO14 371 G6 2
Kensington Pk LYMN SO41 454 B4
Kensington Rd GPORT PO12 19 G5
NEND PO2 399 K6
Kenson Gdns ITCH SO19 344 E4
Kent Gv FHAM/PORC PO16 398 A2
Kentidge Rd WVILLE PO7 376 B3 3
Kentigern Dr CWTH RG45 50 B3
Kentish Rd WSHM SO15 343 G1
Kent La RGWD BH24 334 C7
Kenton Cl FRIM GU16 71 J6
Kent Rd BKME/WDN BH12 446 D2
CHFD SO53 293 H5
FLET GU13 89 G7
BOR GU35 201 J6
LSOL/BMARY PO13 396 F4
PTSW SO17 319 H7
SSEA PO5 21 G6
Kent St PSEA PO1 20 D2
SHAM SO14 13 L1
Kenwith Av FLET GU13 89 H7 1
Kenwood Rd
FHAM/PORC PO16 398 B3
Kenwyn Cl WEND SO18 320 A6
Kenya Rd FHAM/PORC PO16 397 M1
Kenyon Cl PLE BH15 445 K1
Kenyon Rd NEND PO2 399 K6
PLE BH15 445 K1
Kenyons Yd AND SP10 8 C5
Keogh Barracks FRIM GU16 91 K8
Keogh Cl FRIM GU16 91 L7
Keppel Cl RGWD BH24 382 F1
Kerchers Fld OVTN RG25 123 M1
Kerfield Wy HTWY RG27 86 A7 3
Kerley Rd WCLF BH2 22 D7
Kern Cl ROWN SO16 317 L5
Kerrfield WINW SO22 10 A8
Kerrfield Ms WINW SO22 10 B8
Kerry Cl CHFD SO53 293 H2
FARN GU14 89 G3 1
LYMN SO41 440 A5
Kersey Crs NWBY RG14 25 H3
Kersley Crs ODIM RG29 108 B8
Kesteven Wy WEND SO18 319 M8
Kestrel Cl BPWT SO32 296 F8
BPWT SO32 321 M7
FERN BH22 405 M1
FHAM/STUB PO14 395 M4
WINW SO22 238 C4
HORN PO8 328 B4
RFNM GU10 134 A1
NTID SP9 114 F1
ROWN SO16 318 A3
STHA RG19 26 E5 1
TOTT SO40 342 C7
UPTN BH16 428 F8
Kestrel Ct RGWD BH24 358 E8
Kestrel Dr CHCH/BSGR BH23 450 F2
Kestrel Pl CHAM PO6 400 D1
Kestrel Rd ELGH SO50 293 K6
FARN GU14 90 E6
KEMP RG22 103 L7
Kestrel Wy FBDG SP6 333 M3 1
THLE RG7 31 L4
Keswick Av HSEA PO3 399 L8
Keswick Cl CBLY GU15 71 M4
Keswick Rd BOSC BH5 448 E4
ITCH SO19 344 B5
NMIL/BTOS BH25 437 M3
Keswick Wy VWD BH31 356 C3
Ketchers Fld ALTN GU34 223 L2
Ketelbey Ri KEMP RG22 127 L1
Kettering Ter NEND PO2 399 G8
Kevin Cl KSCL RG20 59 L6
Kevins Dr YTLY GU46 69 H1
Kevins Gv FLET GU13 89 G7
Kevlyn Crs HLER SO31 345 K7 2
Kewlake La ROMY SO51 314 C6
Kew La HLER SO31 369 L1
Kew Wk AND SP10 8 C7
Keydell Cl HORN PO8 352 E3
Keyes Cl BKME/WDN BH12 431 K7
CHCH/BSGR BH23 450 E2
LSOL/BMARY PO13 397 G4
Keyes Rd LSOL/BMARY PO13 397 G5
Keyhaven Cl
LSOL/BMARY PO13 396 E6 1
Keyhaven Dr HAV PO9 377 G3
Keyhaven Rd LYMN SO41 454 D4
Keynes Cl FLET GU13 111 G4
Keynsham Rd ITCH SO19 344 F2
Keynsham Wy SHST GU47 50 A6
Keysworth Av
NMIL/BTOS BH25 452 E1
Keysworth Rd UPTN BH16 444 B4
Khandala Gdns WVILLE PO7 376 D4 2
Khartoum Rd PTSW SO17 318 F6
Khyber Rd BKME/WDN BH12 446 C3
Kidmore La WVILLE PO7 351 K2
Kielder Cl CHFD SO53 292 F1
Kielder Gv
LSOL/BMARY PO13 397 H6 4
Kiel Dr AND SP10 118 E4
Kildare Rd BOR GU35 201 J4
Kilford Ct HEND SO30 346 E2
Kilham La WINW SO22 238 A2
Killarney Cl ITCH SO19 345 J5 1
Killinghurst La HASM GU27 229 M2
Kilmartin Gdns FRIM GU16 71 J7 2
Kilmeston Rd NALR SO24 242 C4
Kilmington Wy
CHCH/BSGR BH23
Kilmiston Cl PSEA PO1
Kilmiston Dr
FHAM/PORC PO16
Kilmore Dr CBLY GU15
Kilmuir Cl SHST GU47
Kiln Cl FAWY SO45
WIMB BH21
Kiln Fld LISS GU33
Kiln Flds HASM GU27
Kiln Gdns HTWY RG27
Kiln Hl BPWT SO32
THLE RG7
Kiln La EPSF GU31
NALR SO24
RFNM GU10
ROMY SO51
RSAL SP5
RWIN SO21
TADY RG26
THLE RG7
WVILLE PO7
Kiln Ride EWKG RG40
Kiln Ride Extension EWKG RG40
Kiln Rd CHAM RG24
FHAM/PORC PO16
NWBY RG14
Kilnside WVILLE PO7
Kiln Wy ALDT GU11
GSHT GU26
Kilnyard Cl TOTT SO40
Kilpatrick Cl NEND PO2
Kilwich Wy FHAM/PORC PO16
Kimbell Rd KEMP RG22
Kimber Cl CHAM RG24
Kimberley FLET GU13
Kimberley Cl AND SP10
ELGH SO50
Kimberley Rd ENEY PO4
KEMP RG22
LISS GU33
PSTN BH14
SBNE BH6
Kimbers PSF GU32
Kimbers Dr NWBY RG14
Kimbers La FNM GU9
TADY RG26
Kimbolton Rd HSEA PO3
Kimbridge Crs HAV PO9
Kimbridge La ROMY SO51
Kimmeridge Av
BKME/WDN BH12
Kimpton Cl
LSOL/BMARY PO13
Kimpton Ct HAV PO9
Kineton Rd WSHM SO15
King Albert St PSEA PO1
King Alfred Pl WINC SO23
King Alfred Ter WINC SO23
King Arthur's Ct CHAM PO6
King Arthur's Wy AND SP10
King Charles St PSEA PO1
King Cl RGWD BH24
King Cup Av HLER SO31
Kingcup Cl BDST BH18
King Edward Av
MOOR/WNTN BH9
ROWN SO16
King Edward's Crs
NEND PO2
Kingfisher Cl FARN GU14
FERN BH22
FLET GU13
HAV PO9
HISD PO11
HLER SO31
HORN PO8
KEMP RG22
BOR GU35
THLE RG7
Kingfisher Copse HLER SO31
Kingfisher Dr YTLY GU46
Kingfishers FHAM/PORC PO16
NTID SP9
The Kingfishers VWD BH31
Kingfisher Wk ASHV GU12
Kingfisher Wy
CHCH/BSGR BH23
RGWD BH24
ROMY SO51
TOTT SO40
King George Av EPSF GU31
MOOR/WNTN BH9
King George Rd AND SP10
FHAM/PORC PO16
King George's Av WSHM SO15
King Henry I St PSEA PO1
King John Av BWD BH11
FHAM/PORC PO16
King John Rd KSCL RG20
King Johns Rd ODIM RG29
Kingland Rd PLE BH15
King La PSF GU32
STOK SO20
King Richard 1 Rd PSEA PO1
King Richard Dr BWD BH11
Kings Arms La RGWD BH24
Kings Arms Rw RGWD BH24
King's Av CHCH/BSGR BH23
WINW SO22
HLER SO31
RFNM GU10
PSTN BH14
Kingsbere Av NBNE BH10
Kingsbridge Hl THLE RG7
Kingsbridge Rd NWBY RG14
PSTN BH14
Kingsbury Rd SHAM SO14
Kingsbury's La RGWD BH24
Kingsclear Pk CBLY GU15
Kingsclere Av HAV PO9
ITCH SO19
Kingsclere Cl ITCH SO19
Kingsclere Rd BSTK RG21
DEAN RG23
OVTN RG25
King's Cl CHFD SO53

BH22 380 B7
PO9 353 L6
SO43 363 K3
SO21 266 F1
SO23 191 G7
opse Av HEND SO30 346 B1
Copse Rd FAWY SO45 392 A8
SO30 346 A3
ote Rd CHAM PO6 374 D6
PO8 352 B5
Ct RFNM GU10 113 J8
Crs CBLY GU15 50 F8
SO41 440 B4
BH14 446 D6
roft Ct HAV PO9 16 B5
Croft La HAV PO9 377 G7
own Pl PSEA PO1 21 L2
own Rd WVILLE PO7 352 A6
own Wy WEND SO18 319 L6
Elms RWIN SO21 167 J2
y Av EMRTH PO10 378 C8
ernsden La PSF GU32 275 M3
ld HLER SO31 345 L7
ield LYMN SO41 440 E6
D BH24 382 E1
ield Gdns HLER SO31 345 L7
old Av WEND SO18 319 L5
ord Cl RSAL SP5 285 J3
urlong Dr BSTK RG21 104 E5
ate Rd WINC SO23 238 E3
Hl ALTN GU34 175 J8
Keep FLET GU13 110 F2
GU47 49 L7
and Cl CHAM PO6 375 G7
and Gra NWBY RG14 25 H8
and Rd ALTN GU34 176 D5
a LYMN SO41 413 J8
GU10 158 C2
GU32 246 B6
SO21 239 L2
y Av CBLY GU15 70 F4
y Cl CWTH RG45 49 L5
Y RG14 25 L2
BH6 449 M4
y Gdns TOTT SO40 340 F1
y Pk WHCH RG28 122 B2
y Pl WINW SO22 238 D3
y Rd ENEY PO4 423 M5
GU14 90 C2
RT PO12 421 K1
Y RG27 47 M8
M SO15 342 F1
head ALTN GU34 176 E5
GU14 90 E4
GU16 91 H1
SP11 142 B4
M PO17 349 G1
head Av
/STUB PO14 396 B7
Meadow AND SP10 9 J6
RG25 100 F8
Mede HORN PO8 352 F2
hill Cl GPORT PO12 18 B4
hill Rd BSTK RG21 104 F6
BH17 445 K1
orch DEAN RG23 103 G8
Paddock RSAL SP5 206 D3
Park Dr LTDN BH7 448 D2
Park Rd BMTH BH1 448 D2
M SO15 343 L2
Pightle CHAM RG24 83 L5
Ride CBLY GU15 51 G7
SO45 418 C1
Rd ALDT GU11 6 B3
GU34 176 C6
SO53 293 H2
RG45 49 L4
TH PO10 378 C8
/PORC PO16 15 J6
GU13 89 G7
SO22 238 B2
RT PO12 18 F3
GU27 228 D2
PO11 425 L3
RG22 104 D5
/BMARY PO13 420 C1
SO41 440 B4
/BTOS BH25 438 A4
RG14 2 F5
PO1 422 D2
GU32 275 J4
SP11 119 G1
PO5 20 F5
RG7 42 D7
BH3 447 M1
Rd West NWBY RG14 2 F5
Saltern Rd LYMN SO41 440 E6
Somborne Rd
SO51 235 J7
Ter EMRTH PO10 378 D8
PO1 20 F5
on HLER SO31 369 G1
on Cl AND SP10 8 D9
on Crs NEND PO2 399 H8
on Gdns FHAM PO15 372 B4
on La THLE RG7 30 F2
on Pk LYMN SO41 440 A6
on Rd CBLY GU15 51 K8
RT PO12 18 B1
SN8 32 B6
PO2 399 J8
BH15 445 J4
M SO15 343 H2
EMRTH PO10 378 F5
RT PO12 19 K2
RG29 108 D5
SO14 13 H5
PO5 20 F4
RG7 43 K2
Wk WHCH RG28 122 B3
Wy BPWT SO32 268 D5
T SO32 296 D5
T SO32 324 F3
/PORC PO16 373 K8
SO24 217 L6
SO21 216 D2
SO21 240 C4
SO21 240 F2

WHAM PO17 350 D7
WINC SO23 11 H4
WVILLE PO7 350 D3
Kingsway ALDT GU11 6 C4
BLKW GU17 70 B4
CHFD SO53 293 J1
HISD PO11 401 L5
Kingsway Cl CHCH/BSGR BH23 434 D7
Kingsway Gdns CHFD SO53 265 K8
The Kingsway
FHAM/PORC PO16 374 A8
Kingswell Gdns NBNE BH10 431 M6
Kingswell Gv NBNE BH10 431 M6
Kingswell Rd NBNE BH10 432 A6
Kingswell St PSEA PO1 21 G1
Kingswood TOTT SO40 342 E7
Kingswood Firs GSHT GU26 203 M6
Kingswood La GSHT GU26 203 M6
Kingswood Ri ALTN GU34 196 E6
Kingsworthy Rd HAV PO9 377 K5
King's Yd AND SP10 9 J5
King William St PSEA PO1 422 E2
Kinnell Cl EMRTH PO10 378 D8
Kinross Crs CHAM PO6 399 M1
Kinross Rd TOTT SO40 341 K1
TWDS BH3 447 K2
Kinsbourne Av NBNE BH10 432 B6
Kinsbourne Cl ITCH SO19 345 K2
Kinsbourne Ri ITCH SO19 345 K3
Kinsbourne Wy ITCH SO19 345 J2
Kinson Av PLE BH15 445 M2
Kinson Gv NBNE BH10 432 A2
Kinson Park Rd NBNE BH10 432 B2
Kinson Rd NBNE BH10 431 L7
Kintbury Rd HUNG RG17 34 C2
Kintyre Cl DEAN RG23 102 F6
Kintyre Rd CHAM PO6 375 K7
Kinver Cl ROMY SO51 263 G7
Kipling Cl NTHA RG18 26 F3
YTLY GU46 68 F4
Kipling Ct ITCH SO19 344 D7
Kipling Rd ELGH SO50 293 L5
NEND PO2 399 J5
PSTN BH14 446 A3
Kipling Wk KEMP RG22 104 D5
Kirby Cl PLE BH15 445 L2
Kirby Rd NEND PO2 399 J6
Kirby Wy SBNE BH6 449 J4
Kirkee Rd NTID SP9 114 D3
Kirk Gdns TOTT SO40 341 K3
Kirkham Cl SHST GU47 50 A6
Kirk Knoll BOR GU35 202 C3
Kirkstall Rd ENEY PO4 423 J7
Kirkway BDST BH18 429 M4
Kirkwood Crs THLE RG7 31 J5
Kirtley Cl CHAM PO6 400 A2
Kirton Rd CHAM PO6 400 A1
Kitchener Crs CFDH BH17 429 M6
Kitchener Rd ALDT GU11 113 G2
LISS GU33 225 H6
PTSW SO17 319 H5
Kitchers Cl LYMN SO41 412 F5
Kitcombe La ALTN GU34 198 A7
Kite Cl HORN PO8 352 C4
Kites Croft Cl
FHAM/STUB PO14 371 G7
Kitnocks Hl BPWT SO32 322 D8
Kitscroft Rd NBNE BH10 432 A3
Kittiwake Cl
LSOL/BMARY PO13 396 F6
Kitt's La NALR SO24 244 B6
RFNM GU10 181 J8
Kitwalls La LYMN SO41 454 C3
Kitwood La ALTN GU34 221 H1
Kitwood Rd ALTN GU34 221 G1
Kivernell Rd LYMN SO41 454 B4
Kiwi Cl PLE BH15 445 K5
Knapp Cl CHCH/BSGR BH23 434 E8
Knapp La ROMY SO51 264 C4
TADY RG26 62 A2
Knapp Mill Av
CHCH/BSGR BH23 434 E8
Knapps Hard PSF GU32 272 A3
Knatchbull Cl ROMY SO51 290 E1
Knellers La TOTT SO40 341 H4
Knight Cl FLET GU13 110 B2
WINC SO23 11 G3
Knighton Heath Rd BWD BH11 431 J4
Knighton La BWD BH11 431 H1
Knighton Pk NMIL/BTOS BH25 437 J8
Knighton Rd ITCH SO19 344 D5
RSAL SP5 252 C1
Knights Bank Rd
FHAM/STUB PO14 395 K7
Knightsbridge Dr STHA RG19 38 E5
Knightsbridge Rd CBLY GU15 71 H1
RAND SP11 119 H1
Knights Cl HLER SO31 370 C7
Knights La KSCL RG20 35 M5
Knights Lea KSCL RG20 35 L5
Knights Rd BWD BH11 431 H3
FNM GU9 6 A9
Knightstone Gra FAWY SO45 367 L6
Knight St BSTK RG21 104 E4
Knights Wy ALTN GU34 176 C5
CBLY GU15 71 M4
Knightwood Av HAV PO9 377 L3
LYND SO43 363 K3
Knightwood Cl
CHCH/BSGR BH23 436 C8
LYND SO43 363 K3
TOTT SO40 340 F6
Knightwood Rd FAWY SO45 367 M6
NBAD SO52 264 E8
Knockhundred La GSHT GU26 203 L8
Knockwood La STOK SO20 184 D1
Knole Gdns BMTH BH1 448 C4
Knole Rd BMTH BH1 448 C3
Knoll Cl FLET GU13 88 F6
Knoll Gdns RGWD BH24 381 K4
Knoll La WIMB BH21 428 F1
Knoll Rd CBLY GU15 71 G2
FLET GU13 88 F6
Knollys' Rd ALDT GU11 112 C5
THLE RG7 42 C7
Knottgrass Rd HLER SO31 370 C6
Knott La THLE RG7 29 L4
Knowland Dr LYMN SO41 454 C3

Knowle Crs KSCL RG20 59 J6
Knowle Hl ELGH SO50 294 A1
Knowle La ELGH SO50 295 K8
Knowle Rd BROC SO42 387 J6
Knowles Av CWTH RG45 49 J4
Knowles Cl CHCH/BSGR BH23 450 D1
Knowles Meadow LISS GU33 249 G7
The Knowlings WHCH RG28 122 C4
Knowlton Rd CFDH BH17 430 D6
Knowsley Crs CHAM PO6 399 L1
Knowsley Rd CHAM PO6 399 K1
Knox Cl FLET GU13 110 C3
Knox Rd HAV PO9 16 B4
NEND PO2 399 G7
Knyght Cl ROMY SO51 290 F2
Knyveton Rd BMTH BH1 23 M4
Kohat Cl NTID SP9 114 C1
Kohat Ct ALDT GU11 6 C2
Kohima Cl ALDT GU11 7 H1
Komat Rd NTID SP9 114 D3
Kootenay Av WEND SO18 345 J1
Kooyong Cl ROMY SO51 289 G6
Krooner Rd CBLY GU15 70 E5
Kynegils Rd WINW SO22 10 B3
Kynon Cl GPORT PO12 398 A8
Kyrchil La WIMB BH21 404 C2
Kyrchil Wy WIMB BH21 404 D1
Kytes La BPWT SO32 322 A3

L

Labrador Dr PLE BH15 445 J7
Laburnum Av CHAM PO6 400 A1
Laburnum Cl ALDT GU11 6 E3
FERN BH22 405 M2
NBAD SO52 291 M3
VWD BH31 357 G3
Laburnum Crs FAWY SO45 367 M8
Laburnum Dr LYMN SO41 439 J8
Laburnum Gv ELGH SO50 293 M5
HISD PO11 425 M4
NEND PO2 399 J7
NWBY RG14 2 E1
Laburnum Pas ALDT GU11 6 E3
Laburnum Rd ALDT GU11 6 E3
FHAM/PORC PO16 396 F2
FNM GU9 6 A8
HEND SO30 346 B2
ROWN SO16 319 H4
WVILLE PO7 376 C2
The Laburnums BLKW GU17 69 L3
Laburnum Wy DEAN RG23 104 C2
Lacey Crs PSTN BH14 445 M2
Lackford Av TOTT SO40 341 J2
Lacon Cl WEND SO18 319 K8
Lacy Cl WIMB BH21 404 B2
Lacy Dr WIMB BH21 404 A2
Ladram Rd GPORT PO12 421 J4
Ladwell Cl NWBY RG14 37 G3
Lady Betty's Dr FHAM PO15 371 J2
Ladybridge Rd WVILLE PO7 376 A4
Ladycross Rd FAWY SO45 367 L6
Lady Diana Ct RAND SP11 92 E6
Ladygate Dr GSHT GU26 203 K5
Lady Godley Cl NTID SP9 114 D3
Lady Jane Wk RAND SP11 92 E6
Ladysmith Cl
CHCH/BSGR BH23 450 D1
Ladysmith Pl BOR GU35 201 H3
Ladywell La NALR SO24 218 C1
Ladywood ELGH SO50 293 L2
Ladywood Av FARN GU14 89 M4
Laffan's Rd ALDT GU11 112 C3
ODIM RG29 108 C8
Laffan Tr ALDT GU11 111 M2
Lagado Cl PSTN BH14 446 B8
Lagland St PLE BH15 445 H7
Lagoon Rd PSTN BH14 446 A7
Lahore Cl NTID SP9 114 D1
Lahore Rd NTID SP9 114 D3
Laidlaw Cl BKME/WDN BH12 431 M8
Lainston Cl WINW SO22 214 B6
Lake Av PLE BH15 444 C7
Lake Crs PLE BH15 444 D5
Lake Dr BOR GU35 201 K5
PLE BH15 444 C6
Lake End Wy CWTH RG45 49 K4
Lake Farm Cl HEND SO30 321 H8
Lake Grove Rd
NMIL/BTOS BH25 437 L4
Lakeland Dr FRIM GU16 71 H7
Lakeland Gdns TOTT SO40 342 C7
Lakelands TADY RG26 41 G7
Lakelands Dr WSHM SO15 343 G2
Lake La RFNM GU10 180 B2
Lake Rd BPWT SO32 322 E8
BWD BH11 431 M2
CHFD SO53 265 K8
FRIM GU16 91 K2
ITCH SO19 344 B6
PLE BH15 444 D6
PSEA PO1 423 G2
VWD BH31 356 E4
Laker Sq AND SP10 119 H6
Lakeside ELGH SO50 293 L8
LSOL/BMARY PO13 420 D4
RGWD BH24 383 G2
WHAM PO17 372 C3
Lakeside Av HSEA PO3 423 M2
ROWN SO16 317 K3
Lakeside Cl AND SP10 118 C6
ASHV GU12 113 J4
Lakeside Ct FARN GU14 89 G5
Lakeside Dr HTWY RG27 67 G4
Lakeside Gdns FARN GU14 90 A1
HAV PO9 17 G2
Lakeside Rd ALDT GU11 112 D1
ASHV GU12 113 J4
CCLF BH13 446 F7
The Lake Side BLKW GU17 70 A4
Lakesmere Rd HORN PO8 353 G2
The Lakes BPWT SO32 323 M4
Lakeview Dr RGWD BH24 383 G2
Lakewood Cl CHFD SO53 265 J8
Lakewood Rd
CHCH/BSGR BH23 436 D7

CHFD SO53 265 J8
TOTT SO40 341 G5
Lamb Cl AND SP10 9 L6
NTHA RG18 26 F3
Lambdens Hl THLE RG7 30 B1
Lambdens Wk TADY RG26 41 L8
Lambdown Ap RAND SP11 115 H2
Lambdown Ter RAND SP11 115 G1
Lamberhurst Cl ITCH SO19 344 E8
Lambert Cl WVILLE PO7 376 C3
Lambert Crs BLKW GU17 69 M4
Lamborne Cl SHST GU47 49 K7
Lambourn Cl FHAM/STUB PO14 14 B7
Lambourne Cl FAWY SO45 367 K7
RAND SP11 116 D8
RWIN SO21 213 H5
Lambourne Dr HLER SO31 370 E5
Lambourne La LIPH GU30 251 G5
Lambourne Rd WEND SO18 320 A6
Lambourne Wy RFNM GU10 136 B1
RAND SP11 116 D8
Lambourn Rd KSCL RG20 24 F2
Lambourn Sq CHFD SO53 292 F2
Lambourn Valley Wy
NWBY RG14 2 B4
Lambs Cl CFDH BH17 430 A7
Lambs Rw CHAM RG24 105 L1
Lamden Wy THLE RG7 31 L5
Lamerton Rd BOR GU35 201 H4
Lammas Rd FAWY SO45 367 L6
Lamp Acres NWBY RG14 25 L3
Lampard La RFNM GU10 181 G6
Lampards Cl HTWY RG27 85 L2
Lampeter Av CHAM PO6 375 M8
Lanark Cl FRIM GU16 71 H6
Lancaster Av FNM GU9 134 F8
Lancaster Cl AND SP10 8 E2
ASHV GU12 113 J3
BDST BH18 429 K3
CHCH/BSGR BH23 451 G1
FHAM/PORC PO16 373 M7
HLER SO31 345 L7
LSOL/BMARY PO13 420 F4
NTHA RG18 26 F4
Lancaster Dr BDST BH18 429 J3
CBLY GU15 71 G2
VWD BH31 356 C2
Lancaster Rd BSTK RG21 4 C5
FARN GU14 90 E7
ROWN SO16 317 L5
Lancaster Wy FARN GU14 90 F1
WVILLE PO7 376 D2
Lancer Cl CHCH/BSGR BH23 449 L1
Lancer Ct ALDT GU11 6 A2
Lance's Hl ITCH SO19 344 D1
Landale Cl RAND SP11 119 G1
Lander Cl PLE BH15 445 J7
Landford Wy CHAR BH8 433 H6
Landguard Rd WSHM SO15 343 H2
Landon Rd LSOL/BMARY PO13 397 H8
Landport St PSEA PO1 423 H2
SSEA PO5 20 F4
Landport Ter PSEA PO1 20 F4
Landport Vw PSEA PO1 423 G2
Landsdowne St SSEA PO5 20 F4
The Landsdown Rbt BMTH BH1 23 H5
Landseer Cl BSTK RG21 105 J5
SHST GU47 70 B2
Landseer Ct AND SP10 8 F2
Landseer Rd ITCH SO19 345 G5
Lands End La BOR GU35 201 K3
Lands End Rd HLER SO31 369 M1
Lane End TADY RG26 63 L6
Lane End Dr EMRTH PO10 378 D8
Lanehays Rd FAWY SO45 367 K5
Lanesbridge Cl TOTT SO40 340 D3
Lanes End FHAM/STUB PO14 396 A6
The Lanes NMIL/BTOS BH25 437 L3
Laneswood THLE RG7 43 H3
The Lane ENEY PO4 423 K6
FAWY SO45 392 F5
GPORT PO12 18 D9
TADY RG26 41 L8
Langbar Cl ITCH SO19 344 C2
Langbrook Cl HAV PO9 16 E7
Langdale Av CHAM PO6 399 M1
Langdale Cl FARN GU14 90 B4
ROWN SO16 317 L8
Langdon Cl CBLY GU15 71 M4
Langdon Rd PSTN BH14 446 B4
Langdown Lawn FAWY SO45 367 L6
Langdown Lawn Cl
FAWY SO45 367 L6
Langdown Rd FAWY SO45 367 L5
Langford La RSAL SP5 257 L7
Langford Rd NEND PO2 423 K1
Langham Cl NBAD SO52 291 L4
Langham Rd ALTN GU34 176 D5
Langhorn Rd ROWN SO16 319 H4
Langley Cha RGWD BH24 381 L3
Langley Cl FLET GU13 110 E4
Langley Dr CBLY GU15 71 G2
Langley Gdn FBDG SP6 309 M5
Langley Lodge Gdns
FAWY SO45 418 D1
Langley Rd CHCH/BSGR BH23 436 C7
NEND PO2 399 J8
PSTN BH14 446 E4
WSHM SO15 342 E2
Langrish Cl HAV PO9 377 L2
Langrish Rd ROWN SO16 318 A4
Langside Av BKME/WDN BH12 431 L8
Langstone Av HAV PO9 16 E8
Langstone High St HAV PO9 401 K2
Langstone Rd HAV PO9 16 E9
HSEA PO3 423 L2
Langstone Wk
FHAM/STUB PO14 372 A8
LSOL/BMARY PO13 396 F6
Langton Cl WINW SO22 10 C5
NMIL/BTOS BH25 437 M8
Langton Dr BOR GU35 202 D1
Langton Rd BPWT SO32 297 G8
LTDN BH7 448 E3
Lanham La WINW SO22 213 L8
Lankhills Rd WINC SO23 10 F3
Lansdown Av
FHAM/PORC PO16 398 B2

Lansdowne Av AND SP10 8 D8
WINC SO23 238 E3
WVILLE PO7 375 M5
Lansdowne Cl ROMY SO51 262 D8
Lansdowne Gdns BMTH BH1 23 H3
Lansdowne Hl SHAM SO14 12 F5
Lansdowne Rd ALDT GU11 6 E3
ALTN GU34 176 F3
BMTH BH1 23 G1
FRIM GU16 71 K8
WSHM SO15 342 E1
Lansley Rd BSTK RG21 4 E2
Lantana Cl WVILLE PO7 376 D2
Lanyard Dr LSOL/BMARY PO13 421 H2
Lapin La KEMP RG22 127 G3
Lapthorn Cl
LSOL/BMARY PO13 396 F4
Lapwing Cl GPORT PO12 421 M1
HORN PO8 352 E1
Lapwing Dr TOTT SO40 316 B8
Lapwing Gv
FHAM/PORC PO16 373 K8
Lapwing Ri WHCH RG28 122 A2
Lapwing Rd WIMB BH21 404 E1
Lara Cl CHAR BH8 433 H5
Larch Av FAWY SO45 392 A3
Larch Cl CBLY GU15 51 H7
CFDH BH17 429 J7
HEND SO30 320 C5
LIPH GU30 226 E5
LSOL/BMARY PO13 420 E3
LYMN SO41 438 D5
NWBY RG14 25 G3
RGWD BH24 381 L4
STOK SO20 163 G4
TLHT RG30 31 L4
WINC SO23 191 G8
Larchdale Cl HLER SO31 370 B8
Larch Dr AND SP10 142 B1
KSCL RG20 59 J6
Larches Gdns FHAM PO15 372 A7
Larchfield Rd FLET GU13 110 F1
Larchfield Wy HORN PO8 353 G3
Larch Rd BOR GU35 202 E2
ROWN SO16 317 M5
Larch Rw FBDG SP6 310 C6
Larch Wy FARN GU14 89 M5
FERN BH22 380 A8
HLER SO31 345 K8
Larchwood CHAM RG24 83 L5
Larchwood Av HAV PO9 376 F4
Larchwood Gld CBLY GU15 71 K1
Larchwood Rd TOTT SO40 341 G2
Larcombe Rd PSF GU32 275 J7
Larg Dr WINW SO22 214 B4
Lark Cl AND SP10 119 G6
KEMP RG22 103 L8
NTID SP9 114 E1
Larkfield CHAM RG24 83 L5
Larkfield Rd FNM GU9 134 C5
Lark Hill Ri WINW SO22 238 C4
Larkhill Rd HSEA PO3 399 K4
Lark Ri LIPH GU30 226 D3
Larks Barrow Hl WHCH RG28 99 H6
Larks Cl FERN BH22 405 M1
Larksfield Av
MOOR/WNTN BH9 432 F5
Larkshill Cl NMIL/BTOS BH25 437 M4
Larkspur Cha ITCH SO19 345 J3
Larkspur Cl ALDT GU11 6 F7
BPWT SO32 323 M3
HLER SO31 370 D6
Larkspur Dr TOTT SO40 342 C8
Larkspur Drive NBAD SO52 292 E2
Larkspur Gdns FAWY SO45 391 M4
HEND SO30 346 A2
NTHA RG18 27 J4
Larks Ri FERN BH22 405 M1
Larkswood Cl SHST GU47 49 K7
Larkswood Dr CWTH RG45 49 L3
Larkwhistle Farm Rd
RWIN SO21 148 C7
Larmer Cl FLET GU13 110 C1
Larwood Sq AND SP10 119 H6
Lascelles Rd LTDN BH7 449 G2
Lascombe La RGUW GU3 137 K4
Laser Cl HLER SO31 370 C7
Lashly Meadow WVILLE PO7 326 B5
Latchmore Dr FAWY SO45 367 G4
Latchmore Forest Gv
HORN PO8 352 D5
Latchmore Gdns HORN PO8 352 C5
Latchwood La RFNM GU10 159 G3
Latelie Cl HLER SO31 369 G3
Latham Av FRIM GU16 71 H6
Latham Cl ELGH SO50 295 G6
Latham Ct WSHM SO15 342 F1
Latham Rd ELGH SO50 295 G6
ROMY SO51 262 F8
Latimer Ct HSEA PO3 399 M4
Latimer Rd MOOR/WNTN BH9 432 D8
Latimers Cl CHCH/BSGR BH23 436 D7
Latimer St ROMY SO51 290 D1
SHAM SO14 13 H6
Laud Cl NWBY RG14 26 A3
Lauder Cl EMRTH PO10 379 H6
FRIM GU16 71 H6
Lauderdale FARN GU14 90 A5
Launcelot Cl AND SP10 118 F5
Launcelyn Cl NBAD SO52 291 L5
Launceston Dr ELGH SO50 293 L3
Laundry La CBLY GU15 70 B3
HTWY RG27 66 A3
LYMN SO41 454 D4
Laundry Rd ROWN SO16 318 A6
Laurel Cl CBLY GU15 71 G4
CHCH/BSGR BH23 436 B7
FARN GU14 89 M5
FAWY SO45 367 J5
HLER SO31 370 F4
LYMN SO41 438 C4
ODIM RG29 108 B5
RGWD BH24 381 J4
WIMB BH21 429 H2
Laurel Dr BDST BH18 429 M4
Laurel Gdns ALDT GU11 6 F7
BDST BH18 430 A4
HLER SO31 370 F4

484 Lau - Log

Laurel Gv RFNM GU10 158 C3
Laurel La RGWD BH24 381 J5
Laurel Rd HLER SO31 370 F4
HORN PO8 353 G4
The Laurels AND SP10 8 D3
BSTK RG21 5 H5
FERN BH22 406 A1
FLET GU13 88 F7
FNM GU9 6 C7
Laurence Ct RAND SP11 92 E6
Lauriston Dr CHFD SO53 265 G7 4
Laurus Cl WVILLE PO7 376 E3
Lavant Cl HORN PO8 352 F7
Lavant Dr HAV PO9 17 G1
Lavant St PSF GU32 275 K4
Lavell's La THLE RG7 43 M8
Lavender Cl ITCH SO19 344 D3 3
VWD BH31 357 G3 1
Lavender Gdns BOR GU35 201 J5 1
Lavender La RFNM GU10 158 C4
Lavender Rd CHAR BH8 433 H4
KEMP RG22 126 F1
LYMN SO41 438 C5
WVILLE PO7 376 E2
Lavender Wy BDST BH18 429 H5
Laverock Lea
FHAM/PORC PO16 374 A7
Laverstoke Cl ROWN SO16 317 K2 1
Laverstoke La OVTN RG25 123 H8
WHCH RG28 123 H3
Lavey's La FHAM PO15 371 M2
Lavington Gdns NBAD SO52 291 L5
Lavinia Rd BKME/WDN BH12 446 B1
GPORT PO12 18 D2
Lawday Link FNM GU9 134 D1
Lawday Pl FNM GU9 134 D1 1
Lawday Place La FNM GU9 134 D1
Lawford Crs YTLY GU46 69 G2
Lawford Rd MOOR/WNTN BH9 432 E5
Lawford Wy TOTT SO40 316 D8
Lawn Cl LSOL/BMARY PO13 397 H7 1
LYMN SO41 454 D4
Lawn Dr HLER SO31 370 E6
Lawn Rd ELGH SO50 294 A3
WINW SO22 214 B3 1
LYMN SO41 439 M5
LYMN SO41 454 D4
PTSW SO17 319 G8
Lawns Cl WIMB BH21 405 G2
Lawnside Rd WSHM SO15 317 M8
Lawns Rd WIMB BH21 404 F2
The Lawns CHCH/BSGR BH23 436 F8
FARN GU14 90 B5
Lawn St WINC SO23 11 H7
Lawnswood Cl HORN PO8 352 D6
Lawn Vw CHCH/BSGR BH23 437 H3
Lawrence Av HORN PO8 352 C6
Lawrence Cl AND SP10 8 E1
CHAM RG24 83 H7
Lawrencedale Ct BSTK RG21 4 B9
Lawrence Dr PSTN BH14 446 D7
Lawrence Gv ITCH SO19 344 D6
Lawrence Houses RAND SP11 140 A7
Lawrence La FBDG SP6 334 F4
Lawrence Rd FHAM PO15 14 E4
FLET GU13 88 E8
RGWD BH24 359 G6
SSEA PO5 21 L6
Lawrences La NTHA RG18 27 G2
Lawrence Wy CBLY GU15 70 C4
Lawson Cl HLER SO31 346 B8 1
Lawson Rd BKME/WDN BH12 446 A2
SSEA PO5 21 L4
Laws Ter ALDT GU11 7 J1
Laxton Cl HLER SO31 370 F5
ITCH SO19 344 E6
Layard Dr WIMB BH21 404 B7
Lay Fld HTWY RG27 85 L7
Layton Rd BKME/WDN BH12 446 C3
LSOL/BMARY PO13 397 G5
Lazy Acre EMRTH PO10 379 H8
Lea Cl ASHV GU12 113 K7
BSTK RG21 5 K7
FNM GU9 6 F9
Leacock Cl BPWT SO32 324 A4
Lea Ct FNM GU9 6 D7
Lea Cft CWTH RG45 49 L2
Leaden Vere ODIM RG29 131 J4
Leafy La FHAM PO15 371 J2
Lealand Gv CHAM PO6 376 B8
Lealand Rd CHAM PO6 400 B1
Leamington Crs
LSOL/BMARY PO13 420 D2
Leamington Rd
MOOR/WNTN BH9 447 M1
Leander Cl ELGH SO50 293 M3 1
Lea-oak Gdns FHAM PO15 14 A2
Leaphill Rd LTDN BH7 448 F2
Lea Rd CBLY GU15 70 E6
FAWY SO45 418 C1
Learoyd Rd CFDH BH17 445 J1
Lear Rd GPORT PO12 18 F2
Leaside Wy ROWN SO16 319 H3
Lea Springs FLET GU13 110 C1
The Lea FLET GU13 110 C1
VWD BH31 356 E3
Leatherhead Gdns
HEND SO30 321 J6 1
Lea Wy ASHV GU12 113 J5
BWD BH11 431 J2
The Leaway FHAM/PORC PO16 374 B8
Leawood Rd FLET GU13 110 C1 1
Lebanon Rd WSHM SO15 342 B1
Le Borowe FLET GU13 110 D4
Lechlade Gdns FHAM PO15 372 B4
LTDN BH7 433 L8
Leckford Cl FHAM/PORC PO16 374 A7
WEND SO18 320 C8 2
Leckford La STOK SO20 187 G1
Leckford Rd HAV PO9 377 M2
Ledbury Rd CHAM PO6 375 G7
CHCH/BSGR BH23 450 E3
Lederle La LSOL/BMARY PO13 397 G3
Ledgard Cl PSTN BH14 446 A4
Lee Church La ROMY SO51 290 E8
Lee Ct ALDT GU11 7 J5
Leedam Rd NBNE BH10 432 B4
Lee Dro ROMY SO51 290 F7
Lee Lands LYMN SO41 440 B7
Lee La ROMY SO51 290 F4
Leep La GPORT PO12 18 F8
Lee Rd ALDT GU11 6 A2
GPORT PO12 421 L2
Lees Cl CHCH/BSGR BH23 434 B4
Leesland Rd GPORT PO12 18 C1
Lees La GPORT PO12 18 E1
Leeson Rd LTDN BH7 448 D1
Lefroy Av BSTK RG21 5 G4
Lefroy's Fld RFNM GU10 110 C8
Leger Cl FLET GU13 110 D3
Legge Crs ALDT GU11 6 A3 1
Legg La WIMB BH21 404 B4
Legion Cl PLE BH15 444 D6
Legion La WINC SO23 215 H1
Legion Rd HISD PO11 425 L4
PLE BH15 444 D6
Lehar Cl KEMP RG22 104 C8
Leicester Pl AND SP10 9 G6
Leicester Rd CCLF BH13 446 E5
WSHM SO15 318 C6
Leicester Wy WINC SO23 11 M4
Leigham Vale Rd SBNE BH6 449 J4
Leigh Cl AND SP10 9 L7
Leigh Common WIMB BH21 404 C3
Leigh Fld THLE RG7 43 J2
Leigh Gdns AND SP10 9 L7
WIMB BH21 404 B4
Leigh La FNM GU9 135 H8
WIMB BH21 404 D3
Leigh Pk LYMN SO41 440 A4
Leigh Rd AND SP10 9 L7
CHFD SO53 293 H4
ELGH SO50 293 K5
ELGH SO50 294 A5 1
FHAM/PORC PO16 15 G4
HAV PO9 16 F2
NMIL/BTOS BH25 437 L4
PTSW SO17 318 F7
WIMB BH21 404 A4
Leighton Av WSHM SO15 318 A8
Leighton Rd ITCH SO19 344 C5
Leipzig Barracks FLET GU13 111 G6
Leipzig Rd FLET GU13 111 G5
Leith Av FHAM/PORC PO16 374 B7
Leith Cl CWTH RG45 49 K1
Le Marchant Rd FRIM GU16 71 J5
Lemon Gv BOR GU35 201 H7
Lemon Rd WSHM SO15 342 F1
Lena Cl RAND SP11 92 D6
Lendorber Av CHAM PO6 399 L1
Lendore Rd FRIM GU16 71 G8
Lennel Gdns FLET GU13 111 H2
Lennon Wy KEMP RG22 127 H1
Lennox Cl CHFD SO53 265 K8
GPORT PO12 18 F9
ROWN SO16 317 L3
Lennox Rd South SSEA PO5 21 J8
Lensyd Gdns HORN PO8 352 D2
Lenten St ALTN GU34 176 D5
Lentham Cl CFDH BH17 430 B7
Lentune Wy LYMN SO41 440 B6
Leofric Ct ENEY PO4 424 A5
Leominster Rd CHAM PO6 374 F7
Leonard Cl FRIM GU16 71 G8
Leonard Rd GPORT PO12 19 H2
Leopold Av FARN GU14 90 E3
Leopold Dr BPWT SO32 323 G1
Leopold St ENEY PO4 21 M7
Le Patourel Cl
CHCH/BSGR BH23 450 C1
Lepe Rd FAWY SO45 418 D1
Lerryn Rd LSOL/BMARY PO13 397 H6
Leslie Rd MOOR/WNTN BH9 432 C8
PSTN BH14 445 M5
Leslie Southern Ct NWBY RG14 3 G2
Lester Av HAV PO9 377 G6
Lester Rd GPORT PO12 18 A2
Lestock Wy FLET GU13 89 H7
Levell Ct RAND SP11 92 E6 2
Leven Av WBNE BH4 22 A2
Leven Cl CHFD SO53 264 F8
WBNE BH4 22 A3
Leventhorpe Ct GPORT PO12 19 G4 1
Levern Dr FNM GU9 134 F2 3
Leveson Cl GPORT PO12 18 A6
Leviathan Cl FHAM/STUB PO14 396 B6
Levignen Cl FLET GU13 110 C3
Lewens Cl WIMB BH21 404 A4
Lewes Cl ELGH SO50 293 M2
Lewesdon Dr BDST BH18 429 K4
Lewin Cl RWIN SO21 266 F8
Lewis Cl BSTK RG21 5 H4
FAWY SO45 367 G6
Lewisham Wy SHST GU47 50 A7
Lewis Rd EMRTH PO10 378 E5
Lewis Silkin Wy ROWN SO16 317 M4
Lewry Cl HEND SO30 346 A1
Lexby Rd TOTT SO40 341 L2
Lexden Gdns HISD PO11 425 J4 3
Leybourne Av NBNE BH10 432 B3
WEND SO18 319 L8
Leybourne Cl NBNE BH10 432 A3
Leydene Av CHAR BH8 433 K7
Leydene Cl CHAR BH8 433 K7
Leyland Cl GPORT PO12 18 F6
Leyland Rd BKME/WDN BH12 431 J6
Ley Rd FARN GU14 70 D8
Leys Gdns NWBY RG14 2 D2
Leyside CHCH/BSGR BH23 450 E2
Leyton Rd SHAM SO14 344 A2
Leyton Wy RAND SP11 8 C9
Liam Cl HAV PO9 377 L4
Liberty Rd BPWT SO32 324 F8
The Liberty WVILLE PO7 351 J5
Library Rd BKME/WDN BH12 446 D3
FARN GU14 90 E6
FERN BH22 406 B3
MOOR/WNTN BH9 432 D7
TOTT SO40 341 L1
Lichen Wy TOTT SO40 342 D6
Lichfield Rd FHAM/STUB PO14 371 G5
HSEA PO3 423 L2
Lickfolds Rd RFNM GU10 158 B6
Liddell Cl EWKG RG40 48 B5
Liddel Wy CHFD SO53 292 F3
Liddiards Wy WVILLE PO7 376 C5
Lidiard Gdns ENEY PO4 423 M6
Lightfoot Gv BSTK RG21 105 G6
Lightsfield DEAN RG23 103 G6
Lilac Cl HAV PO9 378 A5
BOR GU35 201 J6
RGWD BH24 358 F8
Lilac Rd ROWN SO16 319 G4
Lilac Wy DEAN RG23 104 C2
Lille Barracks ALDT GU11 91 G8
Lilliput Rd PSTN BH14 446 B8
Lillywhite Crs AND SP10 119 G3 2
Lily Av WVILLE PO7 375 M6
Lily Cl KEMP RG22 126 F1
Limbrey Hl OVTN RG25 130 A3
Lime Av ALTN GU34 176 D3
CBLY GU15 71 K2
ITCH SO19 344 E3
Lime Cl FAWY SO45 367 J6
ITCH SO19 344 E3
NWBY RG14 3 M2
PLE BH15 445 L2
RWIN SO21 266 F8
Limecroft YTLY GU46 68 F3
Lime Dr FARN GU14 89 G4 6
Lime Gdns HEND SO30 320 C5
Lime Gv ALTN GU34 176 D3
CHAM PO6 374 F7
HISD PO11 425 G5
LYMN SO41 439 H8
Lime Kiln La FAWY SO45 391 M4
Limekiln La BPWT SO32 297 L5
PSF GU32 274 A8
PSF GU32 302 B1
Limekiln Rd RAND SP11 94 A3
Lime Rd NALR SO24 218 C3
Limes Av KSCL RG20 57 K1
Limes Cl LIPH GU30 226 F1
LISS GU33 248 E4
Limes Rd FARN GU14 89 M3
The Limes LSOL/BMARY PO13 397 H7
TADY RG26 64 A6
TOTT SO40 342 E7 2
Lime St ALDT GU11 6 D2
SHAM SO14 13 H5
Limetree Av KSCL RG20 56 E6
Lime Tree Cl FBDG SP6 333 K2 1
Limetree Wk WINC SO23 11 M7
Lime Tree Wy CHAM RG24 83 K5
Lime Wk FAWY SO45 367 J6
Limited Rd MOOR/WNTN BH9 432 E7
Linacre Rd ITCH SO19 345 H4
Lin Brook Dr RGWD BH24 359 G6
Linchmere Rd HASM GU27 227 M5
Linch Rd HASM GU27 251 K5
MIDH GU29 279 L3
Lincoln Av BMTH BH1 448 C2
Lincoln Cl ASHV GU12 113 K3
CBLY GU15 71 L4
FHAM/STUB PO14 371 G5
KEMP RG22 127 G1
Lincoln Ct WSHM SO15 318 C6 2
Lincoln Gn ALTN GU34 176 D6
Lincoln Ri HORN PO8 352 E4
Lincoln Rd BKME/WDN BH12 446 C1
FARN GU14 90 D7
PSEA PO1 21 M1
Lincolns Ri ELGH SO50 266 A8
Linda Gv HORN PO8 352 D5
Linda Rd FAWY SO45 392 F5 5
Lindberg Ri FHAM PO15 371 J2
Lind Cl WVILLE PO7 376 D5
Linden Av CHAM RG24 106 A3
ODIM RG29 108 E4
Linden Cl BPWT SO32 323 K5
FERN BH22 406 B7
NWBY RG14 2 C1
RAND SP11 92 F6
Linden Ct CBLY GU15 71 J1
Linden Dr LISS GU33 248 E4
Linden Gdns HEND SO30 346 B3
RGWD BH24 358 D8
Linden Gv CHFD SO53 265 H8
GPORT PO12 22 A5
HISD PO11 425 L5
Linden Lea FHAM/PORC PO16 374 A7
Linden Rd BKME/WDN BH12 446 B2
FERN BH22 406 B7
BOR GU35 202 E3
MOOR/WNTN BH9 432 E5
ROMY SO51 290 E1
ROWN SO16 317 M4
Lindens Cl EMRTH PO10 378 D5
The Lindens CHCH/BSGR BH23 435 H5
FNM GU9 135 G7
Linden Wk NBAD SO52 291 L3
Linden Wy HAV PO9 377 K5 3
HORN PO8 352 F3
LYMN SO41 440 A4
Lindford Cha BOR GU35 201 L3
Lindford Rd BOR GU35 201 K2
Lindford Wey BOR GU35 201 L3
Lindisfarne Cl CHAM PO6 399 L1
Lindley Av ENEY PO4 423 L6
Lindley Gdns NALR SO24 218 C4
Lind Rd GPORT PO12 19 G9
Lindsay Rd CCLF BH13 446 F4
ITCH SO19 345 J2
Lindum Dene ALDT GU11 6 E4
Lindway HLER SO31 370 E2
Lineside CHCH/BSGR BH23 435 G8
The Lines KSCL RG20 59 J5
Linford Cl NMIL/BTOS BH25 437 L4
Linford Ct HAV PO9 377 H1
Linford Crs ROWN SO16 318 C5
Linford Rd RGWD BH24 359 H7
Ling Crs BOR GU35 202 E2
Ling Dl ROWN SO16 318 E1
Lingdale Rd SBNE BH6 449 J2
Lingen Cl AND SP10 118 E5 2
Lingfield Cl CHAM RG24 106 B3
Lingfield Gdns WEND SO18 319 L6 1
Lingfield Rd NWBY RG14 3 J9
Lingmala Gv FLET GU13 111 G3 2
Ling Rd BKME/WDN BH12 430 F7
Lingwood Av
CHCH/BSGR BH23 450 E2
Lingwood Cl ROWN SO16 318 E1
Lingwood Wk ROWN SO16 318 E1 1
Linhorns La NMIL/BTOS BH25 437 L2
Linkenholt Wy HAV PO9 377 G3
Link Ri WIMB BH21 429 J2
Link Rd ALTN GU34 176 F2
CHAM PO6 374 F6
FARN GU14 90 A8
KSCL RG20 59 K6
NWBY RG14 2 E6
RGWD BH24 359 G7
ROWN SO16 317 L5
Links Dr CHCH/BSGR BH23 434 B7
Linkside Av CHAR BH8 433 J8
Linkside East GSHT GU26 203 L1
Linkside North GSHT GU26 203 L1
Linkside South GSHT GU26 203 M2
Linkside West GSHT GU26 203 L1
Links La HAV PO9 353 M5
HISD PO11 425 G5
Links Rd WINW SO22 10 A5
PSTN BH14 446 C6
The Links BOR GU35 201 G7
LSOL/BMARY PO13 397 G7
Links View Av PSTN BH14 446 D7
Links View Wy ROWN SO16 318 E2
Links Wy FARN GU14 89 M5
The Link AND SP10 118 B8
WVILLE PO7 352 E7 2
YTLY GU46 68 F1
Linkway CBLY GU15 70 F4
CWTH RG45 49 J3
FHAM/STUB PO14 396 A7
FLET GU13 110 E2
Link Wy NTHA RG18 26 E4
DEAN RG23 103 G7
Linnet Cl EPSF GU31 276 B6
HORN PO8 352 C4
KEMP RG22 103 M6
RGWD BH24 383 G2 5
Linnet Ct NMIL/BTOS BH25 437 K5 5
Linnet Rd CFDH BH17 429 J8
Linnet Sq ELGH SO50 293 J7
Linnets Rd NALR SO24 218 B4
The Linnets
FHAM/PORC PO16 373 K8 7
TOTT SO40 316 B8 5
Linnets Wy ALTN GU34 176 E3
Linnies La LYMN SO41 438 E1
Linsford La FRIM GU16 91 J5
Linstead Rd FARN GU14 70 B8
Linsted La BOR GU35 202 A1
Linthorpe Rd PLE BH15 445 K4
Linton Cl TADY RG26 61 M1
Linton Dr AND SP10 8 F2
Linwood Cl FAWY SO45 367 L6
Linwood Rd MOOR/WNTN BH9 448 A1
Lion & Lamb Wy FNM GU9 134 E6
Lion Cl OVTN RG25 123 M1
Lionheart Cl BWD BH11 431 H3
Lionheart Wy HLER SO31 345 K7
Lion La GSHT GU26 204 C7
Lion Md HASM GU27 228 C2
Lion Rd FARN GU14 90 E6
Lions Fld BOR GU35 200 C4
Lions Hill Wy RGWD BH24 381 G3
Lions La RGWD BH24 381 H4
Lion St PSEA PO1 20 E1
Lions Wd RGWD BH24 381 J4
Lion Wy FLET GU13 111 G3
Liphook Rd HASM GU27 227 K4
BOR GU35 201 H8
BOR GU35 201 L3
BOR GU35 202 B5
Lipizzaner Flds HLER SO31 346 F8
Lippen La BPWT SO32 271 L5
Lipscombe Cl NWBY RG14 2 A5
Lipscombe Ri ALTN GU34 176 E3
Lisbon Rd WSHM SO15 343 H2
Liskeard Dr FARN GU14 90 D2 3
Lisle Cl WINW SO22 237 M5
LYMN SO41 440 B5
NWBY RG14 25 J3
Lisle Court Rd LYMN SO41 440 F5
Lisle Wy EMRTH PO10 378 C5
Lismoyne Cl FLET GU13 88 E6 1
Liss Rd ENEY PO4 423 K4
Lister Rd KEMP RG22 104 D6
Litchfield Cl AND SP10 118 C5
Litchfield Crs WEND SO18 319 L7
Litchfield Rd WINW SO22 214 C4
WEND SO18 319 L7
Litchford Rd NMIL/BTOS BH25 438 A4
Lith Av HORN PO8 328 B8
Lith La HORN PO8 328 B7
Litle Hyden La HORN PO8 302 A8
Little Abshot Rd
FHAM/STUB PO14 370 F8
Little Aldershot La STHA RG19 40 F6
Little Anglesey Rd GPORT PO12 18 C7
Little Arthur St NEND PO2 423 J1 8
Little Ashton La BPWT SO32 297 J5
Little Austins Rd FNM GU9 135 G8
Little Barn Pl LISS GU33 249 G4
Little Barrs Dr
NMIL/BTOS BH25 437 M4
Little Basing CHAM RG24 105 L1
Little Bull La BPWT SO32 323 J6
Little Copse AND SP10 8 C9
FLET GU13 110 E1
YTLY GU46 68 F1
Little Copse Cha CHAM RG24 83 K6
Little Cnr WVILLE PO7 351 K5
Littlecroft Av
MOOR/WNTN BH9 432 F5
Little Dean La OVTN RG25 130 D3
Little Dene Copse LYMN SO41 439 M6
Little Dewlands VWD BH31 356 B2 1
Littledown Av LTDN BH7 448 D1
Littledown Dr LTDN BH7 448 D1
Little Dro FBDG SP6 310 D1
Little Drove Rd STOK SO20 165 M5
Little Fallow CHAM RG24 83 L8
Littlefield Cl ASHV GU12 113 K7
Littlefield Crs NBAD SO52 292 D2
Littlefield Gdns ASHV GU12 113 K7
Littlefield Rd ALTN GU34 176 F4
Little Forest Rd WBNE BH4 22 B1
Little Frith EWKG RG40 48 F2
Little Gays FHAM/STUB PO14
Little George St PSEA PO1
Little Gn GPORT PO12
Littlegreen Av HAV PO9
Little Green La FNM GU9
Little Hambrook St SSEA PO5
Little Hayes La RWIN SO21
Little Hoddington Cl
OVTN RG25
Little Hyden La HORN PO8
Little Knowle Hl KSCL RG20
STHA RG19
Little Lance's Hl ITCH SO19
Little La GPORT PO12
THLE RG7
Little London Rd THLE RG7
Little Md MARL SN8
WVILLE PO7
Littlemeads ROMY SO51
Littlemill La FBDG SP6
Little Minster St WINC SO23
Little Moor SHST GU47
Littlemoor Av BWD BH11
Little Oak Rd ROWN SO16
Little Paddock CBLY GU15
Littlepark Av HAV PO9
Little Park Cl HEND SO30 34
Little Park Farm Rd
FHAM PO15
Little Quob La HEND SO30
Little Shore La BPWT SO32
Little Southsea St SSEA PO5
Little Thurbans Cl FNM GU9
Littleton Gv HAV PO9
Littleton La RWIN SO21
Little Vigo YTLY GU46
Little Wellington St ALDT GU11
Little Woodfalls Dr RSAL SP5
Littlewood Gdns HEND SO30
HLER SO31 3
Little Woodham La
LSOL/BMARY PO13
Littleworth Rd RFNM GU10
Litton Gdns DEAN RG23
Liverpool Rd
FHAM/STUB PO14
PSEA PO1
Liverpool St SHAM SO14
Livery Rd RSAL SP5
Livia Cl AND SP10
Livingstone Rd
BKME/WDN BH12
BOSC BH5
NWBY RG14
SHAM SO14
SSEA PO5
WIMB BH21
Llangar Gv CWTH RG45
Llewellin Cl UPTN BH16
Lloyd Av TOTT SO40 3
Lloyd's La TADY RG26
Loader Cl WINC SO23
Loane Rd ITCH SO19
Lobelia Rd ROWN SO16
Locarno Rd HSEA PO3
Loch Rd PSTN BH14
Lock Appoach CHAM PO6
Locke Cl RAND SP11
Lockerley Cl LYMN SO41
Lockerley Crs ROWN SO16
Lockerley Rd HAV PO9
ROMY SO51
ROMY SO51
Locke Rd HEND SO30
LIPH GU30
Locke's Dro RAND SP11
Lockhams Rd BPWT SO32
Lockram La THLE RG7
Lock Rd ALDT GU11
Locksash Cl SELS PO20
Locksash La RCCH PO18
Locksbridge La TADY RG26
Locksheath Cl HAV PO9 37
Locksheath Park Rd
HLER SO31
Lockside Ct THLE RG7 2
Lock's La RWIN SO21
Locksley Dr FERN BH22
Locksley Rd ELGH SO50
Locks Rd HLER SO31
Lockway Rd ENEY PO4
Lockswood Rd HLER SO31
Lock Vw CHAM PO6
Lockwood Cl FARN GU14
Lockyers Dr FERN BH22
Loddon Cl CBLY GU15
Loddon Dr BSTK RG21
Loddon Rd FARN GU14
Loddon Wy ASHV GU12
Lode Hl RSAL SP5
Loders Cl CFDH BH17
Lodge Av CHAM PO6
Lodgebury Cl EMRTH PO10
Lodge Cl AND SP10
PSTN BH14
Lodge Ct PSTN BH14
Lodge Dr FAWY SO45
RAND SP11
Lodge Dro RSAL SP5
Lodge Gdns GPORT PO12
Lodge Gv YTLY GU46
Lodge Hill Cl RFNM GU10
Lodge Hill Rd RFNM GU10
Lodge La BROC SO42
HAV PO9
RAND SP11
Lodge Rd CHCH/BSGR BH23
HAV PO9
HLER SO31
LYMN SO41
SHAM SO14
Lodge V ROMY SO51
Lodsworth FARN GU14
Lodsworth Cl HORN PO8 3
Loewy Crs BKME/WDN BH12
Lofting Cl ELGH SO50 2
Logan Cl ROWN SO16
Loggon Rd BSTK RG21

Rd FRIM GU16 … 91 K5
Cl HEND SO30 … 321 H7 2
d Av SBNE BH6 … 449 J3
d St PSEA PO1 … 20 C5 2
dy Cl
BMARY PO13 … 397 J6 1
H31 … 356 F3
dy Ri WVILLE PO7 … 376 D3
a RGWD BH24 … 334 A5
Cl DEAN RG23 … 102 F7
PO2 … 399 H8
orough Rd ENEY PO4 … 21 M5
des FLET GU13 … 110 D4
Av NEND PO2 … 399 H6
La CHCH/BSGR BH23 … 408 D6
Rd ALTN GU34 … 177 G3
P10 … 9 K6
GU17 … 70 B4
G21 … 4 F9
U15 … 70 F2
RG24 … 106 A4
PO6 … 375 K8
U31 … 276 A3
PO8 … 328 B7
RG27 … 87 H3 2
RG27 … 106 F1
J30 … 226 F4
PO2 … 399 J6
RG14 … 2 E2
RG29 … 108 D5
RG25 … 123 L1
SP11 … 119 L8
O19 … 27 H5
O20 … 186 F4
RG28 … 122 D3
O23 … 215 G4
SO15 … 343 K2
PO7 … 352 C8
PO7 … 376 A4
St AND SP10 … 9 J6
RG28 … 122 B3
n La BPWT SO32 … 298 D1
e Dr FERN BH22 … 406 C5
e Wy FERN BH22 … 406 D6
WVILLE PO7 … 376 A5
e ASHV GU12 … 113 K6
RG14 … 25 G8
e Cl LISS GU33 … 248 F4
e Ri CHAM RG24 … 83 K6 2
es FHAM/STUB PO14 … 371 G4
row Cl RWIN SO21 … 190 D3
ech Dr FARN GU14 … 89 M5
O40 … 341 H2
ttom RAND SP11 … 93 L5
FNM GU9 … 134 F6
dge Cl HTWY RG27 … 64 D7
O40 … 316 C6
dge Rd TADY RG26 … 63 L5 2
RSAL SP5 … 256 D8
se Rd HEND SO30 … 346 B1
se West RSAL SP5 … 256 D8
ose FAWY SO45 … 392 C5
ose Cha CHAM RG24 … 83 K6
ose La EMRTH PO10 … 378 D4
ft RFNM GU10 … 156 F3
ft Rd KSCL RG20 … 59 H5
G19 … 27 H6
oss Hl BOR GU35 … 202 B3
oss La KEMP RG22 … 126 F2
tain Rd PSEA PO1 … 20 D6
n Cl CHAM PO6 … 374 E7
e Rd HASM GU27 … 228 E2
wn EPSF GU31 … 276 A4
wn FLET GU13 … 110 E2
wn Cl RFNM GU10 … 158 F2
wn Rd RFNM GU10 … 158 E3
U47 … 49 K7
HEND SO30 … 320 D6
MARY PO13 … 397 G7
RSAL SP5 … 230 C3
d Av FHAM/STUB PO14 … 14 B9
d Cl ENEY PO4 … 424 A3 2
U14 … 70 D8
G25 … 125 K7
d Rd ASHV GU12 … 113 K6
PO10 … 378 C5
O41 … 438 F6
O23 … 215 J8
t Dr WIMB BH21 … 430 E1
t Rd PLE BH15 … 445 K4
d Cl CBLY GU15 … 71 G4 1
rden Wk FNM GU9 … 134 E6 3
rden Wk East
J9 … 134 E6 4
rden Wk West
J9 … 134 E6 5
rden Wy FNM GU9 … 134 E6
TADY RG26 … 41 G6
G7 … 27 L3
RFNM GU10 … 136 B7
e Dr RFNM GU10 … 158 D2
se Gn WINC SO23 … 11 M7
ds Rd EMRTH PO10 … 379 H8
CHAM RG24 … 83 M6
O45 … 392 A3
O31 … 345 L7
RG14 … 25 M1
G29 … 108 E8
O18 … 331 J5
BH24 … 382 F4
O40 … 342 B7
BH21 … 404 B1
e Cl FAWY SO45 … 392 B5
Gdns
TOS BH25 … 437 J5
SO16 … 318 A3
Sq FARN GU14 … 91 H5 3
ze RAND SP11 … 97 H4
Rd FNM GU9 … 135 G7
ad FLET GU13 … 110 F2
O20 … 36 C7
33 … 248 E5
ad Av ELGH SO50 … 294 C4
ad Gdns HAV PO9 … 16 F8
adow FRIM GU16 … 71 J5
adow Gdns
O45 … 367 L4
adow La CFDH BH17 … 429 J7

Longmead Rd RGWD BH24 … 384 D4
WEND SO18 … 319 L6 2
Long Mickle SHST GU47 … 49 K7
Longmoor Dr LIPH GU30 … 226 A4 1
Longmoor La THLE RG7 … 43 K1
Longmoor Rd BSTK RG21 … 104 F4
LIPH GU30 … 225 M4
LISS GU33 … 224 F6
Longmore Av ITCH SO19 … 344 B6
Longmore Crs ITCH SO19 … 344 B6 1
Longmynd Dr
FHAM/STUB PO14 … 14 B8
Longparish Rd RAND SP11 … 165 M1
WHCH RG28 … 121 J7
Long Priors PSF GU32 … 272 A3
Longridge Rd HEND SO30 … 346 A2
Long Rd BPWT SO32 … 325 H2
NBNE BH10 … 432 A4
PSF GU32 … 275 M3
The Long Rd RFNM GU10 … 158 C5
Longroden La OVTN RG25 … 129 G1
Longs Ct WHCH RG28 … 122 B3 3
Longshore Wy ENEY PO4 … 424 B3
Longs La FHAM/STUB PO14 … 396 A5
Longstaff Gdns
FHAM/PORC PO16 … 14 F2
Long Steeple La FBDG SP6 … 283 K6
Longstock Cl AND SP10 … 8 C7 1
CHAM RG24 … 84 A4
ITCH SO19 … 344 E8 1
Longstock Crs TOTT SO40 … 341 H1
Longstock Rd HAV PO9 … 377 M2
RAND SP11 … 164 E4
Long Wk RWIN SO21 … 215 J4
Long Water Dr GPORT PO12 … 19 G9
Longwater La EWKG RG40 … 48 B6
Longwater Rd EWKG RG40 … 48 C6
HTWY RG27 … 48 C8
Longwood Av HORN PO8 … 352 D5
Longwood Dean La
RWIN SO21 … 269 H2
Longwood Rd RWIN SO21 … 268 B4
Lonsdale Av CHAM PO6 … 399 L1
FHAM/PORC PO16 … 398 B2
Lonsdale Rd TWDS BH3 … 447 L1
Loperwood TOTT SO40 … 315 L6
Loperwood La TOTT SO40 … 315 M4
Loraine Av CHCH/BSGR BH23 … 437 G8
Lord Cl CFDH BH17 … 445 L1
Lordington Cl CHAM PO6 … 375 M8 1
Lord Montgomery Wy
SSEA PO5 … 20 F3 2
Lord Mountbatten Cl
WEND SO18 … 319 K4 5
Lordsfield Gdns OVTN RG25 … 100 E8
Lord's Hill Centre East
ROWN SO16 … 317 L3
Lord's Hill Centre West
ROWN SO16 … 317 L4
Lord's Hill Wy ROWN SO16 … 317 L3
Lords St PSEA PO1 … 423 H2
Lordswood ELGH SO50 … 294 D1
THLE RG7 … 42 D8
Lordswood Cl ROWN SO16 … 318 C5 1
Lordswood Gdns ROWN SO16 … 318 C4
Lordswood Rd ROWN SO16 … 318 B4
Loreille Cl ROWN SO16 … 317 K1
Lorne Park Rd BMTH BH1 … 23 G5
Lorne Rd SSEA PO5 … 21 L4
Lorraine Rd CBLY GU15 … 51 J8
Loughwood Cl ELGH SO50 … 293 M2
Louisburg Rd BOR GU35 … 201 J2
Loundyes Cl NTHA RG18 … 26 E4
Lovage Gdns TOTT SO40 … 341 G1
Lovage Rd FHAM PO15 … 371 H1
Lovage Wy HORN PO8 … 328 B7
Lovedean La HORN PO8 … 352 D2
Lovedon La WINC SO23 … 191 H8
Lovegroves CHAM RG24 … 83 M5
Love La AND SP10 … 9 J7
BPWT SO32 … 270 A5
EPSF GU31 … 275 M4
FBDG SP6 … 284 D8
KSCL RG20 … 59 J6
NWBY RG14 … 25 J2
ODIM RG29 … 108 C7
PSF GU32 … 272 B4
ROMY SO51 … 290 D1
RWIN SO21 … 267 G3
Lovell Cl RAND SP11 … 140 C1
RWIN SO21 … 190 D4
Lovells Wk NALR SO24 … 218 B3 1
Loveridge Cl AND SP10 … 119 G4
BSTK RG21 … 104 F6
Lovers La RFNM GU10 … 180 F1
Love's Cl THLE RG7 … 31 J5
Loves Wd THLE RG7 … 43 J3
Lovett Rd HSEA PO3 … 399 K5
Lovington La RWIN SO21 … 217 H4
Lowa Cl NTID SP9 … 114 D3
Lowa Rd NTID SP9 … 114 C2
Lowcay Rd SSEA PO5 … 21 L7
Lowden Cl WINW SO22 … 238 C4
Lower Alfred St SHAM SO14 … 343 M2
Lower Ashley Rd
NMIL/BTOS BH25 … 438 B5
Lower Banister St WSHM SO15 … 343 K2
Lower Bartons FBDG SP6 … 309 L7
Lower Baybridge La
RWIN SO21 … 268 A7
Lower Bellfield
FHAM/STUB PO14 … 395 K1
Lower Bere Wd WVILLE PO7 … 376 D1
Lower Blandford Rd
BDST BH18 … 429 M5
Lower Broadmoor Rd
CWTH RG45 … 50 A4
Lower Brook St BSTK RG21 … 4 A8
WINC SO23 … 11 H7
Lower Brownhill Rd
ROWN SO16 … 317 H6
Lower Buckland Rd
LYMN SO41 … 440 B3
Lower Canal Wk SHAM SO14 … 13 G7
Lower Canes YTLY GU46 … 68 D2
Lower Chase Rd BPWT SO32 … 323 M3
Lower Chestnut Dr BSTK RG21 … 104 E5
Lower Church La FNM GU9 … 134 E6 6

Lower Church Pth PSEA PO1 … 21 H1 3
Lower Church Rd
FHAM/STUB PO14 … 371 G5
SHST GU47 … 49 H7
Lower Common HTWY RG27 … 47 H7
Lower Common La
WIMB BH21 … 380 E1
Lower Common Rd
ROMY SO51 … 288 D6
Lower Crabbick La
WVILLE PO7 … 350 F4
Lower Densome Wd
FBDG SP6 … 284 D8
Lower Derby Rd NEND PO2 … 399 G7
Lower Drayton La CHAM PO6 … 400 A1
Lower Duncan Rd HLER SO31 … 370 F3
Lower Evingar Rd WHCH RG28 … 122 B3
Lower Farlington Rd
CHAM PO6 … 376 C8
Lower Farm Ct STHA RG19 … 26 C7
Lower Farnham Rd ALDT GU11 … 7 J7
Lower Forbury Rd SSEA PO5 … 21 J3 5
Lower Golf Links Rd
BDST BH18 … 429 M3
Lower Gv FBDG SP6 … 283 G6
Lower Grove Rd HAV PO9 … 17 G6
Lower Hanger HASM GU27 … 227 M2
Lower Heyshott EPSF GU31 … 275 M4
Lower Lamborough La
NALR SO24 … 242 C3
Lower La BPWT SO32 … 297 J8
Lower Md EPSF GU31 … 276 A5
Lower Mead End Rd
LYMN SO41 … 412 D8
Lower Moor YTLY GU46 … 69 G3 3
Lower Moors Rd RWIN SO21 … 266 E7
Lower Mortimer Rd ITCH SO19 … 344 B5
Lower Mullin's La FAWY SO45 … 367 J4
Lower Neatham Mill La
ALTN GU34 … 177 K2
Lower Nelson St ALDT GU11 … 6 E1
Lower Newport Rd ASHV GU12 … 7 M5
Lower New Rd HEND SO30 … 320 C7
Lower Northam Rd
HEND SO30 … 346 A1
Lower Paice La ALTN GU34 … 196 B4
Lower Pennington La
LYMN SO41 … 440 B7
Lower Pool Rd HTWY RG27 … 67 G4
Lower Preshaw La BPWT SO32 … 269 L8
Lower Quay Cl
FHAM/PORC PO16 … 15 J8
Lower Quay Rd
FHAM/PORC PO16 … 15 K8
Lower Rd HASM GU27 … 205 J6
HAV PO9 … 376 F7
RSAL SP5 … 256 E4
RWIN SO21 … 190 B4
RWIN SO21 … 190 E4
Lower St Helens Rd
HEND SO30 … 346 A3
Lower Sandhurst Rd
EWKG RG40 … 48 D6
Lower Sandy Down La
LYMN SO41 … 413 M5
Lower South Vw FNM GU9 … 134 F5
Lower Spinney HLER SO31 … 394 A1
Lower St HASM GU27 … 228 E2
ROMY SO51 … 263 G1
Lower Swanwick Rd
HLER SO31 … 346 B8 2
Lower Terrace Rd FARN GU14 … 90 D8
Lower Turk St ALTN GU34 … 176 E5
Lower Vicarage Rd ITCH SO19 … 344 B5
Lower Wardown EPSF GU31 … 276 A4
Lower Wy STHA RG19 … 26 C5
Lower Weybourne La FNM GU9 … 6 C9
Lower Wokingham Rd
EWKG RG40 … 49 G2
Lower Woodside LYMN SO41 … 440 C8
Lower Wote St BSTK RG21 … 4 F7
Lower York St SHAM SO14 … 344 B2
Lowestoft Rd CHAM PO6 … 375 H7
Loweswater Gdns BOR GU35 … 201 J3
Lowford Hl HLER SO31 … 345 K7
Lowicks Rd RFNM GU10 … 181 L2
Lowland Rd WVILLE PO7 … 351 J4
Lowlands Rd BLKW GU17 … 69 M4
KEMP RG22 … 103 M5
Low La FNM GU9 … 7 G9
Lowry Cl SHST GU47 … 70 A2
Lowry Ct AND SP10 … 8 F2
Lowry Gdns ITCH SO19 … 345 G6
Lowther Gdns CHAR BH8 … 23 L1
Lowther Rd CHAR BH8 … 447 M2
Loxwood Av FLET GU13 … 110 D1
Loxwood Rd HORN PO8 … 352 D2
Loyalty La CHAM RG24 … 106 A2
Luard Ct HAV PO9 … 17 J5
Lubeck Dr AND SP10 … 118 E5
Lucas Cl ROWN SO16 … 317 L3 3
YTLY GU46 … 69 G3
Lucas Fld HASM GU27 … 228 B2 1
Lucas Rd BKME/WDN BH12 … 446 B2
Luccombe Pl WSHM SO15 … 318 C6
Luccombe Rd WSHM SO15 … 318 C6
Lucerne Av SBNE BH6 … 449 J3
WVILLE PO7 … 352 B6
Lucerne Gdns HEND SO30 … 345 L2
Lucerne Rd LYMN SO41 … 454 C4
Luckham Rd
MOOR/WNTN BH9 … 432 F6
Lucknow St PSEA PO1 … 21 L2
Lucky La LYMN SO41 … 414 E7
Ludcombe WVILLE PO7 … 351 K3
Ludgershall Rd NTID SP9 … 114 E1
Ludlow Cl DEAN RG23 … 104 B3
FRIM GU16 … 91 K1
NWBY RG14 … 26 B4 2
Ludlow Gdns DEAN RG23 … 104 C3
Ludlow Rd CHAM PO6 … 375 G7
ITCH SO19 … 344 C4
Ludshott Gv BOR GU35 … 202 E3
Ludwell's La BPWT SO32 … 323 L4
Lugano Cl WVILLE PO7 … 352 B7
Luke Rd ALDT GU11 … 6 A5
Luke Rd East ALDT GU11 … 6 B5
Lukin Dr ROWN SO16 … 317 H3

Lulworth Av PLE BH15 … 444 D7
Lulworth Cl CHFD SO53 … 293 G5
FARN GU14 … 90 D1
HISD PO11 … 425 L3
PLE BH15 … 444 D7
ROWN SO16 … 317 K6
Lulworth Crs PLE BH15 … 444 D7
Lulworth Gn ROWN SO16 … 317 K6
Lulworth Rd
LSOL/BMARY PO13 … 420 C2
Lumby Dr RGWD BH24 … 358 F8
Lumby Drive Pk RGWD BH24 … 358 F8 1
Lumley Rd EMRTH PO10 … 378 E7
Lumsden Av WSHM SO15 … 343 G1
Lumsden Rd ENEY PO4 … 424 B5
Lundy Cl CHAM RG24 … 83 J7
ROWN SO16 … 317 K3
Lune Cl BSTK RG21 … 5 J8
Lune Ct AND SP10 … 9 M1 2
Lunedale Rd FAWY SO45 … 367 J8
Lupin Cl BAGS GU19 … 51 M7
KEMP RG22 … 103 M8
Lupin Rd ROWN SO16 … 319 H3
Luscombe Rd PSTN BH14 … 446 B6
Luther Rd MOOR/WNTN BH9 … 432 D8
Lutman St EMRTH PO10 … 378 C4
Luton Rd ITCH SO19 … 344 F4
Lutyens Cl CHAM RG24 … 83 L8
Luxton Cl HEND SO30 … 321 L8
Luzborough La ROMY SO51 … 291 G4
Lyall Pl FNM GU9 … 134 E1
Lyburn Cl ROWN SO16 … 318 B4 2
Lyburn Rd RSAL SP5 … 286 F6
Lych Gate Cl SHST GU47 … 49 J8
Lych Gate Ct RGWD BH24 … 383 G2 2
Lychgate Dr HORN PO8 … 352 F1
Lychgate Gn FHAM/STUB PO14 … 396 A3
Lyde Cl DEAN RG23 … 103 G7
Lydford Cl FARN GU14 … 90 D1 6
FRIM GU16 … 91 K1 2
Lydford Gdns BWD BH11 … 431 L6
Lydford Rd BWD BH11 … 431 L6
Lydgate LYMN SO41 … 453 M3 1
TOTT SO40 … 341 H1 3
Lydgate Cl ITCH SO19 … 345 H4
Lydgate Gn ITCH SO19 … 345 H4
Lydgate Rd ITCH SO19 … 345 H4 3
Lydiard Cl ELGH SO50 … 293 M3
Lydlinch Cl FERN BH22 … 406 B7
Lydlynch Rd TOTT SO40 … 341 J1
Lydney Cl CHAM PO6 … 375 G8
Lydney Rd HLER SO31 … 370 D6
Lye Copse Av FARN GU14 … 70 E8
Lyell Rd BKME/WDN BH12 … 446 B2
Lyeway La NALR SO24 … 220 C4
Lyeway Rd ALTN GU34 … 220 F3
Lyford Rd BSTK RG21 … 4 F5
Lymbourn Rd HAV PO9 … 17 G5
Lyme Cl ELGH SO50 … 293 L3 2
Lyme Crs CHCH/BSGR BH23 … 436 D8
Lymefields LYMN SO41 … 454 D2
Lymer La ROWN SO16 … 317 H2
Lymington Av YTLY GU46 … 68 F3
Lymington Bottom ALTN GU34 … 197 G6
Lymington Bottom Rd
ALTN GU34 … 196 F4
Lymington Cl ALTN GU34 … 196 F6
KEMP RG22 … 127 G2
Lymington Ri ALTN GU34 … 197 G6
Lymington Rd BROC SO42 … 413 L2
CHCH/BSGR BH23 … 451 J1
LYMN SO41 … 441 L3
LYMN SO41 … 454 D1
NMIL/BTOS BH25 … 437 L7
Lymington Road Shelley Hl
CHCH/BSGR BH23 … 451 H1
Lymore La LYMN SO41 … 439 J8
Lymore Va LYMN SO41 … 454 D1
Lynchborough Rd LIPH GU30 … 202 A8
Lynch Cl WINW SO22 … 10 C3
Lynchford La FARN GU14 … 91 H7
Lynchford Rd ALDT GU11 … 90 F8
FARN GU14 … 90 F8 1
Lynch Hl WHCH RG28 … 122 B3
Lynch Hill Pk WHCH RG28 … 122 C3
Lynch La PSF GU32 … 272 B4
Lynch Rd FNM GU9 … 135 G6
The Lynch MARL SN8 … 32 C6
OVTN RG25 … 100 D8
WHCH RG28 … 122 C3
Lyndale Cl LYMN SO41 … 454 D3
Lyndale Dr FLET GU13 … 89 J7
Lyndale Rd HLER SO31 … 370 F4
Lynden Cl FHAM/STUB PO14 … 371 M8
Lynden Ga ITCH SO19 … 344 E5 2
Lyndford Ter FLET GU13 … 110 E1
Lyndhurst Av ALDT GU11 … 7 J9
BLKW GU17 … 69 M2
Lyndhurst Cl WINW SO22 … 214 C4
HISD PO11 … 425 L6
Lyndhurst Dr KEMP RG22 … 127 H2
Lyndhurst Rd BROC SO42 … 387 L6
CHCH/BSGR BH23 … 410 D8
CHCH/BSGR BH23 … 435 M7
GPORT PO12 … 18 C2
NEND PO2 … 399 K6
RGWD BH24 … 384 E5
RSAL SP5 … 287 H5
TOTT SO40 … 339 J1
Lyndock Cl ITCH SO19 … 344 C6 2
Lyndock Pl ITCH SO19 … 344 C6
Lyndsey Cl FARN GU14 … 89 L4
Lyndum Cl EPSF GU31 … 275 L5
Lyneham Rd CWTH RG45 … 49 L3
Lyne Pl HORN PO8 … 352 F2
Lynes La RGWD BH24 … 382 D1
Lynford Av WINW SO22 … 10 C2
Lynford Wy WINW SO22 … 10 D2
Lynn Rd CFDH BH17 … 430 D8
NEND PO2 … 399 K8
Lynn Wy FARN GU14 … 90 C1
WINC SO23 … 215 H2
Lynric Cl NMIL/BTOS BH25 … 452 E1
Lynton Cl FNM GU9 … 158 D1
Lynton Ct TOTT SO40 … 341 J2
Lynton Crs CHCH/BSGR BH23 … 434 B5
Lynton Gdns FHAM/PORC PO16 … 14 E1
Lynton Gv HSEA PO3 … 399 L8

Lynton Meadow STOK SO20 … 165 M4 1
Lynton Rd HEND SO30 … 346 A1
BOR GU35 … 201 J5
PSF GU32 … 275 K4
Lynwood Av WVILLE PO7 … 352 B5
Lynwood Cl FERN BH22 … 406 B1
BOR GU35 … 201 M3 4
Lynwood Dr AND SP10 … 8 D6
FRIM GU16 … 91 K5
WIMB BH21 … 404 D7
Lynwood Gdns HTWY RG27 … 85 M7
Lynx Cl ELGH SO50 … 294 E6
Lyon Av NMIL/BTOS BH25 … 437 M5
Lyon Cl STHA RG19 … 27 J6
Lyon Rd BKME/WDN BH12 … 431 J6
CWTH RG45 … 49 M2
Lyon St SHAM SO14 … 343 L2
Lyon Wy FRIM GU16 … 70 F7
Lysander Cl CHCH/BSGR BH23 … 451 G1
Lysander Wy FARN GU14 … 90 E7
WVILLE PO7 … 352 E8
Lysons Av ASHV GU12 … 91 J8
Lysons Rd ALDT GU11 … 6 F3
Lyster Rd FBDG SP6 … 309 M6
Lystra Rd MOOR/WNTN BH9 … 432 E5
Lytchett Dr BDST BH18 … 429 L5
Lytchett Wy UPTN BH16 … 444 A2 2
Lyteltane Rd LYMN SO41 … 440 B6
Lytham Rd BDST BH18 … 429 L5
WEND SO18 … 319 M8
Lythe La PSF GU32 … 274 F3
Lytton Rd BMTH BH1 … 23 L2
BSTK RG21 … 5 H8
FAWY SO45 … 367 M6

M

Mabbs La HTWY RG27 … 87 H4
Mabey Av NBNE BH10 … 432 B6
Mabey Cl GPORT PO12 … 19 G8
Mablethorpe Rd CHAM PO6 … 375 J7
Macadam Wy AND SP10 … 118 A7
Macandrew Rd CCLF BH13 … 457 L1 3
Macarthur Crs WEND SO18 … 319 M8 3
Macaulay Av CHAM PO6 … 374 D7
Macaulay Rd BDST BH18 … 429 L4
Maccullum Rd RAND SP11 … 96 A8
Macdonald Rd FNM GU9 … 134 E1
Maclaren Rd
MOOR/WNTN BH9 … 432 D5
Maclean Rd BWD BH11 … 431 K5
Macnaghten Rd WEND SO18 … 344 B1
Macrae Rd YTLY GU46 … 68 F2
Madden Cl GPORT PO12 … 18 A6
Maddison St SHAM SO14 … 12 F5 3
Maddocks Hl NALR SO24 … 220 A4
Maddoxford Wy BPWT SO32 … 321 L7
Madeira Cl CHAM RG24 … 83 J7
Madeira Rd BMTH BH1 … 23 G4
NEND PO2 … 399 J5
Madeley Rd FLET GU13 … 111 G2
Madeline Crs
BKME/WDN BH12 … 446 A1
Madeline Rd EPSF GU31 … 275 L4
Madison Av BMTH BH1 … 448 C2
Madison Cl
LSOL/BMARY PO13 … 397 J8 1
Madox Brown End
SHST GU47 … 70 B2 2
Madrid Rd AND SP10 … 9 M3
Mafeking Rd ENEY PO4 … 423 K5
Magazine La TOTT SO40 … 342 E5
Magazine Rd FARN GU14 … 90 A8
Magdala Rd CHAM PO6 … 399 K1
HISD PO11 … 425 J5
Magdalene Rd SHST GU47 … 50 C6
Magdalene Wy
FHAM/STUB PO14 … 371 G7
Magdalen Hl WINC SO23 … 11 J8
Magdalen La
CHCH/BSGR BH23 … 449 M2
Magdalen Rd NEND PO2 … 399 J5
Magennis Cl
LSOL/BMARY PO13 … 421 H1
Magna Gdns BWD BH11 … 431 K2
Magna Rd WIMB BH21 … 404 F8
Magnolia Cl AND SP10 … 8 C7
FAWY SO45 … 367 G4 3
FHAM/STUB PO14 … 14 C7
SHST GU47 … 50 A7 2
VWD BH31 … 357 G4
Magnolia Gv ELGH SO50 … 295 K6
Magnolia Rd ITCH SO19 … 344 D3
Magnolia Wy FLET GU13 … 110 F1
HORN PO8 … 353 G4
Magnus Dr KEMP RG22 … 127 G1
Magpie Cl CHAR BH8 … 433 G5
KEMP RG22 … 103 L8
BOR GU35 … 201 K6 3
RFNM GU10 … 111 G8 1
STHA RG19 … 26 E5
Magpie Dr TOTT SO40 … 341 G1
Magpie Gdns ITCH SO19 … 344 F4
Magpie Gv NMIL/BTOS BH25 … 437 K6 2
Magpie La ELGH SO50 … 293 K6
LSOL/BMARY PO13 … 420 D1 5
Magpie Rd HORN PO8 … 354 A3
Magpie Wk HORN PO8 … 352 B4
Mag's Barrow FERN BH22 … 406 C6
Maguire Dr FRIM GU16 … 71 M5
Mahler Cl KEMP RG22 … 104 E8
Maida Rd ALDT GU11 … 112 E4
Maiden La LYMN SO41 … 440 D7
Maidenthorn La OVTN RG25 … 125 L7
Maidford Gv HSEA PO3 … 400 A4 4
Maidstone Crs CHAM PO6 … 375 J7
Main Dr FAWY SO45 … 417 L2
WHAM PO17 … 374 E2
Main Gate Rd FARN GU14 … 90 E6
Main Rd EMRTH PO10 … 379 G8
FAWY SO45 … 366 E1
FAWY SO45 … 392 A2
WINW SO22 … 213 M2
LSOL/BMARY PO13 … 397 H4
LYMN SO41 … 415 M8
LYMN SO41 … 440 E2

PSEA PO1 20 B1
PSEA PO1 422 D2
RWIN SO21 266 A6
RWIN SO21 266 E6
RWIN SO21 268 A4
RWIN SO21 295 G1
TADY RG26 62 A2
TOTT SO40 341 J4
TOTT SO40 342 D7
Mainsail Dr FHAM/PORC PO16 15 J8
Mainstone ROMY SO51 290 C2
Mainstone Cl FRIM GU16 91 M1 1
Mainstream Ct ELGH SO50 294 C5 1
Main St STHA RG19 38 D3
Maisemore Gdns EMRTH PO10 378 B8
Maitland Rd FARN GU14 90 E8
Maitlands Cl RFNM GU10 136 B2
Maitland St PSEA PO1 423 H1
Majendie Cl NWBY RG14 25 G3 3
Majestic Rd KEMP RG22 126 F3
ROWN SO16 317 G4
Majorca Av AND SP10 9 L2
Malan Cl CFDH BH17 430 C8
Malcolm Cl CHFD SO53 265 K7
HLER SO31 370 F5
Malcolm Rd CHFD SO53 265 K7
Malcomb Cl SBNE BH6 449 M5
Malcroft Ms TOTT SO40 342 E7 3
Maldive Rd CHAM RG24 83 J7
Maldon Cl ELGH SO50 294 C5
Maldon Rd CHAM PO6 375 H8 3
ITCH SO19 344 C4
Malham Gdns KEMP RG22 127 G3
Malham Rd STHA RG19 26 F5
Malibres Rd CHFD SO53 265 L8
Malin Cl FHAM/STUB PO14 395 M5
ROWN SO16 317 K4
Malins Rd NEND PO2 423 H1
Mallard Cl AND SP10 119 G6
ASHV GU12 113 J6
BPWT SO32 296 F8
CHAR BH8 433 G7
CHCH/BSGR BH23 450 F2
HASM GU27 228 B2 2
KEMP RG22 126 E1
LYMN SO41 438 E5
NALR SO24 218 C2
ROMY SO51 262 E8
Mallard Ct NWBY RG14 2 C4
Mallard Gdns HEND SO30 321 H6
LSOL/BMARY PO13 396 F6 2
Mallard Rd CHAR BH8 433 H7
ENEY PO4 423 M3
HAV PO9 353 M7
WIMB BH21 404 E1
Mallards ALTN GU34 176 E3
Mallards Rd HLER SO31 369 K1
The Mallards FHAM/PORC PO16 15 H1
HAV PO9 16 D8
Mallard Wy THLE RG7 29 L5
YTLY GU46 68 E2 2
Mallett Cl HEND SO30 321 K6
Mallory Cl CHCH/BSGR BH23 435 K8
Mallory Crs FHAM/PORC PO16 15 G2
Mallow Cl BDST BH18 429 J5
CHAM PO6 375 K8 1
BOR GU35 201 M3 5
WVILLE PO7 376 D2
Mallow Rd HEND SO30 345 L2
The Mallows NMIL/BTOS BH25 438 B4
The Mall NTID SP9 114 A4
RGWD BH24 384 E5 3
Malmesbury Cl ELGH SO50 295 H6 2
Malmesbury Gdns WINW SO22 10 A3
Malmesbury Park Pl CHAR BH8 23 M1
Malmesbury Park Rd
CHAR BH8 448 A2
Malmesbury Pl WSHM SO15 343 H1
Malmesbury Rd RGWD BH24 381 J5
ROMY SO51 262 D8
WSHM SO15 343 H1
Malmsbury Rd BOR GU35 201 J6
Maloren Wy FERN BH22 380 E7
Malory Cl ITCH SO19 345 H2
Malpass Rd RWIN SO21 190 B6
Malshanger La DEAN RG23 102 F5
Malta Cl CHAM RG24 83 H7
Malta Rd NEND PO2 399 J8
Maltby's ALTN GU34 199 K8
Malthouse Cl FLET GU13 110 D3
ROMY SO51 262 D8 3
RWIN SO21 215 L3
Malthouse Gdns TOTT SO40 342 D7
Malthouse La
FHAM/PORC PO16 15 J5
NALR SO24 195 H7
TADY RG26 62 A2
Malt House La RAND SP11 119 H1
Malthouse Mdw LIPH GU30 226 F4
Malthouse Ms ALTN GU34 177 H2 1
Malthouse Rd NEND PO2 399 H8
Maltings Cl ALTN GU34 176 E6
The Maltings EPSF GU31 275 L5
FHAM/PORC PO16 373 H6 1
LIPH GU30 227 G4
TADY RG26 63 L6
Malt La BPWT SO32 297 H8
Malus Cl FHAM/STUB PO14 396 D1
Malvern Av FHAM/STUB PO14 14 C8
Malvern Cl BPWT SO32 323 J1
KEMP RG22 103 M5
Malvern Ct NWBY RG14 2 D7
Malvern Dr FAWY SO45 367 H5
Malvern Gdns HEND SO30 321 J6
Malvern Ms EMRTH PO10 378 D7
Malvern Rd BLKW GU17 69 J7
FARN GU14 90 A1
GPORT PO12 18 B1
LISS GU33 249 G6
MOOR/WNTN BH9 432 E6
ROWN SO16 318 B6
SSEA PO5 21 J9
Malwood Av ROWN SO16 318 C5
Malwood Cl HAV PO9 377 L2
Malwood Gdns TOTT SO40 316 B8
Malwood Rd FAWY SO45 367 K4
Malwood Rd West FAWY SO45 367 J4
Manchester Rd LYMN SO41 412 F5
PSEA PO1 21 M1
Mancroft Av
FHAM/STUB PO14 396 A7
Mandale Rd BWD BH11 431 K5
Mandela Wy WSHM SO15 12 C1
Manderley LYMN SO41 454 D5
Mandora Rd ALDT GU11 112 E4
Manfield Rd ASHV GU12 113 K6
Manica Cl BOR GU35 201 J5 2
Manley Bridge Rd RFNM GU10 158 B4
Manley James Cl ODIM RG29 108 D5 1
Manley Rd HLER SO31 345 K7
Mann Cl WHCH RG28 122 C4
Manners La ENEY PO4 21 L3
Manners Rd ENEY PO4 21 M3
Manning Av CHCH/BSGR BH23 436 A7
Manningford Cl WINC SO23 11 H1
Mannings Heath Rd
BKME/WDN BH12 430 F6
Mannington Pl WCLF BH2 22 C6
Mannington Wy FERN BH22 380 B6
Manns Cl WEND SO18 320 B6
Mannyngham Wy ROMY SO51 262 C1
Manor Av BKME/WDN BH12 431 G7
Manor Bridge Ct NTID SP9 114 E1
Manor Cl ALTN GU34 176 F2
FBDG SP6 309 L7
FERN BH22 406 C3
HASM GU27 228 B2
HLER SO31 345 K7 3
KEMP RG22 126 F2
LYMN SO41 454 C3
RFNM GU10 136 C1
NTID SP9 138 D1
RAND SP11 141 M5
TOTT SO40 341 J2
WHAM PO17 348 E6
WINC SO23 11 K6
Manor Copse AND SP10 119 G3
Manor Ct FLET GU13 110 F4
RGWD BH24 358 D8
VWD BH31 356 D2 1
Manor Crs CHAM PO6 399 M1
HLER SO31 345 K7
Manor Farm Cl ASHV GU12 113 J7 1
NMIL/BTOS BH25 437 K7 1
RSAL SP5 252 B1
Manor Farm Gn RWIN SO21 266 E3
Manor Farm Gv ELGH SO50 294 D6 2
Manor Farm La ROMY SO51 234 C7
Manor Farm Rd FBDG SP6 309 H7
NBNE BH10 432 A2
WEND SO18 319 J7
Manor Flds LIPH GU30 227 G4
Manor Gdns EMRTH PO10 379 H7
RFNM GU10 159 G3
RGWD BH24 358 D8 1
VWD BH31 356 D2 2
Manor House Av WSHM SO15 342 C2
Manor La CHAM RG24 106 A2
NTHA RG18 26 B4
STHA RG19 40 A1
VWD BH31 356 D3
Manor Lodge Rd HAV PO9 353 M8
Manor Ms CHAM PO6 376 A8
Manor Park Av HSEA PO3 399 L8
Manor Park Dr EWKG RG40 48 A2 1
EWKG RG40 48 B2 2
YTLY GU46 69 G3
Manor Pl NWBY RG14 25 G3
Manor Ri RAND SP11 142 D4
Manor Rd ALDT GU11 6 D5
ALTN GU34 176 F2
AND SP10 8 E3
ASHV GU12 113 J7
BMTH BH1 23 L6
BPWT SO32 322 C1
CHAM RG24 82 D5
CHCH/BSGR BH23 449 M2
ELGH SO50 294 D6
EMRTH PO10 379 H7
FARN GU14 91 G5
FAWY SO45 392 A4
FNM GU9 135 H4
HISD PO11 425 K3
LYMN SO41 454 C2
RFNM GU10 113 J8
NMIL/BTOS BH25 437 M5
PSEA PO1 423 J1
RGWD BH24 382 E1
ROWN SO16 292 C7
RSAL SP5 232 D1
RWIN SO21 266 E3
TOTT SO40 366 E3
VWD BH31 356 D2
Manor Rd North ITCH SO19 344 C4
Manor Rd South ITCH SO19 344 C5
Manorside Cl RFNM GU10 113 J8 1
Manor Wk ASHV GU12 7 G4
Manor Wy EMRTH PO10 379 H7
HISD PO11 425 L6
LSOL/BMARY PO13 420 C2
VWD BH31 356 D1 1
Mans Br WEND SO18 319 L4
Mansbridge Rd ELGH SO50 293 M7
WEND SO18 319 L4
Manse La TADY RG26 62 A2
Mansel Cl BKME/WDN BH12 447 H1
Mansel Ct ROWN SO16 317 K6
Mansell Cl FAWY SO45 367 J8
Mansell Dr NWBY RG14 36 F3
Mansel Rd East ROWN SO16 317 K7
Mansel Rd West ROWN SO16 317 J6
Mansfield Cl FERN BH22 406 B6
Mansfield La WHAM PO17 347 M4
Mansfield Rd KEMP RG22 104 D6
LSOL/BMARY PO13 397 G8
MOOR/WNTN BH9 432 C7
PSTN BH14 446 B4
RGWD BH24 382 D1
Man's Hl THLE RG7 31 M5
Mansion Dr HTWY RG27 67 G4
Mansion Rd ENEY PO4 423 J7
WSHM SO15 343 G2
Mansvid Av CHAM PO6 399 M1
Mantle Cl LSOL/BMARY PO13 421 H1
Mantle Sq NEND PO2 398 F6
Manton Rd PLE BH15 444 D5 5
Maple Cl ALTN GU34 176 E3 2
ASHV GU12 113 J1
BLKW GU17 69 M3
CHCH/BSGR BH23 451 L1
EMRTH PO10 378 D6
FHAM PO15 372 A7
LSOL/BMARY PO13 420 D3 2
NALR SO24 218 B4 1
NMIL/BTOS BH25 453 G1
ROMY SO51 291 H2
SHST GU47 49 J7
STOK SO20 163 G4
Maple Crs BSTK RG21 4 E3
HORN PO8 328 B2
NWBY RG14 2 E1
RAND SP11 93 G6
Maple Dr CWTH RG45 49 M1 1
FERN BH22 380 A8
WINC SO23 191 G8
WVILLE PO7 351 L5
Maple Gdns TOTT SO40 341 G2 3
YTLY GU46 69 G3
Maplehurst Cha KEMP RG22 127 G2
Maple Leaf Cl FARN GU14 90 C5 1
Maple Leaf Dr BOR GU35 201 J4
Maple Rd FAWY SO45 367 M8 2
MOOR/WNTN BH9 432 D8
PLE BH15 445 J5
SSEA PO5 21 J8
WEND SO18 344 C1
Maple Sq ELGH SO50 293 K7 2
The Maples CHFD SO53 265 H8
Mapleton Rd HEND SO30 346 B2 1
Mapletree Av HORN PO8 353 G3
Maple Wk ASHV GU12 7 M6
Maple Wy BOR GU35 202 E2
Maplewood Cl TOTT SO40 341 G2
Maplin Rd ROWN SO16 317 J6
Mapperton Cl CFDH BH17 430 E6
Marabout Cl CHCH/BSGR BH23 450 C1
Maralyn Av WVILLE PO7 376 C2
Marathon Pl ELGH SO50 295 G6
Marbrean Cl FBDG SP6 309 H6 1
Marchant Cl STHA RG19 38 A1 1
Marchant Rd AND SP10 8 D7
March Cl AND SP10 9 K3
Marchwood By-pass
TOTT SO40 341 L3
Marchwood Rd HAV PO9 377 J2
NBNE BH10 432 A5
TOTT SO40 342 A4
WSHM SO15 342 F2
Marconi Rd NWBY RG14 3 G2
Marcus Cl ELGH SO50 295 G6
Mardale CBLY GU15 71 M4
Mardale Rd ROWN SO16 317 J8
Marden Wy EPSF GU31 275 M5
Mardon Cl ELGH SO50 319 K3
Mare La RWIN SO21 267 K1
Mareth Cl ALDT GU11 7 H1
Margam Av ITCH SO19 344 D3
Margards La VWD BH31 356 C3
Margaret Cl WVILLE PO7 352 B7
Margaret Rd KEMP RG22 104 C4
Margarita Rd FHAM PO15 14 C4
Margate Rd SSEA PO5 21 J4
Margery's Ct PSEA PO1 20 D2 2
Margha Rd NTID SP9 114 D2
Marian Cl WIMB BH21 429 G4
Marianne Cl WSHM SO15 342 D2 1
Marianne Rd
BKME/WDN BH12 432 A8
WIMB BH21 404 E1
Marian Rd WIMB BH21 429 G4
Marie Av RSAL SP5 284 C1
Marie Cl BKME/WDN BH12 446 C1
Marie Rd ITCH SO19 345 G5
Marigold Cl CWTH RG45 49 J1
FHAM PO15 14 C4
KEMP RG22 103 M8
Marina Cl EMRTH PO10 378 E8 1
Marina Dr PSTN BH14 446 A7
Marina Gv FHAM/PORC PO16 398 A2
HSEA PO3 423 M2
Marina Keep CHAM PO6 398 E1
The Marina BOSC BH5 448 D5
Marine Ct ENEY PO4 423 L6
Marine Dr NMIL/BTOS BH25 452 D1
Marine Dr East
NMIL/BTOS BH25 452 F2
Marine Dr West
NMIL/BTOS BH25 452 C1
Marine Pde SHAM SO14 13 K4
Marine Pde East
LSOL/BMARY PO13 420 D4
Marine Pde West
LSOL/BMARY PO13 420 B1
Marine Prospect
NMIL/BTOS BH25 452 E1
Marine Rd SBNE BH6 449 J5
Mariner's Cl HLER SO31 369 L4
TADY RG26 62 A2
Mariners Ms FAWY SO45 367 L4 2
Mariners Wk ENEY PO4 423 M3
Mariners Wy GPORT PO12 19 J5
HLER SO31 370 A7
Marine Wk HISD PO11 426 B5
Marino Wy EWKG RG40 47 K2
Marion Rd ENEY PO4 21 M8
Maritime Av TOTT SO40 342 E5
Maritime Wk SHAM SO14 13 J8
Maritime Wy SHAM SO14 13 H7
Marjoram Cl FARN GU14 89 L4 1
Marjoram Crs HORN PO8 352 F5
Marjoram Wy FHAM PO15 371 H1
Markall Cl NALR SO24 242 C3
Mark Cl HSEA PO3 399 K4
WSHM SO15 342 E1
Marken Cl HLER SO31 370 C5
Market Cl PLE BH15 445 H6
Market La WINC SO23 11 G8
Market Pde HAV PO9 16 E4
Market Pl BSTK RG21 4 F9
RGWD BH24 382 D1
SHAM SO14 13 G6
Market Sq ALTN GU34 176 E5
Market St ALTN GU34 176 E5
ELGH SO50 294 A7
NWBY RG14 2 E5
PLE BH15 445 G7
WINC SO23 11 G8
Marketway PSEA PO1 423 G2
Market Wy WIMB BH21 404 B4
Markham Av NBNE BH10 432 B2
Markham Ct CBLY GU15 71 G2 2
Markham Rd
MOOR/WNTN BH9 432 E8
Mark's La NMIL/BTOS BH25 437 L2
Markson Rd RWIN SO21 190 B4
Mark's Rd FHAM/STUB PO14 396 C6
MOOR/WNTN BH9 432 D5
Marks Tey Rd
FHAM/STUB PO14 396 A3
Markway Cl EMRTH PO10 378 B7
Marlborough Cl FLET GU13 89 J8
WVILLE PO7 376 B3 1
Marlborough Ct FAWY SO45 367 J6 1
Marlborough Gdns
DEAN RG23 103 G6 1
HEND SO30 321 H5 3
Marlborough Gv
FHAM/PORC PO16 398 A1
Marlborough Pk HAV PO9 17 K2
Marlborough Pl LYMN SO41 440 B3 2
WIMB BH21 404 B3
Marlborough Ri CBLY GU15 71 H2
Marlborough Rd CHFD SO53 265 K7
GPORT PO12 421 K2
WBNE BH4 447 H5
WSHM SO15 318 A8
Marlborough Rw PSEA PO1 422 E2
Marlborough St AND SP10 9 H4
Marlborough Vw FARN GU14 89 M3
Marldell Cl HAV PO9 377 L3
Marles Cl LSOL/BMARY PO13 421 H1
Marley Av NMIL/BTOS BH25 437 J4
Marley Cl NMIL/BTOS BH25 437 K5
Marley Combe Rd HASM GU27 228 C3
Marley Hanger HASM GU27 228 D5
Marley La HASM GU27 228 B3
Marley Mt LYMN SO41 412 C7
Marlhill Cl WEND SO18 319 L6
Marlin Cl LSOL/BMARY PO13 421 H2
Marline Rd BKME/WDN BH12 446 C2
Marl La FBDG SP6 309 J6
Marlott Rd PLE BH15 445 H3
Marlow Cl FHAM PO15 372 C4
Marlow Dr CHCH/BSGR BH23 434 C5
Marlowe Cl CHAM RG24 5 H1
Marlowe Ct WVILLE PO7 352 B7
The Marlowes NWBY RG14 25 J8
Marlow Rd BPWT SO32 296 F7
Marlpit Dr CHCH/BSGR BH23 436 E6
Marlpit La EMRTH PO10 379 L4
NMIL/BTOS BH25 411 L8
Marl's La CHAM RG24 83 G4
Marls Rd HEND SO30 346 B2 3
Marmion Av SSEA PO5 21 J7 2
Marmion Rd SSEA PO5 21 H7
Marne Rd WEND SO18 344 E1
Marnhull Rd PLE BH15 445 J4
Marples Wy HAV PO9 16 B5
Marram Cl LYMN SO41 440 C2
Marrels Wd WVILLE PO7 376 A4
Marrowbrook Cl FARN GU14 90 D5
Marrowbrook La FARN GU14 90 C6
Marryat Rd NMIL/BTOS BH25 437 K5
Marsden Ct WHCH RG28 123 H2 1
Marsden Rd CHAM PO6 374 F8
Marshall Cl FARN GU14 90 C1
Marshall Gdns BSTK RG21 4 F4
Marshall Rd HISD PO11 426 A6
SHST GU47 70 A1
Marshalls Ct NWBY RG14 25 G3 1
Marshal Rd CFDH BH17 429 M7
Marsh Cl CHAM PO6 400 A2
BOR GU35 201 L5
Marshcourt CHAM RG24 83 L8
Marshfield WIMB BH21 404 D1
Marshfield Cl TOTT SO40 342 B7
Marsh Gdns HEND SO30 321 H5 2
Marshlands Rd CHAM PO6 400 B1
Marsh La CHCH/BSGR BH23 434 D6
FAWY SO45 392 F4
FBDG SP6 283 M8
HTWY RG27 68 B3
LYMN SO41 440 C2
NWBY RG14 2 E3
RCCH PO18 403 L4
SHAM SO14 13 H5
Marsh Rd NTHA RG18 27 H4
The Marsh FAWY SO45 367 L3
Marshwood Av CFDH BH17 430 D6
WVILLE PO7 376 E1
Marston Cl NMIL/BTOS BH25 437 M3 1
Marston Dr FARN GU14 90 E1
NWBY RG14 26 A3
Marston Gv CHCH/BSGR BH23 436 C7
Marston La HSEA PO3 399 M4
Marston Rd FNM GU9 134 C6
ITCH SO19 345 H3
NMIL/BTOS BH25 437 M3
Marsum Cl AND SP10 118 E4 1
Martel Cl CBLY GU15 71 M1
Martello Cl GPORT PO12 421 H5
Martello Pk CCLF BH13 457 L1
Martello Rd CCLF BH13 446 E7
The Martells NMIL/BTOS BH25 453 G1
Martin Av FHAM/STUB PO14 396 B6
WVILLE PO7 351 L4
Martin Cl BPWT SO32 324 A4
BSTK RG21 5 H3
CFDH BH17 444 D1
LSOL/BMARY PO13 420 D1 3
NTID SP9 114 F2
Martindale Av CBLY GU15 71 M5
WIMB BH21 404 F3
Martin Dro End FBDG SP6 280 F3
Martingale Cl UPTN BH16 444 C1
Martingale Ct ALDT GU11 6 B2 3
Martin Rd FHAM/STUB PO14 396 B6
HAV PO9 377 L4
HSEA PO3 399 L8
Martins Cl ALTN GU34 176 F3
BLKW GU17 70 A4
FERN BH22
Martins Dr FERN BH22
Martins Flds RWIN SO21
Martins Hill Cl
CHCH/BSGR BH23
Martins Hill La
CHCH/BSGR BH23
Martins La STOK SO20
Martin's Rd BROC SO42
The Martins ELGH SO50
STHA RG19
Martin St BPWT SO32
Martins Wy FERN BH22
Martins Wd CHAM RG24
Martin Wy AND SP10
FRIM GU16
Martley Gdns HEND SO30
Marvic Ct HAV PO9
Marvin Wy HEND SO30
WEND SO18
Marwell Cl LTDN BH7
Marybridge Cl TOTT SO40
Maryfield SHAM SO14
Maryland EWKG RG40
Maryland Cl WEND SO18
Maryland Gdns LYMN SO41
Maryland Rd UPTN BH16
Mary La ALTN GU34
FERN BH22
OVTN RG25
Mary Rose Cl FHAM PO15
The Mary Rose St PSEA PO1
Masefield Av CHAM PO6
Masefield Cl ELGH SO50
Masefield Crs HORN PO8
Masefield Gn ITCH SO19
Masefield Rd NTHA RG18
Maskell Wy FARN GU14
Mason Cl YTLY GU46
Mason Pl SHST GU47
Mason Rd FARN GU14
Mason Wy ALDT GU11
Masseys La BROC SO42
Masten Crs LSOL/BMARY PO13
Matapan Rd NEND PO2
Matchams La
CHCH/BSGR BH23
RGWD BH24
Matheson Rd ROWN SO16
Mathias Wk KEMP RG22
Matilda Dr KEMP RG22
Matley Gdns TOTT SO40
Matlock Rd FERN BH22
Matthew Rd FNM GU9
Matthews Cl HAV PO9
STHA RG19
Matthews La BROC SO42
Matthews Rd CBLY GU15
Matthews Wy DEAN RG23
Mattock Wy CHAM RG24
Maturin Cl LYMN SO41
Maultway Cl CBLY GU15
Maultway Crs CBLY GU15
Maultway North CBLY GU15
The Maultway CBLY GU15
Maundeville Crs
CHCH/BSGR BH23
Maundeville Rd
CHCH/BSGR BH23
Maunsell Wy HEND SO30
Maureen Cl BKME/WDN BH12
Maurepas Wy WVILLE PO7
Mauretania Rd ROWN SO16
Maurice Rd ENEY PO4
Maurys La ROMY SO51
Mavins Rd FNM GU9
Mavis Crs HAV PO9
Mavis Rd MOOR/WNTN BH9
Maw Cl KEMP RG22
Maxine Cl SHST GU47
Maxstoke Cl SSEA PO5
Maxwell Rd BDST BH18
CCLF BH13
ENEY PO4
ITCH SO19
MOOR/WNTN BH9
May Av LYMN SO41
Maybray King Wy ITCH SO19
Maybrick Cl SHST GU47
Maybrook CHAM RG24
Maybury Cl FRIM GU16
Maybush Dr RCCH PO18
May Bush La BPWT SO32
Maybush Rd ROWN SO16
May Cl CHAM RG24
FAWY SO45
BOR GU35
SHST GU47
May Copse FAWY SO45
May Crs ASHV GU12
FAWY SO45
Maydman Sq HSEA PO3
Mayfair Ct HEND SO30
Mayfair Dr NWBY RG14
Mayfair Gdns BWD BH11
WSHM SO15
Mayfield RFNM GU10
Mayfield Av PSTN BH14
TOTT SO40
Mayfield Cl FERN BH22
FHAM/STUB PO14
FNM GU9
NTID SP9
Mayfield Ct HTWY RG27
Mayfield Dr FERN BH22
Mayfield Rdg DEAN RG23
Mayfield Rd CBLY GU15
FARN GU14
FBDG SP6
GPORT PO12
MOOR/WNTN BH9
NEND PO2
PTSW SO17
Mayfield Wy FERN BH22
Mayflower Cl CHAM RG24
CHFD SO53
FHAM/STUB PO14
LYMN SO41

wer Dr YTLY GU46 68 D1
wer Rd BOR GU35 201 H7 1
M SO15 318 B8 1
wer Rbt WSHM SO15 12 E6
yflowers ROWN SO16 318 F4
Cl FBDG SP6 309 L6 1
rd Rd BKME/WDN BH12 447 G2
dns BWD BH11 431 J5
/BSGR BH23 436 F6
l Rd HSEA PO3 399 L7
La BPWT SO32 298 F8
T SO32 324 C1
ds Av ENEY PO4 423 L4
ds Rd HAV PO9 376 F6
LYMN SO41 414 E7
Cl WHAM PO17 348 E5
La WHAM PO17 348 C7
Rd ENEY PO4 423 M3
gs Farm Rd
/PORC PO16 14 F2
Rd UPTN BH16 428 D6
rd Cl LSOL/BMARY PO13 397 G4
RG18 26 F3
rd Pl HORN PO8 352 F1
rd Rd TOTT SO40 341 K1
rd's Wd CHAM RG24 83 K6
Cl PSEA PO1 423 H1
s La NWBY RG14 2 E5
Cl STHA RG19 27 J6
BSTK RG21 4 F9
ge FHAM/STUB PO14 371 G5
WSHM SO15 343 G1 2
irs FBDG SP6 285 L6
La FHAM/STUB PO14 396 B4
ee Cl WINW SO22 238 B4
e Cl HLER SO31 370 E5
e Gdns HORN PO8 352 C5
ee Rd AND SP10 8 B3
e Rd CHFD SO53 265 H6
/PORC PO16 15 G6
PO8 352 C5
e Cl TOTT SO40 342 D7
od Dr CBLY GU15 71 L1
ney Wk KEMP RG22 127 H1
d Wy WHCH RG28 122 B4
or Barracks ALDT GU11 112 E5
re Rd CHCH/BSGR BH23 407 K8
Cl ALDT GU11 112 F5
ey Rd WBNE BH4 447 H6
ighton Cl FARN GU14 89 M5
am Cl BKME/WDN BH12 432 A8
er Cl TOTT SO40 316 D8 1
rook Gdns CHFD SO53 293 H2
Cl AND SP10 8 E7
BH17 429 L7
SO51 291 G1
rs WEND SO18 319 J5
roft Cl HLER SO31 370 B8
nd Cl HAV PO9 377 M3 2
nd Rd LYMN SO41 412 D7
E PO7 351 L5
Rd RAND SP11 92 F6
am La OVTN RG25 79 G5
awks LISS GU33 248 D3
a FNM GU9 134 E7
w Av HLER SO31 370 E4
wbank Rd FHAM PO15 14 A5
w Cl ASHV GU12 91 J7
GU17 70 A4
T SO32 323 K4 1
/BSGR BH23 434 F1
SP6 309 K6 5
BH22 406 B7
SO30 320 D6
PO11 401 K5
GU30 226 F4
SO24 218 C3 5
SO52 291 M5
BH24 358 F7
BH24 384 D6
RG19 26 F5
SO40 341 K3
w Ct RSAL SP5 259 H4
w Court Cl
/WNTN BH9 432 E5
wcroft Cl RWIN SO21 266 B5 1
w Dr RAND SP11 142 E8
w Edge WVILLE PO7 375 L6
w Gdns BPWT SO32 323 K4
w Gate Rd FARN GU14 90 C7
w Gv VWD BH31 356 F3
whead Rd
SO16 318 E5 1
wland CHAM RG24 83 K5
/BSGR BH23 450 D2
SO23 215 G1
wlands HAV PO9 17 H5
PO9 354 A5
SO41 440 A4
w La CHCH/BSGR BH23 435 G6
SO31 369 L6
RG27 87 H2
PO20 427 M6
wmead Av WSHM SO15 342 E1
w Pound WHCH RG28 122 C3 1
wridge KEMP RG22 127 H3
w Ri BDST BH18 429 K3
PO8 352 F5
RG25 125 L7 2
w Rd BSTK RG21 104 F7
GU14 90 E1
SO41 440 A6
/BTOS BH25 437 M4
RG14 2 D9
BH24 358 F8
ws Cl UPTN BH16 429 G8 1
ws Dr UPTN BH16 444 B1 5
wside Cl WEND SO18 319 K4 5
adows
/PORC PO16 15 L1
RG27 64 C7
SO43 363 L4 1
GU10 181 J7
w St SSEA PO5 20 F5 5
wsweet WVILLE PO7 352 F7
wsweet Cl NTHA RG18 27 H4
wsweet Rd CFDH BH17 429 J8
wsweet Wy CHAM PO6 375 H7

ELGH SO50 321 H2
The Meadow ROMY SO51 262 E7 1
WVILLE PO7 351 K4
Meadow V HASM GU27 228 D2
Meadow Vw FLET GU13 110 D3 5
BOR GU35 201 K5
WHCH RG28 122 A3
Meadow View Rd BWD BH11 431 J4
Meadow Wk LISS GU33 248 E4
LSOL/BMARY PO13 396 F3
Meadow Wy AND SP10 8 A5
ASHV GU12 113 J5
BLKW GU17 69 M3
FAWY SO45 392 F5 5
WINW SO22 238 B4
LIPH GU30 226 F3
RFNM GU10 158 C5
NMIL/BTOS BH25 452 F1
RGWD BH24 358 F8
VWD BH31 356 F4
Mead Rd AND SP10 8 E7
CHFD SO53 293 H2
GSHT GU26 204 C4
LYMN SO41 439 M6
WINC SO23 238 D4
The Meads CHFD SO53 292 F3
HASM GU27 228 C2
ROMY SO51 290 C1
The Mead CHAM RG24 106 A2
FAWY SO45 367 J5
LIPH GU30 226 E3
LISS GU33 248 E4
LSOL/BMARY PO13 396 F5 2
PSF GU32 275 J6
Mead Wy FHAM/PORC PO16 15 J2
Meadway FRIM GU16 71 J6
HASM GU27 228 C2
WVILLE PO7 352 E7
The Meadway
CHCH/BSGR BH23 436 B6
Mears Rd ELGH SO50 295 J6
Meath Cl HISD PO11 426 A7
Mede Cl OVTN RG25 124 A1
Medina Cl CHFD SO53 293 K3 5
Medina Gdns DEAN RG23 103 G7 5
Medina Rd CHAM PO6 375 H8
WSHM SO15 318 A7
Medina Wy CHCH/BSGR BH23 451 H2
Medlar Cl
CHCH/BSGR BH23 435 H7
HEND SO30 346 B2 5
Medlar Dr BLKW GU17 70 C5
Medlicott Wy BPWT SO32 324 A4
Medonte Cl FLET GU13 89 G8 1
Medstead Rd ALTN GU34 175 K7
HAV PO9 377 K5
Medwall Gn ITCH SO19 345 H3
Medway Av DEAN RG23 103 G6
Medway Cl NTHA RG18 26 E3
Medway Ct AND SP10 119 H6
BSTK RG21 5 K8
Medway Dr CHFD SO53 264 F8
FARN GU14 90 B1
Medway Rd FERN BH22 406 E2
Meerut Rd BROC SO42 387 K6
NTID SP9 114 D2
Meeting House La
RGWD BH24 382 D1 5
Megana Wy ROMY SO51 263 H3
Megan Rd HEND SO30 320 C6
Meggeson Av WEND SO18 319 M6
Meitner Cl TADY RG26 63 L4
Melbourne Pl SSEA PO5 20 F3
Melbourne Rd
CHCH/BSGR BH23 434 C7
HEND SO30 346 A2
Melbourne St SHAM SO14 13 K4
Melbury Av BKME/WDN BH12 446 D1
Melbury Cl FERN BH22 406 B4
LYMN SO41 440 B5 1
Melchet Ct ROMY SO51 260 A7
Melchet Rd WEND SO18 320 B8
Meldrum Cl NWBY RG14 36 F2 1
Melford Gdns KEMP RG22 103 M6
Melick Cl TOTT SO40 342 D6
Meliot Ri AND SP10 118 F4
Mellor Cl CHAM PO6 375 H8 5
Mellstock Rd PLE BH15 445 H3
Melrose Av FARN GU14 89 M3
Melrose Cl ENEY PO4 423 M4 2
BOR GU35 201 J6 5
Melrose Ct NMIL/BTOS BH25 438 A5 5
TOTT SO40 316 B7
Melrose Gdns GPORT PO12 421 K1
Melrose Rd WSHM SO15 318 C6
Melverley Gdns WIMB BH21 404 B3
Melville Av FRIM GU16 71 J7
Melville Cl ROWN SO16 318 B3
Melville Rd ENEY PO4 424 A6
GPORT PO12 421 L1
MOOR/WNTN BH9 432 C8
Membury Cl FRIM GU16 91 K1 5
Memorial Rd HTWY RG27 85 M8
Mendip Cl KEMP RG22 103 M5
NMIL/BTOS BH25 437 M6
VWD BH31 356 D3 2
Mendip Gdns FAWY SO45 367 H6 5
Mendip Rd FARN GU14 90 B1
ROWN SO16 317 L8
VWD BH31 356 D2
Mendips Rd FHAM/STUB PO14 14 B8
Mendips Wk FHAM/STUB PO14 14 B8
Mengham Av HISD PO11 425 L6
Mengham La HISD PO11 425 L5
Mengham Rd HISD PO11 425 L5
Menin Wy FNM GU9 135 G7
Menslands La WVILLE PO7 325 L8
Menzies Cl ROWN SO16 317 L3
Meon Cl FARN GU14 90 A2
HORN PO8 328 B4
LSOL/BMARY PO13 396 F6
PSF GU32 275 K4
ROMY SO51 291 H1
TADY RG26 41 K7
Meon Ct WEND SO18 320 C8
Meon Crs CHFD SO53 293 J2
Meon Rd DEAN RG23 103 G7
ENEY PO4 423 M4

LTDN BH7 449 G1
ROMY SO51 291 H1
Meonwara Crs PSF GU32 272 C3
Mercer Cl KEMP RG22 104 B4
Mercer Wy ROMY SO51 262 E8 5
ROMY SO51 262 F8 5
Merchants Pl WINC SO23 11 H7
Merchistoun Rd HORN PO8 352 F1
Mercia Av AND SP10 118 C5
Mercury Cl BOR GU35 201 L5 2
ROWN SO16 317 L4
Mercury Gdns HLER SO31 369 L4
Mercury Pl WVILLE PO7 376 C6
Merdon Av CHFD SO53 265 J8
Merdon Cl CHFD SO53 265 J8
Mere Cft FHAM PO15 371 H5 1
Meredith Cl CHCH/BSGR BH23 450 C1
Meredith Gdns TOTT SO40 341 H2
Meredith Rd NEND PO2 399 J5
Meredun Cl RWIN SO21 265 G1
Merepond La ALTN GU34 245 K5
Merganser Cl GPORT PO12 421 M1
Meriden Cl CCLF BH13 457 L1
Meriden Rd SSEA PO5 20 F3 5
The Meridians
CHCH/BSGR BH23 449 L3
Merino Wy FERN BH22 380 D7
Merivale FLET GU13 88 C8
Merlewood Cl WCLF BH2 22 E2
Merley Dr CHCH/BSGR BH23 436 E8
Merley Gdns WIMB BH21 404 B7
Merley La WIMB BH21 404 B7
Merley Park Rd WIMB BH21 404 A8
Merley Ways WIMB BH21 404 B5
Merlin Cl AND SP10 118 F5
BPWT SO32 297 G8
RGWD BH24 383 G2
Merlin Dr HSEA PO3 399 K4
Merlin Gdns FHAM/PORC PO16 373 M7
HEND SO30 345 M1
Merlin Md KEMP RG22 126 E2
Merlin Rd ALTN GU34 197 G6
FARN GU14 90 E6
Merlins Cl FNM GU9 134 F7 5
Merlin Wy CHCH/BSGR BH23 450 F3
FARN GU14 90 A5
Mermaid Rd FHAM/STUB PO14 396 D3
Mermaid Wy SHAM SO14 13 J7 1
Merriatt Cl BSTK RG21 105 G6
Merrick Wy CHFD SO53 264 E8
Merridale Rd ITCH SO19 344 C4
Merriefield Av BDST BH18 429 M3
Merriefield Dr BDST BH18 429 M2
Merrieleas Cl CHFD SO53 293 H1
Merrieleas Dr CHFD SO53 293 H1
Merriemeade Cl FAWY SO45 367 J7
Merrifield WIMB BH21 404 C1
Merrifield Cl BDST BH18 429 M2
Merrileas Gdns KEMP RG22 103 M8
Merritown La
CHCH/BSGR BH23 433 H1
Merrivale Av SBNE BH6 449 K3
Merrivale Cl FAWY SO45 367 J5
Merrivale Rd NEND PO2 399 J5
Merron Cl YTLY GU46 68 F3 5
Merrow Av BKME/WDN BH12 447 G2
Merrydown La CHAM RG24 83 M6 1
Merryfield CHAM RG24 83 K5
FHAM/STUB PO14 371 G4
Merryfield Av HAV PO9 377 H3
Merryfield Cl
CHCH/BSGR BH23 409 L8
Merryfield Rd EPSF GU31 276 A4
Merry Gdns NBAD SO52 291 M3
Merryman Dr CWTH RG45 49 J2
Merryoak Gn ITCH SO19 344 D3 5
Merryoak Rd ITCH SO19 344 D4
Merrywood Pk CBLY GU15 71 J4
Mersea Gdns ITCH SO19 344 E4
Mersey Wy NTHA RG18 26 E3
Mersham Gdns WEND SO18 344 E1 1
Merstone Rd
LSOL/BMARY PO13 397 G6
Merthyr Av CHAM PO6 375 M7
Merton Av FHAM/PORC PO16 398 B2
Merton Cl FBDG SP6 309 L5 5
SHST GU47 50 C6
Merton Crs FHAM/PORC PO16 398 B2
Merton Rd BSTK RG21 4 B5
PTSW SO17 319 G6
SSEA PO5 21 H7
Meryl Rd ENEY PO4 424 A4
Meryon Rd NALR SO24 218 B4
Mesh Pond RSAL SP5 256 C8
Mesh Rd ROMY SO51 234 B6
Meteor Rd EMRTH PO10 402 E5
Meteor Wy FARN GU14 90 D7
Methuen Cl CHAR BH8 23 L2
Methuen Rd CFDH BH17 429 M6
CHAR BH8 23 J1
ENEY PO4 423 L5
LISS GU33 225 H5
Methuen St SHAM SO14 343 L1
Metuchen Wy HEND SO30 346 A4
Meudon Av FARN GU14 90 E5
Mewsey Ct HAV PO9 377 H1
Mews La WINW SO22 10 D8
The Mews FAWY SO45 418 D1 5
HAV PO9 377 J4
ROWN SO16 317 L2
TADY RG26 64 A6
Mey Cl WVILLE PO7 376 D1
Meynell Cl ELGH SO50 293 L5
Meyrick Cl CHCH/BSGR BH23 435 L1
Meyrick Dr NWBY RG14 36 F3
Meyrick Park Crs TWDS BH3 447 L2
Meyrick Rd BMTH BH1 23 J5
HAV PO9 16 B4
NEND PO2 399 G7
Michael Crook Cl HAV PO9 377 G5
Michaelmas Cl YTLY GU46 69 G4
Michaels Wy ELGH SO50 295 J6
FAWY SO45 367 K4
Micheldever Cl WHCH RG28 122 C5
Micheldever Rd AND SP10 9 K6
WHCH RG28 122 C4
Michelmersh Cl ROWN SO16 317 K3 5
Michigan Wy TOTT SO40 316 A8

Mickleham Cl
BKME/WDN BH12 431 M8
Mickle Hl SHST GU47 49 K7
Midanbury Crs WEND SO18 319 L7
Midanbury La WEND SO18 319 K8
Middle Av FNM GU9 135 G8
Middlebere Crs UPTN BH16 444 B4
Middle Bourne La RFNM GU10 158 E2
Middlebridge St ROMY SO51 290 D2
Middlebrook BPWT SO32 297 H8 2
Middle Brook St WINC SO23 11 H7
Middle Church La FNM GU9 134 E6 7
Middle Cl CBLY GU15 71 M2
NWBY RG14 37 G1
Middle Common Rd
LYMN SO41 439 K5
Middlecroft La GPORT PO12 421 K2
Middlefield FNM GU9 158 D1
SELS PO20 427 L7
Middle Gordon Rd CBLY GU15 70 F3
Middle Hl ALDT GU11 6 F1
Middlehill Dr WIMB BH21 404 F2
Middlehill Rd WIMB BH21 404 E1
Middle La RGWD BH24 382 E1 5
Middle Md FHAM/STUB PO14 371 M8
HTWY RG27 85 M7 5
Middle Meadow LISS GU33 248 F4
Middlemoor Rd FRIM GU16 71 H8
Middle Old Pk FNM GU9 134 C4
Middle Park Wy HAV PO9 377 H2
Middle Rd WINW SO22 10 D6
HLER SO31 370 F3
ITCH SO19 344 E5
LYMN SO41 412 B8
LYMN SO41 412 F6
LYMN SO41 440 B5
NBAD SO52 291 M3
NBNE BH10 432 A3
PLE BH15 445 K2
Middlesex Rd ENEY PO4 423 L5
Middle St CCLF BH13 456 C3
SHAM SO14 343 L1 1
SSEA PO5 21 G3
Middleton Cl FHAM/STUB PO14 14 C9
WEND SO18 319 M6
Middleton Ct NWBY RG14 26 B3
Middleton Gdns BSTK RG21 4 F4
FARN GU14 90 B2
Middleton Ri HORN PO8 328 C4 5
Middleton Rd CBLY GU15 71 H2
NBNE BH10 432 C6
RGWD BH24 358 E8
RSAL SP5 206 E1
The Middleway RAND SP11 120 A8
Midfield Cl FHAM/STUB PO14 396 D1
Midhurst Rd HASM GU27 228 E3
LIPH GU30 226 F5
Midland Rd MOOR/WNTN BH9 432 D7
Midlands Est HEND SO30 320 B6
Midlane Cl BSTK RG21 104 F6
Midlington Hl BPWT SO32 324 F1
Midlington Rd BPWT SO32 325 G1
Midway FAWY SO45 367 K5 5
Midway Rd NEND PO2 399 J3 5
Midways FHAM/STUB PO14 396 A7
Midwood Av CHAR BH8 433 K7
Mike Hawthorn Dr FNM GU9 134 F5 1
Milbeck Cl HORN PO8 352 E5
Milborne Crs BKME/WDN BH12 446 D1
Milbourne Rd FERN BH22 406 A2
Milburn Cl WBNE BH4 447 H4
Milburn Rd WBNE BH4 447 G4
The Milburns ROMY SO51 262 C1 1
Milbury Crs ITCH SO19 344 E2
Milden Cl FRIM GU16 91 K2
Milden Gdns FRIM GU16 91 K2
Mildmay Ct ODIM RG29 108 D6
Mildmay St WINW SO22 238 C3
Milebush Rd ENEY PO4 424 A3
Mile End Rd PSEA PO1 423 G1
Miles Rd ASHV GU12 113 L5
Miles's La RSAL SP5 259 J4
Milestone Rd PLE BH15 445 J2
Milford Cl FERN BH22 380 D6
HAV PO9 377 H5 1
Milford Ct LYMN SO41 454 D4
Milford Crs LYMN SO41 454 D4
Milford Dr BWD BH11 431 K3
Milford Gdns CHFD SO53 293 K2
Milford Rd LYMN SO41 439 K7
NMIL/BTOS BH25 438 A8
PSEA PO1 21 J1
Military Rd FHAM/PORC PO16 373 H6
GPORT PO12 421 J3
GPORT PO12 421 M8
GPORT PO12 422 A7
HSEA PO3 399 K3
PSEA PO1 422 F2
Milkhouse Rd KSCL RG20 24 A2
Milkingpen La CHAM RG24 106 A1
Milkwood Ct TOTT SO40 341 G1 1
Millais Rd ITCH SO19 344 C5
Milland La LIPH GU30 250 D2
Milland Rd LIPH GU30 250 E6
WINC SO23 239 G2
Millard Cl BSTK RG21 4 B3
Millbank St SHAM SO14 13 L1
Millbridge Gdns ITCH SO19 344 F4 5
Millbridge Rd YTLY GU46 48 E8
Millbrook Cl CHFD SO53 293 G3
LISS GU33 248 F4
Millbrook Dr HAV PO9 377 L2
Millbrook Point Rd
WSHM SO15 342 E2
Millbrook Rd East WSHM SO15 343 G3
Millbrook Rd West
WSHM SO15 342 C1
Mill Chase Rd BOR GU35 201 K5
Mill Cl HASM GU27 228 B2 5
HISD PO11 401 K6
ROWN SO16 317 J3
WVILLE PO7 351 M4
Mill Copse Rd HASM GU27 228 E4
Mill Cnr FARN GU14 89 H3 1
Mill Ct FBDG SP6 309 K7 1
Mill End EMRTH PO10 378 F8
FBDG SP6 308 C4
Miller Cl NMIL/BTOS BH25 438 A4

Miller Dr FHAM/PORC PO16 14 F2
Miller Rd CHCH/BSGR BH23 450 C1
Millers La WINW SO22 237 L5
Millers Rd TADY RG26 41 L8
Millfield CFDH BH17 444 F1
Millgreen La STHA RG19 39 J6
Millhams Rd NBNE BH10 431 L1
Millhams St CHCH/BSGR BH23 450 A2
Millhams St North
CHCH/BSGR BH23 450 A2
Mill Hl HEND SO30 346 E1
NALR SO24 218 C1
Mill Hill Cl PSTN BH14 446 A5
Milliken Cl FAWY SO45 392 D6
Millins Cl SHST GU47 50 A7
Mill La ALTN GU34 177 G4
BPWT SO32 299 H6
BPWT SO32 322 C5
BROC SO42 387 M7
CHCH/BSGR BH23 433 M2
CHCH/BSGR BH23 436 F8
EMRTH PO10 378 F6
EPSF GU31 278 C8
EPSF GU31 305 G5
FHAM PO15 371 L7
GPORT PO12 421 M2
HASM GU27 228 F4
HAV PO9 377 G7
HAV PO9 401 J2
HTWY RG27 85 G1
KSCL RG20 58 D4
BOR GU35 201 M4
LISS GU33 223 L8
LYMN SO41 439 J1
LYMN SO41 440 D4 1
LYMN SO41 441 K3
LYND SO43 339 J6
MARL SN8 32 C4
MIDH GU29 279 K6
NALR SO24 218 F3
RFNM GU10 180 E1
NWBY RG14 2 F4
ODIM RG29 108 A3
PSEA PO1 423 G1
PSF GU32 247 K8
PSF GU32 276 A2
PSTN BH14 446 A5
RAND SP11 145 H3
RGWD BH24 385 G3
ROMY SO51 260 D8
ROMY SO51 290 C1
ROWN SO16 316 D4
RSAL SP5 183 G8
TADY RG26 64 B5
THLE RG7 29 M5
THLE RG7 64 B3
WHAM PO17 348 E3
WVILLE PO7 375 J4
YTLY GU46 49 G8
Mill Meadow LYMN SO41 454 B3
Millmere YTLY GU46 69 G1
Mill Pond Rd GPORT PO12 421 M2
The Mill Pond FAWY SO45 391 M2
Mill Quay EMRTH PO10 402 E1
Mill Reef Cl STHA RG19 26 C5
Mill Ri ROMY SO51 233 J8
Mill Rd CHAM RG24 82 B8
CHCH/BSGR BH23 434 E8
EMRTH PO10 378 F4
FHAM/PORC PO16 15 J8
GPORT PO12 421 L2
LISS GU33 248 F3
TOTT SO40 341 L1
WSHM SO15 342 E1
WVILLE PO7 351 L4
WVILLE PO7 376 B2
Mill Rd (North) CHAR BH8 433 H5
Mill Rd (South) CHAR BH8 433 H6
Mill Rythe La HISD PO11 425 L1
Mills Rd NEND PO2 399 H8
Mill Stream FNM GU9 6 B9
Millstream Cl AND SP10 8 F9
CFDH BH17 444 F1
WIMB BH21 404 A4
Millstream Ri ROMY SO51 290 C1
The Millstream HASM GU27 228 B3
Mill St FHAM/STUB PO14 371 L8
Mill Vale Mdw LIPH GU30 250 E5
Millvina Cl TOTT SO40 340 D4
Mill Wy TOTT SO40 341 J3
Millway Cl AND SP10 8 C6
Millway Rd AND SP10 8 C5
Millyford Cl NMIL/BTOS BH25 437 H8
Milne Cl FAWY SO45 367 G6
Milner Ct WSHM SO15 318 B8
Milne Rd CFDH BH17 429 M7
Milner Pl WINW SO22 238 D2
Milner Rd WBNE BH4 447 H6
Milnthorpe La WINW SO22 10 C9
The Milsons STOK SO20 186 E6
Milton Av AND SP10 8 B3
Milton Cl CHAM RG24 5 H1
PSTN BH14 446 C5
Milton Gv HLER SO31 370 F7
NMIL/BTOS BH25 437 M6
Milton Md NMIL/BTOS BH25 437 K6
Milton Pde WVILLE PO7 352 C6
Milton Park Av ENEY PO4 423 M4 5
Milton Rd CHAR BH8 23 H1
ELGH SO50 294 A3 5
ENEY PO4 423 L4
HSEA PO3 423 L1
PSTN BH14 446 C5
WIMB BH21 404 A2
WSHM SO15 343 J2
WVILLE PO7 352 B7
Milverton Cl
CHCH/BSGR BH23 436 C7 2
Milverton Rd WINW SO22 10 C6
TOTT SO40 341 L2
Milvil Rd LSOL/BMARY PO13 420 C3
Mimosa Av WIMB BH21 404 B8
Mimosa Cl BOR GU35 201 M3
Mimosa Dr ELGH SO50 295 K6
Minchens La TADY RG26 63 K5
Mincingfield La BPWT SO32 322 C4
Minden Cl AND SP10 118 E5 5
CHAM RG24 83 K6 5

Minden Wy WINW SO22 238 B3
Minehurst Rd FRIM GU16 91 J4
Minerva Cl WVILLE PO7 376 C6 1
Minerva Rd FARN GU14 90 E7
Ministry Rd STHA RG19 38 D3
Minley Cl FARN GU14 90 B4
Minley Ct HAV PO9 377 M3
Minley Gv FARN GU14 89 G5 1
Minley Rd FARN GU14 69 H7
Minnitt Rd GPORT PO12 19 L3
Minstead Av WEND SO18 320 B8
Minstead Cl WINW SO22 214 C4 3
TADY RG26 61 L2
Minstead Dr YTLY GU46 68 F3
Minstead Rd ENEY PO4 423 M5
NBNE BH10 432 A5
Minsted Rd MIDH GU29 279 J8
Minster Cl FHAM PO15 372 A7
Minster La WINC SO23 11 G8
Minster Vw WIMB BH21 404 A3
Minster Wy UPTN BH16 444 A1
Mintern Cl ELGH SO50 294 C3 3
Minterne Rd CHCH/BSGR BH23 450 D3
PSTN BH14 457 H1
Minters Lepe WVILLE PO7 376 C5
Mint Rd LISS GU33 249 G2
Mirror Cl HLER SO31 370 D7
Mislingford Rd BPWT SO32 324 B5
Missenden Acres
HEND SO30 321 H8 5
Mission Rd BDST BH18 429 L6
Misslebrook La NBAD SO52 292 C4
Mistletoe Rd YTLY GU46 69 G4
Mitcham Rd CBLY GU15 51 K7
Mitchell Av HTWY RG27 87 H3
Mitchell Cl AND SP10 118 A7
NMIL/BTOS BH25 452 F1
Mitchell Dr ELGH SO50 295 H5
Mitchell Gdns KEMP RG22 127 H1 1
Mitchell Rd CFDH BH17 430 D8
ELGH SO50 294 A6
HAV PO9 376 F5
WIMB BH21 405 L1
Mitchells Cl ROMY SO51 290 E1
RSAL SP5 285 J2 3
Mitchell Wy ELGH SO50 319 M1
HSEA PO3 399 M5
Mitford Rd NALR SO24 218 A3
Mitre Copse ELGH SO50 294 E6
Mizen Wy
LSOL/BMARY PO13 421 H2 5
Moat Cl FAWY SO45 391 M5
TADY RG26 63 K4
Moat Dr GPORT PO12 421 H5
Moat Hl WEND SO18 319 L5
Moat La NMIL/BTOS BH25 437 K7
Mockbeggar La RGWD BH24 358 E1
Moffat Rd CHCH/BSGR BH23 450 C1
Moffatts Cl SHST GU47 49 K8
Moggs Md EPSF GU31 275 M5
Mole Cl FARN GU14 90 A2
Mole Hl WVILLE PO7 376 D3
Molesworth Rd GPORT PO12 19 G4 2
Molyneux Rd NMIL/BTOS BH25 438 B5
Momford Rd WINW SO22 238 A5
Monachus La HTWY RG27 87 J1
Monarch Cl HLER SO31 370 E6
KEMP RG22 126 F2
WVILLE PO7 376 E1 5
Monarch's Wy BPWT SO32 296 B1
HAV PO9 354 D7
HORN PO8 353 H3
ROMY SO51 233 L8
RSAL SP5 208 B3
STOK SO20 208 E2
WVILLE PO7 300 F7
Monarch Wy WINW SO22 238 B2
HEND SO30 320 D6 1
Monastery Rd WEND SO18 344 C1
Monckton Rd GPORT PO12 421 M7
HSEA PO3 399 K6
Mon Crs WEND SO18 345 G1
Moneyfield Av HSEA PO3 399 L8
Moneyfield La HSEA PO3 399 L8 2
Moneyfly Rd VWD BH31 356 F3
Mongers Piece CHAM RG24 83 M4
Monier Williams Rd
RWIN SO21 145 G5
Monks Brook Cl ELGH SO50 293 K7
Monks Cl FARN GU14 90 F4
FERN BH22 380 E8
NTID SP9 114 D1
Monkshanger FNM GU9 135 H6
Monk Sherborne Rd TADY RG26 81 J1
Monk's Hl EMRTH PO10 378 E2
Monks La NWBY RG14 37 H1
Monks Orch PSF GU32 275 L3
Monks Pl TOTT SO40 341 H2
Monks Ri FLET GU13 88 C7 1
Monks Rd HLER SO31 368 F2
WINC SO23 11 G5
Monks Wk FAWY SO45 367 J8
RFNM GU10 159 J1
Monks Wy ELGH SO50 293 L7
FHAM/STUB PO14 395 M8
WEND SO18 319 K4
WIMB BH21 431 G3
Monks' Well RFNM GU10 135 M8
Monkswell Gn
CHCH/BSGR BH23 450 C2
Monks Wd PSF GU32 275 L3
Monks Wood Cl ELGH SO50 319 G2
Monkswood Cl NWBY RG14 37 G1 1
Monks Wood Crs TADY RG26 61 L1 3
Monkton Cl FERN BH22 406 B2
Monkton Crs
BKME/WDN BH12 431 J8
Monkton La FNM GU9 135 H3
TOTT SO40 341 G2
Monktons La THLE RG7 43 M3
Monkwood Cl HAV PO9 377 H3 2
Monkworthy Dr RGWD BH24 381 K3
Monmouth Cl CHFD SO53 293 G2
VWD BH31 356 F4
Monmouth Dr VWD BH31 356 F4
Monmouth Rd NEND PO2 399 H6
Monmouth Sq WINW SO22 238 A2 1
Monnow Gdns WEND SO18 320 A7
Monroe Cl GPORT PO12 421 J5
Monsal Av FERN BH22 406 A5
Mons Barracks ALDT GU11 112 F3
Mons Cl ALDT GU11 113 H1
Montacute Cl FARN GU14 91 G4 1
Montacute Dr STHA RG19 27 J6 5
Montacute Wy WIMB BH21 404 C8
Montague Av ITCH SO19 345 H5
Montague Cl CBLY GU15 70 E3 1
ITCH SO19 345 H5 2
Montague Gdns EPSF GU31 276 B5
Montague Pl BSTK RG21 105 G5 1
Montague Rd BOSC BH5 449 G4
NEND PO2 399 J7
Montague Ter NWBY RG14 2 E9
Montagu Rd CHCH/BSGR BH23 452 A1
Monteagle La YTLY GU46 68 D2
Monteray Dr LYMN SO41 438 D4
Monterey Dr HAV PO9 377 L4
HLER SO31 370 E6
Montfort Cl ROMY SO51 291 H1
Montfort Hts ROMY SO51 291 H1 1
Montfort Rd ROMY SO51 291 H2
Montgomerie Rd SSEA PO5 21 J3
Montgomery Av BWD BH11 431 M5
TOTT SO40 316 C8
Montgomery Cl SHST GU47 49 L8 1
Montgomery Rd FARN GU14 90 C5
HAV PO9 17 G4
LSOL/BMARY PO13 397 G4
NWBY RG14 2 A9
WEND SO18 319 M8
Montgomery Wk WVILLE PO7 376 A3
Montgomery Wy CHFD SO53 293 G5
Montpelier Cl HLER SO31 371 G5 3
Montrose Av
FHAM/PORC PO16 374 C7
Montrose Cl FLET GU13 89 G8
FRIM GU16 71 H6 2
HEND SO30 346 C2 1
BOR GU35 201 J7
VWD BH31 356 D2
Montrose Dr NBNE BH10 431 M6
Montserrat Pl CHAM RG24 83 H6 2
Montserrat Rd CHAM RG24 83 H6
LSOL/BMARY PO13 420 C2
Monument Cha BOR GU35 201 K7
Monument Cl NWBY RG14 37 G1 2
Monument La LYMN SO41 440 E3
RCCH PO18 379 K1
WHAM PO17 373 M4
Monxton Rd RAND SP11 140 B7
RAND SP11 141 L1
Moody Rd FHAM/STUB PO14 395 M7
Moody's Hl RSAL SP5 231 H6
Moonhills La BROC SO42 390 F6
Moonrakers Wy
CHCH/BSGR BH23 436 C7
Moonscross Av TOTT SO40 341 K4
Moons Hl RFNM GU10 158 E6
Moor Cl EWKG RG40 48 B1
BOR GU35 201 G5
SHST GU47 50 B7
Moor Court La RWIN SO21 213 G5
Moorcroft Av
CHCH/BSGR BH23 435 G6
Moorcroft Cl RWIN SO21 168 C5
Moordown Cl
MOOR/WNTN BH9 432 E5
Moore Av BWD BH11 431 L5
Moore Cl AND SP10 9 H2
FLET GU13 110 F3
RFNM GU10 113 J8 2
NMIL/BTOS BH25 437 K7 2
Moore Crs HLER SO31 368 F2
Moore Gdns GPORT PO12 18 A3
Moore Rd FLET GU13 110 F3
Moorfield HASM GU27 228 C3
Moorfield Gv
MOOR/WNTN BH9 432 D6
Moorfields Rd CCLF BH13 446 E8 2
Moorfoot Gdns KEMP RG22 104 A5
Moorgreen Rd HAV PO9 377 L3
HEND SO30 320 D7
Moorhams Av KEMP RG22 126 F2
Moorhill Gdns WEND SO18 345 J1
Moorhill Rd HEND SO30 320 C8
RGWD BH24 384 E6
Moorhouse La MIDH GU29 278 F2
The Moorings BSTK RG21 5 K7
FHAM/PORC PO16 396 F1 1
Moorings Wy ENEY PO4 424 A2
Moorland Av NMIL/BTOS BH25 437 K8
Moorland Cl FAWY SO45 367 H5 5
HLER SO31 370 E4
Moorland Crs UPTN BH16 444 A1
Moorland Ga RGWD BH24 382 E3
Moorland Rd BMTH BH1 448 C4
PSEA PO1 423 J2
Moorlands Cl BROC SO42 387 H7
FLET GU13 89 G8 2
GSHT GU26 204 B4
Moorlands Crs WEND SO18 319 M8
Moorlands Ri FERN BH22 380 D5
Moorlands Rd BPWT SO32 323 M2
CBLY GU15 70 D4
FERN BH22 380 C6
VWD BH31 356 D1
Moorland Wy UPTN BH16 444 A1
Moor La RSAL SP5 258 D7
Moor Pk HORN PO8 352 F7
Moor Park La RFNM GU10 135 J5
Moor Park Wy FNM GU9 135 J6
Moor Rd BDST BH18 429 M3
FARN GU14 70 D8
FRIM GU16 71 J8
HASM GU27 227 M3
LISS GU33 225 G7
Moors Cl CHCH/BSGR BH23 433 M1
RWIN SO21 266 E7
Moorside Cl FARN GU14 70 D7
Moorside Rd BWD BH11 431 L5
FERN BH22 380 C6
WIMB BH21 429 H3
WINC SO23 11 M3
The Moors RFNM GU10 136 C1 1
STHA RG19 27 G6
Moortown Av CHAM PO6 376 A7
Moortown Dr WIMB BH21 404 F7
Moortown La RGWD BH24 382 F4
Moorvale Rd
MOOR/WNTN BH9 432 E6
Moor Vw CHAM RG24 106 A1
Moor View Rd PLE BH15 445 K2
Moot Cl AND SP10 119 G4
RSAL SP5 284 F2
Moot Gdns RSAL SP5 284 E2
Moot La FBDG SP6 284 E6
RSAL SP5 284 E2
Mopley FAWY SO45 418 D1
Mopley Cl FAWY SO45 418 D1
Morant Rd RGWD BH24 358 F7
Moraunt Cl GPORT PO12 397 M8 1
Moraunt Dr FHAM/PORC PO16 397 M2
Moray Av SHST GU47 70 A1
Mordaunt Rd SHAM SO14 343 L1
Morden Av FERN BH22 406 A4
Moreland Cl ALTN GU34 176 E6
Moreland Rd GPORT PO12 18 E2
Morelands Rd WVILLE PO7 376 C4
Morestead Rd RWIN SO21 239 G3
Moreton Cl FLET GU13 110 E4
RFNM GU10 181 H7
Moreton Rd MOOR/WNTN BH9 432 F4
Morgan Rd ENEY PO4 424 A4
HEND SO30 346 A3 1
Morgans Dr FHAM/STUB PO14 396 A3
Morgans Rise Rd RSAL SP5 285 J1
Morgans Vale Rd RSAL SP5 285 J2
Morgaston Rd TADY RG26 82 E1
Morland Rd ALDT GU11 7 H8
WSHM SO15 318 B7
Morland's Rd ALDT GU11 113 G3
Morley Cl BOSC BH5 448 F3
CHCH/BSGR BH23 435 G5
ITCH SO19 344 D2
YTLY GU46 68 E3
Morley Crs HORN PO8 352 E5
Morley Dr BPWT SO32 297 H8
Morley Rd BSTK RG21 104 F7
ENEY PO4 423 L6
FNM GU9 134 F7
Morningside Av
FHAM/PORC PO16 374 B7
Mornington Cl AND SP10 142 F3 2
TADY RG26 41 G7
Mornington Dr WINW SO22 214 B6
Mornington Rd BOR GU35 200 F6
Mornish Rd CCLF BH13 446 E6
Morpeth Av TOTT SO40 316 E8
Morris Cl FAWY SO45 367 H4
LSOL/BMARY PO13 397 G4
Morrison Av BKME/WDN BH12 446 E2
Morris Rd FARN GU14 91 G8
WSHM SO15 12 D1
Morris St HTWY RG27 85 K8
Morse Rd KEMP RG22 104 D4
Morshead Crs
FHAM/PORC PO16 14 F2
Mortimer Cl CHCH/BSGR BH23 450 F2
HLER SO31 368 F2
HTWY RG27 87 G4 1
TOTT SO40 316 C7
WINC SO23 215 G2
Mortimer Gdns TADY RG26 61 M1
Mortimer La BSTK RG21 4 D8
THLE RG7 44 A1
THLE RG7 44 A8
Mortimer Rd CHAM PO6 375 G7
CHAR BH8 432 F7
HEND SO30 346 E2
ITCH SO19 344 C4
Mortimers Dr ELGH SO50 295 J6 2
Mortimers La ELGH SO50 295 J6
Mortimer Wy NBAD SO52 291 L5
Mortimore Rd GPORT PO12 421 K2
Morton Cl FRIM GU16 91 J1
Morval Cl FARN GU14 90 B4
Mosaic Cl ITCH SO19 345 K4 1
Mosdell Rd EMRTH PO10 379 H8
Moselle Cl FARN GU14 90 A3
Moss Cl LISS GU33 248 F4
Moss Dr TOTT SO40 342 D6
Mossleigh Av ROWN SO16 317 L3
Mossley Av BKME/WDN BH12 431 K7
Moss Rd WINC SO23 11 K7
Motcombe Rd CCLF BH13 446 F7
Mottisfont Cl WSHM SO15 342 E2 1
Mottisfont Rd ELGH SO50 293 M4
Moulsham Copse La YTLY GU46 68 E1
Moulsham La YTLY GU46 68 E1
Moulshay La HTWY RG27 84 B3
Mound Cl GPORT PO12 18 C5
Mountain Ash Cl WEND SO18 345 G1 2
Mount Av NMIL/BTOS BH25 437 L7
Mountbatten Av ROMY SO51 290 E1
Mountbatten Cl
LSOL/BMARY PO13 397 G4 2
NWBY RG14 25 M3 2
Mountbatten Ct WINW SO22 10 C1
Mountbatten Dr FERN BH22 406 A3
WVILLE PO7 376 A2
Mountbatten Pl WINC SO23 191 H8 1
Mountbatten Ri SHST GU47 49 J7
Mountbatten Rd CCLF BH13 447 G7
ELGH SO50 293 M3 2
TOTT SO40 316 C8
Mountbatten Sq ENEY PO4 423 M6 5
Mount Carmel Rd RAND SP11 161 J3
Mount Cl WINW SO22 10 C1
KSCL RG20 56 C1
NMIL/BTOS BH25 437 L7
NWBY RG14 2 E8
Mount Dr CHFD SO53 293 K4
FHAM PO15 371 M8
Mounters La ALTN GU34 176 C7
Mountfield FAWY SO45 367 J4
Mount Grace Dr PSTN BH14 457 H1
Mount Hermon Rd RAND SP11 161 K2
Mount House Cl FAWY SO45 367 L3 1
Mountjoy Cl WIMB BH21 404 D6
Mount La ROMY SO51 260 E1
Mount Pleasant FNM GU9 134 D6
HTWY RG27 87 J2
RGWD BH24 382 E1 5
SHST GU47 49 K7 1
TADY RG26 41 K8
WINC SO23 215 G2
Mount Pleasant Dr CHAR BH8 433 K7
Mount Pleasant La LYMN SO41 413 K8
Mount Pleasant Rd
GPORT PO12 18 E7
PLE BH15 445 J6
SHAM SO14 343 M1
ALTN GU34 176 E6
ASHV GU12 7 J2
BOR GU35 201 L3
Mount Rd BWD BH11 431 L4
KSCL RG20 56 C1
NTHA RG18 27 G4
PSTN BH14 446 A3
Mountsom's La ALTN GU34 198 E4
Mount Temple ROMY SO51 290 F1
The Mount FLET GU13 88 F6
HASM GU27 205 J6
BOR GU35 202 D2
LSOL/BMARY PO13 397 J7 4
RGWD BH24 359 H8
ROWN SO16 317 M7 1
ROWN SO16 318 E4 1
Mount Vw ALDT GU11 6 E4
ELGH SO50 294 A4
Mountview Av
FHAM/PORC PO16 374 C7
Mountwood Rd EMRTH PO10 379 H7
Mourne Cl KEMP RG22 104 A4
Mousehole La FAWY SO45 367 L5
WEND SO18 319 L8
Mousehole Rd CHAM PO6 374 D7
Mowbray Rd ITCH SO19 344 F4
Moxhams FBDG SP6 309 L7 3
Mozart Cl KEMP RG22 104 D8
Muccleshell Cl HAV PO9 377 L4 2
Muddyford Rd RSAL SP5 257 J7
Mudeford CHCH/BSGR BH23 450 E3
Mudeford La
CHCH/BSGR BH23 450 E2
Mude Gdns CHCH/BSGR BH23 450 F3
Mud La HTWY RG27 47 J7
Mulberry Av CHAM PO6 399 L1
FHAM/STUB PO14 396 A7
Mulberry Cl ASHV GU12 113 K4
CWTH RG45 49 M4
GPORT PO12 18 E4
SHST GU47 50 A8 5
Mulberry Ct ALTN GU34 197 H5
Mulberry Gdns FBDG SP6 309 K8
Mulberry La CHAM PO6 399 L1
Mulberry Rd TOTT SO40 342 D7
Mulberry Wk WSHM SO15 318 B8
Mulberry Wy CHAM RG24 83 L5
Mulfords Hl TADY RG26 41 L7
Mulgrave Rd FRIM GU16 71 J6 1
Mull Cl DEAN RG23 102 F6
Mullen Cl ITCH SO19 344 C4
Mullins Cl BKME/WDN BH12 432 A8
BSTK RG21 4 F2
Mullin's La FAWY SO45 367 K6
Mullion Cl CHAM PO6 398 F1
Mulroy Dr CBLY GU15 71 K2
Mumby Rd GPORT PO12 19 K2
Munday's Boro RGUW GU3 137 K4
Munday's Boro Rd
RGUW GU3 137 K4 1
Mundays Rw HORN PO8 328 B7 5
Munkle Marsh STHA RG19 27 K5 2
Munnings Cl BSTK RG21 105 J5
Munnings Dr SHST GU47 70 A2
Munro Crs WSHM SO15 342 D1
Munster Rd NEND PO2 399 H6
PSTN BH14 446 C5
Murefield Rd PSEA PO1 21 K1 1
Muriel Rd WVILLE PO7 352 C8
Murley Rd MOOR/WNTN BH9 432 E8
Murray Cl AND SP10 142 E3
FHAM PO15 14 D4
ITCH SO19 345 J2
Murray Rd FARN GU14 90 C5
HORN PO8 352 F2
Murray's La PSEA PO1 422 D2
Murray's Rd ALDT GU11 113 G3
Murrell Green Rd HTWY RG27 86 D3
Murrell Rd ASHV GU12 113 K5
Murrells La CBLY GU15 70 E5
Muscliffe Ct HAV PO9 377 M3 10
Muscliffe La
MOOR/WNTN BH9 432 E4
Muscliffe Pk
MOOR/WNTN BH9 433 G4
Muscliffe Rd
MOOR/WNTN BH9 432 D8
Muscott Cl NTID SP9 138 C1 2
Museum Hl HASM GU27 229 G2
Museum Rd PSEA PO1 20 E4
Musgrave Cl KEMP RG22 104 C8 2
Musgrove Gdns ALTN GU34 176 D4
Musket Copse CHAM RG24 105 M2
Mussett Cl TOTT SO40 341 J1
Muss La STOK SO20 210 F5
Mustang Av FHAM PO15 370 F1
Myers Cl BPWT SO32 324 A3
Myland Cl BSTK RG21 5 G3
Mylen Rd AND SP10 8 D4
My Lords La HISD PO11 425 M5
Myrtle Av FHAM/PORC PO16 398 B1
TOTT SO40 341 H2
Myrtle Cl LSOL/BMARY PO13 396 F5 3
LYMN SO41 438 D4 1
THLE RG7 31 M5
Myrtle Dr BLKW GU17 70 A4
Myrtle Gv HSEA PO3 423 M2
Myrtle Rd CHAR BH8 448 B2
ROWN SO16 318 A4
Mytchett Heath FRIM GU16 91 K5
Mytchett Lake Rd FRIM GU16 91 K7
Mytchett Place Rd FRIM GU16 91 K5
Mytchett Rd FRIM GU16 91 J4
Myvern Cl FAWY SO45 392 A5

N

Nada Rd CHCH/BSGR BH23 436 B7
Nadder Rd NTID SP9 1
Nailsworth Rd CHAM PO6 3
Naini Tal Rd NTID SP9 1
Nairn Cl FRIM GU16 7
Nairn Rd CCLF BH13 4
TWDS BH3 4
Naish Ct HAV PO9 3
Naish Dr GPORT PO12 3
Naish Rd NMIL/BTOS BH25 4
Namu Rd MOOR/WNTN BH9 4
Nansen Av PLE BH15 4
Napier Cl ALDT GU11 11
CWTH RG45
NTID SP9
Napier Crs FHAM PO15
Napier Dr CBLY GU15
Napier Rd CWTH RG45
HORN PO8
ITCH SO19
PLE BH15
SSEA PO5
Napoleon Av FARN GU14
Napoleon Dr DEAN RG23 1
Narrow La RGWD BH24
ROMY SO51 29
Narvik Rd NEND PO2
Naseby Ri NWBY RG14
Naseby Rd MOOR/WNTN BH9
Nash Cl BSTK RG21
FARN GU14
FAWY SO45
Nashe Cl FHAM PO15
Nashe Wy FHAM PO15
Nash Mdw ODIM RG29
Nash Rd FAWY SO45
Nasmith Cl LSOL/BMARY PO13
Nately Rd OVTN RG25
Nathen Gdns PLE BH15 44
Nations Hl WINC SO23
Navigator's Wy HEND SO30
Navy Rd PSEA PO1
The Naylors THLE RG7
Nea Cl CHCH/BSGR BH23
Neacroft Cl NMIL/BTOS BH25
Nea Dr RGWD BH24
Nea Rd CHCH/BSGR BH23
Neath Rd BSTK RG21
Neath Wy CHFD SO53
Needles Point LYMN SO41
Neelands Gv CHAM PO6
Neilson Cl CHFD SO53
Nelson Av FHAM/PORC PO16
NEND PO2
Nelson Cl ASHV GU12
FAWY SO45
FNM GU9
NMIL/BTOS BH25
ROMY SO51 26
ROMY SO51 26
STOK SO20
Nelson Ct FHAM/STUB PO14
Nelson Crs HORN PO8 35
Nelson Dr CHCH/BSGR BH23
Nelson La WHAM PO17
Nelson Pl LYMN SO41
Nelson Rd BKME/WDN BH12
ELGH SO50
FNM GU9
GPORT PO12
PSEA PO1
SSEA PO5
WINC SO23
WSHM SO15
Nelsons Gdns HEND SO30
Nelson St ALDT GU11
Nelson Wy CBLY GU15
Nene Ct AND SP10 119
Nepaul Rd NTID SP9
Nepean Cl GPORT PO12
Neptune Rd FHAM PO15
FHAM/STUB PO14
BOR GU35 20
Neptune Wy SHAM SO14
Nerissa Cl WVILLE PO7
Nerquis Cl ROMY SO51 26
Nesbitt Cl LSOL/BMARY PO13 39
Nessus St NEND PO2
Nestor Cl AND SP10
Netherfield Cl ALTN GU34
HAV PO9
Netherhall Gdns WBNE BH4
Nether Hill La BPWT SO32
Netherhouse Moor
FLET GU13 1
Netherton Rd GPORT PO12
Netley Cl CHFD SO53 2
PLE BH15
Netley Firs Rd ITCH SO19
Netley Hill Est ITCH SO19
Netley Lodge Cl HLER SO31
Netley Rd FHAM/STUB PO14
SSEA PO5
Netley St FARN GU14
Netley Ter SSEA PO5
Nettlebeds La NALR SO24
Nettlecombe Av ENEY PO4
Nettlestone HLER SO31 3
Nettlestone Rd ENEY PO4 4
Nettleton Cl CFDH BH17
Neuvic Wy WHCH RG28
Nevada Cl FARN GU14
Neva Rd WEND SO18
Neville Av FHAM/PORC PO16
Neville Cl AND SP10
BSTK RG21
Neville Dr ROMY SO51 2
STHA RG19
Neville Duke Rd FARN GU14
Neville Gdns EMRTH PO10
Neville Rd HSEA PO3
Neville Shute Rd HSEA PO3
Newall Rd RAND SP11
Newark Rd BLKW GU17
New Barn Cl FLET GU13 1
New Barn La ALTN GU34
RAND SP11
Newbarn La RCCH PO18
Newbarn Rd EPSF GU31

P09 ... 377 G5
ld Rd NWBY RG14 ... 25 G3 5
lt Cl HORN P08 ... 352 C5
RG18 ... 26 F3
lt Rd CHAM P06 ... 374 D7
orough Rd WIMB BH21 ... 404 A5
idge HLER S031 ... 369 G2 5
idge Rd TOTT S040 ... 314 E5
idge Wy LYMN S041 ... 440 A7
ighton Rd
H P010 ... 378 D6
oke Rd
BMARY P013 ... 397 J8 2
rgh St WINC S023 ... 10 F6 1
ry Cl ELGH S050 ... 295 G6 2
ry Pl HLER S031 ... 370 D6
ry Rd AND SP10 ... 118 F5
RG20 ... 59 H5
SP11 ... 119 G1
RG28 ... 99 J7
M S015 ... 318 B7 2
ry St AND SP10 ... 9 J5
H RG28 ... 122 B3
urch Rd TADY RG26 ... 41 K7
iffe Gdns HEND S030 .. 345 M3 1
mb Cl AND SP10 ... 142 E3
mbe Rd FERN BH22 ... 380 B5
BH6 ... 449 K2
M S015 ... 343 J2
men Rd NEND P02 ... 399 G6
me Pl ASHV GU12 ... 7 L7
me Rd FNM GU9 ... 6 A8
P01 ... 423 J2
s RAND SP11 ... 92 D7
oft Gdns
/BSGR BH23 ... 434 E8
ut HISD P011 ... 401 K5
awn Cl FARN GU14 ... 90 A5
own La WVILLE P07 ... 375 L6
o RAND SP11 ... 92 D7
ham Rd LYMN S041 ... 440 C6
arm Rd NALR S024 ... 218 A3
S021 ... 170 E5
ld Av FARN GU14 ... 90 B2
ld Rd ASHV GU12 ... 113 K2
U33 ... 248 F2
orest Dr BROC S042 ... 387 H7
undland Dr PLE BH15 ... 445 J7
ate La FHAM/STUB P014 .. 396 E2
arbour Rd South
BH15 ... 445 G7
ouse La RAND SP11 ... 116 F1
n La BROC S042 ... 416 A3
S040 ... 339 M2
n Rd TOTT S040 ... 339 M2
nd Av GPORT P012 ... 18 C3
nds FLET GU13 ... 110 F2
nds Av WSHM S015 ... 343 G1
nds Cl FAWY S045 ... 392 C8
S052 ... 292 D3
GU46 ... 69 G3
nds Copse FAWY S045 ... 392 D7
nds Dr ASHV GU12 ... 113 L4
nds La WVILLE P07 ... 351 L8
nds Rd
/BSGR BH23 ... 450 E1
S045 ... 392 C6
GU16 ... 70 E7
BH7 ... 448 F2
/BTOS BH25 ... 437 M7
LE P07 ... 376 B3
nds Wy BDST BH18 ... 429 H5
EPSF GU31 ... 305 G6
P09 ... 17 G3
S041 ... 454 E5
/BTOS BH25 ... 437 K2
S020 ... 210 F4
ase Rd WVILLE P07 ... 376 D3
Wk ROMY S051 ... 262 F7
Wy BKME/WDN BH12 ... 446 D1
P06 ... 398 E1
an La ALTN GU34 ... 177 G3
ans Cl WIMB BH21 ... 380 C3 1
ans Ct FNM GU9 ... 134 D2
ans Hl WHAM P017 ... 324 B8
an's La FERN BH22 ... 380 A3
an St ROWN S016 ... 318 A8 5
arket Cl ELGH S050 ... 321 J1 2
er Ct HAV P09 ... 377 G2
errifield WIMB BH21 ... 404 D1 1
ll La HTWY RG27 ... 47 H6
ll Rd HTWY RG27 ... 47 H6
orton Rd
R/WNTN BH9 ... 432 E4
y Cl NEND P02 ... 399 K4 5
am Ct HAV P09 ... 377 M3 11
am La CHAM RG24 ... 84 C8
RG27 ... 85 H7
am Pk HTWY RG27 ... 85 L8 2
am Rd HTWY RG27 ... 85 J8
diham Rd ALTN GU34 ... 176 C4
rch PLE BH15 ... 445 G6
addock Cl ALTN GU34 ... 177 H2
ark Rd SBNE BH6 ... 449 H4
rt Cl CHFD S053 ... 292 F4 5
RG14 ... 3 H2
rt La ROMY S051 ... 263 G2
rt Rd ASHV GU12 ... 7 K4
T P012 ... 18 A1
RG14 ... 3 H1
uay Rd PLE BH15 ... 444 F7
d BKME/WDN BH12 ... 446 C2
GU17 ... 70 B4
S032 ... 297 J6
S032 ... 299 J5
S032 ... 323 L4
RG21 ... 4 F9
RG45 ... 49 M3
S050 ... 295 G6
H P010 ... 378 F5
H P010 ... 379 J8
S045 ... 391 M2
S045 ... 392 C7
SP6 ... 282 D7
BH22 ... 406 B3
BH22 ... 432 C1
I/PORC P016 ... 15 H5
GU13 ... 111 G2

WINW S022 ... 213 M2
HASM GU27 ... 228 C3
HAV P09 ... 16 D2
HLER S031 ... 346 D8
HLER S031 ... 368 F2
HLER S031 ... 370 D8
HORN P08 ... 328 B3
HORN P08 ... 352 C2
HTWY RG27 ... 68 B1
HTWY RG27 ... 85 M7
HTWY RG27 ... 87 H2
BOR GU35 ... 201 H7
LYMN S041 ... 454 F4
NBNE BH10 ... 432 C3
NEND P02 ... 423 J1
RFNM GU10 ... 136 C2
NWBY RG14 ... 3 G7
ODIM RG29 ... 108 B4
RGWD BH24 ... 334 F8
ROMY S051 ... 262 C1
ROMY S051 ... 262 F8
RSAL SP5 ... 287 K7
RWIN S021 ... 148 A6
RWIN S021 ... 266 E7
SHAM S014 ... 13 G2
SHST GU47 ... 49 K8
STHA RG19 ... 38 A1
STOK S020 ... 162 B8
TADY RG26 ... 61 K1
TADY RG26 ... 62 B5
TOTT S040 ... 341 G6
New Rd East NEND P02 ... 399 K8
New Road Hl THLE RG7 ... 28 E5
Newstead Rd SBNE BH6 ... 449 J4
New St AND SP10 ... 9 J4
BSTK RG21 ... 4 E9
LYMN S041 ... 440 C4
RGWD BH24 ... 382 E2
STOK S020 ... 186 E6
THLE RG7 ... 44 D8
Newton Cl FHAM/STUB P014 ... 396 A4
RSAL SP5 ... 258 F5
Newton La ALTN GU34 ... 198 D8
ROMY S051 ... 290 D1
RSAL SP5 ... 258 C8
Newton Pl LSOL/BMARY P013 .. 420 C1
Newton Rd CCLF BH13 ... 446 D8
FARN GU14 ... 91 G2
NMIL/BTOS BH25 ... 437 M8
RWIN S021 ... 266 F1
WEND S018 ... 319 K7
Newton Wy RFNM GU10 ... 136 B1
New Town FHAM/PORC P016 ... 374 B8
Newtown TADY RG26 ... 41 K7
Newtown Cl AND SP10 ... 8 D6
Newtown La HISD P011 ... 425 J4 5
RGWD BH24 ... 335 G7
Newtown Rd ELGH S050 ... 293 M4
HLER S031 ... 370 A8
ITCH S019 ... 344 F8
LIPH GU30 ... 226 E5
NWBY RG14 ... 2 E8
ROMY S051 ... 261 G5
SHST GU47 ... 49 L8
VWD BH31 ... 356 E2
New Valley Rd LYMN S041 ... 454 B4
New Wokingham Rd
CWTH RG45 ... 49 K2
Nicholas Cl
CHCH/BSGR BH23 ... 436 F6 2
Nicholas Crs FHAM P015 ... 14 E4
Nicholas Gdns NBNE BH10 ... 432 A6
Nicholas Rd FAWY S045 ... 418 C1
Nicholl Pl LSOL/BMARY P013 .. 397 G6 5
Nichol Rd CHFD S053 ... 265 J7
Nicholson Wk ROWN S016 ... 317 J2
Nicholson Wy HAV P09 ... 16 D1
Nichols Rd SHAM S014 ... 13 K1 2
Nickel Cl WINC S023 ... 11 K6
Nickel St SSEA P05 ... 20 F5 5
Nickleby Gdns TOTT S040 ... 340 F1 1
Nickleby Rd HORN P08 ... 328 A2
Nickson Cl CHFD S053 ... 265 G8
Nideggan Cl STHA RG19 ... 27 G5
Nightingale Av ELGH S050 ... 293 J6
Nightingale Cl FARN GU14 ... 89 M2
WINW S022 ... 238 A2
GPORT P012 ... 421 K2 5
HAV P09 ... 353 L7
ROMY S051 ... 291 G1 5
VWD BH31 ... 356 E3 1
Nightingale Crs BPWT S032 ... 323 L8
Nightingale Dr FRIM GU16 ... 91 K5 1
TOTT S040 ... 316 B8
Nightingale Gdns CHAM RG24 ... 82 B8
HTWY RG27 ... 85 M7
SHST GU47 ... 49 L8
Nightingale Gv WSHM S015 ... 343 G1
Nightingale La RCCH P018 ... 379 L5
THLE RG7 ... 44 A2
Nightingale Pk HAV P09 ... 17 J5
Nightingale Ri OVTN RG25 ... 124 A1
Nightingale Rd ASHV GU12 ... 113 M5
HLER S031 ... 345 K8
BOR GU35 ... 201 K6 11
PSF GU32 ... 275 J6 1
SSEA P05 ... 20 F7
The Nightingales NWBY RG14 ... 2 F9
Nightingale Wk HLER S031 ... 369 G4
Nightjar Cl CFDH BH17 ... 429 J8
HORN P08 ... 352 E2
RFNM GU10 ... 111 G8
Nile Rd PTSW S017 ... 318 F6
Nile St EMRTH P010 ... 378 D8
Nimrod Dr LSOL/BMARY P013 ... 421 H2
Nimrod Wy WIMB BH21 ... 405 K2
Nine Elms La WHAM P017 ... 373 J4
Nine Mile Ride EWKG RG40 ... 48 A2
Ninian Cl ELGH S050 ... 295 H7
Ninian Park Rd HSEA P03 ... 399 L6
Niton Cl LSOL/BMARY P013 ... 397 G6 5
Noads Cl FAWY S045 ... 367 K6 5
Noads Wy FAWY S045 ... 367 J7
Nobbs La PSEA P01 ... 20 D4 2
Nobes Av LSOL/BMARY P013 ... 397 G5
Nobes Cl LSOL/BMARY P013 ... 397 H6
Noble Cl BWD BH11 ... 431 K7
Noble Rd HEND S030 ... 346 B2

Nob's Crook RWIN S021 ... 294 F1
Noel Cl BROC S042 ... 387 L7
Noel Rd NBNE BH10 ... 431 M7
Nogarth Cl ROMY S051 ... 263 G7 2
Nomad Cl WEND S018 ... 320 A7 5
The Nook ELGH S050 ... 294 A3
LSOL/BMARY P013 ... 397 J7
Noon Gdns VWD BH31 ... 356 F2
Noon Hill Dr VWD BH31 ... 356 F2 2
Noon Hill Rd VWD BH31 ... 356 F2
Norbury Cl CHFD S053 ... 293 G1
Norbury Gdns HLER S031 ... 369 J6
Norcliffe Cl BWD BH11 ... 431 M5
Norcliffe Rd PTSW S017 ... 318 F8
Norden Cl BSTK RG21 ... 4 F5
Nordik Gdns HEND S030 ... 346 A3
Nore Crs EMRTH P010 ... 378 B7
Nore Down Wy RCCH P018 ... 330 D8
Nore Farm Av EMRTH P010 ... 378 B7
Noreuil Rd PSF GU32 ... 275 J5
Norfolk Av CHCH/BSGR BH23 ... 434 D7
Norfolk Rd GPORT P012 ... 421 K1
WSHM S015 ... 318 C8
Norfolk St SSEA P05 ... 21 G5
Norgett Wy FHAM/PORC P016 .. 397 M2
Norham Av ROWN S016 ... 318 B6
Norham Cl ROWN S016 ... 318 B6
Norland Rd ENEY P04 ... 21 L5 2
Norlands NTHA RG18 ... 26 F3
Norlands Dr RWIN S021 ... 266 B4
Norley Cl HAV P09 ... 377 J3
Norleywood
CHCH/BSGR BH23 ... 436 D8 2
Norleywood Rd LYMN S041 ... 415 H7
Norman Av BKME/WDN BH12 ... 446 E2
Norman Cl FHAM/PORC P016 ... 398 B2
BOR GU35 ... 201 K5 5
Norman Court La RAND SP11 ... 142 E4
Normandy Cl LYMN S041 ... 412 E6
ROWN S016 ... 317 J2
Normandy Dr
CHCH/BSGR BH23 ... 450 C1
Normandy Gdns GPORT P012 ... 18 B3 2
Normandy La LYMN S041 ... 440 D6
Normandy Rd NEND P02 ... 399 H4
Normandy St ALTN GU34 ... 176 E4
Normandy Wy FBDG SP6 ... 309 K6
PLE BH15 ... 444 C6
TOTT S040 ... 342 D5
Norman Gdns
BKME/WDN BH12 ... 446 F2
HEND S030 ... 345 L3 1
Normanhurst Av CHAR BH8 ... 433 H7
Norman Rd ENEY P04 ... 21 L6
FAWY S045 ... 392 D8
GPORT P012 ... 18 C1
HISD P011 ... 425 M6
WINC S023 ... 238 E2
Normanton Cl
CHCH/BSGR BH23 ... 434 D7
Normanton Rd BSTK RG21 ... 4 F2
Norman Wy HAV P09 ... 377 G6
Normay Ri NWBY RG14 ... 36 F3
Normoor Rd THLE RG7 ... 31 J7
Norn Hl BSTK RG21 ... 5 H5
Norn Hill Cl BSTK RG21 ... 5 H5
Norris Br FARN GU14 ... 89 K8
Norris Cl BOR GU35 ... 201 G7
RGWD BH24 ... 381 J4
ROMY S051 ... 263 H6 2
Norris Gdns HAV P09 ... 17 H6
NMIL/BTOS BH25 ... 437 L7
Norris Hl WEND S018 ... 319 K7
Norris Hill Rd FLET GU13 ... 111 J1
Norrish Rd BKME/WDN BH12 ... 446 B3
Norset Rd FHAM P015 ... 372 A6
Northam Br SHAM S014 ... 344 A2
Northam Ms PSEA P01 ... 21 J1 2
Northampton La FAWY S045 ... 392 C8
Northam Rd SHAM S014 ... 13 K1
Northam St PSEA P01 ... 21 K1 2
PSEA P01 ... 423 H2
Northanger Cl ALTN GU34 ... 176 D4
Northarbour Rd CHAM P06 ... 399 H1
North Av FNM GU9 ... 135 G1
NBNE BH10 ... 432 B2
NEND P02 ... 399 J3
North Battery Rd NEND P02 ... 398 F6
North Bay EMRTH P010 ... 402 E5
North Beta Rd FARN GU14 ... 90 E6
Northbourne Av NBNE BH10 ... 432 B4
Northbourne Cl FAWY S045 ... 367 L7 2
Northbourne Gdns
NBNE BH10 ... 432 C3
Northbrook Av WINC S023 ... 11 K8
Northbrook Cl PSEA P01 ... 423 H1 5
WINC S023 ... 11 L8
Northbrook Rd ALDT GU11 ... 7 G5
BDST BH18 ... 429 L6
SHAM S014 ... 13 J1
Northbrook St NWBY RG14 ... 2 E3
North Charford Crossing
FBDG SP6 ... 284 C4
North Charford Dro FBDG SP6 .. 283 M3
North Cl ASHV GU12 ... 7 M4
FARN GU14 ... 70 D8
GPORT P012 ... 18 A4
HAV P09 ... 17 G6
LYMN S041 ... 440 C4
ROMY S051 ... 263 H7
North Common La LYMN S041 .. 439 K1
RSAL SP5 ... 286 F2
Northcote Av NEND P02 ... 399 K8 1
Northcote Rd ASHV GU12 ... 113 K1
BMTH BH1 ... 23 L2
ENEY P04 ... 21 M6 1
FARN GU14 ... 90 B2
PTSW S017 ... 319 H6
North Crs HISD P011 ... 425 M5
Northcroft La NWBY RG14 ... 2 C3
Northcroft Rd GPORT P012 ... 421 K2
North Cross St GPORT P012 ... 19 K3
Northdene Rd CHFD S053 ... 293 H3
North Downs Wy RFNM GU10 .. 135 K6
RGWW GU3 ... 137 J5
North Dr WINW S022 ... 214 A3
NMIL/BTOS BH25 ... 411 J7
THLE RG7 ... 31 G1

North East Cl ITCH S019 ... 344 F3
North East Rd ITCH S019 ... 344 E4
North End Av NEND P02 ... 399 H6
North End Cl CHFD S053 ... 293 H4
North End Gv NEND P02 ... 399 H6
Northend La BPWT S032 ... 298 F6
North End La FBDG SP6 ... 334 A4
NALR S024 ... 242 C1
Northern Access Rd
FAWY S045 ... 393 H6
Northern Anchorage ITCH S019 .. 13 M5
Northern Av AND SP10 ... 9 H3
NWBY RG14 ... 25 K2
Northern Pde NEND P02 ... 399 H5
Northern Rd CHAM P06 ... 399 K2
Northerwood Av LYND S043 ... 363 J3
Northerwood Cl NBAD S052 ... 291 L4 2
Northey Rd SBNE BH6 ... 449 K2
North Farm Rd FARN GU14 ... 70 B8
Northfield Av
FHAM/STUB P014 ... 396 D1
Northfield Cl ASHV GU12 ... 7 M3
BPWT S032 ... 296 F7
FLET GU13 ... 111 G2 2
HORN P08 ... 328 B6
Northfield La ALTN GU34 ... 176 B8
Northfield Rd FLET GU13 ... 111 G2
HTWY RG27 ... 64 C7
LYMN S041 ... 454 D3
NTHA RG18 ... 26 E4
RGWD BH24 ... 358 E7
WEND S018 ... 319 L5
Northfields Farm La
WHAM P017 ... 348 E3
North Front SHAM S014 ... 13 H2
North Fryerne YTLY GU46 ... 49 G8
Northgate Dr CBLY GU15 ... 71 K1
Northgate La OVTN RG25 ... 128 A7
North Gate Rd FARN GU14 ... 90 F6
North Greenlands LYMN S041 .. 440 A6
North Head LYMN S041 ... 453 M3
North Hl CHAM P06 ... 374 F6
FHAM/PORC P016 ... 15 J1
North Hill Cl WINW S022 ... 10 F3
Northington Rd RWIN S021 ... 193 G7
Northlands Cl TOTT S040 ... 316 C8
Northlands Dr WINC S023 ... 11 G3
Northlands Gdns WSHM S015 ... 343 J1
Northlands Rd ELGH S050 ... 293 M5 2
ROMY S051 ... 291 H2
TOTT S040 ... 316 C8
WSHM S015 ... 343 J1
North La ALDT GU11 ... 113 G5
BROC S042 ... 390 C3
EPSF GU31 ... 303 K3
EPSF GU31 ... 305 G4
HORN P08 ... 302 A7
HORN P08 ... 328 A2
RSAL SP5 ... 207 M8
RSAL SP5 ... 313 H1
Northleigh La WIMB BH21 ... 404 C4
North Lodge Rd PSTN BH14 ... 446 D4
Northmead FARN GU14 ... 90 E4
Northmead Dr CFDH BH17 ... 429 K8
Northmere Dr
BKME/WDN BH12 ... 446 E1
Northmere Rd
BKME/WDN BH12 ... 446 E1
North Millers Dl CHFD S053 ... 264 F7
Northmore Cl HLER S031 ... 370 F3 2
Northmore Rd HLER S031 ... 370 F3
Northney La HISD P011 ... 402 A4
Northney Rd HISD P011 ... 401 M4
Northolt Gdns ROWN S016 ... 317 M4
Northover La LYMN S041 ... 438 C1
Northover Rd HSEA P03 ... 399 M8
LYMN S041 ... 439 L4
North Pde BOR GU35 ... 201 H2
North Poulner Rd RGWD BH24 .. 358 F7
North Rd ALDT GU11 ... 113 G1
ASHV GU12 ... 113 J4
BROC S042 ... 387 L7
FAWY S045 ... 367 H6
HORN P08 ... 328 B6
LTDN BH7 ... 448 D3
PLE BH15 ... 444 F6
PSF GU32 ... 275 L4
PSTN BH14 ... 445 M4
PTSW S017 ... 319 H8
WINC S023 ... 191 G8
WVILLE P07 ... 374 E6
North Rd East WHAM P017 ... 374 E2
North Rd West WHAM P017 ... 374 D2
North Shore Rd HISD P011 ... 425 H3
Northside La NALR S024 ... 219 J1
North St EMRTH P010 ... 378 D7
EMRTH P010 ... 378 F4
HAV P09 ... 16 A3
HAV P09 ... 16 F4
KSCL RG20 ... 59 J6
LYMN S041 ... 440 A6
NALR S024 ... 219 G3
PLE BH15 ... 445 H6
PSEA P01 ... 20 D1
PSEA P01 ... 423 H2
North Stroud La PSF GU32 ... 274 D6
North Town RWIN S021 ... 266 F1
North Trestle Rd FAWY S045 ... 392 F2
Northumberland Rd
BOR GU35 ... 201 J7 2
SHAM S014 ... 13 K1
SHAM S014 ... 343 M2 2
SSEA P05 ... 21 L2 5
North View Rd TADY RG26 ... 62 A1
North Wallington
FHAM/PORC P016 ... 15 M3
North Walls WINC S023 ... 11 J7
North Warnborough St
ODIM RG29 ... 108 A5
North Wy AND SP10 ... 119 K6
Northway FHAM P015 ... 371 J5
North Wy HAV P09 ... 16 D4
Northway NTHA RG18 ... 26 F3
NWBY RG14 ... 3 G6
Northways FHAM/STUB P014 ... 396 B6
North Weirs BROC S042 ... 387 H7
Northwood Cl ROWN S016 ... 318 F2 1
Northwood Dr NWBY RG14 ... 3 J1

Northwood La HISD P011 ... 401 L7
Northwood Rd NEND P02 ... 399 J4
Nortoft Rd CHAR BH8 ... 448 A2
Norton Cl CHCH/BSGR BH23 ... 450 C1
ITCH S019 ... 344 C5
NWBY RG14 ... 36 F2 2
WHAM P017 ... 374 D2
WVILLE P07 ... 376 B1
Norton Dr FHAM/PORC P016 ... 15 H3
Norton Ride CHAM RG24 ... 105 L1
Norton Rd CBLY GU15 ... 71 M4
MOOR/WNTN BH9 ... 432 C7
THLE RG7 ... 45 M6
WHAM P017 ... 374 D2
Norton Welch Cl NBAD S052 ... 292 A4
Norway Rd HSEA P03 ... 399 K4
Norwich Av CBLY GU15 ... 71 H5
WCLF BH2 ... 22 B5
Norwich Av West WBNE BH4 ... 22 A5
Norwich Cl HLER S031 ... 370 C4
Norwich Pl LSOL/BMARY P013 .. 420 C1
Norwich Rd CHAM P06 ... 375 H7
WCLF BH2 ... 22 C6
WEND S018 ... 319 L6
Norwood Pl BOSC BH5 ... 449 G3
Nottingham Pl
LSOL/BMARY P013 ... 420 C1 2
Nouale La RGWD BH24 ... 383 H1
Novello Cl KEMP RG22 ... 127 J1
Novello Gdns WVILLE P07 ... 376 C3
Noyce Dr ELGH S050 ... 295 J7
Noyce Gdns CHAR BH8 ... 433 M6
Nuffield Dr SHST GU47 ... 50 C7
Nuffield Rd CFDH BH17 ... 430 B8
WHIT RG2 ... 47 J1
Nugee Ct CWTH RG45 ... 49 L3 1
Nugent Rd SBNE BH6 ... 449 L4
Nunns Pk RSAL SP5 ... 259 G4
Nuns Rd WINC S023 ... 11 H4
Nuns Wk WINC S023 ... 11 H4
Nunton Dro RSAL SP5 ... 255 J4
Nursery Cl CHAM RG24 ... 83 M5 5
EMRTH P010 ... 378 D5
FLET GU13 ... 89 J8
FRIM GU16 ... 91 J1
HTWY RG27 ... 85 M6 7
LSOL/BMARY P013 ... 396 F5
Nursery Fld LISS GU33 ... 248 D5
Nursery Gdns CHFD S053 ... 293 H5
WINW S022 ... 10 B7
HORN P08 ... 352 E3
ITCH S019 ... 344 F2
ROMY S051 ... 290 F1 2
Nursery Gv HEND S030 ... 346 A3
Nursery La FHAM/STUB P014 ... 396 A7
Nursery Rd ALTN GU34 ... 176 F4
HAV P09 ... 377 G6
MOOR/WNTN BH9 ... 432 E5
NALR S024 ... 218 C3
RGWD BH24 ... 382 E2 5
WEND S018 ... 319 J7
Nursling Crs HAV P09 ... 377 L3
Nursling Gn CHAR BH8 ... 433 H6
Nursling St ROWN S016 ... 317 H3
Nutash FHAM P015 ... 371 G4
Nutbane La RAND SP11 ... 117 L1
Nutbean La THLE RG7 ... 46 C3
Nutbeem Rd ELGH S050 ... 293 M6
Nutbourne FNM GU9 ... 6 B7
Nutbourne Rd CHAM P06 ... 400 B1
HISD P011 ... 426 C7
Nutburn Rd NBAD S052 ... 292 A3
Nutchers Dro STOK S020 ... 210 F5 1
Nutcombe La GSHT GU26 ... 204 B7
Nutfield Ct ROWN S016 ... 317 K5
Nutfield Pl PSEA P01 ... 423 H2
Nutfield Rd ROWN S016 ... 317 J2
Nuthatch Cl CFDH BH17 ... 444 E1
HAV P09 ... 353 M7
RFNM GU10 ... 134 A1
Nutley Cl BWD BH11 ... 431 K4
BOR GU35 ... 201 J6 5
YTLY GU46 ... 69 G3
Nutley La OVTN RG25 ... 126 E7
Nutley Rd HAV P09 ... 377 H3
Nutley Wy BWD BH11 ... 431 K5
Nutmeg Ct FARN GU14 ... 89 M3 5
Nutsey Av TOTT S040 ... 316 C6
Nutsey La TOTT S040 ... 316 D6
Nutshalling Av ROWN S016 ... 317 K3
Nutshalling Cl TOTT S040 ... 316 B7
Nutshell La FNM GU9 ... 134 F2
Nutwick Rd HAV P09 ... 17 K1
Nutwood Wy TOTT S040 ... 316 D6
Nyewood Av
FHAM/PORC P016 ... 374 B7
Nyria Wy GPORT P012 ... 19 J4

O

Oakapple Gdns CHAM P06 ... 376 C8 5
Oak Av CHCH/BSGR BH23 ... 434 B8
SHST GU47 ... 50 A7
Oak Bank AND SP10 ... 9 H8
Oakbank Rd ELGH S050 ... 294 B5
ITCH S019 ... 344 B5
Oak Cl BPWT S032 ... 296 E3
DEAN RG23 ... 103 G7
FAWY S045 ... 367 J7
FERN BH22 ... 406 C7
HORN P08 ... 352 C6
LYND S043 ... 363 K4 5
NTID SP9 ... 114 F1
OVTN RG25 ... 123 M1
RSAL SP5 ... 230 B1
STOK S020 ... 163 G4
WIMB BH21 ... 429 G3
WSHM S015 ... 342 A1
Oak Coppice Cl ELGH S050 ... 294 F6
Oak Ct FNM GU9 ... 134 E7
Oakcroft La FHAM/STUB P014 .. 396 A3
Oakdale Rd PLE BH15 ... 445 K2
Oakdene ALTN GU34 ... 176 D3
LSOL/BMARY P013 ... 397 H7
THLE RG7 ... 31 K5
TOTT S040 ... 340 F1

Oakdene Cl WIMB BH21 404 B3 1
Oakdown Rd
FHAM/STUB PO14 396 B5
Oak Dr ELGH SO50 295 H6
NWBY RG14 2 C6
THLE RG7 31 J6
Oakenbrow FAWY SO45 367 H6
LYMN SO41 412 E5
Oaken Copse CBLY GU15 71 M1
FLET GU13 111 G4
Oaken Copse Crs FARN GU14 90 E1
Oak End Wy THLE RG7 29 M4
Oaken Gv NWBY RG14 25 G8
The Oakes FHAM/STUB PO14 395 M4
Oak Farm Cl BLKW GU17 69 M3
Oakfield Ct HAV PO9 377 M3 12
Oakfield Rd BLKW GU17 70 B4
PLE BH15 445 H2
TADY RG26 42 B7
TOTT SO40 339 M1
TOTT SO40 341 K1
Oakfields ELGH SO50 293 M1
Oakfields Cl KSCL RG20 58 C4
Oak Gdns LYMN SO41 439 H8 5
Oak Green Wy WEND SO18 319 M8
Oak Grove Crs CBLY GU15 70 C2
Oakgrove Rd ELGH SO50 294 D6
Oak Hanger Cl HTWY RG27 86 A7 4
Oakhanger Rd BOR GU35 200 F3
Oakhill HLER SO31 345 M7
Oak Hl NALR SO24 218 C3
Oakhill Cl CHFD SO53 293 K3
HLER SO31 345 M7
Oakhill Rd BOR GU35 202 E3
Oakhurst GSHT GU26 204 A5
Oakhurst Cl FERN BH22 380 D6
HLER SO31 369 G2 4
Oakhurst Dr WVILLE PO7 352 E8
Oakhurst Gdns CHAM PO6 375 M6
Oakhurst La FERN BH22 380 D6
Oakhurst Rd FERN BH22 380 D7
PTSW SO17 318 F5 1
Oakhurst Wy HLER SO31 369 G2
Oakland Av FNM GU9 6 A7
Oakland Dr TOTT SO40 342 D7
Oakland Rd WHCH RG28 122 B3
Oaklands HASM GU27 228 F1 2
RWIN SO21 190 C4
YTLY GU46 69 G2
LYMN SO41 440 D6
Oaklands Av TOTT SO40 341 K1
Oaklands Cl FBDG SP6 309 K6 2
WINW SO22 238 A2
VWD BH31 356 C2
Oaklands Gdns
FHAM/STUB PO14 371 G7
Oaklands Gv HORN PO8 352 C5
Oaklands La CWTH RG45 49 K2
Oaklands Rd HAV PO9 17 H4
PSF GU32 275 K4
The Oaklands CHFD SO53 293 H5 3
Oaklands Wy DEAN RG23 104 B2
FAWY SO45 367 G6
FHAM/STUB PO14 371 G7
ROWN SO16 318 E4
Oakland Wk FERN BH22 406 C7
Oak La RGWD BH24 358 F8
Oaklea ASHV GU12 113 K3
Oaklea Dr HTWY RG27 47 H6
Oaklea Gdns TADY RG26 64 A6
Oakleigh Crs TOTT SO40 341 J2
Oakleigh Dr RSAL SP5 287 J7
Oakleigh Gdns ROMY SO51 290 F1 3
Oakleigh Wy CHCH/BSGR BH23 451 L1
Oakley Cl FAWY SO45 392 A4
Oakley Dr FLET GU13 88 F8
Oakley Hl WIMB BH21 404 B5
Oakley La DEAN RG23 103 G6
WIMB BH21 404 B6
Oakley Rd CBLY GU15 70 E4
HAV PO9 377 H3
BOR GU35 201 J3
NWBY RG14 3 L1
ROMY SO51 233 K6
ROWN SO16 317 L8
TADY RG26 79 L5
WIMB BH21 404 B6
Oakley Straight WIMB BH21 404 C7
Oakmead TADY RG26 63 K4
Oakmead Gdns BWD BH11 431 K4
Oakmeadow Cl EMRTH PO10 378 E5
Oakmead Rd CFDH BH17 444 E1
Oakmont Dr WVILLE PO7 352 D6
Oakmount Av CHFD SO53 293 J4
PTSW SO17 318 F7
TOTT SO40 316 E8
Oakmount Rd CHFD SO53 293 J4
Oak Park Dr HAV PO9 17 G1
Oakridge Rd BSTK RG21 4 B3
WSHM SO15 317 J8
Oak Rd BPWT SO32 297 J8
CHAR BH8 448 B2
FARN GU14 90 F5
FAWY SO45 367 J7
FBDG SP6 333 K3
FHAM PO15 14 A4
HLER SO31 345 J8
HORN PO8 328 B3
ITCH SO19 344 B6
NMIL/BTOS BH25 438 A4
UPTN BH16 444 B2
Oaks Coppice HORN PO8 352 E2
Oaks Dr RGWD BH24 381 H5
Oakshott Dr HAV PO9 377 L3
Oaks Md VWD BH31 356 E2 3
The Oaks ALTN GU34 196 F1
FLET GU13 88 C7
HLER SO31 345 K8
ITCH SO19 344 D3
TADY RG26 41 K8
VWD BH31 356 C1
YTLY GU46 69 G3
Oak St GPORT PO12 19 H3
Oakthorn Cl
LSOL/BMARY PO13 421 G2
Oak Tree Cl ASHV GU12 7 M6
ASHV GU12 91 J7 2
BOR GU35 202 C4
RWIN SO21 266 E8
TADY RG26 41 L7 1
Oak Tree Dr EMRTH PO10 378 C4
HTWY RG27 86 A6
LISS GU33 248 F4
Oak Tree Farm RCCH PO18 379 M7
Oak Tree Gdns HEND SO30 345 M2 3
Oak Tree La HASM GU27 228 A2
Oak Tree Rd BOR GU35 201 H7
STHA RG19 27 H6
WEND SO18 319 J7
Oaktrees ASHV GU12 113 J7
FNM GU9 134 E2 3
Oak Tree Vw FNM GU9 135 G2
Oak Tree Wy ELGH SO50 293 M3
Oaktree Wy SHST GU47 49 K7
Oak V HEND SO30 320 A5
Oakway ASHV GU12 113 H8
RFNM GU10 156 F4
Oakway Dr FRIM GU16 71 H7
Oakwood CHAM RG24 83 L5
FLET GU13 110 F4
Oakwood Av HAV PO9 376 F5
NMIL/BTOS BH25 438 A4
RWIN SO21 266 B5
Oakwood Cl HLER SO31 370 B8
ROMY SO51 263 H7
RWIN SO21 266 B4
Oakwood Ct HEND SO30 320 D6 2
Oakwood Dr ROWN SO16 318 A3
Oakwood Rd
CHCH/BSGR BH23 436 C7
CHFD SO53 265 J8
HISD PO11 425 K5
MOOR/WNTN BH9 432 E6
NEND PO2 399 J4
Oakwood Wy HLER SO31 369 L5 1
Oasthouse Dr FARN GU14 89 H4
Oast House La FNM GU9 135 G3
Oast La ALDT GU11 7 G7
Oates Rd MOOR/WNTN BH9 432 C7
Oatfield Gdns TOTT SO40 316 B7
Oatlands ROMY SO51 262 E8 3
Oatlands Cl BPWT SO32 321 L7
Oatlands Rd BPWT SO32 321 L7
Oban Cl DEAN RG23 102 F6
Oban Rd TWDS BH3 447 K1
O'bee Gdns TADY RG26 41 H7
Obelisk Rd ITCH SO19 344 B6
Obelisk Wy CBLY GU15 70 F2
Oberfield Rd BROC SO42 387 H6
Oberon Cl WVILLE PO7 352 E8
Ober Rd BROC SO42 387 J6
Oberursel Wy ALDT GU11 6 D1 1
Occupation La
FHAM/STUB PO14 395 J1
Ocean Cl FHAM PO15 14 B3
Ocean Rd FHAM/STUB PO14 396 D3
Ocean Wy SHAM SO14 13 J8
Ochil Cl KEMP RG22 104 A5
Ockendon Cl SSEA PO5 21 H4 3
Ocknell Gv FAWY SO45 367 G5
O'connell Rd ELGH SO50 293 K6
O'connor Rd ALDT GU11 113 G1
Octavia Gdns CHFD SO53 293 L1
Octavia Hl WINW SO22 238 C2
Octavian Cl KEMP RG22 127 G1
Octavia Rd WEND SO18 319 K4
Octavius Ct WVILLE PO7 352 F7
Oddfellows Rd NWBY RG14 2 D5
Odell Cl FHAM/PORC PO16 14 E1
Odette Gdns TADY RG26 41 L7
Odiham Cl ROWN SO16 317 L4
Odiham Rd HTWY RG27 46 A7
HTWY RG27 108 F1
RFNM GU10 110 E8
THLE RG7 45 M5
Odstock Rd RSAL SP5 255 K1
Officers Rw TADY RG26 64 A6
Oglander Rd WINC SO23 11 H3
Ogle Rd SHAM SO14 12 F3
O'gorman Av FARN GU14 90 E6
Okeford Rd BDST BH18 429 M6
Okement Cl WEND SO18 320 A6
Okingham Cl SHST GU47 50 A7 3
Olaf Cl AND SP10 119 G4 3
Olave Cl LSOL/BMARY PO13 420 C2 1
Old Acre Rd ALTN GU34 176 D6
Old Agwi Rd FAWY SO45 393 G3
Old Barn Cl OVTN RG25 125 K7 1
RGWD BH24 382 F1
Oldbarn Cl TOTT SO40 316 B6
Old Barn Crs WVILLE PO7 326 B6
Old Barn Farm Rd WIMB BH21 380 E3
Old Barn La RFNM GU10 181 L6
Old Barn Rd CHCH/BSGR BH23 434 B6
Old Bath Rd NWBY RG14 2 B1
Oldberg Gdns KEMP RG22 104 E8 3
Old Bisley Rd FRIM GU16 71 K6
Old Bound Rd UPTN BH16 444 B2
Old Brickfield Rd ALDT GU11 7 G7
Old Brickyard Rd FBDG SP6 309 G6
Old Bridge House Rd
HLER SO31 345 M8
Old Bridge Rd ENEY PO4 21 M8
LTDN BH7 434 B8
Oldbury Cl FRIM GU16 71 J8 1
Oldbury Ct ROWN SO16 317 J6
Oldbury Wy FHAM/STUB PO14 372 A8
Old Canal ENEY PO4 423 M4 4
Old Christchurch Rd BMTH BH1 23 G5
LYMN SO41 439 H7
Old Church La FNM GU9 159 G1
Old Coach Rd NTID SP9 115 G8
Old Coastguard Rd CCLF BH13 457 G4
Old Commercial Rd
PSEA PO1 423 G1 3
Old Common HLER SO31 370 E4
Old Common Gdns HLER SO31 370 E5
Old Common Rd BSTK RG21 105 J4
Old Common Wy RAND SP11 92 E6
Old Compton La FNM GU9 135 H7
Old Copse Rd HAV PO9 16 F2
Oldcorne Hollow HTWY RG27 68 D3
Old Cove Rd FARN GU14 89 G5
Old Cracknore Cl TOTT SO40 342 D6
Old Cross Tree Wy ASHV GU12 113 M8
Old Dean Rd CBLY GU15 71 G1
Old Down RWIN SO21 268 A1
Old Down Cl KEMP RG22 103 M7
Old Down Rd AND SP10 8 E2
Olde Farm Dr BLKW GU17 69 L3
Oldenburg HLER SO31 346 F8
Old English Dr AND SP10 118 E4
Old Farm Cl RGWD BH24 359 G6
Old Farm Dr WEND SO18 319 L6
Old Farm La EMRTH PO10 378 F5
FHAM/STUB PO14 396 A7
Old Farm Pl ASHV GU12 113 J4
Old Farm Rd PLE BH15 445 K2
Old Farm Wk LYMN SO41 440 B5
Old Farm Wy CHAM PO6 400 C1
Old Farnham La FNM GU9 134 F8
RFNM GU10 133 K7
Oldfield Vw HTWY RG27 87 H3 3
Old Forge Rd WIMB BH21 405 K2
Old Frensham Rd RFNM GU10 159 G2
Old Garden Cl
FHAM/STUB PO14 371 G6
Old Gdns WINW SO22 10 F2
Oldgate Gdns NEND PO2 399 K4 3
Old Gosport Rd
FHAM/PORC PO16 15 K8
Old Green La CBLY GU15 70 F1
Old Guildford Rd FRIM GU16 91 L3
Old Ham La WIMB BH21 405 H4
Old Haslemere Rd HASM GU27 228 F3
Old Heath Wy FNM GU9 134 F1 1
Old Hillside Rd WINW SO22 214 B7
The Old Hl RAND SP11 165 L2 1
Oldhouse La HAV PO9 355 H2
ROMY SO51 288 D1
Old Ivy La WEND SO18 320 A6
Old Kempshott La KEMP RG22 103 M5
Old Kennels Cl WINW SO22 237 M5
Old Kennels La RWIN SO21 237 K7
Old Kiln Cl RFNM GU10 181 J6
Old Kiln La RFNM GU10 181 J6
Old Kiln Rd UPTN BH16 444 B1
Old La ALDT GU11 6 E7
ASHV GU12 113 H5
RFNM GU10 180 B4
STHA RG19 40 B7
Old Litten La PSF GU32 247 H5
Old London Rd STOK SO20 186 F5
Old Lyndhurst Rd TOTT SO40 314 E8
Old Magazine Cl TOTT SO40 342 D6
Old Manor Cl WIMB BH21 404 C4
Old Manor Wy CHAM PO6 399 M1
Old Market Rd WIMB BH21 428 C1
Old Micheldever Rd
RAND SP11 143 M3
Old Mill La EPSF GU31 276 A3
HORN PO8 327 G8
Old Mill Pl HASM GU27 228 C1
Old Mill Wy ROWN SO16 317 M7
Old Milton Gn
NMIL/BTOS BH25 437 K7
Old Milton Rd
NMIL/BTOS BH25 437 K7
Old Newtown Rd NWBY RG14 2 D7 1
Old Odiham Rd ALTN GU34 154 C5
Old Orch PLE BH15 445 H7
Old Orchards LYMN SO41 440 D6
The Old Orch FNM GU9 134 C8
ODIM RG29 130 E4
Old Palace Farm STOK SO20 210 F6
Old Park Cl FNM GU9 134 D2
Old Park La FNM GU9 134 C1
Old Park Rd NALR SO24 219 K5
Old Parsonage Ct RWIN SO21 266 B5
Old Pasture Rd FRIM GU16 71 J5
Old Pharmacy Ct CWTH RG45 49 M4 2
Old Pines Cl FERN BH22 406 C4
Old Pond Cl FRIM GU16 70 E7
Old Portsmouth Rd CBLY GU15 71 K4
Old Potbridge Rd HTWY RG27 86 F7
Old Priory Cl HLER SO31 369 L6
Old Priory Rd SBNE BH6 449 L4
The Old Quarry HASM GU27 228 C4
Old Reading Rd BSTK RG21 5 G7
Old Rectory Cl EMRTH PO10 378 F5 2
Old Rectory Dr ASHV GU12 113 L6
Old Rectory Gdns FARN GU14 91 G4 2
WINC SO23 215 J2 1
Old Rectory La RWIN SO21 266 F1
Old Rectory Rd CHAM PO6 376 C8
Old Redbridge Rd WSHM SO15 317 H8
Old Reservoir Rd CHAM PO6 400 B1
Old River WVILLE PO7 351 K5
Old Rd GPORT PO12 19 H5
ROMY SO51 262 F8
SHAM SO14 13 J7
The Old Rd CHAM PO6 399 K2
Old Romsey Rd TOTT SO40 314 D8
The Old Rope Wk PLE BH15 444 E7
Old Salisbury La ROMY SO51 261 K7
Old Salisbury Rd RAND SP11 142 A5
ROMY SO51 315 K1
Old Sawmill Cl VWD BH31 356 C2
Old Sawmill La CWTH RG45 49 M2
The Old Sawmills HUNG RG17 34 B2
Old School Cl ASHV GU12 113 K5
FAWY SO45 391 M2
FERN BH22 406 A3 1
FLET GU13 88 F7 1
HLER SO31 369 H1 1
HTWY RG27 87 J2 1
Old School Dr HISD PO11 425 M6
Old School Gdns HEND SO30 320 D6
Old School La YTLY GU46 68 F2
Old School Rd HTWY RG27 85 K8
LISS GU33 248 E4
Old Shamblehurst La
HEND SO30 321 H6
Old Stacks Gdns RGWD BH24 383 G2 3
Old Star PSEA PO1 20 C1
Old Station Ap WINC SO23 11 K8
Old Station Rd RWIN SO21 216 D1
Old Station Wy BOR GU35 200 F3
Old Stockbridge Rd
RAND SP11 162 A2
STOK SO20 162 F3
Old Stoke Rd RWIN SO21 190 F2
Old St FHAM/STUB PO14 395 M5
Old Timbers HISD PO11 425 K5
Old Tpk FHAM/PORC PO16 15 J2
Old Vicarage La STOK SO20 210 F5
The Old Vineries FBDG SP6 309 J7 1
Old Vyne La TADY RG26 61 J7
Old Wareham Rd
BKME/WDN BH12 445 M1
UPTN BH16 428 E6
The Old Well Cl ITCH SO19 345 G5
Old Welmore YTLY GU46 69 H3
Old Winchester Hill La
BPWT SO32 271 L5
PSF GU32 272 B5
Old Winton Rd AND SP10 9 J7
Old Wokingham Rd CWTH RG45 49 M1
Oldwood Cha FARN GU14 89 L5
Old Worting Rd KEMP RG22 104 B4
Old Wymering La CHAM PO6 375 J8
Oleander Cl CWTH RG45 49 J1
HLER SO31 370 E3
Olive Crs FHAM/PORC PO16 398 B2
Olive Gv RAND SP11 161 K3
Olive Rd ROWN SO16 317 M4
Oliver Ri ALTN GU34 176 E4
Oliver Rd ENEY PO4 423 K5
LYMN SO41 440 A5
WEND SO18 319 J5
Oliver's Battery Crs
WINW SO22 238 A4
Oliver's Battery Gdns
WINW SO22 238 A5
Oliver's Battery Rd North
WINW SO22 238 A3
Oliver's Battery Rd South
WINW SO22 238 A5
Olivers Cl TADY RG26 63 M6
TOTT SO40 340 F1
Oliver's La TADY RG26 63 M4
Olivers Rd WIMB BH21 404 E2
Oliver's Wk CHAM RG24 105 L1
Olivers Wy WIMB BH21 404 E2 2
Olivia Cl WVILLE PO7 352 E7 3
Olympic Wy ELGH SO50 294 F5 1
ELGH SO50 295 G5 2
Omdurman Rd PTSW SO17 318 F6
Omega ALTN GU34 177 G5
Omega St SSEA PO5 21 J2
Omer's Ri THLE RG7 31 K5
Onibury Cl WEND SO18 319 M7
Onibury Rd WEND SO18 319 M7
Onslow Cl CHAM RG24 83 K7
Onslow Gdns WIMB BH21 404 B2
Onslow Rd SHAM SO14 343 L2
SSEA PO5 21 K9
Openfields BOR GU35 202 B2
Ophir Gdns BMTH BH1 23 K2
Ophir Rd CHAR BH8 23 J1
NEND PO2 399 H6
Oracle Dr WVILLE PO7 376 C5
Orange Gv
LSOL/BMARY PO13 397 H7 2
RAND SP11 161 K3
Orange La STOK SO20 162 B6
Orange Rw EMRTH PO10 378 D8 3
Oratory Gdns CCLF BH13 446 E8
Orbit Cl EWKG RG40 48 C2
Orchard Av ELGH SO50 294 E7
PSTN BH14 445 L6
Orchard Cl ASHV GU12 113 K3
CHCH/BSGR BH23 449 M2
EPSF GU31 305 K4
FARN GU14 70 C7
FAWY SO45 392 F5
FBDG SP6 309 L6
FERN BH22 406 C3
FNM GU9 6 F9
GPORT PO12 397 L7
HORN PO8 353 G2
NALR SO24 218 C4
NBAD SO52 291 L3
NWBY RG14 25 M3
RGWD BH24 358 E8
RWIN SO21 190 B4
RWIN SO21 266 E7
THLE RG7 28 F6
TOTT SO40 341 K3
WIMB BH21 429 H1
Orchard Ct HEND SO30 346 C1
VWD BH31 356 E3 2
Orchard End RFNM GU10 158 C5
Orchardene NWBY RG14 3 H2
Orchard Gdns ALDT GU11 7 K6
FBDG SP6 309 L7 4
Orchard Ga SHST GU47 49 L8
Orchard Gv FHAM/PORC PO16 397 L1
HORN PO8 352 D5
NMIL/BTOS BH25 437 L7
Orchard La ALTN GU34 176 F4
EMRTH PO10 378 E8
ROMY SO51 290 D1
SHAM SO14 13 H5
WIMB BH21 429 H1
Orchardlea BPWT SO32 324 A5
Orchard Pl SHAM SO14 13 G7
Orchard Rd AND SP10 8 C3
ELGH SO50 295 H6
ENEY PO4 21 M3
FARN GU14 90 D4
FNM GU9 6 F9
GPORT PO12 422 B2
HAV PO9 16 F6
HISD PO11 425 L6
HLER SO31 370 D6
KEMP RG22 104 B4
RSAL SP5 285 J1
RWIN SO21 190 B4
THLE RG7 43 L3
Orchard St WCLF BH2 22 D6
Orchards Wy HEND SO30 320 C7 3
PTSW SO17 318 F6
The Orchard BWD BH11 431 H2
CHAM PO6 399 K1
HASM GU27 228 C3
LYMN SO41 454 C4
OVTN RG25 100 F8
ROWN SO16 292 D7
TADY RG26 42 A8
WVILLE PO7 351 K4
Orchard Wy ALDT GU11 7 K6
CBLY GU15
FAWY SO45
Orcheston Rd CHAR BH8
Orchid Dr RAND SP11
Ordnance Rd ALDT GU11
GPORT PO12
NTID SP9
WSHM SO15
Ordnance Rw PSEA PO1
Ordnance Wy TOTT SO40
Oregon Cl ITCH SO19
Oregon Wk EWKG RG40
Orford Cl CHCH/BSGR BH23
Oriel Dr FHAM/STUB PO14
Oriel Hl CBLY GU15
Oriel Rd NEND PO2
Orient Dr WINW SO22
Orion Cl FHAM/STUB PO14
ROWN SO16
Orkney Cl CHAM RG24
ROWN SO16
Orkney Rd CHAM PO6
Ormesby Dr CHFD SO53
Ormond Cl ELGH SO50
Ormonde Rd CCLF BH13
Ormsby Rd SSEA PO5
Orpen Rd ITCH SO19
Orsmond Cl WVILLE PO7
Orwell Cl FARN GU14
ROWN SO16
Orwell Crs FHAM/STUB PO14
Orwell Rd PSF GU32
Osborn Crs LSOL/BMARY PO13
Osborne Cl ALTN GU34
BSTK RG21
WVILLE PO7
Osborne Dr CHFD SO53
FLET GU13
Osborne Gdns ELGH SO50
Osborne Rd AND SP10
FARN GU14
GPORT PO12
HLER SO31
LSOL/BMARY PO13
MOOR/WNTN BH9
NMIL/BTOS BH25
PSF GU32
PSTN BH14
SSEA PO5
TOTT SO40
WIMB BH21
Osborne Rd North PTSW SO17
Osborne Rd South PTSW SO17
Osborne View Rd
FHAM/STUB PO14
Osborn Rd FHAM/PORC PO16
FNM GU9
Osborn Rd South
FHAM/PORC PO16
Osborn Wy HTWY RG27
Osier Cl NEND PO2
Oslands Dr HLER SO31
Osler Cl TADY RG26
Osnaburgh Hl CBLY GU15
Osprey Cl CHCH/BSGR BH23
KEMP RG22
ROWN SO16
TOTT SO40
Osprey Dr HISD PO11
Osprey Gdns
LSOL/BMARY PO13
Osprey Quay EMRTH PO10
Osprey Rd KEMP RG22
Ossemsley South Dr
NMIL/BTOS BH25
Osterley Cl HEND SO30
Osterly Rd ITCH SO19
Oswald Cl MOOR/WNTN BH9
Oswald Rd MOOR/WNTN BH9
Othello Dr WVILLE PO7
Otterbourne Crs HAV PO9
TADY RG26
Otterbourne Hl CHFD SO53
Otterbourne Rd RWIN SO21
Otter Cl CWTH RG45
ELGH SO50
UPTN BH16
VWD BH31
Otter Rd PLE BH15
Otters Wk NMIL/BTOS BH25
Ouse Cl CHFD SO53
Ouse Ct AND SP10
Outer Cir ROWN SO16
Outlands La HEND SO30
Outram Rd SSEA PO5
Oval Gdns GPORT PO12
Oval Rd ROMY SO51
The Oval LISS GU33
Overbridge Sq NWBY RG14
Overbrook FAWY SO45
Overbrook Wy NBAD SO52
Overbury Rd PSTN BH14
Overcliff Ri ROWN SO16
Overcombe Cl CFDH BH17
Overdale Ri FRIM GU16
Overdale Wk BOR GU35
Over Links Dr PSTN BH14
Overlord Cl CBLY GU15
Overstand Crs LYMN SO41
Overton Cl ALDT GU11
Overton Crs HAV PO9
Overton Rd RWIN SO21
Oviat Cl TOTT SO40
Ovington Av LTDN BH7
Ovington Gdns LTDN BH7
Owen Cl LSOL/BMARY PO13
Owen Rd ELGH SO50
NWBY RG14
Owen's Rd WINW SO22
Owen St ENEY PO4
Owlsmoor Rd SHST GU47
Owls Rd BOSC BH5
VWD BH31
Owslebury Bottom
RWIN SO21
Owslebury Gv HAV PO9
Oxburgh Cl ELGH SO50
Ox Dro RAND SP11

) SP11 119 M6
/ SO21 190 E4
ve Ri RAND SP11 120 A5
ve Wy NALR SO24 172 C6
/ RG25 173 J2
/ SO21 192 D6
en Ct RFNM GU10 113 H8 2
en Rd RFNM GU10 113 H8
Av SBNE BH6 449 G3
/I SO14 13 H1
Cl FHAM/PORC PO16 14 F3
La BPWT SO32 324 E1
BH11 431 M2
Rd BMTH BH1 23 J4
/ GU14 90 F7
?T PO12 18 A1
Y RG14 2 D1
/ SO21 168 B5
/I SO14 343 L1
GU47 50 B6
PO5 21 L6
St NWBY RG14 2 D2
/I SO14 13 H6
e Cl ROMY SO51 262 F7
e La OVTN RG25 152 D1
Cl FHAM/STUB PO14 371 M8
Ct ENEY PO4 423 M3 3
Cl KEMP RG22 126 F1
Ms PSEA PO1 20 C5 3
Quay CHAM PO6 398 F2
St PSEA PO1 20 C5
d WEND SO18 319 M6

P

Cl SHAM SO14 13 K8
ham Rd BSTK RG21 104 E4
a DEAN RG23 103 C5
? RG22 103 M6
dge La ROMY SO51 291 L7
ay FNM GU9 159 H1
y Cl NEND PO2 399 K4 7
gton Gv BWD BH11 431 H5
gton Rd NEND PO2 399 K7
:k Cl CBLY GU15 71 K2
) BH24 381 K4
SO21 190 D4 2
3 BH21 405 L2
:k Ct HTWY RG27 87 H3 4
:k End WVILLE PO7 351 K5
:k Fld STOK SO20 166 A3
:kfields CHAM RG24 106 A1
:k Gdns LYMN SO41 440 B3
:k Gv VWD BH31 356 E3
:k Rd KEMP RG22 104 C5
/ RG14 2 D8
ddocks FAWY SO45 392 F5 7
ddock BROC SO42 387 K7 2
RG45 49 K2
SO50 294 A2 1
SP6 335 J2
/STUB PO14 396 A4 1
T PO12 18 C5
GU26 203 K4 1
GU27 204 D8
RG27 87 J1
RG20 59 H6
U35 202 B3
/ RG14 3 K5
SO40 316 B6
SO23 215 H2
k Wy HASM GU27 205 K6
U30 226 E3
SO24 218 B4
U32 275 J6
d Cl SBNE BH6 449 K2
Rd RGWD BH24 359 G7 3
Av HORN PO8 352 E6
E PO7 325 L8
Rd HORN PO8 352 F5
w Pl FBDG SP6 309 K8
l Rd SHAM SO14 343 L1
k Av CHAM PO6 375 L8
k Cl BSTK RG21 104 F4
rth La THLE RG7 30 B5
rth Rd THLE RG7 31 H8
l Cl LSOL/BMARY PO13 421 G1
FAWY SO45 392 B6
a BROC SO42 416 A2
l CBLY GU15 71 L1
BH21 404 E1
d BWD BH11 431 L4
T PO12 18 C8
t SHAM SO14 13 K5
n Cl EMRTH PO10 378 E8
n Gdns HISD PO11 426 D6
a ALTN GU34 196 D4
Hl THLE RG7 41 K4
n Av HSEA PO3 399 L8
n Rd ROWN SO16 317 L8
d SSEA PO5 21 J4
ick Cl CHAM PO6 375 G8
SO31 370 D2
s Pightle HTWY RG27 85 L7
Rd SBNE BH6 449 H3
Cl STOK SO20 210 E6
Ga ODIM RG29 108 C5
La BROC SO42 390 E7
HTWY RG27 88 A4
e Rd RAND SP11 161 J2
Rd NBNE BH10 432 B4
HAV PO9 16 B4
Gdns
/PORC PO16 373 H6
ant HAV PO9 16 F4
RWIN SO21 266 E8
HLER SO31 345 K8
Cl BSTK RG21 5 G2
Dr AND SP10 119 J8 2
Pl NMIL/BTOS BH25 437 L4
Rd PLE BH15 445 H3
s Cl ELGH SO50 295 J6 3
s La THLE RG7 31 K6
s Rd EMRTH PO10 378 D7
ston Av
/BSGR BH23 450 C2

FHAM/PORC PO16 15 K5
Palmerston Cl FARN GU14 90 A5 5
UPTN BH16 444 C1 1
Palmerston Dr
FHAM/STUB PO14 396 E1
Palmerston Rd BMTH BH1 448 D3
HISD PO11 425 L4
PSTN BH14 446 C4
SHAM SO14 13 G2
SSEA PO5 21 H8
UPTN BH16 444 B1
Palmerston St ROMY SO51 290 D1 4
ROMY SO51 290 E1 3
Palmerston Wy GPORT PO12 421 J6
Palm Hall Cl WINC SO23 11 L8
Palm Rd ROWN SO16 317 L5
Palmyra Rd GPORT PO12 421 L1
Pamber Heath Rd TADY RG26 42 A8
Pamber Rd THLE RG7 42 D7
Pamela Av CHAM PO6 374 D8
Pamplyn Cl LYMN SO41 440 A4
Pangbourne Av CHAM PO6 399 M1
Pangbourne Cl ITCH SO19 344 E4
Pankridge St RFNM GU10 133 J1
Pannall Rd GPORT PO12 421 L1
Pannells RFNM GU10 159 G3
Panorama Rd CCLF BH13 457 G4
Pan's Gdns CBLY GU15 71 J4
Pan St PSEA PO1 423 G2
Pansy Rd ROWN SO16 318 F4
Pantheon Rd CHFD SO53 293 L1
Pantile Dr HTWY RG27 86 B7
The Pantiles FBDG SP6 309 J7 2
Pantings La KSCL RG20 56 C2
Panton Cl EMRTH PO10 378 C5 2
Panwell Rd WEND SO18 344 E1
Papermakers OVTN RG25 124 A1
Paper Mill La ALTN GU34 176 F4
The Parade PSEA PO1 422 E2
TADY RG26 41 L7 2
Paradise La BPWT SO32 323 K2
EMRTH PO10 378 F4
FHAM/PORC PO16 373 J6
TOTT SO40 340 B2
Paradise St PSEA PO1 21 H1
Paradise Wy THLE RG7 28 F1
Parchment St WINC SO23 11 G7
The Parchment HAV PO9 16 E5
Pardoe Cl HEND SO30 346 A3
Pardown DEAN RG23 126 A1
Parfitts Cl FNM GU9 134 D6
Parham Dr ELGH SO50 293 L4
Parham Rd GPORT PO12 422 A2
NBNE BH10 432 A6
Parish Cl ASHV GU12 113 L7
FNM GU9 134 D2
Parish Rd FARN GU14 90 E8
PLE BH15 445 K5
Park Av CBLY GU15 70 F4
CHAM RG24 106 A3
LYMN SO41 440 B4
NBNE BH10 432 A2
NTHA RG18 27 G4
WINC SO23 11 H6
WVILLE PO7 376 A5
Park Cl BROC SO42 387 L6
CHCH/BSGR BH23 435 G5
DEAN RG23 102 F6
FAWY SO45 367 M4
GPORT PO12 421 K2
HASM GU27 205 J7
BOR GU35 179 H7
LYMN SO41 454 D3
RFNM GU10 157 K6
NMIL/BTOS BH25 438 A3
TOTT SO40 342 B7
WINC SO23 11 G2
Park Close Rd ALTN GU34 176 F3
Park Crs EMRTH PO10 378 B7
Park Dr VWD BH31 356 C1
Park Dro STOK SO20 162 D4
Park End NWBY RG14 2 F2
Parker Cl GPORT PO12 397 L7
Parker Gdns WVILLE PO7 376 A6
Parker Rd MOOR/WNTN BH9 447 L1
Park Farm Av FHAM PO15 372 A4
Park Farm Cl FHAM PO15 14 A1
Park Farm Rd WVILLE PO7 376 B4
Parkfields YTLY GU46 69 G3
Park Gdns BSTK RG21 105 J5
Park Gln FHAM PO15 371 G4
Park Gv CHAM PO6 399 K1
Park Hl FLET GU13 110 E4
Parkhill Cl BLKW GU17 70 A4
Park Hill Cl FAWY SO45 392 A5
Parkhill Rd BLKW GU17 70 A4
Park Homer Dr WIMB BH21 404 D2
Park Homer Rd WIMB BH21 404 D1 2
Park House Farm Wy HAV PO9 376 F3
Parkhouse Rd NTID SP9 138 C1
Parkhurst Flds RFNM GU10 181 J7
Park Lake Rd PLE BH15 445 K6
Parkland Cl VWD BH31 357 H4
Parkland Dr NMIL/BTOS BH25 437 K8
Parkland Gv FNM GU9 6 C6
Parklands HLER SO31 370 E4
WEND SO18 319 K7
Parklands Av HORN PO8 352 E3
Parklands Cl CHFD SO53 293 H1
GPORT PO12 421 M2
Park La ALTN GU34 156 B4
BPWT SO32 298 B7
BPWT SO32 299 G7
CBLY GU15 70 F3 3
CHAM RG24 106 A3
CHAM PO6 399 L1
ELGH SO50 266 A8
EMRTH PO10 354 F8
EWKG RG40 47 K5
FAWY SO45 391 M4
FBDG SP6 333 K2
FHAM/PORC PO16 15 H3
FHAM/STUB PO14 396 A5
HAV PO9 353 G8
HAV PO9 377 G5
HORN PO8 352 E6
LYMN SO41 442 F2
LYMN SO41 454 B4

MFD/CHID GU8 205 H1
NALR SO24 220 A5
NBNE BH10 432 D4
NTHA RG18 27 G3
RAND SP11 139 M4
RSAL SP5 206 F8
RWIN SO21 215 J2
RWIN SO21 266 F3
THLE RG7 43 M6
TOTT SO40 342 A6
WIMB BH21 404 A4
Park Pde HAV PO9 377 J4 3
Park Pl FLET GU13 110 E3
Park Rd ALDT GU11 7 H7
BMTH BH1 23 H3
BPWT SO32 296 F8
CBLY GU15 70 F5
CHFD SO53 265 H8
EMRTH PO10 379 H7
FARN GU14 91 H7
FBDG SP6 309 L6
FNM GU9 135 G4
WINW SO22 10 E2
GPORT PO12 18 F7
HASM GU27 228 F2
HISD PO11 425 G4
LYMN SO41 440 B4
LYMN SO41 454 D4
NMIL/BTOS BH25 437 K7
NMIL/BTOS BH25 438 A3
NTID SP9 114 E2
PLE BH15 445 L5
PSEA PO1 20 D2
PSF GU32 275 L5
SHST GU47 69 M1
WSHM SO15 343 G2
WVILLE PO7 351 K3
WVILLE PO7 376 A4
Park Rd North HAV PO9 16 D3
Park Rd South HAV PO9 16 E5
Park Rw FNM GU9 134 E5
Parkside CHCH/BSGR BH23 436 B7
FNM GU9 134 F2
HAV PO9 377 G6
RGWD BH24 382 D2
TOTT SO40 341 K3
Parkside Av ROWN SO16 317 J8
Parkside La NALR SO24 219 M6
Parkside Rd BSTK RG21 105 H5
NTHA RG18 27 G3
PSTN BH14 446 B4
Parkside Gdns WINW SO22 214 B6
Parkstone Av ENEY PO4 21 L9
PSTN BH14 446 C4
Parkstone Dr CBLY GU15 70 F4
Parkstone Hts PSTN BH14 445 L3
Parkstone Rd NALR SO24 220 C6
PLE BH15 445 K5
Park St CBLY GU15 70 F2
GPORT PO12 18 F2
BOR GU35 201 J5
NWBY RG14 2 E2
ROWN SO16 318 A8
SSEA PO5 20 F4
The Park BPWT SO32 298 F7
NMIL/BTOS BH25 452 B1
Park Vw HEND SO30 345 M1
HEND SO30 346 E1
Parkview Cl AND SP10 8 C1
Parkville Rd ROWN SO16 319 J4
Park Wk SHAM SO14 13 G2
Parkwater Rd RSAL SP5 259 H7
Park Wy FERN BH22 380 C6 5
HAV PO9 16 D4
Parkway CBLY GU15 70 F5
CWTH RG45 49 K3
FHAM PO15 371 K1
Park Wy NWBY RG14 2 E2
Parkway Dr CHAR BH8 433 J8
Parkway Gdns CHFD SO53 293 H1
The Parkway
LSOL/BMARY PO13 396 F6
ROWN SO16 318 F3
Parkwood Cl CHAM RG24 83 L4 2
Parkwood Rd BOSC BH5 448 F4
WIMB BH21 404 A4
Parley Cl FERN BH22 406 D7
Parley La CHCH/BSGR BH23 406 F8
Parley Rd MOOR/WNTN BH9 432 E6
Parliament Pl WINW SO22 238 B4
Parmiter Dr WIMB BH21 404 C4
Parmiter Rd WIMB BH21 404 C4
Parmiter Wy WIMB BH21 404 C4
Parnell La ROMY SO51 234 F6
Parnell Rd ELGH SO50 293 L6
Parr Rd CHAM PO6 375 H8 7
Parr St PSTN BH14 445 M4
Parry Cl CHAM PO6 374 C8
Parry Rd ITCH SO19 345 H4
Parsonage Barn La
RGWD BH24 358 E8
Parsonage Cl ALTN GU34 198 D5
EPSF GU31 276 A3
Parsonage Est EPSF GU31 277 K4
Parsonage Hl RSAL SP5 230 A1
Parsonage La BPWT SO32 322 A2
Parsonage Park Dr FBDG SP6 309 K6
Parsonage Rd BMTH BH1 23 G6
SHAM SO14 343 M2
Parsonage Wy FRIM GU16 71 H7
Parsons Cl FLET GU13 110 E3
HASM GU27 204 F8
HSEA PO3 399 K4
NWBY RG14 2 A5
WHIT RG2 47 K1
Parsons Fld SHST GU47 49 L8
Parsons Gn HASM GU27 204 F8
Parsons La GSHT GU26 203 M2
Part La THLE RG7 45 M5
Partridge Av YTLY GU46 68 E2
Partridge Cl
FHAM/PORC PO16 373 J8 2
FRIM GU16 71 H7
RFNM GU10 111 G8 2
RWIN SO21 167 J1
Partridge Down WINW SO22 238 A5
Partridge Dr PSTN BH14 446 A7
Partridge Gdns HORN PO8 352 B4

Partridge Gn ALTN GU34 176 E3
NMIL/BTOS BH25 437 M2
Partridge Hl RSAL SP5 287 M5
Partridge Rd BROC SO42 387 K8
FAWY SO45 367 K7
Partry Cl CHFD SO53 264 F8
Paschal Rd CBLY GU15 51 J8
Pascoe Cl PSTN BH14 445 M4
Passage La HLER SO31 369 M7
Passfield Av ELGH SO50 293 K6
Passfield Cl ELGH SO50 293 K6 1
Passfield Rd LIPH GU30 202 B8
Passford Hl LYMN SO41 440 B1
Passingham Wk HORN PO8 352 E4
The Pastures
FHAM/STUB PO14 371 G4 3
NALR SO24 242 B2
WINC SO23 191 G7
WVILLE PO7 351 J5 1
Pat Bear Cl WSHM SO15 317 H8
Patchins Rd UPTN BH16 444 A4
Patchway Dr
FHAM/STUB PO14 372 A8
Paternoster Rw WINC SO23 11 H8
Paterson Cl FRIM GU16 71 M5 3
KEMP RG22 127 H1
Paterson Rd LISS GU33 225 H6
Pathfields Cl HASM GU27 229 G1
The Pathfinders FARN GU14 89 M5 3
Patricia Cl HEND SO30 320 C6
Patricia Dr HEND SO30 346 B1
Patrick's Cl LISS GU33 248 F4
Patten Av YTLY GU46 68 F3
Pattinson Crs RAND SP11 141 M1
Paul Cl ALDT GU11 6 B5
Paulet Cl WEND SO18 319 M7
Paulet Lacave Av ROWN SO16 317 J2
Paulet Pl CHAM RG24 106 A2
WINW SO22 238 D3
Pauletts La TOTT SO40 316 A5
Paul's Fld HTWY RG27 48 B8
Paulsgrove Rd NEND PO2 399 K8
Pauls La LYMN SO41 413 H8
Paulson Cl CHFD SO53 265 H8
Pauncefoot Hl ROMY SO51 290 B3
Pauntley Rd CHCH/BSGR BH23 450 D3
Pavan Gdns NBNE BH10 432 A5
Pavilion Cl ELGH SO50 295 H8
Pavilion Rd ALDT GU11 6 A3
ALDT GU11 111 M2
HEND SO30 321 J8
The Pavilions End CBLY GU15 71 G5 1
Pavy Cl STHA RG19 27 J6
Pawley Cl RFNM GU10 136 C1
Pawmers Md FLET GU13 110 C5
Pax Hl RFNM GU10 156 E4
Paxton Cl HEND SO30 346 B3 4
KEMP RG22 127 G1 4
Paxton Rd FHAM/STUB PO14 14 F6
Payne Cl WIMB BH21 380 C3
Paynes Cl STHA RG19 39 H8
STOK SO20 209 G1
Paynesdown Rd STHA RG19 26 E5
Paynes Hay Rd ROMY SO51 235 G8
Paynes La STOK SO20 209 G1
Payne's Rd WSHM SO15 342 F2
Peabody Rd FARN GU14 91 G7
Peace Cl CHCH/BSGR BH23 409 L8
Peachey Dr STHA RG19 27 J6
Peach Gv RAND SP11 161 K3
Peach Rd ROWN SO16 317 M4
Peach Tree Cl FARN GU14 90 D1
Peacock Cl FHAM/PORC PO16 373 J8
Peacock La PSEA PO1 20 D5
Peacock Pl WINC SO23 11 M7
Peak Cl ROWN SO16 317 L8
Peak Dr FHAM/STUB PO14 14 A7
Peake New Rd BPWT SO32 271 L8
Peakfield RFNM GU10 180 F1
WVILLE PO7 351 J4 3
Peak La BPWT SO32 296 F3
FHAM/STUB PO14 14 A8
Peak Rd HORN PO8 327 M3
The Peak HAV PO9 354 A6
Pealsham Gdns FBDG SP6 309 K6 7
Pearce Av PSTN BH14 445 M7
Pearce Ct GPORT PO12 19 H2
Pear Cl BKME/WDN BH12 447 G4
Pearl Gdns NBNE BH10 432 A4
Pearl Rd NBNE BH10 432 A4
Pearman Dr AND SP10 119 J8
Pearson Av PSTN BH14 446 A3
Pearson Gdns NBNE BH10 432 B2
Peartree LYMN SO41 440 C6 3
Pear Tree Av FLET GU13 88 E6 2
Peartree Av ITCH SO19 344 C4
Pear Tree Cl BPWT SO32 321 L6 1
CHCH/BSGR BH23 409 L8
FBDG SP6 333 K2
Peartree Cl
FHAM/STUB PO14 396 B5 2
ITCH SO19 344 B4 1
Pear Tree Cl BOR GU35 201 L4
Peartree Ct LYMN SO41 440 C6 4
Pear Tree Dr RSAL SP5 287 J8
Pear Tree La RFNM GU10 158 C5
NWBY RG14 25 M3
Peartree Rd FAWY SO45 367 J6
ITCH SO19 344 B4
Pear Tree Rd BOR GU35 201 L3
Pease Cft EPSF GU31 305 G5
Peatmoor Cl FLET GU13 88 D6
Peat Moor Cl FLET GU13 88 D6 1
Pebble Cl HISD PO11 425 M6 1
Pebble Ct TOTT SO40 342 D6 1
Pebble Hl HUNG RG17 34 E1
Pebmarsh Rd CHAM PO6 375 H8 8
Peckham Av NMIL/BTOS BH25 437 L6
Pedam Cl ENEY PO4 423 L5 3
Peddlars Gv YTLY GU46 69 H2
Pedula Wy ELGH SO50 294 D3
Peel Av FRIM GU16 91 K1
Peel Cl BKME/WDN BH12 446 B3
ROMY SO51 263 H7
Peel Ct HTWY RG27 87 H2 2
Peel Gdns KSCL RG20 59 H5
Peel Pl SSEA PO5 21 G4
Peel Rd GPORT PO12 19 H2

Peel St SHAM SO14 13 L1
Peewit Hl HLER SO31 345 L5
Peewit Hill Cl HLER SO31 345 L5
Pegasus Av ASHV GU12 113 H5
LYMN SO41 438 E6
Pegasus Cl HASM GU27 228 A3
HLER SO31 369 K6 2
ROWN SO16 317 L4
STHA RG19 26 D4
Pegasus Rd FARN GU14 90 C1 1
FARN GU14 90 E6
Peggotty Pl SHST GU47 50 B6 3
Pelham Cl CHAM RG24 106 A3
CHCH/BSGR BH23 450 C2
BOR GU35 201 J7
Pelham Pl RFNM GU10 158 D4 1
Pelham Rd GPORT PO12 18 E2
SSEA PO5 21 H6
Pelham Ter EMRTH PO10 378 E8 5
Pelican Cl FHAM PO15 14 A3
Pelican Ct AND SP10 9 J3
Pelican La NWBY RG14 2 E2
Pelican Md RGWD BH24 383 G2
Pelican Rd FHAM/STUB PO14 396 D3
TADY RG26 42 B6
Pelton Rd BSTK RG21 4 B6
Pembers Cl ELGH SO50 295 J6
Pemberton Rd LYND SO43 363 L3
Pembrey Cl ROWN SO16 317 L3
Pembridge Rd FBDG SP6 309 M5
Pembroke Broadway
CBLY GU15 70 F3
Pembroke Cl ELGH SO50 293 L3
PSEA PO1 20 D6 1
ROMY SO51 290 E1 4
THLE RG7 31 M5
TOTT SO40 316 F8
Pembroke Crs
FHAM/STUB PO14 395 L6
Pembroke Rd
BKME/WDN BH12 446 C1
DEAN RG23 104 A3 1
WINW SO22 214 B3
ITCH SO19 344 F4
NWBY RG14 2 D3
PSEA PO1 20 E6
WBNE BH4 447 G6
Pembury Rd
FHAM/STUB PO14 396 B4
HAV PO9 17 H6
Pemerton Rd BSTK RG21 5 H4
WINW SO22 10 B1
Penarth Av CHAM PO6 375 M8
Pen Cl AND SP10 9 M6
Pendennis Cl DEAN RG23 104 A2
Pendennis Rd CHAM PO6 374 D8
Pendle Cl ROWN SO16 317 L8
Pendle Gn ROMY SO51 232 E7
Pendleton Gdns FAWY SO45 392 C7 3
Penelope Gdns HLER SO31 345 K6
Penfold Cft FNM GU9 135 J4
Penfords Paddock
BPWT SO32 323 J1 3
Pengelly Av NBNE BH10 432 C3
Pengilly Rd FNM GU9 134 E6
Penhale Gdns
FHAM/STUB PO14 370 F7
Penhale Rd PSEA PO1 21 M1
Penhale Wy TOTT SO40 341 J3
Penhurst Rd HAV PO9 376 F6
Peninsula Rd WINW SO22 10 D9
Penistone Cl ITCH SO19 344 F7
Penjar Av WVILLE PO7 376 A4
Penk Rdg CHAM PO6 376 D8
Pennant Hills HAV PO9 376 F6
Pennant Wy CHCH/BSGR BH23 450 E1
Pennard Wy CHFD SO53 292 F4
Penn Cl NMIL/BTOS BH25 437 J7
Pennefather's Rd ALDT GU11 112 C5
Pennels Cl LIPH GU30 250 E6
Pennerly Ct HAV PO9 377 H1
Penner Rd HAV PO9 16 C8
Penn Hill Av PSTN BH14 446 C5
Pennine Gdns FAWY SO45 367 H6
Pennine Rd ROWN SO16 342 D1
Pennine Wy CHFD SO53 293 J4
FARN GU14 90 A1
KEMP RG22 104 A5
LSOL/BMARY PO13 420 E4
VWD BH31 356 D2 3
Pennington Cl ELGH SO50 266 E8
FERN BH22 380 B7
LYMN SO41 440 A6 2
Pennington Crs FERN BH22 380 B6
Pennington Ov LYMN SO41 439 M6
Pennington Rd FERN BH22 380 B7
Pennington Wy FHAM PO15 14 B1
Penn Rd NWBY RG14 25 G3
Penns Pl EPSF GU31 276 C5
Penns Rd PSF GU32 275 K4
Penns Wd FARN GU14 91 G7
Penns Yd FNM GU9 134 E6 3
Penn Wy GPORT PO12 421 J5
Pennycress HLER SO31 370 C6
Penny Hedge
NMIL/BTOS BH25 437 M8
Penny La EMRTH PO10 378 F8
STOK SO20 186 F7
Penny Pl WVILLE PO7 376 C5 4
Penny's Cl FBDG SP6 309 L5
Penny's Crs FBDG SP6 309 L5
Penny's Hatch KSCL RG20 59 K6
Pennys La FBDG SP6 309 L6
RSAL SP5 230 B1
Penny St PSEA PO1 20 C6
Pennywell Gdns
NMIL/BTOS BH25 438 B4
Penrhyn Cl ASHV GU12 7 G4
ELGH SO50 293 L3
Penrith Cl VWD BH31 356 C3
Penrith Rd BOSC BH5 448 F4
BSTK RG21 4 C9
Penrose Cl NEND PO2 399 H6 3
NWBY RG14 25 J3
Penrose Rd FERN BH22 406 B2
Penryn Dr BOR GU35 202 F3 1
Pensford Cl CWTH RG45 49 L1
Penshurst Ri FRIM GU16 71 J8

Penshurst Wy ELGH SO50 293 M2
The Pentagon FAWY SO45 392 E6
Pentere Rd HORN PO8 352 E2
Pentire Av WSHM SO15 318 C6
Pentire Wy WSHM SO15 318 C6
Pentland Cl FAWY SO45 367 H6 4
KEMP RG22 104 A5
Pentland Ri FHAM/PORC PO16 374 B7
Penton Ct HAV PO9 377 M2
Penton La RAND SP11 117 L2
Penton Rd RWIN SO21 266 F1 2
Pentons Hl FBDG SP6 335 H2
Pentridge Wy TOTT SO40 341 H3
Penwith Dr HASM GU27 228 A4
Penwood Hts KSCL RG20 36 D8
Penwood Rd KSCL RG20 36 F5
Peperham Rd HASM GU27 204 F8
Peper Harow HORN PO8 352 F2
Peppard Cl WEND SO18 344 E1
Peppercorn Wy HEND SO30 321 G5
Pepys Av ITCH SO19 345 H3
Pepys Cl ENEY PO4 423 K5
GPORT PO12 421 M7
Percival Rd NEND PO2 399 K8
Percy Chandler St PSEA PO1 423 H2 5
Percy Cl FAWY SO45 367 K3
Percy Rd BOSC BH5 448 D5
ENEY PO4 21 L4
GPORT PO12 19 G3
ROWN SO16 317 M8
Peregrine Cl TOTT SO40 341 G2 6
Peregrine Rd
CHCH/BSGR BH23 450 F2
The Peregrines
FHAM/PORC PO16 373 K8
Pergin Crs CFDH BH17 445 G1
Pergin Wy CFDH BH17 445 G1
Perham Crs RAND SP11 92 F6
Perins Cl NALR SO24 218 A4
Periwinkle Cl BOR GU35 201 M3 6
Pern Dr HEND SO30 346 E1
Peronne Cl HSEA PO3 399 K3
Peronne Rd HSEA PO3 399 K3
Perowne St ALDT GU11 6 C2
Perran Rd ROWN SO16 317 J7
Perring Av FARN GU14 70 B8
Perring Rd FARN GU14 90 D6
Perry Dr FLET GU13 88 C7
Perry Gdns PLE BH15 445 H7
Perryhill Dr SHST GU47 49 J7
Perryvale Rd NBAD SO52 292 E3
Perry Wy FNM GU9 134 E1
BOR GU35 202 C4
Perrywood Cl FAWY SO45 392 A5
Perrywood Gdns TOTT SO40 316 A8 3
Perseus Pl WVILLE PO7 376 D5
Pershore Cl HLER SO31 370 E5
Pershore Rd CHAM RG24 83 G7
Persian Dr HLER SO31 370 F1
Persley Rd NBNE BH10 432 B4
Perth Cl CHCH/BSGR BH23 434 C7
RAND SP11 115 J1
Perth Rd ENEY PO4 423 M4
LSOL/BMARY PO13 397 H5
Pervin Rd CHAM PO6 399 K1
Peststead La BPWT SO32 325 H4
Peter Ashley Rd CHAM PO6 376 B7
Peterborough Rd CHAM PO6 375 J7
Peter Grant Wy FERN BH22 406 A3
Peterhouse Cl SHST GU47 50 C6
Peters Cl HLER SO31 370 C5
UPTN BH16 444 B2
Peterscroft Av TOTT SO40 340 E7
Petersfield Cl CHAM RG24 84 A4 1
Petersfield La HORN PO8 328 A2
Petersfield Rd EPSF GU31 303 J3
HAV PO9 16 F1
BOR GU35 201 H7 2
LISS GU33 225 G3
LTDN BH7 448 F2
NALR SO24 219 L4
NALR SO24 242 C4
RWIN SO21 239 M2
WINC SO23 11 L9
Petersham Cl WVILLE PO7 352 B7 4
Petersham Rd CFDH BH17 429 K8
Peters Rd HLER SO31 370 C5
Petit Rd MOOR/WNTN BH9 432 E5
Petrel Cft KEMP RG22 103 M8 5
Petrel Wk LSOL/BMARY PO13 396 F6
Petrie Rd LSOL/BMARY PO13 420 D2
Petticoat La RSAL SP5 285 K1
Pettinger Gdns PTSW SO17 319 J8 1
Petty Cl ROMY SO51 290 F2 1
Pettycot Crs
LSOL/BMARY PO13 396 F5
Petty's Brook Rd CHAM RG24 83 L4
Petunia Cl KEMP RG22 103 M8
Petworth Cl FRIM GU16 71 J8 2
KEMP RG22 127 G2 1
Petworth Gdns ELGH SO50 293 M3 5
ROWN SO16 318 A3
Petworth Rd HASM GU27 229 G3
HSEA PO3 423 M2
Petwyn Cl FERN BH22 406 E2
Pevensey Cl ROWN SO16 317 J7
Pevensey Wy FRIM GU16 71 K8
Peverell Rd UPTN BH16 444 A4 1
Peverells Rd CHFD SO53 293 K2
Peverells Wood Av CHFD SO53 293 K1
Peverells Wood Cl CHFD SO53 293 L1
Peveril Cl RGWD BH24 381 K2
Peveril Rd ITCH SO19 344 C4
Pewsey Pl WSHM SO15 318 C6
Pheaben's Fld TADY RG26 63 K5 1
Pheasant Cl KEMP RG22 103 L8
NTID SP9 114 F2 2
RWIN SO21 167 J1
Pheasant Copse FLET GU13 88 C6
Pheby Rd KEMP RG22 104 C6
Phelipps Rd WIMB BH21 429 H1
Pheonix Wy
LSOL/BMARY PO13 397 G7
Philip Rd WVILLE PO7 376 D3
Philips Crs BOR GU35 202 C3
Phillimore Rd ROWN SO16 319 J4
Phillips Cl BOR GU35 202 C3
RFNM GU10 113 H8
ROWN SO16 317 K2
Philpott Dr TOTT SO40 342 D7
Phoenix Cl HLER SO31 345 L7 4
Phoenix Ct HTWY RG27 87 G4
KSCL RG20 59 J6
Phoenix Park Ter BSTK RG21 4 E6
Phoenix Sq NEND PO2 399 J4
Phoenix Ter HTWY RG27 87 G4
Phyldon Cl BKME/WDN BH12 446 A3
Phyldon Rd BKME/WDN BH12 446 A2
Pickard Rd FERN BH22 406 D1
Pickaxe La ODIM RG29 130 E8
Pickering Cl BDST BH18 429 L6
Picket Cl FBDG SP6 309 L6
Picketts Hl BOR GU35 179 M7
Picket Twenty RAND SP11 119 K8
Pickford Rd MOOR/WNTN BH9 432 C7
Pickford St ALDT GU11 7 G2
Pickwick Cl TOTT SO40 340 F1
Picton Cl CBLY GU15 71 M1
Picton Rd AND SP10 142 E3
Pier Head Rd NEND PO2 398 F8
Pierrefondes Av FARN GU14 90 D3
Pier Rd PSEA PO1 20 E7
SSEA PO5 20 E7
Pier St LSOL/BMARY PO13 420 C2
Pigeon Cl TADY RG26 63 M6
Pigeonhouse Fld RWIN SO21 168 B4 1
Pigeon House La WVILLE PO7 375 H5
Pigeons Farm Rd STHA RG19 38 A1
Pig Shoot La CHCH/BSGR BH23 433 K4
Pike Cl ALDT GU11 7 K1
Pikes Hl LYND SO43 363 J1
Pike St NWBY RG14 3 H1
Pilands Wood Rd HLER SO31 345 K8 2
Pilchards Av ELGH SO50 295 G5
Pilcot Rd HTWY RG27 110 A2
Pilford Heath Rd WIMB BH21 404 E1
Pilgrim Cl NMIL/BTOS BH25 438 A4 4
Pilgrim Pk RGWD BH24 359 G8 2
Pilgrim Pl WEND SO18 319 K4 2
Pilgrims Cl FNM GU9 134 D8
NBAD SO52 292 E3
Pilgrims Ga WINW SO22 10 C5
Pilgrims Vw ASHV GU12 113 M8
Pilgrims Wy AND SP10 9 L2
FHAM/STUB PO14 395 M7
BOR GU35 202 B3 1
Pilley Bailey LYMN SO41 414 E6
Pilley Hl LYMN SO41 414 C7
Pilley St LYMN SO41 414 E6
Pill Hl RSAL SP5 258 F4
Pilning Cl FHAM/STUB PO14 372 A8 2
Pilot Hight Rd BWD BH11 431 L5
Pilsdon Dr CFDH BH17 430 C6
Pimpern Cl CFDH BH17 430 C6
Pimpernel Cl HLER SO31 370 C6
Pimpernel Pl NTHA RG18 27 J4 1
Pimpernel Wy CHAM RG24 105 L1
Pinchcut THLE RG7 31 K5
Pinchington La NWBY RG14 37 K1 1
Pindar Pl NWBY RG14 26 B3 2
Pine Av BKME/WDN BH12 446 E1
CBLY GU15 71 G4
SBNE BH6 449 H4
Pine Bank GSHT GU26 204 B4
Pinecliffe Av SBNE BH6 449 H4
Pinecliffe Rd NMIL/BTOS BH25 452 B1
Pinecliff Rd CCLF BH13 446 F8
Pine Cl ASHV GU12 113 K2
CBLY GU15 70 B1
FAWY SO45 367 K6
FERN BH22 406 A1
WINW SO22 238 A5
NBAD SO52 291 L3 2
NMIL/BTOS BH25 437 J8
RSAL SP5 287 J6
RWIN SO21 190 D4
STOK SO20 163 G4
TOTT SO40 341 G5
Pine Crs CHCH/BSGR BH23 436 C8
CHFD SO53 265 H8
Pine Dr BLKW GU17 70 B5
CCLF BH13 446 E5
EWKG RG40 48 D1
RGWD BH24 381 K4
THLE RG7 43 J2
WEND SO18 345 H1
Pine Dr East WEND SO18 345 J1
Pinefield Rd WEND SO18 319 L6
Pinefields Cl CWTH RG45 49 L3 2
Pine Gv FLET GU13 111 G3
HAV PO9 17 H5
RFNM GU10 159 H2
Pinegrove Rd ITCH SO19 344 D5
Pinehill Ri SHST GU47 49 L8
Pinehill Rd CWTH RG45 49 L4
BOR GU35 201 K6
Pineholt Cl RGWD BH24 381 L3
Pinehurst TADY RG26 61 L1
Pinehurst Av
CHCH/BSGR BH23 450 E3
FARN GU14 90 E6
Pinehurst Cl HORN PO8 353 G6
Pinehurst Rd FERN BH22 380 D7
ROWN SO16 318 E1 2
Pinelands Rd ROWN SO16 292 E8
Pine Manor Rd RGWD BH24 381 H3
Pine Mount Rd CBLY GU15 71 G4
Pine Rdg NWBY RG14 25 M3
Pine Ridge Dr RFNM GU10 158 E3
Pine Ridge Rd THLE RG7 31 K6
Pine Rd ALTN GU34 197 H5
BPWT SO32 297 J8
CHFD SO53 265 H7
FBDG SP6 333 K3
MOOR/WNTN BH9 432 D7
ROMY SO51 291 H2
Pinesprings Dr BDST BH18 429 J6
Pines Rd FLET GU13 88 E6
LIPH GU30 226 B4
The Pines AND SP10 8 E4
CBLY GU15 71 J1
FBDG SP6 310 D6
FHAM/PORC PO16 373 L7
Pinetops Cl LYMN SO41 439 L5
Pine Tree Cl WIMB BH21 404 B3
Pine Tree Gdns HORN PO8 352 E6
Pine Tree Gln WBNE BH4 447 H5
Pine Trees Cl FHAM/STUB PO14 14 B7
Pinetree Wk CFDH BH17 429 K8
Pine Vale Crs NBNE BH10 432 D5
Pine Vw BOR GU35 202 E2
Pine View Cl FNM GU9 135 K3
HASM GU27 204 F8
Pineview Cl HLER SO31 345 L7
RSAL SP5 285 J4
Pine View Cl UPTN BH16 444 B2
Pine View Rd VWD BH31 356 B1
Pine Wk HLER SO31 370 E3
LISS GU33 248 F2
ROWN SO16 318 E1
VWD BH31 356 F3
Pine Wy ROWN SO16 318 E1
Pinewood LSOL/BMARY PO13 397 J7
Pinewood Av CWTH RG45 49 M2
HAV PO9 376 F5
NBNE BH10 432 B3
Pinewood Cl CHCH/BSGR BH23 436 E7
FHAM/STUB PO14 396 B4 2
ROMY SO51 263 H7
SHST GU47 49 J8
TADY RG26 41 G7
Pinewood Crs FARN GU14 89 M3 3
FAWY SO45 367 M6 1
Pinewood Dr FAWY SO45 367 M6
KSCL RG20 37 K6
Pinewood Gdns BAGS GU19 51 M5
FERN BH22 406 B1
Pinewood Hl FLET GU13 88 F6
Pinewood Pk FARN GU14 89 M1
ITCH SO19 345 K3
Pinewood Rd CCLF BH13 447 G7
CHCH/BSGR BH23 436 D7
FERN BH22 406 A1
LYMN SO41 438 D5
RGWD BH24 381 K4
Pinkerton Rd KEMP RG22 104 B6
Pinkney La LYND SO43 363 J6
Pink Rd NEND PO2 399 J8 1
Pinks Hl FHAM/PORC PO16 373 H6
Pinks La TADY RG26 41 H7
Pinnell Cl KEMP RG22 126 F2
Pinsley Dr WHAM PO17 374 E2
Pintail Cl KEMP RG22 126 E1 2
Pinto Cl FHAM PO15 370 F1
Pipers Ash RGWD BH24 359 G8 3
Pipers Cl TOTT SO40 341 H2
Pipers Cft FLET GU13 110 F4 1
Pipers Dr CHCH/BSGR BH23 450 F1
Pipers La STHA RG19 27 J7
Pipers Md HORN PO8 327 M3
Pipers Patch FARN GU14 90 E4 2
Pipers Wy STHA RG19 27 K6
Piping Cl RWIN SO21 266 E8
Piping Rd RWIN SO21 266 E8
Pipit Cl GPORT PO12 421 M1
STHA RG19 26 E5
Pippin Cl CHCH/BSGR BH23 434 C6
LYMN SO41 440 C6
Pipsons Cl YTLY GU46 69 G2
Pirbright Rd FARN GU14 90 F5
Pirelli St SHAM SO14 12 E3
WSHM SO15 12 E3
Pirrie Cl WSHM SO15 318 C7
Pitcairn Cl CHAM RG24 83 H6
Pitcairn Ms ENEY PO4 423 M6 2
Pitchponds Rd HLER SO31 370 A8
Pitcot La RWIN SO21 268 A5
Pitcroft La EPSF GU31 303 L3
Pitcroft Rd NEND PO2 399 H7
Pitfield La THLE RG7 43 M4
Pitfold Av HASM GU27 228 A2
Pitfold Cl HASM GU27 228 B2 1
Pither Rd ODIM RG29 108 B8
Pithouse La CHCH/BSGR BH23 408 B8
Pitman Cl KEMP RG22 104 A6
Pitmore Cl ELGH SO50 266 A8
Pitmore La LYMN SO41 413 H6
Pitmore Rd ELGH SO50 266 A8
Pitreavie Rd CHAM PO6 399 L2
Pittard Rd BSTK RG21 104 E5
Pitter Cl WINW SO22 214 A3
Pitt Hill La WVILLE PO7 326 D7
Pitt La RFNM GU10 180 D2
Pittmore Rd CHCH/BSGR BH23 435 G6
Pitton Rd RSAL SP5 206 A8
Pitt Rd WSHM SO15 343 G2
Pitts Deep La LYMN SO41 442 A3
Pitts La AND SP10 9 G8
Pitts Pl NMIL/BTOS BH25 438 B6
Pitt Wy FARN GU14 90 C3
Pit Wk AMSY SP4 160 C1
Pitwines Cl PLE BH15 445 J6
Pitymoor La WHAM PO17 374 F4
Place Crs WVILLE PO7 376 D3
Place House Cl FHAM PO15 372 A7
Place La RWIN SO21 238 C8
Plaitford Gv HAV PO9 377 G4
Plantaganet Crs BWD BH11 431 H3
Plantation Dr
CHCH/BSGR BH23 436 E6
TOTT SO40 342 C7
Plantation Rd AND SP10 8 C6
CFDH BH17 430 A7
CHCH/BSGR BH23 407 M4
LISS GU33 249 G6
NTID SP9 114 E3
ROMY SO51 288 C8
TADY RG26 41 H6
The Plantation BPWT SO32 322 D6
RSAL SP5 206 D3
Plantation Wy BOR GU35 200 F8
Plant Park Rd RGWD BH24 382 A5
Plants Cl ROMY SO51 289 G6
Plassey Crs BWD BH11 431 M3
Plassey Rd NTID SP9 114 D1
Platform Rd SHAM SO14 13 G7
Platoff Rd LYMN SO41 440 C8
Player Ct FBDG SP6 309 L5
Players Crs TOTT SO40 341 J3
Playfair Rd SSEA PO5 21 J4
Playfields Dr
BKME/WDN BH12 446 D2
Pleasance Wy
NMIL/BTOS BH25 437 K5
Pleasant Hl TADY RG26 41 L8
Pleasant La EMRTH PO10 403 H7
Pleasant Rd ENEY PO4 423 M4
Plecy Cl FERN BH22 406 B5
Plemont Cl BKME/WDN BH12 431 J7
Pless Rd LYMN SO41 453 M3
Plough Gdns STOK SO20 209 G2
Plough La BPWT SO32 325 H6
HTWY RG27 66 E5
Plough Rd YTLY GU46 69 H1
Plough Wy WINW SO22 238 C4
Plover Cl AND SP10 119 G6 1
FHAM/STUB PO14 395 M6
KEMP RG22 103 M7
ROWN SO16 318 A3
Plover Dr LYMN SO41 454 E4
Plover Reach ENEY PO4 423 M3 1
Plover Rd TOTT SO40 341 G1
Plovers Down WINW SO22 238 A5
Plovers Rd HORN PO8 352 E2 2
Plovers Wy ALTN GU34 176 F2
P.L.P.H. Rd FAWY SO45 392 F3
Plumer Rd CFDH BH17 429 L7
LISS GU33 225 H5
Plumpton Gdns HSEA PO3 399 M5 2
Plumpton Gv WVILLE PO7 352 F7
Plumpton Rd NWBY RG14 3 J8
Plumpton Wy ALTN GU34 176 E6 3
Plymouth Dr
FHAM/STUB PO14 395 M6
Plymouth St SSEA PO5 21 H3 1
Poachers Fld ODIM RG29 130 F5
Pococks La LISS GU33 247 L1
Poets Wy WINW SO22 10 B6
Poffley Pl STHA RG19 27 K5 3
Pointout Cl ROWN SO16 318 D5
Pointout Rd ROWN SO16 318 D5
Poland La ODIM RG29 108 D2
Polden Cl FARN GU14 90 B1
Polesden Cl CHFD SO53 265 G8 4
Poles La LYMN SO41 440 C7
RWIN SO21 265 G2
Police Station La BPWT SO32 299 G7
Polkerris Wy FLET GU13 111 G4 1
Pollard Gv CBLY GU15 71 M4 1
Pollards Moor Rd TOTT SO40 314 F7
Polmear Cl FLET GU13 111 G4
The Polygon WSHM SO15 12 E1
Pomona Cl FERN BH22 406 B2
Pompeys La FERN BH22 405 L4
Pond Cl NMIL/BTOS BH25 437 L5
NWBY RG14 37 G1
OVTN RG25 123 M2
TOTT SO40 342 D6
Pond Cft YTLY GU46 69 H2
Pondhead Cl FAWY SO45 392 A5 1
Pond La HORN PO8 328 A2
RFNM GU10 180 F4 1
Pond Piece WVILLE PO7 351 K5
Pond Rd FARN GU14 90 E6
HLER SO31 370 D2
BOR GU35 202 D4
TADY RG26 63 M6
Pondside La BPWT SO32 297 H7
Pondtail Cl FLET GU13 89 H8
Pondtail Gdns FLET GU13 89 H8
Pondtail Rd FLET GU13 89 H8
Pondview Cl FLET GU13 89 H6
Ponsonby Rd PSTN BH14 446 C4
Pony Dr UPTN BH16 444 C1
Pook La HAV PO9 17 J6
WHAM PO17 372 F4
Pookles La ALTN GU34 178 A7
Pooksgreen TOTT SO40 342 B6
Poole Hl WCLF BH2 22 B6
Poole La BWD BH11 431 K4
Poole Rd CCLF BH13 446 E4
ITCH SO19 344 C4
UPTN BH16 444 B1
WBNE BH4 447 G5
WCLF BH2 22 B6
WIMB BH21 404 A4
Pool Rd ALDT GU11 7 K8
HTWY RG27 87 H1
Poors Farm Rd CHAM RG24 84 D8
Popes Hl KSCL RG20 59 H6
Popes La BPWT SO32 296 B4
TOTT SO40 341 K1
Popes Md HASM GU27 228 F1
Popes Rd PLE BH15 445 J2
Popham Ct HAV PO9 377 G2
Popham La OVTN RG25 125 K8
Poplar Cl CHCH/BSGR BH23 410 A8
CHCH/BSGR BH23 436 F8
FRIM GU16 91 K5
HTWY RG27 64 C7
TADY RG26 41 G8
WIMB BH21 404 B3
Poplar Crs RGWD BH24 382 F1
Poplar Dr FHAM/STUB PO14 14 C8
TOTT SO40 342 B7
Poplar Gv HISD PO11 425 L4
Poplar La CHCH/BSGR BH23 410 A7
Poplar Pl NWBY RG14 25 K3
Poplar Rd ITCH SO19 344 D2
NMIL/BTOS BH25 438 B4
Poplars Cl FARN GU14 89 M3
The Poplars BPWT SO32 323 J5
Poplar Wk FNM GU9 135 G1
Poplar Wy HEND SO30 346 B1 2
NBAD SO52 291 L3
RGWD BH24 382 F1
Popley Wy CHAM RG24 4 B1
Poppy Cl CHCH/BSGR BH23 435 M8
HLER SO31 370 D6
Poppy Dr NTHA RG18 27 J4
Poppy Flds CHAM RG24 83 M8
Poppyfields NBAD SO52 292 F2 1
Poppyhills Rd CBLY GU15 51 J8
Poppy Rd ROWN SO16 319 H3
Porchester Cl AND SP10 118 C5
Porchester Rd ITCH SO19 344 C5
NWBY RG14 2 E8
Porlock Cl STHA RG19 27 G6 3
Porlock Rd ROWN SO16 317 H7
Portacre Ri BSTK RG21 104 E5
Portal Cl RAND SP11 142 A1
Portal Rd ELGH SO50 294 C5
ITCH SO19
LSOL/BMARY PO13
TOTT SO40
WINC SO23
Portarlington Cl WBNE BH4
Portarlington Rd WBNE BH4
Portchester Ct BMTH BH1
Portchester La WHAM PO17
Portchester Pl BMTH BH1
Portchester Ri ELGH SO50
Portchester Rd CHAR BH8
FHAM/PORC PO16
NEND PO2
Portelet Cl BKME/WDN BH12
Portelet Pl HEND SO30
Porteous Crs CHFD SO53
Porter Cl ODIM RG29
Porter End NWBY RG14
Porter Rd CFDH BH17
KEMP RG22
Portersbridge St ROMY SO51
Porters Cl AND SP10
OVTN RG25
Porter's La SHAM SO14
WIMB BH21
Portesberry Rd CBLY GU15
Portesbery Hill Dr CBLY GU15
Portesham Gdns
MOOR/WNTN BH9
Portesham Wy CFDH BH17
Portfield Cl CHCH/BSGR BH23
Portfield Rd CHCH/BSGR BH23
Portiswood Cl TADY RG26
Portland Dr FLET GU13
GPORT PO12
Portland Gv AND SP10
Portland Rd MOOR/WNTN BH9
SSEA PO5
WVILLE PO7
Portland's Cl PSF GU32
Portland Sq LISS GU33
Portland St FHAM/PORC PO16
PSEA PO1
SHAM SO14
Portland Ter SHAM SO14
Port La RWIN SO21
Portman Crs SBNE BH6
Portman Rd LTDN BH7
Portmore Cl BDST BH18
Portobello Gv
FHAM/PORC PO16
Port Royal St SSEA PO5
Portsdown Av CHAM PO6
Portsdown Hill Rd CHAM PO6
WHAM PO17
Portsdown Rd CHAM PO6
Portsmouth Rd BPWT SO32
CBLY GU15
CHAM PO6
ELGH SO50
FRIM GU16
HLER SO31
HORN PO8
ITCH SO19
LIPH GU30
LIPH GU30
LSOL/BMARY PO13
RWIN SO21
Portsview Av
FHAM/PORC PO16
Portsview Gdns
FHAM/PORC PO16
Portswood Av PTSW SO17
Portswood Pk PTSW SO17
Portswood Rd HAV PO9
NEND PO2
PTSW SO17
Portview Rd WEND SO18
Port Wy CHAM PO6
Portway TADY RG26
THLE RG7
Portway Cl AND SP10
WEND SO18
Portway Pl DEAN RG23
Posbrooke Rd ENEY PO4
Posbrook La
FHAM/STUB PO14
Postern Cl FHAM/PORC PO16
Post Green Rd UPTN BH16
Post Horn La HTWY RG27
Posting House Ms NWBY RG14
Post Office La OVTN RG25
RGWD BH24
TLHT RG30
Post Office Rd HUNG RG17
WCLF BH2
WVILLE PO7
Potbridge Rd ODIM RG29
Pot La CHAM RG24
Potley Hill Rd YTLY GU46
Potteries La FRIM GU16
The Potteries FARN GU14
FHAM/PORC PO16
Potterne Wy WIMB BH21
Potters Av FHAM/PORC PO16
Potters Crs ASHV GU12
Potters Fld LISS GU33
Potters Ga FNM GU9
Potters Heron Cl ROMY SO51
Potters Heron La ROMY SO51
Potters La HTWY RG27
Potters Wy PSTN BH14
Pottery Dro STOK SO20
Pottery La HUNG RG17
RFNM GU10
RCCH PO18
Pottery Rd PSTN BH14
Poulner Cl ITCH SO19
Poulner Ct HAV PO9
Poulner Hl RGWD BH24
Poulner Pk RGWD BH24
Poultons Cl OVTN RG25
Poultons Rd OVTN RG25
Pound Cl BOR GU35
LSOL/BMARY PO13
NALR SO24
RGWD BH24
TADY RG26

d Cottages BPWT SO32 299 H3
d Ga ALTN GU34 176 F3 1
d Gate Dr
AM/STUB PO14 371 G7
d Hl NALR SO24 218 C2
MY SO51 288 B3
d La BPWT SO32 299 J3
OC SP6 308 A3
CL RG20 57 H2
BY RG14 25 G4
E BH15 445 K3
WD BH24 384 C7
MY SO51 264 A6
MY SO51 288 B3
MA RG19 26 D5
T SO40 315 H6
T SO40 341 J5
d Lea HISD PO11 425 L3
d Meadow HTWY RG27 64 D8
d Rd ASHV GU12 7 H3
AM PO6 374 F6
ER SO31 345 K8
MN SO41 439 M5
TN RG25 124 A1
S PO20 427 K7
OK SO20 162 B6
IC SO23 191 H8
d St NWBY RG14 2 D6
ND SO18 344 E1
d Tree Rd SHAM SO14 13 G3
ys Md KSCL RG20 59 K6
ell Crs TOTT SO40 341 K3
ell Rd PSTN BH14 446 A5
er Rd PSEA PO1 423 J2 2
erscourt Rd NEND PO2 399 J8
IL/BTOS BH25 452 C1
s Cl NMIL/BTOS BH25 437 M5
Rd RFNM GU10 136 D1
er Cl FHAM/PORC PO16 15 J3
ings Crs BSTK RG21 105 H6
ings Pl PSEA PO1 20 E5 1
ters Cl AND SP10 8 F1
tz Rd OVTN RG25 100 F8
osa Rd HEND SO30 346 C3
te Wy FHAM/STUB PO14 371 G6
rice Cl FARN GU14 70 E8 1
raw Cl ROWN SO16 318 A4
on Cl UPTN BH16 444 B1 1
on La CHCH/BSGR BH23 435 H5
on Pl NWBY RG14 26 A3 2
on Rd NEND PO2 399 K7
BH15 445 H2
on Wy CHCH/BSGR BH23 436 B8
wick La HASM GU27 205 K6
wood Cl
IL/BTOS BH25 437 K7 3
wood Rd HEND SO30 346 A2
ria Cl LISS GU33 225 H6
ria Rd ENEY PO4 423 K5
ND SO30 345 M3
ND SP11 93 G7
etts Hl BPWT SO32 348 D1
aux-brune Av
L/BMARY PO13 397 G4
Croft Dr FAWY SO45 392 C6
fields FHAM/STUB PO14 371 G6
lands ROMY SO51 262 D8
lands Cl TOTT SO40 340 E2
lands La LYMN SO41 440 A5
lands Rd LYMN SO41 440 A5
La CHCH/BSGR BH23 434 F1
ley Cl TOTT SO40 341 H1 1
ley Cl WEND SO18 344 C3
ley Rd CHAM RG24 104 D1
IE BH10 431 M7
twood Cl WEND SO18 345 H1
te Rd FHAM/STUB PO14 371 H6
ose Cl HEND SO30 346 A3 2
L/BMARY PO13 397 G3
D SO52 292 E4 1
ose Dr HTWY RG27 87 H1
ose Gdns CFDH BH17 429 K7
W GU14 90 B5 1
P RG22 127 G3
ose La LISS GU33 249 J4
L SP5 285 H2
ose Rd RAND SP11 92 E6
VN SO16 318 F4
ose Wy
H/BSGR BH23 436 A8
R SO31 370 D6
MY SO51 263 H7 3
T GU47 49 L7
MB BH21 429 J1
la Rd BOR GU35 201 K5 1
e Albert Rd ENEY PO4 423 L5
e Alfred St GPORT PO12 18 E5
e Charles Cl RAND SP11 92 E5
e Charles Crs FARN GU14 70 E8
e Dr SHST GU47 49 K7
e George's St HAV PO9 16 F4
e George St PSEA PO1 20 C1
e Hold Rd STHA RG19 26 D5
e of Wales Av
M SO15 342 E1
e of Wales Cl
LE PO7 376 E1 3
e of Wales Rd
RT PO12 19 H3 3
IE BH4 447 G4
e Rd FHAM/STUB PO14 396 D2
VN SO16 317 K1
e's Av ALDT GU11 112 F3
e's Cl BPWT SO32 297 G8 3
GU35 201 H7
SP5 285 K1
s Ct SHAM SO14 344 A2 3
s' Crs KEMP RG22 104 D5
SO43 363 L3
s Dr WVILLE PO7 352 E7
s Hl RSAL SP5 285 K1
s Pl WINW SO22 238 D3
/BTOS BH25 438 A4 3
s Rd FERN BH22 406 B2
GU32 275 J4
Y SO51 262 D8
M SO15 343 H2 1
ss Av CHCH/BSGR BH23 450 A2
ss Cl HEND SO30 320 D6

Princess Dr ALTN GU34 176 C5
Princess Gdns HORN PO8 352 F1
Princess Mary Gdns RAND SP11 92 E6
Princess Rd BKME/WDN BH12 446 F4
TOTT SO40 340 F6
WBNE BH4 447 G4
Prince's St PSEA PO1 423 H1
SHAM SO14 344 A2
Princes Wy CBLY GU15 70 F3
Princes Wy ALDT GU11 6 E1
Pringles Cl FERN BH22 406 C3 1
Pringles Dr FERN BH22 406 C3
Prinstead Cl WINC SO23 239 G2 1
Prinsted Crs CHAM PO6 400 B1
Prinsted La EMRTH PO10 403 H1
Prior Croft Cl CBLY GU15 71 K4
Prior End CBLY GU15 71 K3
Prior Rd CBLY GU15 71 L4
Priors Barton WINC SO23 238 E3
Priors Cl CHCH/BSGR BH23 451 H1
EMRTH PO10 379 J7
FARN GU14 70 E8
KSCL RG20 59 J6 2
Priorsdean Av HSEA PO3 423 L2
Priorsdean Crs HAV PO9 377 H4
Priors Dean Rd WINW SO22 214 C4
Priors Keep FLET GU13 89 H8
Prior's La BLKW GU17 69 K3
Priors Leaze La RCCH PO18 379 K7
Priors Rd CFDH BH17 429 L8
TADY RG26 41 K7
Priors Wy WINW SO22 238 A5
Priors Wd CWTH RG45 49 G4
HASM GU27 228 C2
Priory Av PTSW SO17 319 J7
Priory Cl BPWT SO32 297 G8
FLET GU13 88 C8
PTSW SO17 319 J7
Priory Crs ENEY PO4 423 L4
Priory Gdns CHAM RG24 106 A1
FHAM/PORC PO16 374 A8
WVILLE PO7 352 C7
Priory La HTWY RG27 87 H4
RFNM GU10 159 G8
WHCH RG28 122 F1
Priory Pl NWBY RG14 37 L2
Priory Rd ELGH SO50 293 L7
ENEY PO4 423 L6
FERN BH22 380 E8
FHAM PO15 14 A4
HLER SO31 368 F2
NWBY RG14 2 E8
PTSW SO17 319 H8
WCLF BH2 22 E7
WHAM PO17 374 E2
Priory St FARN GU14 91 G4
The Priory BPWT SO32 323 G1
Priory View Pl
MOOR/WNTN BH9 432 E5
Priory View Rd
CHCH/BSGR BH23 435 G6
MOOR/WNTN BH9 432 E5
Pritchard Cl STHA RG19 38 A1 2
Privet La RAND SP11 116 E4
Privet Rd BOR GU35 201 M3
MOOR/WNTN BH9 432 C8
Privett Cl CHAM RG24 83 M8
Privett Pl GPORT PO12 421 J4
Privett Rd FHAM PO15 372 A6
GPORT PO12 421 J4
LSOL/BMARY PO13 421 G5
PSF GU32 246 C6
WVILLE PO7 376 B5
Prochurch Rd HORN PO8 352 F4
Proctor Cl ITCH SO19 345 H3
Proctor Dr NBAD SO52 291 L5
Proctor La PSEA PO1 423 K3
Promenade CCLF BH13 447 G8
The Promenade EMRTH PO10 402 D1
FAWY SO45 367 L3
Propeller Rd FARN GU14 90 E6
Prospect Av FARN GU14 90 E2
Prospect La HAV PO9 377 M3
Prospect Pl CHFD SO53 293 H2 1
FAWY SO45 367 L3
NWBY RG14 2 E7
Prospect Rd ASHV GU12 113 K3
FARN GU14 90 D4
NALR SO24 218 A4
NEND PO2 423 G1
RFNM GU10 158 B5
Provene Cl BPWT SO32 323 K4
Provene Gdns BPWT SO32 323 J4
Providence Hl HLER SO31 345 L6
Provident Wy BSTK RG21 4 E7
Provost St FBDG SP6 309 L8
Pruetts La LISS GU33 248 E7
Prunus Cl FERN BH22 405 M1
ROWN SO16 318 B3
Prunus Dr FERN BH22 405 M1
Puckridge Gate Rd ALDT GU11 112 A2
Puckridge Hill Rd ALDT GU11 112 B3
Puckshott Wy HASM GU27 205 G8
Pudbrooke Gdns
HEND SO30 321 G8 1
Pudding La WINC SO23 215 G4
Puddleslosh La FBDG SP6 309 J5
Puddletown Crs CFDH BH17 430 D6
Puffers Wy NWBY RG14 2 A5
Puffin Cl KEMP RG22 126 E2
ROWN SO16 318 A3
Puffin Crs FHAM/STUB PO14 395 M4
Puffin Gdns
LSOL/BMARY PO13 396 F5 3
Puffin Wk HORN PO8 352 B4
Pug's Hole RSAL SP5 207 M8
Pulens Crs EPSF GU31 276 B4
Pulens La EPSF GU31 276 A4
Pullman Ct FERN BH22 380 B6 1
Pullman Wy RGWD BH24 382 E2
Pump La HORN PO8 352 E3
LSOL/BMARY PO13 397 G7
Punsholt La NALR SO24 244 D5
Purbeck Av PLE BH15 444 D7
Purbeck Cl UPTN BH16 444 A1 1
Purbeck Dr FHAM/STUB PO14 14 A8
VWD BH31 356 D3 3
Purbeck Rd NMIL/BTOS BH25 452 C1
WCLF BH2 22 C6
Purbeck St PSEA PO1 20 E2 1
Purbrook Cl ROWN SO16 318 B4 3
Purbrook Gdns WVILLE PO7 376 A3
Purbrook Heath Rd
WVILLE PO7 375 K3
Purbrook Rd PSEA PO1 21 M2
TADY RG26 41 K8
Purbrook Wy HAV PO9 376 F4
WVILLE PO7 376 D4
Purcell Cl KEMP RG22 104 E7
WVILLE PO7 376 C3
Purcell Rd CWTH RG45 49 L1
ITCH SO19 345 H5
Purchase Rd BKME/WDN BH12 447 H1
Purewell CHCH/BSGR BH23 450 C2
Purewell Cl CHCH/BSGR BH23 450 D2
Purewell Cross Rd
CHCH/BSGR BH23 450 C1
Purkess Cl CHFD SO53 293 J1
Purkiss Cl TOTT SO40 340 A3
Purley Wy FRIM GU16 71 H8
ROMY SO51 288 A5
Purmerend Cl FARN GU14 89 M3 3
The Purrocks PSF GU32 275 L3
Purvis Gdns ITCH SO19 344 F6
Pussex La CHCH/BSGR BH23 407 L8
Putmans La EPSF GU31 304 E2
Puttenham Hl RGUW GU3 137 M3
Puttenham La MFD/CHID GU8 137 M7
Puttenham Rd CHAM RG24 83 M5
RFNM GU10 136 E4
Puttock Cl HASM GU27 228 A3 2
Pycroft Cl HISD PO11 402 A5
ITCH SO19 344 D3
Pye Cl WIMB BH21 429 H1
Pye La WIMB BH21 332 C1
Pyestock Crs FARN GU14 89 M4 2
Pye St PSEA PO1 423 G2
Pyland's La HLER SO31 345 M5
Pyle Cl HORN PO8 352 E4
Pylewell Rd FAWY SO45 367 L4 3
Pyotts Copse CHAM RG24 83 M7
Pyotts Ct CHAM RG24 83 M7
Pyotts Hl CHAM RG24 83 M7
Pyrford Cl GPORT PO12 421 J5
WVILLE PO7 352 B6
Pyrford Ms LYMN SO41 440 C6
Pytchley Cl FHAM/STUB PO14 395 L6

Q

The Quadrangle ELGH SO50 293 M4 2
The Quadrant ASHV GU12 113 K4
Quail Wy HORN PO8 352 E2
Quantock Rd ROWN SO16 317 K8
The Quantocks FAWY SO45 367 H6 3
STHA RG19 27 G6
Quarely Rd HAV PO9 377 G2
Quarrington Cl STHA RG19 27 H6
Quarry La YTLY GU46 69 H3
Quarry Rd WIMB BH21 404 E1
WINC SO23 11 K9
Quarterdeck Av NEND PO2 398 F7
Quarters Rd FARN GU14 90 F6
Quartremaine Rd HSEA PO3 399 M5
Quavey Rd RSAL SP5 285 K2
Quay Hvn HLER SO31 346 B8
Quay La GPORT PO12 397 M7
Quay Rd CHCH/BSGR BH23 450 A3
Quayside Rd WEND SO18 344 B1
Quayside Wk TOTT SO40 342 D5
Quay St FHAM/PORC PO16 15 L7
LYMN SO41 440 D4
The Quay PLE BH15 445 H7
Quebec Gdns BLKW GU17 70 A4 3
HLER SO31 345 K7 1
Queen Anne Dr WIMB BH21 430 C1
Queen Anne's Dr HAV PO9 377 G6
Queen Anne's Ga FNM GU9 135 G1
Queen Elizabeth Av
LYMN SO41 440 B4 1
Queen Elizabeth Dr ALDT GU11 6 D2
Queen Elizabeth Rd CBLY GU15 51 G7
Queen Katherine Rd
LYMN SO41 440 D5
Queen Mary Av BSTK RG21 4 F5
CBLY GU15 70 D3
MOOR/WNTN BH9 432 D6
Queen Mary Cl FLET GU13 88 E6
Queen Mary Rd
FHAM/PORC PO16 398 B1
Queen Rd FHAM/STUB PO14 396 D2
Queen's Av ALDT GU11 112 E3
AND SP10 8 F5
CHCH/BSGR BH23 450 A3
Queensbury Pl BLKW GU17 69 M5
Queen's Cl FARN GU14 90 E8 1
FAWY SO45 367 L5
FERN BH22 380 B7
LSOL/BMARY PO13 420 C2 3
RAND SP11 92 E6
Queens Crs FHAM/STUB PO14 396 B5
HORN PO8 352 F1
SSEA PO5 21 H6
Queensfield OVTN RG25 126 C7
Queens Gdns FBDG SP6 309 L6
WBNE BH4 22 A4
Queen's Gate Rd FARN GU14 112 E1
Queens Gv NMIL/BTOS BH25 438 A4
WVILLE PO7 376 B3
SSEA PO5 21 H7
Queensland Rd LTDN BH7 448 F3
Queens La FNM GU9 134 E1
Queens Md WINW SO22 238 B2 2
Queen's Pde LYND SO43 363 K3
Queen's Park Av CHAR BH8 433 G8
Queen's Park Gdns CHAR BH8 448 B1
Queen's Park Rd CHAR BH8 448 C1
Queen's Park South Dr
CHAR BH8 448 C1
Queen's Park West Dr
CHAR BH8 448 B1
Queen's Pl SSEA PO5 21 H6 2
Queens Ride NBAD SO52 291 K4
Queens Ride CWTH RG45 49 K1
Queens Rd ALDT GU11 6 C3
ALTN GU34 176 D5
BSTK RG21 4 B7
CBLY GU15 70 E4
CHCH/BSGR BH23 450 D2
CHFD SO53 265 J7
FARN GU14 91 G8
FERN BH22 406 B1
FHAM/PORC PO16 15 J6
FLET GU13 110 F1
FNM GU9 134 F2 3
GPORT PO12 19 G2
HLER SO31 370 A8
KSCL RG20 59 K6
LIPH GU30 225 M5
LSOL/BMARY PO13 420 D4
NEND PO2 399 J8
NWBY RG14 3 G6
ODIM RG29 108 B5 1
PSEA PO1 422 D2
PSF GU32 275 J4
PSTN BH14 446 C4
WBNE BH4 22 A5
WHCH RG28 122 C5
WIMB BH21 429 H3
WSHM SO15 318 B6
WVILLE PO7 352 C7
Queens St MIDH GU29 279 K6
Queen's Ter SHAM SO14 13 H6
Queenstown Rd
WSHM SO15 343 H2 2
Queen St ASHV GU12 7 M1
EMRTH PO10 378 E8
FBDG SP6 285 G7
PSEA PO1 20 C1
RWIN SO21 266 E3
Queens Vw HLER SO31 368 F2
Queensway FRIM GU16 91 K1
HISD PO11 401 L5
RGWD BH24 382 F1
Queen's Wy SHAM SO14 13 G6
SSEA PO5 21 H6 3
The Queensway
FHAM/PORC PO16 373 M8
Queenswood Av CHAR BH8 433 J7
Queenswood Dr FERN BH22 406 B1
Queenwood Ri STOK SO20 209 G2
Queenwood Rd STOK SO20 209 G2
Quennells Hl RFNM GU10 158 B2
Querida Cl HLER SO31 346 B8 3
Quilter Cl ITCH SO19 345 H4 1
Quilter Rd KEMP RG22 104 B8
Quince La WIMB BH21 404 B2
Quince Tree Wy HTWY RG27 86 A7
Quintin Cl CHCH/BSGR BH23 436 D8
Quinton Cl SSEA PO5 21 J3 3
Quintrell Av FHAM/PORC PO16 373 L8
Quob Farm Cl HEND SO30 320 D5
Quob La HEND SO30 320 D5
The Quomp RGWD BH24 382 E1 3

R

Racecourse Vw LYND SO43 363 K2 2
Rachel Cl ELGH SO50 295 G6
Rack Cl AND SP10 9 J5
Rack Close Rd ALTN GU34 176 D5
Rackfield HASM GU27 228 A1
Rackstraw Rd SHST GU47 50 A7
SHST GU47 70 A1
Racton Av CHAM PO6 399 M1
Racton Rd EMRTH PO10 378 D5
Radar Rd FARN GU14 90 A7
Radcliffe Cl FRIM GU16 91 J1
Radclyffe Rd FHAM/PORC PO16 15 M3
Radford Cl FNM GU9 135 H3
Radford Gdns BSTK RG21 104 E6
Radical Ride EWKG RG40 48 C1
Radipole Rd CFDH BH17 430 D6
Radleigh Gdns TOTT SO40 316 A8
Radley Cl HEND SO30 321 H7 3
Radnor St SSEA PO5 21 H3
Radstock Rd ITCH SO19 344 C5
Radway Crs WSHM SO15 318 C8
Radway Rd WSHM SO15 318 C8
Raebarn Cl NALR SO24 242 C3
Raeburn Dr HEND SO30 346 A1
Raeburn Wy SHST GU47 70 A2
Rae Rd FARN GU14 90 E7
Raf Gate Rd FARN GU14 90 E7 1
Ragdale THLE RG7 31 K5
Raghill THLE RG7 42 A2
Raglan Cl ASHV GU12 7 J4
CHFD SO53 292 E4
FRIM GU16 71 J8
Raglan Gdns BWD BH11 431 L6
Raglan St SSEA PO5 21 J2
Ragmore La PSF GU32 246 D3
Railside THLE RG7 29 J6
Rails La HISD PO11 425 M6
Railway Rd LISS GU33 225 J5
NWBY RG14 3 G5
Railway Vw PSEA PO1 21 J1
Rainbow Cl CHAM RG24 106 B3
Rainham Cl KEMP RG22 126 E1
Rakemakers ALTN GU34 177 J1 1
Rake Rd LIPH GU30 250 C6
LISS GU33 248 F4
Raleigh Cl CHCH/BSGR BH23 450 E3
NMIL/BTOS BH25 437 K5
RGWD BH24 359 G8 3
Raleigh Wy CBLY GU15 71 J5
Raley Rd HLER SO31 370 E6
Ralph Rd WIMB BH21 429 J1
Ram Aly STHA RG19 39 M8
Ramalley La CHFD SO53 293 C1
Rambler Dr LSOL/BMARY PO13 421 G2
Ramblers Md RAND SP11 117 L5 1
Ramblers Wy HORN PO8 352 F7
Ramillies Cl ALDT GU11 113 H1
Ramley Rd LYMN SO41 439 K3
Rampart Gdns HSEA PO3 399 K3
Rampart Rd WEND SO18 344 B1
The Ramparts AND SP10 8 C9
The Rampart LYMN SO41 440 B3
Rampton Rd WHCH RG28 122 C4
Ramptons La THLE RG7 42 E2
Rampton's Meadow TADY RG26 62 A1
Ramsay Cl CBLY GU15 51 L8 2
Ramsay Pl
LSOL/BMARY PO13 397 G6 3
Ramsay Rd WINC SO23 215 H1
Ramsdale Av HAV PO9 377 G3
Ramsdean Rd PSF GU32 274 C7
Ramsdell Cl TADY RG26 61 L1
Ramsdell Rd TADY RG26 60 B7
TADY RG26 62 A7
Ramsey Rd HISD PO11 425 L5
Ramshill EPSF GU31 275 M4
Ramsholt Cl OVTN RG25 125 K7 2
Rances Wy WINW SO22 238 D3
Randall Cl TOTT SO40 316 B6
Randall Rd CHFD SO53 265 J6
Randalls Hl UPTN BH16 428 D8
Randalls La RGWD BH24 384 B3
Randolph Dr FARN GU14 89 M5
Randolph Rd NEND PO2 399 J5
Randolph St WSHM SO15 343 G1
Ranelagh Gdns
WSHM SO15 343 J1
Ranelagh Rd
CHCH/BSGR BH23 451 L1
HAV PO9 16 B4
NEND PO2 399 G7
WINC SO23 238 D2
Ranfurly Gdns FAWY SO45 367 J6
Range Gdns ITCH SO19 344 F5
Range Gn NEND PO2 399 G5
Range Ride CBLY GU15 70 C1
Range Rd EWKG RG40 48 E1
FARN GU14 89 M7
Range Vw SHST GU47 50 B8
Rankine Cl FNM GU9 6 F9
Rannoch Cl FHAM PO15 14 C2
Ransome Cl FHAM/STUB PO14 395 K1
Ranvilles La FHAM/STUB PO14 395 M1
Rapallo Cl FARN GU14 90 F4 1
Raphael Cl BSTK RG21 105 J5
Rapley Cl CBLY GU15 51 J8
Rapson Cl CHAM PO6 375 G7
Rareridge La BPWT SO32 297 K8
Ratcliffe Rd FARN GU14 70 C8
FAWY SO45 367 K7 1
HEND SO30 346 A1
Ratlake La ROMY SO51 264 E4
Rattigan Gdns HLER SO31 347 G8
Ravel Cl KEMP RG22 104 D7
Ravelin Cl RFNM GU10 133 J3 1
Raven Cl LSOL/BMARY PO13 421 G2
NTID SP9 114 E2
YTLY GU46 68 E2 3
Raven Rd HTWY RG27 85 M7
SHAM SO14 343 M2
Ravens Cl FHAM/STUB PO14 396 B5
Ravenscourt Rd LYMN SO41 440 B5
SBNE BH6 449 H3
Ravens Cft HTWY RG27 86 B7 1
Ravenscroft Cl ASHV GU12 113 M5
HLER SO31 345 K7
Ravenscroft Wy BPWT SO32 321 M7
Raven Sq ALTN GU34 176 E2
ELGH SO50 293 J6 1
Ravens Wy LYMN SO41 454 C4
Ravenswood
FHAM/STUB PO14 371 G5 3
Ravenswood Av CWTH RG45 49 H3
Ravenswood Dr CBLY GU15 71 K3
Ravensworth Rd THLE RG7 43 H2
Raven Wy CHCH/BSGR BH23 450 F3
Ravine Rd BOSC BH5 449 G4
CCLF BH13 446 E8
Rawlings Rd HTWY RG27 86 A8
Rawlinson Rd CBLY GU15 70 C2
Rayleigh Rd BSTK RG21 4 D8
Raymond Cl FAWY SO45 392 B5
HEND SO30 320 E5
VWD BH31 356 F2
Raymond Rd CHAM PO6 374 C7
WSHM SO15 343 H1
Rayners Gdns ROWN SO16 319 J4 2
Raynes Rd LSOL/BMARY PO13 420 D4
Reading Rd BLKW GU17 69 L4
CHAM RG24 5 J1
CHAM RG24 83 K6
EWKG RG40 47 J4
FARN GU14 90 F7
HTWY RG27 48 A8
HTWY RG27 64 C8
HTWY RG27 66 B8
HTWY RG27 68 C1
HTWY RG27 85 M6 3
HTWY RG27 86 A6
THLE RG7 31 J8
THLE RG7 42 C3
TLHT RG30 31 M4
YTLY GU46 68 D1
Reading Rd North FLET GU13 88 D7
Reading Rd South FLET GU13 110 F1
Reading Room La BPWT SO32 322 C8
Readon Cl EPSF GU31 275 M4
Read's Fld ALTN GU34 197 G6
Rebbeck Rd LTDN BH7 448 F3
Rebecca Cl FLET GU13 110 D5
The Recess ELGH SO50 294 A3
Record Rd EMRTH PO10 378 C7
Recreation Cl FARN GU14 70 C7 3
Recreation Rd AND SP10 9 K4
BKME/WDN BH12 446 D2
RFNM GU10 158 B5
ODIM RG29 108 B6
RAND SP11 92 E6
THLE RG7 31 K6
Rectory Av CHAM PO6 376 D7
Rectory Cl FHAM/STUB PO14 396 A5
GPORT PO12 18 D7
NWBY RG14 2 C7
SHST GU47 49 J8 1
TADY RG26 61 M2
Rectory Ct HEND SO30 346 D1
Rectory Hl RSAL SP5 207 M7
RSAL SP5 231 J5
Rectory La BPWT SO32 299 H3
FBDG SP6 284 A7
LIPH GU30 227 G1

RFNM GU10 157 G4
RWIN SO21 192 F8
STOK SO20 209 G2
TADY RG26 59 M8
Rectory Pl RAND SP11 117 J6
Rectory Rd DEAN RG23 102 D7
FARN GU14 90 F4
HAV PO9 16 E6
HTWY RG27 85 M8
PLE BH15 445 H2
THLE RG7 42 C1
Reculver Wy AND SP10 118 C5
Redan Cl CHCH/BSGR BH23 451 L1
Redan Gdns ASHV GU12 7 J2
Redan Rd ASHV GU12 7 J2
The Redan GPORT PO12 19 H9
Red Barn Av
FHAM/PORC PO16 374 A7
Red Barn La FHAM PO15 372 C4
Redbreast Rd
MOOR/WNTN BH9 432 E5
Redbridge Cswy WSHM SO15 317 G8
Redbridge Dr AND SP10 8 E8
Redbridge Gv HAV PO9 377 H5
Redbridge Hl ROWN SO16 317 L7
Redbridge La ALTN GU34 220 F2
CHAM RG24 5 M8
ROWN SO16 317 G6
Redbridge Rd WSHM SO15 317 J8
Redcar Av HSEA PO3 399 L7
Redcliffe Cl CHCH/BSGR BH23 435 G6
Redcote Cl WEND SO18 344 F1 1
Redcrest Gdns CBLY GU15 71 J3
Redcroft La HLER SO31 345 L7
Redenham Dro RAND SP11 93 M8
Redfield Ct NWBY RG14 3 M2
Redfields La RFNM GU10 110 D7
The Redfords TOTT SO40 316 D7
Redgauntlet EWKG RG40 48 B2 3
Redhearne Flds RFNM GU10 181 H6
Red Hl ALTN GU34 197 G3
HTWY RG27 66 D7
KSCL RG20 75 M2
RAND SP11 75 H6
Redhill ROWN SO16 318 D4
Redhill Av NBNE BH10 432 C6
Redhill Cl NBNE BH10 432 C6
ROWN SO16 318 D4
Redhill Crs MOOR/WNTN BH9 432 D5
Red Hill Crs ROWN SO16 318 D4
Redhill Dr NBNE BH10 432 C6
Redhill Rd HAV PO9 353 M7
Red Hill Wy ROWN SO16 318 D5
Redhoave Rd CFDH BH17 430 B6
Redhorn Cl UPTN BH16 444 B4 1
Red House Ct EPSF GU31 277 L4
Redhouse Park Gdns
LSOL/BMARY PO13 421 J1
Redlands BKME/WDN BH12 446 E3
Redlands Dr ITCH SO19 344 D2
Redlands Gv ENEY PO4 424 A4
Redlands La EMRTH PO10 378 D4
FHAM/STUB PO14 14 F6
RFNM GU10 133 J1
Red La BOR GU35 202 E1
OVTN RG25 152 B4
RSAL SP5 231 M1
THLE RG7 42 A3
Red Leaves BPWT SO32 323 K6
Red Lion La BSTK RG21 4 F9
FNM GU9 134 E7
OVTN RG25 100 F8
Red Ldg CHFD SO53 293 G5
Redlynch Cl HAV PO9 377 M4 1
Redmans Vw VWD BH31 356 B2
Redmayne CBLY GU15 71 M4 2
Redmoor Cl ITCH SO19 344 C2
Red Oaks Cl FERN BH22 405 M1
Red Oaks Dr FHAM PO15 370 F3
Redon Wy AND SP10 8 E2
Red Post La RAND SP11 117 K8
Red Rice Rd RAND SP11 142 B7
Redrise Cl FAWY SO45 391 M5
Redshank Cl CFDH BH17 429 K7
Redshank Rd HORN PO8 352 E1
Redvers Buller Rd ALDT GU11 112 F1
Redvers Rd CHCH/BSGR BH23 450 D1
Redward Rd ROWN SO16 317 L3
Redwing Cl KEMP RG22 126 E1
Redwing Ct ENEY PO4 424 A3 3
Redwing Gdns TOTT SO40 316 B8 7
Redwing Rd HORN PO8 328 B3
Redwood Cl FAWY SO45 367 H5
HEND SO30 320 B6
LYMN SO41 440 A3
RGWD BH24 382 F1
Redwood Dr FERN BH22 380 A8
FHAM/PORC PO16 373 M8
Redwood Gdns TOTT SO40 341 G1
Redwood Gv HAV PO9 377 L4
Redwood La ALTN GU34 174 F8
Redwood Rd UPTN BH16 428 E8
Redwoods Wy FLET GU13 111 G4
Redwood Wy ROWN SO16 318 F2
Reed Cl ALDT GU11 113 G2
Reed Dr TOTT SO40 342 D6
Reedmace Cl WVILLE PO7 376 E2 3
Reeds La LISS GU33 249 J2
Reed's Pl GPORT PO12 18 D1
Reeds Rd GPORT PO12 421 M1
The Reeds Rd RFNM GU10 159 G7
Rees Rd RWIN SO21 190 B6
Reeves Cl ROMY SO51 288 D5
Reeves Rd ASHV GU12 7 J3
Reeves Wy HLER SO31 345 K7 5
Regal Cl CHAM PO6 375 K8
Regency Gdns WVILLE PO7 376 B2 1
Regency Pl FHAM PO15 14 C5
Regent Cl FLET GU13 88 F8
RWIN SO21 266 B4
Regent Dr LTDN BH7 433 K8
Regent Pl SSEA PO5 20 F6 2
Regent Rd CHFD SO53 293 J2
Regents Ct HAV PO9 16 E7
Regents Ga HLER SO31 370 C3
Regent's Gv WSHM SO15 318 A8 4
Regent's Park Gdns
WSHM SO15 342 F1 2
Regent's Park Rd WSHM SO15 342 E1
Regents Pl SHST GU47 49 M8
Regent St FLET GU13 88 F8
PSEA PO1 423 G1
SHAM SO14 12 F3
Regent Wy FRIM GU16 71 J7
Regiment Cl FARN GU14 89 M5 4
Reginald Rd ENEY PO4 423 L5
Regnum Dr NWBY RG14 25 L3
Reid St CHCH/BSGR BH23 449 M1
Reith Wy AND SP10 118 A7
Relay Rd WVILLE PO7 352 B8
Reliant Cl CHFD SO53 293 G4 1
Rembrandt Cl BSTK RG21 105 J5
Rememberance Gdns
CHAM RG24 83 L6 2
Remembrance Rd NWBY RG14 2 A6
Rempstone Rd WIMB BH21 404 B7
Renault Dr BDST BH18 429 L7
Renda Rd FAWY SO45 392 A4
Renny Rd PSEA PO1 21 M2
Renoir Cl BSTK RG21 105 J5
Renouf Cl LYMN SO41 440 A5
Renown Cl CHFD SO53 293 G3
Renown Gdns HORN PO8 352 D3
Renown Wy CHAM RG24 83 L4 3
Repton Cl GPORT PO12 421 J4
Repton Gdns HEND SO30 321 J6
Reservoir La HEND SO30 345 L2
PSF GU32 275 L3
Reservoir Rd FARN GU14 90 A7
Rest-a-wyle Av HISD PO11 425 L3
Restormel Cl DEAN RG23 104 A2
Retreat Rd WIMB BH21 404 B4
The Retreat ELGH SO50 294 A4
SSEA PO5 21 H6
TOTT SO40 341 K3
Reuben Dr PLE BH15 444 C6
Reuben's Crs TADY RG26 61 L1
Revelstoke Av FARN GU14 90 E2
Revenge Cl ENEY PO4 424 A2 2
Rewlands Dr WINW SO22 214 B4
Reynards Cl TADY RG26 41 L8
Reynolds Cl BSTK RG21 105 J4
Reynolds Dl TOTT SO40 341 H3
Reynolds Gn SHST GU47 70 A2 2
Reynolds Rd ELGH SO50 295 J7
WSHM SO15 318 B8
Reyntiens Vw ODIM RG29 108 D5 2
Rhine Banks FARN GU14 90 A3
Rhinefield Cl BROC SO42 387 J6
ELGH SO50 294 E6 2
HAV PO9 377 G4 5
Rhinefield Ornamental Dr
BROC SO42 386 D3
Rhinefield Rd
NMIL/BTOS BH25 411 J6
Rhiners Cl LYMN SO41 412 F5
Rhododendron Rd FRIM GU16 71 L8
Rhyme Hall Ms FAWY SO45 392 F5 3
Ribble Cl BDST BH18 429 L6
CHFD SO53 293 J3
Ribble Ct ROWN SO16 317 K7
Ribble Pl FARN GU14 90 B2
Ribble Wy BSTK RG21 5 J8
Ricardo Crs CHCH/BSGR BH23 450 F2
Rice Gdns UPTN BH16 444 C4
Richard Cl FLET GU13 110 D1
UPTN BH16 444 A1 5
Richard Gv GPORT PO12 397 L7
Richards Cl ASHV GU12 113 K3 1
HLER SO31 370 F5
Richborough Dr AND SP10 118 B5
Richlans Rd HEND SO30 346 A2
Richmond Cl CHFD SO53 265 G7
FARN GU14 90 A5
FLET GU13 110 E2
FRIM GU16 71 J7
HISD PO11 425 J4
BOR GU35 201 J7 3
TOTT SO40 316 A7
Richmond Dr HISD PO11 425 H4
Richmond Gdns PTSW SO17 319 G7
WCLF BH2 22 E5
Richmond Hl WCLF BH2 22 E5
Richmond Hill Dr WCLF BH2 22 E5
Richmond Hill Rbt WCLF BH2 22 E4
Richmond La ROMY SO51 262 F7
Richmond Pk RWIN SO21 266 C4
Richmond Park Av CHAR BH8 448 A1
Richmond Park Crs CHAR BH8 448 B1
Richmond Park Rd CHAR BH8 448 B1
Richmond Pl PSEA PO1 20 E2
SSEA PO5 21 H7 1
Richmond Ri
FHAM/PORC PO16 374 A7
Richmond Rd BSTK RG21 4 D5
GPORT PO12 18 C4
LSOL/BMARY PO13 420 B2
PSTN BH14 446 B4
SHST GU47 50 B8
WSHM SO15 343 G2
Richmond St SHAM SO14 13 H5
Richmond Wood Rd
CHAR BH8 448 A1
Richville Rd ROWN SO16 317 M8
Ridding Cl WSHM SO15 318 A8
Riddings La STHA RG19 39 M6
Riders La HAV PO9 377 J4
Rideway Cl CBLY GU15 70 E4
Ridge Cl HORN PO8 328 B4
KEMP RG22 127 H3
Ridge Common La PSF GU32 275 H2
Ridgefield Gdns
CHCH/BSGR BH23 436 B8
Ridge La HEND SO30 347 H5
HTWY RG27 85 K6
ROMY SO51 290 A7
Ridge Moor Cl GSHT GU26 204 B3
Ridgemount Av ROWN SO16 318 E3
Ridgemount Gdns PLE BH15 444 D5 6
Ridges Cl RAND SP11 96 C8 1
The Ridge RSAL SP5 285 J4
Ridge Top La PSF GU32 274 F1
Ridgeway BDST BH18 429 M4
FERN BH22 406 C8
WINW SO22 238 B3
Ridgeway Cl CHAM PO6 374 D7 1
CHFD SO53 293 K3
ELGH SO50 295 H5 1
Ridgeway Hill Rd FNM GU9 134 F8
Ridgeway La LYMN SO41 440 B6
Ridgeway Rd FNM GU9 158 F1
The Ridgeway ALTN GU34 176 E6
FHAM/PORC PO16 373 J7
Ridgewood Cl FAWY SO45 367 G5 1
Ridgway HAV PO9 16 A5
The Ridings BPWT SO32 323 K4
ELGH SO50 294 F6
FRIM GU16 71 L5
LISS GU33 249 G4
NEND PO2 399 K5
Ridley Cl FAWY SO45 392 A4 3
FLET GU13 110 E1
Ridley Rd MOOR/WNTN BH9 432 D8
Ridleys Piece ODIM RG29 130 F4
Ridout Cl NBNE BH10 431 M7
Rifle Wy FARN GU14 89 M5 5
Rigby Rd SHAM SO14 319 G8
Riggs Gdns BWD BH11 431 K6
Rigler Rd PLE BH15 444 F7
Riley La CHAM RG24 106 A1
Riley Rd RWIN SO21 190 D6
Rimbault Cl ALDT GU11 113 G1 2
Rimbury Wy CHCH/BSGR BH23 434 E8
Rimes's La TADY RG26 61 J2
Rimington Rd HORN PO8 352 D5
Ringbury LYMN SO41 440 B2
Ringlet Wy WINC SO23 11 M7
Ringsgreen La PSF GU32 246 F5
Ringshall Gdns TADY RG26 63 K5
The Ring ROWN SO16 318 D1
Ringway East CHAM RG24 5 K3
Ringway North CHAM RG24 104 D1
Ringway South BSTK RG21 105 H5
Ringway West DEAN RG23 104 D1
KEMP RG22 104 D4
Ringwood Dr NBAD SO52 291 K3
Ringwood Rd
BKME/WDN BH12 431 H6
BLKW GU17 69 M2 1
BWD BH11 431 L2
CHCH/BSGR BH23 408 E8
CHCH/BSGR BH23 436 A2
ENEY PO4 423 M5
FARN GU14 90 F1
FBDG SP6 309 M8
FBDG SP6 333 K3
FERN BH22 380 F8
PSTN BH14 445 L2
RGWD BH24 381 K4
RGWD BH24 384 B3
TOTT SO40 340 E1
VWD BH31 356 D1
WIMB BH21 356 C8
WIMB BH21 380 F2
Ripley Gv HSEA PO3 399 L8
Ripon Gdns WVILLE PO7 352 F7
Ripon Rd BLKW GU17 69 J7
MOOR/WNTN BH9 432 E8
Ripplesmore Cl SHST GU47 49 L8
Ripplewood TOTT SO40 342 E7 4
Ripstone Gdns PTSW SO17 319 G5
The Rise BROC SO42 387 K7
CWTH RG45 49 J3
EWKG RG40 47 K6
WVILLE PO7 376 B6
Ritchie Ct ITCH SO19 344 F4
Ritchie Pl FERN BH22 380 B4 1
Ritchie Rd BWD BH11 431 M4
Rival Moor Rd EPSF GU31 276 A6
Rivar Rd MARL SN8 32 B6
River Cl ALTN GU34 197 G6
WIMB BH21 404 A2
Riverdale RFNM GU10 158 B1
Riverdale Av WVILLE PO7 376 E1
Riverdale Cl FBDG SP6 309 L6
Riverdale La CHCH/BSGR BH23 449 M2
Riverdene Pl WEND SO18 319 J8 2
River Gdns LYMN SO41 454 D4
River Gn HLER SO31 369 L6
Riverhead NALR SO24 219 H4
Riverhead Cl ENEY PO4 423 M3
River La FHAM PO15 372 A2
FNM GU9 158 B1
Riverlea Rd CHCH/BSGR BH23 449 M2
Rivermead Cl ROMY SO51 290 C1
Rivermead Gdns
CHCH/BSGR BH23 434 C6
Rivermead Rd CBLY GU15 70 E6
Rivermede BOR GU35 201 K4
River Pde AND SP10 9 L1 1
River Pk NWBY RG14 3 H3
River Rd YTLY GU46 68 E1
Rivers Cl FARN GU14 91 H7
Riversdale Cl ITCH SO19 344 C8 2
Riversdale Rd SBNE BH6 449 M4
Riverside ELGH SO50 294 C5
RGWD BH24 382 D2
Riverside Av
FHAM/PORC PO16 373 H5
LTDN BH7 434 A7
Riverside Cl CHAM RG24 106 A1
FARN GU14 90 C3
LISS GU33 248 E4
OVTN RG25 101 G8
TOTT SO40 340 A2
Riverside Gdns ROMY SO51 290 D2
Riverside Gn STOK SO20 210 F5
Riverside La SBNE BH6 449 L3
Riverside Rd FERN BH22 380 B6
Riverside Wy CBLY GU15 70 D5
River's St SSEA PO5 21 J3
River St EMRTH PO10 378 F4
Riverview TOTT SO40 341 K3
River View Cl STOK SO20 165 L4
River View Rd WEND SO18 319 J6
River Wk WEND SO18 319 K5
River Wy AND SP10 9 K1
CHCH/BSGR BH23 434 B6
HAV PO9 17 G1
R L Stevenson Av WBNE BH4 447 G5
Roads Hl HORN PO8 327 L7
Road Vw NEND PO2 399 G8
Robert Cecil Av WEND SO18 319 K4
Robert Mays Rd ODIM RG29 108 B6 3
Roberts Cl LYMN SO41 439 J7
WHAM PO17 348 E4
WINC SO23 191 G7
Robertsfield STHA RG19 26 C5
Roberts La CFDH BH17 444 F1
Robertson Cl NWBY RG14 25 L8 2
Robertson Rd NALR SO24 218 B4 2
Robertson Wy ASHV GU12 113 J7
Roberts Rd ASHV GU12 7 L3
CBLY GU15 70 D2
CFDH BH17 429 M7
FAWY SO45 367 K4
GPORT PO12 421 K2 4
LISS GU33 225 H6
LTDN BH7 448 F2
RAND SP11 92 D7
RWIN SO21 145 J8
TOTT SO40 341 K3
WSHM SO15 12 B1
Robert Wy FRIM GU16 91 J5
Robert Whitworth Dr
ROMY SO51 262 E7
Robina Cl WVILLE PO7 376 E1
Robin Cl ALTN GU34 176 F2
ASHV GU12 113 J2
KEMP RG22 103 M8
THLE RG7 31 L5 4
Robin Crs NMIL/BTOS BH25 437 H3
Robin Gdns HORN PO8 352 B4
TOTT SO40 316 B8
Robin Gv NMIL/BTOS BH25 437 K6
Robin Hill Dr CBLY GU15 71 K5
Robin Hood Cl FARN GU14 90 D1
Robinia Gn ROWN SO16 318 B3
Robin La SHST GU47 49 M8
Robins Cl FHAM/STUB PO14 396 A5
NWBY RG14 37 J1
Robins Grove Crs YTLY GU46 68 E2
Robins Hl HUNG RG17 34 B2
Robins La MIDH GU29 279 G1
Robins Meadow
FHAM/STUB PO14 371 G7
Robinson Rd
FHAM/STUB PO14 395 M7
Robinson Wy HSEA PO3 400 A5
BOR GU35 201 K6
Robin Sq ELGH SO50 293 H7
Robins Wy CHCH/BSGR BH23 451 G3
Robinswood Dr FERN BH22 380 B8
Robin Wy AND SP10 119 G6
Rochester Cl KEMP RG22 104 A8 4
Rochester Gv FLET GU13 88 E8
Rochester Rd BWD BH11 431 M4
ENEY PO4 423 K5
Rochester St SHAM SO14 13 L2
Rochford Rd BSTK RG21 4 C8
CHAM PO6 375 H8
Rockall Cl ROWN SO16 317 K3
Rockbourne Cl HAV PO9 377 G4 6
Rockbourne Gdns
NMIL/BTOS BH25 437 H8 1
Rockbourne La FBDG SP6 308 D1
Rockbourne Rd WINW SO22 214 C4
Rockdale Dr GSHT GU26 204 A5 1
Rockery Cl FAWY SO45 367 G4
The Rockery FARN GU14 90 A5
Rocket Rd FARN GU14 90 A7
Rockfield Wy SHST GU47 50 A8 4
Rockford Cl SBNE BH6 449 L5
Rock Gdns ALDT GU11 6 C3
Rockingham Rd NWBY RG14 2 C5
Rockingham Wy
FHAM/PORC PO16 373 M8
Rock La RFNM GU10 158 D3
Rockleigh Dr TOTT SO40 341 H4
Rockleigh Rd ROWN SO16 318 C5
Rockley Rd PLE BH15 444 D6
Rockmoor La RAND SP11 53 J6
Rockram Cl TOTT SO40 339 M1
Rockram Gdns FAWY SO45 367 G5 2
Rockrose Wy CHAM PO6 374 E6
Rockstone La SHAM SO14 343 L2
Rockstone Pl WSHM SO15 343 K2
Rockville Dr WVILLE PO7 376 C1
Rodbourne Cl LYMN SO41 439 H7
Rodfield La RWIN SO21 241 G5
Roding Cl BSTK RG21 5 J8
Rodlease La LYMN SO41 414 C6
Rodmel Ct FARN GU14 91 H7
Rodney Cl LSOL/BMARY PO13 421 G2
Rodney Dr CHCH/BSGR BH23 450 E2
Rodney Rd ENEY PO4 423 K3
Rodney Wy HORN PO8 352 F2
Rodway WIMB BH21 404 A4
Rodwell Cl NBNE BH10 432 A2
Roebuck Av FHAM PO15 372 B3
Roebuck Cl CHAM PO6 399 K1 3
NMIL/BTOS BH25 437 M5
Roebuts Cl NWBY RG14 25 J8
Roedeer Copse HASM GU27 228 B2
Roe Downs Rd ALTN GU34 196 E2
Roentgen Rd CHAM RG24 5 M4
Roeshot Crs CHCH/BSGR BH23 436 C7
Roewood Cl FAWY SO45 392 A5 2
Roewood Rd FAWY SO45 392 A5
Rogate Gdns
FHAM/PORC PO16 374 A7
Roger Penny Wy FBDG SP6 310 F5
Rogers Cl ELGH SO50 294 D4
GPORT PO12 421 M2
Rogers Ct ALTN GU34 176 E4
Rogers Md HISD PO11 401 K5
Rogers Rd ELGH SO50 294 D4
Rokeby Cl NWBY RG14 37 K1
Roke La ODIM RG29 108 F8
Roker Wy ELGH SO50 295 G7
Rokes Pl YTLY GU46 68 D2
Roland Cl HORN PO8 352 F2
Rollestone Rd FAWY SO45 391 M5
Rolls Dr SBNE BH6 450 A4
Roman Cl CHFD SO53 293 K1
Roman Dr ROWN SO16 318 D1
Roman Gdns FAWY SO45 367 H7 1
Roman Gv FHAM/PORC PO16 398 B2
Roman Landing SELS PO20 427 J6
Roman Ride CWTH RG45 49 G3
Roman Rd BDST BH18 429 J4
DEAN RG23 104 A3
FAWY SO45 36
FAWY SO45 3
ROWN SO16 2
RWIN SO21 2
STOK SO20 1
Romans Fld THLE RG7 42
Romans Ga THLE RG7
Romans' Rd WINC SO23 2
Roman Wy AND SP10 1
DEAN RG23 1
FAWY SO45 3
FNM GU9 1
HAV PO9 3
NTHA RG18
RWIN SO21 1
The Romany FARN GU14
Romayne Cl FARN GU14
Romford Rd HLER SO31 3
Romill Cl WEND SO18 3
Romney Rd FARN GU14
NBNE BH10 4
Romsey Av FHAM/PORC PO16 3
HSEA PO3 4
Romsey Cl ALDT GU11
BLKW GU17 69
CHAM RG24
ELGH SO50 2
Romsey Rd ELGH SO50 2
WINW SO22
HORN PO8 3
LYND SO43 3
RAND SP11 1
ROMY SO51 2
ROMY SO51 3
ROWN SO16 3
RSAL SP5 2
STOK SO20 1
STOK SO20 2
STOK SO20 2
TOTT SO40 3
Romyns Ct FHAM/STUB PO14
Rookcliff Wy LYMN SO41 4
Rookery Av FHAM PO15 3
HLER SO31 3
Rookery La FBDG SP6 2
STOK SO20 2
The Rookery EMRTH PO10 3
WHCH RG28 12
Rookes Cl HORN PO8 3
Rookes La LYMN SO41 4
Rook Hill Rd CHCH/BSGR BH23 4
Rook La RWIN SO21 1
Rookley HLER SO31 3
Rooksbridge FAWY SO45 36
Rooksbury Cft HAV PO9 37
Rooksbury Rd AND SP10
Rooksdown Av CHAM RG24
Rooksdown La CHAM RG24
Rooks Down Rd WINW SO22 2
Rooksfield KSCL RG20
Rooksnest La HUNG RG17
Rooksway Gv
FHAM/PORC PO16 3
Rookswood ALTN GU34 1
KSCL RG20
Rookswood Cl HTWY RG27 8
Rookwood Av SHST GU47
Rookwood Cl ELGH SO50 29
Rookwood La ALTN GU34 1
SELS PO20 4
Rookwood Rd SELS PO20 4
Rookwood Vw WVILLE PO7 3
Roosevelt Crs BWD BH11
Rope Hl LYMN SO41
Ropers La UPTN BH16
Rope Wk STHA RG19
Ropley Cl ITCH SO19 34
TADY RG26
Ropley Rd ALTN GU34 2
HAV PO9 3
LTDN BH7 4
Rorkes Drift FRIM GU16
Rosamund Av WIMB BH21 4
Rosary Gdns YTLY GU46 6
Roscrea Dr SBNE BH6 4
Rosebank Cl ROWN SO16 3
Rosebay Cl ELGH SO50 32
Rosebay Ct WVILLE PO7 37
Rose Bay Gdns HTWY RG27 8
Roseberry Cl KEMP RG22 1
Rosebery Av CHAM PO6 3
Rosebery Cl VWD BH31 3
Rosebery Crs ELGH SO50 2
Rosebery Rd NALR SO24 2
Rosebury Av FAWY SO45 3
Rose Cl FAWY SO45 36
HEND SO30 3
KEMP RG22 1
Rosecrae Cl
NMIL/BTOS BH25 43
Rose Crs PLE BH15 4
Rosedale ASHV GU12
Rosedale Av ROMY SO51 2
Rosedale Cl FHAM/STUB PO14 3
Rosedale Gdns STHA RG19
Rosedene Gdns FLET GU13
Rosedene La SHST GU47 7
Rose Gdns FARN GU14
MOOR/WNTN BH9 4
Rose Hl HORN PO8 3
Rosehill Dr CHCH/BSGR BH23 4
Rosehip Wy CHAM RG24 1
Rose Hodson Pl DEAN RG23 1
Roselands HEND SO30 32
HORN PO8 3
Roselands Cl ELGH SO50 2
Roselands Gdns PTSW SO17 3
Roseleigh Dr TOTT SO40 3
Rosemary Av ASHV GU12
Rosemary Cl FARN GU14
Rosemary Dr TADY RG26
Rosemary Gdns
BKME/WDN BH12 4
BLKW GU17
FHAM PO15 3
HEND SO30 3
Rosemary La BLKW GU17
RFNM GU10 1

A PO1 20 C2 4
nary Rd
IE/WDN BH12 446 B1
nary Wy HORN PO8 352 F4
noor Gv CHFD SO53 265 G7
nount Rd WBNE BH4 447 G6
ndale Rd CHFD SO53 293 J4 1
Rd SHAM SO14 318 F8
T SO40 341 L2
osery GPORT PO12 18 E9
ta Rd ENEY PO4 423 M4
Wk FLET GU13 88 E6
wall Rd ROWN SO16 317 L5
warne Ct WINC SO23 10 F5
wood LSOL/BMARY PO13 397 J7
wood Gdns HORN PO8 328 B3
L/BTOS BH25 437 K4
T SO40 342 E7
wood Rd BOR GU35 201 M3
Cl STHA RG19 27 J6
a Cl WVILLE PO7 352 F8
Rd TWDS BH3 447 K1
Rd South TWDS BH3 447 J1
nan Rd ITCH SO19 344 D4
n Av HLER SO31 394 B1
Cl BSTK RG21 104 F6 3
Gdns ROWN SO16 317 M6
ngton Av WEND SO18 344 D1
ngton Wy WEND SO18 344 D1
i Cl KEMP RG22 104 D8
ey Cl CHCH/BSGR BH23 436 C6
yn Cl NBAD SO52 291 M4
nore Gdns ALDT GU11 6 B4
nore Rd
IE/WDN BH12 431 G8
Rd RGWD BH24 359 G7
Wy LSOL/BMARY PO13 420 D1
on Cl WEND SO18 319 M5 2
h Rd WEND SO18 344 D1
y Cl WIMB BH21 404 D1
y Ct HLER SO31 368 F2
y Ct BSTK RG21 5 J8
ury Cl ITCH SO19 344 E4 1
T SO40 316 C7
ury Pk
L/BTOS BH25 437 M6 2
rbank Farm La
GU33 248 E2
r Cl EPSF GU31 276 B4
T GU47 49 M8
VD SO18 320 A7
rcombe La PSF GU32 274 F3
r Dl ITCH SO19 345 J5
rfield Rd
H/BSGR BH23 436 E7
r La EPSF GU31 278 D7
r Rd FARN GU14 90 B2
rwick Cl HAV PO9 377 M3
rwick La HTWY RG27 65 G8
rwick Rd TADY RG26 61 L1
say Dr CHCH/BSGR BH23 451 K1
say Rd GPORT PO12 421 L1
S BH3 447 H2
bury Dr CHFD SO53 293 G2
child Cl ITCH SO19 344 C8
ille Pl CHFD SO53 265 G6 2
vell Cl CHAM PO6 374 E7 3
n Green Rd HTWY RG27 88 D2
n Hl OVTN RG25 123 K2
rdam Dr
H/BSGR BH23 450 C1
down La FAWY SO45 392 A7
elia La BOSC BH5 448 D4
oundabouts LISS GU33 248 F3 1
away La RAND SP11 94 D6
Cl YTLY GU46 69 J3
copse FAWY SO45 367 G5 4
End NWBY RG14 37 G3
field THLE RG7 27 L2 1
haye Rd BWD BH11 431 K3
Hl FBDG SP6 309 L7 3
hill Cl WEND SO18 319 M7
house Dr TOTT SO40 340 F2
house Meadow
TH PO10 402 E1
huts Ri WINC SO23 11 M7
mead Rd BSTK RG21 4 C9
way CBLY GU15 71 M2
LE PO7 352 D8
way Cl CBLY GU15 71 M2
way Ct AND SP10 8 C5
on Rd FLET GU13 110 F3
Wy ROWN SO16 317 K1
an Av
/BMARY PO13 396 F7
Av HORN PO8 352 F6
Cha RFNM GU10 158 D3 1
Cl BPWT SO32 324 A4 1
GU15 51 J8
/BSGR BH23 436 B8
GU13 89 H7
SO31 345 K8
/BMARY PO13 420 D3
SO41 412 F7
D BH24 381 H4
Y SO51 291 H2
V SO16 317 L5
SO21 190 D4
SO40 341 H2
Dl FLET GU13 110 E3
Dr CFDH BH17 429 J7
/BSGR BH23 436 B8
H RG45 49 M1
Y RG14 25 K3
BH31 356 F4
Gdns HEND SO30 346 B2
Rd HAV PO9 377 M5
RG26 61 M1
s Cl FARN GU14 70 B7
side Cl BOR GU35 202 F4
s Pk LYMN SO41 440 B5
wans GSHT GU26 204 A6 1
SO40 342 D7
Wy FHAM/STUB PO14 372 A8
RG30 31 L4
rrow Cl CFDH BH17 430 C6
rough Rd WEND SO18 319 L8
ry Rd HAV PO9 377 H2

Rowcroft Cl ASHV GU12 113 K2
Rowcroft Rd WHIT RG2 47 J1
Rowdell Cottages NALR SO24 220 B3
Rowden Cl ROMY SO51 288 D6
Rowe Ashe Wy HLER SO31 370 D5 1
Rowena Rd SBNE BH6 449 L3
Rowes La LYMN SO41 441 M1
Rowhay La BPWT SO32 296 B3
Rowhill Av ALDT GU11 6 C5
Rowhill Crs ALDT GU11 6 C6
Rowhill Dr FAWY SO45 367 G5
Rowhills FNM GU9 6 A6
Rowhills Cl FNM GU9 6 C6
Rowin Cl HISD PO11 426 B6
Rowland Av PLE BH15 445 K3
Rowland Rd CHAM PO6 374 C7 1
FHAM PO15 14 E4
Rowlands Av WVILLE PO7 352 C7
Rowlands Castle Rd
HORN PO8 353 K2
Rowlands Cl CHFD SO53 292 F4
THLE RG7 42 F3
Rowlands Hl WIMB BH21 404 A3
Rowlett Rd LYMN SO41 440 C5
Rowley Cl HEND SO30 321 L8 1
Rowley Dr HEND SO30 321 L8
Rowlings Rd WINW SO22 214 C5
Rowner Cl LSOL/BMARY PO13 397 G7
Rowner La LSOL/BMARY PO13 397 G8
Rowner Rd LSOL/BMARY PO13 396 F7
Rownhams Cl ROWN SO16 317 K2
Rownhams La NBAD SO52 291 L3
ROMY SO51 291 L7
ROWN SO16 317 L1
Rownhams Rd CHAR BH8 433 G5
HAV PO9 377 H3
NBAD SO52 291 M5
ROWN SO16 317 L6
Rownhams Rd North
ROWN SO16 317 L3
Rownhams Wy ROWN SO16 317 K2
Rowse Cl ROMY SO51 262 E7 2
The Row RSAL SP5 285 K1
Row Wood La
LSOL/BMARY PO13 396 F7
Roxbee Cox Rd FARN GU14 89 K7
Roxburgh Cl CBLY GU15 71 M4
Roxburghe Cl BOR GU35 201 J6
Royal Cl DEAN RG23 126 F3
Royal Crescent Rd SHAM SO14 13 J6
Royale Cl ALDT GU11 7 K6 1
Royal Gdns HAV PO9 353 L7
Royal Ga ENEY PO4 423 M6
Royal Oak Rd NBNE BH10 432 A3
Royal Sovereign Av
FHAM/STUB PO14 396 D3
Royal Wy WVILLE PO7 376 E1
Royce Cl AND SP10 118 A7
SELS PO20 427 L7
Royce Wy SELS PO20 427 L7
Royden La LYMN SO41 414 B5
Roydon Cl WINW SO22 238 C3
Roy's La BPWT SO32 325 H6
Royster Cl CFDH BH17 430 A7
Royston Av ELGH SO50 293 M3
Royston Cl PTSW SO17 319 G6
Royston Dr WIMB BH21 404 B3 2
Royston Pl NMIL/BTOS BH25 437 M8
Rozelle Cl WINW SO22 213 M3
Rozelle Rd PSTN BH14 446 B4
Rubens Cl BSTK RG21 105 J6
NMIL/BTOS BH25 437 L4
Ruby Rd ITCH SO19 344 E2
Rudd Hall Ri CBLY GU15 71 G5
Rudd La ROMY SO51 234 C8
ROMY SO51 262 F1
Rudgwick Cl
FHAM/PORC PO16 373 M8 2
Rudland Cl STHA RG19 27 G6
Rudmore Sq NEND PO2 399 G8
Ruffield Cl WINW SO22 214 B5
Rufford Cl ELGH SO50 293 M2
FLET GU13 110 F2
Rufford Gdns SBNE BH6 449 K3
Rufus Cl CHFD SO53 265 K8
ROWN SO16 317 J2
Rufus Gdns TOTT SO40 341 G1
Rugby Cl SHST GU47 50 B7 3
Rugby Rd CFDH BH17 429 L7
SSEA PO5 21 L3
Rumbridge Gdns TOTT SO40 341 L1 1
Rumbridge St TOTT SO40 341 K2
Rune Dr AND SP10 118 E4
Runnymede FHAM PO15 372 B4
HEND SO30 320 C7 4
Runnymede Av BWD BH11 431 H2
Runton Rd BKME/WDN BH12 446 E3
The Runway CHCH/BSGR BH23 451 G1
Runwick La RFNM GU10 134 A7
Rupert Rd NWBY RG14 25 J8
Rushall La WIMB BH21 428 E4
Rushcombe Wy WIMB BH21 429 H2 3
Rushden Wy FNM GU9 135 G1
Rushes Rd PSF GU32 275 K4
The Rushes BSTK RG21 5 K8
TOTT SO40 342 D6
Rushfield Rd LISS GU33 248 E5
Rushford Warren
CHCH/BSGR BH23 450 E4
Rushington Av TOTT SO40 341 K2
Rushington La TOTT SO40 341 J3
Rushmere La WVILLE PO7 351 H1
Rushmere Rd SBNE BH6 449 H1
Rushmoor Cl FLET GU13 110 F1
Rushmoor Rd ALDT GU11 112 B5
Ruskin Av MOOR/WNTN BH9 432 F5
Ruskin Cl BSTK RG21 105 J5
Ruskin Ct CWTH RG45 49 J4 2
Ruskin Rd ELGH SO50 293 M3
ENEY PO4 423 L4
Ruskin Wy HORN PO8 352 D4
Rusland Cl CHFD SO53 293 G1
Russell Cl LSOL/BMARY PO13 420 D2
Russell Cotes Rd BMTH BH1 23 G7
Russell Ct BLKW GU17 70 A3 2
Russell Dr CHCH/BSGR BH23 450 C2
ROMY SO51 233 J8
Russell Gdns RGWD BH24 381 M3 1

UPTN BH16 444 B4
Russell Pl FHAM/PORC PO16 15 J5
PTSW SO17 319 G7
Russell Rd HAV PO9 16 F1
LSOL/BMARY PO13 420 D3
NWBY RG14 2 B5
WINC SO23 11 H3
Russell St GPORT PO12 421 L2
SHAM SO14 13 H5
Russell Wy EPSF GU31 275 M6
Russel Rd NBNE BH10 432 A2
Russet Cl FERN BH22 406 B2
LYMN SO41 440 D6
NALR SO24 218 B4
RFNM GU10 136 B1
Russet Gdns CBLY GU15 71 G5
EMRTH PO10 378 F8
Russet Gld ALDT GU11 6 A4
FNM GU9 112 A8
THLE RG7 31 L6
Russett Cl BPWT SO32 324 A4 2
Russett Rd ALTN GU34 176 F5
Russetts Dr FLET GU13 88 F8
Rustan Cl ELGH SO50 295 J6
HEND SO30 345 M2 5
Rustic Gln FLET GU13 110 E3
Ruth Cl FARN GU14 89 M3
Rutherford Rd CHAM RG24 5 J2
Rutland Cl ALDT GU11 112 D5
Rutland Gdns HLER SO31 345 L7
Rutland Rd CHCH/BSGR BH23 434 D7
MOOR/WNTN BH9 432 F8
Rutland Wy WEND SO18 319 M7
Ruxley Cl FAWY SO45 392 A4
Ryall Dr CFDH BH17 430 B7
Ryan Cl FERN BH22 406 A1
Ryan Gdns FERN BH22 406 A1
Ryan Mt SHST GU47 49 K8
Rydal Cl CHAM PO6 374 F7
CHCH/BSGR BH23 434 B4
FARN GU14 90 A5 5
BOR GU35 201 J3
Rydal Dr FLET GU13 110 D3
STHA RG19 26 D5
Rydal Rd GPORT PO12 397 L8
Ryde Pl LSOL/BMARY PO13 420 E4
Ryde Ter SHAM SO14 13 K5
Ryebeck Rd FLET GU13 110 F3
Rye Cl FARN GU14 89 H3
FARN GU14 90 B2
NBAD SO52 292 E2
Ryecroft FHAM/STUB PO14 371 G6 3
Rye Cft FLET GU13 110 D4
Ryecroft HAV PO9 17 K4
Ryecroft Av BWD BH11 431 J3
Ryecroft Gdns BLKW GU17 70 B4 2
Rye Dl TOTT SO40 341 G5
Ryedown La ROMY SO51 289 H4
Ryefield Cl EPSF GU31 276 B5
Ryeland Cl FARN GU14 89 H3 2
Ryelaw Rd FLET GU13 110 F3
Rye Paddock La FAWY SO45 392 F4
Rylandes Ct ROWN SO16 317 L5
Ryle Rd FNM GU9 134 E8
Ryon Cl AND SP10 118 F4
Ryves Av YTLY GU46 68 D3

S

Sabre Ct ALDT GU11 6 B2
Sabre Rd EMRTH PO10 402 E5
Sackville St SSEA PO5 21 G4
Saddleback Rd CBLY GU15 51 H8
Saddleback Wy FARN GU14 89 G4
Saddle Cl WIMB BH21 405 G2 2
Saddlers Cl ELGH SO50 293 M2
RWIN SO21 168 B4
Saddlers Scarp GSHT GU26 203 K4
Saddlewood CBLY GU15 70 F4
Sadlers La FAWY SO45 367 L7
Sadlers Rd HUNG RG17 33 J2
Sadlers Wk EMRTH PO10 378 E8
Saffron Cl CHAM RG24 83 L4
NWBY RG14 2 D3
Saffron Dr CHCH/BSGR BH23 435 M8
Saffron Wy BWD BH11 431 H5
FHAM PO15 347 H8
Sage Cl WVILLE PO7 376 E2
Sagecroft Rd NTHA RG18 26 F3
Sages La ALTN GU34 245 H3
Sailor's La BPWT SO32 298 B1
Sainfoin La DEAN RG23 103 G8
Sainsbury Cl AND SP10 8 E8
St Agatha's Rd HLER SO31 369 L4 2
St Alban's Av CHAR BH8 448 A1
St Alban's Crs CHAR BH8 448 A1
St Alban's Rd CHAR BH8 448 A1
HAV PO9 377 L4
SHAM SO14 13 K1 3
St Aldhelm's Cl CCLF BH13 446 E5
St Aldhelm's Rd CCLF BH13 446 E4
St Andrew Cl HORN PO8 328 B6
St Andrews Cl CWTH RG45 49 J2
NBAD SO52 291 K3
ROMY SO51 262 C2
St Andrews Pk ELGH SO50 321 H2
St Andrew's Rd CHAM PO6 376 D8
GPORT PO12 18 F4
HISD PO11 425 M6
KEMP RG22 104 C5
BOR GU35 201 G6
NTID SP9 114 D2
SHAM SO14 13 H1
SSEA PO5 21 J5
WIMB BH21 429 L3
St Andrew's Wy FRIM GU16 91 J1
St Anne's Av SBNE BH6 449 K3
St Annes Cl WINW SO22 238 B3
RAND SP11 142 E8
St Anne's Gdns ITCH SO19 344 C6
LYMN SO41 440 B5
St Anne's Gv
FHAM/STUB PO14 396 D1
St Annes La BPWT SO32 348 B1
St Anne's Rd ITCH SO19 344 C6
UPTN BH16 444 A1

St Ann's Cl AND SP10 8 F7
AND SP10 9 G7 1
St Ann's Crs GPORT PO12 421 L2
St Ann's Rd HORN PO8 353 G1
St Anthony's Rd WCLF BH2 22 E2
St Aubin's Av ITCH SO19 344 E3
St Aubins Cl ALTN GU34 197 G6
St Aubin's Pk HISD PO11 425 H5
St Aubyns La RGWD BH24 359 J7
St Augustine Gdns
PTSW SO17 319 J7 1
St Augustine Rd ENEY PO4 423 K5
St Augustine's Cl ASHV GU12 7 M3
St Augustin's Rd WCLF BH2 22 E1
St Austell Cl ELGH SO50 294 D5 1
St Barbara's Cl TADY RG26 64 A6
St Barbara Wy NEND PO2 399 K4 3
St Barbe Cl ROMY SO51 290 F2 2
St Bartholomew's Gdns
SSEA PO5 21 K5 1
St Benedict's Cl ALDT GU11 6 E4
St Blaize Rd ROMY SO51 263 G8 3
St Bonnet Dr BPWT SO32 297 H8 3
St Brelades Av
BKME/WDN BH12 431 H7
St Catherines WIMB BH21 404 A4
St Catherine's Hl THLE RG7 43 H3
St Catherine's Rd ELGH SO50 293 M3
FRIM GU16 71 K7
HISD PO11 425 G5
SBNE BH6 449 K5
WEND SO18 319 K7
WINC SO23 239 G2
St Catherines's Wy LTDN BH7 434 B5
St Catherine St SSEA PO5 21 K9
St Catherines Vw
HEND SO30 345 L2 3
St Catherines Wy
FHAM/PORC PO16 373 J7
St Chad's Av NEND PO2 399 J6
St Christopher Av
FHAM/PORC PO16 15 K2
St Christophers Cl ASHV GU12 7 L1
KEMP RG22 104 B5 3
NBAD SO52 291 L4
St Christophers Pl FARN GU14 90 C5 2
St Christopher's Rd FARN GU14 90 D5
HASM GU27 228 D2
HAV PO9 377 G5
St Clair Rd CCLF BH13 457 K2
St Clares Av HAV PO9 377 H1
St Clements Cl ROMY SO51 262 D8 4
St Clements Gdns BMTH BH1 448 C3
St Clement's Rd BMTH BH1 448 C3
PLE BH15 446 A1
St Clement St WINC SO23 10 F8
St Colman's Av CHAM PO6 375 L8
St Cross Rd FNM GU9 134 F5 2
FRIM GU16 91 K1
RFNM GU10 133 J2
WINC SO23 238 E2
St Cuthberts Cl HLER SO31 370 F4 2
St Cuthberts La HLER SO31 370 F4
St David's Cl FARN GU14 70 C8
FNM GU9 6 B8
ODIM RG29 108 B6 4
TOTT SO40 316 B7
St Davids Rd HLER SO31 370 D5
HORN PO8 328 B3
KEMP RG22 104 D5
NWBY RG14 2 D5
SSEA PO5 21 K4
UPTN BH16 444 A1
St Denys Rd PTSW SO17 319 G7
PTSW SO17 319 G7
St Donats Pl NWBY RG14 2 F6
St Edmund Cl
FHAM/STUB PO14 370 F7
St Edmund's Rd ROWN SO16 318 A8
St Edward's Rd GPORT PO12 18 F4
HLER SO31 368 F1
SSEA PO5 21 G6
St Elizabeth's Av WEND SO18 344 F1
St Evox Cl ROWN SO16 317 L3
St Faith's Cl GPORT PO12 18 C2
St Faith's Rd PSEA PO1 423 H2
WINC SO23 238 E3
St Francis Av WEND SO18 320 A8
St Francis Cl FAWY SO45 418 C1 2
St Francis Ct NEND PO2 399 J4 3
St Francis Pl HAV PO9 377 J5
St Francis Rd FAWY SO45 418 C1
GPORT PO12 19 G9
St Gabriels Lea CHAM RG24 83 M5
St Gabriel's Rd WEND SO18 344 F1
St George Cl HLER SO31 345 K7
St Georges Av CHAR BH8 448 B1
BKME/WDN BH12 430 F8
HAV PO9 17 K4
NWBY RG14 2 B6
St Georges Cl
CHCH/BSGR BH23 409 M8
CHAR BH8 433 G8
CHCH/BSGR BH23 436 B8
FNM GU9 135 L2 2
St Georges Crs FBDG SP6 309 L6 2
St George's Dr FERN BH22 406 A4
St George's Rd ASHV GU12 7 G4
CBLY GU15 71 G2
CHAM PO6 375 K8
ENEY PO4 423 L6
FBDG SP6 309 L6
FNM GU9 135 G7
FNM GU9 135 L2
HISD PO11 425 H5
HLER SO31 370 D5
RFNM GU10 135 L4
NTID SP9 114 D2
PSEA PO1 20 C3
St George's Rd East ASHV GU12 7 H3
St Georges Sq PSEA PO1 20 D2 3
St Georges St SHAM SO14 13 G4
WINC SO23 11 G7
St George's Wy PSEA PO1 20 D2
St Giles Cl WINC SO23 11 K9
St Giles Wy HORN PO8 328 B6
St Helena Gdns WEND SO18 319 L5

St Helena Wy
FHAM/PORC PO16 374 A8
St Helen's Cl ENEY PO4 423 K6
St Helens Crs SHST GU47 49 L8 2
St Helen's Pde ENEY PO4 21 M9
St Helens Rd GPORT PO12 421 J5
HISD PO11 425 H5
St Helier Rd BKME/WDN BH12 431 H7
St Hellen's Rd CHAM PO6 376 B8
St Hermans Rd HISD PO11 426 A6
St Hilda Av HORN PO8 328 B6
St Hubert Rd AND SP10 8 D6
HORN PO8 328 B6
St Ives End La RGWD BH24 381 L3
St Ives Gdns WCLF BH2 22 F2
St Ives Pk RGWD BH24 381 L3
St Ives Wd RGWD BH24 381 M3
St James' Av FNM GU9 135 G4
St James Cl HORN PO8 328 B4
St James' La WINW SO22 10 D8
St James' Rd EMRTH PO10 378 D8
FLET GU13 88 E8
HEND SO30 320 C6
LYMN SO41 413 G6
WIMB BH21 405 L2
St James's Cl WSHM SO15 318 B7
St James's Park Rd
ROWN SO16 318 B6
St James's Rd SSEA PO5 21 G4
WSHM SO15 318 B7
St James's Sq BOSC BH5 448 F3
St James's St PSEA PO1 20 E1 1
St James St RAND SP11 92 D6
St James' Ter FNM GU9 134 F5
WINW SO22 10 E8
St James' Vls WINC SO23 10 E9
St James Wy
FHAM/PORC PO16 374 B8
St John Cl TADY RG26 63 M6
St John's Av WVILLE PO7 376 C4
St John's Cl GPORT PO12 18 E1
HISD PO11 425 J5
HTWY RG27 86 A7 6
ROWN SO16 317 K1
WIMB BH21 404 B4
St Johns Ct TOTT SO40 342 D7 2
St Johns Dr TOTT SO40 342 C7
St Johns Gdns ROMY SO51 262 E8 7
St Johns Glebe ROWN SO16 317 L1
St Johns Gv FNM GU9 158 E1
St John's Hl WIMB BH21 404 B3
St John's Piece DEAN RG23 103 G8
St John's Rd AND SP10 9 J4
BOSC BH5 448 C4
CHAM PO6 375 L8
CHCH/BSGR BH23 449 M2
DEAN RG23 103 G6
ELGH SO50 294 A4
EMRTH PO10 379 G7
FARN GU14 90 B4
FNM GU9 134 E8
HAV PO9 377 G4
HEND SO30 345 L4
HLER SO31 370 F6
HTWY RG27 87 J3
NMIL/BTOS BH25 437 L1
NWBY RG14 2 E7
PLE BH15 445 J4
SHST GU47 69 L1
STHA RG19 26 F5
THLE RG7 43 K3
WINC SO23 11 K7
St John's St FAWY SO45 367 L6
WINC SO23 11 J8
St Joseph's Crs CHAM RG24 83 L6 3
St Joseph's Rd ALDT GU11 6 F4
ASHV GU12 7 G4
St Just Cl AMSY SP4 160 A3
FERN BH22 405 M5
St Lawrence Rd ALTN GU34 176 E4
ELGH SO50 293 M4
SHAM SO14 13 J6
St Ledger's Rd CHAR BH8 448 C1
St Leonards RAND SP11 140 A7 1
St Leonard's Av CHAM RG24 83 M5
HISD PO11 425 L5
St Leonards Cl FHAM PO15 371 J5
St Leonard's Rd CHAR BH8 448 A2
LYMN SO41 415 M8
St Leonards Wy RGWD BH24 381 H3
St Lukes Cl HEND SO30 321 H7 1
St Luke's Rd GPORT PO12 421 L2
TWDS BH3 447 L1
St Margaret's Av
CHCH/BSGR BH23 449 M2
St Margaret's Cl WEND SO18 344 F1
St Margarets La
FHAM/STUB PO14 371 J7
St Margarets Rd HISD PO11 425 L5
PLE BH15 445 H4
St Marks Cl FARN GU14 90 F7 5
GPORT PO12 18 D9
STHA RG19 26 F5
St Marks Pl FNM GU9 134 E1 1
St Marks Rd LYMN SO41 439 M5
BWD BH11 431 M5
GPORT PO12 18 D9
NEND PO2 399 H7 3
St Martin's Cl ROWN SO16 317 K5
WINC SO23 11 K7
St Mary Gv LYMN SO41 438 E6
St Mary's Av GPORT PO12 18 D7
TADY RG26 64 A6
St Marys Cl ALTN GU34 176 E6
CHCH/BSGR BH23 409 M8
RSAL SP5 285 L3
SHST GU47 49 M8
WINC SO23 215 H3
St Mary's Ct BSTK RG21 5 G8
St Mary's Meadow
RAND SP11 141 M4 1
St Mary's Pl SHAM SO14 13 H3
St Mary's Rd ASHV GU12 113 K3
CBLY GU15 70 F2 1
CHAR BH8 448 C2
ELGH SO50 294 C4
FERN BH22 406 A3
FHAM/STUB PO14 396 A4

HISD PO11 425 K5
HLER SO31 369 G2
HTWY RG27 87 H3
KSCL RG20 59 J6
LISS GU33 248 E4
NWBY RG14 2 F2
PLE BH15 445 K4
PSEA PO1 423 J2
SHAM SO14 13 H1
SHAM SO14 343 L2
THLE RG7 43 K3
St Mary's Ter RWIN SO21 266 F2 1
St Mary St WINW SO22 238 C3
SHAM SO14 13 J4
St Mary's Wy THLE RG7 31 M5 1
St Matthews Cl SHAM SO14 13 H1
St Matthew's Rd CHAM PO6 375 K8
WINW SO22 10 B2
St Michaels Av NTID SP9 114 D3
St Michaels Cl FAWY SO45 392 C7
FLET GU13 89 H8
OVTN RG25 125 K7
PLE BH15 444 D5 7
VWD BH31 356 D3 4
St Michaels Ct CHAM PO6 374 F7 5
St Michael's Gdns WINC SO23 10 F9
St Michael's Gv
FHAM/STUB PO14 14 F8
FHAM/STUB PO14 396 D1
St Michaels La THLE RG7 31 G3
St Michael's Rd ASHV GU12 7 G4
CBLY GU15 70 E3 5
FARN GU14 90 E2
HAV PO9 377 G5
HLER SO31 370 D6
KEMP RG22 104 B5
NWBY RG14 2 C6
PSEA PO1 20 F3
SHST GU47 49 J8
TOTT SO40 316 E7
VWD BH31 356 D3
WCLF BH2 22 C6
WINC SO23 238 E2
St Michael's St SHAM SO14 12 F5
St Michaels Wy HORN PO8 328 B6
St Monica Rd ITCH SO19 344 E5
St Neot's Rd HTWY RG27 67 J1
St Nicholas WINC SO23 215 G2
St Nicholas Av
LSOL/BMARY PO13 421 G1
St Nicholas Cl FLET GU13 88 E7
RAND SP11 93 G6 1
St Nicholas Ct KEMP RG22 104 C4
St Nicholas' Rd HAV PO9 377 G5 2
NWBY RG14 2 D5
St Nicholas St PSEA PO1 20 D5
St Omer Barracks ALDT GU11 113 G3
St Osmund's Rd PSTN BH14 446 B5
St Patricks Av NTID SP9 114 C3
St Patrick's La LISS GU33 249 H3
St Patrick's Rd KEMP RG22 104 D5
St Pauls Cl RFNM GU10 136 C1 2
St Paul's Hl WINW SO22 10 E6
St Paul's La BMTH BH1 23 J4
St Paul's Pl BMTH BH1 23 J4
St Pauls Rd BMTH BH1 23 J3
HLER SO31 370 C2
KEMP RG22 104 D5
SSEA PO5 20 F3
St Pauls Rbt BMTH BH1 23 H3
St Paul's Sq SSEA PO5 20 F4 3
St Peter's Av HISD PO11 402 A6
St Peters Cl NTID SP9 138 D1
St Peter's Gdns RFNM GU10 158 C2 4
YTLY GU46 69 G2
St Peter's Gv SSEA PO5 21 J5
St Peters Md ASHV GU12 113 L6
St Peters Pk ALDT GU11 6 A5 1
St Peter's Rd BMTH BH1 22 F5
HISD PO11 402 A6
KEMP RG22 104 B5
PSF GU32 275 L5
PSTN BH14 445 M4
St Peters Rbt BMTH BH1 23 G6
St Peter's Sq EMRTH PO10 378 D8
St Peter's St BPWT SO32 297 H8
St Peter St WINC SO23 11 G7
St Peter's Wy FRIM GU16 91 J1
St Philip's Wy WEND SO18 344 F1 2
St Piran's Av HSEA PO3 423 L1
St Richards Rd NWBY RG14 25 L3
St Ronan's Av ENEY PO4 21 M7
St Ronan's Rd ENEY PO4 21 M7
St Sebastian Crs
FHAM/PORC PO16 15 K1
St Simon Cl HLER SO31 370 F5 2
St Simon's Rd SSEA PO5 21 K8
St Stephens Cl HASM GU27 228 F1
St Stephens La VWD BH31 356 E2
St Stephen's Rd WINW SO22 10 B3
NEND PO2 399 J8 2
WCLF BH2 22 C4
St Stephen's Wy WCLF BH2 22 E4
St Swithun Cl BPWT SO32 297 G8 4
St Swithun's Cl ROMY SO51 263 J7 1
St Swithun's Rd BMTH BH1 23 K3
NEND PO2 399 K6
St Swithun's Rd South
BMTH BH1 23 K4
St Swithun St WINC SO23 10 F9
St Theresas Cl HAV PO9 377 G5
St Thomas Av HISD PO11 425 H5
St Thomas Cl AND SP10 118 D5
BSTK RG21 4 D4
FHAM/PORC PO16 15 L3
St Thomas Pk LYMN SO41 440 B4
St Thomas's Rd GPORT PO12 397 M8
St Thomas's St LYMN SO41 440 B5
PSEA PO1 20 C5
St Thomas St WINC SO23 10 F9
St Tristan Cl HLER SO31 370 F5
St Ursula Gv SSEA PO5 21 J5 2
St Valerie Rd GPORT PO12 18 F6
WCLF BH2 22 E2
St Vigor Wy RWIN SO21 266 E7
St Vincent Crs HORN PO8 352 F2
St Vincent Rd GPORT PO12 421 M2
SSEA PO5 21 J7
St Vincent St SSEA PO5 20 F3 4
St Winifred's Rd ROWN SO16 318 B6
WCLF BH2 22 E2
Salamanca CWTH RG45 49 H3 1
Salcombe Av HSEA PO3 399 L7
Salcombe Cl CHFD SO53 293 G4
Salcombe Crs TOTT SO40 341 J2
Salcombe Rd NWBY RG14 2 A7
TOTT SO40 341 J2
WSHM SO15 342 F1
Salcot Rd WINC SO23 11 G3
Salem St WSHM SO15 318 B7
Salerno Cl ALDT GU11 6 F1
Salerno Dr GPORT PO12 18 B3
Salerno Pl PLE BH15 444 C6 2
Salerno Rd NEND PO2 399 H4
ROWN SO16 318 B4
Salesian Vw FARN GU14 91 H8
Salet Wy WVILLE PO7 352 F7
Salisbury Cl ALTN GU34 176 F6
ELGH SO50 294 A4 1
ODIM RG29 108 B6 5
Salisbury Gdns KEMP RG22 104 B4
Salisbury Gv FRIM GU16 91 K5
Salisbury La STOK SO20 162 B7
Salisbury Rd AND SP10 8 B9
ASHV GU12 113 K6
BLKW GU17 69 M3 2
CHAM PO6 399 L1
CHCH/BSGR BH23 434 F2
ENEY PO4 423 K6
FARN GU14 90 F4
FBDG SP6 309 M6
NALR SO24 218 B3
NTID SP9 138 D3
PSTN BH14 446 B3
PTSW SO17 318 F5
RAND SP11 141 M7
RAND SP11 161 K2
RAND SP11 163 J2
RGWD BH24 334 E7
ROMY SO51 261 K8
RSAL SP5 256 D7
STOK SO20 208 F1
TOTT SO40 316 D7
Salisbury St FBDG SP6 309 L7
WIMB BH21 306 D8
Salisbury Ter FRIM GU16 91 K5
LSOL/BMARY PO13 420 D3
Salmon Dr ELGH SO50 294 E6
Salmond Rd RAND SP11 118 A8
Salmons Rd ODIM RG29 108 B6
Salterns Av ENEY PO4 423 M3
Salterns Cl HISD PO11 426 A5
Salterns Est FHAM/PORC PO16 15 K9
Salterns La FAWY SO45 392 F4
FHAM/PORC PO16 396 F1
HISD PO11 425 M5
HLER SO31 369 L2
Salterns Rd FHAM/STUB PO14 395 M8
PSTN BH14 445 M5
Salterns Wy PSTN BH14 446 A8
Salter Rd CCLF BH13 457 G5
Salters Acres WINW SO22 214 B6
Salters Heath Rd TADY RG26 82 A2
Saltgrass La LYMN SO41 454 F6
Saltings Rd UPTN BH16 444 A2
The Saltings CHAM PO6 400 C1
HAV PO9 401 K2
Salt La BPWT SO32 269 K5
Saltmarsh La HISD PO11 425 J3
Saltmarsh Rd SHAM SO14 13 K6
Saltmead PTSW SO17 319 J7 2
Salt Meat La GPORT PO12 422 B2
Saltram Rd FARN GU14 91 H6
Salvia Cl WVILLE PO7 376 E2 4
Salwey Rd HEND SO30 346 B3
Samarkand Cl CBLY GU15 71 L4
Samber Cl LYMN SO41 440 A4
Sampan Cl HLER SO31 370 C7
Sampson Rd
FHAM/STUB PO14 396 D2
PSEA PO1 422 D2
Samson Cl LSOL/BMARY PO13 421 H1
Samson Rd PLE BH15 444 C5
Samuel Rd PSEA PO1 423 K2
Sam Whites Hl RAND SP11 142 D4
San Carlos Ap ALDT GU11 7 K1
Sancreed Rd BKME/WDN BH12 446 D1
Sandbanks Dr KEMP RG22 127 G1 5
Sandbanks Rd PLE BH15 445 L5
PSTN BH14 445 M5
Sandbourne Rd CCLF BH13 447 G7
PLE BH15 445 J4
WBNE BH4 447 H7
Sandcroft Cl GPORT PO12 421 J5 1
Sandecotes Rd PSTN BH14 446 B5
Sanderling Rd ENEY PO4 424 A3
Sanderlings RGWD BH24 383 G2 6
The Sanderlings HISD PO11 425 L6 1
Sandford Av GPORT PO12 421 H4
Sandford Cl KSCL RG20 59 L6
MOOR/WNTN BH9 433 G5
Sandford Ct ALDT GU11 6 B3
Sandford Rd ALDT GU11 6 D2 1
FNM GU9 134 E1
TADY RG26 41 K8
Sandford Wy BDST BH18 429 K5
Sandheath Rd GSHT GU26 203 M1
Sand Hl FARN GU14 90 E1
Sandhill La LSOL/BMARY PO13 420 E1
Sandhills Cl CFDH BH17 430 B6
Sandhurst Dr WIMB BH21 380 E1
Sandhurst La BLKW GU17 69 L2
Sandhurst Rd CWTH RG45 49 L5
WSHM SO15 343 K2
YTLY GU46 69 H2
San Diego Rd GPORT PO12 421 M2
Sandisplatt
FHAM/STUB PO14 372 A8 3
Sandle Copse FBDG SP6 309 G7
Sandleford Ri NWBY RG14 37 K1
Sandleford Rd HAV PO9 377 H1
Sandleheath Rd FBDG SP6 308 E8
Sandlewood Cl HORN PO8 328 B3
TOTT SO40 316 B8 3
Sandmartin Cl
NMIL/BTOS BH25 452 E1
Sandown Cl ALTN GU34 176 F6 1
BLKW GU17 70 A3
GPORT PO12 421 H5 1
Sandown Crs ALDT GU11 7 G8
Sandown Dr FRIM GU16 71 G6
Sandown Rd CHAM PO6 399 J1
CHCH/BSGR BH23 450 D2
WSHM SO15 318 A7
Sandown Wy NWBY RG14 3 J8
Sandpiper Cl CFDH BH17 429 K7
HORN PO8 352 E1
TOTT SO40 342 C7
Sandpiper Rd ROWN SO16 317 M3
Sandpiper Wy KEMP RG22 126 E1
Sandpit Hl KSCL RG20 36 F5
Sandpit La LYMN SO41 442 C4
THLE RG7 46 E3
Sandport Gv
FHAM/PORC PO16 397 M1
Sandringham Cl ALTN GU34 176 C5 2
MOOR/WNTN BH9 432 F4
NBAD SO52 292 E4
Sandringham Gdns
MOOR/WNTN BH9 432 F4
Sandringham La PSEA PO1 21 L1 1
Sandringham Rd
FHAM/STUB PO14 371 M8
PSEA PO1 21 L1
PSF GU32 275 L4
PSTN BH14 446 A5
WEND SO18 319 K7
Sandringham Wy FRIM GU16 71 J8
Sandrock HASM GU27 228 F2
Sandrock Hill Rd RFNM GU10 158 C2
Sandsbury La PSF GU32 275 G3
Sands Cl RFNM GU10 136 A6
Sands Rd RFNM GU10 135 M6
The Sands BOR GU35 200 F6
Sandy Brow WVILLE PO7 376 B4
Sandy Cl EPSF GU31 276 B5
Sandycroft HLER SO31 370 B8
Sandy Down LYMN SO41 413 M4
Sandy Field Crs HORN PO8 352 C5
Sandy Hill Rd FNM GU9 134 D1
Sandyhurst Cl CFDH BH17 430 A7
Sandy La BPWT SO32 323 H7
CBLY GU15 71 H2
CHCH/BSGR BH23 434 C6
ELGH SO50 295 G6
FARN GU14 89 M2
FHAM/STUB PO14 371 K8
FLET GU13 110 F4
GSHT GU26 204 C6
HASM GU27 205 H7
HASM GU27 227 M1
HTWY RG27 87 J3
LISS GU33 249 K5
LYND SO43 363 K4
MIDH GU29 279 M8
NBAD SO52 292 A3 1
RFNM GU10 158 F7
RFNM GU10 181 K2
RGWD BH24 381 K4
ROMY SO51 262 F5
RSAL SP5 285 K1
SBNE BH6 449 G3
SHST GU47 49 J7
TADY RG26 42 A8
UPTN BH16 428 A2
VWD BH31 356 E2
WIMB BH21 356 C6
Sandy Mead Rd CHAR BH8 433 K7
Sandy Plot CHCH/BSGR BH23 435 G7
Sandy Point Rd HISD PO11 426 C7
Sandys Cl KEMP RG22 104 D5
Sandys Rd KEMP RG22 104 D4
Sandy Wy NBNE BH10 432 C5
Sankey La FARN GU14 89 J4
Sanross Cl FHAM/STUB PO14 395 L7
Santina Cl FNM GU9 112 A8
Saor Ms AND SP10 8 F4
Sapley La OVTN RG25 123 M1
Sapphire Cl WVILLE PO7 376 E1 9
Sapphire Rdg WVILLE PO7 376 E1
Saracen Cl LYMN SO41 440 A7 1
Saracens Rd CHFD SO53 293 L1
Sarah Cl LTDN BH7 433 M8
Sarah Wy FARN GU14 90 E4
Sargood Cl STHA RG19 27 H6 1
Sarisbury Cl TADY RG26 41 K8
Sark Rd BKME/WDN BH12 431 H8
Sarnia Ct ROWN SO16 317 K5
Sarson Cl RAND SP11 141 G2
Sarson La RAND SP11 141 G1
Sarum Av FERN BH22 380 C4
Sarum Cl WINW SO22 238 B1
NTID SP9 114 C8
STOK SO20 162 C8
Sarum Hl BSTK RG21 4 D9
Sarum Rd CHFD SO53 293 K2
WINW SO22 10 A8
WINW SO22 237 J1
TADY RG26 41 K7
Sarum Vw WINW SO22 238 A2
Sarum Wk LYMN SO41 440 B2 3
Satchell La HLER SO31 369 L5
Saturn Cl ROWN SO16 317 L4
Saulfland Dr CHCH/BSGR BH23 436 B8
Saunders La ROMY SO51 261 K3
Saunders Ms ENEY PO4 423 M6 5
Saunton Gdns FARN GU14 90 D2 4
Savernake Cl
LSOL/BMARY PO13 397 H6 5
ROMY SO51 263 G7 3
Savile Crs BOR GU35 201 J5
Saville Cl ELGH SO50 294 C3
GPORT PO12 18 A5
Saville Gdns CBLY GU15 71 L3
FHAM/PORC PO16 14 F1
Savoy Cl AND SP10 9 J6
Savoy Gv BLKW GU17 70 A5
Sawyer Cl WINW SO22 214 B7 2
Saxby Cl THLE RG7 31 L5
Saxholm Cl ROWN SO16 318 E2
Saxholm Dl ROWN SO16 318 E2
Saxholm Wy ROWN SO16 318 E2
Saxley Ct HAV PO9 377 G2
Saxonbury Rd SBNE BH6 449 K2
Saxon Cl FHAM/PORC PO16 373 M7
HLER SO31 370 C7
HORN PO8 328 B4
Saxon Ct STHA RG19 26 D5 3
Saxon Cft FNM GU9 134 F7 5
Saxon Gdns HEND SO30 345 L3
Saxonhurst RSAL SP5 284 F1
Saxonhurst Rd NBNE BH10 432 B4
Saxon King Gdns SBNE BH6 450 A4
Saxon Leas RSAL SP5 206 F2
Saxon Pl LYMN SO41 440 B2
Saxon Rd FAWY SO45 392 D7
WINC SO23 11 G5
WSHM SO15 12 A2
Saxon Wy AND SP10 118 E4
CHAM RG24 105 L1
FBDG SP6 333 L3 5
ROMY SO51 291 G1
Sayers Cl FRIM GU16 91 H1
NWBY RG14 25 L8
Sayers Rd ELGH SO50 294 C6
Sbac Tr ALDT GU11 112 B2
Scafell Av FHAM/STUB PO14 14 B8
Scallows La ROMY SO51 288 C3
Scantabout Av CHFD SO53 293 K1
Scant Road (West) RCCH PO18 379 M6
Scarf Rd CFDH BH17 445 L1
Scarlatti Rd KEMP RG22 104 E8
Scarlet Oaks CBLY GU15 71 H5
Scarlett's Rd ALDT GU11 112 D5
Scholars' Wk CHAM PO6 400 A1
School Cl CHFD SO53 293 G3
LYMN SO41 440 A6
RAND SP11 73 H3
School Flds BOR GU35 179 G7
School Hl BPWT SO32 325 H2
CWTH RG45 50 A4
RFNM GU10 136 E4
RFNM GU10 158 C2
SHST GU47 49 K7
School La BWD BH11 431 M3
CHCH/BSGR BH23 410 C4
CHFD SO53 292 F4
EMRTH PO10 378 F3
HLER SO31 369 L7
LISS GU33 248 E4
LYMN SO41 414 D8
LYMN SO41 440 C4
LYMN SO41 454 D2
MIDH GU29 279 J7
NALR SO24 219 G3
NALR SO24 220 B4
RFNM GU10 157 G3
RFNM GU10 159 G2
PLE BH15 445 H3
PSF GU32 275 M2
RCCH PO18 330 E6
RCCH PO18 403 K1
RGUW GU3 137 M4
RGWD BH24 381 L3
RWIN SO21 216 E1
STOK SO20 162 E8
STOK SO20 208 F1
THLE RG7 31 J6
THLE RG7 42 E7
THLE RG7 46 B5
WIMB BH21 380 D1
WINC SO23 215 G3
WVILLE PO7 351 H3
YTLY GU46 68 E2
School Rd BPWT SO32 324 E6
CHCH/BSGR BH23 410 C4
FAWY SO45 392 E5
GPORT PO12 397 K7
GSHT GU26 203 L5
HASM GU27 228 C3
HAV PO9 16 D5
HLER SO31 345 L8
BOR GU35 201 J4
RFNM GU10 158 B5
ROMY SO51 263 H7
ROMY SO51 288 E6
RSAL SP5 285 L4
RSAL SP5 287 H8
RWIN SO21 266 E2
THLE RG7 30 C7
THLE RG7 46 B4
TLHT RG30 31 M2
TOTT SO40 341 L2
WHAM PO17 348 E5
Schooner Wy HLER SO31 370 C7
HSEA PO3 424 A2
Schroeder Cl BSTK RG21 104 F6
Schubert Rd KEMP RG22 104 D8
The Scimitars
FHAM/STUB PO14 395 M5 9
Scivier's La BPWT SO32 296 B6
Scotland Cl ASHV GU12 113 K3
ELGH SO50 295 K6
Scotland Farm Rd ASHV GU12 113 K3
Scotland Hl SHST GU47 49 K8
Scotland La HASM GU27 228 E3
RSAL SP5 286 F1
Scotlands Cl HASM GU27 228 E3
Scotlands Dr HASM GU27 228 E3 1
Scotney Ct HAV PO9 377 M2 7
Scotney Rd BSTK RG21 4 E3
Scott Cl BKME/WDN BH12 431 K7
FHAM/STUB PO14 396 A4
RWIN SO21 266 F8
STOK SO20 210 F6
Scotter Rd ELGH SO50 294 C5
LTDN BH7 449 G3
Scott Rd BKME/WDN BH12 431 K8
ELGH SO50 293 L6
HSEA PO3 399 K3
ITCH SO19 344 D7
PSEA PO1 422 D2
Scott's Ct FARN GU14 90 E1
Scott's Gn CHCH/BSGR BH23 435 K8
Scotts Hills La
CHCH/BSGR BH23 450 C2
Scratchface La HAV PO9 376 F6
WVILLE PO7 376 D4
Scrivens Md STHA RG19 27 J5
Scrubbs La NALR SO24 218 F5
Scullards La SHAM SO14 12 F3
Scures Rd HTWY RG27 85 L7
Seabird Wy FHAM/PORC PO16
Seabourne Rd BOSC BH5
Seabreeze Wy LYMN SO41
Seacombe Gn ROWN SO16
Seacombe Rd CCLF BH13
Sea Crest Rd
LSOL/BMARY PO13
Seacroft Av NMIL/BTOS BH25
Seafield Cl NMIL/BTOS BH25
Seafield Dr SBNE BH6
Seafield Park Rd
FHAM/STUB PO14
Seafield Rd CHCH/BSGR BH23
FHAM/PORC PO16
HSEA PO3
NMIL/BTOS BH25
ROWN SO16
SBNE BH6
Seafields EMRTH PO10
Seafire Wy FARN GU14
Seaford Cl HLER SO31 3
Sea Front HISD PO11
Seagarth La ROWN SO16
Seager's Ct PSEA PO1
Sea Grove Av HISD PO11
Seagrove Rd NEND PO2
Seagull Cl ENEY PO4 4
KEMP RG22 1
Seagull La EMRTH PO10
Seagull Rd CHAR BH8
The Seagulls
LSOL/BMARY PO13 4
Sea Kings FHAM/STUB PO14 39
Sea La LSOL/BMARY PO13
Seale La RFNM GU10
RGUW GU3
Seale Rd MFD/CHID GU8
Seal Rd BSTK RG21
Seaman's La LYND SO43
Seamead FHAM/STUB PO14
Seamoor Rd CCLF BH13
WBNE BH4
Searing Wy TADY RG26
Searle Rd FNM GU9
Searles Cl NALR SO24 2
Searles Hl RWIN SO21
Searl's La HTWY RG27
Sea Rd BOSC BH5
ITCH SO19
LYMN SO41
NMIL/BTOS BH25
SBNE BH6
Seaton Av HSEA PO3
Seaton Cl CHCH/BSGR BH23
FHAM/STUB PO14
LYMN SO41 4
WEND SO18
Seaton Rd CBLY GU15
CHCH/BSGR BH23
Seatown Cl CFDH BH17
Seaview Av FHAM/PORC PO16
Sea View Rd BKME/WDN BH12
CHAM PO6
Seaview Rd CHCH/BSGR BH23
HISD PO11
NMIL/BTOS BH25
Seaward Av NMIL/BTOS BH25
SBNE BH6
Seaward Dr SELS PO20
Seaward Rd FAWY SO45
ITCH SO19
Seaway NMIL/BTOS BH25 43
Seaway Av CHCH/BSGR BH23
Seaway Crs ENEY PO4
Seaway Gv FHAM/PORC PO16
Seawinds LYMN SO41 45
Sebastian Gv WVILLE PO7 3
Sebastopol Rd ALDT GU11
Second Av CHAM PO6
EMRTH PO10
HAV PO9
THLE RG7
WSHM SO15
Second Marine Av
NMIL/BTOS BH25
Second St FAWY SO45
STHA RG19
Sedbergh Rd ROWN SO16
Sedgefield Cl CHAM PO6
TOTT SO40
Sedgefield Rd NWBY RG14
Sedge Gv NTHA RG18
Sedgeley Gv GPORT PO12
Sedgemead HLER SO31 3
Sedgemoor FARN GU14
Sedgewick Cl
LSOL/BMARY PO13
Sedgewick Rd ELGH SO50
ITCH SO19
Sedgley Cl SSEA PO5
Sedgley Rd MOOR/WNTN BH9
Seebys Oak SHST GU47
Segars La RWIN SO21
Segensworth Rd FHAM PO15
Sek Kong Cl STOK SO20
Selangor Av EMRTH PO10
Selborne Av ALDT GU11
HAV PO9
WEND SO18
Selborne Cl BLKW GU17 6
HTWY RG27
PSF GU32
Selborne Gdns FNM GU9 1
GPORT PO12
Selborne Pl WINW SO22 2
Selborne Rd ALTN GU34
LISS GU33
Selborne Wy BOR GU35
Selbourne Dr ELGH SO50
Selbourne Rd HAV PO9
TOTT SO40 3
Selbourne Ter PSEA PO1
Selby Cl BDST BH18
Seldon Cl WINW SO22
Seldown Br PLE BH15
Seldown La PLE BH15
Seldown Rd PLE BH15
Selfridge Av SBNE BH6

'st Wy ELCH SO50 ... 295 H7
Cl PLE BH15 ... 445 J3
< Cl WIMB BH21 ... 404 C7
ood Rd HLER SO31 ... 369 G2
ood Wy
/BTOS BH25 ... 437 H8
on Av ROMY SO51 ... 263 G8
' Av ENEY PO4 ... 423 L6
RT PO12 ... 397 K8
' Cl HISD PO11 ... 426 D6
VN SO16 ... 317 K6
ore Av HISD PO11 ... 426 A6
ore Rd HISD PO11 ... 425 L5
rth La BPWT SO32 ... 325 C5
rthy Cl PSTN BH14 ... 445 M6
n Dr YTLY GU46 ... 68 E2
n Gdns ELGH SO50 ... 293 M3
ana Cl HEND SO30 ... 346 B2
: Rd ROMY SO51 ... 291 G1
n Pl CHAM PO6 ... 398 E1
nel Cl WVILLE PO7 ... 352 F7
Rd FAWY SO45 ... 392 F4
mber Cl HEND SO30 ... 320 C7
iban Cl STOK SO20 ... 162 F3
Cl TOTT SO40 ... 340 F1
Gdns TOTT SO40 ... 341 H2
on Rd WINW SO22 ... 214 A7
ntine Rd
M/PORC PO16 ... 15 J2
BH15 ... 445 H5
PO5 ... 20 F8
PO5 ... 21 G7
LLE PO7 ... 376 A5
Gdns CHAR BH8 ... 433 J5
Dr HTWY RG27 ... 85 L8
's Cl RWIN SO21 ... 266 E8
orns Rd LYMN SO41 ... 413 G6
Cl ROWN SO16 ... 318 A8
rs Cl PSEA PO1 ... 423 H2
ett YTLY GU46 ... 68 E3
oaks Dr LTDN BH7 ... 433 L8
oaks Rd CHAM PO6 ... 375 J8
th St STHA RG19 ... 38 C3
als Rd MIDH GU29 ... 279 L8
everals CHAM RG24 ... 82 D5
n Cl CHAM PO6 ... 374 F7
M/PORC PO16 ... 373 L8
A RG18 ... 26 E3
T GU47 ... 49 M8
n Ct AND SP10 ... 9 M1
n Gdns DEAN RG23 ... 103 G7
n Rd FARN GU14 ... 90 B2
V BH22 ... 406 E2
VN SO16 ... 317 K8
n Wy BSTK RG21 ... 5 K8
D SO30 ... 320 C7
e Crs AND SP10 ... 9 L3
rd Ri ROMY SO51 ... 263 H8
our Cl CHFD SO53 ... 293 K3
D PO2 ... 423 H1
T SO40 ... 316 B7
our Dr CBLY GU15 ... 51 L8
our La NBAD SO52 ... 291 L4
our Rd KEMP RG22 ... 104 B6
GU35 ... 202 F4
/BMARY PO13 ... 420 D4
D BH24 ... 358 F7
VN SO16 ... 318 B5
leton Rd
/BMARY PO13 ... 397 H8
well Rd NEND PO2 ... 399 J6
Nook FNM GU9 ... 134 E2
esbury Av CHFD SO53 ... 293 H4
W SO17 ... 319 G7
LLE PO7 ... 376 B4
esbury Cl FERN BH22 ... 380 D6
esbury Mt BLKW GU17 ... 69 M5
esbury Rd CHAR BH8 ... 448 B2
V BH22 ... 380 D7
BH15 ... 445 J5
PO5 ... 21 G7
esbury St FBDG SP6 ... 309 K7
sbury Rd GPORT PO12 ... 19 G4
gs Meadow LYND SO43 ... 363 K3
espeare Av AND SP10 ... 8 A3
espeare Dr TOTT SO40 ... 316 C6
speare Gdns
V GU14 ... 90 A3
N PO8 ... 352 C5
espeare Rd CHAM RG24 ... 5 G1
H SO50 ... 293 L3
A RG18 ... 26 F4
PO1 ... 423 J2
IB BH21 ... 404 A2
ourne Ri CBLY GU15 ... 71 G3
ourne Rd GPORT PO12 ... 421 L1
ombe HLER SO31 ... 369 G1
en Rd ASHV GU12 ... 7 L5
on Cl ROWN SO16 ... 318 A4
on Rd HAV PO9 ... 377 M2
on Wy FLET GU13 ... 88 C8
s Rd WEND SO18 ... 344 F1
w La LYMN SO41 ... 414 B8
hallows FBDG SP6 ... 310 B1
oblehurst La HEND SO30 ... 321 H7
oblehurst La North
VT SO32 ... 321 J5
oblehurst La South
D SO30 ... 321 H8
rock Cl FRIM GU16 ... 71 G8
RT PO12 ... 19 J4
rock Rd ITCH SO19 ... 344 B5
rock Wy FAWY SO45 ... 367 L3
lin Ct ASHV GU12 ... 7 K4
lin Crs WSHM SO15 ... 318 C7
lin Rd ENEY PO4 ... 21 M4
M SO15 ... 318 C6
on Cl FHAM PO15 ... 14 A3
on Ct AND SP10 ... 9 M1
on Rd
M/STUB PO14 ... 395 M4
M/STUB PO14 ... 396 D3
on Wy CHFD SO53 ... 293 G2
and Av BWD BH11 ... 431 J3
en Hill La RGWD BH24 ... 384 D6
on Cl FAWY SO45 ... 391 M4
vick Rd PLE BH15 ... 444 F7
Cl VWD BH31 ... 356 E2

Sharf Rd BKME/WDN BH12 ... 446 F1
Sharlands Cl BDST BH18 ... 429 M5
Sharon Rd HEND SO30 ... 320 B6
Sharpley Cl FBDG SP6 ... 309 K5
Sharpness Cl
FHAM/STUB PO14 ... 372 A8
Sharps Cl HSEA PO3 ... 399 M5
Sharps Rd HAV PO9 ... 377 M3
Sharvells Rd LYMN SO41 ... 454 B3
Shavard La BPWT SO32 ... 299 J3
Shaves La NMIL/BTOS BH25 ... 437 L3
Shaw Cl AND SP10 ... 118 B8
TOTT SO40 ... 341 H1
WEND SO18 ... 319 M6
Shaw Farm Rd NWBY RG14 ... 25 L3
Shawfield La ASHV GU12 ... 113 J6
Shawfield Rd ASHV GU12 ... 113 J7
HAV PO9 ... 17 H6
Shawford Cl ROWN SO16 ... 318 D4
TOTT SO40 ... 340 F1
Shawford Gv HAV PO9 ... 377 G3
Shawford Rd CHAR BH8 ... 433 H5
RWIN SO21 ... 266 E2
Shaw Hl MARL SN8 ... 92 A4
NWBY RG14 ... 25 L3
Shaw La TADY RG26 ... 61 J2
Shaw Pk CWTH RG45 ... 49 L5
Shaw Pightle HTWY RG27 ... 85 L7
Shaw Rd NWBY RG14 ... 3 G1
RGWD BH24 ... 359 G6
Sheardley La BPWT SO32 ... 299 L8
Shearer Rd PSEA PO1 ... 423 J1
Shear Hl EPSF GU31 ... 276 A3
Shears Rd ELGH SO50 ... 294 D5
Shearwater Av
FHAM/PORC PO16 ... 373 J8
Shearwater Cl
LSOL/BMARY PO13 ... 396 F6
Shearwater Dr CHAM PO6 ... 400 D1
Sheep Dro STOK SO20 ... 184 C4
Sheep Fair Cl AND SP10 ... 9 L5
Sheephatch La RFNM GU10 ... 159 L3
Sheephouse FNM GU9 ... 134 F8
Sheep Pond La BPWT SO32 ... 298 F5
Sheep St PSF GU32 ... 275 L5
Sheepwash La KSCL RG20 ... 37 K6
SELS PO20 ... 427 M5
TADY RG26 ... 81 J2
WVILLE PO7 ... 351 K8
Sheerlands Rd EWKG RG40 ... 47 H2
Sheffield Cl ELGH SO50 ... 294 C3
FARN GU14 ... 90 C4
Sheffield Rd PSEA PO1 ... 21 L1
Shelbourne Rd CHAR BH8 ... 448 B2
Sheldon's La HTWY RG27 ... 85 M7
Sheldon's Rd HTWY RG27 ... 85 M7
Sheldrake Gdns LYMN SO41 ... 438 F4
ROWN SO16 ... 318 A3
Sheldrake Rd
CHCH/BSGR BH23 ... 450 F3
Shelford Rd ENEY PO4 ... 423 M3
Shellcroft HLER SO31 ... 370 B8
Shelley Av CHAM PO6 ... 374 C7
Shelley Cl CHAM RG24 ... 5 H1
CHCH/BSGR BH23 ... 451 H1
FLET GU13 ... 88 F8
WINW SO22 ... 10 A6
RGWD BH24 ... 381 J3
RWIN SO21 ... 216 D2
WSHM SO15 ... 318 B8
Shelley Ct CBLY GU15 ... 70 F3
Shelley Gdns BMTH BH1 ... 448 D3
HORN PO8 ... 352 C5
Shelley La ROMY SO51 ... 289 K7
Shelley Rd BMTH BH1 ... 448 D3
ELGH SO50 ... 293 L7
ITCH SO19 ... 345 H2
NTHA RG18 ... 26 F4
PSTN BH14 ... 446 C3
TOTT SO40 ... 316 C6
Shelley Rd East BMTH BH1 ... 448 D3
Shelleys La ALTN GU34 ... 177 K7
Shelley Wk YTLY GU46 ... 68 E3
Shell La ALTN GU34 ... 222 A5
Shelly Ri FARN GU14 ... 90 C2
Shelton Rd SBNE BH6 ... 449 H2
Shenley Cl FHAM PO15 ... 372 A6
Shepards Cl FHAM/STUB PO14 ... 372 A8
Shepherd Cl CHCH/BSGR BH23 ... 436 D7
Shepherds Cl WINW SO22 ... 238 A4
TOTT SO40 ... 339 M2
Shepherds Down NALR SO24 ... 218 B4
Shepherds Hey Rd TOTT SO40 ... 316 A7
Shepherd's Hl HASM GU27 ... 228 F2
RGWD BH24 ... 358 A2
Shepherds La RGWD BH24 ... 357 L2
RWIN SO21 ... 265 L2
Shepherds Purse Cl
HLER SO31 ... 370 D6
Shepherds Ri RAND SP11 ... 73 H3
Shepherds Rd TOTT SO40 ... 339 M2
WINC SO23 ... 11 M7
Shepherds Rw AND SP10 ... 9 L6
Shepherds Spring La AND SP10 ... 9 H4
Shepherds Wk FARN GU14 ... 90 B1
Shepherds Wy CWTH RG45 ... 49 H4
LIPH GU30 ... 227 G5
LTDN BH7 ... 448 F1
RFNM GU10 ... 159 M4
ROWN SO16 ... 317 H3
Sheppard Cl HORN PO8 ... 352 E2
WHCH RG28 ... 122 B4
Sheppard Rd BSTK RG21 ... 104 F6
Shepton Br BROC SO42 ... 389 M3
Sheraton Av KEMP RG22 ... 127 G1
Sheraton Cl BLKW GU17 ... 70 B4
Sherborn Crs CFDH BH17 ... 430 D7
Sherborne Ct ELGH SO50 ... 293 L2
Sherborne Dr FERN BH22 ... 406 B4
Sherborne Rd BSTK RG21 ... 4 C4
CHAM RG24 ... 82 E6
FARN GU14 ... 91 G8
PTSW SO17 ... 319 G6
Sherborne Wy HEND SO30 ... 346 A2
Sherbrooke Cl WINC SO23 ... 191 H8
Sherfield Av HAV PO9 ... 377 L3
Sherfield English La
ROMY SO51 ... 288 B2
RSAL SP5 ... 288 A3

Sherfield English Rd RSAL SP5 ... 288 A5
Sherfield Rd TADY RG26 ... 63 L5
Sheridan Cl WINW SO22 ... 238 B3
ITCH SO19 ... 345 G3
Sheridan Crs TADY RG26 ... 41 H7
Sheridan Gdns HLER SO31 ... 347 G8
TOTT SO40 ... 341 H1
Sheridan Rd FRIM GU16 ... 71 G8
Sheringham Rd
BKME/WDN BH12 ... 446 E3
CHAM PO6 ... 375 H7
Sherlock Lea HTWY RG27 ... 68 B1
Shermin's Bank
CHCH/BSGR BH23 ... 450 D3
Sherrardmead NWBY RG14 ... 25 L3
Sherrin Cl PLE BH15 ... 445 J3
Sherringham Cl FAWY SO45 ... 392 F5
Sherwin Crs FARN GU14 ... 70 E8
Sherwood Av FERN BH22 ... 406 A5
HEND SO30 ... 346 A4
PSTN BH14 ... 445 L6
Sherwood Cl
CHCH/BSGR BH23 ... 449 L1
KEMP RG22 ... 127 H2
LISS GU33 ... 248 F1
ROWN SO16 ... 318 D5
Sherwood Dr VWD BH31 ... 356 F2
Sherwood Gdns HLER SO31 ... 370 C4
Sherwood Rd CHFD SO53 ... 265 K7
GPORT PO12 ... 18 D3
Sherwood Wy FAWY SO45 ... 418 C1
Shetland Cl CHAM PO6 ... 375 K7
TOTT SO40 ... 316 A8
Shetland Ri HLER SO31 ... 370 F2
Shetland Rd CHAM RG24 ... 83 H7
Shetland Wy FARN GU14 ... 89 G4
Shillinglee WVILLE PO7 ... 376 C5
Shillingstone Dr
MOOR/WNTN BH9 ... 432 F4
Shillito Rd BKME/WDN BH12 ... 446 C3
Shingle Bank Dr LYMN SO41 ... 454 C4
Ship Aly FARN GU14 ... 90 F2
Shipbuilding Rd PSEA PO1 ... 422 D1
Shipcote La BPWT SO32 ... 297 H6
Ship La FARN GU14 ... 90 F2
Ship Leopard St PSEA PO1 ... 20 C2
Shipley Ct LIPH GU30 ... 226 E5
Shipley Rd RWIN SO21 ... 266 F1
Shipstal Cl UPTN BH16 ... 444 B4
Shipton Wy KEMP RG22 ... 104 B6
Shire Av FARN GU14 ... 89 H5
Shire Cl HLER SO31 ... 370 F1
HORN PO8 ... 352 F7
Shire Ct ALDT GU11 ... 6 A2
Shires Cl RGWD BH24 ... 382 E4
Shires Md VWD BH31 ... 356 E2
The Shires HEND SO30 ... 345 L2
Shires Wy YTLY GU46 ... 49 G8
Shirley Av ENEY PO4 ... 424 A4
WSHM SO15 ... 318 B8
Shirley Cl CHCH/BSGR BH23 ... 409 M7
FERN BH22 ... 380 C6
Shirley High St ROWN SO16 ... 318 A8
Shirley Holms LYMN SO41 ... 413 K7
Shirley Park Rd ROWN SO16 ... 318 A8
Shirley Rd BKME/WDN BH12 ... 446 A2
MOOR/WNTN BH9 ... 432 E7
SSEA PO5 ... 21 L8
WSHM SO15 ... 318 B8
Shoddesden La RAND SP11 ... 92 F8
RAND SP11 ... 116 B2
Shoe La ALDT GU11 ... 112 D2
BPWT SO32 ... 296 E2
Sholing Ct HAV PO9 ... 377 H2
Sholing Rd ITCH SO19 ... 344 C4
Shooters Hill Cl ITCH SO19 ... 344 F5
Shooters Wy BSTK RG21 ... 5 G4
Shoot Hl WHAM PO17 ... 350 B5
Shoot La LSOL/BMARY PO13 ... 396 E8
Shop La HLER SO31 ... 345 J5
NWBY RG14 ... 25 J2
Shore Av HSEA PO3 ... 423 M2
UPTN BH16 ... 444 B2
Shore Cl UPTN BH16 ... 444 B2
Shore Crs BPWT SO32 ... 323 J1
Shorefield Crs LYMN SO41 ... 454 B3
Shorefield Rd LYMN SO41 ... 453 M2
TOTT SO40 ... 342 D6
Shorefield Wy LYMN SO41 ... 454 B3
Shore Gdns UPTN BH16 ... 444 A2
Shorehaven CHAM PO6 ... 374 D8
Shore La BPWT SO32 ... 323 J1
UPTN BH16 ... 444 A3
Shore Rd CCLF BH13 ... 457 J2
FAWY SO45 ... 367 M4
PSTN BH14 ... 457 J1
Shorewell HLER SO31 ... 369 G1
Shorewood Cl HLER SO31 ... 370 E7
Short Cl BKME/WDN BH12 ... 431 L8
Short Dale Rd ALDT GU11 ... 7 K9
Shortfield Rd RFNM GU10 ... 158 F7
Shortheath Crest FNM GU9 ... 158 C2
Shortheath La THLE RG7 ... 31 G5
Shortheath Rd FNM GU9 ... 158 D2
Short Hl ROMY SO51 ... 263 H7
Short La RAND SP11 ... 117 M7
Short Rd FHAM/STUB PO14 ... 395 L6
Short Rw PSEA PO1 ... 422 E2
Shorts Cl CHCH/BSGR BH23 ... 435 G7
Shorts Rd ELGH SO50 ... 295 G6
Short St ALDT GU11 ... 6 E1
RAND SP11 ... 92 E6
Shotterfield Ter LISS GU33 ... 248 E4
Shotters La ALTN GU34 ... 222 E2
Shottsford Rd PLE BH15 ... 445 H3
Shotts La LYMN SO41 ... 441 G4
Shraveshill Cl TOTT SO40 ... 316 C7
The Shrave ALTN GU34 ... 197 K4
Shrivenham Cl SHST GU47 ... 50 A8
Shrubbery Cl
FHAM/PORC PO16 ... 398 A1
The Shrubbery FARN GU14 ... 90 A5
GPORT PO12 ... 421 K1
Shrubb's Av LYMN SO41 ... 440 C4
Shrubbs Hill Gdns
LYND SO43 ... 363 K4
Shrubbs Hill Rd LYND SO43 ... 363 K4
Shrubbs La RFNM GU10 ... 158 C4

Shrubland Cl WEND SO18 ... 320 A8
Shyshack La TADY RG26 ... 41 H7
Sian Cl FLET GU13 ... 111 G3
Sibelius Cl KEMP RG22 ... 127 K1
Sibland Cl FHAM/STUB PO14 ... 14 A8
Sickle Rd HASM GU27 ... 228 C3
Sickles Rd BOR GU35 ... 179 G6
Sidbury Circular Rd NTID SP9 ... 114 C1
Sidestrand Rd ALDT GU11 ... 112 B1
NWBY RG14 ... 25 G8
The Sidings ALDT GU11 ... 112 F5
HLER SO31 ... 369 H3
RSAL SP5 ... 256 F8
Sidlaw Cl KEMP RG22 ... 103 M5
Sidlaws Rd FARN GU14 ... 90 A1
Sidlesham Cl HISD PO11 ... 426 D6
Sidmouth Av HSEA PO3 ... 399 L8
Sidmouth Rd AND SP10 ... 9 M5
Silchester Cl AND SP10 ... 8 C1
WCLF BH2 ... 22 E3
Silchester Rd HSEA PO3 ... 423 M1
TADY RG26 ... 41 L7
TADY RG26 ... 62 D3
TADY RG26 ... 63 G5
Silkin Gdns TOTT SO40 ... 341 H2
Silk Mill La OVTN RG25 ... 100 E8
Silkstead Av HAV PO9 ... 377 K2
Silkstead La RWIN SO21 ... 265 L3
Silkweavers Rd AND SP10 ... 9 J4
Sillen La FBDG SP6 ... 280 F5
Silver Birch Av
FHAM/STUB PO14 ... 14 C7
Silver Birch Cl
BKME/WDN BH12 ... 446 F4
FLET GU13 ... 110 E3
LISS GU33 ... 248 F4
Silver Birches HLER SO31 ... 345 K8
Silver Birch Rd AND SP10 ... 8 C3
Silverdale FLET GU13 ... 110 F2
NMIL/BTOS BH25 ... 437 M8
NMIL/BTOS BH25 ... 453 G1
Silverdale Cl BDST BH18 ... 429 J4
Silverdale Crs FBDG SP6 ... 333 L2
Silverdale Dr WVILLE PO7 ... 352 A6
Silverdale Rd TADY RG26 ... 41 K7
WSHM SO15 ... 343 J1
Silver Dr FRIM GU16 ... 71 M5
Silverglades YTLY GU46 ... 68 F4
Silver Hl SHST GU47 ... 50 B8
WINC SO23 ... 11 H8
Silver La THLE RG7 ... 30 D8
Silverlock Cl NEND PO2 ... 399 H8
Silver Park Cl FLET GU13 ... 111 G2
Silversands Gdns HISD PO11 ... 425 M6
Silvers End FAWY SO45 ... 367 L7
Silver St LYMN SO41 ... 438 D4
LYND SO43 ... 363 H3
SSEA PO5 ... 20 F5
Silvers Wd TOTT SO40 ... 316 B7
Silverthorne Wy WVILLE PO7 ... 352 B8
Silvertrees EMRTH PO10 ... 378 D6
Silver Wy CHCH/BSGR BH23 ... 436 C8
Silverwood Cl WINW SO22 ... 238 C3
WIMB BH21 ... 404 B6
Silverwood Dr CBLY GU15 ... 71 K1
Silvester Cl BSTK RG21 ... 5 H4
Silvester Rd HORN PO8 ... 352 C6
Silvester Wy FLET GU13 ... 110 D4
Silwood Cl WINW SO22 ... 10 B4
Simmondstone La RFNM GU10 ... 181 G6
Simmons Cl HEND SO30 ... 321 H8
Simmons Gn HISD PO11 ... 426 A5
Simms Farm La THLE RG7 ... 43 J4
Simnel St SHAM SO14 ... 12 F5
Simonds Rd RAND SP11 ... 92 D6
Simons Fld NTHA RG18 ... 27 J4
Simons Rd CHAM RG24 ... 83 K6
Simon Wy WEND SO18 ... 345 J1
Simpson Cl FHAM/PORC PO16 ... 374 A8
Simpson Rd NEND PO2 ... 399 G7
Sims Cl TADY RG26 ... 64 A6
Sinah La HISD PO11 ... 425 G5
Sinclair Rd ROWN SO16 ... 317 M3
Sine Cl FARN GU14 ... 70 E8
Singleton Dr NBNE BH10 ... 432 A6
Singleton Gdns HORN PO8 ... 328 C4
Singleton Wy TOTT SO40 ... 316 A8
Sinhurst Rd CBLY GU15 ... 70 E4
Sir Christopher Cl
FAWY SO45 ... 367 M4
Sirdar Rd PTSW SO17 ... 319 H5
Sir Galahad Rd NBAD SO52 ... 292 E2
Sir George's Rd WSHM SO15 ... 343 H2
Sir Lancelot Cl NBAD SO52 ... 292 E2
Siskin Cl BPWT SO32 ... 296 F8
FERN BH22 ... 405 M1
ROWN SO16 ... 317 M3
Siskin Gv WVILLE PO7 ... 376 E2
Sissinghurst Cl ITCH SO19 ... 344 E7
Sissinghurst Rd
FHAM/PORC PO16 ... 397 M1
Six Acre La HUNG RG17 ... 32 C2
Six Oaks Rd NBAD SO52 ... 291 M3
Sixpenny Cl BKME/WDN BH12 ... 446 E1
HLER SO31 ... 370 E7
Sixth Av CHAM PO6 ... 375 J8
Sixth St STHA RG19 ... 38 C3
Sizer Wy FAWY SO45 ... 366 F5
Skates La TADY RG26 ... 62 A3
Skew Rd RAND SP11 ... 140 A5
WHAM PO17 ... 374 A6
Skilman Dr STHA RG19 ... 27 J5
Skinner's Green La KSCL RG20 ... 36 C2
Skinner St PLE BH15 ... 445 H7
Skipper Wy LSOL/BMARY PO13 ... 420 D3
Skippetts La East BSTK RG21 ... 105 H6
Skippetts La West BSTK RG21 ... 105 G6
Skippons Cl NWBY RG14 ... 36 F2
Skipton Cl BDST BH18 ... 429 L6
Skipton Rd CHFD SO53 ... 293 J4
Sky End La LYMN SO41 ... 438 E6
Skylark Mdw FHAM PO15 ... 371 K3
Skylark Ri WHCH RG28 ... 122 A2
Skyllings NWBY RG14 ... 3 J2
Skys Wood Rd NBAD SO52 ... 292 E1
Slab La ROMY SO51 ... 288 C5
RSAL SP5 ... 284 F1
Slade Cl LYMN SO41 ... 438 E5

Slade La EPSF GU31 ... 277 H4
Slades Farm Rd NBNE BH10 ... 432 A7
Slades Hl FAWY SO45 ... 392 D6
Slade's La NBNE BH10 ... 432 A8
Slater Cl TOTT SO40 ... 316 A8
Sleepbrook Cl VWD BH31 ... 356 C2
Sleepers Delle Gdns
WINW SO22 ... 238 D2
Sleepers' Hl WINW SO22 ... 238 C2
WINW SO22 ... 238 C2
Sleepers Hill Gdns
WINW SO22 ... 238 C2
Slepe Crs BKME/WDN BH12 ... 431 K8
Slessor Cl RAND SP11 ... 142 A1
Slim Cl ALDT GU11 ... 113 H1
Slim Rd CBLY GU15 ... 70 E1
Slindon Cl HORN PO8 ... 328 C3
Slindon St PSEA PO1 ... 21 H1
Slingsby Cl PSEA PO1 ... 20 F5
Slinn Rd CHCH/BSGR BH23 ... 450 D1
Slipper Rd EMRTH PO10 ... 402 E1
Slip Wy PLE BH15 ... 445 G6
Sloane Av FAWY SO45 ... 392 B4
Sloane Ct FAWY SO45 ... 392 B4
Sloane Pk BPWT SO32 ... 348 B1
Sloe Tree Cl HLER SO31 ... 371 G6
Smallcutts Av EMRTH PO10 ... 379 H7
Smallfield Dr HTWY RG27 ... 86 B7
Smallridge KSCL RG20 ... 36 F4
Smannell Rd RAND SP11 ... 119 J4
Smay Down La MARL SN8 ... 52 A5
Smeaton Rd AND SP10 ... 118 A6
Smeaton St NEND PO2 ... 399 G6
Smeeton Rd
LSOL/BMARY PO13 ... 420 D2
Smith Cl FAWY SO45 ... 392 D6
Smithe Cl ELGH SO50 ... 293 M5
Smithfield La BOR GU35 ... 180 D7
Smith Gv HEND SO30 ... 346 A3
Smith La EMRTH PO10 ... 403 G7
Smith's Fld ROMY SO51 ... 262 F7
Smiths La BPWT SO32 ... 323 L8
Smith's Md OVTN RG25 ... 125 L7
Smith St GPORT PO12 ... 18 D3
Smithy Cl ALTN GU34 ... 177 J1
Smithy La BOR GU35 ... 180 B6
NMIL/BTOS BH25 ... 437 K2
The Smithy TADY RG26 ... 63 L5
WVILLE PO7 ... 351 J4
Smugglers La NALR SO24 ... 220 F6
Smugglers La North
CHCH/BSGR BH23 ... 436 A8
Smugglers La South
CHCH/BSGR BH23 ... 436 C8
Smugglers' Wy RFNM GU10 ... 136 B8
Smugglers Wood Rd
CHCH/BSGR BH23 ... 436 A7
Smythe Rd ITCH SO19 ... 345 H5
Snailing La LISS GU33 ... 224 C7
LISS GU33 ... 248 A2
Snail's La RGWD BH24 ... 358 E6
Snailslynch FNM GU9 ... 135 G6
Snake La KSCL RG20 ... 24 D2
Snakemoor La BPWT SO32 ... 321 K3
Snapdragon Cl HLER SO31 ... 370 D6
Snape Cl LSOL/BMARY PO13 ... 397 G8
Snellgrove Cl TOTT SO40 ... 316 B6
Snellgrove Pl TOTT SO40 ... 316 B6
Snipe La HASM GU27 ... 228 D7
Snoddington Rd RAND SP11 ... 139 J1
Snode Hl ALTN GU34 ... 175 M5
Snooks La LYMN SO41 ... 440 F2
Snowberry Crs HAV PO9 ... 377 M5
Snowdon Cl STHA RG19 ... 27 G6
Snowdon Dr FHAM/STUB PO14 ... 14 C8
Snowdon Rd FARN GU14 ... 90 B1
WBNE BH4 ... 447 H4
Snowdrop Cl KEMP RG22 ... 103 M8
Snowdrop Copse NTHA RG18 ... 27 J4
Snowdrop Gdns
CHCH/BSGR BH23 ... 435 M7
Soake Rd WVILLE PO7 ... 351 M5
Soalwood La EPSF GU32 ... 246 E7
Soame's La NALR SO24 ... 220 D5
Sobers Sq AND SP10 ... 119 H5
Soberton Rd CHAR BH8 ... 448 C1
HAV PO9 ... 377 J5
Soke Hl ALTN GU34 ... 196 D8
Soke Rd THLE RG7 ... 42 C6
The Soke NALR SO24 ... 218 C1
Solartron Rd FARN GU14 ... 90 D5
Solby's Rd BSTK RG21 ... 4 C8
Soldiers Ri EWKG RG40 ... 49 G1
Soldridge Cl HAV PO9 ... 377 M2
Soldridge Rd ALTN GU34 ... 196 D5
Solent Av ITCH SO19 ... 345 J2
LYMN SO41 ... 440 D5
Solent Cl CHFD SO53 ... 293 K2
LYMN SO41 ... 440 D5
Solent Dr FAWY SO45 ... 367 K4
HISD PO11 ... 425 K6
HLER SO31 ... 394 B2
KEMP RG22 ... 127 G1
NMIL/BTOS BH25 ... 452 F1
Solent Mdw HLER SO31 ... 369 L7
Solent Rd CHAM PO6 ... 376 A8
CHCH/BSGR BH23 ... 436 F6
FAWY SO45 ... 367 J8
FHAM/STUB PO14 ... 395 L7
HAV PO9 ... 16 C5
SBNE BH6 ... 449 M5
Solent Vw FHAM/PORC PO16 ... 373 M7
Solent Wy BROC SO42 ... 391 G3
BROC SO42 ... 416 F1
FHAM/STUB PO14 ... 395 L7
GPORT PO12 ... 19 J7
GPORT PO12 ... 421 J5
HAV PO9 ... 16 A7
HSEA PO3 ... 424 B2
LSOL/BMARY PO13 ... 420 E5
LYMN SO41 ... 454 E6
PSEA PO1 ... 20 D2
SHAM SO14 ... 13 G7
Solly Cl BKME/WDN BH12 ... 446 D1
Solomons La BPWT SO32 ... 323 L6
Solomon Wy PLE BH15 ... 444 C6
Solona Cl CHFD SO53 ... 293 L1
Somborne Dr HAV PO9 ... 377 K3

Somborne Park Rd *STOK* SO20.. 187 H7
Somerby Rd *PLE* BH15 445 J2
Somerford Av
CHCH/BSGR BH23 435 M8
Somerford Cl *ITCH* SO19 344 E2 2
Somerford Rd
CHCH/BSGR BH23 450 E1
Somerford Wy
CHCH/BSGR BH23 450 D1
Somerley Rd
MOOR/WNTN BH9 447 M1
Somerley Vw *RGWD* BH24 358 E8 1
Somers Cl *WINW* SO22 238 C3
Somerset Av *BOR* GU35 201 J5
WEND SO18 345 G1
Somerset Crs *CHFD* SO53 293 H5
Somerset Rd
CHCH/BSGR BH23 449 K1
FARN GU14 90 F7
LTDN BH7 448 E3
PTSW SO17 319 H6
SSEA PO5 21 K9
Somerset Ter *WSHM* SO15 342 F2
Somers Rd *SSEA* PO5 21 K3
Somers Rd North *PSEA* PO1 21 K2
Somerton Av *WEND* SO18 344 F1
Somerton Cl
NMIL/BTOS BH25 438 B5 1
Somerton Gv *STHA* RG19 26 F6
Somervell Cl *GPORT* PO12 18 D8
Somervell Dr *FHAM/PORC* PO16.. 15 G2
Somerville Crs *YTLY* GU46 69 H2
Somerville Rd *RGWD* BH24 359 G8
WCLF BH2 22 B6
WINC SO23 191 H7
Somme Rd *RAND* SP11 92 C8
Sonnet Wy *WVILLE* PO7 352 F8 1
Sonning Cl *KEMP* RG22 126 E1
Sonninge Cl *SHST* GU47 50 A8 6
Soper Gv *BSTK* RG21 4 E5
Sopers La *CFDH* BH17 429 L7
CHCH/BSGR BH23 449 M2
Sopley Cl *NMIL/BTOS* BH25 437 H8
Sopley Ct *HAV* PO9 377 M2 10
Sopwith Cl *STOK* SO20 210 F6
Sopwith Crs *WIMB* BH21 404 C6
Sopwith Pk *AND* SP10 118 A7
Sopwith Wy *HLER* SO31 346 C8
Sorrel Cl *NWBY* RG14 26 A3
ROMY SO51 263 H7
THLE RG7 31 L5 5
WVILLE PO7 376 E2
Sorrel Dr *FHAM* PO15 371 H1
Sorrel Gdns *WIMB* BH21 429 K6
Sorrell Cl *HLER* SO31 370 D6
Sorrell's Cl *CHAM* RG24 83 L5
Sorrell Wy *CHCH/BSGR* BH23 435 M8
Sotherington La *ALTN* GU34 223 L2
South Acre *EPSF* GU31 305 G5
Southampton Cl *BLKW* GU17 ... 69 M2 4
Southampton Hl
FHAM/STUB PO14 371 K7
Southampton Rd *BROC* SO42 413 L3
CHAM PO6 374 D8
ELGH SO50 293 M8
FAWY SO45 367 L5
FBDG SP6 310 A7
FHAM PO15 371 G3
FHAM/PORC PO16 15 J4
FHAM/STUB PO14 371 H6
LYMN SO41 440 B3
LYND SO43 364 A2
RGWD BH24 358 E8
ROMY SO51 290 F2
TOTT SO40 339 M1
Southampton St *FARN* GU14 90 E8
WSHM SO15 343 K2 4
South Atlantic Dr *ALDT* GU11 112 F5
South Av *FAWY* SO45 392 C5
FNM GU9 135 G2
NEND PO2 399 J4
NMIL/BTOS BH25 437 M6
South Baddesey Rd
LYMN SO41 440 F4
South Bay *EMRTH* PO10 402 E5
South Beta Rd *FARN* GU14 90 E6
Southbourne Av *CHAM* PO6 399 M1
EMRTH PO10 378 F8
FAWY SO45 392 A4
Southbourne Coast Rd
SBNE BH6 449 K5
Southbourne Gv *SBNE* BH6 449 G4
Southbourne Overcliff Dr
SBNE BH6 449 H5
Southbourne Rd *LYMN* SO41 440 A5
SBNE BH6 449 G3
Southbrook Cl *CFDH* BH17 430 E6
HAV PO9 16 E7
Southbrook Pl *RWIN* SO21 169 M5 1
Southbrook Rd *HAV* PO9 16 E8
Southby Dr *FLET* GU13 89 G7
South Charford Dro *FBDG* SP6.. 283 M4
Southcliff
LSOL/BMARY PO13 420 C1 5
Southcliffe Rd
CHCH/BSGR BH23 451 G2
NMIL/BTOS BH25 437 H8
Southcliff Rd *SHAM* SO14 343 L1
South Cliff Rd *WCLF* BH2 22 E8
South Cl *GPORT* PO12 19 J4
HAV PO9 17 G6
NALR SO24 218 A3
ROMY SO51 263 H7 6
Southcote Dr *CBLY* GU15 71 K3 2
Southcote Rd *BMTH* BH1 23 L3
South Ct *HLER* SO31 369 J6
Southcroft Rd *GPORT* PO12 18 A1
South Cross St *GPORT* PO12 19 K3
Southdene Rd *CHFD* SO53 293 H3
Southdown Rd *CHAM* PO6 375 L8
HORN PO8 328 B5
RWIN SO21 266 C2
STHA RG19 26 C4 1
TADY RG26 41 K7
Southdowns *NALR* SO24 194 C7
South Downs Wy *BPWT* SO32 270 F8
EPSF GU31 305 K7
HORN PO8 302 B5
NALR SO24 241 J4
PSF GU32 300 D1
WVILLE PO7 325 M4
Southdown Vw *WVILLE* PO7 352 A6
Southdown Wy *FERN* BH22 380 D7
South Dr *WINW* SO22 213 M4
NTID SP9 114 D4
ROMY SO51 262 A5
THLE RG7 31 G1
South East Crs *ITCH* SO19 344 E4
South East Rd *ITCH* SO19 344 E4
Southend *NTHA* RG18 26 F2
South End Cl *RWIN* SO21 265 G2
Southend La *BPWT* SO32 325 J8
South End Rd *AND* SP10 9 K9
Southend Rd *BSTK* RG21 4 C8
Southern Av *FERN* BH22 380 E7
Southern Gdns *TOTT* SO40 341 J1
Southern Haye *HTWY* RG27 87 H3
Southernhay Rd *VWD* BH31 356 F2
Southern La *NMIL/BTOS* BH25 .. 437 K8
Southern Oaks
NMIL/BTOS BH25 437 K7
Southern Rd *BSTK* RG21 105 G4
CBLY GU15 70 F2
HEND SO30 320 C8
BOR GU35 201 J2
LYMN SO41 440 B4
SBNE BH6 449 H4
WSHM SO15 12 C3
Southern Wy *FARN* GU14 90 A5
FNM GU9 134 F7
Southey Rd *CHCH/BSGR* BH23 .. 435 K8
Southfield *RGWD* BH24 382 E2 5
Southfield La *RGWD* BH24 385 G6
Southfield Ms *RGWD* BH24 382 E2 6
Southfields Cl *BPWT* SO32 297 H8
South Front *SHAM* SO14 13 H3
Southgate St *WINC* SO23 10 F8
South Gv *FARN* GU14 89 H4
LYMN SO41 440 D5
South Ham Rd *KEMP* RG22 104 D4
South Haven Cl *UPTN* BH16 444 A4
South Hl *BPWT* SO32 298 F8
FBDG SP6 333 L2
South Hurst *BOR* GU35 201 J7
Southill Av *BKME/WDN* BH12 446 B2
Southill Gdns
MOOR/WNTN BH9 432 E7
Southill Rd *BKME/WDN* BH12 446 B2
MOOR/WNTN BH9 432 E7
Southington Cl *OVTN* RG25 100 D8
Southington La *OVTN* RG25 100 E8
South Kinson Dr *BWD* BH11 431 L4
Southlands *CHAM* RG24 83 K5 2
LYMN SO41 440 A6
Southlands Av *SBNE* BH6 449 L4
WIMB BH21 429 H2
Southlands Cl *ASHV* GU12 113 K7
Southlands Rd *ASHV* GU12 113 K7
South La *ASHV* GU12 113 L7
EMRTH PO10 379 J5
EPSF GU31 303 J4
HORN PO8 328 A3
RSAL SP5 313 H1
Southlawns Wk
NMIL/BTOS BH25 437 K7
Southlea Av *SBNE* BH6 449 L3
Southleigh Gv *HISD* PO11 425 K4
Southleigh Rd *EMRTH* PO10 378 D5
HAV PO9 17 J5
South Ldg *FHAM* PO15 371 M7
South Meadow *CWTH* RG45 50 A5
Southmead Rd *ALDT* GU11 7 G5
FHAM PO15 14 B5
South Millers Dl *CHFD* SO53 293 G1
South Mill Rd *WSHM* SO15 342 D1
Southmoor La *HAV* PO9 16 B8
South Pde *ENEY* PO4 423 H7
South Park Rd
BKME/WDN BH12 431 L8
South Pl *LSOL/BMARY* PO13 420 E4
South Rdg *ODIM* RG29 108 D6
South Rd *ASHV* GU12 113 J4
BMTH BH1 448 D3
CHAM PO6 374 E6
CHAM PO6 400 B1
CWTH RG45 50 B5
HISD PO11 425 K5
HORN PO8 328 B7
KSCL RG20 59 K6
LIPH GU30 226 F7
NALR SO24 218 A3
PSEA PO1 423 J1
PTSW SO17 319 H8
STOK SO20 209 H3
WHAM PO17 374 E2
WIMB BH21 429 H1
Southrope Gn *OVTN* RG25 153 H1
Southsea Ter *SSEA* PO5 20 F6
Southside Rd *RAND* SP11 145 G3
South Sp *CHAM* PO6 374 F6
South St *AND* SP10 9 H8
ELGH SO50 293 M8
EMRTH PO10 378 D8
FARN GU14 91 H7
FAWY SO45 367 L5
FHAM/STUB PO14 371 K8
FNM GU9 134 F6
GPORT PO12 19 J4
HAV PO9 16 F6
LYMN SO41 440 A6
NALR SO24 220 A4
RSAL SP5 252 A1
SSEA PO5 20 F5 11
South Sway La *LYMN* SO41 413 G8
South Ter *PSEA* PO1 20 C1 2
PSEA PO1 422 E2
South Town Rd *ALTN* GU34 196 E2
South Trestle Rd *FAWY* SO45 393 G3
South Vw *WINW* SO22 10 D7
South View Cl *RWIN* SO21 168 C5
South View Cottages
WHCH RG28 122 F1
Southview Gdns *AND* SP10 9 J7
South View Pl *WCLF* BH2 22 C7
Southview Ri *ALTN* GU34 176 D3 1
South View Rd
CHCH/BSGR BH23 449 M2
WINW SO22 238 A5
Southview Rd *BOR* GU35 202 E3
South View Rd *WSHM* SO15 318 C8
South View Ter *RAND* SP11 97 M8
South Wk *ASHV* GU12 7 M1
Southwark Cl *YTLY* GU46 68 F2
South Wy *AND* SP10 119 K6
Southway *CBLY* GU15 70 E4
FHAM PO15 371 J5
Southways *FHAM/STUB* PO14 396 B6
South Weirs *BROC* SO42 413 H1
Southwell Park Rd *CBLY* GU15 .... 70 E3
South West Coast Pth
SWGE BH19 457 G8
South Western Crs *PSTN* BH14.. 446 A5
Southwick Av
FHAM/PORC PO16 374 C7
Southwick Cl *WINW* SO22 214 C4 6
Southwick Ct
FHAM/STUB PO14 396 E2 1
Southwick Hill Rd *CHAM* PO6 375 J7
Southwick Rd *CHAM* PO6 375 G6
SBNE BH6 449 H2
WHAM PO17 349 G5
WVILLE PO7 351 J4
Southwood Av
CHCH/BSGR BH23 436 E7
SBNE BH6 449 H4
Southwood Cl
CHCH/BSGR BH23 436 E7
FERN BH22 406 A3
South Wood Gdns *HLER* SO31 370 D5
Southwood Gdns *THLE* RG7 31 K5
Southwood La *FARN* GU14 89 K5
Southwood Rd *ALTN* GU34 154 A8
FARN GU14 69 H7
FARN GU14 90 B4
HISD PO11 426 A6
NEND PO2 399 J4
Sovereign Crs
FHAM/STUB PO14 370 E7
Sovereign Dr *CBLY* GU15 71 L1
ENEY PO4 424 B3 1
HEND SO30 346 B2
Sovereign La *WVILLE* PO7 376 C5
Sovereign Wy *ELGH* SO50 293 L2
Sowcroft La *ODIM* RG29 154 F3
Sowden Cl *HEND* SO30 345 M1
Sowley La *LYMN* SO41 441 L3
Spackman Cl *STHA* RG19 27 G6
Spain La *ALTN* GU34 152 D5
The Spain *PSF* GU32 275 K5
Spalding Rd *ITCH* SO19 345 H3
Spaniard's La *ROMY* SO51 290 E5
Sparkford Cl *WINW* SO22 238 D2
Sparkford Rd *WINW* SO22 238 D2
Spa Rd *SHAM* SO14 12 F4
Sparrow Cl *HORN* PO8 352 D4
Sparrow Ct
LSOL/BMARY PO13 420 D1 7
Sparrowgrove *RWIN* SO21 266 B4
Sparrowhawk Cl
RFNM GU10 111 G8 5
Sparrow Sq *ELGH* SO50 293 J6
Sparsholt Cl *HAV* PO9 377 G3
Sparsholt Rd *ITCH* SO19 344 D8
RWIN SO21 237 G5
Spartan Cl *EMRTH* PO10 402 E4
FHAM/STUB PO14 396 A3
Spartina Dr *LYMN* SO41 440 C2
Sparvells *HTWY* RG27 48 B8 4
Spats La *BOR* GU35 180 C8
Speakers Corner Rbt
SHAM SO14 13 G4
Spear Rd *SHAM* SO14 318 F8
Speckled Wood Rd *CHAM* RG24 .. 83 G7
Specks La *ENEY* PO4 423 L4
Speedwell Cl *HLER* SO31 370 D6 7
Speedwell Wy *NTHA* RG18 27 J4
Speen Hill Cl *NWBY* RG14 2 A2
Speen La *NWBY* RG14 2 B2
Speen Lodge Ct *NWBY* RG14 2 A1
Speen Pl *NWBY* RG14 2 A1
Speggs Wk *HEND* SO30 346 A2
Speltham Hl *WVILLE* PO7 326 C6
Spencer Cl *ALTN* GU34 197 G5
FLET GU13 111 H3
FRIM GU16 91 H2
HISD PO11 425 L5 1
TADY RG26 42 B7 1
Spencer Ct *FHAM/STUB* PO14 396 C6
Spencer Dr *LSOL/BMARY* PO13 .. 420 D3
Spencer Gdns *HORN* PO8 352 C5
Spencer Rd *BMTH* BH1 23 M3
CCLF BH13 446 D8
ELGH SO50 293 K6
EMRTH PO10 378 C4
ENEY PO4 423 K6
ITCH SO19 345 H2
NMIL/BTOS BH25 437 L5
NWBY RG14 37 G2
Spenlow Cl *NEND* PO2 399 H8 6
Spenser Cl *ALTN* GU34 176 F3
HLER SO31 370 B8 7
Sperrin Cl *KEMP* RG22 104 A5
Spetisbury Cl
MOOR/WNTN BH9 432 F5
Spicer La *BWD* BH11 431 J3
Spicers *ALTN* GU34 176 F5
Spicer's Hl *TOTT* SO40 341 K3
Spicer St *PSEA* PO1 423 G2
Spicer's Wy *TOTT* SO40 341 J2
Spicewood *FHAM* PO15 14 C4
Spiers Cl *TADY* RG26 42 A8
Spiers La *NALR* SO24 172 D5
Spinacre *NMIL/BTOS* BH25 437 M8
Spindle Cl *HAV* PO9 17 L1
WIMB BH21 429 K6
Spindle Warren *HAV* PO9 17 L1
Spindlewood Cl
NMIL/BTOS BH25 437 L7 1
ROWN SO16 318 F2
Spindlewood Wy *TOTT* SO40 342 D8
Spinnaker Cl *HISD* PO11 425 J4 8
LSOL/BMARY PO13 421 H1 2
Spinnaker Dr *NEND* PO2 399 H4
Spinnaker Gra *HISD* PO11 402 A4
Spinnaker Vw *CHAM* PO6 376 E7
Spinners Cl *FERN* BH22 380 C7 1
Spinney Cl *HORN* PO8 352 C5
RGWD BH24 381 H4
Spinney Dl *FAWY* SO45 367 M6
Spinney Gdns *FAWY* SO45 367 M6 2
Spinneys La *FERN* BH22 406 B3
The Spinney *CBLY* GU15 71 M2
ELGH SO50 294 F6
FHAM/PORC PO16 373 K7
FLET GU13 88 C8 5
GSHT GU26 203 K4
HASM GU27 204 F8
HORN PO8 352 E2
HTWY RG27 85 M6
LSOL/BMARY PO13 397 H7 5
NALR SO24 243 H3
RGWD BH24 381 K2
ROWN SO16 318 E2
RWIN SO21 266 B1
TOTT SO40 316 B7
WVILLE PO7 351 K5
YTLY GU46 68 F1
Spinney Wk *WEND* SO18 319 L5
Spinney Wy *NMIL/BTOS* BH25 437 L2
Spitalfields Rd *ALTN* GU34 176 E4
Spitalhatch *ALTN* GU34 177 G5
Spitfire End *WINC* SO23 215 J8 2
Spitfire Loop *ELGH* SO50 319 L1
Spitfire Wy *FARN* GU14 90 B8
HLER SO31 369 K6
Spithead Av *GPORT* PO12 422 A7
Spittlefields *RGWD* BH24 382 F1
Spoil La *RFNM* GU10 136 C1
Spokane Cl *ALDT* GU11 6 D5
Spouts La *ROMY* SO51 288 C2
Sprat's Hatch La *HTWY* RG27 109 K1
ODIM RG29 109 J3
Spray Leaze *RAND* SP11 93 G6
Spray Rd *MARL* SN8 33 H5
Spriggs Cl *STHA* RG19 27 G6
Springbank Rd *LTDN* BH7 433 K8
Spring Cl *CHAM* RG24 82 C5
ELGH SO50 295 H6
ITCH SO19 344 D4
VWD BH31 356 D3
Spring Crs *PTSW* SO17 319 G8
Springcroft
LSOL/BMARY PO13 396 F3
Springcross Av *BLKW* GU17 70 A4 4
Springdale Av *BDST* BH18 429 K3
Springdale Gv *WIMB* BH21 429 J4
Springdale Rd *BDST* BH18 429 K4
WIMB BH21 429 H4
Springfarm Rd *HASM* GU27 228 B3
Springfield *DEAN* RG23 103 G6
Springfield Av
CHCH/BSGR BH23 434 B6
FAWY SO45 392 B6
HTWY RG27 87 H1
SBNE BH6 449 M4
Springfield Cl *AND* SP10 119 J8
HAV PO9 376 F6
LYMN SO41 440 E5
VWD BH31 356 D3
Springfield Crs *PSTN* BH14 446 A4
RSAL SP5 285 J3
Springfield Dr *TOTT* SO40 341 J2 1
Springfield Gdns
NMIL/BTOS BH25 438 B6 1
Springfield Gv *FAWY* SO45 392 B4
Springfield La *FLET* GU13 88 D7
NWBY RG14 25 K8
Springfield Rd *ASHV* GU12 113 K3
CBLY GU15 71 K3
PSTN BH14 445 M3
TADY RG26 42 B7
VWD BH31 356 D3
Springfields Cl *RWIN* SO21 266 E7
Springfield Wy
FHAM/STUB PO14 396 A7
Springford Cl *ROWN* SO16 318 A4
Springford Crs *ROWN* SO16 318 A5
Springford Gdns *ROWN* SO16 318 A4
Springford Rd *ROWN* SO16 318 A5
Spring Garden La *GPORT* PO12 19 H2
Spring Gdns *BKME/WDN* BH12 .. 446 C3
CBLY GU15 71 K3
EMRTH PO10 378 D8
FARN GU14 90 D1 7
NALR SO24 218 A4
NBAD SO52 291 L3
PSEA PO1 20 F2 2
Spring Gv *HLER* SO31 345 L7
Spring Hill La *RAND* SP11 97 L6
Springhill Rd *CHFD* SO53 293 H2
Spring Hills *ITCH* SO19 345 G4
Spring La *BPWT* SO32 324 A3
ELGH SO50 294 C5
FNM GU9 134 D1
KSCL RG20 57 J2
NMIL/BTOS BH25 438 B6
RWIN SO21 266 E7
THLE RG7 41 M2
THLE RG7 43 K1
THLE RG7 45 L3
Spring La West *FNM* GU9 134 D2
Springles La *FHAM* PO15 371 L3
Spring Ms *AND* SP10 9 J3
Spring Pl *ROMY* SO51 290 D1 5
Spring Rd *BMTH* BH1 23 M2
FAWY SO45 367 L4
HLER SO31 370 D2
ITCH SO19 344 D2
LYMN SO41 440 E5
The Springs *THLE* RG7 44 A8
Spring St *PSEA* PO1 21 G1
The Spring *WVILLE* PO7 351 K5
Spring V *BPWT* SO32 323 M4
HORN PO8 352 F4
Springvale Av *LTDN* BH7 433 K8
WINC SO23 215 G2
Springvale Rd *WINC* SO23 215 G3
Springwater Rd *BWD* BH11 431 L5
Spring Wy *NALR* SO24 218 B4
Springwell La *HTWY* RG27 67 J8
Springwood Av *WVILLE* PO7 376 D2
Spring Wood La *THLE* RG7
Spring Woods *FLET* GU13 1
SHST GU47
Spruce Av *BOR* GU35 2
WVILLE PO7 3
Spruce Cl *AND* SP10 14
CFDH BH17 4
HLER SO31 3
RWIN SO21 1
Spruce Dr *ITCH* SO19 3
TOTT SO40 3
Spruce Wy *FLET* GU13
Spur Cl *WIMB* BH21 40
Spurcroft Rd *STHA* RG19
Spurgeon Rd *LTDN* BH7 4
Spur Hill Av *PSTN* BH14 4
Spurlings Rd *WHAM* PO17 3
Spur Rd *CHAM* PO6 3
PSTN BH14 4
WVILLE PO7 3
Spurs Ct *ALDT* GU11
The Spur *GPORT* PO12
WHAM PO17 3
Spybush La *NALR* SO24 1
Square Dr *HASM* GU27 2
Squarefield Gdns *HTWY* RG27 .. 8
The Square *EMRTH* PO10 37
EPSF GU31 3
FAWY SO45 39
GPORT PO12 3
LYMN SO41 4
PSF GU32 2
ROMY SO51 2
STOK SO20 18
WHAM PO17 3
WINC SO23
Squarey Cl *RSAL* SP5 2
Squires Hill La *RFNM* GU10 1
Squires Wk *ITCH* SO19 3
Squirrel Cl *ELGH* SO50 29
SHST GU47
Squirrel Dr *ITCH* SO19 3
Squirrel La *FARN* GU14
Squirrels Drey *CWTH* RG45 4
Squirrels Wk *FAWY* SO45 3
Stable Cl *FHAM/STUB* PO14 3
HTWY RG27
THLE RG7
Stable Ct *NWBY* RG14
Stable Rd *BOR* GU35 2
Stables Rd *NTID* SP9 1
Stable Vw *YTLY* GU46
Stacey Cl *BKME/WDN* BH12 4
Stacey Ct *HAV* PO9 3
Stacey Gdns *CHAR* BH8 4
Staff College Rd *CBLY* GU15
Stafford Rd *BMTH* BH1
PSF GU32 2
SSEA PO5
WSHM SO15 3
Staff Rd *ASHV* GU12
ROMY SO51 2
Stagbrake Cl *FAWY* SO45 391
Stag Cl *ELGH* SO50 2
NMIL/BTOS BH25 4
Stag Hl *KEMP* RG22 1
Stagshorn Rd *HORN* PO8 35
Stags La *RWIN* SO21 2
Stagswood *VWD* BH31 3
Stag Wy *FHAM* PO15 3
Stainer Cl *ITCH* SO19 3
Stainers La *RWIN* SO21 1
Staith Cl *ITCH* SO19 3
Stake La *FARN* GU14
Stakes Hill Rd *WVILLE* PO7 3
Stakes La *BPWT* SO32 2
BPWT SO32 2
Stakes Rd *WVILLE* PO7 3
Stalbridge Dr *FERN* BH22 4
Stalbridge Rd *CFDH* BH17 4
Stalham Rd *BKME/WDN* BH12 4
Stallard Cl *EMRTH* PO10 3
Stallards La *RGWD* BH24 3
Stalybridge Cl *HLER* SO31 3
Stamford Av *FRIM* GU16 7
HISD PO11 4
Stamford Rd *SBNE* BH6 4
Stamford St *PSEA* PO1 4
Stamford Wy *ELGH* SO50 29
Stamshaw Rd *NEND* PO2 3
Stanbridge La *ROMY* SO51 2
Stanbridge Rd *HAV* PO9 3
Stanbury Cl *RAND* SP11 1
Stanbury Rd *RAND* SP11 1
Stancomb Broad La
ALTN GU34 1
Stancombe La *ALTN* GU34 1
ALTN GU34 1
Standard Wy *FHAM/PORC* PO16..
Standen Rd *ROWN* SO16 3
Standford Hl *BOR* GU35 2
Standford La *BOR* GU35 2
Standford St *SHAM* SO14 1
Standing Hl *RSAL* SP5 2
Stanfield *TADY* RG26
Stanfield Rd *BKME/WDN* BH12 .. 4
FERN BH22 4
MOOR/WNTN BH9 4
Stanford Cl *CHAM* PO6 3
Stanford Ct *HAV* PO9 377
Stanford Ri *LYMN* SO41 4
Stanford Rd *KEMP* RG22 1
Stanham Cl *RWIN* SO21 1
Stanhope Rd *CBLY* GU15
PSEA PO1
Stanier Wy *HEND* SO30 3
Stanley Av *HSEA* PO3 3
Stanley Cl *FHAM* PO15
GPORT PO12 3
VWD BH31 3
Stanley Dr *FARN* GU14 8
Stanley Green Rd *PLE* BH15 4
Stanley La *SSEA* PO5
Stanley Rd *BMTH* BH1
CHCH/BSGR BH23 4
EMRTH PO10 3
FAWY SO45 3
LYMN SO41 4

ND PO2 399 G7
/BY RG14 3 G6
E BH15 445 H7
SW SO17 319 H7
TT SO40 316 C7
ley St SSEA PO5 21 H7
more Gdns THLE RG7 43 J3
more La WINW SO22 238 B2
nington Cl
MIL/BTOS BH25 437 M6 3
nington Crs TOTT SO40 316 E8
nington Wy TOTT SO40 316 E8
pit CHCH/BSGR BH23 450 D3
stead Cl HAV PO9 354 A6
stead Rd ELGH SO50 293 L4
sted Crs HAV PO9 377 M2
sted Rd SSEA PO5 21 K4
swood Rd FAWY SO45 418 F4
V PO9 377 H2
ton Dr FLET GU13 88 D8
ton Rd NBNE BH10 432 A6
F GU32 275 K4
SHM SO15 342 D1
water La MIDH GU29 279 H4
ehill Crs WIMB BH21 404 F3
ehill Rd WIMB BH21 405 K3
le Ash La PSF GU32 274 B1
le Cl WVILLE PO7 352 B7
le Close La PLE BH15 445 H2
lecross La
CH/BSGR BH23 435 H8
leford Av FERN BH22 406 D2
leford Cl ROMY SO51 263 G6
leford La BPWT SO32 321 L3
le Gdns WINC SO23 10 F7
lehurst Cl ITCH SO19 344 E8
lers Reach
OL/BMARY PO13 396 F7
leton Cl NWBY RG14 36 F2
leton Rd HSEA PO3 399 L8 3
lewood La TOTT SO40 342 B7
ley La NALR SO24 220 C6
es Cl LSOL/BMARY PO13 421 G1
Hl RFNM GU10 181 G6
Hill Dr RFNM GU10 181 G5
na Gdns WVILLE PO7 352 F8
La ASHV GU12 113 J6
CL RG20 56 C2
ight Farm Cl VWD BH31 356 E1 1
ing Cl KEMP RG22 103 L8
ing Sq ELGH SO50 293 J6 2
Post Rd CBLY GU15 51 H8
ting Gates NWBY RG14 3 J8
on Ap ALTN GU34 197 G5
D SP10 8 E4
HV GU12 113 K1
ST BH18 429 L4
LR SO24 218 C3
EA PO1 20 C2
ND SP11 92 E5
ND SP11 161 L1
on Cl RWIN SO21 216 D2
HAM PO17 348 E4
on Hl ELGH SO50 294 A5
M GU9 134 F6
ND SO30 347 G1
ER SO31 369 M1
LR SO24 219 L3
TN RG25 101 G6
VIN SO21 216 D2
VC SO23 10 F6 2
on La CHFD SO53 293 H2
on Rd ALDT GU11 7 G2
TN GU34 176 F4
WT SO32 323 H1
WT SO32 325 H1
AM PO6 400 A2
CH/BSGR BH23 436 C5
CH/BSGR BH23 449 M1
AN RG23 102 E6
SF GU31 275 L4
RN GU14 90 E4
DG SP6 333 K2
RN BH22 380 B5
AM/PORC PO16 374 B8
M GU16 70 F7
ORT PO12 421 K1
SD PO11 425 J4
ER SO31 368 F3
EA PO3 399 L8
WY RG27 85 M7
H SO19 344 E5
CL RG20 36 D5
R GU35 201 H3
H GU30 226 E6
S GU33 248 E4
MN SO41 412 F6
LR SO24 218 C2
NM GU10 156 F4
MIL/BTOS BH25 437 L6
ID SP9 114 E3
WBY RG14 2 E6
WBY RG14 25 G3
TN RG25 101 G8
TN RG25 128 A1
F GU32 272 B4
F GU32 275 K4
TN BH14 446 A5
ND SP11 161 L1
WD BH24 411 J2
MY SO51 290 D1
WN SO16 316 F3
HA RG19 27 H5
OK SO20 165 L5
LE RG7 28 F6
LE RG7 44 B3
VD BH31 356 B1
AM PO17 348 E4
ICH RG28 122 B2
MB BH21 404 B5
NC SO23 10 E6
SHM SO15 317 H8
on Rd East ASHV GU12 113 J1
on Rd North TOTT SO40 341 L1 2
on Rd South
TT SO40 341 M1 1
on St LYMN SO41 440 D4
EA PO1 21 G1
Station Ter WIMB BH21 404 B4
Station Vw ASHV GU12 91 K8
Station Yd FBDG SP6 333 J2
Staunton Av HISD PO11 425 H5
Staunton Rd HAV PO9 16 C3
Staunton St PSEA PO1 423 G2
Staunton Wy HAV PO9 16 C2
HAV PO9 377 J5
HORN PO8 302 E8
Stavedown Rd RWIN SO21 190 B4
Stead Cl HISD PO11 425 M5
Stedham La MIDH GU29 279 K5
Steele Cl CHFD SO53 293 J4
Steeles Rd ALDT GU11 112 E4
Steels Dro FBDG SP6 310 D1
Steels La FBDG SP6 308 B4
Steel St SSEA PO5 20 F5
Steep Cl FHAM/PORC PO16 374 A7 2
Steepdene PSTN BH14 446 A5
Steeple Cl CFDH BH17 430 B5
Steeple Dr ALTN GU34 176 E4
Steepleton Rd BDST BH18 430 A5
Steeple Wy FHAM/STUB PO14 371 H5
Steepways GSHT GU26 203 L2
Steerforth Cl NEND PO2 423 H1
Steerforth Copse SHST GU47 50 B6 4
Steinbeck Cl FHAM PO15 347 G8
Stein Rd EMRTH PO10 379 H6
Stem La NMIL/BTOS BH25 437 J3
Stenbury Dr OVTN RG25 151 G8
Stenbury Wy HLER SO31 369 D1
Stephen Cl HORN PO8 352 F6
Stephendale Rd FNM GU9 135 G4
Stephen Martin Gdns
FBDG SP6 309 K6 3
Stephen Rd FHAM PO15 14 F5
Stephen's Cl THLE RG7 43 J2
Stephens Firs THLE RG7 43 J2
Stephenson Cl AND SP10 118 B7
GPORT PO12 18 C8 1
NTHA RG18 26 F4
Stephenson Rd TOTT SO40 316 C6
WHIT RG2 47 K1
Stephenson Wy HEND SO30 321 G5
Stephens Rd TADY RG26 41 M8
THLE RG7 43 J2
Steplake Rd ROMY SO51 288 C1
Step Ter WINW SO22 10 D7
Sterling Pk AND SP10 118 B7
Sterte Av PLE BH15 445 G4
Sterte Cl PLE BH15 445 H4
Sterte Rd PLE BH15 445 H4
Steuart Rd WEND SO18 344 B1
Stevens Dro STOK SO20 210 B3
Stevens Gn RAND SP11 97 M7
Stevens Hl YTLY GU46 69 H3
Stevenson Crs PSTN BH14 446 C5
Stevenson Rd RWIN SO21 145 H6
Stevensons Cl WIMB BH21 404 A4
Steventon Rd OVTN RG25 125 K7
WEND SO18 345 C1
Stewart Cl CHAR BH8 23 M1
Stewart Rd CHAR BH8 448 A2
Stewarts Gn WVILLE PO7 326 B5
Stewarts Wy FERN BH22 406 C1
Stibbs Wy CHCH/BSGR BH23 410 A7
Stile Gdns HASM GU27 228 C2
Stiles Dr AND SP10 119 J8
Stillions Cl ALTN GU34 176 F5
Stillmore Rd BWD BH11 431 H5
Stilwell Cl YTLY GU46 69 H2
Stinchar Dr CHFD SO53 292 F3
Stinsford Cl MOOR/WNTN BH9 432 F4
Stinsford Rd CFDH BH17 430 B7
Stirling Av WVILLE PO7 376 D1
Stirling Cl FARN GU14 90 D5
FRIM GU16 71 H6 4
NMIL/BTOS BH25 437 M5
TOTT SO40 316 F8
Stirling Crs HEND SO30 321 H7
TOTT SO40 316 F8
Stirling Rd MOOR/WNTN BH9 447 K1
Stirling St NEND PO2 399 H8
Stirling Wy CHCH/BSGR BH23 451 G2
FARN GU14 112 A1
NTHA RG18 26 D8
Stirrup Cl UPTN BH16 444 C1
WIMB BH21 405 G2
Stirrup Pightle NWBY RG14 37 L1 3
Stoatley Hollow HASM GU27 204 D8
Stoatley Ri HASM GU27 204 D8
Stockbridge Cl CHAM RG24 84 A4
HAV PO9 377 M3 14
Stockbridge Dr ALDT GU11 7 K9
Stockbridge Rd WINW SO22 10 C5
RAND SP11 163 M5
ROMY SO51 262 B1
RWIN SO21 168 B4
RWIN SO21 188 F8
STOK SO20 210 F5
Stockbridge Wy YTLY GU46 69 G4
Stocker Cl BSTK RG21 104 F6
Stocker Pl
LSOL/BMARY PO13 397 H6 3
Stockers Av WINW SO22 10 A3
Stockheath La HAV PO9 16 C2
Stockheath Rd HAV PO9 377 K4
Stockheath Wy HAV PO9 377 K5
Stockholm Dr HEND SO30 346 A3 3
Stock La RSAL SP5 287 K3
Stockley Cl FAWY SO45 392 A5 3
Stocks La ALTN GU34 244 F7
BPWT SO32 299 M4
Stockton Av FLET GU13 88 E6
Stockton Cl HEND SO30 346 B1 3
Stockton Pk FLET GU13 88 E6
Stockwood Ri CBLY GU15 71 J3
Stockwood Wy FNM GU9 6 D7
Stoddart Av ITCH SO19 344 D2
Stodham La EPSF GU31 248 D8
LISS GU33 248 D6
Stoke Charity Rd RWIN SO21 190 F5
Stoke Common Rd ELGH SO50 294 D3
Stoke Gdns GPORT PO12 18 F4
Stoke Hts ELGH SO50 295 G5
Stoke Hl RAND SP11 97 G5
Stoke Hills FNM GU9 134 F5
Stoke La RAND SP11 96 F3
Stoken La HTWY RG27 86 E1
Stoke Park Rd ELGH SO50 294 D4
Stoke Rd GPORT PO12 18 F4
RAND SP11 96 E8
ROWN SO16 317 M7
WINC SO23 11 H1
Stokes Av PLE BH15 445 H4
Stokesay Cl FAWY SO45 367 L8 2
Stokes Bay Rd GPORT PO12 421 H6
Stokes La STHA RG19 40 F7
Stoke Wood Cl ELGH SO50 295 G6 3
Stoke Wood Rd TWDS BH3 447 L1
Stonechat Cl EPSF GU31 276 B6
Stonechat Dr TOTT SO40 316 A8
Stonechat Rd HORN PO8 352 E2
Stone Cl AND SP10 8 C9
RSAL SP5 206 F2 1
Stone Copse NTHA RG18 26 B1
Stone Crop Cl HLER SO31 370 C7
Stonecrop Cl WIMB BH21 429 J6 2
Stonedene Cl BOR GU35 202 E4
Stone Gdns CHAR BH8 433 L6
Stonegate CBLY GU15 71 M2
Stoneham Cemetery Rd
WEND SO18 319 L4
Stoneham Cl PSF GU32 275 J4
ROWN SO16 319 J3 1
Stoneham La ELGH SO50 293 K8
ROWN SO16 319 J3
Stoneham Pk PSF GU32 275 J4
Stoneham Wy ELGH SO50 319 K3
Stonehill Pk BOR GU35 202 E4
Stonehill Rd BOR GU35 202 F4
Stonehills FAWY SO45 393 G6
Stonehouse Ri FRIM GU16 71 H7
Stonehouse Rd LIPH GU30 227 G4
Stone La GPORT PO12 18 F4 2
GPORT PO12 18 F5 2
Stoneleigh Av LYMN SO41 438 D4
Stoneleigh Cl
FHAM/PORC PO16 373 M8 3
Stoneleigh Ct FRIM GU16 71 J7
Stoners Cl LSOL/BMARY PO13 396 F5
Stone Sq HAV PO9 377 K4
Stone St ASHV GU12 7 M5
SSEA PO5 20 F5
Stoney Bottom GSHT GU26 203 M5
Stoney Cl YTLY GU46 69 G4
Stoney Cross RAND SP11 92 E6 3
Stoneyfield THLE RG7 29 K2
Stoneyfields FNM GU9 135 H7
Stoney La ALTN GU34 197 G4
WINW SO22 10 A2
NWBY RG14 26 A2
STHA RG19 27 H5
Stony La CHCH/BSGR BH23 434 F6
FBDG SP6 307 M4
PSEA PO1 422 E2
Stony La South
CHCH/BSGR BH23 450 B2
Stonymoor Cl FAWY SO45 392 A5
Stookes Wy YTLY GU46 68 E4
Stopples La LYMN SO41 438 D4
Storrington Rd HORN PO8 328 C3
Story La BDST BH18 429 M4
Stourbank Rd
CHCH/BSGR BH23 449 M2
Stourcliffe Av SBNE BH6 449 H4
Stour Cl PSF GU32 275 K6
WEND SO18 319 M5
WIMB BH21 405 H4
Stourcroft Dr
CHCH/BSGR BH23 434 B6
Stourfield Rd BOSC BH5 449 G4
Stourhead Cl AND SP10 8 B7
FARN GU14 91 G4
Stourpaine Rd CFDH BH17 430 B6
Stour Rd CHAR BH8 448 C2
CHCH/BSGR BH23 449 M1
DEAN RG23 103 G7
Stourvale Av
CHCH/BSGR BH23 434 B8
Stourvale Gdns CHFD SO53 293 J3
Stourvale Rd SBNE BH6 449 G3
Stour Valley Wy FERN BH22 406 B8
MOOR/WNTN BH9 433 G2
SBNE BH6 449 K1
WIMB BH21 404 A4
Stour Wy CHCH/BSGR BH23 434 B6
Stourwood Av SBNE BH6 449 H4
Stourwood Rd SBNE BH6 449 J4
Stouts La CHCH/BSGR BH23 409 M7
Stovold's Wy ALDT GU11 6 C5
Stowe Cl HEND SO30 321 J7
Stowe Rd ENEY PO4 423 M4
Stradbrook LSOL/BMARY PO13 396 F7
Stragwyne Cl NBAD SO52 291 L2 1
The Straight Mile ROMY SO51 263 K7
Strand SHAM SO14 13 G4
Strand St PLE BH15 445 G7
The Strand HISD PO11 426 A7
Stratfield Av TADY RG26 61 L1
Stratfield Dr CHFD SO53 265 G7 5
Stratfield Pl
NMIL/BTOS BH25 437 J5 3
Stratfield Rd BSTK RG21 4 E2
Stratfield Saye Rd TADY RG26 63 M3
Stratford Pl ELGH SO50 294 A4 2
LYMN SO41 440 B3
Stratford Rd ASHV GU12 91 J8
WVILLE PO7 352 E8
Strathfield Rd AND SP10 142 E3
Strathmore Dr VWD BH31 356 F2
Strathmore Rd GPORT PO12 19 H3
NBNE BH10 432 E4
Stratton Cl CHAM PO6 375 G8
RWIN SO21 170 F4
Stratton La RWIN SO21 171 H7
Stratton Rd BSTK RG21 104 E6
MOOR/WNTN BH9 433 G4
WINC SO23 11 K9
WSHM SO15 318 B7
Stratton Wk FARN GU14 90 D1 3
Strauss Rd KEMP RG22 104 B8
Stravinsky Rd KEMP RG22 104 E8
Strawberry Flds TADY RG26 63 L5
Strawberry Hl HLER SO31 370 D5
NWBY RG14 2 D2
Stream Farm Cl RFNM GU10 159 G1
Streamleaze
FHAM/STUB PO14 371 G7
Streamside FLET GU13 88 F8 2
Stream Valley Rd RFNM GU10 158 F2
Street End HTWY RG27 88 A4
NBAD SO52 292 A3
Streets La RGWD BH24 383 G4
The Street ALTN GU34 178 D1
CHAM RG24 105 M2
FLET GU13 110 C3
HTWY RG27 85 K3
MIDH GU29 279 K7
RFNM GU10 136 C3
RFNM GU10 158 B2
RFNM GU10 180 B2
RFNM GU10 180 F1
ODIM RG29 107 L5
ODIM RG29 131 J5
RGUW GU3 137 L4
RSAL SP5 206 C2
RSAL SP5 230 B1
RSAL SP5 258 F4
TADY RG26 63 J6
THLE RG7 41 K1
THLE RG7 43 L3
THLE RG7 45 M2
Streetway Rd RAND SP11 161 K2
Strettons Copse LIPH GU30 250 E5
Stride Av HSEA PO3 423 M2
Strides La RGWD BH24 382 D1
Strides Wy TOTT SO40 340 F1
Strode Gdns RGWD BH24 381 M3
Strode Rd NEND PO2 399 G6
Strokins Rd KSCL RG20 59 J5
Strongs Cl ROMY SO51 263 G8 3
Stroud Cl CHAM RG24 83 K6
WIMB BH21 404 E2
Strouden Av CHAR BH8 432 F7
Strouden Ct HAV PO9 377 H1
Stroud End PSF GU32 275 G4
Strouden Rd
MOOR/WNTN BH9 432 E7
Stroud La CHCH/BSGR BH23 450 D2
HTWY RG27 110 B3
Stroudley Av CHAM PO6 400 A2
Stroudley Rd CHAM RG24 5 M3
Stroudley Wy HEND SO30 321 J6
Stroud Park Av
CHCH/BSGR BH23 450 D1
Strouds Meadow NTHA RG18 26 F1
The Strouds THLE RG7 29 J2
Stroudwood La BPWT SO32 295 M5
RWIN SO21 295 M3
Stroudwood Rd HAV PO9 377 L5
Struan Ct RGWD BH24 381 L2
Struan Dr RGWD BH24 381 L2
Struan Gdns RGWD BH24 381 K2
Stuart Cl FARN GU14 90 D3
FHAM/STUB PO14 396 A6
UPTN BH16 444 A1
Stuart Crs WINW SO22 238 D3
Stuart Rd CHCH/BSGR BH23 436 F8
NWBY RG14 36 F2
Stubbington Av BOR GU35 201 H7
NEND PO2 399 J7
Stubbington Gn
FHAM/STUB PO14 396 A5
Stubbington La
FHAM/STUB PO14 396 A8
Stubbington Wy ELGH SO50 295 J7
Stubbs Ct AND SP10 8 F2
Stubbs Court Ct AND SP10 8 F2
Stubbs Dro HEND SO30 346 B1
Stubbs Folly SHST GU47 70 A1
Stubbs Moor Rd FARN GU14 90 C3
Stubbs Rd BSTK RG21 105 H6
ITCH SO19 345 G6 3
Stuckton Rd FBDG SP6 309 M8
Studland Cl ROWN SO16 317 J7
Studland Dr LYMN SO41 454 A3
Studland Rd
LSOL/BMARY PO13 420 C2
ROWN SO16 317 J7
WBNE BH4 447 H7
Studley Av FAWY SO45 392 A5
Studley Cl CHCH/BSGR BH23 437 G8
Studley Ct NMIL/BTOS BH25 437 H8 3
Stukeley Rd BSTK RG21 104 E4
Sturdee Cl FRIM GU16 71 H7
Sturt Av HASM GU27 228 C3
Sturt Rd FNM GU9 134 E1
FRIM GU16 91 J3
HASM GU27 228 D4
Sudbury Rd CHAM PO6 375 H8
Suetts La BPWT SO32 323 L1
Suffield La RGUW GU3 137 J8
Suffolk Av CHCH/BSGR BH23 434 D6
WSHM SO15 343 H1
Suffolk Cl CHFD SO53 293 H6
WIMB BH21 405 G2 3
Suffolk Dr CHFD SO53 293 H6
FHAM PO15 370 F1
HLER SO31 370 F1
Suffolk Rd AND SP10 8 F7
ENEY PO4 423 L5
WCLF BH2 22 A5
Suffolk Rd South WBNE BH4 22 A4
Sulhamstead Hl THLE RG7 30 F2
Sulhamstead Rd THLE RG7 31 J4
Sullivan Cl CHAM PO6 374 C8
FARN GU14 90 E4 3
Sullivan Rd CBLY GU15 70 D3
ITCH SO19 345 H5 3
KEMP RG22 104 D7
Sullivan Wy WVILLE PO7 376 C3
Sultan Rd EMRTH PO10 378 D7
NEND PO2 423 G1
Sumar Cl FHAM/STUB PO14 396 B3
Summercroft Wy FERN BH22 380 C5
Summer Down La DEAN RG23 102 D3
Summer Fld WIMB BH21 404 E4
Summerfield Gdns
ROWN SO16 319 J3 2
Summerfield La RFNM GU10 158 D6
Summerfield Rd SELS PO20 427 L6
Summerfields CHAM RG24 83 M4 3
FHAM/STUB PO14 370 F7
LTDN BH7 448 E1
Summer Flds VWD BH31 356 D4
Summer Gdns CBLY GU15 71 M3
Summerhill Rd HORN PO8 352 D5
Summerlands Rd ELGH SO50 295 H6
Summer La BROC SO42 391 J7
Summerleigh Wk
FHAM/STUB PO14 396 B3 1
Summers Av BWD BH11 431 M2
Summers La CHCH/BSGR BH23 435 H7
Summers St SHAM SO14 343 M2
Summertrees Ct
NMIL/BTOS BH25 438 B4
Summit Av FARN GU14 89 M5
Summit Cl EWKG RG40 48 C2
Summit Wy WEND SO18 319 L7
Sumner Rd EPSF GU31 303 J3
FNM GU9 134 F5
Sunbeam Wy GPORT PO12 18 F6
Sun Brow HASM GU27 228 C3
Sunbury Cl BOR GU35 201 K5
Sunbury Ct FHAM PO15 372 C4
Sunderland Pl NTHA RG18 26 F4 2
Sunderton La HORN PO8 328 A4
Sundew Cl CHCH/BSGR BH23 436 A7
NMIL/BTOS BH25 438 B4 3
Sundew Rd WIMB BH21 429 J6
Sundridge Cl CHAM PO6 375 J8
Sunflower Cl KEMP RG22 126 F1 3
Sun Gdns THLE RG7 31 K7
Sun Hill Crs NALR SO24 218 C4
Sun La NALR SO24 218 C4
THLE RG7 45 L6
Sunley Cl NWBY RG14 37 G2
Sunningdale FAWY SO45 367 K6
Sunningdale Cl ELGH SO50 294 E6 1
LSOL/BMARY PO13 397 G7 3
Sunningdale Crs NBNE BH10 432 A4
Sunningdale Gdns
WEND SO18 344 F1 3
Sunningdale Rd
FHAM/PORC PO16 398 B1
HSEA PO3 423 L2
Sunnybank RAND SP11 141 K2
Sunnybank Rd FARN GU14 90 A2
WIMB BH21 404 F2
Sunnydell La FNM GU9 158 D2
Sunnydown Rd WINW SO22 237 M5
Sunnyfield Ri HLER SO31 345 L7 3
Sunnyfield Rd
NMIL/BTOS BH25 437 L8
Sunnyheath HAV PO9 377 J4
Sunny Hill Rd ALDT GU11 112 A6
BKME/WDN BH12 446 C3
Sunnyhill Rd SBNE BH6 449 G3
Sunnylands Av SBNE BH6 449 L4
Sunny Md DEAN RG23 103 G8
Sunnymead Dr WVILLE PO7 352 A6
Sunnymoor Rd BWD BH11 431 L7
Sunnyside FLET GU13 88 D6
Sunnyside Cl AND SP10 118 C6
Sunnyside Rd
BKME/WDN BH12 446 C2
BOR GU35 202 F4
Sunny Wk PSEA PO1 20 B1
Sunny Wy TOTT SO40 341 K1 1
Sun Ray Est SHST GU47 49 J8
Sunridge Cl BKME/WDN BH12 446 F2
Sunset Av TOTT SO40 316 D8
Sunset Rd TOTT SO40 316 D8
Sunshine Av HISD PO11 425 M6 2
Sun St PSEA PO1 20 D2 3
Sunvale Av HASM GU27 228 A2
Sunvale Cl HASM GU27 228 A2 1
ITCH SO19 344 F5
Sunwood Rd HAV PO9 377 H3
Surbiton Rd CBLY GU15 51 K7
ELGH SO50 294 A3
Surrey Av CBLY GU15 70 D4
Surrey Cl CHCH/BSGR BH23 434 D6
TOTT SO40 341 H3
Surrey Gdns WBNE BH4 447 H4
Surrey Rd BKME/WDN BH12 446 F3
CHFD SO53 293 H5
ITCH SO19 344 B6
WBNE BH4 447 H4
Surrey Rd South WBNE BH4 447 H4
Surrey St PSEA PO1 21 G1
Sussex Border Pth
EMRTH PO10 402 D5
EPSF GU31 304 E3
HASM GU27 229 J7
HAV PO9 354 B4
HORN PO8 329 H4
LIPH GU30 226 E8
LISS GU33 249 L2
Sussex Cl MOOR/WNTN BH9 432 F4
Sussex Gdns EPSF GU31 275 L6
FARN GU14 89 G4
Sussex Pl SSEA PO5 21 G6 1
Sussex Rd CHFD SO53 293 J5
EPSF GU31 275 M6
SHAM SO14 13 G3
SSEA PO5 21 G6
Sussex St WINC SO23 10 F7
Sutherland Av BDST BH18 429 J3
Sutherland Cl BOR GU35 201 J7
ROMY SO51 263 G7 1
Sutherland Rd ENEY PO4 21 M5
ROWN SO16 317 L3
Sutherlands NWBY RG14 37 H1 1
Sutherlands Ct CHFD SO53 293 H2 2
Sutherlands Wy CHFD SO53 293 G1
Sutton Cl CFDH BH17 430 E6
HORN PO8 352 B5
HSEA PO3 399 M4
Sutton Fld BOR GU35 201 H7
Sutton Gdns WINC SO23 11 G7
Sutton Pl BROC SO42 387 L7 1
Sutton Rd BSTK RG21 4 E4
CBLY GU15 51 K7
HORN PO8 352 B5
MOOR/WNTN BH9 432 F7
NWBY RG14 25 G3
TOTT SO40 316 C7
Sutton Wood La NALR SO24 195 K8
Swains Cl TADY RG26 41 L8
Swains Rd TADY RG26 41 L8

Swaledale Gdns FARN GU14 89 G4
Swale Dr CHFD SO53 292 F1
Swale Rd FARN GU14 90 A2
Swallow Cl ALTN GU34 176 F2
CFDH BH17 429 K8
HAV PO9 17 J1
KEMP RG22 103 L8
NTID SP9 114 E2
TOTT SO40 340 F2
YTLY GU46 68 E2
Swallow Ct
LSOL/BMARY PO13 420 D1 8
Swallow Dr LYMN SO41 454 E4
Swallowfield Rd THLE RG7 46 D1
Swallowfields AND SP10 119 G6
Swallow Sq ELGH SO50 293 J6 3
Swanage Cl ITCH SO19 344 C5
Swanage Rd
LSOL/BMARY PO13 420 C2
Swan Barn Rd HASM GU27 229 G2
Swan Cl EMRTH PO10 378 E8
HLER SO31 370 B1
Swancote FHAM/PORC PO16 373 K8
Swan Ct HTWY RG27 87 J2 5
Swan Dr THLE RG7 29 L5
Swan La SHST GU47 69 L2
WINC SO23 10 F6
Swanley Cl ELGH SO50 293 M3
Swan Md RGWD BH24 383 G2
Swan Ms ODIM RG29 108 B4 2
Swanmore Av ITCH SO19 344 F5
Swanmore Cl WINW SO22 214 C4 5
Swanmore Rd BPWT SO32 323 L1
HAV PO9 377 H1
LTDN BH7 449 G2
Swansbury Dr CHAR BH8 433 L6
Swan St KSCL RG20 59 H7
PSF GU32 275 K5
Swanton Gdns CHFD SO53 293 G1
Swan Wy FLET GU13 110 C1
Swanwick La HLER SO31 346 B8
Swanwick Shore Rd
HLER SO31 370 B1 1
Swarraton Rd HAV PO9 377 L4
Sway Ct HAV PO9 377 M3 13
Sway Gdns CHAR BH8 433 H6
Sway Rd BROC SO42 413 K1
LYMN SO41 439 J3
NMIL/BTOS BH25 437 M2
Swaythling Rd HAV PO9 377 H2
HEND SO30 320 A6
Swedish Houses TADY RG26 61 M1
The Sweep RGWD BH24 382 D1 7
Sweetbriar CWTH RG45 49 K1 2
Sweetbriar Gdns
WVILLE PO7 376 D3 4
Sweethills Crs HLER SO31 346 F8
Sweetzer's Piece THLE RG7 43 H2
Swelling Hl ALTN GU34 220 F2
Sweyns Lease BROC SO42 416 A2
Swift Cl AND SP10 119 G6
CFDH BH17 429 K8
ELGH SO50 293 J6
WINW SO22 238 C3
HORN PO8 352 E1
LSOL/BMARY PO13 420 D1 9
Swift Gdns ITCH SO19 344 B7
Swift Hollow ITCH SO19 344 B7 2
Swift Rd EMRTH PO10 402 E5
FNM GU9 134 E1
ITCH SO19 344 B7
Swift's Cl RFNM GU10 135 L7
Swinburn Gdns HORN PO8 352 D4
Swincombe Ri WEND SO18 320 A7
Swingate Rd FNM GU9 134 F8
Swing Swang La CHAM RG24 5 L3
Swiss Cl RFNM GU10 158 C4
Swiss Rd WVILLE PO7 376 C1
Switchback La RFNM GU10 158 C4 2
Swivelton La WHAM PO17 373 L5
Sword Cl GPORT PO12 421 J6
HORN PO8 328 A3
Swordfish Wy FARN GU14 112 B1
Sword Sands Rd HSEA PO3 424 A1
Sycamore Av CHFD SO53 265 H7
Sycamore Cl CFDH BH17 429 K7
FHAM/STUB PO14 371 G7 3
FRIM GU16 71 H7
HLER SO31 345 K8
HORN PO8 352 C5
LSOL/BMARY PO13 397 J7 3
LYMN SO41 454 B3
NBAD SO52 291 L3
NTID SP9 114 F2 3
ROMY SO51 291 H2
SHST GU47 69 L1
TLHT RG30 31 L3
Sycamore Crs FLET GU13 110 D2
STOK SO20 163 G4
Sycamore Dr ASHV GU12 113 J1
FAWY SO45 391 M3
FRIM GU16 71 H6
HISD PO11 425 J4
RFNM GU10 158 D2 1
WINC SO23 191 G8
Sycamore Ri NWBY RG14 25 M2
Sycamore Rd BPWT SO32 297 K8
FARN GU14 90 F6
FAWY SO45 367 K5
LYMN SO41 438 D4
ROWN SO16 317 M6
The Sycamores BLKW GU17 69 L3
FARN GU14 91 G5
Sycamore Wy DEAN RG23 104 C1
Sydenham Ter PSEA PO1 21 K2
The Sydings NWBY RG14 25 G3
Sydling Cl CFDH BH17 430 F6
Sydmanton Cl ROMY SO51 290 F2 3
Sydmonton Ct HAV PO9 377 M2 11
Sydney Av HLER SO31 369 J5
Sydney Cl CWTH RG45 49 M1
RAND SP11 115 J1 2
Sydney Rd BDST BH18 429 L5
CHCH/BSGR BH23 434 C7
ELGH SO50 294 C4
GPORT PO12 18 F3
BOR GU35 201 J5
WSHM SO15 318 A7
Sydney Smith Av FARN GU14 90 E7
Syers Rd LISS GU33 248 E4
Sylmor Gdns
MOOR/WNTN BH9 432 E6
Sylvan Av ITCH SO19 345 G2
Sylvan Cl LYMN SO41 438 F6
RGWD BH24 381 H4
Sylvan Dr NBAD SO52 291 L4
Sylvan La HLER SO31 369 L6
Sylvan Rdg SHST GU47 49 K7
Sylvan Rd BKME/WDN BH12 446 A2
The Sylvans FAWY SO45 367 H5 6
Sylvan Vw WVILLE PO7 376 D2
Sylvan Wy FLET GU13 110 E3
Sylvester Cl NWBY RG14 25 H3 1
Sylvia Crs TOTT SO40 316 D7
Symes Rd PLE BH15 444 C4
ROMY SO51 291 G1
Symonds Cl CHFD SO53 293 J4
Symonds St WINC SO23 11 G9
Sympson Rd TADY RG26 42 A7
Syon Pl FARN GU14 91 G4 3
Sywell Crs HSEA PO3 399 M4

T

Tadburn Cl CHFD SO53 293 J3
ROMY SO51 290 F1 4
Tadburn Rd ROMY SO51 290 F2
Tadden Wk BDST BH18 429 K6
Tadfield Rd ROMY SO51 290 F1
Tadham Pl STHA RG19 26 F6
Tadley Common Rd TADY RG26 41 M7
Tadley Hl TADY RG26 61 M1
Tadpole La RFNM GU10 111 G7
Tagdell La HORN PO8 327 L8
Taiping Rd STOK SO20 162 F4 1
Tait Cl CFDH BH17 445 K1
Tait Pl LSOL/BMARY PO13 397 H7
Talbot Ct SHAM SO14 13 K1 2
Talbot Av TWDS BH3 447 K1
Talbot Cl FRIM GU16 91 K4
HAV PO9 377 G5
NWBY RG14 25 H3
ROWN SO16 318 E4
Talbot Dr BKME/WDN BH12 431 M8
CHCH/BSGR BH23 436 D6
Talbot Hill Rd
MOOR/WNTN BH9 432 B8
Talbot Mdw BKME/WDN BH12 431 M8
Talbot Ri NBNE BH10 432 A7
Talbot Rd ENEY PO4 21 M4
FAWY SO45 367 H7
FNM GU9 134 E8
HAV PO9 16 A1
MOOR/WNTN BH9 432 B8
Talgarth Dr FARN GU14 91 G6
Talisman Cl CWTH RG45 49 G3
Talland Rd FHAM/STUB PO14 370 F7
Tallis Gdns KEMP RG22 104 D7
Talmey Cl CHAM RG24 83 K5
Tamar Cl FERN BH22 406 E3
FHAM/PORC PO16 373 L7
Tamar Down WVILLE PO7 376 E1
Tamar Dr DEAN RG23 103 G7
Tamar Gv FAWY SO45 367 J5
Tamarisk Cl ENEY PO4 424 A5
FHAM/STUB PO14 396 A7 4
KEMP RG22 127 H3 1
WVILLE PO7 376 E3 1
Tamarisk Ct NTHA RG18 27 J4
Tamarisk Gdns WEND SO18 319 K8
Tamarisk Rd HEND SO30 345 M1
Tamella Rd HEND SO30 346 C2
Tammys Turn
FHAM/STUB PO14 371 M8 4
Tamorisk Dr TOTT SO40 341 G2
Tamworth Dr FARN GU14 89 G4
Tamworth Rd HSEA PO3 423 L2
Tanfield La WHAM PO17 348 D5
Tanfield Pk WHAM PO17 348 D5
Tangier Ct ALDT GU11 6 C2
Tangier La BPWT SO32 322 E1
Tangier Rd HSEA PO3 423 L1
Tanglewood EWKG RG40 48 D1
FHAM/PORC PO16 15 G1
TOTT SO40 342 E7 5
Tanglewood Cl WVILLE PO7 376 A4 3
Tangmere Cl CHCH/BSGR BH23 451 G2
Tangmere Dr ROWN SO16 317 L4
Tangway CHAM RG24 83 L4
Tangyes Cl FHAM/STUB PO14 396 B5
Tanhouse Cl HEND SO30 346 A3
Tanhouse La ALTN GU34 176 D5
HEND SO30 346 B3
Tan Howse Cl LTDN BH7 433 M8
Tankerdale La PSF GU32 248 B8
Tanker Rd FARN GU14 90 E7
Tankerton Cl CHAM PO6 375 J8 2
Tankerville Rd ITCH SO19 344 B5
Tank Rd CBLY GU15 70 C3
Tanner's Brook Wy
WSHM SO15 342 D2
Tanners Cl THLE RG7 31 J7
Tanners La FBDG SP6 308 E5
FHAM/STUB PO14 396 C2
HASM GU27 228 F1
LYMN SO41 441 L4
ROMY SO51 261 J8
WVILLE PO7 351 K3
Tanner's Rdg WVILLE PO7 376 C5
Tanners Rd NBAD SO52 291 M4
The Tanners
FHAM/STUB PO14 371 G7 3
Tanner St WINC SO23 11 H8
Tanners Wy DEAN RG23 103 G6
Tansy Cl WVILLE PO7 376 E2
Tansy Meadow NBAD SO52 292 E4 2
The Tanyards CHFD SO53 265 G7 6
Taplin Dr HEND SO30 321 H8
Taplings Cl WINW SO22 10 A1
Taplings Rd WINW SO22 10 A1
Taplin's Farm La HTWY RG27 87 K5
Taranto Rd ROWN SO16 318 B4
Tarbat Ct SHST GU47 50 A8 7
Tarbery Crs HORN PO8 353 G1
Target Rd NEND PO2 399 G5
Tarius Cl LSOL/BMARY PO13 397 H6
Tarleton Rd CHAM PO6 374 F7
Tarn Cl FARN GU14 90 B6
Tarn Dr CFDH BH17 429 K7
Tarn La NWBY RG14 2 C9
Tarn Ri HORN PO8 328 B6
Tarn Rd GSHT GU26 204 A5
Tarragon Cl FARN GU14 89 M4
Tarragon Wy THLE RG7 31 L5
Tarrant Cl CFDH BH17 430 C6
Tarrant Gdns HAV PO9 16 B1
Tarrant Rd MOOR/WNTN BH9 432 F5
Taskers Dr RAND SP11 142 B3
Tasman Cl CHCH/BSGR BH23 434 D8
SHAM SO14 13 K8
Tasmania Cl CHAM RG24 83 H6 3
Taswell Rd SSEA PO5 21 K8
Tatchbury La TOTT SO40 315 L7
Tate Rd WSHM SO15 317 H8
Tates Rd FAWY SO45 367 M5 1
FAWY SO45 367 M6 3
Tatnam Rd PLE BH15 445 H4
Tattenham Rd BROC SO42 387 K8
Tattershall Crs
FHAM/PORC PO16 397 M1
Tatwin Cl ITCH SO19 345 H3
Tatwin Crs ITCH SO19 345 H3
Taunton Dr WEND SO18 344 F1
Tavells Cl TOTT SO40 342 C7
Tavell's La TOTT SO40 342 C7
Taverner Cl BSTK RG21 5 J4
Taverners Cl ITCH SO19 345 H5
Tavistock Cl ROMY SO51 263 G7 6
Tavistock Gdns FARN GU14 90 E1
HAV PO9 17 J5
Tavistock Rd FLET GU13 88 C8 6
Tavy Cl CHFD SO53 293 G2
Taw Dr CHFD SO53 293 G1
Tawny Gv ALTN GU34 196 F6
Tawny Owl Cl
FHAM/STUB PO14 395 M4 3
Tay Cl FARN GU14 90 B2
Taylor Dr CHAR BH8 433 H4
TADY RG26 63 M6
Taylors La BOR GU35 201 L3
Teachers Wy FAWY SO45 391 M4 2
Teal Cl FHAM/PORC PO16 373 K8
HISD PO11 425 M5
TOTT SO40 341 G1 7
Teal Crs KEMP RG22 126 E1
Teasel Cl RAND SP11 92 E7
Teasel Wy FERN BH22 380 C7
Teazle Cl EPSF GU31 276 B6
Tebourba Dr GPORT PO12 18 C6
Tebourba Wy WSHM SO15 342 D1
Tedder Cl BWD BH11 431 M5
RAND SP11 142 A1
Tedder Gdns BWD BH11 431 M5
Tedder Rd BWD BH11 431 M5
LSOL/BMARY PO13 397 H5
WEND SO18 319 M8
Tedder Wy TOTT SO40 341 H1
Teddington Rd ENEY PO4 423 L4
Tees Cl CHFD SO53 292 F1
FARN GU14 90 B2
Teg Down Meads WINW SO22 214 A7
Tegg Down Rd NALR SO24 219 K5
Teignmouth Rd GPORT PO12 421 K1
HSEA PO3 399 L8
Tekels Av CBLY GU15 71 G4
Tekels Wy CBLY GU15 71 J5
Telconia Cl BOR GU35 202 F4 2
Telegraph La ALTN GU34 197 J5
EPSF GU31 305 K6
Telegraph Rd HEND SO30 320 D8
Telephone Rd ENEY PO4 21 M3
Telford Gdns HEND SO30 321 J6 2
Telford Rd NEND PO2 399 J5
Teme Crs ROWN SO16 317 K8
Teme Rd ROWN SO16 317 K8 1
Tempest Av WVILLE PO7 352 E8
Templar Cl BKME/WDN BH12 431 K7
SHST GU47 49 K8
Templars Mede CHFD SO53 293 G5
Templars Wy NBAD SO52 292 E4
Templecombe Rd ELGH SO50 294 E7
Temple Gdns ITCH SO19 344 D6 2
Temple La PSF GU32 273 J8
Templemere
FHAM/STUB PO14 396 A1
Temple Rd ITCH SO19 344 D6
LISS GU33 248 F2
Temple's Cl RFNM GU10 135 M7
Temple St PSEA PO1 423 G2
Templeton Cl NEND PO2 399 J5 2
Tenby Cl WEND SO18 319 M8
Tenby Dr CHFD SO53 292 F4
Tenby Rd FRIM GU16 71 K8
Tench Wy ROMY SO51 262 E8
Tennyson Cl BPWT SO32 297 K8
FAWY SO45 391 M3 2
Tennyson Crs WVILLE PO7 352 B7
Tennyson Gdns
FHAM/PORC PO16 15 G4
Tennyson Rd ELGH SO50 293 L6
MOOR/WNTN BH9 432 D6
NEND PO2 399 K8
NTHA RG18 26 F4
PSTN BH14 445 M5
PTSW SO17 319 G8
TOTT SO40 316 C6
WIMB BH21 404 A2
Tennyson's La HASM GU27 229 H4
Tennyson Wy KEMP RG22 104 D5 1
Tensing Cl FHAM/PORC PO16 15 G1
Tensing Rd CHCH/BSGR BH23 450 D1
Tenterton Av ITCH SO19 344 F7
Terence Rd WIMB BH21 429 G3
Terminus Ter SHAM SO14 13 J6
Tern Cl FAWY SO45 367 M6
Tern Ct SBNE BH6 449 J2
Terrace Rd WCLF BH2 22 D6
The Terrace CBLY GU15 70 C3
CWTH RG45 50 A3
Terrier Cl HEND SO30 321 H5
Terrington Av
CHCH/BSGR BH23 436 C7
Terriote Cl CHFD SO53 293 H1
Terwick La EPSF GU31 278 D8
Tesimond Dr YTLY GU46 68 D3
Testbourne Av TOTT SO40 341 H1
Testbourne Cl TOTT SO40 341 H1
Testbourne Rd TOTT SO40 341 H1
Test Cl PSF GU32 275 K7
Testcombe Rd GPORT PO12 18 D6
Testlands Av ROWN SO16 317 J2
Test La ROWN SO16 317 G7
Test Ri STOK SO20 165 M5
Test Rd SHAM SO14 343 M8
WHCH RG28 122 B4
Test Wy BSTK RG21 5 J8
MARL SN8 53 K4
RAND SP11 97 M7
RAND SP11 120 C4
ROMY SO51 233 K5
ROMY SO51 261 M6
STOK SO20 165 L3
STOK SO20 187 G2
STOK SO20 210 B7
TOTT SO40 316 F7
Testwood Av TOTT SO40 316 D7
Testwood Crs TOTT SO40 316 C6
Testwood La TOTT SO40 316 E7
Testwood Pl TOTT SO40 316 F8
Testwood Rd HAV PO9 377 H3 3
WSHM SO15 342 F2
Tethering Dro FBDG SP6 285 J5
Tetney Cl ROWN SO16 317 K5
Teviot Rd CHFD SO53 292 F3
Tewkesbury Av FHAM PO15 372 A5
GPORT PO12 421 L1
Tewkesbury Cl CHAM RG24 83 G7
CHAM PO6 375 H8
Texas Dr WINW SO22 238 A6
Thackeray Rd PTSW SO17 319 G8
Thackham's La HTWY RG27 86 E3
The Thakerays STHA RG19 27 G6 2
Thames Cl FERN BH22 406 E2
WEND SO18 320 A6
Thames Ct AND SP10 119 J6 1
BSTK RG21 5 J7
Thames Dr FHAM PO15 372 B4
Thamesmead Cl
GPORT PO12 421 K1 3
Thames Rd NTHA RG18 26 E3
Thames St PLE BH15 445 G7
Thatchers La
CHCH/BSGR BH23 409 K6
LYMN SO41 415 K8
Theal Cl SHST GU47 50 A8
Theale Rd TLHT RG30 31 L2
Theatre Ms SSEA PO5 21 K7 1
Theatre Rd FARN GU14 90 E8
The Itchen Br ITCH SO19 13 M6
Theobalds Wy FRIM GU16 71 M5
Theobold Rd
CHCH/BSGR BH23 407 L8
Theseus Rd LSOL/BMARY PO13 420 B1
Thetchers Cl NMIL/BTOS BH25 437 M3
Thetford Gdns CHFD SO53 292 F1
Thibet Rd SHST GU47 49 M8
The Thicket FHAM/PORC PO16 373 L8
LSOL/BMARY PO13 397 J7 3
ROMY SO51 291 H2 1
SSEA PO5 21 J6 3
WVILLE PO7 376 B6
Third Av CHAM PO6 375 J8
HAV PO9 17 H3
WSHM SO15 342 D2
Third St STHA RG19 38 C3
Thirlmere ELGH SO50 293 L6 2
Thirlmere Cl FARN GU14 90 B4
FHAM/STUB PO14 396 B4 1
BOR GU35 201 J3 3
Thirlmere Crs FLET GU13 110 D3 1
Thirlmere Rd ROWN SO16 317 K6
Thirlstane Firs CHFD SO53 293 G4 2
Thirsk Ct ASHV GU12 7 M1
Thirt Wy STOK SO20 166 B7
Thistlebarrow Rd LTDN BH7 448 D2
Thistledown HORN PO8 352 F3
Thistledown Cl AND SP10 8 D3 1
Thistledowne Gdns
EMRTH PO10 378 F8
Thistle Rd HEND SO30 345 M2
NBAD SO52 292 E3
Thomas Cl TOTT SO40 341 H2 3
Thomas Lewis Wy
PTSW SO17 319 G8 2
Thomas Rd NBAD SO52 291 M4
Thompson Dr STHA RG19 27 H6 2
Thompson's La RWIN SO21 295 L1
WVILLE PO7 351 G3
Thorburn Cha SHST GU47 70 B2 3
Thoresby Ct
NMIL/BTOS BH25 437 J5 3
Thornbrake Rd GPORT PO12 19 H5 1
Thornbury Av FAWY SO45 392 C8
WSHM SO15 343 J1
Thornbury Cl CWTH RG45 49 L3
FHAM/STUB PO14 372 A8 3
Thornbury Hts CHFD SO53 265 L7
Thornbury Rd SBNE BH6 449 M4
Thornbury Wd CHFD SO53 265 L7
Thorncliffe Cl NEND PO2 399 K4 3
Thorn Cl ELGH SO50 293 M3 3
EPSF GU31 276 B6
RFNM GU10 158 C4 2
Thorncombe Cl CFDH BH17 430 C6
Thorn Ct ALTN GU34 197 G6
Thorn Crs ALTN GU34 197 G6 2
Thorncroft Rd PSEA PO1 21 M2
Thorndike Cl ROWN SO16 317 M6
Thorn Dr ALTN GU34 197 G6 3
Thorne Cl CWTH RG45 49 K1 3
VWD BH31 356 C1
Thorneley Rd KSCL RG20 59 J6 3
Thorness Cl ROWN SO16 317 H7
Thorney Cl FHAM/STUB PO14 14 A8
Thorney Old Pk EMRTH PO10 403 H7
Thorney Rd EMRTH PO10 402 F3
Thornfield STHA RG19 39 G5 1
Thornfield Dr
CHCH/BSGR BH23 436 D7
Thornfield Gn BLKW GU17 70 C5
Thornford Rd STHA RG19 3
Thorngate Wy GPORT PO12 19
Thornham La EMRTH PO10 40
Thornham Rd
NMIL/BTOS BH25 43
Thornhill Av ITCH SO19 34
Thornhill Cl FAWY SO45 392
Thornhill Park Rd WEND SO18 34
Thornhill Rd ALDT GU11 11
FAWY SO45 39
ROWN SO16 31
Thornhill Wy CHAM RG24 8
Thorni Av FHAM PO15 37
Thorn La ALTN GU34 19
Thornleigh Rd ITCH SO19 34
Thornley Rd NBNE BH10 43
Thorn Rd CFDH BH17 43
RFNM GU10 15
Thorns La LYMN SO41 44
Thornton Av HLER SO31 37
Thornton Cl CHAM PO6 375
WIMB BH21 429
Thornton End ALTN GU34 17
Thornton Rd GPORT PO12 39
Thornycroft Av ITCH SO19 34
Thornyhurst Rd FRIM GU16 9
Thorold Rd CHFD SO53 26
FNM GU9 134
WEND SO18 31
Thorpe Gdns ALTN GU34 17
Threadgill Wy NTID SP9 13
Three Acre Dr
NMIL/BTOS BH25 43
Three Acre Rd NWBY RG14 2
Three Acres WVILLE PO7 35
Three Castles Pth HTWY RG27 6
NALR SO24 17
NALR SO24 19
ODIM RG29 10
OVTN RG25 10
RWIN SO21 19
RWIN SO21 21
Three Cross Rd WIMB BH21 38
Threefield La SHAM SO14 1
Three Firs Wy THLE RG7 3
Three Gates La HASM GU27 22
Three Horse Shoes La
ALTN GU34 24
Three Oaks ITCH SO19 34
Three Stiles Rd FNM GU9 13
Three Tun Cl PSEA PO1 2
Thresher Cl HORN PO8 353
Threshers Cnr FARN GU14 89
Throgmorton Rd YTLY GU46 6
Throop Cl CHAR BH8 43
Throop Rd CHAR BH8 43
Throopside Av
MOOR/WNTN BH9 43
Thrush Cl THLE RG7 3
Thrush Rd BKME/WDN BH12 43
Thrush Wk HORN PO8 352
Thruxton Rd HAV PO9 37
Thuillier Rd RWIN SO21 14
Thumwood CHAM RG24 83
Thundery Hl RFNM GU10 13
Thurbans Rd FNM GU9 158
Thurbern Rd NEND PO2 39
Thurmell Cl HEND SO30 34
Thurmond Crs WINW SO22 23
Thurmond Rd WINW SO22 23
Thursby Rd CHCH/BSGR BH23 43
Thursley Rd RFNM GU10 18
Thurston Cl CHFD SO53 29
Thurston Pl BSTK RG21 10
Thurstons ALTN GU34 17
Thwaite Rd BKME/WDN BH12 44
Thyme Av FHAM PO15 34
Thyme Cl CHAM RG24 8
Thyme Ct FARN GU14 8
Tides Reach WEND SO18 31
Tiberius Cl DEAN RG23 10
Tiberius Rd AND SP10 11
Tichborne Cl BLKW GU17 70
Tichborne Down NALR SO24 21
Tichborne Gv HAV PO9 377
Tichborne Pl ASHV GU12
Tichborne Rd ELGH SO50 29
WEND SO18 32
Tichborne Wy
LSOL/BMARY PO13 39
Tichbourne Cl FRIM GU16 7
Tickenor Dr EWKG RG40 4
Tickleford Dr ITCH SO19 34
Tickner Cl HEND SO30 346
Ticonderoga Gdns ITCH SO19 34
Tidemill Cl CHCH/BSGR BH23 43
Tides Wy TOTT SO40 34
Tideway Gdns ENEY PO4 42
Tidworth Rd HAV PO9 37
RAND SP11 9
Tiffany Cl LYMN SO41 438
Tiffield Cl HSEA PO3 40
Tigwells Fld ODIM RG29 13
Tilbrook Rd WSHM SO15 31
Tilburg Rd CHCH/BSGR BH23 45
Tilbury's Cl BOR GU35 201
Tilden Rd RWIN SO21 26
Tile Barn Cl FARN GU14 9
Tilebarn La BROC SO42 41
Tilford Rd FNM GU9 13
GSHT GU26 20
HORN PO8 35
RFNM GU10 15
Tilford St RFNM GU10 15
Tillington Gdns HORN PO8 328
Tilmore Gdns PSF GU32 27
Tilmore Rd PSF GU32 27
Tilney Cl ALTN GU34 17
Timber Bank FRIM GU16 9
Timbercroft Cl ALTN GU34 19
Timberlake Rd BSTK RG21
Timberlane WVILLE PO7 37
Timberley La RSAL SP5 28
Timberley Pl CWTH RG45 49
Timberly Cl FAWY SO45 39
Timbermill Ct HASM GU27 228
The Timbers FHAM PO15 37
Timor Cl HLER SO31 34

Cl *NBNE* BH10 432 B3
Rd *PSEA* PO1 423 J2
y Crs *HAV* PO9 16 C1
y Dr *ROWN* SO16 317 L6
Cl *TOTT* SO40 341 G2 7
n Gdns
/WNTN BH9 432 F4
YTLY GU46 69 G2
Rd *ROWN* SO16 317 K6
ly *ELGH* SO50 319 M1
Cl *RSAL* SP5 285 J4
Cl *AND* SP10 118 F5
RG23 104 B2
Dr *FRIM* GU16 71 J7
Wy *CHAM* PO6 398 F1
Cl *CHAM* RG24 4 B1
PO6 374 D7
Gv *WSHM* SO15 12 C1
Rd *GPORT* PO12 18 D3
n *NEND* PO2 399 G5 1
a *NEND* PO2 398 F5
d *NEND* PO2 399 G6
a *EPSF* GU31 305 G5
dns *KEMP* RG22 104 E8
d *NMIL/BTOS* BH25 412 A7
Cl *ELGH* SO50 293 M3
t *HAV* PO9 377 M3 16
d Cl *TADY* RG26 61 M1 3
d Hl *FHAM/STUB* PO14 371 L8
d La *FHAM* PO15 348 A8
PO17 348 A7
d Park Rd *FHAM* PO15 371 H5
d Rd
/STUB PO14 395 L1
rn *LYMN* SO41 440 C3
ds La *NALR* SO24 243 L4
eadow *KEMP* RG22 127 H3 2
e *WVILLE* PO7 351 K5 1
od Cl *CHFD* SO53 265 G6 3
use La *RAND* SP11 117 H6
ns *WVILLE* PO7 352 E8
Rd *DEAN* RG23 104 B3
CHFD SO53 293 L1
BLKW GU17 70 B4
Cl *CHAM* RG24 83 G7
Cl *RAND* SP11 119 G1
Rd *RAND* SP11 115 J2
PSEA PO1 423 G2 10
e *LISS* GU33 224 E5
ENEY PO4 423 L6
HSEA PO3 399 L7
Gv *AND* SP10 9 L2
Gdns *NBAD* SO52 292 E2 3
Cl *BKME/WDN* BH12 431 J8
Wy *HEND* SO30 320 F8
d Rd *CFDH* BH17 430 B6
CHFD SO53 293 H6
Cl *DEAN* RG23 103 G5
Rd *AND* SP10 8 B2
SO31 346 B8
CHAM RG24 83 M5
le Gdns
/WNTN BH9 432 F4
le Wy *YTLY* GU46 69 J3
Rd *PSTN* BH14 445 M2
Cl *STHA* RG19 27 H6 3
Av *FRIM* GU16 71 J6
Cl *TADY* RG26 61 L1
cote Wy *FRIM* GU16 71 K6
on Dr *EWKG* RG40 48 D2
RGWD BH24 335 L8
ge St *SSEA* PO5 21 H7
d *BWD* BH11 431 M2
n Mdw *RFNM* GU10 136 C1 3
n Rd *ASHV* GU12 7 L6
GU10 135 M4
t Cl
/STUB PO14 396 B7 1
ds Wy *ROWN* SO16 317 J3
Cl *FAWY* SO45 392 D6
Rd *ROMY* SO51 291 H7
r *WVILLE* PO7 352 F8
Gdns *HLER* SO31 370 F4
iary *CHAM* RG24 83 M8
GU14 90 B5
Pl *FNM* GU9 134 F1 5
RGWD BH24 382 E1
race Rd *FARN* GU14 90 D8
Rd *PSTN* BH14 446 B5
y Dr *EPSF* GU31 276 A6
ELGH SO50 295 G6 4
HAM/PORC PO16 373 J7
s Cl *ITCH* SO19 344 C6 3
Ct *ENEY* PO4 424 A5
d *FAWY* SO45 367 K5 5
Gv *NBAD* SO52 291 L4
Pl *GPORT* PO12 18 F2
Rd *NEND* PO2 423 J1
y Av *GPORT* PO12 397 L8
SO15 318 B8
Cl *ITCH* SO19 345 J4
ELGH SO50 293 M2
e Gdns *WEND* SO18 320 A5 1
ton Cl *ITCH* SO19 344 E4 2
GU35 201 M3 7
ton Rd *NEND* PO2 399 J5
FNM GU9 134 C6
rth Cl *FHAM/STUB* PO14 14 A8
EPSF GU31 275 M5
d Gdns *ELGH* SO50 294 E6
Cl *ROWN* SO16 317 K8 2
MIDH GU29 279 K2
La *RFNM* GU10 137 H5
Cl *FARN* GU14 90 D2
SO16 317 K8
Rd *CHAM* PO6 399 J1
BMARY PO13 397 G6
Rd *CFDH* BH17 430 E6
Cl *ELGH* SO50 293 L3
le Cl *NBAD* SO52 291 L5
am Cl *TADY* RG26 63 L4
am Rd *PSEA* PO1 423 J2
am Wk *SHST* GU47 50 A7
own *THLE* RG7 31 J7
La *HTWY* RG27 86 E7
By-pass *TOTT* SO40 341 L2
Cl *ALDT* GU11 113 H1
rbury La *HISD* PO11 425 L4

Tourney Rd *BWD* BH11 431 H2
Tovey Pl *WINC* SO23 191 H8
Tower Cl *AND* SP10 118 C5
GPORT PO12 421 H5
Tower Gdns *HAV* PO9 401 K2
Tower Hl *FARN* GU14 90 D5
Tower La *ELGH* SO50 294 B6
WIMB BH21 404 B2
Tower Pl *HEND* SO30 320 C7
Tower Rd *BMTH* BH1 448 D3
CCLF BH13 447 G7
ENEY PO4 423 K5
GSHT GU26 204 B4
LIPH GU30 226 E4
WINC SO23 10 F6
Tower Rd West *CCLF* BH13 446 F7
Towers Dr *CWTH* RG45 49 L4
Towers Farm *WIMB* BH21 429 H1 2
Tower St *ALTN* GU34 176 D6
EMRTH PO10 378 E8
PSEA PO1 20 B5
WINC SO23 10 F7
Towers Wy *WIMB* BH21 429 H1
Town Cl *NALR* SO24 220 C4
Towngate Br *PLE* BH15 445 H6
Town Hall Rd *HAV* PO9 16 F5
Townhill Wy *WEND* SO18 319 M7
Town La *EPSF* GU31 276 A3
Town Mill La *WHCH* RG28 122 C3
Town Quay *SHAM* SO14 12 F7
Townsend Cl *BSTK* RG21 4 B9
Townsend La *FBDG* SP6 280 D4
Townside Pl *CBLY* GU15 71 G2 3
Townsville Rd
MOOR/WNTN BH9 432 F6
Towpath Md *ENEY* PO4 424 A4 1
Toynbee Cl *ELGH* SO50 293 M5
Toynbee Rd *ELGH* SO50 293 M5
Tozer Cl *BWD* BH11 431 K6
Trafalgar Cl *CHFD* SO53 293 G3
Trafalgar Ct *FHAM/STUB* PO14 396 D1
FNM GU9 134 E7
Trafalgar Pl *PSEA* PO1 423 J2 3
Trafalgar Rd
MOOR/WNTN BH9 447 L1
WSHM SO15 343 G2
Trafalgar Sq *GPORT* PO12 18 E1
Trafalgar St *WINC* SO23 10 F8
Trafalgar Wy *CBLY* GU15 70 C4
FAWY SO45 367 M7
STOK SO20 186 E6
Trafford Rd *FRIM* GU16 71 G8
Trafford Wy *ELGH* SO50 295 G7
Trampers La *WHAM* PO17 349 L7
Tranby Rd *ITCH* SO19 344 C4
Tranmere Cl *LYMN* SO41 440 D6
Tranmere Rd *ENEY* PO4 423 M5 2
Transport Rd *FARN* GU14 90 E7
Travis La *SHST* GU47 69 M1 1
Treadwheel Rd *HORN* PO8 353 L2
Treagore Rd *TOTT* SO40 316 B7 2
Trearnan Cl *ROWN* SO16 317 L8
Treble Cl *WINW* SO22 238 A4
Trebor Av *FNM* GU9 135 G7
Tredegar Rd *ENEY* PO4 423 K5
Tredenham Cl *FARN* GU14 90 F8 2
Tree Av *HASM* GU27 204 C8
Treebys Cl *CHCH/BSGR* BH23 435 H7
Treeside *CHCH/BSGR* BH23 436 A6
Treeside Av *TOTT* SO40 341 L1
Treeside Dr *FNM* GU9 6 A8
Treeside Rd *WSHM* SO15 318 B8
Tree Side Wy *WVILLE* PO7 352 C7
Tree Tops Av *CBLY* GU15 51 K8
Trefoil Cl *HTWY* RG27 87 H1
WVILLE PO7 376 D1
Trefoil Dro *NTHA* RG18 27 J4
Trefoil Wy *CHCH/BSGR* BH23 436 A8
Tregaron Av *CHAM* PO6 399 M1
Tregolls Dr *FARN* GU14 90 F5
Tregonwell Rd *WCLF* BH2 22 D6
Trellis Dr *CHAM* RG24 83 M8
Treloar Rd *HISD* PO11 426 C7
Treloyhan Cl *CHFD* SO53 293 J4
Tremayne Wk *CBLY* GU15 71 M4
Tremona Rd *ROWN* SO16 318 A5
Trenchard Rd *RAND* SP11 142 A1
Trenley Cl *FAWY* SO45 392 A5
Trent Cl *FARN* GU14 90 B2
WEND SO18 319 L7 1
Trent Ct *AND* SP10 9 M1 5
Trent Crs *NTHA* RG18 26 E3
Trentham Av *LTDN* BH7 433 M8
Trentham Cl *LTDN* BH7 433 M8
Trenton Cl *FRIM* GU16 71 K6
Trent Rd *WEND* SO18 319 L7
Trent Wy *BSTK* RG21 5 K8
FERN BH22 406 E2
LSOL/BMARY PO13 420 D2 3
Tresham Crs *YTLY* GU46 68 D2 2
Tresillian Gdns *WEND* SO18 320 A6 2
Tresillian Wy *CHCH/BSGR* BH23 436 F6
Trevis Rd *ENEY* PO4 424 A4
Trevone Cl *TOTT* SO40 341 J3 4
Trevor Rd *ENEY* PO4 21 M6
Trevose Cl *CHFD* SO53 293 J4 2
LSOL/BMARY PO13 397 G7
Trevose Crs *CHFD* SO53 293 J3
Trevose Wy *FHAM/STUB* PO14 370 F7
Triangle La *FHAM/STUB* PO14 395 J4
The Triangle *NWBY* RG14 37 L1
RSAL SP5 259 G4 1
WCLF BH2 22 C6
Tribe Rd *GPORT* PO12 18 D2
Tricketts La *FERN* BH22 406 D2
Trigon Rd *PLE* BH15 445 J1
Trimaran Cl *HLER* SO31 370 C7
Trimaran Rd *HLER* SO31 370 C7 4
Trimmers Cl *FNM* GU9 134 F1 6
Trimmers Wd *GSHT* GU26 204 A2
Trimm's Dro *FBDG* SP6 284 D8
Trinidad Cl *CHAM* RG24 83 G7
Trinidad Crs *BKME/WDN* BH12 431 G8
Trinity *SHST* GU47 50 B6
Trinity Cl *GPORT* PO12 19 K4
Trinity Flds *FNM* GU9 134 D2 5
Trinity Gn *GPORT* PO12 19 L4
Trinity Hl *ALTN* GU34 174 D8

FNM GU9 134 D2
Trinity Ri *RAND* SP11 117 L4
Trinity Rd *ALTN* GU34 174 D7
BMTH BH1 23 H4
SHAM SO14 13 H1
Trinity St *FHAM/PORC* PO16 15 J5
Tristan Cl *FAWY* SO45 419 J1
Triumph Cl *FHAM* PO15 14 B3
Triumph Rd *FHAM/STUB* PO14 396 D3
Troak Cl *CHCH/BSGR* BH23 435 J8
Trojan Wy *WVILLE* PO7 376 D5
Troon Crs *CHAM* PO6 376 A7
Troon Rd *WIMB* BH21 429 L3
Trosnant Rd *HAV* PO9 16 C2
Trotton Rd *EPSF* GU31 278 C8
Trotts La *TOTT* SO40 342 A4
Trotwood Cl *SHST* GU47 50 B6 5
Trout Rd *HASM* GU27 228 B2
Trout Wk *NWBY* RG14 25 L3
Trowbridge Cl *ROWN* SO16 317 K2
Trowe's La *THLE* RG7 45 G4
Truman Rd *BWD* BH11 431 M2
Trunk Rd *FARN* GU14 89 M4
Truro Ri *ELGH* SO50 294 D5
Truro Rd *CHAM* PO6 374 D8
Truscott Av *MOOR/WNTN* BH9 447 M1
Trussell Cl *WINW* SO22 10 A1
Trussell Crs *WINW* SO22 10 A1
Trust Cl *HTWY* RG27 85 L7 4
Tubb's La *KSCL* RG20 56 C2
TADY RG26 61 M8
Tuckers La *PLE* BH15 444 E7
Tucks Cl *CHCH/BSGR* BH23 409 L7
Tuckton Cl *SBNE* BH6 449 J4
Tuckton Rd *SBNE* BH6 449 J4
Tudor Av *EMRTH* PO10 378 C4
Tudor Cl *FBDG* SP6 333 L3
FHAM/PORC PO16 373 M7 2
GSHT GU26 204 A6
HISD PO11 425 K6
LSOL/BMARY PO13 397 H8 2
TOTT SO40 316 B8
Tudor Ct *FHAM/STUB* PO14 396 D1 2
PLE BH15 445 K2
Tudor Crs *CHAM* PO6 399 K2
Tudor Dr *YTLY* GU46 69 G3 4
Tudor Gdns *HEND* SO30 345 L3
Tudor Rd *BDST* BH18 429 M4
NWBY RG14 2 F7
Tudor Wy *FLET* GU13 110 F4
WINC SO23 191 G8
Tudor Wood Cl *ROWN* SO16 318 E4 2
Tuffin Cl *ROWN* SO16 317 H3 3
Tukes Av *LSOL/BMARY* PO13 396 F4
Tulip Cl *KEMP* RG22 126 F1
Tulip Gdns *HAV* PO9 377 G6
HLER SO31 370 D5
Tulip Rd *ROWN* SO16 319 H4 1
Tulls La *BOR* GU35 202 A6
Tumulus Cl *ITCH* SO19 345 K4 2
Tunball La *MARL* SN8 72 B1
Tunbridge Crs *LIPH* GU30 226 E3
Tunbridge La *LIPH* GU30 226 E2
Tunnel Rd *FARN* GU14 90 A7
Tunstall Rd *CHAM* PO6 375 H7
ITCH SO19 345 J4
Tunworth Ct *HAV* PO9 377 M3 17
Tunworth Ms *TADY* RG26 41 M8
Tunworth Rd *OVTN* RG25 106 D4
Tuppenny La *EMRTH* PO10 379 G8
Turbary Cl *BKME/WDN* BH12 431 J8
Turbary Ct *UPTN* BH16 429 G8 2
Turbary Gdns *TADY* RG26 41 L7
Turbary Park Av *BWD* BH11 431 K5
Turbary Rd *BKME/WDN* BH12 446 C1
FERN BH22 406 D1
Turf Hill Rd *CBLY* GU15 51 J8
Turin Ct *AND* SP10 119 G4
Turks La *PSTN* BH14 445 M7
THLE RG7 43 J4
Turk St *ALTN* GU34 176 E5
Turlin Rd *UPTN* BH16 444 B4
Turner Av *LSOL/BMARY* PO13 397 J7
Turner Cl *BSTK* RG21 105 K4
Turner Pl *SHST* GU47 70 A2
Turners Dr *STHA* RG19 27 H5
Turners Farm Crs
LYMN SO41 438 E6 1
Turner's Green La *HTWY* RG27 88 B4
The Turnery *STHA* RG19 26 F5 3
Turnfields *STHA* RG19 27 G5
Turnpike Down *WINC* SO23 11 M7
Turnpike Rd *NTHA* RG18 26 B4
NWBY RG14 3 M1
Turnpike Wy *DEAN* RG23 102 F6
HEND SO30 345 L2
Turnstone End *YTLY* GU46 68 E2 4
Turnstone Gdns *ROWN* SO16 318 A3
Turnworth Cl *BDST* BH18 430 A5
Turtle Cl *FHAM/STUB* PO14 395 M4
Tuscan Wk *CHFD* SO53 293 K2
Tuscany Wy *WVILLE* PO7 352 F8
The Tussocks *TOTT* SO40 342 D6
Tutland Rd *NBAD* SO52 291 L4 3
Tutor Cl *HLER* SO31 369 K5
Tutts La *ROMY* SO51 288 D4
Tweedale Rd
MOOR/WNTN BH9 433 G5
Tweed Cl *CHFD* SO53 292 F1
FARN GU14 90 B2
Tweed La *LYMN* SO41 414 B8
Tweedsmuir Cl *FARN* GU14 90 A5 7
KEMP RG22 104 A4
Twelve Acre Crs *FARN* GU14 90 A3 2
Twemlow Av *PSTN* BH14 445 L6
Tweseldown Rd *FLET* GU13 111 G4
Twiggs End Cl *HLER* SO31 370 D4
Twiggs La *TOTT* SO40 366 B2
Twiggs Lane End *TOTT* SO40 366 A3
Twin Oaks Cl *BDST* BH18 429 M5
Twisell Thorne *FLET* GU13 110 D4
Two Gate La *OVTN* RG25 124 A1
Two Gate Meadow *OVTN* RG25 101 G8
Two Rivers Wy *NWBY* RG14 3 M3
Twyford Av *NEND* PO2 399 H7
WSHM SO15 318 B7
Twyford Cl *CHAR* BH8 433 H6
Twyford La *RFNM* GU10 158 E2

Twyford Rd *ELGH* SO50 294 A2
Twyford Wy *CFDH* BH17 430 E6
Twynham Av
CHCH/BSGR BH23 449 M2
Twynham Cl *RSAL* SP5 284 E2
Twynham Rd *SBNE* BH6 449 K5
Twynhams Hl *BPWT* SO32 323 M8
Tydehams *NWBY* RG14 37 H1
Tyfield *CHAM* RG24 82 D5
Tyler Dr *WHIT* RG2 47 H1
Tylers Cl *LYMN* SO41 440 B3
The Tyleshades *ROMY* SO51 290 F2 4
Tylney La *HTWY* RG27 85 J7
Tylston Meadow *LIPH* GU30 226 E3 2
Tyne Cl *CHFD* SO53 292 F3
FARN GU14 90 B2
Tyne Ct *AND* SP10 119 J6 2
Tynedale Cl *GPORT* PO12 397 K8 3
MOOR/WNTN BH9 433 G4
Tyneham Av *BKME/WDN* BH12 430 F8
Tyne Wy *HEND* SO30 320 D6
NTHA RG18 26 E3
Tyrell Rd *CHFD* SO53 293 H1
Tyrells La *RGWD* BH24 384 C4
Tyrrell Gdns *CHAR* BH8 433 L6
Tyrrells Ct *CHCH/BSGR* BH23 409 M7
Tyseley Rd *SSEA* PO5 21 H3
Tytherley Gn *CHAR* BH8 433 H6
Tytherley Rd *RSAL* SP5 207 H2
WEND SO18 320 B8

U

Uddens Dr *WIMB* BH21 405 J2
Ullswater Av *FARN* GU14 90 B5
WEND SO18 320 A7
Ullswater Cl *FNM* GU9 134 D2 6
BOR GU35 201 J3
STHA RG19 26 D5
Ullswater Gv *NALR* SO24 218 C4 7
Ullswater Rd *ROWN* SO16 317 K7
WIMB BH21 404 A6
Undercliff Dr *BMTH* BH1 23 H7
Undercliff Rd *BOSC* BH5 448 C5
Underdown Av *WVILLE* PO7 376 B6
Underhill La *FNM* GU9 158 E1
Undershore *LYMN* SO41 440 E4
Underwood Av *ASHV* GU12 113 H7
Underwood Cl *ROWN* SO16 318 D4 2
Underwood Rd *ELGH* SO50 294 C4
HASM GU27 228 C1
ROWN SO16 318 D4
Unicorn Rd *LSOL/BMARY* PO13 420 B1
PSEA PO1 422 F2
Union Cl *SHST* GU47 50 B6
Union La *BPWT* SO32 298 F6
KSCL RG20 59 J5
Union Pl *PSEA* PO1 423 H2
Union Ri *LISS* GU33 225 J6
Union Rd *FNM* GU9 134 F6
HAV PO9 16 D4
SHAM SO14 343 M2
Union St *FARN* GU14 90 D4
FHAM/PORC PO16 15 M6
PSEA PO1 20 D1
WINC SO23 11 J7
Union Ter *ALDT* GU11 6 E2
University Crs *PTSW* SO17 319 G5
University Pkwy *ROWN* SO16 292 B7
University Rd *PTSW* SO17 318 F5
Unwin Cl *ITCH* SO19 344 B7
Upfallow *CHAM* RG24 105 M1
Upham St *BPWT* SO32 296 B4
Uphill Rd *WINW* SO22 214 A3
Upland La *LISS* GU33 247 M1
Upland Rd *CBLY* GU15 71 G1
Uplands Av *NMIL/BTOS* BH25 437 L8
Uplands Cl *FERN* BH22 380 E8
HASM GU27 205 G8
SHST GU47 49 L8 3
Uplands Crs *FHAM/PORC* PO16 15 J3
Uplands La *ALTN* GU34 196 F7
Uplands Rd *CHAM* PO6 376 A7
CHAR BH8 433 G6
FERN BH22 380 D6
FNM GU9 135 H7
WINW SO22 10 C1
HAV PO9 354 A6
WVILLE PO7 350 F2
Uplands Wy *PTSW* SO17 318 F6
Uplyme Cl *CFDH* BH17 430 E6
Upnor Cl *RAND* SP11 115 J1
Upper Arundel St *PSEA* PO1 21 H1
Upper Banister St
WSHM SO15 343 K2 5
Upper Barn Copse *ELGH* SO50 295 G5
Upper Bere Wd *WVILLE* PO7 376 D2
Upper Bourne La *RFNM* GU10 158 D3
Upper Bourne V *RFNM* GU10 158 D3 2
Upper Broadmoor Rd
CWTH RG45 49 M3
Upper Brook Dr *HLER* SO31 370 C5
Upper Brook St *WINC* SO23 11 H7
Upper Brownhill Rd
ROWN SO16 317 L5
Upper Bugle St *SHAM* SO14 12 F5
Upper Charles St *CBLY* GU15 70 F2
Upper Chestnut Dr *BSTK* RG21 104 E5
Upper Chobham Rd *CBLY* GU15 71 L4
FRIM GU16 71 K5
Upper Church La *FNM* GU9 134 E6 9
Upper Church Rd *BPWT* SO32 348 C1
Upper College Ride *CBLY* GU15 51 H8
Upper Common Rd
LYMN SO41 439 K4 1
Upper Cornaway La
FHAM/PORC PO16 373 M8
Upper Crabbick La
WVILLE PO7 351 G3
Upper Crescent Rd
NBAD SO52 291 L4
Upper Deacon Rd *ITCH* SO19 344 F2
Upper Dro *AND* SP10 118 B8
Upper Elms Rd *ALDT* GU11 6 E3
Upper Farm Rd *DEAN* RG23 102 F8

Upper Golf Links Rd
BDST BH18 429 M3
Upper Gordon Rd *CBLY* GU15 71 G3
CHCH/BSGR BH23 436 E7
Upper Grove Rd *ALTN* GU34 176 E6
Upper Hale Rd *FNM* GU9 134 E1
Upper Heyshott *EPSF* GU31 275 M5
Upper High St *WINW* SO22 10 E6
Upper Hinton Rd *BMTH* BH1 22 F6
Upper House Ct *WHAM* PO17 348 E5
Upper Lamborough La
NALR SO24 242 D2
Upper Lanham La *NALR* SO24 195 J1
Upper Market St *ELGH* SO50 294 A5
Upper Mead Cl *ELGH* SO50 295 J6 4
Upper Moors Rd *ELGH* SO50 266 E7
RWIN SO21 266 E8
Upper Mt *HASM* GU27 205 J7
LISS GU33 248 D5
Upper Mullin's La *FAWY* SO45 367 J5
Upper Neatham Mill La
ALTN GU34 177 H2
Upper New Rd *HEND* SO30 320 C7
Upper Northam Cl *HEND* SO30 345 L2
Upper Northam Dr
HEND SO30 345 J2
Upper Northam Rd
HEND SO30 345 L1
Upper Norwich Rd *WCLF* BH2 22 B6
Upper Old Park La *FNM* GU9 134 C3
Upper Old St
FHAM/STUB PO14 395 M4
Upper Park Rd *CBLY* GU15 71 G3
Upper Piece *WVILLE* PO7 351 L5
Upper Pinewood Rd
ASHV GU12 113 M5
Upper Rd *BKME/WDN* BH12 446 B2
Upper St Helens Rd
HEND SO30 345 M4
Upper St Michael's Rd
ALDT GU11 7 G5
Upper Shaftesbury Av
PTSW SO17 319 G6
Upper Sherborne Rd *BSTK* RG21 4 C2
Upper Shirley Av *WSHM* SO15 318 B7
Upper Soldridge Rd
ALTN GU34 196 C6
Upper South Vw *FNM* GU9 134 F5
Upper Spinney *HLER* SO31 370 A8
Upper St *FLET* GU13 88 E7
Upper Terrace Rd *FARN* GU14 90 D8
WCLF BH2 22 D6
Upper Toothill Rd *ROWN* SO16 291 K7
Upper Union St *ALDT* GU11 6 D2
Upper Union Ter *ALDT* GU11 6 E2
Upper Verran Rd *CBLY* GU15 71 G5
Upper Wardown *EPSF* GU31 276 A4
Upper Wy *FNM* GU9 134 E8
Upper Weston La *ITCH* SO19 344 E6
Upper Weybourne La
FNM GU9 112 A8
Upper Whf *FHAM/PORC* PO16 15 L7
Uppleby Rd *BKME/WDN* BH12 446 B2
Upron Field Cl *KEMP* RG22 127 G1
Up St *OVTN* RG25 125 K7
Upton Cl *FARN* GU14 91 G5 3
HAV PO9 377 H1
UPTN BH16 444 A1
Upton Ct *UPTN* BH16 444 B1 5
Upton Crs *BSTK* RG21 4 D3
ROWN SO16 317 H1
Upton Grey Cl *WINW* SO22 214 C5
Upton Grey Rd *OVTN* RG25 107 J7
Upton Heath Est *UPTN* BH16 444 C1
Upton La *ROWN* SO16 317 G3
Upton Rd *CFDH* BH17 444 D1
Upton Wy *BDST* BH18 429 J5
Upwey Av *PLE* BH15 444 D5
Urquhart Rd *STHA* RG19 27 G7

V

Vadne Gdns *GPORT* PO12 421 M2 4
Vaggs La *LYMN* SO41 438 C2
Vale Cl *RFNM* GU10 158 F4
Vale Dr *WEND* SO18 319 L7
Vale Gv *GPORT* PO12 421 L1
Valencia Wy *AND* SP10 9 K3
Valentine Av *ITCH* SO19 345 G5
Valentine Cl *FHAM* PO15 372 A5
Valentine Ct *WVILLE* PO7 352 E8 5
Valerian Cl *ELGH* SO50 321 H2 5
Valerian Rd *HEND* SO30 346 A2
Vale Rd *ASHV* GU12 113 K3
BMTH BH1 448 C4
CBLY GU15 70 D4
PSTN BH14 446 D4
RSAL SP5 285 J2
WINC SO23 239 G2
The Vale *DEAN* RG23 102 F7
FAWY SO45 367 K5
HLER SO31 370 F6
HORN PO8 328 B7
SSEA PO5 21 H8
Valetta Pk *EMRTH* PO10 378 C8
Valetta Rd *EMRTH* PO10 403 H7
Valette Rd *MOOR/WNTN* BH9 432 E5
Vale View Dr *THLE* RG7 45 G3
Vale Wy *WINC* SO23 191 G7
Vale Wood Dr *RFNM* GU10 159 G4
Vale Wood La *GSHT* GU26 203 M4
Valewood Rd *HASM* GU27 228 F4
Valiant Gdns *NEND* PO2 399 H4
Valiant Rd *EMRTH* PO10 403 H7
Valiant Wy *CHCH/BSGR* BH23 451 G1
FARN GU14 90 A8
Valley Cl *CHCH/BSGR* BH23 434 C5
FAWY SO45 392 D7 1
RSAL SP5 285 J2
RWIN SO21 266 E8
WVILLE PO7 376 A5
Valleydene *FAWY* SO45 367 K6
Valley Hl *WINW* SO22 214 B3
Valley La *CHCH/BSGR* BH23 410 C4
FNM GU9 158 F1
Valley Md *RAND* SP11 142 B3

Valley Park Dr HORN PO8 328 C5
Valley Ri HLER SO31 370 C4
RAND SP11 142 D4
Valley Rd CHAR BH8 433 K5
CHFD SO53 293 H1
FRIM GU16 71 L8
WINW SO22 214 A3
NWBY RG14 2 A9
NWBY RG14 25 G8
THLE RG7 31 K5
TOTT SO40 341 K3
Valley Side LIPH GU30 226 E3
The Valley WINW SO22 238 C2
Valley Vw BKME/WDN BH12 447 G1
SHST GU47 69 K1
Valley Wk BPWT SO32 269 H6
Valley Wy TADY RG26 42 B7
Vallis Cl PLE BH15 445 J7
Valmeade Cl HTWY RG27 86 A7 2
Valroy Cl CBLY GU15 71 G2
Valsheba Dr FHAM/STUB PO14 395 M7
Vampire Wy FARN GU14 90 B8
Vanburgh Gdns KEMP RG22 127 G1
Vanburgh Wy CHFD SO53 265 G7 2
Van Dyck Cl BSTK RG21 105 K5
Vanguard Hl WINW SO22 214 B2
Vanguard Rd CHAR BH8 433 J7
WEND SO18 319 M8 5
Vanners La KSCL RG20 36 A3
Vanstone Rd
LSOL/BMARY PO13 397 H8
Vardy Cl ITCH SO19 345 H5 5
Varna Rd BOR GU35 201 K5
WSHM SO15 343 G3
Varney Cl FARN GU14 90 B3
Varos Cl GPORT PO12 421 L2
Varsity Rd EMRTH PO10 403 H7
Vaudrey Cl WSHM SO15 318 B7 3
Vaughan Cl ITCH SO19 345 J3
Vaughan Rd FAWY SO45 367 G4 5
Vaughans ALTN GU34 176 F5
Vauxhall Wy PSF GU32 275 K5
Veal's La TOTT SO40 366 F1
Vear's La RWIN SO21 266 F8
Vecta Cl CHCH/BSGR BH23 451 H2
Vectis Cl ALTN GU34 197 G6
Vectis Rd GPORT PO12 421 J5
NMIL/BTOS BH25 452 C1
Vectis Wy CHAM PO6 399 K1
Velder Av ENEY PO4 423 L3
Vellan Ct ROWN SO16 317 H7
Velmead Cl FLET GU13 111 G1
Velmead Rd FLET GU13 110 F1
Velmore Rd CHFD SO53 293 G4
Velsheda Ct FAWY SO45 367 L3
Velvet Lawn Rd
NMIL/BTOS BH25 437 K4
Venator Pl WIMB BH21 404 A2
Venerable Rd
FHAM/STUB PO14 396 E3
Vengeance Rd
LSOL/BMARY PO13 420 C1
Venice Cl WVILLE PO7 352 E8
Venice Ct AND SP10 119 H5
Venning Av BWD BH11 431 J3
Ventnor Rd ENEY PO4 21 M4 2
LSOL/BMARY PO13 396 F5
Ventnor Ter ASHV GU12 7 J4
Ventnor Wy FHAM/PORC PO16 373 J7
Ventry Cl CCLF BH13 446 E4
Ventura Pl UPTN BH16 444 C2
Venture Rd ROWN SO16 292 C7
Verbena Crs HORN PO8 352 F4
Verbena Wy HEND SO30 346 B2 5
Verden Wy AND SP10 118 E5 5
Verdi Cl KEMP RG22 104 C8
Verdon Av HLER SO31 369 J5
Verger Cl FHAM/STUB PO14 371 G5 5
Verity Crs CFDH BH17 430 E7
Vermont Cl ROWN SO16 318 E4
Vermont Woods EWKG RG40 48 B1
Vernalls Cl NBNE BH10 432 B2
Vernalls Gdns NBNE BH10 432 B3
Verner Cl BOR GU35 202 B4
Verne Rd VWD BH31 356 E3
The Verne FLET GU13 110 F3
Verney Cl BWD BH11 431 M5
Verney Rd BWD BH11 431 L5
Vernham Rd WINW SO22 10 B2
Verno La CHCH/BSGR BH23 436 A6
Vernon Av ENEY PO4 423 L4
Vernon Cl GPORT PO12 18 D2
Vernon Hl BPWT SO32 297 H6
Vernon Rd GPORT PO12 18 D2
HSEA PO3 399 L6
Verona Av SBNE BH6 449 J3
Verona Rd CHFD SO53 293 K1
Veronica Cl KEMP RG22 126 F1
Veronica Dr FLET GU13 110 C3
Verran Rd CBLY GU15 71 G5
Verulam Pl BMTH BH1 22 F5
Verulam Rd PLE BH15 445 L4
SHAM SO14 343 M1 5
Verwood Crs SBNE BH6 449 M4
Verwood Rd HAV PO9 377 M2 4
RGWD BH24 357 L7
WIMB BH21 356 D7
Veryan FHAM PO15 14 C6
Vesey Cl FARN GU14 90 D3
Vespasian Gdns CHAM RG24 82 B8
Vespasian Rd AND SP10 119 G4
WEND SO18 344 B1
Vespasian Wy CHFD SO53 293 K2
Vesta Wy CHFD SO53 293 K1
Vestry Cl AND SP10 8 F5
Vetch Cl CHCH/BSGR BH23 435 M8
Vetch Flds HTWY RG27 86 B7
Viables La BSTK RG21 105 G7
Vian Cl LSOL/BMARY PO13 397 G4
Vian Pl WINC SO23 191 H8
Vian Rd WVILLE PO7 376 B2
Vicarage Cl EWKG RG40 48 C2 2
FNM GU9 159 G1
Vicarage Dr HEND SO30 345 M3
Vicarage Gdns FLET GU13 110 E4
GSHT GU26 203 M5
LYMN SO41 438 E6 2
Vicarage Hl ALTN GU34 176 E5
FNM GU9 159 G1
HTWY RG27 87 J3
Vicarage La BPWT SO32 324 B2
FHAM/STUB PO14 396 A5
FNM GU9 134 E6
FNM GU9 134 F1
FNM GU9 159 G1
HASM GU27 228 C2
HTWY RG27 65 L7
LYMN SO41 438 E6
NALR SO24 220 A4
TOTT SO40 315 G7
WVILLE PO7 326 C5
YTLY GU46 68 F1
Vicarage Pk RSAL SP5 285 J2
Vicarage Rd ALTN GU34 176 D6
BFOR GU20 51 M5
BLKW GU17 70 B4
MOOR/WNTN BH9 432 C7
PLE BH15 445 H3
RSAL SP5 285 M3
TOTT SO40 342 D7
VWD BH31 356 D2
YTLY GU46 68 F1
Vicarage Wy CHCH/BSGR BH23 435 H6
Vice La ROMY SO51 313 M4
Viceroy Rd ITCH SO19 344 E5
Vickers Cl CHAR BH8 433 M6
Vickers Rd ASHV GU12 113 J3
Vickery Wy CHCH/BSGR BH23 435 J8
Victena Rd ELGH SO50 295 H6
Victoria Av CBLY GU15 70 D3
HISD PO11 425 K5
MOOR/WNTN BH9 432 C7
WVILLE PO7 375 M5
Victoria Cl HLER SO31 370 E7
WIMB BH21 429 H4
Victoria Ct AND SP10 9 G6
Victoria Crs BKME/WDN BH12 446 C2
Victoria Dr BLKW GU17 69 M4
Victoria Gdns FBDG SP6 309 J7
FERN BH22 406 B2
NWBY RG14 2 F2
RGWD BH24 382 E2 2
Victoria Gld HLER SO31 369 G3
Victoria Gv SSEA PO5 21 K6
Victoria Hill Rd FLET GU13 88 D7
Victoria Park Rd
MOOR/WNTN BH9 432 C7
Victoria Pl BMTH BH1 23 M1
GPORT PO12 18 F4 5
LYMN SO41 440 C6
Victoria Rd ALDT GU11 6 F2
ALTN GU34 176 E4
BKME/WDN BH12 446 B3
BMTH BH1 23 M2
BPWT SO32 297 G8
CHCH/BSGR BH23 450 D3
ELGH SO50 294 A3
EMRTH PO10 378 C7
FARN GU14 90 E4
FBDG SP6 309 J7
FERN BH22 406 B2
FLET GU13 88 D7
FNM GU9 134 F6
HISD PO11 401 K6
HLER SO31 368 E2
ITCH SO19 344 B7 5
LYMN SO41 454 A4
PSEA PO1 422 D2
SHST GU47 50 B7
THLE RG7 43 J2
WINC SO23 10 F5
WVILLE PO7 376 C1 1
Victoria Rd East ALTN GU34 176 F4
Victoria Rd North SSEA PO5 21 L3
Victoria Rd South SSEA PO5 21 J7
Victoria Sq LSOL/BMARY PO13 420 C2
Victoria St BSTK RG21 4 E9
GPORT PO12 19 G2
PSEA PO1 423 G1
SHAM SO14 13 L2
Victoria Tr ALDT GU11 112 A1
Victor Pl THLE RG7 28 F6
Victor Rd EMRTH PO10 403 H7
HSEA PO3 423 K1 1
STHA RG19 27 H5
Victor St WSHM SO15 318 B8 2
Victor Wy FARN GU14 89 M8
Victory Av HORN PO8 352 F6
Victory Cl CHFD SO53 293 G3
Victory Crs WSHM SO15 342 F2 1
Victory Gn NEND PO2 399 G6 1
Victory Rd FHAM/STUB PO14 396 B6
PSEA PO1 20 C2 5
WSHM SO15 342 F2
Victory Rbt BSTK RG21 4 D7
Victory Sq WSHM SO15 342 F2 2
Viewside Cl WIMB BH21 429 G3
Vigo La YTLY GU46 68 F5
Vigo Rd AND SP10 9 L3
Viking Cl FAWY SO45 392 D8
FHAM/STUB PO14 395 M5
ROWN SO16 317 K3
SBNE BH6 449 M4
The Vikings ROMY SO51 291 G1 5
Viking Wy AND SP10 119 G4
CHCH/BSGR BH23 450 F3
HORN PO8 328 B5
SBNE BH6 449 M4
Villa Gdns WVILLE PO7 352 C8
Village Cl FHAM/STUB PO14 396 A6
Village Rd GPORT PO12 18 B7
Village St ALTN GU34 175 G3
PSF GU32 276 A2
STOK SO20 165 M4
The Village EWKG RG40 48 B5
Village Wy YTLY GU46 69 G1
Ville De Paris Rd
FHAM/STUB PO14 396 E3
Villette Cl CHCH/BSGR BH23 434 E7
Villiers Rd FAWY SO45 367 K8
SSEA PO5 21 H8
WSHM SO15 343 G1
Villiers Wy NWBY RG14 36 F2
Vimoutiers Ct FBDG SP6 309 K7 2
Vince Cl BWD BH11 431 M3
Vincent Av ROWN SO16 318 B6
Vincent Cl NMIL/BTOS BH25 437 L6
Vincent Dr AND SP10 9 K6
Vincent Gv FHAM/PORC PO16 398 A1
Vincent Rd NMIL/BTOS BH25 437 K5
NTHA RG18 27 H4
WSHM SO15 318 B8
Vincent's Gv WSHM SO15 318 B8 5
Vincent St WSHM SO15 318 A8
Vincent's Wk SHAM SO14 13 G4
Vindomis Cl ALTN GU34 177 J1
Vine Bank WEND SO18 320 B8
Vine Cl ALDT GU11 112 D2
HLER SO31 370 B5
LTDN BH7 448 F1
RFNM GU10 158 D4
Vine Coppice WVILLE PO7 376 C4
Vine Farm Rd
BKME/WDN BH12 431 M8
Vinegar Hl LYMN SO41 454 C3
Vine House Cl FRIM GU16 91 K5 2
Vineries Cl WIMB BH21 404 D2
The Vineries WIMB BH21 404 D2
Vine Rd ROWN SO16 317 M5
Vinery Gdns ROWN SO16 318 A6
Vinery Rd ROWN SO16 318 B6 1
Vineside LSOL/BMARY PO13 397 J7
Vine St ALDT GU11 6 E3
Vine Tree Cl TADY RG26 62 A1
Vine Wy RFNM GU10 158 D3
Vineyard Cl ITCH SO19 344 B5
The Vineyards NBAD SO52 291 M4
Viney Av ROMY SO51 263 G8
Viney Rd LYMN SO41 440 C7
Vinnells La PSF GU32 272 C1
Vinneys Cl CHCH/BSGR BH23 435 G6
Vinns La OVTN RG25 123 L1
Vinson Rd LISS GU33 248 F4
Violet Av FHAM/STUB PO14 395 M6
Violet Cl KEMP RG22 126 F1
NBAD SO52 292 F2
Violet Gv NTHA RG18 27 H3
Violet La NMIL/BTOS BH25 437 L4
TADY RG26 60 F2
Violet Rd ROWN SO16 318 F4
Virginia Gdns FARN GU14 90 F6
Virginia Park Rd GPORT PO12 421 K2
Viscount Dr CHCH/BSGR BH23 451 G2
Viscount Wk BWD BH11 431 H2
WIMB BH21 431 G3
Vita Rd NEND PO2 399 J5
Vitre Gdns LYMN SO41 440 C6
Vivaldi Cl KEMP RG22 127 K1
Vivash Rd PSEA PO1 21 L2 4
Vivian Cl FLET GU13 111 G2
Vivian Rd BSTK RG21 5 H3
Vixen Cl FHAM/STUB PO14 395 M6
Vixen Wk NMIL/BTOS BH25 437 M3
Vokes Cl ITCH SO19 344 F3
Vulcan Cl WSHM SO15 342 D2
Vulcan Rd EMRTH PO10 403 H7
WSHM SO15 342 D2
Vulcan Wy FARN GU14 89 M8
SHST GU47 69 K1
Vyne Cl ALTN GU34 176 E3 3
Vyne Meadow CHAM RG24 82 E4
Vyne Rd BSTK RG21 4 E5
CHAM RG24 82 E4
Vyse La SHAM SO14 12 F6 2

W

Wade Court Rd HAV PO9 17 G6
Wade La HAV PO9 17 G8
Wade Rd CHAM RG24 5 M1
Wadham SHST GU47 50 C7
Wadham Rd NEND PO2 399 H6
Wadhurst Gdns ITCH SO19 344 E8
Wadhurst Rd HEND SO30 346 A2
The Wad SELS PO20 427 K7
Wadwick Bottom RAND SP11 97 L5
Waggoners Wy GSHT GU26 203 K4
Waggoners Wells Rd
GSHT GU26 203 K6
Wagner Cl KEMP RG22 104 D8
Wagon La HTWY RG27 86 A6
Wagtail Dr NMIL/BTOS BH25 437 K6 3
Wagtail Rd HORN PO8 352 E2
Wagtail Wy FHAM/PORC PO16 373 K8
Wainscott Rd ENEY PO4 423 L6
Wainsford Cl LYMN SO41 439 M5
Wainsford Plantation
LYMN SO41 439 J8 2
Wainsford Rd LYMN SO41 439 J6
Wainwright Cl CHAM PO6 400 A2
Wait End Rd WVILLE PO7 376 C2
Wakefield Av FHAM/PORC PO16 14 F1
NBNE BH10 432 C3
Wakefield Ct WEND SO18 319 M7 5
Wakefield Rd WEND SO18 319 M7
Wakeford Cl TADY RG26 42 B7 2
Wakefords Copse FLET GU13 111 G5
Wakefords Pk FLET GU13 111 G5
Wakefords Wy HAV PO9 377 M2
Wakely Rd BWD BH11 431 M3
Walberton Av CHAM PO6 375 L8
Walburton Wy HORN PO8 328 C4
Walcheren Pl PLE BH15 444 B5
Walcott Av CHCH/BSGR BH23 434 D7
Waldegrave Cl ITCH SO19 344 B7 4
Walden Gdns HORN PO8 352 F1
Walden Rd NEND PO2 399 G6
Walditch Gdns CFDH BH17 430 C6
Waldon Gdns WEND SO18 320 A6 3
Waldorf Hts BLKW GU17 70 A4
Waldren Cl PLE BH15 445 J6
Wales St WINC SO23 11 J7
Walford Cl WIMB BH21 404 A2
Walford Rd CHAM PO6 375 G8
Walhampton Hl LYMN SO41 440 D3
Walker Gdns HEND SO30 321 H7
Walker Pl LSOL/BMARY PO13 397 H7 4
Walker Rd NEND PO2 399 G6
Walkers Cl ELGH SO50 295 J6 5
Walkers La North FAWY SO45 392 D7
Walker's La South FAWY SO45 418 D1
Walker's Rdg CBLY GU15 71 H3
Walkford La NMIL/BTOS BH25 437 H5
Walkford Rd CHCH/BSGR BH23 437 G6
Walkford Wy
CHCH/BSGR BH23 436 F7 2
Walkwood Av LTDN BH7 433 M8
Wallace La BROC SO42 416 A2
Wallace Rd BDST BH18 429 L5
ITCH SO19 344 D7 5
NEND PO2 399 K8
Walldown Rd BOR GU35 201 J8
Walled Meadow AND SP10 9 K6
Waller Dr NWBY RG14 26 B3
Wallington Ct
FHAM/STUB PO14 396 D2 1
Wallington Dr CHFD SO53 264 F8
Wallington Hl
FHAM/PORC PO16 15 L4
Wallington Rd CBLY GU15 51 K7
NEND PO2 399 K7
Wallington Shore Rd
FHAM/PORC PO16 15 M4
Wallington Wy
FHAM/PORC PO16 15 L4
Wallins Copse CHAM RG24 83 L6 4
Walliscott Rd BWD BH11 431 L7
Wallisdean Av
FHAM/STUB PO14 14 E8
HSEA PO3 423 M1
Wallisdown Rd
BKME/WDN BH12 431 H6
Wallis Dr TADY RG26 64 A6
Wallis Gdns WVILLE PO7 352 C7
Wallis Rd BSTK RG21 105 G5
NBNE BH10 431 M7
WVILLE PO7 352 C7
Wall La THLE RG7 42 F6
Wallop Dr KEMP RG22 126 F2
Wallop Dro STOK SO20 184 C4
Wallop Rd RAND SP11 162 A1
STOK SO20 161 M4
Walmer Cl CWTH RG45 49 M3
ELGH SO50 293 M1
FRIM GU16 91 J1
Walmer Rd PSEA PO1 21 M2
Walnut Av WEND SO18 319 K3
Walnut Cl ALDT GU11 6 F6
ALTN GU34 176 E3
CHFD SO53 265 H6
NMIL/BTOS BH25 437 K5
ROWN SO16 317 L7
YTLY GU46 69 G4
Walnut Dr FHAM/STUB PO14 395 M6
Walnut Gv WINW SO22 10 B5
ROWN SO16 317 L8
Walnut Tree Cl HISD PO11 425 K5 1
RWIN SO21 190 C4
Walnut Tree Dr EMRTH PO10 379 J5
Walnut Tree Rd AND SP10 8 E7
Walnwright Gdns HEND SO30 321 H5
Walpole La HLER SO31 370 C1
Walpole Rd BMTH BH1 448 C3
WINW SO22 238 B3
GPORT PO12 19 H3
Walrus Rd FARN GU14 90 A8
Walsall Rd HSEA PO3 423 L2
Walsford Rd WBNE BH4 447 H3
Walsingham Cl CHAM PO6 375 H7 3
Walsingham Dene LTDN BH7 433 K8
Walsingham Gdns WEND SO18 319 K5
Waltham Cl BPWT SO32 298 F6
FHAM/PORC PO16 374 A6
SHST GU47 50 A7 5
Waltham Ct OVTN RG25 101 G8 1
Waltham Crs ROWN SO16 318 A4
Waltham La OVTN RG25 124 D4
Waltham Rd LTDN BH7 449 G1
OVTN RG25 124 A1
Waltham St SSEA PO5 20 F3 5
Walton Cl GPORT PO12 18 D4
WVILLE PO7 376 C3
Walton Ct FHAM PO15 372 B4
Walton Pl WINW SO22 238 C3
Walton Rd CHAM PO6 400 A2
GPORT PO12 18 D4
ITCH SO19 345 H4 5
NBNE BH10 432 A6
PLE BH15 445 M2
Waltons Av FAWY SO45 392 B4
Walton Wy NWBY RG14 3 J1
Walworth Rd RAND SP11 119 L6
Wanborough Hl RGUW GU3 137 M2
Wandesford Pl GPORT PO12 397 L7
Wandle Cl ASHV GU12 113 K7
Wandsdyke Cl FRIM GU16 71 J8
Wangfield La BPWT SO32 322 B7
Wansbeck Cl CHFD SO53 293 G3 2
Wansey Gdns NWBY RG14 26 A3
Wanstead Cl RGWD BH24 358 F8
Wantage Rd SHST GU47 50 A8
Wapiti Wy FARN GU14 90 A8
Warbler Cl HORN PO8 352 E1
ROWN SO16 318 A2
UPTN BH16 428 F8
Warbleton Rd CHAM RG24 83 M5 5
Warblington Av HAV PO9 17 K5
Warblington Cl CHFD SO53 293 G5 3
TADY RG26 61 M1
Warblington Rd EMRTH PO10 402 C1
Warblington St PSEA PO1 20 D4
Warborne La LYMN SO41 440 E1
Warbrook Ct HAV PO9 377 M3 13
Warbrook La HTWY RG27 47 K8
Warburton Cl ITCH SO19 345 J4 1
Warburton Rd CFDH BH17 430 C8
ITCH SO19 345 H3
Ward Cl AND SP10 9 G1
Ward Crs EMRTH PO10 378 E5
Warden Cl HEND SO30 320 C7 6
Wardens Cl HISD PO11 425 K3
Wardle Rd ELGH SO50 294 C1
Ward Rd ENEY PO4 423 L6
Wardroom Rd NEND PO2 398 F7
Wareham Rd WIMB BH21 428 F5
Warehouse Rd STHA RG19 38 C3
Warfield Av WVILLE PO7 376 C1
Warfield Crs WVILLE PO7 376 C1
Wargrove Dr SHST GU47 50 A8
The Warings THLE RG7 29 K1
Warland Wy WIMB BH21
Warlock Cl ITCH SO19
Warmwell Cl CFDH BH17
Warner Ct AND SP10
Warnes La RGWD BH24
Warnford Cl GPORT PO12
Warnford Crs HAV PO9
Warnford Rd LTDN BH7
Warren Av CHCH/BSGR BH23
CHFD SO53
ENEY PO4
HSEA PO3
ROWN SO16
Warren Cl CHFD SO53
FLET GU13
HISD PO11
HTWY RG27
BOR GU35
RGWD BH24
ROWN SO16
SHST GU47
THLE RG7
Warren Cnr RFNM GU10
Warren Crs ROWN SO16
Warren Dr RAND SP11
RGWD BH24
Warren Edge Rd SBNE BH6
Warren La BROC SO42
EWKG RG40
PSF GU32
RGWD BH24
RWIN SO21
Warren Pk LYMN SO41
Warren Pl TOTT SO40
Warren Ri FRIM GU16
Warren Rd LISS GU33
LISS GU33
NWBY RG14
WBNE BH4
WINC SO23
Warren Side EPSF GU31
Warrens La RSAL SP5
The Warren ALDT GU11
FAWY SO45
FNM GU9
TADY RG26
Warrington Ms ALDT GU11
Warrior Cl CHFD SO53
Warrys Cl FAWY SO45
Warsash Cl HAV PO9
Warsash Gv
LSOL/BMARY PO13
Warsash Rd FHAM/STUB PO14
HLER SO31
Warspite Cl NEND PO2
Warton Cl BROC SO42
Warton Rd BSTK RG21
Warwick Av NMIL/BTOS BH25
Warwick Cl ALDT GU11
CBLY GU15
CHFD SO53
LSOL/BMARY PO13
WINC SO23
Warwick Crs SSEA PO5
Warwick Dr NWBY RG14
Warwick Rd ASHV GU12
DEAN RG23
FARN GU14
LTDN BH7
TOTT SO40
WSHM SO15
Wasdale Cl HORN PO8
SHST GU47
Wash Brook HTWY RG27
Washbrook Rd CHAM PO6
Washford La BOR GU35
Washington Av BMTH BH1
Washington Rd EMRTH PO10
NEND PO2
Wash Water KSCL RG20
Wasing La THLE RG7
Watchetts Dr CBLY GU15
Watchetts Lake Cl CBLY GU15
Watchetts Rd CBLY GU15
Watch La WHCH RG28
Watchmoor Rd CBLY GU15
Watcombe Rd SBNE BH6
Waterbeech Dr HEND SO30
Waterberry Dr WVILLE PO7
Watercress Meadow
NALR SO24
Waterditch Rd
CHCH/BSGR BH23
Water End La CHAM RG24
Waterford Cl LYMN SO41
Waterford Gdns
CHCH/BSGR BH23
Waterford La LYMN SO41
Waterford Pl
CHCH/BSGR BH23
Waterford Rd
CHCH/BSGR BH23
NMIL/BTOS BH25
Waterhouse La WSHM SO15
Waterhouse Md SHST GU47
Waterhouse Wy WSHM SO15
Wateridge Rd BSTK RG21
Water La FARN GU14
FAWY SO45
FNM GU9
NALR SO24
RAND SP11
SBNE BH6
STHA RG19
TOTT SO40
WINC SO23
Waterlily Cl BSTK RG21
Waterlock Gdns ENEY PO4
Waterloo Av DEAN RG23
Waterloo Cl CBLY GU15
HORN PO8
Waterloo Ct AND SP10
Waterloo Rd ASHV GU12
CFDH BH17
CWTH RG45
GPORT PO12
HAV PO9
LYMN SO41

R/WNTN BH9 447 L1
3 BH21 428 F2
M SO15 343 G2
oo St SSEA PO5 21 H3
oo Ter WSHM SO15 343 K2
oo Wy RGWD BH24 382 E2 3
nain Rd RGWD BH24 407 L3
nan Cl BOR GU35 201 L6
nans La FAWY SO45 367 J7
nead Rd CHAM PO6 400 C1 1
nill Rd
/BSGR BH23 434 E8
nills Cl AND SP10 8 F9
Rede FLET GU13 110 D5
Ridges DEAN RG23 103 G8
s Edge HEND SO30 345 M2
Edge Gdns
TH PO10 378 D8
edge Rd CHAM PO6 374 E8 2
Gn BROC SO42 387 L6 2
Green Ct BROC SO42 387 L6 3
hip Dr RGWD BH24 383 H2
ide CHCH/BSGR BH23 450 E4
SO45 367 K3
ide Cl BOR GU35 201 K4
BH24 358 F7
ide Ct ALTN GU34 176 F4 2
GU14 89 G5
ide Gdns
1/PORC PO16 373 H7 1
ide La
1/PORC PO16 398 C2
ide Rd ROMY SO51 262 F7 4
meet
1/PORC PO16 396 F2
aters WHAM PO17 372 C3
Tower Rd BDST BH18 430 A4
Wy BSTK RG21 5 K7
vorks Rd CHAM PO6 376 B8
U32 275 M2
SO21 266 B4
La AND SP10 9 K2
/BSGR BH23 435 L7
GU13 110 D5
RG20 35 J3
Rd BOSC BH5 448 E4
SO30 321 K6 1
Cl ROWN SO16 317 J3
La RWIN SO21 213 J4
SO21 267 G2
g End KEMP RG22 127 G1
n Acre AND SP10 8 C4
n Wk TOTT SO40 341 G1 3
n Wy DEAN RG23 104 C1
l AND SP10 118 B7
n Cl CHAR BH8 433 L6
n La BPWT SO32 299 J6
n Rd FAWY SO45 392 A5
Cl ROWN SO16 317 K6
Common Rd ALDT GU11 112 B1
Rd FARN GU14 90 C3
SO30 346 A1
PO1 423 H1
Av CFDH BH17 429 L7
Cl KEMP RG22 104 D6
Rd BWD BH11 431 M4
/BMARY PO13 397 H5
SO18 344 E1
Wy WINW SO22 238 B3
don Av
/BTOS BH25 437 J8
ey Cl
/BMARY PO13 420 D2 9
ey Gn ROWN SO16 317 K7
ley Av BSTK RG21 104 F6
GU13 88 E5
SO31 369 G2
ley Cl CBLY GU15 71 J4
SP6 309 L5
RG29 108 E5
SO51 263 G7 6
ey Ct HLER SO31 369 G3 2
ley Crs PLE BH15 445 J3
ley Dr ASHV GU12 113 K2
GU15 71 H3
SO21 190 D4
ley Gdns ASHV GU12 113 K2 1
ey Gv ENEY PO4 21 L8
ey La FNM GU9 135 M8
ey Rd CHAM PO6 376 A8
GU14 91 G5
SP6 309 L5
/BTOS BH25 437 M6
PO5 21 L7
M SO15 12 A1
averleys NTHA RG18 27 G4 1
er Cl ENEY PO4 424 A3 4
SO31 370 D7
ers LSOL/BMARY PO13 421 H1
er's Wk BPWT SO32 270 B7
RG23 126 D5
PO9 377 G6
V PO8 301 K6
RG20 54 E1
RG20 78 E2
SO24 172 B4
SO24 242 B2
SO24 270 A3
SP11 55 J4
LE PO7 375 M6
nds Pl HEND SO30 345 L4
an Rd FARN GU14 70 B8
3 BH21 429 J2 2
Rd BKME/WDN BH12 446 A2
ete Cl BPWT SO32 297 H8
ete La FNM GU9 134 C6
ete Pl WINW SO22 238 C2 2
nd CBLY GU15 71 H4
le HLER SO31 346 B8
le Cl LYMN SO41 454 C3
le Rd DEAN RG23 104 A3
BH24 381 J7
BH6 449 K4
St CHAM PO6 399 K1
wn Cl CFDH BH17 430 B7
Cl HLER SO31 370 E4
n Rd FARN GU14 90 E6
ale Rd CHFD SO53 293 J4
Weatherby Gdns HTWY RG27 87 J2 5
Weathermore La ALTN GU34 197 J6
Weavers Cl AND SP10 9 J4
FERN BH22 380 C7 2
Weavers Gdns RFNM GU10 158 C1 3
Weavers Gn HAV PO9 17 L1
Weavers Pl CHFD SO53 265 G8
Weavills Rd ELGH SO50 294 F6
Webb Cl CHAM RG24 83 K6
HISD PO11 425 L6
Webb La HISD PO11 425 L6
Webb Rd FHAM/PORC PO16 398 B2
Webbs Acre STHA RG19 27 J6
Webbs Cl RGWD BH24 381 H2
Webbs Farm Cl WHCH RG28 122 B5
Webbs Gn BPWT SO32 325 G5
Webbs La THLE RG7 29 L1
Webburn Gdns WEND SO18 319 M5 3
Webster Rd WINW SO22 214 A7
Wedgewood Cl FAWY SO45 392 A4
FHAM/STUB PO14 396 A6 1
Wedgewood Wy WVILLE PO7 352 C6
Wedgwood Dr PSTN BH14 445 M6
Wedman's La HTWY RG27 85 L1
Wedmore Cl WINW SO22 237 M5
Weeke Cl RSAL SP5 284 C1 1
Weeke Manor Cl WINW SO22 10 A3
Weir Av FARN GU14 90 D5
Weir Cl FARN GU14 90 D5
Weir Rd FARN GU14 89 K6
HTWY RG27 87 G4
The Weir WHCH RG28 122 B5
Welbeck Av PTSW SO17 319 G6
Welbeck Cl FARN GU14 90 C4
Welch Rd ENEY PO4 21 M8
GPORT PO12 421 L1
Welch Wy ROWN SO16 317 K3
Welchwood Cl HORN PO8 352 D2
Weldon Av BWD BH11 431 J3
Weldon Cl FLET GU13 111 G3
Welland Gdns WEND SO18 320 A6
Welland Gn ROWN SO16 317 K8
Welland Rd WIMB BH21 404 B4
Wellands Rd LYND SO43 363 K3 3
Wella Rd KEMP RG22 104 E6
Wellbrooke Gdns CHFD SO53 293 G1
Wellburn Cl SHST GU47 69 L1
Well Cl CBLY GU15 70 E4
NMIL/BTOS BH25 437 K7
OVTN RG25 125 K7
Well Copse Cl HORN PO8 328 B7
Weller Dr CBLY GU15 70 F5
EWKG RG40 47 K2
Wellers Cl TOTT SO40 340 F1
Wellesley Av CHCH/BSGR BH23 451 G1
Wellesley Cl ASHV GU12 113 J1
BAGS GU19 51 M5
WVILLE PO7 376 C1
Wellesley Dr CWTH RG45 49 H3
Wellesley Gdn FNM GU9 134 F1
Wellesley Rd ALDT GU11 112 A5
AND SP10 9 G9
FARN GU14 90 A8
RFNM GU10 181 L2
Welles Rd CHFD SO53 293 J2
Well House Cl FBDG SP6 283 G5
Well House La WINW SO22 214 D3
HTWY RG27 46 E5
Wellhouse Rd ALTN GU34 175 L6
Wellington Av ALDT GU11 6 F1
CHCH/BSGR BH23 451 H1
FLET GU13 89 G6
BOR GU35 201 H6
WEND SO18 344 F1
Wellington Cl FAWY SO45 367 H7
HORN PO8 353 H2
NWBY RG14 25 M3 3
SHST GU47 49 M8
Wellington Crs TADY RG26 41 G7
Wellington Gv
FHAM/PORC PO16 398 A1
Wellingtonia Av EWKG RG40 48 E4
Wellington La FNM GU9 135 G1
Wellington Pk HEND SO30 320 F7
Wellington Rd AND SP10 8 E3
CHAR BH8 23 G1
CWTH RG45 49 M4
PSTN BH14 446 B5
SHST GU47 49 L8
WEND SO18 319 J6
Wellington St ALDT GU11 6 F1
SSEA PO5 21 G3
Wellington Ter DEAN RG23 104 B1
SHST GU47 49 M8 1
Wellington Wy FARN GU14 112 A1
WVILLE PO7 376 C1 2
Well La ALTN GU34 132 A8
ALTN GU34 156 A2
BPWT SO32 324 A1
FBDG SP6 310 D6
HASM GU27 229 G2
HLER SO31 369 L6
PLE BH15 445 H4
Wellmans Meadow KSCL RG20 59 H5
Well Meadow HAV PO9 377 J2
NWBY RG14 25 L3
Wellowbrook Cl CHFD SO53 292 F2 2
Wellow Cl HAV PO9 16 B1
WEND SO18 345 G1
Wellow Dro ROMY SO51 288 D1
Wellow Gdns
FHAM/STUB PO14 371 G6
Wellow Wood Rd ROMY SO51 260 C8
Well Rd RFNM GU10 133 H2
Wells Cottages FNM GU9 158 D1 5
Wellsfield SELS PO20 427 L7
Wellsmoor FHAM/STUB PO14 371 G5
Wells Pl ELGH SO50 293 M6
Wells's La WHCH RG28 122 A4
Well St KSCL RG20 57 K4
Wellswood Gdns HAV PO9 354 A5
Wellsworth La HAV PO9 354 A5
Welsh La THLE RG7 45 K6
Welshman's Rd THLE RG7 42 E3
Welton Ct BSTK RG21 4 C7
Wembley Gv CHAM PO6 399 L2 1
Wendan Rd NWBY RG14 2 D9
Wendover Cl
NMIL/BTOS BH25 437 K7 4
Wendover Dr FRIM GU16 71 M5
Wendover Rd HAV PO9 16 C3
Wenlock Wy STHA RG19 27 G6 7
Wensley Dr FLET GU13 88 F5 2
Wensley Gdns EMRTH PO10 378 D5
Wentwood Gdns
NMIL/BTOS BH25 438 B6
Wentworth Av BOSC BH5 448 F4
Wentworth Cl ASHV GU12 113 K1
BOSC BH5 448 F5
CWTH RG45 49 J2
FNM GU9 6 C9
YTLY GU46 69 G3 5
Wentworth Ct NWBY RG14 3 G7
Wentworth Crs ASHV GU12 113 K2
Wentworth Dr BDST BH18 429 L3
HORN PO8 352 F1
Wentworth Gdns ALTN GU34 176 D4
FAWY SO45 392 B6 1
ITCH SO19 344 F7 1
Wentworth Gra WINW SO22 238 D2
Wentworth Gv FAWY SO45 392 B5
Wesermarsch Rd HORN PO8 352 E4
Wesley Cl CHAR BH8 23 M1
ITCH SO19 345 H4
Wesley Gv HSEA PO3 399 K5
Wesley Rd PSTN BH14 446 B3
WIMB BH21 404 B3
WINC SO23 215 H1
Wessex Av NMIL/BTOS BH25 437 L6
ODIM RG29 108 C7
Wessex Cl BSTK RG21 104 F5
CHCH/BSGR BH23 451 H1
FAWY SO45 392 D7
Wessex Crs ODIM RG29 108 C7
Wessex Dr WINW SO22 10 C2
ODIM RG29 108 C7
Wessex Est RGWD BH24 358 F8
Wessex Gdns AND SP10 8 F4
FHAM/PORC PO16 397 M1
ROMY SO51 291 G1
Wessex La WEND SO18 319 J4
Wessex Pl FNM GU9 134 F7
Wessex Rd FARN GU14 90 C6
HORN PO8 328 B5
PSTN BH14 445 M5
RGWD BH24 358 F8
Wessex Wy CHAR BH8 433 L7
RWIN SO21 266 F8
WBNE BH4 447 G4
WCLF BH2 22 C4
West Ashling Rd RCCH PO18 379 M5
West Av FNM GU9 135 G2
WIMB BH21 356 B8
West Bargate SHAM SO14 12 F4 1
West Battery Rd NEND PO2 398 F7
Westbeams Rd LYMN SO41 412 F6
Westborn Rd FHAM/PORC PO16 15 K5
Westbourne Av EMRTH PO10 378 E6
FAWY SO45 392 A4
Westbourne Cl EMRTH PO10 378 E6 1
WBNE BH4 447 H5
Westbourne Crs PTSW SO17 318 E7
Westbourne Park Rd
WBNE BH4 447 G6
Westbourne Rd EMRTH PO10 378 E5
NEND PO2 399 K8
SHST GU47 70 B1
Westbroke Gdns ROMY SO51 262 E7 3
West Brook Cl DEAN RG23 103 G8
Westbrook Cl HLER SO31 370 E3
Westbrooke Cl AND SP10 9 H6
HORN PO8 352 E2
Westbrooke Rd ALTN GU34 176 D5
Westbrook Gv WVILLE PO7 376 B3
Westbrook Rd
FHAM/PORC PO16 398 B2
Westbrook Wy WEND SO18 319 K4 3
Westburn ALTN GU34 156 B4
Westbury Av FLET GU13 89 J8
Westbury Cl CHAM PO6 374 F7 6
CHCH/BSGR BH23 435 L1
CHCH/BSGR BH23 436 B7
CWTH RG45 49 L2
FLET GU13 89 H8
NMIL/BTOS BH25 437 L8
Westbury Ct HEND SO30 346 A3
Westbury Gdns FLET GU13 89 J8
FNM GU9 135 H4 2
Westbury Rd RGWD BH24 382 F1
WSHM SO15 342 D1
Westbury Wy ASHV GU12 7 L1
Westby Rd BOSC BH5 448 D4
Westcliff Cl LSOL/BMARY PO13 420 C1
West Cliff Gdns WCLF BH2 22 C8
West Cliff Rd WBNE BH4 447 H6
WCLF BH2 22 C7
West Cl FNM GU9 135 G1
LYMN SO41 439 M6
VWD BH31 356 B2
West Common FAWY SO45 418 B1
Westcot Rd FAWY SO45 391 M5 3
Westcroft Pk BDST BH18 430 A4
Westcroft Rd GPORT PO12 18 A1
Westdean Ct BSTK RG21 4 B9
Westdeane Ct BSTK RG21 4 B9
Westdown Rd BWD BH11 431 L3
West Downs Cl
FHAM/PORC PO16 372 E4
West Dr ELGH SO50 294 C4
West End TADY RG26 82 C3
West End Cl WINW SO22 10 D7
West End Gv FNM GU9 134 D6
West End La ALTN GU34 196 A4
RFNM GU10 158 B7
Westend Rd ITCH SO19 344 E1
West End Rd THLE RG7 43 H3
Westend Rd WEND SO18 320 B8
West End Rd HEND SO30 345 K4
WEND SO18 319 M8
West End Ter WINW SO22 10 D7
Westerdale STHA RG19 26 F5
Westerdale Dr FRIM GU16 71 L5
Westerham Cl CHAM PO6 375 J8
Westerham Rd CCLF BH13 447 G5
Westering ROMY SO51 263 H7 7
ROMY SO51 263 H8 2
Westerley Cl HLER SO31 370 C7 5
Western Av AND SP10 9 H7
CCLF BH13 446 D6
EMRTH PO10 378 B8
NBNE BH10 432 B4
NMIL/BTOS BH25 437 H8
NWBY RG14 2 E1
Western Cl NBNE BH10 432 B3
Western District Cut
WSHM SO15 343 H1 1
Western End NWBY RG14 2 A6 1
Western Esp SHAM SO14 12 D2
Western La ODIM RG29 108 C6
Western Pde EMRTH PO10 402 C1
SSEA PO5 20 F6
Western Rd ALDT GU11 6 B3
AND SP10 9 G6
CCLF BH13 446 E8
CHAM PO6 399 J2
CHFD SO53 265 K7
FHAM/PORC PO16 15 J6
WINW SO22 10 D6
HAV PO9 16 C3
HEND SO30 320 C7
BOR GU35 201 H2
LISS GU33 248 E4
LYMN SO41 440 B4
Western Wy FHAM/PORC PO16 15 H6
GPORT PO12 421 J5
KEMP RG22 104 C6
Westfield Av FHAM/STUB PO14 14 F8
HISD PO11 425 J5
Westfield Cl ELGH SO50 321 H1
HLER SO31 369 J6
West Field Cl TADY RG26 42 A8
Westfield Common
HLER SO31 369 H6 1
Westfield Crs CHFD SO53 293 H5
NTHA RG18 26 E4
Westfield Dr BPWT SO32 324 C6
Westfield Dro NALR SO24 241 M8
Westfield Gdns
CHCH/BSGR BH23 435 M7
Westfield La RFNM GU10 158 B2
Westfield Rd BSTK RG21 105 H5
CBLY GU15 70 E6
CHFD SO53 293 H5
ENEY PO4 423 L5
WINW SO22 214 A3
GPORT PO12 18 B2
LYMN SO41 440 D6
NTHA RG18 26 D3
SBNE BH6 449 K4
TOTT SO40 316 E8
West Field Rd WINC SO23 191 H8
Westfield Rd WSHM SO15 342 E1
Westfield Wy NWBY RG14 2 A6
West Fryerne YTLY GU46 69 G1
Westgate FHAM/STUB PO14 396 A7
Westgate Pk WBNE BH4 447 G5
Westgate Rd NWBY RG14 2 A6
Westgate St SHAM SO14 12 F6
Westglade FARN GU14 90 A4 1
West Gn YTLY GU46 68 E1
West Green Rd HTWY RG27 86 E2
Westgrove FBDG SP6 309 K7 3
Westham Cl CFDH BH17 430 C5
West Ham Cl KEMP RG22 104 B4
West Ham La KEMP RG22 104 A4
West Haye Rd HISD PO11 426 B7
West Hayes LYMN SO41 440 D5
Westheath Rd BDST BH18 429 M4
West Heath Rd FARN GU14 90 C4
West Hill Dr FAWY SO45 367 K3
WINW SO22 10 C7
West Hill Pk WINW SO22 10 B7
West Hill Pl WCLF BH2 22 C6
West Hill Rd WCLF BH2 22 C7
West Hill Rd North RWIN SO21 190 D3
West Hill Rd South RWIN SO21 190 D4
West Hoe La BPWT SO32 297 L8
West Horton La ELGH SO50 294 E7
Westland NTHA RG18 26 E4 1
Westland Dr WVILLE PO7 376 C4
Westland Gdns GPORT PO12 18 C6
Westlands Ct
CHCH/BSGR BH23 409 L8
Westlands Gv
FHAM/PORC PO16 398 A1
Westlands Rd NWBY RG14 2 F9
West La HISD PO11 425 J3
LYMN SO41 439 J7 2
NBAD SO52 291 K3
Westley Cl WINW SO22 10 A4
Westley Gv FHAM/STUB PO14 14 E7
Westley La RWIN SO21 213 H4
Westlyn Rd TADY RG26 42 B7
Westman Rd WINW SO22 10 A2
West Marlands Rd SHAM SO14 12 F2
Westmead FARN GU14 90 E5
Westmead Cl HISD PO11 425 H5
Westmead Dr NWBY RG14 25 J8
West Meade LIPH GU30 250 E6
West Mills NWBY RG14 2 D4
Westminister Rd LYMN SO41 454 A4
Westminster Cl FLET GU13 88 F6 1
KEMP RG22 127 G1 6
Westminster Gdns
FHAM/STUB PO14 371 G5 6
Westminster Ga WINW SO22 238 A3 1
Westminster Rd CCLF BH13 447 G7
Westminster Rd East
CCLF BH13 447 G7
West Moors Rd FERN BH22 406 B1
WIMB BH21 380 C1
Westmorland Dr CBLY GU15 71 L5
Westmorland Wy CHFD SO53 293 K3
Weston Av ENEY PO4 423 M4
Weston Cl ITCH SO19 344 D7
Weston Ct RAND SP11 96 A8
Weston Crs WEND SO18 345 G1
Weston Down Rd RWIN SO21 169 K3
Weston Dr BMTH BH1 23 K5
Weston Grove Rd ITCH SO19 344 B6
Weston La ITCH SO19 344 C7
PSF GU32 275 G8
ROWN SO16 316 F4
RSAL SP5 206 E3
Weston Rd ELGH SO50 293 M5
EPSF GU31 275 M5
OVTN RG25 129 M5
WIMB BH21 404 D1 3
West Overcliff Dr WBNE BH4 447 H6
Westover La RGWD BH24 382 B2
Westover Rd BMTH BH1 22 F6
FLET GU13 89 G7
HSEA PO3 399 M8
LYMN SO41 454 C4
ROWN SO16 317 G8
West Pk RAND SP11 117 G2
West Park Dr FBDG SP6 308 C3
West Park La FBDG SP6 308 B3
West Park Rd WSHM SO15 12 E2
West Portway AND SP10 118 A6
West Quay Rd PLE BH15 445 G6
WSHM SO15 12 D3
Westray Cl BSTK RG21 5 J4
Westridge KSCL RG20 56 B4
Westridge Rd PTSW SO17 319 G7
West Rd BOSC BH5 449 G4
CBLY GU15 71 G3
CHCH/BSGR BH23 409 L8
EMRTH PO10 378 C8
FARN GU14 70 D8
FAWY SO45 367 H7
HEND SO30 345 K2
ITCH SO19 344 C6
LYMN SO41 453 M3
RWIN SO21 167 J1
SHAM SO14 13 G7
WHAM PO17 374 E2
Westrow Gdns WSHM SO15 343 J1
Westrow Rd WSHM SO15 343 J1
Westside Cl KEMP RG22 104 C5 1
West Strd SELS PO20 427 J8
West St AND SP10 9 G5
BPWT SO32 325 G3
EMRTH PO10 378 D8
FAWY SO45 367 K3
FBDG SP6 309 K7
FHAM/PORC PO16 15 L6
FHAM/PORC PO16 374 B8
FHAM/STUB PO14 371 K8
FNM GU9 134 C7
HASM GU27 228 F2
HAV PO9 16 B4
KSCL RG20 57 H4
NALR SO24 218 C2
NWBY RG14 2 D3
ODIM RG29 108 B6
PLE BH15 445 G6
PSEA PO1 20 B5
RGWD BH24 382 C1
SHAM SO14 12 F5
TADY RG26 42 A8
WHAM PO17 374 C2
WVILLE PO7 326 B7
West Undercliff Prom
WBNE BH4 447 H7
West View Dr STOK SO20 165 M5
West View Rd
CHCH/BSGR BH23 450 D2
Westview Rd WINW SO22 213 M6
West View Rd BOR GU35 202 F4
PLE BH15 445 H4
Westward Rd HEND SO30 321 H8
West Wy BDST BH18 429 K5
LYMN SO41 440 A6
MOOR/WNTN BH9 432 F6
Westway FHAM PO15 371 J5
Westway Cl ROWN SO16 317 J2
Westways CHAM PO6 376 D8
FHAM/STUB PO14 396 B6
Westways Cl ROWN SO16 317 J3 1
Westwood Av FERN BH22 406 A2
Westwood Cl EMRTH PO10 378 E5
Westwood Gdns CHFD SO53 265 K8
Westwood La RGUW GU3 137 L1
Westwood Rd HLER SO31 368 F1
LYND SO43 363 K2
NEND PO2 399 J4
NWBY RG14 3 H9
PTSW SO17 318 E8
Westwood Vw NALR SO24 242 D7
Wetherby Cl CFDH BH17 429 L6
Wetherby Gdns AND SP10 118 D6
FARN GU14 90 F8 3
TOTT SO40 316 B8
Wetherdown EPSF GU31 275 M5
Wey Bank ALTN GU34 157 H5
Weybank Cl FNM GU9 134 F5 4
Weybourne Rd FNM GU9 135 H3
Weybridge Md YTLY GU46 69 H1
Weybrook Ct TADY RG26 82 C4
Wey Cl ASHV GU12 113 K7
CBLY GU15 70 E3
Weycombe Rd HASM GU27 204 F8
Weydon Hill Cl FNM GU9 134 E8 2
Weydon Hill Rd FNM GU9 134 E8
Weydon La FNM GU9 134 D8
Weydon Mill La FNM GU9 134 E7
Weydown Rd HASM GU27 228 E1
Wey Hl HASM GU27 228 D2
Weyhill Cl FHAM/PORC PO16 374 A7
HAV PO9 377 H3 5
TADY RG26 61 L1
Weyhill Gdns RAND SP11 117 J6
Weyhill Rd AND SP10 8 E6
RAND SP11 117 M7
Weyland Cl LIPH GU30 226 F3
Wey Lodge Cl LIPH GU30 227 G4 2
Weyman's Av NBNE BH10 432 A2
Weymans Dr NBNE BH10 432 A2
Weymouth Av GPORT PO12 397 K8
Weymouth Rd PSTN BH14 446 B3
Weysprings HASM GU27 228 C1
Weysprings Cl BSTK RG21 5 J7
Weywood Cl FNM GU9 6 C8
Weywood La FNM GU9 6 B8
Whaddon Cha
FHAM/STUB PO14 395 M6
Whaddon Ct HAV PO9 377 G2
Whaddon La RWIN SO21 267 M7
Whale Island Wy NEND PO2 399 G7
Whalesmead Cl ELGH SO50 294 E7

Whalesmead Rd ELGH SO50 294 E7
Whaley Rd NEND PO2 398 F7
Wharf Cl BKME/WDN BH12 446 D2
Wharfdale Rd
BKME/WDN BH12 446 C2
WBNE BH4 447 H4
Wharfenden Wy FRIM GU16 91 J2
Wharf Hl WINC SO23 239 G2
Wharf Rd ASHV GU12 113 K4
FRIM GU16 91 J2
NEND PO2 399 G8
NWBY RG14 2 F4
Wharfside THLE RG7 29 M5
Wharf St NWBY RG14 2 E4
Wharf Wy FRIM GU16 91 J2
Wharncliffe Gdns
CHCH/BSGR BH23 451 M1
Wharncliffe Rd BMTH BH1 448 C4
CHCH/BSGR BH23 451 M1
ITCH SO19 344 B5
Whartons La TOTT SO40 341 G4
Whatleigh Cl PLE BH15 445 H7
Wheat Cl NBAD SO52 292 E2
Wheatcroft Dr WEND SO18 320 A7 5
Wheatcroft Rd
LSOL/BMARY PO13 420 D2
Wheatear Dr EPSF GU31 276 B5 2
Wheatears Dr ROMY SO51 288 D5
Wheatland Cl WINW SO22 238 C3
Wheatlands FHAM/STUB PO14 371 G4
Wheatlands Av HISD PO11 426 C7
Wheatlands Crs HISD PO11 426 C7 1
Wheatlands La NWBY RG14 36 E2
Wheatley La ALTN GU34 178 F1
Wheaton Rd LTDN BH7 448 F3
Wheatsheaf Ct HEND SO30 345 M2 5
Wheatsheaf Dr HORN PO8 352 B5
Wheatstone Rd ENEY PO4 21 M6
Wheeler Cl GPORT PO12 421 M2
THLE RG7 31 L5 6
WHCH RG28 122 C4
Wheeler Hl HTWY RG27 86 B7
Wheelers Green Wy STHA RG19 27 H6
Wheelers La BWD BH11 431 G3
Wheelers Wk FAWY SO45 392 C8
Wheelwrights La GSHT GU26 203 K4
Whernside Cl ROWN SO16 317 L8 5
Wherwell Ct HAV PO9 377 M3 10
Whetstone Rd FARN GU14 89 M4
Whichers Cl HAV PO9 353 M8
Whichers Gate Rd HAV PO9 353 M8
Whimbrel Cl ENEY PO4 424 A3
Whinchat Cl FHAM PO15 372 A4
HTWY RG27 87 H1
ROWN SO16 318 A2
Whincroft Cl FERN BH22 406 C1
Whincroft Dr FERN BH22 406 C2
Whinfield Rd FAWY SO45 367 J7
Whin Holt FLET GU13 110 F2
Whins Cl CBLY GU15 70 E4
Whins Dr CBLY GU15 70 E4
Whinwhistle Rd ROMY SO51 289 G6
Whippingham Cl CHAM PO6 375 H8
Whistler Cl BSTK RG21 105 J5
Whistler Gv SHST GU47 70 A2
Whistler Rd ITCH SO19 345 G5
Whistlers Cl CHCH/BSGR BH23 409 M7
Whistlers La THLE RG7 42 E7
Whitaker Crs LYMN SO41 440 A5
Whitby Av BDST BH18 429 L6
Whitby Cl FARN GU14 91 H7 1
Whitby Crs BDST BH18 429 L6
Whitby Rd LYMN SO41 454 A4
Whitchurch Av BDST BH18 430 A5
Whitchurch Cl ALDT GU11 7 L9
Whitcombe Cl TOTT SO40 341 J1 2
Whitcombe Gdns HSEA PO3 423 K2
White Acres Rd FRIM GU16 91 J4
White Av LISS GU33 225 H6
White Barn Crs LYMN SO41 438 E5
Whitebeam Cl
FHAM/STUB PO14 14 C7
HORN PO8 353 G3 1
RWIN SO21 266 F8
White Beam Ri HORN PO8 328 B3
Whitebeam Rd HEND SO30 346 B2
Whitebeams Gdns
FARN GU14 89 M5 7
Whitebeam Wy NBAD SO52 291 M3
VWD BH31 356 F3
Whitechimney Rw
EMRTH PO10 378 F5
White City CWTH RG45 50 A3
Whitecliff Crs PSTN BH14 445 M6
Whitecliffe Av HSEA PO3 423 L1
Whitecliff Rd PSTN BH14 445 L6
White Cliff Rd PSTN BH14 445 M6
White Cloud Pk ENEY PO4 423 K5 1
White Cottage Cl FNM GU9 135 G2
Whitecross Cl CFDH BH17 430 C5
Whitecross Gdns NEND PO2 399 K5
Whitedell La WHAM PO17 373 H4
White Dirt La HORN PO8 328 A6
Whitedown ALTN GU34 176 D6
Whitedown La ALTN GU34 176 C6
Whitedown Rd TADY RG26 41 J8
White Farm Cl NBNE BH10 432 B8
White Farm La MARL SN8 53 G3
Whitefield Rd FAWY SO45 392 A5
NMIL/BTOS BH25 437 L5
PSTN BH14 445 M6
White Gates BPWT SO32 322 A3
Whitehall CHCH/BSGR BH23 450 A3
Whitehall Rd STOK SO20 187 M8
Whitehart Flds RGWD BH24 359 G8 6
White Hart La BSTK RG21 5 G9
FHAM/PORC PO16 397 M1
TADY RG26 61 K8
TOTT SO40 314 E8
White Hart Rd ELGH SO50 295 H7
GPORT PO12 18 F4 2
PSEA PO1 20 C5
Whitehaven
FHAM/PORC PO16 397 M1
HORN PO8 353 H2
Whitehayes Cl
CHCH/BSGR BH23 435 H6
Whitehayes Rd
CHCH/BSGR BH23 435 G7
Whitehead Cl CHAM RG24 105 L1 2
White Heather Ct FAWY SO45 367 L3
White Hl KSCL RG20 57 G6
KSCL RG20 58 C5
ODIM RG29 132 A6
Whitehill Cl CBLY GU15 71 G1
Whitehill La NALR SO24 218 E4
Whitehill Rd BOR GU35 201 L7
Whitehorn Dr RSAL SP5 287 J8
White Horse Dr PLE BH15 445 H3
White Horse La EWKG RG40 47 M3
WVILLE PO7 351 L2
White House Cl KEMP RG22 104 C6
Whitehouse Gdns PSF GU32 275 K3
White House Gdns
WSHM SO15 342 E2
YTLY GU46 68 F1 2
Whitehouse Rd WIMB BH21 404 B6
White House Wk FNM GU9 135 G1 2
White Knights
NMIL/BTOS BH25 452 E1
White Ladies Cl HAV PO9 17 G5
Whitelands CHCH/BSGR BH23 410 B5
Whitelands Rd NTHA RG18 26 F4
White La ASHV GU12 113 M7
RFNM GU10 136 F1
OVTN RG25 107 J6
RWIN SO21 238 F8
TADY RG26 102 B2
Whitelaw Rd WSHM SO15 342 F1
Whiteleaf La WVILLE PO7 326 B1
Whitelegg Wy NBNE BH10 432 C3
Whiteley La FHAM PO15 371 K4
HLER SO31 347 G7
Whiteley Wy FHAM PO15 371 H2
White Lion Wy YTLY GU46 69 G1
Whitemoor La TOTT SO40 315 K4
Whitemoor Rd BROC SO42 387 H6
Whitenap Cl ROMY SO51 291 G2
Whitenap La ROMY SO51 291 H2
White Oak Wy RAND SP11 142 B4
White Post La RFNM GU10 158 D4
White Rd CBLY GU15 70 C2
ELGH SO50 294 C4
White Rose La FNM GU9 158 E1
Whites Cl HTWY RG27 85 L7 5
Whites Hl RWIN SO21 267 L4
THLE RG7 31 H4
Whiteshoot RSAL SP5 285 L4
STOK SO20 209 G1
Whiteshoot Hl RSAL SP5 285 K4
Whiteshute La WINC SO23 238 D4
Whites La FAWY SO45 392 F5 10
Whites Rd FARN GU14 91 H7
ITCH SO19 344 E3
Whitestone Cl ROWN SO16 317 L8 6
Whitestones KEMP RG22 127 H2 3
White Swan Rd PSEA PO1 20 F2
Whitethorn Cl ASHV GU12 113 L7
Whitethorn Rd HISD PO11 425 M5 1
Whitewater Ri FAWY SO45 367 K6
HTWY RG27 86 B6 3
Whitewater Rd ODIM RG29 108 B4
Whiteways WIMB BH21 404 C2
The White Wy BPWT SO32 270 E6
Whitewood CHAM RG24 83 L5
Whitfield Cl HASM GU27 204 F7 1
Whitfield Pk RGWD BH24 381 M3
Whitfield Rd HASM GU27 204 F8
Whithedwood Av WSHM SO15 318 C8
Whitmers La BROC SO42 416 A2
Whitlet Cl FNM GU9 134 E7 2
Whitley Cl EMRTH PO10 378 F3
Whitley Rd HORN PO8 352 D2
YTLY GU46 69 G4
Whitley Wy FARN GU14 90 B7
NMIL/BTOS BH25 437 M3
Whitmarsh La CHAM RG24 84 A5
Whitmoor Vale Rd GSHT GU26 203 J1
Whitmore Cl SHST GU47 50 A8
Whitmore Gn FNM GU9 135 H2
Whitmore V GSHT GU26 203 J2
Whitmore Vale Rd GSHT GU26 203 L4
Whitney Rd CHAM RG24 5 L4
Whitsbury Rd FBDG SP6 309 L5
HAV PO9 377 L3
Whitstable Rd CHAM PO6 375 J8
Whittington Cl FAWY SO45 367 K6
Whittington Ct EMRTH PO10 378 D8
Whittle Av FHAM PO15 371 G3
Whittle Cl EWKG RG40 48 B1
SHST GU47 49 K7 3
Whittle Crs FARN GU14 90 C1
Whittle Rd AND SP10 118 A7
WIMB BH21 405 K1
Whittles Wy PLE BH15 445 G6
Whitwell HLER SO31 369 G1 7
Whitwell Rd ENEY PO4 21 L9
Whitworth Cl GPORT PO12 18 D3
Whitworth Crs WEND SO18 319 J8
Whitworth Rd GPORT PO12 18 D3
NEND PO2 399 K8
WEND SO18 319 J8
WHIT RG2 47 K1
Whynot La AND SP10 8 D5
Whyte Av ASHV GU12 7 L7
Whyte Cl FAWY SO45 391 M5
Whyteways ELGH SO50 293 L4
Wick Cl NMIL/BTOS BH25 437 J6
Wick Dr NMIL/BTOS BH25 437 J6
Wicket Hl RFNM GU10 158 D2
Wicket Rd NBNE BH10 432 A3
The Wicket FAWY SO45 367 K6
Wickfield Av CHCH/BSGR BH23 450 A2
Wickham Cl ALTN GU34 176 C6
FLET GU13 110 D3
TADY RG26 41 L8
Wickham Dr WIMB BH21 429 H4
Wickham Pl FLET GU13 110 D2
Wickham Rd BPWT SO32 324 F4
CBLY GU15 51 H8
FHAM/PORC PO16 15 J1
FLET GU13 110 D2
WHAM PO17 372 F4
Wickham St PSEA PO1 20 C1
Wick Hill La EWKG RG40 48 D2
Wick La CHCH/BSGR BH23 450 A3
RSAL SP5 255 M8
SBNE BH6 449 M3
Wicklea Rd SBNE BH6 450 A4
Wicklow Cl KEMP RG22 104 A5
Wicklow Dr CHFD SO53 292 F3
Wickor Cl EMRTH PO10 378 E6
Wickor Wy EMRTH PO10 378 D5
Wicor Mill La
FHAM/PORC PO16 397 M2
Wicor Pth FHAM/PORC PO16 398 C2
Widbury Rd LYMN SO41 440 A6
Widden Cl LYMN SO41 412 F6
Widdicombe Av PSTN BH14 446 D6
Widecombe Dr FAWY SO45 367 J4
Wide La ELGH SO50 319 L1
WEND SO18 319 K3
Wide Lane Cl BROC SO42 387 K7 3
Widgeon Cl GPORT PO12 421 M1
ROWN SO16 318 A2
Widgeons ALTN GU34 176 E3
Widget Cl BWD BH11 431 M6
Widlers La BPWT SO32 296 D2
Widley Ct FHAM/STUB PO14 396 D2
Widley Court Dr CHAM PO6 399 L1
Widley Gdns WVILLE PO7 376 B5
Widley Rd CHAM PO6 375 L8
NEND PO2 399 G6
Widley Wk CHAM PO6 375 K6
Widmore Rd KEMP RG22 104 B6
Widworthy Dr BDST BH18 429 K3
Wield Cl HAV PO9 377 G4
Wield Rd ALTN GU34 174 A5
Wigan Crs HAV PO9 376 F6
Wigan Rd FARN GU14 90 A8
Wights Wk KEMP RG22 127 G1 7
Wight Wk FERN BH22 406 C6
Wigmore Rd TADY RG26 41 J7
Wilberforce Cl WINW SO22 238 B2 3
Wilberforce Rd GPORT PO12 19 G9
SSEA PO5 21 G5 3
Wild Arum Wy NBAD SO52 292 E3
Wild Briar EWKG RG40 48 C1
Wildburn Cl TOTT SO40 316 B6
Wild Cherry Wy NBAD SO52 292 F2 3
Wilde Cl TOTT SO40 341 H1 3
Wildern Cl HLER SO31 370 D5 2
Wilderness Hts WEND SO18 320 B7
Wilderness Rd FRIM GU16 71 H6
Wildern La HEND SO30 321 G8
Wilders Cl FRIM GU16 71 G5
Wilderton Rd CCLF BH13 446 E5
Wilderton Rd West CCLF BH13 446 E4
Wildfell Cl CHCH/BSGR BH23 434 E7
Wild Herons HTWY RG27 86 B7 5
Wildmoor La HTWY RG27 84 B2
Wildown Gdns SBNE BH6 449 L5
Wildown Rd SBNE BH6 449 M5
Wild Ridings FHAM/STUB PO14 371 M8
Wild Rose Crs HLER SO31 370 C6
Wildwood Gdns YTLY GU46 68 F4
Wilfred Rd BOSC BH5 448 E4
Wilfred Wy STHA RG19 27 J5
Wilkins Cl HORN PO8 328 A2
Wilkinson Dr CHAR BH8 433 L6
Wilks Cl ROWN SO16 317 H3
Willems Av ALDT GU11 6 D1
Willersley Cl CHAM PO6 375 G7
Will Hall Cl ALTN GU34 176 C6
William Cl CHCH/BSGR BH23 436 E6
FHAM/STUB PO14 396 B7
STHA RG19 27 G6
William Farthing Cl ALDT GU11 6 E2
William Macleod Wy
ROWN SO16 317 M8
William Price Gdns
FHAM/PORC PO16 15 J3
William Rd LTDN BH7 448 E1
LYMN SO41 440 C3 4
Williams Cl FAWY SO45 392 B5
LSOL/BMARY PO13 421 H1
Williamson Cl HASM GU27 205 J7 2
RAND SP11 92 D6
Williams Rd HSEA PO3 399 M5
William St SHAM SO14 13 M1
Williams Wy FLET GU13 89 H7
William Wy ALTN GU34 176 F3 2
Willington Cl CBLY GU15 70 E2 1
Willis Av NBAD SO52 292 A4
Willis La ALTN GU34 197 J7
Willis Rd GPORT PO12 19 H3
PSEA PO1 21 G1
ROWN SO16 319 J3
Willis Wy CFDH BH17 445 G2
Willis Waye WINC SO23 215 H3
Willoughby Cl ALTN GU34 176 D4
Willoughby Wy DEAN RG23 104 C2
Willow Av FBDG SP6 309 K6
Willow Cl FRIM GU16 91 H4
HAV PO9 17 G5
HEND SO30 320 D6 3
BOR GU35 201 K5
LIPH GU30 227 G5 2
NWBY RG14 2 D8
RGWD BH24 381 H4
TLHT RG30 31 L3
UPTN BH16 444 C3
Willow Ct FRIM GU16 71 G7
ROWN SO16 317 M5
Willow Crs FARN GU14 90 E1
Willowdale Cl PSF GU32 274 E4
Willowdene Cl HAV PO9 376 F4
NMIL/BTOS BH25 438 A5
Willow Dr CHCH/BSGR BH23 449 M3
RGWD BH24 382 E3
TOTT SO40 342 D8
WIMB BH21 405 G2
Willowford YTLY GU46 69 G2
Willow Gdns EMRTH PO10 378 F4
LIPH GU30 227 G5
NBAD SO52 291 L3
Willow Gn RWIN SO21 266 F8
Willow Gv AND SP10 8 F7
ELGH SO50 295 J6
Willow Herb Cl HLER SO31 370 C6
Willow La BLKW GU17 70 A4
CHCH/BSGR BH23 410 B5
Willow Md CHAR BH8 433 H4
Willowmead Cl NWBY RG14 36 F3
Willow Pk ASHV GU12 113 J6
PSTN BH14 445 L5
Willow Pl GPORT PO12 18 F1
Willow Rd BPWT SO32 323 K1
KSCL RG20 38 C6
LISS GU33 248 E4
TADY RG26 41 L8
Willows End SHST GU47 49 L8 1
The Willows AND SP10 8 E8
RFNM GU10 135 M4
NMIL/BTOS BH25 437 M8
WVILLE PO7 351 J4
Willow Tree Av HORN PO8 352 F6
Willow Tree Gdns
FHAM/STUB PO14 14 C7
Willow Tree Ri BWD BH11 431 M6
Willow Tree Wk ITCH SO19 344 F5
Willow Wy ASHV GU12 113 H8
CHCH/BSGR BH23 449 M3
DEAN RG23 104 C1
FERN BH22 406 B1
FNM GU9 135 G2
HTWY RG27 64 C7
SHST GU47 49 J7
STOK SO20 163 G4
Willow Wood Rd HISD PO11 425 L5 2
Wills Cl WIMB BH21 429 H4
Wills Rd BKME/WDN BH12 446 E3
Wills Wy ROMY SO51 290 F2
Wilmer Rd ELGH SO50 293 M6
Wilmington Cl WEND SO18 319 L5
Wilmot Cl ELGH SO50 294 D3
Wilmott Cl GPORT PO12 18 A2
Wilmott La GPORT PO12 18 A2
Wilmott Wy DEAN RG23 104 C2
Wilmot Wy CBLY GU15 71 J5
Wilmur Crs PLE BH15 445 K2
Wilsom Cl ALTN GU34 176 F5
Wilsom Rd ALTN GU34 177 G5
Wilson Gv SSEA PO5 21 K5
Wilson Rd ASHV GU12 7 M4
BMTH BH1 448 C3
FARN GU14 90 C5 3
NEND PO2 399 G6
PSTN BH14 446 B4
Wilsons Rd BOR GU35 202 E3
Wilson St SHAM SO14 13 L1
Wilton Av WSHM SO15 343 J2
Wilton Cl CHCH/BSGR BH23 434 B7
Wilton Ct FARN GU14 91 G5
Wilton Crs WSHM SO15 318 C7
Wilton Dr HORN PO8 352 E3
Wilton Gdns
NMIL/BTOS BH25 437 K5 3
WSHM SO15 318 C7
Wilton Pl BSTK RG21 4 B8
SSEA PO5 21 H7
Wilton Rd CBLY GU15 70 E5
LTDN BH7 448 E3
WSHM SO15 318 C7
Wilton Ter SSEA PO5 21 J7 3
Wiltshire Av CWTH RG45 49 L2
Wiltshire Gdns
CHCH/BSGR BH23 409 K8
Wiltshire Rd CHCH/BSGR BH23 409 K8
CHFD SO53 293 J5
Wiltshire St SSEA PO5 20 F3
Wilverley Av CHAR BH8 433 K6
HAV PO9 377 L4
Wilverley Pl FAWY SO45 392 C7
Wilverley Rd BROC SO42 387 K7
NMIL/BTOS BH25 411 K5
Wimbledon Cl CBLY GU15 51 J7
Wimbledon Pk Rd SSEA PO5 21 K8
Wimbledon Rd CBLY GU15 51 J7
Wimborne Rd BWD BH11 431 M2
ENEY PO4 423 L4
MOOR/WNTN BH9 432 D4
NBNE BH10 432 E4
PLE BH15 445 H2
TWDS BH3 447 L1
UPTN BH16 428 B4
WCLF BH2 22 F3
WIMB BH21 404 C2
Wimborne Rd East FERN BH22 406 B2
WIMB BH21 405 L2
Wimborne Rd West
WIMB BH21 404 E4
Wimbushes EWKG RG40 48 A2
Wimpole St PSEA PO1 423 H2
Wimpson Gdns ROWN SO16 317 L7
Wimpson La ROWN SO16 317 K8
Wincanton Cl ALTN GU34 176 F6
Wincanton Wy WVILLE PO7 352 F7
Winchcombe Cl FLET GU13 88 F7
Winchcombe Rd BSTK RG21 4 C9
CHAM PO6 374 F7
NWBY RG14 2 F5
Winchester By-pass
RWIN SO21 168 A7
WINC SO23 215 H3
WINC SO23 215 H5
Winchester Gdns AND SP10 9 H9
Winchester Hl ROMY SO51 263 G8
RWIN SO21 168 B5
Winchester Rd ALTN GU34 176 D7
ALTN GU34 197 H5
ASHV GU12 113 K5
BPWT SO32 296 C5
BPWT SO32 321 K5
BSTK RG21 104 F5
CHFD SO53 293 J2
DEAN RG23 126 D4
ELGH SO50 295 H4
KEMP RG22 126 F1
KSCL RG20 79 H1
NALR SO24 217 M3
NEND PO2 399 J8
RFNM GU10 181 L1
NMIL/BTOS BH25 438 A3
PSF GU32 274 A3
RAND SP11 142 F4
RAND SP11 166 B2
ROMY SO51 263 J7 2
ROMY SO51 290 F1
ROWN SO16 317 M7
RWIN SO21 170 A7
RWIN SO21
STOK SO20
STOK SO20
WHAM PO17
WHCH RG28
Winchester St AND SP10
BSTK RG21
FARN GU14
HEND SO30
OVTN RG25
WHCH RG28
WSHM SO15
Winchester Wy BLKW GU17
TOTT SO40
Winchfield Cl ITCH SO19
Winchfield Ct HTWY RG27
Winchfield Crs HAV PO9
Wincombe Dr FERN BH22
Windbury Rd ROWN SO16
Windermere Av
FHAM/STUB PO14
KEMP RG22
ROWN SO16
Windermere Cl FARN GU14
Windermere Gdns
NALR SO24
TOTT SO40
Windermere Rd BOR GU35
NEND PO2
TWDS BH3
WEND SO18
Windermere Wy FNM GU9
STHA RG19
Windfield Dr ROMY SO51
Windham Rd BMTH BH1
Winding Wood Dr CBLY GU15
Windmill Cl HORN PO8
LYMN SO41
RGWD BH24
Windmill Copse FAWY SO45
Windmill Cnr THLE RG7
Windmill Dr BOR GU35
Windmill Fld WVILLE PO7
Windmill Flds ALTN GU34
Windmill Gv FHAM/PORC PO16
Windmill Hl ALTN GU34
Windmill La HLER SO31
RAND SP11
RGWD BH24
THLE RG7
Windmill Rd ASHV GU12
THLE RG7
Windover Cl ITCH SO19
Windrush Gdns WVILLE PO7
Windrush Hts SHST GU47
Windrush Rd ROWN SO16
Windrush Wy FAWY SO45
Windsor Cl ALTN GU34
LYMN SO41
RGWD BH24
Windsor Ct ELGH SO50
Windsor Crs FNM GU9
Windsor Gdns ASHV GU12
KEMP RG22
Windsor Ga ELGH SO50
Windsor Pk ALTN GU34
Windsor Ride CBLY GU15
EWKG RG40
Windsor Ri NWBY RG14
Windsor Rd ALTN GU34
AND SP10
BOSC BH5
CHAM PO6
CHCH/BSGR BH23
FARN GU14
FHAM/PORC PO16
GPORT PO12
BOR GU35
NALR SO24
PSF GU32
PSTN BH14
WVILLE PO7
Windsor Wk BOR GU35
Windsor Wy ALDT GU11
FBDG SP6
FRIM GU16
Windwhistle La RSAL SP5
Winfield Wy EMRTH PO10
Winfrith Crs BKME/WDN BH12
Winfrith Wy ROWN SO16
Wingate Ct ALDT GU11
Wingate Dr ITCH SO19
Wingate Rd ODIM RG29
TOTT SO40
Wingfield Av
CHCH/BSGR BH23
PLE BH15
Wingfield St PSEA PO1
Wingrove Rd TOTT SO40
Wings Cl FNM GU9
Wings Rd FNM GU9
Winifred Cl ELGH SO50
Winifred Rd PLE BH15
WVILLE PO7
Winkfield Rw HORN PO8
Winklebury Wy DEAN RG23
Winkle St SHAM SO14
Winkton Cl CHCH/BSGR BH23
HAV PO9
Winkworth La THLE RG7
Winnall Cl WINC SO23
Winnall Manor Rd WINC SO23
Winnall Valley Rd WINC SO23
Winnards Cl FERN BH22
Winnards Pk HLER SO31
Winnham Dr
FHAM/PORC PO16
Winnington FHAM PO15
Winn Rd PTSW SO17
Winscombe Av HORN PO8
Winsford Av ELGH SO50
Winsford Cl ELGH SO50
Winsford Gdns ELGH SO50
Winslade Rd WINW SO22
HAV PO9
Winsley Av SBNE BH6
Winsor Cl HISD PO11
Winsor La TOTT SO40

r Rd TOTT SO40 339 M1
T SO40 341 L2
it Cl PLE BH15 444 D5
anley Rd NEND PO2 399 G7
VN SO16 317 H3
on Av BKME/WDN BH12 446 F2
Y RG26 62 A1
on Churchill Av SSEA PO5 21 H3
on Cl ELGH SO50 293 M4
I GU16 91 J2
) PO11 425 J5
VN SO16 317 L6
one Crs NBAD SO52 291 M5
on Gdns
E/WDN BH12 446 F2
on Ri ALTN GU34 197 G5
on Rd MOOR/WNTN BH9 432 E5
on Wk RFNM GU10 158 F2 1
on Wy RGWD BH24 358 F8
A RG19 26 C4
rbourne Rd
M PO6 374 D7 2
BH15 445 J4
Y SO51 263 H7 8
rdyne Ms AND SP10 8 E6
rhayes Cl CFDH BH17 430 B5
rhill Rd CHAM PO6 375 H8
r Rd ENEY PO4 423 L5
rs Cl FAWY SO45 392 B5
rs Hl BPWT SO32 296 D8
rslow Dr HAV PO9 377 J2 7
rs Rd BPWT SO32 323 M8
rthur Wy BSTK RG21 4 D7
rton Dr NWBY RG14 25 G3
n Cha AND SP10 119 J8
n Cl LYMN SO41 440 D5 1
SP9 114 E4
n Crs YTLY GU46 69 G3
n Hl STOK SO20 186 F5
n Rd ALDT GU11 6 E4
I GU9 135 G4 1
D PO2 399 K6
GU32 275 L5
n St SHAM SO14 13 H2 2
n Wy NBNE BH10 432 B7
/BTOS BH25 437 M3
nead La RAND SP11 140 F2
ch Wy LYMN SO41 438 D5
rough Rd SSEA PO5 21 K7
s Firs THLE RG7 31 G5
nger La BOR GU35 180 E6
rt Gdns
OR/WNTN BH9 432 F3
noor Cl CBLY GU15 51 H8
noor Rd CBLY GU15 51 H8
l SSEA PO5 21 L7
Gdns FARN GU14 90 A6
Rd AND SP10 8 C7
ria La YTLY GU46 68 F3
ria Dr BOR GU35 201 J6
BH31 357 G4
ria Gdns HAV PO9 377 M4
Cl AND SP10 119 G4
Ct WHCH RG28 122 A2
ampton Cl HAV PO9 377 L3 3
ampton Rd BDST BH18 429 K6
m Cl CHFD SO53 292 F2
rbed La FHAM PO15 371 H4
rmoor Rd
OR/WNTN BH9 432 C8
r Ri DEAN RG23 102 F6
rslack Cl BOR GU35 202 F4 3
s Rd LSOL/BMARY PO13 397 H8
ithies RSAL SP5 207 M8 1
ngham Rd CCLF BH13 446 E5
bed Wy NTHA RG18 27 H3
Cl ROMY SO51 262 E8 3
nsford La LYND SO43 314 B8
ring Rd HISD PO11 426 D6
VN SO16 317 L3
ead Rd FRIM GU16 91 J4
n Hl NALR SO24 218 C4
d ELGH SO50 295 H6
SP5 207 G2
Hl WEND SO18 319 M8
od Rd ALTN GU34 175 H8
ey Cl LYMN SO41 439 M6
n Cl WINW SO22 10 E3
rn Av FARN GU14 91 G4
rn Cl ELGH SO50 293 M2
GU16 71 K7
rn Rd ROWN SO16 318 A3
Cl HORN PO8 328 B5
house Rd ITCH SO19 344 C4
gham Rd CWTH RG45 49 H5
g Rd PSTN BH14 446 B4
Cl WINW SO22 238 B3
Rd ASHV GU12 7 K3
ere La LISS GU33 224 F6
La ALTN GU34 176 D8
ston Rd SBNE BH6 449 L5
on Rd FERN BH22 406 A5
ley Rd ALDT GU11 6 F3
E/WDN BH12 446 C2
M SO15 343 G1
y Wy LYMN SO41 454 C3
ngham Wy STHA RG19 27 G6 3
rton Rd
E/WDN BH12 446 F3
rley Ct ROWN SO16 318 C5 2
rsdene Cl AND SP10 9 L7
rsdene Gdns AND SP10 9 M7
rsdene Rd AND SP10 9 K7
SP10 9 M7 1
rton La TADY RG26 60 C7
rton Rd HAV PO9 377 J3
BH7 448 E3
M SO14 13 K1 5
RG26 60 B6
rton Wy SHAM SO14 13 J1
sey Pl CHFD SO53 292 F4 5
on Cl RWIN SO21 168 C5
on Ct HAV PO9 377 M2 13
on La RWIN SO21 190 B1
on Rd ROWN SO16 318 A4
acre Gdns FERN BH22 406 C4
Barn Rd FHAM PO15 14 A5
y La EMRTH PO10 378 D1

HAV PO9 354 B7
Woodbine Cl SHST GU47 69 L1
Woodbine La KSCL RG20 37 J7
Woodbourne FNM GU9 6 B7
Woodbourne Cl FHAM PO15 14 A6
LISS GU33 248 F4 1
YTLY GU46 69 G2 2
Woodbridge Dr CBLY GU15 71 G1
Woodbridge Rd BLKW GU17 69 L3
Woodbury Av CHAR BH8 433 K6
HAV PO9 16 E7
PSF GU32 275 K3
Woodbury Cl
CHCH/BSGR BH23 434 C5
Woodbury Gv HORN PO8 352 D3
Woodbury Rd KEMP RG22 127 G2
Wood Cl ITCH SO19 345 G5
KEMP RG22 127 G2
Woodcock Cl NTID SP9 114 E2 1
Woodcock La LYMN SO41 438 E5
Woodcocks Crs LTDN BH7 448 F1
Woodcot Crs HAV PO9 377 L2
Woodcote Dr UPTN BH16 444 A2
Woodcote Gn FLET GU13 88 C8
Woodcote La BPWT SO32 296 F1
FHAM/STUB PO14 396 E6
Woodcote Rd MARL SN8 52 F1
PTSW SO17 319 H5 1
Woodcot Gdns FARN GU14 90 A4 2
Woodcot Ter ASHV GU12 7 L5
Woodcroft La HORN PO8 352 D3
Woodcut Rd RFNM GU10 158 C3
Wood End CWTH RG45 49 J4
Woodend FARN GU14 91 G5 4
Woodend Rd FRIM GU16 91 M1
MOOR/WNTN BH9 447 K1
Wood End Rd RGWD BH24 383 J3
Wood End Wy NBAD SO52 292 F1
Wooden House La LYMN SO41 414 F6
Wooderson Cl ELGH SO50 295 G5 3
Woodfern FBDG SP6 310 C6 1
Woodfield BOR GU35 179 G7
Woodfield Av CHAM PO6 376 C7
Woodfield Dr WINW SO22 238 A2
Woodfield Gdns
CHCH/BSGR BH23 436 B7
Woodfield Park Rd
EMRTH PO10 378 F7
Woodfield Rd BWD BH11 431 L3
Woodford Cl RGWD BH24 382 F1
Woodford Rd BMTH BH1 23 L4
Woodgarston Dr KEMP RG22 126 F2
Woodgason La HISD PO11 402 A7
Woodgate FARN GU14 89 H5 3
Wood Glade Cl TOTT SO40 342 D7
Woodgreen Av HAV PO9 16 B2
Woodgreen Dr BWD BH11 431 H4
Woodgreen Rd WINW SO22 214 C4
Woodhall Wy FHAM PO15 14 D1
Woodhayes Av
CHCH/BSGR BH23 436 C6
Wood Hill La ODIM RG29 131 J4
Woodhouse La HAV PO9 354 A4
HEND SO30 321 K8
HORN PO8 353 L2
STHA RG19 40 B5
Woodhouse Rd HORN PO8 353 K1
Woodington Cl HAV PO9 377 L2 3
Woodington Rd ROMY SO51 289 H4
Woodland Av BOSC BH5 448 F4
Woodland Cl ROMY SO51 289 G6
WEND SO18 345 H1
Woodland Dr RFNM GU10 158 E2
RSAL SP5 206 E1 1
TADY RG26 64 A6
Woodland Dro RWIN SO21 266 F5
Woodland Ms HEND SO30 320 C7
Woodland Ri FLET GU13 110 D3
Woodlands CHAM RG24 83 M4 1
CWTH RG45 49 L5
FLET GU13 88 E6
KSCL RG20 56 D1
OVTN RG25 100 F8
YTLY GU46 69 G5
FHAM/PORC PO16 373 H6
Woodlands Av EMRTH PO10 378 C5
FNM GU9 6 C7
PLE BH15 444 D5
THLE RG7 31 K5
Woodlands Cl ASHV GU12 113 K3 2
CHFD SO53 265 J6
FARN GU14 70 B7
FAWY SO45 367 J7
HLER SO31 370 D2
LSOL/BMARY PO13 421 G2
Woodlands Ct FAWY SO45 367 J7 2
SHST GU47 50 C7
Woodlands Crs PLE BH15 444 E5
Woodlands Dr HLER SO31 369 H2
Woodlands Dro TOTT SO40 340 D5
Woodlands Gv WVILLE PO7 376 B3
Woodlands La HASM GU27 228 C1
HISD PO11 425 J3
LISS GU33 249 G6
RCCH PO18 355 J6
Woodlands Rd BROC SO42 413 K1
CBLY GU15 70 E3
FARN GU14 90 A2
NMIL/BTOS BH25 452 D1
TADY RG26 41 G7
TOTT SO40 340 C4
The Woodlands BOR GU35 201 J7
WINC SO23 215 H2
Woodland St PSEA PO1 423 J2
Woodlands Wk FARN GU14 70 B7
Woodlands Wy AND SP10 9 L5
HAV PO9 377 K4 2
HLER SO31 345 K8
NBAD SO52 291 K4
NMIL/BTOS BH25 437 M2
RGWD BH24 381 K4
WSHM SO15 318 E8 3
Woodland Vw HLER SO31 345 K8
HORN PO8 352 D2
Woodland Wk BOSC BH5 448 F4
FERN BH22 406 D1
Woodland Wy
CHCH/BSGR BH23 436 B8

LYMN SO41 454 B4 1
Wood La BWD BH11 431 J2
FARN GU14 90 D5
FLET GU13 89 H7
HTWY RG27 107 H3
LYMN SO41 454 B4
NALR SO24 243 J3
RFNM GU10 136 E4
THLE RG7 45 H3
WHAM PO17 374 E1
Woodlane Cl NALR SO24 243 J3
Woodlark Gdns EPSF GU31 276 B5
Wood Lawn Cl
NMIL/BTOS BH25 437 K8
Woodlea Cl WINW SO22 10 C2
Woodlea Gdns HEND SO30 320 D7
Woodlea Wy ROMY SO51 264 E6
Woodleaze Cl BDST BH18 429 M2
Woodleigh FLET GU13 88 F8
Woodleigh Cl HAV PO9 378 A5
Woodley Cl ROMY SO51 263 H6
Woodley Gdns LYMN SO41 440 B3
Woodley La ROMY SO51 262 F7
Woodley Rd GPORT PO12 19 G4 4
ITCH SO19 344 B5
Woodley Wy ROMY SO51 263 H6 5
Woodling Crs FBDG SP6 310 C6
Woodlinken Cl VWD BH31 356 F4
Woodlinken Dr VWD BH31 356 F4
Woodlinken Wy VWD BH31 356 F4
Wood Ldg TOTT SO40 316 A7
Woodman Cl RWIN SO21 213 J6
Woodmancote La
EMRTH PO10 379 J4
Woodmancote Rd ENEY PO4 423 L4
Woodman La RWIN SO21 213 K5
Woodman's La THLE RG7 31 J5
Woodmere Cft KEMP RG22 126 E1
Woodmill La WEND SO18 319 J5
Wood Moor EWKG RG40 48 C6
Woodmoor Cl TOTT SO40 342 E7 1
Woodpath SSEA PO5 21 H6
Woodpecker Cl HAV PO9 17 J4
KEMP RG22 103 L8
BOR GU35 201 J6
RFNM GU10 111 G8 4
VWD BH31 356 D3 3
Woodpecker Copse
HLER SO31 370 F5
Woodpecker Dr CFDH BH17 429 J8
WINW SO22 214 B6
TOTT SO40 342 C7
Woodpecker Wy ELGH SO50 293 J6
Wood Rdg NWBY RG14 37 H1
Wood Rd CBLY GU15 70 E7
FNM GU9 134 F1
GSHT GU26 204 A2
TOTT SO40 340 F6
Woodroffe Dr KEMP RG22 104 B7
Woodrow WVILLE PO7 351 J4
Woodrush Crs HLER SO31 370 C6
Woodsedge WVILLE PO7 376 E3
Woodside BLKW GU17 69 M5
CBLY GU15 70 C1
NWBY RG14 37 G1
LSOL/BMARY PO13 396 F3
ROWN SO16 292 D6
Woodside Av ELGH SO50 293 L3
LYMN SO41 440 C7
Woodside Cl FERN BH22 406 C2
BOR GU35 201 J5
THLE RG7 27 M3
THLE RG7 43 K2 1
TOTT SO40 342 C7
Woodside Crs BOR GU35 201 J5 4
ROWN SO16 292 C6 1
Woodside Gdns CHAM RG24 83 L4
FLET GU13 89 H6
TOTT SO40 341 G6
Woodside La ALTN GU34 197 M4
LYMN SO41 440 C6
Woodside Pk BOR GU35 201 J5
Woodside Rd ALDT GU11 112 C1
BOSC BH5 449 G4
ELGH SO50 293 K4
FERN BH22 406 C2
FNM GU9 6 A8
NBAD SO52 291 L4 4
PSTN BH14 446 B5
PTSW SO17 319 G8
Woodside Wy HEND SO30 345 L3
Woods La OVTN RG25 127 L1
Woodstock Av HORN PO8 352 E3
Woodstock Cl FHAM PO15 14 C5
HEND SO30 346 B3 3
Woodstock Dr PTSW SO17 318 F7 2
Woodstock La RGWD BH24 382 E2 3
Woodstock Rd GPORT PO12 19 G4
HAV PO9 377 G6
Woodstocks FARN GU14 90 F2
Wood St ASHV GU12 113 K2
Woods View Rd
MOOR/WNTN BH9 432 B8
Woodthorpe Gdns HLER SO31 370 D2
Woodvale FHAM PO15 14 A4
Woodvale Gdns
NMIL/BTOS BH25 438 A4
Woodview Cl ROWN SO16 318 F2
Woodville Cl BLKW GU17 69 L3
Woodville Dr PSEA PO1 20 E5
Woodville Rd FAWY SO45 392 F5
HAV PO9 376 F6
Woodward Cl GPORT PO12 18 A4
Woodway CBLY GU15 70 E3 3
Woofferton Rd CHAM PO6 374 E7
Woolbeding La MIDH GU29 279 L5
Wooldridge Crs ODIM RG29 108 B8
Woolfield La ALTN GU34 246 A5
PSF GU32 246 B6
Woolford Cl WINW SO22 238 B2 1
Woolford Wy DEAN RG23 104 C2
Wool Gv AND SP10 9 L6
Woolhampton Hl THLE RG7 28 F6
Woollards Rd ASHV GU12 113 K4
Woolmead Rd FNM GU9 134 F6
Woolmer Ct HAV PO9 377 M3 20
Woolmer Hill Rd HASM GU27 227 M1
Woolmer La LIPH GU30 202 F8

RGWD BH24 358 D6
Woolmer Rd LISS GU33 225 G5
Woolmer St EMRTH PO10 378 C4
Woolmer Wy BOR GU35 201 H6
Woolner Av CHAM PO6 375 L8
PSF GU32 275 L4
Wool Rd BKME/WDN BH12 430 F8
Wools Br RGWD BH24 381 G2
Woolsbridge Rd RGWD BH24 381 J4
Woolslope Cl FERN BH22 380 C7 3
Woolslope Gdns FERN BH22 380 D7
Woolslope Rd FERN BH22 380 C7
Woolston Rd HAV PO9 377 G2
HLER SO31 344 F8
Woolton Lodge Gdns
KSCL RG20 36 C6 1
Woolwich Cl HLER SO31 345 K6
Wooteys Wy ALTN GU34 176 E3
Wooton Rd LSOL/BMARY PO13 420 E4
Wootton HLER SO31 369 G1 8
Wootton Farm Rd
NMIL/BTOS BH25 411 J6
Wootton Gdns BMTH BH1 23 G5
Wootton Mt BMTH BH1 23 H5
Wootton Rough
NMIL/BTOS BH25 411 M8
Wootton St CHAM PO6 399 K1
Worbarrow Gdns
BKME/WDN BH12 431 G8
Worcester Av KEMP RG22 104 A8
Worcester Cl FARN GU14 90 E1 3
Worcester Pl ITCH SO19 344 F6
LYMN SO41 440 D6 3
Wordsworth Av CHAM PO6 374 C7
CHAR BH8 433 J7
YTLY GU46 68 E4
Wordsworth Cl BPWT SO32 297 K8
CHAM RG24 5 G1
WINW SO22 10 B6
Wordsworth Pl HLER SO31 346 F7
Wordsworth Rd NTHA RG18 26 F4 3
ROWN SO16 318 B7
Worgret Rd PLE BH15 445 J1
Workhouse La PSF GU32 273 J7
Workman's La HLER SO31 394 C3
Workshop Rd WVILLE PO7 374 E6
Worldham Hl ALTN GU34 177 M7
Worldham Rd HAV PO9 377 M2
Wormersley Rd STHA RG19 38 A1
Worrell Dr BKME/WDN BH12 431 G8
Worsley Rd FRIM GU16 91 J1
SSEA PO5 21 H6 11
Worsley St ENEY PO4 423 L6 2
Worthing Av GPORT PO12 397 K8
Worthing Rd SSEA PO5 21 K8
Worthington Crs PSTN BH14 445 M5
Worthy Ct HAV PO9 377 M3 21
Worthy La WINC SO23 10 F5
Worthy Rd NMIL/BTOS BH25 437 L5
WINC SO23 11 G3
Worting Rd BSTK RG21 4 B9
DEAN RG23 103 K4
KEMP RG22 104 C4
Wortley Rd CHCH/BSGR BH23 451 M1
Wote St BSTK RG21 4 F9
Wouldham Cl RAND SP11 115 J1
Wraxhall Cl CFDH BH17 430 B7
Wraysbury Park Dr
EMRTH PO10 378 D4
Wrecclesham Hl RFNM GU10 158 B3
Wrecclesham Rd FNM GU9 158 C1
Wrekin Cl KEMP RG22 104 A5
The Wrekin FARN GU14 91 H7
Wren Cl ALTN GU34 176 F3
CHCH/BSGR BH23 451 G3
WINW SO22 238 C3
NMIL/BTOS BH25 437 K6 4
RGWD BH24 383 G2 7
THLE RG7 31 L5 7
YTLY GU46 68 E2 5
Wren Ct ASHV GU12 113 L5
Wren Crs BKME/WDN BH12 447 G3
Wren Gdns FBDG SP6 333 M2
Wren Rd ELGH SO50 293 K7
Wren Wy FARN GU14 90 C1
FHAM/PORC PO16 373 K8 3
Wrexham Gr HORN PO8 328 A6 1
Wrights Cl RWIN SO21 190 C4
Wright's Hl ITCH SO19 344 E6
Wrights Wy RWIN SO21 190 C4
Wroxham Rd
BKME/WDN BH12 446 E3
Wryneck Cl ROWN SO16 318 A2
Wurford Dr STHA RG19 27 J5
Wyatts Cl WIMB BH21 429 H2
Wyatts La WIMB BH21 429 G2
Wyborn Cl HISD PO11 425 L6
Wych La LSOL/BMARY PO13 396 F4
Wychwood Cl ASHV GU12 113 J6
WCLF BH2 22 D3
Wychwood Dr FAWY SO45 418 C1
WCLF BH2 22 E2
Wychwood Gv CHFD SO53 265 K8
Wychwood Pl CBLY GU15 51 L7
Wyck La ALTN GU34 177 M6
Wycliffe Rd MOOR/WNTN BH9 432 D8
WEND SO18 319 M7
Wycote Rd LSOL/BMARY PO13 396 F4
Wye Ct AND SP10 9 M1
Wyeford Cl HAV PO9 377 M2 14
Wyelands Av WIMB BH21 405 H3
Wykeham Cl ROWN SO16 318 D4 3
Wykeham Ct ODIM RG29 108 C8
Wykeham Dr DEAN RG23 103 M4
Wykeham Fld WHAM PO17 348 E5
Wykeham Pl WINW SO22 238 C3
LYMN SO41 440 C5
Wykeham Rd FNM GU9 134 F5 3
HLER SO31 368 F2
NEND PO2 399 J7
Wykwood LIPH GU30 227 G4 3
Wylde Green La LISS GU33 248 F3
Wylds La PSF GU32 275 H8
Wyllie Rd NEND PO2 399 J4
Wylye Cl WEND SO18 320 A5
Wylye Rd NTID SP9 114 E1
Wymering Ct FARN GU14 91 G5
Wymering La CHAM PO6 375 J8

Wymering Manor Cl
CHAM PO6 375 J8 3
Wymering Rd NEND PO2 399 J8
Wyncombe Rd BOSC BH5 449 G3
Wyndcliffe Rd ENEY PO4 21 M6
Wyndham Cl
CHCH/BSGR BH23 436 F6 3
HORN PO8 352 F4
YTLY GU46 69 G1
Wyndham Ms PSEA PO1 20 D5 2
Wyndham Pl WSHM SO15 12 D1
Wyndham Rd AND SP10 8 D8
CHCH/BSGR BH23 436 F6
NWBY RG14 26 A3
PSTN BH14 446 A5
Wyndham St ASHV GU12 7 J3
Wynfields FRIM GU16 91 J5
Wynford Rd MOOR/WNTN BH9 432 E4
PSTN BH14 446 B5
Wynne Cl BDST BH18 429 K4
Wynne Gdns FLET GU13 111 G3
Wynter Cl LTDN BH7 448 E1
Wynter Rd WEND SO18 320 A8
Wynton Wy FHAM PO15 372 A5
Wynyards Gap NBAD SO52 291 L4
Wyre Cl CHFD SO53 293 G2
Wyvern Cl ASHV GU12 113 J3 1
BKME/WDN BH12 446 C1
CHFD SO53 293 J2

Y

Yaldhurst Ct HAV PO9 377 M2 15
Yaldhurst La LYMN SO41 439 M4
Yale Cl SHST GU47 50 C6
Yapton St PSEA PO1 21 G1
Yarborough Rd SSEA PO5 21 G6
Yardlea Cl HAV PO9 353 M7
Yardley Cl HSEA PO3 400 A4
Yardley Rd HEND SO30 345 M3
Yarmley La RSAL SP5 206 E2
Yarmouth Gdns WSHM SO15 318 A7
Yarmouth Rd
BKME/WDN BH12 446 E2
Yarnhams Cl ALTN GU34 197 G6
Yarrell Md LYMN SO41 439 M4
Yarrells Cl UPTN BH16 444 B2
Yarrells La UPTN BH16 444 B2
Yarrow Cl CHCH/BSGR BH23 435 M8
Yarrow Rd BKME/WDN BH12 430 E8
Yarrow Wy HLER SO31 370 C6
Yateley Cl HAV PO9 377 G3
Yateley Rd YTLY GU46 69 J1
Yatesbury Cl FNM GU9 158 C1
Yates Copse NTHA RG18 26 B3
Yaverland HLER SO31 369 G2
Yeatminster Rd CFDH BH17 430 D6
Yellowhammer Rd
KEMP RG22 126 E2
Yellowhammers ALTN GU34 176 E2
Yelverton Av FAWY SO45 367 L7
Yelverton Rd WCLF BH2 22 E5
Yeo Ct ENEY PO4 424 A5
Yeomans HTWY RG27 68 B1
Yeomans Cl FARN GU14 90 D3
RFNM GU10 113 J8
Yeomans Fld RCCH PO18 379 M7
Yeomans La KSCL RG20 37 K7
LIPH GU30 226 D4
Yeomans Pl BOR GU35 202 B3 2
Yeomans Rd CHAR BH8 433 J5
Yeomans Wy CBLY GU15 71 H3
CHAR BH8 433 J5
TOTT SO40 316 E8
Yeovil Cha WEND SO18 320 A8
Yeovil Cl FARN GU14 91 G7
Yeovil Rd SHST GU47 50 B7
Yeovilton Cl LYMN SO41 439 J7
Yerville Gdns LYMN SO41 438 D5 3
Yetminster Rd FARN GU14 91 G7
Yew Cl KSCL RG20 59 K6
Yew Ga NWBY RG14 25 J2
Yew La NMIL/BTOS BH25 438 A4
Yew Rd WEND SO18 319 M8
Yewside LSOL/BMARY PO13 397 J7 2
The Yews HORN PO8 353 H1
Yewtree Cl FAWY SO45 367 L8
Yew Tree Cl DEAN RG23 103 G8
ELGH SO50 295 H5
FARN GU14 89 M5 3
HEND SO30 345 M2 6
RAND SP11 142 F7
RSAL SP5 206 E2 1
TADY RG26 63 M6
WIMB BH21 404 A3
Yew Tree Dr FHAM PO15 347 G8
HLER SO31 370 F1
Yew Tree Gdns WVILLE PO7 351 J4
Yew Tree La OVTN RG25 125 K7
RSAL SP5 208 A5
Yewtree La ROWN SO16 317 H5
Yew Tree Pl LISS GU33 248 F4
Yew Tree Rd HISD PO11 401 L8
Yew Tree Wk FRIM GU16 71 H7
Yoells Crs HORN PO8 352 D2
Yoells La HORN PO8 352 D2
Yokesford Hl ROMY SO51 262 D3
Yolland Cl FNM GU9 134 F1
Yonge Cl ELGH SO50 294 A5
York Av NMIL/BTOS BH25 437 M5
York Buildings SHAM SO14 13 G4 1
York Cl CHCH/BSGR BH23 449 L1
ELGH SO50 321 J1
KEMP RG22 104 A8
BOR GU35 201 J6
NBAD SO52 292 E4
NWBY RG14 3 G6
PSF GU32 275 J5
SHAM SO14 344 A2
TOTT SO40 316 F8
York Crs ALDT GU11 6 D4
LSOL/BMARY PO13 420 E4
York Dro RSAL SP5 287 H8
WEND SO18 344 F1
Yorke St SSEA PO5 20 F4
Yorke Wy HLER SO31 369 J5

York Gdns *FHAM/PORC* PO16 398 B2
York La *HTWY* RG27 87 H3
York Ms *ALTN* GU34 176 F4
York Pl *CBLY* GU15 71 G1
LTDN BH7 448 F3
PSEA PO1 422 F2
York Rd *ALDT* GU11 6 D4
ASHV GU12 113 K5
BMTH BH1 23 K4
CBLY GU15 71 G1
CFDH BH17 429 L7
ELGH SO50 293 M7
FARN GU14 90 F7
FNM GU9 134 F8
NWBY RG14 3 G6
WSHM SO15 343 G1
Yorktown Rd *SHST* GU47 69 M1
York Wy *SHST* GU47 49 K8
Yorkwood *LISS* GU33 248 E4
Youlden Cl *CBLY* GU15 71 K3
Youlden Dr *CBLY* GU15 71 K3
Young Crs *STHA* RG19 3 M9
Youngs Dr *ASHV* GU12 113 J6
Youngs Paddock *RSAL* SP5 206 F2
Youngs Rd *ALTN* GU34 176 E4
BWD BH11 431 L3
Yves Ms *SSEA* PO5 21 J7

Z

Zamek Cl *BWD* BH11 431 L3
Zetland Rd *CHAM* PO6 400 B1
GPORT PO12 18 E2
Zeus La *WVILLE* PO7 376 D5
Zinnia Cl *KEMP* RG22 126 F2
NBNE BH10 432 C6
Zion Rd *RAND* SP11
Zouch Av *NTID* SP9
Zouch Cl *NTID* SP9
Zouch Farm Rd *NTID* SP9

Index - featured places

The AA - Fanum House *BSTK* RG21 5 K6
Abbey Business Park *FNM* GU9 135 K8
Abbey Chiropractic Clinic *ROMY* SO51 290 D1
Abbey Mead Surgery *ROMY* SO51 290 C1
The Abbey School *FNM* GU9 135 G7
Abbotsford Farm Business Centre *ALTN* GU34 197 J5
Abbotswood Junior School *TOTT* SO40 341 H1
Abbotts Ann Primary School *RAND* SP11 141 L4
ABC Cinema *BMTH* BH1 22 F6
Abraham Gallery *SSEA* PO5 21 H6
Abro Industrial Estate *ALDT* GU11 113 G5
Acorn Business Centre *CHAM* PO6 375 H8
Ad Astra County First School *CFDH* BH17 430 C7
Adelaide Medical Centre *AND* SP10 9 K5
Adeline Road Surgery *BOSC* BH5 448 D4
Admiral Lord Nelson School *HSEA* PO3 399 M7
AFC Newbury Football Ground *NWBY* RG14 3 G3
Airborne Forces Museum *ALDT* GU11 112 D3
Albany Business Centre *WHAM* PO17 372 F1
Alderman Quilley Secondary School *ELGH* SO50 293 L7
Aldermaston C of E School *THLE* RG7 41 J1
Aldermoor Health Centre *ROWN* SO16 318 B4
Alderney Middle School *BKME/WDN* BH12 431 H7
Aldershot & Farnham County Court *ALDT* GU11 7 G2
Aldershot Health Centre *ALDT* GU11 6 D1
Aldershot Military Historical Trust & Museum *ALDT* GU11 112 F1
Aldershot Town Football Club *ALDT* GU11 7 H2
Alexander House Business Centre *ALDT* GU11 7 G2
Alexandra Surgery *ALDT* GU11 6 D1
Allen Gallery *ALTN* GU34 176 E5
All Hallows RC Secondary School *FNM* GU9 6 C8
Allington Manor Business Centre *ELGH* SO50 320 D1
All Saints C of E First School *NFNM* GU10 159 M5
All Saints C of E Junior School *FLET* GU13 88 C8
All Saints C of E Primary School *RSAL* SP5 258 G5
All Saints Community Primary School *WINC* SO23 239 G2
Alma Road Surgery *PTSW* SO17 318 F8
Alma Road Surgery *ROMY* SO51 290 E1
The Alpha Business Park *SHAM* SO14 343 M1
Alresford County Junior School *NARL* SO24 218 C3
Alresford Golf Club *NARL* SO24 218 B5
The Alresford Surgery *NARL* SO24 218 C2
Alton Business Centre *ALTN* GU34 177 G5
Alton College *ALTN* GU34 176 E3
Alton Convent School *ALTN* GU34 176 F2
Alton County Infant School *ALTN* GU34 176 F4
Alton Health Centre *ALTN* GU34 176 F4
Alton Rugby Club *ALTN* GU34 176 F2
Alton Town Football Club *ALTN* GU34 176 F3
Alverstoke C of E Junior School *GPORT* PO12 18 C6
Alverstoke County Infant School *GPORT* PO12 18 C8
Amery Hill Secondary School *ALTN* GU34 176 E4
Amesbury School *GSHT* GU26 204 B7
Amey Industrial Estate *PSF* GU32 275 K5
A M F Bowling *ITCH* SO19 344 D2
A M F Bowling *PSEA* PO1 21 H1
Ampfield Primary School *ROMY* SO51 264 B4
Amport C of E (aided) Primary School *RAND* SP11 140 F3
Anchor Business Centre *CHFD* SO53 293 G2
Andover Football Club *AND* SP10 118 B6
Andover Golf Club *AND* SP10 9 H9
Andover Museum & the Museum of the Iron Age *AND* SP10 9 J4
Andover Road Retail Park *FUFL* SO22 10 E5
The Andrew Isaacs Practice *BMTH* BH1 23 J4
Andrews Endowed Primary School *ALTN* GU34 177 H2
Anne Dale County Junior & Infant School *FHAM/STUB* PO14 396 A6
Anstey County Junior School *ALTN* GU34 176 E4
Anton County Infant School *AND* SP10 9 G9
Anton County Junior School *AND* SP10 9 G9
Anton Trading Estate *AND* SP10 9 G8
The Anvil Concert Hall *BSTK* RG21 4 E7
Apple Industrial Estate *FHAM* PO15 371 G3
Applemore College *FAWY* SO45 367 G6
Applemore Recreation Centre *FAWY* SO45 367 G5
Appleshaw School *RAND* SP11 117 G1
Arch Farm Industrial Estate *FBDG* SP6 309 K5
Arena Leisure Centre *CBLY* GU15 70 E2
The Ark School *THLE* RG7 30 C7
Army Golf Club *ALDT* GU11 112 B2
The Arnewood Practice *NMIL/BTOS* BH25 437 L5
Arnewood School *NMIL/BTOS* BH25 437 K7
Arnhem Barracks *ALDT* GU11 112 D5
Arrow Industrial Estate *FARN* GU14 90 C6
The Art Gallery *EMRTH* PO10 378 F4
Art Space School *PSEA* PO1 423 G1
Arundel Court Junior & Infant School *PSEA* PO1 423 H2
Ashdown Family & Health Centre *NTID* SP9 114 E2
Ashdown School *CFDH* BH17 430 C7
Ashford Hill Primary School *STHA* RG19 40 B7
Ash Grange CP School *ASHV* GU12 113 L6
Ashley County Infant School *NMIL/BTOS* BH25 438 B5
Ashley Heath Industrial Estate *WIMB* BH21 381 G1
Ashley Junior School *NMIL/BTOS* BH25 438 A5
Ash Manor School *ASHV* GU12 113 J8
Ashurst Hospital *TOTT* SO40 340 F7
Ash Vale Health Centre *ASHV* GU12 113 L4
Associated Football Club *TOTT* SO40 316 F8
Atherley House Surgery *WSHM* SO15 343 H2
The Atherley School *ROWN* SO16 317 G2
Avenue Clinic *WSHM* SO15 343 K2
Avenue Shopping Centre *WCLF* BH2 22 D5
Avington Park *RWIN* SO21 216 D3
Avonbourne Girls School *LTDN* BH7 448 F1
Avon Castle *RGWD* BH24 382 B5
Avonlea Preparatory School *RGWD* BH24 358 F8
Awbridge County School *ROMY* SO51 261 J3
Baddesley Park Industrial Estate *NBAD* SO52 292 A4
Baden Powell & St Peters C of E (VC) School *PSTN* BH14 446 A5
Badger Farm Surgery *FUFL* SO22 238 B4
Badgerswood Surgery *LIND* GU35 202 A3
Badshot Lea County First School *FNM* GU9 135 K2
Balksbury County Infant School *AND* SP10 8 B7
Balksbury Industrial Estate *RAND* SP11 142 D3
Ballard College *NMIL/BTOS* BH25 437 L5
Ballard Lake Preparatory School *NMIL/BTOS* BH25 437 L4
Banister School *WSHM* SO15 343 K1
Bargate Museum *SHAM* SO14 13 G4
Bargate Shopping Centre *SHAM* SO14 13 G4
Barncroft Infant School *HAV* PO9 377 H4
Barncroft Junior School *HAV* PO9 377 G4
Barratt Industrial Park *FHAM* PO15 371 G3
Bartley C of E Middle School *TOTT* SO40 339 M1
Bartley Wood Business Park *HTWY* RG27 86 B8
Barton Industrial Estate *NARL* SO24 173 L7
Barton Peveril College *ELGH* SO50 293 L7
Barton Stacey C of E Primary School *RWIN* SO21 145 K8
Barton Surgery *NMIL/BTOS* BH25 437 L7
Basing County Infants School *CHAM* RG24 106 A2
Basingstoke Business Centre *KEMP* RG22 104 D6
Basingstoke College of Technology *BSTK* RG21 4 C8
Basingstoke County Court *BSTK* RG21 5 H7
Basingstoke & Deane Borough Council *CHAM* RG24 5 L2
Basingstoke Ice Rink *KEMP* RG22 104 C3
Basingstoke & North Hants Cricket Club *BSTK* RG21 105 G5
Basingstoke Rugby Club *KEMP* RG22 104 A7
Basingstoke Sports Centre *BSTK* RG21 4 E7
Basingstoke Town Football Club *KEMP* RG22 104 D6
Bassett Green Junior School *ROWN* SO16 319 G4
Baycroft School *FHAM/STUB* PO14 396 B6
Bay House School *GPORT* PO12 421 J6
Baytree Gallery *NARL* SO24 218 B2
BBC South TV & Radio Solent *WSHM* SO15 12 E1
Beacon Hill County Primary School *GSHT* GU26 203 M2
The Bear Museum *EPSF* GU31 275 L6
Bearwood County Primary School *WIMB* BH21 431 G2
Beaucroft School *WIMB* BH21 404 C2
Beaufort Road Surgery *SBNE* BH6 449 H3
Beaulieu CP School *BROC* SO42 390 D7
Beaumont County Junior School *ALDT* GU11 6 C2
Beaver Industrial Estate *LIPH* GU30 226 F5
Bedales School *PSF* GU32 275 K1
Bedenham County Junior & Infant School *LSOL/BMARY* PO13 397 H5
Beech Down County Primary School *KEMP* RG22 104 C8
Beechnut Industrial Estate *ALDT* GU11 7 H3
Beechwood Middle School *WEND* SO18 344 D1
Belbins Business Park *ROMY* SO51 262 F5
Belgrave Industrial Estate *PTSW* SO17 319 H6
Bellemoor Secondary School *ROWN* SO16 318 C6
Belle Vue County Infant School *ASHV* GU12 7 L2
Benham Park *KSCL* RG20 24 D4
Berkshire Business Centre *STHA* RG19 27 K6
Berkshire County Council *NWBY* RG14 2 B8
Berkshire County Council *NWBY* RG14 2 D3
Berkshire County Council *NWBY* RG14 2 E7
Berrywood Primary School *HEND* SO30 321 J7
Bethany C of E (VA) Junior School *BMTH* BH1 448 C3
Bevois Town Primary School *SHAM* SO14 343 L1
Bicknell Boys Residential School *LTDN* BH7 448 F1
Bidbury Junior & Infant School *HAV* PO9 16 A2
Bilton Industrial Estate *CHAM* RG24 83 J7
Binsted C of E Primary School *ALTN* GU34 178 C1
Binswood View Business Centre *ALTN* GU34 200 C4
Birchwood Medical Centre *CFDH* BH17 429 K8
Bishop Challoner RC Secondary School *KEMP* RG22 104 B5
Bishops Waltham County Infant School *BPWT* SO32 297 J8
Bishopswood Co Junior School *TADY* RG26 41 L8
Bishopwood Co Infant School *TADY* RG26 61 L1
Bitterne C of E First School *ITCH* SO19 344 D2
Bitterne C of E Infant School *ITCH* SO19 344 D2
Bitterne Health Centre *WEND* SO18 344 E1
Bitterne Leisure Centre *WEND* SO18 344 E1
Bitterne Manor Primary School *ITCH* SO19 344 B1
Bitterne Middle School *ITCH* SO19 344 D2
Bitterne Park Clinic *WEND* SO18 319 K8
Bitterne Park Junior & Infant School *WEND* SO18 319 J6
Bitterne Park Secondary School *WEND* SO18 319 K6
Bitterne Park Surgery *WEND* SO18 319 K8
Blackbrook Business Park *FHAM* PO15 14 C5
Blackfield Health Centre *FAWY* SO45 392 B6
Blackfield Junior & Infant School *FAWY* SO45 392 C7
Blackmoor Golf Club *LIND* GU35 200 F7
Blackwater & Hawley Leisure Centre *BLKW* GU17 70 A5
Blackwater Industrial Estate *BLKW* GU17 70 B4
Blackwater Trading Estate *ASHV* GU12 113 H8
Bladon Gallery *RAND* SP11 74 D8
Blands Infant School *THLE* RG7 31 J6
Blue Fish Zoo *BMTH* BH1 22 E6
The Boatyard Industrial Estate *FHAM/PORC* PO16 15 H8
Bohunt Community School *LIPH* GU30 226 E4
Bohunt Manor *LIPH* GU30 226 E5
The Bold Gallery *CHCH/BSGR* BH23
Bordon County Junior & Infant School *LIND* GU35
Bordon Trading Estate *LIND* GU35
Boscombe Dental Health Centre *BOSC* BH5
Boscombe Manor Medical Centre *BOSC* BH5
Bosmere Junior School *HAV* PO9
Botley Junior & Infant School *HEND* SO30
Botley Park Hotel & Country Club *BPWT* SO32
Boundaries Surgery *ALTN* GU34
Boundary Oak School *WHAM* PO17
The Bourne Community College *EMRTH* PO10
Bourne County First School *NFNM* GU10
Bourne Mill Industrial Estate *FNM* GU9
Bournemouth Borough Council *BMTH* BH1
Bournemouth Business Centre *BMTH* BH1
Bournemouth College *BMTH* BH1
Bournemouth County Council *BMTH* BH1
Bournemouth County Court *BMTH* BH1
Bournemouth International Airport *CHCH/BSGR* BH23
Bournemouth Magistrates Court *BMTH* BH1
Bournemouth Mosque *MOOR/WNTN* BH9
The Bournemouth Nuffield Hospital *BMTH* BH1
Bournemouth & Poole College *BMTH* BH1
Bournemouth & Poole College *BMTH* BH1
Bournemouth & Poole College *PSTN* BH14
Bournemouth & Poole College of Further Education *PSTN* BH14
Bournemouth School for Boys *CHAR* BH8
Bournemouth School for Girls *CHAR* BH8
Bournemouth Sports Club *CHCH/BSGR* BH23
Bournemouth University *BKME/WDN* BH12
Bournemouth University *BMTH* BH1
Bournemouth University *BMTH* BH1
Bourne Tennis Club *FNM* GU9
Boveridge House School *WIMB* BH21
Boyatt Shopping Centre *ELGH* SO50
Boyatt Wood Surgery *ELGH* SO50
Braemore C of E Primary School *FBDG* SP6
Braishfield CP School *ROMY* SO51
Bramley C of E Primary School *TADY* RG26
Bramshaw Golf Club *LYND* SO43
Branksome Heath Middle School *BKME/WDN* BH12
Bransgore Primary School *CHCH/BSGR* BH23
Breamore House *FBDG* SP6
Brickfield Trading Estate *CHFD* SO53
Brick Kiln Industrial Estate *TADY* RG26
Brickyards Industrial Estate *PSF* GU32
Bridge Gallery *WSHM* SO15
Bridgemary Community School *LSOL/BMARY* PO13
The Bridge Shopping Centre *PSEA* PO1
Brighton Hill Community Schoo *KEMP* RG22

on School RG7 40 C2
County First School GU15 70 E6
halke Primary School SP5 252 B1
ands House Y SO51 290 D3
oor County ary School H RG45 50 A4
noor Hospital H RG45 50 A4
tone First School T BH18 429 M4
tone Middle School T BH18 430 A3
nhurst College C SO42 387 L6
nhurst Primary School C SO42 387 K7
urst County nt School RT PO12 421 K1
urst County or School RT PO12 421 L2
urst Medical Centre RT PO12 421 K1
hurst Manor Golf Club C SO42 413 J2
ton Gallery M SO14 13 H2
s Hill Industrial Estate SO40 316 A4
ield Secondary School R SO31 370 C4
am School GU30 227 H6
de Business Centre F RG7 46 A2
ook Trading Estate GU12 113 H5
wood Industrial Estate I SO50 293 L5
ton County ary School SO20 209 G1
wnhill Surgery SO53 293 J1
ng Barracks GU11 112 D3
sea Open Air Theatre H BH17 429 L8
ad Trading Estate GU35 201 L2
Park Community School /BMARY PO13 397 J8
olme School V BH14 445 M4
nd Medical Centre D PO2 399 H8
bury C of E ary School E RG7 27 M2
ood Surgery RG19 27 H6
rgate School SP6 309 L5
s Road Surgery N SO16 319 H4
lere CP School RG20 57 K2
eld Health Centre E RG7 31 L5
Business Park GU31 303 H1
CP School GU31 303 J3
CP School D BH24 384 E6
Golf Club D BH24 384 F5
m Copse Junior School RG26 41 K7
e Surgery GU13 88 F7
lds Retail Park PO3 399 M7
e Social & Sports Club SO31 346 F6
on C of E Junior & nt School R SO31 345 L8
on Windmill Museum R SO31 345 L6
Primary School H/BSGR BH23 435 G5
lds Infant School M RG29 108 D6
ll D SP11 142 C4
ss Centre M SO14 13 J7
siness Centre K RG21 5 C8
siness Centre SP5 285 J1
siness Centre E RG7 40 C2
tts County Primary ool GU34 176 C6
Business Park LE PO7 351 M6
s Football Club Y SO51 290 E2
n Surgery SO40 339 L1
Roman Antiquity and eum E RG7 42 E7
e County Junior & Infant ool SO40 316 B6
e Industrial Estate SO40 316 D6

Calmore Sports Club *TOTT* SO40 315 M6
Calshot Castle *FAWY* SO45 393 M7
Calthorpe Park School *FLET* GU13 88 B8
Camberley County Infant School *CBLY* GU15 70 E3
Camberley Cricket Club *CBLY* GU15 71 G5
Camberley Health Centre *CBLY* GU15 70 E5
Camberley Heath Golf Club *CBLY* GU15 71 K4
Camberley Magistrates Court *CBLY* GU15 71 G2
Camberley Rugby Football Club *CBLY* GU15 70 F5
Camberley Town Football Club *CBLY* GU15 70 E5
Cambridge Military Hospital *ALDT* GU11 112 E5
Cameleon Theatre *WSHM* SO15 343 H2
Camelsdale County First School *HASM* GU27 228 C3
Campbell Surgery *SSEA* PO5 21 K5
Camp Road Industrial Estate *FARN* GU14 91 G8
Cams Hill School *FHAM/PORC* PO16 373 J8
Canada House Business Centre *NMIL/BTOS* BH25 438 A6
Candover Gallery *NARL* SO24 218 C2
Canford Heath First School *CFDH* BH17 445 K1
Canford Heath Middle School *CFDH* BH17 445 J1
Canford School *WIMB* BH21 404 E6
Cantell Secondary School *ROWN* SO16 318 F4
The Canute Surgery *ITCH* SO19 344 C5
The Carpet Gallery *WBNE* BH4 447 H5
Carter Community School *PLE* BH15 444 E6
Carvers Trading Estate *RGWD* BH24 382 E1
Carwarden House School *CBLY* GU15 71 K5
Castle County Primary School *FHAM/PORC* PO16 398 B1
Castle Court School *WIMB* BH21 428 F1
Castledown Comprehensive School *RAND* SP11 92 B7
Castle Hill Junior School *DEAN* RG23 104 A3
Castle Industrial Park *NWBY* RG14 25 M3
Castle Primary School *RAND* SP11 92 F6
Castle School *NWBY* RG14 25 J2
Catherine Corbett Clinic *HAV* PO9 16 F3
Catherington C of E Controlled Infant School *HORN* PO8 328 A7
The Cedar School *ROWN* SO16 317 K4
Cedars School *THLE* RG7 41 K1
Central Business Park *BMTH* BH1 23 M2
Central Estate *ALDT* GU11 7 H2
Central Trading Estate *SHAM* SO14 13 L3
Centurion Industrial Park *SHAM* SO14 344 A1
Century Galleries *HTWY* RG27 87 J2
Chalkridge School *KEMP* RG22 104 D7
Chamberlayne Park School *ITCH* SO19 344 E7
Chandlers Ford Infant School *CHFD* SO53 293 J1
Chantry Centre Shopping Precinct *AND* SP10 9 H5
Chapel House Gallery *OVTN* RG25 126 C7
Charles Dickens Junior & Infant School *PSEA* PO1 423 H2
Charles Kingsley School *HTWY* RG27 47 M8
Charlton Hill Surgery *AND* SP10 8 D2
Charlton Road Health Centre *AND* SP10 8 D2
Chase Community Hospital *LIND* GU35 201 J6
Chawton House Surgery *LYMN* SO41 440 C5
Chawtown Primary School *ALTN* GU34 198 C1
Chesil Theatre *WINC* SO23 11 J9
Cheswycks School *FRIM* GU16 91 L3
Chevron Business Park *FAWY* SO45 391 M2
Chineham Park Primary School *CHAM* RG24 5 J2
Christchurch Infant School *CHCH/BSGR* BH23 449 M1
Christchurch Junior School *CHCH/BSGR* BH23 449 L1
Christchurch Medical Centre *HAV* PO9 378 A5

Christchurch Ski & Leisure Centre *CHCH/BSGR* BH23 407 M5
Christ the King RC Primary School *BWD* BH11 431 L3
Churchers College *EPSF* GU31 275 M4
Churchers College Junior School *PSF* GU32 275 K5
Church Grange & Bramblys Grange Health Centre *BSTK* RG21 4 D9
Church Grange Lychpit Surgery *CHAM* RG24 105 L1
Churchill Yard Industrial Estate *WVILLE* PO7 352 C7
Church of England Primary School *AND* SP10 9 J6
Church of England School *THLE* RG7 29 G4
City Business Centre *WINC* SO23 11 G5
City Grove Trading Estate *ELGH* SO50 293 K4
City Industrial Park *WSHM* SO15 12 C3
City Museum *PSEA* PO1 20 E5
City Museum & Art Gallery *PSEA* PO1 20 E5
City Offices *WINC* SO23 11 H8
The City of Portsmouth Boys School *NEND* PO2 399 J4
The City of Portsmouth Girls School *PSEA* PO1 423 J2
City of Portsmouth Sports Club *NEND* PO2 399 H5
Civil Service Sports Ground *ENEY* PO4 423 K3
Civil Service Sports Ground *HSEA* PO3 399 L5
Clanfield Junior School *HORN* PO8 328 A1
Clanfield Surgery *HORN* PO8 328 B4
Clarendon County Junior & Infant School *NTID* SP9 114 E1
Clatford Primary School *RAND* SP11 142 F7
Clayfields Sports Centre *FAWY* SO45 367 H4
Clayton Barracks *ALDT* GU11 113 G4
The Clere Secondary School *KSCL* RG20 57 K1
Clewborough House Preparatory School *CBLY* GU15 71 K2
Cliddesden Primary School *OVTN* RG25 127 M3
Cliffdale Primary School *NEND* PO2 399 K6
Clift Surgery *TADY* RG26 63 K4
The Clinic *FNM* GU9 134 F6
Club House *OVTN* RG25 126 D6
The Club House *LISS* GU33 249 K4
Cluster Industrial Estate *HSEA* PO3 423 L3
The Coast Clinic *FAWY* SO45 392 F5
Colden Common Primary School *RWIN* SO21 266 E7
Coliseum Business Centre *CBLY* GU15 70 D5
College Art School *WINC* SO23 238 E2
College Park Infant School *NEND* PO2 399 K6
Collingwood Business Park *FHAM/STUB* PO14 396 F2
Collingwood College *CBLY* GU15 51 K8
Coltwood Business Centre *ALDT* GU11 7 G2
Commercial Business Centre *CHFD* SO53 293 H2
The Community Hospital *ALTN* GU34 176 C7
Comprehensive *YTLY* GU46 68 F4
Compton All Saints C of E Primary School *RWIN* SO21 238 C8
Compton & Upmarden C of E Primary School *RCCH* PO18 330 E6
The Connaught School *ASHV* GU12 136 B1
Continental Ferry Port *NEND* PO2 399 G8
Contour Gallery *LIPH* GU30 226 E4
Copnor Infant School *HSEA* PO3 399 L7
Copnor Junior School *NEND* PO2 399 K7
Copythorne First School *TOTT* SO40 315 G6
Cordwalles County Middle School *CBLY* GU15 51 J8
Corfe Hills School *WIMB* BH21 429 K2
Corhampton Golf Club *BPWT* SO32 298 D4

Cornerways Surgery *RGWD* BH24 381 J4
Corpus Christie School *BOSC* BH5 448 E3
Corpus Christi RC Primary School *NEND* PO2 399 H7
Cosham Health Centre *CHAM* PO6 399 K1
Cottage Grove Primary School *SSEA* PO5 21 H5
County and Magistrates Court *PSEA* PO1 21 G3
County Primary School *NTID* SP9 138 C1
Courthill First School *PSTN* BH14 446 C4
Court Lane Junior & Infant School *CHAM* PO6 399 L1
Court Moor School *FLET* GU13 110 E1
Cove County Infant School *FARN* GU14 90 B2
Cove County Junior School *FARN* GU14 90 B3
Cove County Secondary School *FARN* GU14 90 B3
Cove Cricket Club *FARN* GU14 90 B4
Cove Manor County Junior & Infant School *FARN* GU14 90 C2
Cowplain School *HORN* PO8 352 C6
Coxmoor Farm Light Industrial Estate *NFNM* GU10 110 A6
Cranbourne Secondary School *BSTK* RG21 104 E5
Craneswater Junior School *ENEY* PO4 21 M7
Crawley Ridge First School *CBLY* GU15 71 J2
Crescent Primary School *ELGH* SO50 293 M5
The Crestwood Community School *ELGH* SO50 293 L3
Cricklade College *AND* SP10 9 H4
Cricklade Theatre *AND* SP10 9 G4
Crofton School *FHAM/STUB* PO14 396 C6
Crondall CP School *NFNM* GU10 133 H2
Crookham C of E Infants School *FLET* GU13 110 E4
Crookham County Junior School *FLET* GU13 111 G4
The Crookhorn Community School *WVILLE* PO7 376 D4
Crow Arch Lane Industrial Estate *RGWD* BH24 382 E3
Crowthorne Business Centre *CWTH* RG45 49 M1
Crowthorne C of E Primary School *CWTH* RG45 49 L3
Cumberland Business Centre *SSEA* PO5 21 K2
Cumberland Infant School *ENEY* PO4 423 L5
Cupernham County Junior & Infants School *ROMY* SO51 263 G7
Curdridge Primary School *BPWT* SO32 322 C7
Curtis Museum *ALTN* GU34 176 E4
Cutlers Gallery *BMTH* BH1 22 F5
Daneshill East Industrial Estate *CHAM* RG24 5 L5
Daneshill Industrial Estate *CHAM* RG24 5 M4
Daneshill School *HTWY* RG27 65 J4
David Hart Business Centre *RSAL* SP5 256 D8
Dawkins Business Centre *PLE* BH15 444 C5
D Day Museum *SSEA* PO5 423 G7
Deacon Trading Estate *ELGH* SO50 294 B6
Dean Court (Bournemouth FC) *LTDN* BH7 448 E2
Deanery Campus *SHAM* SO14 13 J5
Deane's Almhouses *BSTK* RG21 105 G4
Dean Farm Estate *WHAM* PO17 372 E3
Dean Surgery *NARL* SO24 219 M4
Delta Business Park *FHAM/PORC* PO16 396 F1
Denmead Health Centre *WVILLE* PO7 351 J3
Denmead Infant School *WVILLE* PO7 351 L4
Denmead Junior School *WVILLE* PO7 351 K4
Derby Road Surgery *NEND* PO2 399 H7
Derry Down Health Clinic *RAND* SP11 97 M7
Devonshire Infant School *ENEY* PO4 21 M4
Devonshire Infant School *ENEY* PO4 423 K4

Devonshire Practice *ENEY* PO4 423 M5
Discover Bible School *WSHM* SO15 343 G2
Diva Gallery *ODIM* RG29 108 D5
Dockyard Apprentice Exhibition *PSEA* PO1 20 B1
Dogmersfield C of E Primary School *HTWY* RG27 109 M1
Donnington Castle *NWBY* RG14 25 H1
Dorset County Council *BMTH* BH1 23 H4
Dorset County Council *FERN* BH22 406 B3
Dorset County Council *WIMB* BH21 404 A3
Dorset County Council *WIMB* BH21 405 K1
Dorset Health Authority *FERN* BH22 406 B3
Dorset Healthcare NHS Trust *WEND* SO18 345 G1
Dorset Magistrates Court *BMTH* BH1 23 G4
Dorset Medical Centre *SHAM* SO14 13 G2
Douai School *THLE* RG7 29 G3
Dove House School *BSTK* RG21 4 F4
Down House *RSAL* SP5 257 J8
Downton C of E Primary School *RSAL* SP5 256 D8
Downton County Secondary School *RSAL* SP5 284 D1
Downton Industrial Estate *RSAL* SP5 256 D8
Dr Gregs Surgery *NTID* SP9 114 E2
Dr Hughes & Partners *RGWD* BH24 382 D1
Dr Munroe & Partners *TOTT* SO40 316 E8
Droxford Junior School *BPWT* SO32 298 F7
Droxford Primary School *BPWT* SO32 298 F7
Dunhurst School *PSF* GU32 275 K2
Dunston Park School *NTHA* RG18 27 G4
Dunwood Manor Golf Club *ROMY* SO51 261 J6
Durley Primary School *BPWT* SO32 321 M2
Durlston Court School *NMIL/BTOS* BH25 452 F1
Eagle House School *PSTN* BH14 445 M3
Eagle House School *SHST* GU47 49 K6
East Barn Surgery *CHAM* RG24 83 L8
East Berkshire Golf Club *CWTH* RG45 49 H3
East Dorset Area Health Authority *FERN* BH22 406 B3
Eastern Industrial Centre *CHAM* PO6 400 A2
Eastfield House Surgery *NWBY* RG14 2 E6
East Hants District Council *PSF* GU32 275 K5
Eastleigh Borough Council *ELGH* SO50 293 L5
Eastleigh College of Further Education *ELGH* SO50 293 M6
Eastleigh Football Club *ELGH* SO50 319 K1
Eastleigh Health Centre *ELGH* SO50 293 M5
Eastleigh Museum *ELGH* SO50 293 M6
Eastleigh Rugby Club *ELGH* SO50 294 B5
East Meon Controlled Primary School *PSF* GU32 273 J7
Eastney Health Centre *ENEY* PO4 423 L5
Eastney Swimming Baths *ENEY* PO4 424 A6
Easton Lane Business Park *WINC* SO23 11 L6
East Shore School *HSEA* PO3 423 M2
East Street Shopping Centre *SHAM* SO14 13 H4
Ebblake Industrial Estate *RGWD* BH24 357 H4
Ecossis Hospital Products *RAND* SP11 116 F6
Edgebarrow School *CWTH* RG45 49 L5
Edgebarrow Sports Centre *CWTH* RG45 49 M5
Edgeborough School *NFNM* GU10 158 F5
Eggars School *ALTN* GU34 177 G2
Eling County Infant School *TOTT* SO40 341 L2
Elliott Industrial Park *ASHV* GU12 113 H6
Elm House Surgery *NTID* SP9 114 D1
Elmhurst Business Park *GPORT* PO12 18 F3

Elmrise Junior & Infant School
BWD BH11 .... 431 K4
Elson County Infant School
GPORT PO12 .... 397 L8
Elson County Junior School
GPORT PO12 .... 397 L8
Elstree School
THLE RG7 .... 29 G4
Embley Park School
ROMY SO51 .... 289 K2
Emsworth Museum
EMRTH PO10 .... 378 D7
Emsworth Primary School
EMRTH PO10 .... 378 C7
Emsworth Surgery
EMRTH PO10 .... 378 D8
Enborne C of E School
KSCL RG20 .... 36 B2
Enborne Lodge (Sch)
NWBY RG14 .... 36 E3
English Gallery
HAV PO9 .... 354 A6
Enterprise Industrial Estate
ASHV GU12 .... 113 J1
Enterprise Industrial Estate
HORN PO8 .... 328 B8
The Epiphany School
MOOR/WNTN BH9 .... 432 F4
Eversley Cricket Club
HTWY RG27 .... 48 C8
Evingar Industrial Estate
WHCH RG28 .... 122 A2
Fairfax Industrial Estate
ASHV GU12 .... 113 H6
Fairfield Infant School
HAV PO9 .... 17 G4
Fairfields Primary School
BSTK RG21 .... 105 C4
Fairisle Junior & Infant School
ROWN SO16 .... 317 K4
Fairlands Montessori School
BPWT SO32 .... 348 C1
Fair Oak Junior & Infant School
ELGH SO50 .... 295 J7
Fairway Business Centre
HSEA PO3 .... 400 A5
Falkland CP School
NWBY RG14 .... 37 G2
Fareham Borough Council
FHAM PO15 .... 371 H3
Fareham Borough Council
FHAM/PORC PO16 .... 15 K5
Fareham Borough Council
FHAM/PORC PO16 .... 397 L1
Fareham College
FHAM/STUB PO14 .... 14 D6
The Fareham Gallery
FHAM/PORC PO16 .... 15 J6
Fareham Leisure Centre
FHAM/PORC PO16 .... 15 H4
Fareham Megabowl
FHAM/STUB PO14 .... 396 F3
Fareham Park C of E
Controlled Junior School
FHAM PO15 .... 372 A3
Fareham Park Infant School
FHAM PO15 .... 372 A3
Far Horizons Gallery
PSF GU32 .... 275 K5
Farleigh House Sch
OVTN RG25 .... 127 K6
Farleigh School
RAND SP11 .... 142 A8
Farley Hill Primary School
THLE RG7 .... 46 F3
Farleys All Saints Primary
School
RSAL SP5 .... 206 B8
Farmhouse Gallery
KSCL RG20 .... 56 E1
Farnborough Business Centre
FARN GU14 .... 90 C6
Farnborough College of
Technology
ASHV GU12 .... 7 H4
Farnborough College of
Technology
FARN GU14 .... 90 E8
Farnborough College of
Technology
FARN GU14 .... 90 F6
Farnborough Grange County
Junior School
FARN GU14 .... 70 C8
Farnborough Hill School
FARN GU14 .... 90 F3
Farnborough Recreation Centre
FARN GU14 .... 90 E5
Farnborough Rugby
Football Club
FARN GU14 .... 90 D2
Farnborough Town
Football Club
FARN GU14 .... 70 D8
Farnham Business Centre
FNM GU9 .... 134 F1
Farnham Business Centre
FNM GU9 .... 134 F5
Farnham Business Park
FNM GU9 .... 134 D7
Farnham Castle
FNM GU9 .... 134 F5
Farnham College
FNM GU9 .... 134 F7
Farnham Golf Club
NFNM GU10 .... 136 A6
Farnham Hospital
FNM GU9 .... 135 H5
Farnham Museum
FNM GU9 .... 134 E6
Farnham Retail Park
FNM GU9 .... 135 H5
Farringdon Industrial Centre
ALTN GU34 .... 198 B6
Farringdon Industrial Estate
ALTN GU34 .... 198 B6

Fawley Business Centre
FAWY SO45 .... 392 E5
Fawley County First School
FAWY SO45 .... 392 E5
Fenwick Hospital
LYND SO43 .... 363 J2
Ferndown First School
FERN BH22 .... 406 A3
Ferndown Medical Centre
FERN BH22 .... 406 B3
Ferndown Middle School
FERN BH22 .... 405 M3
Ferndown Sports Centre
FERN BH22 .... 405 M2
Ferndown Town Council
FERN BH22 .... 406 A2
Ferndown Upper School
FERN BH22 .... 405 M2
Fernhill Comprehensive School
FARN GU14 .... 70 C7
Fernhill Primary School
FARN GU14 .... 70 C7
Fernhurst Junior School
ENEY PO4 .... 423 K4
Fernside Business Park
WIMB BH21 .... 405 L1
Finchampstead C of E
Primary School
EWKG RG40 .... 48 B5
Finchampstead Sports Club
EWKG RG40 .... 48 B5
Finns Industrial Park
NFNM GU10 .... 110 A6
Fir Tree CP School
NTHA RG18 .... 26 B4
Fish Farm
RSAL SP5 .... 256 F5
Flanders Industrial Park
HEND SO30 .... 321 G8
Fleet Business Park
FLET GU13 .... 111 G5
Fleet Community Hospital
FLET GU13 .... 88 D6
Fleet Police Station
FLET GU13 .... 88 E8
Fleming Park Leisure Centre
ELGH SO50 .... 293 K5
Flying Bull Junior &
Infant School
NEND PO2 .... 399 H8
Focus 303 Business Centre
AND SP10 .... 119 J7
Folly Hill County Infant School
FNM GU9 .... 134 D2
Fordingbridge Junior &
Infant School
FBDG SP6 .... 309 L5
Fordingbridge Hospital
FBDG SP6 .... 309 L7
Forest Edge School
TOTT SO40 .... 341 J1
Forest End Surgery
WVILLE PO7 .... 376 B1
Forest Gate Surgery
TOTT SO40 .... 341 G1
Forestside Medical Practice
FAWY SO45 .... 367 J8
Forest Surgery
LIND GU35 .... 201 J5
Fort Brockhurst
LSOL/BMARY PO13 .... 397 K7
Fort Cumberland
ENEY PO4 .... 424 C5
Fort Hill School
DEAN RG23 .... 104 B2
Forthill Surgery
DEAN RG23 .... 104 B2
Forton Road Surgery
GPORT PO12 .... 421 M2
Fort Wallington
Industrial Estate
FHAM/PORC PO16 .... 373 H6
Fosters Business Park
HTWY RG27 .... 107 J1
Foundry Lane Middle &
Primary School
WSHM SO15 .... 318 A8
Foxhills County First School
TOTT SO40 .... 341 H4
France Hill School
CBLY GU15 .... 70 F6
Francis Bailey School
STHA RG19 .... 27 H5
Freeground Junior &
Infant School
HEND SO30 .... 346 B2
Freemantle Business Centre
WSHM SO15 .... 343 G3
Frensham C of E First School
NFNM GU10 .... 159 G8
Frensham Heights School
NFNM GU10 .... 158 D6
Frensham Pond Sailing Club
NFNM GU10 .... 180 F3
Friarsgate Medical Centre
WINC SO23 .... 11 H8
Frimley C of E First &
Middle School
FRIM GU16 .... 91 H1
Frimley Green Medical Centre
FRIM GU16 .... 91 J2
Frimley Park Hospital
FRIM GU16 .... 71 G6
Frobisher Industrial Centre
ROMY SO51 .... 262 C7
Frogmore Community School
BLKW GU17 .... 69 J3
Frogmore County Infant School
BLKW GU17 .... 69 L4
Frogmore Junior School
BLKW GU17 .... 69 L3
Front Lawn GM Junior School
HAV PO9 .... 377 K2
Front Lawn Infant School
HAV PO9 .... 377 K3
Froxfield Endowed
Controlled Infant School
PSF GU32 .... 246 D6

Fryern Junior & Infant School
CHFD SO53 .... 293 K2
The Fryern Surgery
CHFD SO53 .... 293 K1
The Futcher School
CHAM PO6 .... 376 A8
The Gallery
LYMN SO41 .... 412 F7
The Gallery
SHST GU47 .... 49 M8
The Gallery
SSEA PO5 .... 21 H7
Garlands County Junior School
THLE RG7 .... 31 K5
Garrison Theatre
NTID SP9 .... 114 C2
Gasholders
SHAM SO14 .... 13 K2
Gatcombe Park Infant School
NEND PO2 .... 399 K4
George & Dragon Surgery
EMRTH PO10 .... 378 F5
George Street School
Branch Clinic
PSEA PO1 .... 423 K1
Gillies Health Centre
KEMP RG22 .... 104 C8
Glenfield Infant School
WEND SO18 .... 344 D1
Glenhurst School
HAV PO9 .... 17 G4
Glenmoor School for Girls
NBNE BH10 .... 432 B7
Glenwood School
EMRTH PO10 .... 378 C7
Global Adventure Sailing Club
HAV PO9 .... 134 E6
Goldfield Gallery
BPWT SO32 .... 325 H7
Goldfield Gallery
PSEA PO1 .... 20 D5
Goldsmith Infant School
ENEY PO4 .... 21 M5
Golf Club Bungalow
ALTN GU34 .... 154 D7
Gomer County Junior &
Infant School
GPORT PO12 .... 421 J5
Goodway Sea School
GPORT PO12 .... 397 L8
Goodwyn Gallery
SPEA PO1 .... 21 L1
Gordleton Industrial Estate
LYMN SO41 .... 439 K3
Gorse Ride Junior School
EWKG RG40 .... 48 B1
Gosport Health Centre
GPORT PO12 .... 18 C4
Gosport Ice Rink
LSOL/BMARY PO13 .... 397 J7
Gosport Museum
GPORT PO12 .... 19 K3
Gosport War Memorial Hospital
GPORT PO12 .... 18 C4
Grange Comprehensive School
CHCH/BSGR BH23 .... 435 J2
Grange County Junior &
Infant School
LSOL/BMARY PO13 .... 421 G1
Grange Farm Business Park
BPWT SO32 .... 323 H8
The Grange Park
NARL SO24 .... 193 K3
Grateley Business Park
RAND SP11 .... 161 K1
Grateley Junior &
Infant School
RAND SP11 .... 139 M8
Gratton Surgery
RWIN SO21 .... 168 B4
Gravatom Business Centre
BPWT SO32 .... 297 G8
Grayshott Clinic
GSHT GU26 .... 203 L4
Grayshott Council Office
GSHT GU26 .... 204 A5
Grayshott Primary School
GSHT GU26 .... 203 L5
Grayshott Surgery
GSHT GU26 .... 204 A5
Grayswood C of E School
HASM GU27 .... 205 J6
Greatbridge Business Park
ROMY SO51 .... 262 C7
Greatham Primary School
LISS GU33 .... 224 E6
Greenacres School
FUFL SO22 .... 10 E3
Green Croft School
FARN GU14 .... 91 G2
Greenfields Junior School
HTWY RG27 .... 87 H3
Greenham Road Retail Park
NWBY RG14 .... 2 F6
The Gregg School
WEND SO18 .... 319 M5
Greggs School
PTSW SO17 .... 318 F7
Gresham Industrial Estate
ASHV GU12 .... 113 H6
Grey House Private School
HTWY RG27 .... 87 J2
Grey Welles Surgery
HAV PO9 .... 377 K4
Group Practice
NTID SP9 .... 114 E3
Group Surgery
ROWN SO16 .... 319 J4
Grovebell Industrial Estate
NFNM GU10 .... 158 C1
Grove County Primary School
FRIM GU16 .... 71 H6
Grove Medical Practice
WSHM SO15 .... 343 G1
Gudge Heath Surgery
FHAM PO15 .... 14 B2

Guildford Road
Industrial Estate
FNM GU9 .... 135 G5
Guillemont County
Junior School
FARN GU14 .... 89 M1
Gundrymoor Trading Estate
WIMB BH21 .... 380 D3
Gurdwara Sikh Temple
SHAM SO14 .... 343 L2
Hackwood Ho
OVTN RG25 .... 105 J3
Hadleigh Practice
WIMB BH21 .... 429 G4
Hale County First &
Middle School
FNM GU9 .... 134 E1
Hale Primary School
FBDG SP6 .... 285 H5
Hall of Aviation
SHAM SO14 .... 13 K6
Halterworth CP School
ROMY SO51 .... 291 H1
Hamble County Primary School
HLER SO31 .... 369 J4
Hamble County
Secondary School
HLER SO31 .... 369 J3
Hambledon Cricket Club
WVILLE PO7 .... 326 D3
Hambledon Infant School
WVILLE PO7 .... 326 C5
Hambrook Business Centre
RCCH PO18 .... 379 M4
Hammond County
Junior & Infant School
FHAM/STUB PO14 .... 396 A6
Hammond Industrial Estate
FHAM/STUB PO14 .... 396 B7
Hampreston Primary School
WIMB BH21 .... 405 J5
The Hampshire Clinic
CHAM RG24 .... 5 M5
Hampshire County Council
- Basing House
CHAM RG24 .... 105 M2
Hampshire County Council
ELGH SO50 .... 293 M3
Hampshire County Council
ELGH SO50 .... 294 A5
Hampshire County Council
FHAM/PORC PO16 .... 15 G5
Hampshire County Council
GPORT PO12 .... 19 G4
Hampshire County Council
HAV PO9 .... 17 G5
Hampshire County Council
LYMN SO41 .... 440 C4
Hampshire County Council
RGWD BH24 .... 382 E2
Hampshire County Council
TOTT SO40 .... 341 K4
Hampshire County Council
BSTK RG21 .... 4 F8
Hampshire County Council
- Chute House
BSTK RG21 .... 4 E7
Hampshire County Council
WINC SO23 .... 10 E7
Hampshire County
Cricket Club
WSHM SO15 .... 318 E8
Hampshire Gallery
BMTH BH1 .... 23 H4
Hampshire Golf Club
RAND SP11 .... 143 G5
Hamwic College
SHAM SO14 .... 13 H4
Hamworthy Community Clinic
PLE BH15 .... 444 D5
Hamworthy First School
PLE BH15 .... 444 E7
Hamworthy Middle School
PLE BH15 .... 444 E7
Hanway Group Practice
NEND PO2 .... 399 J7
Hanway Surgery
PSEA PO1 .... 423 H1
Harbridge School
RGWD BH24 .... 334 B8
Hardley School
FAWY SO45 .... 392 A3
Harefield Clinic
WEND SO18 .... 344 E1
Harefield Junior &
Infant School
WEND SO18 .... 320 A8
Harestock Infant School
FUFL SO22 .... 214 C5
Harriet Costello School
BSTK RG21 .... 5 H9
Harrison County Primary School
FHAM/PORC PO16 .... 15 K4
Harrow Way Community School
AND SP10 .... 8 B1
Hartley Park Farm
Business Centre
ALTN GU34 .... 199 J4
Hart Plain Infant School
HORN PO8 .... 352 C6
Hart Plain Junior School
WVILLE PO7 .... 352 C6
Hart Sports Centre
FLET GU13 .... 88 B8
Haselworth County
Primary School
GPORT PO12 .... 18 F5
Haslemere District Hospital
HASM GU27 .... 229 G1
Haslemere Health Centre
HASM GU27 .... 229 G1
Haslemere Museum
HASM GU27 .... 229 G1
Haslemere Preparatory School
HASM GU27 .... 229 G1
Hassocks Wood
Industrial Estate
CHAM RG24 .... 5 M3

Hatch Ride Primary School
CWTH RG45 ....
Hatch Warren County
Infant School
KEMP RG22 ....
Hatch Warren County
Junior School
KEMP RG22 ....
Hatch Warren Retail Park
KEMP RG22 ....
Hatch Warren Surgery
KEMP RG22 ....
Hatherden C of E
Primary School
RAND SP11 ....
Havant Business Centre
HAV PO9 ....
Havant College
HAV PO9 ....
Havant Leisure Centre
HAV PO9 ....
Havant Museum
HAV PO9 ....
Havant Retail Park
HAV PO9 ....
Havant Rugby Football Club
HAV PO9 ....
Havant Sports Club
HAV PO9 ....
Havant Town Football Club
HAV PO9 ....
Havant War Memorial Hospital
HAV PO9 ....
Hawley CP School
BLKW GU17 ....
Hawley Lane Industrial Estate
FARN GU14 ....
Hawley Place School
BLKW GU17 ....
The Hawthorns School
KEMP RG22 ....
Hayeswood County
First School
WIMB BH21 ....
Hayling Billy Business Centre
HISD PO11 ....
Hayling Island Health Centre
HISD PO11 ....
Haymarket Theatre
BSTK RG21 ....
Haymoor Middle School
CFDH BH17 ....
Hayward Business Centre
HAV PO9 ....
Hazel Wood First School
TOTT SO40 ....
Headlands Business Park
RGWD BH24 ....
Headley Park Country Club
LIND GU35 ....
Heath End County
Secondary School
FNM GU9 ....
Heatherlands First School
BKME/WDN BH12 ....
Heatherside Surgery
CBLY GU15 ....
Heathfield Infant &
Middle School
ITCH SO19 ....
Heathfield School
FHAM/STUB PO14 ....
Heath Hill Surgery
CWTH RG45 ....
Heathlands Primary School
BWD BH11 ....
Hedge End Business Centre
HEND SO30 ....
Hedge End Retail Park
HEND SO30 ....
Hedge End Town Council
HEND SO30 ....
Henbury View First School
WIMB BH21 ....
Henry Beaufort School
FUFL SO22 ....
Henry Cort Community
School
FHAM PO15 ....
The Heritage Centre &
Museum
TOTT SO40 ....
Herne County Junior School
EPSF GU31 ....
The Herne Farm
Leisure Centre
EPSF GU31 ....
The Herons Swimming and
Fitness Centre
HASM GU27 ....
Highbury College
CHAM PO6 ....
Highbury College
PSEA PO1 ....
Highbury College of
Technology
PSEA PO1 ....
Highbury Primary School
CHAM PO6 ....
Highclere Castle
KSCL RG20 ....
Highcliffe Castle Golf Club
CHCH/BSGR BH23 ....
Highcliffe County Junior School
CHCH/BSGR BH23 ....
Highcliffe GM
Comprehensive School
CHCH/BSGR BH23 ....
Highcliffe Medical Centre
CHCH/BSGR BH23 ....
Highcroft Industrial Estate
HORN PO8 ....
Highfield C of E (A)
Primary School
PTSW SO17 ....
Highfield School
LIPH GU30 ....

rove Industrial Park
EA PO3 399 M5
nds Medical Centre
AM PO15 14 A2
nds Medical Centre
AM PO15 372 A5
own Industrial Estate
WD BH24 382 F2
own Primary School
H SO19 345 J4
urne First School
OH BH17 429 L6
urne Middle School
OH BH17 429 L6
ouse School
MN SO41 414 B7
ne Surgery
HM SO15 343 J1
rk Clinic
AM PO15 14 D1
e County First School
D BH31 356 E1
e Industrial Estate
RN PO8 328 B8
ew First School
NE BH10 432 C5
ew Junior School
NE BH10 432 C5
gbury County Junior &
ant School
FD SO53 265 H7
ead Golf Club
HT GU26 203 L2
Temple
AM SO14 343 M2
ck Gallery
EA PO5 21 H7
oroners Court
TH BH1 23 H4
Victory
EA PO1 422 D2
ook County Junior &
ant School
OL/BMARY PO13 397 G5
ook Recreation Centre
OL/BMARY PO13 397 J7
ry County JMI School
WY SO45 392 A5
brook First School
WN SO16 318 C5
brook Middle School
WN SO16 318 C5
combe School
H GU30 250 F4
Lodge CP School
HV GU12 91 J8
Tree Surgery
NM GU10 158 D4
wood Health Centre
DY RG26 41 K7
ourne Theatre
TN GU34 177 H2
Cross Hospital
SM GU27 228 C1
Family RC Primary School
WN SO16 317 H6
Farm School
LE RG7 29 G5
field School
CH/BSGR BH23 435 G4
opathic Surgery
IIL/BTOS BH25 452 E1
wood Chiropractic
alth Centre
AM/PORC PO16 15 K4
County Junior School
WY RG27 86 A7
Infant School
WY RG27 86 A7
with Warsash
mary School
ER SO31 370 B8
op Kiln
M GU9 134 E7
e C of E GM
mary School
MN SO41 438 E5
e House School
MN SO41 453 M3
dean C of E Junior School
RN PO8 353 G1
dean Community School
RN PO8 352 F1
dean Football Club
RN PO8 352 F1
dean Health Centre
RN PO8 353 H1
dean Infant School
RN PO8 353 G1
s Hill Preparatory School
CL RG20 37 H5
ospital
LY GU15 50 D8
dmills Industrial Estate
TK RG21 104 D1
sdown School
TT SO40 341 K4
rt Junior School
VILLE PO7 376 D2
r Simmonds Gallery
LF BH13 447 G4
bourne Tarrant School
ND SP11 96 D2
urst Community School
DY RG26 41 G7
(C of E Controlled)
mary School
DG SP6 335 H3
CP School
WY SO45 367 L4
Medical Centre
WY SO45 367 K6
alker Odiham Gallery
IM RG29 108 D5
ld School
D SP10 119 J6
Cinema
TH BH1 22 F7

Industrial Estate
DEAN RG23 126 E4
Inhurst House School
STHA RG19 40 F7
Inkpen Primary School
HUNG RG17 34 A2
International Centre &
Leisure Pool
WCLF BH2 22 E8
Isambard Brunel Junior School
NEND PO2 399 J8
Isle of Wight
Car Ferry Terminal
PSEA PO1 20 C4
Itchen Abbas Cp School
RWIN SO21 216 E2
Itchen College
ITCH SO19 344 E3
Jellicoe Theatre
PSTN BH14 445 L3
Jenner House Surgery
FARN GU14 90 B4
The Jigsaw School
FRIM GU16 91 H5
J M L Trading Estate
WSHM SO15 12 C2
John Hanson
Community School
AND SP10 8 E6
John Hunt of
Everest Community School
CHAM RG24 83 H7
John Rankin County
Infants School
NWBY RG14 25 G8
John Rankin Junior
NWBY RG14 25 G8
Jubilee Business Centre
WVILLE PO7 352 C8
Jubilee Surgery
FHAM/STUB PO14 371 K8
Kanes Hill Primary School
ITCH SO19 345 J2
Keble Memorial
Primary School
RWIN SO21 265 G2
Kelseys Doctors Surgery
LISS GU33 248 E4
Kempshott County
Infant School
KEMP RG22 103 M8
Kempshott County
Junior School
KEMP RG22 103 M8
Kennet Secondary School
STHA RG19 27 H5
The Kerridge Industrial Estate
ALTN GU34 176 F4
Kimpton Primary School
RAND SP11 116 C7
King Alfred College
FUFL SO22 10 B8
King Alfreds College of Higher
Education
FUFL SO22 10 C9
King Edward VI School
WSHM SO15 318 D8
King Richard School
CHAM PO6 374 D8
The Kings Centre
ALDT GU11 6 F1
Kingsclere Health Centre
KSCL RG20 59 J6
Kingsclere Primary School
KSCL RG20 59 J6
Kings Copse Primary School
HEND SO30 346 A3
Kings Furlong Infant School
BSTK RG21 104 E5
Kings Furlong Junior School
BSTK RG21 104 E5
Kingsgrove Industrial Estate
FARN GU14 90 D5
Kings Junior School
SBNE BH6 449 L3
Kingsland Market
SHAM SO14 13 H3
Kingsleigh First School
NBNE BH10 432 A5
Kingsleigh Junior School
NBNE BH10 432 A5
Kingsleigh Secondary School
NBNE BH10 432 A5
Kingsley Business Park
LIND GU35 179 H7
Kings Park Primary School
BMTH BH1 448 D2
The Kings Primary School
HEND SO30 320 C5
Kings School
BSTK RG21 4 D9
Kings School
ELGH SO50 295 G7
Kings School
FUFL SO22 238 A2
Kings Somborne C of E School
STOK SO20 210 E6
Kings Theatre
SSEA PO5 21 K6
Kingstons Industrial Estate
ASHV GU12 113 H6
Kingsworthy Primary School
WINC SO23 215 H2
Kin Hon Clinic
SSEA PO5 20 F3
Kinson Primary School
BWD BH11 431 M3
Knights Enham Infants
Infant School
AND SP10 118 F5
Knights Enham Junior School
AND SP10 118 F5
Knightwood Primary School
NBAD SO52 292 E1
Lacey Lodge School
HSEA PO3 423 M2
Lake Road Health Centre
PSEA PO1 423 J2

Lakeside Business Park
SHST GU47 69 K1
Lakeside Country Club
FRIM GU16 91 K2
Lakeside County
Primary School
FRIM GU16 71 J7
Landford C of E
Primary School
RSAL SP5 287 J4
Langdown County
Infants School
FAWY SO45 367 M6
Langdown County
Junior School
FAWY SO45 367 M5
Langrish CP School
PSF GU32 274 F5
Langside School
BKME/WDN BH12 431 L8
Langstone Infant School
HSEA PO3 423 L2
Langstone Junior School
HSEA PO3 423 L1
Lankhills School
WINC SO23 10 F4
Lansdowne Clinic
BMTH BH1 23 H2
Lee on Solent Health Centre
LSOL/BMARY PO13 420 C2
Lee-on-the-solent
Infant School
LSOL/BMARY PO13 420 D3
Lee-on-the-solent
Junior School
LSOL/BMARY PO13 420 D3
Leesland C of E Infant School
GPORT PO12 18 E3
Leesland C of E Junior School
GPORT PO12 18 E3
Leigh House Hospital
CHFD SO53 265 G8
Leisure Centre
AND SP10 9 H4
Leisure Centre
HAV PO9 16 F2
Leisure Centre
SHAM SO14 343 L2
Lido Sports Club
WINC SO23 11 G5
The Lilley Clinic
HUNG RG17 32 E2
Lilliput First School
PSTN BH14 446 B8
Limington House School
KEMP RG22 104 C5
Liner Industrial Estate
WSHM SO15 343 G2
Linsford Business Park
FRIM GU16 91 J5
Linwood School
MOOR/WNTN BH9 447 M1
Liphook County Infant School
LIPH GU30 226 E4
Liphook Golf Club
LIPH GU30 226 D8
Liphook Junior School
LIPH GU30 226 D4
Liss Business Centre
LISS GU33 248 D3
Liss County Infant &
Junior School
LISS GU33 248 E5
Littledown Leisure Centre
LTDN BH7 433 L8
Littlefield School
LIPH GU30 227 G6
Little Green School
RCCH PO18 330 D4
Lockerley C of E (a)
Primary School
ROMY SO51 232 F7
Locksheath County
Infants & Primary School
HLER SO31 370 E7
Locks Road Surgery
HLER SO31 370 E6
Lockswood Surgery
HLER SO31 370 E5
Loddon Business Centre
CHAM RG24 5 M4
London Road School
ODIM RG29 108 D5
Longbridge Industrial Park
SHAM SO14 13 K6
Longdown Estates
TOTT SO40 341 J8
Longfellow Parade Clinic
CHAM RG24 5 H1
Longfleet C of E VC
Combined School
PLE BH15 445 K4
Longparish School
RAND SP11 145 G4
Longspee School
CFDH BH17 445 J1
Longsutton Primary School
ODIM RG29 131 J5
Lord Mayor Treloar
College Lower School
ALTN GU34 156 A6
Lord Mayor Treloar
College Upper School
ALTN GU34 177 G1
Lordshill Health Centre
ROWN SO16 317 L4
Lord Wandsworth College
ODIM RG29 131 K6
Lorraine County First School
CBLY GU15 51 K8
L S U College of
Higher Education
WSHM SO15 343 K1
Lucia Foster Welch College
SHAM SO14 13 J6
Ludgershall Health Centre
RAND SP11 92 E6

Ludgershall Sports Club
RAND SP11 92 D6
Ludlow Infant School
ITCH SO19 344 C5
Ludlow Middle School
ITCH SO19 344 C4
Lulworth Business Centre
TOTT SO40 316 D6
Lydlynch County First School
TOTT SO40 341 J1
Lymington Community
Hospitals
LYMN SO41 440 C4
Lymington County Junior &
Infant School
LYMN SO41 440 B4
Lymington Farm
Industrial Estate
ALTN GU34 196 F5
Lymington Hospital
LYMN SO41 440 B4
Lymington Recreation Centre
LYMN SO41 440 A5
Lyndhurst Infant School
LYND SO43 363 K3
Lyndhurst Junior School
NEND PO2 399 K7
Lyndhurst School
CBLY GU15 70 E3
Lyndhurst Surgery
LYND SO43 363 K3
Lytchett Minster
Upper School
UPTN BH16 428 C8
Magpies Sports Club
WIMB BH21 356 D8
Mainline Business Centre
LISS GU33 248 E4
The Malls/the Walks
Shopping Centre
BSTK RG21 4 F7
Malmesbury Park School
CHAR BH8 23 J1
Malmesbury Park School
CHAR BH8 448 A2
Malvern Business Centre
ROWN SO16 318 C6
Manor Farm Business Centre
NFNM GU10 136 C3
Manorfield Infant School
KEMP RG22 127 K1
Manor Infant School
FAWY SO45 392 A3
Manor Infant School
PSEA PO1 423 J1
Manor Road Surgery
VWD BH31 356 C2
Mansbridge Primary School
WEND SO18 319 K4
The Manse Health Centre
AND SP10 9 J5
Mansel Infant & Junior Schools
ROWN SO16 317 J6
Mansfield Business Park
ALTN GU34 196 F5
Maple Business Park
WIMB BH21 405 K1
Maple Ridge School
BSTK RG21 4 E4
Marchwood C of E
Infant School
TOTT SO40 342 C8
Marchwood Junior School
TOTT SO40 342 D7
Marchwood Priory Hospital
TOTT SO40 366 E1
Maritime Museum
BROC SO42 417 H4
Mark Way School
AND SP10 9 M4
Marlands Shopping Centre
SHAM SO14 12 F3
Marlborough County
Infant School
ALDT GU11 112 F1
Marnel Infant & Junior Schools
CHAM RG24 83 H7
Marsh Farm Business Centre
NFNM GU10 110 C7
The Martin Kemp Welch School
BKME/WDN BH12 431 H8
Marwell Zoological Park
RWIN SO21 267 L8
Marycourt Co-educational
School
GPORT PO12 18 D9
Mary Rose Exhibition
PSEA PO1 20 B1
Mary Rose Ship Hall
PSEA PO1 422 D2
Mason Manor Primary School
ROWN SO16 317 L8
Mayfield Avenue
Industrial Park
RAND SP11 116 F6
Mayfield County
Junior & Infant School
FARN GU14 90 D2
Mayfield Gallery
MOOR/WNTN BH9 432 D6
Mayfield School
ALTN GU34 177 G3
Mayflower Theatre
WSHM SO15 12 D1
Mayhill County Junior School
ODIM RG29 108 D6
May's Bounty
BSTK RG21 105 G5
Mayville High School
SSEA PO5 21 K8
Meadowlands Infant School
HORN PO8 352 C3
Meadowlands Junior School
HORN PO8 352 C3
The Meadow School
LIND GU35 201 M4

Mecca Leisure Bingo and
Social Club
AND SP10 9 G6
Medina Primary School
CHAM PO6 399 J1
Medstead School
ALTN GU34 196 E2
Mengham Infant School
HISD PO11 425 L4
Mengham Junior School
HISD PO11 425 L4
Meoncross School
FHAM/STUB PO14 396 B4
Meon Infant School
ENEY PO4 423 M4
Meon Junior School
ENEY PO4 423 M3
Meonstoke School
BPWT SO32 299 H4
Meon Valley Golf &
Country Club
BPWT SO32 323 J8
Meon Valley Police Station
BPWT SO32 297 J8
Merdon Junior School
CHFD SO53 293 J1
Meredith Infant School
NEND PO2 399 J8
Meridian TV Studios
SHAM SO14 344 A2
Merton County Junior School
CHAM RG24 4 C1
Micheldever Primary School
RWIN SO21 169 M5
Middle Hill Health Clinic
ALDT GU11 112 D5
Middle Park Medical Centre
HAV PO9 377 G4
Milestone Transport Museum
KEMP RG22 104 B3
Milford C of E School
LYMN SO41 454 D2
Millbrook Clinic
ROWN SO16 317 K8
Millbrook Community School
ROWN SO16 317 K5
Millbrook Secondary School
ROWN SO16 317 K5
Millbrook Trading Estate
WSHM SO15 342 C1
Mill Chase County
Secondary School
LIND GU35 201 L5
Millers Dale Surgery
CHFD SO53 265 G8
Millhouse Business Centre
ITCH SO19 344 B4
Millstream Trading Estate
RGWD BH24 382 D3
Milton Park Infant School
ENEY PO4 423 M4
Milton Park Junior School
ENEY PO4 423 M4
M L S College
BMTH BH1 22 E5
Monks Brook Industrial Park
CHFD SO53 293 G3
Moordown C of E
Primary School
MOOR/WNTN BH9 432 D7
Moorgreen Hospital
HEND SO30 320 E6
Moorings Way Infant School
ENEY PO4 424 A2
Moorlands College
CHCH/BSGR BH23 434 F2
Moorlands Infant School
WEND SO18 319 M7
Moor Park College
NFNM GU10 135 K7
More House School
NFNM GU10 158 F6
Morelands Primary School
WVILLE PO7 376 C6
Moreton House School
PSF GU32 275 K5
Morgans Vale &
Woodfalls Primary School
RSAL SP5 285 J1
Morland Surgery
TADY RG26 61 L1
Mortimers Farm
Industrial Estate
ROMY SO51 315 K2
Mortimer Surgery
THLE RG7 43 J2
Mottisfont Abbey
ROMY SO51 233 L5
Mottisfont Club House
ROMY SO51 233 K6
Mountbatten Business Centre
WSHM SO15 12 B1
Mountbatten Secondary School
ROMY SO51 291 H2
The Mount Hospital
ELGH SO50 294 C3
Mount Pleasant
Industrial Estate
SHAM SO14 343 M1
Mount Pleasant Junior School
SHAM SO14 343 M1
Moyles Court School
RGWD BH24 359 G2
Mudeford County
Primary School
CHCH/BSGR BH23 450 D2
Mudeford Junior School
CHCH/BSGR BH23 450 E2
Murrell Green Business Park
HTWY RG27 86 D6
Muscliff C Primary School
MOOR/WNTN BH9 433 G5
Museum of Army Flying
STOK SO20 162 F5
Music Gallery
MOOR/WNTN BH9 432 F8
Mylen Business Centre
AND SP10 8 D3

Mytchett County First School
FRIM GU16 .... 91 J4
National Motor Museum
BROC SO42 .... 390 D6
National Museum of Artillery
WHAM PO17 .... 373 M5
The Natural Health Centre
NWBY RG14 .... 37 G2
Natural Sciences Museum
ENEY PO4 .... 423 K7
Nelson Industrial Park
HEND SO30 .... 321 G7
Nethercliffe School
FUFL SO22 .... 10 D5
Netley Abbey Infant School
HLER SO31 .... 368 F1
Netley Court School
HLER SO31 .... 368 F3
Netley Marsh C of E
    Controlled Infant School
TOTT SO40 .... 340 E1
Neville Lovett Community
    School
FHAM/STUB PO14 .... 14 E8
New Ashgate Gallery
FNM GU9 .... 134 E6
Newbridge Junior School
NEND PO2 .... 423 K1
Newbury Business Park
NWBY RG14 .... 3 J2
Newbury College of Further
    Education
NWBY RG14 .... 2 C1
Newbury District Council
NWBY RG14 .... 3 G6
Newbury District Council
WHCH RG28 .... 122 B2
Newbury District Hospital
NWBY RG14 .... 2 D7
Newbury District Museum &
    Tourist Information Centre
NWBY RG14 .... 2 F4
Newbury Retail Park
NWBY RG14 .... 37 L1
Newbury Rugby
    Football Club Ltd
NWBY RG14 .... 37 J2
Newbury Town Council
NWBY RG14 .... 2 E4
The New Chineham Surgery
CHAM RG24 .... 83 L6
New Forest District Council
NMIL/BTOS BH25 .... 437 L6
New Forest District Council
RGWD BH24 .... 382 D2
New Forest Golf Club
LYND SO43 .... 363 M2
New Forest Museum &
    Visitors Centre
LYND SO43 .... 363 L3
New Greenham Park
    Leisure Centre
STHA RG19 .... 38 D4
Newlands CP School
YTLY GU46 .... 68 F3
Newlands Infant &
    Middle School
ROWN SO16 .... 317 K7
New Milton Junior School
NMIL/BTOS BH25 .... 437 L7
New Milton Recreation Centre
NMIL/BTOS BH25 .... 437 K6
New Milton Sports Club
NMIL/BTOS BH25 .... 438 A5
New Milton Town Council
NMIL/BTOS BH25 .... 437 L6
Newport County
    Junior & Infant School
ASHV GU12 .... 7 L4
New Scotland Hill CP School
SHST GU47 .... 49 K6
New Street Football Club
RAND SP11 .... 118 C3
New Street Medical Centre
AND SP10 .... 9 K3
New Theatre Royal
PSEA PO1 .... 20 F2
The Newton Health Clinic
SHAM SO14 .... 343 L2
Newton Toney School
AMSY SP4 .... 160 A3
Newtown Soberton County
    Primary School
WHAM PO17 .... 349 M2
Newtown Surgery
LIPH GU30 .... 226 E6
Nightingale County Junior &
    Infant School
ELGH SO50 .... 293 J7
Nightingale Surgery
ROMY SO51 .... 262 F8
Nomansland & Hamptworth
    C of E Primary School
RSAL SP5 .... 287 G8
Norman Court School
RSAL SP5 .... 207 K6
The Norman Gate School
    (acorns)
AND SP10 .... 9 M3
Northam Business Centre
SHAM SO14 .... 344 A2
Northam Primary School
SHAM SO14 .... 13 L1
North Baddesley County Infants
    School
NBAD SO52 .... 292 A4
North Baddesley Junior School
NBAD SO52 .... 292 A4
Northbrook Industrial Estate
ROWN SO16 .... 318 B6
Northcroft Surgery
NWBY RG14 .... 2 D4
Northern County Junior &
    Infant School
FHAM/PORC PO16 .... 374 A7
Northern Parade Clinic
NEND PO2 .... 399 J4

Northern Parade Infant
    School
NEND PO2 .... 399 J5
Northern Parade Junior
    School
NEND PO2 .... 399 J5
North Farnborough County
    Infant School
FARN GU14 .... 91 G3
North Hampshire Hospital
CHAM RG24 .... 82 D8
North Hants Golf Club
FARN GU14 .... 88 F4
North Lane Practice
ASHV GU12 .... 113 H7
Northtown Trading Estate
ASHV GU12 .... 113 H7
Northview Gallery
HLER SO31 .... 346 A8
North Waltham Business
    Centre
OVTN RG25 .... 126 A6
North Waltham School
OVTN RG25 .... 125 K7
Norwood CP School
ELGH SO50 .... 293 M5
Nova Business Park
NMIL/BTOS BH25 .... 437 J8
Nuffield Theatre
PTSW SO17 .... 318 F5
Nursling C of E Primary School
ROWN SO16 .... 317 J3
Nursling Industrial Estate
ROWN SO16 .... 317 G5
Oakdale South Road
    Middle School
PLE BH15 .... 445 J3
Oak Farm Community School
FARN GU14 .... 90 D2
Oakfield Primary School
TOTT SO40 .... 316 D8
Oaklands Community School
ROWN SO16 .... 317 J3
Oaklands County Junior &
    Infant School
CWTH RG45 .... 49 K2
Oaklands RC School
WVILLE PO7 .... 376 D3
Oakley C of E Junior School
DEAN RG23 .... 102 F7
Oakley County Infant School
DEAN RG23 .... 102 F7
Oak Lodge School
FAWY SO45 .... 367 G5
Oakmead College of
    Technology
BWD BH11 .... 431 K3
Oak Park Golf Club
NFNM GU10 .... 133 K2
Oakridge County Junior School
BSTK RG21 .... 4 C3
Oakwood First School
ROWN SO16 .... 318 A3
Oakwood Junior School
ROWN SO16 .... 318 A3
Oakwood School
HTWY RG27 .... 87 J3
Oatlands House Health Clinic
ROWN SO16 .... 318 B6
Oceanographic Centre
SHAM SO14 .... 13 K8
Odeon Cinema
BMTH BH1 .... 22 F6
Odeon Cinema
NEND PO2 .... 399 H7
Odeon Cinema
WSHM SO15 .... 12 D4
Odiham Castle
ODIM RG29 .... 108 A4
Odiham Cottage Hospital
ODIM RG29 .... 108 D6
The Odiham Health Centre
ODIM RG29 .... 108 C5
Oil Refinery
FAWY SO45 .... 392 D4
O Jays Industrial Park
HSEA PO3 .... 399 L6
Old Anchor Inn Surgery
ELGH SO50 .... 294 B5
Old Basing Surgery
CHAM RG24 .... 106 A3
Old Dames School
FBDG SP6 .... 285 H5
Oldfield Gallery
SSEA PO5 .... 21 H5
The Old Fire Station Surgery
ITCH SO19 .... 344 C5
Old Hambledonians
    Cricket Club
HORN PO8 ....*.... 301 K6
Old Thorns Golf &
    Country Club
LIPH GU30 .... 226 A6
Olivers Battery Primary School
FUFL SO22 .... 238 B5
The Omni Business Centre
ALTN GU34 .... 177 G5
On Line Gallery
WSHM SO15 .... 343 K4
Orchard County Infant &
    Junior School
FAWY SO45 .... 367 J6
Orchard Lea Junior &
    Infant Schools
FHAM PO15 .... 372 C4
Oriel Business Park
ALTN GU34 .... 177 G5
Orion Business Centre
WEND SO18 .... 319 K3
The Osborn Clinic
FHAM/PORC PO16 .... 15 L5
Osborne Practice Surgery
SSEA PO5 .... 21 G7
Osborn Way Industrial Estate
HTWY RG27 .... 85 M8
Otterbourne Primary School
RWIN SO21 .... 266 A6

Our Lady & St Joseph RC
    Primary School
LYMN SO41 .... 440 D4
Our Ladys Preparatory
    School
CWTH RG45 .... 49 K3
Overbridge Surgery
KEMP RG22 .... 104 D4
Overton C of E Primary
    School
OVTN RG25 .... 100 E7
Overton Gallery
OVTN RG25 .... 100 F8
Overton Surgery
OVTN RG25 .... 101 G8
Owlsmoor Primary School
SHST GU47 .... 50 B7
Owsleby CP School
RWIN SO21 .... 267 M4
Padnell Infant School
HORN PO8 .... 352 E6
Padnell Junior School
HORN PO8 .... 352 F5
Padworth College
THLE RG7 .... 30 B7
Palace House
BROC SO42 .... 390 C7
Palmerston Business Park
FHAM/STUB PO14 .... 396 E1
Park Community School
HAV PO9 .... 377 G3
Park Gate Business Centre
HLER SO31 .... 370 F2
Park Gate Junior School
HLER SO31 .... 370 F3
Park House Primary School
HAV PO9 .... 377 G3
Park House School
NWBY RG14 .... 37 H2
Parklands Business Park
WVILLE PO7 .... 351 K5
Park Lane Medical Centre
HAV PO9 .... 377 H5
Park Primary School
ALDT GU11 .... 7 J7
Parkstone Grammar School
    for Girls
CFDH BH17 .... 429 M8
Park View Infant School
KEMP RG22 .... 104 B6
Park View Junior School
KEMP RG22 .... 104 B5
Parkway Retail Park
BMTH BH1 .... 23 J2
Parley First School
FERN BH22 .... 406 B5
Parsons Down Infant School
STHA RG19 .... 26 E5
Parsons Down Junior School
STHA RG19 .... 26 D5
The Pascoe Practice
PSEA PO1 .... 20 E4
Passfield Mill Business Park
LIPH GU30 .... 202 A7
Paulsgrove Industrial Centre
CHAM PO6 .... 374 F8
Paulsgrove Primary School
CHAM PO6 .... 374 F8
Pavilion
BMTH BH1 .... 23 G3
Pavilion Theatre
BMTH BH1 .... 22 E6
Pavillion Theatre
BMTH BH1 .... 22 F7
Peacock Trading Estate
ELGH SO50 .... 293 L3
Peel Common County Junior &
    Infant School
LSOL/BMARY PO13 .... 396 E6
Pegham Industrial Park
FHAM PO15 .... 371 M2
Pendulum Gallery
ALTN GU34 .... 199 K8
Penhale Infant School
PSEA PO1 .... 21 M1
Pennington County Junior &
    Infant School
LYMN SO41 .... 440 A5
Perins County Secondary
    School
NARL SO24 .... 218 B3
Peter Dyer Gallery
SSEA PO5 .... 21 H7
Petersfield Business Park
PSF GU32 .... 275 J5
Petersfield Community
    Hospital
PSF GU32 .... 275 K5
Petersfield County Infant
    School
EPSF GU31 .... 275 L5
Petersfield Golf Club
PSF GU32 .... 248 B8
Petersfield Rugby
    Football Club
EPSF GU31 .... 276 C4
Petersfield School
PSF GU32 .... 275 K6
Petersfield Swimming Pool
EPSF GU31 .... 275 L5
Petersfield Town Council
EPSF GU31 .... 275 M5
Petersfield Town
    Football Club
EPSF GU31 .... 275 M4
Petersgate Infant School
HORN PO8 .... 328 B4
Peter Symonds College
FUFL SO22 .... 10 E4
The Pheasant Hotel
AMSY SP4 .... 182 D6
Phoenix Industrial Park
ELGH SO50 .... 294 B6
Pierreponte School
NFNM GU10 .... 159 H7
Pier Theatre
BMTH BH1 .... 22 F8

Pilgrims School
WINC SO23 .... 11 H9
Pilgrims Way Infants School
FNM GU9 .... 134 E8
Pinehill Surgery
LIND GU35 .... 201 J6
Pineridge County First School
CBLY GU15 .... 51 K7
Pinewood Infants School
FARN GU14 .... 90 A1
Pipers Industrial Estate
STHA RG19 .... 27 J7
Pipers Wood Industrial Park
WVILLE PO7 .... 352 A8
Pitmore School
CHFD SO53 .... 265 L8
Plaza Theatre
ROMY SO51 .... 290 E1
Pokesdown Primary School
BOSC BH5 .... 449 G3
The Polygon School
WSHM SO15 .... 343 J2
Poole Grammar School
CFDH BH17 .... 430 B6
Poole Road Medical Centre
WBNE BH4 .... 22 A6
Poole Technical High School
PLE BH15 .... 445 H4
Portcastrian R F C
SBNE BH6 .... 449 K2
Portchester Castle
FHAM/PORC PO16 .... 398 C3
Portchester Community
    School
FHAM/PORC PO16 .... 398 A1
Portchester Health Centre
FHAM/PORC PO16 .... 374 A8
Portchester School
LTDN BH7 .... 448 F1
Portesbery School
CBLY GU15 .... 71 G2
Portsdown Group Practice
WVILLE PO7 .... 376 C5
Portsmouth City Council
CHAM PO6 .... 374 F7
Portsmouth City Council
CHAM PO6 .... 375 K8
Portsmouth City Council
CHAM PO6 .... 399 J1
Portsmouth City Council
HAV PO9 .... 377 K4
Portsmouth City Council
PSEA PO1 .... 20 D5
Portsmouth City Council
PSEA PO1 .... 423 J1
Portsmouth City Council
SSEA PO5 .... 21 G6
Portsmouth City Council
SSEA PO5 .... 21 H2
Portsmouth City Council
SSEA PO5 .... 21 J5
Portsmouth County Court
PSEA PO1 .... 21 G2
Portsmouth Crown Court
PSEA PO1 .... 21 G3
Portsmouth Grammar School
PSEA PO1 .... 20 E4
Portsmouth High School
SSEA PO5 .... 20 F6
Portsmouth Natural
    Health Centre
SSEA PO5 .... 20 F4
Portsmouth Rugby
    Football Club
HSEA PO3 .... 399 L4
Portsmouth Sixth
    Form College
HSEA PO3 .... 424 A1
Portswood Primary School
PTSW SO17 .... 319 H6
Portswood Road Surgery
PTSW SO17 .... 319 G7
Portway County Infants School
AND SP10 .... 8 A4
Portway Junior School
AND SP10 .... 118 B8
Potley Hill County
    Primary School
BLKW GU17 .... 69 K3
Potters Gate Primary School
FNM GU9 .... 134 D6
Poulner Junior & Infant School
RGWD BH24 .... 359 G6
The Practice Doctors Surgery
FHAM/PORC PO16 .... 15 H5
Premier Business Park
FHAM/STUB PO14 .... 14 C7
Preston Candover
    Primary School
OVTN RG25 .... 151 G8
Preston Ho
OVTN RG25 .... 151 G7
Priestlands County
    Secondary School
LYMN SO41 .... 440 A5
Priets House Museum
WIMB BH21 .... 404 A4
Princes Hall
ALDT GU11 .... 6 E1
Princes Mead School
RWIN SO21 .... 215 K2
Princess Anne Hospital
ROWN SO16 .... 318 A5
Prior Heath School
CBLY GU15 .... 71 K3
Priory C of E VA
    Primary School
CHCH/BSGR BH23 .... 450 A2
The Priory Primary School
TADY RG26 .... 62 A7
Priory School
SSEA PO5 .... 21 L3
Private Medical Centre
BMTH BH1 .... 23 G5
Prospect Business Centre
NARL SO24 .... 218 B4
Purbrook Cricket Club
WVILLE PO7 .... 375 M4

Purbrook Junior &
    Infant School
WVILLE PO7 .... 3?
Purbrook Park School
WVILLE PO7 .... 3?
Puttenham C of E School
RGUW GU3 .... 13?
Queen Alexandra Hospital
CHAM PO6 .... 3?
Queen Marys College
BSTK RG21 .... 1?
Queens Enclosure
    Primary School
WVILLE PO7 .... 35?
Queens Road Surgery
NEND PO2 .... 3?
Raceview Business Centre
NWBY RG14 .... 3?
Rachel Madocks School
HORN PO8 .... 3?
Rake C of E Controlled
    First School
LISS GU33 .... 2?
Ranvilles Junior &
    Infant School
FHAM/STUB PO14 .... 3?
Red Barn County
    Primary School
FHAM/PORC PO16 .... 3?
Redbridge Community School
ROWN SO16 .... 3?
Redbridge Primary School
ROWN SO16 .... 3?
Redfields Industrial Estate
FLET GU13 .... 1?
Redfields Industrial Park
FLET GU13 .... 1?
Red Funnel Ferry Terminal
SHAM SO14 .... 3?
Red Gallery
SSEA PO5 .... 3?
Red House Museum & Gardens
CHCH/BSGR BH23 .... 4?
Redlands County
    Primary School
FHAM/PORC PO16 .... 3?
Red Lodge School
ROWN SO16 .... 3?
Redlynch C of E
    Primary School
RSAL SP5 .... 3?
Redwood Park School
CHAM PO6 .... 3?
Regents Park Girls School
ROWN SO16 .... 3?
Regents Park Surgery
WSHM SO15 .... 3?
Regional Film Theatre
SHAM SO14 .... 3?
Retail Park
NWBY RG14 .... 3?
Rex Industrial Estate
CHFD SO53 .... 2?
Richard Aldworth
    Community School
KEMP RG22 .... 3?
Richard Martin
    Gallery & Bookshop
GPORT PO12 .... 2?
Richmond Surgery
FLET GU13 .... 1?
Riders Junior & Infant School
HAV PO9 .... 3?
Ridgemede Junior School
BPWT SO32 .... 2?
Ridgeway House
    Special School
ITCH SO19 .... 2?
Ridgeway School
FNM GU9 .... 3?
Ringwood C of E
    Infant School
RGWD BH24 .... 3?
Ringwood County
    Junior School
RGWD BH24 .... 3?
Ringwood Recreation Centre
RGWD BH24 .... 3?
Ringwood School
RGWD BH24 .... 3?
Ringwood Town Council
RGWD BH24 .... 3?
Ringwood Trading Estate
RGWD BH24 .... 3?
Ringwood Waldorf School
RGWD BH24 .... 3?
Riverpark Industrial Estate
NWBY RG14 .... 3?
River Park Leisure Centre
WINC SO23 .... 3?
Riverside Business Park
FNM GU9 .... 3?
Riverside Business Park
LYMN SO41 .... 3?
Riverside Close Surgery
LISS GU33 .... 2?
Riverside Park
    Industrial Estate
FNM GU9 .... 3?
Riverside School
WVILLE PO7 .... 3?
Riverwey Industrial Park
ALTN GU34 .... 3?
Robert King Gallery
LYMN SO41 .... 4?
Robert Mays School
ODIM RG29 .... 3?
Rogate C of E
    Controlled School
EPSF GU31 .... 3?
Romans Business Park
FNM GU9 .... 3?
Roman Way Primary School
AND SP10 .... 3?
Romsey Abbey C of E
    Primary School
ROMY SO51 .... 3?

y County Junior School Y SO51 262 F8
y Cricket Club Y SO51 290 E2
y Hospital Y SO51 290 F1
y Industrial Estate Y SO51 262 D7
y Infant School Y SO51 290 E1
y Rugby Football Club Y SO51 290 E2
msey School Y SO51 262 D8
y Sports Centre Y SO51 290 E2
sbury Park School M PO17 349 H4
C of E Primary School L SO24 220 B3
dge C of E First School M GU10 158 A5
ans House strial Estate N SO16 317 K2
r County Infant School /BMARY PO13 397 H7
r County Junior School /BMARY PO13 397 H7
r Health Centre /BMARY PO13 397 G8
r Swimming Centre /BMARY PO13 421 G2
rmy Medical Corps GU11 113 G4
ampshire nty Hospital SO22 10 B8
ampshire ment Museum C SO23 10 F8
ospital Haslar RT PO12 19 K7
arines Museum Y PO4 423 M6
aval Museum PO1 20 A1
avy Submarine Museum ces RT PO12 19 L6
yal School M GU27 204 D6
outh Hants Hospital M SO14 343 L2
Winchester Golf Club SO22 238 A1
all County hary School K RG21 105 J5
mbe County t School B BH21 429 H2
gton Business Park SO40 341 J3
oor Borough Council V GU14 90 E5
Cotes Art Gallery & eum H BH1 23 G7
Hicks & Temple Y SO51 290 D1
ns C of E Primary School PO9 377 L5
elms C of E bined School E/WDN BH12 446 F2
ews Surgery H SO50 293 M6
es Catholic ary School P RG22 104 C5
es School /BMARY PO13 420 C1
s Hospital BH13 457 K2
onys RC Primary School M/STUB PO14 371 H6
e Museum N SO41 440 C4
holomews C of E ool M GU27 204 F8
holomews nt School) Y RG14 2 B7
holomews School Y RG14 2 B8
es Catholic Primary ool M RG24 82 F7
es C of E Primary School C SO23 11 H6
edicts Convent School D SP11 117 M5
adettes RC ary School V GU14 90 D3
erines RC ary School B BH21 404 E2
erines Road or School H SO50 293 M3
erines School GU15 70 F4
stophers Hospital M/PORC PO16 15 L2
stophers School D SO18 319 K8
ents C of E School H BH1 448 C3
mans School H GU29 279 K2
ys Primary School V SO17 319 H7
unds Catholic School PO1 21 J1

St Edmunds School GSHT GU26 204 A5
St Edward Comprehensive School PLE BH15 445 L1
St Edwards School ROMY SO51 258 M7
St Faiths Primary School WINC SO23 238 E3
St Francis Primary School NBAD SO52 292 E3
St Francis School FHAM/STUB PO14 372 A7
St Gabriels School KSCL RG20 37 L2
St Georges Beneficial C of E Primary School PSEA PO1 20 D2
St Georges Business Centre PSEA PO1 20 D2
St Georges Catholic Boys School ELGH SO50 319 H2
St Georges Hospital LYMN SO41 454 B4
St Georges Industrial Estate CBLY GU15 70 E5
St Georges Industrial Estate ENEY PO4 423 L3
St Georges University School of Medicine WINC SO23 11 G7
St Ives CP School RGWD BH24 381 L3
St James C of E Primary School EMRTH PO10 378 C6
St James C of E Primary School LTDN BH7 449 G3
St James C of E (VC) First School FBDG SP6 333 L2
St James Hospital ENEY PO4 423 M3
St James Primary School HEND SO30 320 E6
St Johns Cathedral PSEA PO1 422 F2
St Johns Cathedral Primary School PSEA PO1 21 K1
St Johns C of E First School NFNM GU10 181 H7
St Johns C of E Infant School HLER SO31 371 G6
St Johns C of E Primary School GPORT PO12 421 M1
St Johns C of E Primary School HAV PO9 353 M8
St Johns College SSEA PO5 21 J6
St Johns School BSTK RG21 104 F5
St Johns School NWBY RG14 2 D9
St Johns School THLE RG7 43 K3
St Johns School WIMB BH21 404 B4
St John the Baptist RC Primary School AND SP10 8 B6
St John the Baptist School BPWT SO32 323 K6
St Josephs Gm RC Primary School ALDT GU11 6 F6
St Josephs RC Primary School NWBY RG14 3 H1
St Josephs RC School BKME/WDN BH12 446 D1
St Josephs RC School CHCH/BSGR BH23 435 L8
St Jospehs RC Junior School ALDT GU11 6 F5
St Judes Catholic Primary School FHAM/STUB PO14 14 C6
St Judes C of E Primary School PSEA PO1 20 E5
St Katherines C of E Primary School SBNE BH6 450 A4
St Lawrence C of E (Controlled) Primary School ALTN GU34 176 D4
St Leonards Hospital RGWD BH24 381 G7
St Lukes C of E School MOOR/WNTN BH9 432 D8
St Lukes C of E School SSEA PO5 21 H2
St Lukes Surgery HEND SO30 321 G7
St Marks C of E County Infant School CHCH/BSGR BH23 436 D7
St Marks C of E Junior School WSHM SO15 343 H1
St Marks C of E Primary School FARN GU14 91 G8
St Marks C of E Primary School NBNE BH10 432 A7
St Marks Primary School KEMP RG22 127 G2
St Martins East Woodhay C of E Primary School KSCL RG20 55 K1
St Mary Bourne School RAND SP11 97 L6
St Marys C of E Junior School CHAM RG24 106 A2
St Marys C of E Junior School NTHA RG18 27 G4
St Marys C of E Primary School SHAM SO14 13 J2

St Marys C of E Primary School SHAM SO14 13 K2
St Marys College WEND SO18 319 K8
St Marys First School FERN BH22 380 B5
St Marys Hospital HSEA PO3 423 L2
St Marys Primary School ALTN GU34 175 G3
St Marys Primary School TLHT RG30 31 M2
St Marys RC Primary School GPORT PO12 18 C1
St Marys RC School PLE BH15 445 K3
St Marys School THLE RG7 44 A3
St Marys Surgery AND SP10 9 J4
St Marys Surgery SHAM SO14 13 J3
St Matthews C of E Primary School LIND GU35 200 F8
St Michaels Abbey FARN GU14 90 F3
St Michaels C of E Controlled Secondary School ALDT GU11 7 J6
St Michaels C of E Infant School ALDT GU11 7 H6
St Michaels C of E Primary School SHST GU47 49 H8
St Michaels C of E School WCLF BH2 22 B6
St Michaels Middle School WIMB BH21 404 C1
St Michaels School KSCL RG20 57 J2
St Monica Infant School ITCH SO19 344 E5
St Monica Middle School ITCH SO19 344 E5
St Neots Preparatory School Ltd HTWY RG27 47 H8
St Nicholas C of E School NWBY RG14 2 D6
St Nicholas School NFNM GU10 110 D6
St Omer Barracks ALDT GU11 113 G4
St Patricks RC Primary School ITCH SO19 344 C5
St Patricks RC School FARN GU14 91 G4
St Pauls C of E First School NFNM GU10 136 D1
St Pauls Hospital FUFL SO22 10 E6
St Pauls RC Primary School CHAM PO6 374 F8
St Peter's Church BMTH BH1 22 F6
St Peters C of E Middle School FNM GU9 158 C2
St Peters Gm C of E School YTLY GU46 69 G2
St Peters Junior School FARN GU14 90 F4
St Peters School FUFL SO22 238 A3
St Peters School LTDN BH7 433 M8
St Peters School SBNE BH6 449 L4
St Polycarps RC Primary School FNM GU9 135 G7
St Swithuns RC Primary School SSEA PO5 21 K8
St Swithuns School RWIN SO21 215 J8
St Swithun Wells RC Primary School CHFD SO53 293 J3
St Thomas Clinic LYMN SO41 440 B5
St Thomas Infant School KSCL RG20 36 B8
St Thomas Mores RC Primary School HAV PO9 16 A1
St Vincent College GPORT PO12 18 F1
St Walburgas RC Primary School MOOR/WNTN BH9 432 F6
Salesian College FARN GU14 91 G7
Salterns School TOTT SO40 316 F8
Sampson Business Park CBLY GU15 70 E5
The Samuel Cody School ALDT GU11 112 E1
The Sanatorium Canford School WIMB BH21 404 E7
Sandford Springs Golf Club TADY RG26 59 M6
Sandhurst College Town County Junior School SHST GU47 50 B8
Sandhurst School SHST GU47 50 A8
Sandhurst Sports Club SHST GU47 69 M1
Sandhurst Surgery SHST GU47 69 L1
Sandleford Hospital NWBY RG14 25 K8
Sandleheath Industrial Estate FBDG SP6 309 G5
Sandle Manor School FBDG SP6 309 J6

Sarisbury Green C of E Primary School HLER SO31 370 C3
Sarisbury Infant School HLER SO31 370 C4
Sarum Road Hospital FUFL SO22 238 B1
Saxon Shore Infant School CHAM PO6 374 C8
Saxonwood School for the Handicapped DEAN RG23 82 A8
Scantabout Primary School CHFD SO53 293 L1
Scaplens Court Museum PLE BH15 445 G7
Selborne Primary School ALTN GU34 199 J8
Shakespeare Business Centre ELGH SO50 294 A4
Shakespeare County Infant School ELGH SO50 293 M4
Shalbourne C of E School MARL SN8 32 B4
Shamblehurst CP School HEND SO30 321 H8
Sharps Copse Junior & Infant School HAV PO9 377 M3
Shawcross Industrial Park HSEA PO3 399 L3
Shaw-cum-donnington School NWBY RG14 25 K2
Shawfield County Infant School ASHV GU12 113 K5
Sheet CP School PSF GU32 276 A2
Shelley Museum BOSC BH5 448 E4
Shepherds Down School RWIN SO21 266 B2
Shepherd Spring Medical Centre AND SP10 119 G5
Shepherds Spring County Infants School AND SP10 119 G5
Sherborne House School CHFD SO53 265 J8
Sherborne St John Primary School CHAM RG24 82 D4
The Ship House Surgery LIPH GU30 226 E5
Shirley Business Park WSHM SO15 343 G1
Shirley First & Middle School WSHM SO15 318 B7
The Shirley Health Centre WSHM SO15 343 G1
Shirley Swimming Pool WSHM SO15 343 G1
Shirley Warren Primary School ROWN SO16 317 M6
Sholing First School ITCH SO19 344 E4
Sholing Girls School ITCH SO19 344 E4
Sholing Infants School ITCH SO19 344 E3
Sholing Middle School ITCH SO19 344 E3
Shottermill County Middle School HASM GU27 228 C1
Sidings Industrial Estate HLER SO31 369 H3
Sikh Temple SSEA PO5 21 J4
Silchester Primary School THLE RG7 42 E7
Simcoe Clinic WSHM SO15 343 J1
Sinclair First & Junior School ROWN SO16 317 M3
Siskin County Junior & Infant School LSOL/BMARY PO13 421 H2
The Sixth Form College FARN GU14 90 E1
Slades Farm Special School NBNE BH10 432 B7
Smannell & Enham Primary School RAND SP11 119 K1
Solent Business Centre WSHM SO15 342 F2
Solent Industrial Centre WSHM SO15 343 G1
Solent Industrial Estate HEND SO30 321 G7
Solent Infant School CHAM PO6 376 B8
Solent Junior School CHAM PO6 376 B8
Solent Peoples Theatre ITCH SO19 345 G5
Somerford County Infant School CHCH/BSGR BH23 450 D1
Somerford County Junior School CHCH/BSGR BH23 450 D1
Somers Park Primary School SSEA PO5 21 J2
Somers Town Health Centre SSEA PO5 21 J3
Sopley CP School CHCH/BSGR BH23 409 G7
Southampton Airport Parkway Station ELGH SO50 319 L2
Southampton Central Mosque SHAM SO14 343 M2
Southampton City College SHAM SO14 13 J4

Southampton City Council PTSW SO17 319 H6
Southampton City Council ROWN SO16 317 H6
Southampton City Council ROWN SO16 318 A7
Southampton City Council ROWN SO16 318 C3
Southampton City Council SHAM SO14 12 F5
Southampton City Council SHAM SO14 12 F6
Southampton City Council SHAM SO14 13 J2
Southampton City Council SHAM SO14 13 K3
Southampton City Council WSHM SO15 12 C2
Southampton Football Club WSHM SO15 343 J2
Southampton General Hospital ROWN SO16 318 A5
Southampton Institute & Millais Gallery WSHM SO15 13 G1
Southampton Magistrates Court WSHM SO15 343 L2
Southampton & New Forest Magistrates Courts WSHM SO15 12 D1
Southampton Sports Centre ROWN SO16 318 C4
Southampton Sports Club ROWN SO16 317 H6
Southampton Technical College SHAM SO14 13 M5
Southampton University ROWN SO16 292 B7
South Baddesley C of E Primary School LYMN SO41 441 H2
Southbourne County Junior & Infant School EMRTH PO10 379 J8
Southbourne Surgery EMRTH PO10 379 J8
Southdown School RWIN SO21 266 B2
The South Downs College WVILLE PO7 376 E5
Southern Electric Museum CHCH/BSGR BH23 450 A1
South Farnborough County Junior School FARN GU14 91 G6
South Farnborough Infant School FARN GU14 91 G8
South Farnham Middle School FNM GU9 135 H7
South Ham Medical Centre KEMP RG22 104 B5
South Hants Country Club WHAM PO17 349 L7
Southlands School LYMN SO41 440 C1
Southlea Surgery ALDT GU11 7 H7
South Parade Pier PSEA PO1 423 J7
Southsea Castle Museum SSEA PO5 423 G7
Southsea Infant School SSEA PO5 21 L7
South West Health Authority HEND SO30 345 M4
Southwick Park Naval Recreation Centre WHAM PO17 374 E3
South Wonston Primary School RWIN SO21 190 C4
Southwood Golf Club FARN GU14 90 B6
Sparsholt College Hampshire RWIN SO21 212 F4
Sparsholt Primary School RWIN SO21 213 J5
Spectrum Sports Club SBNE BH6 449 H4
Speenhamland Cp School NWBY RG14 2 D1
Spitfire Court Surgery SHAM SO14 13 M6
Springdale First School BDST BH18 429 J4
Springfield School CHAM PO6 400 A1
Springhill RC Primary School WSHM SO15 343 J2
Springlake Country Club ASHV GU12 113 H4
Spurcroft Primary School STHA RG19 27 G6
Staff College CBLY GU15 70 F1
Stag Business Park RGWD BH24 382 E3
Stakes Hill Infant School WVILLE PO7 376 D2
Stakes Lodge Surgery WVILLE PO7 376 E2
Stamshaw Infant School NEND PO2 399 H6
Stamshaw Junior School NEND PO2 399 G5
Stamshaw & Tipner Leisure Centre NEND PO2 399 G6
Stanbridge Earls School ROMY SO51 262 A5
Stanley Green First School PLE BH15 445 H2
Stanmore Primary School FUFL SO22 238 D3
Stanton Industrial Estate WSHM SO15 342 E1

Stapehill Abbey
  WIMB BH21 .... 405 J3
Station Industrial Estate
  FLET GU13 .... 89 G5
Station Road Surgery
  FRIM GU16 .... 71 G8
Station Theatre
  HISD PO11 .... 425 H4
Staunton Park
  Community School
  HAV PO9 .... 377 M1
Stedham CP School
  MIDH GU29 .... 279 J7
Steep School
  PSF GU32 .... 275 K1
Stephen's Castle
  VWD BH31 .... 332 E8
Sterling Industrial Estate
  NWBY RG14 .... 3 G5
Stockbridge CP School
  STOK SO20 .... 186 F5
Stockcross School
  KSCL RG20 .... 24 B2
Stoke Gallery
  GPORT PO12 .... 18 F5
Stoke Park County
  Junior School
  ELGH SO50 .... 294 D5
Stoke Park Infant School
  ELGH SO50 .... 294 D6
Stokewood Surgery
  ELGH SO50 .... 294 F6
Stourfield First School
  SBNE BH6 .... 449 J2
Stratfield Saye
  THLE RG7 .... 65 G1
Stroud School
  ROMY SO51 .... 263 K6
Stubbs Industrial Estate
  ALDT GU11 .... 113 H3
Summerbee First School
  CHAR BH8 .... 433 G7
Summerbee Junior School
  CHAR BH8 .... 433 G7
Summerbee Secondary School
  CHAR BH8 .... 433 H7
Sun Hill Infant School
  NARL SO24 .... 218 C4
Sunnyside Doctors Surgery
  PSEA PO1 .... 21 L1
Sun Valley Business Park
  WINC SO23 .... 11 M5
Super Bowl
  BMTH BH1 .... 23 G5
Super Bowl
  WSHM SO15 .... 342 D1
Superstore
  BMTH BH1 .... 23 J3
Superstore
  BSTK RG21 .... 4 A8
Superstore
  SHAM SO14 .... 12 C1
Superstore
  SHAM SO14 .... 12 E3
Surrey Hampshire Borders
  Nhs Trust
  BSTK RG21 .... 5 G8
Surrey House First School
  ITCH SO19 .... 345 H5
Surrey House Health Centre
  ITCH SO19 .... 345 H5
Swallowfield Medical Practice
  THLE RG7 .... 45 M1
Swanmore Business Park
  BPWT SO32 .... 323 L3
Swanmore C of E School
  BPWT SO32 .... 324 A2
Swanmore County
  Secondary School
  BPWT SO32 .... 323 M3
Swan Street Surgery
  PSF GU32 .... 275 K5
Swanwick Business Park
  HLER SO31 .... 370 B1
Sway Park Industrial Estate
  LYMN SO41 .... 412 F7
Sway St Lukes Primary School
  LYMN SO41 .... 412 F6
Swaythling Clinic
  PTSW SO17 .... 319 H5
Swaythling Primary School
  PTSW SO17 .... 319 G5
Sylvan First School
  BKME/WDN BH12 .... 446 A2
Synagogue
  BMTH BH1 .... 23 G5
The Synagogue
  PTSW SO17 .... 343 K1
Tadley CP School
  TADY RG26 .... 61 M2
Tadley Police Station
  TADY RG26 .... 41 L7
Talavera County Junior &
  Infant School
  ALDT GU11 .... 112 C4
Talbot Heath School
  WBNE BH4 .... 447 H3
Talbot House
  Preparatory School
  MOOR/WNTN BH9 .... 432 C8
Talbot School
  BKME/WDN BH12 .... 431 M8
Talisman Business Centre
  HLER SO31 .... 370 F2
Tankerville School
  ELGH SO50 .... 294 A5
Tanners Brook Infant School
  WSHM SO15 .... 342 D1
Tanners Brook Junior School
  ROWN SO16 .... 342 D1
Tatchbury Manor House
  TOTT SO40 .... 315 L7
Tatchbury Mount Hospital
  TOTT SO40 .... 315 M6
Tauntons College
  WSHM SO15 .... 318 D7

Tavistock County
  Infant School
  FLET GU13 .... 88 C8
Tempus Business Centre
  BSTK RG21 .... 4 A4
Tennis Club
  FLET GU13 .... 110 E5
Terminus Industrial Estate
  PSEA PO1 .... 21 J2
Testbourne Community School
  WHCH RG28 .... 122 C5
Test Vale Surgery
  TOTT SO40 .... 316 E8
Test Valley Business Centre
  TOTT SO40 .... 317 G6
Test Valley County
  Secondary School
  STOK SO20 .... 186 C5
Testwood School
  TOTT SO40 .... 316 E7
Thatcham Bowling Club
  NTHA RG18 .... 27 G4
Thatcham Health Centre
  NTHA RG18 .... 26 F4
Thatcham Town Council
  NTHA RG18 .... 26 F4
Thatcham Town Football Club
  STHA RG19 .... 27 J8
Thornden School
  CHFD SO53 .... 265 L8
Thorney County
  Primary School
  EMRTH PO10 .... 402 E5
Thorneycroft Industrial Estate
  BSTK RG21 .... 4 A9
Thorngrove School
  KSCL RG20 .... 56 B1
Thornhill Clinic
  ITCH SO19 .... 345 H3
Thornhill First School
  ITCH SO19 .... 345 G3
Thornhill Junior School
  ITCH SO19 .... 345 G3
Thornhill Park Surgery
  ITCH SO19 .... 345 H2
Three Legged Cross
  Country First School
  WIMB BH21 .... 356 C7
Tidworth Garrison Golf Club
  NTID SP9 .... 114 B4
Tidworth Health Centre
  NTID SP9 .... 114 E2
Tiptoe CP School
  LYMN SO41 .... 412 B8
Titchfield County
  Primary School
  FHAM/STUB PO14 .... 371 K7
Tomlinscote School
  FRIM GU16 .... 71 J6
Totton College
  TOTT SO40 .... 316 C8
Totton College
  TOTT SO40 .... 341 J3
Totton Recreation Centre
  TOTT SO40 .... 316 C8
Tower Hill CP School
  FARN GU14 .... 90 C5
Tower Industrial Estate
  ELGH SO50 .... 294 B6
Townhill Infant School
  WEND SO18 .... 319 M6
Townhill Middle School
  WEND SO18 .... 319 M6
Townhill Park Health Clinic
  WEND SO18 .... 319 M6
Townhill Surgery
  WEND SO18 .... 320 A5
The Toynbee School
  CHFD SO53 .... 293 J3
Treadgold Museum
  PSEA PO1 .... 20 D1
Trinidad First School
  BKME/WDN BH12 .... 431 G8
Trinity Business Centre
  TOTT SO40 .... 316 D6
Trinity Industrial Estate
  WSHM SO15 .... 342 D1
Trinity School
  NWBY RG14 .... 25 L3
Trojans Sports Club
  ELGH SO50 .... 319 H1
Tudor House Museum
  SHAM SO14 .... 12 F5
Tunworth Ho
  OVTN RG25 .... 106 C8
Turlin Moor First School
  UPTN BH16 .... 444 B4
Turlin Moor Middle School
  UPTN BH16 .... 444 B4
Turnpike Business Park
  FHAM/PORC PO16 .... 15 K3
Turnpike Gallery
  PSF GU32 .... 275 L5
Tweseldown Infant School
  FLET GU13 .... 111 G4
Two Riversmeet
  Leisure Centre
  CHCH/BSGR BH23 .... 450 B2
Twyford C of E
  Primary School
  RWIN SO21 .... 266 E2
Twyford School
  RWIN SO21 .... 266 F2
Twyford Surgery
  RWIN SO21 .... 266 E7
Twynham
  Comprehensive School
  CHCH/BSGR BH23 .... 449 M2
Tylney Park Golf Club
  HTWY RG27 .... 85 J4
Ufton Nervet
  Parochial Primary School
  THLE RG7 .... 30 F4
Unicorn Trading Estate
  HASM GU27 .... 228 E1
Union Buildings Playschool
  ALDT GU11 .... 112 D5

United Services Cricket Ground
  PSEA PO1 .... 20 D3
United Services Rugby Club
  PSEA PO1 .... 20 E2
University of Portsmouth
  ENEY PO4 .... 423 M4
University of Portsmouth
  HISD PO11 .... 424 D4
University of Portsmouth
  PSEA PO1 .... 20 D1
University of Portsmouth
  PSEA PO1 .... 20 D4
University of Portsmouth
  PSEA PO1 .... 20 E2
University of Portsmouth
  PSEA PO1 .... 20 E3
University of Portsmouth
  PSEA PO1 .... 21 K2
University of Portsmouth
  SSEA PO5 .... 20 F6
University of Portsmouth
  SSEA PO5 .... 21 G3
University of Portsmouth
  SSEA PO5 .... 21 H4
University of Southampton
  PTSW SO17 .... 319 G5
University of Southampton
  ROWN SO16 .... 318 E5
University Practice
  SSEA PO5 .... 20 F4
Upham School
  BPWT SO32 .... 296 D3
Uplands County
  Primary School
  FHAM/PORC PO16 .... 15 G2
Uplands CP School
  SHST GU47 .... 49 L8
Uplands School
  PSTN BH14 .... 446 B5
Upton Grey Ho
  OVTN RG25 .... 129 M2
Upton Health Centre
  UPTN BH16 .... 444 B1
Venture Industrial Park
  LSOL/BMARY PO13 .... 397 H5
Vermont School
  ROWN SO16 .... 318 D4
Vernham Dean School
  RAND SP11 .... 73 J3
Verwood C of E First School
  VWD BH31 .... 356 C3
Verwood C of E School
  VWD BH31 .... 356 C3
Verwood Industrial Estate
  VWD BH31 .... 356 F2
Verwood Leisure Centre
  VWD BH31 .... 356 D2
Verwood Sports Centre
  VWD BH31 .... 356 E2
Verwood Town Council
  VWD BH31 .... 356 D1
Viables Industrial Estate
  KEMP RG22 .... 104 F7
Vicarage Lane Clinic
  HASM GU27 .... 228 C2
Vickers Business Centre
  CHAM RG24 .... 82 D8
Victoria Cottage Hospital
  EMRTH PO10 .... 378 D8
Victoria Park
  Swimming Centre
  PSEA PO1 .... 20 F1
Victor Street Surgery
  WSHM SO15 .... 318 A7
Victory Business Centre
  PSEA PO1 .... 21 L2
Victory Retail Park
  PSEA PO1 .... 423 G1
Victory Trading Estate
  HSEA PO3 .... 399 M6
Vigo County Infant School
  AND SP10 .... 9 M3
Vigo County Junior School
  AND SP10 .... 9 M3
Village Medical Practice
  FERN BH22 .... 380 B6
The Vine School
  BPWT SO32 .... 322 C8
Vintage Motorcycle Museum
  NMIL/BTOS BH25 .... 437 J3
Virgin Cinemas
  SHAM SO14 .... 13 J7
Wallisdean County
  Infant School
  FHAM/STUB PO14 .... 14 D7
Wallisdean County
  Junior School
  FHAM/STUB PO14 .... 14 E7
Wallop CP School
  STOK SO20 .... 184 E1
Walsh C of E First &
  Middle School
  ASHV GU12 .... 113 J7
Waltham Business Park
  BPWT SO32 .... 323 M4
Warblington School
  HAV PO9 .... 17 J4
War Memorial Hospital
  AND SP10 .... 8 D1
War Memorial Hospital
  LYMN SO41 .... 454 D4
Warren Avenue
  Industrial Estate
  ENEY PO4 .... 423 M3
Warren Park Primary School
  HAV PO9 .... 377 H1
Warrior Business Centre
  CHAM PO6 .... 400 C1
Watchetts County
  Middle School
  CBLY GU15 .... 70 F6
Waterfront Garden Surgery
  FAWY SO45 .... 367 L3
Waterfront Museum
  PLE BH15 .... 445 G7
Waterloo Industrial Estate
  HEND SO30 .... 321 G7

The Waterloo School
  WVILLE PO7 .... 376 C1
Waterlooville Football Club
  WVILLE PO7 .... 352 C8
Waterlooville Health Centre
  WVILLE PO7 .... 352 B6
Watermill Theatre &
  Restaurant
  KSCL RG20 .... 24 E1
Watermill Theatre
  STHA RG19 .... 38 C3
The Waterside Health Centre
  FAWY SO45 .... 367 L6
Waterside School
  FHAM/PORC PO16 .... 398 F5
The Wavell School
  ALDT GU11 .... 112 E1
Waverley Abbey C of E School
  NFNM GU10 .... 159 M3
Webb Peploe House Surgery
  LYMN SO41 .... 440 C5
Weeke CP School
  FUFL SO22 .... 10 A2
Weford County Infants School
  LIND GU35 .... 201 L4
Wellington Business Park
  CWTH RG45 .... 49 H4
Wellington College
  CWTH RG45 .... 49 K5
Wellington Shopping Centre
  ALDT GU11 .... 6 F2
Wellington Sports Centre
  CWTH RG45 .... 49 J4
Wellington Sports Club
  ELGH SO50 .... 319 J1
Wellow County Primary School
  ROMY SO51 .... 288 E5
Wellum House Dental
  Health Centre
  AND SP10 .... 9 J7
Wentworth College
  BOSC BH5 .... 448 F4
Wessex Bowl
  KEMP RG22 .... 104 B3
Wessex Downs Golf Club
  THLE RG7 .... 29 H4
Wessex Nuffield Hospital
  CHFD SO53 .... 265 L7
Wessex Nuffield Hospital
  ELGH SO50 .... 294 A5
Wessex Regional
  Health Authority
  HEND SO30 .... 321 G7
Wessex Superbowl
  CHAM PO6 .... 376 E7
West Berkshire Council
  NWBY RG14 .... 2 D5
West Berkshire District Council
  NWBY RG14 .... 2 D3
West Berkshire District Council
  NWBY RG14 .... 2 E4
West Berkshire District Council
  NWBY RG14 .... 2 E5
West Berkshire District Council
  NWBY RG14 .... 3 G2
Westbourne County
  Primary School
  EMRTH PO10 .... 378 F4
Westbourne Galleries
  CCLF BH13 .... 447 G5
Westbourne Surgery
  EMRTH PO10 .... 378 F5
West Cliff Medical Centre
  WCLF BH2 .... 22 C8
Westend County Infant School
  ALDT GU11 .... 6 D3
West End Surgery
  HEND SO30 .... 320 D6
Western Community Hospital
  ROWN SO16 .... 317 M7
Western Downland
  Primary School
  FBDG SP6 .... 308 C4
Western Downland School
  FBDG SP6 .... 282 E7
Western Primary School
  FUFL SO22 .... 10 B6
Westfield County Junior School
  YTLY GU46 .... 68 E3
Westfield Junior School
  CHAM PO6 .... 374 C8
The Westgate School
  FUFL SO22 .... 10 C5
West Hill Park School
  FHAM/STUB PO14 .... 371 J8
Westlands Medical Centre
  FHAM/PORC PO16 .... 398 A1
West March Business Centre
  AND SP10 .... 9 J1
West Meon Controlled
  Primary School
  PSF GU32 .... 272 A3
West Moors Group Practice
  FERN BH22 .... 380 B6
West Moors Middle School
  FERN BH22 .... 380 D7
Weston Park Boys School
  ITCH SO19 .... 344 F7
Weston Park First School
  ITCH SO19 .... 344 E7
Weston Park Junior School
  ITCH SO19 .... 344 E7
Weston Shore First School
  ITCH SO19 .... 344 D8
Westover Gallery
  BMTH BH1 .... 22 F6
Westover Primary School
  HSEA PO3 .... 399 M8
West Point Business Park
  AND SP10 .... 118 A7
West Portway
  Industrial Estate
  RAND SP11 .... 117 M7
West Quay Retail Park
  WSHM SO15 .... 12 D3
West Quay Shopping Centre
  SHAM SO14 .... 12 E3

West Suuex County Council
  CBLY GU15 ....
West Tytherley Primary School
  RSAL SP5 ....
West Wittering
  Parochial School
  SELS PO20 ....
Westwood Business Park
  TOTT SO40 ....
Weybourne County
  Infant School
  FNM GU9 ....
Weydon County
  Secondary School
  FNM GU9 ....
Weydown Industrial Estate
  HASM GU27 ....
Weyford County Junior School
  LIND GU35 ....
Wherwell School
  RAND SP11 ....
Whitchurch C of E
  Primary School
  WHCH RG28 ....
Whitchurch Medical Centre
  WHCH RG28 ....
Whitedown Special School
  ALTN GU34 ....
White Hart Gallery
  OVTN RG25 ....
White Hart Industrial Estate
  BLKW GU17 ....
Whitelands Park CP School
  NTHA RG18 ....
Whiteley County
  Primary School
  FHAM PO15 ....
The Whiteley Surgery
  HLER SO31 ....
Whiteparish Surgery
  RSAL SP5 ....
Whitewater C of E (Controlled)
  Primary School
  HTWY RG27 ....
Wickham C of E
  Controlled Primary School
  WHAM PO17 ....
Wickham Park Golf Club
  WHAM PO17 ....
Wickham Riding School
  WHAM PO17 ....
Wickham Surgery
  WHAM PO17 ....
Wick 1 Industrial Estate
  NMIL/BTOS BH25 ....
Wick 2 Industrial Estate
  NMIL/BTOS BH25 ....
Wicor County Primary School
  FHAM/PORC PO16 ....
Wildern Clinic
  HEND SO30 ....
The Wildern School
  HEND SO30 ....
Wildground County
  Infant School
  FAWY SO45 ....
Wildground County
  Junior School
  FAWY SO45 ....
William Cobbett County
  Junior School
  FNM GU9 ....
William Gilpin C of E
  Primary School
  LYMN SO41 ....
Willink Leisure Centre
  THLE RG7 ....
Willink School
  THLE RG7 ....
Willis Museum
  BSTK RG21 ....
Willments Industrial Estate
  ITCH SO19 ....
Willowdene Play School
  CHAM PO6 ....
Wimbledon Park Sports Centre
  SSEA PO5 ....
Wimborne Industrial Estate
  WIMB BH21 ....
Wimborne Junior &
  Infant School
  ENEY PO4 ....
Winchcombe CP Infant School
  NWBY RG14 ....
Winchcombe Junior School
  NWBY RG14 ....
Winchester Agricultural
  Museum
  WINC SO23 ....
Winchester City Museum
  WINC SO23 ....
Winchester College
  WINC SO23 ....
The Winchester Gallery
  ROWN SO16 ....
Winchester Lawn Tennis Club
  FUFL SO22 ....
Winchester Recreation Centre
  WINC SO23 ....
Winchester Road
  Industrial Estate
  BSTK RG21 ....
Winchester Rugby
  Football Club
  WINC SO23 ....
Winchester School of Art
  WINC SO23 ....
Winklebury Infant School
  DEAN RG23 ....
Winklebury Junior School
  DEAN RG23 ....
Winklebury Medical Centre
  DEAN RG23 ....
Winnall CP School
  WINC SO23 ....
Winnall Farm Industrial Estate
  WINC SO23 ....

slow Primary School
  SP5 .... 206 E2
Play School
  SP10 .... 9 L4
nton School
  SP10 .... 119 J8
shing Well Gallery
  H/BSGR BH23 .... 409 M7
shing Well Gallery
  VD BH24 .... 384 E5
s School
  M GU27 .... 204 F7
dene School
  SP10 .... 9 K7
sey Palace
  C SO23 .... 11 H9

Woodhill Preparatory School
  CHFD SO53 .... 293 J1
Woodhills School
  HEND SO30 .... 346 D1
Woodlands Community School
  WEND SO18 .... 320 C8
Woodlea Primary School
  LIND GU35 .... 201 J7
Wool House Maritime Museum
  SHAM SO14 .... 12 F6
Woolmer Hill School
  HASM GU27 .... 228 A1
Woolmer Surgery
  LIND GU35 .... 201 J5
Woolsbridge Industrial Estate
  WIMB BH21 .... 380 F2

Woolsbridge
  Small Business Centre
  WIMB BH21 .... 380 E2
Woolston First School
  ITCH SO19 .... 344 C6
Woolston School
  ITCH SO19 .... 344 D5
Woolton Hill County
  Junior School
  KSCL RG20 .... 56 B1
Wordsworth Infant School
  WSHM SO15 .... 318 B7
Worldham Park Golf Club
  ALTN GU34 .... 177 H6
Worting County Infant School
  DEAN RG23 .... 103 M4

Worting County Junior School
  KEMP RG22 .... 104 A4
Wykeham Gallery
  STOK SO20 .... 186 E5
Wykeham House School
  FHAM/PORC PO16 .... 15 M5
Wykeham Industrial Estate
  WINC SO23 .... 11 L4
Wynford Farm Industrial Estate
  ROMY SO51 .... 262 E4
The Wyvern Community
  Secondary School
  ELGH SO50 .... 295 H7
Yarrells Preparatory School
  UPTN BH16 .... 444 A1

Yateley County Infant School
  YTLY GU46 .... 69 G2
Yateley Health Centre
  YTLY GU46 .... 69 G2
Yateley Manor
  Preparatory School
  YTLY GU46 .... 69 G1
Yateley School
  YTLY GU46 .... 68 F3
Yeoman Industrial Park
  TOTT SO40 .... 317 G6
Youngs Industrial Estate
  THLE RG7 .... 41 J4